edition

7

MANAGING HUMAN RESOURCES

A PARTNERSHIP PERSPECTIVE

SUSAN E. JACKSON
RUTGERS UNIVERSITY

RANDALL S. SCHULER
RUTGERS UNIVERSITY

South-Western College Publishing
Thomson Learning™

Australia • Canada • Denmark • Japan • Mexico • New Zealand • Philippines
Puerto Rico • Singapore • South Africa • Spain • United Kingdom • United States

Managing Human Resources: A Partnership Perspective
by Susan E. Jackson and Randall S. Schuler

Publisher: Dave Shaut
Executive Editor: John Szilagyi
Developmental Editor: Atietie Tonwe
Marketing Manager: Joseph A. Sabatino
Production Editor: Kelly Keeler
Manufacturing Coordinator: Dana Began Schwartz
Internal Design: Jennifer Martin-Lambert
Cover Design: Joe Devine
Cover Illustrator: ©99 SIS/Campell Laird
Production House: settingpace
Printer: West Publishing

Printed in the United States of America
1 2 3 4 5 02 01 00 99

For more information contact South-Western College Publishing, 5101 Madison Road, Cincinnati, Ohio, 45227 or find us on the Internet at http://www.swcollege.com

For permission to use material from this text or product, contact us by
• **telephone: 1-800-730-2214**
• **fax: 1-800-730-2215**
• **web: http://www.thomsonrights.com**

Library of Congress Cataloging-in-Publication Data
Jackson, Susan E.
   Managing human resources : a partnership perspective / Susan E.
Jackson, Randall S. Schuler.
      p.   cm.
   Includes bibliographical references and index.
   ISBN 0-324-00415-X
   1. Personnal management.   I. Schuler, Randall S.   II. Title.
HF5549.J254   1999
   658.3--dc21
                                                    99-22218
                                                       CIP

This book is printed on acid-free paper.

Contents

Contents

Chapter 2
THE ENVIRONMENTAL CONTEXT FOR MANAGING HUMAN RESOURCES   46

Contents

Chapter 3
MANAGING EMPLOYEES FAIRLY   86

Contents

Chapter 4
THE INTERNAL ENVIRONMENT: CREATING STRATEGIC ALIGNMENT   127

Contents

Chapter 5
ORGANIZATIONAL CHANGE AND LEARNING   176

Contents

Chapter 6

JOB AND ORGANIZATIONAL ANALYSIS: UNDERSTANDING THE WORK TO BE DONE   215

Contents

Chapter 7
RECRUITMENT: ATTRACTING QUALIFIED CANDIDATES   256

Contents

Chapter 8
SELECTION AND PLACEMENT: CHOOSING THE WORKFORCE 299

Contents

Chapter 9
SOCIALIZATION, TRAINING, AND DEVELOPMENT: ENSURING WORKFORCE CAPABILITY 348

Contents

Chapter 10
TOTAL COMPENSATION: DEVELOPING AN OVERALL APPROACH   397

Chapter 11
PERFORMANCE MANAGEMENT: APPRAISAL AND FEEDBACK   450

Contents

Chapter 12
PERFORMANCE MANAGEMENT: REWARDING EMPLOYEES' CONTRIBUTIONS   499

Contents

Chapter 13

INDIRECT COMPENSATION: PROVIDING BENEFITS AND SERVICES   542

Contents

Chapter 14

OCCUPATIONAL SAFETY AND HEALTH:
MANAGING THE INCIDENCE OF DEATHS, INJURIES, AND DISEASES   579

Contents

Chapter 15
UNIONIZATION AND COLLECTIVE BARGAINING: NEGOTIATING THE EMPLOYMENT CONTRACT   610

Contents

Today, it's become commonplace to hear managers from the very largest multinational firms to the smallest domestic firms claim that managing people effectively is vital to success in today's highly competitive marketplace. "The most important thing I do is hire bright people," says Microsoft's CEO Bill Gates. "Hire people smarter than you and get out of their way," says Howard Schultz, CEO of Starbucks. "Without the right people in place, strategies can't get implemented," says General Electric's CEO Jack Welch. In fact, the challenge of effectively managing human resources is recognized throughout the world. According to Floris Maljers, CEO of the British-Dutch company Unilever, "Limited human resources, not unreliable capital, are the biggest constraint when companies globalize." These CEOs know that it's people that are the core of any organization. In order to succeed, they must have the best people available working productively throughout their companies.

PURPOSES OF THIS BOOK

Managing Human Resources: A Partnership Perspective, Seventh Edition, offers a detailed picture of how successful organizations manage human resources in order to compete effectively in a dynamic, global environment. Because organizations differ from each other in so many ways—including their locations, technologies, products and services, and corporate cultures—we use many different companies as examples in this text. Included are Kinkos, Sears, AT&T, Microsoft, Gateway, Hallmark, Kodak, Southwest Airlines, McDonald's, Mrs. Fields, Ritz Carlton, Marriott, General Electric, Eaton, Avon, Levi Strauss, Dell, Chrysler, Coca-Cola, Disney, Lincoln Electric, Aetna, Weyerhaeuser, Federal Express, UPS, PepsiCo, Aid Association for Lutherans, and many others. By combining a respect for established principles of human resource management with a willingness to experiment and try new approaches, these companies succeed year after year.

Despite the many differences between companies, those that succeed seem to share a few things in common. Perhaps most importantly, they recognize that there's more to "success" than just a good bottom line. The best companies balance their concerns over short-term, bottom-line results with the recognition that long-term success requires satisfying a variety of stakeholders. In addition to satisfying the demands of shareholders, the best organizations also address the concerns of their employees and their families, customers, local communities, government regulators, unions, public interest groups, as well as other organizations that they do business with. These various stakeholders often care deeply about how businesses conduct themselves, and in particular, about how they treat their employees. Thus, throughout this textbook, we explicitly consider how alternative approaches to managing human resources are likely to be viewed by various stakeholders. Although it's not always possible to satisfy all stakeholders equally well, effective organizations make a habit of analyzing the available alternatives from multiple perspectives and seeking solutions that meet as many concerns as possible.

Another quality shared by successful companies seems to be the belief that managing human resources is everyone's responsibility. Naturally, HR professionals carry much of the responsibility for ensuring an organization is managing people as effectively as possible, but their responsibility is shared with line managers and all other employees in the organization. This view—that managing human resources is a shared responsibility—is what we mean by the "partnership perspective." This textbook was written with all three of the key HR partners in mind: HR professionals, line managers, as well as all other employees within an organization. Within each chapter, the unique roles and responsibilities of these three partners are detailed in a feature titled "The HR Triad." The 21st century will witness even greater cooperation among HR managers, line managers, and employees, as teams strive to make their organizations more capable of success. Thus, this book is written for everyone working in organizations, as well as those who will eventually.

A third quality shared by successful organizations is responsiveness to a dynamic and increasingly global environment. Rapid changes in technologies, as well as economic, political, and social conditions mean that few organizations can effectively compete today by just using the old tried-and-true approaches of yesterday. As the best organizations realize, continuous change requires continuous learning. Finding new and better ways of doing things is the only way to get ahead and stay ahead of the competition—and that includes learning new and better ways of managing human resources. Throughout this text, we focus on five challenges that require new approaches to managing human resources:

- managing strategically,
- managing globalization,
- managing diversity,
- managing teams, and
- managing change.

As described in Chapter 1, organizations of all types now face these five challenges. Furthermore, addressing these five challenges almost always requires rethinking and revising older, traditional approaches to managing human resources. Because these challenges are relatively new, even the experts don't yet know the answers to many of the questions that come up. The research that will one day help answer some of those questions is just now being conducted as leading companies experiment with various new HR policies and practices. To give readers a feel for how organizations are addressing these challenges, in each chapter boxed features highlight the relevant HR policies and practices of those at the leading-edge.

ORGANIZATION OF THIS BOOK

The field of human resource management is exciting today because it is undergoing so much change. Driving the changes in this field are changes in the external and internal environments of organizations. Managing people effectively is not something done in isolation. It begins with an understanding of how a variety of converging forces are reshaping the design and functioning of modern organizations. Because we believe that understanding the context of work is so important to managing human resources effectively, we devote several chapters to describing that dynamic context. Chapter 1 provides an overview of the many aspects of the environment that can affect an organization's approach to managing human resources. Chapters 2 and 3 then describe in more detail the external environment, including globalization, the changing labor market, new technologies, restructuring due to mergers and acquisitions, laws and regulations, and employees' evolving view of what constitutes fair employment practices. As described in Chapter 4, changes in the external environment put pressure on organizations to change internally. In addition to developing and focusing on new competitive strategies, organizations may redesign their internal structures, create new types of jobs, and fundamentally alter both where and how work gets done. Entering the new millennium, HR professionals now realize that one of their most important responsibilities is facilitating the process of change. While the specific changes occurring today are new, the need for change has always been around. Thus, we know a great deal about how to manage change successfully. Chapter 5 describes several basic principles for managing change and illustrates how these can be used to facilitate many types of specific change now occurring in organizations.

Having described the environment that shapes how organizations manage human resources, we then turn to descriptions of several activities involved in managing human resources. The first activity is simply to develop an understanding of the nature of the work that needs to be done in an organization. Chapter 6 describes how jobs can be analyzed in order to understand what tasks they involve and the qualities that employees need to perform the jobs. Chapters 7 and 8 go on to describe how companies, using the information of the nature of jobs, as well as the entire context of company and its environment, recruit and select job applicants. Chapter 9 describes the socialization, training and development practices that follow induction into an organization. Training and retraining are critical issues in an information era. With rapid changes in job requirements, existing employees must learn new sets of skills. Chapters 10, 11, 12 and 13 describe the human resource activities that relate to appraising and compensating employees. Employees need fair and clearly stated performance standards. They deserve useable feedback and the support needed to identify and correct performance deficiencies. When these are combined with well-designed compensation and rewards, capable individual employees can become part of a high-performance, team-oriented workforce. As many organizations have discovered, retaining a high performance workforce can be a major challenge. The best companies often become targets for recruitment by competitors. Offering innovative benefits packages that address a wide array of employees' concerns is one tactic for warding off such poaching, as described in Chapter 14. Chapters 14 and 15 examine other ways to further improve work environments—by ensuring a safe and healthy workplace and by developing cooperative relationships with unions and other employee representatives

Finally, Chapter 16 considers the HR profession itself. This chapter is written specifically for readers who wish to pursue a career in human resource management, working either as a staff member within an organization or as a consultant. What competencies will you need to succeed in this field? What professional standards will you need to meet? How are HR activities organized in different organizations? And what is the future likely to hold? The last chapter explores these questions from the perspective of HR professionals.

FEATURES OF THIS EDITION

Several features are incorporated into this edition:

Managing Through Partnership at . . . : As an introduction to each chapter, this feature describes in some detail the human resource activities of a company familiar to most readers. They are used to illustrate how HR professionals, line managers and employees work together to achieve effective approaches to managing human resources.

The HR Triad: To further elaborate the partnership perspective, each chapter contains an exhibit that describes the roles and responsibilities of each partner in the HR triad—HR professionals, line managers, and employees. The roles and responsibilities listed within each chapter tie directly into the material discussed in the text. Thus, The HR Triad feature helps summarize some of the key points raised in the chapter.

In each chapter, real world examples of current HR practices are illustrated under the titles, Managing Globalization, Managing Strategically, Managing Change, Managing Teams, and Managing Diversity. These features reinforce two important lessons. First, successful companies follow basic well-established principles for managing human resources, and second, they also are willing to experiment with new ideas in order to improve upon what is known. Through these examples, we hope to convince readers that effectively managing human resources requires mastering what is known and then having the confidence to venture into the unknown.

Margin Notes: Throughout the chapters, margin notes reinforce and extend key ideas. The fast facts offer tidbits of information that are sometimes surprising. The quotes illustrate the perspectives of real managers and HR professionals. Some quotes are from well-known executives or public figures; others from names you may not recognize. In either case, we think you'll agree their insights are worth remembering.

Terms to Remember: A list of key terms and concepts appears at the end of each chapter. Its purpose is to allow you to check whether you recall and understand the key vocabulary associated with the content of the chapter. If you see a term you aren't sure about, you may want to go back and review that section of the chapter again, or ask the instructor to help clarify the meaning for you.

Discussion Questions: The discussion questions at the end of each chapter seek to determine your understanding of the material found in the chapter. They include material in the body of the chapter and in the "Managing..." features. By the time you finish reading and studying all the chapters, you should know a great deal about human resource management, about what particular companies are doing today to manage their human resources, and about what companies should be preparing to do as they begin the 21st century.

Projects to Extend Your Learning: The projects at the end of the chapters reinforce the key themes of managing strategically, managing globalization, managing teams, managing change, and managing diversity. Some of these projects direct you to investigate human resource practices in companies in your neighborhood. Many others ask you to gather information from the Internet. Finally, one project in each chapter focuses your attention on the human resource activities used by the three companies portrayed in the end-of-text integrative cases.

End-of-Chapter Case Studies: The case studies at the end of chapters offer challenge and variety. It is up to you to analyze what is going on and suggest improvements. In some instances, discussion questions are presented to guide your thinking; in other instances, you are on your own to determine the issues most relevant to the material in the chapter. Except in the three end-of-textbook integrative case studies, many of the companies in these cases are disguised, although their problems and challenges are not.

End-of-Text Integrative Case Studies: At the end of the textbook we present three longer case studies. They describe various human resource activities at Lincoln Electric, Southwest Airlines, and Aid Association for Lutherans. By studying each case, you should gain an appreciation for how the many aspects of human resource management described throughout the text work together as a total system. By necessity, any particular chapter focuses on only one small piece of the total HR puzzle. In the real world, the pieces must fit together into a meaningful whole. The end-of-text integrative cases illustrate three very different total HR systems found in three very successful organizations. They are provided so that you can see examples of how firms are systematically managing all their human resource activities through partnership consistent with the characteristics of their organizations and the concerns of their stakeholders.

SUPPLEMENTARY MATERIALS

Supplementary materials for *Managing Human Resources: A Partnership Perspective*, Seventh Edition include:

An Instructor's Manual, ISBN 0-324-00686-1, which contains
- Chapter outlines
- Lecture enhancements, including experiential and skill-building exercises and end-of-chapter case notes

A printed *Test Bank,* ISBN 0-324-00687-X, which includes multiple-choice, true-false, and short essay questions with answers referenced to pages in the text

A computerized version of the test bank, Thomson Learning Testing Tools™, ISBN 0-324-00688-8.

Transparency Acetates, ISBN 0-324-00690-X, containing some of the key charts and graphs from the text.

Power Point slides, ISBN 0-324-00689-6.

Additional materials include *Managing Organizations and People: Cases in Management, Organizational Behavior* and *Human Resource Management,* Sixth Edition, by Paul F. Buller and Randall S. Schuler; *Applications in Human Resource Management: Cases, Exercises, and Skill Builders,* Fourth Edition, by Stella Nkomo, Myron D. Fottler, and R. Bruce McAfee; and *Personal Computer Projects for Human Resource Management,* Second Edition, by Nicholas J. Beutell. All these materials are available from South-Western College Publishing Company.

ACKNOWLEDGMENTS

As with the previous editions, many fine individuals were critical to the completion of the final product. They include Paul Buller at Gonzaga University; Peter Dowling at the University of Tasmania in Australia; Hugh Scullion at the University of Newcastle in England; Paul Sparrow at Manchester Business School in England; Shimon Dolan at the University of Montreal; Stuart Youngblood at Texas Christian University; Gary Florkowski at the University of Pittsburgh; Bill Todor at the Ohio State University; Nancy Napier at Idaho State University; Vandra Huber at the University of Washington; John Slocum at Southern Methodist University; Lynn Shore at Georgia State University; Mary Ahmed at Grand Forks; Ed Lawler at the Center for Effective Organizations, University of Southern California; Hrach Bedrosian at New York University; Lynda Gratton and Nigel Nicholson at the London Business School; Chris Brewster and Shaun Tyson at the Cranfield Management School; Michael Poole at the Cardiff Business School; Paul Stonham at the European School of Management, Oxford; Jan Krulis-Randa and Bruno Staffelbach at the University of Zurich; Albert Stahli and Cornel Wietlisbach at the GSBA in Zurich; David Ricks at Thunderbird; Mark Mendenhall at the University of Tennessee, Chattanooga; Helen De Cieri and Denise Welch of Monash University; Yoram Zeira of Tel-Aviv University; Dan Ondrack, the University of Toronto; Moshe Banai, Baruch College; Steve Kobrin, Wharton School; Steve Barnett, York University; Carol Somers, Harvard University; Christian Scholz, University of Saarlandes; Pat Joynt, Henley Management College; Reijo Luostarinen, Helsinki School of Economics and Business Administration; Mickey Kavanagh, SUNY, Albany; Wayne Cascio, University of Colorado, Denver; Ricky Griffin, Texas A&M University; Ed van Sluijs, University of Limberg; Joy Turnheim, New York University; and Mark Huselid and Paula Caliguiri, Rutgers University.

The following individuals provided many good ideas and suggestions for changes and alterations in their roles of reviewers and evaluators: Samuel Adekunle, Albany State University; Richard Grover, University of Southern Maine; Mary A. Klayton-Mi, Mary Washington College; Edward H. Meyer, The college of Mount St. Vincent; Shirley L. Teeter, California State University, Northridge; James E. Welch, Kentucky Wesleyan College.

Several human resource managers, practicing line managers, and publishers also contributed in many important ways to this edition, particularly with examples and insights from their work experiences. They include Mike Mitchell, Judith Springberg, Tom Kroeger, Patricia Ryan, Margaret Magnus, Betty Hartzell, Don Bohl, Bob Kenny, Jack Berry, Steve Marcus, Paul Beddia, Mark Saxer, John Fulkerson, Cal Reynolds, Jon Wendenhof, Joan Kelly, Michael Losey, Jo Mattern, Larry Alexander, Nick Blauweikel, Mike Loomans, Sandy Daemmrich, Jeffery Maynard, Lyle Steele, Rowland Stichweh, Bill Maki, Rick Sabo, Bruce Cable, Gil Fry, Bill Reffett, Jerry Laubenstein, Richard Hagan, Horace Parker, and Johan Julin.

The following individuals graciously provided case and exercise materials: George Cooley, Bruce Evans, Mitchell W. Fields, Hugh L. French, Jr., Peter Cappelli, Anne Crocker-Hefter, Stuart Youngblood, Ed Lawler, John Slocum, Jeff Lenn, Hrach Bedrosian, Kay

Contents

Stratton, Bruce Kiene, Martin R. Moser, James W. Thacker, Arthur Sharplin, and Jerry Laubenstein.

The support, encouragement, and assistance of many individuals were vital to the production of this work. They include Ilysa Riemer, who worked carefully in the preparation of the many parts of the final chapter drafts; Barbara Lee, HRM Department Chair, and John F. Burton, Jr., Dean of the School of Management and Labor Relations at Rutgers University; Ari Ginsberg, Management Department Chair and George Daly, Dean, of the Stern School of Business. Also, several people at South-Western College Publishing deserve our special thanks for their help and support: John Szilagyi, executive editor, Atietie Tonwe, developmental editor, Kelly Keeler, production editor. Without their professional dedication and competence, this book would not have been possible.

Susan E. Jackson and Randall S. Schuler
Piscataway, New Jersey

MANAGING HUMAN RESOURCES FOR COMPETITIVE ADVANTAGE

"We pay just as good wages and benefits as other airlines, but our costs are lower because our productivity is higher, which is achieved through the dedicated energy of our people. We've got exactly the same equipment. The difference is, when a plane pulls into a gate, our people run to meet it."

Herb Kelleher
CEO
Southwest Airlines Company[1]

Chapter Outline

MANAGING THROUGH PARTNERSHIP

at Southwest Airlines

For nearly 30 years Southwest Airlines' successful low-cost, on-time, no-frills, no-allocated seats, no-meals approach to air travel has helped the company fly high above its competitors with hefty profit gains. In contrast with the industry as a whole, which has lost billions of dollars, Southwest's lean, mean flying machine has carved out 25 consecutive years of profits and has risen to become the eighth largest U.S. airline. This profitability has fueled Southwest's tremendous stock success over the years. Since Southwest began selling stock to the public in 1972, its value has increased more than 21,000 percent!

Texas businessman Rollin King and lawyer Herb Kelleher founded Air Southwest Company in 1967 as an intrastate airline, linking Dallas, Houston, and San Antonio. In 1978, Kelleher became president. Regarded as something of an industry maverick, Kelleher went on to introduce advance-purchase "Fun Fares" in 1986 and a frequent-flyer program based on the number of flights, rather than mileage, in 1987. To help keep costs low, the airline uses only fuel-efficient Boeing 737s. Since any airline can buy these planes, competitors have tried to muscle into this low-frills, short-haul market. For example, United Airlines introduced its shuttle service on the West Coast in October 1994. Shuttle by United was a copy of Southwest. It had a 45-plane fleet of Boeing 737s and adopted a low-cost operating strategy. Like Southwest, most Shuttle employees were unionized, but United seemed to have an advantage because it was able to effect looser union work rules. And it aimed to approach the low operating costs that are a key factor in Southwest's success. Ultimately, Shuttle by United was unable to beat Southwest at its low cost game and within 16 months it had retreated from head-to-head competition. Five years later, US Airways took on Southwest Airlines again with their new MetroJet. Time will tell whether they will succeed.

Southwest's workforce is probably the most productive and most motivated in the business. Southwest has 81 employees per airplane and the major airlines have up to 157. The number of passengers per Southwest employee is nearly double that of the industry average. It also provides excellent service. Nine times it has won the industry's triple crown, 1) best on-time performance, 2) fewest lost bags, and 3) fewest passenger complaints in the same month. No competitor has achieved that even once!

These outstanding productivity and service figures result from a well-managed organization that starts with CEO Herb Kelleher and continues with Elizabeth Pedrick Sartain, vice president of the people department, and every other Southwest employee. Herb Kelleher is famous for his strong belief that people make the difference, and it's in how you manage that makes that difference. Southwest Airlines has a sustainable competitive advantage over its rivals, and this advantage comes from its approach to managing human resources.[2]

To learn more about Southwest Airlines visit the company home page at **www.iflyswa.com**

THE STRATEGIC IMPORTANCE OF HUMAN RESOURCES

Successful leaders see human resources as assets that need to be managed conscientiously and in tune with the organization's needs. Tomorrow's most competitive organizations are working now to ensure they have available tomorrow and a decade from now employees who are eager and able to address competitive challenges. Increasingly this means attracting superior talent and then stimulating employees to perform at peak levels. Analyzing the evolutionary changes in our economy since the dawn of the industrial revolution, economist Lester C. Thurow has shown that competitive success has become increasingly dependent on human resources—and in particular, the intellectual resources that people bring to their work. "Consider what are commonly believed to be the seven key industries of the next few decades— microelectronics, biotechnology, the new materials industries, civilian aviation, telecommunications, robots plus machine tools, and computers plus software. All are brainpower industries."[3] If brainpower drives the business, attracting and keeping great talent becomes a necessity—even for nonprofit organizations and companies in industries other than the seven referred to by Thurow.

Gaining and Sustaining Competitive Advantage

A firm has a competitive advantage when all or part of the market prefers the firm's products and/or services. Because competition is the name of the game, companies seek ways to compete that can last a long time and cannot easily be imitated by competitors. That is, they seek to gain a sustainable competitive advantage.[4] Firms can establish a competitive advantage in many ways: Wal-Mart Stores uses rapid market intelligence so that the right products are always available in the right amounts. McDonald's Corporation enters into agreements with shopping mall developers to secure prime locations in their facilities. Au Bon Pain and Starbucks negotiate special supplier arrangements to ensure that they receive some of the best coffee beans. Mrs. Fields Corporation has a great information system that enables the firm to carefully monitor and enhance the service of each store outlet on a daily basis.

As part of their strategies, some firms use their approaches to managing human resources to gain a *sustainable competitive advantage*. Exhibit 1.1 illustrates conditions an organization must meet in order to gain sustainable competitive advantage through human resources.

Employees Who Add Value. One means through which employees can add value to the organization is by enhancing customers' perceptions of the products and services their organization has to offer. Investors seek companies with satisfied employees. These investors recognize that satisfied employees result in satisfied customers, especially in the services sector. Managers and employees who hate their jobs can't give the best possible service to customers. Conversely, when customers are happy, employees feel a sense of pride and satisfaction at being part of the company.[5]

Employees Who Are Rare. To be a source of sustainable competitive advantage, human resources must also be rare. If competitors can easily access the same pool of talent, then that talent provides no advantage against competitors. By being an employer of choice, organizations can gain access to the best available talent. In other words, "The Best Get the Best." And by managing that talent well, employers can further enhance their advantage.

The general public pays attention to whether a company has a good reputation for effectively managing its human resources. Books and articles that purport to identify the "best" places to work are especially popular among students graduating from college, who view firms high in the rankings as desirable places to land their first post-graduation job. Dissatisfied workers

"At other places managers say that people are their most important resource, but nobody acts on it. At Southwest, they have never lost sight of the fact."

Alan S. Boyd
Retired Chairman
Airbus North America

"The company views each employee's performance strategically as a means to help Chaparral gain competitive advantage."

Gordon E. Forward
President
Chaparral Steel Company

"If we treat employees the right way, they'll naturally treat our customers the right way."

Elizabeth Pedrick Sartain
VP of the People Department
Southwest Airlines

Exhibit 1.1
Gaining a Sustainable Competitive Advantage Through Human Resources

Resources for Gaining a Sustainable Competitive Advantage Must Be:	Implications for Managing Human Resources
A Source of Value	Employees have a positive impact on the way customers perceive the organization's products and services. For example, they • Offer excellent services • Generate innovative ideas for new products • Serve as ambassadors of goodwill Employees help the firm gain access to other resources that can be used for competitive advantage. For example, they • Recruit other excellent talent • Help the organization understand and gain access to new markets Employees facilitate organizational change and adaptation. For example, they • Anticipate major environmental changes in advance of others • Are capable of making rapid changes
Rare	Employees have unusually high levels of technical knowledge and skill. Employees have unusually high levels of organization-specific knowledge. For example, they • Understand the organization as a total system • Know the organization's history and are unlikely to repeat mistakes Employees are committed to the organization and highly motivated to contribute to its success.
Difficult to Copy	All aspects of managing human resources fit together to provide a clear, consistent guide for behavior. Authentic attitudes, values, and habits guide behavior more than do rulebooks and manuals. Approaches to managing human resources represent solutions created by the organization to address its specific needs.

■■□ *fast fact*

Portfolio investment managers rank attracting and retaining talented employees as the fifth of 39 most important factors when deciding where to invest.

who are looking for better employment situations read these lists too. Over time, a good reputation for attracting, developing, and keeping good talent acts like a magnet drawing the best talent to the firm.

When Lincoln Electric Company in Cleveland, Ohio, announced it was planning to hire 200 production workers, it received over 20,000 responses. When BMW Incorporated announced that it had selected Spartanburg, South Carolina as the site for its first U.S. production facility, it received more than 25,000 unsolicited requests for employment. Numbers this large make it more feasible for Lincoln Electric and BMW to hire applicants who are two to three times more productive than their counterparts in other manufacturing firms.

Besides hiring only people who fit Southwest's unique culture, Southwest Airlines makes sure employees understand the company's strategy and are motivated to do every thing possible to achieve outstanding company success. When a gate supervisor was asked what makes Southwest different from other airlines she said, "We're empowered to make on-the-spot decisions. For example, if a customer misses a flight, it's no sweat. We have the latitude to take care of the problem. There's no need for approvals." A profit-sharing program is one reason why Southwest's employees stay focused on the company's performance. An incident in Los Angeles illustrates the point: An agent from another airline asked to borrow a stapler. The Southwest agent went over with the stapler, waited for it to be used, and brought it back. The other agent asked, "Do you always follow staplers around?" The Southwest agent replied, "I want to make sure we get it back. It affects our profit sharing." Setting goals and targets for the performance of the company as a whole and never setting separate departmental goals is another way to insure employees are all pulling together. "At Southwest, we all work toward the same goal, and setting up different goals for different areas is likely to create a schism within the company," he asserts.[6]

Recently, Continental Airlines has begun to look like it could become a serious competitor for Southwest. As described in Managing Change: Continental Goes From Worst to First,[7] a new CEO has adopted an approach to managing human resources that looks a lot like Herb Kelleher's.

A Culture That Can't Be Copied. Business practices that are easy for competitors to copy don't provide sources of sustained competitive advantage. Similarly, a corporate culture that's easily duplicated provides little advantage. The most difficult corporate cultures to copy are those that have evolved over a period to suit the specific needs of the organization. Some companies continually scrutinize their approaches to managing human resources in order to improve continuously. Federal Express Corporation is one such company. Years of relentless attention to how people are managed have helped Federal Express maintain a position of leadership in a highly competitive industry.

In 1990, as the United States' largest express transportation company, Federal Express was the first service company to win the coveted Malcolm Baldrige National Quality Award. Since day one, its basic philosophy of doing business, as stated by founder and Chief Executive Officer Frederick W. Smith, has been People, Service, and Profit. Its motto is 100 Percent Customer Satisfaction. In a business that relies on individuals delivering packages overnight to customers anywhere, 100 percent customer satisfaction comes only from managing human resources as if they really matter. Highlighting its concern for managing human resources, Federal Express formulated a philosophy of managing people based upon these cornerstones

- no layoffs;
- guaranteed fair treatment;
- survey, feedback, action;
- promotion from within;
- profit sharing; and
- an open-door policy.

■□*fast fact*

The Baldrige Award is named for Malcolm Baldrige, who served as Secretary of Commerce from 1981 until his tragic death in a rodeo accident in 1987. His managerial excellence contributed to long-term improvement in efficiency and effectiveness of government.

MANAGING CHANGE

Continental Goes From Worst to First

You know times are bad when even the vice-president of corporate communications admits things like, "This airline was probably, candidly, one of the least-respected airlines in corporate America. It could *not* get any worse than Continental in 1994." Then some mechanics ripped the company logo off their uniforms so that they could run errands after work without being identified as Continental employees. Two years later, Continental was celebrating its highest pretax profits ever. Within four years, it had moved up to third place in *Fortune*'s rankings for the airline industry. How did the company do it? With the leadership of a new CEO whose battle cry was "From worst to first." The Go Forward plan set out the following strategic goals.

1. *Fly to win.* The goal was to achieve top-quartile industry margins.
2. *Fund the future.* To do so required reducing interest expense by owning more hub real estate.
3. *Make reliability a reality.* Specific goals included ranking among the top airlines on the four measurements used by the U.S. Department of Transportation (DOT).
4. *Working together.* Have a company where employees enjoy working and are valued for their contributions.

When Gordon Bethune took over as CEO, he let nearly every vice president go. That's one way to reduce resistance to change! Eventually, some 7,000 of the 40,000 employees were cut, leaving the others a bit concerned. But Bethune was not just cutting costs, he was also trying to change a culture. "No matter what [the old] management told employees they were supposed to do, it was a pretty fair guess it was a lie," he explained. To signal that a new future lay ahead, the 800-page corporate policy manual was hauled out to a parking lot and set aflame with a torch as employees, managers, and executives watched. Burning a policy manual was a good way to embark on a change process, but it was just a beginning. Specific goals, linked to specific rewards, were what made the strategy meaningful.

In 1995, one goal was to be ranked in the top five of the DOT on-time performance ratings. For each month the goal was reached, employees would earn an extra $65. Two months later, Continental was in first place. The next year, the goal and the reward were changed. Now employees could earn $100 for each month the company ranked first and $65 for each month it ranked second or third. These goals and rewards were still in place as of 1998. Executives have goals and associated rewards, too. Employees regularly rate their managers on an employee survey. How well does the manager communicate the plan to employees? Does the manager treat employees with respect and dignity? An outside consulting group analyzes the results and executives' bonuses reflect their performance.

Performance measured against these goals isn't the only type of information given to employees. In a complete shift from the past, the company now disseminates data about baggage handling performance, on-time performance, complaints, and stock performance daily. The data are faxed to 350 locations, e-mailed to 2,000 locations, and available through voice mail from any location an employee happens to be. Though not yet perfect, Continental is proud of the fact that its customer satisfaction was high enough in 1997 to earn it the number one spot among major airlines for flights of 500 or more miles and the "Airline of the Year" title from a leading industry magazine. Besides that, wages went up; and sick leave, turnover, workers' compensation, and on-the-job injuries all went down.

To learn more about Continental Airlines, visit the company's home page at **www.flycontinental.com**

The company also has a pay-for-knowledge program, which is based on interactive video training and job knowledge testing for its 35,000 customer-contact employees. Before couriers ever deliver a package, they receive at least three weeks of training. Because Federal Express is constantly making changes or additions to its products and services, it also must continually update its training programs. Employees at hundreds of Federal Express locations around the United States can readily access a 25-disk training curriculum that covers topics such as customer etiquette and defensive driving. Customer-contact employees take a job knowledge test every six months; the company pays each employee for four hours of study and preparation and for two hours of test taking. The knowledge required to do well on the test is so job related that performance on the test essentially reflects performance on the job. As an incentive for employees to get serious about doing well on the test, the company links their compensation to performance on the test. Employees who excel in applying their knowledge to job performance become eligible for additional proficiency pay. Federal Express dedicates an enormous amount of time, money, and effort to managing its human resources because it knows that doing so gives it an edge over its competitors when it comes to satisfying customers. By continuously changing and improving various practices within its human resource management system, Federal Express strives to stay ahead of competitors who might try to copy its system, thereby maintaining its competitive advantage.[8]

Like Southwest Airlines, Federal Express has developed a complex and integrated system of human resource practices, all designed to keep employees focused on the needs of customers and the business. Its system was not simply copied intact from another company, nor did the firm develop it by applying some formula that could guarantee a correct solution. Rather, through a period of many years, Federal Express developed its own unique philosophy, policies, and practices. Like national cultures, the corporate cultures at both Southwest Airlines and Federal Express are difficult for outsiders to fully understand, and thus they're nearly impossible to copy.

The Best Places to Work Are the Best Places to Invest

As indicated in the description of Southwest Airlines, business analysts pay attention to how people are being managed. Their judgments of a company's current and future success take into account many aspects of effective human resource management. For example, the *Fortune* magazine's annual ratings of America's "Most Admired Companies" considers *the ability to attract, develop, and keep talented* people a primary performance dimension, along with long-term investment value, financial soundness, use of corporate assets, quality of products and services, innovation, quality of management, and community and environmental responsibility.[9] The *Fortune* staff conducts extensive interviews with employees in order to evaluate the best companies to work for.

Do companies with happy workers also make shareholders happy? To determine just how important happy workers were for achieving higher shareholder returns, *Fortune*'s research staff studied the 61 publicly traded firms on their 1987 list of 100 Best Companies to Work For in America. They compared shareholder returns for the 100 Best to that of the Russell 3000, an index that includes comparable companies. Looking at returns five and ten years out (1992 and 1997), they concluded that investing in their Best Companies increased wealth substantially more than investing in the Russell

3000, on average. Over the five-year time period, the Best Companies averaged annual returns of 27.5 percent, compared to 17.3 percent for the Russell 3000. A similar pattern emerged for the ten-year time frame. The bottom-line? If you invested $1,000 in the Russell 3000 in 1987, you would have had $3,976 in 1997, but if you had invested the same amount in the Best Companies to Work For, you would have had $8,188 by 1997—more than twice as much.[10]

From the mid-1980s to the mid-1990s, large-scale research projects generated substantial evidence linking human resource management practices to bottom-line profitability and productivity gains. To help draw attention to this evidence, in 1993, the U.S. Department of Labor summarized much of it in a report titled *High Performance Work Practices and Firm Performance.*[11] For example, one study involved asking thousands of employees to describe their job and their organizations. The responses were used to form an index to reflect how much emphasis was placed on human resources. The research results showed a strong association between profitability and emphasizing human resources, as measured by average return on assets over a five-year period.[12] An international study focusing on 62 automobile plants, 18 located in North America, also demonstrated the importance of managing human resources. This study found a strong relationship between productivity and systematically integrating human resources management with a flexible production system (e.g., coordinating recruitment practices, the use of work teams, job rotations, training, and compensation). For similar vehicles produced in plants with similar technology, the use of modern integrative approaches to managing human resources resulted in faster production and higher quality.[13] Several other recent studies also have shown that the approaches companies take to managing their human resources can translate into greater profitability, higher annual sales per employee (productivity), higher market value, and higher earnings-per-share growth.[14]

MULTIPLE STAKEHOLDERS SHAPE HOW ORGANIZATIONS MANAGE HUMAN RESOURCES

Managers have many responsibilities that engage them in a wide range of activities. One way to organize these activities is according to the groups of people who are affected by the decisions made by managers and the actions they take. That is, a manager's job can be thought of as a series of attempts to address the concerns of multiple stakeholders.[15]

Stakeholders are individuals or groups that have interests, rights, or ownership in an organization and its activities. Stakeholders who have similar interests and rights are said to belong to the same stakeholder group. Customers, suppliers, employees, and strategic partners are examples of stakeholder groups, as illustrated in Exhibit 1.2. Each stakeholder group has an interest in how an organization performs and is interdependent with it. These stakeholder groups can benefit from a company's successes and can be harmed by its failures and mistakes. Similarly, the organization has an interest in maintaining the general well being and effectiveness of these stakeholder groups. If one or more of the stakeholder groups were to break off their relationships with the organization, the organization would suffer.

For any particular organization, some stakeholder groups may be relatively more important than others. The most important groups—the primary stakeholders—are those whose concerns the organization must address in order to ensure its own survival. Customers, employees, shareholders, and

Exhibit 1.2

Organizational Stakeholders and Examples of Their Concerns

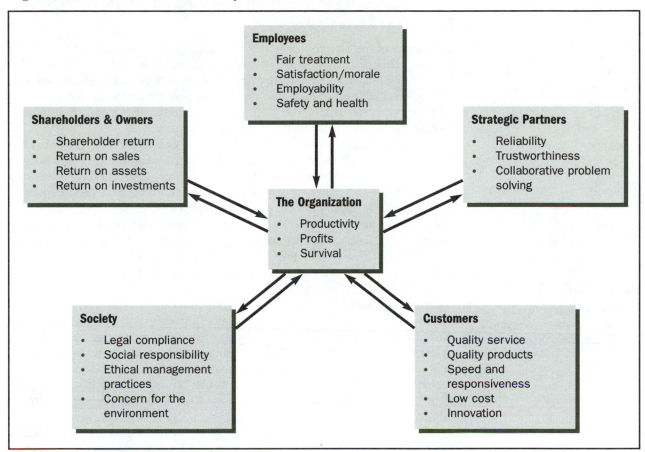

society are primary stakeholders for most U.S. companies. Secondary stake-holders are also important because they can take actions that can damage—but not destroy—the organization. Public opinion leaders, political action groups, and the media are secondary stakeholders for many organizations.[16] When success is defined as effectively serving the interests of these groups, their needs define a firm's fundamental objectives. These objectives, in turn, drive the organization's approaches to managing employees. Thus, under-standing the concerns of various stakeholder groups is essential to effective-ly managing human resources.

Each group of stakeholders has somewhat different concerns, and each organization weighs these concerns somewhat differently. In general, how-ever, many observers believe that we are in a period of transition—or per-haps a revolution. Executives who once enjoyed enormous autonomy and wielded considerable personal power in running their companies now focus increasingly on maximizing shareholder value. Companies that once attend-ed little to customers now find that in almost every industry it's a buyers' market, and sellers have become captives of the customer. Employers who once acted as if they were in charge of the employment relationship are now so desperate for good people that they're beginning to let employees decide where company offices should be located, what hours they'll work, and under what conditions.[17] This new model of business activity is sometimes referred to as "stakeholder capitalism."[18]

Owners and Shareholders

Most owners and shareholders invest their money in companies for financial reasons. This is true for both privately held and publicly traded firms. It's true for owners employed by the firm as well as those whose investment is limited to stock ownership. At a minimum, owners and shareholders want to preserve their capital for later use. To achieve this goal, their capital should be invested primarily in profitable companies.

During the past decade, the majority of publicly traded shares have moved from the hands of individual investors to institutional investors, who trade on behalf of individuals.[19] Because the job of institutional investors is to make money by choosing which companies to invest in, their perspective on corporate issues is to make profit generation the firm's top priority. This has become increasingly complex as intangible and difficult-to-measure assets—which include such things as reputation, brand recognition, employee talent and loyalty, and the company's ability to innovate and change—become increasingly important to success.

The value of most intangibles doesn't appear on a balance sheet. Yet, as described earlier in this chapter, intangibles such as how employees feel and behave can be used to predict financial performance. Susan M. Smith knows this from experience. She was "vice president of knowledge-based industries" for four years at Royal Bank of Canada and subsequently became CEO of Royal Bank Growth Company, one of the lead bankers for knowledge-based companies. "It truly is a new economy," she says, "and the rules aren't written. We have to learn as we go and lend based on intellectual and intangible assets."[20]

Creating systematic rules to apply in order to estimate in dollar terms the value of investments such as training and long-term efforts to change an organization's culture is a topic of increasing interest to accountants. Until such rules are developed however, investors and shareholders must rely on their own judgments of how well a company manages its intangible assets. In organizations such as investment banks, consulting firms, and advertising agencies, there is almost nothing there except intangible human assets. Investing in these companies often means buying a customer list, some product brands, and to a large extent the hope that the best people working there will stay and invest their talents.[21] As one study of initial public offering (IPO) companies showed, companies that attend to human resource management issues are rewarded with more favorable initial investor reactions as well as longer-term survival.[22]

Investors' judgments about the value of intangible assets often are informed by analyzing reputation rankings, such as those published by business magazines, and by considering other forms of the public recognition for excellence. For example, the Catalyst Award is given to organizations with outstanding initiatives that foster women's advancement into senior management. In 1998, Catalyst conferred the award on Procter & Gamble and Sara Lee, noting that these companies understand the bottom-line business reasons for tapping into women's talents. Another form of recognition for excellence in managing human resources is receipt of an Optima Award, sponsored by *Workforce* magazine. In 1998, Trident Precision Manufacturing received the Optima Award for Financial Impact. The award recognized the company's success in using better recruitment methods, increased training, employee involvement, and numerous other approaches to managing human resources to increase productivity 73 percent and quadruple revenue over a ten-year period.[23]

Customers

As Southwest Airlines, Federal Express, and others have found, improving customer satisfaction is a primary means through which human resource management practices affect success. Reducing costs and improving product quality are two ways we generally think of improving customer satisfaction. But, as many companies have now learned, customers react to more than just these.[24]

Exhibit 1.3 shows the results from a study of 1,936 customers who purchased goods and services from five different service companies. When asked to allocate 100 points to the five characteristics shown in the exhibit, on average, customers gave only 11 points to the tangible product or service (e.g., the food purchased or the report delivered). The remaining points were allocated to characteristics that more directly reflect the interactions with service providers.[25] With nearly 80 percent of current U.S. gross domestic product (GDP) being generated in the service sector, few companies can be satisfied with this situation.

■□ *fast fact*

Averaging only seven hours per employee per year, the retail industry spends less on training than all other business sectors.

Exhibit 1.3
Customer Satisfaction Ratings of Service Components

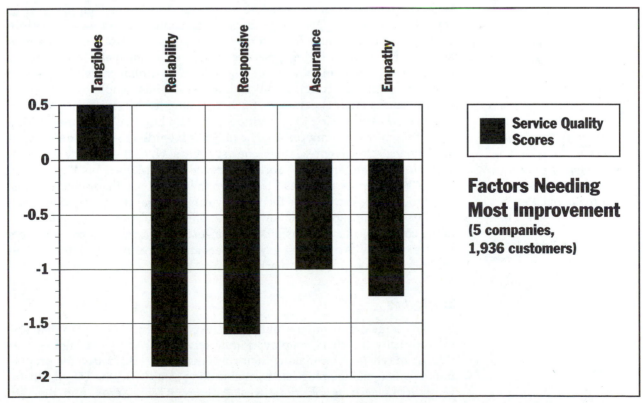

Service Quality Scores

Factors Needing Most Improvement
(5 companies, 1,936 customers)

Service companies win or lose during the time of contact between employees and customers. This time of contact is now referred to by many people as the moment of truth—a coin phrased by Jan Carlzon, as he was writing about his experiences as CEO and Chairman of Scandinavia Airlines System.[26] The moment of truth, it turns out, is often the moment when customers get a glimpse of how a firm manages its human resources. When the internal climate of the organization is positive, with employees generally getting along well and not leaving the company at too rapid a pace, customers report they're more satisfied and intend to return.[27]

Because frontline employees—such as the Federal Express delivery people, the attendants at Disney's theme parks, the sales clerks at Nordstrom, or the flight attendants of Southwest Airlines—are so important to service delivery, some experts have argued that service companies should be literally turned upside down. Service providers should control important decisions, and everyone else should provide secondary support. Marketing campaigns, operations management systems, and practices for managing human resources should all be coordinated with customers' needs in mind.[28]

For many organizations, addressing the concerns of their customers or clients means using total quality management (TQM) principles to improve the quality of products while keeping costs in check. TQM efforts engage both external customers who purchase the product or service and internal customers from other departments in continuously finding solutions to quality problems. These programs extend throughout the entire company and frequently involve suppliers as well as customers.

Even when customers aren't involved in helping solve quality problems, a company may find that addressing customers' concerns requires finding ways to improve the company's ability to communicate with customers and understand their perspective. Recognizing that being able to communicate with customers is fundamental to satisfying them, some employers see human resource management practices as the solution to improved communication with customers. In particular, they see hiring practices as a key to success. Through its hiring practices, a company can make sure that the employees in the company are demographically similar to customers. The assumption is that communication improves when employees and customers share similar experiences. Such reasoning led Mark Willes, chairman of the Times Mirror Co., to pay editors partly on how well they meet hiring goals for women and minorities. The policy is intended to increase the diversity of perspectives represented in newspapers such as the *Los Angeles Times*, the *Baltimore Sun*, and New York's *Newsday*. He explained his logic as follows, "When our readers read the paper, they don't see themselves. People want to feel like the paper's theirs. They can't do that if it's a fundamentally white-male newspaper."[29] American Express has a similar view of how to better communicate with customers. To insure that gay and lesbian investors feel welcomed, it's recruiting gay planners and educating its advisers about the special needs of the gay market.[30]

"If a company depends on employees for a competitive advantage, you've got to create an environment to attract people from all segments of the population."

**Jim Porter
Vice President for Human Resources
Honeywell**

Employees

In many large organizations, employees express their concerns to management directly. In others, employees may rely heavily on union representatives as the channel for making their concerns known. Although the proportion of union membership has been shrinking steadily in the U.S. for many years, firms such as GE, Southwest Airlines, AT&T, Xerox, and the U.S.

automakers look to the unions for joint discussion on issues such as productivity gains, the quality of working life, and outsourcing. Unions still play a vital role in companies that strive to be globally competitive and profitable, as described in detail in Chapter 15. Regardless of whether employees inform their employers through informal conversations or through union representatives, the concerns they're likely to mention include pay and benefits, quality of work life, security, and the impact of work on family life.

Pay and Benefits.   Pay is one area of concern to many employees. Not only do employees want to be paid well, they want to be paid fairly. The desire to receive equal pay for equal work is among the most important workplace issues, according to a national survey of 40,000 women. The *Equal Pay Act of 1963* makes it illegal to pay men and women differently for doing equivalent work. Nevertheless, many women feel that their employers don't live up to the principle on which this law is based. Of nearly equal importance were a desire for secure and affordable health insurance, paid sick leave, and assured pension and retirement benefits. Some people were surprised that child-care issues were considerably less important than these other concerns for the majority of women surveyed.[31] Progressive companies monitor the concerns of their employees and recognize that meeting such concerns is a responsibility they should take seriously.

Quality of Work Life.   Besides earning a good living, many employees also want to enjoy a good quality of life while on the job. Starbucks' CEO Howard Schultz grew up knowing his father felt beaten down by his work. At Starbucks, Schultz strives to make sure that workers have self-esteem no matter what the nature of their jobs. Providing a stock option program and generous health insurance benefits for everyone—even part-timers—are part of the strategy.[32] Many aspects of human resource management contribute to a good quality of work life, including

- training and development to improve employees' skills and knowledge,
- job designs that allow employees to really use their knowledge and skills,
- management practices that give employees responsibility for important decisions,
- selection and promotion systems that ensure fair and equitable treatment,
- safe and healthy physical and psychological environments, and
- work organized around teams.

Such practices increase employee commitment, satisfaction, and feelings of empowerment, which in turn result in greater customer satisfaction.[33] In general, cultures characterized by greater employee involvement and participation generate higher returns on sales and investments in subsequent years.[34]

Security.   In addition to wanting to feel respected and respectable, many of the concerns that employees have today reflect changes in the structure of organizations and the fact that work is a major activity in their lives. During the past decade, the changing economy and its effects on the workplace have introduced tremendous uncertainty creating feelings of insecurity and anxiety for employees and their families. When IBM restructured its organization in the early 1990s, it terminated more than 100,000 employees, many at the middle management level. The company had long been known for its

"Our policies say that all requests from employees deserve due consideration and should not be rejected without a full review process."

Daniel Burger
President
DuPont—Europe

"The relationship we have with our people and the culture of our company is our most sustainable competitive advantage."

Howard Schultz
CEO
Starbucks Corp.

policy of job security, so employees were shocked when IBM replaced some of its managers with temporary people hired to finish ongoing projects. Just as the economy was absorbing the shock of layoffs at IBM, AT&T announced that it expected to lay off 40,000 employees. Like IBM, AT&T had been known for job security. Employees felt betrayed, and the media vilified AT&T's CEO Bob Allen (who eventually resigned). In the end there were fewer layoffs than he had originally announced. Many people believe that Allen decided against laying off so many people because of the public's adverse reaction. It sent a clear message that laying off so many people was ethically untenable.

After more than a decade of corporate restructuring and the layoffs that often follow, there are few U.S. employees left who feel a sense of job security. In fact, now many employers spend time and energy making sure employees aren't misled into expecting job security. In place of job security, companies like IBM now strive to develop a sense of security by helping employees develop the skills and knowledge they need to be employable should they lose their current job and providing outplacement assistance when appropriate.

Work and Family.   For employees who move to other countries as part of their job, almost all aspects of their work and personal lives become areas of concern. As companies expand globally, helping expatriate employees and their families deal successfully with issues such as spousal employment, housing arrangements, schooling for children, tax filings, and a host of other daily concerns suddenly becomes a strategic imperative.[35] Increasingly, organizations are finding that even domestic employees look to employers for help in dealing with personal and family issues. No longer can organizations assume that employees' concerns are limited to pay, job security, and working conditions.[36]

Society

For organizations such as public schools, nonprofit foundations, and government agencies, the concerns of owners—that is, taxpayers and contributors—often are essentially those of society at large. But for privately owned companies and those whose shares are publicly traded, the concerns of owners—that is, shareholders—may be quite different from those of society in general. When a large employer in a community is forced to downsize because of declining sales and profits, the organizational change can affect the entire community. Eastman Kodak, headquartered in Rochester, New York, was the biggest employer in the region and the country's best known name in photography. But when its main competitor, Tokyo-based Fuji, reduced the price of its color film by as much as 30 percent, Kodak's profits plummeted. To cut costs, Kodak announced that it would reduce its workforce by more than 10,000 people worldwide. Worried about job security, some of the 34,000 local employees cut back on their lunches at local restaurants, and when they did go to lunch they brought fewer smiles with them. CEO George Fisher, who had been praised for his pro-growth strategy just a few years earlier, acknowledged the pain: "The anxiety that we create when we do things like we're doing is immense, and you can't help but generate some degree of ill will."[37] Many legal regulations are intended to insure some balancing of stakeholder interests. In addition, some companies make a point of addressing basic societal concerns even when this isn't required by law and perhaps even reduces profitability.

"One thing that surprised me was how involved you get with an employee's family and personal life. Employees look to HR to know about all things that affect their families."

Jeanne Dennison
HR Director, International
Telecommunications Group
Bell Atlantic

Legal Compliance.   Codes of conduct for some aspects of business behavior take the form of formal laws, and many of these have implications for managing human resources. In addition, businesses are subject to regulation through several federal agencies and various state and city equal employment commissions and civil rights commissions. Finally, multinational corporations (MNCs) must be aware of the employment laws in other countries. By complying with legal regulations, firms establish their legitimacy and gain acceptance and support from the community. Ultimately, they increase their chances for long-term survival.[38] Because they affect virtually all human resource management activities, many different laws, regulations, and court decisions are described throughout this book, beginning with an overview in Chapter 3.

Community Relations.   Formal laws and regulations establish relatively clear guidelines for how society expects a company to behave, but effective companies respond to more than simply the formal statements of a community's expectations. The most effective companies understand that the enactment of formal laws and regulations often lags behind public opinion by several years. Indeed, unless a community's most strongly held values are being violated, legal restrictions are unnecessary. Long before legislation is agreed to, communities communicate their expectations and attempt to hold organizations accountable for violations of those expectations. In turn, proactive organizations stay attuned to public opinion and use it as one source of information that may shape their own management practices. With heightened public interest in corporate social responsibility, many companies are discovering that they can't avoid having people evaluate how well they perform in this respect.[39]

A commitment to community involvement and development can have major implications for managing human resources, because often voluntary labor is a community's biggest need. For example, Walt Disney World employees also serve as teachers to students who take on-site classes to learn about leisure and entertainment industries. At Epcot Teachers' Center, schoolteachers learn to use entertainment and communication techniques to improve student learning.[40] UPS recently celebrated the 30th anniversary of its Community Internship Program, a four-week program in which managers live in poor neighborhoods while working in soup kitchens and women's shelters. One of the most ambitious volunteer programs—one which often serves as a benchmark for other companies—is the We Are Volunteer Employees (WAVE) program, supported by the Fannie Mae and Freddie Mac Foundation. Key components of this program are described in Exhibit 1.4.[41] Clearly, being socially responsive in these and other ways has many implications for managing human resources. Among its impacts are

- the type of employees the company chooses to hire,
- the criteria used to evaluate their performance,
- the scheduling and coordinating of activities within work units, and
- compensation practices associated with paying employees for time spent in the community.

To encourage companies to become involved in their communities, in 1997 the federal government established the Ron Brown Award for Corporate Leadership, which rewards leadership in employee and community relations. Named after the late Secretary of Commerce, who died in an airplane accident while on government business in Bosnia, the Ron Brown Award

■□*fast fact*

On average, volunteers serving in formal programs donate an average of 4.2 hours per week.

Exhibit 1.4
The WAVE Program

Key Components of the

We Are Volunteer Employees (WAVE) Program

• Volunteer matching service that helps employees connect with volunteer opportunities
• Group projects that are coordinated by "issues" committees (e.g., AIDS/HIV, homelessness)
• Corporatewide and regional recognition programs
• "Dollars for Doers" grants that match the hours employees work with donations for the agencies they serve
• Team building for executives based on volunteer service
• 10 hours paid leave time per month for volunteer activities

To learn more about Fannie Mae, visit
www.fanniemae.com

To learn more about Freddie Mac, visit
www.freddiemac.com

complements the Malcolm Baldrige National Quality Award. The Ron Brown Award defines excellence in terms of three basic principles, namely

• top management must demonstrate commitment to corporate citizenship,
• corporate citizenship must be a shared value of the company that's visible at all levels, and
• corporate citizenship must be integrated into a successful business strategy.

When evaluating companies, a select committee of judges looks for employee and community centered programs that meet five criteria.

• The programs are distinctive, innovative, and effective. They represent "best practices" when compared to competitors.
• They have had a significant, measurable impact on the people they were designed to serve.
• The programs offer broad potential for social and economic benefits for U.S. society.
• They're sustainable and feasible within a business environment and mission.
• They can be adapted to other businesses and communities.

The Ron Brown Award encourages business leaders to move away from the traditional, utilitarian model of business and take a more proactive stance with respect to contributing to society. Rather than deny their social responsibility, or resist it by doing the least possible amount, many companies are choosing to do everything that's required and to look for areas in which they can do even more.

Preserving the Environment.   For many industries, being profitable while addressing society's need for a healthy environment has been a difficult challenge. For those that depend on the environment to sustain their businesses, meeting this challenge is a strategic imperative. Companies such as 3M, McDonald's, Kodak, Volvo, and many of the leading chemical companies now include principles of industrial ecology in their strategic plans. For example, 3M's strategic policy formalizes the company's commitment to

- solve its own pollution and conservation problems beyond compliance requirements;
- prevent pollution at the source, whenever possible;
- conserve natural resources through waste reclamation and other methods;
- assist regulatory and government agencies concerned with environmental activities; and
- develop products that have a minimal negative effect on the environment.

If a company commits to being environmentally friendly, what are the implications for managing human resources? At Patagonia, a company that designs and manufactures specialty sportswear, social responsibility and activism seem to be more important than financial success. A recent visit to Patagonia's home page revealed that the company wanted to fill two positions: Director of Supply Chain Integration and Internet Program Manager. Hundreds of possible job applicants could have the technical skills and managerial competencies needed for these jobs, but how many would fit this description: "Demonstrated Environmental Activism is a requirement"? And as long as founder and entrepreneur Yvon Chouinard is still around, that's not likely to change at this privately held company. Chouinard spends most of his time far away from the company, leaving day-to-day management tasks to professional managers who have been carefully screened to ensure that their values are in line with those of the activist founder. A CFO who thinks the bottom line is all she needs to worry about might find it difficult to adjust to working in a company that's used as a tool for social change.

For years, Patagonia did extremely well, growing steadily to reach $24 million in annual sales by the mid-1980s. Then it quickly tripled in size. Chouinard had set a goal of $250 million in annual sales because he wanted more funds in order to pursue his social causes. To encourage growth, he seemed to hire everyone he met whose values fit the company's goal, despite warnings from his professional management team. Eventually, the financial problems mounted to a point where they could no longer be ignored. In 1991, Patagonia was forced to lay off 20 percent of its workforce and Chouinard was forced to rethink his approach to business. Could a company that wants to make the best quality outdoor clothing in the world become the size of Nike? Was the idea of improving the environment incompatible with manufacturing clothing—when the process of producing such goods is itself a process that pollutes the environment? Which is the more socially responsible course of action: trying to use a business to lead the process of change or getting out of business altogether?

Back in 1991, Chouinard spent several months thinking long and hard about questions such as these. In the end, he decided to stay in business and continue to use Patagonia as a tool for creating change. He also committed his company to a course of action that was intended to ensure the company's survival for another 100 years. It dropped 30 percent of its clothing lines, reduced its advertising, and began making major changes in its manufacturing processes. Because Chouinard owns Patagonia, he can run the company in a way that's consistent with his values and passion for the environment, even if doing so means being somewhat inefficient. Nevertheless, some people wonder whether Patagonia can continue to stay in business as a clothes manufacturer and, at the same time, have a net positive impact on the environment.[42]

Opposition to Corporate Social Spending.   In the U.S. economic system, the principles of capitalism have long defined the social contract that governs business decisions. Under capitalism, the primary managerial obligation is to maximize shareholders' profits and their long-term interests. Nobel Prize-winning economist Milton Friedman is probably the best-known advocate of this approach.[43] Friedman argues that using resources in ways that do not clearly maximize shareholder interests amounts to spending the owners' money without their consent—and is equivalent to stealing. According to Friedman, a manager can judge whether a decision is right or wrong by considering its consequences for the company's economic needs and financial well being. If it improves the financial bottom line it's right, but if it detracts from the financial bottom line, it's wrong. Thus, for example, a company would be justified in hiring long-term welfare recipients if an analysis showed that this paid off given that government tax incentives and wage subsidies are available. But it could not justify such action simply by asserting it's the right thing to do. Similarly, no firm *unilaterally* should go beyond what the law requires for the sake of helping preserve the environment. Doing so would only reduce that firm's profits and would do nothing to eliminate the pollution caused by its competitors. Some managers apply this logic to all firm activities—even so-called "charitable" contributions. A recent survey of contributions managers found that two-thirds were struggling to show how the company's donations and community service programs contribute to corporate goals.[44]

Many people might agree with Chrysler Chairman Robert Eaton, who says, "The idea of corporations taking on social responsibility is ridiculous. You'll simply burden industry to a point where it is no longer competitive." But the average American rejects the idea that making money is the only role of business. In fact, socially responsible corporations are the more attractive alternative to prospective employees.[45]

THE PARTNERSHIP PERSPECTIVE FOR MANAGING HUMAN RESOURCES

In the U.S., we tend to think of firms as autonomous organizations, with clear boundaries separating one from another. However, as our discussion of how organizations relate to a variety of stakeholders reveals, such an image is overly simplistic. A more realistic image portrays firms as nodes in a web of relationships that link together multiple organizations and their employees, communities, government agencies, unions, and so forth. In the long run, the organization and its stakeholders are highly interdependent. Clearly, the primary concerns of the stakeholder groups differ somewhat, and conflict among stakeholders is common. But shared interests aren't unusual. Effective managers determine the interests of key stakeholders and work with them to find a solution that addresses each set of concerns. They recognize cooperative partnerships with stakeholders benefit both the stakeholder groups and the organization.

Partnership and Stakeholder Satisfaction

By working together in partnership, each helps insure its own future good. For example, even when it's costly in the short-term, paying attention to the concerns of employees is good for business in the long term. When Aaron Feuerstein, owner, president, and CEO of Malden Mills, spent $15 million to pay wages and benefits to 1,000 employees who weren't even working, some observers thought he was acting more like a saint than an intelligent businessman. Malden Mills, located in Lawrence, Massachusetts, suffered a catastrophic fire, forcing the plant to close for several months. Rather than close the old plant permanently, or take the opportunity to move it to a lower cost site, the 70-year-old Feurerstein chose to rebuild the plant and keep his employees on the payroll while the plant was being rebuilt. "Why would I go to Thailand to bring the cost lower when I might run the risk of losing the advantage I've got, which is superior quality?" he asked. Corporate customers—including Land's End, L.L. Bean, Patagonia, and North Face—rely on Malden Mills to manufacture and supply high-tech fabrics created in its R&D labs. This CEO believes that the financial success of his company depends on consistently producing high-quality products, which in turn requires employing superior technology and employees.[46]

Increasingly, a company's access to stockholder capital also will depend on its ability to satisfy multiple stakeholders—including unions! The events leading up to a settlement between the United Steelworkers and Wheeling-Pittsburgh Steel Co. illustrates the point. When steelworkers struck the company, the union put pressure on the company's major stockholders. The source of the influence was its pension funds. Over $10 billion in pension funds were managed by one of the steel company's major stockholders. After this stockholder publicly expressed support for management's position, the union sent a message. They said, "If this is your philosophy, maybe you shouldn't be managing worker money." When the dispute was resolved, the chairman of the company that was managing the pension fund took some credit for encouraging the company to reach a satisfactory agreement with the union.[47]

In the chapters that follow, we argue that approaches to managing human resources can often provide organizations with effective solutions to the problem of how best to align the organization with the concerns of its multiple stakeholders, even when the concerns of different stakeholder groups seem to conflict. For example, shareholder and employee interests often seem to conflict, especially over restructuring and downsizing. Decisions to reduce layers of management or sell off a poorly performing division usually are made to improve efficiency and profitability in order to satisfy shareholders. The employees who lose their jobs in the process are victims of the conflict between their needs for employment and shareholders' desire for financial gain. However, when the compensation system is used to insure that employees are owners themselves, managers and other employees may put more effort into finding a solution that minimizes disruption while also meeting the organization's financial goals.

As another example, consider how an organization's approach to managing human resources can address community concerns. Providing employees with continuous training not only improves immediate job performance, it also prepares the workforce for change and develops employees' confidence in their own abilities to continuously learn new ways of working. Regular employee assessments, feedback, and career management activities provide the information employees need to understand their strengths and weaknesses and to prepare for the future. Such practices improve employees' long-term employability. Ultimately, by developing their employees, employers help ensure that the workforce is employed in good jobs that pay well enough to maintain the high standard of living to which Americans have grown accustomed. Full employment, in turn, gen-

◼☐ fast fact

Union pension holdings, most of which are invested in the stock market, exceed $1.3 trillion.

◼☐ fast fact

Data collected by the U.S. Census Bureau indicate that one out of four employers provide work-based learning experiences for students in their community.

erates tax dollars for the community and reduces the need to spend tax dollars providing for government assistance to residents.

Partnership and Strategic Management Processes

The partnership perspective for managing human resources is consistent with a relatively new, but increasingly popular approach to strategic decision making, organizational performance evaluation, and strategic realignment—the *balanced scorecard*. Using the balanced scorecard approach, companies can begin to shift away from their habit of building operational and management control systems that address financial considerations exclusively. As illustrated in Exhibit 1.5, the balanced scorecard combines financial performance with three other broad areas of concern: customers, internal processes, and the capacity of the organization for learning and growth.[48] Excellent performance in these four domains is presumed to be required in order for any organization to succeed in implementing its stated vision and strategy.

To use the balanced scorecard approach, an organization develops indicators of success in each of the four domains and then assesses itself against these performance indicators. Specific indicators typically reflect the concerns of a variety of stakeholders. Financial indicators typically reflect the shareholders' perspective, and often include measures of revenue growth and mix, cost reduction and productivity improvement, and asset utilization. Core measures often used to assess performance in the customer domain include market share, account share, customer acquisition, customer retention, and customer satisfaction. For the domain of internal business processes, managers identify the internal processes that are most central to their value chain, thus they vary greatly depending on whether the organization competes on the basis of excellent customer service, innovation, providing low cost products and services, and so on. Finally, in the domain of learning and growth would be indicators that tap the organization's capacity for renewal and change. Employee-based measures such as level of satisfaction, retention rates, training opportunities, and skill development usually fall in this domain.

Exhibit 1.5

Performance Indicators Used in the Balance Scorecard Approach

External Performance	
Financial	Objectives, measures, targets, initiatives intended to affect the shareholders' perceptions of the organization's success
Customers	Objectives, measures, targets, initiatives intended to affect customers' perceptions of the organization's success
Internal Performance	
Business Processes	Objectives, measures, targets, initiatives intended to insure the organization excels in the areas of importance to customers
Learning and Growth	Objectives, measures, targets, initiatives intended to insure the organization sustains its ability to change and improve in the future

Identifying the criteria to include in each performance domain is only the first step involved in using the balanced scorecard approach. More important to the success of this approach is understanding how to improve performance on the key indicators once they're identified. Fundamentally, performance improvement in all of these domains involves

- clarifying the organizational vision and gaining consensus around this vision,
- communicating the vision and aligning the behavior of all employees with the vision,
- setting targets, allocating and establishing milestones, and
- using feedback and learning to make adjustments in the system.

These processes, in turn, often have implications for numerous aspects of the organization's approach to managing human resources. As many organizations soon discover, one way or the other, employees turn up at the center of most of the activities involved in implementing the balanced scorecard approach to strategic management and organization performance. Who the company hires, the training they receive, performance goals and the reward systems that motivate performance, performance assessment and feedback systems, executive development strategies—all of these activities can affect customer satisfaction and retention, the value added by internal operations, and the organization's capacity for future growth and learning.

Consider a typical manufacturer who uses employee turnover as one indicator of internal processes. Among U.S. companies, the average annual turnover rate is about 20 percent. There is considerable variation in average turnover rates across industries, however. For example, Trident once took pride in its turnover rate of 41 percent because it was below the industry average of 52 percent. When Thomson, the French electronics company, first set up operations in Juarez, Mexico, turnover at its average factory was about 20 percent *per month*. Despite the relatively low labor costs in the region, managers recognized that this high level of turnover was intolerable because it cut so deeply into productivity. To raise productivity, Thomson focused on lowering turnover. Managers learned to treat employees with respect and break down communication barriers. Employees' skills were upgraded, which gave them greater career advancement opportunities. The company even lobbied Mexican officials to get workers day passes to shop across the border in Texas and to speed up the process of mortgage applications so employees could obtain state-subsidized housing. Within a year, monthly turnover dropped to 6 percent. Juarez can now boast that it's home to Thomson's most efficient factory, producing television sets at four-fifths the cost of its next best plant in France and at half the cost of a plant in Beijing, where labor costs are even lower.[49] Research on hundreds of U.S. companies indicates that Thomson's experience isn't unique. Excellence in managing human resources is central to improving both internal processes and financial performance.[50]

The relationship between HR practices and customer satisfaction is explicit in the guidelines used to evaluate organizations vying for the Malcolm Baldrige National Quality Award. To meet customers' demands for higher quality, companies such as Weyerhaeuser, Southwest Airlines, and Federal Express maintain an environment conducive to full participation and personal and organizational growth for their employees. This is the criterion for human resource utilization used by the committee that determines award recipients. Specific suggestions for how to create this environment are also offered in guidelines. These include:

"U.S. industry viewed Mexico's labor as a cheap input, something for a quick gain. Then you woke up and with this turnover, you realized that the gains you achieved in labor costs were offset with pretty shoddy quality."

Edward Boyd
Plant Manager
Thomson Televisores de Mexico SA

■□ fast fact

Our rate of productivity growth actually fell in the 1970s and 1980s. Recently it has been going up, and U.S. workers are still the most productive in the world.

- Promote cooperation such as internal customer-supplier techniques or internal partnerships.
- Promote labor-management cooperation, such as partnerships with unions.
- Use compensation systems based on building shareholder value.
- Create or modify recognition systems.
- Increase or broaden employee responsibilities.
- Create opportunities for employees to learn and use skills that go beyond current job assignments.
- Form partnerships with educational institutions to develop employees or to help ensure the future supply of well-prepared employees.

A sample of Baldrige National Quality Award finalists was used to examine the change in financial performance of firms after they implemented comprehensive changes in work practices. Altogether, 15 companies considered exemplary in their customer-driven approach to quality, strong leadership, continuous improvement, and employee involvement were analyzed. The adoption of the exemplary practices listed above were associated with better employee relations, improved operating procedures, greater customer satisfaction, and enhanced operating results. The average annual increase in market share after implementing new practices was 13.7 percent. Operating results, such as return on assets and return on sales, improved for all but two of the reporting companies after the adoption of these practices. [51]

Partnership and Corporate Social Responsibility

In addition to adopting a balanced scorecard approach to evaluating their firm's performance, many companies also undertake a social audit. Like the balanced scorecard approach, a *social audit* attempts to identify, measure, evaluate, report on, and monitor performance using information not covered in traditional financial reports.[52] Whereas the balanced scorecard focuses attention on the concerns of stakeholders who most organizations consider to be primary, a social audit assesses how well the organization addresses the concerns of stakeholders that many organizations consider secondary. Exhibit 1.6 shows some of the areas assessed by the social audits conducted at firms such as Levi Strauss & Company, AT&T, the Body Shop, McDonald's, and Johnson & Johnson.[53] Used in combination, the balanced scorecard and social audit provide a comprehensive approach to assessing the quality of partnerships an organization maintains with a wide range of stakeholders.

THE HR PARTNERSHIP TRIAD

Managing to Achieve Productivity Engages Everyone

"In many ways, I can't divorce the primary responsibilities of the CEO from the responsibilities of the senior HR person."

**Irv Hockaday
CEO
Hallmark Cards**

Companies like Southwest Airlines draw upon the skills and knowledge of line managers, human resource (HR) professionals, and every other employee. In these firms, the special expertise of HR professionals is used by, and in cooperation with, line managers, other administrative staff, and all first-line employees in every department. In other words, in the best companies, managing human resources is done through partnership.

The responsibility for effectively managing human resources does not rest with those in the human resources department. All company managers are responsible for leading people. No department alone can effectively

Exhibit 1.6
Performance Criteria Considered By Levi Strauss & Company

Stakeholder Group	Examples of Concerns Considered When Assessing Performance
Owners and investors	Financial soundness
	Consistency in meeting shareholder expectations
	Sustained profitability
	Average return on assets over five-year period
	Timely and accurate disclosure of financial information
Customers	Product/service quality, innovativeness, and availability
	Responsible management of defective or harmful products/services
	Safety records for products/services
	Pricing policies and practices
	Honest, accurate, and responsible advertising
Employees	Nondiscriminatory, merit-based hiring and promotion
	Diversity of the workforce
	Wage and salary levels and equitable distribution
	Availability of training and development
	Workplace safety and privacy
Community	Environmental issues
	Environmental sensitivity in packaging and product design
	Recycling efforts and use of recycled materials
	Pollution prevention
	Global application of environmental standards
	Community involvement
	Percentage of profits designated for cash contributions
	Innovation and creativity in philanthropic efforts
	Product donations
	Availability of facilities and other assets for community use
	Support for employee volunteer efforts

manage a company's human resources. So, regardless of whether a line manager ever holds a formal position in human resource management, she or he will be accountable for the task of managing people. There's a saying at Merck that goes like this, "human resources are too important to be left to the HR department." At Merck, fully one-third of every manager's performance evaluation is related to people management."[54]

Line Managers Have Always Been Responsible

In small businesses, the owner must have HR expertise because he or she will be building the company from the ground up. This reality is clearly reflected in the various popular magazines targeted to small-business owners—for example, *Inc., Money, Success,* and *Entrepreneurship.* These publications devote a great deal of space to discussing issues related to managing

■□ fast fact

At Gillette, the CEO personally conducts 800 performance reviews annually.

"Best Management Decision: Appointing the right people. Biggest Management Mistake: Appointing the wrong people."

Richard Goldstein
Unilever, United States CEO

the people who make up a small company. Eventually, as a company grows, the owner may contract out some of the administrative aspects related to managing people (e.g., payroll), or delegate some of the responsibilities to a specialist, or both. As the company grows larger, more specialists may be hired—either as permanent staff or on a contract basis to work on special projects, such as designing a new pay system. As with other business activities, these specialists won't bear all responsibility for the project. For example, many companies have a marketing department; nevertheless, they employ people outside that department to conduct marketing activities. Similarly, most companies have a few people with special expertise in accounting; nevertheless, employees throughout the company perform accounting activities. The same is true for managing human resources.

This book treats managing human resources as a responsibility shared by everyone in the company—line employees *and* professionals in the human resources department *and* top-level executives *and* even entry-level new hires. Consistent with the stakeholder model in Exhibit 1.2, the partnership can even extend to people outside the organization, such as managers in supplier firms, customers, and members of community organizations. Although numerous people are involved in the partnership, the ultimate responsibility is with line managers. Those who recognize the importance of this responsibility work in partnership with HR professionals who have specialized knowledge and skills, as described more extensively in Chapter 16.

HR Professionals Provide Special Expertise

HR professionals refer to people with substantial specialized and technical knowledge of HR issues, laws, policies, and practices. The leaders of HR units and the specialists and generalists staff who work within the function usually are HR professionals, although this isn't always the case. Sometimes organizations fill the top-level HR position with a person who has a history of line experience but no special expertise in the area of HR. According to one survey of 1,200 organizations, this is a growing trend, reflecting increasing recognition of the importance of people to business success. Line managers who are doing a "tour of duty" in the HR department would be appropriately referred to as HR managers, but they would not be considered HR professionals—at least not until they gained substantial experience and perhaps took a few executive development courses devoted to HR. External experts who serve as consultants or vendors for the organization may be HR professionals also. But don't assume that a consultant or vendor is an HR professional on the basis of the products or services he or she offers.

In addition to a record of substantial HR experience, other things that might indicate that a consultant or vendor has special expertise would include a college level degree in the field and/or accreditation from a professional association. For example, the Society for Human Resource Management provides certification for two levels of expertise for HR generalists: basic and senior. The American Compensation Association is an example of a professional organization that provides certification in a specialized area of HR. Whether employed on the staff or hired as a consultant or vendor, HR professionals play many important roles in managing people effectively.

Employees Are Sharing the Responsibility

The responsibilities of line managers and HR professionals are especially great, but partnership involves even more sharing of responsibility.

Employees in an organization, regardless of their particular jobs, share some of the responsibility for effective human resource management. For example, employees commonly write their own job descriptions. Some even design their own jobs. Employees may also be asked to provide input for the appraisal of their own performance or the performance of their colleagues and supervisors, or both. Perhaps most significant, employees assess their own needs and values and must manage their own career in accordance with these. Doing so effectively involves understanding many aspects of their employer's human resource management practices. As we move forward, we all need to position ourselves for the future. For all of us, learning about how effective organizations are managing human resources is an essential step for getting into position.

This theme of partnership, of working together to manage human resources, is highlighted throughout this book in two ways. First, each chapter opens with a feature called Managing Human Resources Through Partnership, which illustrates the partnership perspective at a particular organization. In addition, each chapter includes a feature titled The HR Triad: Partnership Roles

THE HR TRIAD

Partnership Roles and Responsibilities for Managing Human Resources

Line Managers	HR Professionals	Employees
Work closely with HR professionals and employees to develop and implement HR philosophies, policies, and practices.	Work closely with line managers and employees to develop and implement HR philosophies, policies, and practices.	Work closely with line managers and HR professionals to develop and implement HR philosophies, policies, and practices.
Include HR professionals in the formulation and implementation of business strategy.	Stay informed of the latest technical principles for managing human resources.	Accept responsibility for managing their own behavior and careers in organizations.
On a daily basis, consider the implications of business decisions for managing human resources.	Develop the skills and competencies needed to support change processes.	Recognize the need for personal flexibility and adaptability.
Accept shared responsibility for managing human resources strategically and work to reduce barriers to this objective.	On a daily basis, consider how well the organization's approaches to managing human resources fit with its current and possible future business strategies.	Learn about and apply basic accepted principles for managing human resources for HR activities in which they participate (e.g., selecting team members, appraising supervisors, and training coworkers).
Learn about and apply basic accepted principles for managing human resources.	Work with employees to help them voice their concerns effectively, and serve as their advocate when appropriate.	Voice their concerns and work with managers and HR professionals to develop solutions to address them.
	Be proactive in learning about how leading companies are managing human resources, and what they're learning from their experiences.	

and Responsibilities for Managing Human Resources, which summarizes several major roles and responsibilities for the HR partners.

LOOKING AHEAD: RECURRING THEMES

Activities related to managing human resources occur in all companies, from the smallest to the largest. At a minimum, every company has jobs which comprise a set of responsibilities. To get these jobs done, the firm hires people and compensates them in return for the work they do. To hire, the company generally finds that it must recruit a few potential employees and then select among them. Few companies continue to pay a person who cannot or won't perform satisfactorily, so at least some measurement of performance generally occurs—even if it's just to keep track of how many hours were worked. To ensure that people know what they're supposed to do, some instruction and training are usually given, though these may be minimal. Employees' work is carried out in a physical context, which may be plush or dangerous and is increasingly off-site. Their work also occurs in an interpersonal context, which may be informal or governed by an explicit contract. Eventually, of course, employees are dismissed, retire, or simply leave voluntarily. Because no employee stays forever, every company must manage the process of exit.

Although these major activities occur in all organizations that employ a workforce, the specific ways in which they're conducted varies greatly across organizations. Used wisely, human resource management activities can transform a lackluster company into a star performer. Used unwisely, they can create havoc. In some companies, existing approaches to managing human resources reflect chance and happenstance. Instead of analyzing how their HR systems affect all aspects of the business, some organizations continue to do things the same way year after year. Ask why salespeople in the shoe section are paid on commission and people in toys are not, and you are likely to be told, "That's just the way we've always done it." When companies do change the way they manage people, they may do so for the wrong reason. Why did that small retail food chain just send all its middle managers to off-site wilderness training? "Everybody in the industry's doing it—we can't be the only ones who don't." Why did your insurance company start randomly listening in on calls from customers? "The new telecommunications system we installed last year included it as a no-cost feature, so we decided we should use it." Whether a company chooses its human resource practices carefully or somewhat haphazardly, those practices can be powerful influences on behavior.

Managing Strategically

Using input from multiple stakeholders plus thoughtful and systematic analysis, leading organizations are rapidly learning from this experimentation and gaining a competitive advantage. Firms that are relatively successful wisely choose and implement the appropriate human resource activities, policies, and practices. This requires taking a strategic approach. A *strategic approach* has five defining characteristics. It

1. reflects state-of-the-art knowledge,
2. integrates all of the major activities for managing human resources,
3. is tailored for the specific organization,
4. is flexible and responsive to changing conditions, and
5. is evaluated continuously.

State-of-the-Art Knowledge.   As a result of thousands of research studies, we know a great deal about designing effective methods for selecting people, assessing performance, designing training programs, designing pay systems, and implementing other HR activities. This technical information should be the foundation of any organization's HR activities. Employing well-trained HR professionals is one means an organization can ensure that its approaches to managing human resources are technically up-to-date. Until very recently, when organizations began outsourcing all sorts of technical expertise, most large organizations employed HR professionals as members of their core staff. Increasingly, large and small organizations alike rely on external vendors to provide such expertise. In addition, many organizations use benchmarking practices to learn about the most successful approaches used in other organizations. Winners of the Malcolm Baldrige Award for Quality are one excellent benchmarking resource. As a condition for accepting the award, organizations must agree to share their learning experiences as a way of facilitating improvement in other organizations.

Integrated HR Activities.   A strategic approach involves considering how all the specific practices for managing people *together* affect the attitudes and behaviors of employees working in various jobs. Human resource policies and practices that are consistent with each other and coordinated with each other communicate the same message to employees.[55] A performance appraisal system that evaluates employees on the basis of the attainment of long-term goals, coupled with a compensation system that rewards employees on the same basis sends a clear message to employees. On the other hand, a human resource policy that describes employees as the most valuable resource, coupled with constant layoffs and little training sends conflicting messages. Exhibit 1.7 illustrates many of the choices available when designing a system for managing human resources. Consistency across all human resource policies and practices results in consistency and clarity about what is expected, what is rewarded, and what is important.

Tailored to a Specific Organization.   A strategic approach involves taking into account the unique characteristics of the company, including the company's history, top management's goals and the strategies they intend to pursue, the corporate culture, the size of the company and the way it's structured, the technologies people use, and so on. Just as different companies in the same industry can compete for different customers, using different competitive strategies successful firms in the same industry can have rather different human resource activities.[56] For example, Nordstrom is a retail department store that competes on the basis of customer service, whereas Sears, which is in the same industry, competes largely on the basis of low cost and brand names. Although both organizations are successful in the same industry, they have substantially different HR practices and philosophies. They reflect the firms' different approaches to retailing and the needs that result from these.

In firms that manage their employees strategically, managers know why they lead their people the way they do: their entire set of HR practices has been explicitly developed to match the needs of their employees and customers and the strategies of the business. Ideally, the organization's approach to managing human resources has been considered in all strategic discussions.

Flexible and Responsive to Change.   Because so many internal and external elements must be considered when choosing how to manage human

Exhibit 1.7
Choices for Managing Human Resources

Planning Practice Choices

Informal	- - - - -	Formal
Short-Term	- - - - -	Long-Term
Explicit Job Analysis	- - - - -	Implicit Job Analysis
Job Simplification	- - - - -	Job Enrichment
Low Employee Involvement	- - - - -	High Employee Involvement

Staffing Practice Choices

Internal Sources	- - - - -	External Sources
Narrow Paths	- - - - -	Broad Paths
Single Ladder	- - - - -	Multiple Ladders
Explicit Criteria	- - - - -	Implicit Criteria
Limited Socialization	- - - - -	Extensive Socialization
Closed Procedures	- - - - -	Open Procedures

Appraising Practice Choices

Behavioral Criteria	- - - - -	Results Criteria
Purposes: Development, Remedial, Maintenance		
Low Employee Participation	- - - - -	High Employee Participation
Short-Term Criteria	- - - - -	Long-Term Criteria
Individual Criteria	- - - - -	Group Criteria

Compensation Practice Choices

Low Base Salaries	- - - - -	High Base Salaries
Internal Equity	- - - - -	External Equity
Few Perks	- - - - -	Many Perks
Standard, Fixed Package	- - - - -	Flexible Package
Low Participation	- - - - -	High Participation
No Incentives	- - - - -	Many Incentives
Short-Term Incentives	- - - - -	Long-Term Incentives
No Employment Security	- - - - -	High Employment Security
Hierarchical	- - - - -	Egalitarian

Training and Development Practice Choices

Short Term	- - - - -	Long Term
Narrow Application	- - - - -	Broad Application
Productivity Emphasis	- - - - -	Quality-of-Work-Life Emphasis
Spontaneous, Unplanned	- - - - -	Systematic, Planned
Individual Orientation	- - - - -	Group Orientation
Low Participation	- - - - -	High Participation

SOURCE: Adapted from R. S. Schuler, "Human Resource Management Practice Choices," in R. S. Schuler, S. A. Youngblood, and V. L. Huber, eds., *Readings in Personnel and Human Resource Management,* 3rd ed., St. Paul, MN: West Publishing, 1988

resources, there is no "one best way" that will be effective under all circumstances. As conditions change, new approaches to managing human resources may be needed. Changes in labor market conditions, the actions of competitors and strategic partners, new laws or new interpretations of existing laws, union initiatives, and pressure from political action groups may all signal the need for new approaches to managing people. Chapter 2 considers the changing environment in more detail.

Continuously Evaluated. The need for change leads to the fifth defining feature of a strategic approach: continuous evaluation. Like any body of knowledge, our understanding of how to manage people effectively is based on what has worked in the past. As conditions change, some of our knowledge may become obsolete. Thus, a strategic approach must be driven by information and data, from beginning to end. Information and data are gathered before changes are made and used to decide what changes to make; continued monitoring during the change process facilitates midstream adjustments; and after a change is in place, data are used to evaluate the intended and unintended consequences. In other words, a strategic approach ensures that the organization and its employees learn from their mistakes and successes.

The importance of continuous monitoring and evaluation can't be overemphasized. When Sears began its turnaround efforts in 1992, the CEO engaged everyone in the effort. As described in Managing Strategically: A Turnaround at Sears,[57] enthusiasm for the turnaround effort was so great that attention to internal processes distracted employees from serving customers well. Because *managing strategically* is essential to managing human resources effectively, it's illustrated repeatedly throughout this book in the Managing Strategically feature.

MANAGING STRATEGICALLY

A Turnaround at Sears

The 1980s were a decade of declining sales at Sears, but the 1990s seemed to be a much better time for the company. Old rules had been stripped away, and employees had been both empowered and intensively trained. Stock prices rose steadily for three years running, following the appointment of CEO Arthur C. Martinez in 1992. Then, suddenly, Sears' stock prices took a plunge, tumbling almost ten percent. Sluggish sales, flattening customer service ratings, complaints from overworked store managers, and a weak profit picture all led investors to wonder whether the company had lost its focus again. In an interview about how he planned to respond to recent events, Martinez shared his plan. "I want to revisit and intensify the theme of our customer being the center of our universe," he explained. "There will be no new initiatives, no new big ideas." He just wanted to send a clear, simple message.

In recent years, Martinez had learned how difficult it was to communicate even a very simple message. Misunderstandings were common in the company. Random surveys of employees revealed that many thought their main function was to protect the assets of the company, not to be obsessive about customer service. These surveys also revealed that employees knew little about the company's performance. When Sears was earning only two cents on the dollar, many employees thought it was earning fifty or sixty cents on the dollar.

With these facts in hand, Martinez shifted into overdrive in an effort to achieve a key strategic objective: "develop a winning culture." Employees were soon being bombarded with information from headquarters. Training programs intended to teach employees about the company's products and goals mushroomed. The company completely revamped its approach to communicating with employees. Store managers began receiving e-mail messages about everything that was going on in the company, even if it had little relevance to them. Morale improved at first, energizing managers to intensify their customer service efforts. But soon everyone was frustrated by information overload. To make the point that too much information was as bad as too little, one executive went to a meeting pushing a wheelbarrow filled with memos, surveys, videos, and various other communiqués received during the past month.

The point was made. With so many messages flooding the workplace, focusing on the customer had become difficult. According to Anthony Rucci, executive vice president of administration, headquarters promptly responded to the feedback. More than 100 planned initiatives were removed from the 1997 fourth-quarter agenda and e-mail was shut down entirely during the busy holiday season. Consistent with putting customers first, future holiday seasons will be free from surveys, product training sessions, and benefits requiring managers' attendance. Store managers also have been assured that they can respond to mundane messages from headquarters as their time permits.

To learn more about Sears, Roebuck & Company, visit the company's home page at **www.sears.com**

Managing Teams

In a recent study of U.S. and Canadian companies, half the managers responding believed that improving teamwork processes to focus on customers was the strategic initiative with the greatest potential for ensuring their organizations' success.[58] According to a survey conducted by the Conference Board, innovation and on-time delivery were the two most common reasons for the increasing use of work teams. Exhibit 1.8 lists several of the other reasons for organizing employees into work teams instead of having them work on small tasks that they can complete alone.[59]

Exhibit 1.8
Why Organizations Use Work Teams

The Most Common Reasons For Having Employees Work in Teams

- Improve on-time delivery of results
- Improve customer relations
- Facilitate innovation in products and services
- Facilitate management and employee development and career growth
- Reinforce or expand informal networks in the organization
- Improve employees' understanding of the business
- Reduce costs and improve efficiency
- Improve quality
- Increase employee ownership, commitment, and motivation

Signicast Corporation is an example of a company that adopted a team-based organizational design as a strategic move. The company was poised for continued growth, except that it needed more space in order to do so. When management decided to build new facilities, it also rethought the firm's strategy and the logic of its operations. As described in Managing Teams: Signicast Creates a Team-Based Learning Organization, the design of the new facilities was based on utilization of work teams.[60]

The increasing popularity of team-based organizational structures reflects the belief that teamwork can achieve outcomes that could not be achieved by the same number of individuals working in isolation. But as many organizations are discovering, the payoff from teams isn't automatic. Although teams offer great potential for increased innovation, quality, and speed, that potential isn't always realized. Even when teams do fulfill their potential in these areas, team members and their organizations may experience unanticipated negative side effects, such as lingering unproductive conflicts and turnover.[61]

MANAGING TEAMS

Signicast Creates a Team-Based Learning Organization

Headquartered in Milwaukee, Signicast Corporation is a manufacturer of castings. Using the blueprints supplied by customers such as Harley Davidson and John Deere, it manufactures precision metal parts. In 1992, top management decided to build a new facility, which would allow the company to grow. These executives decided not just to replicate the existing plant. Instead, they wanted to design the best facility in the world. To guide their decisions, they first investigated their customers' concerns arising from Signicast's history of long lead times, high costs, and unreliable delivery dates. To respond to these concerns, top management adopted speed, low cost, and flexibility as its strategic goals. Achieving these goals would require that production be switched from the batch process design of the old plant to an automated, continuous-flow process.

To take advantage of the employees' expertise, Signicast's executives involved them in designing the new facilities. A team of five executives would develop an idea and then ask employees to evaluate it and suggest revisions. The employees were volunteers from each department in the Milwaukee facility, and when asked for suggestions they had plenty to say. "Sometimes those meetings would go on for hours," recalled Robert Schuemann, a member of the executive team. "Sometimes there were even multiple meetings to discuss one item. Employees would come up with suggestions; we'd implement them, and bring them back [to employees] for confirmation."

This approach was new to the company, so some learning was expected. Rather than build one huge facility that could handle all the processes and products involved, the company decided to build small modules that could operate independently. The first module has been operating since 1993, and in 1998, the second module was under construction. In the first module, one supervisor oversees the entire plant, which is organized into two day teams and two night teams. Many of the plant's policies and procedures were adopted only after the teams had an opportunity to vote on them. Supporting the new team design are a new pay system that rewards employees for developing a variety of skills, extensive cross-training for technical skills, and a ten-week team-building course that's mandatory for team leaders and open to everyone else.

To learn more about Signicast Corporation visit the company home page at **www.signicast.com**

An organization's human resource management practices can make the difference between success and failure for organizations using teams. To create and orchestrate teams, people need to be selected, appraised, compensated, and trained in ways that reflect the unique relationships that develop between employees who work together. Most companies know—or at least believe—that people working in teams should not be managed just the same as people who work more or less independently. Nevertheless, teamwork really is a somewhat new phenomenon in the American workplace, so considerable experimentation in how best to manage teams is still taking place around the country. Some practices now viewed as experimental will undoubtedly become commonplace within the next decade.

Because teams are rapidly becoming more prevalent in organizations, examples of how organizations are using human resource practices to maximize team effectiveness are highlighted throughout this book in the Managing Teams feature.

Managing Diversity

At about the same time that organizations began to recognize the benefits of teamwork, they discovered that the people who were being put into teams were more diverse than ever before. More and more women are working, for example, resulting in a new gender mix that's nearly balanced instead of being male-dominated. Throughout this century, immigration patterns also have changed, resulting in more diversity in terms of national heritage. In the 1990s, awareness of increasing workforce diversity has grown steadily. A Department of Labor report, *Workforce 2000*, initially drew attention to this issue by highlighting the changing demographics of the U.S. labor force. Then, a follow-up report by the Department of Labor's Glass Ceiling Commission showed that women and non-Caucasian men were advancing up the corporate ladder more slowly than Caucasian men were. In the Big Five accounting firms, for example, women comprise about one-quarter of the workforce, but less than ten percent of partners are women. With approximately equal numbers of men and women now obtaining degrees in accounting, accounting firms are now under considerable pressure to improve these statistics. Failing to do so will greatly impair their appeal as employers for fully one-half of all entry-level accountants.

Many of the approaches to managing people that are prevalent in today's organizations reflect old habits, developed when the workplace was more homogeneous. To the extent diversity was present years ago, different demographic groups were segregated by level in the organization and job categories. Segregation within organizations is declining, albeit slowly, and with this desegregation comes the new challenge of managing workforce diversity. *Workforce diversity* is a general term that refers to the mix of people from various backgrounds in today's labor force. *Demographic diversity* is a more specific term that reflects the degree and mix of characteristics such as age, sex, race, and national origin. An organization that employs mostly high school students or mostly workers who have returned to work from retirement would have very little age diversity. An organization that employs people of all ages in approximately equal numbers would have a great deal of age diversity. Equal Employment Opportunity and other employment laws and regulations generally address demographic diversity; thus, the issues associated with managing demographic diversity are somewhat different from those associated with managing cultural diversity.

■☐*fast fact*

Five years after the Defense Department adopted its "Don't ask, don't tell" policy for gay men and lesbians in the military, the armed forces discharged more people as homosexuals than in any year during the prior decade.

In today's progressive atmosphere, it may seem hard to believe glass walls (real but invisible barriers between occupational groups) and glass ceilings (real but invisible barriers between levels within the organization) still persist in corporate America. But it takes considerable effort and time to change some of the old patterns of managing human resources that created these phenomena.[62] Segregation within organizations is due, in part, to job sex-typing. That is, a job takes the image of being appropriate only for the sex that dominates the job. Once a job becomes sex-typed, it attracts mostly persons of that sex. Job sex-typing, combined with sex-role stereotyping, has traditionally restricted perceived job choices and preferences for both men and women.

Evidence now indicates that the range of perceived job choices and preferences is expanding for both men and women. Indeed, one out of every four American workers is employed by a business owned by a woman, and employment growth in these companies is 50 percent greater than for all the U.S. firms.[63] This trend has been facilitated by the gradual changes in attitudes in our society as a whole. In addition, some of the job sex-typing has been reduced due to the use of sex-neutral job titles and the increasing number of women graduating from professional schools, especially business schools.[64] Finally, because health care and other social services are among the fastest growing occupations, men will increasingly move to where the jobs are—i.e., to occupations traditionally perceived as "women's work."[65] Projections being made now for the future workplaces are looking better. Trend forecasters say that besides growing up more environmentally conscious and achievement oriented, Generation Y (born between 1979 and 1994) is growing up with far more tolerance for differences.[66]

An organization's *cultural diversity* refers to the full mix of the national cultures and domestic subcultures to which members of the workforce belong. Subcultures with which employees may identify include those associated with ethnicity, religion, sexual orientation, marital and family status, and other unifying life experiences.[67] A decade after the term workforce diversity was coined, about three-fourths of all *Fortune* 500 companies have started so-called diversity initiatives.

At Dayton Hudson, a Minneapolis-based retailer, appreciating the cultural diversity of customers is as important as appreciating employee diversity. Consequently, the company thinks of diversity very broadly and uses this thinking in ways linked to buying behaviors. For example, management and buyers recognize that people who are unusually large or small may have different perspectives from those who are of average size when it comes to pricing, merchandise selection, and the physical layout of stores.

The multicultural organization, with a workforce that includes the full mix of cultures found in the population at large and a commitment to full utilization of its human resources, requires finding new ways of managing human resources. The increasing diversity of the workforce, combined with changing attitudes about differences that may have been ignored in the past (including religious traditions and life-style choices) presents both challenges and opportunities for organizations and their employees. As described in the feature Managing Diversity: Creating an Harassment-Free Workplace,[68] ensuring that employees feel respected and free of harassment is one such challenge. Because managing diversity is so important in today's work environment, we highlight it throughout this book in a recurring Managing Diversity feature.

"The burden is on us, not the employee, to change, For many of us, that's a new recognition."

**Charles R. Romea
Employee Benefits Director
ConAgra**

■□*fast fact*

The term *Hispanic* is used to refer to people with national origins from numerous different countries and cultures, including: Mexico, Cuba, Spain, Puerto Rico, and the countries of Central and South America.

MANAGING DIVERSITY

Creating an Harassment-Free Workplace

Many organizations didn't begin to consider sexual harassment to be a significant problem until Anita Hill testified against Supreme Court Justice Clarence Thomas during his Senate confirmation hearings. If Thomas's eventual appointment left doubt in some people's mind about the seriousness of the problem, the record settlement agreed to by Mitsubishi Motor Manufacturing in 1998 should have convinced them that workplace harassment is bad for business. Mitsubishi agreed to pay a record $34 million after an investigation by the EEOC found that 300 women employed in the Normal, Illinois plant had been subjected to sexual harassment and that plant managers did nothing to intervene. "There have been some problems involving sexual harassment in our plant, which required correction," conceded executive vice president Kohei Ikuta. Some women would receive as much as $300,000. To prevent future problems, the company also agreed to begin several intervention programs, including annual training for all supervisors.[69]

By the time Mitsubishi acknowledged it had a problem, Delaware-based E.I. du Pont de Nemours (DuPont) had already been battling sexual harassment for several years as part of its efforts to improve the company. It didn't set out to be on the cutting edge of this issue; it was just trying to do what was right for DuPont. Nevertheless, its program won *Workforce* magazine's Optimas Award for *Vision.* Called "A Matter of Respect," the program's centerpiece is its sexual harassment workshops. Gender-balanced groups of 20 to 25 employees view and discuss a variety of workplace incidents that involve communications with various possible interpretations. The workshops are given in Japan, China, Mexico, Puerto Rico, and throughout Europe and the United States, with each country adapting the specific material to fit the local cultural context. More than 65 percent of DuPont's workforce have attended the workshops.

The following vignettes are taken from videos that employees watch and discuss. Key questions for them to consider are whether the vignette represents sexual harassment and how they would have handled the situation.

- A DuPont employee is dining with a customer. He proposes signing the final contract in his hotel room.
- A female employee is waiting for her male counterpart to give her instructions on a lab procedure. Instead, he comments on how good she smells and comments that his wife wouldn't want the two of them to go together on a business trip. When she tries to change the subject, he tells her how smart and pretty she is.
- A female employee appears to proposition a male employee.
- While considering whether to give a woman a particular assignment, two male managers discuss her looks and her divorce.

Janet Staats, who serves as one of the discussion facilitators, says that employees struggle to draw conclusions, going back and forth in their opinions. For one employee, the situation may definitely be viewed as harassment, but for another it isn't. By exposing employees to people's differing perspectives, the company seeks to make everyone more sensitive to some of the emotional consequences that their actions can have on other people.

The workshops sometimes stimulate memories of previous incidents of harassment, and for a few participants they confirm that uncomfortable experiences they're currently experiencing need not be tolerated. Such employees often need someone to talk to. With that in mind, DuPont has trained more than 100 facilitators in how to listen, how to talk to worried employees, how to guide employees to toward professional help, and how to conduct the early stages of the investigative process that's followed when a formal complaint is made.

Managing Globalization

During the past fifty years, technological advances in transportation and communications have spurred the growth of international commerce. As a result, many firms evolved from purely domestic to truly global. The first step in this evolution was simply to export goods for sale in one or two foreign markets. The next step was to manufacture those goods overseas because it was more efficient than shipping products to foreign markets. Setting up operations close to foreign markets also helped a company better understand its customers. For example, Mercedes-Benz, the German automaker, recently opened its first foreign plant in Alabama, where it produces its first sports utility vehicle. The company hopes that this sportier model will appeal to younger, less affluent buyers, who are the key to the company's future growth.[70]

Mercedes is just beginning to evolve into a global company; other companies started years ago. Many that succeeded with their initial foreign ventures continued to evolve to the point of becoming transnational. A transnational firm has "headquarters" in several nations, and no single national culture is dominant in the firm.[71] Customers in various countries may not even think of such firms as being foreign owned. For example, many U.S. customers don't think of Shell Oil Company as a Dutch firm.

Globalization creates several challenges for managing human resources. Effectively managing U.S. expatriates who are sent abroad is one challenge. Increasingly, expatriates come from all levels of the organization, and it's not always easy to know who to send where, as illustrated in Managing Globalization: An International Staffing Dilemma.[72] Mercedes sent 160 Alabamans to Germany, where they learned their jobs working alongside their German counterparts. In addition, 70 Germans were sent to Alabama to help train the rest of the new U.S. employees. According to a worldwide survey of 351 companies, 43 percent of them plan to increase the number of employees sent on overseas assignments; only 13 percent plan to reduce overseas assignments in the near future. About 80 percent of companies with expatriates send their employees to Asia and Europe. North, Central, and South America receive expatriates from about 50 percent of the companies.[73]

Managing foreign workers who are located in the U.S. is another challenge. In the United States, domestic labor shortages in certain fields mean that some organizations cannot succeed unless they consider the entire world as their labor market. Similarly, the changing political and economic landscape in Europe means that workers can now more freely move across national borders to find desirable jobs. Thus, more and more employees are being hired from other countries. Many middle managers are working with a global workforce without even leaving home. This workforce brings with them values, expectations, and patterns of behavior that reflect, in part, the HR philosophies, policies, and practices that they experienced in their home countries.

For truly global organizations, deciding which approaches to managing human resources should be applied universally and which should reflect local practices is another key challenge. As the Lincoln Electric Company discovered, approaches to managing human resources that are effective in the U.S. may be ineffective in other countries. In fact, they may even be illegal, just as some common practices in other countries are illegal in the U.S.

Throughout this book, we return repeatedly to issues of how globalization affects how organizations manage their human resources. Although detailed treatment of this topic is beyond the scope of this text, many of the issues that global organizations face are illustrated in the Managing Globalization

MANAGING GLOBALIZATION

An International Staffing Dilemma

Suppose that you are a senior partner in Midland Ashby, a consulting firm. You are writing a proposal for an assignment halfway around the world, and as part of the proposal you need to describe the members of the team that would work with your client. The client is located in a country with very "traditional" views about men and women. The person with the most expertise on the client's problem is a woman, so you list her as one of the team members. Your potential client comments on this aspect of the proposal, stating that a woman team member is unacceptable. What should you do? Should you remove the woman from consideration and give her another assignment, or should you refuse to play by the client's rules?

When a panel of managers was asked this question, here's how they responded.

- One manager commented, "Business is business. Leave her on the team, where you need her. It would be ridiculous to assume that she could not be on the team even in a culture with very different attitudes about women."
- Two other managers chose to begin by trying to persuade the client to accept the woman. But if the client would not accept her, they would take her off the team in order to respect the culture of the client.
- Acknowledging that this is one of the toughest business decisions, another manager said that the consulting company's principles against discrimination should not be compromised. He would leave her on the team and let her make presentations to the client to prove her expertise. He thought that this would probably result in loss of the contract, but that was better than discriminating against his employee.
- Two managers thought that the woman's suggestions and input should be sought before she was written into the proposal. If she was interested in the assignment knowing the extra challenges she would face, these managers would keep her on the team. They would handle the client by stressing the importance of making a sound business decision—in this case, that means making use of the expert on the topic.
- One manager agreed that the consultant should be responsive to the cultural norms of clients. But she noted that the consultant might want to reconsider where and with whom they were willing to do business.
- One manager proposed handling the situation by explaining the situation to the woman and asking her to serve as a ghost member of the team. Her input would be sought and used by the team, but the client would never see her.
- One manager stated that legally, the consultant had no option but to use the best qualified person. Under Title VII, denying her the assignment because she was a woman would be illegal.

What's your opinion?

Note that the name of the company is fictitious but that the situation reflects a common problem.

To learn more about issues in international human resources management, visit the home pages of the International Association for Human Resource Information Management at
www.ihrim.org

the International Personnel Management Association at
www.ipma-hr.org

and the Institute for International Human Resources at
www.shrmglobal.org

feature. Readers who are particularly interested in cross-cultural and international human resource management should consult the relevant sources referenced throughout the chapters.

Managing Change

Current approaches to managing people within any particular company reflect both the past and the process of letting go of the past in order to prepare for the future. As environmental change quickens, more and more companies are concluding that some of the traditional approaches to managing human resources must be modified. A shortage of qualified employees may lead an organization to change its human resources management system in order to attract more job applicants. A never-ending stream of new technologies makes possible new approaches to recruiting—not to mention the possibility of a virtual organization. Changing laws and regulations may threaten old practices or create new opportunities. Merging with another firm, spinning off a business unit, and flattening the hierarchical structure all involve changing who does what and how. Chapters 2 through 4 describe some of the implications for managing human resources of these and other environmental changes.

A dynamic, changing environment makes innovation and change as important—if not more important—for established organizations as they are for new organizations. Even the most successful organizations can't rest on prior successes. They must continually change. If they become complacent, competitors will woo away employees as well as customers. Decline and even extinction result when organizations fail to adapt.

Most people—whether students, employees, managers, or consultants—are involved with organizations that need to change. To be effective, organizations and their managers, employees, and contractors must learn how to deal creatively with day-to-day conditions that require adaptation. Successful organizational change almost always involves changing some approaches to managing people. Chapter 5 describes in depth several principles for successful change management. In addition, throughout the other chapters, the feature Managing Change appears as a recurring reminder of the importance and difficulty of using human resource practices to facilitate organizational change.

P.S.: WHAT *ARE* HUMAN RESOURCES?

This book is about managing human resources. So far, we have spent a great deal of time talking about the subject, but we have not yet provided a definition of the term *human resources*. Is it just a fancy way to refer to *people* or *employees*? Does it mean anything different than the older term, *personnel*? How are human resources different from *human assets*? Although these sound like simple questions, we do not have simple answers. The term *human resources* gets used in a variety of ways by business journalists, managers, HR professionals, and even professors who write HR textbooks! Sorting out all the potential nuances suggested by this group of terms is a task for another time and place. Here we simply wish to state what we mean when we use the term:

> **Human resources:** *the available talents and energies of people who are available to an organization as potential contributors to the creation and realization of the organization's mission, vision, strategy, and goals.*

SUMMARY

Managing human resources is critical to the success of all companies, large and small, regardless of industry. The more effectively a firm manages its human resources, the more successful the firm is going to be.

Organizations define success by how well they serve their stakeholders. Stakeholders include those who have a claim on the resources, services, and products of the companies. Although stakeholders influence all parts of an organization, they affect some aspects more than others, and some aspects are affected by more stakeholders. The primary stakeholders who shape the typical organization's approach to managing human resources include (but aren't limited to) the organization itself, the shareholders and owners, society, the customers, and the employees. It is, in part, the existence of these powerful stakeholders that makes managing human resources such a challenging and important task.

There is no one best way to manage employees. Organizations need to manage human resources to fit their unique situation. This involves coordinated human resource activities. Every activity sends a message to employees. If all these activities are sending different messages, the employees are likely to respond in rather unpredictable ways. To insure that all HR activities are coordinated with each other and that they fit an organization's unique situation, a strategic approach should be taken. Data should drive decisions about what new approaches to try and data should be used to monitor how well the HR system is functioning.

The complexity of managing human resources means that no one person can manage this task alone. Instead, a partnership is needed, involving line managers, HR professionals and all other employees working in the organization. In the following chapters, this partnership theme appears repeatedly. Other recurring themes include teams, diversity, globalization, and organizational change. Organizational change is emphasized for two reasons: (1) rapid change is everywhere, in technology, in the workforce, in the world, and in the customers; and (2) for virtually all organizations, positioning for maximum competitiveness will require a change in the way they manage their human resources.

TERMS TO REMEMBER

Balanced scorecard	Partnership perspective
Cultural diversity	Social audit
Demographic diversity	Stakeholders
HR partnership triad	Strategic approach
HR professionals	Sustainable competitive advantage
Human resources	Workforce diversity

DISCUSSION QUESTIONS

1. What has Southwest Airlines been doing that demonstrates the value of managing human resources?
2. Why is managing human resources important?

3. Refer to the list of stakeholders and their concerns in Exhibit 1.2. For each stakeholder group, add at least one additional concern that you think may shape how organizations manage human resources. Then, for each stakeholder group, give at least one specific example of how that group's concerns could affect a major HR activity (e.g., planning, staffing, appraisal, compensation, or training).

4. Explain the meaning of a "partnership perspective for managing human resources."

5. Is it realistic to expect organizations to be strategic in managing human resources? What organizational and individual barriers are likely to make it difficult to adopt a strategic approach?

PROJECTS TO EXTEND YOUR LEARNING

1. **Managing Strategically.** As the general public puts more pressure on businesses to behave in socially responsible ways, new business opportunities are created. For example, numerous consulting firms now offer assistance to organizations that are interested in developing and implementing ethics policies. Investigate the types of consulting services being offered. Can an organization significantly change its culture by utilizing this type of consulting service? Can an ethical culture be a source of sustainable competitive advantage for an organization? Are there some industries in which such a culture is more likely to be of value, rare and difficult to copy? Explain. For an example of what one consulting firm, KPMG, offers, visit its home page at **www.usserve.us.kpmg.com/ethics**

2. **Managing Change.** In the engine-building business, many joint ventures have been attempted, and almost as many have failed. On paper, joint ventures between companies with different strengths promise big rewards. But, in reality, establishing cooperative relationships between former rivals often proves difficult. Despite its history of modest success with joint ventures, GE decided to enter into a new joint venture with United Technologies' Pratt & Whitney unit. Ironically, the same competitive forces that kept these two companies apart in the past are now responsible for them getting together.

   Boeing, a potential buyer of large quantities of the engines these companies make, had announced that it would require new engines to meet a stricter standard. Operating costs for new 747s would have to be reduced by ten percent. While at an air show in Singapore, employees of the two companies were complaining about this new standard. But being engineers, their conversation eventually moved toward speculation that a new type of engine might be the solution. Someone apparently said, "let's do it together," and soon officials from the two companies were exploring the possibilities.

   Time will tell whether managers and other employees can set aside the past and begin to trust each other enough to share information and work together effectively. Each company suspects the other of spreading information about defects in its rival's engines. The suspicions may be valid. According to one newspaper account, a GE executive once showed a reporter a video of a Pratt engine backfiring and belching flames.

Whether this venture succeeds will depend in part on whether employees can overcome their distrust of each other. How might human resource practices be useful for ensuring that employees who work in the new joint venture cooperate with each other? Describe specific HR practices that you think should be adopted as well as any that you think should be avoided.

To learn more about these two companies, visit their home pages at
www.ge.com
www.pratt-whitney.com

3. **Managing Strategically.** One way that organizations can contribute to the community is by encouraging employees to participate in community activities. Genentech, a biotech company that uses human genetic information to develop and manufacture pharmaceuticals, is an example of a company that takes this approach. Investigate the specific types of community activities that Genentech supports. Does this company's approach to corporate responsibility represent a sincere concern about its role in society, or are the motives behind the company's activities primarily commercial. To learn about Genentech's involvement in community activities, visit its home page at
    www.gene.com

4. **Managing Globalization.** Many U.S. companies have located some or all of their manufacturing facilities in other countries. As described in this chapter, employment conditions at those facilities may not meet the standards we have come to expect in the United States. Nike, the athletic apparel manufacturer, is an example of a company that received a great deal of criticism for the actions of its foreign suppliers. Nike responded to this criticism by extending various U.S. protections to all employees globally? How did Nike's competitors respond? Compare Nike at
    www.nike.com
    to Reebok and New Balance at
    www.reebok.com
    www.newbalance.com

5. **Integration and Application.** Read the three cases at the end of this textbook, entitled "The Lincoln Electric Company," "Southwest Airlines," and "Aid Association for Lutherans (AAL)." Then, using the stakeholder framework illustrated in Exhibit 1.2, make an illustration that identifies the stakeholders of each company and shows the relative importance of each stakeholder to each company. Here, as in the chapters to follow, you can gather your information from materials in the chapter, the cases at the end of the text, and from other sources including newspapers, magazines, the Internet, and your experience. If you are unable to obtain information you feel is relevant, make assumptions based on your best judgment. Be sure to note any major assumptions you make.

    To learn more about these organizations, visit their home pages at
    www.lincolnelectric.com
    www.iflyswa.com
    www.aal.org

CASE STUDY

Levi Strauss & Company

In 1872, Levi Strauss received a letter from Jacob Davis. A Nevada tailor, who had been buying bolts of fabric from Strauss's dry goods company, Davis wrote to explain how he used metal rivets to strengthen the construction of the overalls he made. Because Davis couldn't afford to file for a patent, he invited Strauss to become a partner. Strauss knew a good idea when he saw it and the two were granted the patent in 1873. Today, Levi Strauss & Company is still privately owned, and the company's approach to ethical management is as familiar to business leaders as its jeans are to teenagers. Its mission statement begins, "The mission of Levi Strauss & Co. is to sustain responsible commercial success as a global marketing company of branded apparel." Its Aspiration Statement goes on to say, "We all want a company people can be proud of, . . ." which includes "leadership that epitomizes the stated standards of ethical behavior." At Levi Strauss, ethical leadership extends well beyond company walls, to its dealings with some 500 cutting, sewing, and finishing contractors in more than 50 countries. Despite cultural differences in what is viewed as ethical or as common business practices, the company seeks business partners "who aspire as individuals and in the conduct of all their businesses" to ethical standards compatible with those of Levi Strauss. In addition to legal compliance, the company will do business only with partners who share a commitment to the environment and conduct their business consistent with its own Environmental Philosophy and Guiding Principles. In the area of employment, partners must pay prevailing wage rates, require less than a sixty-hour week, not use workers under age fourteen and not younger than the compulsory age to be in school, not use prison labor, and not use corporal punishment or other forms of coercion. Levi Strauss regularly conducts contractor evaluations to ensure compliance. It helps companies develop ethical solutions when noncompliance is discovered.

Closer to home, Levi Strauss actively promotes ethical business practices through activities such as membership in Business for Social Responsibility—an alliance of companies that share their successful strategies and practices through educational programs and materials. The company's domestic employment policies are known for being ahead of the times. For example, it was among the first companies to offer insurance benefits to its employees' unmarried domestic partners. Through this and other policies, the company has taken a strong stance for the diversity that employees bring to the workplace.[74]

QUESTIONS

1. Suppose that Levi Strauss were a public company. Knowing that its managers are willing to trade some economic efficiencies in order to operate according to their collective view of what is "ethical," would you buy shares of stock in this company? Why or why not?

2. Managers at Levi Strauss believe that they run an ethical company, but critics view their liberal employment and benefits policies as immoral. These critics object to the policies as inconsistent with the critics' religious views. Analyze the pros and cons of adopting socially liberal employment policies that are viewed by some members of society (including potential employees and potential customers) as immoral.

3. Suppose you are looking for a new job. You have two offers for similar positions—one at Nike and one at Levi Strauss. Both organizations have indicated that they would like you to work for a year in one of their production plants somewhere in southeast Asia. The two salary offers are similar, and in both companies you would be eligible for an annual bonus. The bonus would be based largely on the productivity of the production plant where you will be located. Which offer would you accept? Explain why.

To learn more about managing human resources at Levi Strauss & Company, visit the company's home page at
www.levi.com

ENDNOTES

[1] T. A. Stewart, "America's Most Admired Companies: Why Leadership Matters," *Fortune* (March 2, 1998): 70–82.

[2] J. Pfeffer, *Competitive Advantage Through People* (Boston: Harvard Business School Press, 1995): 4; "The Hoover 100," *Hoover's Company Profile Database* (Austin, TX: The Reference Press, Inc., 1996); S. McCartney and M. J. McCarthy, "Southwest Flies Circles Around United's Shuttle," *The Wall Street Journal* (February 20, 1996): BI, 9; F. E. Whittlesey, "CEO Herb Kelleher Discusses Southwest Airlines' People Culture: How the Company Achieves Competitive Advantage from the Ground Up," *ACA Journal* (Winter 1995): 8–25; K. Labich, "Is Herb Kelleher America's Best CEO?" *Fortune* (May 2, 1994): 50; B. Paik Sunoo, "How Fun Flies At Southwest Airlines," *Personnel Journal* (June 1995): 62–8.

[3] L. C. Thurow, *Head to Head* (New York: William Morrow & Co., 1992): 45.

[4] M. E. Porter, *Competitive Advantage* (New York: Free Press, 1985); J. Barney, "Firm Resources and Sustained Competitive Advantage," *Journal of Management* 17 (1) (1991): 99–120; S. A. Snell, M. A. Youndt, and P. M. Wright, "Establishing a Framework for Research in Strategic Human Resource Management: Merging Resource Theory and Organizational Learning," *Research in Personnel and Human Resource Management* 14 (1996): 61–90; I. Dierickx and K. Cool, "Asset and stock accumulation and sustainability of competitive advantage," *Management Science* 35 (1989): 1504–1511.

[5] S. Shellenberg, "Investors Seem Attracted to Firms with Happy Employees," *The Wall Street Journal* (March 19, 1997): B1; M. J. Schmit and S. P. Allscheid, "Employee Attitudes and Customer Satisfaction: Making the Theoretical and Empirical Connections," *Personnel Psychology* 48 (1995): 521–536; C. A. Lengnick-Hall, "Customer Contributions to Quality: A Different View of the Customer-oriented Firm," *Academy of Management Review* 21 (1996): 791–824; and P. S. Goodman, M. Fichman, F. J. Lerch, and P. R. Snyder, "Customer–Firm Relationships, Involvement, and Customer Satisfaction," *Academy of Management Journal* 38 (1995): 1310–1324.

[6] F. E. Whittlesey, "CEO Herb Kelleher Discusses Southwest Airlines' People Culture: How the Company Achieves Competitive Advantage from the Ground Up," *ACA Journal* (Winter 1995): 8–25.

[7] G. Bethune and S. Huler, *From Worst to First: Behind the Scenes of Continental's Remarkable Comeback* (New York: John Wiley & Sons, 1998); G. Flynn, "A Flight Plan for Success," *Workforce* (July 1997): 72–78.

[8] P. Cappelli and A. Crocker-Hefter, *Distinctive Human Resources Are the Core Competencies of Firms*, report no. R117Q00011-91 (Washington, DC: U.S. Department of Education, 1994).

[9] E. A. Robinson, "The Ups and Downs of the Industry Leaders," *Fortune* (March 2, 1998): 86–87; E. Brown, "America's Most Admired Companies," *Fortune* (March 1, 1999): 68–73.

[10] L. Grant, "Happy Workers, Happy Returns," *Fortune* (January 12, 1998): 81. Also see G. E. Fryzell and J. Wang, "The Fortune Corporation 'Reputation' Index: Reputation for What?" *Journal of Management* 20 (1994): 1–14.

[11] *High Performance Work Practices and Firm Performance* (U.S. Department of Labor: Washington, DC, 1993).

[12] G. S. Hansen and B. Wernerfelt, "Determinants of Firm Performance: Relative Importance of Economic and Organizational Factors," *Strategic Journal of Management* 10 (1989): 399–411.

[13] J. P. MacDuffie and J. Krafcik, "Integrating Technology and Human Resources for High-Performance Manufacturing," *Transforming Organizations*, eds. T. Kochan and M. Useem, (New York: Oxford University Press, 1992): 210–226. See also J. B. Arthur, "Effects of Human Resource Systems on Manufacturing Performance and Turnover," *Academy of Management Journal* 37 (1994): 670–687.

[14] For descriptions of other studies that show the linkage between managing human resources and organizational effectiveness, see B. E. Becker, M. A. Huselid, P. S. Pinkus and M. F. Spratt, "HR as a Source of Shareholder Value: Research and Recommendations," *Human Resource Management*, 36 (1) (Spring 1997): 39–48; B. E. Becker and M. A. Huselid, "High Performance Work Systems and Firm Performance: A Synthesis of Research and Managerial Implications," *Research in Personnel and Human Resources Management*, G. Ferris, ed. (Greenwich, CT.: JAI Press, 1998); and the following articles, which all appeared in the *Academy of Management Journal's* "Special Research Forum on Human Resource Management and Organizational Performance," Vol. 39 (4), (August 1996): B. Becker and G. Gerhart, "The Impact of Human Resource Management on Organizational Performance: Progress and Prospects," 779–801; J. E. Delery and D. H. Doty, "Modes of Theorizing in Strategic Human Resource Management: Tests of Universalistic, Contingency, and Configural Performance Predictions," 802–825; M. A. Youndt, S. A. Snell, J. W. Dean, Jr., and D. P. Lepak, "Human Resource Management, Manufacturing Strategy, and Firm Performance," 836–867; R. D. Banker, J. M. Field, R. G. Shroeder, and K. K. Sinha, "Impact of Work Teams on Manufacturing Performance: A Longitudinal Field Study," 867–890; T. M. Welbourne and A. O. Andrews, "Predicting the Performance of Public Offerings: Should Human Resource Management be in the Equation?" 891–919.

[15] For a review of this perspective, see T. Donaldson and L. E. Preston, "The Stakeholder Theory of the Corporation: Concepts, Evidence, and Implications," *Academy of Management Review* 20 (1995): 65–91.

[16] M. B. E. Clarkson, "A Stakeholder Framework for Analyzing and Evaluating Corporate Social Performance," *Academy of Management Review* 20 (1995): 92–117; R. E. Freeman, *Strategic Management: A Stakeholder Approach* (Boston:

Pittman/Ballinger, 1994); T. M. Jones, "Instrumental Stakeholder Theory: A Synthesis of Ethics and Economics," *Academy of Management Review* 20 (1995): 404–437; D. J. Wood, "Social Issues in Management: Theory and Research in Corporate Social Performance," *Journal of Management* 17 (1991): 383–405.

[17] G. Colvin, "Naked Power: The Scoreboard," *Fortune* (April 27, 1997): 449–451.

[18] E. Freeman and J. Liedtka, "Stakeholder Capitalism and the Value Chain," *European Management Journal* 15 (3) (June 1997): 286–296.

[19] M. Useem, "Shareholders as a Strategic Asset," *California Management Review* (Fall 1996): 8–27.

[20] T. A. Stewart, "Real Assets, Unreal Reporting," *Fortune* (July 6, 1997): 207–208.

[21] C. Handy, "A Better Capitalism," *Across the Board* (April 1998): 16–22.

[22] T. M. Welbourne and A. O. Andrews, "Predicting the Performance of Initial Public Offerings: Should Human Resource Management Be in the Equation?" *Academy of Management Journal* 39 (1996): 891–919.

[23] J. J. Laabs, "Quality Drives Trident's Success," *Workforce* (February 1998): 44–49.

[24] A. Wilkinson, G. Godfrey, and M. Marchington, "Bouquets, Brickbats and Blinkers: Total Quality Management and Employee Involvement in Practice," *Organization Studies* 18 (5) (1997): 799–819; J. D. Olian and S. L. Rynes, "Making Total Quality Work: Aligning Organizational Processes, Performance Measures, and Stakeholders," *Human Resource Management* (Fall 1991): 303–334; A. Parasuraman, L. L. Berry, and V. A. Zeithaml, "Perceived Service Quality as a Customer-Based Performance Measure: An Empirical Examination of Organizational Barriers Using an Extended Service Quality Model," *Human Resource Management* (Fall 1991): 335–364.

[25] J. L. Heskett, W. R. Sasser, Jr., and C. L. W. Hart, *Service Breakthroughs: Changing the Rules of the Game* (New York: Macmillan, 1990).

[26] J. Carlzon. As quoted in C. Grunroos, *Service Management and Marketing* (Lexington, MA: Lexington Books, 1990): xv.

[27] J. W. Johnson, "Linking Employee Perceptions of Service Climate to Customer Satisfaction," *Personnel Psychology*, 49 (1996): 831–846; J. W. Wiley, "Customer Satisfaction: A Supportive Work Environment and Its Financial Cost," *Human Resource Planning* Vol. 9 (1991): 117–128.

[28] J. L. Heskett, W. E. Sasser, Jr., and L. A. Schlesinger, *The Service Profit Chain* (New York: Free Press, 1997); B. Schneider and D. Bowen, *Winning the Service Game* (New York: Harvard Business School Press, 1995).

[29] L. Bannonm "The Publisher Plans New Type Faces for the L. A.Times," *The Wall Street Journal* (May 15, 1998): A1; A8.

[30] R. Abelson, "Welcome Mat is Out for Gay Investors," *New York Times* (September 1, 1996): Section 3: 1, 7.

[31] T. Lewin, "Equal Pay for Equal Work is No. 1 Goal for Women," *New York Times* (September 5, 1997): A20.

[32] K. F. Clark, "Leaders of the Pack," *Human Resource Executive* (May 6, 1997): 80–82.

[33] A. J. Rucci, S. P. Kirn, and R. T. Quinn, "The Employee-Customer-Profit Chain at Sears," *Harvard Business Review* (January-February 1998): 83–97; E. E. Lawler III, *The Ultimate Advantage: Creating the High Involvement Organization* (San Francisco: Jossey-Bass, 1992); E. E. Lawler III, S. A. Mohrman, and G. E. Ledford, *Employee Involvement in America: An Assessment of Practices and Results* (San Francisco: Jossey-Bass, 1992).

[34] D. Denison, *Corporate Culture and Organizational Effectiveness* (New York: John Wiley & Sons, 1990); E. E. Lawler III, et al., *Employee Involvement and Total Quality Management* (San Francisco: Jossey-Bass, 1992).

[35] For international employees, leaving one's home country is just the beginning. Research shows that returning home also is fraught with difficulties to which employers should attend. For a discussion of these, see H. B. Gregersen and L. K. Stroh, "Coming Home to the Arctic Cold: Antecedents to Finnish Expatriate and Spouse Repatriation Adjustment, *Personnel Psychology* 50 (1997): 635–654.

[36] S. A. Lobel, "In Praise of the Soft Stuff: A Vision for Human Resource Leadership," *Human Resource Management* (1996): 91–99.

[37] Associated Press, "Kodak's Hometown Feels Little Security," *Dallas Morning News* (November 13, 1997): 4D.

[38] J. W. Meyer and B. Rowan, "Institutionalized Organizations: Formal Structure as Myth and Ceremony," *American Journal of Sociology* 72 (1977): 340–363; W. R. Scott, "The Adolescence of Institutional Theory," *Administrative Scientific Quarterly* 32 (1987): 493–511; and L. G. Zucker, "Institutional Theories of Organization," *Annual Review of Sociology* 13 (1987): 443–464.

[39] To learn how researchers attempt to measure corporate social performances, see B. M. Ruf, K. Muralidhar, and K. Paul, "The Development of a Systematic, Aggregate Measure of Corporate Social Performance," *Journal of Management* 24 (1998): 119–133.

[40] J. J. Laabs, "Disney Helps Keep Kids in School," *Personnel Journal* (November 1992): 58–68.

[41] B. Leonard, "Supporting Volunteerism," *HRM Magazine* (June 1998): 84–93.

[42] Adapted from the company's home page; A. Adelson, "Casual, Worker-friendly, and a Money-maker, Too," *New York Times* (June 30, 1996): F8; C. Callicott, "How Green Is Your Gear?" *Hudson Valley Sports* (September/October 1996); M. Katakis and R. Chatham, *Sacred Trusts: Essays on Stewardship and Responsibility* (Mercury House, New York, 1993); and E. O. Wells, "Lost in Patagonia," *Inc.* (August 1992): 91–95.

[43] M. A. Friedman, "Friedman Doctrine: The Social Responsibility of Business Is to Increase Its Profits," *New York Times Magazine* (September 13, 1970): 32ff.

[44] L. Holyoke, "How HR Measures Impact of Corporate Donations," *Workforce* (June 1997): 23.

[45] K. H. Hammonds, W. Zellner, and R. Melcher, "Writing a New Social Contract," *Business Week* (March 11, 1997): 60–61.

[46] T. Teal, "Not a Fool, Not a Saint," *Fortune* (November 11, 1996): 201–204.

[47] A. Berstein, "Working Capital: Labor's New Weapon?" *Business Week* (September 29, 1997): 110–112.

[48] Adapted from E. P. Marquardt, "Aligning Strategy and Performance with the Balanced Scorecard," *ACA Journal* (Autumn 1997): 18–27; R. S. Kaplan and D. P. Norton, "Using the Balanced Scorecard as a Strategic Management System," *Harvard Business Review* (January-February 1996): 75–85; R. S. Kaplan and D. P. Norton, "Linking the Balanced Scorecard to Strategy," *California Management Review* 39 (Fall 1996): 53–79.

[49] J. Millman, "High-tech Jobs Transfer to Mexico with Surprising Speed: How One Electronics Firm Boosts Productivity by Addressing Workers' Needs," *The Wall Street Journal* (April 9, 1998): A18.

[50] M. A. Huselid, "The Impact of Human Resource Management Practices on Turnover, Productivity, and Corporate Financial Performance," *Academy of Management Journal* 38 (1995): 635–672; B. Schneider, S. S. White, and M. C. Paul, "Linking Service Climate and Customer Perceptions of Service Quality: Test of a Causal Model," *Journal of Applied Psychology* 83 (1998): 150–163; J. B. Arthur, "Effects of Human Resource Systems on Manufacturing Performance and Turnover," *Academy of Management Journal* 37 (1994): 670–687; S. A. Snell and M. A. Youndt, "Human Resource Management and Firm Performance: Testing a Contingency Model of Executive Controls," *Journal of Management* 21 (1995): 711–737.

[51] General Accounting Office, *Management Practices: U.S. Companies Improve Performance through Quality Efforts*, GAO/NSIAD-91-190 (1991). Eleven companies reported data on market share, nine reported return on assets, and eight reported return on sales. The Baldrige finalists are not necessarily representative of all the firms that adopted the identifying work practices.

[52] M. Franssen, "Going Beyond Profits: The Body Shop Does," *Business Quarterly* (Autumn 1993): 14–20.

[53] M. B. E. Clarkson, "A Stakeholder Framework for Analyzing and Evaluating Corporate Social Performance," *Academy of Management Review* 20 (1995): 92–117.

[54] R. S. Schuler and J. W. Walker, "Human Resources Strategy: Focusing on Issues and Actions," *Organizational Dynamics* (Summer 1990): 4–19.

[55] R. S. Schuler, "Strategic Human Resources Management: Linking the People with the Strategic Needs of the Business," *Organizational Dynamics* (1992): 18–32; R. S. Schuler and S. E. Jackson, "Linking Competitive Strategies with Human Resource Management Practices," *Academy of Management Executive* (August 1987): 207–219; G. E. Ledford, Jr., J. R. Wendenhof, and J. T. Strahley, "Realizing a Corporate Philosophy," *Organizational Dynamics* (Winter 1995): 5–19.

[56] D. P. Lepak and S. A. Snell, "The Human Resource Architecture: Toward a Theory of Human Capital Allocation and Development," *Academy of Management Review* 24 (1999): 31–48; P. Cappelli and A. Crocker-Hefter, *Distinctive Human Resources Are the Core Competencies of Firms*.

[57] J. Steinhauer, "Time to Call a Sears Repairman: A Turnaround Is Sidetracked By Its Own Oversell," *New York Times* (January 15, 1998): D1, D3; G. Buck, "Revitalized Sears Sings Happy Tune Yet Again," *Chicago Tribune* (January 24, 1997; accessed online at **www.chicago.tribune.com**; and G. Crawford, "Credit Woes Are Sears' Big Q4 Questionmark," Reuters Limited (January 16, 1998; accessed online at **biz.yahoo.com/finance/980116/credit_woe_1**).

[58] *The Hay Report: Compensation and Benefits Strategies for 1997 and Beyond* (New York: Hay Group, 1997).

[59] H. Axel, "Teaming in the Global Arena," *Across the Board* (February 1997): 56; R. D. Banker, J. M. Field, R. G. Schroeder, and K. K. Sinha, "Impact of Work Teams on Manufacturing Performance: A Longitudinal Field Study," *Academy of Management Journal* 36 (1996): 867–890; and S. A. Mohrman and A. M. Mohrman, Jr. *Designing and Leading Team-based Organizations: A Workbook for Organizational Self-design* (San Francisco: Jossey-Bass, 1997).

[60] B. Nagler, "Recasting Employees Into Teams," *Workforce* (January 1998): 101–106.

[61] I. D. Steiner, *Group Process and Productivity* (New York: Academic Press, 1972); S. E. Jackson, K. E. May, and K. Whitney, "Understanding the Dynamics of Diversity in Decision Making Teams," in R. A. Guzzo and E. Salas (eds.) *Team Effectiveness and Decision Making in Organizations* (San Francisco: Jossey-Bass, 1995); S. E. Jackson and R. N. Ruderman (eds.), *Diversity in Work Teams: Research Paradigms for a Changing Workplace* (Washington, DC: American Psychological Association, 1995).

[62] P. D. Jennings, "Viewing Macro HRM From Without: Political and Institutional Perspectives," *Research in Personnel and Human Resource Management* 12 (1994): 1–40.

[63] *Manpower Argus* (August 1996) 335:6.

[64] "Economic Trends: The Amazing U.S. Labor Pool," *Business Week* (May 26, 1997): 30; "U.S. Department of Labor Women's Bureau: Facts on Women Workers," *Bulletin to Management* (April 14, 1994): 118.

[65] M. Minehan, "Futurist Task Force," *HRM Magazine: 50th Anniversary Issue* 50 (1998): 77–88.

[66] M. Beck, "Generation Y: Next Population Bulge Shows Its Might," *The Wall Street Journal* (February 3, 1997): B1, B5;

E. Neuborne and K. Kerwin, "Generation Y," *Business Week* (February 15, 1999): 80–88.

[67] For a description of the cultural experiences of Latino Americans, see R. Suro, *How Latino Immigration is Transforming Us* (New York: Knopf, 1998).

[68] G. Flynn, "A Pioneer Program Nurtures a Harassment Free Workplace," *Workforce* (October 1997): 38–24.

[69] J. P. Miller, "Mitsubishi Will Pay $34 Million In Sexual-Harassment Settlement," *The Wall Street Journal* (June 12, 1998): B4.

[70] B. Vlasic, "In Alabama, the Soul of a New Mercedes?" *Business Week* (March 31, 1997): 70–71.

[71] N. Adler and S. Bartholomew, "Managing Globally Competent People," *Academy of Management Executive* 6 (1992): 52–65.

[72] Adapted from: "More Ticklish Questions," *Across the Board* (May 1996): 38–43.

[73] "International Assignments," *Bulletin to Management* (February 8, 1996): 44–45.

[74] Adapted from J. Makower, *Beyond the Bottom Line: Putting Social Responsibility to Work for Your Business and the World* (New York: Simon & Schuster, 1994).

THE ENVIRONMENTAL CONTEXT FOR MANAGING HUMAN RESOURCES

"The technology business has a lot of twists and turns. That makes you wake up every day thinking, 'Hmmm, let's try to make sure today's not the day we miss the turn in the road.'"

**Bill Gates
CEO
Microsoft**[1]

Chapter Outline

MANAGING THROUGH PARTNERSHIP

at BMW

On June 23, 1992, the Bavarian Motor Works (BMW) of Munich, Germany announced that it was building a plant in Spartanburg, South Carolina. This was the first time a German auto company decided to build a manufacturing plant in the U.S. In 1993, Mercedes-Benz announced plans to build a manufacturing plant in Alabama. In both cases, some of the factors convincing these firms to move to the U.S. were the combined costs of labor, shipping, and components. At that time, the hourly costs of the German auto worker were about $42 versus $24 in the U.S. After lengthy investigation and negotiations, both companies selected rural areas in the South as the locations for their plants.

While BMW officials wanted to locate near a deep water port, many locations would have met this condition. What factors swayed the decision in favor of Spartanburg? The $35 million in incentives offered certainly helped the case. The work climate and perceived work ethic of the people in South Carolina were important also. The HR representative from BMW in Germany insisted on the availability of training and funding for training. As a result, the state provides up to 400 hours of on-the job training for each employee at BMW. According to Susan Crocker, vice president of HR at the plant, it was the entire package offered by the state and the area that made the difference.

Interestingly, the BMW officials were not concerned with the fact that the workers in the area had never worked in an automobile factory. Says Crocker: "We're of the philosophy that people don't have to know how to make cars before they come to work for us. We'll train them to do that. We need people who are flexible, who can think, who can use their brains, and are willing to work in a team environment."

BMW was interested in workers who were able and willing to adapt to the BMW way of operating. In Spartanburg, the company has found workers who are very capable and willing to train, to adapt, and to learn. They're also willing to work for wages that are substantially below their counterparts in Munich. In fact, BMW has found that workers in South Carolina are much more flexible and adaptable than the workers in Munich. In Germany, tradition and independence prevail: workers can still enjoy a beer on the job, and they refuse to wear standard blue uniforms with their names on them.[2]

To learn more about BMW visit the company home page at
www.bmw.com

MANAGING HUMAN RESOURCES IN CONTEXT

As is true of many aspects of managing organizations, approaches to managing human resources have been influenced by the external conditions of its environment. Exhibit 2.1 illustrates a general framework for understanding how environmental conditions exert their influence.[3]

In this chapter we describe a few aspects of the environmental context, including

- intense domestic competition,
- expanding global markets,
- domestic and global labor markets,
- technologies, and
- the structure of interfirm relationships.

Exhibit 2.1

The Contexts of Managing Human Resources

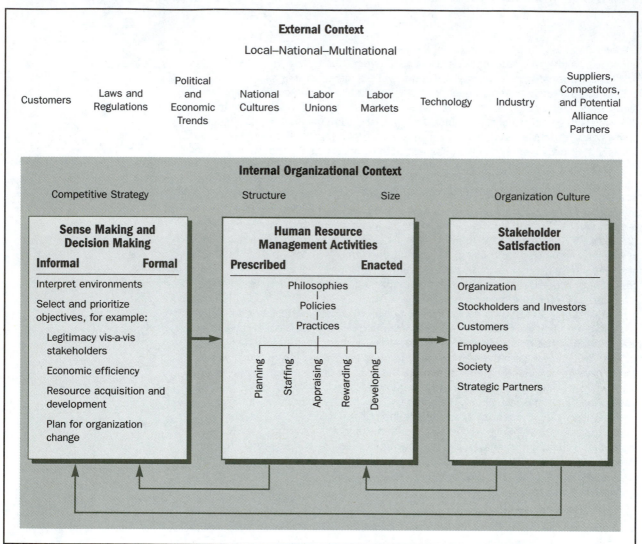

Other important aspects of the environment that are described in depth in subsequent chapters include

- the legal laws and regulations, described in Chapter 3;
- a firm's specific industry and competitors, described in Chapter 4; and
- unions, described in Chapter 15.

For any specific business, competition within the industry as a whole and the actions of specific competitors have very direct and immediate consequences. These aspects of the competitive landscape are generally monitored quite closely and are continuously used in strategic planning and decision making. This topic is addressed in Chapter 4.

Changes in a firm's competitive micro-environment can often be anticipated by looking at the broad trends in domestic and global competition. The U.S. is a vast and highly competitive marketplace. Almost no industry is excluded from intense domestic competition. But the global market is far more vast, and increasingly U.S. companies depend on it for continued growth. We consider these broader issues here.

Domestic Competition

Within the U.S., an open market and deregulated industries combine to create intense competition—even for companies that serve only the domestic market.

An Open Market. Depending on your perspective, you may believe the U.S. is either too open to foreign competition or not open enough. Regardless of one's perspective, however, it's clear that the size and wealth of the U.S. market make it a desirable target for foreign competitors. And, in comparison to other markets of similar size, it has remained relatively open regardless of which political party was in power. Imports of shoes, textiles, and electronics continue to increase, even as the intense pressure they create for domestic producers threatens to put them out of business. Less than ten years ago, U.S. companies dominated the office copier business here and abroad. Today their share of the domestic market is approximately 50 percent. Similar trends have occurred in several other industries during the last 25 years.

Deregulation. Electric utilities, once thought of as essential natural monopolies that had to be regulated by the government, are facing less regulation and more open environments. To consumers, this means more choices about where to purchase power supplies. For utility companies, it means shifting their focus from worrying about the concerns of regulators to worrying about the actions of competitors and the preferences of consumers.

The telecommunications industry, once highly regulated, now changes every day, as competitors battle for individual and institutional customers with increasingly sophisticated needs. A century ago, farmers were content to use the barbed wire on their fences as the wires that enabled them to take advantage of the newest technology—telephones.[4] Today, customers want a fully integrated communication system, combining the benefits of the TV cable system, computer software capabilities, and satellite technology. To give them what they want, telecommunications companies are changing the very definition of an industry by acquiring and merging with cable TV providers, satellite operations, and software companies.[5] The competitive environment is filled with many competitors, including many small and entrepreneurial firms, and it's changing very rapidly.[6] As recently as 1997, mergers such as those now occurring in the telecommunications industry were described by the Federal Communications Commission (FCC) chairman as "unthinkable." A year later, the new FCC chairman viewed them as "eminently thinkable," and even desirable as a means to encourage greater competition.[7] The financial services industry is undergoing a similar transformation.

Together, an open market and deregulation have created intense competition, making it more and more difficult to grow and prosper. One response to such pressures is to look for other markets. In addition to the desire for continued growth, numerous other forces pull many U.S. companies into global expansion. These include a rapidly expanding market for the goods and services they provide and foreign labor markets that meet the needs of some companies better than the domestic labor market.

■□ *fast fact*

In Denver, the starting pay for a phone equipment salesperson is $40,000— twice what it was in 1992.

■□ *fast fact*

McDonalds opens two outlets every three days in Europe.

Chapter Two

Expanding Into Global Markets

To compete effectively, many U.S. companies can no longer depend on the domestic market as their sole source of customers. To thrive, they must expand to serve a global market that's growing at a much faster pace. In some industries, it's now typical that foreign sales for the entire industry account for between one-third and two-thirds of a U.S. company's total sales. These industries include

- computers and office equipment (59 percent foreign sales),
- machinery (51 percent foreign sales),
- autos and auto parts (44 percent foreign sales),
- chemical products (39 percent foreign sales), and
- transportation equipment (34 percent foreign sales).[8]

Within many other industries that have lower foreign sales overall, particular firms can be found that depend heavily on foreign sales. Coca Cola, for example, generates 80 percent of its sales in other countries; for Gillette, the figure is 65 percent.

Services also are being offered to expanding global markets, although in many cases they aren't "exported" in the way products are exported. Products can be produced in one location and then shipped elsewhere for distribution. Services, however, are produced, distributed, and consumed on the spot. Consulting firms, for example, cannot produce their service in the U.S. and then ship it abroad, to be bought and consumed by a customer. The meaning of a consulting service requires that the customer be intimately involved with the process. Nor can a hotel produce its services in the U.S. and then distribute them in another country. They must locate their hotel services at the location the service is "consumed." Thus, for service firms expanding into global markets usually means setting up operations in those markets. Examples of U.S. service firms that generate substantial sales in other countries include Hilton Hotels, KMPG Peat Marwick, and EDS.

LABOR MARKET CONDITIONS

Domestic labor shortages and attractive foreign labor markets also contribute to globalization. Just as firms must compete for customers, so must they compete for employees. Like customers, employees can be sought in the domestic market only or employers can broaden their horizons to include the entire global labor market.

Domestic Labor Market

With a population of more than 275 million today, projections indicate that the U.S. population will continue to grow, reaching 383 million by 2050. Despite this growth, labor shortages could become severe due to the lack of needed skills. A large portion of the U.S. workforce now is from the baby-boom generation (those born between 1946 and 1961). Between 1990 and 2000, the number of people aged 35 to 47 will increase by 38 percent, and the number between 48 and 53 will increase by 67 percent. The size of the baby-boom generation created a huge workforce influx. In the late 1970s, for instance, about three million people entered the 18- to 24-year-old age group each year. But, in 1990, only 1.3 million new workers were in this age group, and this number continues to shrink.

■□ fast fact

The number of Americans trained in engineering and computer sciences has dropped by more than 30 percent.

■□ fast fact

Approximately 25 percent of U.S. adults are functionally illiterate, compared to 5 percent in Japan.

Some people have argued that it's the age distribution of computer programmers and systems analysts that creates the labor shortage in that industry, not a shortage in the number of skilled programmers. Their logic? To fill the 350,000 jobs now open in the industry, critics charge that employers prefer younger workers who are willing to put in 80-hour weeks and accept temporary status as contract workers. Whereas younger workers seem to feel their temporary employment status gives them more control over their careers, older workers with families to support find such work contract unacceptable.[9]

In industries experiencing worker shortages, many companies cannot find workers with the needed skills. After installing millions of dollars worth of computers in its Burlington, Vermont factories, the IBM Corporation discovered, much to its dismay, that it had to teach high school algebra to thousands of workers before they could run the computers. Similarly, Andre Miles has applied for a job at Lincoln Electric Co. three times in the past three years, but he has never gotten past a screening interview. "It's frustrating that I don't even have a chance," says the 22-year-old construction worker. He isn't alone. Most of the 1,000+ applications submitted to Lincoln each month are rejected. Yet the maker of motors and welding products still has positions to fill and can't find the workers it needs. The company needs many skilled tool-and-die makers, mold makers, and machinists. But few of the thousands of applicants who apply for jobs at Lincoln can do high school trigonometry or read technical drawings, and many don't show an aptitude for learning how to operate computer-controlled machines—skills that Lincoln says even entry-level workers need.[10]

Global Labor Market

The lack of skilled labor in the domestic market has led many U.S. companies to look elsewhere for their employees. There is no shortage of people when one considers the global market as a potential source of employees. Currently there are six billion people on this planet. Projections indicate that the labor force in developing nations alone will expand by about 700 million people by the year 2010, while the U.S. labor force will grow by only 7.5 million. To get a sense of the characteristics of this population, study the figures presented in Exhibit 2.2.[11]

As the data shown in Exhibit 2.3 suggest, employers can find workers with higher levels of math and science skills in many other countries.[12] Increasingly, well-educated entry-level workers can be found in developing countries. Furthermore, educational gains are being made more rapidly in developing countries. In 1970, less than 25 percent of all college students were in developing countries. Today, about 50 percent of all college students are in developing countries. For employers seeking flexible and adaptable workers, the young and newly educated workforces in developing countries are particularly attractive. Workers from other countries fill professional level jobs, also. U.S. companies are increasingly hiring highly skilled workers in Asia, the former Soviet bloc, and Europe to perform jobs once reserved for American professionals. Texas Instruments Inc., IBM, and scores of other companies have contracted with Indians, Israelis, and others to write computer programs. Film and TV producers increasingly bring in foreign film professionals.

Implications for Managing Human Resources

The forces putting pressure on U.S. companies to globalize are being felt around the world. Just as U.S. companies are expanding into other markets,

"Over the last quarter century, there has been a decline in the blue-collar professions. Now we're paying the price. There aren't enough skilled trade workers."

Joel Kotkin
Senior Fellow
Pepperdine University

■□ *fast fact*

Since 1995, Asia's workforce has grown by 240 million, while Europe's has grown by only 6 million.

"Whereas kids in America are mostly practicing math problems, kids in Japan are inventing different ways to solve them."

James Stigler, PhD
Professor and Education Expert
University of California–Los Angeles

Exhibit 2.2

Selected Characteristics of the World Population

If the world's population were shrunk to a village of 100 people but the existing ratios remained the same, the population breakdown would be as shown below:

	1990	2025 (Est.)
Asians	57	61
Europeans	21	9
North and South Americans	14	13
Africans	8	17
	100	100
Nonwhite	70	80
White	30	20
	100	100

Exhibit 2.3

A Sampling of Test Scores from a 41-Nation Study of Eighth Graders

Math Scores		Science Scores	
Singapore	643	Singapore	607
Japan	605	Czech Republic	574
Czech Republic	564	Japan	571
Slovak Republic	547	Australia	545
Australia	530	Slovak Republic	544
Ireland	527	Ireland	538
Germany	509	United States	534
United States	500	Germany	531
Latvia	493	Spain	517
Spain	487	Greece	497
Greece	484	Latvia	485

To Warner Bros., when it was trying to recruit in Europe: *"You offer bad jobs: poorly paid seasonal work. Plus, you insist that the workers smile!"*

Sabine Burzler
Local Official
Ruhr Valley, Germany

so too are foreign companies relocating some of their operations to the United States. These dynamics have many implications for all aspects of managing human resources, including staffing, training, appraising performance, giving feedback, and designing compensation and reward systems. Here we illustrate this point briefly; other challenges created by intense competition and globalization will be described in subsequent chapters.

More Intensive Domestic Recruiting. The situation at Lincoln Electric has forced this 100-year-old company to adopt some unusual tactics to find employees. Along with advertising on local radio stations, managers have met with local ROTC units and the Interchurch Council of Greater Cleveland to discover candidates. Lincoln won't specify how much it spends on recruiting, but says it has spent more in the past two years than it has in the previous 98 years put together. The company holds frequent open houses for high-school teachers, career counselors, and students and has sent recruiting teams to neighboring counties in Ohio and Pennsylvania. When Lincoln asked the Ohio Bureau of Employment Services to search its databases for candidates for the tool-and-die openings, the bureau couldn't come up with a single candidate in the entire state—even though Ohio has one of the highest numbers of machine-tool companies in the country.

An International Workforce. For U.S. companies that require high skill levels in areas such as science and engineering, adopting an international approach is no longer questioned. Declining test scores and lack of interest among U.S. students mean these companies must seek needed talent in other countries and among recent immigrants. Muffin Head Productions is typical. Owner Haim Ariav describes his small company as the United Nations of multimedia because five of his sixteen employees are immigrants.[13] Because of the skills shortage at home and the resulting high wages demanded by skilled Americans, each year some 35,000 U.S. companies request visas, especially for physical therapists, civil engineers, and people in computer-related jobs. These requests do not represent a search for cheaper labor: According to a study by the U.S. Department of Labor, 99 percent of employees holding work visas are paid the prevailing wage rate.[14] And if companies can't move needed workers to the U.S., they move the jobs abroad. In many cases this solves the skill shortage and reduces payroll costs.

More Training. In addition to more intensive and global recruiting, firms are energetically training and retraining their workforces. It's estimated that in the next five years, four out of five people in the industrial world will be doing jobs differently from the way they have been done in the last 50 years. Most people will have to learn new skills. In the year 2000, 75 percent of all employees will need to be retrained in new jobs or taught new skills. To meet this high level of demand, corporate trainers are exploring alternative and faster methods of delivering new skills and learning, including interactive video, audiotapes, take-home videodiscs, computer-based instruction, and expert systems.

The Virtual Workforce. Companies such as VeriFone, Price Waterhouse, and Whirlpool have questioned the assumption that people who work together need to be together. They're among a growing number of organizations that are using new technologies to address the challenge of drawing on the ideas and knowledge of people who happen to live all over the world. In the past, face-to-face meetings were the only feasible way to bring such talent to bear on a project or problem. But today, people who are geographically dispersed can be readily formed into an electronically-connected team that will work together for as long as needed. Of course, such teams are possible only because of recent developments in technology.

TECHNOLOGY

Technology generally refers to the process of making and using tools and equipment plus the knowledge used in this process. In early civilization, the available technology was limited to simple tools—hammers, levels, pulleys, shovels, picks, spears—and related knowledge about how to use them. The relatively simple technology of ancient civilization, combined with a system of organizing the people who used it, made possible the creation of objects

■□ *fast fact*

The Senate overwhelmingly endorsed legislation to increase the cap on H1-B visas, which go to workers with at least the equivalent of a bachelors degree, from 65,000 to 95,000 for 1998.

■□ *fast fact*

A projected 20 percent of households will have at least one adult working full time from home by 2002.

■□ *fast fact*

Approximately 90 percent of medium and large companies provide employees with access to e-mail.

that continue to inspire awe centuries later—the pyramids, fireworks, and Stonehenge are just a few familiar examples. Technology has been evolving for thousands of years, but the rate of evolution greatly accelerated after reliable technology was created for generating power. The steam engine, introduced in the late 1700s, was a revolutionary technology. By powering ships and trains, it greatly expanded the speed and reach of trade and commerce. By powering machines such as the "spinning jenny," it lowered production costs, lowered prices, and in doing so expanded markets for the goods produced. To meet the expanding demand required more workers, more machines, and a larger scale of production, and soon the factory system—another fundamentally new technology—evolved.

The Age of Factories and Mass Production Technologies

With the factory system came myriad new challenges related to managing human resources. Organizations were not new—churches, governments, the military—all predated factories. Nevertheless, factories presented special problems. First, people had to be convinced to leave their farms or small workshops and move near the factory—usually a large city and often far away. Once recruited to the factory, people had to be convinced to work in a completely new way. On their farms and in their small shops, workers had previously enjoyed a great deal of personal autonomy and flexibility in their approach to the work. Now they had to accept the authority of factory owners and their agents and they had to accept the highly standardized procedures used to complete the work. Whereas the quality or creativity or speed of their previous work had created some feelings of personal pride, factory work was highly routine and depersonalized. What motivated people to accept this change in their work life? Usually it was the prospect of more income and/or more reliable income.

Finally, factory owners had to address the issue of skills. Most of the existing labor force had little education. They were unable to read instruction sheets or procedures manuals. They had little experience with complex machinery. They knew little about how to plan large-scale production processes or how to manage other workers. The skills they had simply didn't match those needed in the factory. All of these challenges had to be addressed in order to run a factory.[15]

Approaches to solving these human resource challenges has evolved and changed, just as the technology used has continued to evolve and change. A full appreciation of current approaches requires some understanding of their historical evolution. Exhibit 2.4 presents a thumbnail sketch of the changing concerns of human resource management within the United States.[16]

At the beginning of the 20th century, Frederick W. Taylor helped shape management practices. Trained as an engineer, Taylor emphasized the importance of developing precise analytical schemes to select, train, evaluate, and reward production workers for the purposes of motivating them, controlling their behaviors, and improving productivity. During the second quarter of the century, the focus shifted somewhat to acknowledging the importance of the work group's influence on employees. Elton Mayo and his work at the Hawthorne plant (the "Hawthorne studies") focused on improving individual productivity by experimenting with changing the work group's composition and incentive schemes, in addition to its environmental conditions, such as the lighting and physical arrangements. World War II

"The factory of the future will have only two employees, a man and a dog. The man will be there to feed the dog. The dog will be there to keep the man from touching the equipment."

Warren Bennis
Author and Distinguished Professor
University of Southern California

Exhibit 2.4

Evolution of Approaches to Managing Human Resources

Changing Concerns of Human Resource Management

Time Period	Primary Concerns	Employee Perceptions	Techniques of Interest
Before 1900	Production technologies	Indifference to needs	Discipline systems
1900–1910	Employee welfare	Employees need safe conditions and opportunity	Safety programs, English-language classes, inspirational programs
1910–1920	Task efficiency	Need high earnings made possible with higher productivity	Motion and time study
1920–1930	Individual differences	Employees' individual differences considered	Psychological testing, employee counseling
1930–1940	Unionization	Employees as adversaries	Employee communication programs, anti-unionization techniques
	Productivity	Group performance	Improving conditions for groups
1940–1950	Economic security	Employees need economic protection	Employee pension plans, health plans, fringe benefits (pensions, etc.)
1950–1960	Human relations	Employees need considerate supervision	Foremen training (role playing, sensitivity training)
1960–1970	Participation	Employees need involvement in task decision	Participative management techniques
	Employment laws		
1970–1980	Task challenge and quality of working life	Employees from different groups should be treated equally	Affirmative action, equal opportunity
1980–1990	Employee displacement; quality, cost, and customers	Employees need work that is challenging and congruent with abilities	Job enrichment, integrated task teams
1990–present	Productivity Competitiveness Globalization	Employees need jobs—lost through economic downturns, international competition, and technological changes	Outplacement, retraining, total quality management, organizational learning
	Change	Employees need to balance work and nonwork and make contributions; need to be flexible	Linking the needs of the business, training, ethics, diversity, and workplace accommodation

refocused attention on the importance of improving selection procedures for people doing more complex jobs (e.g., for fighter pilots and secret service agents). During the 1950s and 1960s, practices developed for military applications, such as assessment centers, spread into the private sector.

Throughout most of this time, a bureaucratic view—shaped by the needs of factories—predominated. By the 1970s, however, issues such as safety and health, stress, and employee satisfaction began to draw more attention. By then, technologies and the nature of work had changed substantially from the early factory days. Increasingly, employers wanted people to do more that just routine, mostly manual work; they wanted people to use their intellectual and creative talents to solve problems and create new products and services. Today, these very *human* resources are recognized as sources of potential competitive advantage.

The Age of Computers and Information Technology

"As you walk through cubicle land and you look at a bunch of people staring at computer screens, you really don't know what they're doing."

Jeffrey Rayport
Professor
Harvard Business School

By 1990, there were fewer manufacturing jobs than government jobs in this country. Those who still work in factories, like the employees at Lincoln Electric, now do so along side sophisticated robots. In many cases, the robots are being used to produce the computers that will help design the next generation of products to be manufactured—by the robots!

Clearly, computers have become the foundation of a new information age. Mass production systems were useful for producing standardized, low-cost goods. In his time, Henry Ford could produce a standard black Model T and count on people buying it, regardless of how well they actually liked that particular design and color. But now consumers demand more specialized products. Thanks to computers, modern production systems are highly flexible, allowing companies to efficiently produce small batches of customized designs.[17]

By the early 1990s, U.S. businesses had invested over $500 billion in new computer equipment.[18] In some industries, such as banking and insurance, business simply cannot be conducted without the use of computers. With computer-driven technology, many jobs have become more complex. Like the early factory owners, U.S. employers again face a shortage of the skills they need to leverage the newest technology. The fact that computers are now widely used at home as well as at work, as shown in Exhibit 2.5,[19] should

Exhibit 2.5
Percent of Households in Region with Personal Computers (1998 Estimates)

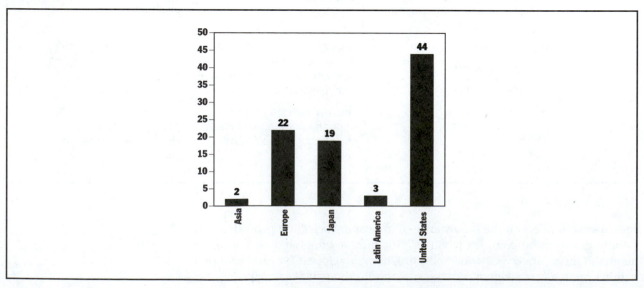

mean that this problem will ease somewhat with time, but until then, employers will have to find other ways to address this problem. The strong demand for computers within the U.S. helps account for the fact that, since the 1980s, computer manufacturing has accounted for one-third of the total productivity growth in the private sector. This is remarkable considering that the computer producing sector accounts for only three percent of total GDP.

It's inevitable that computer technology as we know it will eventually become obsolete. But in the foreseeable future, it will continue to transform the nature of work, the structure of organizations, and organizational approaches to managing human resources. As described in the feature, Managing Change: Do Executives Need More IT Training?,[20] just because employees have access to new technologies and are willing to use them is no guarantee that they have the skills needed to use them to full advantage.

Technology in the Services Industries

Currently, the technologies used in manufacturing industries are quite different from those used in the services industries. Most services involve something intangible that's produced and consumed during an interaction between the service provider and the customer. Clearly, some types of services are more intangible and simultaneous than others. The dinner at a nice restaurant includes a tangible product (the food), as well as some intangibles (the ambiance, the server's manner, etc.). In general, service work has involved a relatively high degree of social interaction. Until the advent of internet-based services, most service organizations were relatively low-tech (medical services are a notable exception, however). It was through social skills and technical knowledge that employees created value for the company and developed a sense of personal accomplishment. Technology was used primarily as a record keeping tool. However, changes in technologies may have profound implications for services in the future. Increasingly, technical knowledge is being captured by "expert systems" (also called, appropriately, artificial intelligence) that can be used by non-experts. In addition, technologies are increasingly being used to mediate transactions between service providers and customers. As customers of service organizations, we often must negotiate an electronic menu before speaking with a person. Employees, on the other hand, are increasingly being asked to create a positive service interaction with someone they will never see.

Knowing how new technologies will affect the service sector is difficult to predict. For some services, new technologies may have consequences that are as profound as those of mass production in the manufacturing sector. Jobs will increasingly involve narrow, simple, and routine transactions. Alternatively, new technologies may soon eliminate the most simple and routine aspects of service, leaving only those jobs that require relatively high levels of skill and expertise. This would be comparable to the effects on the factory floor of new manufacturing technologies and robotics. Regardless of which direction the changes occur, the services sector can expect to face new challenges for managing human resources.

Using Information Technologies to Manage Human Resources

New technologies change not only the nature of work in organizations, but also change the way workers are managed. When computer technologies are used to gather, analyze, and distribute information about the people in an organization, the resulting systems are referred to as human resource infor-

"The more technology you have in your office and at home, the more you need to balance that with the high touch of a personal meeting."

Patricia Brudick
Coauthor of Megatrends 2000

■□*fast fact*
Computer power is now 8,000 times less expensive than it was 30 years ago. If the same were true for automobiles, you could buy a Lexus for about $2.

MANAGING CHANGE

Do Executives Need More IT Training?

When information technologies (IT) were first introduced into the office environment, many executives were slow to use them. They were accustomed to dealing with people on a face-to-face basis, and often relied on their support staff for activities that involved such things as using a keyboard. Things have changed, however, and now many executives use these technologies regularly. To learn just how much executives were using information technology, and their views about its effectiveness, the Academy of Management polled 350 executives from a wide variety of organizations. The percentages of executives who were using each of several types of technology were as follows.

Type of Information Technology	Percentage Using It
E-mail	90%
Voice mail	88%
Fax	82%
Internet	53%
Cellular phone	46%

Although they were experienced users of information technologies, many of these executives expressed frustration and skepticism about their overall effectiveness. The following table shows the percentage of executives who indicated each type of concern listed.

Type of Concern	Percentage Who Expressed the Concern
IT has made our lives busier, but not better	58%
ITs ability to add value is vastly overrated	55%
IT produces more misunderstandings than real-time human conversation	54%
IT has caused relationships to deteriorate	51%
IT means serious information overload and redundancy for me	50%
IT has caused the work environment to become too cold and impersonal	44%

Often when technology is introduced, it's viewed as a technical improvement that will have little effect on how people relate to each other on a personal basis. As these results reveal, however, if people aren't trained to understand the potential misuses and negative consequences of a new technology, it can have unintended consequences. Many organizations are learning this lesson the hard way, after personal relationships have already been damaged. Nevertheless, many companies have successfully used new information technologies to improve their performance. Debbie Fields, CEO and president of Mrs. Fields is an example. She uses information technology to coach her managers on how to make and sell cookies. The technology helps her convey both business information and her charismatic leadership style, making her presence felt throughout the organization.

To learn more about the Academy of Management, visit their home page at **www.aom.pace.edu**

mation systems (HRIS). Several global companies have developed quite sophisticated human resource information systems for keeping track of who's doing what and where. For example, Citibank maintains a database that provides basic information about all employees in the 98 countries where it does business. In addition, it has more detailed information for about 10,000 key managers who are considered to be part of the company's global talent pool. When openings occur within the company, the database can be searched for potential internal candidates to fill the position.[21] As a preview to subsequent discussions, Exhibit 2.6 presents data showing which specific HR activities are currently most affected by information technologies, based on a study of 122 major corporations located around the world.[22]

The results in Exhibit 2.6 are particularly interesting when compared to predictions made by a human resource executive a decade earlier. Then, the introduction of new technologies was not considered a major concern. Its anticipated effects were limited primarily to the computerization of employee records. At the time, companies didn't yet have e-mail systems, intranets, and Internet access to the World Wide Web. With these new technologies already in place, implementing fully integrated global human resource management systems has become the next frontier for half of these companies. Such systems, they anticipate, are essential for such activities as recruitment and staffing, succession planning, and career tracking and development.

Exhibit 2.6 shows only *which* HR activities are most affected by new technology, not *how* they're affected. With time, the way technology is used will change, as well as the frequency with which it's used. Currently, most organizations use only low-level applications that essentially allow employees to access general information. For example, policies and procedures may be provided on a company intranet. A bit more complex are systems that allow employees to access specific information contained in their own employee records, such as retirement plan balances and vacation days accrued. Sometimes referred to as employee self service, such systems may also han-

Exhibit 2.6

Percent of Respondents Who Said Technology Has a "Major" Impact on the HR Activity

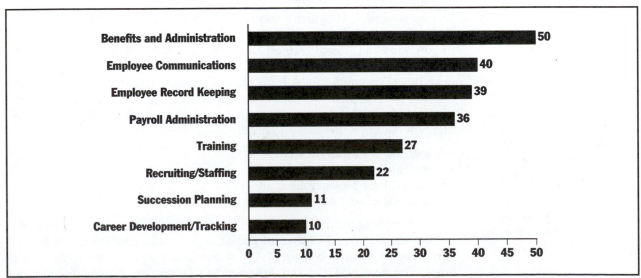

dle purchase requisitions and other simple requests. Much more complex are systems that give employees and managers a way to administer their own HR data and processes, without paperwork or administrative support. For example, advanced systems allow employees and managers to enter performance data, display and analyze it for trends over time, and use the data as input for both the employee's personal development plan and the organization's longer-term workforce and succession planning. When appropriate, third-party vendors (e.g., pension-fund managers, insurance providers, accountants) can be brought into the process also. As they become more common, sophisticated applications will greatly facilitate cooperative planning and problem solving by the HR partnership triad.[23]

It's interesting to note that the types of systems needed for sophisticated HR applications are quite similar to those already being used to meet the needs of customers. For example, trucking companies give customers access to their computerized tracking systems so they can check the status of their shipments. Retail chains are linked with their suppliers so they can give their suppliers up-to-date information about the the timing and the nature of needed shipments. Through computers, banks and brokerage firms already allow customers to conduct financial transactions and conduct what-if scenarios as part of their financial planning. In these and other ways, technology is dissolving many of the walls that previously defined the boundaries between various stakeholders.

THE STRUCTURE OF INTERFIRM RELATIONSHIPS

The media often portrays business organizations as warring enemies who define their own success by the demise of their competitors. Executives sometimes use similar imagery to motivate their "troops." What such images ignore are the strong interdependencies among business organizations and the degree to which cooperation results in mutual gains. Phrases such as strategic alliances and joint ventures, mergers and acquisitions, network organization, and multinational organization may not be eloquent, but they accurately describe the new organizations in which most people work.

Mergers and Acquisitions

During the 1990s, U.S. firms restructured through mergers and acquisitions (M&As) at a dizzying pace, and they remain a popular strategy for improving organization effectiveness.[24] Determining whether a deal was actually a merger or an acquisition is often difficult. In a merger, the two firms supposedly are on equal footing after the deal is closed, while in an acquisition it's clear that one firm will take control of the other's resources. For a variety of political and marketing reasons, however, acquisitions often are called mergers. Through mergers and acquisitions, firms seek to

- increase their market share,
- increase their geographic reach,
- fill out their product lines, and
- respond to new deregulation.[25]

In the computer industry (hardware and software), a major objective of a merger or acquisition is to gain access to the skills and talents of people employed by another company. Any technology that a company owns will quickly become outdated. But if the people who created that technology stay and remain energized, they're likely to create new products that will continue to succeed in the market place.

Before companies gained their current level of experience with M&As, the objectives that originally drove the deal were seldom fully realized. Research indicates that these deals fail to achieve their intended value in over two-thirds of the cases.[26] Plans that looked logical on paper, often fell apart when managers tried to implement them. People, it seemed, got in the way. More specifically, differing cultures often got in the way. When a firm with a fairly uniform culture introduces diversity in the form of another organizational culture, the culture clash can be so severe that the financial benefits of a merger can't be realized. As organizations began to experience the importance of different organizational cultures, they began to consider this issue more carefully before closing M&A deals. Novell, which was an aggressive participant in M&As, was one of the first companies to take a strategic approach to managing human resources during restructurings. To ensure that executives thought through all the HR issues when merging companies, Novell developed the Merger Book. Its two thousand questions pertaining to HR served as a road map for all Novell's M&A activities. Information gathering and analysis are the heart of the process.[27]

GE Capital Services took this idea a step further to create their Pathfinder model, which is described in Managing Diversity: GE Capital's Pathfinder Model for Cultural Integration.[28]

Downsizing

Throughout the 1990s, mergers and acquisitions were often accompanied by downsizing—the process of reducing the size of a firm by laying off or retiring workers early. The primary objectives of downsizing are to

- cut costs,
- spur decentralization and speed up decision making,
- cut bureaucracy and eliminate layers of hierarchy, and
- improve customer relations.

The ranks of middle managers have been especially hard hit by downsizing. According to a study by the Conference Board, about 72 percent of companies have fewer middle managers today than they did five years ago. One consequence of this trend is that today's managers supervise larger numbers of subordinates who report directly to them. In 1990, only about 20 percent of managers supervised 12 or more people and 54 percent supervised six or fewer. By 1995, 40 percent of managers supervised twelve or more people and only 15 percent supervised six or fewer.[29] More recent figures aren't available, but it's safe to assume the trend has continued in the same direction.

Because of downsizing, first-line managers have had to assume greater responsibility for the work of their departments. At Muratec Business Systems, which makes fax machines, specialists in quality control, human resources, and industrial engineering provide guidance and support. First-line managers participate in the production processes and other line activities, and coordinate the efforts of the specialists as part of their jobs. At the same time, the workers that first-line managers supervise are less willing to put up with authoritarian management. Employees want their jobs to be more creative, challenging, fun, and satisfying and want to participate in decisions affecting their work. One solution is self-managed work teams that

MANAGING DIVERSITY
GE Capital's Pathfinder Model for Cultural Integration

GE Capital Services has made the successful management of acquisitions a corner-stone of its strategy for growth. Every business group has a business development officer whose job is to find potential acquisition targets. The company has made more than 100 acquisitions during the past five years, growing by 30 percent in the process. GE Capital's experience has shown that acquisitions are much more likely to be successful if the employees who end up working together share the same values and mindsets. Therefore conducting a cultural audit and identifying cultural barriers are tasks that GE Capital's managers complete before an acquisition decision is finalized.

Its cultural audits identify cultural differences at all levels—societal, industry-wide, and organizational. Regarding industry-level similarities and differences, the companies are compared in terms of costs, brands, technologies, and customers. If the differences seem so great that they could cause the acquisition to fail, GE drops the planned acquisition. If the differences seem manageable and an acquisition deal is finalized, a systematic process for integrating the cultures then begins.

One of the first steps is to appoint an integration manager, who is responsible for integrating the cultures and the business and operational systems. As soon as the deal is finalized, key people from the two businesses are brought together to socialize, exchange information, and share their feelings about the new situation. Managers of the acquired company are quickly informed of GE Capital's twenty-five central policies and practices. Integration goals are developed, a 100-day deadline is set, and managers from the two companies meet for a three-day session devoted to exploring the cultural differences. Managers tell each other about their companies' histories, folklore, and heroes. Other topics include approaches to market penetration, the amount of focus on cost, and reliance on authority versus shared decision making.

These discussions culminate in a written plan for the next six months or more. Such plans generally include short-term projects that require people from the two companies to work together to achieve some quick results, such as reducing costs. The plans, as well as other information related to the integration process, are posted on the company's intranet, where managers throughout the company can study them and learn from each new acquisition experience.

Information about GE Capital Services can be accessed from the home page of General Electric at
www.ge.com

bring together employees and first-line managers who make joint decisions to improve the way they do their jobs.[30]

Spinoffs

When people consider the consequences of mergers and acquisitions, they often think of the downsizing that occurs through layoffs and the drive for efficiency. Layoffs almost always mean that large numbers of people lose their employment. Downsizing sometimes occurs without people losing their jobs, however. Sometimes entire divisions of a firm are simply spun off from the main company to operate on their own as new, autonomous companies. In spinning off divisions, the firm seeks to become more focused. For

"With the possible exception of GE—or maybe it's just Jack Welch—most companies cannot manage disparate businesses."

Larry White
Professor of Economics
New York University

example, in 1997, PepsiCo decided to spin off its 30,000 Taco Bell, KFC, and Pizza Hut restaurants in order to focus on its soft drink and snack foods businesses. The restaurants are still doing business, but now they're owned by Tricon Global Restaurants.[31] When Sears, Roebuck & Company recently restructured, it sold off interests in insurance (Allstate Insurance Company), real estate (Coldwell Banker), and finance (Dean Witter Reynolds). The objective was to refocus on merchandising.

Spinoffs aren't expected to compete with the original parent firm, but the parent is very likely to become a customer. That happened when AT&T "downsized" the old Bell Labs unit, which is now Lucent Technologies. Rather than having its research carried out in-house by Bell Labs, AT&T contracts with Lucent for the work. Lucent, in turn, is free to enter into contracts with companies other than AT&T. Thus, in this scenario it's more accurate to say that AT&T outsourced its research unit rather than to say it laid off these valuable employees. As organizations outsource functions, they become flatter and smaller. Unlike the behemoths of the past, the new, smaller firms are less like autonomous fortresses and more like nodes in a network of complex relationships. Outsourcing is one of many activities that creates interdependencies among companies. Nike outsources the production of its shoes to low-cost plants in South Korea and China and imports the shoes for distribution in North America. These same plants also ship shoes to Europe and other parts of Asia for distribution. A company that's really a set of highly interdependent but legally separate businesses is known as a modular corporation. They're most common in the apparel, auto manufacturing, and electronics industries.[32] The most commonly outsourced function is production. By outsourcing production, a company can switch suppliers as necessary to use the supplier best suited to a customer's needs.

Decisions about what to outsource and what to keep in-house are fundamental strategic decisions that define the organization. Most experts believe that the decision to contract production to another company is a sound business decision, at least for U.S. manufacturers. It appears to hold down the unit cost of production by relieving the company of some overhead, and it frees the company to allocate scarce resources to activities for which the company holds a competitive advantage. Chrysler's compact car, the Neon, is manufactured as a modular project. The entire car is shipped to Neon assembly plants in four easy-to-assemble modules from separate suppliers. Other U.S. car manufacturers are expected to follow its lead. In the future, a car may be designed on the super CAD/CAM system at IBM's Boca Raton facility, built by suppliers in various countries, and assembled for delivery at a site closest to its targeted customer.

This new mode of operating seems to be a solution to various problems in the rapidly changing business environment. But it isn't a cure-all, and, in fact, the trend may have already gone too far. Some companies that outsourced key functions such as human resource management and information technology are now reconsidering those decisions as they realize how essential these functions are to their business.[33]

Strategic Alliances and Network Organizations

A strategic alliance involves two or more firms agreeing to cooperate as partners in an arrangement that's expected to benefit both firms. Sometimes strategic alliances involve one firm taking an equity position on another

■□ fast fact

In 1982, AT&T agreed to spin off 22 Bell System telephone companies in return for being allowed to expand into previously prohibited areas of competition, ending a 13-year lawsuit against them.

firm. Ford, for example, has equity in both foreign and U.S. auto parts producers. It also owns 49 percent of Hertz, the car rental company that's also a major customer. Other alliances do not affect legal ownership. In the airline industry, a common type of alliance is between an airline and an airframe manufacturer. For example, Delta agreed to buy all its aircraft from Boeing. Boeing has a similar deal, valued at billions of dollars, with American Airlines. Through these agreements, Boeing guarantees that it will be able to sell specified models of its aircraft for several decades to come. The airlines, in turn, can develop a schedule for retiring old aircraft and can begin to adapt their operations to the models they will be flying in the future.[34]

To understand how complex and global interdependencies among strategic partners can become, consider the following factual example:

> *Natural gas owned by Indonesia's oil agency, Pertamina, flows out of a well discovered by Royal Dutch Shell into a liquification plant designed by French engineers and built by a Korean construction company. The liquified gas is loaded onto U.S.-flagged tankers, built in U.S. shipyards after a Norwegian design. The ships shuttle to Japan and deliver the liquid gas to a Japanese public utility, which uses it to provide electricity that powers an electronics factory making television sets that are shipped aboard a Hong Kong-owned container ship to California for sale to American farmers in Louisiana who grow rice that's sold to Indonesia and shipped there aboard Greek bulk carriers. All of the various facilities, ships, products, and services involved in the complex series of events are financed by U.S., European, and Japanese commercial banks, working in some cases with international and local government agencies. These facilities, ships, products, and services are insured and reinsured by U.S., European, and Japanese insurance companies. Investors in these facilities, ships, products, and services are located throughout the world.[35]*

In high-tech industries, strategic alliances allow older, established firms to gain access to the hot new discoveries being made by scientists in universities and in small, creative organizations. For example, the U.S. biotechnology industry is characterized by networks of relationships between new biotechnology firms dedicated to research and new product development and established firms in industries that can use these new products, such as pharmaceuticals. In return for sharing technical information with the larger firms, the smaller firms gain access to their partners' resources for product testing, marketing, and distribution.[36] Big pharmaceutical firms such as Merck or Eli Lily gain from such partnerships because the smaller firms typically develop new drugs in as little as five years, versus an eight-year average development cycle in the larger firms.[37]

As a firm enters into more and more strategic alliances, it becomes enmeshed in a web of relationships and interdependencies—that is, it becomes a part of a larger network. The term *network organization* often is used to refer to a large group of interconnected companies. In Japan, such networks, called *keiretsu*, have pervaded the economy since about World War II.[38] In the U.S., biochips, which blend computer technology with biological science, are among the most exciting products being created through new network organizations. Taking advantage of a computer's ability to process massive amounts of information, biochips are being developed to scan people's genetic makeups and analyze risks associated with various genetically transmitted diseases.[39] The Acer Group refers to its network of affiliated companies as a federation. Its slogan, "21 in 21," is used to remind people that their goal is to have at least 21 members in this federation of cooperating firms by the 21st century. Included are organizations that specialize in R&D, marketing, manufacturing, and so on.[40]

CREATING A FOUNDATION FOR MANAGING IN THE GLOBAL ARENA

Poorly managed human resources account for many business failures in the international arena. The primary causes of failure in multinational ventures stem from a lack of understanding of the essential differences in managing human resources in foreign environments—differences due to culture as well as those due to political and economic trends.

Understanding National Cultures

Societal values have many far-reaching consequences for managing organizations.[41] For example, at 3Com, the 65 nations represented present significant barriers to communication. Explained one worker, "Around here you point a lot." Besides making conversation difficult, cultures shape the preferences and behaviors of customers, employees, and all other members of the communities in which an organization operates. For example, in individualistic cultures, people are more comfortable being given straightforward feedback about their individual strengths and weaknesses; in collectivistic cultures feedback is given in more subtle and indirect ways and focuses less directly on the individual. At Microsoft, differences such as these mean that the company's U.S. managers must understand a variety of societal cultures and be able to work with the local managers who run sales offices in some 60 countries. Expatriates who lack cultural sensitivity experience problems in communication and feelings of isolation. Managers working in a culture that they don't understand are likely to make poor decisions about how to staff their organizations and motivate employees.[42]

Are you wondering where you're most likely to be sent on your next expatriate assignment? Exhibit 2.7 reports on a study by the National Foreign Trade Council and Windham International that reveals the 15 countries emerging as the most likely destinations for expatriates.[43] Of course, these projections were based on current conditions; major political or economy changes can occur rapidly and significantly change the desirability of any of these locations for significant foreign investment.

Certain management philosophies and techniques have proven successful in the domestic environment. They're successful in part because they were developed and honed to fit the peculiarities of our domestic conditions, including a culture characterized as highly individualistic and democratic. Conversely, when foreign companies set up operations here, they bring along approaches to managing that fit well in their own home environment. Exporting approaches to managing human resources to foreign environments often leads to frustration, failure, and underachievement. This is one reason why expatriates who have been sent abroad to manage a firm's foreign operations often fail, despite the exceptional financial and marketing skills that made them seem like the ideal candidates for such conditions.[44]

Experienced travelers and managers alike know that societal cultures don't necessarily change suddenly when they cross the border between countries. Conversely, even within the same country cultures often change dra-

■☐ *fast fact*

National flags from 65 countries wave at a 3Com plant in Illinois. Each represents the nation of a worker hired in the three years since the plant opened.

Exhibit 2.7
The 15 Top Destinations for Expatriates

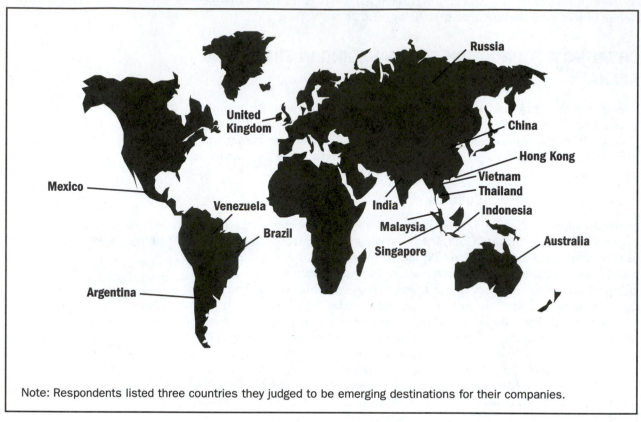

Note: Respondents listed three countries they judged to be emerging destinations for their companies.

matically from one side of a mountain range to the other, from north to south, and from the seashore to the landlocked interior within countries. For example, China's billion plus people comprise many distinct ethnic groups who speak many dialects and follow myriad local customs. A study of 700+ managers in large cities in each of the country's six major regions suggests that there are at least three distinct subcultures in China: one in the southeast, another in the northeast, and a third covering much of the central and western parts of the country. The subculture of the southeast region is the most individualistic, whereas the subculture of the central and western areas is the most collectivistic. The culture of the northeast region falls between these two extremes. Bridging this and other differences among the regions, however, is a shared commitment to traditional Confucian values of societal, interpersonal, and personal harmony.[45] In China, the U.S., and many other countries, distinct regional subcultures are present, and thinking that all members of a society share the same attitudes, values, and norms is a mistake.

Understanding Global Political and Economic Trends

In addition to the cultural differences among countries, vast differences in political and economic conditions affect how organizations manage human resources. And these can change quite rapidly. For example, at the beginning of 1997, Indonesia was experiencing 10 percent GDP growth. But by the end of the year, the value of the rupiah and the stock market had both plunged 50 percent while GDP slowed to nearly zero. Student protests against political corruption forced Indonesia's president of 30 years to step down in 1998, creating great political uncertainty. The rupiah plunged another 25 percent. Most foreign businesses vacated the country, including the many Chinese enterprises that served as the foundation of the economic engine, and by mid-year GDP growth hit minus four percent.[46] Will future business in Indonesia be marked by the political corruption and cronyism of the past, or will political reforms open this huge market to more open competition? It's too soon to tell, but the two possible futures have vastly different consequences for human resource management practices in that country.

Entire volumes have been devoted to describing cultural and economic differences,[47] and the space here isn't nearly sufficient to summarize this work. Instead, we will highlight conditions in just three regions: China, Mexico, and Europe. In subsequent chapters, we return to these regions to examine the implications of some of these conditions for managing human resources.

China. U.S. businesses have invested approximately $18 billion in mainland China. They are counting on government officials to make good on a plan to reduce the civil servant workforce by four million, reform the banking system, revive large state enterprises and privatize many smaller state enterprises, and build private health insurance and pension schemes from scratch. Currently, the private sector accounts for only about 20 percent of this country's economy, and even the vice minister of the China's State Economic and Trade Commission admits that up to half the 75 million state-enterprise workers aren't needed. Significant reform would mean unemployment for millions more Chinese people. In a country where tens of millions of people already are unemployed, and lower-level state officials are widely assumed to be corrupt, political and economic stability are far from certain.[48]

Of course, any generalizations about China greatly oversimplify conditions in this diverse country. Conditions in poverty-stricken rural areas are worlds apart from those in the dynamic urban centers of Shanghai, Beijing, and Hong Kong. Generational differences also are significant. Chinese who are currently about 50 years old came of age during the country's violent and repressive Cultural Revolution in the late 1960s and early 1970s, and have spent much of their adult life cocooned in a closed political and economic system. Subsequent generations have been increasingly exposed to Western capitalism—largely through television but also through Western business education.

To glimpse what the China of the future might be like, it's useful to look at the business practices of Chinese people living in other countries throughout Southeast Asia. The family enterprise is the basic unit of economic activity in Southeast Asia, and 90 percent of the billionaires in the region are ethnic Chinese. For example, Liem Sioe Liong, as founder of the Salim Group, controls Indonesia's largest ethnic Chinese enterprise. It accounts for five percent of Indonesia's gross domestic product, and its $3 billion in assets span 75 companies in 24 countries.

The rapid growth of Chinese family businesses reflects their entrepreneurial approach. Unlike the traditional large U.S. business, a Chinese family enterprise often consists of a vast network of businesses. Despite their size, however, these businesses bear little similarity to a complex corpora-

"In almost every state enterprise, between 30 percent and 50 percent of the workers are redundant."

Denis Simon
Head of Andersen Consulting in

"China is moving from one kind of orderly system, socialism, to another, free-market capitalism. In between, you have a chaotic period."

Dong Tao
SC First Boston, China

tion. They're managed more like small businesses, held together by strong personal ties instead of formal structures, policies, and procedures. Close relatives fill most top management positions and other strategic posts. These managers accept the authority of the family head, deferring to his decisions. Professional managers (outsiders) are almost never entrusted with the business. Financial arrangements and connections among these companies are kept secret, and strategic planning activities take the form of family discussions, with the head of the family making the key decisions. Even when one of these enterprises decides to sell stock on a major stock exchange, the owners release as little information as necessary. The constant, circuitous flow of assets makes these enterprises difficult for western financial analysts to understand.

Although highly successful, this form of organizing does have its downside. For one thing, effectiveness may be needlessly limited when incompetent and untrained relatives are given jobs that require professional expertise. Even if nonfamily members are eventually hired, they may not be very productive. They have little real authority, even over those who report to them. So it isn't surprising that they generally are dissatisfied and spend their energy thinking about leaving to start their own companies. Increasingly, however, professional managers may be found within the family, as Chinese sons and daughters take their western business-school training back home. Their challenge will be to find ways to blend professional management techniques with the highly successful family approach that has worked so well for hundreds of years of Chinese enterprise.[49]

Mexico. In 1993, the Canadian Parliament, the U.S. Congress, and the Mexican Congress each approved an historical agreement designed to allow for eventual free trade among these three countries. The North American Free Trade Act (NAFTA) went into effect the following year, marking the first time that a developing country entered into a free trade agreement with developed countries. Immediately all tariffs were removed for some classes of goods (e.g., computers, telecommunications, aerospace and medical equipment) as well as for all new services. Tariffs for other goods and services were scheduled to decrease gradually over a period of years, with nearly all tariffs being eliminated within 15 years.[50] The same year that NAFTA went into effect, Mexico became the 25th member of the Organization for Economic Cooperation and Development (OECD)—the first Latin American country to join. Exhibit 2.8 shows how Mexico compares on several indicators to several other OECD countries. Of the countries shown, the one whose state of economic development is most similar to Mexico's is Turkey.[51]

Since passage of the North American Free Trade Agreement (NAFTA), dozens of major U.S. manufacturing companies have expanded operations in Mexico. In many cases, this has meant moving low-skill, low-pay jobs from one side of the border to the other. According to a 1997 Department of Labor study, jobs paid at an average hourly rate of $7.71 in El Paso, Texas, would be paid only $1.36 in Mexico. (Note, however, that U.S. workers would pay a larger share of that in taxes, compared to the Mexican counterparts, as shown in Exhibit 2.8.) Predictably, unemployment levels in U.S. border towns went up, often to levels that were two and three times higher than the national average. On the brighter side, growth is now on the rise in towns on both sides of the border, as warehouses, distribution centers, and truck depots are expanded to support the growing trade traffic. But most observers agree that U.S.

Exhibit 2.8

Comparing Mexico to Selected OECD Countries

	Mexico	United States	Canada	Japan	Turkey
Self employment as percent of total employment	58	65	68	70	62
Percent employed in services	52	73	73	60	33
Personal income taxes:					
Lowest rate	3	15	17	10	25
Highest rate	35	31	29	50	50
Average after-tax disposable income of production worker, as percent of gross pay					
Unmarried	89	74	74	85	84
Married with two children	89	81	85	90	82

workers in the border region will be able to lift their standard of living to the national average only after extensive retraining and skill development.[52]

Meanwhile, manufacturing companies from around the world are setting up state-of-the-art manufacturing plants in Mexico to produce goods that will eventually be sold in the U.S. Since 1994, auto manufacturers and parts suppliers from around the world have invested nearly $15 billion in Mexico. For Volkswagen, Mexico offers not only higher levels of worker productivity but also a growing market for its old-style Beetles. GM now uses its facilities in Cuidád Juarez, just across the border from El Paso, as a basic training location for its network of global managers. While many of the plant managers that GM will eventually send to other countries are Mexican nationals, managers from all over the world also receive their training in Mexico.[53]

European Union. The countries that belong to the European union differ from each other in many political, economic, and cultural ways. Unemployment rates, for example, range from around 2 percent in Luxembourg to 12 percent in Germany (its highest level in 50 years), and 19 percent in Spain. Nevertheless, they share some similarities. For example, government spending as a percent of GDP averages more than 45 percent, compared to just over 30 percent in the U.S. Unlike Americans, who save only about 4 percent of their annual income, Europeans save more than 10 percent of their annual income.[54]

Assuming the European peoples actually accept the plans put in place by their government leaders, as outlined in Exhibit 2.9, the new euro establishes participating countries as the second largest economic zone (after the U.S.), with countries linked together through common economic policies. In the longer term, government spending and individual savings rates may decline, and at the same time, they're likely to become even more uniform across the region. Governments have already begun deregulating industries such as telecommunications and airlines. Companies have already begun merging and streamlining, following the pattern established a decade earlier in the United States. Corporate executives are getting a taste of performance-based pay agreements—a change that other employees can anticipate, too.

Thus, like China, major changes are afoot in Europe, and the transition period is likely to be bumpy. Compared to the U.S., workers in Europe are

"The single most important regulatory change anywhere in the world is the European Monetary Union."

**Mac Heller
Head of M&A
Goldman Sachs**

Exhibit 2.9

Key Scheduled Milestones on the Road to the Euro

May 1998	Governments pick European union members and set exchange rates for entry
January 1999	European Central Bank takes over monetary policy. National currencies remain but stocks, government debt, bank accounts, credit cards, and prices will be measured in euros.
January 2002	Euro physically replaces national currencies. Retail payments allowed only in euros.
July 2002	National currencies cease to exist, replaced by euros.

*"When I want to call
Europe, who do I call?"*

**Henry Kissinger,
when he was Secretary of State**

eligible for more social benefits and live in greater economic egalitarianism. Centralized wage-setting institutions have kept wage disparities down relative to the U.S., and educational and work apprenticeship programs generally ensure high levels of skills. In addition, various laws protect workers from layoffs. Monetary union is likely to change all that as soon as an economic downturn hits part, or all of, the region. Major battles are likely to be fought over tax policies and subsidies to poorer countries within the European union. Proposed rules limiting budget deficits may force cuts in health and welfare benefits, widening the disparities between rich and poor. As foreign countries move into Europe to exploit the consumer market, competitive pressures on domestic companies may force some to move to lower-cost Central Europe, repeating the NAFTA dynamics described above. Competitive pressures may also detract from the relatively high standards of corporate social responsibility to which European businesses are currently held. Whether the people will consider the pain to be worth the gain is an open question.

Managing Diversity

Perhaps the greatest challenge to managing human resources in a global economy is learning to manage across different cultures. Cultures come in many varieties: national cultures, regional cultures, industry cultures, corporate cultures, occupational cultures, and so on. Increasingly, a firm's total diversity is created by a variety of these influences.

Diversity created through organizational restructuring can be particularly difficult to management. Cultures often go unnoticed until they clash. Such clashes often occur when organizations merge or enter into other types of deep strategic alliances. For companies with little experience, the clash of cultures often is more disruptive than anticipated. The process of learning to manage such diversity can be painful, as illustrated in the feature Managing Globalization: Culture Clash at Pharmacia & Upjohn, Inc.[55] This company was created through a merger of U.S. and Swedish pharmaceutical firms. Because they were in the same industry, the two firms shared some common assumptions and values, but these commonalities seemed small in light of their cultural differences.

To many outsiders, societal-level cultural differences created the conflicts within Pharmacia & Upjohn. But some of the firm's managers argue that differing management philosophies and organizational cultures caused the problems. Most likely, both types of differences contributed to the problems. For the new company to function effectively, managers and employees alike must learn to manage the organization's total diversity more effectively.

MANAGING GLOBALIZATION

Culture Clash at Pharmacia & Upjohn

Shortly after the merger, the headquarters of Pharmacia & Upjohn was just a stone's throw from England's Windsor Castle. For the managers who had to travel from Stockholm, Kalamazoo, and Milan—the locations of the company's main operations and 30,000 employees—the headquarters decision was just one of many sources of stress. Among the others were the following.

- The hard-driving U.S. approach clashed with the consensus-oriented Swedish approach. While the U.S. managers at Upjohn focused on ambitious cost-cutting goals and numerical accountability, the Swedish managers at Pharmacia kept their employees informed and sought feedback about how to carry out changes.
- Upjohn managers scheduled meetings throughout the summer and couldn't comprehend that Pharmacia managers spent all of August on vacation.
- Managers in many European companies are accustomed to working across borders and tend to be more flexible and adaptable than U.S. managers. Upjohn's strict policies subject all workers to drug and alcohol testing and ban smoking.
- At Pharmacia's Milan location, wine is poured freely in the company dining room and the boardroom in Stockholm is well-stocked with humidors.
- The Upjohn-based CEO required frequent reports, budgets, and staffing updates. The Swedes viewed these tasks as a waste of time and eventually stopped taking them seriously.

These conflicts hurt the company's bottom line. Everyone had hailed the merger as a wise strategic decision to expand the scale and scope of both firms. The new firm had greater international presence and more products than either firm had alone. But earnings in the first two years were below expectations, resulting in the resignation of the firm's CEO.

One approach that began to bridge the cultures among members of the research units was moving managers back and forth across the Atlantic. According to Research Executive Vice President Goran Ando, doing so helped speed cultural learning and development of mutual respect. But the basic styles of the managers were slow to change. "I am a Swede who has lived in both Britain and the United States for a number of years," explained Ando. "I see in Americans a more can-do approach to things. They try to overcome problems as they arise. A Swede may be slower on the start up. He sits down and thinks over all the problems, and once he is reasonably convinced he can tackle them, only then will he start running." Guy Grindborg, a technical trainer for the Swedish firm Ericsson, Inc., observed similar differences, causing him to adjust the way he conducts training sessions when he's in the United States. "The Swedish approach is more the engineering approach: 'Tell my why and how this thing works.' The American approach is much more direct. Their attitude is: 'Don't teach me to be an expert, just tell me what I need to know to do my job.'"

Given the challenges of managing the different cultures in the new company, adding even more diversity by locating headquarters in another cultural context was a novel idea. In the long-run, it proved to be ineffective; headquarters has since been moved. Where would you locate this company's headquarters, and why?

To learn where Pharmacia & Upjohn is now headquartered, visit the company's home page at
www.pharmacia.se

Developing a strong corporate culture is one approach to this challenge. When a company's operations are flung across great distances and many national cultures, a consistent and strong corporate culture glues the pieces together. The Swiss-Swedish firm Asea Brown Boveri (ABB) is one global firm with a strong corporate culture. "We think of ABB as a company without regard to national boundaries. We just operate on a global basis," explains Richard Randazzo, vice president of human resources. The corporate culture—focused on making money, taking action, using a hands-on approach, and traveling to wherever business opportunities arise—isn't insensitive to national cultures, however. Indeed, the firm insists that its 213,000 employees working in 1,300 national companies adapt the corporate culture to blend with the local cultural scene. Local activities, in turn, influence the ABB corporate culture because local learning is shared across borders. For example, ABB's approach to equal employment opportunity in Europe reflects its U.S. experience. This is because European countries have become actively concerned with issues of equal employment opportunity only recently, whereas the United States has many years of experience addressing these concerns.

It has taken years for ABB to learn to manage effectively as a global corporation. Ultimately, Pharmacia & Upjohn will develop its own unique corporate culture—one that blends elements of the U.S. and Swedish approaches to doing business. The sooner that happens, the easier it will be for everyone in the company to work together productively. In the mean time, however, ABB's skills at managing the diversity within its organization are a source of competitive advantage.[56]

In the future, other organizations may be able to use new research findings to help them define a corporate culture that's likely to be effective across many cultures. The Global Leadership and Organizational Behavior Effectiveness Research Program, which is referred to as the GLOBE project, was the brainchild of Wharton Professor Robert House. This massive study is a collaborative effort involving 170 social scientists and management scholars who have been collecting data on the behavior they prefer from organization leaders. Results from this project are just beginning to be made public. Some of the earliest conclusions from this project are described in the feature, Managing Strategically: Research Points the Way to Defining an Effective Global Corporate Culture.[57]

Preliminary results from the GLOBE project suggest that managers with a few essential behavioral styles—charismatic/value based, team-oriented, and humane—can be reasonably effective in many different countries and cultures. Many culturally specific behaviors must be learned by leaders working in various cultures also. Can a manager give performance-related feedback the same way in every country? Probably not. In the U.S., supervisors usually provide negative feedback directly in a face-to-face conversation. But in Japan, supervisors usually channel negative feedback through a peer of the subordinate's. Nevertheless, the GLOBE results indicate that supervisors working in either country can be effective by attending to the administrative aspects of performance evaluation and then using the information they gather to give feedback in a diplomatic way, given the cultural norms.

Unilever, often described as one of the foremost transnational companies, views its approach to managing human resources as central to its ability to operate its 500 or so businesses around the world as a cohesive organization. Explained CEO and Co-Chairman Floris Maljers, "Of course, we

MANAGING STRATEGICALLY

Research Points the Way to Defining an Effective Global Corporate Culture

The GLOBE project seeks to address several interesting questions about the nature of leadership in organizations around the world. One key question under investigation is whether some leader behaviors are considered effective by managers worldwide. To answer this question, the project collected data from approximately 16,000 middle managers working in more than 800 organizations in 64 countries. They were asked to describe behaviors that facilitated or impeded effective leadership. Leadership behaviors were grouped into six general patterns. Specific behaviors and attributes associated with each category also were identified. Middle managers' responses were analyzed to determine which leadership behavior patterns were universally considered positive or universally considered negative. The following table shows the results of the study.

General Leadership Behavior Patterns	Specific Leader Behaviors and Attributes	Universally Positive or Negative?
Charismatic/value-based	Visionary Inspirational Self-sacrificing Shows integrity Decisive Performance-oriented	Universally positive
Team-oriented	Collaborative team orientation Team integrator Diplomatic Not malevolent Administratively competent	Universally positive
Humane	Modest Generous Compassionate	Positive in most countries
Participative	Not dictatorial Not bossy Not elitist	Mixed; somewhat positive in some countries and somewhat negative in other countries
Autonomous	Individualistic Independent Unique	Mixed; somewhat positive in some countries and somewhat negative in other countries
Narcissistic	Self-centered Status conscious Conflict inducer Face saver Procedural	Universally negative

did not design our extensive system of recruitment, training, and attachments [international assignments] with the idea of forming a 'transnational network.' However, in practice, this network—as represented by both the company's formal structure and the informal exchanges between managers—may well be one of the ingredients in the glue that holds Unilever together."[58]

MANAGING THROUGH PARTNERSHIP IN A DYNAMIC ENVIRONMENT

As shown in Exhibit 2.1, a process of sense making and decision making determines how the many aspects of a dynamic environment affect the organization's approach to managing human resources. To meet the challenges created by a dynamic environment, partners in the HR triad must work together to gather relevant information about the environment, share it with all relevant stakeholders, and collaboratively develop action plans to address the challenges. Having a respected HR professional on the top management team facilitates the partnership processes. Even when this isn't the case, members of the HR triad should integrate issues related to managing human resources into the firm's planning processes by attending to the roles and responsibilities shown in the feature, The HR Triad: Partnership Roles and Responsibilities for Environmental Scanning and Analysis.

Formal Processes

Formal and systematic analysis of the environment generally includes[59]

1. scanning all segments of the environment to detect changes that are already underway and to identify early signals of potential changes,
2. regular monitoring of key aspects of the environment in order to more precisely determine the nature of changes as they unfold,
3. using forecasting techniques to make projections about what might actually happen and when, and
4. assessing the timing and significance of environmental changes for key decisions related to managing the firm (e.g., strategy selection).

In many organizations, managers engage in these formal activities according to a regular schedule, e.g., annually. Often, however, key events that are judged to be of special importance—such as an unexpected and major new action by a competitor or a military coup—can trigger a formal analysis.

Whenever possible, objective information about the environment should be used in these formal analyses. However, for many aspects of the environment, objective data are either not available or they're available but only as indicators of what has already happened—not what is about to happen. For example, although there are objective milestones that have been set for Europe's monetary union, there are many uncertainties that could change the dates by which key milestones are reached. In deciding how to respond to Europe's shift to the euro, therefore, decision makers are likely to use their own judgments about the actual process of consolidation into a single monetary union.

Informal Processes

Often the process of conducting a formal analysis ensures that the analysis is reasonably systematic. That is, a structure is imposed on the process to

"High-level managers won't waste their time with you if you can't talk about the same goals."

Ken Carrig
Vice President of HR
Continental Airlines

The HR Triad: Partnership Roles and Responsibilities for Environmental Analysis

Line Managers	HR Professionals	Employees
Stay informed about economic conditions and their possible implications for the organization.	Stay informed about economic conditions and their possible implications for the organization.	Stay informed about economic conditions and their possible implications for the organization.
Investigate potential new markets for products and services. Encourage discussion of the potential implications that you learn.	Investigate foreign labor market qualifications and conditions. Encourage discussion of the potential implications that you learn.	Develop a basic understanding of how global conditions are likely to affect your organization and career.
Investigate new technologies relevant to the business to learn how they can be used to gain competitive advantage. Advocate their use as appropriate.	Learn to use advanced HRIS technologies and understand how they can be used to gain competitive advantage. Advocate their use as appropriate.	Take responsibility for continuously developing skills needed to use new technologies. Be proactive and creative in thinking about how available technologies can be used advantageously in your own work area.
Develop an understanding of the culture of selected countries of likely importance to the business. Develop language and interpersonal skills for working in a multicultural environment. Encourage and facilitate the development of cross-cultural skills among employees.	Educate the organization about the new issues to be addressed as the organization expands beyond domestic borders. Provide resources for managers and other employees to learn about cultural differences and to develop skills in cross-cultural interaction.	Develop an understanding of at least one culture other then your own. Develop an understanding of the unique aspects of your own culture and how people from other cultures view it. Help employees from other cultures learn about your culture.
Develop an understanding of newly emerging structural forms and their implications for managerial jobs. Develop skills needed for managing alliances.	Provide information to managers and employees about the skills needed in newly emerging organizational structures and provide the resources needed to develop those skills.	Develop teamwork skills needed for working across organizational boundaries.
Keep employees and HR professionals informed of environmental trends that are likely to have a significant impact on the business.	Keep line managers and employees informed about the implications of environmental trends for individual skills development, career management, and changes in approaches to managing human resources.	Recognize that changes in the environment can have unpredictable consequences for your employment situation and be prepared for unexpected disruptions.

ensure that all of the available information is used and considered. As any experienced manager understands, however, there are many informal processes that influence how the information collected through formal analysis is eventually translated into decisions. Internal politics and simple habits from the past can shape the decisions made almost as much as the information itself. Perhaps most fundamental is simply who is asked to participate in the process. In a company where marketing is viewed as the most important activity, people who are viewed as relevant to marketing activities may have more influence than others; if research and innovation are key concerns, then people who have little expertise about R&D issues may be excluded from the process.

To the extent that human resource management issues aren't viewed as central to the success of the business, an organization may be less likely to ensure that information about labor markets and cultural conditions are taken into account. Increasingly, however, HR issues *are* being recognized as essential to business success. This is reflected in the changing status of HR managers within organizations, and in the way HR managers spend their time. According to a recent survey of more than 900 HR managers in positions at all levels, about one out of six spends 25 percent of their time—or more than one full day per week—on strategic planning.

SUMMARY

The environment in which organizations operate is complex and dynamic, creating a constant flow of new opportunities and challenges for organizations and the people who work there. We began this chapter by briefly describing the nature of competition within the borders of the United States. The intensity of this competition is one reason many U.S. companies become involved in international activities. Labor market conditions at home and abroad are a second reason.

Whereas competition and labor market conditions are forces that push organizations into the global arena, new technology facilitates the process. New technologies mean that there are always new possibilities for how to respond to the changing global conditions. Just as new technologies are beginning to make new forms of organizing possible in the future, the technology of the past played a major role in shaping today's organizations. A brief overview of how mass production systems shaped current approaches to managing human resources was provided as a basis for understanding the profound changes that are needed as the old production systems become obsolete.

In order to maximize their competitiveness and exploit the opportunities created by a dynamic global environment, collaboration among several firms may be needed. These collaborative arrangements can take many forms, including strategic alliances, mergers, outsourcing relationships, and so on. In some industries, complex networks or interdependent organizations have evolved.

One consequence of the ways that firms have responded to the many environmental forces described in this chapter has been an increase in the amount of diversity within an organization. Learning how to manage their increasing internal diversity has become one of the major challenges for managing human resources. Because this is so difficult and so important, the firms that meet this challenge most quickly will gain a source of sustainable competitive advantage. To meet this and the other challenges created by a dynamic environment, partners in the HR triad must work together to gather relevant information about the environment, share it with all relevant stakeholders, and work collaboratively to develop action plans to address these challenges.

TERMS TO REMEMBER

Corporate culture	International workforce
Domestic labor market	Mass production technology
Downsizing	NAFTA
European union	Network organization
Flexible manufacturing technology	Open markets
Global labor market	Outsourcing
Human resource information system (HRIS)	Spinoff
	Strategic alliance
Information technology (IT)	Virtual workforce

DISCUSSION QUESTIONS

1. Why did BMW locate in Spartanburg, South Carolina? How could this decision help them gain a sustainable competitive advantage?

2. Choose an industry of interest to you. How would you rate the relative level of domestic and international competition in this industry at the current time? Explain your evaluation. What are the specific indicators of competitiveness in the industry? Is the level of competitiveness likely to intensify in the next five years? Why or why not?

3. Which characteristics of the domestic and global labor markets are most significant for a consumer products company like Coca Cola? Which are most significant for a pharmaceutical company like Merck? Describe the nature of the effects.

4. You are working at a local bank in a mid-level management position. You learn on the evening news that your company has agreed to a merger with a competitor. The rationale that's given for the merger is, "There are many synergies that a merger will allow us to exploit. This merger isn't about becoming more efficient—it's about growing revenues." Assume this is true. What will be the three most significant HR issues for the new organization? Why?

5. Do you agree or disagree with the following statement: "As long as a company is careful to base employment decisions (such as who to hire and how much to pay them) on merit, it shouldn't need to invest a lot of resources in special diversity initiatives."

PROJECTS TO EXTEND YOUR LEARNING

1.   **Managing Strategically.**   Your company is exploring the idea of acquiring another firm. It has never completed an acquisition before, and everyone wants to make sure they make the right decision. After learning about GE Capital Service's Pathfinder model, you are convinced this is just what your company needs to do. You need much more information in order to actually use the model, however, so you have arranged a one-hour interview the Director of Human Resources at GE Capital Services. What are the most important things you need to learn during your interview with this person? If you could interview one other person, who would it be, and what would you want to learn? Explain your rationale.

2.   **Managing Teams.**   You work in an organization that uses many temporary teams to work on projects. The projects usually last three or four months, and then the team disbands. After reading about the results of the Academy of Management's executive survey concerning the uses and consequences of information technology, the vice president of marketing suggests that your company put together a training program. You are a member of the task force put in charge of this. Answer the following questions:
    a.   What are the most important objectives of the training program?
    b.   Should the program be required or mandatory, and for whom?
    c.   Could the program be delivered electronically over the company's intranet, or should it be delivered in person? Why?
    d.   Explain how the company could determine whether the program has achieved its objectives.

3.   **Managing Globalization.**   Working with a class partner, choose two countries of interest to you and learn as much as you can about the characteristics of the labor markets in those two countries. What are the biggest differences between the labor forces in the two countries? How would these differences be likely to affect approaches to managing human resources in these countries? To begin your investigation, you may find it useful to visit the following web sites:
    www.worldculture.com
    www.euen.co.uk
    www.ilo.org

4.   **Managing Change.**   For years, IBM was known as a company that treated people well, including a near-guarantee of job security. The 1990s were a time of significant change. When IBM first announced there would be layoffs, people were stunned. There were several years of trauma, but after the downsizing the company rebounded. By 1996 it was growing again, with much of its new growth coming from acquisitions. Read the chairman's letter to shareholders in IBM's most recent annual report. Identify one or two *current* strategic issues facing IBM and explain how these issues are likely to affect human resources practices at the company. You can view an online version of IBM's annual report at **www.ibm.com/AnnualReport**

5.   **Managing Diversity.**   An organization called the Shorter Work Time Network of Canada maintains a web site that documents experiments

with altered work weeks in the United States and Canada. Visit the site and then write a paragraph describing three advantages and three disadvantages that have been found to be related to the use of alternative work schedules. In addition, list one key information source that you would recommend to an organization interested in considering alternative schedules. The address for this site is www.vcn.bc.ca/timework/worksite.htm

6. **Integration and Application.**   Review the end-of-text cases. Then,
   a. describe the impact/relevance of the following environmental factors for AAL's approach to managing human resources
      • the global economy,
      • the national culture of the U.S., and
      • changes in technology.
   b. describe the impact/relevance of the following possible events for Southwest Airlines' approach to managing human resources
      • The unemployment rate continues to decline, putting pressure on wages.
      • A tax law change makes it more difficult for business travelers to treat airfare as a deductible expense.
      • OPEC members agree to substantially reduce oil production in an attempt to boost prices.

CASE STUDY

Implications of a Competitive Environment for Managing Human Resources at the Barden Corporation

The largest segment of the Barden Corporation is the Precision Bearings Division. It manufactures high-precision ball bearings for machine tools, aircraft instruments and accessories, aircraft engines, computer peripherals, textile spindles, and medical and dental equipment. Currently, the division employs about 1,000 people and includes a marketing department and a small corporate staff. It was founded during World War II to manufacture the special bearings needed for the Norden bombsight and has been nonunion since the beginning. Mr. Donald Brush, vice president and general manager of the Precision Bearings Division, gives the following description of his division:

Reporting directly to me is a small staff comprising a manufacturing manager, a quality manager, an engineering manager, a director of manufacturing planning, and a manager of human resources (see Case Exhibit 1). We meet several times a week to discuss current problems, as well as short- and long-range opportunities and needs. On alternate weeks, we augment this group by including the supervisors who report to the senior managers listed above. I might interject here that all supervisors meet with hourly employees on either a weekly or biweekly basis to review specific departmental successes and failures, and to otherwise keep employees informed about the business and to encourage ownership of their jobs. The managers themselves meet on call as the Employee Relations Committee to discuss and recommend approval of a wide range of issues that include the evaluation and audit of hourly and salaried positions, as well as the creation and modification of all divisional personnel policies.

A few words about our Human Resource Department: There are six employees who together provide the basic services of employment, affirmative action, employee activity support, labor relations, interpretation of the federal and state laws, benefits administration, wage and salary administration, records preparation and maintenance, cafeteria supervision, and so on. There are, in addition,

Case Exhibit 1
Precision Bearings Division

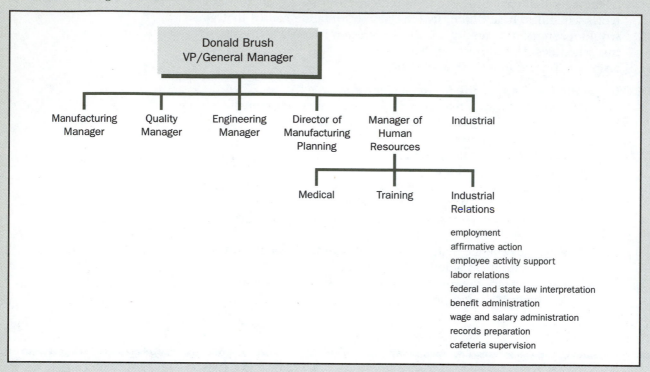

two people who coordinate our rather extensive training activities.

As currently organized, the Medical Department comes under the supervision of the manager of human resources. Its authorized staff includes a medical director, the manager of employee health and safety (who is an occupational health nurse), a staff nurse, a safety specialist, and secretary/clerk.

The development and execution of plans and programs, including those of a strategic nature, almost invariably involve the active participation of HR. And that's how we want it to be. On the other hand, the HR Department doesn't run the business. By this I mean they don't hire or fire, promote or demote. They don't write job descriptions or determine salaries or wages. All these things are done by the line managers with the HR Department providing a framework to ensure consistency and that all actions are appropriate to company goals. You might say that HR is our "Jiminy Cricket"—they're there for advice, consent, and, importantly, as a conscience.

BUSINESS OBJECTIVES

During the past several months, we have been running into many issues that affect the very essence of our business objectives: growth, profits, survival, and competitiveness. Because the issues involve our human resources, these must be our major HR objectives. Would you please give us your experience, expertise, and suggestions as to how we can solve them? Thanks! The following briefly describes the nature of each of the four HR objectives.

Recruiting and Training New Hourly Employees. The need to recruit and train approximately 125 new hourly workers to respond to a surge in business is very challenging. By mid-year, it became evident that we had an opportunity to significantly increase our business. In order to achieve otherwise attainable goals, we need to increase our hourly workforce by a net of about 125 employees (that is, in addition to normal turnover, retirements, etc.) in one year. I have asked HR to test the waters, recognizing the unemployment in the Danbury labor market for skilled workers has reached an unprecedented low of about 2.5 percent.

Safety and Occupational Health Improvement. The need to create a heightened awareness by the workforce for safety and occupational health considerations is very important. This is an evolving mission born of a dissatisfaction on our part about "safety as usual." Over the years, Barden employees have assumed that, because we are a metalworking shop, people were just going to get hurt. But we cannot afford to have people get hurt and miss work anymore. Yet, as our workforce ages, the employees seem to get out of shape and become more injury and illness prone.

Managing Health Costs of an Aging Workforce. The spiraling health costs of an aging and, sometimes, out-of-shape workforce are very costly. All employers face this. Barden's problem is a little unique in that hourly employees tend to stay with the company and retire from the company. For example, we still have several employees whose careers began with us 45 years ago, shortly after the company was founded. Our average age approaches 45 for employees and their dependent spouses. Generally, our jobs do not require much physical effort, and it's easy to become out of shape. As a consequence, employees get sick, use hospitals, and have accidents.

New Machines and the Development of Qualified Workers. The technological evolution of increasingly complex machinery and related manufacturing equipment, and the development of trained workers to operate and maintain this equipment, are important facts of life. This process is unceasing and requires a good deal of planning for both the short- and the long-run. For example, what should we do in the next year, or five years out, in order to remain competitive in terms of cost, quality, and service? Buying and rebuilding machines is part of the story. Running them efficiently is quite another. As you know, modern equipment of this sort requires operational people who aren't only knowledgeable about the turning or grinding of metals, but also conversant with computerized numerical controls. The employee who sets up and operates a $500,000 machine must be well trained. Yet finding trained people is getting more difficult.

SUMMARY

Mr. Brush knows that these HR objectives all reflect the increasing diversity of the workforce. Because of this, he knows these issues will be around for a long time. He requests that you provide him with your general ideas and suggestions. He doesn't want details at this time.

QUESTIONS

1. Which of the HR objectives facing Mr. Brush are really the most important to the success of the business? Prioritize them and justify your list.

2. Now consider this list of objectives from the perspective of employees. Using the employees' perspective, how would you prioritize the list? What are the implications in any differences in the two lists of priorities for Mr. Brush?

3. Choose two objectives. For each, describe the key roles and responsibilities of the HR manager, the line managers, and other employees.

4. Visit the company's website at **www.nai.net/~barden01/home**

   Based on the types of products it offers, describe the nature of the environment and its implications for remaining competitive.

SOURCE: This case was prepared by Randall S. Schuler, who expresses his appreciation for the cooperation of Donald Brush.

CASE STUDY

The Sherwin-Williams Company: Power of the Environment

Spread throughout the United States and North America, the Cleveland, Ohio-based Sherwin-Williams Company has claimed for years that it sells enough paint to cover the earth. Perhaps you have seen its logo of the earth being covered with a can of red paint. Well, this is just part of the 18,000 person, $3 billion company. Its largest business unit is the Stores Group, which operates about 2,000 paint stores across the United States. These stores sell to do-it-yourself retail customers, as well as professional painters and industrial customers. They're the exclusive channel of distribution for Sherwin-Williams–brand products. The Coatings Group is responsible for product development and manufacturing and also sells other brands of paint products to major retail customers such as hardware stores, home centers, and mass merchandisers. The Automotive Division is a major player in the automotive aftermarket; it provides a variety of specialty coatings to original equipment manufacturers.

Sherwin-Williams felt the effect of the external environment back in 1977, the first year in its 111-year existence that it lost money. Shortly after that, the reigning CEO, Walter Spencer, resigned. For the first time in its history, the company went outside to recruit a new CEO. John G. Breen quickly took the company into a significant cultural and organizational change. Beginning in 1979 and through the 1980s, the culture altered dramatically from paternalistic to performance based. The management style became aggressive and demanding. A centralized structure was replaced with a decentralized, autonomous one. These changes occurred while the organization went through two major strategies. The first strategy was a turnaround; the business had to be saved. The key business issue during this period, from 1979 into the early 1980s, was survival and was characterized by the slogan "Cash Is King." Management emphasis was on expense control, working capital management, financial controls and systems, and divestiture of nonprofitable businesses. The planning horizon was one day at a time. Once the financial stability of the organization had been secured, the second strategy was set in place. This strategy emphasized growth. From the mid-1980s forward, the growth strategy was evidenced

by the business goals of profitable growth, sales development and market share, product quality, acquisitions in the core business, and longer-term planning. During this period, the saying that captured the spirit became "Paint Is King."

These business changes in turn greatly affected the company's approach to managing human resources. Driven by the new corporate culture and structure, new HR policies and practices were rolled out. Here are some typical examples of how HR practices changed from the time of the turnaround to the time of new growth:

- HR planning went from short-term survival concerns to longer-term development concerns.
- Staffing went from heavy outplacement to ongoing hiring at all levels.
- Performance appraisal criteria shifted from an emphasis on short-term, bottom-line results to a focus on longer-term issues such as leadership development and feedback.
- Compensation for top management went from high risk, high reward to above-average pay for high performance.

The only constants during these times of perpetual change were the beliefs and values of the company. These included a fundamental belief that managers are paid for improvement and that smart people plus hard work equals success. Other cornerstones of the Sherwin-Williams culture included these beliefs:

- Winning is better than losing.
- Truth is what you can put a number on.
- Problems are to be faced, not avoided.
- Personal integrity above all is essential.

During these times, the HR department had to deal with its own structure. The key to the effectiveness of the HR strategy at Sherwin-Williams was an effective partnership between the HR professionals and operating managers. Human resource responsibilities continued to be pushed out into the divisions and to the line managers while the corporate HR staff became smaller and shifted to a group of highly specialized professionals providing technical expertise to the division staffs in such areas as employment law, compensation, benefits, labor relations, management development and HR planning, and consulting.

These changes, made in response to developments in the environment (competition at the business level and a new business strategy, culture, and structure at the HR level), were successful. Yet, neither Sherwin-Williams nor any other firm is able to assume that the environment will ever again be relatively constant and predictable. To this day, the HR staff at Sherwin-Williams continues to make changes and adjustments in the HR operations because of changes in the environment, and the line managers continue to act in true partnership by actually taking responsibility for many HR activities.

QUESTIONS

1. In addition to the change in leadership and business strategy, what other forces in the environment were probably influencing how Sherwin-Williams was managing human resources during the 1980s and early 1990s?

2. In what ways can companies like Sherwin-Williams monitor their environment to anticipate what, if any, changes may be needed in their approaches to managing human resources?

3. Visit the company's homepage at **www.sherwinwilliams.com**

   Then describe the international marketplace for Sherwin-Williams's products.

4. If Sherwin-Williams expands globally, what new issues are likely to affect its approach to managing human resources?

ENDNOTES

[1] "The Bill and Warren Show," *Fortune* (July 20, 1998): 48–64.

[2] G. Jaffe and O. Suris, "Audi May Join Car Makers' Caravan to Southern States," *The Wall Street Journal* (March 13, 1997): B1, B10; M. Tennesen, "HR Faces Distinct Issues in Rural Areas," *Personnel Journal* (June 1994): 112–120; C. Scholz, *Human Resource Management in Germany* (Universitat des Saarlandes, November 1994). For additional information about labor relations within Germany, see K. S. Wever, "Political Economic Institutions, Labor Relations, and Work," A. Howard, ed., *The Changing Nature of Work* (San Francisco: Jossey-Bass, 1995).

[3] Adapted from S. E. Jackson and R. S. Schuler, "Understanding Human Resource Management in the Context of Organizations and Their Environments," *Annual Review of Psychology* (1995): 254.

[4] D. B. Sicilia, "How the West Was," *Inc.* (January 1997): 74–78.

[5] P. Elstrom, C. Arnst, and R. Crockett, "At Last, Telecom Unbound," *Business Week* (July 6, 1998): 24–27.

[6] M. McNamee, W. Zellner, R. A. Melcher, B. Javetski, et.al., "Industry Outlook," *Business Week* (January 13, 1997): 86–132; E. E. Gordon, R. R. Morgan, and J. A. Ponticell, *Futurework: The Revolution Reshaping American Business* (Westport, CT: Praeger Publishers, 1996); I. Morrison, *The Second Curve: Managing the Velocity of Change* (New York: Ballentine Books, 1996); L. C. Thurow, *The Future of Capitalism: How Today's Economic Forces Shape Tomorrow's World* (New York: William Morrow & Company, 1996); R. Ruggiero, "The High Stakes of World Trade," *The Wall Street Journal* (April 28, 1997); M. Mandel, K. Naughton, G. Burns and S. Baker, "How Long Can This Last?" *Business Week* (May 19, 1997): 29–34.

[7] C. Yang, "This Could Be the Breakthrough Merger," *Business Week* (July 6, 1998): 29.

[8] P. Coy, E. Neuborne, W. Zellner, A. Reinhardt, et.al., "Industry Outlook," *Business Week* (January 12, 1998): 80–134.

[9] A. Bernstein and S. Hamm, "Is There Really a Techie Shortage? Yes, But It's Not as Dire As the Computer Industry Says," *Business Week* (February 15, 1998): 15–17.

[10] H. Gleckman, "High–Tech Talent: Don't Bolt the Golden Door," *Business Week* (March 16, 1998): 30; R. Beck, *The Case Against Immigration* (Norton, NY, 1996); "Dearth of High-Tech Workers Cited," *Bulletin to Management: Policy Guide* (July 24, 1997): 240.

[11] "Earth Population Breakdown," *ACA News* (July/August 1996): 17; "World Population to Hit Six Billion Next Year," *The Sunday Times* (July 12, 1998): 15.

[12] B. Murray, "America Still Lags Behind in Mathematics Test Scores," *APA Monitor* (January 1997): 44.

[13] J. Messina, "A Gift of Tongues: New Immigrants Drive High-Tech in NY," *Crain's New York Business* (April 6, 1996): 1–41.

[14] "Five Myths of Today's Labor Market," *Workforce* (March 1998): 48.

[15] D. A. Wren, *The Evolution of Management Thought* (New York: John Wiley & Sons, 1994).

[16] Portions of this exhibit were adapted from S. J. Carroll and R. S. Schuler, "Professional HRM: Changing Functions and Problems in the 1980s," in S. J. Carroll and R. S. Schuler, eds., *Human Resource Management in the 1980s* (Washington, DC: Bureau of National Affairs, 1983): 8–10. Also see A. Howard, "A Framework for Work Change," in A. Howard, ed., *The Changing Nature of Work* (San Francisco: Jossey-Bass, 1995).

[17] For discussions of new manufacturing technologies and the many ways in which they change organizations, see T. D. Wall and P. R. Jackson, "New Manufacturing Initiatives and Shopfloor Job Design," in A. Howard, ed., *The Changing Nature of Work* (San Francisco: Jossey-Bass, 1995); P. S. Adler, ed., *Technology and the Future of Work* (New York: Oxford University Press, 1992).

[18] R. H. McGuckin, K. J. Stiroh, and B. van Ark, *Perspectives on a Global Economy* (New York: The Conference Board, 1997).

[19] T. Peterson, "The Euro," *Business Week* (April 27, 1998).

[20] Adapted from J. F. Veiga and K. Dechant, "Wired World Woes: www.help," *Academy of Management Executive* 11(3) (1997): 73–79.

[21] L. Stroh, S. Grasshoff, A. Rude, and N. Carter, "Integrated HR Systems Help Develop Global Leaders," *HRM Magazine* (April 1998): 15–17.

[22] *HR Executive Review: Technology's Role in HR Management* (New York: Conference Board, 1998).

[23] J. F. LeTart, "A Look At Virtual HR: How Far Behind Am I?," *HRM Magazine* (June 1998): 33–42; S. Greengard, "Building a Self-Service Culture that Works," (July 1998): 60–64.

[24] A. Harrington, R. M. Rao, and T. Maroney, "Mergers: Why This Historic Boom Will Keep Making Noise," *Fortune* (April 7, 1998): 148–156; L. M. Holson, "The Deal Still Rules," *The New York Times* (February 14, 1999): Section 3, 1 and 10.

[25] G. Colvin, "M&A and You: Career Power," *Fortune* (June 22, 1998): 173–175.

[26] D. A. Nadler, *Champions of Change* (San Francisco: Jossey-Bass, 1998).

[27] D. Anfuso, "Novell Idea: A Map for Mergers," *Personnel Journal* (March 1994): 48–55; "Doing Mergers by the Book Aids Growth," *Personnel Journal* (January 1994): 59; A. F. Buono and J. L. Bowditch, *The Human Side of Mergers and Acquisitions: Managing Collisions between People, Cultures, and Organizations* (San Francisco: Jossey-Bass, 1989).

[28] R. N. Ashkenas, L. J. DeMonaco, and S. C. Francis, "Making the Deal Real: How GE Capital Integrates Acquisitions," *Harvard Business Review* (January–February 1998): 165–178.

[29] G. H. Axel, *HR Executive Review: Redefining the Middle Manager* (New York: The Conference Board, 1995).

[30] A. Mohrman and A. M. Mohrman, Jr., K. B. Evans and H. P. Sims, Jr., "Mining for Innovation: The Conceptual Underpinnings, History, and Diffusion of Self-Directed Teams," in C. L. Cooper and S. E. Jackson, eds., *Creating Tomorrow's Organizations: A Handbook for Future Research in Organizational Behavior* (Chichester, England: John Wiley & Sons, 1997): 269–292. G. M. Parker, *Cross-Functional Teams* (San Francisco: Jossey-Bass, 1994); and C. C. Manz and H. P. Sims, Jr., *Business Without Bosses* (New York: John Wiley & Sons, 1994).

[31] For more discussion about spinoffs see: *Beyond the Break-up: The Special Challenges for Leaders of New Spinoffs* (New York: Delta Consulting Group, 1998); D. C. Hambrick and K. Stucker, "Breaking Away: Executive Leadership of Corporate Spinoffs," in J. Conger, et al., *The Leader's Change Handbook* (San Francisco: Jossey-Bass, 1998).

[32] G. Dess, A. M. A. Rasheed, K. J. McKaughlin, and R. L. Priem, "The New Corporate Architecture," *Academy of Management Executive* 9 (3) (1995): 7–20.

[33] Adapted from M. E. McGill and J. W. Slocum, Jr., *The Smarter Organization* (New York: John Wiley & Sons, 1994).

[34] M. Brannigan and J. Cole, "Delta to Buy All Its Planes from Boeing Co.," *The Wall Street Journal* (March 20, 1997): B2.

[35] T. Peters, *Thriving on Chaos* (New York: Alfred Knopf, 1987): 123.

[36] J. P. Liebeskind, A. L. Oliver, L. Zucker, and M. Brewer, "Social Networks, Learning, and Flexibility: Sourcing Scientific Knowledge in New Biotechnology Firms," *Organization Science* 7 (1996): 428–443.

[37] E. Schonfeld, "Merck vs. the Biotech Industry: Which One Is More Potent?," *Fortune* (March 31, 1997): 161–162; and I. Sager, "The New Biology of Big Business," *Business Week* (April 15, 1996): 19.

[38] For an historical account of Japanese keiretsu, see J. R. Lincoln, M. Gerlach, and C. Ahmadjian, "Evolving Patterns of Keiretsu Organization and Action in Japan," *Research in Organizational Behavior* 20 (1998): 303–345.

[39] D. Stipp, "Gene Chip Breakthrough," *Fortune* (March 31, 1997): 56–73.

[40] R. E. Miles, C. E. Snow, J. A. Mathews, G. Miles, and H. J. Coleman, Jr., "Organizing in the Knowledge Age: Anticipating the Cellular Form," *Academy of Management Executive* 11(4) (1997): 7–24.

[41] S. C. Schneider and J. L. Barsoux, *Managing Across Cultures* (New York: Prentice-Hall, 1997); Hofstede, *Cultures and Organizations: Software of the Mind* (New York: McGraw Hill, 1995); G. Hofstede, B. Neuijen, D. D. Ohayv, and G. Sanders, "Measuring Organizational Cultures: A Qualitative and Quantitative Study of Twenty Cases," *Administrative Science Quarterly* 30 (1990): 286–316; P. C. Earley and M. Erez, eds., *New Perspectives in International Industrial/Organizational Psychology* (San Francisco: New Lexington Press, 1997).

[42] B. Schlender, "Microsoft: First America, Now the World," *Fortune* (August 18, 1997): 214–217; R. Tung and V. Worm, "East Meets West: Northern European Expatriates in China," *Business and the Contemporary World* 9 (1997) 137–148; and N. Rogovsky and R. S. Schuler, "Managing Human

Resources Across Cultures," *Business and the Contemporary World* 9 (1997): 63–75.

43 C. M. Solomon, "Hot New Markets," *Global Workforce* (January 1998): 13–22.

44 M. A. Shaffer and D. A. Harrison, "Expatriates' Psychological Withdrawal from International Assignments: Work, Nonwork, and Family Influence," *Personnel Psychology* 51 (1998): 87–118; W. A. Arthur, Jr. and W. B. Bennett, Jr., "The International Assignee: The Relative Importance of Factors Perceived to Contribute to Success," *Personnel Psychology* 48 (1995): 99–114; D. C. Thomas and E. C. Ravlin, "Responses of Employees to Cultural Adaptation By a Foreign Manager," *Journal of Applied Psychology* 80 (1995): 133–146.

45 D. A. Ralston, Y. Kai-Cheng, X. Wang, R. H. Terpstra, and H. Wei, "The Cosmopolitan Chinese Manager: Findings of a Study on Managerial Values Across the Six Regions of China," *Journal of International Management* 2 (1996): 79–109.

46 M. Landler, "Gloom Over Asia Economies Spreads as Yen Drops Again," *New York Times* (June 12, 1998): D1, D6.

47 R. B. Freeman, ed., *Working Under Different Rules* (New York: Russell Sage, 1997); P. R. Sparrow & J. M. Hiltrop, *European Human Resource Management in Transition* (New York: Prentice Hall, 1995); P. J. Dowling, D. E. Welch, and R. S. Schuler, *International Dimensions of Human Resource Management,* 3rd ed. (Cincinnati: South-Western/ITP, 1999).

48 R. Thomlinson, "The China that Clinton Won't See," *Fortune* (June 6, 1998): 130–134; L. Kelley and Y. Lud, *China 2000: Emerging Business Issues* (Thousand Oaks, CA: Sage, 1998).

49 M. Weidenbaum, "The Chinese Family Business Enterprise," *California Management Review* (Summer 1996): 141–156; L. W. Busenitz and C. M. Lau, "A cross-cultural cognitive model of new venture creation," *Entrepreneurship Theory and Practice* (Summer 1996): 25–40.

50 For a full discussion of cultural differences among the three NAFTA countries, see R. T. Moran and J. Abbott, *NAFTA: Managing the Cultural Differences* (Houston, TX: Gulf Publishing, 1994).

51 *Manpower Argus* (December 1995) 327: 10.

52 S. H. Verhoveck, "Free Trade's Benefits Bypass Border Towns," *New York Times* (June 23, 1998): A1, A16.

53 M. Gowan, S. Ibarreche, and C. Lackey, "Doing Things Right in Mexico," *Academy of Management Executive* 10 (1996): 74–81; J. Millman, "Mexico is Becoming Auto-Making Hot Spot," *The Wall Street Journal* (June 23, 1998): A17.

54 Much of the information in this section about the European Community was reported in a *Business Week* special report, "The Euro," (April 27, 1998): 90–110, which included the following individual articles: T. Peterson, "The Euro;" J. Warner, "Mix us culturally? It's Impossible;" W. Echickson, "Workplace Earthquake?"; G. Edmondson, "Industrial Revolution;" and J. Warner, "The Great Money Bazaar."

55 Adapted from A. Friedman, "A Case of Corporate Culture Shock in the Global Arena," *International Herald Tribune* (Zurich ed.) (April 23, 1997): 1, 11; R. Frank and T. M. Burton, "Cross-border Merger Results in Headaches for a Drug Company," *The Wall Street Journal* (May 1, 1997): A1, A13; D. Stamps, "Welcome to America. Watch Out for Culture Shock," *Training* (November 1996): 22–30; and R. Calori and B. Dufour, "Management European Style," *Academy of Management Executive* 9(3) (1995): 61–73.

56 L. S. Csoka, B. Hackett, R. J. Kramer, K. Troy, and M. L. Wheeler, *Global Management Teams: A Perspective* (New York: The Conference Board, 1996); and K. J. Fedor and W. B. Werther, Jr., "The Fourth Dimension: Creating Culturally Responsive International Alliances," *Organizational Dynamics* (Autumn 1996): 39–52.

57 R. J. House, P. J. Hanges, S. A. Ruiz-Quintanella, P. W. Dorfman, M. Javidan, M. Dickson, and 170 GLOBE country co-investigators, "A Global Study of Leadership," W. Mobley, ed., *Advances in Global Leadership*, Volume 1 (Greenwich, CT: JAI Press, 1998).

58 F. A. Maljers, "Inside Unilever: The Evolving Transnational Company," *Harvard Business Review* (September–October 1992): 46–51.

59 M. A. Hitt, R. D. Ireland, and R. E. Hoskisson, *Strategic Management: Competitiveness and Globalization* (Cincinnati, OH: Thomson, 1999).

MANAGING EMPLOYEES FAIRLY

"Eighty percent of the ethics issues that came across my desk were human-resources related [involving] people who thought they should have been allowed to try for a particular job opening, or someone who thought they were unfairly disciplined, where the boss yelled at them unfairly in front of others, showing a lack of mutual respect."

Bill Prachar
Former Ethics Officer
Teledyne Inc.[1]

Chapter Outline

MANAGING THROUGH PARTNERSHIP

at Coors

The Coors Brewing Company, headquartered in Golden, Colorado, is famous for its beer and for its procedures for managing employees fairly. Headed by the family heir, Peter Coors, Coors Brewing Company realized in 1978 that it had to develop better relations with employees. A bitter confrontation between the union that had represented the employees for nearly fifty years and the management preceded a failed strike against the company. Furthermore, the employees voted to decertify the union representation. Naturally, this left the employees without protection from what they saw were the "potential abuses of management."

Employees were afraid that management would take control from them and give them no recourse in such matters as employee discipline. To their way of thinking, "if management wants to get us out of here, they'll do it and do it without a fair hearing." According to Richard Kellogg, who was involved in the grievance process at that time and later became Coors HR director, representatives for the workers told Bill Coors, who was head of the company: "Our employees are frightened because they've had this union here that was taking care of our needs and making sure that discipline was meted out fairly. Now we don't have that and we've got to either find a way to provide it or ultimately the employees will bring in another union."

The company, specifically the HR department, acted swiftly. Borrowing from a Coors subsidiary, Coors Container Company, the HR department set up a peer review system designed to give employees a chance to air their complaints and have their peers take part in evaluating whether their complaints were legitimate. HR believed that such a system would benefit employees and management alike. Others in senior management, including the Coors family members, were not so positive. They feared that every disciplinary action would be considered unfair. So disciplinary actions would always be reviewed by the peer review system. This, in turn, would mean that the disciplinary action would always be reversed. Despite their concerns, they agreed to put the system in place. To appease senior management's fears, HR said it would use the system only for debates over termination actions. According to Kellogg: "We found out early on, however, that some employees get very upset about a first written warning." As a result, the company expanded the system to include hearings for all forms of discipline including first warnings, final warnings, suspensions without pay, and terminations. Coors' peer review system works like this:

Step 1   An employee who's unsatisfied with the application of a company policy—but not the policy itself—may file an appeal with his or her employee relations representative within seven working days. The employee relations representative then sets up an appeal board by randomly selecting two members of management and three employees from the same job category as the appellant.

Step 2   A hearing is held, orchestrated by the employee relations representative. At the hearing, the supervisor describes the circumstances surrounding the discipline. The employee then explains why the supervisor's action was unfair. Board members may ask questions of both parties during the proceedings and also may request testimony from witnesses.

Step 3   When the board members are satisfied that they have all the information that they need, they privately discuss the case. They decide by majority vote on one of three outcomes: to uphold the action; to reduce the severity; or to overturn the action completely. The board's decision is final. The employee relations representative notifies both the supervisor and the appellant of the decision through a brief, written summary, signed by all the board members.

The results thus far indicate that management's fears were unfounded: for the past ten years, an average of only nine percent of management's decisions have been overturned by the review boards. Management now recognizes an added value of the review board: Coors has never lost a wrongful termination case in court. According to Ed Cruth, employee relations manager for the company: "If we can't substantiate or uphold a termination internally with an appeal board, we can almost guarantee it wouldn't be upheld in front of a jury. And if it's upheld internally, then we feel comfortable that it's going to be upheld in front of a jury." Cruth goes on to add that the peer review system is also consistent with the Civil Rights Act of 1991 that specifically provides for and encourages the use of alternative dispute resolutions. Over time, employees learn to accept, trust, and use a grievance and appeal system even when the majority of decisions are not made in their favor! The experience of Coors, as well as a great deal of research on the topic, shows that the process and procedures used to make decisions are as important to employees as are the decisions themselves.[2]

To learn more about Coors, visit the company's home page at:
www.coors.com

"If the only thing we do is reside in the rules-based, compliance-based legal focus, I don't think we challenge our organizations to revise and grow."

Keith Darcy
Senior Vice President
IBJ Schroder Bank and Trust

FAIRNESS: A KEY CONCERN FOR MULTIPLE STAKEHOLDERS

In a capitalistic economic system, managers on behalf of shareholders seek to maximize profits free of non-economic external constraints—that is, without constraints other than those imposed by consumers and competitors. In the real world, effective U.S. businesses address the concerns of many stakeholders. However, as noted in Chapter 1, companies vary greatly in this regard. Some take a proactive stance in their relationship toward society and employees, going beyond codified laws and regulations in order to live up to society's ethical principles. At the other extreme, some companies allow managers and other employees to flagrantly violate existing laws and regulations. For example, Dayton-Hudson considers issues of managing diversity effectively in their department stores to be essential to their business success, while Dillard's department store has been criticized severely for racially-biased practices in its Kansas City stores. As part of a recent lawsuit, police officers who worked while off duty as security guards for the company, testified that the company instructed them to follow black customers and that some guards used special codes over the walkie-talkie system to alert the store to the presence of black shoppers. After losing the case, which was brought by a black human resources manager who was searched by a security guard at an upscale suburban store, Dillard issued no apologies and is appealing the verdict. Meanwhile, the Mayor has asked the city's pension managers to ensure that the city doesn't own any Dillard's stock.[3] As Dillard has learned, fairness is a topic that concerns society, the labor force and various legal institutions.

Society

At the societal level, a fundamental concern is that employees be treated fairly. People believe that fairness is a desirable social condition—we want to be treated fairly, and we want others to view us as being fair.[4] Companies that rank high as the best places to work generally emphasize fairness as part of their corporate culture because fairness creates the feeling of trust that's needed to "hold a good workplace together."[5]

The concept of fairness has many connotations, so ensuring fair treatment can be a major challenge for employers.[6] Furthermore, society's view of what constitutes fair treatment of employees is in constant flux, so companies must continually adjust. Practices that were considered fair at the beginning of the 20th century had become illegal by the middle of the 20th century. Similarly, practices considered fair today may no longer be legal in five or ten years. For companies operating internationally, being responsive to multiple societal concerns becomes particularly complex.

What does it mean to be treated fairly? Do we automatically feel that we have been treated unfairly when things do not turn out in our favor? What do people do when they have been treated unfairly? We address these and related questions in this chapter. The chapter begins by explaining how employees evaluate whether they have been treated fairly and how this affects their behavior at work. Next, we describe workplace policies, procedures, and practices that employers use to ensure fair treatment of employees. As you will see, some approaches to workplace fairness mirror the procedures used in the U.S. courts. In the United States, the legal system helps define and interpret for society the meaning of fair treatment within employment settings. Thus, this chapter concludes with an overview of the legal rights and responsibilities of employers and employees.

The concerns of our broader society are communicated through, and supported by, the actions of two primary stakeholders: the labor force and legal institutions.

The Labor Force

Members of the workforce communicate their concerns directly and indirectly. As free agents, they communicate their concerns to employers directly. For example, when deciding which company to work for, a potential employee evaluates whether a company pays a fair wage, whether it offers desirable benefits, whether the corporate culture is appealing, and so on. When making these evaluations, perceptions of what is "fair," "desirable," and "appealing" reflect the potential employee's concerns. The free agency of job applicants, combined with the diversity of the U.S. labor force, means that companies must consider a broad array of labor force concerns in order to attract and hire the best talent.

Once hired, employees continue to express their concerns, and they also evaluate whether their employer is addressing those concerns. Indirectly, or informally, employees may voice their concerns in daily conversations at work. If they feel unfairly treated, they may also "vote with their feet" and seek employment elsewhere.[7] To avoid such departures and surface problems before they become severe, many companies also offer formal channels of expression, such as employee surveys and employee grievance systems.

Finally, union members voice their concerns directly when they collectively bargain with employers over working conditions and compensation.

Legal Institutions

Legal institutions provide indirect channels for the labor force to use in communicating their concerns to employers. Through elected government representatives, members of the labor force initiate and ultimately create federal and state laws. Through their tax payments, employees pay for the operations of a vast array of government agencies and courts, which are responsible for interpreting and enforcing the laws. Thus, employment laws should be thought of not only as legal constraints; they're also sources of information about the issues that potential employees are likely thinking about as they decide whether to join or leave an organization.

WHAT FAIRNESS MEANS TO EMPLOYEES

Imagine that you are the employees involved in the following two situations. How do you feel? And what will you do?

A Missed Promotion   *Michelle Chang graduated with her MBA five years ago. Since then, she has worked for a large financial services company as an industry analyst. Her performance reviews have always been positive. She and her peers assumed she was on the company's informal fast track. But recently, she has begun to wonder. After the manager of her unit left last month for a better opportunity at another firm, Michelle applied for the job. She didn't get the promotion. To her surprise, the person chosen to be the new boss for her unit was Jim Johnson, a twenty-year veteran of the firm who was transferred from another unit. After three weeks at his new job, it was obvious that Jim's previous experiences had not provided him with the knowledge he needs. Michelle feels that the company's decision to give Jim the job is a signal that her future may not be as bright as everyone thought. Perhaps it's time to look into possibilities at other companies.*

An Unexpected Layoff   *Bill Markham works for the same firm as Michelle and Jim. He has been with the organization about seven years, coming there after working for twelve years at a large computer company and for eight years as an independent consultant. As manager of the Information Services Department, he has been responsible for managing all the company's computer specialists. Last week, the firm unexpectedly disclosed plans for a major reorganization of Information Services. To "improve efficiency," the company has decided to decentralize several staff activities. In the new structure, the activities of the Information Services Department will be carried out by generalists who will work within each of the firm's several divisions. Of course, everyone knew that the words* improve efficiency *were code, meaning the size of the Information Services staff will be reduced. But Bill was not worried when he heard the announcement; he expected to be assigned to the largest division and had already begun discussing the idea of a major move with his family. He was shocked when he learned that he was going to be let go. He appreciated the firm's offer to pay for outplacement counseling, but he wondered whether he should accept its decision as final. As a fifty-something white male, he imagined that finding a new job would be pretty tough. Maybe he should put up a fight.*

How much trust in their employer do Michelle and Bill feel. Has each person been treated fairly? What other information might you want before deciding whether this company is treating employees fairly?

Since the mid-1970s, social and organizational scientists have conducted numerous studies designed to improve our understanding of concepts such as fairness and justice. This research has shown that people's perceptions of fairness reflect at least two features of the situations they find themselves in: the actual *outcomes* and the *procedures* used in arriving at these outcomes. These two features are referred to as distributive justice and procedural justice, respectively.[8]

Distributive Justice

Not surprisingly, people prefer favorable outcomes for themselves. In the cases of Michelle and Bill, a promotion is better than no promotion and a transfer is better than being let go. In another case, nonsmokers will view a new policy banning smoking at work as more fair than will smokers.[9]

Nevertheless, we do not necessarily feel that we have been treated unfairly when we do not get the best possible outcome. Instead, perceptions of fairness hinge on how our own outcomes compare with the outcomes of other people, taking into account our own situation and the situations of others. In evaluating the fairness of her situation, for example, Michelle compares her outcome with Jim's. If Michelle felt that the outcomes she and Jim experienced reflected their relative qualifications, then Michelle probably would accept the situation as fair even though she didn't get promoted. Furthermore, Michelle and Jim's coworkers use similar heuristics in evaluating their employer. When Michelle's coworkers see that she has been unfairly treated, they not only feel bad about what happened to Michelle, they may also conclude that their employer generally treats employees unfairly.[10]

Consider how you evaluate whether people are paid fairly on two counts: the level of pay people receive and changes in pay over time (e.g., due to raises). Generally, people see pay as fair when they believe that the distribution of pay across a group corresponds to the relative value of the work being done by each person. Similarly, when the relative sizes of raises correspond to the relative performance levels of people in the unit, people are likely to feel fairly treated. As these examples illustrate, in the workplace, distributive fairness is perceived under conditions of equity, or merit-based decision making.[11]

Recently, issues of equity were salient in the ongoing public discussion about CEO compensation, when critics began asking some tough questions: Is it fair that the average CEO's pay is forty times as much as the average engineer, teacher and factory worker? Is it fair that CEO pay has been growing at a pace that's seven times the rate of growth in pay for these other workers? What arguments would convince you that this distribution of outcomes is fair?[12]

Typical American employees generally consider equity when evaluating fairness at work; employees from other countries and cultures may see things quite differently. American culture is individualistic, whereas many other cultures are more collectivistic. In collectivistic cultures, concern for social cohesion is greater than in the United States. Going along with a perspective that focuses more on groups, people from collectivistic cultures value *equality* of treatment and treatment based on *need*, and they allocate rewards accordingly.[13] Thus, from a collectivistic perspective, Michelle might be viewed as having been treated fairly. Michelle was treated the same as her coworkers (equally), and perhaps Jim needed the job more than did Michelle. What implications might these differences across countries have for managing human resources in a global organization?

Procedural Justice

Perceptions of justice depend on more than the relative distribution of outcomes: beliefs about the entire process used to determine outcomes also come into play. The term *procedural justice* refers to perceptions about fairness in the process. For example, Michelle and Bill might wonder *how* their company made its decisions in their situations. Research suggests that in American culture, a formal procedure is considered fair if it meets the conditions shown in Exhibit 3.1.[14] With the criteria shown in Exhibit 3.1 in mind, how would you design a procedure for detecting harassment and disciplining those involved? For deciding who to fire or lay off? How would you design drug-testing procedures? Before addressing such issues, it's useful to consider how employees react when they feel they have been treated unfairly, and to consider possible legal constraints.

It's important to keep in mind that the formal system is only one aspect of the procedures that employees react to, however. Employees also take into account how they personally are treated in their interactions with the managers who carry out the formal procedures. If employees feel that the managers are sensitive to their situation and treat them politely and respectfully, they're more likely to feel the procedures are fair. In addition, employees respond more favorably when they feel they were given a full and reasonable account of what happened.[15]

Reactions to Unfair Treatment

When employees feel they have been treated unfairly, they can react in many different ways. Consider again the situation of Michelle. If you were Michelle, you would probably consider actions that fall into one of the following categories:

A. Exit the organization and put the incident behind you;
B. Stay and simply accept the situation as something you must tolerate;
C. Stay but engage in negative behaviors that help you restore your sense of fairness (e.g., shorten your hours a bit; stop attending unnecessary meetings and functions);
D. Voice your concern to people inside the organization (e.g., discuss the situation with your colleagues; talk about it with a mentor; talk to someone in the employee relations office); or
E. Voice your concern to external authorities (e.g., explore possible legal action; talk to the press).[16]

Exhibit 3.1
Employees' Views of Fairness

Conditions To Be Met In Order for Employees to Perceive Formal Procedures as Fair

- The information used to make the decision is appropriate and accurate.
- The basis for making the decision is clearly explained.
- All legitimately interested parties are given the opportunity to have input into the decision process.
- Attention is paid to ensuring that the less powerful parties are protected from abuse by the more powerful parties.
- All interested parties have equal and open access to the system.
- The system is relatively stable and consistent over time.
- The system is flexible enough to be responsive to changing conditions and unique circumstances.

Quit? For high performers like Michelle, choice A, quitting, may be the best alternative. From the organization's perspective, however, having Michelle leave and perhaps join the competition may be the least desirable alternative. From society's perspective, turnover caused by feelings of injustice is undesirable because it tends to reduce productivity.[17]

Stay and Accept the Situation? Alternative B would be better for Michelle's employer, but it's probably not very common because few people easily shrug off injustices suffered at the hands of their employers. Instead, their outlook sours. Employees who stay in situations that they believe are unfair lose confidence in the competence of management and feel they cannot trust management.[18] Employees who feel unfairly treated also report feeling dissatisfied and uncommitted to both their employers and the goals their employers set for them.[19]

Seek Revenge? Feelings of injustice affect behavior, not just attitudes, even for employees who decide not to quit because of unfair treatment. Therefore, reactions that fall into categories C and E are possible. Employees attempt to maintain a sense of balance in their relationship with employers. If legal issues are involved, employees may seek legal solutions. Often, however, feelings of unfairness arise in response to perfectly legal management behavior. This was illustrated quite dramatically in a company that temporarily cut employees' pay. The company was a large manufacturer of aerospace and automotive parts.

Owing to the loss of two contracts, temporary pay cuts were required at two of the company's three plants. Everyone at the two plants took a 15 percent pay cut for ten weeks, including management. The situation created a natural opportunity for the company and a researcher to learn more about how best to implement pay cuts, so a small experiment was conducted. In one plant, the company tried to convey how much it regretted the pay cuts, explained that the pay cuts would eliminate the need for layoffs, and assured employees that no favoritism would occur. At a full meeting with the employees, top management spent an hour answering employees' questions. At the second plant involved, the pay cut was announced at a brief fifteen-minute meeting with no apology and very little explanation. The third plant was used as a control group. Employees' reactions were assessed in terms of theft rates, turnover, and responses to a survey.

At both the plants taking pay cuts, theft rates went up during the weeks the cuts were in effect and then went back down again when full pay was restored, particularly at the plant where the inadequate explanation was given. Turnover in this plant also soared, from five percent to 23 percent. Survey results confirmed that employees at this plant didn't understand how their pay cut was determined and felt they were treated unfairly.[20] As this company found out, people are sensitive to changes that disturb their sense of equity, and will seek ways to rebalance the scales if they're tipped.[21]

Talk to Others in the Organization? The way companies manage situations can greatly influence how employees react.[22] One aspect of managing situations effectively involves using formal organizational systems to deal with conflicts and disputes. By fully explaining how decisions are made and by offering employees opportunities to voice their concerns and have their questions answered (choice D), employers can minimize negative employee reactions. In well-managed companies, employees' feelings of dissatisfaction

■□ fast fact

Employers lose $40 billion per year due to theft, most of which is committed by employees.

are intentionally surfaced and used to stimulate positive changes that actually benefit both employees and employers.[23]

MANAGING TO ENSURE FAIR TREATMENT

Managers use a variety of procedures, policies, and practices to ensure fairness. In Chapters 8 and 11, for example, you will learn about specific, proactive means for insuring fairness when making selection decisions and evaluating performance. Here we focus on procedures aimed to redress a perceived incident of unfair treatment. As you read about these, keep in mind that good systems are not enough. The interpersonal relationships between members of the organization also influence the management of fairness. Inevitably, employees sometimes feel that a decision or procedure is unfair. Sensitive supervisors and managers who acknowledge these situations and express their concern can minimize the disruptive effects of the situations. As simple as it seems, apologies reduce anger.[24]

Grievance Procedures

Formal grievance procedures are one way to encourage employees to voice their concerns and seek constructive resolutions. In unionized settings, the presence of such procedures had already become nearly universal by 1950.[25] Almost all public and private unionized employees are covered by contracts that specify formal written grievance procedures, and most of these culminate in final and binding arbitration by a third-party arbitrator.[26] Historically, the picture has been quite different for nonunion employees. In 1950, formal procedures were almost never available to these employees. Now more than half of America's largest corporations have some type of formal complaint resolution system.[27]

The growing popularity of formal complaint resolution is consistent with managers' beliefs that employees have a right to fair treatment.[28] Such systems seem to be more common in younger organizations and in those that have adopted other HR policies that favor employees.[29] They help establish a positive corporate culture in which conflicts are resolved through compromises that acknowledge the legitimate interests of both disputing parties. Fairness systems like the one at Coors are particularly helpful in environments where employees lack the representation and negotiating power of a union.[30] Coors's appeal process gives employees a voice in how they're treated. This voice combined with peer review ensures a better balance of power, which may in turn result in employees being more willing to continue working for an organization even if they have some complaints.[31] Of course, as is true of most administrative systems, the specific details of the system itself are not as important as the way the system is used. When they work well, grievance systems not only help lower the legal costs associated with resolving disputes in the courts, they also increase employee loyalty.[32]

Proactive Prevention of Grievances

Is the absence of a formal system for processing employees' complaints necessarily bad business? It may seem so at first, but some companies may choose not to support such systems for good reasons. Grievance systems are reactive. They focus the attention and energy of disputants on the past, and formalize a process for *naming* an injured party, *blaming* someone or something for the injury, and *claiming* a remedy.[33] Given limited resources, some organizations choose to develop and promote proactive policies and practices designed to prevent the need for formal grievance procedures.

Hallmark Cards does a great job of providing proactive policies and practices for their employees, as described in the feature Managing Strategically: Employees Get Fair Treatment at Hallmark Cards.[34]

MANAGING STRATEGICALLY
Employees Get Fair Treatment at Hallmark Cards

If the measure of employees' job satisfaction is the length of time they stay with a company, Kansas City, Missouri-based Hallmark Cards Inc. has some seriously satisfied people. Once a year, the company hosts a celebration for Quarter-Century Club Members—those who've put in 25 years or more with Hallmark. In 1995, more than 25 percent of the workforce—3,600 employees—received an invitation.

In these days, when job-hopping is the norm for most employees, Hallmark keeps its workforce safely snuggled in its fold. Start with its work-life approach. Perhaps Hallmark has a little more insight into the work-family balance, being a family-run business itself (founding family, the Halls, still own about two-thirds of the stock). Whatever the reason, the company devotes a lot of time and energy to the issue. Even before it was legally required, new parents could take advantage of a six-month leave. Adopting parents receive reimbursement of up to $5,000—one of the most generous in the country. In addition, sick children get a little TLC through a partnership Hallmark forged with six area hospitals—the first day of care is free; every day after costs only $3.00 to $3.50 an hour.

But Hallmark also wants to treat employees themselves to a little extra. To start with, the company does its best to alleviate worries over continued employment. It has basically a spotless history as far as layoffs go. Even with terminations, employees know they'll get a fair shake: The director of employee relations must sign off on any termination of an employee who's been at Hallmark two to five years; for those with five or more years' service, two vice presidents must approve the termination. Hallmark also shares. Since 1956, employees have received an average of 9 percent to 10 percent of their pay a year in profit sharing. The profit-sharing plan is worth $1.4 billion; Hallmark stock comprises 67 percent of the plan, making employees one-third owners of the company.

Hallmark doesn't just share money. It shares information through a variety of communications, including an employee newsletter, "Noon News," published daily since 1957. In addition, a monthly CEO forum allows groups of employees to speak their mind with no managers present. Diversity also enjoys dialogue through the Multicultural Exchange, of which CEO Irvine O. Hockaday is a member.

Perhaps most important, though, Hallmark just has a friendly, energetic environment. "There's something about this place I felt the first day I walked in here," says Jerry Kenefake, director of compensation and benefits. "People genuinely mean it when they say, 'Have a good day.' People work hard, but they have a good time doing it. The management of this company for years has encouraged that kind of feeling, and I think it's resulted in deep-seated loyalty. I think people, by and large, enjoy coming here every day."

To learn more about Hallmark Cards, visit the company's home page at:
www.hallmark.com

Proactive approaches to ensuring fair treatment might include formal performance appraisals, frequent informal feedback, progressive discipline policies, annual surveys to monitor employees' attitudes and perceptions, benefits packages designed to meet the diverse needs of employees, employee involvement in managerial decision making, management training in how to treat employees fairly, and frequent use of communication channels.

Hallmark Cards treats employees fairly, legally, and with respect. Such treatment stems from Hallmark's values, culture, and top management. To its 35,000 employees worldwide, Hallmark provides an attractive, energetic environment in which many job applicants would like to work; low turnover among employees; an excitement and dedication to working hard; and a sense of loyalty among the employees. Hallmark Cards fosters loyalty and uses it as a competitive advantage to attract and retain the best employees.

LEGAL MEANS TO ENSURE FAIR TREATMENT

Laws are simply society's values and standards that are enforceable in the courts. The legal environment communicates society's concerns through state and federal laws, regulations, and court decisions. In general, the legal system is designed to encourage socially responsible behavior.[35] That is, it considers the outcomes of all parties concerned and attempts to impose decisions and remedies that balance the perspectives of employees, employers, and other stakeholders.[36] Failure to comply with societal expectations as defined by this environment may result in monetary fines, imprisonment, and court orders that constrain future activities.

The legality of actions and decisions doesn't necessarily make them ethical, however. At one time, for example, U.S. organizations could legally discriminate against women and minorities in hiring and promotions. As a consensus developed that such discriminatory practices were unethical, laws such as the *Civil Rights Act of 1964* were passed to stop the practices and ensure equal employment opportunities for all citizens. In addition, the federal government issued regulations requiring government agencies and federal contractors to work at correcting the effects of past discrimination. As shown in Exhibit 3.2, discrimination laws and regulations are one of four major categories of regulatory influences that affect how organizations manage human resources.

U.S. companies must act in accordance with several different types of laws, including constitutional laws, statutory laws, administrative regulations, executive orders, and common laws. To understand how the legal environment affects the way companies manage human resources, it's helpful to understand the U.S. legal system in general. What types of laws and regulations exist? How do disputes move through the system? What types of remedies can the system offer? It's also helpful to understand the many specific laws and regulations that are promulgated and enforced by this system.

Constitutional Laws

In countries that have one, the constitution is the fundamental law of the land. The U.S. Constitution is the oldest written constitution still in force in the world. It defines the structure and limits of the federal government and allocates power among the federal government and the states. All 50 states also have written constitutions. State and federal laws must be consistent with the U.S. Constitution.

Exhibit 3.2

Significant Legal and Regulatory Influences on Human Resource Management in the United States

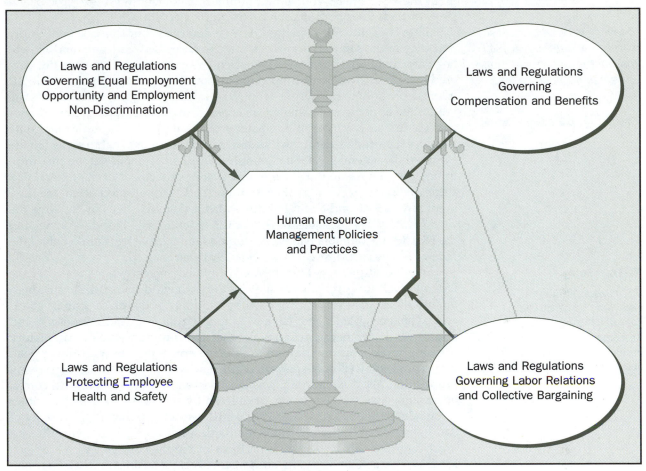

In the area of employment, one section of the U.S. Constitution that's particularly important is the Fourteenth Amendment, which guarantees due process and equal protection. This amendment also prohibits state actions that are inconsistent with federal law. Because of its equal protection clause, the Fourteenth Amendment often plays a role in cases involving reverse discrimination.

Statutory Laws

The U.S. Constitution gives Congress all power to make laws on behalf of the federal government. Paralleling the federal instrument, state constitutions give lawmaking power to state-level governmental bodies. The resulting federal and state laws are called *statutes*.

One especially important federal employment law has been Title VII of the *Civil Rights Act*. As originally enacted in 1964, Title VII prohibited discrimination by employers, employment agencies, and unions on the basis of race, color, religion, sex, or national origin. A 1978 amendment prohibited discrimination against pregnant women. In 1991, a new version of the *Civil Rights Act* went into effect. The new law reinforces the intent of the *Civil Rights Act of 1964* but states more specifically how cases brought under the

■□ *fast fact*

Surveys show that 90 percent of Americans believe that hiring persons with disabilities is good.

act should proceed.[37] Key statutory laws that affect the employment relationship are summarized in Appendix A. Although we cannot fully discuss all of these laws here, you should familiarize yourself with the basic provisions of these laws in preparation for future chapters.

State laws must be consistent with federal law, but this does not imply that they're the same. Two important differences between state and federal laws are common. First, state laws often cover companies that are not covered by federal laws. For example, federal employment laws such as Title VII often apply only to businesses with 15 or more employees, but similar state laws often apply to even smaller businesses. In general, federal laws do not supersede state laws that offer greater protection to employees. Second, state laws often precede federal laws and in this sense tell us what to expect in the future at the federal level. For example, Massachusetts passed the first minimum wage legislation in 1912, which was a predecessor of the federal *Fair Labor Standards Act of 1938* (FLSA). New York had adopted a fair employment law in 1945 and about half the states had similar laws by the time the *Civil Rights Act of 1964* was passed at the federal level. Florida, Maine, and the District of Columbia had each adopted family leave legislation before the federal *Family and Medical Leave Act of 1993* was enacted.

Two recently enacted California laws may suggest what's ahead at the federal level. Research shows that investors reward companies with high quality affirmative action programs by bidding up the price of their stock, and punish companies that have been found guilty of discrimination.[38] But opponents of affirmative action argue that such programs are discriminatory (causing reverse discrimination). California voters agreed with the opposition. They outlawed *state*-sponsored affirmative action programs by passing Proposition 209. A similar law was later passed by Washington state voters; other such laws are now being considered by several other states. Another recent California initiative that affects businesses more directly is the City of San Francisco's requirement that companies that do business with the city must offer benefits to domestic partners of employees. Cities such as San Francisco argue that imposing such restrictions on business is their prerogative. If companies want to take advantage of such benefits as the tax incentives that cities often offer to businesses, they may have to be responsive to local social issues that are important to city residents and that influence their local regulations.[39]

Administrative Regulations

At both the federal and state levels, the legislative and executive branches of government can delegate authority for rule making and enforcement to an administrative agency. For example, the federal *Equal Employment Opportunity Act of 1972* gave power to enforce *Title VII of the Civil Rights Act* to the Equal Employment Opportunity Commission (EEOC). The EEOC also administers the *Equal Pay Act of 1963* and the *Age Discrimination in Employment Act of 1967* (ADEA). In carrying out their duties, agencies such as these make rules—often called standards, guidelines, or decisions; conduct investigations; make judgments about guilt; and impose sanctions. In practice, this means these federal agencies have the responsibility and authority to prosecute companies they believe are in violation of the law. Affirmative action programs were one outcome of such regulations.

Federal agencies generally require companies to monitor their own behavior and file reports, either at preset time intervals or following partic-

---

"Slavery is one of history's worst moments, but it isn't just history when you look at some of these cases."

Janet Reno
U.S. Attorney General

■□ *fast fact*

U.S. citizens employed elsewhere by a firm that's controlled or owned by an American parent are protected by the ADEA, ADA, and Title VII.

■□ *fast fact*

It's perfectly legal for managers to discriminate against young people under the ADEA, using whatever stereotypes they might have.

ular types of events. For example, the Occupational Safety and Health Administration (OSHA) conducts safety and health inspections, investigates accidents and alleged hazardous conditions, issues citations for violations, levies fines, collects mandatory reports prepared by employers, and compiles statistics on work injuries and illnesses.

Agencies can also acquire information directly through inspections and audits. Recently, the EEOC announced a new approach to getting information about employers' practices. In addition to requiring reports and conducting audits, they'll use undercover "testers." Pairs of job applicants with equivalent qualifications but who differ on gender, race, age, or disability, will apply for the same jobs. The EEOC will then analyze hiring rates for the testers to learn more about patterns of discrimination.

Executive Orders

U.S. presidents shape the legal environment by approving and vetoing bills passed by Congress and by influencing how vigorously administrative agencies carry out their duties and responsibilities. In addition, the President can create law by issuing executive orders that specify rules and conditions for government business and for doing business with the government. Organizations that do work for the federal government are referred to as government contractors. In the area of employment, the actions of government contractors are most affected by Executive Order 11246, issued in 1965 by President Lyndon B. Johnson. Like Title VII, Executive Order 11246 prohibits discrimination on the basis of race, color, religion, or national origin. It applies to federal agencies and to federal contractors and subcontractors. In 1966, Executive Order 11375 was issued to prohibit discrimination based on sex by these employers.

Whereas Executive Orders 11246 and 11375 parallel federal law that applies to all employers, Executive Order 11478, issued in 1969, has no parallel in federal statutory law. Executive Order 11478 requires that employment policies of the federal government be based on merit.

Common Laws

Common laws are rules made by judges as they resolve disputes between parties. The U.S. system of common law is rooted in English common law, which was established after the Normans conquered England in 1066. To help unify the country, William the Conqueror established the King's Court. Its purpose was to develop a common set of rules and apply them uniformly throughout the kingdom. Decisions were based on the opinions of judges. Important decisions were recorded and subsequently referred back to as *precedent* (examples) for making future decisions. When new types of disputes arose, judges created new law to resolve them. This system is still in effect today in England.

Unlike English judges, U.S. judges do not make laws, they only interpret and apply them. But their interpretations continue in the tradition of setting precedent to decide new cases. The use of precedent to decide cases helps employers anticipate how the courts might rule should they find themselves involved in a similar case. When interpreting the implications of court decisions, keep in mind that rulings made by the Supreme Court carry the most weight because the decisions of all other federal and state courts are subject to review by the Supreme Court. Appendix A lists several Supreme Court rulings of particular importance for managing human resources within employment settings.

fast fact

The vast majority of age discrimination lawsuits are brought by men.

fast fact

Approximately 70,000 companies are federal government contractors.

REMEDIES TO DISPUTES IN CIVIL LITIGATION

Most civil suits never actually reach the stage of a formal trial. Instead, they're resolved privately. For cases that are resolved in court, two common remedies are monetary damages and settlement agreements.

Monetary Damages

If a legal right has been violated and has resulted in injury, the defendant may be required to pay monetary damages to the plaintiff. Compensatory monetary damages are intended to help victims retrieve what they have lost, for example, back pay and attorneys' fees. Punitive damages are intended specifically to punish wrongdoers and deter future wrongdoing.

Firing employees and making examples out of them can prove costly for employers if such actions are not based on clear facts. This point is illustrated starkly in a Texas case, where damages in excess of $15 million were awarded a former Procter & Gamble employee who was fired after being accused of stealing a $35 telephone. The employee had worked for P&G for 41 years and, according to his attorney, had an unblemished record. He had purchased the phone with his own money and was not reimbursed because he had lost the receipt. Later, a security guard stopped the employee as he was leaving work and discovered the phone in his belongings. After an internal investigation, P&G fired the employee and announced through internal notices that he had committed a theft. The employee sued for libel, saying P&G used him as an example to prevent other thefts.

Procter & Gamble committed actual malice in falsely accusing the employee of stealing the phone, the jury in the case decided. The jury awarded the employee $14 million in punitive damages and more than $1 million for actual damages to the employee's character and damages to his mental and physical well-being (*Hagler v. Procter & Gamble Manufacturing Co.* 1993).[40]

Settlement Agreements

Court proceedings can be lengthy and costly—sometimes outrageously so. When the objective is correcting employer wrongdoing, court procedures often are not the most expedient. The U.S. Justice Department and administrative agencies can speed the process of ensuring that employers engage in responsible behavior by negotiating a settlement. When lawsuits are resolved by a settlement agreement, the defendant (employer) usually does not admit to wrongdoing. Nevertheless, it may agree to pay money to the plaintiff or plaintiffs. And it may agree to conduct itself according to the court's specific directives. The first settlement agreement regarding unfair employment practices was negotiated with AT&T and its 24 operating companies. In 1973, the firm agreed to (a) pay $15 million to 13,000 women and 2,000 men of color who had been denied pay and promotion opportunities, and (b) develop goals for employing women and people of color in all jobs in all of its 700 establishments.

In another settlement, the courts recognized that the circle of victims in organizations that engage in unfair employment practices can be surprisingly large. In 1993, Shoney's restaurant chain agreed to pay $105 million to victims of the company's blatant racial discrimination. Most of the plaintiffs were African-American employees, but some settlement money also was awarded to white managers and supervisors who were dismissed because they refused to follow orders to terminate African-American employees.[41] More recently, Mitsubishi agreed to pay $34 million to several hundred women who alleged that their reports of incidents of sexual harassment were ignored by the company's managers over a period of several years.

ALTERNATIVE DISPUTE RESOLUTION

A growing number of businesses are using alternative dispute resolution (ADR) to resolve charges of employment discrimination or wrongful termination. Alternative dispute resolution procedures include an agreement to forego litigation and instead resolve disputes by either internal or external mediation or arbitration. Working out a dispute before it reaches litigation can promote goodwill between management and employees and reduce the adverse publicity often associated with legal disputes.[42] It can also reduce legal costs to both employers and society.

Mediation and arbitration are the two most common forms of alternative dispute resolution. Internal review procedures, such as those used at Coors, can also be thought of as alternative dispute resolution systems.

■□*fast fact*

Federal Express handles sexual harassment complaints through the Guaranteed Fair Treatment program, often cited as one of the best grievance procedures in the U.S.

Mediation

Mediation is the most popular form of ADR, partly because its format is more flexible than that of other proceedings. All concerned parties come before a third-party neutral (the mediator), who may be appointed by a judge or selected by the parties or their attorneys. Parties to a civil dispute may be ordered into mediation by the court, or they may volunteer to submit to the process in an effort to settle the dispute without litigation.

Arbitration

Arbitration, another popular method of alternative dispute resolution, has skyrocketed in use since the early 1990s. Many employers ask employees to sign contracts upon being hired stating that they'll accept arbitration as a means to settle any potential future discrimination complaint. Arbitration may be binding or nonbinding. If the award is nonbinding, the process could lead to a trial. More often, however, employees are asked to agree to binding arbitration in which the arbitrator's decision is final, subject to a very limited right of appeal. In most cases, employees who sign agreements to use binding arbitration give up their right to a court hearing. While the courts have generally upheld arbitration decisions, both the EEOC and the NLRB have taken positions against their use.[43]

Compared to mediation, arbitration is more formal, yet not so formal that the rules of a court must be followed. Attorneys must present their cases in a formal manner, but arbitrators do not need to provide a written decision or use previous cases in rendering their decisions. Because arbitrators are selected by employers, their neutrality may be questionable. For example, Wall Street firms usually have used industry executives as arbitrators. The practice appears to be so biased in favor of the employer that a federal judge ruled that Merrill Lynch couldn't force a former financial consultant to arbitrate her claim instead of using the courts. In stating her decision, the judge noted that she was "deeply troubled" by the "structural bias" in the industry's arbitration system.[44] But in 1997, in order to settle a discrimination lawsuit without going to court, Smith Barney agreed to use a panel of professional arbitrators rather than industry executives.[45]

In part because it's relatively new, the approach to resolving disputes is still quite controversial. Exhibit 3.3 summarizes the argument for and against mandatory arbitration practices.[46] The idea that employers can ask employees to waive their right to a trial is one that worries members of Congress. As they watched the escalation of layoffs during the 1990s, they became concerned that older employees were being asked to sign waivers as a condition for accepting benefits that their employer was offering as inducement to early retirement and voluntary resignations. Congress stepped in to ensure that employees understand the full implication of such waivers. In an effort to deter unscrupulous practices, Congress passed the *Older Workers Benefit Protection Act*. This act includes strict guidelines for the conditions under which such waivers will be treated as valid. These include:

- The benefits being offered to employees must be greater than what they would otherwise be entitled to.
- Employees must *know* they're signing away their right to participate in any subsequent age discrimination lawsuit; this fact can't be buried somewhere in fine print.
- Employees much sign such waivers *voluntarily*.
- The waiver must be written in language that's easy to understand.
- The waiver must explicitly state the rights that the employee is agreeing to waive.
- Employees must be notified that they should consult an attorney before signing the waiver.
- Employers must give employees at least 21 days to consider the agreement.
- Employees must be given seven days to revoke the agreement after signing.[47]

Exhibit 3.3

Weighing the Pros and Cons of Using Mandatory Arbitration to Settle Disputes

Pros	Cons
Quick dispute resolution	Requires employees to relinquish their statutory right to a trial as a condition of employment
Lower personal, professional, and financial costs for both parties	Availability of "user-friendly" arbitration may stimulate a flood of claims
Reduction in employer's advantage in litigation by outspending and outlasting an employee	May prevent better guidance for future action since courts are better able to provide consistent and clear interpretations of law
More business-related experience and expertise of professional arbitrators	Arbitrators may not be competent or impartial
Reduction in exposure to unpredictable jury awards for emotional distress and punitive damages	Small monetary penalties may reduce their effectiveness as remedies in the case of a wronged employee
Permits disputes to remain private	Confidentiality of the process may reduce its deterrence effect; conversely, confidentiality isn't guaranteed
May improve communication and employee relations	May deter some talented employees from accepting employment

MANAGERS' RESPONSIBILITIES FOR ENSURING FAIRNESS

The task of managing to ensure fairness in the workplace is complex. To succeed, managers must behave in ways that are consistent with societal expectations regarding employee and employer rights and responsibilities. Failure to do so jeopardizes the success of their companies.

During the 20th century, society's expectations gradually shifted, hinting at trends for the future. At one time, the doctrine of employment-at-will seemed to give employers the right to treat employees in almost any way they wished. However, a more balanced approach to employment relations is evolving. Early in the century, the rights of most concern to employees were basic conditions of work. Both the rhetoric of union organizers and early workplace legislation reflected these concerns. In comparison, from the mid-1970s to the mid-1990s, much attention focused on the right to equal opportunities in employment: women's opportunities should equal men's, and members of minority groups should have the same opportunities as members of the majority. As we begin the 21st century, concerns about equal opportunity remain salient. Nevertheless, several shifts in perspective are apparent.

Fairness for All Groups

Eliminating discrimination on the basis of race and gender had been the focus of most attention in the recent past. It's increasingly evident, however, that members of many other demographic groups sometimes are victims of unfair discrimination. Gradually, legal protections have been extended to prohibit more and more types of discrimination. Nevertheless, for members of some groups, no legal protection is currently available, and it's probably safe to predict that regardless of how broadly the reach of legal protection eventually extends, some groups of employees will always remain vulnerable to legal unfair treatment.

What has become increasingly apparent is that simply trying to "obey the law" is not a very effective way for employers to stay out of court or to ensure that they'll win if they end up there. A better approach to meeting employees' and society's concerns about fairness is to create a corporate culture in which all employees respect each other and in which decisions are made on the basis of merit rather than personal demographic attributes. If an employer isn't able to make reasonable progress toward that goal, then the courts will step in and specify corrective actions. The feature, Managing Diversity and Change: Texaco's Plan for a Cultural Shift, describes the conditions agreed to by Texaco as part of its lawsuit settlement.[48] The change initiatives imposed on Texaco are similar to voluntary change efforts adopted by other organizations.

Implementing such changes will take many years, and many challenges will arise along the way. Perhaps the biggest challenge to managers is understanding that cultural diversity can have many organizational consequences. For example, on the one hand diversity can enhance a team's ability to solve problems creatively. On the other hand, the price of such creativity may be heightened conflict within the team. Similarly, changing the mix of men and women in a team or department toward a 50–50 split may improve the attitudes of the women involved while irritating the men. Managers shouldn't expect that diversity-related initiatives affect members of the organization in uniformly positive ways. They should be prepared to weigh carefully which costs they're willing to incur in order to achieve other gains.

MANAGING DIVERSITY AND CHANGE

Texaco's Plan for a Cultural Shift

In 1990, in the process of its normal monitoring activities, the Department of Labor found that Texaco was deficient in its minority representation, and in 1995 the EEOC issued a similar finding. Although the company's employment numbers indicated it had been making some progress in terms of hiring a more diverse workforce, promotion and pay rates lagged other companies in the industry. The problem was that too many managers within the company ignored the company's nondiscrimination policies. They often allowed their personal prejudice to affect their actions at work. The seriousness of Texaco's problems became public in 1996, when secretly recorded conversations revealed that senior executives used racial epithets and plotted to destroy documents demanded by the courts in a discrimination case. Other evidence presented during the case revealed that it was common for supervisors to refer to members of racial subgroups in derogatory terms. Many employees did nothing to protest such treatment, for fear of losing their jobs. Others quit. And eventually, some took their evidence to court. As part of the settlement, Texaco agreed to pay $140 million—the largest settlement ever for a case of racial discrimination. The massive cultural change effort that the company agreed to initiate is outlined below.

Components of Texaco's Cultural Change Initiatives

Recruitment and Hiring
- Ask search firms to identify wider arrays of candidates
- Enhance the interviewing, selection, and hiring skills of managers
- Expand college recruitment at historically minority colleges

Identifying and Developing Talent
- Form a partnership with INROADS, a nationwide internship program that targets minority students for management careers
- Establish a mentoring process
- Refine the company's global succession planning system to improve identification of talent
- Improve the selection and development of managers and leaders to help ensure that they're capable of maximizing team performance

Ensuring Fair Treatment
- Conduct extensive diversity training
- Implement an alternative dispute resolution process
- Include women and minorities on all human resources committees throughout the company

Holding managers accountable
- Link managers' compensation to their success in creating "openness and inclusion in the workplace"
- Implement 360-degree feedback for all managers and supervisors
- Redesign the company's employee attitude survey and begin using it annually to monitor employee attitudes

Improve Relationships with External Stakeholders
- Broaden the company's base of vendors and suppliers to incorporate more minority- and women-owned businesses
- Increase banking, investment, and insurance business with minority- and women-owned firms
- Add more independent, minority retailers and increase the number of minority managers in company-owned gas stations and Xpress Lube outlets

To learn more about Texaco, visit the company home page at:
www.texaco.com

Fairness Must Be Reciprocated

It's easy to emphasize the responsibility of employers to treat employees fairly. Fairness is a two-sided coin, however, and the other side is the responsibility of employees to treat their employers fairly.

In many firms, the responsibilities of employees are spelled out in policy statements on conflicts of interest. Conflict-of-interest policies are intended to ensure ethical business conduct and high standards of integrity. Generally, such policies specify that the best interests of the company must be employees' foremost concern in all business dealings. For example, J. P. Morgan's statement of Guiding Principles states the expectation that all employees will abide by the "highest standards of personal and professional conduct so that we will be deserving of our clients' and colleagues' trust." More specifically, *employees* are expected to

- act with personal and professional integrity;
- understand and comply fully with the letter and spirit of laws and regulations, as well as the firm's rules and policies;
- safeguard the firm's reputation; and
- preserve the confidentiality of information about clients, colleagues, and the firm.

In exchange, the *company* agrees to

- engage in business activities that are consistent with its reputation for integrity;
- articulate its standards and rules clearly;
- provide support in making legal and ethical decisions; and
- refuse to tolerate illegal, unethical, or unprofessional conduct.

Perhaps the best indicator of how fairly employees feel they're being treated is the degree to which they're willing to accept responsibility for behaving fairly in all dealings with their employers.

CURRENT CONCERNS ABOUT FAIRNESS

Managers will always need to be alert to employees' concerns about fairness. Yet, at particular times in history and in particular organizations or industries, specific fairness issues are particularly salient and in need of attention. Today, these concerns include harassment, employment-at-will, privacy, and understanding fairness in other cultures.

Harassment in the Workplace

In 1980, the EEOC issued guidelines stating that sexual harassment is a form of sex discrimination. This view was consistent with several earlier court decisions (*Tomkins v. Public Service Electric and Gas Company*, 1977; *William v. Saxbe*, 1976; *Barnes v. Costle*, 1977; *Heelen v. Johns-Manville Corporation*, 1978). In the original guidelines, remarks or behavior of a sexual nature were defined as harassment if

- submission to such conduct is either explicitly or implicitly made a term or condition of an individual's employment;
- submission to, or rejection of, such conduct by an individual is used as the basis for employment decisions affecting that individual; and

■■□ *fast fact*

The EEOC received more than 14,000 sexual harassment complaints in 1998, twice the number they received a decade earlier.

- such conduct has the purpose or effect of substantially interfering with an individual's work performance or creating an intimidating, hostile, or offensive working environment.

Despite these guidelines, many organizations didn't begin to consider sexual harassment to be a significant problem until Anita Hill testified against Supreme Court Justice Clarence Thomas during his Senate confirmation hearings. But by then, Delaware-based E.I. duPont de Nemours (DuPont) had already been battling sexual harassment for several years as part of its efforts to improve the company.

In 1993, the EEOC issued regulations that broadened the types of harassment considered illegal.[49] Under the new regulations, employers have a duty to maintain a working environment free of harassment based on race, color, religion, gender, national origin, age, or disability. Furthermore, conduct is harassment if it creates a hostile, intimidating, or offensive work environment; unreasonably interferes with the individual's work; or adversely affects the individual's employment opportunities. Harassing conduct includes such things as racist epithets, raunchy jokes, and ethnic slurs, and usually, though not always, it has to be systematic. In several cases, the offending behavior has taken the form of inappropriate e-mail or Internet messages.[50] For example, in one well-publicized case, Salomon Smith Barney discharged two managing directors for sharing X-rated material on their office computers. A month earlier, Morgan Stanley Dean Witter settled a lawsuit brought against them by two African-American employees who charged that they lost out on promotions because they had complained about the distribution of e-mail messages containing racist jokes.[51]

"Smart employers will stop sexual harassment in their shop because they realize the worst thing they can do to hurt their self interest is to do nothing."

Ellen Bravo
Executive Director of 9-to-5
National Organization of
Working Women

The Consequences of Harassment. Harassment creates an offensive, hostile, and stressful work environment that prohibits effective performance; leads to expensive financial settlements and negative publicity; and, ultimately, interferes with the ability of the organization to attract and retain the best talent. Indeed, whole industries can be hurt when the public learns about unfavorable workplace climates.[52] After extensive media coverage of Lew Lieberbaum & Co.'s exploitative culture (which included lewd language, racist jokes, hiring strippers for office parties, and promising promotions in exchange for sexual favors), the company saw its business drop off dramatically, which is perhaps what led Lieberbaum to change the firm's name to First Asset Management.[53]

On Wall Street, the perpetrators of such actions would undoubtedly feel that women were overreacting to men who were just having a little fun and trying to relieve some of the stress that builds up in this high-pressure environment. But such explanations carry little weight. The 1993 regulations clarify that the standard for evaluating harassment is whether a "reasonable person" in the same or similar circumstances would find the conduct intimidating, hostile, or abusive. The perspective of the victim—reflecting her or his race, gender, age, place of origin, and so forth—has an important place in the evaluation. This is an expansion of the "reasonable-woman" standard articulated in *Ellison v. Brady* (1991). There the court said that "unsolicited love letters and unwanted attention . . . might appear inoffensive to the average man, but might be so offensive to the average woman as to create a hostile working environment." The "average woman" in this case became the "reasonable woman," and this standard was reaffirmed later in *Harris v. Forklift Systems* (1993).[54] In 1998, in the case of *Oncale v. Sundown Offshore Service,*

Commenting on how male MBA students treat female MBA students, *"In the real world, people would be fired for this sort of behavior."*

Karin Kissane
1997 Graduate
Harvard Business School

Inc., the court further clarified the rules by stating that employers could be held liable for same-sex harassment.[55]

The 1993 EEOC guidelines also clearly state that employers are liable for the acts of those who work for them if they knew or should have known about the conduct and took no immediate, appropriate corrective action. Employers who fail to develop explicit, detailed anti-harassment policies and grievance procedures may put themselves at particular risk.

A 1998 Supreme Court ruling (*Faragher v. City of Boca Raton*) goes further in providing guidance to employers. It says companies can be held liable for incidents that aren't reported if there are no readily available means for such reporting to occur. In other words, if no procedures for dispute resolution are in place, employers can't plead innocent by reason of being uninformed. Conversely, according to the ruling, employees may forfeit their right to pursue a legal case against the company if they fail to use the procedures that are in place to detect and eliminate offensive behavior. In other words, if a company develops a good internal reporting process, employees who experience harassment are obligated to use it.[56]

Preventing Harassment. The Supreme Court's 1998 rulings also clearly stated that employers can protect themselves against complaints by having and enforcing a "zero tolerance" policy. When Salomon Smith Barney discharged two top executives, it signaled that the firm was serious about adopting a "zero tolerance" approach to dealing with harassment. At Northern States Power, a letter from CEO James J. Howard to employees reads, in part: "All of us have the right to be treated fairly, with dignity and respect. Any violation of this right simply won't be tolerated. We will continue to enforce a 'Zero Tolerance' approach to all forms of discrimination and harassment. Inappropriate behavior will result in the strict use of our Positive Discipline program with the possibility of termination. . . . Join me in making this a company that respects men and women of all ages, races, backgrounds, affectional orientations and physical abilities."[57] For such values to have meaning, companies need clear policies, effective training to teach employees about what is and isn't acceptable, and strong enforcement. Exhibit 3.4 describes the components that should be part of a sexual harassment policy.[58] Such policies may not eliminate harassment, but they do help communicate the company's expectations and provide a fair means for enforcing appropriate behavior.[59]

Training programs further support efforts to prevent harassment. Awareness-training programs such as DuPont's can help employees understand the pain and indignity of harassment. If they're comprehensive and used aggressively, such programs can be highly effective. According to one study, the estimated cost for training ranges from $5,000 for a small company to $200,000 for a large one. These bargain rates compare favorably against the costs of losing key employees, incurring negative publicity, and handling expensive lawsuits. According to one attorney who specializes in defending companies against sexual harassment lawsuits, employers spend an average of $200,000 on each complaint that's investigated in-house and found not to be valid. For claims that are valid and end up in court, you can add the cost of the average court verdict for sexual harassment, which is $225,000. Given that 90 percent of the *Fortune* 500 companies have dealt with sexual harassment complaints, and 25 percent have been sued repeatedly, it's easy to see why one labor lawyer compares the total cost of harassment to the cost of asbestos cleanups—in the $1 billion range.[60] And, like asbestos's, harassment's true cost can never be adequately expressed in dollar terms.

■□ fast fact

Companies can be held liable for a supervisor's harassing behavior even if the offense was never reported.

■□ fast fact

If an outside contractor sends into a workplace employees who sexually harass the on-site workers, those workers can sue their employer who hired the outside contractor.

Exhibit 3.4

Preventing Sexual Harassment in the Workplace

Guidelines for Effective Sexual Harassment Policies

1. Raise affirmatively the issue of harassment. Acknowledge that it may be present in the organization, and make all employees aware of the company's position on harassment.

2. Provide a clear and broad statement defining what constitutes harassment.

3. State that employees who experience or witness harassment are required to report it.

4. Set up reporting procedures for harassed employees to use; include a list of names and positions to whom complaints can be made. The list should make it clear that employees who are harassed by supervisors have alternative reporting options.

5. Specify that offenders will be subject to appropriate discipline, up to and including discharge.

6. Establish procedures for investigating and corroborating an harassment charge.

7. Give the person accused of harassment opportunity to respond immediately after charges are made. Due process must be provided the alleged perpetrator as well as the alleged victim.

8. Build in checkpoints designed to detect harassment. For example, review all discharges to ensure that the employee was clearly performing poorly and had been given adequate opportunity to improve.

9. Specify a set of steps in a framework of progressive discipline for perpetrators of harassment. These could be the same steps used by the organization in treating any violation of organizational policies.

10. Assure employees that they won't be subjected to retaliation for reporting incidents of harassment.

Employment-at-Will

As the industrial era was beginning, employers managed their businesses under the assumption that they had the right to terminate employees for any reason. This right is known as the employment-at-will rule. It's a common-law rule with historical roots in medieval England. In the United States, one Tennessee court explained it as follows:

> "All may dismiss their employee(s) at will, be they many or few, for good cause, for no cause, or even for cause morally wrong without being thereby guilty of legal wrong." *(Payne v. Western and A.R.R Company, 1884)*

The courts still recognize the force of at-will employment. Exhibit 3.5 lists several specific reasons that the courts have upheld it as within the employers' rights. But numerous regulations and court decisions also acknowledged that employers shouldn't have absolute autonomy to end a person's employment. Giving employers too much self-government would be harmful to employees and essentially nullify all employee rights. The *Civil Rights Act*, the *Age Discrimination in Employment Act*, and the *Americans with Disabilities Act* curtail employers' use of the employment-at-will doctrine by stating that certain personal characteristics cannot be used as justification for employment decisions of any kind, including termination. In addition, the *National Labor Relations Act* prohibits discharge for union-organizing activities or for asserting rights under a union contract, even if the employee in question had a record of poor performance (*National Labor Relations Board v. Transportation Management*, 1983).[61] Other examples of reasons for termination that the court has found to be unacceptable are listed in the second column of Exhibit 3.5.[62]

▮▯fast fact

A statement about job security in an employee handbook can become an enforceable legal contract that protects the employees.

Exhibit 3.5
Court Interpretations That Have Defined the Meaning of Employment-at-Will

Permissible Reasons for Employee Dismissal

- Incompetence in performance that does not respond to training or to accommodation
- Gross or repeated insubordination
- Civil rights violations such as engaging in harassment
- Too many unexcused absences
- Illegal behavior such as theft
- Repeated lateness
- Drug activity on the job
- Verbal abuse
- Physical violence
- Falsification of records
- Drunkenness on the job

Unacceptable Reasons for Employee Dismissal

- Blowing the whistle about illegal conduct by their employers (for example, opposing and publicizing employer policies or practices that violate laws such as the antitrust, consumer protection, or environmental protection laws)
- Cooperating in the investigation of a charge against the company
- Reporting Occupational Safety and Health Administration (OSHA) violations
- Filing discrimination charges with the Equal Employment Opportunity Commission (EEOC) or a state or municipal fair employment agency
- Filing unfair labor practice charges with the National Labor Relations Board (NLRB) or a state agency
- Filing a workers' compensation claim
- Engaging in concerted activity to protest wages, working conditions, or safety hazards
- Engaging in union activities, provided there is no violence or unlawful behavior
- Complaining or testifying about violations of equal pay, wage, or hour law
- Complaining or testifying about safety hazards or refusing an assignment because of the belief that it's dangerous

Note: These decisions apply to nonunion situations. When employees are represented by a union, the union contract replaces the termination-at-will doctrine and specifies the conditions under which an employee may be fired.

Decisions of the past ten years emphasize the value of procedural justice. That is, termination of employment should be the last step in a series of documented steps designed to ensure that an employee understood that performance problems existed and had opportunity to improve. Furthermore, all evidence and material relevant to each step should be documented and filed. Even though an employer may have the right to discharge an employee, the employer may be required to show evidence indicating that none of the protections against wrongful termination were violated.

Employee Privacy

Simply stated, the right to privacy is the right to keep information about ourselves to ourselves. Nowhere in the Bill of Rights are private-sector employees directly guaranteed a right to privacy. Perhaps this is why Henry Ford faced no resistance from the government when he sent social workers to the homes of employees to investigate their personal habits and family finances. He and other early industrialists were free to monitor whether employees went to church and to check up on the dating habits of their young female employees. Such invasions of privacy went hand in hand with the doctrine of employment-at-will.

Although the U.S. Constitution does not guarantee us the right to privacy, in 1965, the U.S. Supreme Court concluded that various guarantees stated in the Constitution (e.g., the Fourth Amendment's protection against illegal search and seizure) have the effect of creating zones of privacy. Since then, new state and federal legislation has begun to address employee privacy rights more explicitly. The best example of this at the federal level is the *Family Education Rights and Privacy Act of 1974*, also known as the Buckley Amendment. It allows students to inspect their educational records and prevents educational institutions from supplying information without students' consent. Employee rights to control private information were also a consideration in the passage of the *Employment Polygraph Protection Act of 1988*, which gives individuals the right to refuse to take a polygraph test as a condition of employment for most jobs.

Other privacy legislation is of a much weaker form. Rather than giving individuals control over who gets what information, most statutes simply give individuals a right to access and verify the information others already have. The *Privacy Act of 1974* was the first major statute to address issues of privacy directly. This act, which applies only to federal agencies, gives individuals the right to verify information collected about them and used in selection and employment decisions. It allows individuals to determine which records pertaining to them are collected, used, and maintained; to review and amend such records; to prevent unspecified use of such records; and to bring civil suit for damages against those intentionally violating the rights specified in the act. The *Privacy Act* is consistent with the *Freedom of Information Act of 1974*, which allows individuals to see all the material a federal agency uses in its decision-making processes.

In contrast to federal employees and citizens affected by the decisions of federal agencies, private-sector employees are relatively unprotected against employers, who have the ability to access and use information, often without the knowledge or consent of employees or job applicants. Two laws establish exceptions to this generalization. The *Fair Credit and Reporting Act of 1970* gives job applicants the right to know the nature and content of credit files. The *Employee Exposure and Medical Records Regulation of 1980* gives employees the right to access their on-the-job medical records and records that document their exposure to toxic substances.

Concerns about privacy also are addressed by state-level legislation. Several state laws—for example, in California, Connecticut, Maine, Michigan, Oregon, and Pennsylvania—give employees access to their human resource files and define what information employees are and are not entitled to see, as well as where, when, and under what circumstances employees may view their files.

Issues of privacy continue to be debated. How much access should employers have to medical records? Is there any nonmedical information that employers shouldn't have the right to obtain, and are all methods of monitoring employees acceptable? Should employers have the right to use information about employees' behavior off the job when making employment decisions? Does the company have a right to monitor use of the e-mail?

Access to Medical Information.   Health insurance costs grew so dramatically from the mid-1980s to the mid-1990s that many employers now feel

■□ *fast fact*

Employees have more privacy rights in the public sector than in the private sector.

pressure to do whatever is necessary to reduce them. One way to lower these costs is to employ people who make little use of health care services, because insurance for such employees is less expensive. Like insurance companies, employers can predict how much health care a person is likely to need if they have information about variables that put people into high-health-risk categories: Does she smoke? Is he overweight? Does she abuse alcohol? Other drugs? Does he exercise regularly? Like to bungee jump or drive too fast?

A study of 4,000 employees by DuPont documented the following additional annual costs associated with several personal behaviors and conditions:[63]

- Average smoking habit $960
- Excessive weight $401
- Alcohol abuse $369
- Elevated cholesterol $370
- High blood pressure $343

Data like these support General Mills' policy of lowering workers' insurance premiums if they lead healthy lives, as measured by behaviors such as not smoking, drinking little to no alcohol, controlling blood pressure and cholesterol, and wearing seat belts. They also support Turner Broadcasting System's policy of not hiring people who smoke, and help explain why drug testing has quickly gone from a rare to a routine practice: whereas in 1987, only about 20 percent of employers conducted drug testing, now more than 90 percent do so.[64]

It appears that employers can penalize or even terminate employees because of some types of conditions associated with high health care costs. But other employee conditions are clearly protected. The *Americans with Disabilities Act of 1990* (ADA) protects anyone with a history of drug use who has successfully completed or is currently engaged in rehabilitation —with some exceptions, especially when public safety may be at risk. The ADA also states that a medical exam may be given only after a conditional job offer has been made. Then, the offer may be rescinded only if the exam reveals a condition that would prevent the applicant from performing the job, and cannot be accommodated. Under the ADA, medical records are supposed to be kept separate from other human resource records and treated as confidential.

The ADA protects primarily people with disabilities. It does not address directly the question of how employers might use information about genetic makeup. Advances in our understanding of the link between genetics and disease susceptibility raise new concerns about medical privacy. Should a 25-year-old applicant for a sales job be required to undergo genetic screening for diseases that may be experienced in middle age? Is it fair to penalize workers with high cholesterol, given that genes as well as diet affect cholesterol levels?

Access to Nonmedical Information. Employers who seek medical information usually do so for good reasons. They may be concerned about how to keep health insurance costs as low as possible, which benefits the company's bottom line and may ultimately mean that healthy employees see a bigger paycheck. Or they may be concerned about protecting employees and customers from contagious diseases or unsafe behavior by employees carrying out their duties. Medical information seems to be directly relevant to such concerns.

What about other concerns? For example, research has shown linkages between watching violent TV and movies and engaging in violent behavior.[65] With violence in the workplace becoming a major issue in our society, should employers be allowed, perhaps even expected, to attempt to screen out employees whose viewing behaviors suggest they're likely to be violent?[66] Or suppose an employer wants to ensure that employees do not engage in illegal behaviors of various sorts, such as industrial espionage, drug dealing, or insider trading: Does this give the employer the right to listen in on employees' telephone calls? Do employers have the right to access and use all computer files on employees' office PCs? May employers monitor all employee e-mail communications?[67]

Do employers have the right to obtain all possible information about on-the-job behavior? Are all methods of monitoring on-the-job behavior acceptable? How would you feel if you discovered that your employer, as part of an effort to detect the illegal behavior of another employee, made a video-tape of you while you were in the bathroom or locker room, installed a monitoring device to learn what magazines you were reading during your lunch break, and hired undercover agents to pose as employees as a way to keep tabs on workers? This is what the Campbell Soup Company did—before terminating 62 employees.[68]

Unlike a journalist who might use such tactics to get story material for a TV "news" exposé, employers are not invading people's privacy to get rich. In their view, they're merely trying to keep costs down and profits up. Even when employees acknowledge that employers have a right to prevent certain types of employee behavior, however, most resent the idea of being so closely monitored. Thus, the challenge is finding approaches to monitoring that employees agree are legitimate and acceptable.[69] As technology continues to make such monitoring both easy and unobtrusive, employers are likely to continue increasing their use of it, absent new legal restrictions.

Fairness in the Global Context

Clearly, keeping up with both legal requirements and employees' attitudes about various employment practices requires substantial time as well as expertise. Laws relevant to almost every imaginable aspect of the employment relationship exist, and they take dozens of different forms in countries around the world. To provide a flavor for the international legal environment, here we touch on three topics: staffing and compensation, terminations, and informal expectations for supervisors' behaviors.

Staffing.   Deciding whether to offer someone a job is usually the first step in establishing an employment relationship—and it offers many opportunities for taking a misstep. Consider the magnitude of the hiring responsibilities of employers such as Cirque du Soleil. As described in the feature, Managing Globalization: Staffing Is No Laughing Matter for Cirque du Soleil, this company must continuously and quickly restaff as it travels around the world.[70]

The example of Cirque du Soleil illustrates the need to adhere to local labor laws. As clothing manufacturers have learned, it's not just the locals who are watching what employers do either. Most U.S. apparel manufacturers rely heavily on the low production costs in developing countries. Taking full advantage of low-cost offshore suppliers has its drawbacks, however. Public interest groups concerned about human rights have protested conditions in offshore apparel manufacturing, affecting a wide range of

■□ *fast fact*

The *U.S.-Japanese Treaty of Friendship* states that foreign corporations are allowed to discriminate in favor of citizens from their own country in filling specified high-level positions within the U.S.

MANAGING GLOBALIZATION
Staffing Is No Laughing Matter for Cirque du Soleil

Remember the last time you sat under the big top, watching clowns entertain and acrobats tumble across the floor? Perhaps you've even seen a performance of Cirque du Soleil—one of the most unique acts in the world. With corporate headquarters in Montreal and offices in Las Vegas and Amsterdam, Cirque du Soleil is an international entertainment company that employs more than 1,200 people representing 17 nationalities and speaking at least 13 different languages. Its major "products" include a permanent show that runs in Las Vegas and three touring shows—an American tour, an Asian tour, and a European tour. Growth plans include adding permanent shows at Disney World and in Berlin. These shows highlight the talents of Cirque's 230 full-time artists. But these artists could not have delighted more than 10 million spectators worldwide without the efforts of the company's other 1,000 employees.

In a business where people are clearly its most important asset, managing human resources effectively is essential. Success is possible only with careful planning, recruitment, and selection. For its tours, Cirque relies heavily on temporary staff (temps). In each city where it performs, Cirque hires 125 to 150 people to work as ushers, ticket sellers and takers, and security personnel. For a year of tours, that adds up to some 1,800 temps. Although Cirque employs them for only a few days, good temps are essential to the company's reputation because they have the most direct personal contact with customers. To be hired, applicants must conduct themselves well during an interview designed to assess attitude, experience, and skills. For positions in the touring groups, the selection process is more intensive. "When a person applies for a touring position, it's not just a job, but a way of life," explains one of Cirque's managers. These positions involve traveling 50 percent of the time and working with performers from many different cultures. For them, the selection process involves multiple stages of interviews—some that are one-on-one and others with a whole group of Cirque employees posing "what if" and "how would you handle this" questions. Throughout all of these activities, the company must ensure that it adheres to all local labor laws. Exhibit A illustrates differences in discrimination laws—just one aspect of employment conditions. Ideally, they'll also be sensitive enough to local conditions to be able to avoid engaging in practices that, while legal, are considered undesirable within the local culture.

Exhibit A Who's Protected Where?

Country	Age	Sex	National Origin	Race	Religion	Marital Status
U.S.	Yes	Yes	Yes	Yes	Yes	No
France	Some	Yes	Yes	Yes	Yes	Yes
Venezuela	No	No	No	No	No	No
Canada	Yes	Yes	Yes	Yes	Yes	Yes
Hong Kong	No	No	No	No	No	No
Japan	No	Yes	Yes	Yes	Yes	No
Vietnam	No	Yes	No	Yes	Yes	No
Germany	No	Yes	Yes	Yes	Yes	No
Indonesia	No	No	No	No	No	No
United Kingdom	No	Yes	No	No	No	No
Singapore	No	No	No	No	No	No
Greece	No	Yes	No	Yes	Yes	Yes

To learn more about Cirque du Soleil, visit the company's home page at
www.cirquedusoleil.com

■□ *fast fact*

The Haymarket Massacre refers to the day when hundreds of U.S. workers were shot at in Chicago as they rallied for eight-hour work days.

companies. Conditions in a shoe manufacturing plant in Donguann, China, illustrate the problem. Some 50,000 employees, many of them younger than the Chinese minimum age of 16 for working in factories, make products for Nike, Adidas, Reebok, LA Gear, Puma, and New Balance. Many weren't even being paid the Chinese minimum wage of $1.90 per day, with no benefits. They work under conditions that are typical in the region but are harsh by global standards. Mandatory overtime hours typically amount to 80 hours per month, or double the amount allowed by Chinese law. Meal breaks last only 10 to 15 minutes. At other factories in the area, conditions are even worse. To manage the high turnover rates, some local employers require employees to pay a "deposit" equivalent to two weeks' pay. Employees forfeit the deposit if they leave before their contracts expire. Other employers confiscate migrant workers' identification papers so that they can't job hop or even remain in the city.[71] Eventually, the pressure of public interest groups led Nike to agree to provide its workers worldwide with the protection of various American health and safety standards (e.g., air quality), and to include representatives from labor and human rights groups in a team of independent auditors for monitoring compliance with the standards globally. Extending the protection of U.S. laws to non-U.S. citizens is not legally required, but Nike has nevertheless concluded that going beyond what is required by law is good business practice.[72]

Termination.   Whereas some developing countries have few laws to protect employees' rights, the laws of many other countries protect employees more aggressively than do U.S. laws. In many countries, for example, termination of employment is viewed as a harsh action that's potentially harmful to employees. Consequently, in fairness to employees, employers are held responsible for minimizing its negative consequences. Most countries have some traditional or legally required practices that come into play in the event of a plant closing or a substantial reduction of the workforce. In general, these practices create more extensive and costlier employer obligations than do layoffs in the United States and Canada. One such obligation is the payment of cash indemnities that are in addition to individual termination payments required by law, collective bargaining agreements, or individual contracts.

Furthermore, in many countries, a company that wishes to close down or curtail operations also must develop a "social plan" or its equivalent, typically in concert with unions and other interested stakeholders. The plan may cover continuation of pay, benefit plan coverage, retraining allowances, relocation expenses, and supplementation of statutory unemployment compensation. Frequently, a company planning a partial or total plant closing must present its case to a government agency. In the Netherlands, for example, authorities may deny permission for a substantial workforce reduction unless management is able to demonstrate that the cutback is absolutely necessary for economic reasons and that the company has an approved social plan.

Informal Expectations.   When operating abroad, as when operating at home, complying with legal regulations is one step toward managing fairly. To be truly effective, however, managers need to realize that perceptions of fairness reflect cultural assumptions and values—not just legal realities. Managers who are insensitive to the broader social fabric will find it difficult to anticipate employees' reactions to how they're treated. Unenlightened managers run the risk of triggering negative employee reactions. To illustrate this, consider the culture of Mexico.

Mexico's social structure is similar to its family structure, and its institutions—whether government, business, or church —resemble an authoritarian, paternalistic family. A plant manager, like the president of Mexico, fills a fatherly role, rather than a mere organizational function. Mexico's history and legal institutions reflect the Mexican view that the employer has a moral and paternal responsibility for all its employees, even when the workers have a union. Mexican employees are not just working for a paycheck: they tend to expect to be treated as the "extended family" of the boss; they're accustomed to receiving a wide range of services, including food baskets and medical attention for themselves and their families, apart from social security. Medical benefits are not considered "an extra" or discretionary; they simply fulfill the employer's role and responsibilities. Corresponding to these expectations, employees have a reciprocal obligation to be loyal, to work hard, and to be willing to do whatever is requested of them. American managers who accept the Mexican sense that a job is more than a paycheck and who try to fulfill the expectations of their employees can reap the benefits of this form of partnership.

SUMMARY

Workplace fairness is a complex issue that touches all employees and all employers. When managing human resources, the question "What is fair?" may be difficult to answer. Historically, the power to determine workplace conditions rested largely in employers' hands. Gradually, society recognized that this was unfair and a shift in the power balance was needed. Numerous laws now sanction some employer actions because they're clearly unfair to employees. Some practices that employers once considered fair are now illegal.

A first step toward ensuring workplace fairness, therefore, is legal compliance. By following the laws, employers should at least be able to protect themselves from losing lawsuits alleging unfair employment practices. However, workplace fairness is more than an issue of legal compliance. Even legal employer actions may be considered unfair by employees. Drug-testing practices are becoming routine. They're accepted as legal by the courts. Does this mean employees agree that drug testing is fair? Not necessarily. Employees tend to evaluate whether drug testing is fair on a case-by-case basis. They weigh issues of invasion of privacy, threats to safety and health, the specific procedures used to conduct the drug tests, and the penalties associated with failing a drug test.

Managing human resources fairly requires an understanding of how employees evaluate fairness. Managing in ways that meet the principles of distributive and procedural justice is one approach to creating fair employment conditions. Managers also need to understand that the same policy and the same outcome can be perceived as relatively fair or unfair depending on the attitudes they display and the amount of respect they show personally for the concerns of employees. In addition, because perceptions of fairness constantly change with time and vary across cultures, employees' attitudes about fairness should always be determined and taken into account when establishing policies and procedures. These and other responsibilities of members of the HR Triad are summarized in The HR Triad: Partnership Roles and Responsibilities to Ensure Fairness.

THE HR TRIAD: PARTNERSHIP ROLES AND RESPONSIBILITIES TO ENSURE FAIRNESS

Line Managers	HR Professionals	Employees
Be informed about laws and regulations protecting employees' rights and behave in accordance with them.	Be informed about laws and regulations protecting employees' rights and behave in accordance with them.	Be informed about laws and regulations protecting employees' rights and behave in accordance with them.
Set policy for fair treatment of employees in workplace issues in collaboration with HR professionals.	Set policy for fair treatment of employees in workplace issues in collaboration with line managers.	Work with HR professionals in establishing procedures for dealing fairly with workplace issues.
Learn the steps involved in the organization's procedures for due process and follow them.	Encourage managers to use societal views of fairness as guides to policies and behaviors rather than adopting a legalistic model.	Report discriminatory or other illegal behavior among subordinates, colleagues, or superiors to an HR professional.
Be proactive in attempting to understand and respond to employees' views about fairness.	Assist in developing and implementing policies and practices that support and are consistent with fair and ethical behavior by everyone in the organization.	Accept and fulfill responsibilities to behave fairly toward the employer and the organization's assets.
Be proactive and intervene if you observe discriminatory or other illegal behavior among subordinates, colleagues or superiors.	Help keep employer and employee rights and responsibilities in balance.	Recognize that laws differ across countries and may account for some behaviors of people from other countries.
Keep accurate and current records regarding employee problems and performance.	Identify sources of legal advice and seek advice as needed.	Help educate employees from other cultures about U.S. employment laws.

TERMS TO REMEMBER

Age Discrimination in Employment Act of 1967 (ADEA)
Alternative dispute resolution
Americans with Disabilities Act
Arbitration
California Proposition 209
Civil Rights Act of 1964 and 1991, Title VII
Distributive justice
Employment-at-will
Equal Employment Opportunity Act of 1972

Equal Employment Opportunity Commission (EEOC)
Equal Pay Act of 1963
Executive orders
Fair Labor Standards Act of 1938 (FLSA)
Fairness
Family and Medical Leave Act of 1993 (FMLA)
Grievance procedures
Mediation
National Labor Relations Act

National Labor Relations Board
Occupational Safety and Health
    Administration (OSHA)
Older Workers Benefit Protection Act
Privacy Act of 1974

Procedural justice
Settlement agreement
Sexual harassment
"Zero tolerance" policy

DISCUSSION QUESTIONS

1. Why does the peer review system at Coors Brewing Company work so well?

2. Why should companies be concerned about managing employees fairly?

3. What is the employment-at-will doctrine? Why were courts in the late 1880s more willing to uphold the doctrine than are courts today?

4. How would you distinguish a just from an unjust dismissal? Is this distinction easier to make for low-level jobs than for high-level or managerial jobs? Explain.

5. The industrial, occupational, and demographic composition of the labor force shifted from the mid-1970s to the mid-1990s. How might these specific shifts coincide with the heightened interest in employee rights in the 1990s?

6. Develop counterarguments for the following arguments in support of the employment-at-will doctrine:
   a. If the employee can quit for any reason, the employer can fire for any reason.
   b. Because of business cycles, employers must have the flexibility to expand and contract their workforce.
   c. Discharged employees are always free to find other employment.
   d. Employers have economic incentives not to discharge employees unjustly; therefore, their power to terminate shouldn't be restricted by laws.

7. What workplace policies and procedures would you recommend for firms to be fair in their efforts to downsize and lay off employees?

8. What kinds of behaviors might constitute sexual harassment? How can an organization prevent those types of behaviors from occurring?

9. Due process has been interpreted as the duty to inform an employee of a charge, solicit employee input, and provide the employee with feedback in regard to the employment decision. How can a grievance procedure ensure this type of due process for an employee accused of sexual harassment? How can the grievance procedure protect the victim of the alleged harassment?

PROJECTS TO EXTEND YOUR LEARNING

1. **Managing Teams.** As organizations begin to use more and more teams, employees become more interdependent with each other. Teams are usually staffed with just enough people to get the job done. If a team

member is absent, other members of the team must pick up the slack. The *Family and Medical Leave Act of 1993* requires some employers to grant up to 12 weeks of unpaid leave for various family-related situations (e.g., the birth or adoption of a child). The law states only the minimum leave that employers must allow. Some employers have more generous policies. How are extended leaves likely to affect the functioning of work teams? Suppose you were a member of a team and needed to take a 12-week leave. How would you manage this situation with your teammates?

Visit the home pages of three companies that interest you. Based on the information provided, what is each company's philosophy concerning the relationship between work demands and family needs? Do any of the companies seem to have policies that address the issue of how teams are expected to deal with an extended absence of one of their members? To see the full text of the *Family and Medical Leave Act*, visit **www.dol.gov/dol/esa/fmla**

2. **Managing Diversity.**   The following ten questions might be asked during an employment interview. Some of them are illegal and should never be asked. Employers who ask illegal questions may be subject to legal prosecution for employment discrimination. Place a check mark in the appropriate column to indicate whether the question is legal or illegal. Before taking this quiz, visit the home page of the Equal Employment Opportunity Commission (EEOC) at **www.eeoc.gov**

Quiz Questions

		Legal	Illegal
1.	How old are you?	_____	_____
2.	Have you ever been arrested?	_____	_____
3.	Do any of your relatives work for this organization?	_____	_____
4.	Do you have children, and if you do, what kind of child-care arrangements do you have?	_____	_____
5.	Do you have any handicaps?	_____	_____
6.	Are you married?	_____	_____
7.	Where were you born?	_____	_____
8.	What organizations do you belong to?	_____	_____
9.	Do you get along well with other men [or women]?	_____	_____
10.	What languages can you speak and/or write fluently?	_____	_____

NOTE: Answers appear at the end of this chapter.

3. **Managing Globalization.**   Many U.S. companies have located some or all of their manufacturing facilities in other countries. As described in this chapter, employment conditions at those facilities may not meet the standards we have come to expect in the United States. Nike, the athlet-

ic apparel manufacturer, is an example of a company that has received a great deal of criticism for the actions of its foreign suppliers. How has Nike responded to this criticism? Compared to some of its competitors, does Nike seem to be more or less concerned about issues of fairness? Compare Nike at
www.nike.com
to Reebok at
www.reebok.com
and New Balance at
www.newbalance.com

4. **Managing Change.**   Consult the Bureau of National Affairs's (BNA's) *Fair Employment Practices, Labor Relations Reporter,* or *Labor Arbitration Reports* to find two recent cases that involved a charge of unjust dismissal. Address the following issues: On what basis did the employee contest the discharge? Did the dismissal appear to occur in an organization that was undergoing major change—such as a reengineering effort, a change in strategy, the introduction of new technology, a merger or other organizational restructuring , or downsizing? If so, what role did the change appear to have in the employee's dismissal? Did the company have a grievance procedure? What did the judge or arbitrator rule? Why? State whether you agree with the outcome of the case, and why.

    To learn more about the BNA and these publications, visit the company's home page at
    www.bna.com

5. **Integration and Application.** Review the end-of-text cases before answering the following questions.

    A.   Lincoln Electric
    *   What is the evidence that Lincoln Electric manages employees fairly? Are there any aspects of Lincoln's practices that you would consider unfair? Why?
    *   Describe what Lincoln's management appears to expect from employees. What does Lincoln agree to give employees in return? How do the expectations and responsibilities of Lincoln's management relate to notions of distributive and procedural justice?

    B.   Southwest Airlines
    *   What is the evidence that Southwest Airlines manages employees fairly? Are there any aspects of Southwest's practices that you would consider unfair? Why?
    *   Describe what Southwest's management appears to expect from employees. What does Southwest agree to give employees in return? How do the expectations and responsibilities of Southwest's management relate to notions of distributive and procedural justice?

CASE STUDY

What's Wrong With What's Right?

Stuart Campbell, now 35, moved slowly down the front steps of the courthouse and squinted as the last rays of sunlight pierced through downtown Cleveland. It had been a long day in the life of Stuart Campbell, who had spent the entire day in court recalling the details of his past employment with Nako Electronics, a major marketer of audio tapes in the U.S. Nako Electronics had—and still has—a considerable stake in Stuart Campbell. The arbitrator's decision and the award of $500,000 plus interest of $82,083.50 was a bitter pill for Nako to swallow for having terminated their Midwest sales representative.

Stuart had agreed to meet his attorney, Jim Baldwin, for a couple of drinks and to unwind from the courtroom tension. His spirits began to pick up as he maneuvered through the city traffic, but he couldn't help thinking how, within a year's time, his good job had soured.

Five years ago, Stuart Campbell was riding high as the Midwest representative for Nako covering Ohio, West Virginia, and Pennsylvania. Stuart, a hard worker, contracted with Nako Electronics and then boosted the sluggish sales of Nako audio tapes from less than $300,000 to a $2-million business in about 14 months. In fact, business was going so well for Stuart that he began driving a Mercedes-Benz sports utility vehicle. But that's when Mike Hammond, vice president of marketing at Nako Electronics, took notice of Campbell. On one of his visits to Campbell's territory, Hammond commented to Stuart that he really liked his car. Mike remarked that he was making a trip to California soon. "I distinctly remember Mike saying he would like to have a Buick," Stuart testified. "He didn't want anything as fancy as I had, because a new Buick would be adequate and, after all, he wanted me to bear the expense!"

Mike Hammond unfortunately couldn't be in court that day to defend himself; Hammond died unexpectedly last year of a heart attack. During the trial, though, Nako Electronics had to defend a number of allegations made against Mike Hammond. It seems that some of Stuart Campbell's co-workers suffered a similar fate. Not only had Stuart refused to go along with Hammond's car scheme, but he also refused to invest in a cartridge business begun by Hammond, which Stuart believed was a phony. Hammond, in fact, had approached all the sales representatives of Nako Electronics to invest in the cartridge company at $1,250 a share, a company for which Hammond and two other associates paid $1 a share for 80 percent of the stock. Stuart's attorney, Jim Baldwin, made sure that two of Stuart's former fellow sales representatives testified at the court proceedings that they were mysteriously fired after refusing Mike Hammond's demands to invest in his side company.

In the year following Stuart's successful boost in the sales of Nako audio tapes and Hammond's thwarted attempts at commercial shakedown, Nako increased Campbell's sales quota by more than 75 percent. As Campbell further testified, Nako sabotaged a substantial proportion of his sales by refusing to give his large customers promotional assistance. In the fall of that year, Nako fired Stuart without explanation. Nako argued in court that it didn't need a reason to fire Campbell and, besides, Campbell wasn't meeting his new, increased sales quota. Moreover, the company argued, Mr. Hammond could not defend himself against the charges of Campbell and others.

Stuart rehashed these details many times with his attorney, both during the private arbitrator hearing and during numerous rehearsals for the trial. As he arrived at the restaurant, he hoped he could put these memories behind him. As they talked, Jim summarized the day's proceedings and expressed cautious optimism for the final outcome. "But you know, Stuart," mused Jim, "If you would have kicked in the $10 or $15K that Hammond demanded, you would have outlived him, you'd have a business worth over $4 million in sales today, and we wouldn't be having this drink!"

QUESTIONS

1. Why did the arbitrator award Stuart so much money?

2. Was the arbitrator's decision a just and fair one?

3. Did Nako have to give Stuart a reason for firing him?

4. If his firing was due to his failure to invest in Hammond's side company, could this be defended in court?

5. Do you think there was anything Stuart could have done, legally, to avoid being fired?

6. How do you think Stuart's old co-workers at Nako would react to what happened to Stuart?

Source: Stuart A. Youngblood, Texas Christian University

Additional information about employee rights can be obtained by visiting the Teamsters home page at **www.teamster.org**

CASE STUDY

The Payback

Lucy Pascal was hired by ABC Jobbers, Inc., two months ago. ABC had wooed Lucy away from her previous employer because of her outstanding sales record. Enticed by a substantial boost in pay, commissions, and perks, Lucy was looking forward to widened professional contacts and increased income. Also, she was thrilled at having been one of the first women to be directly hired for sales work at ABC.

Lucy liked working for her new company even though she was certainly a rarity there. Virtually all of the other professionals and salespeople were male. Most were macho types, often joking and talking about their latest exploits with "a little number" met while on the road. When Lucy was around, they enjoyed teasing her to see what her reaction would be. She would change the subject pleasantly, but their conversations bothered her, and then there were all the centerfold pictures prominently displayed in a lot of the offices, which Lucy did her best to ignore. Yet, even with all this, she was still pleased she had made the job move because of its growth potential.

On one of her initial sales calls in her newly assigned district, Lucy visited Frank Grumman, a major client who was responsible for signing off on all sales contracts for his company. Lucy gave Frank Grumman a sales pitch in her typically persuasive and professional manner. Frank responded that he was most impressed not only with the product, but also with Lucy herself. He cajoled her to go out with him so they "could get to know each other better." Lucy began feeling increasingly uncomfortable with Frank's comments. It was obvious he was more interested in her as a woman than as ABC's sales representative.

Finally, in response to his insistent urgings that they take off together for the evening, Lucy, as nicely as she could, gave him a firm no. She, with a forced smile, advised him she had to catch an early flight.

Frank, feeling rejected, testily replied that Lucy really must not want the contract very much if she wasn't going to "entertain" him. Angered, Lucy told him in no uncertain terms what he could do with the contract if "entertaining" was part of the price she had to pay in order to get it. She stormed out of Frank's office.

Upon returning to her district office, Lucy related to James Roberts, her first-line supervisor and the district sales manager, what had happened on her sales call. James reacted with laughter. He said to Lucy, "There are certain things we all have to do to keep our clients happy."

"If you knew all the rounds of golf I've played with some real creeps for business purposes, then you'd realize what I was talking about." Lucy said "James, I'm not talking about playing golf. That's not the type of game he wanted me to play." James grew chilly. He told Lucy "You better not lose that contract. You do, and you'll lose your district and all its fat commissions!"

Lucy had been placed in a no-win situation by both her client and her boss. As she pondered over her dilemma, the chief executive officer of ABC saw her in the hall. "Lucy," said Donald Stubbs, "what's my favorite new sales gal looking so worried about? Come on into my office and tell me how things are going." The grandfatherly Mr. Stubbs gently ushered Lucy into his office. After only a few moments, Lucy blurted out her situation. Losing control, and to her great embarrassment, she broke into tears. Concerned, Mr. Stubbs placed his arms around Lucy to console her. Lucy soon calmed down enough to apologize for her behavior. Mr. Stubbs advised her he would place some phone calls and try to smooth things over. As he led her to the door, he admonished her. "You have to realize, Lucy, that men will be men. You'll just have to get used to these things in this business."

Lucy wandered down the hall wondering what was going to happen now. Samuel Kindel, a fellow salesperson, spotted Lucy and asked her if she'd like to have some coffee. Lucy replied she needed to talk to someone about the things that were happening to her. In the cafeteria, she told Samuel the entire story and the frustration she felt. Samuel became furious. He told her that "those guys are all no-good skunks." Lucy was relieved to have such a sympathetic ear to bend. As they continued their talk, Samuel said, "You know, I've been wanting to get to know you better ever since you got here, Lucy. What do you say we take in a movie tonight and forget this place?"

QUESTIONS

1. What sorts of measures could ABC Jobbers take with its clients to prevent this situation?

2. Samuel Kindel asked Lucy for a date. Was she being sexually harassed by him? How do you think she should have responded?

3. How could Lucy have dealt with the situation differently?

4. What type of company policies would you recommend that ABC Jobbers institute for its employees to forestall sexually harassing behaviors?

To learn more facts about the meaning and legal consequences of sexual harassment, visit the Equal Employment Opportunity Commission's home page at
www.eeoc.gov

ENDNOTES

1 T. Kelley, "Charting a Course to Ethical Profits," *New York Times* Section 3 (February 8, 1998): 1, 12.

2 D. Anfuso, "Coors Taps Employee Judgment," *Personnel Journal* (February 1994): 56.

3 L. Louise, "Dillard's is Meeting with Minorities to Talk of Diversity: Years of Silence End as a Store Chain Acts to Resolve Race-Bias Allegations," *The Wall Street Journal* (April 8, 1998): B4.

4 J. Greenberg, "Looking Fair vs. Being Fair: Managing Impressions of Organizational Justice," B. M. Staw and L. L. Cummings, eds., *Research in Organizational Behavior*, vol. 12 (Greenwich, CT: JAI Press, 1990): 111–157.

5 W. C. Kim and R. Maugorgne, "Fair Process: Managing in the Knowledge Economy," *Harvard Business Review* (July–August 1997): 65–75; R. Levering, *A Great Place to Work* (New York: Random House, 1988); see also F. Fukuyama, *Trust: The Social Virtues and the Creation of Prosperity* (New York: Free Press, 1995).

6 B. M. Ferdman, "Values About Fairness in the Ethnically Diverse Workplace," *Business & the Contemporary World* 9 (1997): 191–208.

7 M. A. Donovan, F. Drasgow, and L. J. Munson, "The Perceptions of Fair Interpersonal Treatment Scale: Development and Validation of a Measure of Interpersonal Treatment in the Workplace," *Journal of Applied Psychology* 83 (1998): 683–692; J. C. Morrow, P. C. Morrow, and E. J. Mullen, "Intraorganizational Mobility and Work-related Attitudes," *Journal of Organizational Behavior* 17 (1996): 363–374.

8 For good reviews of research on these topics, see R. Folger and R. Cropanzano, *Organizational Justice and Human Resource Management* (Thousand Oaks, CA: Sage, 1998); J. Greenberg, *The Quest for Justice on the Job: Essays and Experiments* (Thousand Oaks, CA: Sage, 1997); T. R. Tyler and E. A. Lind, "A Relational Model of Authority in Groups," *Advances in Experimental Social Psychology* 25 (1992): 115–191; R. Cropanzano, ed., *Justice in the Workplace: Approaching Fairness in Human Resource Management* (Hillsdale, NJ: Lawrence Erlbaum Associates, Publishers, 1993); B. H. Sheppard, R. J. Lewicki, and J. W. Minton, *Organizational Justice: The Search for Fairness in the Workplace* (New York: Lexington Books, 1992).

9 K. James, "The Social Context of Organizational Justice: Cultural, Intergroup, and Structural Effects on Justice Behaviors and Perceptions," in Cropanzano, *Justice in the Workplace*.

10 D. M. Mansour-Cole and S. G. Scott, "Hearing it Through the Grapevine: The Influence of Source, Leader-relations,

and Legitimacy on Survivors' Fairness Perceptions," *Personnel Psychology* 51 (1998): 25–53.

[11] M. P. Miceli, "Justice and Pay System Satisfaction," R. Cropanzano, *Justice in the Workplace*; R. L. Heneman, D. B. Greenberger, and S. Strasser, "The Relationship Between Pay-for-Performance Perceptions and Pay Satisfaction," *Personnel Psychology* 41 (1988): 745–761; M. P. Miceli, et al., "Predictors and Outcomes of Reactions to Pay-for-Performance Plans," *Journal of Applied Psychology* 76 (1991): 508–521.

[12] For a full discussion of these and related issues, see *CEO Pay: A Comprehensive Look* (Scottsdale, AZ: American Compensation Association, 1997); D. M. Gold, "Pressing the Issue of Pay Inequality," *The New York Times* (February 7, 1999): 11.

[13] James, "Social Context of Organizational Justice"; H. C. Triandis, "Cross-Cultural Industrial and Organizational Psychology," H. C. Triandis, M. D. Dunnette, and L. M. Hough, eds., *Handbook of Industrial and Organizational Psychology*, vol. 4 (Palo Alto, CA: Consulting Psychologists Press, 1994): 103–172; H. C. Triandis, "The Self and Social Behavior in Differing Cultural Contexts," *Psychological Review* 96 (1989): 506–520; Y. Kashima, et al., "Universalism in Lay Conceptions of Distributive Justice: A Cross-Cultural Examination," *International Journal of Psychology* 23 (1988): 51–64.

[14] Cropanzano, *Justice in the Workplace*; Sheppard, Lewicki, and Minton, *Organizational Justice*; Tyler and Lind, "A Relational Model of Authority in Groups."

[15] R. J. Bies and J. S. Moag, "Interactional Justice: Communication Criteria for Fairness," in B. Sheppard, ed. *Research on Negotiation in Organizations*, vol. 1 (Greenwich, CT: JAI, 1986): 43–55.

[16] See C. E. Rusbult, et al., "Impact of Exchange Variables on Exit, Voice, Loyalty and Neglect: An Integrative Model of Responses to Declining Job Satisfaction," *Academy of Management Journal* 31 (1988): 599–627.

[17] R. B. Freeman and J. L. Medoff, *What Do Unions Do?* (New York: Basic Books, 1984).

[18] T. R. Tyler and R. Schuler, "A Relational Model of Authority in Work Organizations: The Psychology of Procedural Justice" (manuscript, American Bar Foundation, 1990).

[19] D. B. McFarlin and P. D. Sweeney, "Distributive and Procedural Justice as Predictors of Satisfaction with Personal and Organizational Outcomes," *Academy of Management Journal* 35 (1992): 626–637; R. Kanfer, and P. C. Earley, "Voice, Control, and Procedural Justice: Instrumental and Noninstrumental Concerns in Fairness Judgments," *Journal of Personality and Social Psychology* 59 (1990): 952–959.

[20] J. Greenberg, "Employee Theft as a Reaction to Underpayment Inequity: The Hidden Cost of Pay Cuts," *Journal of Applied Psychology* 75 (1990): 561–568.

[21] See Freeman and Medoff, *What Do Unions Do?*; D. G. Spencer, "Employee Voice and Employee Retention," *Academy of Management Journal* 29 (1986): 488–502; S. Alexander and M. Ruderman, "The Role of Procedural and Distributive Justice in Organizational Behavior," *Social*

Justice Research 1 (1987): 117–198; G. E. Fryxell and M. E. Gordon, "Workplace Justice and Job Satisfaction as Predictors of Satisfaction with Union and Management," *Academy of Management Journal* 32 (1989): 851–866.

[22] R. H. Moorman, "Relationship Between Organizational Justice and Organizational Citizenship Behaviors: Do Fairness Perceptions Influence Employee Citizenship?" *Journal of Applied Psychology* 76 (1991): 845–855.

[23] M. P. Miceli and J. P. Near, *Blowing the Whistle: The Organizational and Legal Implications for Companies and Employees* (New York: Lexington Books, 1992).

[24] J. Greenberg, "The Social Side of Fairness: Interpersonal and Informational Classes of Organizational Justice," Cropanzano, ed., *Justice in the Workplace*.

[25] "Arbitration Provisions in Union Agreements in 1949," *Monthly Labor Review* 70 (1950): 160–165.

[26] See M. E. Gordon and G. E. Fryxell, "The Role of Interpersonal Justice in Organizational Grievance Systems," in Cropanzano, *Justice in the Workplace*.

[27] R. Ganzel, "Second-Class Justice?" *Training* (October 1997) 84–96; A. J. Conti, "Alternative Dispute Resolution: A Court-Backed, Mandatory Alternative to Employee Lawsuits," *Fair Employment Practices Guidelines* (October 10, 1997): 1–15; P. Feuille and J. T. Delaney, "The Individual Pursuit of Organizational Justice: Grievance Procedures in Nonunion Workplaces," *Research in Personnel and Human Resources Management* 10 (1992): 187–232.

[28] D. W. Ewing, "Who Wants Employee Rights?" *Harvard Business Review* 49 (November–December 1971): 22–35.

[29] J. T. Delaney and P. Feuille, "Grievance and Arbitration Procedures Among Nonunion Employers" (paper presented at the Forty-Fourth Annual Meeting of the Industrial Relations Research Association, New Orleans, 1992), J. F. Burton, Jr., ed., Proceedings of the Forty-Fourth Annual Meeting (Madison, WI: Industrial Relations Research Association, 1993).

[30] B. S. Klaas and A. DeNisi, "Managerial Reactions to Employee Dissent: The Impact of Grievance Activity on Performance Ratings," *Academy of Management Journal* 41 (1998): 445–458; D. Lewin, "Dispute Resolution in the Nonunion Firm: A Theoretical and Empirical Analysis," *Journal of Conflict Resolution* 31 (1987): 465–502; R. B. Peterson, "The Union and Nonunion Grievance System," in *Research Frontiers in Industrial Relations and Human Resources*, D. Lewin, O. S. Mitchell, and P. D. Sherer, eds. (Madison, WI: Industrial Relations Research Association, 1992): 131–164.

[31] J. B. Olson-Buchanan, "Voicing Discontent: What Happens to the Grievance Filer After the Grievance?" *Journal of Applied Psychology* 18 (1996): 52–63; C. Handy, "A Better Capitalism," *Across the Board* (April 1998): 16–22.

[32] M. T. Miklave, "Why 'Jury' is a Four Letter Word," *Workforce* (March 1998): 56–64; K. Aquino, R. F. Griffeth, D. G. Allen, and P. W. Hom, "Integrating Justice Constructs into the Turnover Process: A Test of a Referent Cognitions Model," *Academy of Management Journal* 40 (1997): 1208–1227; M. Schminke, M. L. Ambrose, and T. W. Noel, "The Effect of Ethical Frameworks on Perceptions of

Organizational Justice," *Academy of Management Journal* 40 (1997): 1190–1207; S. P. Schappe, "Bridging the Gap Between Procedural Knowledge and Positive Employee Attitudes: Procedural Justice as Keystones," *Group & Organization Management* 21(3) (September 1996): 337–364; J. Giacobbe-Miller, "A Test of the Group Values and Control Models of Procedural Justice from the Competing Perspectives of Labor and Management," *Personnel Psychology* 48 (1995): 11–141; D. J. Mesch and D. R. Dalton, "Unexpected Consequences of Improving Workplace Justice: A Six-Year Time Series Assessment," *Academy of Management Journal* 35 (1992): 1099–1114; M. E. Gordon and R. L. Bowlby, "Reactance and Intentionality Attributions as Determinants of the Intent to File a Grievance," *Personnel Psychology* 42 (1989): 309–329; B. S. Klaas, "Determinants of Grievance Activity and the Grievance System's Impact on Employee Behavior: An Integrative Perspective," *Academy of Management Review* 14 (1989): 445–458.

[33] W. L. F. Felstiner, R. L. Abel, and A. Sarat, "The Emergence and Transformation of Disputes: Naming, Blaming, Claiming. . . ," *Law and Society Review* 15 (1980): 631–654; P. Feuille and J. T. Delaney, "The Individual Pursuit of Organizational Justice: Grievance Procedures in Nonunion Workplaces," *Research in Personnel and Human Resources Management* 10 (1992): 187–232.

[34] G. Flynn, "Hallmark Cares," *Personnel Journal* (March 1996): 50–61; G. Flynn, "A Satisfied Work Force Is in Hallmark's Cards," *Personnel Journal* (January 1996): 44–48; "Optimas Awards Celebrate Exemplary HR," *Personnel Journal* (January 1996): 50.

[35] This discussion is based mostly on Ringleb, Meiners, and Edwards, *Managing in the Legal Environment*. Useful overviews also appear in R. D. Arvey and R. H. Faley, *Fairness in Selecting Employees*, 2nd ed. (Reading, MA: Addison-Wesley Publishing Co., 1988); and A. Gutman, *Law and Personnel Practices* (Newbury Park, CA: Sage Publications, 1993).

[36] J. Ledvinka, "Government Regulation and Human Resources," A. Howard, ed., *The Changing Nature of Work* (San Francisco: Jossey-Bass, 1995).

[37] P. E. Varca and P. Pattison, "Evidentiary Standards in Employment Discrimination: A View toward the Future," *Personnel Psychology* 46 (1993): 239; D. Seligman, "What's Your Job-Bias Liability?" *Forbes* (February 8, 1999): 21–22.

[38] P. Wright, S. P. Ferris, J. S. Heller, and M. Kroll, "Competitiveness Through Management of Diversity: Effects on Stock Price Valuation," *Academy of Management Journal* 38 (1995): 272–287.

[39] L. Himmelstein, "Going Beyond City Limits?" *Business Week* (July 7, 1997): 98–99.

[40] "Firing Proves Costly," *Bulletin to Management* (May 13, 1993): 145.

[41] R. Smothers, "$105 Million Poorer Now, Chain Mends Race Policies," *New York Times* (January 31, 1993): L16.

[42] V. C. Smith, "Sign of the Times," *Human Resource Executive* (April 1997): 57–63; S. Caudron, "Blow the Whistle on Employment Disputes," *Workforce* (May 1997):

51–57; R. Furchgott, "Opposition Builds to Mandatory Arbitration at Work," *New York Times* (July 20, 1997): F11; "Employee Relations," *HR Reporter* 14 (12) (December 1997): 1–12; "NASD Votes To Nix Mandatory Arbitration," *Fair Employment Practices* (August 21, 1997): 99.

[43] G. Glynn, "Mandatory Binding Arbitration—Ensure Your Plan is Usable," *Workforce* (June 1997): 121–127.

[44] M. A. Jacobs, "Judge Finds Merrill Lynch Can't Force Ex-Consultant to Arbitrate Case," *The Wall Street Journal* (January 27, 1998): B8.

[45] P. Truell, "Smith Barney Plaintiffs Agree to Incentives for Settlement," *The Wall Street Journal* (November 7, 1997): D1, D7.

[46] M. L. Bickner and C. Feigenbaum, "Developments in Employment Arbitration," *Dispute Resolution Journal* (January 1997): 234–251.; S. Caudron, "Blow the Whistle on Employment Disputes."

[47] P. J. Kennedy, "Take the Money and Sue," *HRM Magazine* (April 1998): 105–108.

[48] K. Eichenwald, "The Two Faces of Texaco: The Right Policies Are on the Books, But Not Always on the Job," *New York Times* (November 10, 1996): A1–A3; A. Bryant, "How Much Has Texaco Changed? A Mixed Report Card on Anti-Bias Efforts," *New York Times* (November 2, 1997): 3-1, 3-16, 3-17; V. C. Smith, "Texaco Outlines Comprehensive Initiatives," *Human Resource Executive* (February 1997): 13; and "Texaco's Workforce Diversity Plan," as reprinted in *Workforce* (March 1997): Supplement.

[49] "Liability for Sexual Harassment Still in the Air," *Fair Employment Practices Guidelines*, Number 441 (October 10, 1997); "EEOC Proposes Harassment Guidelines," *Fair Employment Practices Guidelines* (July 29, 1993): 87.

[50] A. M. Townsend, M. E. Whitman, and R. J. Aalberts, "What's Left of the Communications Decency Act?" *HRM Magazine* (June 1998): 124–127.

[51] P. McGeehan, "Two Analysts Leave Salomon in Smut Case," *The Wall Street Journal* (March 31, 1998): C1, C25.

[52] "A Question of Ethics," *Bulletin to Management* (July 9, 1992): 211.

[53] B. Weiser, "Brokerage Settles Lawsuit on Racial and Sexual Bias: Firm to Pay $1.75 in Federal Case," *New York Times* (April 9, 1998): B5.

[54] J. Steinhauer, "If the Boss is Out of Line, What's the Legal Boundary," *New York Times* (March 27, 1997): D1, D4; "Reasonable Woman Standard Gains Ground," *Fair Employment Practices Guidelines* (June 25, 1993): 4.

[55] K. M. Jarin and E. K. Pomfert, "New Rules for Same Sex Harassment," *HRM Magazine* (June 1998): 115–123.

[56] S. R. Garland, "Finally, A Corporate Tip Sheet on Sexual Harassment," *Business Week* (July 13, 1998): 39; S. G. Gibson and H. Roberts-Fox, "Supreme Court Rulings on Sexual Harassment Disputes," *The Industrial-Organizational Psychologist* 36 (2) (October 1998): 33–36.

[57] *What Is Harassment?* (Brochure of the Northern States Power Co., St. Paul, MN: Company Publication, 1993): 1.

58 "Preventing Sexual Harassment: Helpful Advice and Another Reason," *Fair Employment Practices* (February 19, 1998): 21; M. Raphan and M. Heerman, "Eight Steps to Harassment-Proof Your Office," *HR Focus* (August 1997): 11–12; D. E. Terpstra and D. D. Baker, "Outcomes of Federal Court Decisions on Sexual Harassment," *Academy of Management Journal* 35 (1992): 181–190; B. A. Gutek, A. G. Cohen, and A. M. Konrad, "Predicting Social-Sexual Behavior at Work: A Contact Hypothesis," *Academy of Management Journal* 33 (1990): 560–577.

59 E. Peirce, C. A. Smolinski, and B. Rosen, "Why Sexual Harassment Complaints Fall on Deaf Ears," *Academy of Management Executive* 12 (3) (1998): 41–54.

60 "$10 Million Sexual Harassment Settlement," *Fair Employment Practices* (February 19, 1998): 24; A. B. Fisher, "Sexual Harassment: What to Do," *Fortune* (August 23, 1993): 84–88.

61 J. D. Aram and P. F. Salipante, "An Evaluation of Organizational Due Process in the Resolution of Employee/Employer Conflict," *Academy of Management Review* 2 (1977): 197–204; B. H. Sheppard, R. J. Lewicki, and J. W. Minton, *Organizational Justice: The Search for Fairness in the Workplace*.

62 "Policy Guide: What Constitutes 'Good Cause' for Firing?" *Bulletin to Management* (January 22, 1998): 24; "How Employers Can Use Employment-at-Will Disclaimers Effectively," *Fair Employment Practices Guidelines* (November 10, 1997): 6–8; "A Pledge of Job Security Can Alter At-Will Status," *Bulletin to Management* (August 14, 1997); "Whistleblower Costs Employer Buckets," *Bulletin to Management* (November 27, 1997): 379; "Termination and the McKennon Decision," *Fair Employment Practices Guidelines* (April 25, 1996): 5; C. Roberson, *Hire Right/Fire Right: A Manager's Guide to Employment Practices that Avoid Lawsuits* (New York: McGraw-Hill, 1992); S. A. Youngblood and L. Bierman, "Due Process and Employment-at-Will: A Legal and Behavioral Analysis," K. M. Rowland and G. R. Ferris, eds., *Research in Personnel and Human Resources Management* (Greenwich, CT: JAI Press, 1985): 185–230.

63 L. Smith, "What the Boss Knows about You," *Fortune* (August 9, 1993): 88–93.

64 W. L. Holstein, "From Rare to Routine," *New York Times* (November 28, 1993): 3–11.

65 W. Wood, F. Y. Wong, and J. G. Chachere, "Effects of Media Violence on Viewers' Aggression in Unconstrained Social Interaction," *Psychological Bulletin* 109 (1991): 371–83; F. S. Andison, "TV Violence and Viewer Aggression: A Cumulation of Study Results," *Public Opinion Quarterly* 41 (1977): 314–331.

66 H. F. Bensimon, "Violence in the Workplace," *Training and Development Journal* (January 1994): 27–32; M. Braverman and O. M. Kurland, "Workplace Violence," *Risk Management* 40 (1993): 76–77; D. J. Peterson and D. Massengill, "The Negligent Hiring Doctrine—A Growing Dilemma for Employers," *Employee Relations Law Journal* 15 (1989–90): 419–432; *A Post Office Tragedy: The Shooting at Royal Oak* (Report of the Committee on Post Office and Civil Service, United States House of Representatives, 1992).

67 R. Behar, "Who's Reading Your E-Mail?" *Fortune* (February 3, 1997): 57–70; "Telephone and Electronic Monitoring: A Special Report on the Issues and the Law," *Bulletin to Management* 48(14) (April 3, 1997): 1–8; P. D. Samuels, "Who's Reading Your E-Mail? Maybe the Boss," *New York Times* (May 12, 1996): F11; "Policy Guide: Curbing the Risks of E-Mail Use," *Bulletin to Management* (April 10, 1997): 120; M. J. Cronin, "Tough Rules for Web Access," *Fortune* (August 4, 1997): 218–219; D. F. Linowes, "Maintaining Privacy in the Electronic Technology Age," *HR Reporter* 13 (8) (August 1996): 6–8.

68 "Video Surveillance Withstands Privacy Challenge," *Bulletin to Management* 48(16) (April 17, 1997): 121; "Secret Video OK'd as Inspection Tool," *Bulletin to Management* (February 12, 1998): 44.

69 W. S. Hubbartt, *The New Battle Over Workplace Privacy* (New York: AMACOM, 1998).

70 G. Flynn, "Acrobats, Aerialists, and HR: The Big Top Needs Big HR," *Workforce* (August 1997): 38–45. Table 1 is adapted from L. B. Pincus and J. A. Belohlav, "Legal Issues in Multinational Business Strategy: To Play the Game You Have to Know the Rules," *Academy of Management Executive* 10(3) (1996): 52–62; J. P. Begin, *Dynamic Human Resource Systems: Cross-National Comparisons* (New York: de Gruyter, 1997); R. Orzechowski and B. Berret, "Setting Up Shop in Vietnam," *Global Workforce* (May 1998): 24–27.

71 Verena Dobnik. "Study: Chinese Workers Abused While Making Nike, Reebok Shoes," Associated Press, *Corpus Christi Caller-Times* (September 21, 1997): p. A8; A. Chan, "Boot camp at the shoe factory," *Washington Post* (November 3, 1996): C1, C4.

72 W. A. Carmell, "U.S. Law Heads Abroad," *International HR Update* (July 1998): 5.

73 P. J. Dowling, R. S. Schuler, and D. E. Welch, *International Dimensions of Human Resource Management*, 3rd ed. (Cincinnati: South-Western/ITP, 1999).

Answers to Item #2 Under Projects to Extend Your Learning

The following evaluations provide clarification rather than strict legal interpretation because employment laws and regulations are constantly changing.

1. *How old are you?*
    This question is legal but inadvisable. An applicant's date of birth or age can be asked, but telling the applicant that federal and state laws prohibit age discrimination is essential. Avoid focusing on age, unless an occupation requires extraordinary physical ability or training and a valid age-related rule is in effect.

2. *Have you ever been arrested?*
    This question is illegal unless an inquiry about arrests is justified by the specific nature of the organization—for instance, law enforcement or handling controlled substances. Questions about arrests generally are considered to be suspect because they may tend to disqualify some groups. Convictions should be the basis for rejection of an applicant only if the number, nature, or recent occurrence renders the applicant unsuitable. In that case the question(s) should be specific. For example: Have you ever been convicted for theft? Have you been convicted within the past year on drug-related charges?

3. *Do any of your relatives work for this organization?*
    This question is legal if the intent is to discover nepotism.

4. *Do you have children, and if you do, what kind of child-care arrangements do you have?*
    Both parts of this question are currently illegal; they shouldn't be asked in any form because the answers would not be job-related. In addition, they might imply gender discrimination.

5. *Do you have any handicaps?*
    This question is illegal as phrased here. An applicant doesn't have to divulge handicaps or health conditions that don't relate reasonably to fitness to perform the job.

6. *Are you married?*
    This question is legal, but may be discriminatory. Marriage has nothing directly to do with job performance.

7. *Where were you born?*
    This question is legal, but it might indicate discrimination on the basis of national origin.

8. *What organizations do you belong to?*
    As stated, this question is legal; it's permissible to ask about organizational membership in a general sense. It's illegal to ask about membership in a specific organization when the name of that organization would indicate the race, color, creed, gender, marital status, religion, or national origin or ancestry of its members.

9. *Do you get along well with other men [or women]?*
    This question is illegal; it seems to perpetuate sexism.

10. *What languages can you speak and/or write fluently?*
    Although this question is legal, it might be perceived as a roundabout way of determining an individual's national origin. Asking how a particular language was learned isn't permissible.

THE INTERNAL ENVIRONMENT: CREATING STRATEGIC ALIGNMENT

Chapter Outline

"In three years, Ameritech has gone from a sleepy, bureaucratic company to a nimble, market-driven global communications company. We tapped new leadership and recruited new people. We compressed management layers. We pushed for those closest to customers to drive major company decisions. We outsourced and trimmed our workforce. We reorganized and consolidated. And the change continues."

**William M. Oliver
Senior VP, Human Resources
Ameritech[1]**

MANAGING THROUGH PARTNERSHIP

at General Electric

General Electric (GE) Company's dramatic changes during the 1980s and early 1990s reflect a company adjusting to an increasingly competitive environment in innovative ways that mesh its human resource policies with the needs and strategy of the business. During the 1970s, CEO Reginald H. Jones, the highly regarded "financial wizard," built the firm into a strong financial performer. He also led a diversification effort that put the company into about 100 different businesses, ranging from manufacturers of appliances and lightbulbs, to coal mines and producers of TV sets and computer chips. Company earnings per share rose an average of 4.9 percent yearly.

In the process of building a profitable and diverse conglomerate, Jones also created a massive organization mired in bureaucracy. Reporting requirements were legendary. One manager finally had to stop computers from generating seven daily reports on sales of hundreds of thousands of products; the paper from just one of those reports stood twelve feet high!

In 1981, Jack Welch assumed the post of GE's chief executive officer. In picking Welch as his successor, Jones supported Welch's objective of making the $27-billion GE a "world-class competitor," able to thrive in an increasingly global marketplace. Welch took the helm of a strong yet somewhat complacent firm. A key task would be to "instill in … managers a sense of urgency when there is no emergency," and prepare the company to meet the challenges of the future.

Welch saw the world marketplace as a tough and increasingly competitive playing field that eventually would be dominated by a few large firms. To compete effectively, Welch believed, GE had to operate only in markets in which it could be the first or second player worldwide. This led to a major restructuring: GE exited all but about 14 businesses and quickly reduced its 420,000-person labor force by 25 percent.

To increase productivity in the remaining businesses, Welch shifted responsibility for decision making down the line and consolidated the layers of line management. Managerial spans of control went from an average of six or seven subordinates to an average of about 15. Welch's reasoning? "Overstretched" managers perform better on important tasks because they have no time for trivia and no time to interfere with subordinates' tasks. Larger spans of control mean people down the line take on more responsibility and show their ability to perform. Welch also reduced corporate staff and forced remaining staff units to ask how they could help people on the line "be more effective and competitive." By the mid-1990s, GE had reduced its workforce to 200,000 employees through layoffs, attrition, and divestiture of businesses.

Under Welch's leadership, GE continues to change. In recent years, improving quality has been a primary focus for the firm. Welch understands that one way to beat competitors and maximize a company's profitability is by improving quality control. To focus his managers' attention on quality control, Welch tied 40 percent of executive bonuses to implementing a quality improvement initiative. By the year 2000, the company plans to train a cadre of 10,000 "Black Belts" in quality control techniques. After completing the training, each Black Belt will go to a plant or office to set up and organize quality improvement projects. Welch is investing hundreds of millions of dollars to carry out the training, run projects, and put in place the computer systems needed to measure quality and analyze problems.

According to Welch, managing human resources effectively is part of the solution for managing GE into the future. To improve communication and further reduce bureaucracy, GE initiated a program called Work-Out in late 1989. The heads of the business units meet regularly with subordinates to identify and eliminate unnecessary activities—meetings, reports, and unproductive work. The process also seeks to identify better ways to evaluate and reward managers. Training is another top priority. Welch takes his message directly to employees during training sessions at GE's in-house university in Crotonville, New York, which trains 5,000 employees annually. In planning and staffing business units, Welch seeks business leaders who are open and willing to change. This means they must be able to "create a vision, articulate the vision, passionately own the vision, and. . . relentlessly drive it to completion." In the current environment, managers who don't become Black Belts and lead the company's quality improvement efforts know they don't have much future at GE. Identifying and preparing future leaders is so important that Welch regularly reviews files of selected employees from the time they join the firm, and evaluates each person's potential for future positions.[2]

For more about General Electric, visit the company's home page at **www.ge.com**

COMPONENTS OF THE INTERNAL ENVIRONMENT

In Chapter 2, the external environment was portrayed as having an important influence on how organizations manage human resources. Yet the external environment does not fully determine an organization's approach—a more accurate portrayal is to think of the external environment as a set of constraints and opportunities. Each organization's response to these is unique, depending on the organization's internal strengths and weaknesses. Effective organizations seek to create an internal environment that fits well with the current external environment yet is also capable of changing for the future. An organization's internal analysis includes the competitive strategy, organizational design, and organizational culture. These aspects of the internal environment provide an immediate context for managing human resources. Because the external environment changes constantly, changes in the internal environment often are needed. The ability of an organization to manage change is, therefore, a key determinant of its long-term success.

As is true of the external environment, components of the internal environment are highly interdependent. At GE, competitive forces in the external environment stimulated a change in the firm's strategy. The new strategy, in turn, stimulated GE's restructuring efforts. But a new structure alone would not automatically improve the firm's competitiveness—new processes were also needed. Now GE is learning about and adopting TQM processes in all of its businesses. Structure and processes are two key elements of an organization's design. Implementing TQM, in turn, requires adopting not only a new set of technical skills but also a new philosophy about how to manage people. Thus, more change is in GE's future as its culture and approaches to managing human resources are aligned to fit the new strategic imperatives.

INDUSTRY

As noted in Chapter 2, the industry in which a company competes is an important aspect of the external environment. Changes occurring in the general external environment may have different implications for different industries. For example, changes in national policies regarding tariffs or wages may be viewed as favorable for one industry and unfavorable for another. As another example, an overall trend in the direction of increasing productivity at the national level can mask the fact that some industries are enjoying substantial gains while other industries may actually be declining.

An industry's boundaries are both fuzzy and unstable, so the question "What industry are we in?" isn't always easy to answer. Furthermore, some companies compete by constantly pushing at the boundaries of the industry and, eventually, redefining the industries in which they compete. Nevertheless, at any point in time, the relevant industry for most organizations is comprised of a group of companies that offer similar products and services. Companies within an industry generally experience similar patterns of growth, and eventually a common industry culture may develop. Furthermore, companies within the same industry generally are a firm's most significant competitors. Not surprisingly, then, the industry context of an organization has a strong influence on managers' perceptions of the external environment.[3]

Industry Life Cycles

■□ *fast fact*

The typical life span of a company is about 12.5 years.

Like people and the organizations they work in, industries have life cycles. This is illustrated in Exhibit 4.1 Companies within the same industry may experience these life cycles in tandem, which creates certain similarities in the issues they face and the solutions they adopt. Factors such as changes in the industry's price-cost-profits economics, customer needs and expectations, and technology may make a particular industry either very attractive or very unattractive. As industry conditions change, external opportunities for growth may be created and external threats to the company's competitive position may emerge. When there are many opportunities for growth (e.g., because of strong demand or government deregulation), many firms can thrive within the industry. How to capture opportunities for growth and ward off threats to the company's competitive position in the industry are key strategic decisions. Eventually, however, competition is likely to intensify, and eventually growth of the industry levels off or even contracts. Then strategic decisions may focus more on whether and how to exit the industry, and perhaps create or enter another industry.[4]

Nascent. During the nascent stage of an industry's life cycle, firms are competing to establish a distinctive reputation and to create customer loyalty. At this stage, there are relatively few competitors, so each company has many options. Since the industry isn't yet well established, there is a great deal of risk associated with this stage of an industry's life cycle. Many start-up companies will fail, so simply surviving is the primary concern for the company. Internet service providers are an example of an industry in the nascent stage.

Growth. Companies that survive this first stage usually enjoy a period of rapid growth. If the new product offered by the industry can be easily standardized, this growth phase may be characterized as a period of rapid franchising. For example, during the 1980s, the franchising of premium quality coffee bars resulted in extremely rapid growth of that industry. Most industries do not grow through franchising, however. Instead, the dominant firms each grow their market share by developing new products to meet consumers' evolving demands. As organizations grow, issues of acquiring and

Exhibit 4.1
Industry Life Cycle

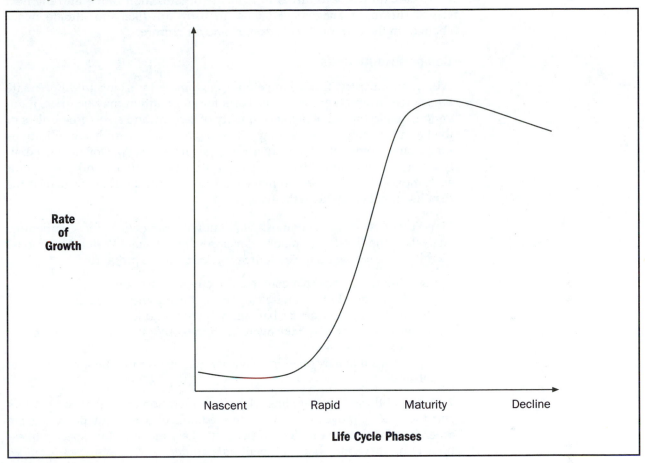

Life Cycle Phases

retaining talent and coordinating the activities of the expanding enterprise often become central.

Mature. Eventually, in most industries, the rate of growth eventually slows and the industry moves into a mature stage. Now there are a few large firms all striving to become more efficient while also improving the quality of their products. Often it's at this stage that companies begin to expand into international markets, which are viewed as opportunities for continued growth. Industry maturity may also stimulate consolidation through mergers and acquisitions, as is currently occurring in the financial services industry.[5]

Decline. Finally, an industry may go into decline as the products and services on which it's based become obsolete. At this stage, companies in the industry must eventually go out of business or transform themselves to offer new products and services and, effectively, enter a new industry.

Changing managerial priorities characterize organizations in these various developmental stages.[6] In addition, companies within the same industry tend to draw upon the same labor pool for people working in the technical areas that define the industry, thus common approaches to managing human resources tend to evolve within industries. At the senior level, for example, changes in the role of the CEO and top management team correspond to changes in the stage of the industry's life cycle and often organizations seek outside executives to help the organization move into the next stage. The top management teams, in turn, are likely to initiate major changes in the firm's strategy, design, and/or culture.

Competitive Analysis

Within an industry, firms compete for customers by trying to differentiate themselves from other firms. The basis for competition may be price, innovation, quality, speed of delivery, quality of service, and so on. Regardless of the basis for competition, a competitive move by one firm has implications for all other competitors. If Burger King cuts its prices, McDonald's generally must follow. Competitive analysis is used to anticipate and prepare for such moves. It's also used to make decisions about the basis on which the firm itself will compete in the future.

Five-Forces Model. The most well-known framework for competitive analysis is the five-forces model, developed by Michael Porter. This model identifies the following major sources of competitive pressure:

- existing rival firms that compete directly for customers,
- suppliers' ability to exercise bargaining power and leverage,
- buyers' ability to exercise bargaining power and leverage,
- other firms that may take away customers by offering substitute products or services, and
- new firms that may enter into competition by offering the same products of services.

While all of these forces are important, consideration of current competitors and their likely moves is the most immediate concern. Understanding the other four forces help predict competitors' likely moves. More specific questions to be answered about competitors include:

- What drives the competitor? That is, what are their objectives? Answering this question involves understanding who the competitor defines as their key customers and the basis on which the competitor tries to attract and retain customers.
- What is the competitor's current strategy and what strategy could they adopt?
- What assumptions does the competitor make about the industry? Answering this question involves discerning whether the competitor seems to be operating in a status quo mode or is preparing for major changes, and if so, the nature of change they anticipate.
- What are the competitor's capabilities?[7] Included here is information about marketing strategies, distribution methods, size of the sales force, terms and conditions of sales, size and location of operations, research and development activity, and just about every other aspect of doing business.

Answers to these questions can also be used to organize competitors into strategic groups. A strategic group includes all of the firms in the industry that are competing on the same basis.[8]

Competing for Labor.   Just as firms compete for customers in the product market, they engage in similar competition in the labor market. To attract and retain the best talent, firms may try to differentiate themselves from others on the basis of compensation or benefits, flexibility of work schedules, opportunities for skill development and use, and so on. If one firm begins to offer signing bonuses of several thousand dollars to new MBAs, the competitors will be under considerable pressure to match that competitive move. If one firm gives middle managers more degrees of autonomy or more influence in key strategic decisions, other firms may find their best talent is soon hired away unless they match these working conditions.

Although similar dynamics among competitors hold in the labor market, however, the systematic use of competitive analysis for understanding competition for labor isn't widely used. A related activity that *is* quite common is *benchmarking*. Benchmarking differs from competitor analysis in several important ways, however. Competitor analysis focuses specifically on understanding one's direct competitors; as a consequence the process tends to be covert and involves little cooperation between the competing firms. In contrast, benchmarking usually is a collaborative effort among several firms that, ostensibly, aren't in direct competition. In addition, benchmarking studies usually focus on one or two specific aspects of human resource management, such as recruiting practices *or* use of flexible schedules *or* use of team-based job designs. Thus, benchmarking does not yield a complete, integrated picture of a particular competitor.

As the discussion above makes clear, firms within the same industry attend carefully to each others' actions, and they use the information they gather as input when making key decisions, such as the formulation of a competitive strategy.

COMPETITIVE STRATEGIES

Throughout this book, we often refer to a firm's competitive strategy using one of the following a simple label, such as "innovation," "total quality," or "low cost." These simple descriptors oversimplify the complexity of the competitive strategies of some firms, but they're nevertheless useful for drawing comparisons between firms.

Levels of Strategy

One type of complexity that our labels ignore is the level at which strategies are formulated. Three common levels for strategy formulation are the *business*, *corporate*, and *international* levels. In addition, in some companies, *functional* strategies may be developed.

Business Strategy. A business-level strategy is firm-specific. It describes how a firm competes against other direct rivals offering the same products and services. Several business-level strategies are described below. In addition to these, large corporations that operate several businesses formulate corporate level strategies.

Corporate Strategy. A corporate-level strategy describes how the corporation will select and manage a portfolio of businesses to ensure that the whole is greater than the sum of its parts.[9] The central issue addressed is usually how much diversification (low, high) and what type of diversification (related, unrelated) to pursue. Corporate-level strategies often have implications for how the human resources function is structured. This topic is addressed in Chapter 16.

"We strive to create an environment where employees can achieve company goals and personal goals simultaneously."

Paul Beddia
Vice President, Human Resources
Lincoln Electric

International Strategy. Historically, most new business start-ups have begun with a domestic focus, with an international expansion occurring as a way to continue growing in an untapped new market. But increasingly, entrepreneurs found their firms as global enterprises. Logitech—which many people know as the firm that manufactures a widely used computer mouse—is a well-known global start-up. Founded in 1982, by a Swiss and two Italians, this firm was headquartered in California and Switzerland and then spread to Ireland and Taiwan. Within seven years, it had captured 30 percent of the computer mouse market. A full description of all the strategic options pursued by firms competing in the international arena is beyond the scope of this text.[10] Instead, simply note that the key decisions affecting the management of human resources are those concerning when to adopt local practices and when to develop a single integrated approach that's uniformly followed in every country.

Functional Strategy. In organizations with strong, centralized functional departments, functional strategies may be developed to support the business strategy. For example, the heads of marketing, R&D, finance, and human resources may each develop strategies intended to support the business strategy. For example, if the intended business strategy is to grow through acquisitions, then the human resource functional strategy will focus on evaluating the work forces and corporate cultures of potential acquisition candidates and developing HR practices that facilitate integration of newly acquired firms. Alternatively, if the business strategy calls for internally-driven growth, the human resource functional strategy will focus on recruiting, hiring, and perhaps training a sufficient number of new employees to meet the expected demand for labor.

Internal Resources, Capabilities, and Core Competencies

Strategy development considers not only threats and opportunities within the industry environment, but also the strengths and weaknesses of the firm. The analysis of this combination of factors is often referred to as a *SWOT analysis*. The process through which firms develop their competitive strategies vary greatly. Although most large companies eventually adopt a fairly systematic approach to strategy formulation, the strategy of smaller firms may reflect the founder's intuitions and passions as much as his or her formal analysis. Here we consider currently popular prescriptions about what firms should consider when developing their competitive strategies, while recognizing that many firms may be somewhat unsystematic or they may use a systematic approach that considers different issues than the ones noted here.

Firms generate profits by pursuing strategies that give them a sustainable competitive advantage, as described in Chapter 1. That is, they produce, deliver, and/or sell products and services for which customers will pay a price that's above the firm's total costs. They do this by capitalizing on their own strengths and, whenever possible, exploiting the weaknesses of competitors. One approach to evaluating a firm's strengths and weaknesses is to consider the firm's available resources, capabilities, and core competencies.

Resources. Tangible assets such as equipment, real estate holding, and access to financial capital are a firm's most visible resources. In addition, a firm may have a variety of intangible assets, including a reputation for excellence, a widely recognized brand name, patents, trademarks, and other types of intellectual capital. Resources that are unique to the firm can serve as a basis for creating a sustained competitive advantage.

Capabilities.   When managed well, the integration of all resources creates a capability that enables the organization to accomplish a task or achieve an outcome. Capabilities that are rare, valuable, difficult to imitate, and for which there are no substitutes serve as the foundation for a sustainable competitive advantage. Capabilities are often associated with specific functional areas. For example, Motorola's effective and extensive training programs represent its exceptional capability in the area of human resources. Sony's miniaturization of electronic components represents its capability in the areas of R&D and manufacturing.[11] As described in the feature, Managing Globalization: Virtual Teams are a Competitive Advantage, Verifone's electronic and technical networking capabilities are essential to its ability to operate as a global organization.[12]

> *"I've tried to figure out why Mickey appealed to the whole world. Everybody's tried to figure it out. So far as I know, nobody has."*
>
> **Walt Disney**
> **Creator of Mickey Mouse**
> **Founder of Walt Disney Co.**

MANAGING GLOBALIZATION
Virtual Teams Are a Competitive Advantage

For some people just mentioning global organizations conjures up images of homesick expatriates and travel-weary managers who spend as much time in airports as at home. Although shuffling people around the world is one way to staff a global company, it's not the only way. In fact, it isn't even a very good way if speed and efficiency are top priorities. William Pape, cofounder of Verifone, has a different idea. He's built his company into a global competitor by structuring people into virtual teams.

At Verifone, some virtual teams may last for only a day or two—just long enough to solve a pressing problem. Other teams are more permanent. The interesting thing about Verifone teams is employees create them on an as-needed basis. Any employee can establish a virtual team as long as he or she follows a few simple rules. First, there must be a clear and specific purpose for the team. This is the foundation that guides the design of the team and its work: who should be on it, what information will they need, and how will they evaluate their effectiveness. Second, the teams must be kept small—usually only three to five people. The small size is important because it keeps communication and coordination problems in check. Third, the team should be designed to leverage differences in time zones. This means that the ideal design is one where everyone on the team is in a different time zone. The logic here is that these teams don't spend a lot of time chatting to each during conference calls. Instead, each member has certain tasks to do, and often there is some sequencing of tasks that makes the most sense. Another rule is that the duration of the team must be stated. This makes individual planning much easier and helps ensure that people don't join a team that they can't stay with until the task is accomplished. The final rule is that employees must match the technology they use to the type of task they're working on. They understand that e-mail is a good way to send information to each other, but if much discussion is needed, then telecommunication technology should be used, or, if it's not available, a "live" team might be the best solution.

Here's an example of how a Verifone global team works: When an employee was trying to sell the company's services in Greece, the prospective customer expressed some doubt in the ability of the company to deliver the service as described. He needed some convincing. Immediately after leaving his meeting with the prospective customer, the employee found the nearest telephone, hooked up his laptop, and sent an e-mail SOS to other employees around the world. The purpose of his message was to recruit a team to help him make the sale. He wanted testimonials from other customers who could vouch for Verifone's performance, and he was open to any other advice about how to make the sale. It was near the end of the Greek day, so he was looking for people who could work on this while he slept. A San Francisco employee took up the challenge and organized a conference call with marketing employees in Atlanta and Hong Kong. These three people agreed on a plan for what type of data they should collect from customers. By the end of their day, the two Americans had drafted a sales presentation. They forwarded it to Hong Kong so the Asian data could be added. When the Greek rep was ready to get started the next day, he retrieved the presentation from his e-mail account and used his laptop to present it to the prospective client, who was so impressed by what had been accomplished while he was asleep that he placed an order with Verifone.

To learn more about Verifone, visit the company's home page at **www.verifone.com**

■□ *fast fact*

McDonald's founder Ray Kroc specified that its hamburgers weigh exactly 1.6 ounces, measure exactly 3.875 inches, and be served with exactly .25 ounces of onions.

Core Competencies. The term core competency is often use interchangeably with the term capability. Originally, however, capabilities were conceptualized as being relevant to a single business unit or division of a firm, while core competencies were viewed as capabilities that support multiple businesses.[13] Like a capability, a core competency reflects a firm's unique knowledge about how to accomplish something and its effectiveness in using this knowledge to satisfy customers.[14] Some of the core competencies needed for success in the financial services industry include relationship management, foreign exchange, transaction processing, and management. Canon uses its core competencies in precision mechanics, fiber optics, microelectronics, and electronic imaging to produce cameras, printers, copiers, and laser imagers. Successful firms understand what their own core competencies are, which competencies are essential for success in their industry given a particular strategy, and also how to leverage their existing competencies to move into new areas of business. They also understand that some of their core competencies will become obsolete with time, and new ones will be needed to replace them.[15] A core competency is central to the strategic intent of the firm as well as its success. Is Motorola's training system central to its strategy? The firm's executives would undoubtedly say yes; otherwise they should probably outsource this activity, like most of their competitors do.

Primary Business-Level Strategies

Firms choose a competitive strategy based on its analysis of the external environment; competitors; and internal resources, capabilities, and core competencies. Organizations continually develop strategies to beat their competitors. Firms describe their competitive strategies using a variety of terms, but basically competitive strategies reflect two decisions. Who are the customers and what is the *relative* importance attached to each of the following?

- Innovation
- Total Quality
- Low Cost[16]

A firm can't compete by focusing on any one of these areas and completely ignoring the others. There are few products or services that customers will buy based solely on price, for example. Some minimal level of quality must also be maintained. Conversely, there are few products or services for which quality or innovation is so important that customers will pay any price to have it.

Associated with each of these business strategies are several unique challenges for managing human resources. That is, for competitive strategies to be successfully implemented, employees have to behave in certain ways. The needed behaviors flow from the business imperatives of the strategy as well as features of organization design that tend to be associated with the strategy. In this section, the business imperatives for each strategy are described.

Innovation.   Innovation is a strategy that involves differentiating the firm's products and services from those of competitors by having something new that competitors cannot offer, usually because the new product or service is protected by trademarks, copyrights, or patents. Innovations often are the impetus for the creation of new organizations and even new industries. Alexander Graham Bell's invention of the telephone predated a similar prototype developed by Thomas Edison by only a short time, yet because Bell established patent rights this innovation was eventually worth billions of dollars to the Bell telephone system of companies.[17]

When a desirable new product or service is created, its uniqueness and limited availability mean that a company can charge a premium price and a sufficiently large number of customers will be willing to pay it. However, this opportunity arises only if the firm also has the capabilities needed to develop the new invention into a marketable product and then bring that product into the marketplace. Celtrix, a California biotech firm, holds patents on a cell-regulating protein that may prove useful in helping cells heal. However, Genentech was able to more quickly develop the process for producing this protein. This situation effectively forced Celtrix to enter into a joint venture with Genentech in order to realize at least a portion of the future profits from their invention.

Firms pursuing innovation generally serve a narrow customer base—the company seeks to satisfy those customers who are most likely to appreciate and purchase the new product or service. From its founding in 1938 until the mid-1960s, Hewlett Packard focused on creating new electronic measuring instruments that "made important technical contributions to the advancement of science, industry, and human welfare."[18] Their original products were designed for and appealed to sophisticated engineers. They got into the computer business because computer technology offered a means for improving the accuracy of measurement instruments. As recently as the early 1980s most business users of computers were not yet familiar with the HP name because the company's products were designed only for businesses that required very sophisticated systems. At that time, the printers it sold were about the size of a refrigerator and cost $100,000. Home consumers first became familiar with the Hewlett Packard name in the mid-1980s after it introduced its first LaserJet printer.

Continuing to innovate over long periods of time turns out to be rather difficult. The success of early innovations usually results in the organization growing in size. As the organization becomes larger, they develop procedures and impose rules in an attempt to minimize the chaos that accompa-

"Fairchild was steeped in an east coast, old-fashioned, hierarchical structure; I never wanted to be a part of a company like that."

Robert Noyce, commenting on his ex-employer Co-Founder Intel

nies rapid growth. Ways of doing things that succeeded in the past become institutionalized as "the best way" of doing things, creating rigidities that can become unproductive.[19] Usually, bureaucracy and standardization are at odds with innovation and change. Employees come to take the working environment for granted, and individual efforts to foster change may be met with resistance. Solutions to such problems can be found in both the organization's design and human resource management practices that support a creative culture.

Total Quality. Another basic way to differentiate one's products and services from those of others is to offer outstanding quality. Organizations are continually confronted and challenged with the need to deliver quality goods and services. In the international arena, the standards of quality keep going up: what was acceptable quality yesterday is unacceptable today. Thus, many organizations continue to pursue quality improvement with a vengeance. Delivering total quality depends on all parts of the organization working together. Increasingly, these efforts are guided by feedback from customers, because quality is in the eyes (and ears and hands and taste buds!) of customers.[20] The specific aspects of products and service that go into customers' judgments of quality are listed in Exhibit 4.2.[21]

The beneficial outcomes of pursuing total quality strategies are greater than mere survival, as shown in Exhibit 4.3. The desirability of these and related outcomes provide strong incentives for undergoing the necessary organizational design and cultural changes and dealing with the implications for managing human resources.[22]

■□ *fast fact*

During the 1970s, quality problems at Harley-Davidson were so bad that they set up "hospitals" where bikes that came off the line incomplete were patched up before being shipped to dealers.

Exhibit 4.2
What Does Quality Mean to Customers?

Products
- *Performance:* A product's primary tangible operating characteristic. Examples are a car's ability to accelerate and a television set's picture clarity.
- *Features:* Supplements to a product's basic functioning characteristics, such as one-touch power windows on a car.
- *Reliability:* A probability of not malfunctioning in a specified time period.
- *Conformance:* The degree to which a product's design and operating characteristics meet established standards.
- *Durability:* A measure of product life.
- *Serviceability:* The speed and ease of repairing a product.
- *Aesthetics:* How a product looks, feels, tastes, and smells.
- *Perceived Quality:* Quality as defined and judged by the individual customer.

Services
- *The Tangibles:* The appearance of the physical setting for the service, including the location, people, communication materials, and equipment.
- *Reliability:* The ability to perform the promised service dependably and accurately.
- *Responsiveness:* The extent to which an employee helps customers and provides prompt service.
- *Assurance:* An employee's knowledge, courtesy, and ability to convey trust and confidence.
- *Empathy:* Caring, individualized attention.
- *Insight:* The ability to anticipate the customer's needs.
- *Problem-solving:* The ability to diagnose problems with the customer and develop solutions the customer finds appropriate.

Exhibit 4.3
The Deming Chain Reaction

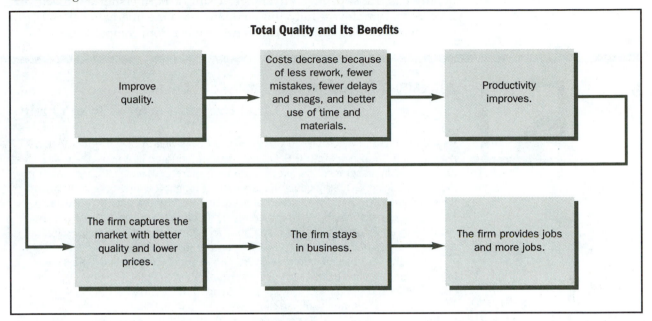

The Ford Motor Company, which has become a leader in quality improvement programs, pursues total quality by following the principles of W. Edwards Deming. The 14 principles that guide Ford's quality strategy efforts, as well as those of many other companies that have been influenced by Deming's philosophy and methods, are shown in Exhibit 4.4.[23]

Exhibit 4.4
Achieving Total Quality

W. E. Deming's 14 Principles

1. Create consistency and continuity of purpose.
2. Refuse to allow a commonly accepted level of delay for mistakes, defective material, or defective work.
3. Eliminate the need for and dependence upon mass inspection.
4. Reduce the number of suppliers. Buy on statistical evidence, not price.
5. Search continually for problems in the system and seek ways to improve it.
6. Institute modern methods of training, using statistics.
7. Focus supervision on helping people to do a better job, and provide the tools and techniques for people to have pride of work.
8. Eliminate fear. Encourage two-way communication.
9. Break down barriers between departments. Encourage problem solving through teamwork.
10. Eliminate the use of numerical goals, slogans, and posters for the workforce.
11. Use statistical methods for continuing the improvement of quality and productivity, and eliminate all standards prescribing numerical quotas.
12. Remove barriers to pride of work.
13. Institute a vigorous program of education and training to keep people abreast of new developments in methods, materials, and technologies.
14. Clearly define management's permanent commitment to quality and productivity.

The Case Swayne Co., described in the feature, Managing Strategically: Case Swayne Achieves Total Quality, took a different approach to gaining a quality-based competitive advantage. Using a partnership approach that involved all employees fully, this company used the international ISO certification process as a means to differentiate itself from competitors.[24]

MANAGING STRATEGICALLY

Case Swayne Achieves Total Quality

Based in Corona, California, the Case Swayne Co. is one of only five food companies in the U.S. to achieve ISO 9001 registration. Initiated by Kathy Ware, vice president of quality assurance, the process took 18 months. Ware first suggested the idea of obtaining ISO certification because she thought it would be a good way to assure customers that the company offered only the highest quality products. Furthermore, because so few of the company's competitors had ISO certification, Ware believed it could give them a competitive advantage. It would help differentiate the company as being "the best," not just "equal to" the others.

From the very beginning of the effort, HR vice president Yoland Guibert was involved. Her responsibilities included communicating to employees the value of obtaining certification and facilitating the change process. Guibert also asked employees to nominate candidates to be members of the team that would guide the certification process. The 36 nominees put together resumes and were screened by Ware and President Keith Swayne using an interview process. "We selected 10 very energetic, motivated people from different departments, including sales, operations, and quality assurance," Guibert explained. Then a consultant with special expertise in ISO registration was hired to assist the team.

An example of one of the requirements for certification is that the company must have complete documentation of all systems and procedures, including detailed descriptions of every job function and expectation, as well as training procedures. The committee prepared all of these materials, but once they were created, every employee still had to show they understood and could use them. During the certification visit, the ISO team could be expected to quiz any employee about any aspect of the procedures, from the janitor on up. This meant every employee had to learn a great deal of material. To make sure everyone was prepared, employees helped each other learn the material. Some employees held question-and-answer sessions for their colleagues. Others prepared tutoring aids during their off-hours as a way to make the ISO concepts easier to grasp. Non-English speaking employees enlisted the help of their children, who served as translators for them. Although the process of preparing and learning all of these materials was extremely time consuming, employees ultimately benefited from the improved clarity of expectations that they developed. The new skills they acquired also allowed them to be more autonomous, so they could rely less on instructions from their supervisors.

Was the achievement of ISO registration worth the effort? Ware thinks so: "One of the most impressive things we've seen is that it affects our customers and potential clients. Our customers now have a high level of confidence in our system because we've achieved ISO registration." In addition, communication between departments within the company and between management and employees has improved greatly, creating a more positive atmosphere for everyone. Guibert agrees. She feels that the team spirit created through this process "has been an enriching experience for our employees—they no longer feel they're coming in just to do their jobs. They feel they're part of a bigger process."

To learn more about the Case Swayne Co., visit its homepage at:
www.case-swayne.com

Low Cost.   Also called cost leadership, this strategy involves offering no-frills, standardized products and services with acceptable features at the lowest price. Wal-Mart is well-known for its success using this strategy. The most common approach to pursing a low-cost strategy is to generate a high volume of sales to make up for the low margin associated with each sale, so companies usually seek the broadest possible customer base. Appealing to the typical or average customer is the objective. Dollar General has put a new twist on this traditional approach, however, using a strategy that has been referred to by some as an "extreme-value" strategy. Prices at Dollar General are so low that they make Wal-Mart look expensive. To be successful at this strategy, Dollar General targets a more narrow customer base. It seeks to serve lower-income shoppers who are shopping simply to obtain basic products (e.g., toothpaste, detergents), who prefer to do so in a smaller store that's conveniently located in their neighborhood, but who won't pay extra for the convenience of the location.[25]

The central business objective for firms pursuing a low-cost strategy is reducing their costs. Investments in more efficient production systems, tight cost monitoring and controls, low investment in R&D, and a minimal sales force are characteristic of this strategy. Highly efficient systems that link the firm to its suppliers and distributors and "trouble-free" products and services that keep recalls and customer returns low also are important for success. In the retail business, links to suppliers who will sell at rock-bottom prices also are especially important.[26]

The importance of cost considerations generally increases as an industry matures. During the growth phase, customers may be more concerned with continuous improvements in quality and/or new innovations. But as gains in quality and newness begin to level off and become less perceptible, price considerations are given more weight. As pressure to reduce prices intensifies, aggressive cost cutting efforts may be pursued. Three common cost-cutting tactics are reengineering, offshore production, and mergers and acquisitions. Offshore production and the increasing pace of mergers and acquisitions were described in Chapter 1. Reengineering is fundamentally a change in the organization's design, and is discussed in the next section of this chapter.

Other Business Strategies.   The strategies described above represent three primary competitive strategies used by firms to create a sustainable competitive advantage. As economist Michael Porter has pointed out, however, firms can seek to differentiate their products and services in many other ways. For example, they can seek to create a superior or unique image for their products and services. Firms pursuing this strategy include Nike, Ralph Lauren, Rolex, and McKinsey & Co. Maytag has sought to differentiate its products as being the most reliable. Arizona Iced Tea uses its unique packaging to differentiate its products, and so on. Many of these alternative differentiation strategies succeed or fail primarily on the basis of the firm's marketing efforts, or salesmanship. Issues of cost, quality, and innovation may be very important as secondary business imperatives, however. Nike cannot sell new products based on image alone; customers also expect continuous innovation in its products. McKinsey & Co. may be able to charge a premium price because of its image as a superior consulting firm, but this continues to be possible only if they maintain a reasonably high level of quality in the services they offer.

Changes in Business Strategy.   At any point in time, effective organizations have a clearly defined business strategy, but strategies may change in

"Sure it's cheaper here. They don't call it a dollar store for nothing."

**John Brown
Customer
Dollar General Store No. 2392**

■□ *fast fact*

Wal-Mart's founder, Sam Walton, flew first class only once in his life—on a trip to Africa.

response to changes in the external environment. For example, when the Hunter Fan Company started up in 1886, it had an innovative new product—large ceiling fans that could be used to cool factories. Continuous improvement in the design of the product allowed the company to maintain a large market share. But changes in technology—the invention of air conditioning—cut sharply into their business and the firm went into decline. When energy prices rose rapidly in the 1970s, however, Hunter Fan was able to use its capabilities to exploit a new market for high-quality ceiling fans for home use. Thus, while strategic change may be stimulated by the environment, the direction of change should be strongly influenced by a firm's existing capabilities and competencies.[27]

ORGANIZATION DESIGN

Defining a clear business strategy to guide the organization and give all employees a clear sense of direction is an important activity for any organization, but it's just the beginning. To support and implement the strategy effectively, the entire organization must be aligned with the strategy.[28]

Organizational Structure

Organizational structure describes the allocation of tasks and responsibilities among individuals and departments; a structure designates the nature and means of formal reporting relationships as well as the groupings of individuals within the organization.[29] The structural forms generally recognized for domestic firms include functional departmentalization, divisionalization based on products or geographic location, and matrix organization. As an organization grows and ages, it may progress through all of these forms.[30] In addition, as described in Chapter 2, many organizations are linking up with other firms to create various network forms. Different structures arise in response to a variety of internal and external forces, including technological demands, organizational growth, environmental turbulence, and business strategy. Furthermore, each structural form poses different challenges for managing human resources.[31] The feature, Managing Change: Kinko's Grows into a Major Corporation, illustrates a typical evolutionary path for successful young companies.[32]

Departmentalization. Departmentalization involves subdividing work into tasks and assigning them to *specialized* groups within the organization (e.g., sales, manufacturing, accounting, etc.). Businesses with a single product or service often have a departmental structure. Decision making is centralized at the top of the organization, and a clear vertical chain of authority is used to communicate decisions downward.[33] Sales and operations departments often wield the most power. Careers in these types of companies generally focus narrowly on developing single-function, "silo-like" expertise.

Ben & Jerry's Homemade, the ice cream company, was in business for ten years before its structure first broke into two departments. By that time, the company had grown so large that professional managers had to be brought in to oversee some of the tasks. A director of retail operations oversaw the franchisees; a controller supervised the accounting and finance functions, and a director of manufacturing oversaw plant operation. In recalling the change from one big family to a departmentalized organization, the former CEO remarked, "The up side was that more work was getting done. The

MANAGING CHANGE

Kinko's Grows into a Major Corporation

Ever wonder where the name Kinko's came from? The nickname was given to Paul Orfalea, inspired by his red hair. In 1970, Orfalea founded Kinko's, the copy shop company, by setting up one copier in a converted taco stand. Until 1996, Kinko's culture was as casual as its name suggests. Decisions were made by consensus, which took a lot of time but also seemed to build a committed community of partners. But much has changed during the past couple of years.

To celebrate Kinko's twenty-sixth birthday, CEO Orfalea decided to sell a 30 percent stake of the privately held company to Clayton, Dublier & Rice (CDR), a New York investment firm. Before CDR came on the scene, Kinko's was owned by 128 partners, who operated a total of 851 stores. There was little attempt to impose a formal structure onto all of the dispersed parts of the organization. Now, however, partners own an estimated 35 percent of the company, with Orfalea holding the remaining 35 percent of shares. Orfalea compared that day to his wedding day: "It's scary and happy at the same time," he said.

Kinko's was phenomenally successful under Orfalea's leadership. A champion of innovation, he gave annual awards (e.g., all-expense-paid vacations to Disneyland) to the employees of the copy shop that came up with the most innovative idea during the year. While the employees enjoyed their reward, Orfalea and his board would stay behind to attend to customers. Among the new services developed was digitized document services, allowing customers to send electronic text and image documents over the Internet for instant printing anywhere in the world. Charlotte McManus and C. Rollin Buchanan, owners of a Kinko's store in Irvine, California, started and developed this service, which has grown to become a division of Kinko's. In Atlanta, Kinko's stores operate a center for learning and training, which can be accessed via the Internet.

Some stores grew rapidly as a result of the innovations they made, but others lagged behind. In 1996, nearly a third of the stores were unprofitable. To cut costs, CDR consolidated partners' debts, centralized purchasing, and is financing overseas expansion. Daily management of the firm is in the hands of professional outside managers. This leaves Orfalea with more time to think up new ideas, but it removes much of the autonomy previously enjoyed by the managers of each shop. Kinko's partners know that the change from entrepreneurial autonomy to corporate oversight won't always be easy. "There will be turmoil in the transition," observed Orfalea's cousin, who also was one of the first Kinko's partners. "Once in a while you have a twinge, but the other side is we can gain a lot."

To learn more about Kinko's, visit the its corporate home page at
www.kinkos.com

its Atlanta learning center home page at
www.tlckinkos.com

and its document solution division home page at
www.edp.com

down side was that as people became more task-oriented, they began to lose their connection to the whole of the organization."[34]

Departmentalization can easily engender feelings of commitment and loyalty to functional groups (accounting, marketing, R&D), and turn organizational decision-making into a competitive sport in which departments battle over turf and resources.[35] Customers are almost always the losers of these battles. According to Richard C. Palermo, a vice president for quality and transition at Xerox, "If a problem has been bothering your company and your customers for years, that problem is the result of a cross-functional dispute." He calls this Palermo's law. And Palermo's corollary is "People who work in different functions hate each other."[36] Nevertheless, a departmental structure can work well for organizations that strive to maximize efficiency and are in a fairly stable environment that does not require rapid organizational change and flexibility.

Divisionalization. Multiproduct or multiservice firms often take a divisionalized structure, with each division serving a different customer need (product-based divisions) or a different customer base (geographic divisions). Divisionalized firms tend to be more externally focused than are firms structured around functional departments, and they emphasize bottom-line results over smooth internal functioning. They tend to serve broad markets and in general must respond to an environment characterized by considerable complexity.[37] In the 1970s, GE reorganized into 43 divisions, with each division being essentially a complete business that could clearly identify its potential customers and competitors, could design strategies to address them, and could be held accountable for achieving business objectives. These divisions were called Strategic Business Units (SBUs). Since the 1980s, this structure has been adopted by several other large corporations and the term SBU is now widely used to refer to highly autonomous divisions.[38] Different SBUs may adopt different business strategies and coordination between divisions may be modest, at best.

For many years, Colgate-Palmolive was organized around regional divisions: North America, Latin America, Eastern Europe, and so on. In 1997, however, the firm reorganized as part of its new strategic plan. In the new structure, the type of business strategies being pursued are the basis for organizing. These strategies differ according to whether the market for a product is relatively mature or newly emerging.[39] For example, issues of establishing brand-name recognition would be more important in emerging markets, while reducing costs may be more important in mature markets. In addition, goals related to market share and sales growth would differ among divisions despite the fact that they're selling the same product.

Until the mid-1960s, Unilever was organized according to location, also. Because the business was driven by the raw foods that were the inputs to its products, it made sense to allow each country to operate autonomously. In 1966, however, the company drastically reorganized around products. Product groups were responsible for profits and country managers were essentially demoted into advisory roles. Although such a change may sound simple, it took the firm several years to complete the reorganization.

As is true in departmentalized organizations, too little coordination among the major groups—in this case, divisions—can create problems for the total corporation. Or, as Unilever discovered, lack of coordination may simply not be the most efficient use of resources and capabilities. For Unilever, brand names were an important intangible resource, and their food processing and consumer research skills were important capabilities. To offset this problem, many large companies began to adopt matrix structures during the 1970s and 1980s. Unilever, however, chose to reorganize again around product divisions. In their new structure, the divisions represent broad groups of products: edible fats, ice cream, beverages, meals, and professional markets (e.g., caterers and bakeries).[40]

Matrix. The matrix form of organization began to emerge in the 1960s and 1970s as corporations faced markets that demanded both efficiency (strength of the functional form) and responsiveness (the strength of the divisional form).[41] In a matrix structure, employees report to more than one boss, with each boss responsible for a different aspect of the organization.[42] For example, a clothes designer artist might report to the vice president of marketing and the vice president of outerwear. These vice presidents, in turn, might report to a general manager for manufacturing and a general manager for the North American region. In this type of structure, managers enjoy a great deal of autonomy, but they also must coordinate with each other in assigning work to their subordinates, evaluating employee performance, and so on.

The vast majority of medium and large companies in the U.S. are structured around functional departments, divisions, or some hybrid of these. One common modification, for example, is the inclusion of skunkworks within an organization that otherwise takes one of the three basic forms just described. Structural arrangements are imposed as a way to create order and minimize chaos. Orderliness has its virtues, but also its drawbacks. When innovation is the objective, stable structures can hinder more than help, so innovative organizations intentionally allow some disruption in their otherwise orderly forms by supporting "skunkwork" operations.

A skunkwork unit is a new venture team that has considerable leeway in their activities. Often they even move to another location that's out-of-sight and out-of-mind, where they can more easily operate outside the normal model. Within these islands of entrepreneurial activity, formal rules and procedures are ignored in favor of experimentation and innovation. Top management may tolerate violations of reporting policies and review procedures, as long as the team stays focused on helping the company bring new products and services to market ahead of competitors.[43] Of course, a large organization isn't likely to support a particular skunkworks operation forever. If the effort succeeds, operations will be formalized, and the team might become the nucleus around which a new department is formed. If the effort fails to meet expectations, it might be closed down. A third possibility is to spin off the skunkworks and allow it to operate as a separate division or subsidiary. This approach allows the parent organization to obtain a return on its investment while keeping the entrepreneurial spirit alive.

As noted in Chapter 2, innovation also is often the strategic reason that's driving many organizations into totally new structures that link parts of one firm with parts of other firms, forming complex networks. This new structural form has evolved as yet another attempt to create a form that meets the needs of a changing environment in another firm.

As companies move into the international arena, they face the same problems of how to organize tasks and how to integrate and coordinate the parts of the organization, but structural options for achieving these objectives differ, as described next.

Structures That Cross Country Borders. Many terms can be used to describe global organizational structures, including international, multinational, transnational, and multidomestic.[44]

Briefly, a *multidomestic* structure describes a firm that operates mostly as a domestic company but has foreign operations. As operations spread to other countries, each country operates fairly autonomously. Eventually, however, multidomestic companies usually seek to have more coordination among the parts. At this point, they may adopt a *multinational* structure. With this structure, activities are reorganized around products or lines of business. As Unilever discovered, just as lack of coordination across countries can be problematic, too little coordination among product divisions has its drawbacks. Unilever concluded that having too many product-based divisions resulted in an inefficient use of resources and capabilities. For Unilever, brand names were an important intangible resource, and the food processing and consumer-research skills they had developed in some areas of the company were important capabilities that were not being fully utilized throughout the entire organization. To offset this problem, Unilever reorganized again—this time around three broad product divisions. They have since reorganized yet again in an effort to find a structure that best leverages their capabilities yet permits decision making to be sufficiently decentralized to allow for quick reactions to changes in the marketplace.[45] Like other large, complex firms operating around the world (e.g., 3M),[46] Unilever has gradually evolved toward a network-form of organization, referred to as a *transnational* structure. In the network are several core nodes of activity, and these are all connected together through a variety of linking mechanisms.

These are just a few of the basic forms of organizational structures found in global firms. There are many other possible arrangements and permutations.[47] Each structure has unique implications for how people are managed, but the fundamental challenge that's common across these alternatives is how to coordinate the dispersed units while also adapting to the societal requirements of host societies. Many companies find that global teams are an essential tool for coordinating their dispersed operations.

"We had to resolve conflicts with individuals who felt their position was to defend their home country or their particular function. On a global team, you are a voice, an expert on that topic."

**Barry Simmonds
Senior VP, Personnel
Corange London Limited**

Global Teams.   For many companies, making the transition from a multidomestic to a multinational structure, or from a multinational to a transnational structure, proves to be a significant challenge. Regardless of how the company is structured—e.g., by country or by products—the autonomous units become focused on succeeding in the domain over which they have authority. Coordinating with other units for the good of the company as a whole seems to fall to the bottom of the priority list. To deal with this problem, many companies are using teams as cross-cutting structures for linking together autonomous units. According to a recent study by the Conference Board, this practice is especially prevalent in the manufacturing sector and in companies based outside the U.S. For example, General Motors has used global teams in its R&D activities to examine the feasibility of producing "global" cars. Coopers & Lybrand has been using global teams to serve its clients since the 1960s, but they have seen rapid growth in the need for such teams in the last decade as the clients served by the firm have globalized. The feature, Managing Global Teams: State-of-the-Art Practices, describes some of the major findings from the Conference Board's research on global teaming.[48]

Organizational Processes

Whereas structure describes the way tasks and responsibilities are distributed across the organization, process describes methods used to get tasks accomplished. Two types of process interventions that have received a great deal of attention within the U.S. in recent years are Total Quality Management (TQM) and process reengineering.[49]

MANAGING GLOBAL TEAMS

State-of-the-Art Practices

In their study of 90 companies, approximately one-third were located outside the U.S. The Conference Board set out to determine just how prevalent global teams really are, and the issues that such teams raise for managing human resources. A few of the major findings from the study are summarized below.

Why Use Teams?

Companies use global teams to overcome traditional organizational barriers between countries or business units. Most companies that have at least one global team reported having many global teams. When evaluating what outcomes from global companies they most value, the respondents identified six outcomes as very important:

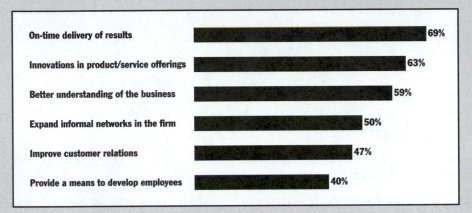

On-time delivery of results	69%
Innovations in product/service offerings	63%
Better understanding of the business	59%
Expand informal networks in the firm	50%
Improve customer relations	47%
Provide a means to develop employees	40%

What Types of Global Teams Are Most Common?

Team composition varies greatly, but the following summary of characteristics shows the general trends:

Type of Team Composition	% Companies Who Reported Having this Type of Team
Crosses borders, but all members from the same function	82%
Crosses borders and functions	76
Formal and ongoing	74
Formal and short term	74
Informal networks	62
Mixes across job levels	57
Senior and middle managers only	54
Professional and technical employees only	40
Includes outsiders (e.g., suppliers, customers)	31

Barriers to Effectiveness

Given all the global teaming that's going on—and that will be going on in the future—it's important to understand what conditions in an organization create barriers to team effectiveness and what conditions can help the team's functioning. The study identified many barriers to effectiveness. Not surprisingly, the most frequently cited barrier was *geographical distances and time zones*. Perhaps more interesting is the fact that less than half the companies reported that differences *in culture and language skills* were problems. In fact, the barrier of *organization structure* was cited as frequently as cultural barriers (about 40 percent). One out of three companies reported that inappropriate team assignments and the need for face-to-face meetings created problems for global teams. Issues that could have been barriers but apparently were seldom a problem included competing priorities, technology, and compensation issues.

Making Global Teams More Effective

What can organizations do to help global teams be more effective? Four things stood out: Top management needs to be actively involved, top management should set the example for how to work as part of a global team, team members should have experience in international assignments, and team members should have experience working in teams. Companies such as Otis Elevator and Becton Dickinson understand how important it is to staff global teams with people who have appropriate international experience and who have demonstrated that they work well in teams, so their HR groups are heavily involved in the selection of team members.

A Growing Trend?

When asked whether they expected the use of global teams to grow in the next few years, fully 96 percent said yes.

"What you're after is congruence among strategic direction, organizational design, staff capabilities, and the processes you use to ensure people are working together to meet the company's goal."

Paul Allaire
Former Chairman and CEO
Xerox

Total Quality Management. Since its inception in 1987, the Malcolm Baldrige National Quality Award has been used by hundreds of U.S. companies to redesign the processes used to produce and deliver high quality goods and services. This award is given to companies that excel in several domains of business activity. These are shown in Exhibit 4.5. Notice that five out of the seven major categories of criteria assess managerial processes that are believed to result in excellent quality. Only two focus directly on the results of these processes.

Somewhat similar to the Baldrige Award criteria for quality are the standards of the International Organization for Standardization (ISO) in Geneva, Switzerland. Any company that meets the set of specified standards receives ISO certification—it isn't a contest. Nevertheless, the standards are very difficult to meet. The ISO standards, which are identified by numbers (e.g., ISO 9000), have been adopted by many companies within the European Union. Most of the areas addressed in the 150 ISO 9000 criteria are covered in category 6.0 of the Baldrige criteria, Process Management.[50]

Although not directly specified as a criterion for the Baldrige Award, many firms pursuing total quality rely heavily on empowerment to accomplish important tasks. Empowered employees have the autonomy and responsibility to make key decisions about how work gets done, without seeking approval from their supervisors. Miller Brewery has a fully empowered workforce at its plant in Trenton, Ohio, which gives the company

Exhibit 4.5
Scoring the Baldrige Award

1999 Examination Criteria and Point Allocations

General Category and Specific Items	Item Point Values	Total Category Points
1 Leadership		**125**
1.1 Organizational Leadership	85	
1.2 Public Responsibility and Citizenship	40	
2 Strategic Planning		**85**
2.1 Strategy Development	40	
2.2 Strategy Deployment	45	
3 Customer and Market Focus		**85**
3.1 Customer and Market Knowledge	40	
3.2 Customer Satisfaction and Relationships	45	
4 Information and Analysis		**85**
4.1 Measurement of Organizational Performance	40	
4.2 Analysis of Organizational Performance	45	
5 Human Resource Focus		**85**
5.1 Work Systems	35	
5.2 Employee Education, Training, and Development	25	
5.3 Employee Well-Being and Satisfaction	25	
6 Process Management		**85**
6.1 Product and Service Processes	55	
6.2 Support Processes	15	
6.3 Supplier and Partnering Processes	15	
7 Business Results		**450**
7.1 Customer Focused Results	115	
7.2 Financial and Market Results	115	
7.3 Human Resource Results	80	
7.4 Supplier and Partner Results	25	
7.5 Organizational Effectiveness Results	115	
Total		**1000**

To learn more about the Baldrige Award, visit
www.quality.nist.gov/

several sources of competitive advantage: *no* supervision (and its associated costs), reduced need for quality management (the employees do it), minimal maintenance staffing, and fewer administrative workers. At first, the employees were hesitant to use their new power, but when they realized that management was serious about giving them more autonomy, they began to come up with great ideas. After making the mistake of over-pasteurizing 3,000 cases of beer, one employee developed a new pasteurization system that prevents such mishaps. The system is now used on every line in the plant.[51]

Empowering workers appears to be critical to getting employees more committed and involved. In fact, employers that mesh total quality programs with empowerment efforts are twice as likely to report significant improvements in their products and services, according to a survey of 126

"We realized that a capability comes only by combining a competence with a reliable process."

Jan Leschy
CEO
SmithKline Beecham

companies by the Wyatt Company and the Manufacturers Alliance for Productivity and Innovation. At these companies, "[e]mpowerment measures included increased use of functional or cross-functional work teams, decentralization of decision-making, and redesign of jobs, functions, and work groups."[52] Empowerment has been found to be one of the core competencies needed to use TQM to produce a competitive advantage. Compared to many other aspects of TQM procedures, empowerment is much more difficult to imitate; thus, organizations that learn to use empowerment effectively cannot be easily copied by competitors.[53] A similar argument has been made about the role of collaboration, which generally goes hand-in-hand with empowerment.[54]

For the A. W. Chesterton Co. in Shoneham, Massachusetts, empowered employees may be what it will take to ensure the firm survives. The company produces mechanical seals, pumps, and other flow-control products. Recently, its competitors have been consolidated through mergers and acquisitions, and now the firm is facing pressure to do likewise. But the CEO of this privately held firm isn't interested in putting the company up for sale. Instead, he's decided to share with employees confidential financial information and seek their help in developing new ways to improve efficiency and reduce costs. The approach has yielded impressive results. By redesigning one key part so that it required less metal to produce, the company was able to begin saving $200,000 a year. Employees also helped design a program that encourages safety by sharing with employees 25 percent of any savings achieved from reduced accidents. In 1997, the savings amounted to $500,000.[55]

Process Reengineering.   Reengineering also focuses on creating new ways to get work done. It most often involves the redesign of processes related to logistics, manufacturing, and distribution. The goal is to design the most effective process for delivering a service or product.[56] Effective processes are those that cost the least while at the same time producing goods and providing services of excellent quality rapidly.

Successful reengineering requires managers and employees to examine the breadth of activities to be redesigned and the depth of the changes needed. In terms of *breadth*, although reengineering a single activity or function may be important to an organization, including more activities is likely to extend its benefits throughout the organization.[57] Often, reengineering a process is interrelated with other key activities. Recall that many organizations are structured by function and that employees' ideas about change typically are based on its effect on their departments. However, reengineering requires employees to think across functions. Reengineering can reduce the amount of "hand-offs" between departments by increasing the amount of resources that are brought together simultaneously to meet customers' needs. Benefits may include faster delivery time, more accurate billing, and fewer defective products that must be returned.

The *depth* of a reengineering effort is measured by the number of roles, responsibilities, rewards, incentives, and information technologies to be changed. Successful reengineering requires in-depth changes. If reengineering efforts are sufficiently deep, the old support systems (e.g., accounting, performance measurement, training, and compensation) will become obsolete. Starting from scratch, in effect, the organization can redesign itself and new support systems will emerge. In the short run, the change process may create excess capacity and financial stress. Unless the organization is growing, such pressures can lead to layoffs.[58]

"What drove our reengineering effort was the recognition that we couldn't rest on our past success at delighting customers. Most of our reengineering dealt with how we could do things faster."

Louis Zambella
Senior VP, Operations
L.L. Bean

Firms capable of growth can undergo changes to improve efficiency without having to suffer this short-term side effect. With 85 percent of Banca di America's (BAI) revenues coming from retail banking, its managers chose reengineering as the way to improve customer satisfaction. Two teams of BAI employees analyzed customer transactions and categorized them as payments, deposits, withdrawals, money orders, and the like. By carefully documenting the processes for each transaction (e.g., depositing a check drawn on another bank in a customer's account), they discovered that a simple deposit transaction required sixty-four activities and nine forms. After reengineering this process, the same transaction required only twenty-five activities and two forms. The average number of employees per branch has dropped from nine to three or four. These savings allowed BAI to open 50 new branches and increase revenues by 24 percent without adding personnel.[59]

Structures Built Around Processes

Traditionally, industrial organizations have organized around tasks, with like tasks being grouped into departments, and departments being grouped into SBUs or a business. These organizations were managed by giving supervisors responsibility for assigning tasks to individuals and then monitoring their work. More recently, organizations that have focused on processes such as those needed to ensure total quality or those needed to maximize the cycle times and efficiency with which a set of tasks is performed have begun to adopt a new approach to structure. In this new structure, an entire process or work flow—i.e., everything that occurs between the point at which the organization receives inputs from suppliers until it satisfies a customer—replaces a task as the fundamental building block. This new structure is more accurately described as horizontal, rather than vertical.[60]

In the horizontal organization structure, work is performed by teams, who are held accountable for performance indicators that relate to their assigned process. For example, the performance of a team that handles order generation and fulfillment might be evaluated using cycle time as the primary criterion. Another key principle for horizontal structures is to combine managerial and nonmanagerial activities whenever possible. In other words, process teams should be self-managing and empowered to make decisions and take quick action, as needed. Training should be offered to help members of the team improve this process, and career progression is likely to occur first within the process, as members master all of the tasks required, and then between processes. It's interesting to note that the horizontal structure incorporates many principles that are similar to those suggested by the motivational approach to job design, described later in this chapter. In other words, horizontally-structured process-based organizations are likely to offer jobs that many employees may find more rewarding and enjoyable than the jobs offered in traditional organizations based on a bureaucratic model.

JOB DESIGN

Job design is the process by which the characteristics and qualities of jobs are determined and created. As described in Chapter 2, technology is one major factor that affects the design of a job,[61] but even after the technology has been decided on, there remain many other questions to answer when designing jobs: Should the nurses at the hospital work rotating shifts, or is it better to always have the same staff on the graveyard shift? After the layoffs, will everyone just be expected to work harder, or is there a smarter way to design the work? If everyone is fully connected electronically, is there really any need for people to all work in an office?

Since the times of Frederick W. Taylor and scientific management, jobs have been designed for technical efficiency (finding the one best way to produce a product) and productivity (obtaining maximum use of human and physical resources).[62] Today, in addition to improving the efficiency and productivity of workers, the objectives of job design include

* organizing work to fit new business strategies that call, increasingly, for more teamwork;
* attracting, accommodating, motivating, and retaining a workforce that's diverse in terms of age, gender, lifestyle, and capability; and
* fully leveraging new technologies.

"Teamwork is the essence of life."

Pat Riley
Coach
Miami Heat Basketball Team

Companies such as Xerox and GE have empowered employees working in teams designed to support total quality cost strategies. At TIE/Communications, a supplier of telecommunications equipment, technical specialists function as "ambassadors to the customers." Technicians interact with the customers, learn about their problems, and recommend solutions.[63] Even the San Diego Zoo has redesigned its jobs. In the old days, jobs were narrow and specific: a keeper did the keeping and a gardener did the gardening. Today the zoo is organized around "bioclimatic zones," into which visitors enter and enjoy a naturalistic combination of plants and animals and where employees work in teams and share a variety of tasks.[64]

Although the scientific management approach to job design is still used in some companies, three other popular approaches to job design are the human factors approach, the motivational approach, and alternative work arrangements. Often, these different approaches are used in combination to achieve multiple objectives. A recent study of over 200 companies suggests that the three most common objectives of job design efforts were to encourage the organization to stay focused on important performance outcomes, rather than who does what; to enhance employee growth and learning; and to increase flexibility of task assignments.[65]

Scientific Management Approach

Also sometimes referred to as the mechanistic approach, scientific management methods apply principles of mechanical engineering to job design. Job designers (typically, industrial engineers) use time-and-motion studies to determine the most efficient method to perform and sequence job tasks. Usually, the jobs of interest involve mostly physical activity rather than mental activity. For the sake of efficiency, work is often portioned into small, simple, standardized tasks that can easily be performed with little training. A job comprises a very limited number of tasks, which are performed over and over by the worker. Each job is highly specialized, as are the tools and procedures associated with it. Traditional assembly line jobs and modern fast-food jobs are mechanistically designed.

Taylor believed such jobs would improve productivity because the performance of the workers was less dependent on employee initiative: "Under the old type of management, success depends almost entirely upon getting the 'initiative' of the workmen, and it's indeed a rare case in which this initiative is really attained. Under scientific management the 'initiative' of the workmen (that is, their hard work, their goodwill, and their ingenuity) is obtained with absolute uniformity and to a greater extent than is possible under the old system."[66] In Taylor's system, the responsibilities of managers included dividing work into tasks; selecting and training people to do the tasks; ensuring that the work was done in accordance with the rules; and taking over any of the work for which they, the managers, were "better fitted." Taylor's philosophy was to clearly separate back work from brain work. The intent wasn't to demean in any way the work of laborers, nor was it to work people beyond their limits. Rather, the philosophy stressed the idea that the systematic collection and analysis of data was the best way to learn how to get work done as efficiently as possible. Employees could not be expected to collect such data and analyze it while also doing the work.

When used today, the scientific management approach still includes the core idea of applying mechanical engineering principles to designing jobs that can be performed efficiently, but much of Taylor's philosophy about the role of managers versus workers has been replaced. In particular, workers—not managers—are recognized as the ones who have the most expertise and useful insights about how to improve the design of specific tasks.

Disney Theme Parks. Successful use of the scientific management approach can be found at the Disney theme parks, where ride operators perform perfectly scripted roles repeatedly and predictably throughout their days and nights. Consistent with a view that high-quality service is reliable service—that is, the same regardless of time, place, or customer—Disney employees learn to anticipate every eventuality. New employees are taught the ropes not by managers, but by veterans in the job, who have experienced just about every possible situation the new employee is likely to encounter and knows how Disney guests are likely to react. They know which jokes work reliably as well as which ones just elicit groans. Such a mechanistic approach may seem counterintuitive for service-based companies, but it makes sense when the success of the business depends on high volume and low costs. These business imperatives are also common in fast-food restaurants and convenience stores.

UPS. Meticulous application of mechanical engineering principles has helped UPS thrive, despite stiff competition. In the business where "a package is a package," this method has been the key to gains in efficiency and productivity since the privately held company was founded in 1907. In the 1920s, UPS engineers cut away the sides of UPS trucks to study how the drivers performed. Changes in equipment and procedures were then made to enhance workers' efficiency. In the 1990s, the study of workers' behavior on the job continues. In one project, more than one thousand industrial engineers used a time study to set standards for a variety of closely supervised tasks. In return, the UPS drivers, all of whom are Teamsters, earn good wages and receive generous benefits. Because of the company's success, it has also been able to offer employees good job security.

Human Factors Approach

The objective of the human factors approach, which is also referred to as *ergonomics*, is to design equipment that fits the full range of physical features found in the population of people likely to be using the equipment. Rather

fast fact

The National Labor Relations Act requires that employers provide information related to job design programs to the union, if a union represents the employees.

than maximize efficiency, the goal is to minimize the amount of stress and fatigue experienced as a result of doing work. This approach focuses on the physical dimensions of the human body, the mechanical principles that govern physical movements, and physiology.[67] For example, with an understanding of the biomechanics of the wrist, arm, and shoulder, both office equipment and price scanners can be designed to minimize the development of the painful carpal tunnel syndrome, which is characterized by numbness, tingling, soreness, and weakness in the hand and wrist. An understanding of the physiology of circulation, respiration, and metabolism allows work tasks to be designed to maximize the efficient use of energy.

The human factors approach to job design has proved useful in automobile factories, where the physical capabilities of the workforce have changed as this workforce has aged. On average, U.S. autoworkers are now more than a decade older than their counterparts in Japan. This makes it increasingly difficult to achieve productivity gains using the old approach of just speeding up the assembly line. To thrive, the auto industry has had to redesign its plants, installing ergonomic equipment to ease the strain. For example, overhead conveyor belts tilt auto bodies at angles that make assembly work less physically demanding, and the air guns used to drive screws are designed to reduce the stresses that cause carpal tunnel syndrome. Gyms have been installed, and workers have taken "back classes" to learn how to lift without injuring themselves.

The office of the future may reflect design principles developed by a new branch of ergonomics—dubbed *cognitive ergonomics*. Cognitive ergonomics deals with the challenge of creating spaces where the mind does its best work. The objective is to better understand how people think as they're going through their workday and then design spaces that facilitate both thinking and remembering. Michigan-based Haworth Inc., a furniture company, already sees companies applying this approach to job design as they experiment with open office layouts and virtual-office arrangements.[68]

Motivational Approach

If the mechanistic approach to job design focuses on tasks and the human factors approach focuses on the body, what is left for the focus of the motivational approach? The mind and heart. Of course, this is the terrain of psychologists.

The motivational approach assumes that jobs can be designed to stimulate employee motivation and increase job satisfaction. The Hackman-Oldham theory is the most well-established framework for designing jobs that people find highly motivating.[69] Briefly, the theory states that three critical psychological states are needed to create high levels of motivation in the workplace. Experienced meaningfulness refers to whether employees perceive their work as valuable and worthwhile. Experienced responsibility refers to whether employees feel personally responsible for the quantity and quality of their work. Knowledge of results refers to the extent to which employees receive feedback about how well they're doing. Feedback can come from the task itself or from other sources, such as supervisors and customers. These three psychological states, in turn, are affected by five key job characteristics:

- *Skill variety:* the degree to which the job involves many different work activities or requires several skills and talents.
- *Task identity:* this is present when a job involves completing an identifiable piece of work, that is, doing a job with a visible beginning and outcome.

- *Task significance:* this is present when a job has a substantial impact on the goals or work of others in the company.
- *Autonomy:* this is present when the job provides substantial freedom, independence, and discretion to the individual in scheduling work and determining the procedures to be used in carrying out tasks.
- *Feedback:* this is present when work results give the employee direct and clear information about his or her performance.

Hackman and Oldham also believed that individual differences play a role in how people respond to the design of their jobs. In particular, they identified the strength of an employee's growth needs as an individual difference that would influence how people reacted to enriched jobs. Growth-need strength refers to a desire for personal challenges, a sense of accomplishment and learning. Employees with strong growth needs are likely to respond positively to enriched jobs. However, employees with weak growth needs may experience enriched jobs as frustrating and dissatisfying. This point is illustrated by a study in which autoworkers from Detroit worked in Sweden as engine assemblers in a SAAB plant. These jobs allowed the workers a great deal of freedom and responsibility. After a month, however, 75 percent of the U.S. workers reported that they preferred their traditional assembly-line jobs. As one worker said, "If I've got to bust my a__ to have a meaningful job, forget it; I'd rather it be monotonous."[70]

Several different strategies can be used to design jobs with the motivating core characteristics. With *job rotation*, each job remains the same but employees move from one job to another over a period of time. This increases task variety and, depending on the jobs involved, may also increase skill variety and boost job identity. Job rotation introduces variety into work that consists of narrowly defined jobs without actually changing the design of the jobs. *Job enlargement* expands the number of tasks in a job—it's the opposite of scientific management. The objective of job enlargement is increasing skill variety. Job identity may also improve because employees in enlarged jobs often complete a "whole and identifiable piece of work." This approach may increase skill variety, but it's also likely to foster resentment because the employee is expected to do more of the same, which eventually becomes boring again.

Job enrichment uses vertical loading of responsibility. This approach increases the number and variety of tasks assigned to a worker, and in addition it gives the worker more control over the work. Responsibility for activities such as planning and controlling the work flow are shifted from the supervisor to the person performing the work. In Germany, all of these design principles are applied in factories where workers perform in "work islands." They avoid boredom by rotating jobs, socializing, and working in cycles of up to 20 minutes rather than a few seconds. In assembling electronics products, automobiles, and appliances, the Germans appear to be well ahead of other countries in modifying or reducing the conventional assembly line and its simple, repetitive jobs. This enlightened position in alternative job design is a product of the work-humanization movement in Germany, initially funded by the German government in 1974 and maintained by the cooperative relationship between labor and management.

Does designing jobs according to the Hackman and Oldham model really improve productivity *and* employee satisfaction? Dozens of studies involving thousands of employees in many types of jobs indicate that the answer to this question is yes. Both performance and job satisfaction go up after jobs are redesigned to provide more skill variety, task identity, signifi-

■□*fast fact*

Research in Germany shows that workers become markedly dissatisfied when the cycle time for repeating job tasks is less than 1.5 minutes.

cance, autonomy, and feedback.[71] These beneficial outcomes are especially likely to be seen among employees with high growth needs. Such people enjoy challenges, like to be creative and innovative, and are comfortable being in positions where they have high levels of responsibility.[72]

The motivational approach to job design is consistent with the growing use of work teams. Although teamwork may be unusual for some employees, it appears that most employees are able to adapt to it. It may take time to install teams and attain high levels of teamwork, but the benefits can be substantial, as illustrated in the feature, Managing Teams: Kodak's Team Zebra.[73]

Managing Teams

Kodak's Team Zebra

There was a time when the black-and-white film division of the Eastman Kodak Company was regarded by employees as the worst place in the company to work. The division, which produces 7,000 products from 250 product lines, suffered from budget overruns, huge inventories, waste, and late delivery of products. It was actually losing money for the company when "Mother" Kodak stepped in and gave the division 18 months to turn around its financial performance. Failure to do so would mean shuttering the division.

Led by a 15-member team of managers from the division, the employees reengineered their workplace from a traditional manufacturing process organized by functions to a team-driven process organized by work flow. The flow system flattened out the organization, breaking down the boundaries between functions and eliminating the every-function-for-itself mentality. It created a seamless process for the manufacture of film and paper from raw materials at one end to finished goods at the other.

The transformation involved more than just redesigning jobs, of course. An entirely new culture and mindset also were created. Stephen J. Frangos, manager of Kodak's black-and-white division at the time of the reorganization, credits the HR strategy as key to the successful transformation. That strategy involved leveraging the company's intangible human assets rather than investing in new equipment and technical programs, or cutting costs and dropping product lines. At the heart of the strategy was the assumption that empowered teams of employees could and would be much more productive than individuals working in narrow jobs with close supervision.

Employees and managers alike had to change. It required employees to become more comfortable with risk taking, and it required managers to use positive reinforcement to unleash creativity. It also meant improving the company's approach to recruitment and selection, rewards and recognition, performance measurement and feedback, capability building, and communications. Martha Britt, human resource manager for the black-and-white division at the time of the reorganization, says, "We had to put together a strategy that would build the capability, the understanding, and the desire of the 1,500 partners to play a key role in turning the business around."

The plan worked. Product quality, customer satisfaction, and overall operating efficiency rose dramatically. Within the first two years, the division cut inventories in half, saving $50 million; and reduced waste by 75 percent, generating $40 million in cost reductions without eliminating any product lines. Overall, productivity increased by 15 to 20 percent each year.

To learn more about Eastman Kodak, visit the company's home page at: **www.kodak.com**

Being Successful.   Getting to the point where a team is self-managed and is capable of making decisions and performing related activities requires change and commitment in several organizational areas. According to one large study of intact work teams, the biggest barriers have little to do with the team process itself, and a lot to do with organization practices that do not fit the design of the work. For example, most teams operate in companies that continue to use individual-based compensation and performance-appraisal systems. Teams also feel hampered by their inability to access crucial information from their own companies, which are concerned about leakage of proprietary information. Perhaps most important, employees feel they need new skills in areas such as leadership and conflict management, but their employers seldom provide it. In some organizations, lack of support from all line managers and union representatives create additional problems.[74] Ultimately, the success of a team depends on effective partnership.

Alternative Work Arrangements

Standard work schedules include day, evening, and night sessions as well as overtime, part-time, and shift work. The vast majority of U.S. employees still work standard schedules, but changes are afoot. The growing number of single-parent families, the high costs of commuting, the desire for larger blocks of personal time, and the desire of older workers to reduce their hours, all create conflict for today's workers. Alternative work arrangements can reduce the stresses caused by such conflict between job demands, family needs, leisure values, and educational needs. Offering flexibility in time schedules, job sharing, and telecommuting arrangements are also ways to comply with the *Americans with Disabilities Act of 1990* (ADA). For organizations with 15 or more employees, the ADA "prohibits bias against qualified individuals with disabilities in all aspects of employment and requires employers to make reasonable accommodations for such individuals so long as the accommodations do not pose an undue hardship to the employer's business."[75] For the Philip Morris Company, accommodating the scheduling needs of a valued employee who suffered a spinal injury meant installing a computer in his hospital room during his extended recovery, working with the hospital rehabilitation staff to facilitate his recovery, and hiring couriers to bring him materials.[76]

Accommodating to employees' schedule needs and preferences is especially challenging for organizations that either must or simply prefer to operate 24 hours a day, seven days a week. The possible combinations of shift lengths, shift rotations, and days-on/days-off is almost limitless. Years of research on shift workers has sought to answer the question, "What shiftwork schedules are best?" Are some arrangements easier for employees to adjust to? Are some schedules more likely to result in employees being sleepy and more accident- or error-prone while at work? With 20 million Americans employed as shiftworkers, the answers to such questions are important not only to employers and employees, but also to the many families who are affected by shiftwork schedules. But no simple answers seem to apply to all situations, as is often true with managing people. While all shiftworkers are affected by biological, circadian rhythms, these may be less significant in determining reactions than an employee's family and social life in determining reactions to alternative shift arrangements. Thus, the "best" schedule is the one the employees prefer. In addition, some types of people seem to adjust more easily to shiftwork than others. For example, according to Circadian Technologies, Inc., highly effective shiftworkers tend to exercise; normally stay awake very late, even when not working shifts; can fall asleep easily at different times of the day; tend to have a somewhat relaxed attitude; and have a sense of internal control.[77]

Just as some employees appreciate having more flexibility, employers prefer more flexibility. To achieve greater organization flexibility, many companies have reduced the size of their core workforce and increased their reliance on contingent workers. Contingent workers enter their employment contract with the understanding that their job is temporary. Because there is no agreed-upon definition of precisely what it means to say that the work is temporary, estimates of the number of temporary employees vary widely. The Bureau of Labor estimates that 5 percent of the workforce works on a contingent basis, which it defines as those who have no contract and expect their jobs to last less than one year. Some contingent workers are part-timers who receive reduced benefits, others are full time. According to some estimates, fully 30 percent of the workforce currently is employed as contract labor.[78] Contract laborers may be self-employed consultants, freelance workers or contractors, or they may be paid by a temporary-help agency or an employee-leasing firm. The trend toward increased use of contingent workers and contract workers isn't limited to the U.S. The same is occurring throughout most of Europe. And on both continents, it's a growing concern of labor unions.[79] In 1997, for example, a dispute over the use of contingent workers caused UPS to suffer a two-week strike that cost the company more than $700 million in lost revenue. Eventually, UPS agreed to convert 10,000 part-time jobs to full-time jobs at double the hourly rate of pay.[80]

To avoid such confrontations, many other companies have addressed their need for flexibility by adopting policies of forced overtime as a way to deal with increased demand without having to hire more workers.[81] According to a survey conducted by William M. Mercer, Inc., three-fourths of the nearly 3,400 responding mid- to large-size companies have restructured jobs to offer non-standard arrangements to some employees. The most common alternatives offered were contingent workers; job-sharing arrangements, in which two part-time employees fill what would otherwise be one full-time job; flexible work schedules, such as a workweek of four 10-hour days rather than the traditional five 8-hour days; and telecommuting programs.[82] Employers and employees alike seem to benefit from flexible work arrangements. A study of IBM employees found that teleworkers perceived their situation as favorable in terms of their productivity and flexibility. Surprisingly, telecommuters were no more or less favorable in terms of the issue of work/life balance. And, there was one clear disadvantage reported by this group of employees: when it came to teamwork, telecommuting made it more difficult to communicate with team members and develop a sense of camaraderie.[83]

Finally, alternative work arrangements can benefit the broader community by reducing traffic and the accidents and pollution associated with it. Many communities now offer tax incentives to employers to encourage them to find ways to reduce the number of miles their workforce accumulates driving to work. While some companies earn such credits by increasing their employees' use of public transportation, other companies earn the credits by simply having fewer employees come in to the office.[84]

Which Approach Is Best?

Clearly, no single job-design approach is the best approach. Each approach has some advantages and disadvantages, as shown in Exhibit 4.6. To meet all

■☐ *fast fact*

The United States' contingent workforce—consisting of roughly 45,000,000 temporaries, self-employed, part-timers, or consultants—has grown 57 percent since 1980.

■☐ *fast fact*

One-third of large Japanese firms use temporary workers and nearly as many report they will hire more temporary workers in the future.

"Through virtual-office programs, we might be able to attract people with proven records of success who can't or won't move to our office sites."

Richard Karl Goeltz
Vice Chairman and CFO
American Express

Exhibit 4.6
Comparison of Job Design Approaches

Approach	Advantages	Disadvantages
Scientific Management	• Ensures predictability • Provides clarity	• May be boring • May result in absenteeism, sabotage, and turnover
Human Factors	• Accommodates jobs to people • Breaks down physical barriers • Makes more jobs accessible to more people	• May be costly for some jobs • Is impractical if structural characteristics of the organization make job change impossible
Motivational	• Can satisfy needs for responsibility, growth, and knowledge of results • Provides social interaction • Provides growth opportunity • Reduces boredom • Can improve quality, customer service and other indicators of productivity • Reduces absenteeism problems • Improves morale	• May not work for people who prefer routine • May not work for people who prefer to work alone • Often requires additional training • May require higher pay • Requires a more complex performance measurement system • Requires managers to coach and facilitate rather than control employees
Alternative Work Arrangements	• Helps attract a broader range of workers • Can reduce stress and improve quality of life • Some alternative arrangements reduce employers' costs • Provides a means to assure legal compliance with ADA regulations	• Many new alternative arrangements require experimentation to learn what works best • If only some workers are offered alternative arrangements, others may feel resentment • Can be more difficult to manage a workforce with a variety of arrangements • Arrangements that involve working offsite require new approaches to supervision and performance measurement

of the desired objectives in any particular situation, a combination of approaches often is needed. Decisions about job design must take into account each of the other elements of the internal environment described in this chapter. The approach a company ultimately chooses for a particular job will also depend in part on needs, costs, and the available technology. Because it believed it had found an unusually effective employee, UPS spent $11,000 for equipment that enabled a blind man to work as a computer-programming instructor. Job design choices may also depend on the history of the company. UPS and Lincoln Electric have long histories of using the scientific management and human factors approaches to job design. Because they have first-hand knowledge of the benefits of these approaches, it may be easier for employees to accept some of their disadvantages. Design choices

■☐*fast fact*

The productivity level of the Lincoln Electric worker is almost three times as much as the average manufacturing worker.

also depend on the task. For example, one study of 45 projects at a dozen large companies revealed that teams are especially effective for developing and launching new products, but product modification is better done by individuals.[85]

Management's views of its responsibility to society as a whole may also play a role in choosing how to design work. Since 1985, the Chicago Marriott has teamed up with the International Association of Machinists Center for Administering Rehabilitation and Employment Services (IAM CARES) to provide training and jobs for people with severe disabilities. Many of the jobs have been designed according to principles of scientific management, and this approach seems to work quite well as a way of creating jobs that are manageable for this portion of the workforce. Marriott's partnership with the IAM CARES staff is essential to success, too, because the IAM CARES staff will jump in to resolve problems. IAM CARES agrees that partnership is essential; it needs support from Marriott's CEO, HR, and direct supervisors.[86]

ORGANIZATIONAL CULTURE

A culture is the unique pattern of shared assumptions, values, and norms that shape the socialization activities, language, symbols, rites, and ceremonies of a group of people. One way to think about culture is to compare it to personality. Like personality, culture affects in predictable ways how people behave when no one is telling them what to do.[87] As we have seen, cultures develop at the level of very large groups of people, such as nations, as well as at the level of smaller groups.

The Importance of Culture

At Amy's Ice Creams in Austin, Texas, having a fun culture is key to the strategy. Back in 1984, when Amy's first opened, super-premium ice cream shops were hard to find, but today competitors are everywhere. To survive, owner Amy Miller needed to differentiate her shop from all the others. How? Miller's strategy is to give customers a memorable "experience" with every scoop of ice cream. Examples of some of the experiences customers look forward to are Sleep-Over night (when employees dress in pajamas), Disco night (with strobe lights going), and Romance night (when the store is lit with candles). The strategy may sound crazy, but it's working. Annual sales for her seven-store chain have topped $2 million and continue to grow at about 20 percent per year.

Miller's strategy requires a special organizational culture. To make her strategy work, Miller keeps close tabs on her company's culture. In Amy Miller's hands, for example, job interviews are a powerful tool. When hiring she wants creative types, so she tests for creativity by giving job applicants a white paper bag and telling them do something interesting with it. They have a week to work on their creations. If job applicants can't be creative with the bag, she figures they won't be entertaining on a hot night with a long line of customers waiting for service. For those who are eventually hired, the interview clearly signals the high value Miller places on fun. To remind current employees how many creative people are out there looking for jobs, Miller occasionally passes around some of the best creations of applicants. Such reminders seem to stimulate employees to come up with new entertainment ideas on their own. If the line is long, time seems to go by more quickly when customers are doing their best imitations of barnyard animals in order to win free ice cream. When they have to wait while an empty ice cream tub is replaced with a refill, customers seem to mind less when they're trying to think of the answer to a pop trivia quiz or watching someone break-dance on a freezer top. Of course, fun isn't the only reason people come to Amy's Ice Creams. They also know that the fun doesn't cost them more or interfere with the speed or quality of customer service.[88]

Amy's Ice Creams is a small company with a uniform culture throughout. In most large organizations, multiple cultures exist side-by-side. In firms with a functional structure, different cultures may be found in different departments. In divisionalized firms, each division may be unique.

A prominent example of an organization with two cultures is Andersen Worldwide, which has experienced debilitating internal conflicts between its accounting and consulting units. Like a person with a "split personality," the presence of two sharply contrasting cultures has proved difficult. Since its founding in 1913, the accounting firm of Arthur Andersen had built a reputation for being so internally cohesive that employees were sometimes referred to as "Androids." Its consulting activities, which focus on information technology, didn't begin until 1954. During the first years of its existence, the mature accounting business helped smooth out the ups and downs of the entrepreneurial consulting business. For years, people who specialized in accounting and consulting coexisted in relative peace, relying on give and take to resolve conflicts. New recruits were hired straight out of college and socialized through rigorous training and mentorship programs. They were taught to believe that the firm as a whole was greater than the sum of its parts. Consultants, who didn't need in-depth knowledge of accounting, were expected to pass the CPA exam nevertheless. Most of the people who became partners had been with the firm their entire careers.

By the 1980s, the culture had become fragmented. Some partners came to the firm later in their careers and weren't CPAs. The consultants began to question the assumption that the two businesses were better off combined than they would be as separate firms. According to a former board member, "They began to think, 'well, we'd rather not be in one pot.'" In 1989, after several key partners from the consulting business left, the remaining partners negotiated a compromise that established Andersen Consulting as a separate business unit.

Since then, the two business units have continued to grow apart, each with its own culture and vision of the future. News stories have chronicled the in-fighting, and some competitors have tried to use the feud to their own advantage. Deloitte & Touche Consulting Group, for example, ran full-page advertisements that read, "Andersen Consulting: Distracted by infighting. Deloitte Consulting: Focused on our clients. When you hire a consulting firm, you can't afford for them to be more concerned with their own problems than they are with your well-being . . . since we're not wasting time fighting with each other, we give every client our undivided attention."[89]

Types of Organizational Cultures

There are many ways to describe organizational cultures. Of the many frameworks that have been proposed, one useful one is presented in Exhibit 4.7.[90] The vertical axis reflects the relative formal control orientation, ranging from stable to flexible. The horizontal axis reflects the relative focus of attention, ranging from internal functioning to external functioning. The

Exhibit 4.7
Framework of Types of Cultures

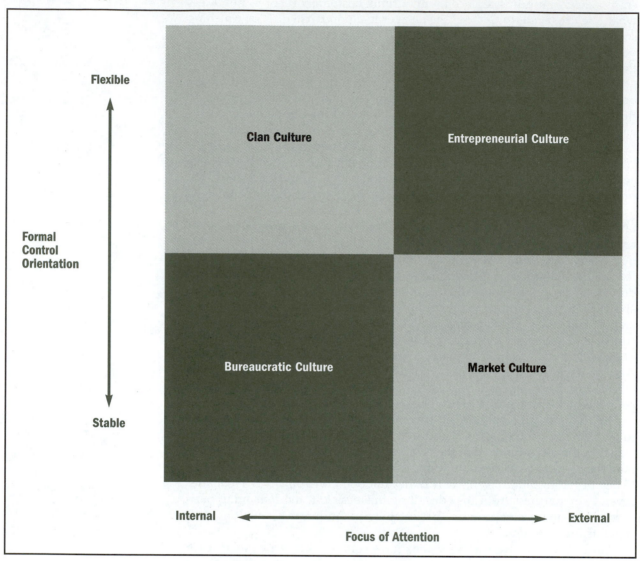

extreme corners of the four quadrants represent four pure types of organizational cultures: bureaucratic, clan, entrepreneurial, and market.[91] In a culturally homogeneous organization, one of these basic types of culture will be predominant. In a culturally fragmented organization, multiple cultures are likely not only to exist but also to compete for superiority.

As is true of organization designs, different organizational cultures may be appropriate under different conditions, with no one type of culture being ideal for every situation. Regardless of how appropriate they may be, however, the different cultures tend to coincide with different types of strategies and organizational designs. Furthermore, some employees may prefer one culture over another. Employees who work in organizations with cultures that fit their view of an ideal culture tend to be committed to the organization and optimistic about its future.[92]

Bureaucratic Culture. An organization that values formalization, rules, standard operating procedures, and hierarchical coordination has a bureaucratic culture. Recall that the long-term concerns of a bureaucracy are predictability, efficiency, and stability. Its members highly value standardized goods and customer service. Behavioral norms support formality over informality.[93] Managers view their roles as being good coordinators, organizers, and enforcers of written rules and standards. Tasks, responsibilities, and authority for all employees are clearly defined. The many rules and processes are spelled out in thick manuals, and employees believe that their duty is to "go by the book" and follow legalistic procedures. Most local, state, and federal governments have bureaucratic cultures, as do many companies organized by specialized functions.[94]

Clan Culture. Tradition, loyalty, personal commitment, extensive socialization, teamwork, self-management and social influence are attributes of a clan culture. Its members recognize an obligation beyond the simple exchange of labor for a salary. They understand that contributions to the organization (e.g., hours worked per week) may exceed any contractual agreements. The individual's long-term commitment to the organization (loyalty) is exchanged for the organization's long-term commitment to the individual (security). The clan culture achieves unity with a long and thorough socialization process, such as the one used at Arthur Andersen. Long-time clan members serve as mentors and role models for newer members. These relationships perpetuate the organization's values and norms over successive generations of employees. The clan is aware of its unique history and often documents its origins and celebrates its traditions in various rites. Members have a shared image of the organization's style and manner of conduct. Public statements reinforce its values.

Fel-Pro, an auto-parts maker in Skokie, Illinois, had a clan culture. Maintaining that culture was made a condition of selling the company to Federal-Mogul. The Fel-Pro culture valued having a family atmosphere. It operated a summer camp for children of its employees, always sent parents a Treasury Bond upon the arrival of a new child, and funded scholarships for employees and their children. Teamwork among employees was promoted, and turnover was unusually low. The family programs cost the company 57 cents per worker hour, and company data indicated that employees who took advantage of the programs were more likely to participate in team problem solving and offer suggestions for operational improvements. When Chairman Richard Snell of Federal-Mogul approached Fel-Pro about buying the company, he was told that a deal could be worked out only if Fel-Pro's culture was protected. Although he worried about how Federal-Mogul's employees might react, Snell agreed to continue operating Fel-Pro's summer camp for at least two years and to continue the scholarship fund for at least five years.[95]

Entrepreneurial Culture. High levels of risk taking, dynamism and creativity characterize an entrepreneurial culture. There is a commitment to experimentation, innovation and being on the leading edge. This culture doesn't just quickly react to changes in the environment, it creates change. Effectiveness means providing new and unique products and rapid growth. Individual initiative, flexibility, and freedom foster growth and are encouraged and well rewarded. This is the type of culture large firms expect to see develop within the skunkworks they create to foster innovation.

"One thing that eroded our culture very fast was bringing in a huge amount of new people from blue chip corporations."

Anita Roddick
Founder
The Body Shop

"A duck who is tamed will never go anywhere anymore. We are convinced that any business needs its wild ducks. And in IBM we try not to tame them."

Thomas J. Watson, Jr.
Former CEO and Chairman
IBM

Entrepreneurial cultures usually are associated with small- to middle-sized companies that are still run by a founder. Nordstrom, one of the West Coast's premier department store chains, is an example of a large company that has kept its entrepreneurial culture. Sales personnel are expected to do whatever it takes to please the customer. Writing thank you notes to customers and reminding them of special occasions that may require gift purchases are tasks often done during a salesperson's days off. Stories of heroic deeds are part of the company's culture, too. Examples include changing a customer's flat tire in the parking lot, driving for three hours to deliver a holiday gift, and buying a shirt that met the customer's style preference from a competitor in order to give the customer what he wanted. These heroic deeds are considered part of doing the job, which is meeting customers' needs so that they'll return to buy more. Incentive pay plans motivate everyone at Nordstrom to approach their jobs as opportunities for entrepreneurial risk taking and rewards.[96]

Market Culture.   The achievement of measurable and demanding goals, especially those that are financial and market-based (e.g., sales growth, profitability, and market share) characterize a market culture. Hard-driving competitiveness and a profits orientation prevail throughout the organization. Colgate-Palmolive is an example of an organization with a market culture.

In a market culture, the relationship between individual and organization is contractual. The individual is responsible for some level of performance, and the organization promises a specified level of rewards in return. Increased levels of performance are exchanged for increased rewards. Rather than promoting a feeling of membership in a social system, the market culture values independence and individuality and encourages members to pursue their own financial goals and, by so doing, to help each other. For example, the salesperson who increases sales will make more money, and the firm will earn more profits through the salesperson's greater sales volume.

The market culture doesn't exert much informal, social pressure on an organization's members. Superiors aren't formally judged on their effectiveness as role models or mentors, for example, and few economic incentives are tied directly to cooperating with peers. Managers are expected to cooperate with managers in other departments only to the extent necessary to achieve their performance goals.

Creating a Strong Culture

Regardless of the specific type of culture an organization has, a strong culture that's well matched to an organization's objectives and criteria for measuring success can enhance organizational performance as well as individual performance and satisfaction. Strong cultures provide clear guidelines for how people in the organization should behave. In a strong market culture, for example, people understand that ultimately their performance will be judged in terms of quantifiable, bottom-line results. In a strong clan culture, people understand that focusing on the bottom line and ignoring interpersonal relationships is a recipe for disaster. In and of itself, however, a strong culture is of no particular usefulness for achieving business objectives. This is because culture addresses the question of "*How* do we do things around here?" A culture becomes useful when paired with a clear answer to the question, "*Where* are we going?"

CREATING ALIGNMENT IN THE INTERNAL ENVIRONMENT

As this brief synopsis of the components of an organization's internal environment reveals, organizations are exceedingly complex. To achieve excellence requires creating an organization that's both aligned internally and well-suited to the conditions in the external environment. A clear strategic direction, an integrated HR system, and the partnership perspective all facilitate alignment.

Clear Strategic Direction

To keep people focused on what everyone is striving for, many organizations use a vision statement (also sometimes referred to as a mission statement). In a study of over 300 chief executives, when asked to write down their vision statement, all but one was able to do so.[97] At the 35,000-employee Weyerhaeuser lumber and paper company, the vision is to be *The Best Forest Products Company In The World*. At Southwest Airlines, the vision is to be *The Airline of Choice*. While a company's vision statement may seem very general to outsiders, if formulated with the deliberation and input of many employees, it can take on great meaning. A company's approach to managing human resources can further facilitate internal and external alignment, or contribute to misalignment.

Integrated HR System

In addition to a general vision or mission statement that relates to the business objective of the company, many companies also have a formal statement describing how people are to be treated and managed. Systems for selecting new employees, socializing them, managing their performance, providing rewards and recognition should all be designed to support the behaviors needed to innovate, deliver high quality goods and services, and/or continuously increase efficiency and reduce costs, as called for by the competitive strategy.

Weyerhaeuser Company uses an HR philosophy statement to describe what employees mean to the company. The following is an excerpt:

- People are mature, responsible individuals who want to contribute.
- People hold themselves to high standards of integrity and business ethics; they're responsible stewards of the land and environment.
- Our work environment is based on mutual respect, personal satisfaction, and growth opportunities for everyone.
- People recognize that teamwork, cooperation, and a clean, safe, well-maintained workplace are essential to fulfilling our customer commitments.
- Continuing education is an ongoing commitment that involves everyone.[98]

At Levi Strauss, a company known for its strong, values-based culture, the company's philosophy about how to treat employees is spelled out in an Aspirations Statement. The specific aspirations of the company include:

- For management to exemplify "directness, openness to influence, commitment to the success of others, and willingness to acknowledge our own contributions to problems."
- To value "a diverse workforce (age, sex, ethnic group, etc.) at all levels of the organization; diversity will be valued and honestly rewarded, not suppressed."

> *"We don't care that much about education and expertise, because we can train people to do whatever they have to do. We hire attitudes."*
>
> **Herb Kelleher**
> **CEO**
> **Southwest Airlines**

- The company will "provide greater recognition—both financial and psychic—for individuals and teams that contribute to our success [including] those who create and innovate and those who continually support day-to-day business requirements."
- Management should epitomize "the stated standards of ethical behavior. We must provide clarity about our expectations and must enforce these standards throughout the corporation."
- Management must be "clear about company, unit, and individual goals and performance. People must know what is expected of them and receive timely, honest feedback."
- Management must "increase the authority and responsibility of those closest to our products and customers. By actively pushing responsibility, trust, and recognition into the organization, we can harness and release the capabilities of our people."[99]

Formal statements such as these may help large companies keep their HR systems aligned with the broader vision, but they aren't essential. More important than the formal statements are the way people are treated and the messages they're sent about the importance of innovation, quality, costs, and other key issues. As is true at Amy's Ice Creams, most employees learn about a company's culture and its HR philosophy through the way they're selected, the formal and informal training they receive, the aspects of their performance that seem to receive most attention during performance reviews, and the behaviors they see rewarded or punished on a daily basis.

Partnership Perspective

As forces in the external environment stimulate companies to reassess their competitive strategies and organizational structures, the challenge of creating internal alignment is becoming a top priority. To achieve this objective, large scale organizational changes may be needed. Planning and implementing such change processes is the topic of Chapter 5. Regardless of whether an organization is undergoing fundamental change or merely needs to continually fine tune the elements of its internal environment, success depends on the cooperation of managers, HR professionals, and all other employees. The implications of the partnership perspective are summarized in The HR Triad: Partnership Roles and Responsibilities for Creating Internal Alignment.

SUMMARY

Many of the forces from the external environment described in Chapters 2 and 3 influence organizations directly, but some of the effects of these forces are transmitted to the organization through their effects on the industry as a whole. When customers' preferences change, it affects all the firms competing for those customers. Thus, when deciding how to respond to customers, a firm must take into account not only their own actions but also the actions of competitors. Firms that can take actions which create the most value for customers can gain market share. Well-chosen actions also increase profitability. To create customer value that's difficult for competitors to match, a company must be able to use some unique resources, capabilities, and core competencies. Thus, identifying and developing resources, capabilities, and

THE HR TRIAD: PARTNERSHIP ROLES AND RESPONSIBILITIES FOR CREATING INTERNAL ALIGNMENT

Line Managers	HR Professionals	Employees
Understand the competitive dynamics of the industry and their implications.	Understand the competitive dynamics of the industry and their implications.	Understand the competitive dynamics of the industry and their implications.
Know the firm's resources, capabilities, and core competencies and strive to enhance them.	Develop approaches to managing human resources that enhance the firm's resources, capabilities, and core competencies.	Understand how your job relates to the firm's resources, capabilities, and core competencies.
Assist HR professionals in determining the behaviors needed to implement the firm's strategy, and encourage these behaviors among employees.	With line managers, determine the behaviors needed to implement the firm's strategy and develop policies and practices to support the needed behaviors.	Learn which behaviors are needed to implement the firm's strategy; develop the skills needed for strategy implementation; assist other employees with needed behaviors and skills.
Recognize the importance of organizational culture for firm performance and direct efforts to building an appropriate culture.	Help line managers and other employees understand the importance of organizational culture; develop HR practices that send a clear and consistent message about the desired culture.	Seek to understand the organization's culture and its implications for your own behavior; adapt to changing conditions, if appropriate.
Understand and hone the new managerial behaviors needed for an empowered workplace.	Help line managers and employees adjust to empowerment and teamwork.	Accept the need for job design improvements; assist in job redesign efforts by providing input for improvements and feedback about the effects of changes to job design.
Treat employees with disabilities fairly, recognizing that job accommodations are a means for ensuring that all qualified employees have equal employment opportunities.	Be familiar with and use the many resources available to help organizations fully utilize the talents of employees with disabilities through appropriate job accommodations.	Request job accommodations, if needed.
Continuously monitor the internal environment to ensure the many components are aligned.	Assist in monitoring the alignment of the human aspects of the internal environment; recommend and help implement changes when needed.	Monitor one's own needs and requirements and seek changes as needed.

core competencies is essential to a firm's long-term success and survival. Like all other activities within a firm, approaches to managing human resources should be considered with this objective in mind.

Firms formulate competitive strategies based on their assessments of the competitive environment and their capabilities and core competencies.

Typical strategies include offering low prices, excellent quality or highly innovative products, and services to domestic customers and/or customers in foreign markets. The choice of strategy and markets, in turn, are likely to influence the way the organization structures its activities and the design of jobs within the organization. Job designs also are influenced by consideration of employees' preferences, as well as biological and physiological abilities and limits. As will be described in subsequent chapters, job designs have many important implications for managing human resources, beginning with the types of people the organization should hire and continuing throughout all aspects of the employment relationship.

All the elements of an organization's internal environment, as they have evolved throughout the life of the organization, give rise to a distinct organizational culture. A strong culture provides clear guidelines for how people in the organization should behave. When matched with the organization's objectives and the concerns of multiple stakeholders, a strong culture can enhance organizational performance as well as individual performance and satisfaction. HR practices usually reflect the current culture, and they also can be used to create a new culture. As organizations change their strategies, structures, and job designs, changes in the culture may also be needed. The process of organizational change is addressed next in Chapter 5.

TERMS TO REMEMBER

Bureaucratic culture
Business strategy
Capabilities
Clan culture
Competitive analysis
Competitive strategy
Contingent workers
Core competencies
Corporate strategy
Deming's 14 principles
Divisional structure
Entrepreneurial culture
Five-forces model
Functional strategy
Functional structure
Hackman-Oldham theory of job design
Horizontal structure
Human factors
Industry life cycle
Innovation strategy
Internal alignment
International strategy
ISO registration
Job enrichment
Job rotation
Low cost strategy
Market culture
Matrix structure
Multidomestic structure
Process reengineering
Resources
Scientific management
Skunkwork unit
Strategic Business Unit (SBU)
Strategic group
SWOT analysis
Total quality management
Total quality strategy
Transnational structure

DISCUSSION QUESTIONS

1. How would you describe Kinko's sources of competitive advantage? What are its core capabilities? Did these change as the company grew? After referring to Exhibit 4.7, explain how the new structure of Kinko's is likely to affect its culture.

2. To what degree did the job changes made in Kodak's Team Zebra fit the motivational approach to job design. Do you think the new design is likely to have any negative consequences on the psychological states of employees?

3. Many companies are making greater use of teams, while at the same time allowing people to have more flexible schedules. How is technology making flexible schedules and teamwork possible? What are the disadvantages of using technology to facilitate flexible schedules? Be specific about the issues that are likely to arise for the team.

4. What type of organizational culture do you think you would prefer? Explain your reasoning. How are employees likely to behave when they work in an organizational culture that does not fit their personal preferences? What are the implications for organizations—should they try to have only employees who fit into the corporate culture, or are there advantages to having some employees who do not fit in well with the culture?

PROJECTS TO EXTEND YOUR LEARNING

1. **Managing Strategically.** Select an industry of interest to you and visit the websites of three companies within that industry. Based on the information provided, how does each company seem to prioritize concerns about cost, quality, and innovation? Describe how each company is organized (by departments, divisions, matrix, etc.). Some companies may show an organization chart of their structure, but for other companies you will need to look at the titles of the top management team to determine the structure. Is HR represented on the top management team?

2. **Managing Globalization.** Compare the organizational structures of two great competitors: PepsiCo (www.pepsico.com) and Coca Cola (www.cocacola.com). How does the structure of each company compare to Unilever's structure? What do the formal structures of these companies suggest about the type of culture you could expect to find in each company?

3. **Managing Change.** For IBM, the past decade has been a time of significant change. After downsizing during the early 1990s, the company had rebounded by 1996. Much of its new growth came from acquisitions. Read the Chairman's letter to shareholders in IBM's most recent annual report. Identify one or two current strategic issues facing IBM and speculate about the challenges for managing human resources that these issues are likely to create. You can view an online version of IBM's annual report at
www.ibm.com/AnnualReport

4. **Managing Strategically.**   Interview one of the overnight delivery carriers (you might have to interview them as they're walking!), and ask them to describe their company's competitive strategy. Try to determine how much the employees seem to focus on reducing costs, delivering top quality service, and coming up with new ideas for how the company can beat the competitors. Try to determine which human resource management practices are used to support the strategy. For example, does the strategic focus affect the way the company trains employees, its pay system, or the way it measures performance? Report your findings to the class.

5. **Integration and Application.**   Review the Lincoln Electric Company and AAL cases, and then answer the following questions.
   a. What are the key characteristics of the company's industry?
   b. What is the company's competitive strategy?
   c. Describe the basic structure of the company and the principles that it seems to follow when designing jobs.
   d. How does the company's job design approach relate to the company's selection, training, performance measurement, and compensation systems?
   e. Which elements of the internal environment do you think are most likely to change within the next five years? Why?

CASE STUDY

Improving Internal Customer Service

You are the manager of the data management department at a large retail store. Your unit's major responsibility is to organize information into a format that can then be used by line managers to analyze various trends occurring in the business. Some analyses are performed monthly, some are done quarterly, and some grow out of particular issues facing the managers at the particular point in time. The unit is essentially a support function. It's centralized in the company because the company's various specialized information systems (accounting, personnel, customer service, etc.) aren't integrated. Managers ask for many types of information to be entered into the system so they can use it in their analyses. Some of the information is printed, some is handwritten, and some of it's in electronic form. Employees use a variety of technologies. Some data must be entered essentially by hand, some data are moved electronically from the company's intranet to the central data processing system, some data can be scanned into the system, and so on.

The unit has 15 data-entry employees reporting to one supervisor. They handle a wide variety of work supplied by various departments and groups. Some jobs are small; others are quite large and may take weeks to complete. Some work involves innovative problem solving, but much of it's quite routine; some work comes with a due date; the remainder has been prescheduled to be done on a regular basis.

The work is supplied to the employees in the unit by an assignment coordinator, who attempts to see that each employee gets exactly one-fifteenth of the work. The assignment coordinator looks at each project before assigning it to a data-entry employee, and makes sure the request is understandable. If it isn't clear what the unit is being asked to accomplish, the assignment coordinator gives the request to you, and you return it to the originating department with a request for clarification. Because of the exactness required for this work and the cost of doing it, the completed data files are sent to verifiers to review, to help keep errors to a minimum. Nevertheless, some errors aren't discovered until after the finished job is returned to the client. Turnover is high, and many due dates aren't met. You are concerned that your unit is becoming a source of frustration for some of the line managers, so you need to do something to improve its performance.

Questions

1. Write a statement that clearly states the business imperatives for your unit. Be clear about what it means for your unit to be highly effective.

2. Currently, your unit is a specialized department in an organization structured along functional lines of specialization. Is this the best arrangement for your department? What are some other options, and what do you think is the ideal structure? Do you think you could convince the other managers in the organization to consider restructuring? What arguments could you use to make the case for an alternative structure?

3. Regardless of whether you can convince the organization to consider a major change in its structure, you need to do something now to improve your unit's performance. You are considering three options: reengineering, total quality management, and the motivational approach to job design. Which one would you choose? Why?

CASE STUDY

Redesign or Relocate?

During the past five years, productivity and worker satisfaction at the Jackson Toy Company have been declining. Productivity is now so low that Dr. Helen Jackson, the company's founder and president, is considering closing the plant and moving south. She's heard that several auto manufacturers have chosen various southern locations for their new plants and is pretty sure they would not make such a decision without first doing plenty of research on the quality of the labor force. Perhaps they've discovered that workers in the south are simply more motivated than they seem to be in the north these days.

When Jackson, a mechanical engineer, started the company in 1980, she installed an assembly line so that workers could become specialized at their jobs and, hence, very productive. The employees were quite productive during the first ten years of operation. Then, several younger, newly hired employees began complaining about the repetitive, boring nature of the work. About that time, Jackson began to notice a decline in productivity. Her response was to assume that pay was too low. Many of the original employees were essentially "second-income earners," so perhaps they didn't mind hold-

ing low-paying jobs. The newly hired employees were younger, however, and she discovered that several were moonlighting at other jobs in order to earn more money. That seemed to explain why so many seemed to be coming to work too tired to work efficiently. Jackson decided to raise everyone's salary by 20 percent. Since she had 75 employees, this represented a substantial increase in payroll expenses. Nevertheless, she was concerned about productivity as well as the "plight" of the workers. Besides, she knew that increasing the base pay of the workers she had would cost less overall than hiring more workers.

About two months after the salary increase, Jackson noted that the level of productivity had not increased. In fact, it had actually declined slightly. Disappointed, but resolved to do something, Jackson called the local university. Professor Erin Brief, a specialist in job redesign, suggested that Jackson either completely redesign the jobs for the employees or implement a job rotation program. Although it would be more costly to completely redesign the jobs, Professor Brief recommended that alternative. Jackson wondered if it would be more trouble than it was worth.

QUESTIONS

1. On what basis would Brief recommend completely redesigning the jobs? What did she mean by it anyway?

2. Was increasing salaries by 20 percent a valid way for Jackson to test her assumption about the cause of the productivity problems? What would you have done?

3. Does Jackson's competitive strategy have any impact on how the jobs are designed? That is, would she choose a different approach depending on whether she was more concerned about keep costs low versus making toys of the best possible quality? Explain.

ENDNOTES

1 J. J. Laabs, "Change," *Personnel Journal* (July 1996): 57.

2 W. M. Carley, "Charging Ahead: To Keep GE's Profits Rising, Welch Pushes Quality Control Plan," *The Wall Street Journal* (January 13, 1997): A1, A8; P. M. Gunther, "How GE Made NBC No. 1," *Fortune* (February 3, 1997): 92–100; S. G. Richter, "General Electric's Victory in Europe," *New York Times* (November 30, 1997): B11; J. Curran, "GE Capital: Jack Welch's Secret Weapon," *Fortune* (November 10, 1997): 116–134; A. Bernstein, S. Jackson, and J. Byrne, "Jack Cracks the Whip Again," *Business Week* (December 15, 1997): 34–35; Koenig, "If Europe's Dead, Why is GE Investing Billions There?" *Fortune* (September 9, 1996): 114–118; J. F. Welch, "A Master Class in Radical Change," *Fortune* (December 13, 1993): 83.

3 K. M. Sutcliffe and G. P. Huber, "Firm and Industry as Determinants of Executive Perceptions of the Environment," *Strategic Management Journal* 19 (1998): 793–807; G. Hamel and C. K. Prahalad, *Competing for the Future: Breakthrough Strategies for Seizing Control of Your Industry and Creating the Markets of Tomorrow* (Boston: Harvard Business School Press, 1994).

4 M. E. Porter, *Competitive Strategy: Techniques for Analyzing Industries and Competitors* (New York: Free Press, 1980).

5 See M. A. Hitt, R. D. Ireland, and R. E Hoskisson, *Strategic Management: Competitiveness and Globalization* (Cincinnati: South-Western, 1999); C. M. Grimm and K. G. Smith, *Strategy as Action* (Cincinnati: South-Western, 1997).

6 P. Cappelli and A. Crocker-Hefter, "Distinctive Human Resources Are the Core Competencies of Firms," Report No. R117 Q00011–91 (Washington, D.C.: U.S. Department of Education, 1994); M. Gerstein and H. Reisman, "Strategic Selection: Matching Executives to Business Conditions," *Sloan Management Review* 24 (1983): 33–49.

7 M. E. Porter, *Competitive Strategy: Creating and Sustaining Superior Performance* (New York: Free Press, 1985); T. Eisenhart, "Where Do You Go When You Need to Know," *Business Marketing* 74 (11) (1989): 40.

8 M. E. Porter, *Competitive Strategy: Creating and Sustaining Superior Performance.*

9 M. E. Porter, "From Competitive Advantage to Corporate Strategy," *Harvard Business Review* 65 (3) (1987): 43–59.

10 See M. A. Hitt, R. D. Ireland, and R. E. Hoskisson, *Strategic Management,* for a more complete discussion.

11 R. M. Grant, *Contemporary Strategy Analysis* (Cambridge, England: Blackwell Business, 1991).

12 W. Pape, "Group Insurance," *Inc. Tech* 2 (1997): 29–31.

13 C. K. Prahalad and G. Hamel, "The Core Competence of the Corporation," *Harvard Business Review* 68 (May–June 1990): 79–91.

14 For a review see R. Sanchez and A. Heene, "Reinventing Strategic Management: New Theory and Practice for Competence-Based Competition," *European Management Journal* 15 (3) (1997): 303–317.

15 G. Hamel and C. K. Prahalad, *Competing for the Future.*

16 D. Miller, "Generic Strategies: Classification, Combination, and Context," *Advances in Strategic Management* 8 (1992): 391–408.

17 G. S. Smith, *The Anatomy of a Business Strategy: Bell, Western Electric, and the Origins of the American Telephone Industry* (Baltimore: Johns Hopkins University, 1985).

18 D. Packard, *The HP Way: How Bill Hewlett and I Built Our Company* (New York: HarperCollins, 1995): 93.

19 D. Leonard-Brown, "Core Capabilities and Core Rigidities: A Paradox in Managing New Product Development," *Strategic Management Journal* 13 (Summer, 1992): 111–126; D. Dougherty, "Interpretive Barriers to Successful Product Innovation in Large Firms," *Organization Science* 3 (1992): 179–202.

20 G. Tucker and B. Shearer, "Winning Over Main Street and Wall Street," *Across the Board* (October 1996): 33–35; W. M. Carley, "To Keep GE's Profits Rising, Welch Pushes Quality-Control Plan," *The Wall Street Journal* (January 13, 1997): A1, A8. See also W. E. Deming, *Quality, Productivity,*

and *Competitive Position* (Cambridge: MIT Center for Advanced Engineering Study, 1992); W. E. Deming, *Out of Crisis* (Cambridge: MIT Press, 1986): 23–24; J. M. Juran, *Juran on Quality by Design* (New York: Free Press, 1992).

[21] R. B. Lieber, L. Grant, and J. Martin, "Now Are You Satisfied? The 1998 American Customer Satisfaction Index," *Fortune* (February 16, 1998): 161–168; T. A. Stewart, "A Satisfied Customer Isn't Enough," *Fortune* (July 21, 1997): 112–113; D. A. Garvin, "How the Baldrige Award Really Works," *Harvard Business Review* (November–December 1991): 80–95; V. A. Zeithaml, A. Parasuraman, and L. L. Berry, *Delivering Quality Service* (New York: Free Press, 1990).

[22] R. S. Schuler and D. L. Harris, *Managing Quality* (Reading, MA: Addison-Wesley, 1992), 32.

[23] Deming, *Quality, Productivity, and Competitive Position*, 23–24.

[24] Information for this feature was obtained from the company's home page at **www.case-swayne.com**

[25] A. Faircloth, "Value Retailers Go Dollar for Dollar," *Fortune* (July 6, 1998): 164–166.

[26] M. E. Porter, *Competitive Strategy*.

[27] J. B. Barney, "Looking Inside for Competitive Advantage," *Academy of Management Executive* 9 (4) (1995): 49–61.

[28] D. A. Nadler and M. B. Nadler, *Champions of Change: How CEOs and Their Companies are Mastering the Skills of Radical Change* (San Francisco: Jossey-Bass, 1998).

[29] W. A. Randolph and G. G. Dess, "The Congruence Perspective of Organization Design: A Conceptual Model and Multivariate Research Approach," *Academy of Management Review* 9 (1984): 114–127.

[30] L. E. Greiner, "Evolution and Revolution as Organizations Grow," *Harvard Business Review* (May–June 1998): 55–67. [An earlier version of this classic article appeared in 1972.]

[31] L. Baird and I. Meshoulam, "Managing Two Fits of Strategic Human Resource Management," *Academy of Management Review* (1988): 116–128.

[32] Adapted from N. Byrnes, "Kinko's Goes Corporate," *Business Week* (August 19, 1996): 58–59; and information provided on the Web sites **www.kinkos.com**; **www.tlckinkos.com**; and **www.edp.com** (November 10, 1997).

[33] P. V. Marsden, C. R. Cook, and A. L. Kallenberg, "Bureaucratic Structures for Coordination and Control," A. L. Kallenberg, D. Knoke, P. V. Marsden, and J. L. Spaeth, eds., *Organizations in America: Analyzing Their Structures and Human Resource Practices* (Thousand Oaks, CA.: Sage, 1996).

[34] F. C. Lager, *Ben & Jerry's: The Inside Scoop* (New York: Crown Trade, 1994): 143.

[35] P. Cappelli and A. Crocker-Hefter, "Distinctive Human Resources Are the Core Competencies of Firms," Report No. R117 Q00011–91 (Washington, D.C.: U.S. Department of Education, 1994).

[36] R. Jacob, "The Search for the Organization of Tomorrow," *Fortune* (May 18, 1992): 95.

[37] P. V. Marsden, C. R. Cook, and A. L. Kallenberg, "Bureaucratic Structures for Coordination and Control."

[38] D. Channon, "SBU Structure," C. L. Cooper and C. Argyris, eds., *The Concise Blackwell Encyclopedia of Management* (Malden, MA: Blackwell, 1998).

[39] T. Parker-Pope, "Colgate Gives Management New Structure," *The Wall Street Journal* (January 15, 1997): B6.

[40] F. A. Maljers "Inside Unilever: The Evolving Transnational Company," *Harvard Business Review* (September–October 1992): 46–51.

[41] R. E. Miles and W. E. D. Creed, "Organizational Forms and Managerial Philosophies: A Descriptive and Analytic Review," *Research in Organizational Behavior* 17 (1995): 333–372.

[42] S. M. Davis and P. R. Lawrence, *Matrix* (Reading, MA: Addison-Wesley, 1977).

[43] M. E. McGill and J. W. Slocum, Jr., *The Smarter Organization: How to Adapt to Meet Marketplace Needs* (New York: John Wiley & Sons, 1994); G. T. Lumpkin and G. G. Dess, "Clarifying the Entrepreneurial Orientation Construct and Linking It To Performance," *Academy of Management Review* 21 (1996): 135–172. Note, however, that this approach to innovation structures is more pronounced in some cultures than others—see S. Shane, S. Venkataraman, and I. MacMillan, "Cultural Differences in Innovation Championing Strategies," *Journal of Management* 21 (1995): 931–952.

[44] S. Ghoshal and C. A. Bartlett, "The Multinational Corporation as an Interorganizational Network," *Academy of Management Review* 15 (1990): 603–625; A.V. Phatak, *International Dimensions of Management* (Boston: PWS-Kent, 1992); also see L. Eden, *Multinationals in North America* (Calgary, Alberta: University of Calgary Press, 1994).

[45] F. A. Maljers "Inside Unilever: The Evolving Transnational Company," *Harvard Business Review* (September–October, 1992): 46–51.

[46] For a description of 3M's evolution, see M. Ackenhusen, D. Muzyka, and N. Churchill, "Restructuring 3M for an Integrated Europe. Part One: Initiating the Change," *European Management Journal* 14 (1) (1996): 21–36; M. Ackenhusen, D. Muzyka, and N. Churchill, "Restructuring 3M for an Integrated Europe. Part Two: Implementing the Change," *European Management Journal* 14 (2) (1996): 151–159.

[47] Y. L. Doz and C. K. Prahalad, "Managing DMNCs: A Search for a New Paradigm," R. P. Rumelt and D. J. Teece, eds., *Fundamental Issues in Strategy: A Research Agenda* (Boston: Harvard Business School Press, 1994): 495–526.

[48] H. Axel, *HR Executive Review: Company Experiences with Global Teams* (New York: Conference Board, 1996).

[49] D. A. Garvin, "Leveraging Processes for Strategic Advantage: A Roundtable with Xerox's Allaire, USAA's Herres, SmithKline Beecham's Leschley, and Pepsi's Weatherup," *Harvard Business Review* (September–October 1995): 77–90.

[50] J. Conkling, "A Firm Reaches for and Achieves Excellence," *Workforce* (May 1997): 87–90; M. G. Brown, *The Pocket Guide to the Baldrige Award Criteria* (New York: Quality Resources, 1994).

[51] "Miller Brewery's Sociotech Ohio Brewery Becomes Model for Change," *Manpower Argus* No. 330 (March 1996): 6.

52 Giving Quality Programs a Boost," *Bulletin to Management* (July 22, 1993): 225. For reviews of research on this topic, see D. J. Glew, R. W. Griffin, and D. D. Van Fleet, "Participation in Organizations: A Preview of the Issues and Proposed Framework for Future Analysis," *Journal of Management* 21 (1995): 395–421; J. L. Cotton, *Employee Involvement: Methods for Improving Performance and Work Attitudes* (Newbury Park, CA: Sage, 1993): 16; E. E. Lawler, S. A. Mohrman, and G. E. Ledford, Jr., *Employee Involvement and Total Quality Management: Practices and Results in Fortune 1000 Companies* (San Francisco: Jossey-Bass, 1992); E. A. Locke and D. M. Schweiger, "Participation in Decision-Making: One More Look," *Research in Organizational Behavior* 1 (1979): 265–339.

53 T. C. Powell, "Total Quality Management as Competitive Advantage: A Review and Empirical Study," *Strategic Management Journal* 16 (1995): 15–37; also see M. R. Kelley, "Participative Bureaucracy and Productivity in the Machined Products Sector," *Industrial Relations* 5 (3) (1996): 374–399; F. K. Pils and J. P. MacDuffie, "The Adoption of High-Involvement Work Practices," *Industrial Relations* 35 (3) (1996): 423–455.

54 J. M. Liedtka, "Collaborating Across Lines of Business for Competitive Advantage," *Academy of Management Executive* 10 (2) (1996): 20–37.

55 W. C. Symonds, "Where Paternalism Equals Good Business," *Business Week* (July 20, 1998): 16E4–16E8.

56 E. Brynjolfsson, A. A. Renshaw, and M. V. Alstyne, "The Matrix of Change," *Sloan Management Review* (Winter 1997): 37–54; M. Hammer and J. Champy, *Reengineering the Corporation* (New York: HarperCollins, 1993); M. Hammer, *Beyond Reengineering: How the Process-Centered Organization Is Changing Our Lives* (New York: HarperBusiness, 1996); and J. Champy, *Reengineering Management: The Mandate for New Leadership* (New York: HarperBusiness, 1996).

57 A. Majchrzak and Q. Wang, "Breaking the Functional Mind-set in Process Organizations," *Harvard Business Review* (September–October 1996): 93–99.

58 J. D. Sterman, N. P. Repenning, and F. Kofman, "Unanticipated Side Effects of Successful Quality Programs: Exploring a Paradox of Organizational Improvement," *Management Science* 43 (1997): 503–521; R. L. Harmon, *Reinventing the Business: Preparing Today's Enterprises for Tomorrow's Technology* (New York: Free Press, 1996).

59 Adapted from G. Hall, J. Rosenthal, and J. Wade, "How to Make Reengineering Really Work," *Harvard Business Review* (November–December 1993):124–126; A. Nahavandi and E. Aranda, "Restructuring Teams for the Reengineered Organization," *Academy of Management Executive* 87 (4) (1994): 58–68; H. Lancaster, "Managing Your Career," *The Wall Street Journal* (January 17, 1995): 1B. Also see D. Santos, B. L. Dos, and K. Peffers, "Rewards to Investors in Innovative Information Technology Applications: First Movers and Early Followers in ATMs," *Organization Science* 6 (1995): 241.

60 F. Ostroff and D. Smith, "The Horizontal Organization," *McKinsey Quarterly* 1 (1992): 148–168.

61 The impact of technology on office jobs is described in M. D. Coovert, "Technological Changes in Office Jobs," A.

Howard, ed., *The Changing Nature of Work* (San Francisco: Jossey-Bass, 1995).

62 R. Kangel, *The One Best Way* (New York: Viking, 1997); P. S. Adler, "Time and Motion Regained," *Harvard Business Review* (January–February 1993): 97–108.

63 B. Singer, "It's 7 P.M., and 5 Percent of Omaha is Calling. Want 28 Steaks and a Radio?" *New York Times Magazine* (December 3, 1995): 68–71.

64 K. Labich, "Elite," *Fortune* (February 19, 1996): 90–99; T. J. Hackett, "Giving Teams a Tune-Up," *HR Focus* (November 1997): 11.

65 C. Fay, H. Risher, and D. Mahoney, "The Jobless Organization: Survey Results of the Impact of New Job Design on Compensation," *ACA Journal* (Winter 1997): 29–44.

66 F. W. Taylor, "The Principles of Scientific Management," *Scientific Management* (New York: Harper, 1947).

67 W. C. Howell, "Human Factors in the Workplace," M. D. Dunnette and L. M. Hough, eds., *Handbook of Industrial-Organizational Psychology*, Vol. 2 (Palo Alto, CA: Consulting Psychologists Press, 1991): 209–270.

68 G. Flynn, "An Ad Agency Pitches for the Virtual Office," *Workforce* (November 1997): 56–63; also see G. R. Oldham, A. Cummings, and J. Zhou, "The Spatial Configuration of Organizations: A Review of Literature and Some New Research Directions," *Research in Personnel and Human Resources Management* 13 (1995): 1–38.

69 Adapted from J. R. Hackman and G. R. Oldham, *Work Redesign* (Reading, MA: Addison-Wesley, 1980): 77.

70 R. B. Goldman, *A Work Experiment: Six Americans in a Swedish Plant* (New York: Ford Foundation, 1976).

71 B. T. Loher, et al., "A Meta-Analysis of the Relation of Job Characteristics to Job Satisfaction," *Journal of Applied Psychology* 70 (1985): 280–289; L. R. Berlinger, W. H. Glick, and R. C. Rodgers, "Job Enrichment and Performance Improvement," J. P. Campbell and R. J. Campbell, eds., *Productivity in Organizations* (San Francisco: Jossey-Bass, 1988): 219–254; Y. Fried, "Meta-Analytic Comparison of the Job Diagnostic Survey and Job Characteristics Inventory as Correlates of Work Satisfaction and Performance," *Journal of Applied Psychology* 76 (1991): 690–697.

72 J. R. Hackman and G. R. Oldham, "Development of the Job Diagnostic Survey," *Journal of Applied Psychology* 60 (1975): 159–170. B. Gerhart, "How Important Are Dispositional Factors as Determinants of Job Satisfaction? Implications for Job Design and Other Personnel Programs," *Journal of Applied Psychology* 72 (1987): 366–373; J. R. Rentsch and R. P. Steel, "Testing the Durability of Job Characteristics as Predictors of Absenteeism Over a Six-Year Period," *Personnel Psychology* 51 (1998): 165–190; R. P. Steel and J. R. Rentsch, "The Dispositional Model of Job Attitudes Revisited: Finding of a 10-Year Study," *Journal of Applied Psychology* (1997): 873–879; J. L. Xie and G. Johns, "Job Scope and Stress: Can Job Scope be Too High?" *Academy of Management Journal* 38 (1995): 1288–1309; R. W. Renn and R. J. Vandenberg, "The Critical Psychological States: An Underrepresented Component in the Job Characteristics Model Research," *Journal of Management* (1995): 279–303.

73 Adapted from "Team Zebra Changes Kodak's Stripes," *Personnel Journal* (January 1994): 57; D. Anfuso, "Xerox Partners with the Union to Regain Market Share," *Personnel Journal* (August 1994): 46–53; D. Anfuso, "Kodak Employees Bring a Department into the Black," *Personnel Journal* (September 1994): 104–112; L. Grant, "Can Fisher Focus Kodak?" *Fortune* (January 13, 1997): 76–79.

74 "The Problem with Teams: Individuals and Organizations," *HR Reporter* (April 1993): 3–6.

75 T. L. Jones, *The Americans with Disabilities Act: A Review of Best Practices* (New York: American Management Association, 1993); "Employers' ADA Responses—Concerned but Waiting," *Fair Employment Practices* (July 30, 1992): 87. See also "Discrimination Charges Filed under ADA," *Bulletin to Management* (June 2, 1994): 172–173.

76 An excellent source of information about what companies are doing to accommodate the needs of disabled employees is J. W. Spechler, *Reasonable Accommodation: Profitable Compliance with the Americans with Disabilities Act* (Del Ray Beach: St. Lucie Press, 1996).

77 C. R. Maiwald, J. L. Pierce, J. W. Newstrom and B. P. Sunoo, "Workin' 8 p.m. to 8 a.m.," *Workforce* (July 1997): 30–36.

78 M. N. Wolfe, "Classification of Workers: Independent Contractor vs. Employee," *ACA Journal* (Summer 1998): 6–14; R. J. Grossman, "Short-term Workers Raise Long-term Issues," *HR Magazine* (April 1998): 81–89; see also J. Pfeffer and J. N. Baron, "Taking the Workers Back Out: Recent Trends in the Structuring of Employment," *Research in Organizational Behavior* 10 (1988): 257–303; C. L. Hulin and T. M. Glomb, "Contingent Employees: Implications for Individuals and Organizations," D. R. Ilgen and E. Pulakos, eds., *The Changing Nature of Work Performance: Implications for Staffing, Personnel Actions, and Development* (San Francisco: Jossey-Bass, 1999).

79 C. von Hippel, S. L. Mangum, D. B. Greenberger, R. L. Heneman, and J. D. Skoglind, "Temporary Employment: Can Organizations and Employees Both Win?" *Academy of Management Executive* 11 (1) (1997): 93–104; C. Brewster, L. Mayne, and O. Tregaskis, "Flexible Working in Europe," *Journal of World Business* 32 (2) (1997): 133–151.

80 S. Caudron, "Part-timers Make Headline News: Here's the Real HR Story," *Workforce* (November 1997): 41–50.

81 S. Babbar and D. J. Aspelin, "The Overtime Rebellion: Symptom of a Bigger Problem?" *Academy of Management Executive* 12 (1) (1998): 68–76.

82 "Earnings and Benefits of Workers in Alternative Work Arrangements: Datagraph," *Bulletin to Management* (January 30, 1997): 36–37; "More Employers Are Providing Flexibility Through Job Restructuring," *Personnel Journal* (March 1994): 16.

83 E. J. Hill, B. C. Miller, S. P. Weiner, and J. Colihan, "Influences of the Virtual Office on Aspects of Work and Work/Life Balance," *Personnel Psychology* (1998): 667–683.

84 S. Greengard, "How Technology Will Change the Workplace," *Workforce* (January 1998): 78–84; M. Apgar, "The Alternative Workplace: Changing Where and How People Work," *Harvard Business Review* (May–June 1998): 121–136.

85 G. Flynn, "Workforce 2000 Begins Here," *Workforce* (May 1997): 78–84.

86 J. J. Laabs, "Individuals with Disabilities Augment Marriott's Work Force," *Personnel Journal* (September 1994): 46–53.

87 D. R. Denison, "What Is the Difference Between Organizational Culture and Organizational Climate? A Native's Point of View on a Decade of Paradigm Wars," *Academy of Management Review* 21 (1996): 619–654; C. A. O'Reilly and J. A. Chatman, "Culture as Social Control: Corporations, Cults, and Commitments," B. M. Staw and L. L. Cummings, eds., *Research in Organizational Behavior* 18 (1996): 157–200.

88 J. Case, "Corporate Culture," *Inc.* (November 1996): 42–52.

89 Advertisement. *The Wall Street Journal* (February 26, 1998): p. A9; A. Bryant, "The Andersen Family Feud: Two Units Split on New Leadership," *New York Times* (June 28, 1997): B35, B37; and D. Whitford, "Arthur, Arthur. . . .," *Fortune* (November 10, 1997): 169–178.

90 Adapted from R. Hooijberg and F. Petrock, "On Cultural Change: Using the Competing Values Framework to Help Leaders Execute a Transformational Strategy," *Human Resource Management* 32 (1993): 29–50; R. E. Quinn, *Beyond Rational Management: Mastering the Paradoxes and Competing Demands of High Performance* (San Francisco: Jossey-Bass, 1988).

91 R. Hooijberg and F. Petrock, "On Cultural Change: Using the Competing Values Framework to Help Leaders Execute a Transformational Strategy."

92 S. G. Harris and K. W. Mossholder, "The Affective Implications of Perceived Congruence with Culture Dimensions During Organizational Transformation," *Journal of Management* 22 (1996): 527–547.

93 D. A. Morand, "The Role of Behavioral Formality and Informality in the Enactment of Bureaucratic Versus Organic Organizations," *Academy of Management Review* 20 (1995): 831–872.

94 P. V. Marsden, C. R. Cook, and A. L. Kallenberg, "Bureaucratic Structures for Coordination and Control."

95 R. A. Melcher, "Warm and Fuzzy, Meet Rough and Tumble," *Business Week* (January, 26, 1998): 38.

96 P. Spector and P. D. McCarthy, *The Nordstrom Way: The Inside Story of America's #1 Customer Service Company* (New York: John Wiley & Sons, 1995).

97 L. Larwood, C. M. Falbe, M. P. Kriger, and P. Miesing, "Structure and Meaning of Organizational Vision," *Academy of Management Journal* 38 (1995): 740–769.

98 R. S. Schuler, "Strategic Human Resource Management: Linking People with the Strategic Needs of the Business," *Organizational Dynamics* (Summer 1992): 32.

99 R. Mitchell and M. Oneal, "Managing By Values: Is Levi Strauss' Approach Visionary—or Flaky?" *Business Week* (August 1, 1994): 46–52.

Chapter

5

"Most companies go to great lengths to avoid any kind of change. For them, change is like a snakebite—one hit and they're paralyzed. For MCI, change has always meant new opportunities."

Gerald H. Taylor
CEO
MCI Communications Corp.[1]

ORGANIZATIONAL CHANGE AND LEARNING

Chapter Outline

MANAGING THROUGH PARTNERSHIP

at XBS

In 1996, Xerox gave its prestigious President's Award to Chris Turner, XBS's Learning Person. In 1997, President Clinton awarded Xerox the 1997 Malcolm Baldrige National Quality Award. Winning the Baldrige award wouldn't have been possible without the years of effort devoted to changing the 40-year-old XBS organization. XBS is Xerox Business Services—a billion-dollar, fast-growing division of the Xerox company. Unlike other Xerox employees, 80 percent of the 15,000 employed by XBS go to work at the sites of the customers' businesses. Their jobs involve operating on-site document processing centers for companies that outsource this function to XBS. It already has 40 percent of the market share for document outsourcing, and its customers give XBS a 95 percent satisfaction rating. But its employees want more, and they view learning and continuous change as their keys to greater success.

To get where it is today, XBS had to change. And for XBS to change, the behaviors of its employees had to change. Turner is careful to point out that the goal was not to fundamentally change the people: "A change strategy doesn't have to be about changing people, because everything is already there. It's about creating conditions where it can all come out," she says. Turner describes the XBS change strategy as "creating a community of inquirers and learners." Unlike most change efforts, this one had no senior team leading the effort, no formal plan or performance goals. What kept the change process on track was Turner's vision of an environment that produces business results and also supports personal growth.

The XBS community is global, working in 4,000 companies in 36 countries. Those companies include large organizations, such as Intel, Microsoft, General Electric, and Motorola, as well as many small companies. At some sites, there is just one XBS employee operating one machine, while at other sites there are 200 XBS employees operating 2,000 machines. But the real challenge is created by the company's rapid growth. In 1981, there were about 3,000 employees. By 1997, there were about 15,000 employees. By 2000, XBS expects to have about 35,000 employees. In this environment, Turner says there are three key issues:

- being clear about how they can differentiate themselves from the competitors,
- finding ways for employees to participate in such a large and unwieldy organization, and
- having in place the necessary knowledge and infrastructure.

On the topic of how to differentiate XBS from the competition, Turner says it comes down to three questions:

- If you were a customer, would you rather do business with someone who has done things the same way for 15 years, or someone who is doing cutting-edge thinking that you can learn from?
- If you were a talented person looking for a job, who would you rather work for?
- If you were a company president, would you rather try to succeed by having a few top managers doing all the thinking, or by having 15,000 people all contributing to the business?

For Turner, the answers are obvious, and she has anecdotes to make her point. She recalls talking to one potential customer about the XBS strategy and seeing a light go on in the person's head. "That's your competitive advantage. Everyone can do anything else, but nobody else is doing this. Can we learn from you?" the person asked. Turner replied, "You can if you're our customer. I don't think we'll share much if you go with a competitor." They got the business.[2]

To learn more about XBS, visit its home page at
www.xerox.com/XBS

THE NATURE OF CHANGE

Organizational change refers to any transformation in the structure or functioning of an organization. It can be stimulated by conditions in the external environment, or by people within the organization who have a vision about how to do things differently. It can be revolutionary or evolutionary.[3] And it can be a one-time event or continuous.

Revolutionary Change

When an organization changes its fundamental assumptions about how to compete, revolutionary change is likely to be the result. Revolutionary change touches everyone and everything in the organization. It changes the daily lives of every employee, as well as other key stakeholders, such as customers, suppliers, and alliance partners. At XBS, the structure of the business was well-defined, but the business could be run in a variety of ways. Turner exploited the opportunity to do things in a revolutionary way. Another organization that experienced revolutionary change is Nucor. When employees told Nucor Steel's CEO Ken Iverson about a new low-cost technology for making steel, he studied the idea carefully and then decided to build a $270 million plant for a thin-slab, mini-mill. The decision to build the new plant represented a fundamental shift in Nucor's assumptions about how to succeed in the steel business. The old way relied on efficiently producing large volumes of a standard product. The new way is to make small batches of customized products that meet customers' special needs. Nucor's decision to adopt a new model for how to compete had consequences for almost every aspect of steel making. Jobs of production workers and managers alike have changed significantly, as have the competencies needed to perform those jobs. Nucor now makes a ton of sheet steel in forty-five minutes, versus three hours for other big steelmakers.[4] Nucor not only reinvented itself; it reinvented the U.S. steel-making industry.

Evolutionary Change

Not every organization needs, or could survive, revolutionary change. More often organizational change involves smaller adjustments. When Frito-Lay created a new low-fat chip, only minor modifications in production and sales activities were required. Though small in magnitude, those changes were essential to customer acceptance of the new product. A shortage of qualified employees may lead an organization to begin changing aspects of its compensation system, offer more developmental experiences, and allow for more flexibility in work arrangements. Gradually with such changes a new culture may begin to emerge, even though that may not have been the original intent.

   Most organizations go through evolutionary changes as a normal part of steady growth. As departments get too big to manage, additional layers of supervision are added, and gradually the organization turns into a hierarchical bureaucracy. As opportunities in other countries arise, a company may slowly begin selling in foreign markets, then producing there, and gradually a global organization is built. Successful companies are adept at managing both evolutionary change and revolutionary change.

Learning Organizations

Whether revolutionary or evolutionary, successful change isn't an event with a clear-cut beginning and ending. Rather, it's a process that ebbs and flows. In some of the best organizations, keeping the process of change flowing continuously has become a top priority. In recent years, such organizations have been referred to as *learning organizations*. When the environment is complex and dynamic, learning may require a lot of exploration and experimentation. When the environment is more stable, learning is more likely to occur through a systematic process of testing alternative approaches.[5] In either case, learning and change are continuous.

A great deal has been written recently about the characteristics of a learning organization. Exhibit 5.1 summarizes the major components that define a learning organization.[6] While all the elements shown are important, we focus here on the learning activity itself and activities that support that learning—namely the culture and associated HR practices.

A learning organization is capable of learning from past experience, learning across parts of the company, and learning from other companies. Through continuous change, a learning organization creates sustainable competitive advantage in its industry. Learning and change occur at the organizational level as well as at the individual employee level, supported by a culture of partnership and empowerment and appropriate HR practices.

Learning From Past Experience.   If companies are changing for the purpose of getting better, they should avoid making the same mistakes over and over. When something new is learned, it should be incorporated into the way things get done in the future. In this age of downsizing, as companies lose employees, they lose knowledge of past successes and failures. Walking out the door with the employees is the knowledge and wisdom they have

■▪▫ *fast fact*

Tandem Computer has an online repository that tracks past, current, and planned benchmarking studies, summarizes results, and includes contact names for more information.

Exhibit 5.1

Characteristics of a Learning Organization

accumulated during their time with the company. Learning organizations are finding ways to keep this knowledge from being lost.[7] The feature, Managing Strategically: Remembering What We Already Know, describes some possible solutions to this problem.[8]

Learning From Other Parts of the Company.   Many times employees in different parts of an organization are working on the same challenge, but are completely unaware of each other. They don't discuss common problems as they try to solve them, and they don't share solutions once they've been discovered. Learning organizations find ways to prevent this. At XBS, the learning laboratories were set up partly to address this issue. XBS also uses a variety of large, planned learning "events" designed to bring people together to share what they've been learning.

Great Harvest Bread Company also encourages sharing across parts of the business. The philosophy at Great Harvest is the opposite of McDonalds. What links the 151 Great Harvest Bread stores is little more than the fact that each one bakes the company's signature honey-wheat bread on the premises, using whole wheat flour ground on site. Anything else that a franchisee wants to try is up to the individual. Franchisees have developed everything from new breads to new approaches to child care. The owners of the 150+ franchise stores share most of their ideas by e-mail or telephone, but they also can have 50 percent of their travel costs reimbursed if they make a trip to visit another franchise location to learn about recent innovations.[9]

By sharing information about the problems they face and the solutions they discover, employees minimize the number of times they reinvent the wheel and speed up the process of organizational learning. Coopers & Lybrand (which has since merged with Price Waterhouse) identified a way to increase the amount and effectiveness of soft information sharing as one of its key strategic challenges. Its clients were scattered around the world, and they all demanded service that reflected cutting-edge practice. In this environment, Coopers & Lybrand knew that its success depended on finding ways to transfer quickly the learning that occurs. With each consulting engagement, employees gain new insights and experiment with new solutions. The learning that occurs is useful for that specific engagement, and it may also be useful to another team sometime in the future. But transferring the lessons learned by one team to other teams working elsewhere around the world isn't easy. These lessons can't be taught with numbers alone. Detailed narrative explanations also are needed. The challenge is to find effective ways to record and transmit narrative explanations of what has been learned.

Several companies now use computer-aided systems for managing narrative information. Companies such as Texas Instruments use computer-aided systems for best-practice sharing. Like e-mail, these systems allow for rapid and wide distribution of information. In addition, they enable the organization to store shared solutions in an electronic library. Later, users can access the library, using index catalogs in which problems and solutions are grouped in meaningful categories. Although this technology is in its infancy, it promises to enhance organizational learning even when knowledge is widely dispersed in both space and time.[10]

Learning From Other Companies.   GE claims that it learned from Wal-Mart about the importance of a speedy distribution system and the importance of rapid inventory turnover. Many companies have visited Lincoln Electric in Cleveland, Ohio in order to hear and see first-hand how their

MANAGING STRATEGICALLY
Remembering What We Already Know

After a decade of downsizing by U.S. organizations, many employees have come to accept the idea that they'll be moving from one organization to another several times during their careers. Professionals who enter the job market today can expect to change jobs about every five years, working for as many as ten different employers during their careers. In each job, the professional learns a great deal. Some of the learning is of a technical nature, which will probably be useful regardless of where the next job happens to be. But much of the professional's learning will be specific to the organization left behind: What are the rules of behavior that characterize the organization culture? How are decisions made in the organization? What was the real reason that the last client wasn't completely satisfied? Where are the inefficiencies in the system that should be eliminated? Unless this knowledge has somehow been captured by the employer and passed on to others, it walks out the door when the professional leaves. Soon, the organization finds itself left with mainly new employees, all of whom are struggling to learn their jobs and, at the same time, how the organization really operates. Few people—including managers at the top of the organization—personally remember what happened at the organization more than five years ago. When decisions have to be made, they're likely to rely on their experiences with previous employers. Often the result is poor decision making. When McKinsey & Co., a consulting firm, studied this problem at an automotive company, it discovered that 30 percent of the time spent solving problems was wasted. The problems had been solved before. The real problem, it seemed, was that no one was around who remembered!

Organizational memory loss is particularly severe when turnover is high. However, reducing turnover isn't the only way to preserve what employees learn. Many organizations try to retain what employees have learned by capturing that knowledge before they leave. One approach is to use intensive exit interviews. A skilled interviewer can probe and record an employee's knowledge and recollections. N. M. Rothschild PLC, a London-based firm, used this approach when its director of corporate affairs left before a successor had been found. The interview was recorded, edited for clarity, and then made widely available in the company.

Learning audits are another technique used to capture organizational memories. Kraft General Foods has used this technique for years, accumulating huge archives of information in the process. Learning audits typically center on a project. Throughout the project, key people periodically record what they're doing and thinking. The records capture their reasoning and can be studied by others in the company, enabling them to draw important lessons and inferences about the project.

A government-owned research center in New Mexico didn't conduct learning audits during the many years it carried out nuclear weapons testing, but now it wishes that it had. Weapons testing has stopped, and management is concerned that the knowledge and skills of weapons specialists eventually will be lost. To avoid that possibility, in case testing is ever resumed, management at the facility decided to interview its retired engineers and technicians. The director of nuclear weapons technology explained, "We don't want to press the erase button on our memory and go back to where we were 50 years ago."

To learn more about McKinsey & Co., visit the company's home page at
www.mckinsey.com

To learn more about Kraft General Foods, visit the company's home page at
www.kraftfoods.com

famous incentive system works. This practice, referred to as benchmarking, enables companies to learn from other companies how things might be done differently.

Porsche, the German auto maker famous for its fast sports car, learned from employees at Toyota. Through extensive training and teaching by the Japanese, Porsche has reduced the time it takes to produce a car from 120 hours to 72 hours and manufacturing flaws from six per car to three per car. But according to Wendelin Wiedeking, Porsche's chief executive officer, what is ultimately revolutionary about what the Japanese have done is redefine craftsmanship for the Germans:

> *"The traditional craftsmanship for which Germany became famous was filing and fitting parts so that they fit perfectly. But that was wasted time. The parts should have been made right the first time. So the new craftsmanship is the craftsmanship of thinking up clever ways of making things simpler and easier to assemble. It is the craft of creating an uninterrupted flow of manufacturing."[11]*

How effective is benchmarking? Some critics have argued that benchmarking doesn't create competitive advantage because at best it indicates what lagging companies need to do in order to catch up with the best firms. But a field experiment designed to test the effectiveness of benchmarking revealed that this practice does lead to productivity improvements. The practice is especially effective when combined with aggressive goal setting.[12] The point that critics often miss is that learning what other companies are doing does not imply that the learners will simply copy the best practices they observe. More likely, the benchmarking activity opens their eyes to many new possibilities and stimulates them to design new practices that exceed those they observed elsewhere.

HR Practices to Support Individual Learning and Change. A learning organization can't succeed without employees who are willing to learn. Learning organizations use human resource management practices to create an environment that encourages and enables individual learning. A flat, team-based structure facilitates learning by involving employees in a broad range of activities and exposes them to others from whom they can learn. Formal training is another way to ensure continuous learning. For managers in particular, continuous learning is essential to develop the competencies needed by generalists who are knowledgeable in several areas, as opposed to specialists who understand only finance, production, marketing, or some other function. Training doesn't benefit just the person on the receiving end, however. When employees are used as the trainers, the teaching experience ensures that people reflect on what they have learned and record it in a systematic form (e.g., lecture notes, visual aids) that is accessible to others. Performance appraisals that include progress achieved on learning goals and pay practices that reward learning also support the behaviors needed in learning organizations.

Partnership, Empowerment, and Community. In learning organizations, everyone is encouraged to find ways to improve products and services and to experiment with new methods to serve the organization. At Yahoo!, a provider of Internet search engines and other services, all employees experiment constantly to satisfy customer demand. Yahoo! receives thousands of suggestions and comments from users who are eager for sites that suit their

■□ *fast fact*

Interest in benchmarking against Walt Disney World in Orlando, Florida is so strong that Disney created the Disney Institute, which offers seminars such as "The Walt Disney Approach to HR Management" to interested professionals.

particular needs. Employees who read these submissions are fully empowered to make changes as they see fit. The sharing of decision making and leadership creates a culture that fully supports the goals and efforts of a learning organization. Empowerment provides a way to integrate tasks and allow employees to buy into the organization's goals. A sense of community and trust is also an important aspect of the culture in learning organizations. Everyone needs to work together, respecting each other and being able to communicate openly and honestly. Problems can't be avoided or handled by just passing them along to another department or up the hierarchy. Conflict and debate are accepted as responsible forms of communication. A sense of community also gives employees the feeling that they're important and are being treated fairly. Employees cooperate because they want to, not because they have to.[13]

Max Depree, former CEO of the Herman Miller Company, believes that leaders in learning organizations should liberate employees. Leaders can do so by removing roadblocks that keep employees from doing their jobs to the best of their abilities and supporting those who experiment with new approaches to satisfy customers. Herb Kelleher, CEO of Southwest Airlines, shares this view. At Southwest, empowered employees are always looking for better ways to meet customers' needs for low-cost, reliable air travel. When clerks suggested doing away with tickets, Kelleher encouraged them to experiment with the innovative idea on selected routes. Now, a customer calling for a reservation receives a PIN number. When the passenger arrives at the gate, an attendant asks for that PIN number and issues a plastic, reusable, boarding pass that's color coded for seat selection (first come, first served). Passengers who need a receipt get one promptly through the mail.[14]

A FRAMEWORK FOR PLANNED CHANGE EFFORTS

Change can be somewhat chaotic or planned and relatively smooth. By its very nature, chaotic change is difficult to describe. Large-scale organizational changes seldom occur without a bit of chaos. Indeed, a few organizations seem to thrive on chaos. But most organizations strive to keep chaos under control during change efforts by imposing some order on the change process. Change is likely to be more orderly when it has been planned. This chapter focuses on planned change, which is the approach to change advocated by most change experts.

Overview of the Phases of Planned Change

The process of planned organizational change comprises the nine steps shown in Exhibit 5.2. Although planned changes don't always proceed exactly as shown, these steps constitute the basic components of a change process, regardless of the sequence.[15] Exhibit 5.2 isn't intended to be a precise map that shows all the alleys and valleys of change. It's more like a snapshot of a famous skyline. You can see most of the landmarks, but you recognize it would take several days to explore them all.

Human Resource Planning in the Context of Change

Human resource issues are a major part of any change effort—whether the change leaders recognize that or not. Changes in how an organization manages human resources seldom occur in isolation, however. HR issues are necessarily considered in the context of issues related to other tangible and

"In IBM, HR is right there at the table whatever the issues are—shutting a plant down, hiring workers, downsizing. We work with management on the decision, help craft the action plan, and then implement it with line management."

**Laura Russell
Resource Program Director
IBM**

Exhibit 5.2
Phases of Planned Change

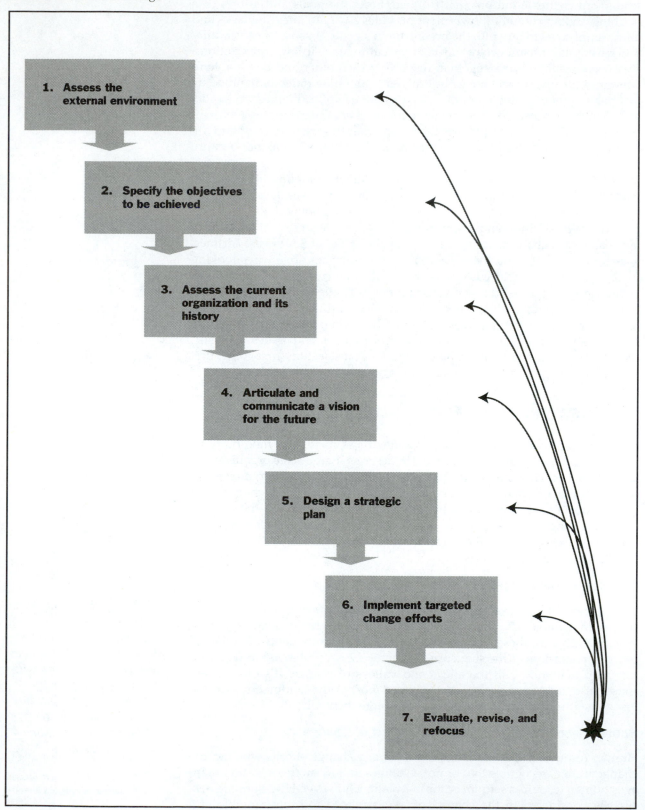

intangible resources, including finances, technology, physical resources, and the firm's current and desired reputation. The term *human resource planning* refers to the efforts of firms to identify the human resource implications of the key issues posed by the changing environment, in order to align their human resources with needs resulting from those issues.[16]

Earlier, in times of greater environmental stability, human resource planning focused on matching human resource demand with human resource supply. At that time, forecasting human resource needs and planning the steps necessary to meet those needs was largely a numbers game. This process typically consisted of developing and implementing plans and programs to ensure that the right number and type of people were available at the right time and place to serve relatively predictable business needs. For example, if the business was growing at ten percent, top management would continue to add to the workforce by ten percent: it worked before, it would work again.

Today, because the environment is changing organizations so dramatically, human resource planning has become a more dynamic, volatile issues game.[17] Yes, human resource planning still involves numbers, but it often also involves

- crafting and communicating mission and value statements;
- ensuring that managers as well as all other employees understand and buy into the process of change;
- systematically designing and aligning HR activities to address the concerns of multiple stakeholders;
- developing methods to monitor the effects of change;
- being alert to signals indicating that plans should be reconsidered or modified; and
- integrating all of these activities with other change efforts in areas such as finance, marketing, and operations.

Effective human resource planning considers change from both long- and short-term perspectives, paralleling the typical cycles for business planning.[18] In many organizations the planning process begins with a vision of where the organization needs to be in five (or even ten) years, and then works back to the implications of those goals for the present. In other organizations, the longer-term view might play little role in the planning process. Several reasons may explain inattention to the long-term, but two common ones are (a) a belief that the future is so unpredictable that trying to predict it is a waste of time, or (b) an implicit assumption that the future will be pretty much the same as the present.

For either long- or short-term planning, the phases of change shown in Exhibit 5.2 seldom unfold linearly. Nevertheless, planning activities generally precede implementation. Although even this distinction—between planning change and implementing change—isn't clear-cut, we use it here to organize our discussion.

PLANNING FOR CHANGE

For complex organizations undergoing large-scale, revolutionary or evolutionary change, the planning process is likely to take several months, and may even stretch across a period of a year or two. In many organizations, preparation and presentation of annual business plans is a ritual that many managers dread. This was true at Coca Cola until CEO M. Douglas Ivester succeeded Roberto Goizueta as Chairman and CEO. Ivester sees his role as managing evolutionary change. He describes it this way: "It's constant layering and refinement, constantly adding polish over a period of time." One of his refinements involves changing the company's approach to planning. In the past, managers spent weeks preparing to give their presentation; some even hired speech coaches. "It was 45 days of hell," according to one participant. Ivester wants to move away from the Broadway-production approach to business planning and replace it with a system of continuous planning and dialog. He hopes to make the organization more flexible and improve its capacity for quick response.[19]

Assess the External Environment and Specify Objectives

The first phase of planning for change involves gathering data to learn about and understand all aspects of the organization's external environment, as depicted in Exhibit 2.1. The four environmental factors most responsible for stimulating organizational change are customers, technology, competitors, and the labor force.

Understanding labor market conditions is essential for organizations that hope to experience significant growth. The Boeing Company, based in Seattle, was hiring 150 to 200 employees each week in an effort to keep up with the growth in demand for aircraft. To meet their needs, they even began hiring people away from some of their suppliers—a move they eventually regretted. Many employers who need skilled workers point their fingers at the educational system as part of the problem. "Cutbacks in education and a lack of emphasis on the skill sets needed for the information age are taking a toll. Finding people with both the aesthetic and technical capabilities is becoming more difficult all the time," according to John Hughes, President of a Los Angeles-based animation company called Rhythm and Hues. A novice digital animator makes about $80,000 a year, which helps explain why Hughes gets about 140 applicants for each job opening, but he says "there are precious few qualified applicants."[20]

Other factors that may pressure organizations to change include globalization and the actions of important stakeholders, such as shareholders, government regulators, unions, and political action groups.[21] Concerns about global competitiveness, for example, are especially salient for large companies ($1 billion in sales or more), those with operations overseas, and those in the manufacturing sector.[22] But this general issue translates into many different change efforts. For some companies, globalization translates into cost-cutting or productivity-enhancing efforts. For other companies, globalization represents an opportunity for rapid growth, and concerns turn to how to staff that growth. At Texas Instruments, improving individual development has been identified by its Strategic Leadership Team as one of the top three business priorities, and each business is evaluated annually on its progress on this and other people issues.[23]

Consideration of technology, the labor force, consumer markets, community and labor relations, economic and political stability, as well as the likely action of competitors and alliance partners, all affect how managers translate their expectations for the future into a set of objectives for the firm. Regardless of the source of pressures for change, it's the strategic implications that give shape to the change effort. Questions to be addressed include: How will the changes affect our ability to compete successfully given our current strategy? Do we need to craft a new strategy? Should we stay in the business we're in? Should we move into other businesses?

■□ *fast fact*

Service Marine Industries, a shipbuilding company, offers $50 just for qualified applicants to show up and take a craft test.

"We want to be here for the long haul, and the only way you do that is by balancing the needs of customers, employees, and shareholders. I know everyone gives that lip service, but we really try to [do it]."

B. J. Smith
Human Resources
Duke Power

To get managers thinking seriously about such questions, Motorola designed coursework experiences at Motorola University, its training and development facility. Over a period of six months, 30 teams of managers spent a week each in places like Mexico City, Sao Paulo, and Santiago. Their assignments included interviewing customers, suppliers, and employees; holding discussions with bankers and government officials; and immersing themselves in the local culture. These experiences helped develop the managers' understanding of how the markets in these locations work, and that enabled them to think more meaningfully about possible new approaches to competing effectively in those markets.[24]

Assess the Organization and Its History

An organizational assessment is often referred to as "organizational diagnosis." The aim of diagnosis is to fully understand the current situation before taking action. The idea that diagnosis should precede action may seem obvious, but its importance is often underestimated.[25]

Review Existing Data.   All too often results-oriented managers begin the change process prematurely and impatiently push for solutions without taking into account their starting point and the history that led to the current situation. Reviewing a variety of information is the best approach during this phase. In addition to information about the supply and productivity of employees, data about skills, competencies, education levels, turnover and absenteeism rates, and attitudes may all be useful. Organizations often hire outside consultants to assist with organizational diagnosis, which may require gathering sensitive information from employees. Outside consultants may be better able to conduct interviews and interpret data in an unbiased manner. In addition, consultants often have the expertise that the organization lacks to conduct and analyze attitude surveys properly.[26]

Short-Term Forecasting.   In addition to assessing the current state of human resources, the assessment phase may include making forecasts about probable conditions for the next one to three years. Forecasts can be used to project the labor supply and demand.[27] Two basic types of forecasting techniques are judgmental and statistical. Exhibit 5.3 provides more details about forecasting techniques. Once made, the supply forecast can be compared with a demand forecast and used as input in setting specific goals for change. Forecasting human resource supply for specific managerial positions in the organization is referred to as replacement planning. It involves developing replacement charts to show the names of the current and potential occupants of positions. Potential promotions can be estimated by the performance levels of employees currently in jobs and their development needs. Incumbents are listed directly under the job title. Individuals likely to fill potential vacancies are listed directly under the incumbent. When planning change efforts, it's useful to know specifically who is likely to be available to help lead the change (or resist it).

Historical Trends.   When change efforts are expected to affect the culture of the organization, an historical perspective is especially important. Change efforts involving increasing and leveraging workforce diversity provide one example of the role of history. Traditional organizational practices tend to minimize cultural diversity in various ways. Recruiting practices emphasize finding candidates from "reliable" sources. Interviews screen out candidates

Exhibit 5.3
HR Forecasting: Sophisticated Methods for an Uncertain Science

A variety of forecasting methods—some simple, some complex—can be used to predict an organization's demand for human resources and the likely supply that'll be available to meet the demand. The type of forecast used depends on the time frame and the type of organization, the organization's size and dispersion, and the accuracy and certainty of available information. The time frame used usually parallels that used in forecasting other business trends. Comparing the demand and supply forecasts then determines the firm's short-, intermediate-, and long-term needs.

Forecasting involves approximations, not absolutes or certainties. The forecast quality depends on the accuracy of information and the predictability of events. The shorter the time horizon, the more predictable the events and the more accurate the information. For example, organizations are generally able to predict how many graduates they need for the coming year, but they're less able to predict how many they'll need for the next five years. And predicting the behavior of new college graduates is easier than predicting the behavior of people at the other end of their employment cycle. You can count on new graduates to be looking for jobs, but at what age should you expect older workers to be thinking about retirement?

A recent study titled "Workforce 2020—Work and Workers in the 21st Century" suggests that patterns of behavior observed in the prior generation will not be repeated by the baby boomers. Baby boomers are healthier and expected to live longer than their parents' generation. They also are less financially secure due to employers' shifting from defined benefit to defined contribution pension plans. Uncertainties about the future viability of the social security system further deteriorate their financial security. Despite this, three-fourths of this generation have no savings goals or retirement goals. So what will they do? When asked now, about half of them *want* to retire by age 55, but few expect to be able to. Nevertheless, predicting the conditions under which they'll keep working, and for how long is sheer guesswork. HR planners often call it "judgmental forecasting."

Judgmental forecasting relies on informed experts (usually managers) to provide data on current and projected productivity levels, market demand, and sales, as well as current staffing levels and mobility information. One way to arrive at estimates is the Delphi technique. At a Delphi meeting, experts take turns at presenting their forecasts and assumptions to the others, who then make revisions in their own forecasts. This combination process continues until a viable composite forecast emerges. The composite may represent specific projections or a range of projections, depending on the experts' positions. Although judgmental forecasts rely on less data than those based on statistical methods such as linear and multiple linear regressions, they tend to dominate in practice.

Even when using the most sophisticated forecasting techniques, the results should be considered rough estimates, at best. Accurate forecasts depend on the ability to predict both changing conditions in the external labor market and current employees' future employment attitudes and behaviors. The reality is that no one has the ability to predict either of these very well! Thus, it's not surprising that there have been many spectacular goofs, some of which have become quite public. For example, Bell Atlantic North launched an aggressive cost-cutting and reengineering effort to boost productivity. In anticipation of a slowdown in demand for new telephone lines, it also offered a generous buy-out package to encourage voluntary attrition. Based on their expectations for productivity gains and the projected decrease in business, they projected a large surplus of labor. But the productivity gains never materialized, and customer demand didn't slow as much as expected. The buy-out package was so attractive that many employees decided to accept it and look for new jobs. Unemployment rates were near record-setting lows, so employees expected to be able to find other work. Suddenly Bell Atlantic North found itself trying to convince the union to agree to increasing pension benefits by 25 percent in an effort to prevent employees from leaving. Suddenly the union was in a position of power, so before signing off on the deal, they demanded that the same generous pension benefits be offered to their colleagues at Bell Atlantic South. By the time the dust settled, this cost-cutting effort cost a bundle.

who "don't fit." Socialization and training practices produce uniform ways of thinking and behaving. Attendance policies and pay practices standardize work schedules. Many such practices were adopted by organizations for good reasons. For example, standardization was viewed as a way to increase efficiency and fair treatment of employees. As organizations consider how to change their cultures to be more accepting of diversity, practices that create uniformity within the organization often become targets. Resistance to the diversity-related changes may then arise not because of negative attitudes about diversity per se, but because managers have been trained over many years to equate uniformity with efficiency, and to value both.

Diagnosis at Sears.   When Sears set out to design a turnaround strategy to pull the firm back from the brink of extinction, it conducted a highly sophisticated organizational diagnosis. Sears knew it needed to improve customer satisfaction, but what caused customers to be satisfied or dissatisfied? Instead of relying on the hunches, Sears conducted research, as described in the feature, Managing Change: Ailing Sears Uses Self-Diagnosis.[28]

MANAGING CHANGE

Ailing Sears Uses Self-Diagnosis

Like many U.S. retailers, it wasn't long ago that Sears had lost track of how important customer satisfaction is to success in this industry (see Chapter 1). When Anthony Rucci, Sears Chief Administrative Officer, walked around and asked employees, "What do you think is the primary thing you get paid to do here?" more than half said it was to protect the assets of the company. No wonder Sears was getting some of the lowest customer satisfaction ratings in the industry. In the mid-1990s, the company committed to regaining its reputation as a world-class retailer. A group of 120 top executives were organized into task forces. Their objective was to define what world class meant—to shareholders, employees, and customers. These task forces helped Sears develop a new vision, which is to become "A compelling place to shop, work, and invest." They also developed measures that the company could use to assess its performance against its vision. Then they developed a theory about what caused performance to rise and fall. Their theory viewed employee and customer attitudes as the primary causes of financial performance.

Their theory seemed reasonable, but they decided they should test it before engaging in a massive change effort. The data came from the records they kept at all 820 of their full-line stores. Included were "13 financial performance measures, hundreds of thousands of employee-satisfaction data points, and millions of data points on customer satisfaction," explains Rucci. They gave their data to statisticians and asked them to test it. The statistical model confirmed the general sequence of effects, but added some more specific information. The two particular types of employee satisfaction that were predictors of how employees behaved with customers were attitudes about the job itself and attitudes about the company. These predicted customer retention and customers recommending Sears to other shoppers. Furthermore, they learned that increasing employee satisfaction by five points on their survey would translate into a two-point increase in customer satisfaction the following quarter, which in turn would improve financial performance by .5 percent. That small percentage improvement is worth millions.

Based on this diagnosis, Sears changed its compensation plan for its top executives, and eventually it'll change the compensation system throughout the company. It also developed a new way to get customer satisfaction data to individual employees. It even instituted town meetings that serve as a forum for educating employees about such things as how the competitive environment has changed during the past few decades and how the revenue generated by the sales employees is related to profit figures.

To learn more about Sears, visit the company home page at
www.sears.com

Articulate and Communicate a Vision for the Future

Successful change efforts are guided by a clear vision for the future. Articulating and communicating the vision is equally important. Until leaders formulate a clear vision and persuade others to join them in being dedicated to that vision, they won't be able to generate the enthusiasm and resources needed for large-scale cultural change. Chris Turner at XBS explained the importance of vision to her change efforts: "We knew the first piece of our change strategy—to create a shared vision. To me, a vision is an ongoing conversation. It's the way we think, individually and collectively, about the community we're creating. What's important to us. How we want to be with each other. It's never frozen, it's never set. It's energy—or spirit."[29]

Vision is also important at Manugistics, where change is constant because of its growth-through-acquisition strategy. The software that Manugistics sells is used to integrate planning activities for product demand, distribution, manufacturing, and transportation throughout the supply chain. It integrates operations both within a firm and among separate entities. Guiding Manugistics through all the changes that have accompanied its growth are its Elements of Excellence.

- We treat others as we would like to be treated.
- Partnership with our clients results in superior products.
- Team success is more important than personal glory.

The company focuses on instilling these values—its vision—in the companies it acquires. Doing so usually means changing the culture of the acquired company. "It's critical that whatever company we're involving ourselves with internationally is going to embrace, can embrace, and must embrace our Elements of Excellence, our values," explains a manager. "Being the same in terms of processes and procedures isn't so important."[30] At XBS and Manugistics, their vision isn't simply a slogan that's printed on corporate souvenirs. It's an internalized standard for what people are striving to achieve, and against which all plans and actions are evaluated.

Design a Strategic Plan

The strategic plan is the blueprint for action. For major change efforts, the strategic plan for the organization as a whole can be quite complex because it includes plans for all levels and all units involved in the change effort. If an organization is structured along functional departments, then each department develops a strategic plan; if it's organized by region, then plans for each region are developed, and so on. Thus, depending on the specific circumstances, the human resources component of the strategic plan may be prepared as a plan for the functional area of human resources management, or HR issues may be addressed within the strategic plan for the entire division. As is true for any organizational effort, the design process must include mechanisms for coordinating all of this planning. Regardless of which approach is used, the following elements should be included:

- a guiding philosophy for the change process,
- full consideration of a wide range of alternative ways to proceed,
- clearly articulated goals and specific measures for monitoring and evaluating progress toward those goals, and
- a time table for implementation and evaluation.

Although there is good evidence showing that investments made in human resource planning produce significant improvements in productivity,[31] there is also good evidence showing that most companies begin major change efforts without a thoughtful, integrated plan.[32]

Guiding Philosophy.   A guiding philosophy sets the tone for how change will occur. If the organization already has identified its core values, then it's important to manage the change process in a way that is consistent with those values. For example, when Consumer Goods Group initiated its change effort, it systematically translated the corporate values into a list of implications for the change effort. Some examples are shown below.[33]

Corporate Values (selected examples)	Implications for Change Process
Integrity	Open and honest communication throughout the change effort, even when the implications were unclear.
Respect for the Individual	Headcount reduction program based solely on voluntary separations and early retirements. No employees were "fired."
Fairness	Employees who accepted voluntary separation packages were treated in the same manner as employees who stayed, not as "second-class" citizens.

In developing a guiding philosophy, three issues that are useful for any organization to address are *communication, involvement,* and *responsibility*.

The importance of a clear vision that serves to act as a guide throughout the change effort has already been noted. But it's important to keep in mind that a vision is useful only to those who see it. Thus, *communicating the vision* should be a top priority. Messages should be sent consistently and repeatedly through varying channels. In describing the change processes that have been underway for several years at American Express, CEO Harvey Golub noted that about the time he was completely sick of repeating the same message, people were just starting to hear it. Recognizing that different people prefer different modes of communication, Golub made sure his vision for change was put in every form possible: memos, employee newspapers, videos, speeches, "white-papers" that provided supporting analysis, and so on.

Just as important as communicating the vision to employees is listening to reactions from employees. GE's well-known "Work-Out" sessions were created for just this purpose. After several years of trying to create change primarily through top-down directives, Jack Welch concluded that top management was too insulated from the reactions of the people working in the trenches. At Work-Out sessions, employees throughout the company are brought together for a session of intense and frank discussion with a selected manager. Trained facilitators help run the sessions, which ensures that employees do most of the talking and managers do most of the listening. Like trips to the gym, Work-Out sessions usually cause managers to work up a good sweat. By creating a new channel for two-way communications, GE also facilitated employee involvement.

For a plan to be effective, those who are affected must buy into it. The best way to ensure that is through *early involvement*. It seems obvious that employees should be involved when planning change, but often this principle is forgotten—even by experienced managers. Xerox has a long record of enlightened diversity management. One of its earliest successes involved a caucus group for African-American employees. In fact, it was so successful that the company decided to create a caucus group for female employees. However, the first attempt to establish a women's caucus—in the mid-1970s—failed. One explanation for the failure was that the women's caucus was designed to duplicate the existing African-American caucus instead of being designed specifically to address the concerns of female employees. A few years later, female employees at Xerox began to establish caucus groups on their own. Eventually there were a dozen different women's caucuses: Some are national, some are regional, and some are specific to one location; some are for minority women and others aren't; some are for exempt employees and others are for nonexempt employees. At Xerox, women have several caucus groups that meet their needs because *they* designed them.

Task forces, focus groups, surveys, hot lines, and informal conversations are just a few of the ways managers can involve employees and other stakeholders in planning change efforts. There is little disagreement among change experts about the importance of involvement. How you get people involved is less important than doing it. However, it *is* important to be clear about what involvement means. If employees are led to believe that they'll have the final say when in fact their opinions are just one of many factors that will affect decisions, involvement can backfire.

Finally, *responsibility* is the third important issue that can be addressed by a guiding philosophy. Questions to deal with here include: Who will ultimately be held responsible for success and failure? If the change is a success, will only managers reap the rewards? If things don't go well, will the lower-level employees be the ones who suffer most? Involvement is likely to be most effective when people are not merely asked for input. They should also have a stake in the outcomes that result.

Considering Alternatives.   For almost any set of objectives, the list of alternative ways to move toward the objective is likely to be long and varied. For example, the Components of Texaco's Cultural Change Initiatives described in Chapter 3 lists many of the alternatives organizations consider when developing a plan to change their approach to managing diversity. As long as the Texaco list is, it represents just a portion of all the things companies are doing in the area of managing diversity.[34]

Some of the alternatives available to employers who face a shortage of skilled workers are listed in Exhibit 5.4. As this exhibit also reveals, every alternative has its disadvantages. Solutions that might work in the short term may create new problems in the long term. Solutions that might work in the long term may do little to address short-term needs. Similarly, different alternatives have different advantages. Some alternatives contribute by lowering costs, while others contribute more by increasing skill levels. For example, retaining current workers is an excellent way to reduce costs. According to a study of over 200 companies, conducted by consulting firm William M. Mercer, turnover costs reach $40,000 per person for 10 percent of all vacancies when you take into account lost productivity due to the vacancy, search fees, management time used to interview, and training costs. For 30 percent of all vacancies, the costs range between $10,000 and $40,000.[35] For highly technical work in fields that change rapidly, however, the skills of new college graduates may be much more current than those of current employees.

When developing a strategic plan, all possible alternatives should be considered, along with the pros and cons. Major issues usually require multi-pronged solutions. All chosen solutions can't usually be implemented en masse, however, so priorities must be decided upon, taking into account both short- and long-term needs. The feature, Managing Strategically: GE Medical Learns How to Fill Jobs, describes how one company deals with its need for more skilled workers.[36]

Goals and Measures.   As the GE Medical example illustrates, effective change efforts have a clear link to the business strategy. GE did not simply need to hire more technical workers, it needed workers with skills that precisely matched the type of work that would be done for the specific new products being developed. Because the company is always innovating, it was important to have very specific recruiting goals. And because cost considerations were also important, new approaches to measuring the effectiveness of the new approach were important.

> *"Being a strategic leader means you can show evidence that you have actually influenced the direction of the business."*
>
> **Chuck Nielson**
> **Vice President, HR**
> **Texas Instruments**

Exhibit 5.4
Alternatives to Coping With Labor Shortages

Possible Solution to a Labor Shortage	Possible Negative Consequences
Raise base wages to attract more applicants	May attract more applicants, but new applicants may not be any more qualified. Recruiting costs per hire go up as number of applicants to be screened goes up.
Offer more financial incentives in an effort to motivate employees to boost their productivity	If productivity increases don't keep up with increased labor costs, margins will shrink unless consumers are willing to pay higher prices.
Reduce turnover rates to lessen the need for new hires	May drive up labor costs if wages tend to increase with time at the company. Too little turnover may stifle creativity. Skills obsolescence may become a problem.
Hire people without the skills needed and train them	Productivity of new hires is low. Increased supervision is required of new workers, which raises costs. Can be costly, takes time, and, once trained, workers may leave to work for competitors.
Buy up other companies to acquire their workforce	The challenge of integrating the acquired company may cause productivity declines in the short-term. Success rates for mergers and acquisitions are only about 50 percent.
Buy new technologies that reduce the number of people needed	Major changes in technology require major organizational changes, which take time. New technologies may require even higher levels of skill to operate.
Utilize foreign labor markets	The organization learning curve is steep for domestic firms with no prior international experience. Competition for labor in the global market may be just as stiff as in the domestic market.
Make business decisions that reduce the need for more skilled workers	May be possible, but would probably involve major changes in strategy and even changing the businesses in which the company competes.

MANAGING STRATEGICALLY

GE Medical Learns How to Fill Jobs

A recent survey by the American Management Association found that 60 percent of companies are finding it takes longer to fill professional and technical jobs now than it did three years ago; only 9 percent of companies say they can fill these jobs faster now than in the past. Research shows that understaffing is associated with lower group performance for professional workers, so ignoring the problem doesn't appear to be a good alternative for this particular challenge. GE Medical needed a solution that would improve its ability to attract the workers it needs. How did this company in Milwaukee, Wisconsin manage to hire as many as 500 new technical workers per year, while cutting the cost of hiring 17 percent and reducing the time it takes to fill positions by 25 percent? Why would qualified technical workers choose to work for this company instead of Intel, Microsoft, or Hewlett Packard?

According to Stephen Pascott, head of GE Medical staffing and leadership development, it wasn't the money. Many of the people he hires could have gone to work for a high-tech start up or an established firm with generous stock options and have a much greater chance of becoming a youthful millionaire. So GE needed to find people that would prefer to use their talents to invent lifesaving devices. To develop its approach to finding such workers, the HR group began with an internal benchmarking study of procurement and supplier management practices elsewhere in the business. "We know everything about acquiring wires and screws and boards and computers. But our most important asset is the human asset, and we [didn't] measure that process. It's shame on us as HR people," Pascott recalled.

Learning from how the company acquired the physical supplies it needed, a new staffing process was developed. The process begins with a companywide "multigenerational product plan" that specifies exactly what skills will be needed for each phase of a product's development and production life cycle. This is then used to prepare a multigenerational staffing plan to match the skills needed. For example, a CT product plan may indicate that in two years, the company will need 30 "absolute algorithm" experts to write code for real-time imaging. Such specs are then used throughout the recruiting process—by the internal staff as well as professional recruiters who work with the firm. "We get a real good spec—not just for technical skills but also for interpersonal skills," explained professional recruiter Ron Roth.

To further increase the efficiency of the recruiting process, GE Medical has made it clear that it wants to work only with the most talented suppliers—whether that means schools, professional recruiting firms, or employee referrals.

Recruiters.   To judge the efficiency of professional recruiters, GE calculates yield figures. To improve recruiters' performance, GE provides feedback on why they didn't choose to hire someone they interviewed, and they offer bonuses to the most productive recruiters.

School Internship Programs.   To improve school-based recruiting, GE revamped its summer intern program. Former summer interns are twice as likely to accept a job offer as other applicants, so hiring interns is more efficient than using other sources of talent. To get more interns procedures were developed to weed out bosses who used interns for menial tasks like photocopying and put managers in a position of having to earn good evaluations from past interns in order to be able to get more interns in the future.

Employee Referrals.   After some research, GE Medical discovered that resumés submitted by people who were referred to the company by an employee were ten times more likely to lead to an interview and an eventual hire. To increase this source of resumés, small incentives like gift certificates are offered simply for referring a candidate to the company. If a referral results in a hire, the employee receives up to $3000, depending on the category of talent being hired. Compared to headhunter fees of $15,000 to $20,000, that's a real bargain for the company.

When goals related to recruiting and hiring are established, measures that might be used to assess progress toward goals can include the number of minimally qualified applicants who apply for jobs, the skill levels of applicants, the length of time needed to fill vacancies, yield rates such as those used by GE Medical, turnover rates for employees who have been with the company less than a year, and so on. Such measures can generally be created and tracked with ease. For some other types of goals, measures of progress are less easily developed.

Customer satisfaction. In many companies, change efforts are stimulated by the company's desire to better satisfy customers. A study by The Conference Board found that customer-driven changes were common in the manufacturing and service sectors. Exhibit 5.5 summarizes some of the findings from that study.[37] For the goals listed, how would you measure the organization's progress?

Family friendly. Hiring more workers is one way to deal with a labor shortage. Increasing the productivity of the current workforce is another. At Xerox, retaining productive workers is an important goal, and it's supported by their system called "Managing for Results." Each manager, supervisor, and front-line associate has goals, action plans, and performance measures that flow directly from the company's strategic goals. Monthly customer reviews help the company assess employees. Xerox's *family-friendly policies*—which include child-care subsidies, leaves of absence, and flexible work arrangements, among other things—are an essential part of their approach to maximizing results. These policies incorporated what the company had

Exhibit 5.5

The Most Common Goals When Changing HR Practices

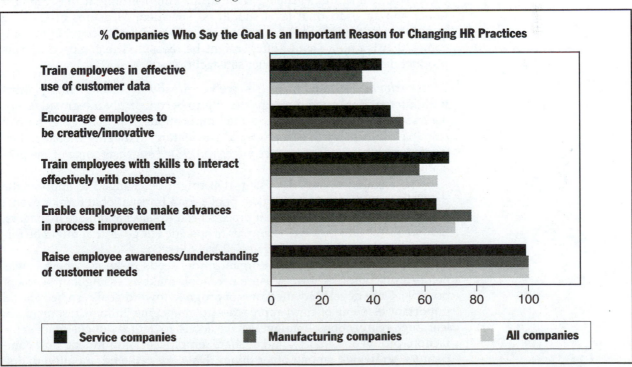

learned from its research on the causes of inefficiency and nonproductive work practices. By adopting the new policies that addressed work-family conflicts, Xerox reaped the benefits of reduced absenteeism and increased customer satisfaction. Every year, when *Working Mother* magazine publishes a list of the best companies for working mothers, Xerox is on the list, and being on that list is considered important to the company's success.[38] In this example, goals might include improving productivity and becoming an "employer of choice" as a means to facilitate recruiting efforts. As indicators of the effectiveness of the changes, Xerox used objective measures, such as their ranking in *Working Mother* magazine, absenteeism rates, and customer satisfaction data.

Team Effectiveness.   As another example, suppose an organization is convinced of the need to change from its old command-and-control management approach to an empowerment approach. The long-term vision includes an organization run by self-managed teams. How will the organization know when they've succeeded with this effort? How will they know if they're making progress toward it? Will they simply count how many people are working in teams instead of working alone? Probably not.

More important than how many teams are in place is how well they function. But what does *that* mean? As Exhibit 5.6 shows, team functioning includes many things.[39] No team is likely to be outstanding on all dimensions of performance that might be measured. In order to decide which aspects of team performance to measure, goals for the teams must first be established. These goals, in turn, should reflect strategic concerns. Then appropriate measures can be selected. If reducing cost and speeding up order fulfillment are important to the strategy, one set of measures might be suggested. But if the strategy calls for teams that can develop creative solutions, a very different set of measures would be appropriate. Or, perhaps the vision is to become a learning organization, and teams are viewed as a vehicle to facilitate learning. Then goals that indicate learning at the organizational and/or individual level should be specified. Measures of learning might then be developed (e.g., product and customer knowledge) or the outcomes that learning should affect might be measured (e.g., speed of new product development or customer satisfaction).

Transnational Organization.   As we've already described, many firms with international operations are striving to become truly integrated, *transnational organizations*. What are the implications for managing human resources of this type of change effort? The feature, Managing Globalization: Goals for Managing Human Resources (p. 198),[40] suggests some of the possibilities.

One element of the HR system that might be changed to support the development of a managerial talent pool—for a transnational firm or even a domestic firm—is the assessment process used to select and place managers. Exhibit 5.7 (p. 198) provides examples of specific HR goals that might be formulated to meet a variety of strategic objectives.[41]

To judge improvement, an organization needs to know where it was before and where it is now. Measurement tools make assessing improvement possible. Once developed, measures of progress toward goals can become an important element of new approaches to managing human resources. In learning organizations, employees have access to data about customer satisfaction, profits and losses, market share, employee commitment, and competitors' strategies, among other things. Data are gathered, monitored, dis-

"I'm more interested in anecdotal evidence than hard data. If you get 1,000 anecdotes and they all begin to fit together, then you've got a pattern that makes sense."

Chris Turner
Learning Person
XBS

Exhibit 5.6
Possible Goals for Work Teams and Team Members

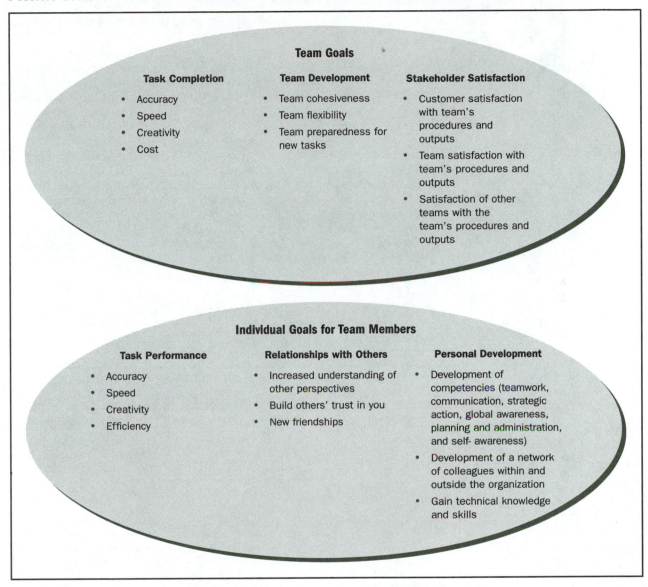

seminated and used throughout the organization. At Springfield Remanufacturing, managers make available all production and financial figures, and employees are encouraged to ask tough questions about them. Employees also have access to daily printouts that provide detailed cost information on all products. In learning organizations, the days of managers hoarding information are long gone.[42] The motivational value of goals accompanied by feedback about progress toward the goals is well documented by years of organizational research.[43] Many managers also understand this basic principle and use it to create organizational change. As described in Chapter 1, Gordon Bethune is one example of a CEO who used a systematic approach to goal setting as part of the massive organizational change effort that helped Continental Airlines go "From Worst to First."

MANAGING GLOBALIZATION

Goals for Managing Human Resources

As organizations globalize, managing the human system is a major challenge. The question isn't *what* needs to be done—there's general agreement on the need to integrate the diverse parts and leverage the full pool of human talent—but *how* to do it. Meeting the leadership challenge is often a top priority. When the transnational operations are in place, who will manage them? Who will be available for the senior leadership roles, and how can the firm ensure that these people will have the competencies needed? As Exhibit A, below, suggests, managers who competently perform traditional international roles can do so without having developed the skills needed in a transnational organization.

Because transnational organizations are a relatively recent development, there are few managers in the world with fully developed transnational skills. Even if an organization was prepared to pay any price to hire such managers, it would not be able to find them. They have to be grown by the organization, and then retained long enough to reap the rewards of a long-term investment.

Developing transnational managers requires a transnational human resource system. Such systems

- approach all HR activities (e.g., recruitment, hiring, training) with a global frame of mind, not from the perspective of a particular region or country;
- yield a portfolio of mobile executives and managers that is just as multinational as the firm's production, financing, sales, and profits; and

Exhibit A   Examples of Differing Skill Levels Needed by International and Transnational Managers

Skill	International Managers	Transnational Managers
Global Perspective	Understand a single foreign country and manage relationships between headquarters and that country.	Understand worldwide business and manage relationships among parts located in dozens of countries.
Synergistic Learning	Work with and coach people in each foreign culture separately or sequentially.	Work with and facilitate learning among people from many cultures simultaneously.
Collaboration	Interact within clearly defined hierarchies of structural and cultural dominance.	Interact with all foreigners as equals and facilitate the same behavior in others.
Career Perspective	Expatriation and repatriation occur primarily to get a specific job done.	Transpatriation experiences are accepted in anticipation of long-term career and organizational development.
Cross-cultural Interaction	Use cross-cultural skills primarily on foreign assignments.	Use cross-cultural skills on a daily basis throughout one's career.

- include decision making and planning processes that reflect and achieve synergy with those of all the countries represented in the company. Practices from the headquarter country are not simply exported and adjusted. Instead, new practices are created to fit the transnational environment.

According to one study of 1500 executives in 50 different transnational companies, the degree to which the human resource system is transnational lags far behind that of the other systems. For example, on average, these firms generated 40 percent of their business from other countries, yet only 8 percent of their top 100 executives were from other countries. Furthermore, only one-third of the executives in the study reported having any expatriate experience and less than 20 percent spoke a second language. Clearly, to begin developing their talent pool of the future, these firms must examine all of the HR activities with the goal of developing new practices to encourage and support the development of transnational leaders.

Exhibit 5.7
Translating Strategic Concerns into Specific HR Goals: Selected Examples.

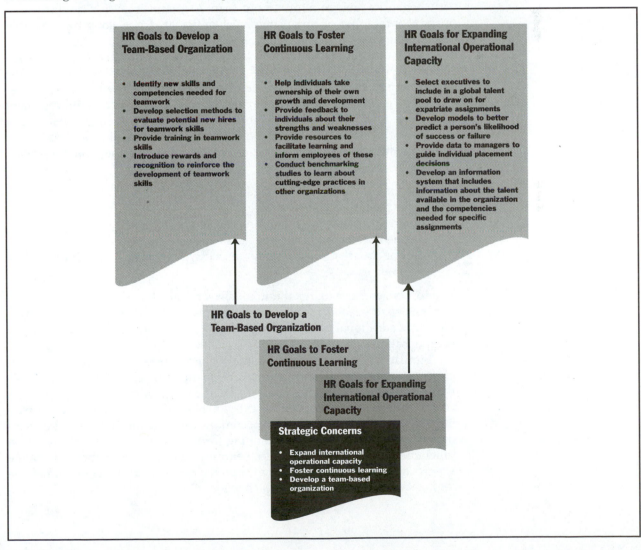

HR Goals to Develop a Team-Based Organization

- Identify new skills and competencies needed for teamwork
- Develop selection methods to evaluate potential new hires for teamwork skills
- Provide training in teamwork skills
- Introduce rewards and recognition to reinforce the development of teamwork skills

HR Goals to Foster Continuous Learning

- Help individuals take ownership of their own growth and development
- Provide feedback to individuals about their strengths and weaknesses
- Provide resources to facilitate learning and inform employees of these
- Conduct benchmarking studies to learn about cutting-edge practices in other organizations

HR Goals for Expanding International Operational Capacity

- Select executives to include in a global talent pool to draw on for expatriate assignments
- Develop models to better predict a person's likelihood of success or failure
- Provide data to managers to guide individual placement decisions
- Develop an information system that includes information about the talent available in the organization and the competencies needed for specific assignments

HR Goals to Develop a Team-Based Organization

HR Goals to Foster Continuous Learning

HR Goals for Expanding International Operational Capacity

Strategic Concerns

- Expand international operational capacity
- Foster continuous learning
- Develop a team-based organization

Timetables.   In the early 1990s, L. L. Bean began a major change effort to improve customer service. After he had five years of experience under his belt, the senior vice president of operations was asked, "If you had to start your reengineering all over again, what would you do differently?" His reply, "We would specify a time limit on when we needed an end result. We should have set specific dates for individuals and departments to make the changes."[44]

Change is tough work that often involves making difficult and sometimes painful decisions. If people can put it off, they will. Building deadlines and scheduled check points into the change process is one way to keep the process moving ahead. The challenge is to set deadlines that are challenging but achievable. Realistic expectations about how quickly change will occur are important to the long-term success of change efforts. Changes designed to help employees balance their work and nonwork commitments might be effective within only a year or two. More fundamental changes can require much longer. Usually even changes that seem relatively simple occur more slowly than expected. Xerox began changing its culture to be more receptive of diversity more than 30 years ago and continues to do so. Digital Equipment Corporation (DEC), another leader in terms of managing diversity, began its change efforts more than 20 years ago.[45] It's doubtful that managers in either of these companies anticipated how long their companies' change efforts would continue to evolve.

When a computer manufacturing company that produced leading-edge specialty products for business decided to change its strategy to include the consumer market, it knew it would also need managers with a different set of skills. The company estimated it would need five years to build the talent pool. The first year was spent analyzing the environment, developing a model of the skills that would be needed, and developing a strategy for building the talent pool. The initiatives taken during the next four years included

- assessing their current managers to determine who had the skills needed for the new business strategy,
- training managers on the meaning of the new strategy,
- externally recruiting new managers with the needed skills, and
- meeting quarterly with senior executives to keep them informed of progress.

In addition, as these planned initiatives were rolled out, it became clear that changes were needed in most other aspects of the HR system, including a variety of additional training programs, the organizational structure, and the compensation system.[46]

Similarly, transforming an international organization into a transnational one is a very long-term project. Complete cultural transformations like these take many years and many different change initiatives occur over the course of those years. Sometimes the slowness of change is merely frustrating. At other times, unrealistic expectations cause change efforts to be abandoned prematurely. Whether planning for two years or twenty, however, a timetable helps guide the process. Learning from the experiences of change experts and other organizations may be the best way to develop a timetable for creating major organizational changes.

IMPLEMENTING CHANGE

The focus so far has been on developing a plan. Eventually, the time comes to move from planning to action. We turn next to issues that arise when plans are taken out of the drafting room and onto the shop floor.

The Change Has Already Started

If the people who are responsible for drawing up the blueprint for change have followed the principles of communication and involvement as part of their guiding philosophy, the implementation stage is actually already well under way by the time the plans have been fully developed. People already have a good grasp of the vision—they had to understand it in order to be involved in the planning process. Although a leadership team may have been responsible for getting the plan put together, many of the specifics of the plan (goals, timetables) were developed using substantial input from the people who will be expected to implement the plan. If honest two-way communication has occurred throughout the planning process, major obstacles to implementing change have already been identified and removed. If empowered employees have been energized by the challenges identified, some are already experimenting with new approaches to their work. To the extent this is true, problems of resistance—the major barrier to implementing change—will be lessened. Even in the best of circumstances, however, pockets of resistance will be found.

Resistance to Change

Few planned organizational change efforts proceed smoothly. Most run into some amount of resistance. The various forms that resistance can take include immediate criticism, malicious compliance, sabotage, insincere agreement, silence, deflection, and in-your-face defiance.[47] The reasons for such resistance include fear, misunderstandings, and interorganizational agreements.[48]

Fear. Some people resist change because they fear that they'll be unable to develop the competencies required to be effective in the new situation. When Mercedes-Benz Credit Corporation set out to restructure its operations in the United States, employees seemed to have good reason to be fearful of the future. Weren't layoffs sure to follow? The company's president, Georg Bauer, knew that fear could be a problem and would make getting needed help from employees difficult. "It was absolutely essential to establish a no-fear element in this whole change process," he said. Rather than resist change, he wanted employees to help create a new, more efficient organization by expressing their ideas about where to cut and how to do work differently. Besides empowering employees to make decisions about how to change their work, he offered an incentive to convince employees that even cutting their own jobs wouldn't harm them financially. The incentive was to offer the security of a new—and probably better—job to anyone bold enough to eliminate his or her current position. The approach worked. Four entire layers of management vanished at the suggestion of the employees themselves.[49]

Misunderstandings. People resist change when they don't understand its implications. Unless quickly addressed, misunderstandings and lack of trust build resistance. Top managers must be visible during the change process to spell out clearly the new direction for the organization and what it will mean

> *"By not spending a lot of time trying to force a square peg into a round hole, you can concentrate your efforts on the vast group of people who can change and want to change but require some help to do so."*
>
> **Louis V. Zambello, III**
> **Senior Vice President, Operations**
> **L. L. Bean**

for everyone involved. Getting employees to discuss their problems openly is crucial to overcoming resistance to change.[50]

Managers sometimes initiate change believing that anyone with the same information would make the same decision. This assumption isn't always correct. Often top-level managers see change as a way to strengthen the organization. They may also believe that change will offer them new opportunities to develop their own competencies as they tackle new challenges. In contrast, employees may view proposed changes as upsetting the implicit and explicit compacts between themselves and their employer. In particular, they may expect increased workloads and longer hours to be the only rewards for staying around to help implement a major organizational change.[51]

Interorganizational Agreements. Labor contracts are the most common examples of interorganizational agreements that create resistance and limit options for change. Actions once considered major rights of management (e.g., to hire and fire, assign personnel to jobs, and promote) have become subjects of negotiation. Advocates of change also may find their plans delayed because of agreements with competitors, suppliers, public officials, or contractors. Although agreements sometimes are ignored or violated, the legal costs of settlement can be expensive.

When Sir Colin Marshall, CEO of British Airways (BA), declared that the company would become the "world's favourite airline," many employees saw little reason to change. They felt secure in their jobs at this government-subsidized airline. Before its turnaround in the late 1980s, the airline had been dubbed by customers as BA for "Bloody Awful." Sir Colin needed to convince BA's employees that their jobs would be secure only when their customers were satisfied. Being best in customers' eyes meant everything from making sure that the concourse lights were always on to making sure that meals on short flights were easy to deliver and unwrap. It also meant that employees had to change their attitudes toward customers from that of moving "packages" to a concern for passengers as human beings.

To make the changes needed, customer-service training was provided to all employees. Flight crews attended language-training classes to help them become proficient in French, Italian, German, or Spanish. The trainers themselves were crew members who flew half the year and taught the other half. Thus they knew and understood customer-service problems, the questions most likely to be asked, and the vocabulary most often used. This program helped British Airways attain its goal of being one of the best airlines in the world.[52]

Reducing Resistance. Resistance to change will never disappear completely; in fact, some resistance to change may actually be useful. The first lesson in reducing resistance is to not be afraid of it. Employees can operate as a check-and-balance mechanism to ensure that management properly plans and implements change. Justifiable resistance that causes management to think through its proposed changes more carefully may result in better decisions. One particularly useful method for managing resistance is participation. Research shows that participation usually leads to commitment, especially when it's voluntary.[53] Exhibit 5.8 lists several other methods for reducing resistance to change, along with some of their advantages and drawbacks.[54] The feature, Managing Teams: Training for Change at Motorola (p. 204), describes how one company used training to address the problem of resistance to change.[55]

Exhibit 5.8
Methods of Overcoming Resistance to Change

Method	Situations	Advantages	Drawbacks
Education	When there is a lack of information or inaccurate information and analysis.	Once persuaded, people will often help implement the change.	Can be very time-consuming if many people are involved.
Participation	When the initiators do not have all the information they need to design and others have considerable power to resist.	People who participate will be committed to implementing change, and any relevant information they have will be integrated into the change plan.	Can be very time-consuming if participants design an inappropriate change.
Negotiation	When someone or some group will clearly lose out in a change and that person or group has considerable power to resist.	Sometimes it's a relatively easy way to avoid resistance.	Can be expensive in many cases if it alerts others to negotiate for compliance.
Cooptation	When other tactics will not work or are too expensive.	It can be a relatively quick and inexpensive solution to resistance problems.	Can lead to future problems if people feel manipulated.

Evaluate, Revise, Refocus

When a company offers a product to the external marketplace, it's almost certain to evaluate the success of that product using some type of objective indicator. Likewise, the success of products and services offered in the company's internal marketplace should be monitored closely. At this point, the goals for change and the measures developed to track progress toward goals again come into play. The measures define the criteria to be used in evaluating whether a program or initiative is successful or is in need of revision. For example, if personal self-development is the only goal one hopes to achieve from holding diversity-awareness workshops, then asking employees whether the workshop experience was valuable may be the only data that should be collected. However, when large investments are made for the purposes of reducing turnover, attracting new or different employees to the firm, or improving team functioning, or all three, then data relevant to these objectives should be examined. A human resource information system (HRIS) facilitates evaluation by allowing for more thorough, rapid, and frequent collection and dissemination of data. Based on what is learned, people can make informed decisions about whether to stay the course as planned, or revisit and perhaps revise the original plan. Overall objectives for the change effort are not likely to be changed at this point, but new goals might be added and timetables might be adjusted.

Change expert John Kotter believes that change can be facilitated by virtually guaranteeing that the evaluation process will produce some positive results, which can then be used as a cause for celebration. He calls these "short-term wins." The slowness of change can be demotivating. After sev-

MANAGING TEAMS

Training for Change at Motorola

Christopher Galvin, CEO of Motorola, is a firm believer in teamwork. As the company's third-generation leader, he has been reshaping a corporate culture long based on internal competition. His predecessors were so confident that competitive behavior was needed for success that they urged units to try to steal business away from each other. From a company where employees felt that the different business units were best described as "a loose confederation of warring camps," Galvin wanted to build a global giant with a cohesive strategy and corporate culture to match. Galvin has succeeded in instilling a culture based on teamwork. As general manager of paging during the 1980s, he used teamwork and quality improvement techniques to reduce from twenty-eight to two days the time required to manufacture pagers. In the mid-1980s Galvin coined the phrase "an answering machine in your pocket" and used it as the vision statement for his group's goal. Since then, pagers and paging devices have become an integral part of the 1990s telecommunications revolution. No longer limited to medical doctors and emergency personnel, these small devices are used by dual-career families who need to maintain contact with each other and their children, salespeople who must be on call to their customers, and millions of others in all walks of life.

At Motorola's plant in Boynton Beach, Florida, all pagers are custom built in unique job lots for the purchaser. They are built by robots and teams of workers. The robots tune the crystals inside the pagers to the proper frequencies and inspect the finished products. The workers monitor the robots. Several minifactories exist within the larger "plant." Each factory produces a specialized type of pager. One group, for example, builds a wristwatch pager that has little attraction for the Western consumer but that is extremely popular with the Japanese.

This plant didn't always function as well as it does now. In 1987, the Paging Division was producing large numbers of defective products. The company decided to use its Boynton Beach plant as an experiment. To be fair to those who were going to become part of the experiment, all employees were permitted to stay on the payroll as long as they met the basic human resources requirement of third-grade reading and writing skills. Rather than fire those who didn't have the skills needed to work with the high-tech robots, the company trained workers in how to monitor robots and take full responsibility for the product as it was assembled. Their quality target was to lower the defect level to *six sigma* (about one defect in 14 million pagers).

As the number of defects fell toward targeted levels, management expanded the project to include interdepartmental teams that volunteered to solve problems involving nonproduction issues. Now Galvin is pushing the rest of Motorola to work together as a team. His brother Michael observes, "Chris is very, very committed to the team process. He's always saying that the essence of successful partnerships in life, whether it's marriage, business, or sports, is trust."

To learn more about Motorola, visit the company's homepage at
www.motorola.com

eral months of all-out effort, employees will be almost certainly be asked to rededicate themselves for another several months of effort. Without some evidence that the new ways of doing things are paying off, too many people may give up and join the ranks of the resisters. Rather than leave to chance the question of whether there will be anything to celebrate after a year or two of effort, Kotter suggests specifically assigning a few excellent people to the task of creating a short-term win. And when they meet the challenge, be sure to involve everyone in the celebration.[56]

Whether or not the evaluation of progress against goals is accompanied by celebration, pausing to reflect on the process is an essential part of any effective change process. It ensures the change process will be self-correcting and should prevent most misjudgments made during the planning process from turning into major fiascos.

CREATING READINESS FOR CHANGE

Organizational change is a complex undertaking. For the process to lead to desired outcomes, each step must be completed satisfactorily, even if the order of the steps is different from that shown in Exhibit 5.2. There is one additional step that organizations can take to improve the effectiveness of their change efforts, however. This step—creating readiness for change— should be taken even before the decision to undertake a specific change has been made. Of course that takes great forethought and planning!

For organizations that anticipate the need for eventual change, taking steps to enhance organizational readiness for change is a wise investment. Exhibit 5.9 describes several actions that managers should take in order to create an organization that is in a continual state of readiness.[57]

Exhibit 5.9
Guidelines for Creating Organizational Readiness for Change

Develop a Pro-Learning Orientation Among Employees

- Provide frequent opportunities for employees to take responsibility for problem identification and problem solving.
- Develop open communication channels and ensure that they're used frequently to inform employees of organizational successes and failures.
- Do everything possible to keep employees informed of customers' preferences and the evaluations of the services and products offered by the organization.
- Encourage small-scale experimentation to produce solutions to emerging problems before large-scale solutions are needed.

Develop a Resilient Workforce

- Use resilience-to-change as a basis for hiring and promotion decisions.
- Educate the workforce about the fundamentals of organizational change processes.
- Train employees to understand the symptoms and causes of resistance and cynicism, and train managers in effective means for reducing resistance and cynicism.
- Celebrate successful change efforts—large and small—to build confidence in the organization's capacity for change.

Build the Architecture to Support Change Initiatives

- Develop a means for recording lessons learned from change efforts and ensuring these lessons are used to guide future change efforts.
- Train managers in structured approaches to change rather than allowing them to rely on their intuition and instincts.
- Create opportunities for employees to work in cross-functional teams as a means of developing the teamwork and communication competencies often needed for large-scale change efforts.
- Identify key measures that can be used to regularly measure organizational performance. Regularly assess the organization against these measures to establish a baseline against which future change can be assessed.

Working together, managers and HR professionals can prepare their organizations for successful organizational change by following these guidelines prior to initiating a change effort. The objective should be to ensure that the organization maintains a state of readiness for change so that it can move quickly and effectively when major changes are needed and then learn from its experiences.[58] Like all other activities involved in successful organizational change, developing a state of organizational readiness requires collaboration. The many opportunities for collaboration among line managers, HR professionals, and employees during change processes are described in The HR Triad: Partnership Roles and Responsibilities for Planned Organizational Change.

SUMMARY

A dynamic external environment creates the need for both evolutionary and revolutionary change in most organizations. Increasingly, employees are being asked to expect and accept continual change as part of their normal work situation. Learning organizations thrive in such an environment. They're adept at learning from the past, transferring learning from one part of the organization to the rest of the organization, and learning from other organizations. For them, a capability for successful change and continuous learning is a sustainable competitive advantage. Essential to this capability is maintaining a constant state of readiness for change. This involves developing a prolearning attitude among employees, developing a resilient workforce, and building an architecture that provides support for change initiatives.

Most large-scale organizational changes affect the people in the organization. Therefore, the process of planning for organizational change should almost always include planning for the human resource implications of change. The term human resource planning refers to the efforts of firms to identify the short- and long-term human resource implications of the key issues created by the changing environment. A variety of sophisticated statistical forecasting techniques can be used when the focus of HR planning is on ensuring the right numbers of capable people are available to work at pre-specified times and places. But many of the issues that require HR planning are not easily quantified. Thus, managers and HR professionals also must become adept at using more subjective, qualitative data as part of their planning efforts.

Planning and implementing change involve several phases of activity, which can be described linearly but seldom are experienced linearly. Significant change almost always involves unforeseeable sources of resistance and unintended consequences. Although these can't be avoided, their detrimental effects can be minimized by involving the entire organization in planning for and evaluating the change process. Managers and other employees who'll be affected by a major organizational change should be involved in developing a strategic plan and in monitoring the outcomes of changes made. Monitoring the key indicators of effectiveness throughout the change process makes it possible for an organization to quickly detect when corrective action is needed, as well as detect when key milestones have been reached and can be celebrated.

THE HR TRIAD: PARTNERSHIP ROLES AND RESPONSIBILITIES FOR PLANNED ORGANIZATIONAL CHANGE

Line Managers	HR Professionals	Employees
Articulate the types of learning that are important to the organization's long-term survival and effectiveness.	Develop and oversee the implementation of HR practices that enable and encourage organizational learning.	Engage in activities that ensure personal learning.
Learn about effective change processes and act as a role model for effective learning and change.	Seek out opportunities for the HR unit to learn from other units within the firm.	Willingly share own knowledge and pass own skills on to others.
Identify opportunities for useful benchmarking and participate in benchmarking studies.	Identify opportunities for useful benchmarking and participate in benchmarking studies.	Identify opportunities for useful benchmarking and participate in benchmarking studies.
In the early phases of planned change, participate by providing information about the current environment and forecasting the labor needs.	Identify the need for change and take responsibility for managing the organization's HR planning activities, including forecasting labor demands and supplies.	Provide input during the early phases of planning for change as needed.
Participate in the process of generating and evaluating alternative approaches to change.	Participate in the process of generating and evaluating alternative approaches to change.	Participate in the process of generating and evaluating alternative approaches to change.
With HR professionals, participate in the development of specific HR goals.	With line managers, participate in the development of specific HR goals.	Understand the firm's HR goals and their implications for your current job and future opportunities in the firm.
Collaborate in the collection and interpretation of data to assess progress toward HR goals.	Develop, collect, and analyze measures to assess progress toward HR goals.	Collaborate in the collection and interpretation of data to assess progress toward HR goals.
Communicate constantly with employees concerning planned changes using formal and informal means.	Work with line managers to develop and disseminate formal communications about planned changes in HR activities.	Take personal responsibility for ensuring own understanding of planned changes and their implications.
	Respond promptly and candidly to questions about planned changes in HR activities.	

TERMS TO REMEMBER

Benchmarking

Change goals and measures

Continuous change

Diagnosis

Evolutionary change

Guiding philosophy

Human resource planning

Learning organizations

Phases of planned change

Readiness for change

Resistance to change

Revolutionary change

Short-term forecasting

Strategic plan

Timetables

Vision

DISCUSSION QUESTIONS

1. Review Chapters 2 through 4, which describe several aspects of the external and internal environments of organizations. Which aspects of the environment are more likely to lead to revolutionary vs. evolutionary change? Explain.

2. What are the characteristics of a learning organization? What are some of the key employee behaviors needed in an organization that seeks to learn?

3. A thorough approach to planning for change can take a great deal of time. When time is short, which steps in the planning process can be eliminated most readily? What are the potential risks of skipping these steps? Explain your logic.

4. Describe one of your own experiences with organizational change. What evidence of resistance was evident during the change? What were the reasons for the resistance you observed? What could have been done to reduce the resistance?

5. Throughout your career you will often be expected to participate in evolutionary and revolutionary organizational changes. What can you personally do now to be prepared for being effective during such change situations?

PROJECTS TO EXTEND YOUR LEARNING

1. **Managing Strategically.** *FastCompany* publishes a business magazine that describes itself as the "Handbook of the Business Revolution." This company is based on two ideas: A global revolution is underway that is changing the world of business, and business is changing the world. The company's founders believe that the current revolution will be as far-reaching as the industrial revolution. Besides having fun, *FastCompany*'s founders set out to chronicle this revolution and stimulate conversations about it. Through their magazine, they hoped to disseminate innovative best practices and leading ideas, identify the values of the revolution, debunk old myths, and discover new legends. What are the newest ideas

being discussed in this handbook? What are the implications of these ideas for managing human resources? To find out, visit the electronic version of *FastCompany* at
www.fastcompany.com

2. **Managing Change.** The process of organizational change requires extensive communication among all parts of an organization. For global organizations, communications can be particularly challenging. First, explain why communication is important to change efforts and describe how differences in cultures, locations, and time zones can interfere with effective communication during the process of a planned organizational change. Second, describe how information technology can be used to address these issues. To learn about the current capabilities of communication technology, visit the home page of *Computer Mediated Communications Magazine* at
www.december.com/cmc/mag

3. **Managing Globalization.** As domestic companies begin to expand overseas, they face many new challenges. Among these is managing expatriates. Because the international environment is so complex, many employers rely on consulting companies to provide expatriation and repatriation services. Review Exhibit 5.2, and then explain when in the planning process a decision about whether to outsource this activity would be made. After visiting the following Web sites, describe the various human resource management services available to firms sending employees overseas. Under what conditions should a company outsource these services to a consulting firm?
Hewitt Associates: **www.hewittassoc.com/resc**
Windham World: **www.windham.com/expat**
Arthur Andersen: **www.arthurandersen.com/bus-info/services/IES**

4. **Managing Diversity.** Imagine you were recently appointed to a task force charged with conducting a benchmarking study to identify state-of-the art approaches to leveraging diversity to enhance your organization's performance. The CEO has asked the task force to prepare a report describing the key HR practices that are used to leverage diversity in at least six outstanding companies. Identify the six companies that you would recommend for participation in the benchmarking study. Then, focusing on the issue of how to plan and implement change, prepare a list of questions that you would seek to answer as part of the benchmarking study.

5. **Integration and Application.** Review the end-of-text cases before proceeding.

   a. Lincoln Electric has had experience with operating overseas, but it has not always been positive. Nevertheless, they realize that survival depends on learning to operate effectively in a global environment. Imagine you are a member of the planning committee that has been charged with setting up operations in Shanghai. The company has decided to build a new plant and staff it entirely with local nationals. Develop a strategic plan complete with objectives, goals, measures, and timetables for the staffing process.

b. Refer to Exhibit 5.6, which lists several possible goals for work teams. Using this exhibit in conjunction with the information provided in the AAL case, list the team-level and individual-level measures used to assess the effectiveness of AAL's work teams. Then describe how each measure relates to the team's goals and the organization's strategic objectives.

c. To what extent did AAL employees resist change? How was their resistance to change expressed in terms of behavior? AAL knows it will eventually need to implement more changes in the IPS department as new technologies become available. What could AAL managers begin doing now to increase the organization's readiness for such changes? Be specific.

CASE STUDY

Managing Change at Weyerhaeuser Company

With yearly sales of about $12 billion, Weyerhaeuser Company is one of the largest paper and forest products companies in the world. Headquartered in Federal Way, it spreads most of its 40,000 employees throughout North America. Its major competitors include Georgia-Pacific Corporation, International Paper Company, and Westvaco Corporation.

Today, the Weyerhaeuser Company is successful in many respects, yet it continually strives to improve. Its guiding vision is "To be the best forest products company in the world." Leading the company toward this vision is Steven Rogel, chief executive officer, who describes the company's key strategies as

- making total quality the Weyerhaeuser way of doing business,
- relentlessly pursuing full customer satisfaction,
- empowering Weyerhaeuser people,
- leading the industry in forest management and manufacturing excellence, and
- producing superior returns for our shareholders.

The company's vision and these key strategies are in clear focus today, but before competition intensified to its present level, their importance was not so apparent. Through the 1970s, the firm enjoyed fairly consistent growth and financial success. Then, in the 1980s, things began to change: global and domestic competition roared in at the same time the national economy went into recession and the housing industry entered a major slump. These conditions created overcapacity in the paper industry. Suddenly the company's long-successful strategy of being a large-commodity lumber and paper business was no match against the tactics of new, smaller, and speedier competitors who focused more on the customer.

Faced with a do-or-die crisis situation in the 1980s, top management decided to decentralize operations and concentrate attention on the customer. They created three major divisions, or strategic business units: forest products, paper products, and real estate. The decentralized operating structure was motivating for those running the independent business units. But decentralization created new problems, too. In decentralized firms, it's easy to lose a feeling of identity with the larger company; inefficiencies due to duplication creep into the operation, and potential synergies may not be realized, so resources are underutilized.

The challenge of reducing the disadvantages of decentralization without losing its advantages was tackled by Jack Creighton upon becoming CEO. He and a new senior management team established the company's new vision. Shared by everyone in the company, this vision helps align business objectives across the strategic business units. Supporting this vision and the company's key strategies is a set of common values, which are also shared by everyone in the company:

Customers: We listen to our customers and improve our products and services to meet their present and future needs.

People: Our success depends upon people who perform at a high level working together in a safe and healthy environment where diversity, development, and teamwork are valued and recognized.

Accountability: We expect superior performance and are accountable for our actions and results. Our leaders set clear goals and expectations, are supportive, and provide and seek frequent feedback.

Citizenship: We support the communities where we do business, hold ourselves to the highest standards of ethical conduct and environmental responsibility, and communicate openly with Weyerhaeuser people and the public.

Financial Responsibility: We are prudent and effective in the use of the resources entrusted to us.

The vision and these common values facilitate coordination and cooperation between the people spread out across the different divisions.

Restructuring has helped Weyerhaeuser focus on its customers, be innovative, and become more efficient. But according to Creighton and his senior management team, ultimately it's the people—not the organizational structure—that make the company successful. In the preceding list of values, Weyerhaeuser's people have a prominent position. Furthermore, the values list describes how senior management expects people to behave in order to drive the business objectives. Managers' behaviors should support safety and health, diversity, teamwork, high performance, and total quality. Managers should empower employees, talk with customers,

team with others in the company and communicate effectively with everyone. Human resource practices play a central role in changing managers' old behaviors to be consistent with the new organization and the new expectations. Compensation, training and development, and performance management systems all must be aligned to deliver a clear and consistent message that encourages and supports the behaviors that can drive the business objectives.

The past ten years of change haven't been easy for Weyerhaeuser. But through the cooperation of everyone in the company and with a new way of managing human resources, considerable success has been achieved. Yet the company is seeking ways to improve and move into an even better position for even more intense global competition.

QUESTIONS

1. Describe the business objectives and goals of Weyerhaeuser today.

2. Describe the human resource objectives and goals of Weyerhaeuser today. How do these relate to the company's business objectives?

3. As described in Chapter 4, Weyerhaeuser has also developed a formal statement of its HR philosophy. Describe the implications of each of the company's common values and each component of its HR philosophy for the design and implementation of planned change efforts. Which phases of the change process are most affected by the values and HR philosophy?

To learn more about Weyerhaeuser, visit the company's home page at
www.weyerhaeuser.com

ENDNOTES

[1] G. H. Taylor, "Knowledge Companies," W. E. Halal, ed., *The Infinite Resource: Creating and Leading the Knowledge Enterprise* (San Francisco: Jossey-Bass, 1998): 97–109.

[2] Adapted from: N. Morgan, "My Days at Camp Lur'ning," *FastCompany* (October–November 1996): 115–124; A. M. Webber, "XBS Learns to Grow," *Fast Company* (October–November 1996): 112–125; and Malcolm Baldrige National Quality Award 1997 Winner Services Category: Xerox Business Services, **www.nist.gov/public-affairs/bald97** (November 7, 1997).

[3] Revolutionary change is also referred to as discontinuous or fundamental change, retrofit, transformation, radical change, and reinvention. Evolutionary change is also referred to as incremental change. See R. Beckhard and W. Pritchard, *Changing the Essence: The Art of Creating Fundamental Change in Organizations* (San Francisco: Jossey-Bass, 1992); A. Howard and Associates, *Diagnosis for Organizational Change: Methods and Models* (New York: Guilford, 1994); J. A. Neal and C. L. Tromley, "From Incremental Change to Retrofit: Creating High-Performance Work Systems," *Academy*

of Management Executive 9 (1) (1995): 42–92; D. A. Nadler and M. B. Nadler, *Champions of Change: How CEOs and Their Companies are Mastering the Skills of Radical Change* (San Francisco: Jossey-Bass, 1998).

[4] E. O. Welles, "Bootstrapping for Billions," *Inc.* (September 1994): 78–86.

[5] Y-T. Cheng and A. H. Van de Ven, "Learning the Innovation Journey: Order Out of Chaos," *Organization Science* 7 (1996): 593–614.

[6] D. Hellriegel, S. E. Jackson, and J. W. Slocum, Jr., *Management* (Cincinnati: South-Western, 1999).

[7] To learn more about downsizing and its consequences for employees, see M. K. Gowing, J. D. Kraft, and J. C. Quick, *The New Organizational Reality: Downsizing, Restructuring, and Revitalization* (Washington, DC: American Psychological Association, 1998).

[8] A. Kransdorrf, "Fight Organizational Memory Lapse," *Workforce* (September 1997): 34–39.

[9] T. Petzinger, Jr., "Bread-store Chain Tells Its Franchisees: Do Your Own Thing," *The Wall Street Journal* (November 21, 1997): B1.

[10] P. S. Goodman and E. D. Darr, "Exchanging Best Practices Through Computer-Aided Systems," *Academy of Management Executive* 10 (2) (1996): 7–19.

[11] N. C. Nash, "Putting Porsche in the Pink: German Craftsmanship Gets Japanese Fine-Tuning," *New York Times* (January 20, 1996): 35, 38.

[12] L. Mann, D. Samson, and D. Dow, "A Field Experiment on the Effects of Benchmarking and Goal Setting on Company Sales Performance," *Journal of Management* 24 (1998): 73–96.

[13] C. Kim and R. Maubourgne, "Fair Process: Managing in the Knowledge Economy," *Harvard Business Review* (July–August 1997): 65–75; and R. Pascale, M. Millimann, and L. Gioja, "Changing the Way We Change," *Harvard Business Review* (November–December 1997): 127–139.

[14] T. Maxon, "Southwest To Go 'Ticketless' on All Routes January 31," *Dallas Morning News* (January 11, 1995): 1D; M. E. McGill and J. W. Slocum, Jr., *The Smarter Organization: How to Build an Organization That Learns to Adapt to Marketplace Needs* (New York: John Wiley & Sons, 1994); and M. DePree, *Leadership Is an Art* (New York: Doubleday, 1992).

[15] S. J. Jackson, "Stepping Into the Future: Guidelines for Action," S. E. Jackson, ed., *Diversity in the Workplace: Human Resources Initiatives* (New York: Guilford, 1993); A. H. Van de Ven and M. S. Poole, "Explaining Development and Change in Organizations" *Academy of Management Review* 20 (1996): 510–540; P. J. Robertson, D. R. Roberts, and J. I. Porras, "Dynamics of Planned Change: Assessing Empirical Support for a Theoretical Model," *Academy of Management Journal* 36 (1993): 619–634; and M. L. Tushman and C. A. O'Reilly III, *A Practical Guide to Leading Organizational Change and Renewal* (Boston: Harvard Business School Press, 1997).

[16] J. W. Walker, "The Ultimate Human Resource Planning: Integrating the Human Resource Function with the Business," G. R. Ferris, ed., *Handbook of Human Resource Management* (Oxford, England: Blackwell, 1995); B. J. Smith, J. W. Boroski,

and G. E. Davis, "Human Resource Planning," *Human Resource Management* (Spring–Summer 1992): 81–94; M. London, E. S. Bassman, and J. P. Fernandez, eds., *Human Resource Forecasting and Strategy Development: Guidelines for Analyzing and Fulfilling Organizational Needs* (Westport, CT: Quorum Books, 1990); E. H. Burack, "Linking Corporate Business and Human Resource Planning: Strategic Issues and Concerns," *Human Resource Planning* 8 (1985): 133–146; D. Ulrich, "Strategic Human Resource Planning," R. S. Schuler, S. A. Youngblood, and V. L. Huber, eds., *Readings in Personnel and Human Resource Management*, 3rd ed., (St. Paul: West Publishing Co., 1988): 57–71.

[17] R. S. Schuler and J. W. Walker, "Human Resources Strategy: Focusing on Issues and Actions," *Organizational Dynamics* (Summer 1990): 5–19; E. H. Burack, "A Strategic Planning and Operational Agenda for Human Resources," *Human Resource Planning* 11 (2) (1988): 63–69; L. Dyer, "Strategic Human Resources Management and Planning," in *Research in Personnel and Human Resource Management* (Greenwich, CT: JAI Press, 1985):1–30; G. Milkovich, L. Dyer, and T. Mahoney, "The State of Practice and Research in Human Resource Planning," S. J. Carroll and R. S. Schuler, eds., *Human Resource Management in the 1980s* (Washington, DC: Bureau of National Affairs, 1983).

[18] Adapted from S. E. Jackson and R. S. Schuler, "Human Resource Planning: Challenges for I/O Psychologists," *American Psychologist* (February 1990): 223–239.

[19] N. Deogun, "Ivester Alert: Advice to Coke People from their New Boss: Don't Get too Cocky," *The Wall Street Journal* (March 9, 1998): A1, A11.

[20] S. Greengard, "HR Can Unlock a Prosperous Future," *Workforce* (March 1998): 45–54.

[21] S. B. Bacharach, P. Bamberger, and W. J. Sonnenstuhl, "The Organizational Transformation Process: The Micropolitics of Dissonance Reduction and the Alignment of Logics of Action," *Administrative Science Quarterly* (1996): 477–506; P. H. Mirvis, "Human Resource Management: Leaders, Laggards, and Followers," *Academy of Management Executive* 11 (2) (1997): 43–56; and M. Hammer and S. A. Stanton, "The Power of Reflection," *Fortune* (November 24, 1997): 291–296.

[22] P. H. Mirvis, "Human Resource Management: Leaders, Laggards, and Followers."

[23] G. Flynn, "Texas Instruments Engineers a Holistic HR," *Workforce* (February 1998): 30–35.

[24] T. T. Baldwin, C. Danielson, and W. Wiggenhorn, "The Evolution of Learning Strategies in Organizations: From Employee Development to Business Definition," *Academy of Management Executive* 11 (4) (1997): 47–58.

[25] G. P. Huber and W. H. Glick, *Organizational Change and Redesign* (New York: Oxford University Press, 1993). See also A. Howard and Associates, *Diagnosis for Organizational Change: Methods and Models*.

[26] Technical advice about conducting surveys can be found in A. I. Kraut, ed., *Organizational Surveys: Tools for Assessment and Change* (San Francisco: Jossey-Bass, 1996) and J. E. Edwards, M. E. Thomas, P. Rosenfeld, and S. Booth-Kewley, *How to Conduct Organizational Surveys: A Step-by-Step Guide* (Thousand Oaks, CA: Sage, 1997).

27 For a special report on retirement and the baby boomers, see the December 1997 issue of *Workforce*, or visit them online at **www.workforceonline.com/boomers**. See also *Workforce 2020—Work and Workers in the 21st Century* (Indianapolis: Hudson Institute, 1997); G. Flynn, "New Skills Equal New Opportunities," *Personnel Journal* (June 1996): 77–79; A. Bernstein, "Oops, That's Too Much Downsizing," *Business Week* (June 8, 1998): 38; J. A. Talaga and T. A. Beehr, "Are There Gender Differences in Predicting Retirement Decisions?" *Journal of Applied Psychology* 80 (1995): 16–28.

28 "Bringing Sears Into the New World: An Interview with Anthony Rucci," *Fortune* (October 13, 1997): 183–184.

29 A. M. Webber, "XBS Learns to Grow."

30 G. Flynn, "It Takes Values to Capitalize on Change," *Workforce* (April 1997): 27–34.

31 M. J. Koch and R. G. McGrath, "Improving Labor Productivity: Human Resource Management Policies Do Matter," *Strategic Management Journal* 17 (1996): 335–354.

32 J. E. McCann, III and M. Buckner, "Redesigning Work: Motivations, Challenges and Practices in 181 Companies," *Human Resource Planning* 17 (4) (1994): 23–41.

33 M. Orgland and G. von Krogh, "Initiating, Managing, and Sustaining Corporate Transformation: A Case Study," *European Management Journal* 16 (1998): 31–38.

34 For information about what many other companies are doing in this area, see M. L. Wheeler, *Corporate Practices in Diversity Measurement: A Research Report* (New York: Conference Board, 1996).

35 "Job Turnover Tab," *Business Week* (March 20, 1998): 8.

36 T. A Stewart, "In Search of Elusive High Tech Workers," *Fortune* (February 16, 1998): 171–172; D. C. Ganster and D. J. Dwyer, "The Effects of Understaffing on Individual and Group Performance in Professional and Trade Occupations," *Journal of Management* 21 (1995): 175–190.

37 K. Troy, *Change Management: Striving for Customer Value: A Research Report* (New York: Conference Board, 1996).

38 B. Laymon, "Xerox Chairman Makes Business Case for Family-Friendly Work Culture: Allaire Delivers Keynote at 'CEO Summit on Rethinking Life and Work.'" Xerox Press Release, **www.xerox.com/PR/NR970915-family** (September 15, 1997).

39 Adapted from S. E. Jackson, K. E. May, and K. Whitney, "Understanding the Dynamics of Diversity in Decision Making Teams," R. A. Guzzo, E. Salas, and Associates, eds., *Team Effectiveness and Decision Making in Organizations* (San Francisco: Jossey-Bass, 1995): 204–261; "A Seven-Step Model to Develop Team Measures," *ACA News* (November–December 1996): 15–16; D. C. Borwhat, Jr., "How Do You Know if Your Work Teams Work?" *Workforce* (May 1997): 7; D. R. Denison, S. L. Hart, and J. A. Kahn, "From Chimneys to Cross-Functional Teams: Developing and Validating a Diagnostic Model," *Academy of Management Journal* 39 (1996): 1005–1023; and M. Cianni and D. Wnuck, "Individual Growth and Team Enhancement: Moving Toward a New Model of Career Development," *Academy of Management Executive* 11 (1997): 105–113.

40 N. J. Adler and S. Bartholomew, "Managing Globally Competent People," *Academy of Management Executive* 6 (3) (1992): 52–64; see also P. R. Sparrow and J. M. Hiltrop, *European Human Resource Management in Transition* (New York: Prentice Hall, 1994).

41 Adapted from S. L. Davis, "Assessment as Organizational Strategy," R. Jeanneret and R. Silzer, eds., *Individual Psychological Assessment: Predicting Behavior in Organizational Settings* (San Francisco: Jossey-Bass, 1998).

42 J. Stack, "The Great Game of Business," *Inc.* (June 1992): 53–66.

43 E. A. Locke, "Toward a Theory of Task Motivation and Incentives," *Organizational Behavior and Human Performance* 3 (1968): 157–189; E. A. Locke and G. P. Latham, *A Theory of Goal Setting and Task Performance* (Englewood Cliffs, NJ: Prentice-Hall, 1990). For a study involving roofers, see R. Austin, M. L. Kessler, J. E. Riccobono, and J. Bailey, "Using Feedback and Reinforcement to Improve the Performance and Safety of a Roofing Crew," *Journal of Organizational Behavior Management* 16 (1996): 49–75. A study of pizza deliverers is described in T. D. Ludwig and E. S. Geller, "Assigned Versus Participative Goal Setting and Response Generalization: Managing Injury Control Among Professional Pizza Deliverers," *Journal of Applied Psychology* 82 (1997): 253–261. See also G. P. Latham and J. J. Baldes, "The Practical Significance of Locke's Theory of Goal Setting," *Journal of Applied Psychology* 60 (1975): 122–124.

44 "Growing Pains," *Across the Board* (February 1997): 43–48.

45 S. E. Jackson, ed., *Diversity in the Workplace: Human Resource Initiatives*.

46 R. Silzer, "Shaping Organizational Leadership: The Ripple Effect of Assessment," R. Jeanneret and R. Silzer, eds., *Individual Psychological Assessment: Predicting Behavior in Organizational Settings*.

47 R. Maurer, *Beyond the Wall of Resistance* (Austin, Texas: Bard Books, 1996).

48 K. Skoldberg, "Tales of Change," *Organization Science* 5 (1994): 219–238.

49 T. Petzinger, Jr., "Georg Bauer Put Burden of Downsizing into Employees' Hands," *The Wall Street Journal* (May 10, 1996): B1.

50 C. Heckscher, White-Collar Blues (New York: Basic Books, 1995).

51 P. Strebel, "Why Do Employees Resist Change?" *Harvard Business Review* (May–June 1996): 86–106.

52 Adapted from C. H. Lovelock, "What Language Shall We Put It In?" *Marketing Management* (Winter 1994): 41; J. Valente, "British Airways Sees Strong Gains, Challenges Ahead," *The Wall Street Journal* (November 8, 1994): B4; and P. Dwyer, "British Air: Not Cricket," *Business Week* (January 25, 1993): 50–51.

53 J. E. Mathieu and D. M. Zajkac, "A Review and Meta-Analysis of the Antecedents, Correlates, and Consequences of Organizational Commitment," *Psychological Bulletin* 108 (1990): 171–194; J. F. Brett, W. L. Cron, and J. W. Slocum, Jr., "Economic Dependency on Work: A Moderator of the Relationship Between Organizational Commitment and Performance," *Academy of Management Journal* 38 (1995):

261–271; R. E. Allen, M. A. Lucero, and K. L. Van Norman, "An Examination of the Individual's Decision to Participate in an Employee Involvement Program," *Group & Organization Management* 22 (1997): 117–143; and W. C. Kim and R. Mauborgne, "Fair Process: Managing the Knowledge Economy," *Harvard Business Review* (July–August 1997): 65–75.

54 Adapted from J. P. Kotter and L. A. Schlesinger, "Choosing Strategies for Change," *Harvard Business Review* (March–April 1979): 111.

55 R. Tetzeli, "And Now for Motorola's Next Trick," *Fortune* (April 28, 1997): 130. See also, Q. Hardy and J. I. Rigdon, "Motorola Overhauls Staff Structure; Top Management's Pay Dropped in '96," *The Wall Street Journal* (March 24, 1997): B2; and P. Elstrom, "Does Galvin Have the Right Stuff?" *Business Week* (March 17, 1997): 102–105.

56 J. P. Kotter, "Leading Change: Why Transformation Efforts Fail," *Harvard Business Review* (March–April 1995): 59–67.

57 J. L. McCarthy, *A Blueprint for Change: A Conference Report* (No. 1149-96-CH) (New York: Conference Board, 1996); T. J. Galpin, *The Human Side of Change* (San Francisco: Jossey-Bass, 1996); Price Waterhouse, *Better Change: Best Practices for Transforming Your Organization* (Burr Ridge, IL: Irwin, 1995); and B. Schneider, A. P. Brief, and R. A. Guzzo, "Creating a Climate and Culture for Sustainable Organizational Change," *Organizational Dynamics* 24 (4) (1996): 6–19; P. M. Wright and S. A. Snell, "Toward a Unifying Framework for Exploring Fit and Flexibility in Strategic Human Resource Management," *Academy of Management Review* 23 (1998): 756–772.

58 For a detailed discussion of the role of human resource management in maintaining organizational flexibility and readiness for change, see P. M. Wright and S. A. Snell, "Toward a Unifying Framework for Exploring Fit and Flexibility in Strategic Human Resource Management," *Academy of Management Review* 23 (1998): 756–772.

JOB AND ORGANIZATIONAL ANALYSIS: UNDERSTANDING THE WORK TO BE DONE

Chapter

6

Chapter Outline

"With the job families, we're trying to get rid of all the extraneous details and allow managers and their employees to do what is needed to serve their customers extremely well."

Mary Fitzer
Director of Base Salary
Development
Aetna Life and Casualty
Company[1]

MANAGING HUMAN RESOURCES THROUGH PARTNERSHIP
at MetLife

MetLife Auto and Home is a subsidiary of Metropolitan Life Insurance Company, based in Rhode Island. In the early 1990s, it was a traditional company with a traditional culture. "We loved job titles and job descriptions," explained Carolyn MacDonald, the Director of Human Resources. "There was a sense of security with our job titles." With 732 job descriptions, there seemed to be more than enough security to go around. But competition was heating up in the insurance industry and MacDonald sensed the need for change.

After studying what was needed to succeed in the future, MacDonald and her staff concluded that employees should be valued and rewarded based on their individual contributions rather than job titles. An approach called "broadbanding" seemed to offer one solution. With a broadbanding approach, MacDonald could reduce hundreds of narrowly defined jobs to a few dozen more broadly defined jobs. After several months of research aimed at better understanding both the needs of the organization and employees' concerns, MacDonald and her staff concluded that simply having fewer categories of more broadly defined jobs wasn't the answer. Typically, broadbanded job categories merely lessen the amount of hierarchy and rigidity in the structure—they do not eliminate it. They had a grander vision. They wanted a system that moved as far as possible toward emphasizing workers' contributions over job-defined tasks.

To achieve their vision, MacDonald and her staff eventually decided to completely eliminate job descriptions and salary ranges. The new approach would give managers the flexibility needed to move employees around the organization, and it would give employees opportunities to accept new challenges without worrying about whether taking a new position would result in lower pay or status.

A new organizational architecture was designed to meet their objective. Its four key elements are career bands, corporate profiles, functional profiles, and employee development continuums.

Career bands describe the general types of careers followed by most employees. Five careers were identified: leadership, professional, technical, management, and administrative.

Corporate profiles describe an array of competencies that all employees should display. For all jobs, seven areas of competency are expected: knowledge, customer relations, impact/execution, decision making, innovation, communication, and ethics/quality. For each career band, a corporate profile details the responsibilities of people who are moving along that career ladder. For example, for the domain of "Innovation," professionals "encourage and foster a learning environment that encompasses a theoretical or scientific area of expertise and its applicability to MetLife Auto and Home." Within this system, no profile is superior to the other, and there are no salary ranges associated with the profiles.

Function profiles describe departmental roles and are used in place of traditional job descriptions. The function profiles do not include tasks. Instead, they describe what's to be achieved and the competencies needed to achieve it. For example, the function of a trainer is to "develop and/or administer programs that will educate claims personnel and enhance the skills necessary to facilitate individual personal and professional development." Performing this function requires knowledge of the company's claims procedures, state regulations, basic understanding of learning and instructional techniques, effective communication skills, the ability to work independently, as well as several other specified competencies.

An *employee development continuum* describes how employees can continuously develop their competencies. For example, by studying these guidelines employees learn that the continuum for partnership behavior begins with simply becoming oriented to the organization and department and developing customer-relations skills. As employees develop themselves, however, they'll eventually begin to influence their work environment and participate in special projects. Next on the continuum comes acting as a mentor and educator to departmental peers, initiating and directing special projects, and enhancing customer service. Finally, when fully developed, partnership involves developing corporatewide strategic initiatives that have a positive impact on both internal and external customers.

In this new culture, titles do little more than indicate one's general function. An employee's level of development is what determines his or her value to the organization, regardless of one's career track or departmental affiliation.[2]

To learn more about MetLife, visit the company home page at
www.metlife.com

THE STRATEGIC IMPORTANCE OF JOB AND ORGANIZATIONAL ANALYSIS

At MetLife, job analysis provided the foundation for establishing congruence between business objectives and approaches to managing human resources. Consistent with a partnership philosophy, job families allow managers to match employees to work assignments without being constrained by salary grades and meaningless status markers. Employees can decide which new tasks to take on without being penalized for their willingness to switch departments or move to a new line of business. With less bureaucracy getting in the way, managers and all other employees get more involved in important decisions about how people are managed.

Redesigning work to achieve strategic objectives and mapping career paths are just two of the many uses for job analysis. Others include

- identifying redundant jobs that can be merged or eliminated during organizational restructuring,
- specifying the competencies needed to perform a job,
- redesigning jobs to accommodate employees with disabilities,
- developing measures of job performance,
- designing training programs and approaches to evaluating them, and
- developing a compensation structure that's internally equitable.

Job analysis provides a foundation upon which to build all of these components of the HR system. Thus, job analysis can be used to ensure that an organization's entire system for managing people is internally consistent and appropriate for the organization's context.

Partnership in Job and Organizational Analysis

Perhaps the term *job analysis* brings to mind images of a technician walking around in a white coat, making entries into the latest palm-sized computer—but this is not what job analysis is really like. The people who work in a job and the people who observe a job being done day in and day out are the experts. A thorough job analysis means that all of these people must be actively involved in the process of job analysis. At MetLife, for example, the cooperation of nearly everyone in the organization was needed to restructure the organization and redefine the way work was to be done. Job analysis was a central activity that both guided the process and ensured that the new system was fully documented so it could be understood by each person whose job was affected. The feature, The HR Triad: Partnership Roles and Responsibilities in Job and Organizational Analysis, summarizes the major ways that HR professionals, managers, and other employees get involved in job analysis.

This chapter describes the methods organizations use to conduct job analysis and some of the ways that changes in the organizational environment can affect job analysis. Subsequent chapters illustrate how job analysis results are used for the specific components of the HR system listed above.

BASIC TERMINOLOGY

In everyday conversations, people often use the word *job* whenever they refer to an employment situation. But when an entire system for managing human resources depends on understanding the jobs in an organization, more specific terminology is needed. More precise use of several related terms facilitates clear communication.

THE HR TRIAD: PARTNERSHIP ROLES AND RESPONSIBILITIES IN JOB AND ORGANIZATIONAL ANALYSIS

Line Managers	HR Professionals	Employees
Participate in strategic planning and organizational change planning. (See Chapters 4 and 5.)	Participate in strategic planning and organizational change planning. (See Chapters 4 and 5.)	Participate in strategic planning and organizational change planning. (See Chapters 4 and 5.)
Work with HR managers to determine whether jobs need to be analyzed or reanalyzed.	Communicate with line managers and employees about the importance of job analysis.	Understand the purposes and importance of job analysis.
Help decide who should conduct the job analysis and for what purposes.	Work with line managers to determine whether jobs need to be analyzed or reanalyzed and for what purposes.	Help line managers recognize when major changes in a job indicate the need for job analysis or reanalysis.
Help identify incumbents to participate in job analysis.	Serve as a job analysis expert, or help select an external vendor to conduct job analysis.	Provide accurate information for the job analysis process.
Provide technical documents to the job analyst.	Ensure that line managers and employees are aware of legal considerations.	Adapt to the changing nature of the job and be willing to show flexibility in performing new job tasks.
Participate in job analysis through interviews and questionnaires.	Prepare and update job descriptions with line managers and employees.	Use job analysis results for career planning and job choice decisions.
Facilitate job incumbents' participation in job analysis.	Keep up-to-date on new techniques and changing trends in job analysis.	

Organizational Analysis

Most jobs exist in the context of a larger organization. As described in Chapter 4, the internal environment of an organization can be described as having many different aspects. The organization's size, structure, strategy, and culture all combine to create a unique organizational environment. The objective of an *organizational analysis* is developing a comprehensive understanding of this environment.[3] The focus of an organizational analysis is on identifying system-wide features of the environment that are relatively similar across all jobs. At MetLife, the organizational analysis involved understanding what was needed in order for the company to thrive in the future. The organizational analysis conducted by MacDonald and her colleagues indicated that the current organization was too rigid, and that more flexibility would be needed in the future. The organizational analysis of Sears that was conducted by CEO Martinez and his top managers (see Chapter 5) revealed a culture in which employees were too concerned with protecting the assets of the company and not concerned enough with satisfying their customers. An organizational analysis of XBS (see Chapter 5) revealed a well-aligned system of strategy, structure, and culture all focused on providing total quality and continual improvement.

The work of conducting an organizational analysis is intertwined with the work of strategic planning and planning for organizational change. Here the important point to note is that a complete organizational analysis should include identifying the common role behaviors needed by employees throughout the organization. Human resource management practices can then be developed to ensure that all employees carry out their work in a manner that's consistent with the ideal role behaviors. For example, at Southwest Airlines, the importance of having fun and satisfying customers is clearly understood by employees in all jobs. The CEO, pilots, engine maintenance crews, and flight attendants have very different job responsibilities, but they all share responsibility for maintaining an environment in which employees and customers have fun and are completely satisfied with their flying experiences.

Positions, Jobs, and Job Families

Human resource professionals use the term *position* to refer to the activities carried out by any single person. They use the term *job* to refer to positions that are functionally interchangeable in the organization. In small organizations, each job may have only one position associated with it; no two employees are expected to do the same thing. An example of this situation would occur if Raol's position is Account Manager and the job of Account Manager is held only by Raol.

As organizations grow, the number of positions associated with some jobs increase. For example, a family bakery may eventually hire more people to work as bakers as well as more people to work at the sales counter. This type of expansion involves adding positions without increasing the number of jobs. If the bakery continues to grow, new jobs are likely to be added. For example, if the bakery decides to add seating and coffee service for customers, the job of waiter might be added. Additional jobs could also be created through increased specialization. For example, in the small bakery, the job of baker would include baking breads as well as pies and cakes, but as the organization grows, this job might be replaced by two jobs: bread baker and pastry maker.

A *job family* refers to a group of jobs that can be treated as similar for administrative purposes. Usually, jobs in the same family involve similar but not identical tasks and require similar competencies. Job families are closely related to what many people think of as occupational categories. In the bakery example, the jobs of bread baker and pastry maker would likely fall into the same job family.

Job Analysis

Job analysis is the process of describing and recording information about job behaviors and activities.[4] Typically, the information described and recorded includes the

- purposes of a job;
- major duties or activities required of job holders;
- conditions under which the job is performed; and
- competencies (i.e., skills, knowledge, abilities, and other attributes)[5] that enable and enhance performance in the job.

In contrast to an organizational analysis, which focuses on the commonality across jobs, job analysis aims to explain the distinct features of particular jobs.

Job Descriptions

Often, the most immediate use of job analysis results is the writing of job descriptions. A *job description* details what the jobholder is expected to do and the competencies needed for the job. Job descriptions are part of the written contract that governs the employment relationship. A thorough job description includes information generated by an organizational analysis and a job analysis. Exhibit 6.1 shows an example of a job description.

During recruitment and job search, clear job descriptions are helpful because they provide job applicants with realistic information. For example, when Southwest Airlines posted a recruiting announcement on their home page, they described the job of flight attendant like this:

> *Fight Attendants ensure that Customers' safety and comfort come first, and create a memorable experience by providing friendly, enthusiastic, courteous and fun service.*[6]

Also listed were several required qualifications and pay information.

Once on the job, employees use their job descriptions as guides to their behavior, directing their energies to the aspects of the job and organizational role that seem most important. Supervisors use job descriptions in evaluating performance and providing feedback. Well-written job descriptions can also guide supervisors in writing references and incumbents in preparing resumes. Typically, a well-written job description includes the elements listed in Exhibit 6.2.[7]

SOURCES OF INFORMATION

Information about a job and the organization can be obtained from anyone who has specific information about what the work involves. The people used as sources of information about specific jobs are often referred to as subject matter experts (SMEs). They can include current incumbents, supervisors, trained job analysts, and/or customers. Each of these sources sees the

"I've learned Windows 3.1, Windows 95, and Windows 98. I'm not sure I have another Windows in me."

Tom
A 50-something executive

Exhibit 6.1
Job Description

Title: Corporate Loan Assistant   Department: Corporate Banking
Date: June 2000   Location: Head Office

Note: *Statements included in this description are intended to reflect in general the duties and responsibilities of this classification and are not to be interpreted as being all inclusive.*

Relationships

Reports to: Corporate Account Officer or Sr. Corporate Account Officer
Subordinate staff: None
Internal customers: Middle and Senior Managers within the Corporate Banking Department
External contacts: Major bank customers

Summary Description

Assist in the administration of commercial accounts to ensure maintenance of profitable Bank relationships.

Domains

A. Credit Analysis (Weekly)
   Under the direction of a supervising loan officer, analyze a customer company's history, industry position, present condition, accounting procedures, and debt requirements. Review credit reports, summarize analysis and recommend courses of action for potential borrowers; review and summarize performance of existing borrowers. Prepare and follow-up on credit reports and Loan Agreement Compliance sheets.

B. Operations (Weekly)
   Help customers with banking problems and needs. Give out customer credit information to valid inquirers. Analyze account profitability and compliance with balance arrangements; distribute to customer. Direct Loan Note Department in receiving and disbursing funds and in booking loans. Correct internal errors.

C. Loan Documentation (Weekly)
   Develop required loan documentation. Help customer complete loan documents. Review loan documents immediately after a loan closing for completeness and accuracy.

D. Report/Information System (Weekly)
   Prepare credit reports, describing and analyzing customer relationship and loan commitments; prepare for input into Information System. Monitor credit reports for accuracy.

E. Customer/Internal Relations (Weekly)
   Build rapport with customers by becoming familiar with their products, facilities, and industry. Communicate with customers and other banks to obtain loan-related information and answer questions. Prepare reports on customer and prospect contacts and follow-up. Write memos on events affecting customers and prospects.

F. Assistance to Officers (Monthly)
   Assist assigned officers by preparing credit support information, summarizing customer relationships, and accompanying on calls or making independent calls. Monitor accounts and review and maintain credit files. Coordinate paper flow to banks participating in loans. Respond to customer questions or requests in absence of assigned officer.

G. Assistance to Division (Monthly)
   Represent Bank at industry activities. Follow industry/area developments. Help Division Manager plan division approach and prospect for new business. Interview loan assistant applicants. Provide divisional back-up in absence of assigned officer.

H. Competencies (Any item with an asterisk will be taught on the job)
   Oral communication, including listening and questioning. Intermediate accounting proficiency. Writing. Researching/reading to understand legal financial documents. Organizational/analytical skills. Social skills to represent the Bank and strengthen its image. Sales. Knowledge of Bank credit policy and services.* Skill to use Bank computer system.* Knowledge of bank-related legal terminology. Independent work skills. Work efficiently under pressure. Knowledge of basic corporate finance.

I. Physical Characteristics
   See to read fine print and numbers. Hear speaker twenty feet away. Speak to address a group of five. Mobility to tour customer facilities (may include climbing stairs).

J. Other Characteristics
   Driver's license. Willing to: work overtime and weekends occasionally; travel out of state every three months/locally weekly; attend activities after work hours; wear clean, neat businesslike attire.

Exhibit 6.2
Elements of a Job Description and What They Should Specify

Element	What Should Be Specified
Job title	Defines a group of positions that are interchangeable (identical) with regard to their significant duties.
Department or division	Indicates where in the organization the job is located.
Date the job was analyzed	Indicates when the description was prepared and perhaps whether it should be updated. A job description based on a job analysis conducted prior to any major changes in the job is of little use.
Job summary	An abstract of the job, this is often used during recruitment to create job postings or employment announcements and in setting the pay levels.
Supervision	Identifies reporting relationships. If supervision is given, the duties associated with that supervision should be detailed under work performed.
Work performed	Identifies the duties and underlying tasks that make up a job. A *task* is something that workers perform or an action they take to produce a product or service. A *duty* is a collection of related, recurring tasks. Duties should be ranked in terms of the time spent on them as well as their importance. Specified duties are used to determine whether job accommodations for individuals protected under the Americans with Disabilities Act are reasonable, whether the job is exempt from overtime provisions of the Fair Labor Standards Act, and whether two jobs with different titles should be treated as equal for purposes of compliance with the Equal Pay Act.
Job context	Describes the physical environment that surrounds the job (e.g., outdoors, in close quarters, in remote areas, in extremely high or low temperatures, exposure to dangerous conditions such as fumes and diseases) as well as the social environment in which work is performed (e.g., teamwork, flexibility, and continuous learning). Increasingly, the degree of change and uncertainty associated with the job, the corporate culture, and elements of the organizational mission or vision statement are specified.

job from a different perspective, and associated with each source are different advantages and disadvantages. Indeed, a recent review of the literature identified 16 social and cognitive sources of potential inaccuracy in job analysis.[8] Some common job analysis errors and the conditions that can cause them are described in Exhibit 6.3. To conduct the most comprehensive job analysis, the best strategy is to include each type of source.

Job Incumbents

"The auto worker is almost a scientist in a technical way. He's required to know so many trades, he's required to know so much."

Joe Lo Galbo
Machinery repairman turned trainer
Ford Motor Company

Job incumbents—the people who are currently doing the job—have the most direct knowledge. Incumbents usually provide data through participation in an interview or by responding to a questionnaire.

One concern in job analysis is selecting the particular job incumbents to include. For example, if your publishing firm employs 30 copyeditors, do you need to obtain information from them all? Many companies feel that it would be inefficient to survey everyone, so they select only a sample. These companies have to be sure a representative sample of incumbents participates: men and women, members of different ethnic groups and nationalities, younger people as well as older ones, people who work in different divisions or regions, and so on.[9]

Exhibit 6.3
Job Analysis Inaccuracy

Source of Error	Conditions Likely to Cause Error	Possible Consequences
Low accuracy motivation	Tasks aren't meaningful, the group is large, individuals do not feel accountable.	Incomplete information about job
Impression management	Job incumbents feel the job analysis results will be used to evaluate them as individuals.	Inflated descriptions of job or competency requirements
Demand effects	Supervisors convey their preference for employees to portray their jobs as challenging and/or as more complex than in the past.	Inflated agreement and inflated descriptions of job or competency requirements
Reliance on heuristics and job stereotypes	Too many items on a questionnaire, creating fatigue and loss of ability to differentiate among similar tasks.	Incomplete and unreliable task ratings
Use of extraneous and irrelevant information	Extraneous information about things such as employees' salaries and tenure levels are known.	Inaccurate ratings; they may be either inflated or deflated
Halo	The rater has insufficient job information available, little personal knowledge of the job, or low motivation.	All job tasks are given similar ratings
Leniency and severity	Leniency is more likely when it can result in benefits for the raters (e.g., a possible pay raise). Severity may occur if the job analyst thinks it may benefit the organization (e.g., help justify elimination of a job or low wages).	All job tasks are given high (lenient) or low (severe) ratings

Line managers and incumbents usually agree about whether an incumbent performs specific tasks and duties. However, incumbents tend to see their jobs as requiring greater skill and knowledge than do line managers or outside job analysts. One reason for this difference is that job-specific information is more salient to incumbents who perform the work than it is to outsiders. The difference may also be due to self-enhancement. Because job analysis is related to many human resource outcomes—for example, performance appraisal and compensation—incumbents, and, to a lesser extent, their supervisors, may exaggerate job duties in order to maximize organizational rewards and self-esteem.[10]

Although incumbent ratings may be slightly enhanced, there are still good reasons to include them in the job analysis process. First, they're the source of the most current and accurate information about the job. Second, their inclusion allows line managers and incumbents to gain a shared perspective about job expectations. Third, their inclusion can increase perceptions of procedural fairness and reduce resistance to changes that might be introduced on the basis of job analysis results.

Supervisors

Like incumbents, supervisors have direct information about the duties associated with a job. Therefore, they're also considered SMEs. Yet, because

*"They do everything
through computers. The
supervisor says you have
to do 20.2 stops an hour
and you can only do 15.
Next day the supervisor
tells you it took you two
hours longer than the
computer says it should
take; it's terrible."*

**Edward Martin
Package Truck Driver
UPS**

they're not currently performing the job, supervisors may find it more difficult to explain all the tasks involved in it. This is especially true of tasks the supervisors cannot observe directly, such as mental tasks or tasks performed out in the field. On the other hand, supervisors who have seen more than one job incumbent perform a job bring a broader perspective to the job analysis process. Whereas an incumbent provides information about what she or he in particular does, supervisors can provide information about the tasks typically associated with the job. Supervisors also may be in a better position to describe what tasks should be included in the job, and what tasks could be included if the job is to be redesigned.[11]

Trained Job Analysts

Some methods of job analysis require input from trained job analysts. Supervisors or incumbents can be taught to serve as job analysts, but usually outside consultants or members of the company's HR staff perform this role.

An advantage of enlisting the help of trained job analysts is that they can observe many different incumbents working under different supervisors and in different locations. Trained job analysts also can read through organizational records and technical documentation and provide information culled from these indirect sources. Furthermore, trained experts are more likely to appreciate fully the legal issues associated with conducting job analysis, which are described later in this chapter. Nevertheless, like every other source of information, trained job analysts are imperfect. One drawback to using their skills is that, like supervisors, they cannot observe all aspects of a job. Also, they may rely too much on their own stereotypes about what a job involves, based on the job title, rather than attending to all the available information. Finally, especially in the case of outside consultants, their services may be expensive.

Customers

If satisfying customers is a key strategic objective, it seems obvious that customers should also be used as subject matter experts. In actuality, this is seldom done. Collecting information from customers has been considered to be a marketing activity rather than an HR activity. But consider the following facts: In most convenience stores, 25 inches separate a cashier and customer, 80 inches separate two cashiers, and managers are far from the work floor. Furthermore, cashiers spend 78 percent of their time interacting with customers and only 13 percent of their time interacting with managers.[12] For jobs like these, it seems obvious that using customers as job analysis SMEs is likely to become more common as organizations increasingly incorporate the perspectives of customers when designing jobs and assessing employee performance.

COLLECTING INFORMATION

Just as many sources provide information about jobs and the organization as a whole, many methods are used to obtain that information. Four common ways to collect job and organizational analysis information are observations, interviews, questionnaires, and diaries.

Observations

As Frederick Taylor understood quite well, observing workers as they perform their work provides rich information about the tasks involved.

Observation may include videotaping, audiotaping, and even electronic monitoring. Physical measurements of activities performed, such as measuring objects that must be moved, and descriptions of how equipment is operated often require some observation of the job as it's being performed. Through observation of a "filler" in the original Ben & Jerry's Homemade ice cream factory, an observer could learn that this job involved two basic tasks. At a time when hand-filled pints of ice cream were unusual in the industry, the filler job at Ben & Jerry's required holding a pint container under a pipe that exuded ice cream and then pulling the pint away at just the moment it was filled. At the same time the filler moved another container under the pipe. As the second container filled, the other hand was used to print a production code on the bottom of the filled container and slide it along a table to the next work station. Fillers did this over and over again, all day long.[13]

Observation can be very time consuming, especially if the work tasks and conditions change depending on the time of day or on a seasonal basis. To be practical, the use of observation generally requires sampling. A haphazard approach—which yields equally haphazard results—is to simply observe the work being performed when it's convenient for the job analyst. Systematic work sampling yields better information. Work sampling refers to the process of taking instantaneous samples of the work activities of individuals or groups of individuals. The job analyst can observe the incumbent at predetermined times, or cameras can take photographs at predetermined times, or electronic records can be sampled.

One disadvantage of close monitoring is that employees may feel as if they're under surveillance. Their privacy is invaded by close observation, and they may feel their judgments will be called into question. As competition in the freight delivery business intensifies, managers have begun using high-tech observation methods to analyze every aspect of a truck driver's job. Often the results of the job analysis are used to make efficiency-enhancing changes in how truckers perform their jobs. To resist such intrusions, some drivers put buckets or aluminum foil over their satellite dishes. Others seek shelter by parking beneath a wide overpass when they feel they need a short nap. "It's getting worse and worse all the time," according to one experienced driver. "Pretty soon they want to put a chip in the drivers' ears and make them robots."[14]

Interviews

Some jobs include tasks that are difficult to observe. The components of the larger system—the structure, culture, and strategy—also may be difficult to discern through simple observation. A better way to understand some jobs and the organizational context may be to conduct interviews with the various people touched by them. For example, to really understand the job of a software designer who develops customized graphics programs for commercial printers, you might interview job incumbents, their supervisors, members of their product design teams, staff members who write the computer codes to implement their design, and the customers who ultimately define their objectives.

Questionnaires

Questionnaires are useful for collecting information from many different people because they're more economical than interviews or observations. This is especially true when the questionnaires are administered electroni-

■□ *fast fact*

Compared to their older siblings, modern looms require half the number of workers to produce five times the fabric.

■□ *fast fact*

Almost all freight trucks are fitted with electronic engines programmed to control speed and gear-shifting and satellite dishes used to monitor the trucks' exact location at all times.

■■□ *fast fact*

SAP software means that technicians at Colgate-Palmolive's factory and fragrance plant can instantaneously inform suppliers and customers of a soap shipment's status using no phones, no faxes, no paper, and barely any human interaction.

cally (e.g., using the organization's intranet). Questionnaires may be developed for specific circumstances, or standardized questionnaires may be purchased from external vendors. Standardized questionnaires are more economical. Often an added benefit is that the vendor can also provide useful information from a larger database. On the other hand, customized questionnaires usually yield information that's much more specific to the particular jobs involved. This feature is especially useful for writing meaningful job descriptions and for developing performance measures.

Diaries

One drawback of observations, interviews, and questionnaires is that the information they yield is likely to be dependent on the time it happens to be collected. Whatever is most salient at the time of the interview is most likely to find its way into the job and organizational analysis results. Diaries offer one solution to this problem. If job incumbents and supervisors keep a diary over a period of several weeks, the results are less likely to be biased by the timing of the analysis. For jobs that vary at different times of the year, diaries may be especially valuable.

SPECIFIC JOB ANALYSIS TECHNIQUES

Despite the value of conducting an organizational analysis, HR experts have paid relatively little attention to developing systematic methods for such an analysis. Thus, an organizational analysis usually is relatively subjective and impressionistic. In contrast, HR experts have devoted a great deal of attention to developing systematic job analysis techniques. Why the difference? It's most easily explained by the fact that government regulations and the courts have emphasized the importance of job analysis while showing little concern about organizational analysis. Legal issues related to job analysis are described later in this chapter.

The most common and widely used job analysis techniques include methods analysis, functional job analysis, standardized job analysis questionnaires, customized task inventories, and integrated approaches to job analysis. All of these techniques can yield useful information for redesigning work, developing selection procedures, designing performance measures, planning for training programs, and setting pay levels.

Methods Analysis

Methods analysis focuses on analyzing job elements, the smallest identifiable components of a job. It's most often used in conjunction with the scientific management approach to job design. Methods analysis can be used to assess minute physical movements. These movements can then be assessed to determine whether they're efficient and whether they cause undue strain. UPS successfully used methods analysis to discover how drivers naturally carried packages and how they handled money received from customers. Job design experts then determined the best way to carry packages (under the left arm) and how to handle money (place it face-up before folding). Training programs now incorporate this information to maximize the company's operational efficiency.

Computerized manufacturing technology. Although many organizations have shifted away from methods analysis, it's still used by companies that rely heavily on human labor to carry out repetitive and routine tasks accurately and efficiently. Paradoxically, new manufacturing technologies also increase the need for methods analysis. New manufacturing technologies may require a quantum jump in a manufacturing organization's precision and integration. To prevent process contamination, for example, it's no longer possible to rely on people who have a "feel" for their machines, or just to note on a blueprint that operators should "remove iron filings from the part." Automated machine tools can produce parts to more exacting specifications than can the most skilled human machinist, but to do so, they need explicit, unambiguous instructions: Where is the blower that removes the filings, and what's the orientation of the part during operation of the blower?[15] These instructions are given in the form of computer programs. Therefore, the new hardware makes it increasingly important to study and document work processes.

Reengineering.   The popularity of process reengineering has also stimulated greater use of methods analysis. Flow process charts are familiar to anyone who has participated in a reengineering effort. Such charts detail the overall sequence of an operation by focusing on either the movement of an operator or the flow of materials. Flow process charts have been used in hospitals to track patient movements, in grocery stores to analyze the checkout process, in small-batch manufacturing facilities to track the progress of material from machine to machine, in banks to examine the sequence associated with document processing, and to track supervisor-incumbent interactions during a performance appraisal interview.

Functional Job Analysis

The U.S. Training and Employment Service developed functional job analysis (FJA) to improve job placement and counseling for workers registering at local state employment offices. As in methods analysis, trained observers conduct FJA. However, with FJA, the observers use a complex rating system to describe the activities of jobs, rather than measuring activities directly.

Data, People, and Things.   The trained analysts describe jobs in terms of the extent to which they involve three types of activities: working with data, dealing with people, and handling things. For each of these aspects, the analysts provide a rating of the level of functioning required by the job. This is illustrated in Exhibit 6.4.[16]

■□ *fast fact*

Business investment in computers doubled in the last five years.

"The first 25 years of our history we provided data to people. For the next 25 years, we'll handle interactions between people."

Hasso Plattner
Co-Chairman
SAP

Exhibit 6.4
Functional Job Analysis Ratings

Data	People	Things
0 = Synthesizing	0 = Mentoring	0 = Setting Up
1 = Coordinating	1 = Negotiating	1 = Precision Working
2 = Analyzing	2 = Instructing	2 = Operating, Controlling
3 = Compiling	3 = Supervising	3 = Driving, Operating
4 = Computing	4 = Diverting	4 = Manipulating
5 = Copying	5 = Persuading	5 = Tending
6 = Comparing	6 = Speaking, Signaling	6 = Feeding, Offbearing
	7 = Serving	7 = Handling
	8 = Taking Instructions, Helping	

FJA is both a conceptual system for defining the dimensions of worker activity and a method of measuring worker activity levels. Its basic premises are as follows:

1. A fundamental distinction must be made between what gets done and what workers do to get it done. Bus drivers do not carry passengers; they drive vehicles and collect fares.

2. All jobs require workers to relate to data, people, and things to some degree.

3. In relation to things, workers draw on physical resources; in relation to data, on mental resources; and in relation to people, on interpersonal resources.

4. Although workers' behaviors or the tasks they perform can apparently be described in an infinite number of ways, only a few definitive functions are involved. Thus, in interacting with manufacturing machines, workers feed, tend, operate, and set up; in interacting with vehicles or related machines, they drive or control them. Although these functions vary in difficulty and content, each draws on a relatively narrow and specific range of worker characteristics and qualifications for effective performance.

5. The functions appropriate to dealing with data, people, or things are hierarchical and ordinal, proceeding from the complex to the simple. Thus, to indicate that a particular function—say, compiling data—reflects the job requirements is to say that it also includes lower-function requirements, such as comparing, and excludes higher-function requirements, such as analyzing.[17]

Dictionary of Occupational Titles.   The U.S. Department of Labor has used FJA as a basis for describing thousands of jobs. These results have been made available to the public in the *Dictionary of Occupational Titles (DOT)*. An example of a *DOT* job description follows:[18]

> *166.267-018 JOB ANALYST (profess. & kin.) alternate titles: personnel analyst*
>
> *Collects, analyzes, and prepares occupational information to facilitate personnel, administration, and management functions of organization. Consults with management to determine type, scope, and purpose of study. Studies current organizational occupational data and compiles distribution reports, organization and flow charts, and other background information required for study. Observes jobs and interviews workers and supervisory personnel to determine job and worker requirements. Analyzes occupational data, such as physical, mental, and training requirements of jobs and workers, and develops written summaries, such as job descriptions, job specifications, and lines of career movement. Utilizes developed occupational data to evaluate or improve methods and techniques for recruiting, selecting, promoting, evaluating, and training workers, and administration of related personnel programs. May specialize in classifying positions according to regulated guidelines to meet job classification requirements of civil service system and be known as Position Classifier.*

The identification codes in the *DOT* provide a significant amount of information. For a job analyst, this code is 166.267-018. The first three digits (166) are the occupational code, which in this case means Professional, Technical, and Managerial Occupations. The next three digits (267) represent the degree to which a jobholder typically has responsibility for and judgment over data (2 - Analyzing), people (6 - Speaking, Signaling) and things (7 - Handling). The final three digits (018) indicate the alphabetic order of titles within the occupational group having the same degree of responsibility and judgment.

Occupational Information Network (*O*NET*)

By the year 2000, the *Dictionary of Occupational Titles* will have been replaced by the U.S. Department of Labor's new job analysis service titled the *Occupational Information Network*, also known as *O*NET*. *O*NET* was first released to the public in the fall of 1998. The function of O*NET is similar to the *DOT*—it's "to provide a comprehensive database system for collecting, organizing, describing and disseminating data on job characteristics and worker attributes."[19] *O*NET* can be accessed online, but it's not just a new electronic version of the *DOT*. It represents a new conceptual framework for categorizing jobs. Development of the *DOT* was heavily influenced by the dominance of traditional manufacturing jobs earlier in the 20th century. As jobs changed, the *DOT* has gradually become obsolete. The need to reconceptualize and update the job descriptions that are used and disseminated by the U.S. government stimulated developmental work that eventually culminated in the creation of *O*NET*. *O*NET* better captures the role of advanced technologies and the increasing importance of service-based jobs. This new framework describes jobs as having six content areas, as shown in Exhibit 6.5.

Exhibit 6.5

*O*NET*s Content Model for Describing Jobs

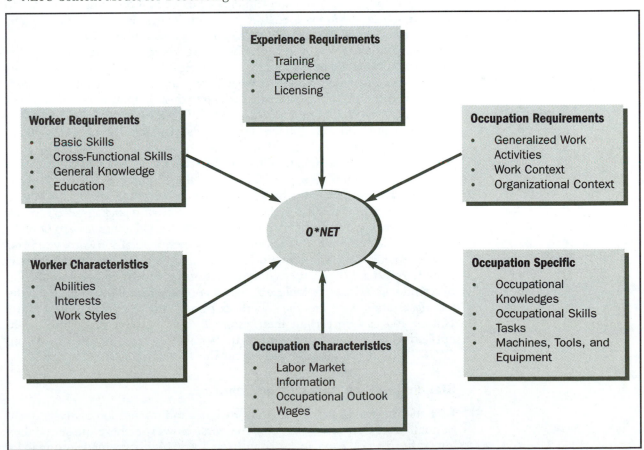

■□ *fast fact*

Approximately half of all
actuaries who are wage and
salary workers are employed
in the insurance industry.

Like the *DOT*, *O*NET* is intended to be a resource for employers, but an added objective of *O*NET* is to serve as a resource for anyone who seeks to make informed employment decisions. People will be able to get facts about occupations and jobs by visiting *O*NET*'s homepage and searching the database. Currently such information is provided by the Bureau of Labor Statistics *Occupational Outlook Handbook*, which can now be accessed through *O*NET*. For example, a search for information about the occupation of "actuaries" yielded five full pages of descriptive information about this occupation. Included were details about

- specific tasks actuaries perform,
- work conditions of typical jobs,
- education that's needed to become an actuary (including recommendations that can be used when selecting college courses),
- examinations and occupational certifications that are required for advancement in the profession,
- predictions about the job outlook through the year 2006,
- average salaries for actuaries at different stages of their careers, and
- suggestions about where to get additional information about this occupation.

In addition, the *Occupational Outlook Handbook* continues to list the FJA-based *DOT* codes, which are still used by both governmental agencies and many employers.

O*NET is likely to become an important resource for private and public employers. Suppose you're a line manager in a small business. You want to provide job descriptions for all of your employees. How can you do this given your limited resources? *O*NET* offers one solution. *O*NET* provides job descriptions for thousands of jobs. There you could find a detailed job description and then adapt it to fit the specific conditions in your company. *O*NET* could also help you describe jobs that do not yet exist in your organization. This would make it easier for you to describe future jobs to the new talent you'll need to recruit as you expand. *O*NET* is quick, and it's essentially free. Furthermore, the job descriptions available through *O*NET* are based on hundreds of observations.[20]

With a bit of research, you'll soon discover that *O*NET* is not the only resource of this kind, however. You also could purchase a commercial software product that includes hundreds of job descriptions, ready for you to edit and tailor to your needs. The commercial software package also is quick and inexpensive. The software package may be a good alternative to *O*NET*, but before deciding whether to purchase the commercial software, you need to know whether the information used to generate the job descriptions is equally reliable. What sources of information were used to generate the job descriptions? Were acceptable job analysis procedures followed to create the job descriptions, or are the job descriptions just convenient examples? Unless you can be certain that systematic job analysis procedures were applied to very large samples of incumbents in each job of interest to you, *O*NET* is probably the best solution for this hypothetical small business.

Standardized Job Analysis Questionnaires

Like the functional job analysis approach, standardized job analysis questionnaires rely on ratings of job behaviors. However, these questionnaires generally do not need to be completed by a highly trained job analyst.

Instead, they rely primarily on incumbents' and supervisors' responses, or perhaps the ratings of a human resource manager.

The items on standardized questionnaires are intentionally written to be generally applicable to a wide variety of jobs. For example, consider the job of salesperson in an ice cream parlor. Relevant items from a standardized questionnaire might read "Works in an enclosed area that is cold" and "Chooses among items that differ in terms of color." The value of using such general statements is that it allows you to analyze all types of jobs using the same items. For example, you could use the same questionnaire to analyze the jobs performed by the production workers who make ice cream, packers who prepare it for shipping, drivers who deliver it to locations around town, and salespeople who eventually serve it to customers.

Two of the most widely used standardized job analysis questionnaires are the Position Analysis Questionnaire (PAQ) and the Job Element Inventory (JEI).

Position Analysis Questionnaire.   The Position Analysis Questionnaire (PAQ) is often described as a worker-oriented method of job analysis. The term *worker-oriented* was coined to describe the idea that the items on the PAQ can be applied to the activities and behaviors of all workers, regardless of the specific jobs they perform. The creator of the PAQ, Ernest J. McCormick, started with two assumptions: (a) relatively few work behaviors exist across all jobs, and (b) all jobs can be described in terms of how much they involve each of these behaviors. Based on these assumptions, he developed a structured questionnaire containing 194 statements that describe worker behaviors. Each statement is rated on scales such as extent of use, importance to the job, and amount of time spent performing the job. The statements are organized into the six divisions shown in Exhibit 6.6.[21] These divisions are somewhat abstract, but not as abstract as the *DOT*'s grouping of data, people and things.

The PAQ has been used to analyze hundreds of jobs held by thousands of people. The results from many of these job analyses have been centrally stored in a database to allow comparisons between similar jobs in different organizations. Using the very large data set generated with the PAQ, research has been conducted to determine whether a small number of dimensions of work behaviors can be used to describe all jobs. The results of this research suggest that work involves five basic dimensions:

- having communication, decision-making, or social responsibilities (e.g., working with people, supervising and planning activities);
- performing skilled activities (e.g., using technical devices or tools, doing manual precision work);
- being physically active, and related environmental conditions (e.g., performing activities that require full use of the body and the setting in which this occurs, such as loading pallets in a factory);
- operating vehicles and equipment (e.g., working with machines that require the use of sensory and perceptual processes); and
- processing information (e.g., working with data of all types, which may or may not involve using machines such as computers).

The PAQ database also contains information about the relationships between PAQ responses, job aptitudes, and pay rates for the labor market. Thus, the PAQ can be used to decide what selection criteria to use when making hiring decisions, and it can be used to design pay packages.

Exhibit 6.6
The PAQ's Six Divisions for Organizing Work Behaviors

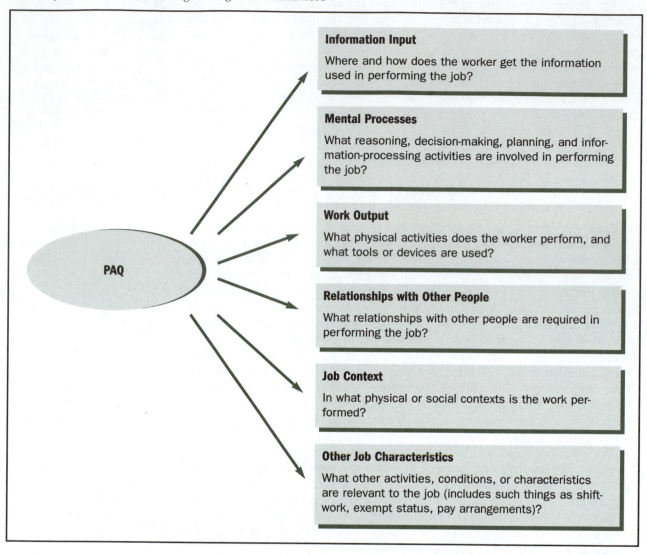

However, the PAQ must be bought from a consulting firm; consequently, direct costs appear high. Another potential drawback to using the PAQ is that it requires a postcollege reading comprehension level. Thus, the PAQ shouldn't be given to raters who have lower levels of reading skill or English fluency.[22]

Job Element Inventory. Closely modeled after the PAQ, the 153-item Job Element Inventory (JEI) has a readability index estimated to be at the tenth-grade level and is explicitly designed for completion by job incumbents. For example, the PAQ item "Dirty Environment (situations in which workers and/or their clothing easily becomes dirty, greasy—environments often associated with garages, foundries, coal mines, highway construction, furnace cleaning)" is "Work where you easily become dirty" on the JEI. The dimensional structure of the JEI is similar to that of the PAQ. Another advantage of the JEI lies in the cost savings associated with having incumbents rather than trained analysts complete the instrument.[23]

Management Position Description Questionnaire. The Management Position Description Questionnaire (MPDQ) is a standardized questionnaire containing 197 items related to managers' concerns, responsibilities, demands, restrictions, and miscellaneous characteristics.[24] These items have been condensed into 13 essential components of managerial jobs, as illustrated in Exhibit 6.7.

The MPDQ is designed for analyzing all managerial positions, so responses are expected to vary by managerial level in any organization and also across different organizations. The MPDQ is appropriate for creating job families and placing new managerial jobs into the right job family; developing selection procedures and performance appraisal forms; determining the training needs of employees moving into managerial jobs; and designing managerial pay systems.

Exhibit 6.7
Components of Managerial Jobs Assessed by the Managerial Position Description Questionnaire

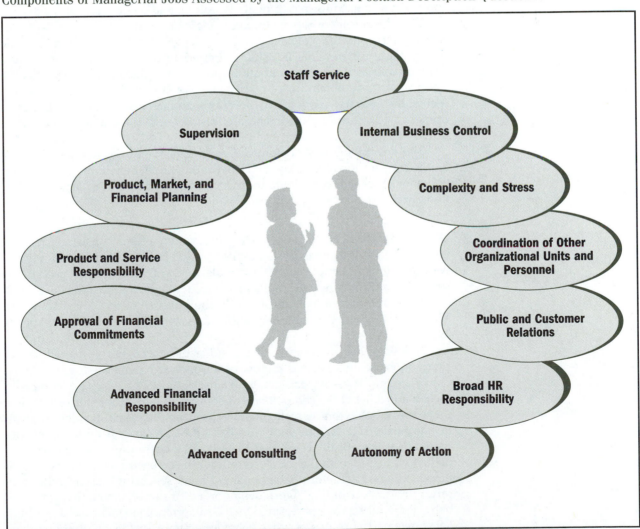

Customized Task and Work Behavior Inventories

A customized inventory is a listing of tasks or work behaviors, called items, for the jobs or group of jobs being analyzed, with a provision for various types of ratings to be made for each item listed. Usually, tasks or work behaviors are rated in terms of importance, frequency, and difficulty.[25] These inventories are customized in that they're developed from the ground up for each new customer, such as a company or a unit within a company or a manager. In a task inventory, the items are very specific. It's therefore not unusual to have 200 to 300 items on a task inventory. In comparison, a work-behavior item refers to a larger chunk of work, which usually involves doing several specific tasks. As a consequence, customized inventories based on work-behavior items are shorter and more user-friendly. The trade-off is that the results are somewhat less specific.

When responding to a task or work-behavior inventory, the job incumbent, supervisor, or job analyst checks the appropriate scale responses for each item listed. If the job of HR analyst were analyzed using a customized work-behavior inventory, a part of the inventory might look like Exhibit 6.8. Because the inventory method is based on a structured questionnaire, it's easy and quick to score and analyze. The results can be readily processed by computer and used for recruitment, selection, and compensation.

The development of customized task or work-behavior inventories requires large numbers of employees and complex statistical analysis, so the use of these instruments is usually limited to organizations that employ many people in the same occupation (police, firefighters, data entry clerks). The use of these inventories is fairly widespread in city and state governments, the military, and large corporations. In fact, much of the early development work carried out to generate this method of job analysis was conducted by the U.S. Air Force and AT&T.

The development of customized behavior inventories depends heavily on the cooperation of employees. Usually, they must be willing to have their behavior observed, participate in interviews, and respond to lengthy questionnaires.

Observation and Interviews.   The observation phase consists of on-site visits in which the job analysts observe the job being performed by incumbents and review samples of the materials, forms, and equipment used in the job. Brief, informal interviews may be conducted during this phase, if needed, to clarify observations and identify the purpose of employee activities. This step is intended to familiarize job analysts with various aspects of the job.

Following the observation phase, subject matter experts—usually experienced job incumbents and their supervisors—are invited to a group interview meeting. These experts generate a list of work behaviors performed on the job and a list of the competencies necessary for adequate performance of those work behaviors, which then are used as the items in a job analysis questionnaire like the one shown in Exhibit 6.8. Ratings from the questionnaire are arithmetically combined to arrive at a description of the job. Work behaviors included in the job description are screened based on their combined ratings. Each work behavior must meet several minimum criteria in order to be a "qualifying" work behavior. For instance, a "qualifying" work behavior would be one performed by the majority of job incumbents. Exhibit 6.9 shows partial results of work behavior ratings for the job of HR analyst.

Exhibit 6.8

Job Analysis Questionnaire for Human Resource Analyst I

Work Behaviors	A. Is the work behavior performed in the position? 1 = Yes 0 = No	B. Indicate the percentage of time spent performing it. The percentages must total exactly 100.	C. How important is it that this work behavior be performed acceptably? 4 = Critical 3 = Very important 2 = Moderately important 1 = Slightly important 0 = Of no importance	D. Is it necessary that employees new to the position be able to perform this work behavior? 1 = Yes 0 = No
1. *Counsels employees* on various matters (career opportunities, insurance and retirement options, personal problems relating to employment, etc.) by listening, asking relevant questions, and noting alternative courses of action.	(circle one) 1 0	(circle one) _____ %	(circle one) 4 3 2 1 0	(circle one) 1 0
2. *Disseminates information* (job vacancies and requirements, insurance and retirement programs, merit system rules, etc.) to applicants, employees, and the public verbally through written materials and/or using electronic means.	1 0	_____ %	4 3 2 1 0	1 0
3. *Prepares reports* (e.g., management reports, HUD reports) by collecting, organizing, and summarizing statistical data, historical documents, or verbal records, or all three.	1 0	_____ %	4 3 2 1 0	1 0
4. *Interviews applicants or employees* in a structured or unstructured manner to investigate applicant or employee complaints, grievances, or adverse action appeal cases and, to identify qualified applicants for specific job vacancies.	1 0	_____ %	4 3 2 1 0	1 0
5. *Conducts job analyses* by reviewing written records (e.g., job descriptions, class specifications), observing and interviewing job experts, and administering questionnaires.	1 0	_____ %	4 3 2 1 0	1 0

Statement 5 would now be eliminated because it doesn't qualify as being part of the job for most incumbents.

The Critical Incident Technique. The critical incident technique (CIT) is another approach that can be used to create task statements. It involves having people who are knowledgeable about a job describe the critical job incidents that represent effective or ineffective performance.[26] Those describing the incidents are also asked to describe what led up to the incidents, what

Exhibit 6.9
Job Analysis Results for Human Resource Analyst I

		Work Behavior		
Item	Work Behavior	Percentage Who Perform	Mean Percentage of Time Spent	Median Importance Rating*
1	Counsels employees	100	5	2
2	Disseminates information	100	33	3
3	Prepares reports	100	33	3
4	Interviews applicants	100	14	2
5	Conducts job analyses	0	0	0

Note: Importance ratings are based on the responses of only SMEs who perform the task.

*Scale for median importance rating: 3 = Critical
                                      2 = Very important
                                      1 = Moderately important
                                      0 = Of slight or no importance

the consequences of the behavior were, and whether the behavior was under the incumbent's control. Here is a critical incident report written by a librarian, as an example of effective job performance:

> "A person who was apparently somewhat disturbed came into the library and started yelling obscenities. When I heard the commotion, I came out of my office and tried to calm him down. I was really afraid he might hurt someone or cause some damage to our collection. I spoke with him for about ten minutes and finally convinced him to step outside. As soon as he did so, I had a staff member call the police and I went outside to try to keep him from leaving the area until the police arrived. Luckily, nothing more happened once we went outside. Later that day, however, a reporter from the local TV news came by and wanted the full story. I told her the basic flow of events but tried not to say anything that would reflect poorly on the library or compromise the rights of our intruder. We were all happy to see that the story wasn't carried on the ten o'clock news that evening."

After the critical incident reports are gathered (often, several dozen are obtained from incumbents in the job), the job analyst writes task statements. For example, the librarian's critical incident report was used to create task statements like these:

- Handles serious disturbances created by users of the library.
- Represents the library to members of the news media (e.g., reporters).

Advantages and Disadvantages of the Customized Approach.   A major advantage of customized task inventories is that they generate vivid descriptions of the job. By reading a job description developed using this method, it's easy to picture what the job involves. Rather than generating abstract descriptions that could apply to any job, this method creates specific descriptions that clearly outline the tasks required. This advantage also makes it easier to develop training programs for people who will do the job.[27]

The major disadvantages of customized task inventories are the time required to gather the critical information used to develop the task statements and the complex data analysis required after task ratings have been obtained. For example, one job analysis conducted for an organization with 120 positions (i.e., 120 employees) involved 106,000 task ratings; another job analysis for an organization with 3,600 positions involved 1.8 million ratings. Desktop computers, intranets, and even artificial intelligence systems can ease the task of collecting and analyzing data sets like these. Therefore, this disadvantage is not as significant as it was just a few years ago.[28]

Analyzing Needed Competencies

Recall that competencies are the skills, knowledge, abilities, and other characteristics that someone needs to perform a job effectively. Information about required competencies is essential if job analysis results are going to be used to develop procedures for selecting people to perform jobs. This information can also be very helpful for developing recruitment strategies and for designing training programs. Competency information can be obtained using either a standardized or customized approach.

Standardized Approach. A well-known, standardized approach to assessing ability requirements is the Ability Requirements Approach.[29] This approach can be used to assess the level of ability needed in a job using 50 different ability dimensions. Usually, job incumbents are trained to understand what each ability involves, and then they use a rating scale to report the level of ability required in their work.

Customized Approach. The example of a job analysis questionnaire for a human resource analyst shown in Exhibits 6.8 and 6.10 reflects a customized approach. In addition to the information generated by the customized work-behavior inventory, this customized procedure also yielded information about the competencies relevant to the job. The procedure involves asking subject matter experts (usually incumbents and supervisors) to identify all the skills, knowledge, attitudes, values, and so on that they think may be necessary to perform the work. A group interview meeting may be held to create the list of possible competencies to examine. Based on the results of the group interview meeting, a competency rating questionnaire is created and distributed to subject matter experts. Respondents rate the competencies along a number of dimensions: importance, whether a new incumbent needs the competency upon entry to the job, and the extent to which the competency distinguishes a superior incumbent from an adequate one. Exhibit 6.10 shows a portion of a competency rating questionnaire.

Exhibit 6.11, on page 239, shows results for the competency items. Based on these results, the organization may conclude that it should ensure that new hires have a good knowledge of HR procedures and good computer skills, as well as some familiarity with relevant laws and ethical standards. To maximize performance, the organization may also want to offer additional training in both HR procedures and legal and ethical standards. Investing in computer training for new hires may not pay off as much, however. While computer skills are necessary, they do not contribute much to outstanding performance. More likely, all employees learn whatever computer skills are needed to do the job.

"When you're working counter to your values, it's like putting the wrong shoes on your feet every day."

Martha I. Finney
Co-Author of
Find Your Calling, Love Your Life

Exhibit 6.10

Questionnaire to Identify Competencies Needed for Human Resource Analyst I

Competencies	E. Is the competency used in the position? 1 = Yes 0 = No	F. How important is this competency to acceptable job performance? 4 = Critical 3 = Very important 2 = Moderately important 1 = Slightly important 0 = Of no importance	G. Is it necessary that employees new to the position possess this competency? 1 = Yes 0 = No	H. To what extent does this distinguish between superior and adequate new employees? 3 = To a great extent 2 = Considerably 1 = Moderately 0 = Not at all
	(circle one)	**(circle one)**	**(circle one)**	**(circle one)**
A. *Knowledge of HR procedures:* Knowledge of the working rules and regulations. Included are policies on overtime, absences, vacations, holidays, sick leave, court leave, selection, promotion, reassignment, disciplinary actions, terminations, grievance procedures, performance appraisals, and so forth, as outlined in relevant manuals.	1 0	4 3 2 1 0	1 0	3 2 1 0
B. *Knowledge of organizational structure:* Knowledge of whom to contact when various situations arise. Included is the knowledge of interrelationships between organizational units, lines of authority, and responsibility within organizational units.	1 0	4 3 2 1 0	1 0	3 2 1 0
C. *Knowledge of laws and ethics:* Knowledge of legal and ethical standards to be maintained in HR work. Included are ethical considerations governing general professional practice (e.g., confidentiality of records) as well as state and federal regulations governing fair employment practices (e.g., EEO legislation and the Uniform Guidelines on Employee Selection Procedures).	1 0	4 3 2 1 0	1 0	3 2 1 0
D. *Computer skill:* Skill in the use of a computer terminal. Included is a basic knowledge of the keyboard and of computer terminology.	1 0	4 3 2 1 0	1 0	3 2 1 0

JOB FAMILIES AND CAREER PATHS

The initial results of job analyses are typically many separate and unique job descriptions and employee specifications—as many as there are unique jobs. Often, however, these unique jobs aren't greatly different from each other. That is, employees who perform one job may be able to perform several others. And increasingly, this flexibility is what employers need. This is why

Exhibit 6.11

Competency Rating Results for Human Resource Analyst I

Item	Competency	Percentage Who Use It	Median Importance Rating*	Percentage Rating it Necessary at Entry	Median Rating for Distinguishing Superior Employees**
		Competency Ratings			
A	Knowledge of HR procedures	100	2.5	70	3.0
B	Knowledge of organizational structure	100	2.0	0	2.0
C	Knowledge of laws and ethical standards	100	2.0	60	2.5
D	Computer skill	100	2.5	80	0.5

Note: Ratings provided by job incumbents. Results are shown for SMEs who reported they use the competency, only.

*Scale for importance ratings: 3 = Critical
2 = Very important
1 = Moderately important
0 = Of slight or no importance

**Scale for extent to which competency distinguishes superior from average employees in the job: 3 = To a great extent
2 = Considerably
1 = Moderately
0 = Slightly or not at all

organizations group jobs into families. Jobs are placed in the same family to the extent that they require similar worker specifications or have similar tasks or are of similar value to the organization.[30]

When BPX recognized the value of having a more flexible organization, they used job analysis to restructure the work organization and, consequently, the way people within the organization behave. In their new structure, BPX has job families that group together jobs of similar content. They used competency information to link together jobs in different families. Thus, job content and worker specifications form the warp and woof of the organization's total job fabric, as described in Managing Change: BPX Employees Get Back on Track.[31]

Broadbanding

When jobs are grouped into only a very small set of categories, as they did at BPX, the term "broadbanding" is used. Broadbanding involves clustering jobs (or even job families) into wide tiers for the purposes of managing employee career growth and administering pay. Broadbanding has become an attractive alternative to traditional job and pay structures. It fits flatter organizational structures well because it collapses multiple salary grades with narrowly defined pay ranges into fewer salary grades with more pay potential. Broadbanding clusters more jobs into broader job family categories. Job descriptions are still used, but they encompass a broad class of jobs rather than specific jobs.[32]

As described earlier in this chapter, MetLife Auto and Home used a modified broadbanding approach to support a new corporation culture that placed less emphasis on rules and more emphasis on flexibility. Although

fast fact

A 1998 study of firms that use broadbanding found that it neither increased nor decreased costs.

MANAGING CHANGE

BPX Employees Get Back on Track

Like so many other successful organizations, the Exploration Division of British Petroleum (BPX), the third-largest oil company in the world, had accumulated many layers of bureaucracy over the years. "Careers" were defined by a time-in-grade system, and career success was equated with management titles. Individual contributors, such as engineers and other technology experts, had to switch over to management if they wanted to advance to the top levels of the company. For BPX to realize its vision of success, this needed to change. Senior management wanted a more dynamic system that would challenge employees constantly to gain and apply the new skills needed by the business.

The framework the company devised for creating this strategic shift was a set of competency matrices. Each matrix describes steps in the career ladder—from the lowest level to the highest—along the vertical axis, and the competencies that were required for each step across the horizontal axis. BPX needed talented individual contributors to support its technology mission as much as it needed managers to support its business mission. Therefore, it created competency matrices for two types of employees: (1) people who want to go into management and (2) people whose talents and expertise lie elsewhere (individual contributors). The management matrix is common across all the job families, but the individual contributor path is unique to each job family.

This dual-track system was designed by multidisciplinary teams of BPX staff members from various locations around the globe. On the teams were representatives of all the types of employees who would be affected by the shift: managers, individual contributors, human resource staff, and senior executives. Together they developed the descriptors for competencies and levels of performance that applied globally to each particular job family. Drilling managers in Aberdeen, South Dakota, would have the same career path as drilling managers in Alaska.

To bridge the gap between existing competencies and what the business needed, the teams created development matrices. These were designed to stimulate each individual's thinking about how his or her skills might be developed through formal training, coaching, on-the-job experimentation, self-study, and so on. The matrices are so detailed that employees can see precisely what types of roles are available in BPX and what levels of performance are required at each level.

In addition to opening up new avenues for increasing productivity, the matrices provide support for other human resource initiatives. For example, BPX launched an upward feedback program, in which employees rate their bosses' people management skills—one important competency needed for most managerial jobs. The matrices also are linked to a personal development planning system that individuals use for professional growth and self-marketing within the company.

To learn more about British Petroleum, visit the company home page at **www.bp.com**

the reasons were different, a similar approach was taken by one of MetLife's competitors. As described in Managing Strategically: Aetna Uses Job Analysis to Achieve Greater Profitability, the use of job analysis to reduce bureaucracy and broaden the domain of employees' work activities is common in organizations that are transforming themselves in order to compete more effectively.[33]

MANAGING STRATEGICALLY
Aetna Uses Job Analysis to Achieve Greater Profitability

Aetna Life and Casualty Company is a leading provider of insurance and financial services. Its lines of business include health care, casualty coverage for commercial and personal property, life insurance, and asset management. After years of great success, Aetna's profits started to decline in 1987. This happened partly because the company had a product line that was too large and too diversified and because some of its businesses were unprofitable. Also, overhead expenses exceeded the industry average in many cases.

In the early 1990s, then-CEO Ronald E. Compton set about the task of making the company more profitable. Like other large insurers in the industry, such as ITT Corporation, Hartford Fire Insurance Company, and Cigna Corporation, Aetna started eliminating unprofitable lines of businesses. These included its individual health and reinsurance operations. Soon Compton announced plans to stop selling guaranteed investment contracts (GICs) and single-premium annuities to pension plans. At the same time, he announced that ten percent of the workforce would be laid off.

In addition to eliminating people and lines of business, Aetna reengineered many areas of the business and introduced new technologies. Throughout the process, corporate HR staff partnered with managers to implement the new strategy. Specifically, it sought to ensure that the new work environment is consistent with Aetna's vision:

> *"Aetna's employees have worked together to create one of the world's leading providers of insurance, financial and health care services. We strive to offer unmatched customer service and to achieve superior financial performance. To attain greatness, we have become a multi-niche company that is quick, flexible and right in a challenging environment. Our employees demonstrate the highest levels of integrity and competency. In all we do, our policy is to go beyond the expected."*

Aetna's three core values are invest in people, build trust, and inspire excellence. The first core value—invest in people—influences how work is structured throughout the company. Specifically, Aetna's commitment is to be sure that all employees have the opportunity to reach their potential. This implies that careers progress along logical paths within the company. With all the changes that were occurring, employees found it hard to see how what they were being asked to do in this time of turmoil might relate to their own longer term career objectives. To address this issues, new career paths were developed using job analysis and broadbanding.

The human resource professionals helped the company reduce more than 7,000 individual job titles to 200 job families. In effect, they redesigned jobs to give more latitude to the employees and to managers. The old job classification system specifically delineated the tasks that employees were supposed to do. This discouraged employees from taking on additional responsibilities. With the new job families, employees can perform many tasks and be rewarded for doing so, without having to go through a promotion procedure and without having to revise the job description. Aetna used job analysis to define the boundaries and content of its job families.

Broader job families are particularly useful in organizations like Aetna that have reduced the layers of management and, in the process, reduced the opportunities for advancement through promotion. Job families give employees and line managers more, but not unlimited, flexibility. Like kinship families, job families describe groupings of related members. But in this case, the members are tasks, related through their common reliance on particular skills and abilities. Identification of these group-ings of related tasks is consistent with the core value "Invest in people" because it shifts the focus to a consideration of each person's current and potential capabilities.

Today, Aetna is rapidly expanding through mergers and acquisitions. As it does so, it'll continue to use job analysis as a tool for organizing. Job analysis can be used to identify similarities and differences in the content of jobs that exist in differ-ent companies, identify areas of redundancy, and provide a blueprint for the cre-ation of new positions.

To learn more about Aetna, visit the company home page at **www.aetna.com**

TRENDS IN JOB AND ORGANIZATIONAL ANALYSIS

At some organizations, such as AT&T and Microsoft, technological changes occur so rapidly that traditional job analysis is all but impossible. And increasingly, job requirements are hard to specify because companies expect employees to do "whatever the customer wants." In these situations, job analysis becomes much more dynamic and fluid. Here, the HR profession-als, line managers, and employees all need to value flexibility and adapt-ability. These changes in the nature of "jobs" have major implications for vir-tually all other HR activities as organizations enter the fast-paced world of the 21st century, but they pose particularly great challenges for traditional job analysis procedures.

"The shelf-life of job analysis results is only as long as the duration of the current job configurations."

Karen E. May
Partner
Human Resource Solutions

Decreased job specialization, increased job sharing and the increased prevalence of work teams are just a few of the reasons that people have begun to question the usefulness of traditional job analysis techniques. Traditional techniques force boundaries to be drawn between jobs and are inconsistent with the trend toward increased sharing of responsibilities across jobs and across levels in the organization.[34]

The apparent inconsistency between the assumptions of traditional job analysis and new approaches to managing employees is so great that it has even led some human resource professionals to raise the question: "Do we need job analysis anymore?" Karen May of Human Resource Solutions, a consulting firm that includes job analysis among the services it offers, thinks the answer to this question is a qualified yes. Although traditional job analy-sis techniques may not be useful in all situations, job analysis provides value for organizations that have at least some jobs that are structured around spe-cific and relatively stable tasks and organizations that are concerned about legal compliance and their ability to defend their employment practices. Furthermore, in many cases, traditional techniques can be modified and suc-cessfully adapted to current organizational realities. One type of modifica-tion is to adapt job analysis techniques for the purpose of conducting an organizational analysis.

Future-Oriented Job and Organizational Analysis

By examining several years of traditional job analysis results for the job of store managers, CORE, an HR consulting company, was able to map the changes that have occurred in this particular type of work. CORE conducted hundreds of job analyses for this position during the 1980s and 1990s, using a semi-custom/semi-standard approach. The standard aspect of their approach was that they always assessed the six domains of store managers jobs shown in Exhibit 6.12.[35] As the exhibit reveals, customer service and human resource management activities are now a much larger part of the job, while store operations, administration, and expense control are now a smaller part of the job.

Corresponding to the changes in job tasks are changes in the competencies required to perform these job effectively. Specific competencies that have increased in importance are managing relationships, leadership, and communication.

To address the reality of constant change, traditional analysis procedures can be easily modified to provide information about the likely nature of future job tasks and the competencies that employees are likely to need to perform those new tasks. In a future-oriented job analysis, the emphasis shifts from *descriptions* of the present to *prescriptions* about what the future should be like. For example, suppose an organization has decided to downsize. Traditional job analysis could be used to identify all the tasks currently performed by employees. Then, a future-oriented job analysis could be conducted to focus attention of the question of which tasks the organization *should* continue doing, and which they should eliminate or outsource. This same approach can be used to guide other types of organizational change.

"At one point we were hiring hands and arms and legs, and now we are hiring total people—with minds more important than the other."

Robert J. Eaton
Co-Chairman
DaimlerChrysler

Exhibit 6.12
The Changing Job of Store Manager

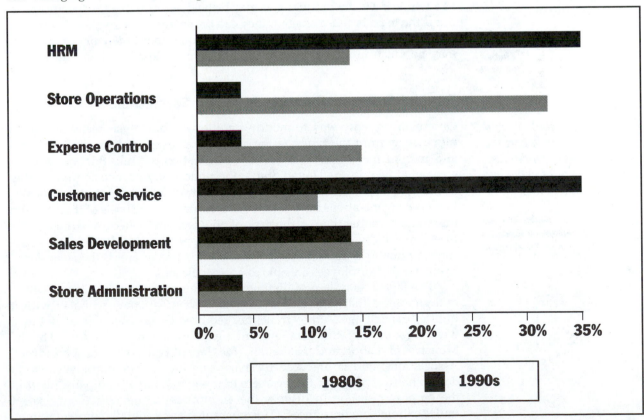

For example, future-oriented job analysis was used to help a fashion retailer redesign its floor layout, redesign jobs and create new ones, and alter its work processes.[36]

From "My Job" to "My Work"

Today's environment requires that organizations be adaptable and that individuals be flexible. Job analysis techniques were developed in a time when organizations and jobs were more stable and predictable. People could be hired to do a particular job, and they could expect to do basically the same job in the same way for many months or even years. This arrangement was convenient for management and workers, except when management wanted the workers to change or do something "not in their job descriptions."

Today, organizations focus on how they can get flexibility without worker resistance, while also satisfying workers' needs for comfort. Organizations such as Nissan and Honda hire applicants to work for the company rather than to do a specific job. At Southwest Airlines, Libby Sartain, vice president of people, likes to say that they hire people to do work, not jobs. Thus, we are seeing a shift in employee's attention—from only thinking about doing "my job" to thinking about doing whatever is necessary to accomplish the organization's work.[37] Corresponding to this, some human resource professionals have argued that the term *work analysis* should be used in place of the term job analysis.[38]

This shift from a focus on "the job" to "the work" is almost inevitable in organizations where work is organized around teams instead of individuals. In a team environment, the tasks performed by a particular individual may depend on the talents and interests of the other people in the team. The team as a whole is assigned duties and may be held accountable for specific tasks, but if the team is self-managed, they can organize the team's work any way they wish. In such situations, asking individuals about the work of the team may be much more useful than asking them to describe their "individual job."[39]

From Job Tasks and Behaviors to Worker Specifications

One relatively easy way to modify traditional job analysis techniques is to move away from the typical approach of emphasizing tasks and behaviors and instead focus more on worker specifications. While this approach is somewhat new in the United States, the philosophy of focusing on worker attributes rather than specific jobs has a long tradition in Japan. Traditionally, Japanese organizations have selected individuals on the basis of their fit with the company rather than on the basis of how well they can do a particular job. In essence, individuals are organizational applicants rather than job applicants. Continuous training rather than selection procedures is the means used to ensure that employees are able to do specific jobs.

The Japanese system of lifetime employment, *shushin koyo*, comes close to a guarantee that once employees join a company, they will stay with it until retirement age. Although neither required by law nor formalized by a written contract, lifetime employment is encouraged by and endorsed by the Ministry of Labor and Nikkeiren (the Japan Federation of Employers' Associations) and is practiced by major employers. The employees won't decide halfway through their careers to move to another company, nor will the employer decide to dismiss the employees before retirement, except under extreme circumstances. (This guarantee has generally applied to men

"The job is just a social artifact. Most societies since the beginning of time have done fine without jobs. In the preindustrial past, people worked very hard, but they did not have jobs."

William Bridges
Author
Job Shift

"We no longer look at a job as a function or a certain kind of work. Instead, we see it as a set of skills and competencies."

Marile Robinson
Redeployment Managers
Intel Corporation

only; women have usually left their jobs once they were married or pregnant.) With lifetime employment, practices of selecting people for the company and not the job help provide flexibility.[40] In effect, the traditional Japanese approach to managing human resources is competency-based, rather than job-based.

In the United Kingdom, job analysis procedures have been used to detail the competencies needed for a wide variety of jobs. As described in the feature, Managing Globally: Competency Modeling Takes the UK by Storm, a decade of intensive effort has been dedicated to determining the competencies needed to perform currently available jobs.[41] The goal is to use the information to design more effective education and training programs.

Job Analysis for Customers

A desire to maximize customer satisfaction drives many organizations to look for new approaches to managing. Having nearly run out of new ideas, some progressive companies began to realize that there are many parallels between managing customers and managing employees. Peter Mills, a business professor and service management expert, even suggested that customers should be thought of as "partial employees" of the organization.

If one thinks of customers as partial employees, the next logical step is to consider how human resource management practices might be used with customers. Professors Benjamin Schneider and David Bowen have done just that. They advise organizations to use job analysis techniques to assess their

"How do I know what customers want? I ask them every chance I get."

Richard L. Huber
Chairman and former CEO
Aetna, Inc.

MANAGING GLOBALLY
Competency Modeling Takes the UK by Storm

Within the United Kingdom, the public's concern over how employers do, and should, develop their employees has focused attention on competencies. Traditionally in the UK, the status of one's family within the class structure largely determined educational opportunities and educational achievement, and in turn was often *presumed* to result in competence at work. Demonstration of one's job skills often wasn't required to land good managerial jobs.

In 1981, the Manpower Services Commission published a report that suggested a strategy for improving vocational education standards to align them more closely with competencies needed to perform modern jobs. The objective was nothing short of developing a more flexible and highly skilled national workforce. Subsequent documents emphasized the need for major reform and began to sketch out the details of a new national policy. One stated that "vocational qualifications need to relate more directly and clearly to the competence required (and acquired) at work." In 1986, the National Council for Vocational Qualifications was formed to develop national occupational competency standards.

Responsibility for developing managerial competencies and standards was given to the National Forum for Management Education and Development. To accomplish this task, they analyzed the roles of thousands of managers from hundreds of organizations using interview and questionnaire techniques. Its work was guided by a well-specified set of procedures developed and disseminated by the Manpower Services Commission. The set of procedures closely approximates the procedures for the customized approach to job analysis described in this chapter.

current customer role and to develop a description of the ideal role that customers could play.

For many organizations, customers are given tasks to do before they arrive on site (e.g., mortgage companies send forms for customers to complete and checklists of items to attach to the forms; surgical outpatient clinics give patients dietary instructions to follow the day before they're to have surgery, etc.). Once on site, the organization is likely to want customers to engage in some behaviors and avoid others. Job analysis procedures can help the organization identify customer behaviors and/or competencies that increase or decrease the probability of a successful service encounter.

For example, many banks have installed ATMs and drastically reduced the number of tellers available to customers. For this new model of banking to succeed, it's important for customers to use the ATMs for as many of their transactions as possible. If they choose instead to go to a teller, a long queue begins to form, creating dissatisfaction for customers and employees alike. What explains why some customers resist using the ATMs, even when they can provide faster service? A job analysis may reveal that customers don't understand, or simply don't have, the competencies needed to operate an ATM. Having such information is the first step to solving the problem.

Detailed "job" analysis results describe the behaviors and competencies needed from customers. The organization can then decide whether customer behaviors are best modified by

- selecting different customers (e.g., sell to a different market),
- training customers (e.g., give them better instructions), and/or
- increasing their motivation to engage in the desired behaviors (e.g., change the service fee structure).

LEGAL CONSIDERATIONS

Jobs and job analysis are changing. Like all aspects of managing human resources, they're evolving and adapting to environmental conditions. These conditions include not only changes in the nature of competition and technology, but also changes in the legal landscape.

Because it serves as the basis for selection decisions, performance appraisals, compensation, and training, job analysis has received considerable attention from legal and regulatory bodies. Principles for conducting appropriate job analyses have been articulated in the *Uniform Guidelines* and several court decisions. For example, Section 14.C.2 of the *Uniform Guidelines* states that "there shall be a job analysis which includes an analysis of the important work behaviors required for successful performance." Any job analysis should thus focus on work behavior(s) and the tasks associated with them.[42]

Where job analysis has not been performed, selection decisions have been successfully challenged (*Kirkland v. New York Department of Correctional Services*, 1974; *Albemarle Paper Company v. Moody*, 1975). Numerous court decisions regarding job analysis and promotion and performance appraisal also exist. For example, in *Brito v. Zia Company* (1973), the court states that the performance appraisal system of an organization is a selection procedure and therefore must be validated—that is, it must be anchored in job analysis. And in *Rowe v. General Motors* (1972), the court ruled that to prevent discriminatory practices in promotion decisions, a company should have written objective standards for promotion. In *U.S. v. City of Chicago* (1978), the court stated that, in addition to having objective standards for promotion, the standards should describe the job to which the person is being considered for promotion. These objective standards can be determined through job analysis.[43]

The *Americans With Disabilities Act of 1990* (ADA) draws attention to the importance of job analysis also. The law itself doesn't require written job descriptions, but when the EEOC investigates an employer's compliance with ADA, written job descriptions are one of the first documents they ask to see. To comply with ADA requirements, employers should conduct analyses to identify essential functions and formulate job descriptions to facilitate compliance with the law. Written job descriptions may provide evidence, although not conclusive, of the job's "essential functions" and serve as baselines for performance reviews. It's important, therefore, that written job descriptions be accurate and correspond to the current requirements of the job.[44]

■□ *fast fact*

Workplace participation of the 17 million U.S. adults with less severe disabilities has actually fallen during the last decade.

SUMMARY

The creation and maintenance of effective organizations require a comprehensive understanding of the work that needs to be done and the way work is structured into jobs. Job analysis can provide information about the duties associated with jobs, the behaviors required to fulfill those duties, and the competencies needed by job holders. In turn, this information is helpful for determining hiring criteria, designing training programs, developing measures of performance, creating career paths, and setting pay policies. Thus, job analysis results serve as a basis for linking together all human resource activities and also linking these activities to the needs of the business.

Job analysis can be conducted in a variety of ways. When choosing a method for conducting job analysis, the best choice depends on the intended purpose. Standardized methods make it easy to compare the results for a particular job with results found for many other similar or dissimilar jobs—including jobs in other organizations. Thus, it can be useful for setting pay schedules and creating career ladders. Compared to standardized approaches, customized job analysis methods provide more job-specific details. Such details are particularly useful for designing training programs and creating performance measurement and feedback systems. Regardless of the approach, job analysis serves as the backbone for nearly all the human resource activities described in the chapters ahead.

TERMS TO REMEMBER

Broadbanding
Career paths
Competencies
Critical Incident Technique (CIT)
Customized task inventories
Dictionary of Occupational Titles (DOT)
Functional Job Analysis (FJA)
Future-oriented job analysis

Job
Job analysis
Job description
Job Element Inventory (JEI)
Job families
Job incumbent
Management Position Description Questionnaire (MPDQ)
Methods analysis

Occupational Information Network
   *(O*NET)*
Position
Position Analysis Questionnaire
   (PAQ)
Standardized job analysis

Subject matter experts (SMEs)
Task inventories
Uniform Guidelines
Work sampling
Worker specifications

DISCUSSION QUESTIONS

1. How does the use of job families improve Aetna Life and Casualty's ability to achieve its mission?

2. Describe the possible uses of job analysis results. What does it mean to say that job analysis serves as a foundation for an organization's integrated HR system?

3. What are the advantages and disadvantages of time-and-motion studies? Name three types of jobs that could be usefully studied using this approach to job analysis.

4. Despite the decreasing emphasis on Taylor's scientific management in organizations, why should today's organizations have a firm understanding of the elemental motions that constitute many jobs?

5. Can job analysis make human resource practices—such as recruitment, performance appraisal, and compensation—less legally vulnerable? Explain.

6. What are the implications of continual organizational change for job analysis?

7. How does the use of job families give companies more flexibility with their employees?

8. How does BPX benefit from replacing job descriptions with a matrix reflecting skills and behaviors?

PROJECTS TO EXTEND YOUR LEARNING

1. **Managing Teams.** In a local organization (e.g., businesses, hospitals, or service organizations), identify one or more jobs that seem to require a great deal of team work. Obtain the job descriptions for these jobs. First, analyze each job description in terms of its completeness, as described in this chapter. To what extent do they provide information regarding performance standards, worker activities, equipment used, job context, job characteristics and worker specifications, or personality requirements? Then interview the job incumbents to get their views about whether the job description is complete. Find out what job analysis methods were used by the organization to collect the information in the descriptions, who provided the information, and how long ago the information was collected. Suggest specific improvements in the job analysis methods used to create the job description.

2. **Managing Globalization.**   Conduct a future-oriented job analysis focusing on how globalization is likely to affect the way an existing job might be performed in the future. Follow these steps:

   a.   Select a job you might like to perform during some stage of your career. Pick a professional job (e.g., manager, financial analyst, chemical engineer, museum curator, dietician), not a skilled or semiskilled job.

   b.   Select a method to conduct your job analysis. To do this exercise, you will have to modify whatever technique you choose in order to make it a future-oriented job analysis.

   c.   Select a person or persons to interview, observe, and so forth. Identify that person and give her or his telephone number.

   d.   Conduct a future-oriented job analysis. Focus on learning how the job is likely to change during the next five years. What changes might result in the job becoming more globally oriented? What implications would greater globalization have for the competencies needed to do the job?

   e.   Prepare a complete job description for the position as it's likely to exist in five years. Rank the job duties in order of their importance. Indicate the amount of time spent on each task. Also indicate the criticality of error if this task is performed incorrectly.

   f.   On a separate typed sheet, explain the method of job analysis you used, why you chose it, and its strengths and weaknesses.

   g.   Respond to this question: "From the perspective of (1) an employee and (2) the employee's manager, why is it important to conduct future-oriented job analysis?"

3. **Managing Strategically.**   You are an HR consultant who has just been contacted by an up-and-coming fashion designer, based in New York City. Her specialty is designing clothes for young teens, and business is booming. Until now, she has sold her products through small specialty shops. For labor, she has relied on a few friends and family members who were happy to have part-time work they could do at home. For the business to grow, this small operation must change. Investors have provided funds for the designer to set up a factory operation, but she is uncertain about how to set up the work in the factory and what competencies will be needed by her new employees. You have been hired to provide expert advice. You've agreed to:

   a.   investigate how work is organized in other similar production facilities,

   b.   make recommendations about how to set up the new factory (with an eye to helping the designer gain a competitive advantage),

   c.   prepare two or three prototypic job descriptions for new employees, and

   d.   specify the qualifications the designer should look for when hiring her new employees.

   You've heard about *O*NET*, so you plan to begin by visiting their web site at
   www.doleta.gov/programs/onet/

4. **Integration and Application.**   After reviewing the end-of-text cases of Lincoln Electric and Aid Association for Lutherans, answer the following questions:

a.   Compare the objectives of job analysis in these two cases.
b.   Explain how job analysis helps each organization meet its strategic objectives.
c.   For each company, describe the advantages and disadvantages of using standardized versus customized job analysis techniques.

CASE STUDY

Job Descriptions at HITEK

Jennifer Hill was excited about joining HITEK Information Services after receiving her BA. Her job involved examining compensation practice, and her first assignment was to review HITEK's job descriptions. She was to document her work and make recommended changes, which would include reducing more than 600 job descriptions to a manageable number.

BACKGROUND

To its stockholders and the rest of the outside world, HITEK is a highly profitable, highly aggressive company in the computer business. In addition to its numerous government contracts, it provides software and hardware to businesses and individuals. From its inception in the late 1970s, it has maintained its position on the leading edge by remaining flexible and adaptable to the turbulent environment in which it operates. It's a people-intensive organization that relies enormously on its human resources; therefore, it's in HITEK's best interests to establish policies and procedures that nurture productivity and enhance the satisfaction of its employees.

Because the computer industry is growing at an incredible pace, opportunities for placement are abundant, and the competition for high-quality human resources is tremendous. HITEK has grown about 30 percent in the last three years, and its management knows that, as easily as it attracts new employees, it can lose them. However, its turnover rate (14 percent) is about average for its industry.

HITEK remains relatively small at 1,000 employees, and it prides itself on its "small team company culture." This culture is maintained partly by the use of a computer mail system that can put any employee in touch with anyone at HITEK and by the utilization of open office spaces. The relative-ly flat lean organizational structure (shown in Case Exhibit 1) and the easy accessibility of all corporate levels also promotes an open-door policy. All in all, employees enjoy working for HITEK, and management is in touch with the organization's "pulse."

With the notable exception of the HR department, there are few rules at HITEK. In other departments, employees at all levels share the work, and positions are redefined to match the specific competencies and interests of the incumbent. "Overqualified" and "overachieving" individuals are often hired but are then promoted rapidly. Nothing is written down; and if newcomers want to know why something is done a certain way, they must ask the person(s) who created the procedure. There is extensive horizontal linkage between departments, perpetuating the blurring of distinctions between departments.

THE HR DEPARTMENT

The HR department stands in stark contrast to the rest of HITEK. About thirty people are employed in the department, including the support staff members, or about one HR employee per thirty-three HITEK employees. The vice president for human resources, Isabel Rains, rules the department with an "iron fist." Employees are careful to mold their ideas to match Rains' perspective. When newcomers suggest changes, they're told that "this is the way things have always been done" because "it's our culture." Written rules and standard operating procedures guide all behavior. Department employees know their own job descriptions well, and there is little overlap in employees' duties.

With the exception of one recruiter, all twelve of the incumbents whose positions are represented in Case Exhibit 2 are women. Only half of them have

Case Exhibit 1
HITEK's Organizational Chart

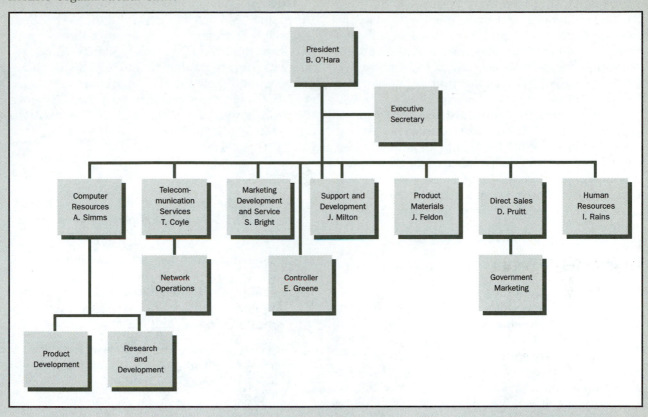

Case Exhibit 2
The Structure of the Human Resource Department at HITEK

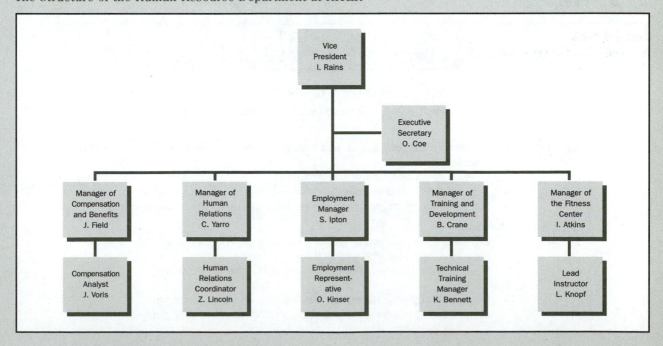

degrees in industrial relations or HRM, and only one-fourth have related experience with another company. Most of them have been promoted from clerical positions. In fact, some employees view the vice-presidency as a "gift" given to Isabel, a former executive secretary, the day after she received her bachelor's degree at a local college. In other departments, it's widely believed that professional degrees and related experience lead to expertise.

One incident that conveyed the department's image to Jennifer Hill occurred during her second week on the job. While preparing a job description with Dave Pruitt, Jennifer explained that she would submit the job description to Janet Voris for final approval. Dave became confused and asked, "But Janet is only a clerical person; why would she be involved?"

Jennifer Hill's Duties

At HITEK, the pool of job descriptions had grown almost daily as newcomers were hired, but many of the old job descriptions were not discarded, even when obsolete. Other job descriptions needed updating. Jennifer spent some time thinking about how to proceed. She considered the uses of the job descriptions and what steps she would need to take to accomplish all that was expected of her. Support from within the department was scarce because other employees were busy gathering materials for the annual review of HITEK's hiring, promotion,

and development practices conducted by the Equal Employment Opportunity Commission.

After six harried months on the job and much frustration, Jennifer had revised all the descriptions that were still needed (examples of "old" and "new" job descriptions appear in Case Exhibits 3 and 4). She was also beginning to develop some strong opinions about how the HR department functioned at HITEK and what needed to be done to improve its effectiveness and its image. She decided to arrange a confidential lunch with Billy O'Hara, HITEK's president.

Questions

1. What are the goals of HITEK? Of the HR department? Why does the conflict create problems for HITEK?

2. Organization members can draw from several kinds of power, such as referent power and reward power. Is the HR department powerful? Why is it important for HITEK to maintain a professional, competent HR function?

3. Jobs change frequently at HITEK. Shouldn't the HR department simply discontinue the practice of job analysis and stop writing job descriptions?

4. What steps should Jennifer Hill take in performing the tasks assigned to her? How do your answers to the earlier questions affect your answer?

Case Exhibit 3
An "Old" Job Description

Associate Programmer

Basic Objective	Perform coding, testing, and documentation of programs, under the supervision of a project leader.
Specific Tasks	• Perform coding, debugging, and testing of a program when given general program specifications. • Develop documentation of the program. • Assist in the implementation and training of the users in the usage of the system. • Report to the manager, management information services as requested.
Job Qualifications	Minimum: • BA/BS degree in relevant field or equivalent experience/knowledge • Programming knowledge in FORTRAN • Good working knowledge of business and financial applications Desirable: • Computer programming experience in a time-sharing environment • Some training or education in COBOL, PL1, or assembler languages.

Case Exhibit 4
A "New" Job Description

Associate Programmer

General Statement of Duties	Performs coding, debugging, testing, and documentation of software under the supervision of a technical superior or manager. Involves some use of independent judgment.
Supervision Received	Works under close supervision of a technical superior or manager.
Supervision Exercised	No supervisory duties required.
Examples of Duties	(Any one position may not include all the duties listed, nor do listed examples include all duties that may be found in positions of this class.)

Examples of Duties:

- Confers with analysts, supervisors, and/or representatives of the departments to clarify software intent and programming requirements.
- Performs coding, debugging, and testing of software when given program specifications for a particular task or problem.
- Writes documentation for the program.
- Seeks advice and assistance from supervisor when problems outside of realm of understanding arise.
- Communicates any program specification deficiencies back to supervisor.
- Reports ideas concerning design and development back to supervisor.
- Assists in the implementation of the system and training of end users.
- Provides some support and assistance to users.
- Develops product knowledge and personal expertise and proficiency in system usage.
- Assumes progressively complex and independent duties as experience permits.
- Performs all duties in accordance with corporate and departmental standards.

Minimum Qualifications:

- Education: BA/BS degree in relevant field or equivalent experience/knowledge in computer science, math, or other closely related field.
- Experience: No prior computer programming work experience necessary.
- Knowledge, skills, ability to exercise initiative and sound judgment.
- Knowledge of a structured language.
- Working knowledge in operating systems.
- Ability to maintain open working relationship with supervisor.
- Logic and problem-solving skills.
- System flowchart development skills.

Desirable Qualifications:

- Exposure to FORTRAN, C++ and object-oriented programming languages.
- Some training in general accounting practices and controls.
- Effective written and oral communication skills.

5. Is the "new" job description (Case Exhibit 4) better than the "old" one (Case Exhibit 3)? Why or why not?

6. What should Jennifer suggest to the president concerning the image and operation of the HR department?

Source: Written by M. P. Miceli, Ohio State University, and Karen Wijta, Macy's.

ENDNOTES

[1] S. Caudron, "Master the Compensation Maze," *Personnel Journal* (June 1993): 64D.

[2] L. Sierra, "The Next Generation of Broadbanding: Insurance Company Overhauls Hierarchy with CareerBanding," *ACA News* (February 1998): 21–24; For a similar account of another organization's use of this approach see W. DeCaporale, "Switching to Broadbanding: One Company's Experience," *ACA News* (April 1996): 8–12; see also D. Gilbert and K. S. Abosch, *Improving Organizational Effectiveness through Broadbanding* (Scottsdale, AZ: American Compensation Association, 1996).

[3] I. L. Goldstein, *Training in Organizations* (Pacific Grove, CA: Brooks/Cole, 1993).

[4] R. J. Harvey, "Job Analysis," M. D. Dunnette and L. M. Hough, eds., *Handbook of Industrial Organizational Psychology*, 2nd ed. (Palo Alto, CA: Consulting Psychologists Press, 1991).

[5] Throughout this book, we use the term competency to refer to a cluster of related knowledge, skills, abilities, and other personal characteristics and qualities that affect performance on the job. For a detailed discussion of several competency studies, see S. B. Parry, "The Quest for Competencies," *Training* (July 1996): 48–56.

[6] From the Southwest Airlines home page at **www.iflyswa.com/people/fltattend.html** (October 3, 1998).

[7] *How to Analyze Jobs* (Stanford, CT: Bureau of Law & Business, 1982); Equal Employment Opportunity Commission, "Uniform Guidelines on Employee Selection Procedures," *Federal Register* 43 (1978): 38290–38315; J. Ledvinka and V. G. Scarpello, *Federal Regulation of Personnel and Human Resource Management*, 2nd ed. (Boston: Kent Publishing, 1990).

[8] F. P. Morgenson and M. A. Campion, "Social and Cognitive Sources of Potential Inaccuracy in Job Analysis," *Journal of Applied Psychology* 82 (1998): 627–655.

[9] M. K. Lindell, C. S. Clause, C. J. Brandt, and R. S. Landis, "Relationship Between Organizational Context and Job Analysis Task Ratings," *Journal of Applied Psychology* 83 (1998): 769–776; F. J. Landy and J. Vasey, "Job Analysis: The Composition of SME Samples," *Personnel Psychology* 44 (1991): 27–50.

[10] R. D. Arvey, "Sex Bias in Job Evaluation Procedures," *Personnel Psychology* 39 (1986): 315–335; A. P. O'Reilly, "Skill Requirements: Supervisor-Subordinate Conflict," *Personnel Psychology* 26 (Spring 1973): 75–80.

[11] B. Schneider and A. M. Konz, "Strategic Job Analysis," *Human Resource Management* 28 (1989): 51–63.

[12] D. E. Bowen and D. A. Waldman, "Customer-driven Employee Performance," D. R. Ilgen and E. Pulakos, eds., *The Changing Nature of Work Performance: Implications for Staffing, Personnel Actions and Development* (San Francisco: Jossey-Bass, 1999).

[13] F. C. Lager, *Ben & Jerry's: The Inside Scoop* (New York: Crown Trade Paperbacks, 1994).

[14] A. W. Mathews, "New Gadgets Trace Truckers' Every Move," *The Wall Street Journal* (July 14, 1997): B1, B2.

[15] R. H. Hayes and R. Jaikumar, "Manufacturing's Crisis: New Technologies, Obsolete Organizations," *Harvard Business Review* (September–October 1988): 77–85.

[16] Adapted from U.S. Department of Labor, Employment Service, Training and Development Administration, *Handbook for Analyzing Jobs* (Washington, DC, 1972): 73; S. A. Fine and M. Getkate, *Benchmark Tasks for Job Analysis: A Guide for Functional Job Analysis (FJA) Scales* (Hillsdale, NJ: Lawrence Erlbaum, 1995).

[17] S. A. Fine, "Functional Job Analysis: An Approach to a Technology for Manpower Planning," *Personnel Journal* (November 1974): 813–818. See also S. A. Fine, *Functional Job Analysis Scales: A Desk Aid* (Milwaukee: Sidney A. Fine, 1989); S. A. Fine and W. Wiley, *An Introduction to Functional Job Analysis* (Washington, DC: Upjohn, 1971); U.S. Department of Labor, *Dictionary of Occupational Titles*, 4th ed. (Washington, DC, 1991).

[18] U.S. Department of Labor, *Dictionary of Occupational Titles*, 4th ed. (Washington, DC, 1991).

[19] Information about *O*NET* is provided by the Department of Labor at **www.doleta.gov/programs/onet/**.

[20] Fundamental changes to the *DOT*—a monumental undertaking—has been underway for several years. Our description of the *DOT* doesn't reflect changes that were still pending in 1999.

[21] The PAQ is published by Consulting Psychologists Press. Our description of the PAQ and its development is based on E. J. McCormick, P. R. Jeanneret, and R. C. Mecham, "A Study of Job Characteristics and Job Dimensions as Based on the Position Analysis Questionnaire," *Journal of Applied Psychology* 56 (1972): 347–367; E. J. McCormick and J. Tiffin, *Industrial Psychology*, 6th ed., (Englewood Cliffs, NJ: Prentice Hall, 1994); E. J. McCormick and D. R. Ilgen, *Industrial Psychology* (Englewood Cliffs, NJ: Prentice-Hall, 1980).

[22] For additional discussion of the PAQ, see E. T. Cornelius III, A. S. DeNisi, and A. G. Blencoe, "Expert and Naive Raters Using the PAQ: Does it Matter?" *Personnel Psychology* (Autumn 1984): 453–464; E. J. McCormick, A. S. DeNisi, and B. Shaw, "Use of the Position Analysis Questionnaire for Establishing Job Component Validity of Tests," *Journal of Applied Psychology* 64 (1979): 51–56.

[23] R. J. Harvey, et al., "Dimensionality of the Job Element Inventory, A Simplified Worker-Oriented Job Analysis Questionnaire," *Journal of Applied Psychology* 73 (1988): 639–646.

[24] W. W. Tornow and P. R. Pinto, "The Development of a Managerial Job Taxonomy: A System for Describing, Classifying, and Evaluating Executive Positions," *Journal of Applied Psychology* 61 (1976): 410–418.

[25] J. I. Sanchez and S. L. Fraser, "On the Choice of Scales for Task Analysis," *Journal of Applied Psychology* 77 (1992): 545–553; M. A. Wilson and R. J. Harvey, "The Value of

Relative Time-Spent Ratings in Task-Oriented Job Analysis," *Journal of Business and Psychology* 4 (1990): 453–461.

26 J. C. Flanagan, "The Critical Incident Technique," *Psychological Bulletin* 51 (1954): 327–358.

27 I. L. Goldstein, *Training in Organizations: Needs Assessment, Development, and Evaluation* (Pacific Grove, CA: Brooks/Cole Publishing Co., 1993).

28 R. J. Harvey, "Job Analysis."

29 E. A. Fleishman and M. D. Mumford, "Ability Requirement Scales," S. Gael, ed., *The Job Analysis Handbook for Business, Industry, and Government*, Vol. 2 (New York: John Wiley & Sons, 1988).

30 Detailed discussions of issues related to creating job families are provided in J. Colhan and G. K. Burger, "Constructing Job Families: An Analysis of Quantitative Techniques Used for Grouping Jobs," *Personnel Psychology* 48 (1995): 563–586; M. K. Garwood, L. E. Anderson, and B. J. Greengart, "Determining Job Groups: Application of Hierarchical Agglomerative Cluster Analysis in Different Job Analysis Situations," *Personnel Psychology* 44 (1991): 743–762; J. Hogan, "Structure of Physical Performance in Occupational Tasks," *Journal of Applied Psychology* 76 (1991): 495–507; K. Pearlman, "Job Families: A Review and Discussion of Their Implications for Personnel Selection," *Psychological Bulletin* 87 (1980): 1–27.

31 Reengineering the Organization, *Bulletin to Management* (November 1993): 360.

32 ACA/Hewitt Associates, *Life with Broadbands* (Phoenix, AZ: American Compensation Association, 1998); K. S. Abosch, "Confronting Six Myths of Broadbanding," *ACA Journal* (Autumn 1998): 28–35.

33 J. B. Treaster, "Aetna is Said to Seek Deal in Health Care," *New York Times* (February 28, 1998): D1; J. B. Treaster, "Aetna Deal for New York Life's Health Unit is Expected Today," *New York Times* (March 16, 1998): D1; S. Jackson, "Aetna's Brave New World," *Business Week* (March 30, 1998): 180; S. Caudron, "Master the Compensation Maze," *Personnel Journal* (June 1993): 64D; C. Roush, "Aetna's Heavy Ax," *Business Week* (February 14, 1994): 32. *Aetna Life and Casualty Company, Our Vision and Our Values* (internal company document, Hartford, CT, 1994). Equal Employment Opportunity Commission, "Uniform Guidelines on Employee Selection Procedures," *Federal Register* 43 (1978): 38290–38315.

34 R. B. Morgan and J. E. Smith, *Staffing the New Workplace: Selecting and Promoting Quality Improvement* (Milwaukee: ASQC Quality Press, 1996); K. P. Carson and G.

L. Stewart, "Job Analysis and the Sociotechnical Approach to Quality: A Critical Examination," *Journal of Quality Management* 1 (1996): 49–64.

35 L. Fogli and K. Whitney, "Assessing and Changing Managers for New Organizational Roles," in R. Jeanneret and R. Silzer, eds., *Individual Psychological Assessment: Predicting Behavior in Organizational Settings* (San Francisco: Jossey-Bass, 1998).

36 L. Fogli and K. Whitney, "Assessing and Changing Managers for New Organizational Roles."

37 W. Bridges, *Job Shift: How to Prosper in a Workplace Without Jobs* (Addison-Wesley, 1995).

38 J. I. Sanchez, "From Documentation to Innovation: Reshaping Job Analysis to Meet Emerging Business Needs," *Human Resource Management Review* 4 (1) : 51–74.

39 For a discussion of how to analyze the work of teams, see S. A. Mohrman, S. G. Cohen, and A. M. Mohrman, Jr., *Designing Team-Based Organizations: New Forms for Knowledge Work* (San Francisco: Jossey-Bass, 1995).

40 M. S. O'Conner, "Report on Japanese Employee Relations Practices and Their Relation to Worker Productivity" (prepared for a study mission to Japan, November 8–23, 1983); K. J. Duff, "Japanese and American Labor Law: Structural Similarities and Substantive Differences," *Employee Relations Law Journal* (Spring 1984): 629–641; R. Marsland and M. Beer, "The Evolution of Japanese Management: Lessons for U.S. Managers," *Organizational Dynamics* (Winter 1983): 49–67.

41 G. Lane and A. Robinson, "The Development of Competency Standards for Senior Management," *Executive Development* 8 (6) (1995): 13–18.

42 The essence of the *Civil Rights Acts of 1964 and 1991*, the *Equal Opportunity in Employment Act of 1972*, and various court decisions is that employment decisions be made on the basis of whether the individual will be able to perform the job. Chapter 8 expands on the job relatedness of selection procedures. For more legal review, see D. E. Thompson and T. A. Thompson, "Court Standards for Job Analysis in Test Validation," *Personnel Psychology* 35 (1982): 865–874.

43 "Objective Employee Appraisals and Discrimination Cases," *Fair Employment Practices* (December 6, 1990): 145–146.

44 M. Harris, "Practice Network: ADA and I-O Psychology," *The Industrial–Organizational Psychologist* 36 (1) (1998): 33–37; "Job Analyses and Job Descriptions Under ADA," *Fair Employment Practices* (April 22, 1993): 45.

Chapter 7

RECRUITMENT: ATTRACTING QUALIFIED CANDIDATES

"Any solution you provide to our staffing needs is like bringing a bucket of ice cubes into hell. The demands are just so great."

Don Goodman
Vice President for Business Development
Chubb Computer Services[1]

Chapter Outline

MANAGING HUMAN RESOURCES THROUGH PARTNERSHIP
at Microsoft

Microsoft Corporation is one of the biggest success stories in America today. Chairman and CEO William H. Gates has grown the company from its birth in 1975 to a healthy young adulthood in which it employed more than 18,000 people, with an average age of about 31 years, in 2000. Based in Redmond, Washington, Microsoft is continually ranked among the most admired companies and often singled out as the most innovative company in the United States. It's not at all unusual for the firm to introduce as many as 50 new products in one year, including many international versions. The success of Microsoft has made millionaires of many current and past employees, including Gates, who is the richest person in America.

According to many observers and Microsoft vice president Jeff Raikes, the firm is "high horse-power, high energy." Gates is described by most as "brilliant and totally focused on the company." He expects the same in others and serves as a role model for most. As CEO, he stays abreast of what is happening within Microsoft while also continually seeking opportunities to work closely with other manufacturers. For example, Microsoft and Xerox are jointly developing a new generation of printers and fax machines. Microsoft also works closely with its customers. According to Dorothy Cooney, Aetna's director of information technology and a customer of Microsoft, "Our joint commitment with Microsoft is important to us; it's a big part of how we're making quantum leaps in effectively using technology to improve customer service and reduce expenses, while bringing increased order to our technology environment, which all brings bottom-line benefits to our customers, users, and shareholders."

To achieve all this success and involvement in an industry in which total product lines become obsolete within five years, Microsoft needs great people, and it needs a lot of them. Acting on the premise that a company succeeds only because of its people, Gates gets involved in the recruitment at Microsoft. Indeed, ask Gates what was the most important thing he did last year and he answers, "I hired a lot of smart people." This means that Microsoft did a lot of recruiting, too.

With revenues approaching $10 billion, Microsoft hires almost 100 people per week. During the course of a year, managers and the HR staff recruit at more that 100 campuses. They review 120,000 résumés per year and interview 7,400 recruits. They eventually hire fewer than two percent of their applicants."[2]

To learn more about Microsoft, visit the company's home page at
www.microsoft.com

RECRUITMENT ACTIVITIES

Recruitment involves searching for and obtaining qualified job candidates in such numbers that the organization can select the most appropriate person to fill its job needs. At Microsoft, getting the right people into the organization is so important that the chairman gets personally involved in the firm's recruiting and selection. At Microsoft, managers devote time and attention to recruiting because they believe it's vital to the success and long-term survival of the business. Effective recruitment attracts individuals to the organization *and* also increases the chance of retaining the individuals once they are hired. Thus, recruitment efforts seek to satisfy the needs of job applicants as well as the needs of managers.[3]

Recruitment includes most, but not all, of the activities that occur between an employer and potential employee. In everyday conversation, people often refer to the term "recruiting" to refer to the entire process of hiring employees. HR professionals usually describe this entire process as *recruitment and selection*. Recruitment and selection are closely related activities. The objective of recruitment is creating a pool of potential employees. Recruitment stops short of making decisions about which particular applicants should be hired. That's where the selection process begins. Described in Chapter 8, selection involves sorting and ranking potential employees and making decisions about which individuals will receive offers of employment. A recent survey by the Bureau of National Affairs revealed that recruitment and selection activities were the *top* HR priority in the late 1990s.[4]

Effective recruitment begins during the strategic planning process when managers determine the organization's immediate and long-term labor needs. Domestic labor market conditions—and perhaps global labor market conditions—are then analyzed from the perspective of the organization's needs. Analysis of the labor market identifies potential sources of qualified applicants. Methods for informing potential applicants of employment opportunities are then developed.

With the involvement and cooperation of line managers and other employees who will work with new recruits, HR professionals usually take the lead in designing a systematic and integrated program of recruitment. However, as shown in Exhibit 7.1, responsibility for implementing the recruitment plan often is shared.[5]

Exhibit 7.1

Shared Roles and Responsibility for Recruitment

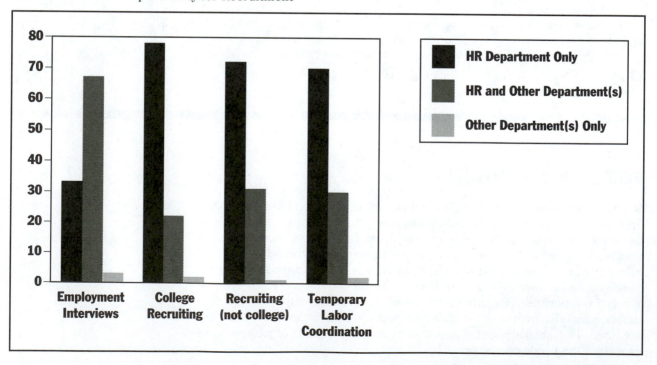

At Cisco Systems, the active involvement of employees is essential to the company's recruiting efforts. Employees participate in focus groups designed to brainstorm ideas about where to find qualified applicants. These folks aren't spending their time looking through want ads. They're more likely to be found surfing the net or attending local art festivals and garden shows. So Cisco recruiters go to these events and work the crowds. When an interested prospect is identified, Cisco pairs the person with a current employee who has similar interests and skills—a "friend." Friends help screen out unsuitable applicants and serve as advocates to convince the best applicants to accept Cisco's job offers.[6] Other ways that employees and managers can be involved in recruitment are summarized in the The HR Triad: Partnership Roles and Responsibilities for Recruitment feature.

Obtaining a pool of qualified applicants is the primary objective of recruiting, but legal compliance is also very important. Legal compliance requires careful record keeping. Although managers sometimes deride such record-keeping as a bureaucratic nuisance, the records used to document legal compliance can also be very useful for evaluating the effectiveness of recruitment efforts and for linking recruitment activities to other aspects of

> *"Our philosophy is simple—if you have the best people in the industry to fit into your culture and you motivate them properly, then you're going to be an industry leader."*
>
> **John Chambers**
> **CEO**
> **Cisco Systems**

THE HR TRIAD: PARTNERSHIP ROLES AND RESPONSIBILITIES FOR RECRUITMENT

Line Managers	HR Professionals	Employees
Work with HR staff to develop recruitment objectives and plans that meet the organization's strategic needs and address employees' concerns.	Work with line managers to develop recruitment objectives and plans that meet the organization's strategic needs and address employees' concerns.	Openly discuss your short-term and long-term objectives in order to facilitate the development of recruitment plans that address your concerns.
Help disseminate information about open positions to all potentially qualified internal candidates.	Develop recruitment plans that meet legal guidelines and that generate a pool of qualified internal and/or external candidates	Use knowledge of competitors' recruitment approaches to help develop innovative and more effective practices.
Stay informed of labor market trends in order to anticipate their implications for recruitment.	Be innovative in developing new sources and methods of recruiting to ensure a sufficient number of qualified applicants.	Participate in recruitment efforts such as referring the company to others.
Understand and abide by relevant legal regulations.	Provide training as needed to line managers and employees involved in recruitment activities.	Work with HR professionals and line managers in the organization's efforts to effectively manage workforce diversity.
Facilitate retention efforts through effective management and employee development.	Monitor recruitment activities for effectiveness and use the information to suggest future improvements.	Seek out information about openings within the company and actively pursue those that fit your personal career objectives.

the human resource management process. A study of 3,200 employers in Atlanta, Boston, and Los Angeles supports this view. The results indicated that employers who actively engaged in affirmative action efforts, which require extensive recording keeping, were also more likely to carefully evaluate performance and provide training to new hires. Furthermore, the study indicated that effective *recruitment*—not preferential selection—was the key to the success.[7]

THE STRATEGIC IMPORTANCE OF RECRUITMENT

When designing a recruitment program, the first step is establishing the objectives. Recruitment objectives should flow directly from the organization's strategic planning process. Questions addressed at that stage might include:

- How many new hires do we need in the near term and three to five years from now?
- Do we want to recruit people who will stay with the company for a long time, or are we looking for a short-term commitment?
- Are we prepared to pay top dollar, or should we look for people who will be attracted to our company despite the modest compensation we offer?
- Are we interested in finding people who are different from our current employees to bring in new perspectives, or is it important to maintain our status quo?

"Companies are so focused on hiring that many forget the point of the exercise. The goal is to recruit and retain the best."

Barbara Beck
Sr. V. P. Human Resources
Cisco Systems

Effective recruitment efforts are consistent with the strategy, the vision, and the values of the company. The feature, Managing Strategically: Recruitment That Fits Business Needs Ensures Success, illustrates this point.[8] To implement its business strategy, Chubb aims its recruitment efforts at inexperienced undergraduates and graduates who mirror Chubb's customers. Chubb looks for applicants who have good interpersonal competencies because these are important and very difficult to develop. The technical competencies needed by Chubb employees are unique to the firm, so Chubb can't expect to find applicants who already have the expertise they need. Instead, Chubb seeks out applicants who are capable of learning, and then invests in training programs to develop the firm-specific skills it needs. To reap satisfactory returns on their investments, Chubb must be able to retain new recruits. Chubb's recruitment approach wouldn't work at AIG. Because it enters and exits markets so quickly, AIG doesn't have time to train inexperienced employees. So its recruitment efforts seek to create a pool of applicants who already know the industry and can quickly jump into a new job and perform it well.

"While there is some concern for numbers, it is primarily the concern for skills that [line managers] are worried about."

Frank Berardi
Corporate Human Resources
Allstate Insurance

Strategic discussions focus on the general needs of the organization. Once those needs are understood, the focus turns to defining the needs of specific units or departments and the requirements for specific positions. At this stage, job analysis results become relevant. An appropriate job analysis yields answers to questions such as:

- What are the characteristics of the ideal recruit?
- Which competencies must people have when they first enter the organization, and how important is it that new hires be eager to learn new competencies?
- What career opportunities can we discuss with applicants?

MANAGING STRATEGICALLY
Recruitment That Fits Business Needs Ensures Success

The property and casualty business of the insurance industry is based on knowledge and skills. Identifying and assessing risk in unique situations is central to success. The competencies of employees drive success in the insurance business. The approaches firms use to obtain and maintain employee competencies vary widely across firms, apparently in response to different competitive strategies. Chubb Corporation and American International Group (AIG) are two property and casualty firms that illustrate this point. Both rank among the most profitable firms in the entire insurance industry.

Chubb

Competitors often describe Chubb as being the best at what it does. Chubb doesn't create new markets or expand the ones it's in through low prices; instead, it tries to find the very best risks that will provide high returns on its premiums. Chubb often goes after customers of other firms who it believes are good risks, identifies "gaps" or problems in their coverage, and offers them superior insurance protection. The core competency that makes these efforts possible is superior underwriting skill. Chubb looks for customers who are willing to pay a premium for superior service. It has a reputation for being the insurer of choice for the very wealthy.

Human Resource Practices. Chubb invests heavily in managing its human resources. Their investment begins with recruiting. Historically, Chubb has gone to the most prestigious undergraduate schools and hired graduates who, regardless of major, have good interpersonal and communication skills upon which insurance-specific skills can be built. It has been argued that the recruiters search for applicants who are similar to Chubb's customers. Applicants who come from backgrounds similar to those of customers may be better able to create contacts and establish a comfortable rapport with the monied class.

New hires complete several months of intensive training and testing before beginning work in the branch into which they were hired. For the next six to twelve months, they work with established underwriters who provide a great deal of supervision in an apprentice-like system in the field.

The company goes to great lengths, through career planning, to ensure that the new workers stay around long enough so that this substantial investment in skills can be recouped. It keeps its underwriters from the boredom of desk jobs, which often produces turnover elsewhere, by making them agents. Sending the underwriters to the field to do the selling is key. It eliminates communication problems that otherwise exist between sales and underwriting functions, by eliminating the intermediary role of agents. The underwriter gets better information for assessing risks and also provides customers with better service, including better information about their risks. The superior abilities of the employees make it possible to combine the sales role with the underwriting job.

Chubb fills vacancies internally, moving people frequently and retraining them for new jobs. The pace of work eventually results in some people voluntarily leaving the organization, but they rarely go to other insurance companies and more typically become independent agents, helping to expand the network for Chubb's business. This turnover has the added benefit of expanding what would otherwise be very limited career opportunities for those remaining.

AIG

American International Group (AIG) achieves its high level of profitability in a different way than Chubb, but it also relies on its human resources. AIG is a market maker. It identifies new areas of business, creates new products, and benefits from "first-mover" advantages in getting to those markets. It was the first insurer allowed into Communist China and later moved into Russia. AIG thrives in markets where it has little competition, often insuring high-risk operations that competitors avoid. Once companies that compete on price enter its markets, AIG may move on to another market.

Human Resource Practices.   AIG's core competencies are identifying new business opportunities and then quickly changing as needed to exploit them. To support this strategy, AIG uses an approach to managing human resources that's quite different from Chubb's. AIG's managers and HR staff operate in a highly decentralized manner. The corporation creates literally hundreds of subsidiary companies, each targeted to a specific market. The executives in each company are managed through a series of financial targets—with generous rewards for meeting them—and are otherwise given considerable autonomy in running the businesses. The companies typically hire experts from other firms in the industry. It has been known to hire away entire operations from competitors. Higher pay rather than opportunities for career development are what attract people to AIG. When a market dries up or tough competition arrives, a company in that market may close down. Employees are let go to return to the industry's labor market. The need to quickly acquire employees with the competencies required in new markets means that AIG can't rely on internal sources when staffing new companies. The quick changes make it difficult for AIG to recoup the investment it would need to develop necessary market-specific skills, so it relies on the external labor market instead.

To learn more about Chubb and AIG, visit the company's home pages at **www.chubb.com**

and
www.aig.com

At GE Medical Systems, the strategic planning process links recruitment planning directly with product development planning. When developing new products, managers draw up a "multigenerational product plan" *and* a "multigenerational staffing plan." These clarify the skills that will be needed as a product moves through three iterations of development. For example, suppose a development plan for a CT scanner that will complete 1-second scans in its first generation, 3/4-second scans in the second generation, and 1/2-second scans in the third generation is drawn up. A recruitment plan is then drawn up that specifies the number of "absolute algorithm" experts who will be needed to write code for each product generation.

Events that occur during recruitment can determine whether the best applicants happily accept the organization's employment offer, or choose to reject it. Recruitment activities should create positive experiences for all applicants—even those who aren't offered positions. If the firm's recruitment methods promote a favorable image of the company, rejected applicants may try again in the future and encourage their friends to view the company as an employer of choice. In other words, recruitment addresses current labor needs while also anticipating future labor needs. Effective recruiting leads all applicants—whether they're hired or not—to perceive the organization as an employer of choice.

Entering the 21st century, concerns about recruitment and retention are salient for many employers. Even as many companies continue to downsize, finding the talent needed remains a concern. A survey conducted by the

Conference Board found that nearly all companies believe that being an "employer of choice" is an important objective today if they're to remain viable in the years ahead. At the same time, 43 percent of them reported having problems in achieving this objective. Recruiting problems were slightly worse among service companies than manufacturers, perhaps due to their faster growth rates and relatively lower rates of compensation. The occupational groups that accounted for most of the concerns were technical workers and senior managers. Both of these groups were difficult to recruit and difficult to retain.[9] The feature, Managing Diversity: Attracting the World to Work at McDonald's, describes how one service-based company addresses its recruitment challenges.[10]

"All the things that make you an employer of choice are the same things that make you a successful company."

Derek Smart
Personnel Director
Nuclear Electric PLC

RECRUITMENT METHODS AND SOURCES

Once the recruitment objectives are specified and job analysis results have been considered, specific recruitment activities can be planned and implemented. In designing recruitment activities, two central issues to address are the methods to use and the sources to target.

MANAGING DIVERSITY
Attracting the World to Work at McDonald's

Every eight hours, somewhere in the world, another McDonald's restaurant opens its doors. More than 17,000 golden arches decorate the landscape in more than 80 countries. In Beijing, China, one restaurant served 50,000 people the first day it was open. As do many service-oriented firms, McDonald's faces problems finding the variety of employees it needs—those who staff its restaurants as well as those intended for management positions, either as restaurant managers or franchise owners.

For its restaurant staff positions, McDonald's has used a variety of recruiting approaches. First, rather than rely on its traditional labor pool, McDonald's has looked to new groups to hire, such as retirees and mothers with young children. To attract these groups, the firm offers flexible working hours. In the past, the firm has been able to recruit and hire young people, particularly from inner-city locations, but has been unable to retain them. The company found that inner-city teenagers would often work for a few months and then quit. The teenagers worked just long enough to earn money to buy specific items such as new clothes or a boom box. To retain such employees, McDonald's sought ways to make the jobs more fun. In some parts of the country, the young people are allowed to choose the music played in the restaurant or to wear favorite clothes on particular days, rather than the standard McDonald's uniforms. Such flexibility in company practices has made it a more attractive employer for different groups in the workforce. Finally, to attract employees with potential for restaurant management, McDonald's sponsors summer internships and management training programs for minority students.

Its recruitment of franchise operators, particularly those for overseas restaurants, has been easier because of the opportunities the company offers. In many countries, the franchisees provide a unique and welcome opportunity to be an entrepreneur. Thus, "recruitment" varies greatly depending on the area and type of employee the firm needs.

To learn more about McDonald's, visit the company home page at
www.mcdonalds.com

Employers inform potential applicants about employment opportunities using a variety of methods. They place ads, post notices on the company bulletin board, accept applications from people who simply walk in to their recruiting offices, and so on. Different methods may reach different sources of applicants. Posting announcements on company bulletin boards is a good way to recruit employees. Employees are called *internal sources*. Potential applicants who don't work for the organization are called *external sources*. Placing ads in local newspapers or trade publications are common methods used to reach external sources.

Many studies have considered whether recruiting from different sources results in different employee outcomes, such as performance, turnover, loyalty, and job satisfaction. If different sources of applicants were found to have different outcomes, companies could target their recruitment efforts to the most appropriate sources, given their strategic needs. Overall, however, research shows no clear differences in the employment experiences of new employees recruited from different sources.[11]

Instead of targeting one source of applicants, most employers recruit from multiple sources using multiple methods. This approach helps the organization generate a large applicant pool. In addition, recruiting from multiple sources is a good way to increase the diversity of the applicant pool.

Recruiting from the Organization's Internal Labor Pool

For jobs other than those at entry level, current employees may be a source of applicants. They become candidates for promotions, transfers, and job rotations. Current employees usually become applicants by informing their employer of their interest in an announced opening. That is, employees learn about appropriate job openings and express their interest in a position in order to be considered. Having expressed their interest in a position, internal applicants typically go through the recruitment process in much the same was as external applicants.

Internal applicants for job vacancies can be located using several methods. Some (e.g., the grapevine and job postings) assume that potential applicants should take most of the responsibility for learning about opening positions and applying for those they find interesting. Others (e.g., using talent inventories) place more responsibility on the HR staff and line managers.

Job Postings.   Job postings prominently display current job openings to all employees in an organization. They're usually found on bulletin boards (cork as well as electronic). Other than word-of-mouth, job postings are the most commonly used method for generating a pool of internal applicants. Job postings usually provide complete job descriptions. A well-constructed job description communicates organizational goals and objectives. By also including information about compensation and performance standards, job postings send signals to employees about what is valued. Astute employees realize that observing postings over time yields information about turnover rates in various departments, as well as information about the competencies that are most in demand.

Job postings can reduce turnover by communicating to employees that they don't have to go elsewhere in order to find opportunities for advancement and development. Posting jobs also creates an open recruitment process, which helps to provide equal opportunity for advancement to all employees. Job posting has many advantages, but it's not foolproof. If hiring decisions are already made when postings appear, the system will soon lose

"Online job hunting is going to be the standard approach of the emerging workforce."

Bruce Skillings
Executive Vice President
Hodes Advertising

credibility. Managers who merely go through the motions of posting jobs generate ill will and cynicism.

Talent Inventories. Almost every organization has a pool of internal talent that it can tap when recruiting to fill open positions. Like savings accounts, internal talent pools contain easily accessed resources that can be "withdrawn" as needed. In addition, the future value of the organization's talent pool can be enhanced through investments in selection procedures, training programs, and retention efforts.

Although all organizations have talent pools, not all organizations have a systematic method for keeping track of the pool of talent and ensuring that it's used wisely. Rather than rely on employees to identify appropriate openings in the organization, proactive employers systematically monitor their internal talent and facilitate the process of matching internal applicants to suitable opportunities. By maintaining a talent inventory, proactive employers can ensure that they consider all internal candidates with the necessary qualifications, regardless of whether taking the open position would involve a promotion, transfer, or temporary job rotation.

A *talent inventory* is a database that contains information about the pool of current employees. Talent inventories usually include employees' names, prior jobs and experiences, performance and compensation histories, and demonstrated competencies. The employees' work-related interests, geographic preferences, and career goals also should be included. With an up-to-date talent inventory to consult, there is no need to rely on employees to nominate themselves for job openings. Instead, qualified potential applicants can be identified and encouraged to apply when jobs become available. Citibank uses its talent inventory to identify suitable positions for staff members who wish to transfer or who are seeking another job because of technological displacement or reorganization. The system ensures that suitable internal candidates won't be overlooked before recruiting begins outside the organization.

Promotions. Regardless of how an employee becomes an applicant, recruitment activities can result in three types of career moves within the organization. A *promotion* generally involves moving into a position that's recognized as having higher status—and often, higher pay. To plan for employee promotions, some organizations use replacement planning charts in addition to maintaining a talent inventory. *Replacement planning charts* list the current and potential occupants of positions in the firm. The charts also list each person's promotion potential and developmental needs. An example of a replacement chart is shown in Exhibit 7.2. Replacement charts can alert the organization to critical talent shortages. If a key position has only one potential replacement available, the organization is vulnerable—if the key person suddenly resigns or is incapacitated, the organization would be unable to quickly replace him or her. If the company in Exhibit 7.2 used a talent inventory, the employees wouldn't be stacked in small divisional and functional jobs; instead, all of these individuals would be in one big grouping, differentiated only in terms of job levels and perhaps job families.

Transfers. A *transfer* involves moving into a position that's of similar status, often with no increase in pay. Chapter 6 explained that many organizations have replaced the traditional system of jobs that are organized into clear status hierarchies with job families. With job families, taking a new

■■□ *fast fact*

At Hallmark, 90 percent of management positions are filled internally.

Exhibit 7.2
Sample Employee Replacement Chart

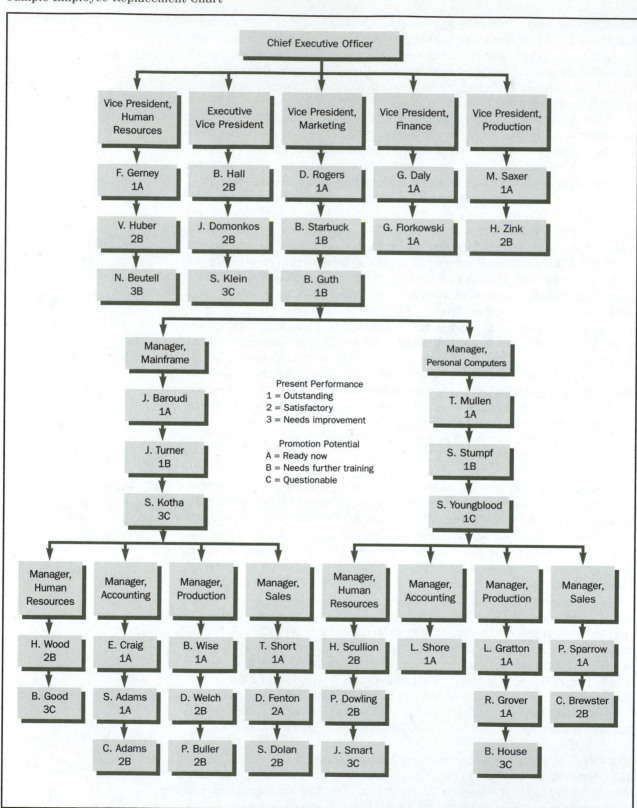

position within the company often involves a lateral job transfer rather than a promotion. After several transfers, employees develop a broader perspective and can better understand how the entire organization functions as a system.

Some organizations schedule two or three years of planned job transfers to help employees develop a broad array of competencies. When they're included as part of a planned development process, transfers often last for only a few months. Some organizations refer to such transfers as job rotations. Everyone involved realizes that the assignment is intended to be temporary, and that employee development is one of the primary objectives. Unlike other job openings and placements, those associated with job rotation programs seldom involve formal recruitment and competition among applicants.

Pros and Cons of Internal Recruitment.   There are several potential benefits associated with recruiting applicants who are eligible for promotions and transfers. Perhaps most importantly, employees are likely to feel more secure and to identify their long-term interests with an organization that provides them the first choice of job opportunities. Gaining a reputation for excellent employee development is one of the best ways to become an "employer of choice," according to a recent study conducted by the Conference Board.[12]

Compared to external recruitment, internal recruitment can reduce labor costs. Outside recruits tend to receive higher salaries. The organization may also pay a one-time signing bonus to external recruits. In addition to reducing these monetary costs, internal recruitment is valued by employees. Recruiting externally can reduce employee morale and diminish employees' willingness to maximize their productivity in order to be eligible for future career opportunities.

Counterbalancing these advantages are several disadvantages. If internal recruitment is used in place of external recruitment, the most qualified candidates may never be considered. Other disadvantages include infighting between candidates vying for a position, and inbreeding. Inbreeding exists when someone who is familiar with the organization has come to accept its ways of doing things. Such people are less likely to come up with creative and innovative ideas for improvement.

Recruiting from the External Labor Market

Rapidly growing organizations and those that require large numbers of highly skilled professionals and managers seldom can meet their labor needs without recruiting from the external labor market.[13]

For growing organizations, internal recruitment simply can't produce the numbers of people needed to sustain continued growth. During one of its growth spurts, for example, Cisco Systems was taking on about 1,000 new hires each quarter, which amounted to nearly ten percent of total job growth in Silicon Valley.[14] Companies that aren't growing, or are perhaps even shrinking, may be able to generate large numbers of internal applicants, but those applicants may not have the skills needed for changing business conditions. If internal candidates would require training in order to be qualified, it may be cheaper, easier, and quicker to hire people with the competencies needed. In addition, recruiting from the outside brings in people with new ideas, which is especially important for organizations that require innovation and creativity.[15]

External applicants come from many sources and are recruited through a variety of means. Under tight labor market conditions, employers generally

■☐ *fast fact*

In 1950, 71 percent of 65-year-old men were in the labor force; by 1985, their employment had dropped to only 33 percent; in 1995, this trend started to reverse itself.

■□ *fast fact*

Warmer metropolitan areas
attract job seekers far more
than seasonal environments,
according to the Department
of Labor.

must adopt a more proactive approach to external recruitment. As described in the feature, Managing Change: Gateway Outgrows Its Midwestern Home,[16] labor shortages sometimes even force a company to pull up roots and move to the location of the talent. When demand is low, however, job applicants become more proactive in the process.

Walk-in Applicants.   Some individuals become applicants by simply walking into an organization's employment office. Before the Internet explosion, walk-ins were especially prevalent for clerical and service jobs; managerial, professional, and sales applicants were seldom walk-ins.[17] New technology is quickly changing that. Now, applicants for almost any type of job can "walk-in" to an organization through its electronic, cyberspace doors. Virtually all major employers now have electronic home pages that describe their operations and list available employment opportunities. Many employers also accept—even encourage—electronic applications.[18]

MANAGING CHANGE
Gateway Outgrows Its Midwestern Home

From 1985 to 1998, North Souix City, South Dakota, was home for Gateway, Inc., the world's second largest direct marketer of personal computers. Now San Diego is called home. CEO Theodore Waite, who grew up in South Dakota and still has family there, says the company's recruiting needs dictated the move. During its early years, Gateway's business strategy required people to assemble and ship products, and little else. Within a dozen years of its founding, the company employed 5,500 assembly workers, which helped to substantially reduce the region's unemployment rate. This simple strategy could not sustain continued growth forever. Eventually, Waite decided to expand in new directions. Following the success of his competitors, the company began to supplement its direct sales business with retail outlets—called "Country Stores." Waite also plans to reinvent the company's image and give up its trademark Holstein cow spots. More significant, however, are his plans to develop new software and cutting edge product designs.

To implement the new strategy, Gateway needs highly talented engineers as well as managers with competencies in marketing and finance. Attracting the best people in these fields to South Dakota proved difficult. After a year of trying to fill 250 such job openings, Waite concluded that the company would have to move in order to attract the caliber of talent needed. "We need to get a better blend of people than we have here, with people who have more experience," explained Waite. Manufacturing operations will remain in South Dakota.

Knowing the time to move is one thing—knowing where to move is another. To choose the company's new location, Gateway hired Coopers and Lybrand (now part of PriceWaterhouseCoopers) to do a labor market study of several cities. San Diego came out on top as a location with a large pool of available high tech workers. Waite's plan calls for hiring about 200 engineers and managers within the first year and eventually expanding to as many as 1,000. Shortly after Gateway's decision to move was announced, Waite could see the results. As he interviewed applicants, he realized that he suddenly was seeing "a whole new level of candidate."

To learn more about Gateway, Inc., visit the company home page at
www.gateway.com

Advertising encourages walk-in and mail-in applications. Mirage Resorts gets great results with well-placed newspaper ads. Several months before they open a new facility, they open their employment offices and put image advertising in the local newspaper. One ad proclaimed, "We're looking for 5,000 people who wouldn't mind working in a tropical rain forest with live sharks and a volcano that erupts every 30 minutes." They received 57,000 applications for the 6,500 open positions Another said: "We're looking for roughians [sic], scalawags and other people who don't mind a good fight while they're working." That yielded nearly 70,000 applications.[19] Online advertising works too. A job opening listed on electronic employment boards such as E-Span, FedWorld, and Monster Board can quickly generate hundreds of applicants from around the world.

Holding an open house is another excellent way to attract walk-in applicants. An open house can serve to introduce the organization to the community and attract individuals who might not otherwise become applicants. Such events give the firm a chance to look at potential applicants in a fairly informal setting.

Employee Referrals. Employee referrals occur when a current employee informs someone they know about an opening and encourages them to apply. Informal referral programs consist of informing current employees about job openings and encouraging them to have qualified friends and associates apply for positions. This is a very low-cost approach. Formal referral programs reward employees for referring qualified applicants. The financial incentives may be linked to a recruit's completion of an application, acceptance of employment, or completion of work for a specified time period.

Compared with other external recruiting methods, for most occupations, employee referrals result in the highest one-year survival rates. One explanation for this success is that employees provide a balanced view of organizational life. The more information that's available, the better the referral decision is likely to be. Another explanation is that employees tend to recruit applicants who are similar to them in interests and motivations. Since employees are already adjusted to the organizational culture, this matching process increases the likelihood that applicants also will fit into the environment.[20]

The referral approach seems to be good for applicants as well as employees. At Citibank, referral applications present more appropriate résumés, are more likely to apply under favorable market conditions, perform better in the interview, and are more likely to get hired.[21] A potential disadvantage of referrals is that employees tend to refer others who are similar in age, gender, ethnicity, and religion. If relied on too heavily, this recruiting approach may be detrimental to equal employment opportunity goals.

Employment Agencies. Public and private employment agencies are good sources of temporary employees and permanent employees. American public employment agencies operate under the umbrella of the U.S. Training and Employment Service; it sets national policies and oversees the operations of state employment agencies, which have branch offices in many cities. State employment agencies offer counseling, testing, and placement services to everyone and provide special services to military veterans, members of some minority groups, colleges, and technical and professional people. Their services are supported by employer contributions to state unemployment funds. The *Social Security Act* provides that, in general, workers who have

"Our intention in HR was to get a giant applicant pool and then screen for several traits: personality, stability and some type of experience."

Arte Nathan
HR Manager
Mirage Resorts

■■□ *fast fact*

The *Personal Responsibility and Work Opportunity Act of 1996* requires that adult welfare recipients return to work within two years after they start receiving welfare.

been laid off from a job must register with the state employment agency in order to be eligible for unemployment benefits. Thus, most state agencies have long rosters of potential applicants.

Private employment agencies—sometimes called headhunter or search firms—serve professional, managerial, and unskilled job applicants. Agencies dealing with unskilled applicants often provide job candidates that employers would have a difficult time finding otherwise. Many employers looking for unskilled workers do not have the resources to do their own recruiting or have only temporary or seasonal demands for these workers.

Private agencies play a major role in recruiting professional and managerial candidates. Between the mid-1980s and the mid-1990s, the executive recruiting industry grew phenomenally. Employees in companies known for their outstanding managers provide a talented pool of potential candidates for other companies to raid. Headhunter firms are the agents who perform the raids. The General Electric Company is a favorite hunting ground. So many companies have been rejuvenated by the arrival of a new chief executive drawn from GE's management that many investors feel as if they've hit a jackpot when their companies announce such recruiting coups.

The fees charged by executive search firms may be as high as one-third of the first year's total salary and bonus package for a job that's filled. Thus, this can be an expensive recruitment method for the employer. More troublesome are the hidden costs of using search firms. A search firm generally can't approach executives it has recently placed, and it may have agreements with its clients that limit its ability to approach the clients' employees. This restricts the pool of applicants considered by a search firm and runs counter to the objective of creating the large pool of qualified applicants. In addition, search firms typically present employers with very few possible candidates to consider. They prescreen heavily before letting the employer and applicant meet. This protects applicants' privacy and saves the employer time. It also places a great deal of weight on the judgment of the search firm. Because search firms have much less information about the needs of the organization, compared to managers, search firms are more likely to err by rejecting a candidate who would do well.[22] To minimize such costs, close monitoring of the search firm's activities is necessary. In spite of these drawbacks, headhunter firms are doing well, especially when it comes to helping talented people who work in troubled companies find new positions. Exhibit 7.3 offers suggestions for how to select a search firm when one is needed.[23]

School Placement Services and Trade Associations.   Schools are important sources of recruits for most organizations, although their importance varies depending on the type of applicant sought. If an organization is recruiting managerial, technical, or professional applicants, then colleges and universities are the most important source. These institutions become less important when an organization is seeking production, service, office, and clerical employees (see Exhibit 7.4 on page 272).[24]

For some jobs, the recruitment process begins in the high schools even though the hiring process doesn't kick in until college graduation. Gannett, owner of *Detroit News*, *Asheville Citizen-Times*, and 80 other newspapers, targets high school students who show even a glimmer of interest in journalism. Editors speak with the students, talking up the glamorous aspects of a career in journalism. In addition to sponsoring workshops for the staff working on high school newspapers, Gannett's editors offer to critique the papers and invite students into their newsrooms to give them exposure to

"I get calls from headhunters and such, offering bigger salaries, signing bonuses and such. But the excitement of what I'm doing here is equal to a 30 percent pay raise."

Jorgen Wedel
Executive Vice President
Gillette

■□ *fast fact*

To guard against trivial assignments being given to student interns, who may then get turned off, Chase requires supervisors to describe intern projects to the HR staffers who oversee recruiting.

Exhibit 7.3

Tips for Selecting an Executive Search Firm

- Learn about the search industry; be sure to understand its weaknesses.

- Investigate the firm's "completion" rate. Some firms fill the positions they're hired for more than 90 percent of the time. Others fill the positions less than 70 percent of the time.

- Be sure you know how many restrictions the firm is under. If a firm you want to use is obligated to not recruit from a long list of clients, you may need to hire more than one firm.

- Determine the ratio of "lions" (the partners who often are essential to arranging a meeting and closing a deal) to "squirrels" (researchers and recruiters who help put together a list of possibilities). Be sure you meet the squirrels before hiring the lions.

- Understand and carefully consider the fee structure. Most fee structures are designed to benefit the search firm making few performance commitments to clients. Negotiate a flat fee rather than a fee based on the new hire's compensation, and insist on a refundable retainer.

- Understand the search process used by the firm and evaluate how likely it is that the process will yield candidates who meet your recruitment objectives.

---

the excitement. For college students, working as an intern provides additional experience. These and other efforts help Gannett compete effectively for college graduates despite the fact that the publishing industry pays much less than many others.[25]

Many trade and professional associations also provide recruiting opportunities. Often jobs can be announced through their newsletters and/or through links to the association's website. Annual trade conferences provide a more personal forum where employers and potential job applicants can meet. Communities and schools have adopted this idea and now bring together large numbers of employers and job seekers at job fairs.

Increasingly, job fairs incorporate electronic screening in order for employers to use their time at the fairs more efficiently. Employers set up an electronic site that contains information about openings and a link to the company website, where applicants can learn more. The site is active for a two- to four-week period just prior to a scheduled job fair. Interested candidates use the site to submit their applications. Employers can then screen applicants in advance and contact those they're most interested in to schedule a meeting at the job fair.

Foreign Nationals. In some professions—such as chemical engineering, software engineering, and others that involve high-tech skills—labor shortages cause employers to recruit foreign nationals. Foreign nationals may be employed in operations in the United States or abroad. When they work abroad, they serve as *host-country nationals* (persons working in their own country, not the country of the parent company) or *third-country nationals* (persons working in a country that's neither their own nor that of the parent company). Under the *Immigration Reform and Control Act of 1986* and the *Immigration Act of 1990*, it's unlawful for employers to hire foreign nationals to work in the U.S. unless they're authorized to do so. Those hired must be paid the prevailing wage. For professional-level workers, employers typically spend an additional $100,000 to $200,000 in relocation costs.[26]

fast fact

Merck committed to giving $10 million to the United Negro College Fund for scholarships and internships in an effort to expand the pool of outstanding minority researchers.

fast fact

Costa Rica requires high school students to take English; its workforce includes 12,000 engineering students, and its per-capita computer usage rate is higher than the U.S. and Canada.

Exhibit 7.4

Recruiting Sources and Methods Used by Companies (%) by Occupation

(Number of companies)	Any Job Category* (245)	Office/ Clerical (245)	Production/ Service (221)	Professional/ Technical (237)	Commissioned Sales (96)	Managers/ Supervisors (243)
Internal Sources						
Promotion from within	99%	94%	86%	89%	75%	95%
Advertising						
Newspapers	97	84	77	94	84	85
Journals/magazines	64	6	7	54	33	50
Direct mail	17	4	3	16	6	8
Radio/television	9	3	6	3	3	2
Outside Referral Sources						
Colleges/universities	86	24	15	81	38	45
Technical/vocational institutes	78	48	51	47	5	8
High schools/trade schools	68	60	54	16	5	2
Professional societies	55	4	1	51	19	37
Community agencies	39	33	32	20	16	9
Unions	10	1	11	1	—	1
Employee referrals	91	87	83	78	76	64
Walk-in applicants	91	86	87	64	52	46
Employment Services						
State employment services	73	66	68	38	30	23
Private employment agencies	72	28	11	58	44	60
Search firms	67	1	**	36	26	63
U.S. Employment Service	22	19	20	11	7	7
Employee leasing firms	20	16	10	6	2	**
Computerized résumé service	4	**	—	4	—	2
Video interviewing service	2	**	**	1	—	1
Special Events						
Career conferences/job fairs	53	20	17	44	19	19
Open house	22	10	8	17	8	7
Other	9	5	5	7	6	7

**Percentages for each job category are based on the number of organizations that provided data for that category, as shown by the number in parentheses.

Recruiting for foreign nationals successfully requires making an extra effort to understand other cultures from which applicants are sought. For example, whereas U.S. applicants can be expected to recognize the names of many large companies, the names of those companies may be very unfamiliar to applicants outside the U.S. Or, even if the name is recognizable, applicants may have little information about what it would be like to work in a particular U.S. city. Many French students recognize Coca-Cola's brand name, but few are likely to have a clear image of what it would be like to work in their Atlanta headquarters. The job searching approaches used in other countries are another factor to consider when recruiting outside the U.S. In Japan, for example, a tradition of long-term employment security means that many excellent potential applicants have had little need to hone their job seeking skills. Also, they're less likely than U.S. applicants to use the internet for job hunting, and more likely to rely on magazines and newspapers for information.[27]

Acquisitions and Mergers.   In contrast with other external methods, acquisitions and mergers can facilitate the immediate implementation of an organization's strategic plan. Cisco Systems has used this strategy to help them keep growing.[28] When an organization acquires a company with skilled employees, this ready pool may enable the organization to pursue a business plan—such as entering a new product line—that would otherwise be infeasible. However, the need to displace employees and to integrate a large number of them rather quickly into a new organization means that the human resource planning and selection process becomes more critical than ever.

Contingent Employees, Rehires, and Recalls

As large U.S. companies scramble to get leaner and more efficient, they're shedding thousands of workers. Like the tolling of an iron bell, a gloomy statistic has begun to resonate with many Americans: by some calculations, more than one out of four of us is now a member of the contingent workforce.

Contingent workers are people hired by companies to cope with unexpected or temporary challenges—part-timers, freelancers, subcontractors, and independent professionals. Usually, employers hire contingent workers from the external labor market, but AT&T put a new twist on the trend toward greater reliance on contingent workers. It created Resource Link as a mechanism to manage a pool of internal contingent workers. Through this program, displaced managers and professionals who qualified were retained by the company to serve as temporary staff for managers who needed help on projects. The temporary assignments generally last three to twelve months. More recently, AT&T has joined with other companies to create an "internal" pool of contingent workers that includes employees from all the cooperating companies. Each company contributes employees to the pool, and each can recruit people from the pool to work on temporary assignments.

Members of the contingent workforce understand that they'll be frequently entering into and exiting from employment relationships. Therefore, even when they're working on temporary assignments, they nurture their connections to a wide range of possible future employers. In effect, contingent workers must continually maintain their status as a member of the applicant pool in order to ensure their continued employment.[29]

Some contingent workers are recruited directly, but many are recruited indirectly by using the services of temporary help agencies. As more and more companies find it preferable to hire temporary workers, temporary help agencies have experienced a real boom. Organizations are using temporary help agencies more than ever because some hard-to-get skills are available nowhere else. This is especially true for small companies that aren't highly visible or can't spend time recruiting. Getting short-term employees without an extensive search is an obvious advantage of temporary help agencies.

Strategic Objectives.   Many employers recruit from the contingent workforce as part of a planned strategy. Rehiring and recalling are particularly

■□ *fast fact*

In the U.S., 1.3 million people work for temporary help agencies. About 55 percent of these people have no health insurance coverage.

fast fact

Manpower, which is based in
Milwaukee and has 2,400
franchises and independent
offices, is the world's largest
temporary services firm.
About 50 percent of revenues
come from overseas.

fast fact

The U.S. Postal Service, which
is the largest U. S. employer,
starts recruiting in August for
the 40,000+ temporary
workers needed to handle the
holiday mail.

beneficial to organizations that have seasonal fluctuations in the demand for workers, such as department stores, canneries, construction companies, and ski resorts. Each summer and fall during the apple harvest, canneries in eastern Washington State recall large numbers of employees—some who have been on the payroll for more than twenty years. Mail-order companies like L.L.Bean continually bring back a large share of their laid-off workforces between September and December, the busiest months of the year.

Recalls and rehires aren't always planned, however. American Express had not planned to recall its retired head of the Travel-Related Services unit, but this is just what it did when it found it had been weakened by a steady drain of its marketing talent. Recalls and rehires also occur in organizations coping with unexpected staffing problems created by downsizing. A survey of large U.S. companies conducted by the American Management Association found that more than half of the respondents who had downsized said they had lost so many talented people that their ability to compete had been severely damaged. When this happens, many downsized companies end up rehiring as temporary employees the people they just laid off. Indeed, an estimated 17 percent of contingent employees were previously regularly employed by the same company that now employs them on an as-needed basis. At some companies, as many as 80 percent of contingent workers were previously working as regular employees.[30]

Advantages and Disadvantages. Rehiring former or laid-off employees is a relatively inexpensive and effective method of recruiting. The organization already has information about the performance, attendance, and safety records of these employees. Rehires are already familiar with job responsibilities, so they need less time to settle in—*unless* the job has changed substantially while they were away.

The growing reliance on contingent employment is often considered a negative trend for employees, however. As the name suggests, such workers lead uncertain lives, and they almost never receive benefits. Nevertheless, some employees prefer contingent arrangements because it allows them to work on a schedule of their own choosing. Highly skilled temporary workers often are paid more on an hourly basis than are permanent employees doing similar work. Temporary employment also provides a way to preview different jobs and work in a variety of organizations. For employees, temporary work is a good way to learn about possible new careers. Good temporary employees often receive permanent job offers. Contingent employment also serves the needs of core employees because it facilitates implementation of temporary leave policies.

Recalls, rehires and contingent employees have some unique disadvantages, however. The commitment of rehired employees who would have preferred to keep a steady, full-time job, may be low. Alternatively, permanent employees who know they're paid less per hour than comparable temporary hires may feel resentful. For these and other reasons, conflict between permanent and temporary employees is common. L.L.Bean is very aware of these possible disadvantages and realizes that relying on rehires would backfire if all employees weren't fully committed to providing high quality service. To prevent this, it works very hard to recruit employees who prefer seasonal employment, and then establish positive employment relationships.

In order for a strategy of using recalls and rehires to be effective, employees who have left the company must be eager to return if an opportunity arises. Treating departing employees well is one way to set the stage for their subsequent re-recruitment. Exhibit 7.5 offers advice for employers who want to say "good-bye" to applicants with style. Of course, employees will appreciate a dignified send-off even if they're never recalled.[31]

RECRUITMENT FROM THE APPLICANT'S PERSPECTIVE

Imagine that you own a toy company. With the baby boomlet in full swing, orders are growing at a fast pace. To keep up, you need to expand your manufacturing facility and hire a couple of good managers. When you offer the best applicants a job, what will determine whether they say yes? Does it make a difference whom you choose to do the job of recruiting, or can you just give this task to whomever is most easily spared? Does the recruitment process itself really make much difference?

For organizations to effectively attract potentially qualified candidates, they need to understand the behaviors and preferences of the diverse workforce. How do candidates differ in their job search activities? Where do they get their information regarding job availability, and what do they react to the most?[32]

Timing of Recruitment Procedures

In markets where recruiting occurs in well-defined cycles, as in college recruiting, organizations can enhance their chances of obtaining high-potential candidates by starting early. High-technology companies involve high-potential college juniors in summer internships or cooperative education programs. Progressive organizations also bypass traditional second-semester campus interviews and invite high-potential candidates directly to corporate headquarters early in their senior year. Most major accounting firms

> *"A lot of new hires said our managers are so responsive that they'd been hired before other companies even called them back."*
>
> **Cara Jane Finn**
> **Vice President, Employee Relations**
> **Remedy Corp.**

Exhibit 7.5
Tips for Saying Good-Bye to Applicants

DO	DON'T
• Ask employees how they prefer to spend their time on their last day.	• Assume employees will want a party to celebrate their departure; ask.
• Treat all departing employees the same.	• Wait until the employees' last day to plan the employees' exit; think this through in advance.
• Let departing employees know their work has been appreciated.	• Cut-off access to supplies and resources prior to the employees' last day, unless it's necessary for security reasons.
• Give employees plenty of opportunity to say good-bye to friends, coworkers, and mentors.	• Be stingy when deciding what the employees are entitled to (e.g., number of vacation days) upon departure; it's better to err in favor of the employees.
• Conduct a thorough exit interview.	• Expect the employees to continue to be available to offer assistance after they leave, unless you pay for that assistance.
• Be flexible in addressing the needs of individual employees.	• Make departing employees feel like they're just a statistic being processed by an uncaring bureaucracy.

have job offers out and accepted by the end of the calendar year. Such strategies are designed to induce commitment from top graduates before they're exposed to competing firms. Organizations that rely on traditional second-semester senior year interviews and long selection processes may find themselves in a less competitive position.

Making a Good Impression

To develop an understanding of how job applicants view recruiting practices, one team of researchers decided to conduct intensive, open-ended interviews with a few job hunters. The researchers asked placement directors from four colleges of a large university to identify job seekers who were as different from each other as possible in terms of sex, race, grade point average, and so on. Forty-one job seekers were identified and then interviewed early in the campus recruiting season and again near the end, eight to ten weeks later. The interviews were recorded, transcribed, and then content analyzed.

The results showed that job seekers' early perceptions of how well they fit a job were affected most by job and company characteristics, then by contacts with recruiters, and then by contacts with other people in the company besides recruiters. In many instances, recruiters made jobs that initially appeared unattractive seem attractive. Positive impressions were created by the status of recruiters and whether recruiters made applications feel "specially" treated. On the other hand, almost all job seekers reported that some recruiters or recruiting practices, or both, created poor impressions and made some jobs seem less attractive. Timing was especially important here, with slow or late decisions being a major reason for negative impressions.

Recruiters were viewed as more important by job seekers who had more job offers to choose from. Also, women (compared with men) viewed recruiters as more important. Many women (50 percent) reported some "offensive" interactions with recruiters, including remarks made about their personal appearance, negative comments about "minority" groups other than women (e.g., older workers), and mail addressed to "Mr." even after the initial interview. Another interesting finding was that the best applicants were more likely than weaker applicants to interpret recruiting practices as indications of what the employing organization was like rather than assuming the practices were just a poor reflection on the particular recruiter involved.[33]

This and several other studies show that the behaviors of the recruiters make a big difference. Effective recruiters show sincere interest in applicants, and, in return, applicants show more interest in the job.[34] A national study of recruitment for engineering graduates revealed that students not only responded to the interpersonal skills of recruiters but also preferred recruiters who were similar to them in terms of gender and education. Contrary to conventional wisdom, recruits did not respond more favorably to line managers or engineers than to human resource personnel.[35] Given that recruiters sell the organization to employees, perhaps they should be trained just as if they were selling the firm's products. Instead, whereas salespeople generally receive several weeks of training, recruiters seldom receive more than a few hours.

Making an Offer Applicants Will Find Attractive

Recruiters and the recruitment process help create a good (or bad) impression, but other things matter too. Especially for younger applicants, deciding

"I was impressed that these women executives would take the time out to interview me, a mid-level person. I was delighted to find people that embrace the same values I embrace."

Teri Robinson
Vice President
Darden Restaurants

whether to accept an employment offer may be entangled with choosing an occupation. These choices are influenced by economic issues, including the realities of the labor market; psychological issues, such as individual needs, interests, and abilities; and sociological issues, including exposure to the occupation through parents and relatives.[36]

It's often assumed that the attractiveness of an offer depends in part on what other offers the applicant is considering. This line of thinking follows from the image of a job seeker who invests a great deal of time and effort to generate as many options as possible and then simultaneously evaluates them. In reality, except for new college graduates, job seekers have only a hazy notion of their options.[37] The objective of most job seekers is to find an acceptable, rather than ideal, job. They usually evaluate opportunities sequentially. If an offer meets minimum criteria, it's accepted; if it doesn't, the sequential search process continues. In other words, alternative offers are less important than past experiences and beliefs about what is realistic to expect.

Location, perceptions that the organization's values match the applicant's own, job attributes, and company attributes all influence an applicant's decision.[38] Important job and company characteristics include status of the functional area the job is in, company reputation and management ethics as presented in the media, attitudes toward the product, and HR practices—such as whether the company is hiring new managers and at the same time laying some people off.[39]

Another important consideration is the applicant's *noncompensatory reservation wage*, which is the minimum pay necessary to make a job offer acceptable. Prior compensation levels, length of unemployment, and the availability of accurate salary information all affect an individual's reservation wage. In general, males have higher reservation wages than females. Females tend to undervalue their work abilities.[40] Another may be that males are exposed to more job opportunities. Increasingly, when applicants evaluate compensation offers, they consider the value of signing bonuses in addition to salary, benefits, and incentive offers. In 1998, corporate recruiters offered Cornell business school graduates signing bonuses that averaged $17,500. Even Burger King offers signing bonuses when it's recruiting new managers in some cities. Currently, the value of signing bonuses is rising more quickly than are salaries.[41]

Once a reservation wage is met, job seekers adopt a *compensatory approach*. They make trade-offs between different job attributes.[42] In one large study, more than 50,000 male and female applicants to the Minnesota Gas Company were asked to rank the importance of ten job attributes. Both sexes tended to rank the importance of company and coworkers higher than benefits, hours, and pay. Job applicants agreed that pay was important to others but were less willing to admit that it was important to them. Females ranked the type of work as most important, whereas males ranked job security more highly.[43] Both sexes prefer companies that offer more flexibility and opportunity to learn quickly.[44]

Giving Applicants the Information They Need

In their efforts to attract a large pool of applicants, many employers oversell their virtues and cover over their flaws. Just as applicants work to create the best possible impression,[45] so do employers. Some recruiters tell job applicants only about the positive aspects of a job and the company. This tactic

■ □ *fast fact*

Today, most people have chosen an occupational career by age 27.

■ □ *fast fact*

The Society for Human Resource Management estimates that signing bonuses are offered by 40 percent of employers.

■□ *fast fact*

According to the Bureau of Labor Statistics, the average worker holds nine different jobs between the ages of 18 and 32.

■□ *fast fact*

A survey of 400 international assignments in 80 companies around the world revealed that 40 percent wouldn't take another international assignment after learning what it was like.

follows from a desire to increase offer acceptances. In the short run, this tactic may work.[46] Longer-term, it's counterproductive. Describing both the positive and negative aspects of a job and organization—that is, providing a realistic job preview—is a better approach. Research shows that using realistic job previews actually increases the number of eventual recruits. In addition, recruits who receive both types of information are more committed and less likely to quit once they accept the job.[47]

Being overly optimistic also is questionable from an ethical perspective. Accepting a job offer can have far-reaching implications for a person's life—it can affect where the person lives, how much stress the person experiences commuting to work, where the person's children attend school, where a partner works, income levels, and so on. Viewed in this light, persuading a person to take a job becomes a big responsibility. Clearly, the only ethical approach is to engage in an honest exchange of information with job applicants. If a firm's representatives make false promises to job candidates, the firm can face costly lawsuits. Truth-in-hiring lawsuits have yielded damage awards as high as $10 million.[48] Withholding information is just as dangerous as making false statements. In one case (*Berger v. Security Pacific Information Systems*), Colorado's highest court upheld a jury's award of $451,600 because a company withheld information about its financial difficulties from a prospective employee.

Realistic job previews take many forms, including advertisements, formal job descriptions, film or video presentations, and samples of the actual work. A study involving several large companies found that potential applicants are attracted to companies that provide more information in their ads. When ads tell about the company, the job, and the job benefits, job seekers are more likely to follow up and apply for the job.[49] Another study found that applicants who obtained information through both formal and informal means had more knowledge about the job than those who relied on only one type of information.[50] In general, more information is better, and informal means of communicating about the job often produce more accurate perceptions.[51]

More accurate information allows employees to make better decisions about whether a situation is right for them. By helping applicants who won't be satisfied self-select out of the hiring process, organizations prevent unnecessary turnover. Applicants and employers both benefit. New or potential employees usually have inflated ideas or expectations about what a job involves. A realistic preview usually reduces these overly optimistic expectations. In other words, a realistic preview serves primarily to acquaint prospective employees with the negative aspects of a job.[52] Of course, employees share responsibility for getting a realistic job preview. In order to make sure they know what they're getting into, applicants should ask questions until they get detailed answers about things such as the expected results, the timetable available to achieve the results, and the resources available to them.[53]

Rejecting with Tact

When Mirage Resorts received 57,000 applications for 6,500 job openings, they had to tell thousands of applicants they wouldn't be hired. Southwest Airlines sends the same message to thousands of applicants year after year. If rejected candidates feel angry, they may never again purchase services from the organization. If recruiting procedures are viewed as unfair, too lengthy, or too impersonal, rejected candidates may share their dissatisfaction with friends and associates. Like many other "high-demand" organizations, Mirage Resorts and Southwest Airlines must find a way to reject applicants with tact.

Most applicants receive the news of their rejection in written form. Whether it's a traditional letter or a more modern e-mail message, the same basic principles apply. To leave a positive impression, a rejection letter should include statements that are friendly, a personalized and correct address and salutation, and a summary of the applicant's job qualifications. Including statements about the size and excellence of the application pool reduces disappointment and increases perceptions of fairness.[54] Applicants also appreciate timely rejection notices. A recruitment and selection timetable should be specified for applicants and the organization should meet its self-imposed deadlines.

REDUCING RECRUITMENT NEEDS THROUGH RETENTION

For some organizations, rapid growth is the primary reason that new employees must be recruited. But the need to replace workers who have left is a far more common factor driving recruitment activities. Turnover, not growth, is the reason behind most recruitment pressures. Some turnover is unavoidable, of course. People retire or move for non-job related reasons. But the lion's share of turnover—that caused by layoffs and dissatisfied employees, may be avoidable. At Ernst & Young, for example, voluntary turnover among women at the senior management level was reduced by 7 percent after the company began making a serious effort to increase retention rates. At this firm, offering more flexible work arrangements has been particularly helpful for retaining their best female employees.[55] Other firms may need to find other ways to reduce voluntary turnover. If they succeed, recruiting costs are sure to go down.

After a decade of downsizing that inflicted severe pain on millions of employees, some observers find it difficult to muster any sympathy for employers who now face a worker shortage. Perhaps if employers hadn't been laying off nearly three million people per year as a solution to competitive pressures, they would be in better shape to take advantage of today's growth opportunities. If they were more effective at creating change in their existing workforces, there would be less pressure to search for new employees to replace the ones that are let go. If they were more attentive to employees' concerns, perhaps fewer would leave to take similar jobs with competitors. At the very least, they might not take such great pleasure in walking out. When layoffs and turnover are absolutely necessary, a bit of foresight can prevent the feelings of betrayal that keep many downsized and demoralized workers from applying for open positions with their past employers.

Reduce Turnover

Exhibit 7.6 illustrates some of the known causes of turnover.[56] From the exhibit, it's easy to see that some causes of turnover aren't under employers' control. But many causes of turnover can be controlled by employers. Examples of unfair HR practices that increase turnover rates include electronic monitoring and travel schedules that require extended time away from home. Lower compensation and poor benefits also increase the rate at which employees voluntarily leave their employers.[57] Furthermore, many of the conditions that cause people to leave also make it difficult to attract new

■□ *fast fact*

When Ernst & Young learned that women were much more likely than men to leave this firm to work elsewhere, they created an Office of Retention.

"This upswing in the economy is a blessing. I'm getting out. I feel like, hey it's my turn to make you guys sweat."

David Mitchell
Middle Manager
(Employer Name Withheld)

■□ *fast fact*

In the fast-food industry, turnover of hourly workers averages 140 percent annually.

Exhibit 7.6

The Process of Employee Turnover

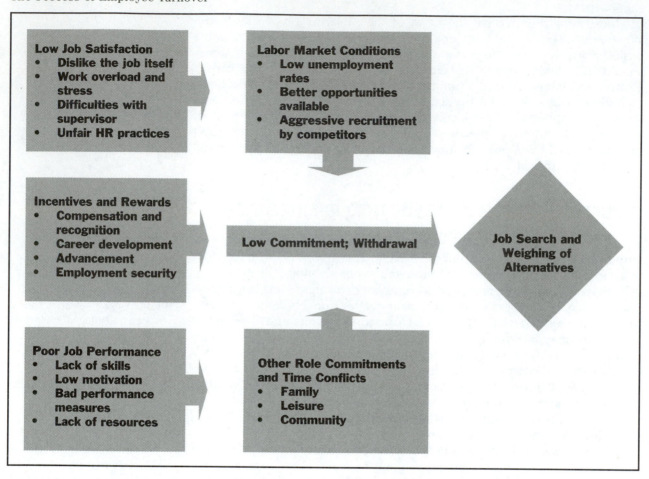

applicants to replace them. For example, if employees are leaving a company due partly to their inability to manage both work and nonwork demands, that company will also have a more difficult time recruiting new employees with the same concern.

Turnover can be extremely costly for an organization. According to research by the Saratoga Institute, the average company loses about $100,000 for every professional or managerial employee who leaves.[58] The feature, Managing Diversity: Eddie Bauer Satisfies Employees' Needs, illustrates how one company ensures the commitment of current employees and attracts the interest of new applicants.[59] In general, however, keeping good employees involves nothing less than doing an excellent job in all aspects of managing human resources.

Manage Layoffs Carefully

Facing the threat of job loss and seeing others lose their jobs can be a traumatic and bitter experience.[60] This is one reason why many excellent companies do everything possible to avoid layoffs. Instead, they work to maintain an internal labor market from which to recruit applicants for job openings.[61]

■■☐ *fast fact*

Autodesk began allowing employees to bring pets to work in 1982, and it's still a unique part of their culture.

MANAGING DIVERSITY
Eddie Bauer Satisfies Employees' Needs

To most people, the Eddie Bauer Company brings to mind images of outdoor clothing and casual business wear. Located in Redmond, Washington, Eddie Bauer is a rapidly growing catalog and retail company. The past five years have seen double-digit revenue growth for the catalog division, which brings in about 30 percent of the company's $1.5 billion in annual sales. Retail stores selling clothing and furniture make up the rest of the business. Throughout this growing company, employee satisfaction is given high priority, earning it a spot among *Business Week*'s top ten places to work as well as inclusion in *Working Mother* magazine's list of Top 100 Employers.

Among the many Eddie Bauer strategies for attracting new employees (called associates) and keeping the current workforce satisfied is the firm's family-friendly approach. Dealing with family issues is a part of the company's strategic business plan. Its success in this regard is part of what led *Business Week* to conclude that it's such a good place to work." "The pay isn't great," the magazine acknowledged, "but employees like the hours and say management demonstrates impressive family support." Company spokeswoman Liz Gorman elaborates: "Balance is at the core of what Eddie Bauer is all about. We believe there really is a need to have a balance in work and life." How does the company help associates achieve work and life balance for 12,000 people working in more than 450 locations throughout the United States, Canada, Japan, and Germany? They offer

- a flexible work day that allows workers at the corporate headquarters to choose an 8 a.m.-to-5 p.m. workday or a 6:30 a.m.-to-3:30 p.m. workday;
- a cafeteria that prepares takeout food for associates who work into the evening;
- special summer hours that allow associates to work a four-day week, so they can have long weekends;
- one "Balance Day" per year, in addition to normal vacations and holidays, intended to encourage employees to schedule "call in well" absences;
- a casual dress code, which has been in place for more than a decade;
- job sharing and telecommuting arrangements;
- a 40 percent subsidy of transportation costs for associates who use a vanpool;
- emergency child-care services;
- child- and elder-care consulting and referral services;
- dry cleaning services that pick up and deliver at the associate's place of work;
- special in-home health services for new parents;
- an Outdoor Experience Allowance, which provides 50 percent subsidies for a variety of activities, ranging from golf lessons to horseback riding; and
- a Group Mortgage HOME program that assists employees with financial transactions associated with selling or purchasing a home.

These are just a few of the many practices developed by Eddie Bauer in response to its associates' preferences. Five years ago, when the company decided to aim for being an employer of choice, management held focus group sessions with associates to get their input. What became clear was that juggling work and nonwork activities was a struggle for a large portion of the workforce. President Rick Fersch responded to employees' concerns by giving his full support to creating change quickly and with as little red tape as possible. Management believes that these benefits pay for themselves because many of them result in lower health-care costs. In addition, the programs enable associates to be more focused and productive at work because they know that they'll have the resources they need to manage their personal needs.

To learn more about Eddie Bauer, visit the company's home page at
www.eddiebauer.com

The 3M company, based in St. Paul, Minnesota, works hard to keep employees even when its own business units eliminate jobs. Instead of being fired, displaced employees are given first consideration for other job openings within the unit. If no suitable placement can be found, they're put on the Unassigned List, which makes them eligible for jobs in other units. They can stay on the list for six months. During that time, finding employment is the employee's responsibility. The company supports their efforts, however. Before recruiting externally to fill open positions, managers first check the qualifications of people on the Unassigned List. The company also sponsors an optional three-day workshop that covers topics such as outplacement, coping with job loss, résumé writing, and interviewing skills. For the first four months that they're on the Unassigned List, employees have the option of taking a severance package and leaving the company. Approximately 50 percent of the people on the list find other jobs at 3M within the four-month window. When that happens, employees and the company are both winners.[62]

Internal transfers are just one of many alternatives to massive layoffs. Others include:

- Restricting overtime
- Reducing the hours in a standard workweek
- Not renewing contracts for temporary and part-time workers
- Temporary leaves
- Job sharing
- Retraining
- Providing seed funds and entrepreneurship training and encouraging employees to start their own businesses
- Transferring staff to other companies (e.g., suppliers, customers)
- Early retirement with preferential conditions
- Reducing executive salaries and incentive pay
- Partnering with government agencies and professional societies to find jobs for displaced employees
- Voluntary turnover
- Employee buyouts of the company[63]

When employees must be let go, the process by which jobs are eliminated can make a difference. Loss of attachment, lack of information, and a perception of apparent managerial capriciousness as the basis for decisions about who will be terminated cause anxiety and an obsession with personal survival.[64] The negative cycle of reactions may not be inevitable. If survivors feel that the process used to decide who to let go was fair, their productivity and the quality of their job performance may not suffer as much. It's not the terminations per se that create bitterness—it's the manner in which the terminations are handled. Survivors often express feelings of disgust and anger when their friends and colleagues were fired. If they believe their own performance is no better than those who are let go, survivors may feel guilty that they have kept their jobs.[65] Statistics showing that older displaced workers who find new work earn about one-third less than they did in their old job contribute to the survivors' angst.[66] Thus, in developing human resource policies, procedures, and practices for effective downsizing and layoffs, even the needs of survivors require attention.

As with any major organizational change, the steps of diagnosing the current situation and developing a careful plan to implement change are essential. But the process of change isn't just about strategies and plans; it's also about relationships between the people in a company, and it's about personal character. The greatest challenges for managers are maintaining employee morale and regaining their trust while the actions of the company seem to say, "You are not valuable."[67] A manager who had the challenge of maintaining the morale and performance of employees until the closing of more than six General Motors auto plants offers the tips shown in Exhibit 7.7 for how to be effective in such situations.[68]

AFFIRMATIVE ACTION PLANS

Legal considerations play a critical role in the recruitment and hiring process-es of most companies in the United States. Global companies must abide by the relevant laws in all countries of operation. The feature, Managing Globally: Recruitment in Russia, describes the legal environment of one coun-try in which several U.S. companies have recently set up operations.[69]

The U.S. employment laws most directly relevant to recruitment are those describing affirmative action programs (AAPs). Affirmative action programs are intended to ensure proportional representation or parity, or to correct underutilization, of qualified members of protected groups in an organization's relevant labor market. Title VII of the *Civil Rights Act of 1964* identifies the following as protected groups: women, African Americans, Hispanics, Native Americans, Asian Americans, and Pacific Islander Americans. As Exhibit 7.8 on page 285 shows, most firms have AAPs.[70]

■□*fast fact*

In 1997, non-Hispanic white males were the largest group hired by state agencies under federally mandated affirmative action programs.

Exhibit 7.7

Tips for How to Manage the Process of Layoffs

Communicate

Give notice as far in advance as possible—certainly before workers read it in the paper. Be thorough and repeti-tious, because they may not be able to absorb everything the first time.

Be visible

Take personal responsibility for guiding people through the change. Don't just have an "open door" policy; wan-der around outside your office.

Be honest

False hope isn't helpful for anyone. Be blunt about the plant closing, even if you don't know the exact date.

Be positive

Reward top performers and implement worker ideas for improvements. Also, encourage plant tours by school-children and customers. They imply that workers are worth showing off.

Demand more

Remind workers that improving skills will help the plant today and make them more marketable later.

Keep the building looking good

Clean it, paint it. Don't let the equipment deteriorate. Morale is iffy enough already.

MANAGING GLOBALLY

Recruitment in Russia

Since the breakup of the Soviet Union in 1991, Russia and its neighbors have attracted considerable interest and increasing amounts of foreign investment. The region is rich in natural resources and is home to a well-educated population. But years of communism have left a legacy of management practices that are poorly suited to the capitalist economy that's slowly reemerging. Recruitment practices in Russia illustrate the point. Word-of-mouth recruiting is still the most common method for filling vacancies—especially outside the major cities and for lower-level jobs. Employees inform friends and relatives, and they're usually the ones who get the job. For higher level jobs, newspaper ads may be used.

Few Russians—especially older applicants—present résumés when applying for jobs. Instead, they carry a *trudovaya knizhka*. It lists the names and addresses of everyone the person has worked for, along with the dates of employment and reasons for termination. Employers generally give departing workers a reference letter to use in seeking a new job, but these seldom include useful information about prior job performance. Nor do most Russian employers ask applicants to fill out application forms or take any tests designed to assess the competencies. Instead, information about candidates usually is passed around informally among colleagues. For foreign firms just entering this environment, effective recruitment and selection can be extremely difficult unless the company is operating in partnership with a local company that's plugged into the informal communication network.

Compared to the volume of laws, regulations, and court decisions that affect U.S. employment practices, Russia's legal environment seems easy to navigate. The entire Code of Laws of Labor is less than 100 pages long. With the exception of a few rules prohibiting employment discrimination against pregnant women, the Code has little to say about equal employment opportunity. The lack of government regulations coincides with the use of more formal employment contracts that spell out the rights and responsibilities of employers and employees and a preference for resolving conflicts through informal means rather than through court action.

To learn more about international employment laws, visit the home page of the International Labour Organization at
www.ilo.org

Federal Contracts

█ ▢ fast fact

There are about 65,000 companies that are federal contractors.

If a company has a federal contract greater than $50,000 and has 50 or more employees, it's referred to as a federal contractor. Executive Order 11246, which became effective in 1965, requires federal contractors to

1. have and abide by an equal employment policy;
2. analyze its workforce to assess possible underutilization of women and ethnic minorities; and
3. when underutilization is revealed, develop a plan of action to eliminate it and make a good faith effort to implement the plan.

Regulatory guidelines and subsequent Supreme Court decisions make it clear that such plans must not include strong preferential treatment or strict quotas. Instead, plans should emphasize recruitment activities that increase the representation of protected groups and employment practices that eliminate bias.

In addition to protecting members of the groups identified in Title VII, federal contractors are required to take affirmative action to employ and advance qualified disabled individuals (section 503 of the *Rehabilitation Act*

Exhibit 7.8

How Prevalent Are Affirmative Action Programs?

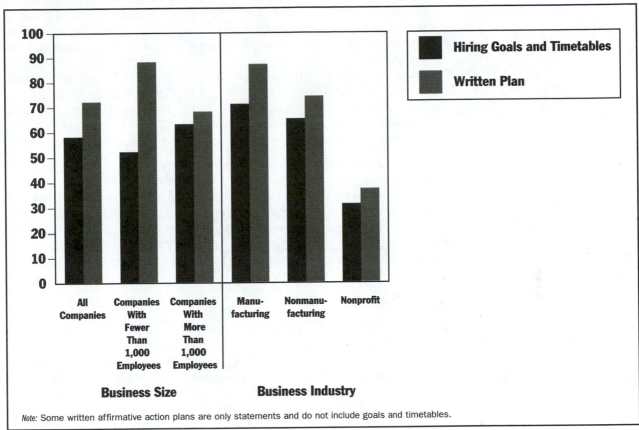

Note: Some written affirmative action plans are only statements and do not include goals and timetables.

of 1973). The rules further provide that employers with 50 or more employees who hold federal contracts totaling more than $50,000 must prepare written affirmative action programs for disabled workers *in each of their establishments*—for example, in each plant or field office. This condition must be met within 120 days after the contractor receives the federal contract. Those who hold contracts or subcontracts of less than $2,500 aren't covered by this act. Those with federal contracts that range from $2,500 to $50,000 are required to include an affirmative action clause in their contracts, but they do not need a written affirmative action plan.

The *Rehabilitation Act,* as amended in 1980 and in 1990 by the *Americans with Disabilities Act,* identifies three categories of protected disabled persons:

1. any individual who has a physical or mental impairment that greatly limits one or more of life's major functions;
2. any individual who has a history of such an impairment; or
3. any individual who is perceived as having such an impairment.

Federal contractors are required to file written affirmative action plans with the Office of Federal Contract Compliance Program (OFCCP). The Department of Labor specifies the required components of the written plans:

1. A *utilization analysis.* The analysis determines the number of minorities and women employed in different jobs within an organization.

■□ *fast fact*

More than 20 percent of the U.S. workforce is covered by OFCCP affirmative action regulations.

2. An *availability analysis.* This measures how many members of minorities and women are available to work in the relevant labor market of an organization. The relevant labor market is generally defined as the geographic area from which come a substantial majority of job applicants and employees. If an organization is employing proportionately fewer members of protected groups than are available, a state of *underutilization* exists.

3. *Goals and timetables.* These specify how the organization plans to correct any underutilization. Because goals and timetables become the organization's commitment to equal employment, they must be realistic and attainable. When a protected group is found to be underutilized, the timetable for addressing the problem is likely to stretch over several years.

These plans are intended to reduce discriminatory practices among employers who receive federal funds. Several studies indicate that for federal contractors, representation of black males and black females has grown rapidly.[71] A review of the status of women and minorities in these firms suggests that AAPs may not eliminate discrimination, however. In summarizing their findings, an OFCCP official concluded, "In nearly every review we do, we're finding inequities in the compensation for women and minorities compared to white men."[72]

Consent Decrees

Employers that aren't federal contractors may nevertheless be subject to a government-regulated affirmative action plan. A federal court may require an AAP if it finds evidence of past discrimination in a suit brought against the organization through the Equal Employment Opportunity Commission. The evidence that leads to such conclusions often comes from a utilization analysis conducted by the EEOC. Consent degrees specify the affirmative action steps the organization will take.

Since the 1960s, hundreds of consent degrees have put AAPs into place. Their effectiveness to date is difficult to judge, however. Women and minorities have made some progress in their employment status. Whether progress would have been faster or slower in the absence of consent decrees is impossible to know. When *Fortune* put together its list of the 50 Best Companies for Asians, Blacks and Hispanics, the vast majority of the 50 companies selected had aggressive EEOC recruiting plans in place.[73] Some programs were put in place years ago in response to consent decrees. It's likely that many others were developed to avoid lawsuits or minimize the damages that would be caused by a lawsuit. One thing is clear, however: perceptions of unfair discrimination persist even among African Americans who are generally optimistic about their futures.[74]

Voluntary Action

If a company develops a reputation for being a difficult place for minorities to work, it's likely to make recruiting in a tight labor market all the more challenging. Elgin Clemons described an incident he experienced while working as an attorney at the prestigious law firm of Shearman & Sterling. A graduate of Princeton University and New York University Law School, Clemons worked as an associate for the law firm for two years. One day he decided not to call for a messenger and instead personally delivered to the firm's mail room a stack of work to be sent to a client. A mail clerk told him he would have to get an attorney's signature. "What makes you think I'm not an attorney?" Clemons, who is black, asked. He knew that the mail clerk was reacting to his race. The stereotyping was even more painful because the mail clerk also was black.

A mail clerk's stereotyping habits may have little consequence for an attorney, but when the firm's partners engage in stereotyping the consequences are significant. At Shearman & Sterling, the partners, all of whom were white, acknowledged that they assumed that blacks as a group have more problems with legal writing than whites. When stories such as this spread—through the informal grapevine as well as national newspapers—they naturally reduce the size and diversity of the firm's applicant pool.[75]

The content of a voluntary AAP depends on the organization and the extent to which various groups are underrepresented. It may also depend on the company's business objectives. Xerox, for example, is proactively recruiting Hispanic managers in particular, recognizing that their bilingual skills are a particularly valuable asset.

The EEOC publishes guidelines for organizations that wish to establish voluntary affirmative action programs, and it offers the annual Exemplary Voluntary Efforts Award to recognize companies with the best voluntary programs. Winning the award appears to have value beyond simply good public relations. A study of firms that have won this award showed that investors bid up the stock prices of the winning companies after the award was announced. By comparison, stock prices fell following announcements of discrimination settlements.[76]

Despite such findings, mandatory and voluntary AAPs have come under increasing political attack. It's unclear how long they'll remain legal. Employers who thought they were being socially responsible by taking affirmative actions have lost lawsuits for taking measures that the courts viewed as reverse discrimination. The case of *Piscataway Board of Education v. Taxman*, 1997, illustrates this legal trend. The case involved a layoff affecting two equally qualified teachers who had been hired on the very same day and so had identical job tenure. A white teacher (Sharon Taxman) was laid off while an African-American teacher (Debra Williams) was retained in order to maintain the school's racial diversity. The courts ruled that the Board of Education engaged in illegal employment practice because under Title VII employers may not use race as a basis for employment decisions except for compelling reasons. Because the school district had no record of past discrimination or underutilization, maintaining a diverse workforce was not viewed as a sufficiently compelling reason to consider race in the layoff decision.[77]

When deciding whether to implement a voluntary affirmative action plan, employers must consider the threats posed by the shifting legal and political landscape. Many employers remain supportive of affirmative action, despite the controversy surrounding it. Some of the nation's largest broadcasters decided to continue their affirmative action efforts even after a court ruled that they were no longer required to follow guidelines published by the Federal Communications Commission (FCC). The guidelines essentially stated that, as a condition for keeping their license, broadcast companies make good-faith efforts to recruit and hire minorities. When the court ruled that such guidelines were not enforceable, ABC, NBC, CBS, Fox, and Time Warner all chose to continue their current efforts voluntarily. Presumably, they realized that such efforts serve the public interest as well as their own business interests.[78]

Some opponents of affirmative action argue that preferential treatment often backfires, causing harm to the intended beneficiaries of AAPs. Consis-

"It hurt her self-esteem. With all she had put into education, and then to be told that the only reason she has her job is because she's black."

**Alvin Williams
Husband of Debra Williams**

tent with this argument, studies have shown that affirmative action hires are *perceived* as being less competent than *equally qualified* employees not hired under an AAP.[79] During the 1990s, organizations began developing new approaches to managing diversity. These include offering cultural awareness training programs and the development of decision making procedures that reduce the impact of any individual's personal prejudices and biases. According to numerous opinion polls, Americans strongly support efforts designed to ensure equal opportunity and eliminate bias, and they oppose practices that they believe involve giving any group preferential treatment.[80]

Breaking the Glass Ceiling

"The critical factor for the advancement of women is commitment from the top."

**Sheila Wellington
President
Catalyst**

Regardless of why organizations develop AAPs, their presence often stimulates people to think more systematically about their recruitment efforts. Until recently, the disciplined approach associated with AAPs—that is, defining the relevant labor market and tracking how recruitment efforts affect both who is offered a position and who accepts job offers—was used only for lower-level positions and external recruitment efforts. One consequence is the apparent existence of glass ceilings, which the Department of Labor defines as "artificial barriers based on attitudinal or organizational bias that prevent qualified individuals from advancing upward in their organizations."

Many companies have found that a decade or two of affirmative action recruiting at lower levels ensured that by the late 1980s there were plenty of women in the pipeline for higher-level positions. Yet, women still seem to be trapped below a glass ceiling. The challenge for these companies is how to balance their desire to recruit the best available talent with their desire to break the glass ceiling. For Colgate-Palmolive, focusing the firm's recruitment efforts on women seemed like a reasonable solution. When one of the four regional vice presidents stepped down, Colgate's CEO decided he wanted to fill the position with a woman. According to CEO Reuben Mark, the company "wanted the best person we could possibly get, but that person had to be a woman." Colgate hired Lois Juliber in 1988 and put her in charge of its Far East and Canada Operations. A decade later, she was promoted to Executive Vice President and put in charge of North America and Europe, which constitute half of the company's worldwide operations. The appointment was widely viewed as a signal that she was being considered as a top contender for the CEO position.[81]

Based on its intensive study of nine large corporations, the Department of Labor concluded that the recruitment methods typically used to hire managerial talent contributes to the problem of glass ceilings. Exhibit 7.9 lists the specific problems identified by the Department of Labor.[82] Colgate's approach was one way to overcome these problems.

"If you stick to hiring the best and brightest, diversity will take care of itself. That's not to say that people don't have to be trained to develop a comfort level. That's what we're working on."

**Archyne Woodward
Diversity Coordinator
The Chubb Corporation**

To remedy these problems, which are now more widely recognized than they were when the Department of Labor's Glass Ceiling Commission first began its investigation, several actions can be taken. One company developed a management intern program aimed at recruiting recent minority and female college graduates, as well as sponsoring scholarships for minorities and women in disciplines related to the company's business. Others try to remedy problems related to the glass ceiling and affirmative action with better use of search firms and other forms of recruitment, record keeping, and internal monitoring. Other approaches include awareness training for top executives and cultural audits, which can be used to identify obstacles or barriers that hinder individuals from meeting their career goals. Important

Exhibit 7.9
Recruiting Practices That May Create a Glass Ceiling

Reliance on Networking—Word-of-Mouth

In some companies, mid- and upper-level positions were filled by senior executives through word-of-mouth referrals. In some of these instances, corporate executives had learned of individuals, interviewed them casually (at luncheons or dinners), and made them an offer, outside the formal recruitment process. The net result of these activities was a diminished opportunity for the career advancement of women and members of minorities.

Reliance on Networking—Employee Referrals

In some companies, elaborate employee referral systems are in place. In one company reviewed by the Department of Labor, the review team could not establish if this system was discriminatory, but no members of minorities or women were hired into mid-levels and upper levels of the company through this process. Moreover, no minorities or women were in mid-level or upper-level positions doing the referring

Use of Executive Search Firms

All companies reviewed by the Department of Labor used search firms during the period under review. One company appeared to fill almost every upper-level management position through search firms. Most of the companies failed to make executive recruitment firms aware of their equal employment and affirmative action obligations under the law. When these companies asked a search agency for a candidate pool, many of them did not make any effort to ensure that the search firm reached out to identify qualified minorities and women. In addition, when the search firm sent forward a slate with no minorities or women, the contractors did not demonstrate any good-faith effort to broaden the pool of candidates.

Job Postings

In some companies, vacancies were posted for lower-level jobs, but not for mid- to upper-level jobs. At the higher levels, employees learned about an opening only through their informal networks. Informal communications tend to flow more intensely among people who are demographically similar, which means that members of many protected groups are less likely to hear about openings for higher-level positions.

Interview Process

In addition to the type of recruitment used, the recruitment process itself can, at times, be a barrier for women. For example, when recruiting occurs at a conference for a trade or professional association, it often is scheduled to take place in a hotel room. A professional office is not usually available. A Wellesley College Center for Research on Women study found that holding job interviews in hotel rooms is intimidating for many women and reduces the possibility of finding qualified women applicants.

---

to the success of all such interventions is maintaining merit as the actual and perceived basis for employment decisions.[83]

SUMMARY

Organizations are dynamic, and the need to attract the right number of people at the right time and place is perpetual. Two important HR activities that guide effective recruitment are the strategic planning process and job analysis. Planning establishes close linkages between longer-term strategic objectives and recruitment activities. Job analysis enables the organization to convey information accurately (via job descriptions and job specifications) to applicants so that both individuals and organizations are well-matched. Selection also is closely connected to recruitment. Decisions about who to hire are constrained by the size and quality of the applicant pool, which is created through recruitment activities.

Recruitment involves internal and external searches. Although organizations vary considerably in terms of the types of jobs available, both external and internal labor markets exist for the recruitment of suitable applicants. Over time, organizations weigh costs and benefits of internal and external methods in order to choose the most effective ones for a given job. The choice of recruitment methods and the implementation of a recruiting plan should take into account the perspective of applicants, as well as the needs of the organization. For applicants, the recruitment is fundamentally a search for information. Applicants deserve to be given accurate and complete information in order to make the best possible employment decisions. Employers also benefit from this approach, as it reduces post-hire dissatisfaction and premature turnover.

Retaining employees is one way to reduce the need for extensive recruiting and its associated costs. The development of an effective human resource management system requires understanding the causes of voluntary turnover. In addition to reducing voluntary turnover, many organizations now realize that reducing mandatory turnover—especially layoffs—is another approach to managing recruitment. With so many available alternatives to layoffs, layoffs should be a practice of last resort.

The legal environment plays an important role in recruitment, primarily in requiring organizations to meet federal and state fair-employment regulations in their staffing activities. Affirmative action programs, though usually designed explicitly for legal compliance, encourage organizations to systematically measure and monitor their recruiting activities. In addition to improving equal employment opportunities, this disciplined approach is consistent with a growing interest in managing human resources strategically.

TERMS TO REMEMBER

Affirmative action
Affirmative Action Programs
    (AAPs)
Applicant pool
Availability analysis
Consent decree
Contingent employees
Employee referrals
Employment agencies
External labor market
Glass ceiling
Goals and timetables

Host-country nationals
Internal labor pool
Promotion
Realistic job preview
Recruitment
Relevant labor market
Replacement planning chart
Talent inventory
Third-country nationals
Transfer
Underutilization
Utilization analysis

DISCUSSION QUESTIONS

1. Is the strategic importance of recruitment greater in some industries than others? Explain.

2. Compare and contrast the recruiting methods and philosophies of Chubb Insurance and AIG. Explain the reasons for similarities and differences.

3. After reviewing Chapter 4 describe how a SWOT analysis could be used in developing a recruitment plan.

4. Do you think Gateway's decision to move its headquarters to San Diego will have any impact on its ability to recruit people to fill its manufacturing jobs in South Dakota? Explain why or why not?

5. According to some estimates, one-third of all executive-level hires prove to be unsatisfactory. What role might executive recruitment practices play in creating this situation?

6. Why do some organizations use mostly external searches, whereas others use mostly internal searches?

7. What information should be contained in a realistic job preview by a firm seeking to attract the best MBA students? Does your answer depend on the type of industry? The geographic location of the job? On whether it involves an overseas assignment?

8. Do you think firms such as Colgate-Palmolive should address the glass ceiling problem by explicitly stating that they want to fill a specific managerial position with a woman? Explain your opinion.

PROJECTS TO EXTEND YOUR LEARNING

1. **Managing Strategically.**   Employers can easily advertise their employment opportunities over the web. They can list openings on the company website and/or list them on public sites. Visit several available public recruiting sites. Compare and contrast the features of these sites from the perspective of employers and applicants. What are the major strengths and weaknesses of the sites you visited? If you were an employer and could list an opening on only one public site, which one would you choose? Explain your choice. Here are some of the sites that were popular at the time this book went to press:
    The Monster Board at **www.monster.com**
    Online Career Center at **www.occ.com**
    Career Mosaic at **www.careermosaic.com**
    HispanStar at **www.hispanstar.com**

2. **Managing Diversity.**   Shearman & Sterling is an international law firm headquartered in New York City, with offices in Abu Dhabi, Beijing, Dusseldorf, Tokyo, Paris, and elsewhere. Like other law firms, much of the work that must be done is carried out by entry-level professionals, including student interns and associates who have just completed law school. The firm is dependent on these sources of labor and is eager to attract the best and the brightest. Visit the website for Shearman & Sterling to investigate the professional opportunities described (e.g., summer programs, continuing education, and career development). Analyze the firm's formal communication. What messages are conveyed through the website? Describe the specific cues that you react to as part of the message. Prepare a one-page memo to Shearman & Sterling describing the strengths and weaknesses of its approach to communicating via the World Wide Web. How could improving its website con-

tribute to its recruitment effectiveness? Visit Shearman & Sterling's employment opportunities at
www.shearman.com

3. **Managing Teamwork.**   Visit the Hire Quality home page at
www.hire-quality.com
(or visit the site of a similar service) to learn about how employment firms help match job candidates and employers. Click on the box addressed to employers seeking qualified candidates and read the description of how the service identifies suitable candidates. Describe the basic steps in the company's approach. If you were an employer looking for highly motivated employees to work in a team-based organization, would you use this service to find them? Why or why not?

4. **Managing Globally.**   Hiring qualified employees is a key strategic action for high-tech firms. Unless these firms can attract the very best talent, they won't be able to compete successfully. Due to the domestic shortage of engineers and programmers, these firms recognize that their recruitment efforts must extend beyond U.S. borders. Many of these firms also are eager to ensure that their workforces reflect the diversity of their customer base. Visit the home pages of several high-tech companies. Evaluate how effective these companies are likely to be in getting people to apply for jobs with them and eventually accepting job offers from them. Select one company and offer suggestions for how they could improve their electronic job posting and recruiting efforts. Be sure to include suggestions for how to enhance their appeal to women, North Americans from a wide range of ethnic backgrounds, and potential applicants from overseas. Three companies that you might visit are Etec Systems at
www.etec.com
IBM at
www.ibm.com
and Microsoft at
www.microsoft.com
For additional information about the legal issues involved in recruiting foreign workers, visit
www.immigrationlaw.com

5. **Integration and Application.**   After reviewing the three end-of-text cases, answer the following questions by comparing and contrasting the recruitment efforts of the three firms.

   a. Which company do you think needs to be most concerned about recruitment? Why?
   b. What should be the objectives of each company's recruitment efforts? Relate the recruitment objectives to each company's strategic objectives.
   c. Which company is likely to have the most difficult time creating a large pool of qualified applicants? Explain your reasoning.

CASE STUDY

Downsizing: Anathema To Corporate Loyalty?

Jim Daniels was unprepared for the dilemma facing Defense Systems, Inc. (DSI). Jim, Vice President of Human Resources for DSI, joined the company one year ago when he was pirated away from one of the company's major competitors. DSI manufactures electronic components used in weapons supplied to the Air Force and many other firms. In addition, DSI makes semiconductors used in many of the weapons systems as well as in personal computers and automotive computers.

When Jim joined DSI, a major drive to build up the staff in engineering was undertaken in anticipation of a major upturn in the semiconductor market. Unfortunately, industry analysts' projections were optimistic, and the semiconductor market failed to pick up. DSI had recently completed an aggressive hiring policy at the major universities around the U.S., wherein the company had selected 1,000 engineers who were among the cream of the crop with an average GPA of 3.4. Without a pickup in business, however, DSI is confronted with some fairly unpleasant alternatives.

From one point of view, potential cutbacks at DSI fit the overall pattern of cutbacks, restructuring, and downsizing of major U S. companies during the past few years. The motives among firms who have trimmed their workforces vary—some to please Wall Street and the stockholders, others to keep pace with foreign competitors or to shrink an unwieldy organizational structure. To Jim, the DSI layoffs or terminations were poor alternatives to dealing with a turbulent environment.

The major problem, as Jim saw it, was to preserve as many of these jobs as possible until business picked up. To terminate these new hires would irreparably harm DSI's future recruitment efforts. On the other hand, underemploying these talented recruits for very long was bound to lead to major dissatisfaction. Although terminations would improve the balance sheet in the short run, Jim worried about the impact of such a move on corporate loyalty, a fragile and rare commodity at other major firms that have had to cut their white-collar workforce.

Jim is scheduled to meet with the executive committee of DSI in three days to discuss the overstaffing problems and to generate alternatives. In preparation for this meeting, Jim is trying to draw on his experience with his past employer to generate some ideas. A number of differences between DSI and Jim's old employer, though, makes comparisons difficult.

For one, DSI does not employ nearly the number of temporaries or student interns as did his old employer. Nor does DSI rely on subcontractors to produce parts needed in its assembly operation. Because of extra capacity, DSI can currently produce 50 percent of the parts it purchases, whereas Jim's ex-employer could produce only 5 percent.

Another major difference is the degree of training provided by DSI. At Jim's old employer, each employee could expect a minimum of 40 hours of additional training a year; at DSI, however, training consists of about 10 hours per year, much of it orientation training.

Jim wondered whether there might be some additional ways to remove slack from the system and at the same time preserve as many jobs as possible. For example, overtime hours are still paid to quite a few technicians. Would the engineers be willing to assume some of these duties in the interim until business picked up? Some older employees have accumulated several weeks of unused vacation. Could employees be encouraged to take unpaid leaves of absence? Perhaps early retirement incentives could be offered to make room for some of the bright young engineers. DSI also has 14 other geographic locations, some in need of additional workers.

As Jim thought about these options, one thing was clear: he needs to organize and prioritize these ideas concisely if he is to be prepared for his upcoming meeting.

QUESTIONS

1. Why is Jim sensitive to DSI's recruitment efforts?
2. What are some potential problems for the current class of engineers recruited at DSI?
3. How could the use of temporaries, student interns, or subcontractors potentially help DSI?
4. Evaluate Jim's alternatives for reducing DSI's labor surplus.

CASE STUDY

The New Recruit

General Instruments (GI), a defense contractor, employs nearly 1,000 engineers, and designs and manufactures a number of electronic systems for nuclear submarines. Recruiting qualified engineers has been difficult for GI because of the competitive market in Palo Alto and the substantial cost-of-living increase for anyone relocating to the area. Stan Fryer, project leader at GI, knew that today would be one of those proverbial Mondays that managers so often fear. Stan's boss and group manager, Harry Hoskinsson, had left town on business the previous Friday and would not return until the following week.

Stan's problem this morning concerns a new engineer recruit, June Harrison, a single, 25-year-old systems engineer who was hired three weeks ago upon graduation from San Diego State University. Much to Stan's surprise, June has submitted a letter of resignation, stating personal reasons as the cause of her departure. In addition to the letter of resignation, Stan also has a memo from June's supervisor, Lou Snider, describing the events leading up to June's resignation.

As Stan reconstructed these events, it seemed that June was expecting overtime payment in this week's paycheck because of the extra hours she had put in over the previous three weeks. Lou Snider, however, had neglected to file the proper payroll paperwork so that June could receive her overtime in the current pay period. This did not surprise Stan, given Lou's prior history in other supervisory positions. Apparently, Harry Hoskinsson had spoken to Lou about filing so much overtime for his section. So Lou decided to spread out some of the overtime charges over several pay periods.

What Lou hadn't realized was that June had finally secured an apartment in Palo Alto (she had been renting a room in a nearby hotel) and had committed to making a three-month payment and deposit with her paycheck and the additional overtime payment she was expecting. When June realized what was going to happen, she called Harry Hoskinsson to set up a meeting to discuss how she could cover her housing expense. June remembered that when she was being recruited, Harry had emphatically told her to contact him if she ever needed anything or had any problems settling into her new job at GI. Harry was in a bit of a rush to make a staff meeting, so he agreed to see June early the following day. When June reported to Harry's office the next morning, she was understandably upset when Harry's secretary told her that Harry had left town on a business trip. With that, she returned to her office and drafted her resignation letter.

As Stan contemplated how to resolve his "Monday morning" problem, he recalled the speech Harry had given him two years ago when he joined GI. Harry had made clear his distaste for young engineers who tended to live beyond their means and to count on bonuses and overtime as if they were regular and assured components of their paycheck. Nonetheless, Stan decided, despite Harry's speech, that GI must try to arrange for a loan covering June's housing expenses and, more importantly, to persuade her to reconsider her hasty decision.

No sooner had Stan decided on a course of action when June appeared in his doorway. She had done some thinking over the weekend after talking with another GI project engineer, a temporary employee hired only for the duration of his project. It seemed that temporary employees earned about 20 percent more than comparable permanent employees at GI, although they received considerably fewer benefits (such as retirement and health insurance). June made a proposal to Stan: she would retract her resignation letter if GI would permit her, in effect, to quit and be rehired as a temporary project engineer. Otherwise she planned to leave GI and accept a standing offer she had received from an engineering firm in her home city of San Diego. As Stan listened, he wondered how Harry would handle this situation. To Stan, June's proposal sounded like blackmail.

QUESTIONS

1. Should June have resigned over the overtime issue?
2. Should GI accept June's proposal of rehiring her as a temporary employee?
3. How could the recruiting process for June have been done better?
4. Was the socialization process for June lacking something? What?

ENDNOTES

[1] D. Sears, "Staffing the New Economy: Shortage or Myth?" *HR Magazine* (June 1998): 130–138.

[2] S. Hamm, A. Cortese, and S. B. Garland, "Microsoft's Future," *Business Week* (January 19, 1998): 58–68; B. Schlender, "Microsoft: First America, Now the World," *Fortune* (August 18, 1997): 214–217; R. Lieber, "Wired for Hiring: Microsoft's Slick Recruiting Machine," *Fortune* (February 5, 1996): 123–124; R. E. Stross, "Mr. Gates Builds His Brain Trust," *Fortune* (December 8, 1997): 84–98; D. Coupland, "Microserfs: Seven Days in the Life of Young Microsoft," *Wired* (January 1994): 87–95.

[3] J. A. Breaugh, *Recruitment: Science and Practice* (Boston: PWS-Kent, 1992); B. Schneider and N. Schmitt, *Staffing Organizations*, 2nd ed. (Glenview, IL: Foresman, 1986).

[4] *Special Survey Report: Human Resources Outlook* 49 (4) (Washington, DC: Bureau of National Affairs, 1998).

[5] Data shown in Exhibit 7.1 were reported in "SHRM-BNA Survey No. 63: Human Resource Activities, Budgets, and Staffs, 1997–1998," *Bulletin to Management* (June 18, 1998): 2. See also Breaugh, *Recruitment*; M. S. Taylor and C. M. Giannantonio, "Forming, Adapting, and Terminating the Employment Relationship: A Review of the Literature from Individual, Organizational, and Interactionist Perspectives," *Journal of Management* 19 (1993): 461–515. See also S. L. Rynes, "Recruitment, Job Choice, and Post-Hire Consequences: A Call for New Research Directions," in *Handbook of Industrial and Organizational Psychology*, vol. 2, M. D. Dunnette and L. M. Hough, eds. (Palo Alto, CA: Consulting Psychologists Press, 1991): 399–444.

[6] P. Nakache, "Cisco's Recruiting Edge," *Fortune* (September 29, 1997): 275–276; D. Anfuso, "Humana Pushes Down Recruitment Costs—and Raises Quality," *Workforce* (March 1999): 36-40.

[7] "Does Hiring Minorities Hurt?" *Business Week* (September 14, 1998): 26.

[8] Based on P. Cappelli and A. Crocker-Hefter, *Distinctive Human Resources Are the Core Competencies of Firms*, Report No. RQ00011-91 (Washington, DC: U.S. Department of Education, 1994).

[9] H. Axel, *HR Executive Review: Competing as an Employer of Choice* (New York: The Conference Board, 1996).

[10] D. Leonhardt, "McDonald's: Can It Regain Its Golden Touch?" *Business Week* (March 9, 1998): 70–77; G. Flynn, "McDonald's Serves up HR Excellence," *Personnel Journal* (January 1996): 54–55.

[11] A. E. Barber, *Recruiting Employees: Individual and Organizational Perspectives* (Thousand Oaks, CA: Sage, 1998); R. P. Vecchio, "The Impact of Referral Sources on Employee Attitudes: Evidence from a National Sample," *Journal of Management* 21 (5) (1995): 953–965.

[12] H. Axel, *HR Executive Review: Competing as an Employer of Choice* (New York: The Conference Board, 1996).

[13] T. A. Stewart, "In Search of Elusive Tech Workers," *Fortune* (February 16, 1998): 171–172; S. Baker, G. McWilliams, and M. Kripalani, "Forget the Huddled Masses: Send Nerds," *Business Week* (July 21, 1997): 110–113; G. DeGeorge, "Sign of the Times: Help Wanted," *Business Week* (November 10, 1997): 60–61; C. Lee, "The Hunt for Skilled Workers," *Training* (December 1997): 26–33.

[14] P. Nakache, "Cisco's Recruiting Edge."

[15] K. A. Bantel and S. E. Jackson, "Top Management and Innovations in Banking: Does the Composition of the Top Management Team Make a Difference?" *Strategic Management Journal* 10 (Summer Supplement 1989): 107–124.

[16] R. O. Crockett, "Gateway Loses the Folksy Shtick," *Business Week* (July 6, 1998): 80–84.

[17] For information about sources in recruiting salespeople, see S. L. Martin and N. S. Raju, "Determining Cutoff Scores That Optimize Utility: A Recognition of Recruiting Costs," *Journal of Applied Psychology* 77 (1992): 15–23.

[18] C. Patton, "Searching in Space," *Human Resource Executive* (October 6, 1997): 36–38; B. P. Sunoo, "Thumbs Up for Staffing Web Sites," *Workforce* (October 1997): 67–72; S. Greengard, "Rating HR Online," *Personnel Journal* (June 1996): 168–171; "Datagraph: Internet Recruitment Survey," *Bulletin to Management* (May 22, 1997): 164–165; J. Dysart, "Web Fever," *Human Resource Executive* (March 6, 1997): 30–39; J. Martin, "Changing Jobs? Try the Net," *Fortune* (March 2, 1998): 205–208; J. Waldrop and T. Butler, "Finding the Job You Should Want," *Fortune* (March 2, 1998): 211–214; S. Kucznski, "You've Got Job Offers," *HR Magazine* (March 1999): 50-58.

[19] S. Peters, "HR Helps Mirage Resorts Manage Change," *Personnel Journal* (June 1994): 22–30.

[20] T. A. Judge and D. M. Cable, "Applicant Personality, Organizational Culture, and Organizational Attraction," *Personnel Psychology* 50 (1997): 359–394; A. M. Saks and B. E. Ashforth, "A Longitudinal Investigation of the Relationships Between Job Information Sources, Applicant Perceptions of Fit, and Work Outcomes," *Personnel Psychology* 50 (1997): 395–426.; R. W. Griffeth, P. W. Hom, L. S. Fink, and D. J. Cohen, "Comparative Tests of Multiple Models of Recruiting Sources Effects," *Journal of Management* 23 (1997): 19–36.

[21] R. M. Fernandez and N. Weinberg, "Sifting and Sorting: Personal Contacts and Hiring in a Retail Bank," *American Sociological Review* 17 (December 1997): 883–902.

[22] For a detailed discussion of these errors in recruiting decisions, see S. Rubenfeld and M. Crino, "Are Employment Agencies Jeopardizing Your Selection Process?" *Personnel* (September–October 1981): 70–78.

[23] C. McCreary, "Get the Most Out of Search Firms," *Workforce* (Supplement) (August 1997): 28–30.

[24] Bureau of National Affairs, "Personnel Policies Forum, survey no. 146," *Recruiting and Selection Procedures* (Washington, DC: 1988; updated 1999): pp. 4–5. Reprinted by permission.

[25] R. S. Johnson, "The 50 Best Companies for Asians, Blacks & Hispanics," *Fortune* (August 3, 1998): 94–122.

[26] P. Brotherton, "Employers Lighten Worker Shortage Burden by Going Abroad," *International Update* (May 1993): 1–8.

[27] J. L. Laabs, "Recruiting in the Global Village," *Workforce* (April 1998): 30–33.

[28] "Cisco Systems' HR is Wired for Success," *Personnel Journal* (January 1996): 59; D. M. Schweiger, J. M. Ivancevich, and F. R. Power, "Executive Actions for Managing Human Resources Before and After Acquisitions," *Academy of Management Executive* (May 1987): 127–238.

[29] See C. von Hippel, S. L. Mangum, D. B. Greenberger, R. L. Heneman, and J. D. Skoglind, "Temporary Employment: Can Organizations and Employees Both Win?" *Academy of Management Executive* 11 (1) (1997): 93–104.

[30] D. G. Albrecht, "Reaching New Heights: Today's Contract Workers are Highly Promotable," *Workforce* (April 1998): 42–48.

[31] Adapted from R. Kessler, "Say Good-bye with Style," *HR Magazine* (June 1998): 171–174.

[32] S. L. Rynes and A. E. Barber, "Applicant Attraction Strategies: An Organizational Perspective," *Academy of Management Review* (1990): 286–310; R. E. Herman, *Keeping Good People: Strategies for Solving the Dilemma of the Decade* (New York: McGraw-Hill, 1991); K. G. Connolly and P. M. Connolly, *Competing for Employees: Proven Marketing Strategies for Hiring and Keeping Exceptional People* (Lexington, MA: Lexington Books, 1991): C. L. Cooper and I. T. Robertson, eds., *International Review of Industrial and Organizational Psychology*, vol. 6 (New York: John Wiley & Sons, 1991); S. L. Rynes, R. D. Bretz, Jr., and B. Gerhart, "The Importance of Recruitment in Job Choice: A Different Way of Looking," *Personnel Psychology* 44 (1991): 487–521; J. M. Grant and T. S. Bateman, "An Experimental Test of the Impact of Drug-Testing Programs on Potential Job Applicants' Attitudes and Intentions," *Journal of Applied Psychology* (1990): 127–131; K. R. Murphy, G. C. Thornton III, and D. H. Reynolds, "College Students' Attitudes toward Employee Drug Testing Programs," *Personnel Psychology* 43 (1990): 615–631; T. J. Hutton, "Increasing the Odds for Successful Searches," *Personnel Journal* (September 1987): 140–152; M. S. Taylor and T. J. Bergmann, "Organizational Recruitment Activities and Applicants' Reactions at Different Stages of the Recruitment Process," *Personnel Psychology* (Summer 1987): 265–285.

[33] S. D. Maurer, V. Howe, and T. W. Lee, "Organizational Recruiting as Marketing Management: An Interdisciplinary Study of Engineering Graduates," *Personnel Psychology* 45 (1992): 807–833.

[34] R. Ganzel, "Putting Out the Welcome Mat," *Training* (March 1998): 54–62; D. B. Turban and T. W. Dougherty, "Influences of Campus Recruiting Applicant Attraction to Firms," *Academy of Management Journal* 35 (1992): 739–765.

[35] S. D. Maurer, V. Howe, and T. W. Lee, "Organizational Recruiting as Marketing Management."

[36] J. O. Crites, *Vocational Psychology* (New York: McGraw-Hill, 1969); J. P. Wanous, *Organizational Entry: Recruitment, Selection, and Socialization of Newcomers* (Reading, MA: Addison-Wesley, 1980); K. G. Wheeler and T. M. Mahoney, "The Expectancy Model in the Analysis of Occupational Preference and Occupational Choice," *Journal of Vocational Behavior* 19 (1981): 113–122.

[37] D. P. Schwab, S. L. Rynes, and R. A. Aldag, "Theories and Research on Job Search and Choice," K. Rowland and G. Ferris, eds., *Research in Personnel and Human Resource Management* 5 (1987): 129–166.

[38] A. E. Barber and M. V. Roehling, "Job Postings and the Decision to Interview: A Verbal Protocol Analysis," *Journal of Applied Psychology* 78 (1993): 845–856; T. A. Judge and R. D. Bretz, Jr., "Effects of Work Values on Job Choice Decisions," *Journal of Applied Psychology* 77 (1992): 261–271.

[39] S. D. Maurer, V. Howe, and T. W. Lee, "Organizational Recruiting as Marketing Management."

[40] M. A. Plater, D. R. Rahtz, and J. P. Katz, "Compensation Package Alignment," *ACA Journal* (First Quarter 1999): 28–33; C. E. Jergenson, "Job Preference: What Makes a Job Good or Bad?" *Journal of Applied Psychology* 63 (1978): 267–276; B. Major and E. Konar, "An Investigation of Sex Differences in Pay in Higher Education and Their Possible Cause," *Academy of Management Journal* 4 (1986): 777–792; Schwab, Rynes, and Aldag, "Theories and Research," 129–166.

[41] L. Uchitelle, "Signing Bonus Now a Fixture Farther Down the Job Ladder," *New York Times* (June 10, 1998): A1, D2; J. S. Lublin, "Now Butchers, Engineers Get Signing Bonuses," *The Wall Street Journal* (June 2, 1997): B1.

[42] R. D. Bretz, Jr., J. W. Boudreau, and T. A. Judge, "Job Search Behavior of Employed Managers," *Personnel Psychology* 47 (1994): 275–301.

[43] Jergenson, "Job Preference"; Schwab, Rynes, and Aldag, "Theories and Research"; S. L. Rynes, H. Heneman III, and D. P. Schwab, "Individual Reactions to Organizational Recruiting: A Review," *Personnel Psychology* 33 (1980): 529–542.

[44] S. Branch, "MBAs: What They Really Want," *Fortune* (March 16, 1998): 167; N. Munk, "Organization Man," *Fortune* (March 16, 1998): 63–74; T. A. Stewart, "Gray Flannel Suit?" *Fortune* (March 16, 1998): 76–82.

[45] C. K. Stevens and A. L. Kristof, "Making the Right Impression: A Field Study of Applicant Impression Management During Job Interview," *Journal of Applied Psychology* 80 (1995): 587–606.

[46] R. D. Bretz and T. A. Judge, "Realistic Job Previews: A Test of the Adverse Self-Selection Hypothesis," *Journal of Applied Psychology* 83 (1998): 230–337.

[47] J. P. Wanous, et al., "The Effects of Met Expectations on Newcomer Attitudes and Behaviors: A Review and Meta-Analysis," *Journal of Applied Psychology* 77 (1992): 288–297; J. M. Phillips, "Effects of Realistic Job Previews on Multiple Organizational Outcomes: A Meta-Analysis," *Academy of Management Journal* 41 (1999): 673–690.

[48] M. R. Buckley, D. B. Fedor, and D. S. Marvin, "Ethical Considerations in the Recruiting Process: A Preliminary Investigation and Identification of Research Opportunities," *Human Resource Management Review* (1997): 101–134; "Truth in Hiring Gains Importance," *Bulletin to Management* (July 28, 1994): 5.

[49] R. D. Gatewood, M. A. Gowan, and G. J. Lautenschlager, "Corporate Image, Recruitment Image, and Initial Choice Decisions," *Academy of Management Journal* 36 (1993): 414–427.

[50] C. R. Williams, C. E. Labig, Jr., and T. H. Stone, "Recruitment Sources and Posthire Outcomes for Job Applicants and New Hires: A Test of Two Hypotheses," *Journal of Applied Psychology* 78 (1993): 163–172.

[51] A. M. Saks, "A Psychological Process Investigation for the Effects of Recruitment Source and Organization Information on Job Survival," *Journal of Organizational Behavior* 15 (1994): 225–244.

[52] P. W. Hom, R. W. Griffeth, L. E. Palich, and J. S. Bracker, "An Exploratory Investigation into Theoretical Mechanisms Underlying Realistic Job Previews," *Personnel Psychology* 51 (1998): 421–451; J. P. Wanous, *Organizational Entry*, 2nd ed. (Reading, MA: Addison-Wesley, 1992); J. P. Wanous, T. D. Poland, S. L. Premack, and K. S. Davis, "The Effects of Unmet Expectations on Newcomer Attitudes and Behaviors: A Review and Meta-Analysis," *Journal of Applied Psychology* 77 (1992): 288–297; D. Arvey and J. G. Campion, "The Employment Interview: A Summary and Review of the Recent Literature," *Personnel Psychology* 35 (1982): 281–322; see also J. A. Breaugh, "Realistic Job Previews: A Critical Appraisal and Future Research Directions," *Academy of Management Review* (October 1983): 612–623.

[53] A. Fischer, "Don't Blow Your New Job," *Fortune* (June 22, 1998): 159–162.

[54] K. Tyler, "The Art of Saying No," *HR Magazine* (January 1999): 8–11; M. J. Aamodt and D. L. Peggans, "Rejecting Applicants with Tact," *Personnel Administrator* (April 1988): 58–60.

[55] B. P. Sunoo, "Initiatives for Women Boost Retention," *Workforce* (November 1998): 97–100.

[56] Hundreds of studies have examined the reasons for voluntary employee turnover. A detailed discussion is beyond the scope of this chapter. Interested readers can begin to learn more by consulting J. D. Shaw, J. E. Delery, G. D. Jenkins, and N. Gupta, "An Organizational-Level Analysis of Voluntary and Involuntary Turnover," *Academy of Management Journal* 41 (1998): 511–525; R. W. Griffeth and P. W. Hom, "The Employee Turnover Process," *Research in Personnel and Human Resources Management* 13 (1995): 245–293.

[57] J. D. Dawson, J. E. Delery, G. D. Jenkins, Jr., and N. Gupta, "An Organizational-Level Analysis of Voluntary and Involuntary Turnover," *Academy of Management Journal* 41 (1998): 511–525.

[58] C. M. Solomon, "Keep Them! Don't Let Your Best People Get Away," *Workforce* (August 1997): 46–52.

[59] D. Hellriegel, S. E. Jackson, and J. W. Slocum, Jr., *Management,* 8th ed. (Cincinnati: South-Western College Publishing, 1999). Used with permission.

[60] R. L. Knowdell, E. Branstead, and M. Moravec, *From Downsizing to Recovery—Strategic Transition Options for Organizations and Individuals* (Palo Alto, CA: CPP Books, 1994); G. E. Prussia, A. J. Kinicki, and J. S. Bracker, "Psychological and Behavioral Consequences of Job Loss: A Covariance Structure Analysis Using Weiner's (1985) Attribution Model," *Journal of Applied Psychology* 78 (1993): 382–394; C. R. Leana and D. C. Feldman, *Coping with Job Loss: How Individuals, Organizations, and Communities Respond to Layoffs* (New York: Lexington Books, 1992).

[61] A detailed discussion of internal labor markets can be found in L. T. Pinfield and M. F. Berner, "Employment Systems: Toward a Coherent Conceptualization of Internal Labor Markets," *Research in Personnel and Human Resource Management* 12 (1994): 41–78.

[62] B. P. Sunoo, "Initiatives for Women Boost Retention," *Workforce* (November 1998): 97–99; M. Nealy Martinez, "Retention: To Have and To Hold," *HR Magazine* (September 1998): 131–138.

[63] T. Mroczkowski and M. Hanaoka, "Effective Rightsizing Strategies in Japan and America: Is there a Convergence of Employment Practices?" *Academy of Management Executive* 11 (2) (1997): 57–67; M. London, "Redeployment and Continuous Learning in the 21st Century: Hard Lessons and Positive Examples from the Downsizing Era," *Academy of Management Executive* 10 (4) (1992): 67–79; W. N. Davis, III, D. L. Worrell, and J. B. Fox, "Early Retirement Programs and Firm Performance," *Academy of Management Journal* 39 (4) (1996): 970–984; R. Maurer, "Alternative to Downsizing," *Solutions* (October 1996): 40–48.

[64] E. W. Morrison, "When Employees Feel Betrayed: A Model of How Psychological Contract Violation Develops," *Academy of Management Review* 22 (1997): 226–256; E. M. Mervosh, "Downsizing Dilemma," *Human Resource Executive* (February 1997): 50–53; C. R. Leana and D. C. Feldman, "When Mergers Force Layoffs: Some Lessons about Managing the Human Resource Problems," *Human Resource Planning* 12 (2) (1989): 123–240; K. S. Cameron, S. J. Freeman, and A. K. Mishra, "Best Practices in White Collar Downsizing: Managing Contradictions," *Academy of Management Executive* 5 (3) (1991): 57–73; W. F. Cascio, "Downsizing: What Do We Know? What Have We Learned?" *Academy of Management Executive* 7 (1) (1993): 95–104.

[65] D. M. Schweiger, J. M. Ivancevich, and F. R. Power, "Executive Actions for Managing Human Resources Before and After Acquisition," *Academy of Management Executive* 1 (2) (1986): 127–138.

[66] G. Koretz, "Downsizing's Painful Effects," *Business Week* (April 13, 1998): 23.

[67] H. Axel, *HR Review: Implementing the New Employment Compact* (New York: The Conference Board, 1997).

[68] J. B. Treece, "Doing It Right, Till the Last Whistle," *Business Week* (April 6, 1992): 58–59.

[69] D. M. Bostwick, *Human Resources Management: Practices in Post-Soviet Russia: Observations and Recommendations for US/Western HR Managers* (Alexandria, VA: Society for Human Resource Management, 1998); A. Kim, "Employment Practices in Russia," in *International Trade Administration: BISNIS Bulletin*

(Washington, DC: U.S. Department of Commerce, April 1997).

[70] Data provided by the Bureau of National Affairs. For a discussion of how to calculate EEO statistics in the temporary help industry, see A. M. Ryan and M. J. Schmidt, "Calculating EEO Statistics in the Temporary Help Industry," *Personnel Psychology* 49 (1996): 167–180.

[71] J. S. Leonard, "The Impact of Affirmative Action Regulation on Employment," *Journal of Economic Perspectives* 3 (1990): 47–63.

[72] L. Micco, "Wilcher Describes Changes Under Way at OFCCP," *HR News* (April 1998): 6.

[73] Johnson, "The 50 Best Companies for Asians, Blacks & Hispanics."

[74] N. Munk, "Hello Corporate America," *Fortune* (June 6, 1998): 136–146.

[75] P. M. Barrett, "Legal Separation: Prestigious Law Firm Courts Black Lawyers, But Diversity Is Illusive," *The Wall Street Journal* (July 8, 1997): A1, A9; see also E. White, "'We're Wild and Wacky'" Law Firms Tell Recruits," *The Wall Street Journal* (June 24, 1998): B1.

[76] P. Wright, S. R. Ferris, J. S. Hiller, and M. Kroll, "Competitiveness Through Management of Diversity: Effects of Stock Price Valuation," *Academy of Management Journal* 38 (1995): 272–286.

[77] "Piscataway Settlement Hangs Heavy Over Affirmative Action," *Fair Employment Practices* (February 25, 1998): 1–2; B. Pulley, "A Reverse Discrimination Suit Upends Two Teachers' Lives," *New York Times* (August 31, 1997): A1, A18.

[78] S. A. Holmes, "Broadcasters Vow to Keep Affirmative Action," *New York Times* (July 30, 1998): A12.

[79] M. E. Heilman, C. J. Block, and P. Stathatos, "The Affirmative Action Stigma of Incompetence: Effects of Performance Information Ambiguity," *Academy of Management Journal* 40 (1997): 603–625.

[80] For a full review of this and other research on affirmative action, see D. A. Kravitz, D. A. Harrison, M. E. Turner, E. L. Levine, W. Chaves, M. T. Brannick, D. L. Denning, C. J. Russell, and M. A. Conrad, *Affirmative Action: A Review of Psychological and Behavioral Research* (Bowling Green, OH: Society for Industrial and Organizational Psychology, 1997).

[81] T. Parker-Pope, "Colgate Puts Lois Juliber in Line for Top," *The Wall Street Journal* (January 20, 1997): B5.

[82] J. P. Fields, *Women and the Corporate Ladders: Corporate Linkage Project* (Wellesley, MA: Wellesley College Center for Research on Women, July 31, 1994); U.S. Department of Labor, *A Report on the Glass Ceiling Initiative* (Washington, DC, 1991).

[83] Chicago Area Partnerships, *Pathways & Progress: Corporate Best Practices to Shatter the Glass Ceiling* (Chicago: Chicago Area Partnerships, 1996).

SELECTION AND PLACEMENT: CHOOSING THE WORKFORCE

Chapter

8

"What we are looking for, first and foremost, is a sense of humor. We look for attitude. We'll train you on whatever you need to do, but the one thing we can't do is change inherent attitudes."

**Herb Kelleher
CEO
Southwest Airlines**[1]

MANAGING HUMAN RESOURCES THROUGH PARTNERSHIP
at Brush Wellman

Cleveland-based Brush Wellman produces specialty metal products. When it opened a new facility on Ohio's North Coast, it had a vision that included low overhead, high employee involvement, and a very capable workforce. To create a pool of candidates who fit this vision, Brush Wellman teamed up with a local vocational school. The school's primary role was to provide training to potential new employees. But before ever putting someone into a training program, they first assessed whether the person had the basic aptitudes and knowledge required for Brush Wellman's new plant. Only people who passed this initial hurdle could eventually be considered for employment at Brush Wellman.

After passing the initial screening, prospective employees entered an intensive 100-hour classroom-training program, which they paid for themselves. The vocational school worked jointly with Brush Wellman to design the curriculum, and the school's regular faculty conducted the classes. At the end of the training, faculty recommended candidates to Brush Wellman based on criteria such as attendance records and class participation. Brush Wellman supplemented this information with reference checks and interviews before making a final hiring decision.

Brush Wellman managers and new hires both seem to like this approach to selection. Employees are proud of their achievements and feel a sense of belonging. They also feel good about their co-workers, knowing that they were among the best in their training class. Managers say employees perform well and seem more committed to their jobs. With such positive outcomes, the fact that the new program was paid for partly with state and federal funds is viewed as just icing on the cake.

To learn more about Brush Wellman, visit the company home page at **www.brushwellman.com**

Selection and placement procedures provide the essence of an organization—its human resources. When done well, these procedures ensure that a company has employees who perform well, resulting in high productivity. *Selection* is the process of obtaining and using information about job applicants in order to determine who should be hired for long- or short-term positions. *Placement* involves matching individuals to jobs, based on the demands of the job and the competencies, preferences, interests, and personality of the individual. Together, selection and placement yield a match between the organizations' needs for qualified individuals and the various needs of employees that determine the type of work that's satisfying for them.[2] Although generally not thought of as such, the selection process also plays a role in decisions about whom to fire, layoff, or ease into retirement.[3]

THE STRATEGIC IMPORTANCE OF SELECTION AND PLACEMENT

As Exhibit 8.1 shows, there are many significant consequences that result from making correct versus incorrect selection and placement decisions. Recognizing the importance of these decisions, effective organizations invest substantial amounts of time, effort, and money to select their workforces. Toyota (USA) screened 50,000 applications for 3,000 factory jobs in the initial

Exhibit 8.1
The Consequences of Correct and Incorrect Selection and Placement Decisions

	How Employee Does/Would Perform → **Do Not Offer Applicant the Open Position**	**Offer Applicant the Open Position**
High Performance	• Applicant and employee continue to pay costs of continued searching, unnecessarily. • Applicant may decide to accept alternative job that's less well suited to his or her competencies and interests. • Applicants may remain unemployed unnecessarily and forego rewards they could have earned. • Applicant may file discrimination lawsuit. • Employees may be required to carry an overload until job is filled. • Customers' expectations may not be met while employer is understaffed.	• Employee performs well. • Employee receives rewards associated with good performance. • Employee enjoys work. • Peers benefit from employee's good performance and high morale. • Managers achieve their objectives. • Customers receive products and services that meet their expectations.
center boxes	**Reject a Qualified Candidate (Incorrect decision)**	**Accept a Qualified Candidate (Correct decision)**
center boxes	**Reject an Unqualified Candidate (Correct decision)**	**Accept an Unqualified Candidate (Incorrect decision)**
Low Performance	• Applicant continues to look for more suitable work. • Employer continues to search for more suitable employee. • Applicant may decide to get more training. • Employer may decide to offer more training so that more applicants can be accepted. • Customers do not suffer from the mistakes of a poor performer. • Employees may continue to carry an overload while search continues, but they do not suffer from the errors produced by an ineffective peer.	• Employee performs poorly. • Employee loses self esteem due to poor performance, and forgoes the rewards associated with good performance. • Peers suffer consequences of poorly performing employee. • Customers' expectations aren't met due to employee's poor performance. • Managers fail to meet their objectives. • Injuries, accidents, and other serious problems may occur due to employee's poor job performance. • Employee eventually must find new job, creating additional costs associated with turnover.

Employer's Selection Decision

staffing of its plant in Georgetown, Kentucky. By the time they were actually hired, each applicant had spent at least 18 hours in the selection process. Included as part of that process were an exam on general knowledge, a test of attitudes toward work, an interpersonal skills assessment center, a manufacturing exercise designed to provide a realistic job preview of assembly work, an extensive personal interview, and a physical exam. Toyota used all of these techniques to achieve one thing—they wanted to be sure they hired the best applicants and rejected those who were not suitable for the available jobs.

By making good selection decisions, employers help ensure that their financial investments in employees pays off.[4] The value of using several methods to make selection decisions was demonstrated in a study of 201 companies from several industries. Companies reported their use of practices such as conducting validation studies, using structured interviews, and administering cognitive tests. The researchers showed that companies that used these practices had higher levels of annual profit, profit growth, and overall performance. The relationship between use of these practices and bottom-line performance was especially strong in the service and financial sectors, as defined by SIC codes.[5]

Many factors contribute to the relationship between investments in selection and company performance. Perhaps most importantly, selecting the best person improves productivity. For example, when the job to be filled is that of general manager for a division or business unit, the evidence from a few studies suggests that matching the experience profiles of applicants to the defined strategy leads to better performance.[6] Effective selection also minimizes the risk of lawsuits brought by victims of criminal, violent, or negligent acts perpetrated by employees who shouldn't have been hired or kept in their jobs. By using fair and legal procedures when making selection decisions, employers also can minimize the risk of discrimination lawsuits.

PARTNERSHIP IN SELECTION AND PLACEMENT

To achieve its strategic objectives, selection and placement must be congruent with the internal and external environment. The involvement of line managers and other employees helps ensure congruence. During strategic planning, line managers identify the jobs to be filled, and perhaps the jobs to be eliminated. They participate in the job analysis activities that are used to identify the qualifications employees must have in order to perform current and future jobs. They evaluate job applicants and may coordinate the involvement of other employees during the interview process. Eventually, line managers and the employee's peers evaluate employee performance, which may serve as a basis for decisions about who should be asked to leave the organization. All these activities engage line managers and other employees in the selection and placement process, regardless of whether hiring is from external or internal applicant pools.

The feature, The HR Triad: Partnership Roles and Responsibilities for Selection and Placement, summarizes the key roles that line managers and employees play in deciding who will be hired and which jobs they will perform. HR professionals, in turn, help coordinate the entire process and ensure that it results in the best possible decisions.

Role of Managers in Promotion and Transfer

In some organizations and under some circumstances, immediate supervisors have limited control in deciding whom to promote or transfer out of their unit, but they usually have considerable say in who will move into the unit. In many companies, immediate supervisors have almost total control over selection decisions, especially promotion and transfer decisions. They search for qualified candidates and help choose the best candidate.

Because line managers often have so much influence, it's important that they understand how to ensure that their selection decisions truly result in the most qualified person filling an open position. It's easy for a manager's personal preferences to get in the way of placing the best person in a job. When a new job is being created, managers may be able to determine exactly who will be promoted by writing the job description to fit only one person. This isn't necessarily a fair practice, but it's common. Managers can also con-

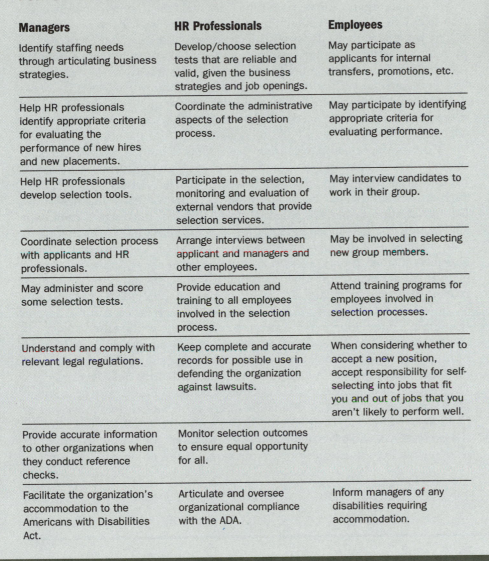

The HR Triad: Partnership Roles and Responsibilities for Selection and Placement

Managers	HR Professionals	Employees
Identify staffing needs through articulating business strategies.	Develop/choose selection tests that are reliable and valid, given the business strategies and job openings.	May participate as applicants for internal transfers, promotions, etc.
Help HR professionals identify appropriate criteria for evaluating the performance of new hires and new placements.	Coordinate the administrative aspects of the selection process.	May participate by identifying appropriate criteria for evaluating performance.
Help HR professionals develop selection tools.	Participate in the selection, monitoring and evaluation of external vendors that provide selection services.	May interview candidates to work in their group.
Coordinate selection process with applicants and HR professionals.	Arrange interviews between applicant and managers and other employees.	May be involved in selecting new group members.
May administer and score some selection tests.	Provide education and training to all employees involved in the selection process.	Attend training programs for employees involved in selection processes.
Understand and comply with relevant legal regulations.	Keep complete and accurate records for possible use in defending the organization against lawsuits.	When considering whether to accept a new position, accept responsibility for self-selecting into jobs that fit you and out of jobs that you aren't likely to perform well.
Provide accurate information to other organizations when they conduct reference checks.	Monitor selection outcomes to ensure equal opportunity for all.	
Facilitate the organization's accommodation to the Americans with Disabilities Act.	Articulate and oversee organizational compliance with the ADA.	Inform managers of any disabilities requiring accommodation.

trol the final decision by stacking the deck to confirm their favorite candidate. To make the selection process appear legitimate, a manager may select several candidates, in addition to the favorite, for others to evaluate. The catch is that the other candidates are far less qualified than the favorite. The whole selection process becomes superficial, allowing only one "real" choice.

It's not only the managers who will supervise a new employee who get involved in a selection decision, however. Line managers from other units also play a role. Whether acting as formal mentors or informal sponsors, managers in other units can help to ensure that others notice their protégé's strengths. They can also withhold information about an employee's poor performance, in order to increase the likelihood of that person being moved to another unit. In the end, however, managers who control selection and placement decisions should accept responsibility for making wise decisions.

Role of HR Professionals

In very small organizations, no HR professionals may be involved in selection decisions. But when small organizations grow rapidly, they often turn to HR professionals to assist with recruitment and selection processes. In large organizations, human resource professionals usually gather detailed information about applicants and arrange interviews between job applicants and line managers. They may also administer standardized tests to assess the applicants' competencies and select the most qualified applicants for managers to interview. As detailed in Exhibit 8.2, centralization of some aspects of selection benefits both the organization and the applicants.

Multi-business companies often have several human resource departments, with each serving the unique needs of its own business. The decentralization is intended to produce a closer congruence between HR activities such as selection and the strategy and culture of each business unit. Decentralization does have potential disadvantages, however. If each division or unit operates independently, it's likely to select only from among its own employees and not from the whole workforce. Decentralization may also mean that each unit relies on its own performance appraisal system, so even if candidates from other divisions become internal applicants, they may be difficult to evaluate. This reality is magnified in global firms: regions of the world may become virtually unrelated to each other, and the human resources of one region may be completely off limits to the others.

Fundamentally, the role of a company's HR professionals is helping ensure that the best candidates available fill open positions. They ensure that the organization has the information it needs to identify the best candidate. They should also make sure the selection decision is based only on relevant information and that the most qualified person does not lose out because of prejudice and stereotyping that are irrelevant to job qualifications. Finally, HR professionals help persuade applicants to accept job offers. To fulfill this responsibility requires sensitivity to the perspectives of job applicants.

Exhibit 8.2

How Centralizing Selection and Placement Activities Can Benefit Job Applicants and Employers

Benefits for Applicants	**Benefits for Employers**
• Applicants go to only one place to apply for all jobs in the company, which is convenient.	• The company can consider each applicant for a variety of jobs, which is efficient.
• Specialists trained in staffing techniques do hiring, so the selection decisions are often better, resulting in better employee performance.	• Specialists trained in staffing techniques do hiring, so the selection decisions are often better, resulting in better employee performance.
• People who know about the many legal regulations relevant to selection handle a major part of the hiring process, which improves both legal compliance and fairness to job applicants.	• Operating managers can concentrate on their operating responsibilities, which is especially helpful during peak hiring periods.

Role of Employees

As organizations rely more and more on teamwork, they also are likely to make sure employees get more and more involved in selecting new coworkers. Often the role of employees is to help determine how well an applicant is likely to fit into the company's culture. At Rosenthal International, a travel-management company, applicants for managerial jobs might be asked to play a game of softball with the company team or help repair a broken fence. The objective isn't to test the applicant's skill at softball or fence mending—it's to learn whether the applicant is able and willing to be nice. At Worthington Industries, an Ohio-based steel processor, employees play an even bigger role. There the final selection decision is made after the applicant has completed a 90-day "probation period." At the end of the probation, an employee council of about ten peers formally votes on whether the new hire should be allowed to stay on. Presumably, at Worthington, peers make their judgments primarily on the basis of the new hire's performance level. At Worthington, profit sharing accounts for about 40 percent of each employee's total pay. Knowing that a good hiring decision translates into more profits, current employees are motivated to help ensure that only productive people are allowed to join the company.[7]

Involving employees in the selection process is generally a good idea and is a practice that seems to be growing. When employees are involved in the selection of new team members, they seem to become more committed to making sure the new hires succeed. As employees become more involved in this important decision process, it's essential that they understand the process and receive training about how to make appropriate decisions. Just as managers can be influenced by many factors other than an applicant's ability to perform well, so too are employees susceptible to making decisions for the wrong reasons.[8]

THE PERSPECTIVE OF APPLICANTS

Applicants almost always care deeply about the outcomes of selection decisions and can have strong reactions to their experiences. Consider the following stories:

> A married graduate student with a 3.9+ grade point average reported that the first three questions in one company's psychological assessment procedure involved inquiries about her personal relationships with her husband and children. Although the company asked her what she thought of the procedure before she left, she lied because she was afraid that telling the truth would eliminate her from further consideration. Because of dual-career constraints, she continued to pursue an offer, but noted that if she got one, her first on-the-job priority would be to try to get the assessor fired.

> A male MBA told how he had originally planned to refuse to submit to psychological testing, but was persuaded by his girlfriend that it would be a more effective form of protest to pursue the offer and then pointedly turn it down.

> The first interview question asked of a female MBA student was, "We're a pretty macho organization. . . . Does that bother you?" Unfortunately, it did, and she simply wrote the company out of her future interviewing plans. (When this incident was later relayed to an audience of corporate recruiters, a male recruiting director raised his hand and asked, "What's wrong with that?")[9]

"Peers need an opportunity to weigh in on a candidate. They need a chance to ask whether they want to split the pie with a particular individual."

Eric Smolenski
Personnel Manager
Worthington Industries

■□ *fast fact*

Southwest Airlines flies some of its best customers to Dallas and involves them in the flight attendant hiring process, believing that they probably know best what makes a good employee.

Applicants' reactions to selection processes clearly affect their decisions about whether to pursue job opportunities in a company. Equally important, these early experiences serve as an organization's first steps in a socialization process that will continue for several months after an applicant is eventually hired.[10] At the heart of applicants' concerns is the desire to be treated fairly. Applicants judge fairness by the content of the measures used to select people, the administration of the process, and the outcomes of the process.[11]

Content of Selection Measures

Applicants prefer a process that involves them in activities that have obvious relevance to the job opening. Work samples and simulations usually seem more relevant to applicants than cognitive paper-and-pencil tests and handwriting analysis, for example, and, perhaps for this reason, applicants consider them to be fairer.[12] Applicants react negatively to poorly conducted interviews. Offensive or discriminatory questions obviously send negative messages, but so do questions that appear to be superficial or not clearly related to the job.[13]

Administration of the Selection Process

> "You cannot expect to delight your customers unless you as an employer delight your employees."
>
> **Carla Paonessa**
> **Partner**
> **Andersen Consulting**

Applicants also attend to the process: Did the company tell them what it was evaluating and why? Did it provide feedback about how they scored? Did it appear to respect their desire for confidentiality? Did the company representatives behave professionally and appear to take the task seriously? Was the company respectful of their time and need for information about their chances for a positive outcome? Did it seem to treat all candidates equally, or did it treat some more equally than others? Did the process appear to recognize the potential for applicants to misrepresent themselves, and take steps to ensure that honesty was not penalized? Effective selection includes managing these and many other aspects of the process.[14]

Outcomes of the Selection Process

Whereas applicants primarily experience the content and administrative features of a selection process, the outcomes are visible to a broader array of people. These include the acquaintances and coworkers of applicants who tell stories about the process, the new coworkers of successful applicants, the managers inside an organization who participated in the process, and people who served as references for applicants. Based on who is selected and who is rejected, all these constituencies form opinions about whether a company uses fair procedures and makes wise choices about who to hire or promote. Even the news media offer comments about executive selection decisions. They publish reports concerning the demographic characteristics of successful applicants at specific companies. Consider, for example, the results of a study conducted by the *The Wall Street Journal*, which compared the percentages of women hired into managerial jobs for companies in several different industries. These results clearly suggested that within any given industry, some companies appear to be more "fair" in terms of selecting women to fill managerial jobs.

OVERVIEW OF THE SELECTION PROCESS

The selection process generally involves the following basic steps:

1. Assess the job demands and organizational needs to establish the criteria of interest.
2. Establish the predictors that are likely to be useful by inferring the type of person needed.
3. Design a method or process that allows both the organization and the applicant to gather job-related information.
4. Synthesize the information collected and make selection decisions.

The selection process does not end when the organization makes its decision. The candidate must ultimately make a final decision about whether to accept the new position and under what conditions. As the person enters the new position, accommodation, socialization, and training activities may all be involved. As time passes, both the organization and the new job incumbent will reevaluate their decisions.

Assess the Job Demands and Organizational Needs

An understanding of the specific tasks required by a job and the organizational context surrounding the job develops from job analysis as well as, more generally, human resource planning. Ideally, a systematic job analysis would be conducted for all jobs in an organization. In reality, job analysis is more likely to be conducted for lower-level and mid-level jobs and for jobs that encompass many positions. For positions near the top of the organization, "job analysis" may or may not be systematic and very likely will be subjective rather than quantitative. At the level of CEO, for example, it may consist of a discussion among members of the board of directors.[15]

Whether it's formal or informal, based on quantitative data or "soft" judgments, the objective of all this analysis is to establish the relevant *criteria* for making selection and placement decisions. Often, the criteria used are closely linked to the critical elements of job performance. For example, in a corporate loan assistant's job, accurately documenting decisions is probably more critical than keeping the office desks clean and organized. Increasingly, employers consider the criteria of interest to be more than just ability to perform in an immediate job. They're looking for employees who have the competencies needed to perform a broad range of jobs and roles in an organization that's continually changing.[16]

Infer the Type of Person Needed

Organizations make selection decisions on the basis of information about one or more predictors of future performance. Predictor information serves as the basis for estimating how well applicants will perform if placed in a particular job. Generally, these predictors fall within three broad categories:

- competencies,
- personality and values, and
- other characteristics essential to job performance.

Competencies are the most often assessed predictors. But some firms care more about a person's personality and basic values. If used appropriately in combination with information about the culture and strategy of the firm, personality and values may be good predictors of future satisfaction in the job, as well as future performance and long-term career success.[17] When the Walt Disney Company selects people to work in their theme parks, current employees judge the personalities of applicants and assess their ability to fit into the Disney culture. The Disney approach is described in the feature,

"What seniors do best for us is give us a good work ethic. They're on time; they show up; they care."

Dottie Justice
Director of Human Resources
Days Inn and Knights Inn

Managing Strategically: Walt Disney Selects for Crowd Appeal. When jobs are ambiguous and supervision is minimal, knowing that the job incumbent has the appropriate values can be reassuring. Presumably, the person's character can be relied on to function like a trustworthy compass, pointing him or her in the right direction.

Employers can also gather information about other characteristics. They can ask about information relevant to the terms and conditions of employment, including willingness to obtain licenses required by law; willingness to travel or to work split shifts, weekends, or under adverse conditions such

MANAGING STRATEGICALLY
Walt Disney Company Selects for Crowd Appeal

The next time you visit Walt Disney World in Florida or Disneyland in California, consider the complexity of finding more than 25,000 people needed to fill more than 1,000 types of jobs that make the entertainment complexes so effective. With over 50 million visitors to Disney World and Disneyland yearly, the company is a reigning star in the entertainment business. Since the mid-1980s, when it went through a major change in senior management and strategic direction, the Walt Disney Company has developed a reputation for creativity, strong financial management, and very effective approaches to managing people.

The managers and employees of the Walt Disney Company view themselves as part of a large show or production. This is reflected in the way they speak of themselves, their activities, and the process of selecting new members. Eager applicants to the firm are cast for a role, rather than hired for a job. Rather than being employees, applicants who join the firm become cast members in a major entertainment production. A casting director interviews applicants.

For hourly jobs, a casting director spends about ten minutes interviewing every applicant. The interviewer's (casting director's) major objective is to evaluate the applicant's ability to adapt to the firm's very strong culture. Does the applicant understand and accept the fact that Disney has strict grooming requirements (no facial hair for men, little makeup for women)? Is the applicant willing to work on holidays—even ones that almost everyone else will have off? After the first screening, the remaining applicants are assessed as they interact with each other and judged as to how well they might fit with the show.

Once people join the firm, they become cast members whose inputs and talents are highly valued by the Walt Disney Company. The company fills 60 to 80 percent of its managerial positions by promoting existing cast members. In addition, the firm draws on suggested referrals from current cast members for help in hiring the 1,500 to 2,000 temporary employees required during particularly busy periods—Easter, Christmas, and summers.

Every newly hired cast member participates in an orientation and training program at Disney University. Cast members first receive an overview of Walt Disney Company and learn about its traditions, history, achievements, and philosophy. They also learn about the key Disney product—happiness—and their roles in helping to provide it. Current employees who are experts in their roles participate in this entire process, assess the applicants' behaviors and attitudes while also providing firsthand information about his or her role in the production.[18]

To learn more about the Walt Disney Company, visit the company home page at **www.disney.com**

as in confined facilities and with high noise levels; willingness to adhere to uniform requirements or business-related grooming codes; willingness to supply tools required on the job but not provided by the employer; and willingness to complete required training. Being willing to do these things provides no guarantee candidates will perform. However, if applicants are unwilling to comply with job requirements, they can be disqualified from further consideration.

Choose Job-Related Predictors

A great deal of information often *can* be gathered and used to evaluate candidates; whether that information *should* be gathered and used depends on the likelihood that it will lead to better selection decisions. Information that predicts the subsequent outcomes of concern—that is, the criteria—should be used, and information that won't predict these outcomes should be avoided.

The Concept of Validity.   The term validity refers to the usefulness of a predictor for correctly inferring the future job behavior of applicants. High validity means that low predictor scores translate into low scores on the specified criteria and high predictor scores translate into high scores on the criteria. For example, interviewers who take notes that focus on the applicants' behaviors have been shown to be more accurate in their predictions of performance compared to interviewers who take more general notes.[19]

For most predictors, validity depends on what you want to predict. A personality test that assesses gregariousness might be valid for predicting performance as a fund-raiser for the city ballet company, but it's probably useless for predicting performance as a highway landscape designer. How can you be sure that a given measure is valid for the situation of interest? Three basic strategies are used to ascertain whether inferences based on predictor scores will be valid:

- content validation,
- criterion-related validation, and
- validity generalization.

All these strategies begin with a job analysis to determine tasks and working conditions. Ideally, an organizational analysis will also have been conducted. Then, the three strategies diverge. (For more detailed information on these strategies, consult Appendix B.)

Content Validation.   Content validation is the most commonly used strategy. Based on job analysis information, it involves building a rational argument to link job content to predictors. In the simplest case, an expert job analyst determines which predictors appear to map onto the content of the job. For example, if the job analysis reveals that 70 percent of the job involves data entry, the job analyst might conclude that an appropriate selection tool is a work simulation test that involves data entry. Suppose a board of directors concludes that a new CEO will spend 50 percent of his or her time identifying partners for new joint ventures. The job analyst, in this case a member of the board, might conclude that past experience in establishing joint ventures is a reasonable predictor to use for the selection decision.

This basic content validation strategy can be substantially improved by involving a wider range of people in judging whether a predictor is likely to be job related. Integrated job analysis procedures serve this purpose. As described in Chapter 6, more rigorous job analysis relies on structured procedures. Using questionnaires or structured interviews, job incumbents and supervisors rate the extent to which specific competencies are needed to perform the job. Although such judgments are necessarily subjective, one's confidence is increased when several subject matter experts agree that a particular skill is needed.[20]

When an organization is creating new jobs and experiencing major organizational change, a content validation strategy may be the only feasible validation approach. It's the approach Levi Strauss & Co. used when it recently began the biggest change effort in the company's history. As described in the feature, Managing Change: The New Look at Levi's, when hundreds of new jobs were created at the company, employees were asked to facilitate the change process by actively seeking new job placements.[21]

MANAGING CHANGE

The New Look at Levi's

A decade ago, Levi Strauss & Co. adopted its much-publicized Aspirations Statement, which detailed a management philosophy grounded in participation, diversity, accountability, teamwork and open communication. These values affect everything the company does, including the way it transformed itself. Selection and placement activities were a central component of the company's change efforts.

In the early 1990s, Levi's market value was an estimated $10 billion—more than four times what it was a decade earlier. Recognized as one of the world's most successful company's, Levi's top management recognized that success wouldn't last unless the company underwent significant change. Levi's had great products and great marketing skills. So why the need for change? Because its customers—store managers and purchasing agents—were saying they had poor service. It took a year to move from a new design idea to delivering the product to customers. Once the product was available, customers still couldn't count on Levi's to ship it when they said they would—they missed their shipping dates 60 percent of the time. One customer told them, "Your lead times are the worst. If you weren't Levi's, you'd be gone." One big customer complained of delivery errors: "We trust many of our competitors implicitly," they said. "We sample their deliveries. We open all Levi's deliveries."

Leading the change effort was a team of 200 people, organized into 20 teams. Their task was to reinvent the supply chain. Current employees applied to become members of this change team and were selected based on several criteria believed to be important for change agents: courage, flexibility, balance, and humor. Over a period of several months, this group redefined the way Levi's would operate. They invented thousands of new jobs, specifying everything from the title and formal job description to the required competencies. Examples of some new titles include: process leader, performance consultant, source relations manager, and system relationship coordinator. Such jobs would require many new behaviors. People would need to understand the big picture, work in a team, and think in terms of the entire organizational system.

They also designed a new staffing process. Consistent with their philosophy of participation and accountability, the new jobs would be staffed using procedures that depended on current employees to apply for the new jobs. Job descriptions were posted via e-mail. Employees submitted applications and were screened in order to determine whether they qualified for a panel interview. The procedures were described in a document that came to be known as "The Lunch Box." It explained the principles behind the design of the new organization, included posters that traced the steps in the interview and evaluation process for making selection and placement decisions, and developed a career-planning workbook. Levi's distributed 4,500 lunch boxes in English and Spanish and followed them up with workshop sessions. One employee who found the material helpful spent 60 hours working through it. Eventually, he successfully landed a new job as vice president in the Dockers organization.

Many Levi's employees had not been on the job market for years. Some may have thought they would never again have to look for a new job. The change team realized that such people would need support in order to be successful in their job search efforts. Help for employees who felt unprepared to succeed in a new job search was offered in the form of a handbook titled *Individual Readiness for a Changing Environment*. It included

- diagnostic tools to assess personal values, interests, talents, and attitudes;
- advice about how to upgrade skills; and
- a refresher course on résumés and interviews.

Even with this help, many employees applied for new jobs and didn't get them. Sometimes the process was painful. Long-term employees began to worry about whether there would be a place for them in the new organization. But the process was also enlightening. Employees were forced to assess their strengths and weaknesses and consider how they could add value. As managers participated in selecting people to staff their new organizations, they discovered that many employees had talents and skills that were underutilized and even unknown to the company. By placing such employees into new jobs, Levi's supported its change initiative while also managing human resources more effectively.

To learn more about Levi Strauss & Co., visit the company's home page at **www.levistrauss.com**

Criterion-Related Validation. Criterion-related validation uses more definitive data to establish a relationship between predictor scores and criteria. It involves assessing people on the predictor and also assessing their actual performance in the job. If a ballet company wanted to decide whether gregarious people are better fundraisers, it could ask all its current fundraisers to take a personality test. Then it could correlate the fundraisers' scores on gregariousness with their performance as fundraisers. If gregariousness and fundraising performance were correlated, criterion-related validity would be established. Criterion-related validity replaces judgments about which predictors are most useful with statistical analyses that demonstrate the predictive usefulness of criteria.

Validity Generalization. Validity generalization is a relatively new approach that has been gaining acceptance during the past decade and may continue to gain popularity in the 21st century. The validity generalization strategy assumes that the results of criterion-related validity studies conducted in other companies can be generalized to the situation in your company. For example, suppose ten other organizations have already shown that gregarious people tend to be more successful fundraisers. Even if the correlation between this personality characteristic and fundraising performance was not strong in all those organizations, and even if the type of fundraising was quite different, you might nevertheless conclude that gregariousness is likely to be a valid predictor of fundraising success for your ballet company. If you accepted this conclusion, then your company should evaluate gregariousness and use it when selecting people whose roles include fundraising.

In fact, validity generalization analyses have been conducted for a large number of applicant characteristics that an employer might assess during the selection process. The results indicate that each of the techniques described in this chapter can be effective predictors of performance across a variety of jobs.[22] Whether or not a technique such as a mental ability test or a structured interview is actually a good predictor of performance for a particular job in a particular organizational setting depends on many things, however. First, the predictors must be selected because they're relevant to the job. Job analysis results can be used to select appropriate predictors. Second, sound measurements are essential. Consider as an example the assessment center technique. Assessment centers have been shown to be effective for identifying employees who will perform well in their jobs. Naturally, most of the studies of assessment centers that have been used for validity generalization involved professionally designed assessment centers. An employer who takes shortcuts when designing or conducting an assessment center shouldn't assume that the resulting selection technique *will* be valid, regardless of how many other studies have shown that assessment centers *can* be valid.

Advantages and Disadvantages.   Each of these strategies has associated advantages and disadvantages. The criterion-related validation strategy has the advantage of documenting empirically that a predictor is correlated with performance in a particular job in a particular organization. However, the strategy can be costly and isn't applicable for jobs that have only a few incumbents (e.g., CEO). Content validation strategies are more feasible, but they also depend more on subjective judgment. Validity generalization may be cost-effective, but you won't know whether results from other organizations will hold in your organization until after you make a selection decision. Furthermore, whereas the legal credibility of the other strategies is well established, validity generalization has not been sufficiently tested in the courts.

Design a Method for Selection

fast fact

Circle K convenience stores have computers in them to allow customers to apply for a job.

For each predictor of interest (each competency, personality characteristic, and so forth), many means can be used to assess applicants. Information can be obtained using application forms, résumés, reference checks, written tests, interviews, physical examinations, and other measurement approaches.

Identify Possible Measures.   Most organizations use interviews of some type at one or more steps in the process. Who should conduct these interviews? At what stage in the process should they be conducted? What exactly should be assessed through the interview? If paper-and-pencil tests are to be given, which characteristics will be assessed: personality? cognitive ability? both? For internal candidates, past performance will undoubtedly be of some interest. How should this be assessed: sales volume figures? ratings and evaluations from supervisors and peers? How far back in the records should you go? These and many similar questions arise during the process of designing a selection method and process. Exhibit 8.3 illustrates how a company might use several different methods to capture all the information it wishes to use in selecting a corporate loan assistant (refer to Chapter 6 for information about what is involved in this job).

Exhibit 8.3
Selection Matrix: Possible Selection Methods for Several Competencies

Corporate Loan Assistant

Code	Competencies	Used to Rank?	Methods Used to Assess							
			SAF	WKT	WS	PCD	SPI	DMI	BI/REF	PAF
MA	1. Communication	Yes	X				X	X	X	X
MQ	2. Math		X		X					
MQ	3. Writing		X							X
MQ	4. Reading		X		X					X
MQ	5. Researching		X							
MQ	6. Organizing	Yes	X							X
MQ	7. Listening	Yes	X				X			X
MQ	8. Social skills		X				X			X
MQ	9. Sales	Yes								X
MQ	10. Interpreting	Yes					X			
WT	11. Bank policy									
WT	12. Bank services	Yes	X	X				X		X
MT	13. Computer					X				

MQ	=	Is a minimum qualification
MT	=	May be acquired through training or on the job (desirable); preference may be given to those who possess this competency
MA	=	Can be accommodated within reason
WT	=	Will be acquired through training or on the job; not evaluated in the selection process.
SAF	=	Supplemental Application Form
WKT	=	Written Knowledge Test
WS	=	Work Sample
PCD	=	Physical Capability Demonstration
SPI	=	Structured Panel Interview
DMI	=	Departmental Manager Interview
BI/REF	=	Background Investigation/Reference Check
PAF	=	Performance Appraisal Form (internal hires only)

Choose Reliable Measures. Because each bit of information contributes to the final selection decision, the quality of information used determines the quality of the final outcome. One aspect of information quality that's especially important is reliability. The *reliability* of a measure (e.g., an interview, a mathematical reasoning test, or a work simulation) is the degree to which the measure yields dependable, consistent results. Unreliable measures produce different results depending on the circumstances. Different circumstances could include having different people administer and score the measure (e.g., having several different interviewers screen applicants), or administering the measure while different events are occurring (e.g., giving a mathematical reasoning test in August versus during the week immediately after everyone files their tax returns).

Reliable measurement tools yield equivalent results time after time regardless of incidental circumstances; this is referred to as *test-retest reliability*. Reliable tools also yield equivalent results regardless of who uses them; this is referred to as *inter-rater reliability*. Unreliability translates into greater measurement error. Greater measurement error, in turn, translates into decision errors concerning whom to hire, promote, transfer, and so on. When purchasing any test from a vendor, information about reliability should be requested. Reputable test developers can demonstrate that they have performed and documented all of the steps needed to create a reliable and valid test. For many published tests, information about reliability and validity can be found in sources such as *Tests in Print* and *The Mental Measurements Yearbook*.[23]

Decide When to Measure Each Predictor. Often, selection decisions progress through several steps, with each progression to a new step based on some information about how the candidate scores in terms of one or more predictors. Exhibit 8.4 illustrates a typical progression. Clearly, each piece of information used throughout this process has the potential to determine the final outcome. Perhaps less clearly, information used early in the process is, in effect, weighted the most heavily—applicants who fail to do well early in the process fail by default on all the later steps. For example, suppose an applicant for a systems analyst position in a life insurance company scores poorly on a mathematical reasoning ability test given to all applicants who pass the initial interview. This person may never be given the opportunity to show her or his skills by completing a work simulation.

Consider Economic Utility. In general, the economic value of using a specific predictor is a function of the cost of acquiring the information and the value of performance gains that can be expected as a result of using that information. Information gleaned from résumés and brief screening interviews costs relatively little to acquire compared with information from multiple interviews, background investigations, and medical exams. Nevertheless, expensive information may be worth acquiring if it enables the organization to make better decisions *and* if substantial consequences are attached to making better decisions. More expensive procedures may be justified when

- tenure in the job is expected to be relatively long,
- incremental increases in performance reap large rewards for the organization, and/or
- many applicants are available to choose among.

Expensive procedures may not be justified if

- progressively higher tax bites are associated with increased profits,
- labor costs are variable and rise with productivity gains, and/or
- labor markets are tight, which makes it less likely that the best candidates, once identified, can be enticed to take the position.[24]

For details about how to conduct an economic utility analysis, consult Appendix B.

Evaluate Legal and Social Acceptability. The acceptability of the selection methods and process must be designed with legal regulations and social norms clearly in mind.[25] These can vary greatly from one country to the

"You can't spend too much time or effort on hiring smart. The alternative is to manage tough, which is far more time consuming."

Pierre Mornell
Independent Consultant

fast fact

A poor hiring decision can cost as much as five times the employee's salary, due to lost productivity, unemployment insurance costs, and poor morale among coworkers.

Exhibit 8.4

Possible Steps in the Selection Process

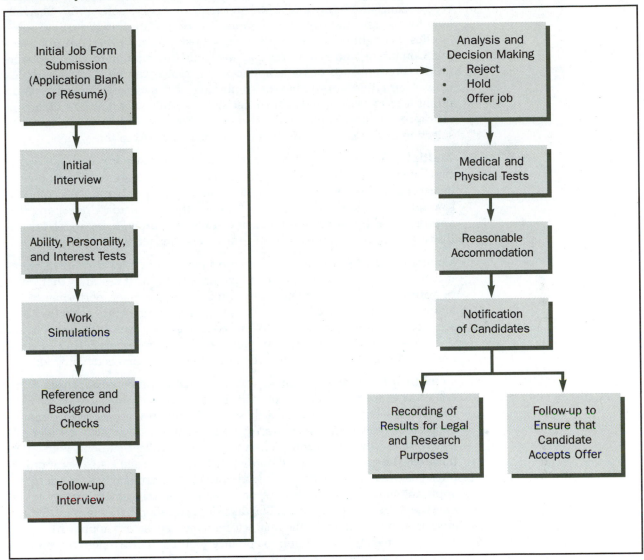

next, from state to state within the United States, and from year to year. For example, in 1998, California passed a new law that prohibits discrimination against people who have a genetic tendency toward disease, and Congress was discussing the possibility of similar legislation at the national level.[26]

Legal acceptability does not ensure social acceptance. Although the courts may agree that an employer's procedures are legally defensible, members of the public, including potential employees and customers, may not accept them. To compete effectively in a tight labor market, employers must move beyond the minimum standards for fairness defined by legal regulations and strive to meet the more complex standards for fairness held by potential employees and interested members of the general public.

Synthesize Information and Choose Appropriate Candidates

Upon reaching this final step, a large amount of information of many types—some of it easily quantified and some of it very "soft"—may be available for a large number of applicants. To complicate things further, some applicants might be considered simultaneously for more than one job opening. Combining and synthesizing all available information to yield a yes-or-no decision for each possible applicant-job match can be a fairly complex task. Alternative approaches to combining and synthesizing information might lead to very different final decisions, so this step takes on great significance for both applicants and the organization. When more than one selection device is used, information can be combined in three ways.

Multiple-Hurdles Approach. In the multiple-hurdles approach, an applicant must exceed fixed levels of proficiency on all the predictors in order to be accepted. A higher-than-necessary score on one predictor can't compensate for a score lower than the cutoff on another predictor. Underlying this approach is the assumption that some skills or competencies are so critical that inadequacy guarantees the person will be unsuccessful on the job.

Compensatory Approach. Because most jobs do not have absolute requirements, a compensatory approach is commonly used. It assumes that good performance on one predictor can compensate for poor performance on another—for instance, a high score on an interview can compensate for a low score on a written examination. With a compensatory approach, no selection decisions are made until the completion of the entire process. Then, a composite index that considers performance on all predictors is developed.

Combined Approach. Many organizations use a combined approach. First, one or more specific requirements—for instance, pass the state bar or the CPA examination—must be met. Once these hurdles are met, scores on the remaining predictors are combined into an overall measure of suitability. Consider college recruiting. Many organizations interview only college students with GPAs that exceed a specific level (first hurdle). To be offered a site visit, the candidate must pass a campus interview (second hurdle). At corporate headquarters, the applicant must take aptitude tests, participate in an assessment center, and be interviewed. A composite index that takes into consideration scores in all three areas is then used to make the final selection (compensatory approach).

Companies that are trying to enhance their competitiveness by improving quality seem to agree that the employees at the front line—for example, the production workers—are key to improving and delivering quality. Thus, they devote considerable time and effort to selecting production workers. In high-quality manufacturing environments, work is organized around teams, so selecting people who can be effective as team players is essential. Exhibit 8.5 lists several types of competencies that are likely to be needed in team-based organizations.[27] To assess these competencies, some organizations use very sophisticated approaches, including those listed in Exhibit 8.6. In this exhibit, each box represents one step in a series of multiple hurdles. A compensatory approach is used to combine the information within each step and decide whether to involve the applicant in the next step.

TECHNIQUES FOR ASSESSING JOB APPLICANTS

A variety of selection techniques are available for assessing an applicant's competencies, personality, values, and other relevant characteristics.

Exhibit 8.5
Competencies Required for Teamwork

I. Communication
    A. Understand verbal and nonverbal communications
    B. Listen without evaluation
    C. Give feedback to others that can be used
    D. Encourage others to contribute
    E. Facilitate communication across teams

II. Problem Solving
    A. Identify problems with others
    B. Gather data to diagnose
    C. Propose and analyze alternative solution
    D. Implement solutions
    E. Evaluate results

III. Group Member
    A. Understand group stages of development
    B. Manage group dynamics
    C. Understand social, task, and individual roles
    D. Understand team project planning, goals setting, execution, evaluation, and learning
    E. Manage group conflict
    F. Understand interaction styles of group members
    G. Recognize the variety of types of teams used in organizations

IV. Performance Management
    A. Understand need for team mission and objectives
    B. Monitor and measure group performance
    C. Understand self and team management concepts
    D. Have ability to learn from the past

Exhibit 8.6
An Approach to Selecting Team Workers in a Total Quality Manufacturing Plant

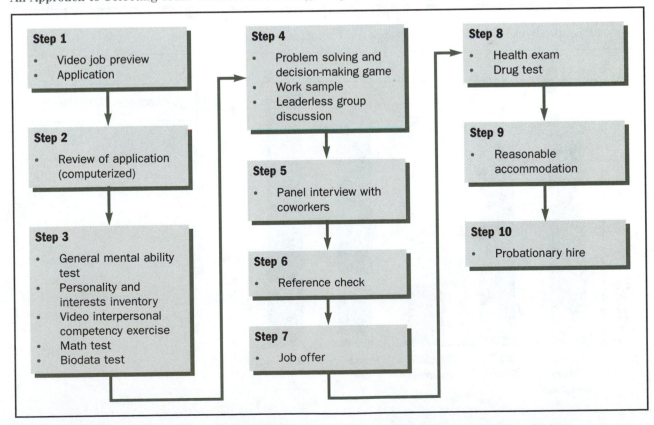

Exhibit 8.7 summarizes the results of a survey of assessment professionals who were asked which techniques they used in their work.[28] The available techniques vary greatly in their frequency of use. They also differ in cost and their usefulness for predicting various outcomes.

Personal History Assessments

Premised on the assumption that past behavior is a good predictor of future performance, personal history assessments seek information about the applicant's background. Application blanks and biodata tests are two commonly used methods of assessing personal histories. Application blanks usually are quite short, asking for the most basic information. Biodata tests often include 200–300 items and delve much more deeply into the applicant's past experiences.

Application Blanks. Application blanks usually seek information that the employer uses to screen candidates and assess whether they meet the *minimum* job requirements. In other words, it often is the first hurdle applicants must clear. Application blanks often ask for details of educational achievements and work experience, as well as a variety of other background information. Validity evidence indicates that educational requirements are predictive of job tenure. Both educational and experience requirements may be useful in selecting individuals for high-level, complex jobs, not jobs that require a short learning period.[29] Application blanks may also request the applicant's willingness to work split shifts, work on weekends, or work

Exhibit 8.7
Percentage of Assessors Who Reported Using Each Technique

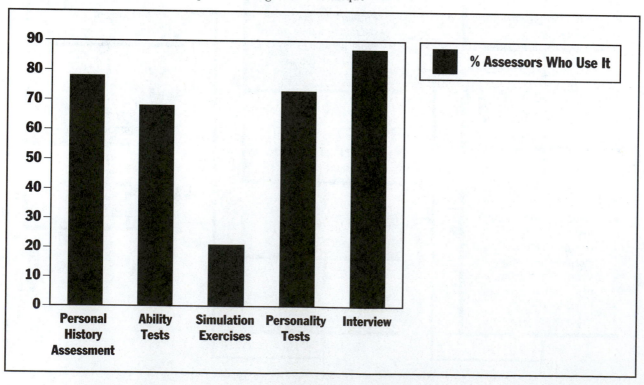

alone. If the job does require split-shift work, items that inquire about shift preferences tend to be good predictors of turnover.[30]

In smaller companies that rely heavily on managers to select their employees, the application blank may also be used simply as an initial document that's useful for keeping track of applicants. When using the application blank in this manner, employers should be especially cautious to avoid asking for information that's not directly relevant to the job. The feature, Managing Diversity: Designing Application Blanks with Fairness in Mind, lists several items that might be included on an application blank. Which items do you think might be avoided because they might lead to unfair discrimination?

MANAGING DIVERSITY
Designing Application Blanks with Fairness in Mind

Instructions

Indicate whether each item below is something to do or not to do in interviews and on job applications.

Do	Don't	Item
		1. Ask about marital status
		2. Ask about the number of children
		3. Ask about skills to do the job
		4. Ask for a woman's maiden name
		5. Ask the age of the applicant
		6. Ask for driver's license
		7. Ask about religious affiliation
		8. Ask about birthplace of applicant
		9. Ask about club memberships
		10. Ask if planning to have children
		11. Ask about preferred hours of work
		12. Ask about disabilities
		13. Ask about other names applicant has used
		14. Ask about arrest record
		15. Ask about height and weight
		16. Ask about nature of military discharge
		17. Ask about friends or relatives with the firm
		18. Ask for clergy as references
		19. Ask questions about credit history
		20. Ask if the applicant is willing to travel

Answers appear later in this chapter.

Biodata Tests.   Biodata tests are a variation on this theme of obtaining information about past and current activities. They ask autobiographical questions on such subjects as extracurricular activities (e.g., "Over the past five years, how much have you enjoyed outdoor recreation?"), family experiences as a child, and recent and current work activities (e.g., "How long were you employed in your most recent job?"). Responses to these questions are empirically keyed based on research that usually involves hundreds of respondents.[31] Biodata information alone can be quite effective as a predictor of overall performance, and it can also be effective when used in combination with an interview or general mental ability test.[32] Besides overall performance, other criteria that biodata can predict include turnover, customer service, coping with stress, learning rate, teamwork, and promotability.[33]

Despite their validity, biodata tests do have a downside: Applicants often react to them as being unfair and invasive.[34] The major reason for this reaction is that many biodata items do not appear to be job-related. This reaction is easy to understand when you consider some of the questions that appear on biodata tests. Here are some actual examples:

What is your weight?
a)   Under 135 pounds
b)   136-155 pounds
c)   156-175 pounds
d)   176-195 pounds
e)   Over 195 pounds

When are you most likely to have a headache?
a)   When I strain my eyes
b)   When I don't eat on schedule
c)   When I am under tension
d)   January first
e)   Never had headaches

Reference and Background Verification

The information obtained from application blanks and biodata tests has proved to be useful in a variety of settings. But increasingly, employers question the accuracy of applicant-generated background information. Verified Credentials reports that almost 30 percent of the résumés it checks contain false information. Distortions vary from a wrong starting date for a prior job to inflated college grades to actual lies involving degrees, types of jobs, and former employers. The most common distortions relate to length of employment and previous salary.

Because some job applicants falsify their qualifications and misrepresent their past, employers have stepped up efforts to check references thoroughly. Instead of relying on unstructured reference letters, which are seldom negative, some organizations hire outside investigators to verify credentials. Other employers personally contact prior employers to get reference information firsthand. Unfortunately, the potential for defamation-of-character suits has made getting information from past employers more and more difficult. Reference checks of an applicant's prior employment record aren't an infringement on privacy if the information provided relates specifically to work behavior and to the reasons for leaving a previous job. Nevertheless, to avoid possible lawsuits many employers strictly limit the type of information they give out about former employees.[35]

■■□*fast fact*

About 5 percent of the people Ford hires today have college degrees, compared to 1.2 percent in the 1980s.

■■□*fast fact*

American Eagle hired M. P. Hillis as a pilot without checking his job reference. When his plane crashed four years later, killing him and 14 others, an investigation revealed a record of poor performance at his previous employer.

Written Tests

The most common types of written tests measure knowledge, ability, and personality.

Ability Tests. Ability tests measure the potential of an individual to perform, given the opportunity. Used in the United States and Europe since the turn of the 20th century, numerous studies document the usefulness of such tests for a wide variety of jobs.[36] Bank tellers need motor skills to operate a computer and finger dexterity to manipulate currency. Sensory tests that measure the acuity of a person's senses, such as vision and hearing, may be appropriate for such jobs as wine taster, coffee bean selector, quality control inspector, and piano tuner. The number of distinct abilities of potential relevance to job performance is debatable, but generally they fall into three broad groupings: cognitive (e.g., verbal, quantitative), psychomotor (perceptual speed and accuracy), and physical (e.g., manual dexterity, physical strength and ability).[37]

Personality Tests. Personality refers to the unique blend of characteristics that define an individual and determine her or his pattern of interactions with the environment. A variety of approaches for psychological assessment can be used to measure personality, but paper-and-pencil tests are probably the most common.[38]

Although most people believe that personality plays an important role in job success or failure, for many years U.S. employers shied away from measuring it largely because research indicated that personality seldom predicted performance. But this early conclusion may have been inaccurate.[39] Recent advances in the academic community's understanding of the nature of personality suggest that employers may have abandoned personality measures too early. The most significant advance has been the realization that most aspects of personality can be captured using only a few basic dimensions. Often referred to as the Big Five, these are

- extraversion (sociable, talkative, assertive),
- agreeableness (good-natured, cooperative, trusting),
- conscientiousness (responsible, dependable, persistent, achievement oriented),
- emotional stability (not being overly tense, insecure, or nervous), and
- openness to experience (imaginative, artistically sensitive, intellectual).[40]

One important dimension for predicting job performance across a variety of jobs and a variety of occupational groups is conscientiousness. In general, conscientious people perform better, and this seems to be even truer for managerial jobs characterized by high levels of autonomy. Not surprisingly, extraversion is somewhat predictive of performance in jobs that involve social interaction, such as sales and management, but these linkages are actually not very strong.[41]

Personal integrity and honesty is another personality characteristic that's attracting a lot of attention among employers. Employee theft is often cited as a primary reason for small-business failures, with some estimates suggesting it's the cause of up to 30 percent of all failures and bankruptcies. In retailing, inventory shrinkage (unexplained losses in cash, tools, merchandise, and supplies) is a major problem, requiring companies to invest large amounts in security systems. In a survey of 9,000 employees by the Justice Department,

"There is no getting around [the fact] that, in terms of IQ, you've got to be elitist in picking people to write software."

**Bill Gates
CEO
Microsoft**

■□ fast fact

In France, graphology (handwriting analysis) often is used for making selection decisions.

one-third admitted stealing from their employers. White-collar crime involving millions of dollars regularly makes the news.

Problems of this scope and magnitude help explain why employers administer millions of integrity tests annually. Undoubtedly, not all these tests are equally valid, but the better ones can predict dishonest and disruptive work behaviors—for instance, theft and disciplinary problems.[42] Applicants favor paper-and-pencil integrity tests over more invasive procedures, such as background checks and lie detectors (which were found to be highly unreliable and banned as selection tools under the *Employee Polygraph Protection Act of 1988*).[43]

Sometimes simply giving a test can help solve a company's problems. A convenience store chain gave an honesty test to a few hundred employees and told them how to correct the test themselves. The employees' exposure to the test and the process of self-correction prompted an immediate two-thirds reduction in inventory theft. Thus, carefully developed personality assessments can be inexpensive additions to the selection process.

Interest and Preference Inventories.   Interest inventories assess applicants' preferences for different types of work and work situations. Interests and preferences are reflected in the behaviors people engage in voluntarily. Thus, these inventories help match people to jobs they'll enjoy. Here are two representative items from an interest inventory:

> For each set, put an *M* next to the activity you *most* like and an *L* next to the activity you *least* like.
>
> 1. _____ Go to a concert.
>   _____ Play tennis.
>   _____ Read a book.
> 2. _____ Work in the garden.
>   _____ Go hiking.
>   _____ Paint a picture.

Interest and preference inventories are most often used to assist people during their early struggles with deciding which types of occupations or careers suit them. For example, high school and college counselors often advise students based on results from the *Strong Vocational Interest Blank*, which can be taken in computerized form. With massive downsizing, outplacement counselors serving unemployed adults also use such inventories to help people develop midlife career strategies and evaluate potential changes in occupation. In all these settings, the assumption is that people will be both more satisfied and more likely to perform satisfactorily in jobs that match their interests. Some evidence supports this idea, and also shows a tendency for satisfied jobholders to remain in their jobs longer.[44] Thus, wise employers use interest inventories as part of their placement activities.

Work Simulations

Work simulations, often referred to as work sample tests, require applicants to complete verbal or physical activities under structured "testing" conditions. Rather than measure what an individual knows, they assess the individual's ability to do. For example, applicants for factory jobs at an auto plant might be asked to assemble a headlight within a specified time. Applicants for the job of retail associate at a department store might be asked to watch a videotape that shows a typical customer and then describe how

fast fact

When hiring managers for its stores in China, McDonald's requires potential management candidates to work in a restaurant for three days before making a final selection decision.

they would handle the situation. Interactive video assessments of conflict resolution skills can be used to predict the performance of managers.[45]

Work sample tests are somewhat artificial because the testing situation itself tends to promote anxiety and tension. On the positive side, however, these tests are very difficult to fake. They tend to be more valid than almost all other types of selection devices and are the least likely to create problems due to unfair discrimination. Unfortunately, they're usually expensive to develop so they're only cost-effective when large numbers of applicants are to be examined. Since work sample tests are also expensive to administer, the total price is lower if they're placed at the end of a selection process, when the number of applicants tested is smaller.[46]

Assessment Centers

Assessment centers evaluate how well applicants or current employees might perform in a managerial or higher-level position. Assessment centers usually involve six to twelve attendees, although they may involve more. Customarily, they're conducted off the premises for one to three days. Usually managers from throughout the organization are trained and asked to assess the employees or job applicants. Increasingly, team members who will work with new hires also assess the participants.[47] At Cummins Engine and Libbey-Owens, the opinions of peers are just as important as those of managers. The reason? According to an HR representative at Libbey-Owens, "We want their buy-in on the candidate, and also they often look for different characteristics than we do."[48] Assessment centers can be particularly effective at selecting team-oriented candidates, and their use grows each year.[49]

At a typical assessment center, candidates are evaluated using a wide range of techniques. One activity, the *in-basket exercise*, creates a realistic situation designed to elicit typical on-the-job behaviors. Situations and problems encountered on the job are written on individual sheets of paper and set in an in-basket. The applicant is asked to arrange the papers by priority and note any actions that should be taken. To simulate a typical day, the task must be completed under time pressure. The problems or situations described to the applicant involve different groups of people—peers, subordinates, and people outside the organization. As the applicant is working through this task, he or she is interrupted often by phone calls or other distractions meant to create more tension and pressure.

Other tests used in assessment centers include business games and leaderless group discussions. Business games are living cases. They ask individuals to live assigned roles, make decisions, and deal with the consequences of those decisions over the course of several hours or days. In a *leaderless group discussion (LGD)*, a group of individuals is asked to discuss a topic for a given period of time. For example, participants might each be asked to make a five-minute oral presentation about the qualifications of a candidate for promotion, and defend their nomination in a group discussion with several other participants. Participants are rated on their selling ability, oral communication skill, self-confidence, energy level, interpersonal competency, aggressiveness, and tolerance for stress. LGD ratings are useful predictors of managerial performance in a wide range of business areas.

Because in-basket exercises, business games, and LGDs tend to be useful in managerial selection, they're often used together in an assessment center. As candidates go through these exercises, a trained team of assessors—usually managers—rates their performance. After the program ends, the

fast fact

Assessments were invented in the 1950s at AT&T.

"Teams spend a lot of energy on the hiring process, and they want the new person to succeed."

Deborah Harrington-Mackin
President
New Directions Corporate
Consulting Group

fast fact

The United Nations uses assessment centers to select managers for its operations all around the world.

assessors discuss the candidates and prepare written evaluations based on their combined judgments of the candidates. Frequently assessed competencies include organizing, planning, analyzing, decision making, controlling, oral communications, interpersonal relations, influencing, and exhibiting flexibility. The composite performance on the exercises and tests is often used to determine an assessment center attendee's future promotability. It may also be used to develop the organization's human resource planning and training needs and to make current selection and placement decisions. Assessment center participants usually receive feedback about the results of the experience and are encouraged to use it for personal career planning.

Assessment centers appear to work because they reflect the actual job environment and measure performance on multiple job dimensions, and because two or more trained raters with a common frame of reference evaluate each participant's behavior. Although assessment centers are expensive to operate, the cost seems to be justified. The annual productivity gains that are realized by selecting managers through assessment centers average well above administrative costs.[50] In addition, assessment centers appear to be nondiscriminatory as well as being valid across cultures.[51] Thus, their higher cost may be further justified by lower costs related to lawsuits.[52]

Selection and Placement Interviews

Job offers go to the applicants who *appear* most qualified, because it's often impossible to determine from available data who *really* is most qualified. Although appearances can be deceiving, the job interview and the perceptions gained from it still constitute the tool most heavily used to determine who gets a job offer. As shown in Exhibit 8.4, interviews occur both at the beginning and during the selection process.

At Southwest Airlines, candidates for flight attendant jobs are first interviewed by a panel of representatives from the People Department and the Inflight Department. Before the selection process is finished, they'll also have one-on-one interviews with a recruiter, a supervisor from the hiring department, and a peer. Interviews that follow sound procedures can be quite useful. Poorly conducted interviews may yield very little useful information, and may even damage the organization's image. Southwest Airlines' interview process was developed in collaboration with Development Dimensions International, a consulting firm that specializes in designing sound selection procedures. Thus, the procedures at Southwest Airlines adhere to the basic principles of good interview design: structured questions, systematic scoring, multiple interviewers, and interviewer training.[53]

Structure. An *unstructured selection interview* involves little preparation. The interviewer merely prepares a list of possible topics to cover and, depending on how the conversation proceeds, asks or does not ask them. Although this provides for flexibility, the resulting digressions, discontinuity, and lack of focus may be frustrating to the interviewer and interviewee. More important, unstructured interviews result in inconsistencies in the information collected about the candidates.

In a *structured selection interview*, all the applicants are asked the same questions in the same order. Usually, the interviewer also has a prepared guide that suggests which types of answers are considered good or poor. Although structuring the interview restricts the topics that can be covered, it ensures that the same information is collected on all candidates. As a result, managers are less likely to make snap and possibly erroneous judgments.

Two types of approaches to designing structured selection interviews are the situational approach and the experienced-based approach. The situational approach asks candidates to imagine a hypothetical situation that's described by the interviewer, and then state how they would behave in that situation. The experience-based approach asks the candidate to describe examples of behaviors that actually occurred. Although either approach can be effective, the experience-based approach appears to have higher validity.[54]

Computerized interviewing is one way to ensure the interview process is structured. Computer-aided interviewing does not replace face-to-face interviewing; it complements it by providing a base of information about each applicant before the interviewer meets the applicant. This helps ensure that the interviewer's first impression is based on information that's job relevant rather than anecdotal. Another advantage of computer-aided interviewing is that it provides an automatic record of answers so that they can be compared across applicants. Computer-aided interviews have been validated in a number of settings, including the manufacturing and service industries.

Another approach that minimizes snap judgments is the *semistructured selection interview*. Questions are prepared in advance, the same questions are asked of all candidates, and responses are recorded. However, follow-up questions are allowed to probe specific areas in depth. This approach provides enough flexibility to develop insights, along with the structure needed to acquire comparative information. In general, structured and semistructured interviews are more valid than unstructured interviews.[55] Structured interviews also appear to be less likely to unfairly discriminate against members of ethnic minority groups.[56]

CORE is a consulting firm that specializes in the design and implementation of human resource systems. When designing interview questions for clients to use in their selection process, CORE writes questions that focus the interview on past behavior that's job relevant. Exhibit 8.8 lists some of the types of questions CORE has designed to assess an applicant's competency in the area of relationship building.[57] Based on the job analyses it has conducted in many different companies, CORE identified relationship building as one of several important competencies required of managers. Depending on the client's preference, these questions could be used as a basis for a structured or semi-structured interview.

Systematic Scoring. Job interviews also vary in the degree to which results are scored. At one extreme, an interviewer merely listens to responses; forms an impression; and makes an accept, reject, or hold decision. Alternatively, raters are given specific criteria and a scoring key to evaluate responses to each question. This approach helps ensure that applicants are evaluated against the same criteria. Systematic scoring also tends to minimize halo bias, in which an interviewer judges an applicant's entire potential on the basis of a single characteristic, such as how well the applicant dresses or talks.

Number of Interviewers. Typically, interviewers meet with applicants one person at a time. Unfortunately, managers sometimes overlap in their coverage of some job-related questions and miss others entirely. This is a time-consuming process in which the interviewer's and applicant's impressions vary, depending on what was discussed. These problems can be overcome by using a panel interview, in which several individuals simultaneously interview one applicant. Because all interviewers hear the same responses, panel

■□ *fast fact*

An interview that would take two hours to complete with a human interviewer can be completed in about 20 minutes using a computerized interview.

"A candidate may be able to fool one interviewer, but he or she isn't likely to fool three people at once."

Antonio Fulk
HR Specialist
Rohr Inc.

Exhibit 8.8

Examples of Questions to Use in a Structured Interview

Competency Being Assessed: Relationship Building

Interview Questions Designed to Focus on Behavioral Descriptions

1. Sketch out two or three key strengths you have in dealing with people. Can you illustrate the first strength with a recent example? [Repeat same probes for other strengths.]

    Probes:
    - When did this example take place?
    - What possible negative outcomes were avoided by the way you handled this incident?
    - How often has this situation arisen?
    - What happened the next time this came up?

2. Tell me about a time when you effectively used your people skills to solve a customer problem?

    Probes:
    - When did this take place?
    - What did the customer say?
    - What did you say in response?
    - How did the customer react?
    - Was the customer satisfied?

3. Maintaining a network of personal contacts helps a manager keep on top of developments. Describe some of your most useful personal contacts.

    Probes:
    - Tell me about a time when a personal contact helped you solve a problem or avoid a major blunder.
    - How did you develop the contact in the first place?
    - What did you do to obtain the useful information from your contact?
    - When was the next time this contact was useful?
    - What was the situation at that time?
    - How often in the past six months have personal contacts been useful to you?

---

interviews produce more consistent results. They may also be less susceptible to the biases and prejudices of the interviewers, especially if panel members come from diverse backgrounds.[58] On the other hand, panel interviews are expensive because many people are involved. However, if applicants are to be interviewed by more than one person anyway, panel interviewing can be efficient, reliable and cost-effective.[59]

fast fact

Firms using total quality management approaches typically spend nearly 20 hours per applicant in selection.

Interviewer Training. Left on their own, interviewers tend to form their own impressions based on whatever criteria are most important or salient to them. An applicant might be rejected by one interviewer for being "too aggressive," but accepted by another for being "assertive." In fact, interviewers' recommendations about whether to hire an applicant are strongly influenced by how much the interviewer likes the applicant and physical attractiveness.[60] Consequently, interviewers must be trained to use job-relevant information and to apply it consistently across applicants.[61] Frame-of-reference training involves teaching interviewers a common nomenclature for defining the importance of each component of behavior that's to be observed in the interview.[62] This can be accomplished by having potential interviewers develop questions and a scoring key. Alternatively, an interviewer's ratings for "practice" interview questions can be compared with normative ratings given by other interviewers. Such training brings individual perceptions into closer congruence with those of the rest of the organization.

Medical and Physical Tests

Although not all organizations require medical exams or physical tests, these are being given in increasing numbers. As concerns about privacy and fear of discrimination based on medical conditions mount, however, opposition to such testing grows.

General Health Examinations. Because of their high cost, health examinations have often been among the final steps in the selection process. But since the enactment in 1990 of the *Americans with Disabilities Act* (ADA), these exams may be given only after a job offer has been made.[63] Before the offer is made, employers should only describe the job's functions and ask if the applicant is capable of performing the job. Employers can't inquire at this stage about any disabilities. Post-offer physical and medical exams that tend to screen out people with disabilities must be job related. Attempts at accommodation should be made and documented.

Guidelines for assessing physical abilities have been developed that detail the sensory, perceptual, cognitive, psychomotor, and physical requirements of many jobs, including police officer, firefighter, electrical powerplant worker, telephone line worker, steel mill laborer, paramedic, maintenance worker, and numerous mechanical jobs. When applied carefully, these physical requirements—not physical examinations per se—are extremely useful in predicting job performance, worker's compensation claims, and absenteeism. Non-job-related exams are legal as long as everyone must have them and the results don't screen out members of protected groups at a higher rate than members of non-protected groups.

Genetic Screening. Each year, hundreds of thousands of job-related illnesses and deaths occur. Many of these are attributable to chemical hazards. Genetic screening identifies individuals who are hypersensitive to harmful pollutants in the workplace. Once identified, these individuals can be screened out of chemically dangerous jobs and placed in positions in which environmental toxins do not present specific hazards. Genetic screening isn't prohibited by the ADA and several major firms use it. As scientific research on genetic screening continues, the debate over the ethics of basing employment decisions on immutable traits is likely to grow. It also seems probable that organizations will be pressured to develop engineering controls that minimize or eliminate workplace pollutants. These controls would be the preferred alternative to genetic screening, a selection criterion over which an individual has no control.[64]

Drug and Alcohol Testing. Drug and alcohol abuse cost U.S. industry more than $100 billion annually. That helps explain why more than 15 million applicants and employees are tested for drugs annually. Of those tested, between six percent and eight percent test positive. Consequently, firms are likely to continue drug testing. Federal contractors have no choice. According to the *Drug-Free Workplace Act of 1988*, firms that do business with the federal government must have written drug use policies. Regardless of what methods are used for drug testing, a key issue in adopting a drug policy is establishing a disciplinary procedure: "If a drug policy does not state specifically that disciplinary actions will be taken when an employee tests positive for drug use, there's no reason to test. Drug testing doesn't make sense if you're not willing to take disciplinary action based on a confirmed positive test result. A policy calling for discipline in such a circumstance doesn't have to require termination. Rehabilitation can be required as an alternative."[65] The *Americans with Disabilities Act* protects applicants and employees who are in recovery programs, but not current drug and alcohol users. Testing for illegal drugs isn't considered a medical exam under the ADA and is, therefore, permissible.

Pre-Certification

A comprehensive approach to selecting employees is expensive and fraught with legal risks. When employers make poor selection decisions—hiring someone who doesn't work out or not hiring someone who would have performed well—both the employer and the applicant lose. As finding competent employees becomes increasingly difficult, employers may begin to adopt new approaches to selection. Pre-certification selection is one approach that may become more common in the future.

The opening feature describing the experiences of Brush Wellman illustrated this approach. In contrast to most other selection procedures, pre-certification requires employers to form significant partnerships with local schools and colleges. These partnerships allow employers to influence the curricula of those institutions. Such influence carries with it significant responsibility. Employers must take care to base their recommendations to schools on accurate job analysis information that describes the jobs they want to fill and the competencies needed to perform those jobs. Employers using pre-certification also must be able to project their future needs accurately and be able to time their hiring activities to fit with the timing of pre-certification training schedules. In return, employers using pre-certification may gain a significant competitive advantage by hiring a workforce that has been tailor-trained to their needs using state and federal funds. Exhibit 8.9 describes some of the other important differences between traditional selection procedures and pre-certification.[66]

GUIDELINES AND STANDARDS FOR SELECTION AND PLACEMENT

Numerous acts, executive orders, guidelines, professional standards, and agencies affect selection practices in most organizations. Their effect isn't

Exhibit 8.9
Traditional vs. Pre-Certification Selection Approaches

Traditional Approaches	Pre-certification Approach
• Job and education history implies skills.	• Skill is demonstrated.
• Applicants invest little in order to be considered.	• Applicants make commitment prior to the selection decision.
• Employers hope new hires will be continuous learners.	• Employees have demonstrated their willingness to continuously learn.
• Applicants may accept a position with little thought about long-term goals.	• Applicants have time to reflect on their career goals prior to accepting a position.
• New hires enter new jobs with unclear expectations.	• New hires enter new jobs with clear expectations and well-learned behaviors.
• New hires enter new jobs with new associates.	• New hires enter new jobs with familiar classmates.

direct in the sense of mandating procedures to be used. Rather, legal constraints operate by defining what constitutes illegal discrimination and specifying how employers can successfully defend themselves if they're charged with illegal discrimination. The effects of numerous acts and executive orders were described in Chapters 3 and 7. Here we describe the effects of federal guidelines and professional standards.

Federal Guidelines

Federal guidelines describe the procedures that organizations should use to comply with acts and orders. They explain how to develop and use selection tools, such as tests, and how organizations can assess whether their procedures may be considered discriminatory.

The first set of federal guidelines addressing selection and placement was issued in 1970 by the EEOC. The intent was to provide a workable set of ideal standards for employees, unions, and employment agencies. Those guidelines defined tests as being "all formal, scored, qualified or standardized techniques of assessing job suitability, including . . . background requirements, educational or work history requirements, interviews, biographical information blanks, interview rating scales and scored application blanks."

Following the issuance of the guidelines, the courts began using them as a sort of checklist of *minimum* standards for test validation, rather than as a flexible set of *ideal* standards, as intended. Concern over this trend prompted the Equal Employment Opportunity Coordinating Council to develop a set of uniform guidelines, to be used by all federal agencies, that were based on sound psychological principles and were technically feasible. As a result, the *Federal Executive Agency (FEA) Guidelines* were published in 1976, followed by the *Uniform Guidelines on Employee Selection Procedures* in 1978. The *Uniform Guidelines* were issued in a 14,000-word catalog of do's and don'ts and questions and answers for hiring and promotion. It contains interpretation and guidance not found in earlier EEOC guidelines and is generally considered the most complete and useful legal document relevant to selection and placement.

The EEOC also has published many other guidelines relevant to selection, as well. In 1980, it issued *Guidelines on Discrimination Because of Sex.* These guidelines are premised on the assumption that sexual harassment is a condition of employment if women are exposed to it more frequently than men are. That same year, the EEOC issued its *Guidelines on Discrimination Because of National Origin.* These guidelines extended earlier versions of this protection by defining national origin as a *place* rather than a *country*. It also revised the "speak-English-only rules." This means employers can require that English be spoken if they can show a compelling business-related necessity. In 1981, the EEOC issued guidelines on age discrimination, in essence, identifying what the *Age Discrimination in Employment Act* meant to do and what it should mean to employers and employees. Under the *Guidelines on Discrimination Because of Religion,* an employer is obliged to accommodate the religious preferences of current and prospective employees unless the employer demonstrates undue hardship. Regarding interpretive guidelines for compliance with the *Americans with Disabilities Act,* the best currently available document is the *Technical Assistance Manual on Employment Provisions,* published by the EEOC in 1992. This document provides valuable guidance in such areas as explaining how to identify essential job functions,

■□*fast fact*

A "no-beard" employment policy may discriminate against African-American men who have a predisposition to pseudofolliculitis barbae unless the policy is job related and consistent with business necessity.

acceptable interviewing strategies, and the appropriate timing and use of medical examinations.[67]

Professional Standards

Selection processes are also monitored by the American Psychological Association (APA), which includes among its members many experts in testing and individual assessment. In 1966 and again in 1974, the APA released its *Standards for Education and Psychological Tests*. These were updated in 1985 and were again revised in 1998. In 1975 and again in 1987, the Society for Industrial-Organizational Psychology (SIOP) published its *Principles for the Validation and Use of Personnel Selection Procedures*. Drawing from relevant research, these help clarify issues regarding test fairness and discrimination.[68]

ILLEGAL DISCRIMINATION

Although federal laws explicitly prohibit discrimination, nowhere in the law is discrimination defined. Usually, the court system decides whether or not illegal discrimination has occurred. Broadly speaking, however, the law prohibits differential treatment of employees on the basis of membership in particular groups defined by race, color, religion, national origin, sex, age, physical and mental handicap, and status as a disabled or Vietnam-era veteran. Discrimination on all other bases or qualifications is untouched by federal law, except when it appears to be a disguise for illegal discrimination.[69] In other words, it's not sufficient to avoid asking directly about an applicant's religion, for example. Employers should avoid asking for any information that's likely to reveal the applicant's religion. Regardless of whether they appear on an information blank, in a biodata test, in a personality test, or during an interview, many traditional questions inquiring about an applicant's background are considered "red flags" of discrimination. Exhibit 8.10 lists several areas of inquiry that should be avoided.

Prima Facie Cases

In a typical discrimination lawsuit, a person alleges discrimination due to unlawful employment practices. The person may first go to the Equal Employment Opportunity Commission (EEOC) office. The EEOC may seek out the facts of the case from both sides, attempting a resolution. Failing a resolution, the person may continue the case and file a suit. In the first phase of the suit, the person filing it (the plaintiff) must establish a prima facie case of discrimination. This is done by showing disparate treatment or disparate impact.

Disparate Treatment. Illegal discrimination against an individual is referred to as disparate treatment. A prima facie case of disparate treatment exists when an individual can demonstrate that

- the individual belongs to a protected group;
- the individual applied for a job for which the employer was seeking applicants;
- despite being qualified, the individual was rejected; and
- after the individual's rejection, the employer kept looking for people with the applicant's qualifications.

For individual applicants, demonstrating a case of disparate treatment can be difficult. One reason is that discrimination can be subtle, so the applicant

Exhibit 8.10
Types of Inquiries into Personal Background That Should be Avoided

Type of Information	Reasons for Caution
Demographic Information	Questions related to race should be avoided because essentially no conditions legally allow one to make an employment decision on the basis of race. An exception to this may arise if a firm needs to fulfill a legally mandated affirmative action plan. Age, gender, religion, and national origin may be considered if they're related to a bona fide occupational qualification, but this can be difficult to prove, so questions regarding them should be avoided. Proof of age and citizenship can be required after hiring.
Commitments	It's acceptable to ask if applicants have any social, family, or economic responsibilities that would prevent them from performing job duties. However, questions about marital status, dependents, spouse's job, and child-care arrangements need to be asked of both men and women and given equivalent weight for both if they're asked at all.
Arrests and Convictions	Inquiries about arrest records aren't permissible under any conditions, but employers may ask about convictions.
Disabilities	Disabilities may be considered after the job offer is made. The guidelines contained in the *Americans with Disabilities Act* must be followed closely.
Physical Requirements	Height and weight may be queried for a few jobs. Care should be taken to ensure that physical requirements are valid, because they tend to discriminate against some ethnic groups (Hispanics, Asians) and against women.
Affiliations	Catchall questions about organization affiliations (e.g., country clubs, fraternal orders, and lodges) must be avoided. However, it's acceptable to ask about professional memberships that relate to specific jobs.

may never really realize that a decision was made on the basis of personal characteristics. Also, most of the decision processes aren't visible to applicants. Rejected applicants, especially external ones, seldom know how other applicants performed or even who was eventually hired. In part for these reasons, the law also provides other means for establishing a case of illegal discrimination—specifically, the logic of disparate impact.

Disparate Impact.   Unfair discrimination against an entire protected group is called disparate impact. The Supreme Court specified the basic criteria for establishing a prima facie case of disparate impact in *Griggs v. Duke Power*. Cases of disparate impact can be brought on the basis of three types of statistical evidence.

One type of evidence is comparative statistics showing the rates at which members of protected versus nonprotected groups have been hired, fired, promoted, transferred, or demoted. The *Uniform Guidelines* state that disparate impact, also called adverse impact, is demonstrated when the selection rate "for any racial, ethnic, or sex subgroup is less than four-fifths or 80 percent of the highest selection rate for any group." This so-called bottom-line criterion, which focuses on the consequences of a selection decision rather than on its intent, applies to *each part* of the selection process as well as to the process as a *whole* (*Connecticut v. Teal*, 1982). For enforcement purposes, employees file EEO-1 report forms reporting their sex, race, religion, and so on. The EEOC has authority to audit these forms and use them as evidence of possible discrimination.[70]

Disparate impact can also be based on the demographic statistics of the labor market. That is, an employer's selection procedures can be shown to be discriminatory in a prima facie sense if the employer's workforce fails to reflect parity with the race or sex composition of the relevant labor market. Organizations may determine their relevant labor market in several ways. One is by identifying where 85 percent of current employees reside. Another is by identifying where job applicants reside. A third approach—preferred by the EEOC—is by identifying where potentially qualified applicants reside, even if the organization's current recruitment efforts do not reach this market. Employers can successfully defend prima facie cases of this type if they can show that statistical parity exists, that is, that the proportions of protected group members in their organization's workforce mirror the proportions in the relevant labor market.

The third basis for establishing a case of disparate impact is concentration statistics. The argument here is that a prima facie case of illegal discrimination exists to the extent that protected group members are located in one particular area or job category in the organization. For example, equal numbers of male and female employees may be hired into entry-level jobs in the organization, but the females may be placed predominately in secretarial jobs. This type of practice creates "glass walls" between job categories and job families. Furthermore, because the route to the top of an organization often begins in jobs dominated by men, these glass walls contribute to the problem of "glass ceilings."

Bases for Defending Discriminatory Practices

> *"I will fire you if you discriminate. Anyone who doesn't like the direction this train is moving had better jump off now."*
>
> **Jim Adamson**
> **CEO Flagstar**
> **Parent Corporation of Denny's**

Once a prima facie case of disparate treatment or disparate impact has been established, the employer is given the opportunity to defend itself.[71] An organization accused of illegal discrimination may be able to successfully defend its employment practices by showing that the demonstrated discrimination is legally justified. Discriminatory employment practices can be acceptable if they're used on the basis of

- job relatedness,
- business necessity,
- bona fide occupational qualifications,
- bona fide seniority systems, and
- voluntary affirmative action programs.

Job Relatedness. In discrimination cases, the employer bears the burden of showing that a selection decision is based on job-related information. To demonstrate job relatedness, the company must show that the information used (e.g., interviews, ability tests, education requirements) to make decisions about who to hire or how to place a new hire is related to an employee's being successful on the job (*Watson v. Fort Worth Bank and Trust*, 1988). Employers can use either a logical argument or statistical evidence to demonstrate job relatedness. To be effective, either type of defense requires evidence that the important components of the job were determined through job analysis. For example, a typing test is arguably an appropriate selection device for an administrative assistant if a job analysis shows that people in this job spend 60 percent of their time typing. It may not be an appropriate selection device if people in the job actually spend less than 5 percent of their time typing. When using interviews for selection, employers are more likely to be able to successfully defend themselves against litigation if the interview is structured and it covers job-related information.[72]

Business Necessity. Showing the job relatedness of a selection procedure isn't always possible. The law recognizes this, and allows companies to defend their selection procedures by showing business necessity—that is, they must show that the selection decision was based on a factor (e.g., pregnancy) directly related to the safe and efficient operation of the business. In cases where the logic for arguing business necessity is strong, demonstrating that a specific selection procedure is job related may not be necessary (*Spurlock v. United Airlines*, 1972). However, the courts and the language of the *Civil Rights Act of 1991* define this exception in very narrow terms. Employers must demonstrate that selection procedures having adverse effect on members of protected groups are essential to the safe and efficient operation of the business.

Bona Fide Occupational Qualifications. The defense of *bona fide occupational qualifications (BFOQ)* is permitted for decisions based on sex, religion, and national origin only—not race or color. To use this defense, the employer must show that the discriminatory practice is "reasonably necessary to the normal operation of that particular business or enterprise." For example, women can be barred from contact positions in an all-male, maximum-security prison (*Dothard v. Rawlinson*, 1977).

Bona Fide Seniority Systems. As long as a company has established and maintained a seniority system without the intent to discriminate illegally, it's considered bona fide. Thus, promotion and job assignment decisions can be made on the basis of seniority. In a major decision, the U.S. Supreme Court ruled that seniority can also be used in the determination of layoffs, even if doing so reverses effects of affirmative action hiring (*Firefighters Local Union 1784 v. Stotts*, 1984).

Voluntary Affirmative Action Programs. As described in Chapter 7, the status of voluntary affirmative action programs is increasingly uncertain, due to a variety of new laws being enacted at the state level. Nevertheless, past court decisions have held that voluntary affirmative action programs can be a defense against illegal (reverse) discrimination if they're remedial in purpose, limited in duration, restricted in effect, flexible in implementation, and minimal in harm to innocent parties (*Wygant v. Jackson Board of Education*, 1986; *International Association of Firefighters Local 93 v. City of Cleveland*, 1986; *Black Fire Fighters Association of Dallas v. City of Dallas*, 1994; *Ensley Branch, NAACP v. Seibels*, 1994).

SELECTION AND PLACEMENT FOR U.S. COMPANIES OPERATING ABROAD

The number of American expatriate employees is relatively small, but their importance to companies operating in the international markets is relatively large. Without effective expatriates, U.S. companies are essentially unable to operate successfully abroad. Nevertheless, the ineffectiveness of expatriate employees—also called parent-country nationals (PCNs)—is alarmingly commonplace.

■□*fast fact*

A PriceWaterhouseCoopers Survey revealed that 96 percent of expatriates are men.

Managing Relationships

Expatriate managers perform their daily activities in the context of the parent company's headquarters, the host country's government, the parent company's government, and a local culture that's often quite different from their home culture. In addition, expatriate managers typically operate in a culture with a different language—a major obstacle for many of them.[73] For expatriate managers to be successful, they need the competencies required to perform their specific job as well as those needed to effectively manage six major types of relations:

- internal relations with their coworkers,
- relations with their families,
- relations with the host government,
- relations with their home government,
- external relations with the local culture, and
- relations with the company's headquarters.

Using these success characteristics for selection can go a long way toward increasing the likelihood of expatriate managerial success.[74] For example, one study of expatriates found that the quality of their relationships with family members predicted expatriates' adjustment to the host country six months later.[75] Assessing a candidate's competencies in all of these relationship domains is a major challenge for organizations. Encouraging employees to carefully think through their own competencies is one approach to dealing with this challenge. Paula Caligiuri is a specialist who advises companies on how to manage expatriates. As described in Managing Globally: Self-Selection for Global Assignments, she recommends engaging candidates in a process of self-selection.[76]

MANAGING GLOBALLY

Self-Selection for Global Assignments

It takes a special person to thrive personally and professionally outside his or her home country. While this fact has been widely recognized for many years, many employers continue to select their expatriate workforce based on only their technical competencies. After experiencing the human and economic costs of having expatriates return home before satisfactory completion of their overseas assignments, many employers have adopted new selection procedures, which may include four phases.

Phase I: Self-Selection

This phase begins by creating an initial pool of the potential candidates for global assignments. Experts suggest casting a wide net for the purpose of identifying the largest possible number of candidates with the requisite technical competencies. Potential candidates are then encouraged to consider their own suitability for an international assignment. To help facilitate their self-evaluation, they might complete an instrument such as The Self-Assessment for Global Endeavors (The SAGE). Exercises in The SAGE encourage employees to critically evaluate three critical dimensions: personality and individual characteristics, career issues, and family issues. The goal is to help employees make a thoroughly informed and realistic decision about whether to become a candidate for a global assignment.

EDS encourages self-assessment by making a self-selection instrument available on their Intranet. Deloitte and Touche LLP gives a workbook version of a self-selection instrument to its targeted employees. Regardless of the method, a decision counselor (either internal or external to the organization) should be available to talk with the employees about the issues raised during the self-evaluation process. HR professionals also should become involved by providing accurate information about company policies for overseas assignees and the likely career implications of taking such an assignment.

Phase II: Create a Talent Pool

The objective of Phase II is to systematize the information about self-selected candidates to create a talent pool that can be accessed as needs arise. The general qualifications of self-selected candidates are recorded and organized in a database. Information kept in this central database may include: specific dates of availability, language capabilities, the countries preferred by the candidate, and basic information about technical competencies. All interested employees should be included in the database.

Phase III: Assess Technical Competencies

Next, the open global assignments are analyzed in order to determine the technical and logistical requirements of the positions. When the job requirements are established, the database can be searched for all possible candidates who meet the requirements. Typically, the list of candidates and information about their qualifications is given to the relevant line managers, who evaluate the candidates' technical and managerial readiness.

Phase IV: Make a Mutual Decision

By Phase IV, the pool of candidates often is narrowed down to one or two people who have been tentatively "selected." Given the high stakes associated with global assignments, the organization may now offer additional opportunities for self-selection (de-selection). Some companies send candidates to the host country for a visit before making a final commitment. A less expensive option is matching repatriated families with the selected families. Repatriated families (those who have been-there, done-that) can provide realistic previews about the challenges of the assignment as well as advice about how to cope with those challenges.

This four-part process facilitates the success of global selection in three ways. First, it starts early by engaging employees to consider the desirability of global assignments long before specific openings must be filled. Second, it involves the family as early as possible in the process. Research on expatriates shows that each family member can influence an expatriate's success, for better or worse. Third, the process allows for and even encourages deselection. The best selection decision reflects a mutual agreement between the employee, the employer, and the employee's family.

For more information about self-selection for global assignments and The SAGE, visit
www.caligiuri.com.

Expatriate employees fill a few positions in U.S. companies operating abroad, but most employees abroad are host-country nationals (HCNs). Usually HCNs are selected using host-country practices.[77] A U.S. company may also employ third-country nationals (TCNs). TCNs are individuals from neither the host country nor the parent country. Firms often select TCNs using practices similar to those used in selecting expatriates. The pros and cons of selecting these three types of individuals are listed in Exhibit 8.11.[78]

Legal Considerations for Global Selection

In the *Civil Rights Act of 1991*, Congress affirmed its policy that American civil rights laws apply to the employment practices of American multinationals relative to U.S. citizens employed in their foreign operations. The U.S. District Court in Washington, D.C., has ruled that U.S. law can even replace the laws of other nations. The case involved a non-profit U.S. corporation well known for two of its broadcast services—Radio Free Europe and Radio Liberty, which employed more than 300 U.S. citizens at its Munich facility. Consistent with most collective bargaining agreements in Germany, the company had a mandatory retirement policy. When the employer discharged two employees because of their age, the employees filed a bias suit under the *Age Discrimination in Employment Act* (ADEA). The employer argued that ADEA's "foreign laws" exemption—allowing actions taken in order to avoid violating the laws of a foreign country—applied. But the U.S. district court disagreed, stating that a German labor policy of mandatory retirement at age

---

Exhibit 8.11

Selecting Managers: Pros and Cons of PCNs, HCNs, and TCNs

Parent-Country Nationals

Advantages
- Organizational control and coordination is maintained and facilitated.
- Promising managers are given international experience.
- PCNs are the best people for the job.
- The subsidiary will likely comply with the company objectives, policies, and so forth.

Disadvantages
- The promotional opportunities of HCNs are limited.
- Adaptation to the host country may take a long time.
- PCNs may impose an inappropriate headquarter style.
- Compensation for PCNs and HCNs may differ.

Host-Country Nationals

Advantages
- Language and other barriers are eliminated.
- Hiring costs are reduced, and no work permit is required.
- Continuity of management improves, since HCNs stay longer in positions.
- Government policy may dictate the hiring of HCNs.
- Morale among HCNs may improve as they see the career potentials.

Disadvantages
- Control and coordination of headquarters may be impeded.
- HCNs have limited career opportunities outside the subsidiary.
- Hiring HCNs limits opportunities for PCNs to gain overseas experience.
- Hiring HCNs could encourage a federation of national rather than global units.

Third-Country Nationals

Advantages
- Salary and benefit requirements may be lower than for PCNs.
- TCNs may be better informed than PCNs about the host-country environment.

Disadvantages
- Transfers must consider possible national animosities.
- The host government may resent the hiring of TCNs.
- TCNs may not want to return to their own countries after assignment.

65 does not mean the U.S. employers can violate the ADEA for American workers in Germany. The court did not consider the policy to carry the weight of a foreign law. In explaining it logic, the court stated that "where a foreign labor union policy collides" with a law of the United States, the U.S. law "cannot be expected to bow down" (*Mahoney v. RFE/RL*, 1991).[79] Some say that this is a rather ethnocentric policy.

The U.S. also holds foreign companies operating within the U.S. accountable for adhering to U.S. employment laws. There are some exceptions to this general rule, however. For example, a treaty between the U.S. and Japan permits companies of either country to prefer their own citizens for executive positions in subsidiaries based in the other country. Japanese firms usually select parent-country (i.e., Japanese) executives to run their American subsidiaries, and they provide few opportunities for promotion to the top management slots for their American managers.[80] U.S. employees often consider this practice to be discrimination based on national origin. But according to the ruling in *Fortino v. Quasar Co.*, *Title VII* of the *Civil Rights Act* was preempted by a subsequent trade treaty.

■□ *fast fact*

Foreign companies operating in the U.S. must abide by U.S. employment laws.

SUMMARY

Through selection and placement procedures, organizations strive to fill job openings with the most appropriate people. By the same token, job applicants strive to obtain jobs that are appropriate to their personal objectives. Effective selection and placement systems result in the assignment of individuals to jobs (and even career paths) that match the individuals' technical competencies, personalities, interests, and preferences. In order to achieve an effective match between individuals and job situations, organizations and job applicants need to exchange information. Organizations need to obtain information about the applicant and clearly communicate information about the job and the work setting. Applicants, on the other hand, need to seek information about the job and the work setting and also share information about their qualifications and preferences. This exchange of information begins during recruitment and continues throughout all phases of the selection process.

Applicants often use a fairly informal and unstructured approach to gathering information about organizations and jobs. In contrast, effective organizations are quite systematic in their efforts to learn all they can about applicants. They begin with a clear understanding of the work to be performed and then develop techniques for assessing how well particular individuals are likely to perform the work. Application forms, interviews, written and physical performance tests, work samples, and assessment centers are among the techniques organizations use to evaluate applicants. Managers, HR professionals, the future colleagues of a new hire and even customers may be involved in using these techniques to assess a job applicant.

Few organizations, if any, rely on a single predictor when making selection and placement decisions. Typically, the selection process involves gathering several types of information using a variety of methods. The information obtained may be considered sequentially, using the multiple-hurdles approach. Or, a compensatory approach to decision making may be followed. Regardless of the approach, managing human resources effectively involves an assessment of both validity and the potential disparate impact associated with each bit of information that's used. An extensive framework of legal regulations provides employers with guidelines for how to conduct the selection process in a manner that reduces unfair discrimination. These regulations were designed to ensure that the information collected, retained, and used respects the individual's right to privacy and the organization's right to select individuals on the basis of likely job performance.

Increasingly, U.S. organizations are operating in other countries. Globalization presents many challenges for selection and placement. For organizations, the challenge is to understand how working in a foreign culture affects the nature of the work required of expatriates. For individuals who are considering a cross-cultural assignment, the challenge is to understand how working in another culture may affect both performance in the job and the quality of daily life outside of work. The high rate of expatriate failures is one indication of the difficulties associated with expatriate selection. One approach to reducing expatriate failures is to improve the process used to select expatriates. Engaging applicants more actively in the selection process is one type of improvement that's being tried by a few companies. By encouraging employees to systematically consider all of the implications of an international assignment, some companies hope to stem the tide of expatriates who return home prematurely.

TERMS TO REMEMBER

Application blank
Assessment center
Biodata tests
Bona fide occupational
    qualifications (BFOQ)
Bona fide seniority systems (BFSS)
Business necessity
Combined approach
Compensatory approach
Content validation
Criteria
Criterion-related validation
Disparate impact
Disparate treatment
Economic utility
Genetic screening
Host-country nationals
In-basket exercise
Integrity tests
Interest inventories
Job-related predictors
Leaderless group discussion (LGD)

Multiple-hurdles approach
Panel interview
Parent-country nationals
Personality inventories
Placement
Predictor
Principles for the Validation and Use of
    Personnel Selection Procedures
Reference verification
Reliability
Selection
Self-selection
Standards for Education and
    Psychological Tests
Structured interview
Third-country nationals
Uniform Guidelines on Employee
    Selection Procedures
Validity
Validity generalization
Work sample tests
Work simulations

DISCUSSION QUESTIONS

1.   A frequent diagnosis of an observed performance problem organization is, "This person was a selection mistake." What are the short- and long-

term consequences of so-called selection mistakes? If possible, relate this question to your own experiences with organizations.

2. Successful selection and placement decisions are dependent on other human resource activities. Identify these activities, and explain their relationships to selection and placement.

3. Given all the weaknesses identified with unstructured interviews, why do they remain so popular? How could you improve the typical job interview to overcome some of its potential weaknesses?

4. Describe the meaning of the partnership perspective for selection and placement.

5. What are some of the benefits to employers who are responsive to the applicant's perspective throughout the selection process? Consider the process of selecting employees in as well as the process of selecting them out.

6. Do you think employers should be allowed to use the results of genetic tests in their selection decisions? Explain the rationale for your opinion.

7. What characteristics should companies consider when selecting expatriates?

PROJECTS TO EXTEND YOUR LEARNING

1. **Managing Globalization.** When entrepreneur Doug Mellinger had difficulty finding computer programmers to work for his company, he solved the problem by moving to a location to which people from all over the world might be willing to move—Barbados. He has been able to hire programmers from Germany, India, Ireland, China, and many other counties. What are the selection challenges faced by a global company like Mellinger's, which selects employees from such a diverse labor pool? What competencies do you think would be most important to assess when selecting programmers for this company? Why? To learn more about Doug Mellinger and PRT (his company), visit the company home page at
   www.prt.com

2. **Managing Strategically.** Federal Express and UPS are two companies that compete in the same industry using very different approaches to managing. What are the implications of these differences for the selection criteria that should be used when hiring first-level supervisors? To learn more about these companies, visit their home pages at
   www.ups.com
   and
   www.fedex.com

   For each company, address the following issues:
   a. Identify up to five competencies that you think would be important for supervisors.
   b. List the selection procedures you would use to assess these competencies. If you will use a cognitive ability test, identify which one. If you will use a situational interview, describe the questions

that will be asked. If you will use a personality test, identify the specific test. Provide a rationale for the choice of each selection device.

c.   Outline the order in which the selection devices will be administered and explain the rationale for the ordering.

d.   Specify how information will be combined: using a compensatory, multiple hurdles, or combination approach. Detail how the selection devices will be scored.

e.   In what ways are the differences between these two companies reflected in the selection procedures you described?

3.   **Managing Diversity.**   Although the workforce of many companies includes a diverse mix of people, this diversity isn't yet well represented in high-level leadership positions of Fortune 500 companies. To assist companies interested in improving representation of all types of people in top-level positions, the U.S. government's Glass Ceiling Commission developed and published several recommendations. What are the implications of these recommendations for the design and implementation of selection and placement systems? The commission's recommendations are described at

www.dol.gov/dol/_sec/public/media/reports/ceiling

4.   **Managing Teams.**   America's Job Bank is a recruiting service that was established by Employment Services and is owned by the Department of Labor. Employers post job openings with detailed job descriptions, and prospective employees can use AJB to search and apply for jobs. Visit America's Job Bank at

www.ajb.dni.us

Find at least ten position announcements for jobs that involve teamwork. Based on these position announcements, what characteristics do employers seem to look for when hiring employees into team-oriented jobs? How does your list compare to the one shown in Exhibit 8.5?

5.   **Application and Integration.**   Review the end-of-text cases of Lincoln Electric and Southwest Airlines. Then, describe, evaluate, and compare the selection and placement procedures used at Lincoln Electric and Southwest Airlines. In preparing your answer, consider the following issues:

a.   the objectives of selection and placement;

b.   the criteria used;

c.   the methods used to assess the competencies and other characteristics of individual candidates;

d.   the apparent effectiveness of the selection and placement process;

e.   the roles and responsibilities of managers, HR professionals, and other employees; and

f.   the relationship between the selection and placement process and other aspects of the HRM system (e.g., training received by employees, the pay system).

CASE STUDY

Selecting Soldiers for the Cola War

Few products appear to be more similar than soft drinks, yet the "cola wars" between Coca-Cola and Pepsi show how even organizations with highly similar products can be differentiated by their business strategies.

COKE'S DOMINANCE

Coke is the most recognized trademark in the world. First marketed some 70 years before Pepsi, Coke is, literally, part of American history and culture. In World War I, for example, Coca-Cola bottling plants went to Europe along with the U.S. armed forces. With such enormous recognition in the market, Coke's business strategy centers on maintaining its position and building on its carefully groomed image. Compared with other companies its size, Coca-Cola owns and operates few ventures—especially now that its brief fling with Columbia Pictures is over—and has relatively few bottling franchises with which to deal. Indeed, the largest franchisee, which controls 45 percent of the U.S. market, is owned by Coca-Cola itself.

Given its dominance, the Coke trademark is something akin to a proprietary technology, and Coca-Cola's business strategy turns on subtle marketing decisions that build on the trademark's reputation. This isn't to suggest that running Coke's business strategy is easy. Rather, the decisions are highly constrained within a framework of past practices and reputation. (One reason New Coke was a debacle, it can be argued, was that it broke away from the framework represented by Coke's tradition.)

Managing Coca-Cola therefore requires a deep firm-specific understanding and feel for the trademark that can't be acquired outside the company or even quickly inside it. What Coke does, then, is both teach that culture and hang onto it. Coke typically hires college graduates—often liberal arts majors and rarely MBAs—with little or no corporate experience and provides them with intensive training. Jobs at Coke are very secure, virtually lifetime positions for adequate performers, and a system of promotion from within and seniority-based salary increases provides the carrot that keeps employees coming back day after day. The organizational culture is often described as familylike with a high degree of employee loyalty. Decision-making is very centralized; the people management system ensures that only career Coke managers who have been thoroughly socialized into worrying about the company as a whole get to make decisions affecting the company. The company allows little autonomy and has a low tolerance for individual self-aggrandizement: no one wants an unsupervised, low-level decision backfiring on the trademark. To reinforce the centralized model, performance is evaluated at the company or division level.

PEPSI'S CHALLENGE

Pepsi is not Coke. Pepsi has prospered by seeking out the market niches where Coke isn't dominant and then differentiating itself from Coke. From its early position as a price leader ("Twice As Much for a Nickel") to contemporary efforts at finding a "New Generation" of consumers, Pepsi cleans up behind the Coke trademark. Pepsi markets more aggressively to institutional buyers like hotels and restaurants than does Coke, which is focused on individual consumers. Pepsi also has many more bottling franchises that operate with some autonomy.

Given its marketing strategy, Pepsi faces a much more diversified and complicated set of management challenges. It needs more innovative ideas to identify market niches, and it needs the ability to move fast. Its people management system makes this possible. Pepsi hires employees with experience and advanced degrees, high-performing people who bring ideas with them. In particular, Pepsi brings in advanced technical skills. Within the company, Pepsi fosters individual competition and a fast-track approach for those who are successful in that competition. The company operates in a much more decentralized fashion, with each division given considerable autonomy, and performance is evaluated at the operating and individual levels. Restructuring in the early 1990s moved the firm toward further decentralization and introduced a stock option program, designed to push entrepreneurial action down to individual employees.

Pepsi employees have relatively little job security, and the company does not have a strong promotion-from-within policy. One Pepsi insider commented, "Whenever anybody is either over 40 or has been in the same Pepsi job for more than four or five years, they tend to be thought of as a little stodgy." In part because of higher turnover, Pepsi employees have significantly less loyalty to the company than do their counterparts at Coke. Indeed, the main issue that unites them, some say, is their desire to "beat Coke."

What Pepsi gets from this system is a continuous flow of new ideas (e.g., from experienced new hires), the ability to change quickly (e.g., by hiring and firing), and the means for attacking many different markets in different ways (e.g., decentralized decision making with individual autonomy).[81]

QUESTIONS

1. How do the different strategies of Coke and Pepsi affect the types of competencies these two companies need in their managerial staff?

2. If you worked for Coke, would you consider experience as a Pepsi manager to be a positive feature for a job applicant applying for a managerial job? Explain.

3. If you worked for Pepsi, would you consider experience as a Coke manager to be a positive feature for a job applicant applying for a managerial job? Explain.

4. Although Pepsi generally gives employees little security, CEO Craig Weatherup moved into that position from the inside, after serving in a variety of managerial roles over several years. When Weatherup first arrived at Pepsi, he was assigned to a position in Japan, despite the fact that he had no experience with the type of job he was assigned to, he had never before visited Japan, and he spoke no Japanese. Placing people in very challenging "stretch" assignments is typical for Pepsi. What competencies should Pepsi consider when assigning managers to jobs for which they have little direct relevant experience? What are the implications of this approach to selection and placement for employees, for the company's long-term performance, and for other aspects of the company's HRM system?

ENDNOTES

[1] B. P. Sunoo, "How Fun Flies at Southwest Airlines," *Personnel Journal* (June 1995): 62–71.

[2] For detailed reviews, see N. Schmitt and D. Chan, *Personnel Selection: A Theoretical Approach* (Thousand Oaks, CA: Sage, 1998); N. Anderson and P. Herriot, eds., *International Handbook of Selection and Assessment* (Chichester, UK: John Wiley and Sons, 1997); R. M. Guion, *Assessment, Measurement, and Prediction for Selection Decisions* (Mahwah, NJ: Lawrence Erlbaum Associates, 1997); W. Borman, M. Hanson, & J. Hedge, "Personnel Selection," *Annual Review of Psychology* 48 (1997): 299–337; H. G. Heneman, III, R. L. Heneman, and T. A. Judge, *Staffing Organizations*, 2nd ed. (Homewood, IL: Irwin Publishing, 1996); N. Schmitt, W. C. Borman & Associates, *Personnel Selection in Organizations* (San Francisco: Jossey-Bass, 1993).

[3] V. C. Smith, "Staffing Strategies," *Human Resource Executive* (January 1998): 44–45; C. Patton, "Natural Bedfellows," *Human Resource Executive* (January 1998): 62–63; S. M. Colarelli and T. A. Beehr, "Selection Out:

Firings, Layoffs, and Retirement," *Personnel Selection in Organizations*, N. Schmitt et al. (1993): 341–384.

[4] C. C. Snow and S. A. Snell, "Staffing as Strategy," *Personnel Selection in Organizations*, N. Schmitt et al., (1993): 448–478.

[5] D. E. Terpstra and E. J. Rozell, "The Relationship of Staffing Practices to Organizational Level Measures of Performance," *Personnel Psychology* 46 (1993): 27–48.

[6] A. K. Gupta, "Contingency Linkages Between Strategy and General Manager Characteristics: A Conceptual Examination," *Academy of Management Review* 9 (1984): 399–412; A. K. Gupta and V. Govindarajan, "Business Unit Strategy, Managerial Characteristics, and Business Unit Effectiveness at Strategy Implementation," *Academy of Management Journal* 27 (1983): 25–41; A. D. Szilagyi and D. M. Schweiger, "Matching Managers to Strategies: A Review and Suggested Framework," *Academy of Management Review* 9 (1984): 626–637.

[7] J. Martin, "So, You Want to Work for the Best..." *Fortune* (January 12, 1998): 77–78.

[8] For example, see L. M. Graves and G. N. Powell, "The Effect of Sex Similarity on Recruiters' Evaluations of Actual Applicants: A Test of the Similarity–Attraction Paradigm," *Personnel Psychology* 48 (1995): 85–97.

[9] S. L. Rynes, "Who's Selecting Whom? Effects of Selection Practices on Applicant Attitudes and Behavior," *Personnel Selection in Organizations*, N. Schmitt et al., (1993): 242.

[10] For excellent reviews of this literature, see Rynes, "Who's Selecting Whom?"; S. L. Rynes, "Recruitment, Job Choice, and Post-Hire Consequences: A Call for New Research Directions," *Handbook of Industrial and Organizational Psychology*, vol. 2, M. D. Dunnette and L. M. Hough, eds. (Palo Alto, CA: Consulting Psychologists Press, 1991): 399–444.

[11] R. D. Arvey and P. R. Sackett, "Fairness in Selection: Current Developments and Perspectives," *Personnel Selection in Organizations*, N. Schmitt et al. (San Francisco: Jossey-Bass, 1993): 171–202; see D. Chan, N. Schmitt, J. M. Sacco, and R. P. DeShon, "Understanding Pretest and Posttest Reaction to Cognitive Ability and Personality Tests," *Journal of Applied Psychology* 83 (1998): 471–485.

[12] See R. D. Arvey and P. R. Sackett, "Fairness in Selection: Current Developments and Perspectives;" S. W. Gilliland, "Effects of Procedural and Distributive Justice on Reactions to a Selection System," *Journal of Applied Psychology* 79 (1994): 691–701.

[13] D. Chan, "Racial Subgroup Difference in Predictive Validity Perceptions on Personality and Cognitive Ability Tests," *Journal of Applied Psychology* 82 (1997): 311–320; D. Chan, N. Schmitt, R. P. DeShon, C. S. Clause, and K. Delbridge, "Reactions to Cognitive Ability Tests: The Relationships Between Race, Test Performance, Face Validity Perceptions, and Test-Taking Motivation," *Journal of Applied Psychology* 82 (1997): 300–310; J. W. Smither et al., "Applicant Reactions to Selection Procedures," *Personnel Psychology* 46 (1993): 49–76; J. Schwarzwald, M. Koslowsky, and B. Shalit, "A Field Study of Employees' Attitudes and Behaviors after Promotion Decisions," *Journal of Applied Psychology* 77 (1992): 511–514; R. D. Bretz, Jr., and T. A. Judge, "The Role of Human Resource Systems in Job Applicant Decision Processes," *Journal of Management* 20 (1994): 531–551.

[14] See Rynes, "Who's Selecting Whom?"

[15] For a detailed review of what is known about this very special selection process, see G. P. Hollenbeck, *CEO Selection: A Street-Smart Review* (Greensboro, NC: Center for Creative Leadership, 1994) and V. I. Sessa, R. Kaiser, J. K. Taylor, and R. J. Campbell, *Executive Selection: What Works and What Doesn't* (Greensboro, NC: Center for Creative Leadership, 1998).

[16] E. E. Lawler, III, "From Job-Based to Competency-Based Organizations," *Journal of Organizational Behavior* 15 (1994): 3–15.

[17] A. J. Vinchur, J. S. Schipmann, F. S. Switzer, III, and P. L. Roth, "A Meta-Analytic Review of Predictors of Job Performance for Salespeople," *Journal of Applied Psychology* 83 (1998): 586–597; D. E. Bowen and D. A. Waldman, "Customer-Driven Employee Performance," *The Changing Nature of Performance*, D. R. Ilgen and E. D. Pulakos, eds. (San Francisco: Jossey-Bass, 1999); R. Hogan and R. J. Blake, "Vocational Interests: Matching Self-Concept with the Work Environment," *Individual Differences and Behavior in Organizations*, K. R. Murphy, ed. (San Francisco: Jossey-Bass, 1996): 89–144; J. A. Chatman, "Matching People and Organizations: Selection and Socialization in Public Accounting Firms," *Administrative Science Quarterly* 36 (1991): 459–484; R. Dunifon and G. J. Duncan, "Long-run Effects of Motivation on Labor-market success," *Social Psychology Quarterly* 61 (1998): 33–48.

[18] R. Grover and E. Schine, "At Disney, Grumpy Isn't Just a Dwarf," *Business Week* (February 24, 1997): 38; R. Grover, "Michael Eisner Defends the Kingdom," *Business Week* (August 4, 1997): 73–75; V. C. Smith, "Spreading the Magic," *Human Resource Executive* (December 1996): 28–31; J. Pfeffer, *Competitive Advantage Through People* (Boston: Harvard Business School Press, 1994).

[19] J. R. Burnett, C. Fan, S. J. Motowidlo, and T. DeGroot, "Interview Notes and Validity," *Personnel Psychology* 51 (1998): 375–396.

[20] I. L. Goldstein, S. Zedeck, and B. Schneider, "An Exploration of the Job Analysis-Content Validity Process," *Personnel Selection in Organizations*, N. Schmitt et al., eds. (1993): 3–34.

[21] D. Sheff, "Levi's Changes Everything," *FastCompany* (1997): 24–31.

[22] See F. L. Schmidt and J. E. Hunter, "The Validity and Utility of Selection Methods in Personnel Psychology," *Psychological Bulletin* 124 (1998): 262-274.

[23] Both of these resources are regularly updated and published by the Buros Institute.

[24] W. F. Cascio, "Assessing the Utility of Selection Decisions: Theoretical and Practical Considerations," *Personnel Selection in Organizations*, N. Schmitt, et al., eds. (1993): 310–340; J. W. Boudreau, "Economic Considerations in Estimating the Utility of Human Resource Productivity Improvement Programs," *Personnel Psychology* 36 (1983): 551–557; J. W. Boudreau, "Utility Analysis for Decisions in Human Resource Management," *Handbook of Industrial and Organizational Psychology*, Dunnette and Hough, eds. (1991): vol.2; K. M. Murphy, "When Your Top Choice Turns You Down: The Effect of Rejected Offers on the Utility of Selection Tests," *Psychological Bulletin* 99 (1986): 133–138.

[25] W. F. Cascio, "Reconciling Economic and Social Objectives in Personnel Selection: Impact of Alternative Decision Rules," *New Approaches to Employee Management: Fairness in Employee Selection* 1 (1992): 61–86; M. E. Baehr et al., "Proactively Balancing the Validity and Legal Compliance of Personal Background Measures in Personnel Management," *Journal of Business and Psychology* 8 (Spring 1994): 345–354; S. E. Maxwell and R. D. Arvey, "The Search for Predictors with High Validity and Low Adverse Impact: Compatible or Incompatible Goals?" *Journal of Applied Psychology* 78 (1993): 433–437.

[26] L. Micco, "California Bans Employment Bias Based on Genetic Testing," *HR News* (August 1998): 13.

27 Based on M. J. Stevens and M. A. Campion, "The Knowledge, Skill and Ability Requirements for Teamwork: Implications for Human Resource Management," *Journal of Management* 20 (1994): 505–530; B. Dumaine, "The Trouble with Teams," *Fortune* (September 5, 1994): 86–92; N. R. F. Maier, "Assets and Liabilities in Group Problem Solving: The Need for an Integrative Function," *Psychological Review* (April 1967): 239–249; D. Hellriegel, S. E. Jackson, and J. W. Slocum, Jr., *Management*, 8th ed. (Cincinnati, OH: South-Western College Publishing, 1999).

28 A. M. Ryan and P. R. Sackett, "Individual Assessment: The Research Base," *Individual Psychological Assessment: Predicting Behavior in Organizational Settings*, R. Jeanneret and R. Silzer, eds. (San Francisco: Jossey-Bass, 1998).

29 D. G. Lawrence, et al., "Design and Use of Weighted Application Blanks," *Personnel Administrator* (March 1982): 53–57, 101.

30 C. J. Russell et al., "Predictive Validity of Biodata Items Generated from Retrospective Life Experience Essays," *Journal of Applied Psychology* 75, no. 5 (1990): 569–580; H. R. Rothstein et al., "Biographical Data in Employment Selection: Can Validities Be Made Generalizable?" *Journal of Applied Psychology* 75, no. 2 (1990): 175–184; M. A. McDaniel, "Biographical Constructs for Predicting Employee Suitability," *Journal of Applied Psychology* 74, no. 6 (1989): 964–970; A. Childs and R. J. Klimoski, "Successfully Predicting Career Success: An Application of the Biographical Inventory," *Journal of Applied Psychology* (February 1988): 3–8.

31 A. F. Snell et al, "Adolescent Life Experiences as Predictors of Occupational Attainment," *Journal of Applied Psychology* 79 (1994): 131–341; G. Stokes, M. Mumford, and W. Owens, eds., *Biodata Handbook: Theory, Research, and Use of Biographical Information for Selection and Performance Prediction* (Palo Alto, CA: Consulting Psychologists Press, 1994).

32 M. D. Mumford, D. P. Costanza, M. S. Connelly, and J. E. Johnson, "Item Generation Procedures and Background Data Scales: Implications for Construct and Criterion-Related Validity," *Personnel Psychology* 49 (1996): 361–398; A. T. Dalessio and T. A. Silverhart, "Combining Biodata Test and Interview Information: Predicting Decisions and Performance Criteria," *Personnel Psychology* 47 (1994): 303–319.

33 F. A. Mael and B. E. Ashforth, "Loyal From Day One: Biodata, Organizational Identification, and Turnover Among Newcomers," *Personnel Psychology* 48 (1995): 309–333; R. D. Gatewood and H. S. Field, *Human Resource Selection* (Orlando: Harcourt Brace, 1994).

34 R. Folger and R. Cropanzano, *Organizational Justice and Human Resource Management* (Thousand Oaks, CA: Sage, 1998); F. A. Mael, M. Connerley, and R. A. Morath, "None of Your Business: Parameters of Biodata Invasiveness," *Personnel Psychology* 49 (1996): 613–650.

35 L. Walley and M. Smith, *Deception in Selection* (New York: John Wiley, 1998); E. A. Robinson, "Beware—Job Seekers Have No Secrets," *Fortune* (December 29, 1997): 285; "Positive Reference Leads to Claim of Negligence," *Fair Employment Practices Guidelines*, No. 430 (April 25, 1997):

1; "Supreme Court Decision Possible Setback to Employee Reference," *Human Resource Executive* (April 1997): 8; "Background Checks: Advantages and Risks," *Fair Employment Practices Guidelines*, No. 373 (December 10, 1994): 3.

36 F. L. Schmidt and J. E. Hunter, "The Validity and Utility of Selection Methods in Personnel Psychology: Practical and Theoretical Implications of 85 Years of Research Findings;" J. C. Hogan, "Physical Abilities," *Handbook of Industrial and Organizational Psychology*, Dunnette and Hough, eds. (1991): 753–831; R. M. Guion, "Personnel Assessment, Selection, and Placement," *Handbook of Industrial and Organizational Psychology*, Dunnette and Hough, eds. (1991): 327–398.

37 E. A. Fleishman and M. K. Quaintance, *Taxonomies of Human Performance* (New York: Academic Press, 1984).

38 R. Hogan, J. Hogan, and B. W. Roberts, "Personality Measurement and Employment Decisions," *American Psychologist* 51 (1996): 469–477; R. T. Hogan, "Personality and Personality Measurement," *Handbook of Industrial and Organizational Psychology*, Dunnette and Hough, eds. (1991): 873–890.

39 D. V. Day and S. B. Silverman, "Personality and Job Performance: Evidence of Incremental Validity," *Personnel Psychology* 42 (1989): 25–36; R. P. Tett, D. N. Jackson, and M. Rothstein, "Personality Measures as Predictors of Job Performance: A Meta-Analytic Review," *Personnel Psychology* 44 (1991): 703–742.

40 L. M. Hough and R. J. Schneider, "Personality Traits, Taxonomies, and Applications in Organizations," *Individual Differences and Behavior in Organizations*, K. R. Murphy, ed. (San Francisco: Jossey-Bass, 1996): 31–88; J. M. Collins and D. H. Gleaves, "Race, Job Applicants, and the Five-Factor Model of Personality: Implications for Black Psychology, Industrial/Organizational Psychology, and the Five-Factor Theory," *Journal of Applied Psychology* 83 (1998): 531–544; R. R. McCrae and P. T. Costa, Jr., "Personality Trait Structure as a Human Universal," *American Psychologist* 52 (1997): 509–535; M. R. Barrick and M. K. Mount, "The Big Five Personality Dimensions and Job Performance: A Meta-Analysis," *Personnel Psychology* 44 (1991): 1–26. For an alternative view, see R. J. Schneider, L. M. Hough and M. D. Dunnette, "Broadsided by Broad Traits: How to Sink Science in Five Dimensions or Less," *Journal of Organizational Behavior* 17 (1996): 639–655.

41 M. K. Mount and M. R. Barrick, "The Big Five Personality Dimensions: Implications for Research and Practice in Human Resources Management," *Research in Personnel and Human Resources Management* 13 (1995): 153–200; M. R. Barrick and M. K. Mount, "The Big Five Personality Dimensions and Job Performance." For an alternative view, see R. P. Tett, "Is Conscientiousness Always Positively Related to Job Performance?" *The Industrial-Organizational Psychologist* (July 1998): 24–29; D. F. Caldwell and J. M. Burger, "Personality Characteristics of Job Applicants and Success in Screening Interviews," *Personnel Psychology* 51 (1998): 119–136.

42 K. R. Murphy, Honesty in the Workplace (Pacific Grove, CA: Brooks/Cole Publishing Co., 1993); D. S. Ones, C.

Viswesvaran, and F. L. Schmidt, "Comprehensive Meta-Analysis of Integrity Test Validities: Findings and Implications for Personnel Selection and Theories of Job Performance," *Journal of Applied Psychology* 78 (1993): 679–703; W. J. Camara and D. L. Schneider, "Integrity Tests: Facts and Unresolved Issues," *American Psychologist* 49 (1994): 112–119; J. M. Collins and F. L. Schmidt, "Personality, Integrity, and White Collar Crime: A Construct Validity Study," *Personnel Psychology* 46 (1993): 295–311; L. R. Burris, "Integrity Testing for Personnel Selection: An Update," *Personnel Psychology* 42 (1989): 491–529; P. R. Sackett and M. M. Harris, "Honesty Testing for Personnel Selection: A Review and Critique," *Personnel Psychology* 37 (1984): 221–246.

43 W. G. Iacono and D. T. Lykken, "The Validity of the Lie Detector: Two Surveys of Scientific Opinion," *Journal of Applied Psychology* 82 (1997): 426–433; A. Mello, "Personality Tests and Privacy Rights," *HR Focus* (March 1996): 22–23.

44 See R. Dawis, "Vocational Interests, Values, and Preferences," *Handbook of Industrial and Organizational Psychology*, Dunnette and Hough, eds., (1991): 833–872.

45 J. A. Weekley and C. Jones, "Video-Based Situational Testing," *Personnel Psychology* 50 (1997): 25–49; J. B. Olson-Buchanan, F. Drasgow, P. J. Moberg, A. D. Mead, P. A. Keenan, and M. A. Donovan, "Interactive Video Assessment of Conflict Resolution Skills," *Personnel Psychology* 51 (1998): 1–24.

46 For an extensive review of and guide to these tests, see L. P. Plumke, *A Short Guide to the Development of Work Sample and Performance Tests*, 2nd ed. (Washington, DC: U.S. Office of Personnel Management, February 1980). Note the interchangeability of the terms work sample and performance test.

47 For a discussion of assessment center history and future trends, see B. T. Mayes, "Insights into the History and Future of Assessment Centers: An Interview with Dr. Douglas Bray and D. William Byham," *Journal of Social Behavior and Personality [Special Issue]* (1997): 3–12.

48 S. Caudron, "Team Staffing Requires New HR Role," *Personnel Journal* (May 1994): 88–94.

49 A. C. Spychalski, M. A. Quinnones, B. A. Gaugler, and K. Pohley, "A Survey of Assessment Center Practices in Organizations in the United States," *Personnel Psychology* 50 (1997): 71–90; J. N. Zall, "Assessment Centre Methods," *Handbook of Work and Organizational Psychology*, Vol. 3; P. J. D. Drenth, H. Theirry, and C. J. DeWolff, eds. *Personnel Psychology* (Basingstoke, UK: Taylor & Francis Press, 1998);] R. J. Campbell, "Use of an Assessment Center as an Aid in Management Selection," *Personnel Psychology* 46 (1993): 691–699; A. Howard and D. W. Bray, *Managerial Lives in Transition: Advancing Age and Changing Times* (New York: Guilford Press, 1988); J. R. Kauffman et al., "The Construct Validity of Assessment Centre Performance Dimensions," *International Journal of Selection and Assessment* 1 (1993): 213–223; G. C. Thornton, *Assessment Centers in Human Resource Management* (Reading, MA: Addison-Wesley, 1992); S. J. Motowidlo, M. D. Dunnette, and G. W. Carter, "An Alternative Selection Procedure: The Low-Fidelity Simulation" *Journal of Applied*

Psychology 75, no. 6 (1990): 640–647; J. S. Schippmann, E. P. Prien, and J. A. Katz, "Reliability and Validity of In-Basket Performance Measures," *Personnel Psychology* 43 (1990): 837–859.

50 L. M. Donahue, D. M. Truxillo, J. M. Cornwell, and M. J. Gerrity, "Assessment Center Construct Validity and Behavioral Checklists," *Journal of Social Behavior and Personality* 12 (5) (1997): 85–108; B. B. Gaugler et al., "Meta-Analysis of Assessment Center Validity," *Journal of Applied Psychology* 72 (1987): 493–511; R. Klimoski and M. Brickner, "Why Do Assessment Centers Work? The Puzzle of Assessment Center Validity," *Personnel Psychology* 40 (1987): 243–260.

51 D. R. Briscoe, "Assessment Centers: Cross-Cultural and Cross-National Issues," *Journal of Social Behavior and Personality [Special Issue]* (1997): 261–270.

52 C. C. Hoffman and G. C. Thornton, III, "Examining Selection Utility Where Competing Predictors Differ in Adverse Impact," *Personnel Psychology* 50 (1997): 455–470.

53 B. P. Sunoo, "How Fun Flies at Southwest Airlines."

54 E. Pulakos and N. Schmitt, "Experience-Based and Situational Interview Questions: Studies of Validity," *Personnel Psychology* 48 (1995): 289–308.

55 M. A. Campion, D. K. Palmer, and J. E. Campion, "A Review of Structure in the Selection Interview," *Personnel Psychology* 50 (1997): 655–702; M. A. McDaniel et al., "The Validity of Employment Interviews: A Comprehensive Review and Meta-Analysis," *Journal of Applied Psychology* 79 (1994): 599–616; S. J. Motowidlo et al., "Studies of the Structured Behavioral Interview," *Journal of Applied Psychology* 77 (1992): 571–587; M. A. Campion, E. D. Pursell, and B. K. Brown, "Structured Interviewing: Raising the Psychometric Properties of the Employment Interview," *Personnel Psychology* (Spring 1988): 25–42; A. I. Huffcutt and W. Arthur, Jr., "Hunter and Hunter (1984) Revisited: Interview Validity for Entry-Level Jobs," *Journal of Applied Psychology* 79 (1994): 184–190.

56 A. I. Huffcutt and P. L. Roth, "Racial Group Difference in Employment Interview Evaluations," *Journal of Applied Psychology* 83 (1998): 179–189.

57 L. Fogli and K. Whitney, "Assessing and Changing Managers for New Organizational Roles," *Individual Psychological Assessment: Predicting Behavior in Organizational Settings*, R. Jeanneret and R. Silzer, eds. (San Francisco: Jossey-Bass, 1998).

58 T. Lin, G. H. Dobbins, and J. Farh, "A Field Study of Race and Age Similarity Effects on Interview Ratings in Conventional and Situational Interviews," *Journal of Applied Psychology* 77 (1992): 363–371; see also A. J. Prewett-Livingston, H. S. Field, J. G. Veres, III, and P. M. Lewis, "Effects of Interview Ratings in a Situational Panel Interview," *Journal of Applied Psychology* (1996): 178–186.

59 E. D. Pulakos, N. Schmitt, D. Whitney, and M. Smith, "Individual Differences in Interviewer Ratings: The Impact of Standardization, Consensus Discussion, and Sampling Error on the Validity of a Structured Interview," *Personnel Psychology* 49 (1996): 85–102.

[60] D. M. Cable and T. A. Judge, "Interviewers' Perceptions of Person-Organization Fit and Organizational Selection Decisions," *Journal of Applied Psychology* 82 (1997): 546–561; C. M. Marlowe, S. Schneider, and C. E. Nelson, "Gender and Attractiveness Biases in Hiring Decisions: Are More Experienced Managers Less Biased?" *Journal of Applied Psychology* 81 (1996): 11–21.

[61] C. K. Stevens, "Antecedents of Interview Interactions, Interviewers' Ratings, and Applicants' Reactions," *Personnel Psychology* 51 (1998): 55–85.

[62] H. J. Bernardin and R. W. Beatty, *Performance Appraisal: Assessing Human Behavior at Work* (Boston: Kent, 1984), 258–260; W. C. Borman, "Format and Training Effects on Rating Accuracy Using Behavior Scales," *Journal of Applied Psychology* 3 (1979): 103–115.

[63] "EEOC Issues Final Guidance for Medical Examinations Under ADA," *Fair Employment Practices Guidelines* (January 25, 1996): 5; "Past Accommodations Do Not Always Determine the Future," *Fair Employment Practices Guidelines*, No. 436 (July 25, 1997): 1; A. Bryant, "Seeing What Really Matters," *New York Times* (December 24, 1997): D1, D4; R. R. Faden and N. E. Kass, "Genetic Screening Technology: Ethical Issues in Access to Tests by Employers and Health Insurance Companies," *Journal of Social Issues* 49 (1993): 75–88.

[64] "Growing Sophistication in Genetic Testing Raises Insurance and ADA Concerns," *Fair Employment Practices Guidelines* (February 10, 1998): 5; S. Greengard, "Genetic Testing: Should You Be Afraid? It's No Joke," *Workforce* (July 1997): 38–44; D. Stipp, "Gene Testing Starts to Pay Off," *Fortune* (April 4, 1997): 25; N. Wade, "Testing Genes to Save a Life Without Costing You a Job," *New York Times* (September 14, 1997): 5; R. Cropanzano and K. James, "Some Methodological Considerations for the Behavioral Genetic Analysis of Work Attitudes," *Journal of Applied Psychology* 75 (1990): 433–439.

[65] W. L. Kornreich, "Employee Drug Testing: More Employers Are Testing, Fewer Employees Are Testing Positive," *Fair Employment Practices Guidelines* (September 10, 1997): 6–8; "New Guide Examines State Drug Testing Laws," *Bulletin to Management* (September 15, 1994): 289; J. Normand, S. D. Salyards, and J. J. Mahoney, "An Evaluation of Preemployment Drug Testing," *Journal of Applied Psychology* 75 (1990): 629–639.

[66] D. A. Lambillote, "Brush Wellman Tries New Twist on Screening Job Applicants," *HR News* (August 1998): 17.

[67] Equal Employment Opportunity Commission, "Americans with Disabilities Act," *Technical Assistance Manual on Employment Provisions* (Title I) (Washington, DC, 1992).

[68] For the most recent information about relevant changes in the Standards and the Principles, consult current issues of the SIOP's newsletter, *The Industrial-Organizational Psychologist*. For information about the SIOP and its newsletter, visit this organization's web site at www.siop.org.

[69] R. D. Arvey and R. H. Faley, *Fairness in Selecting Employees* (Reading, MA: Addison-Wesley, 1988).

[70] For discussions about how the design of selection procedures can affect adverse impact, see R. P. DeShon, M. R. Smith, D. Chan, and N. Schmitt, "Can Racial Difference in Cognitive Test Performance Be Reduced by Presenting Problems in a Social Context?" *Journal of Applied Psychology* 83 (1998): 438–451; K. Hattrup, J. Rock, and C. Scalia, "The Effects of Varying Conceptualizations of Job Performance on Adverse Impact, Minority Hiring, and Predicted Performance," *Journal of Applied Psychology* 82 (1997): 656–664; P. R. Sackett and J. E. Ellington, "The Effects of Forming Multi-Predictor Composites on Group Differences and Adverse Impact," *Personnel Psychology* 50 (1997): 707–722.

[71] J. Ledvinka and V. G. Scarpello, *Federal Regulations in Personnel and Human Resource Management* (Boston: PWS-Kent, 1990).

[72] L. G. Williamson, J. E. Campion, S. B. Malos, M. V. Roehling, and M. A. Campion, "Employment Interview on Trial: Linking Interview Structure with Litigation Outcomes," *Journal of Applied Psychology* 82 (1997): 900–912.

[73] P. J. Dowling, D. E. Welch, and R. S. Schuler, *International Human Resource Management: Managing People in a Multinational Context*, 3rd ed. (Cincinnati: South-Western College Publishing, 1999).

[74] C. Reynolds, "Strategic Employment of Third Country Nationals," *Human Resource Planning*, Vol. 20, No. 1, (1997): 33–39; E. M. Mervosh, "Around the World," *Human Resource Executive* (June 6, 1997): 42–44; C. M. Solomon, "One Assignment, Two Lives," *Personnel Journal* (May 1996): 36–47; C. A. Bartlett and S. Ghoshal, "What Is a Global Manager?" *Harvard Business Review* (September–October 1992): 132; A. K. Gupta and V. Govindarajan, "Knowledge Flows and the Structure of Control within Multinational Corporations," *Academy of Management Review* 16, no. 4 (1991): 768–792; R. L. Tung, *The New Expatriates* (Cambridge, MA: Ballinger, 1988).

[75] P. M. Caligiuri, M. M. Hyland, A. Joshi, and A. S. Bross, "Testing a Theoretical Model for Examining the Relationship Between Family Adjustment and Expatriates' Work Adjustment," *Journal of Applied Psychology* 83 (1998): 598–614.

[76] The information described here was provided by Paula Caligiuri, personal correspondence, October 1998. See also V. Frazee, "Selecting Global Assignees," *Global Workforce* (July 1998): 28–29.

[77] M. E. Mendenhall, E. Dunbar, and G. R. Oddou, "Expatriate Selection, Training and Career-Pathing: A Review and Critique," *Human Resource Management* (Fall 1987): 331; J. S. Black, M. Mendenhall, and G. Oddou, "Toward a Comprehensive Model of International Adjustment: An Integration of Multiple Theoretical Perspectives," *Academy of Management Review* 16, no. 2 (1991): 291–317.

[78] P. J. Dowling, D. E. Welch, and R. S. Schuler, *International Human Resource Management*.

[79] "Age Bias in Germany," *Fair Employment Practices Guidelines* (December 17, 1992): 145.

[80] R. Kopp, *The Rice Paper Ceiling: Breaking Through Japanese Corporate Culture* (New York: Stone Bridge Press, 1994).

[81] D. Greising, *I'd Like the World to Buy a Coke: The Life and Leadership of Roberto Goizueta* (New York: John Wiley, 1998); P. Sellers, "Where Coke Goes From Here," *Fortune* (October 13, 1997): 88–91; J. Huey, "In Search of Roberto's Secret Formula," *Fortune* (December 29, 1997): 230–234; G. Collins, "Left Alone at the Food Fight," *New York Times* (July 16, 1997): D1, D4; L. Bongiorno and S. Anderson, "Fiddling with the Formula at Pepsi," *Business Week* (October 14, 1996): 42; P. Sellers, "Pepsico's New Generation," *Fortune* (April 1, 1996): 110–118; P. Sellers, "Pepsi Opens a Second Front," *Fortune* (August 8, 1994): 70–75. P. Cappelli and A. Crocker-Hefter, *Distinctive Human Resources Are the Core Competencies of Firms*, Report No. R117 Q00011-91 (Washington, DC: U.S. Department of Education, 1994).

Answers to Managing Diversity: Designing Application Blanks with Fairness in Mind

In most situations, it's probably fine to ask questions 3, 6 (when driving is required on the job), 11 and 20 (if job requires travel). Question 12 could be asked in this way, "Is there any condition you have that might make it impossible to perform 'essential job functions' even after some accommodation?" Even here, however, the applicant should be volunteering this information. It's probably best to ask this after a decision to hire has been made. Forget about the rest. They are questions that shouldn't be asked.

Chapter

9

> "There's no magic. What will make all the difference in business will be how well you train your workforce, how well you motivate—and how well you empower."
>
> **Robert Eaton**
> **CEO**
> **Chrysler Corporation**[1]

SOCIALIZATION, TRAINING, AND DEVELOPMENT: ENSURING WORKFORCE CAPABILITY

Chapter Outline

MANAGING THROUGH PARTNERSHIP

at General Motors

Bill Lovejoy, the general manager of the Service Parts Operations (SPO) division of General Motors, didn't believe that his division's employees were performing at their highest levels of productivity potential. Performing to their highest levels meant serving the needs of their customers, the GM dealers, AC Delco distributors and other retailers—all folks who depend upon "having the right part at the right time at the right price." While the division had already achieved productivity gains through changes in systems and processes, Lovejoy believed that the employees still had not maximized their potential for productivity gains.

To prove his point, Mr. Lovejoy brought in some of the division's customers to hear their views on the quality of the service SPO was delivering. In addition to hearing that the customers weren't satisfied, Lovejoy and his top management team read the results of a survey that SPO had participated in for warehousing and parts supplier companies. The results indicated that SPO came in tenth place out of ten companies in their service provided. Lovejoy and his management team believed that achieving higher levels of customer satisfaction and employee productivity would require better supervisory and leadership competencies.

So, Lovejoy and others at SPO invited in the consulting firm of Development Dimensions International (DDI) to: (1) assess the desired leadership competencies, including personal leadership characteristics, and communication and implementation competencies; (2) assess the level of competencies currently possessed by the SPO managers; (3) provide training; and (4) offer personal coaching. Although the SPO wanted to make changes affecting all 12,350 of its employees, it decided to start with a pilot location. As it turned out, one location, a facility in Fort Worth, Texas, wanted to assess the business impact of its HR initiatives, so this DDI program would fit with their needs exactly.

The General Motors unit and DDI developed an assessment center in 1995 for the 100 employees of the pilot location. The center, which then ran for two days, used a variety of management tools such as in-box exercises, to identify the strengths and weaknesses of the desired leadership competencies. Using the results of the assessment center, each supervisor developed an individualized development plan in consultation with the DDI staff. The general manager of the pilot location, Aubrey Woodfolk, was very supportive of the desired leadership competencies that Lovejoy and senior management wanted, namely those focusing on empowerment and individual and team accountability. The pilot location manager and Lovejoy wanted to see the behaviors of their managers change as a result of the DDI development programs. They also wanted to see a favorable impact on the business as a consequence. Rod Driggett, the director of operations effectiveness, took the lead in evaluating the impact and success of the development programs.

Using a variety of employee satisfaction measures, SPO concluded that the culture of the pilot location had changed in the right direction and that employees were more satisfied with their working conditions, their feelings about the company and their satisfaction with their supervisors. While these were desirable, Lovejoy wanted to know the impact of these changes on the rest of the business. So the pilot location was compared with rest of the locations (which served as the control group for the study). Starting from being fifteen percent less favorable than the control group locations, by the end of 1996, the pilot location was better on the following business criteria:

(1) scheduling attainment;

(2) quality (errors per order line);

(3) productivity (lines shipped per hour);

(4) health and safety (recordable injuries per 200,000 hours worked); and

(5) absenteeism.

The overall conclusion, based on the above findings was that the Fort Worth facility improved its organization culture and its business performance during the time the leadership intervention was being implemented. SPO leadership concluded that the positive changes were in fact due to the leadership development intervention. Aubrey Woodfolk further developed measures of the business impact of the leadership development intervention. Woodfolk concluded that of the facility's 21 percent improvement in productivity from 1994-1996, at least 30 percent could be attributed to the intervention. This represented approximately $1.2 million savings in its operating budget. To cost justify the intervention, management had estimated that the productivity improvement from the intervention would have to be seven percent. Thus the leadership development intervention was regarded as a success and has since been expanded to the other facilities within SPO.[2]

To learn more about General Motors, visit the company home page at **www.gm.com**

GM's leadership development process is representative of what many outstanding organizations are doing today. Namely, these firms are using training and development to become more productive and align behaviors with their overall strategy, in this case high quality, customer satisfaction, but at a low cost. The General Motors example also highlights the importance of leadership training in changing a company's culture and its business performance. It also shows how systematically training and development is being done. First GM did a pilot test. Then it carefully evaluated its impact, both on the culture and the business. Finally this example highlights the extensive partnership involved in delivering development programs: senior line managers, customers, HR professional, and outside consultants all worked together to achieve the results.

STRATEGIC IMPORTANCE OF SOCIALIZATION, TRAINING, AND DEVELOPMENT

Employee socialization, training, and development are an organization's *intentional* efforts to improve current and future performance by increasing capabilities.[3] Specifically, *socialization* refers to teaching the corporate culture and philosophies about how to do business, *training* refers to improving competencies needed today or very soon, and *development* refers to improving competencies over the long term. In practice, of course, these apparently clear distinctions become blurred, since the three types of activities are components of an (ideally) integrated system. This system is referred to simply as a training system, even though it encompasses all three components.

Upon entry into a new job or a new organization, all employees initially need to "learn the ropes." Through socialization, they learn how things are done in the new environment, including things they can't find written in any policy-and-procedures manual.[4] In addition, new hires may have insufficient skills. For other employees, technological changes and job redesign may create the need for new job skills. Employees who are transferred or promoted may require new skills and knowledge. A new product may require technologies not before used by employees. Changes in company strategy may mean that senior management needs to adopt new leadership behavior and acquire new business knowledge. In some of these cases, the need for socialization, training, and development can be immediate; in others, future needs can be anticipated and planned.[5]

Socialization, training, and development serve many strategic purposes. Perhaps most importantly, they create shared experiences and understanding among employees with many different histories and so help speed the development of organizational cohesiveness and employee commitment. Of course, they also arm employees with the competencies they need to perform well in both their current and future positions. As the feature Managing Strategically: Trident Trains for Quality Improvement[6] explains, the adoption of a total quality management philosophy often demands investing in training in order to ensure operational success.

■□ fast fact

Before Merrill Lynch employees can become telecommuters, they complete a grueling training program that includes spending two weeks in a simulation lab.

MANAGING STRATEGICALLY
Trident Trains for Quality Improvement

Based in Webster, New York, Trident Precision Manufacturing fabricates sheet metal for customers such as Xerox, Kodak, and IBM. The company seemed to be humming along back in the late 1980s. Customers were happy and profits were good. But employees were leaving the company at a brisk pace. "The irony of it all was that people were leaving for as little as a nickel [more] down the street," recalled April Lusk, the company's total quality manager. CEO Nick Juskiw knew there must be a better way. After attending a Xerox presentation titled "Leadership Through Quality," Juskiw ended up spearheading the company's total quality approach. Within ten years, Trident was awarded the Malcolm Baldrige National Quality Award. The company attributes much of their success to a clear vision that focused on improving their approach to managing their human resources.

When the top executives began analyzing the company's weaknesses, they realized that they needed to start valuing employees more. A decade ago, Trident's managers didn't care who they hired so long as they were breathing and could do the job. The approach clearly wasn't working. Far too many products came off the line with major defects that required them to be redone completely. A change in the corporate culture was needed. Their informal motto seemed to sum up the problem: "We make it nice because we make it twice."

Top management officially recognized the importance of having truly committed employees when they identified their five key business drivers:
- Supplier partnerships
- Operational performance
- Customer satisfaction
- Shareholder value
- Employee satisfaction

To achieve their goal of completely reshaping the corporate culture would require a major investment in education and training. They set as a goal delivering a 25-hour quality training course to every employee. In addition to basic problem solving and communication skills, employees learned to read blueprints and solve problems using trigonometry. During the past decade, Trident has spent 4.7 percent of its payroll costs on training—more than three times as much as the industry average.

Trident's investment in training has brought handsome returns. In one year, employees typically make over 2000 process improvement suggestions, of which about 98 percent are implemented. Defects dropped from 3 percent to .007 percent. Turnover dropped from 41 percent to 3.5 percent, creating enormous saving due to reduced recruitment and selection costs. And, according to recent surveys, over 90 percent of employees report being satisfied with their work.

Commitment

When done well, socialization, or orientation creates intensely loyal employees. Companies that have perfected the socialization process include IBM, Wal-Mart, Procter and Gamble, and Morgan Guaranty Trust Company of New York. Often, the socialization process begins before the employee is hired.[7] At Procter and Gamble (P&G), for example, an elite cadre of line managers trained in interviewing skills probes applicants for entry-level positions in brand management, for qualities such as the "ability to turn out high volumes of excellent work." Through the interviewers' questions, applicants begin to learn about the organization's culture. Only after successfully completing at least two interviews and a test of general knowledge are applicants flown to P&G headquarters in Cincinnati, Ohio, where they endure a day-long series of interviews. These interviews are two-way communications that continue the socialization process at the same time that selection decisions are being made. If applicants pass the extensive screening process, they then confront a series of rigorous job experiences calculated to induce humility and openness to new ways of doing things. Typically, this phase of socialization involves long hours of work in a pressure cooker environment. Throughout this phase, new employees learn transcendent company values and organizational folklore, including the importance of product quality and stories about the dedication and commitment of employees long since retired. Intense socialization such as this increases employees' commitment to the success of the company. Commitment, in turn, translates into a greater willingness to work long hours, less absenteeism and lower turnover rates.

Performance

After the initial socialization period come training and development. A major purpose of training is to remove deficiencies, whether current or anticipated, that cause employees to perform at less than the desired level. Training for immediate performance improvement is particularly important to organizations with stagnant or declining rates of productivity. It's also important to organizations that are rapidly incorporating new technologies and consequently increasing the likelihood of employee obsolescence. With their longer-term focus, development activities prepare employees for future

■□ fast fact

Andersen Consulting spends six percent of revenues on education. Professional employees complete at least 130 hours of training each year.

career moves, even if these haven't yet been identified. Development activities also ensure that employees are qualified for the positions to which they aspire.

Training and development are vital to organizations adapting to the new, more competitive business environment. Like socialization, training and development can strengthen the level of commitment of employees to the organization and magnify their perceptions that the organization is a good place to work. Stronger commitment can result in less turnover and absenteeism, thus increasing an organization's productivity. More and more, experts are recognizing that training and development can benefit society by enabling individuals to be productive and contribute to their organizations. These are among the reasons why U.S. corporations spend an estimated $60 billion annually on formal employee training programs that use an estimated 1.5 billion hours of time for the more than 56 million employees who participate.[8]

In some companies, managers view socialization, training, and development as too costly and too long-term to justify.[9] At other companies, annual training budgets register in the millions. For example, at Motorola, training represents four percent of total payroll and about one percent of annual sales. Motorola gives all employees at least forty hours of training a year, and hopes to quadruple this number by the year 2000. A commitment to training investment by past leaders such as Sam Walton of Wal-Mart, Robert Galvin of Motorola, and D. Wayne Calloway of PepsiCo is critical to the success of an organization's efforts. The rewards for top management's support are impressive: "Motorola calculates that every $1 it spends on training delivers $30 in productivity gains within three years."[10]

THE PARTNERSHIP PERSPECTIVE

Without top management support and commitment, the major focus of an organization is likely to be on other activities. This is particularly true when the organization has short-term goals and desires immediate results; this situation allows too little time to wait for the benefits of training and development. Top managers at Motorola, Dell, Microsoft, GE, GM, Coca-Cola, Ritz-Carlton, the Four Seasons, and PepsiCo began to emphasize training and development at the same time they recognized that they had to develop their people and businesses in order to be effective.[11]

Although a few exceptional companies recognize the value of training investments, most U.S. companies invest much less than their competitors in other regions of the world. A study of seventy auto-assembly plants from twenty-four companies in seventeen countries showed that newly hired production workers in U.S.-owned plants received an average of only about forty hours of training during their first six months on the job. That compares with an average of about 300 hours for similar workers in plants owned by citizens of Japan and about 260 hours for similar workers in plants headquartered in the newly industrialized countries of Korea, Mexico, Taiwan, and Brazil.[12]

Role of Employees

The effectiveness of an organization's training system requires the support and cooperation of all employees in the system—top management's support alone isn't sufficient. For example, self-managed teams often take responsi-

■□ fast fact

Intel, which makes computer chips, spends more than $120 million a year on training, an average of $3,000 per worker, more than double the national average.

"The development of our best people is the personal responsibility of management."

Robert C. Goizueta
Former CEO
Coca-Cola

bility for training their own members.[13] Similarly, as organizations begin to embrace a philosophy of continuous learning and improvement, more active participation in the design and delivery of the organization's training system by all stakeholders is seen as both desirable and necessary. The feature, The HR Triad: Partnership Roles and Responsibilities in Socialization, Training, and Development, shows some activities for the line manager, the HR professional, and the employee.

   Although most employees aren't actively involved in designing and delivering training systems, most organizations depend heavily on employees seeking opportunities to use the available system to their advantage. For example, many companies sponsor informal events designed to provide employees opportunities to meet other people in the company, develop informal networks and support groups, and even establish mentoring relationships. By participating in such activities, employees facilitate their own socialization into the organization, and potentially reap longer-term benefits

THE HR TRIAD: PARTNERSHIP ROLES AND RESPONSIBILITIES IN SOCIALIZATION, TRAINING, AND DEVELOPMENT

Line Managers	HR Professionals	Employees
Cooperate with HR professionals in identifying the implications of business plans for socialization, training, and development.	Identify socialization, training, and development needs in cooperation with line managers.	Identify their own training and development needs with HR professionals and line managers.
Participate in the delivery of socialization, training, and development programs.	Assist employees in identifying their individual training and development needs.	Accept responsibility for learning about training and development opportunities.
Work with employees to determine individual needs.	Communicate with employees regarding training and development opportunities and the consequences of participating in them.	Evaluate employment opportunities from the perspective of the potential for personal learning and development.
Support employees' participation in training and development opportunities and reinforce the transfer of newly learned behaviors to the job.	Develop and administer the socialization, training, and development opportunities.	Actively participate in socialization, training, and development opportunities.
Do much of on-the-job socialization and training.	Train the line managers and employees in how to socialize, train, and develop employees.	Assist with the socialization, training, and development of coworkers.
Participate in efforts to assess training effectiveness.	Evaluate the effectiveness of socialization, training, and development activities.	Participate in efforts to assess the effectiveness of socialization, training, and development activities.

such as greater income, job satisfaction, and a better sense of personal identity.[14] Formal activities may also be offered to employees on a voluntary basis. For example, career-planning workshops, tuition reimbursement for job-related course work, and support for attending professional conferences are often available. Research indicates that these opportunities are more likely to be used by employees who acknowledge their own needs for improvement and have developed a specific career plan.[15]

Linking with the Needs of Customers

Organizations can use their socialization, training, and development activities to link with the needs of customers. Siemens USA—one of the world's leading manufacturers of high-technology equipment—conducts a variety of training programs for its 27,000 employees, as well as for its customers. Courses are designed to meet the special needs of customers and their markets. For example, on-the-job training for customers ensures that all the capabilities of the company's technologically advanced systems are fully utilized, and all their benefits are fully realized.

Similarly, in the low-margin, highly competitive world of department store sales, Seattle-based Nordstrom has turned exacting standards of customer service into a billion-dollar annual business. A major ingredient in Nordstrom's success is the quality of the salesclerks. They're paid about 20 percent better than those of competitors, and they're selected, trained, and encouraged to do almost anything within reason to satisfy customers.[16]

The growing importance of a business philosophy focused on the customer means training activities are on the rise in many companies across America today. As these companies are discovering, effective training is a relatively complex and challenging activity, owing in part to the multitude of relationships training and development have with other human resource activities, and the fact that it's never ending. New people are always joining the company and technology is continually changing.

> *"No nation can thrive in the modern world without investing in its people. This is why national statistics on savings should include the cost of investing in human capital."*
>
> **Gary S. Becker**
> **The 1992 Nobel Laureate teaches at the University of Chicago**

DETERMINING TRAINING AND DEVELOPMENT NEEDS

Socialization is needed by almost any new employee and by current employees moving into new jobs or to new units within the company. Therefore, formal assessments of an individual's need for socialization are seldom undertaken. Formal assessments may occur, however, based on employees' individual circumstances. Whether accurate or not, for example, companies or managers may assume that applicants recruited from sources that have yielded good performers in the past need little socialization. They may also assume that internal placements require less socialization than new hires.

Most often training is offered on the basis of need—to rectify skill deficiencies, to provide employees with job-specific competencies, or to prepare employees for future roles they may be given.[17] Employees, however, sometimes receive training for reasons other than need. For example, in some organizations, attendance at an executive training program serves as a reward for past performance. In other organizations, participation in training programs is a ritual that signals to newly promoted employees as well as to members of their former work groups that a change in status has occurred (e.g., a rank-and-file employee is now a manager).

A formal needs assessment is a vital part of a training system.[18] Without determining the need for training, an organization can't guarantee that the right training will be provided for the right trainees. The role of needs assessment in the overall training model is detailed in Exhibit 9.1.[19]

Exhibit 9.1
Training Program Model

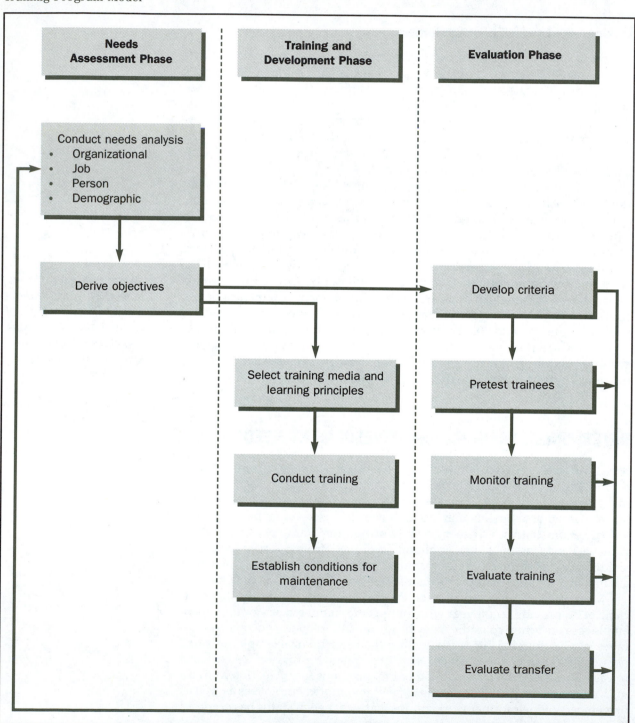

Organizational Needs Analysis

According to many training experts, attaining the objectives of the business should be the ultimate concern of any training and development effort. Therefore, conducting an organizational needs analysis should be the first step in effective needs assessment. It begins with an examination of the short- and long-term objectives of the organization and the trends that are likely to affect these objectives. It can include a human resource analysis, analyses of efficiency indexes, and an assessment of the organizational climate.

The organizational needs analysis should translate the organization's objectives into an accurate estimate of the demand for human resources. Efficiency indexes including cost of labor, quantity of output (productivity), quality of output, waste, and equipment use and repairs can provide useful information. The organization can determine standards for these indexes and then analyze them to evaluate the general effectiveness of training programs.

Organizational analysis also can address the organization's performance in the "softer" domains that constitute the corporate culture. For example, it may reveal a misalignment between the current value system in the organization and the values espoused by top management. Many companies today espouse values such as focusing on customers, following ethical business practices, and supporting diversity, yet behavior within these companies may fail to reflect those values. In such cases, training for everyone in the company, regardless of their specific job, may be needed.[20]

Different Strategies, Different Needs.   Even if they're in the same industry, two companies with different business strategies may adopt very different training systems, as illustrated in the feature, Managing Strategically at Boston Consulting Group vs. McKinsey and Company.[21]

MANAGING STRATEGICALLY
Boston Consulting Group vs. McKinsey and Company

Boston Consulting Group (BCG) and McKinsey and Company are among the world's leading strategic consulting firms. Both have worldwide operations, and their reputations for thoughtful leadership and quality service to management are comparable. Both hire from the best undergraduate and MBA programs, competing for the top students. Both have rigorous selection procedures and exceptional compensation. Yet the characteristics of the people the two firms hire and the way these employees are managed differ in line with the ways the companies approach their markets.

Boston Consulting Group

BCG tends to attract candidates with very broad perspectives on business. Some previously started their own companies, and others leave BCG to found new companies. BCG also maintains something of a revolving door with academia, hiring business school professors as consultants and sometimes losing consultants to faculty positions in business schools. Once hired, consultants jump right into work, although they're closely supervised, and the formal training they receive is likely to be from outside courses.

BCG has an entrepreneurial environment, expecting each project team to come up with its own innovative approach. Each office is even thought to have a slightly different culture. BCG pays less than many of its competitors but offers more individualized incentive pay, reinforcing the entrepreneurial culture.

Although BCG has some "products," such as time-based competition and capabilities-based strategies, these approaches aren't the source of its competency. Indeed, some of them, like the Growth-Share matrix, are well publicized and basically given away. The value added comes from a customized application to the client's situation. Many of BCG's projects start not with these products but rather with a blank-slate approach. What clients buy, therefore, are original solutions and approaches to their problems. And these approaches begin with consultants whose varied backgrounds and entrepreneurial spirit help produce a unique product.

McKinsey and Company

McKinsey has historically hired all its new employees from on-campus recruiting and rarely hired from other employers. It tends to prefer candidates with backgrounds in technical areas, such as engineering and computer science, who have depth in some functional area of business. Its new entrants vary little in terms of management experience and come in with few consulting ideas. If McKinsey consultants leave, they're more likely to take senior line management positions in corporations than to move into entrepreneurial positions.

McKinsey provides new consultants with extensive training on the company's method of project execution and management, even though this is highly tailored to each client's situation. McKinsey's size—it employs 3,000 consultants, compared with 800 at BCG—may create scale economies in training new entrants that make it easier for the firm to provide programs itself. The firm expects the career path to the highest position, senior partner, to take approximately twelve years—versus six to eight years at BCG—which gives the consultants a long time to learn how to fit in.

In terms of its consulting product, the company is known for the "McKinsey way." McKinsey strives to provide its clients with consistent services; its clients know what to expect from the project teams. The firm's products and techniques are regarded as proprietary and aren't publicized. Its core competency, therefore, is in the consistent products and techniques that constitute the McKinsey way. To have consultants deliver that product in the same way across companies and countries, McKinsey takes bright people with strong skills and adapts them to the product. This standardization is especially notable given the far-reaching nature of McKinsey's empire. Half its senior partners are abroad, and 27 of the 33 offices it has opened since 1980 were outside the United States in 1994.

To learn more about these companies, visit their home pages at **www.mckinsey.com and www.bcg.com**

Increasingly, companies are recognizing that by establishing a new strategy and a new set of objectives, they create an immediate need for a major training and development initiative. Here, the organizational analysis begins by identifying the demands of the new strategy on human resources. Only after this is done can implications for training and development be identified. As companies such as Weyerhaeuser, GE, Eaton, Dell, GTE, Ameritech Corporation, Motorola, and AT&T have discovered, significant training and development needs often arise from strategy-driven changes in the nature of managerial jobs.

Job Needs Analysis

The specific content of present or anticipated jobs is examined through job analysis. For existing jobs, information on the tasks to be performed (contained in job descriptions), the skills necessary to perform those tasks (drawn from job qualifications), and the minimum acceptable standards (gleaned from performance appraisals) are gathered. This information can then be used to ensure that training programs are job specific and useful.

The process of collecting information for use in developing training programs is often referred to as job needs analysis. In this situation, the analysis method used should include questions specifically designed to assess the competencies needed to perform the job. Therefore, an integrated job analysis approach is appropriate.

For jobs that have yet to be created, expert information and predictions can be made relevant to their anticipated content and complexity. For example, in 1985, it was predicted that the next generation of manufacturing managers would need to know computer-aided design and computer-aided manufacturing (CAD/CAM), computer-integrated manufacturing (CIM), group technologies, flexible manufacturing, "just-in-time" inventory control, manufacturing resource planning (MRP), robotics, and a whole litany of other techniques and technologies in manufacturing. In addition, it was already clear back then that these new technologies would require managers who understand systems thinking and have a well-developed understanding of corporate strategies.[22] Companies that began preparing for this situation in 1985, by developing their future managerial talent, have a reasonable chance at surviving in today's hypercompetitive manufacturing environment.

Finally, the new technology would require a great deal of teamwork and cooperation. The growing importance of teamwork is changing the required competencies, and thus the training needs, for employees in many companies. Exhibit 9.2 profiles the competencies needed for employees in a team-oriented, total-quality, modern manufacturing plant.[23]

Person Needs Analysis

After information about the job has been collected, the analysis shifts to the person. A person needs analysis identifies gaps between a person's current capabilities and those identified as necessary or desirable. Person needs analysis can be either broad or narrow in scope. The broader approach compares actual performance with the minimum acceptable standards of performance. The narrower approach compares an evaluation of employee proficiency on each required skill dimension with the proficiency level required for each skill. The first method is based on the actual, current job performance of an employee; therefore, it can be used to determine training needs for the current job. The second method, on the other hand, can be used to identify development needs for future jobs.

Whether the focus is on performance of the job as a whole or on particular aspects of the job, several approaches can be used to identify the training needs of individuals.[24]

Output Measures. Performance data (e.g., productivity, accidents, customer complaints, as used in SPO division of General Motors), as well as performance appraisal ratings, can provide evidence of performance deficiencies. Person needs analysis can also consist of work sample and job

Exhibit 9.2
Team Member Competencies

Team member competencies

=

Ability to learn

+

Motivation to
- Work in participative environment
- Cooperate with management
- Seek feedback and recognition
- Exhibit high work standards
- Take on new responsibilities
- Work as a member of a team
- Solve work-related problems

+

Personal strengths
- Energy
- Physical ability and health

+

Job skills
- Technical knowledge
- Technical proficiency
- Analysis and decision making skills
- Personal organization skill

+

Interaction skills
- Influence
- Meeting membership
- Trainer–coach
- Communication

+

Action skills
- Initiative
- Innovation

Exhibit 9.3

Sample Questions from a Self-Administered Training Needs Survey

Please indicate in the blanks the extent to which *you* have a training need in each specific area. Use the scale below. To what extent do you need training in the following areas?

To no extent 1	2	3	4	To a very large extent 5

Basic Management Skills (Organizing, Planning, Delegating, Problem Solving)

_____ 1. Setting goals and objectives
_____ 2. Developing realistic time schedules to meet work requirements
_____ 3. Identifying and weighing alternative solutions
_____ 4. Organizing work activities

Interpersonal Skills

_____ 1. Resolving interpersonal conflicts
_____ 2. Creating a development plan for employees
_____ 3. Identifying and understanding individual employee needs
_____ 4. Conducting performance appraisal reviews

Administrative Skills

_____ 1. Maintaining equipment, tools, and safety controls
_____ 2. Understanding local agreements and shop rules
_____ 3. Preparing work flowcharts
_____ 4. Developing department budgets

Quality Control

_____ 1. Analyzing and interpreting statistical data
_____ 2. Constructing and analyzing charts, tables, and graphs
_____ 3. Using statistical software on the computer

identify which competencies are important for managerial effectiveness. Differences in opinions can serve as a basis of discussion about what is really necessary for managerial success in today's environment. Generally, the results of attitude surveys can contribute significantly to the design of a training program, as they did in the case of the SPO division of General Motors.

Demographic Needs Analysis

Organizations should conduct demographic studies to determine the training needs of specific populations of workers. More generally, research indicates that different groups have different training needs. Demographic needs analysis can also be used to assess whether all employees are given equal access to growth experiences and developmental challenges, which are known to be useful on-the-job methods for promoting skill development. For example, one large study of managers compared the developmental career experiences of men and women. In general, men were more likely to have been assigned to jobs that presented difficult task-related challenges (e.g., operation start-ups and "fix-it" assignments), whereas women were

knowledge tests that measure performance capability and knowledge. Major advantages of such measures are that

- they can be selected according to their strategic importance,
- they often are easily quantified, and
- when they show improvements, the value of training investments is readily apparent.

For example, a study of Michigan manufacturing firms that received state training grants showed that increasing training from fifteen to thirty hours reduced scrap by seven percent.[25] A major disadvantage is that such indicators reflect the past and may not be useful for anticipating future needs.

Self-Assessed Training Needs. The self-assessment of training needs is growing in popularity. At Motorola, for example, top managers require the employee and his or her supervisor to identify what the business needs are for the department and the business, as well as the skill needs and deficiencies of the individual. Many major U.S. firms allow managers to nominate themselves to attend short-term or company-sponsored training or education programs. Self-assessment can be as informal as posting a list of company-sponsored courses and asking who wants to attend, or as formal as conducting surveys regarding training needs.

Exhibit 9.3 shows sample questions from a managerial self-assessment survey.[26] Surveys are convenient tools for self-assessment, but more time-consuming methods may be needed in some circumstances. For example, if an organization is conducting a needs analysis on the topic of ethics, it might use interviews to ask managers to identify the issues that were most troubling to them. The themes identified by managers can then be used to create teaching cases that reflect the real-life ethical dilemmas that employees are likely to encounter.

Self-assessment is premised on the assumption that employees, more than anyone else, are aware of their weaknesses and performance deficiencies. Therefore, they're in the best position to identify their own training needs. One drawback of self-assessment is that individuals may not be aware of their weaknesses, especially if the organization does a poor job of providing honest feedback during performance appraisals. Also, employees may be fearful of revealing their weaknesses and so may not accurately report their training needs. In both cases, reliance on self-assessment may result in individuals not receiving education that's necessary for them to remain current in their fields. On the other hand, employees who are forced to attend programs that they believe they don't need or that don't meet their personal training needs are likely to become dissatisfied with training and to lack the motivation to learn and transfer competencies.

Attitude Surveys. Attitude surveys completed by a supervisor's subordinates or by customers or by both also can provide information on training needs. For example, when one supervisor receives low scores regarding her or his fairness in treating subordinates, compared with other supervisors in the organization, the supervisor may need training in that area.[27] Similarly, if the customers of a particular unit seem to be particularly dissatisfied compared with other customers, training may be needed in that unit. Thus, customer surveys can serve a dual role: providing information to management about service and pinpointing employee deficiencies.

Surveys can also be completed by higher-level managers to identify the development needs of the cadre below them. Such surveys can be used to

"People instin[c]
to lear[n]

Chairman and

more likely to have been assigned to jobs that presented challenges caused by obstacles to performance (e.g., a difficult boss or a lack of support from top management).[28] Presumably, successful performance in the face of task-related challenges is the more valuable currency in work organizations. Therefore, if a company finds demographic differences such as these, it might conclude that an intervention is needed to assure men and women equal access to valuable developmental challenges—and equal exposure to debilitating obstacles.

SETTING UP A TRAINING SYSTEM

Successful implementation of training and development programs depends on selecting the right programs for the right people under the right conditions.

Who Participates?

The answer to the question "Who will participate?" depends in part on the results of the person needs analysis. It also depends on how many employees are to be trained simultaneously. If only one or two employees are to be trained, then on-the-job approaches such as coaching are generally cost-effective. If large numbers of individuals need to be trained in a short period of time, then programmed instruction may be the most viable option.

When larger groups are to be trained, questions arise concerning how to sequence participation across groups and how to compose the groups. When everyone has been targeted as needing training, as is often the case with major corporate change efforts, top managers often participate first, and other employee groups are scheduled in hierarchical sequence. But as Medtronic learned when it introduced diversity training throughout the company, this common approach may not be the best: "[W]hen we trained [the] first corporate group, the managers told us they wished they had gone through with employees at other levels, so now we do that. We mix different levels of managers and supervisors in the same group, since that is a part of diversity as well."[29]

Decisions about who participates in a group training session may influence how much learning occurs during the session. Furthermore, when employees who work side by side attend training sessions together, they may find it easier to transfer their learning back to the work site because coworkers can provide feedback and friendly coaching.[30]

Who Provides?

Socialization, training, and development activities may be provided by any of several people, including

- the supervisor;
- a coworker, such as a lead worker or a buddy;
- an internal or external subject matter expert; and
- the employee.

The person or people selected to teach often depends on where the program is held and what skills or competencies are taught. Literacy and technical competencies are usually taught by the immediate job supervisor or a coworker, although technical competencies may also be taught by internal or external subject matter experts. A basic organizational orientation is usually handled by a member of the HR staff. Interpersonal, conceptual, and integrative competencies for management are often taught by training specialists, university professors, or consultants.

A concern with relying on supervisors and coworkers as trainers is that although they may perform adequately, they may not be able to instruct others. They may also teach others their own shortcuts rather than correct procedures. On the other hand, immediate supervisors or coworkers may be more knowledgeable than anyone else about work procedures. If coworkers or managers are to be trainers, they should receive instruction on how to train and should be given sufficient time on the job to work with trainees.

Subject matter experts may not be familiar with procedures in a specific organizational culture. As a result, they may be respected for their expertise but mistrusted because they aren't members of the work group. Still, if no one in the immediate work environment possesses the knowledge needed, or if large numbers of individuals need to be trained, the only option may be to hire experts.

Self-paced instruction is also an option. Trainees benefit from this method by learning at a speed that maximizes retention. However, if they aren't given incentives to complete the instruction in a specified period of time, they may place it on the back burner.

DEVELOPING PROGRAM CONTENT

A training program must have content congruent with its learning objectives. Three types of learning objectives that the organization may be concerned about are cognitive knowledge, skill-based outcomes, and affective outcomes.[31]

Cognitive Knowledge

Cognitive knowledge includes the information people have available to themselves (what they know), the way they organize this information, and their strategies for using this information. Of these, what people know is by far the type of cognitive knowledge that most organizations try to address through training systems.

Company Policies and Practices. Orientation programs are frequently used for building cognitive knowledge. These programs brief new employees on benefit programs and options, advise them of rules and regulations, and explain the policies and practices of the organization.

Typically, orientation programs inform new employees about equal employment opportunity practices, safety regulations, work times, coffee breaks, the structure and history of the organization, and perhaps the products or services of the organization. Usually, they don't tell employees about the politics of the organization—for example, that the organization may soon be going out of business, that it may be merging with another company, or even that an extensive layoff may soon occur.

Basic Knowledge and the Three Rs. Increasingly, organizations are concerned about cognitive knowledge of a more basic nature: the three Rs (reading, writing, and arithmetic). Training programs designed to correct basic skill deficiencies in grammar, mathematics, safety, reading, listening, and writing are still necessary in today's organization. In particular, as the movement toward total quality management grows, the importance of basic math and statistical knowledge grows. The feature, Managing Change: Improving Quality at Ritz-Carlton, shows how this applies to service-oriented firms.[32]

Statistical tools are fundamental to W. Edwards Deming's approach to quality, which is improvement by the numbers. To improve quality, one must know the causes of poor quality. *Statistical process control (SPC)* techniques provide employees a means for determining these causes. SPC is the practice of using the tools of statistics to help control the quality of operating processes.

Also basic to total quality is knowledge about how to diagnose and solve problems. A fishbone diagram (see Exhibit 9.4) provides a cognitive strategy

MANAGING CHANGE

Improving Quality at Ritz-Carlton

It seems clear that the training function in Ritz-Carlton Hotels has earned a healthy respect as the major force in quality improvement. While this may be partly—or even mostly—a result of being in the hospitality industry, the company still serves as an interesting model for close quality/training interface.

At a time when the company had no training positions in the hotels, one of the regional vice presidents implemented a training position and presented the description of it to the president of the company. Since then, training has been a critical part of the organization, with a training manager in each hotel. Like many other organizations, the Ritz-Carlton's training program has undergone changes as a result of the company's journey into quality management. Their decision to go for the Baldrige Award for Quality had a particularly big influence. "The Baldrige application forced us to take a look at business process design in a way that we had never really done before," explained one manager. "Right now we are looking at cycle time, such as how long it takes from the moment guests walk in, until they're in their rooms. We've done customer surveys and are studying eighteen cycle times throughout our systems to see where we are as an organization. Then we will be able to judge how to decrease cycle times by taking out the nonvalued elements from jobs. Using the check-in example, if we want to reduce cycle time to two minutes, we may discover we can have the desk receptionists skip an explanation of the in-room bar service and have the bell staff do that job. Of course, then we must retrain." Another way that the quality initiatives feed into training is through the hotels' feedback forms. Internal Defect Reports are to be completed by any employee when systems go wrong.

"When the information is compiled and supplied to the hotel's general manager (gm) on a daily basis, it gives the manager a valuable look at what actually went on in the hotel that day. Otherwise a gm might look at the dollar and guest numbers and think, 'Well, we had a bang up day.' This way, the gm can get all the information about the hotel. And the beauty of the system is that it's tracked over time. So, something like the problem of the availability of nonsmoking rooms could be pinpointed to a certain pattern. Maybe there's a shortage only on Sundays because that's when the rooms are taken out for deep cleaning. The objective in all our work with the defect reports is to better serve guests and internal customers. The more problems we can detect, the fewer there are to be seen by guests." And, of course, the more new processes put in place to detect problems, the more training employees need in order to use those new processes effectively.

To learn more about Ritz-Carlton Hotels, visit the company home page at **www.ritzcarlton.com**

Exhibit 9.4
Fishbone Diagram for Total Quality Management

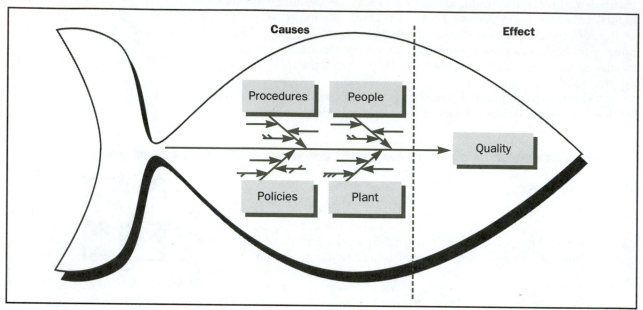

and a way of structuring information that facilitates effective use of available information. Thus, basic knowledge about fishbone diagrams can help employees analyze the procedures, people, policies, and plant characteristics that are helping or hindering a company's efforts to improve its quality.

The Big Picture.   Employees striving for or currently in managerial positions may need knowledge about the organizational structure, the organization's products and services, the organization's business strategies, and changing conditions in the environment. Much of this type of knowledge is learned through standard job assignments as well as through temporary developmental learning experiences, such as serving on a task force or taking an overseas assignment. Adapting to complex and changing environments is often a responsibility for top and middle managers, and conceptual training helps such employees make new associations. Cognitive knowledge is at the heart of today's emphasis on creativity and entrepreneurship, and on making major changes in an organization's strategy, objectives, vision, and values at firms such as Microsoft, GE, GTE, Dell, GM, Weyerhaeuser, and Eaton.

Improved Skills

Skill-based outcomes of training programs include the development of technical and motor skills.[33] Whereas cognitive knowledge is, essentially, inside the head, skills are evident in behaviors. Whereas cognitive learning often involves studying and attending to information, skill-based learning generally involves practicing desired behaviors.

Owing to rapid changes in technology and the implementation of automated offices, industrial and managerial systems, technological updating and skill building have become a major thrust in training. Skills in communication, conducting performance appraisals, team building, leadership, and negotiation are also increasingly in demand. The development of interpersonal competencies is essential for lower- and middle-level managers as well as for employees who interface with the public, such as sales associates.

Affective Outcomes

When the desired result of socialization, training, or developmental experiences is a change in motivation, attitudes, or values, or all three, the learning objectives of interest are affective outcomes.

At the Walt Disney Company, all newly hired "cast members" participate in an orientation and training program at Disney University. New hires first receive an overview of the company and learn about its traditions, history, achievements, and philosophy. In addition, they learn about the key Disney "product"—happiness—and their roles in helping to provide it. Next, each cast member learns about the benefits—health, social, recreational—of being part of the Disney "family"; gains more direct information about his or her role in the production; and has a tour of the complex. Tailored to reflect the needs of each type of cast member and group, the initial orientation and subsequent training have a theme of bringing new hires into the family and developing a team spirit, as well as a focus on courtesy to guests, safety, and putting on a good show (entertainment).[34]

The objectives of building team spirit and socializing employees into the corporate culture aren't the only affective outcomes of a training system. In fact, training activities often are designed in part to develop employees' feelings of mastery and self-confidence. For example, mentoring programs not only provide information, they also provide the feedback and supportive encouragement that give employees confidence in their ability to take on new tasks and make decisions that might otherwise seem too risky. Self-confidence enhances task performance. This is a point not lost on athletes, their coaches, or sportscasters—nor, apparently, is it lost on the many companies now providing wilderness training. Although the evidence is sparse, testimonials and some research indicate that participating in outdoor group adventures boosts self-confidence.[35]

CHOOSING A PROGRAM LOCATION

Three types of locations for training activities are on the job, on-site but not on the job, and off-site. Decisions about location may be constrained by the type of learning that's to occur—cognitive, skill based, or affective—as well as by cost and time considerations. Exhibit 9.5 summarizes the advantages and disadvantages of several learning formats according to their location.

On the Job

On-the-job training (OJT) occurs when employees learn their jobs under direct supervision. Trainees learn by observing experienced employees and by working with the actual materials, personnel, or machinery, or all three, that constitute the job. An experienced employee trainer is expected to provide a favorable role model and to take time from regular job responsibilities to provide job-related instruction and guidance.

One advantage of OJT is that transfer of training is high. That is, because trainees learn job skills in the environment in which they will actually work, they readily apply these skills on the job. Assuming the trainer works in the same area, the trainee receives immediate feedback about performance.

Exhibit 9.5

Advantages and Disadvantages of Training Programs by Location

Type of Program	Advantages	Disadvantages
On the Job		
Job instruction training	Facilitates transfer of learning	Interferes with performance
	Does not require separate facilities	Damages equipment
Apprenticeship training	Does not interfere with real job performance	Takes a long time
		Is expensive
	Provides extensive training	May not be related to job
Internships and assistantships	Facilitate transfer of learning	Are not really full jobs
	Give exposure to real job	Provide vicarious learning
Job rotation	Gives exposure to many jobs	Involves no sense of full responsibility
	Allows real learning	Provides too short a stay in a job
Supervisory assistance and mentoring	Is informal	Means effectiveness rests with the supervisor
	Is integrated into job	
	Is inexpensive	May not be done by all supervisors
On-Site But Not on the Job		
Programmed instruction	Provides for individualized learning and feedback	Is time-consuming to develop
	Provides for fast learning	Is cost-effective only for large groups
Videotapes	Convey consistent information to employees in diverse locations	Are costly to develop
	Are more portable than film	Do not provide for individual feedback
Videodisks	Store more information than tapes	Are extremely costly to develop
	Allow for fast-forward	Offer limited courseware
	Are portable	
Interactive video training	Draws on more senses	Is costly to develop and implement
	Provides for self-paced learning and feedback	Requires diverse staff to develop
Telecommunication training	Provides for latest insights and knowledge	Is costly and difficult to set up
	Speeds up communications	Is not feasible for small firms
	Is standardized	
Off the Job		
Formal courses	Are inexpensive for many	Require verbal skills
	Do not interfere with job	Inhibit transfer of learning
Simulation	Helps transfer of learning	Cannot always duplicate real situations exactly
	Creates lifelike situations	
Assessment centers	Provide a realistic job preview	Are expensive to develop
	Creates lifelike situations	Take time to administer
Role playing	Is good for interpersonal skills	Cannot create real situations exactly; is still playing
	Gives insights into others	
Sensitivity training	Is good for self-awareness	May not transfer to job
	Gives insights into others	May not relate to job
Wilderness trips	Build teams	Are costly to administer
	Build self-esteem	Are physically challenging

However, on-site training is appropriate only when a small number of individuals need to be trained and when the consequence of error is low. Also, the quality of the training hinges on the skill of the manager or lead employee conducting it.[36]

Job Instruction Training. The disadvantages of on-the-job training can be minimized by making the training program as systematic and complete as possible. Job instruction training (JIT) was developed to provide a guide for giving on-the-job training to white-collar and blue-collar employees as well as technicians.[37] Because JIT is a technique rather than a program, it can be adapted to training efforts for all employees in off-the-job as well as on-the-job programs.

JIT consists of four steps: (1) careful selection and preparation of the trainer and the trainee for the learning experience to follow; (2) a full explanation and demonstration by the trainer of the job to be done; (3) a trial on-the-job performance by the trainee; and (4) a thorough feedback session to discuss the trainee's performance and the job requirements.

Apprenticeship Training, Internships, and Assistantships. Another method for minimizing the disadvantages of on-the-job training is combining it with off-the-job training. Apprenticeship training, internships, and assistantships are based on this combination.

Apprenticeship training is mandatory for admission to many skilled trades, such as plumbing, electronics, and carpentry. These programs are formally defined by the U.S. Department of Labor's Bureau of Apprenticeship and Training and involve a written agreement "providing for not less than 4,000 hours of reasonably continuous employment . . . and supplemented by a recommended minimum of 144 hours per year of related classroom instruction." The Equal Employment Opportunity Commission allows the United States' 48,000 skilled trade (apprenticeship) training programs to exclude individuals aged 40 to 70, because these programs are part of the educational system aimed at youth.[38] To be most effective, the on- and off-the-job components of an apprenticeship program must be well integrated and appropriately planned and must recognize individual differences.

Somewhat less formalized and extensive are the internship and assistantship programs. Internships are often part of an agreement between schools and colleges, and local organizations. As with apprenticeship training, individuals in these programs earn while they learn, but at a lower rate than that paid to full-time employees or master crafts workers. Internships are a source not only of training but also of realistic exposure to job and organizational conditions. Hewlett-Packard's internship program enables the company to evaluate college students and prepare them for future jobs.[39]

Assistantships involve full-time employment and expose an individual to a wide range of jobs. However, because the individual only *assists* other workers, the learning experience is often vicarious. This disadvantage is eliminated by programs that combine job or position rotation with active mentoring and career management.

Job Rotation. Job rotation programs are used to expose employees to and train them in a variety of jobs and decision-making situations. The extent of training and long-run benefits it provides may be limited, because employees aren't in a single job long enough to learn very much and may not be motivated to work hard since they know they will move on in the near future.

Supervisory Assistance and Mentoring.   Often the most informal program of training and development is supervisory assistance or mentoring. Supervisory assistance is a regular part of the supervisor's job. It includes day-to-day coaching, counseling, and monitoring of workers on how to do the job and how to get along in the organization. The effectiveness of these techniques depends in part on whether the supervisor creates feelings of mutual confidence, provides opportunities for growth, and effectively delegates tasks.

Mentoring, in which an established employee guides the development of a less-experienced worker, or protégé, can increase employees' competencies, achievement and understanding of the organization.[40] At AT&T, for example, protégés are usually chosen from among high-potential employees in middle- or entry-level management. Each executive is encouraged to select two people to mentor, and must decide how to develop the relationships. Usually, executives counsel their protégé on how to advance and network in the company, and they sometimes offer personal advice.

Coaching.   For high-level executives and other employees who hold visible and somewhat unique jobs, traditional forms of on-the-job training are impractical. Yet, these employees often need to develop new competencies in order to be fully effective. In recent years, more and more executives have turned to personal coaches to address their training needs. A coach might sit in on a meeting to observe the employee in action, and later provide feedback and guidance for how to improve their interaction skills in the future. Most coaches also encourage their "trainees" to discuss difficult situations as they arise and work through alternative scenarios for dealing with those situations. Although coaching is rapidly growing in popularity, it's a relatively new technique. Evidence of its effectiveness has not yet been documented and few guidelines are available to evaluate whether a potential coaching relationship is likely to succeed.[41]

On-Site but Not on the Job

Training at the work site but not on the job is appropriate for required after-hours programs and for programs in which contact needs to be maintained with work units but OJT would be too distracting or harmful. It's also appropriate for voluntary after-hours programs and for programs that update employees' competencies while allowing them to attend to their regular duties.

For example, when a major Northeast grocery store chain switched to computerized scanners, it faced the problem of training thousands of checkers spread out across three states. The cost of training them off-site was prohibitive. Yet management also was fearful about training employees on the job, lest their ineptitude offend customers. To solve the problem, the grocery chain developed a mobile training van that included a vestibule model of the latest scanning equipment. Checkers were trained on-site but off the job in the mobile unit. Once the basic skill of scanning was mastered, employees returned to the store, and the trainer remained on-site as a resource person. According to one store manager, the program was effective because employees could be trained rapidly and efficiently, yet no customers were lost owing to checker errors or slowness.

Company Schools and Executive Education Programs. A growing trend in the United States is the development of company schools and executive education programs tailored to the needs of the company. Company schools focus on the education of employees and sometimes customers. McDonald's Hamburger University, begun in 1961, is among the oldest corporate universities. Started in a basement, the center now trains more than 2,500 students annually in the fine details of restaurant and franchise operations. General Electric, an advocate of training and development for years, has an up-to-date facility in Croton-on-Hudson, New York, that it uses for divisional and group training. Corporate schools have also been developed by such diverse firms as AT&T, Ford, Arthur Andersen, General Motors, Motorola, United Airlines, Chase Bank, Kodak, Dell, and Harley-Davidson.

Motorola dedicated its $10 million Galvin Center for Continuing Education in 1986. The facility contains 88,000 square feet of classrooms, individual instruction centers, an auditorium, lounges, dining facilities, and a fitness center. In affiliation with the National Technological Union, a consortium that teaches by satellite, Motorola offers courses leading to three master's degrees. It has also opened Motorola University, where it teaches total quality management to its own employees. In addition, it teaches TQM to faculty from business and engineering schools.

Like a growing number of corporations, Motorola is committed to company-based education. In fact, recent research suggests that 65 percent of all major firms offer some form of executive education. Today, many corporate colleges offer degrees, and hundreds of corporations offer courses leading to degrees.

In providing company schools and executive education, corporations, large and small, can help their employees obtain state-of-the-art knowledge, both technical and managerial. In the process, employees develop an ability to adapt continuously to changing conditions. This can then make it easier for organizations to institute major changes such as a movement to total quality management. While not always the case, the executive programs at companies may be under the direction of the chief learning officer.[42]

Programmed Instruction. Programmed instruction (PI) is an old on-site training method. Here, the instructional material is broken down into frames and programmed for the computer. Each frame represents a small component of the entire subject to be learned, and each frame must be learned successfully before the next one can be tackled.

An advantage of PI is that large numbers of employees can be trained simultaneously, with each learner free to explore the material at her or his own pace. In addition, PI includes immediate and individualized feedback. The downside is that development costs are high, especially for computerized PI. Although the development of several authoring systems has eased the burden of developing PI modules, instruction still must be carefully planned. It's estimated that one hour of programmed instruction requires 50 hours of development work. Consequently, this approach is effective only if off-the-shelf programs (e.g., word processing and database tutorials) are used or if large numbers of employees are to be trained so that development costs for an original program can be justified. Increasingly, the use of personal computers and intranets is making large-scale use practical.[43]

Interactive Video and Web-based Training. Interactive video programs, typically formatted on a CD-ROM, present a short video and narrative pre-

"If we are to build an organization that people want to come to and do great things, we have to allow them the opportunity to learn."

**Richard F. Teerlink
CEO**

sentation and then require the trainee to respond to it. Usually, the video program is attached to a personal computer, and the learner responds to video cues by using the keyboard or by touching the screen. This sequence—packaged program, learner response, and more programmed instruction—provides for individualized learning. The latest Web-based technology courses are built on a model similar to interactive video training. But a major difference is that multiple trainees can all be connected to each other. Rather than working solo at the PC, they can use the Internet to ask questions of a "live" instructor and discuss issues with their "classmates." Now in its infancy, Web-based training may soon become the industry standard.[44]

Teleconferencing.   Teleconferencing allows people at different locations to see and talk to each other in real time. A cost study conducted by Kodak estimates that a new product training program beamed by satellite to three cities costs $20,000. It would cost five to six times that amount to send engineers and managers on the road to do the same training. More important, teleconferencing saves six weeks of training time, which is invaluable in a competitive industry.[45]

Off the Job

When the consequence of error is high, it's usually more appropriate to conduct training off the job. For example, most airline passengers would readily agree that it's preferable to train pilots in flight simulators rather than have them apprentice in the cockpit of a plane. Similarly, it's usually useful to have a bus driver practice on an obstacle course before taking to the roads with a load of schoolchildren.

Off-the-job training is also appropriate when complex competencies need to be mastered or when employees need to focus on specific interpersonal competencies that might not be apparent in the normal work environment. For example, it's difficult to build a cohesive management work team when members of the team are constantly interrupted by telephone calls and subordinate inquiries. Team building is more likely to occur during a retreat, when team members have time to focus on establishing relationships.

However, the costs of off-the-job training are high. Transfer of knowledge to the workplace is also a concern. Research has shown that the more dissimilar the training environment is to the actual work environment, the less likely trainees will be to apply what they learn to their jobs. For example, the transfer-of-knowledge problem is minimal for vestibule training, in which trainees work with machines that are comparable to the ones in their actual work environment. However, it may be difficult to apply teamwork competencies learned during a wilderness survival program to a management job in a large service organization.

Formal Courses.   Formal courses can be directed either by the trainee—using programmed instruction, computer-assisted instruction, reading, and correspondence courses—or by others, as in formal classroom courses and lectures. Although many training programs use the lecture method because it efficiently and simultaneously conveys large amounts of information to large groups of people, it does have several drawbacks. Perhaps most importantly, except for cognitive knowledge and conceptual principles, the transfer of learning to the actual job is probably limited. Also, the lecture method does not permit individualized training based on individual differences in

fast fact

Ameritech Corporation puts executives to work for an afternoon in soup kitchens, housing projects, and AIDS clinics as team-building exercises.

fast fact

According to the Department of Labor, U.S. businesses spend $50 billion annually on formal training plus $70 billion on wages paid to workers attending training.

ability, interests, and personality. Because of these drawbacks, the lecture method is often complemented by other training methods.

Simulation.　Simulation, which presents situations that are similar to actual job conditions, is used for both managers and nonmanagers.[46] A common simulation technique for nonmanagers is the vestibule method, which simulates the environment of the individual's actual job. Because the environment isn't real, it's generally less hectic and more safe than the actual environment; as a consequence, trainees may have trouble adjusting from the training environment to the actual environment. However, the arguments for using a simulated environment are compelling: it reduces the possibility of customer dissatisfaction that can result from on-the-job training, it can reduce the frustration of the trainee, and it may save the organization a great deal of money because fewer training accidents occur. Not all organizations, even in the same industry, accept these arguments. Some banks, for example, train their tellers on the job, whereas others train them in a simulated bank environment.

Assessment Centers.　An increasingly popular simulation technique for managerial assessment and development is assessment centers. Assessment centers are especially useful for identifying potential training needs, as illustrated in the opening feature of General Motors but they can also be used as a training method.[47] Management games and in-basket exercises are two assessment center components that work especially well as training tools.[48]

Regardless of where they're used, *management games or business games* can be used to develop a variety of competencies, such as teamwork in a group setting. In contrast, *in-basket exercises* are more solitary. The trainee sits at a desk and works through a pile of papers found in the in-basket of a typical manager, setting priorities, recommending solutions to problems, and taking any necessary action in response to the contents.

Although assessment center exercises tend to be enjoyable and challenging, the extent to which they improve a manager's ability depends in part on what takes place afterward. An analysis of what happened and what should have happened in business games and in-basket exercises, when done by upper-level managers in the organization, should help trainees learn how to perform like managers. The opportunity for improvement may be drastically reduced if the trainees are left to decide what to transfer from the games or exercises to the job.

Role-Playing and Sensitivity Training.　Whereas simulation exercises may be useful for developing conceptual and problem-solving skills, two other types of training are used for developing human relations or process skills. Role-playing and sensitivity training develop managers' interpersonal insights—awareness of self and of others. Such insight may encourage attitude change.

Role-playing generally focuses on understanding and managing relationships rather than facts. The essence of role-playing is to create a realistic situation, as in the case discussion method, and then have the trainees assume the parts of specific personalities in the situation. The usefulness of role-playing depends heavily on the extent to which the trainees get into the parts they're playing. If you have done any role-playing, you know how difficult this can be and how much easier it is to simply read the part. However, when the trainee does get into the role, the result is a greater sensitivity to the feelings and insights that are presented by the role.

In sensitivity training, individuals in an unstructured group exchange thoughts and feelings on the "here and now" rather than the "there and then." Although being in a sensitivity group often gives individuals insight into how and why they and others feel and act the way they do, critics claim that these results may not be beneficial because they aren't directly transferable to the job. Despite such criticism, both role playing and sensitivity training are frequently included as part of training programs.

Wilderness Trips and Outdoor Training.   To improve employees' attitudes about the here and now and raise their self-esteem, organizations sometimes use programs that involve physical feats of strength, endurance, and cooperation. These can be implemented on wilderness trips to the woods or mountains or water. Whereas many firms such as General Electric, General Foods, Knight-Ridder, Xerox, and Burger King use some variation of outdoor experiences in their management training with success, many others, such as Microsoft, question the degree of transfer to the job that these experiences offer. Firms using outdoor experiences recognize this concern and thus articulate the link between the competencies developed in the experiences and the competencies needed by the managers on the job. They are sensitive to employee differences in physical ability and fitness, and they are careful about choosing experiences that accommodate an increasingly diverse workforce.[49]

MAXIMIZING LEARNING

Even when the training technique is appropriate, learning may not take place if the experience isn't structured appropriately. Exhibit 9.6 details learning principles that increase the success of training.[50]

Setting the Stage for Learning

Before launching a training program, a trainer or manager needs to consider how information will be presented. In addition, he or she must consider the beliefs of trainees regarding task-specific competencies.

"If, when holding a gun to an employee's head, he or she will perform, the problem isn't a training problem."

Alice Pescuric
Vice President
DDI

Clear Expectations.   If task instructions are unclear or imprecise, learning is hampered. Employees must know what is expected in order to perform as desired. Clear instructions establish appropriate behavioral expectations. Training expectations should be stated in specific terms. The conditions under which performance is or isn't expected should be identified, along with the behavior to be demonstrated. It's also useful to specify up front what the reward will be for performing as desired. Trainees are more likely to be motivated if they know that successful performance can lead to positive reinforcement (e.g., promotion, pay raise, or recognition) or can block the administration of negative reinforcement (e.g., supervisory criticism or firing).[51]

Behavioral Models.   Even when instructions are clear, the desired behavior still may not occur if the trainee does not know how to perform it. This problem can be overcome through *behavioral modeling*, which is a visual demonstration of desired behavior. The model can be a supervisor, coworker, or subject matter expert, and the demonstration can be live or videotaped. The

Exhibit 9.6
Learning Principles to Increase the Effectiveness of Training

---

Setting the Stage for Learning

1. Provide clear task instructions.
2. Model appropriate behavior.

Increasing Learning During Training

1. Provide for active participation.
2. Increase self-efficacy.
3. Match training techniques to trainees' self-efficacy.
4. Provide opportunities for enactive mastery.
5. Ensure specific, timely, diagnostic, and practical feedback.
6. Provide opportunities for trainees to practice new behaviors.

Maintaining Performance After Training

1. Develop learning points to assist knowledge retention.
2. Set specific goals.
3. Identify appropriate reinforcers.
4. Train significant others in how to reinforce behavior.
5. Teach trainees self-management skills.

Following up on Training

1. Evaluate effectiveness.
2. Make revisions as needed.

---

important thing is to show employees what needs to be done before asking them to do it. Care is needed in choosing an appropriate behavioral model. If the model makes the task look too simple, trainees may quit the first time they encounter a difficulty. Thus, models should show not only how to achieve desired outcomes but also how to overcome performance obstacles.

Increasing Learning During Training

Although employees should be responsible for their own learning, organizations also can do much to support employees

Active Participation. Individuals perform better if they're actively involved in the learning process. Organizational help in this area can range from encouraging active participation in classroom discussions to establishing a set of programs to assist managers in a major strategic change. Participation may be direct (e.g., hands-on training) or indirect (e.g., role-plays and simulations). The important point is to hook the individual on learning. Through active participation, individuals stay more alert and are more likely to feel confident.[52]

Self-Efficacy. Even with modeling, learning may not occur if people have feelings of low self-efficacy. Self-efficacy is a trainee's beliefs about a task-specific ability. If individuals dwell on their personal deficiencies relative to the task, potential difficulties may seem more formidable than they really are. On the other hand, people who have a strong sense of self-efficacy are likely to be motivated to overcome obstacles.

The choice of an appropriate training method is critical to self-efficacy. In a recent study, a group of trainees was taught how to use computer spreadsheets. People low in self-efficacy performed better when one-on-one tutorials were conducted; individuals with high self-efficacy (who believed they could easily learn how to use spreadsheets) performed better when appropriate behavior was merely modeled. Consequently, before choosing training techniques, the level of self-efficacy for each trainee should be determined.[53]

Enactive Mastery.   Self-efficacy increases when experiences fail to validate fears and when competencies acquired allow for mastery of once-threatening situations. This process is called enactive mastery. To facilitate task mastery, trainers should arrange the subject matter so that trainees experience success. Whereas this may be easy when tasks are simple, it can be quite difficult when tasks are complex. Solutions include segmenting the task, shaping behavior, and setting proximal goals.

Task segmentation involves breaking a complex task into smaller or simpler components. For some jobs (e.g., laboratory technician), the components (e.g., drawing blood, culturing a specimen, and running a blood chemistry machine) can be taught individually and in any order. For other jobs (e.g., engineer, chauffeur, and interviewer), segments must be taught sequentially because task B builds on task A and task C builds on task B.[54]

Shaping includes rewarding closer and closer approximations to desired behavior. For example, when managers are learning how to conduct a selection interview, they can be reinforced for making eye contact and for asking situational questions.

The setting of *proximal goals*, or intermediary goals, also increases mastery perceptions. Consider a software developer with an overall objective of developing a new word processing package. Proximal goals might include meeting a project specifications deadline, developing algorithms for fonts by a set deadline, developing an algorithm for formatting paragraphs, and so on. These proximal goals all lead to the attainment of the distal, or overall, objective.[55]

Feedback.   For individuals to master new concepts and acquire new competencies, they must receive accurate diagnostic feedback about their performance. When feedback isn't received or is inaccurate, the wrong behaviors may be practiced. Feedback can be provided by a supervisor, coworkers, customers, computers, or the individual performing the task. It must be specific, timely, based on behavior and not personality, and practical. If a performance discrepancy exists, the feedback should also be diagnostic and should include instructions or modeling of how to perform better.[56] The Weyerhaeuser Company, American Express, GE, and Eaton Corporation use surveys to make sure managers get a lot of feedback on how well they're doing as managers. It now appears that feedback from more sources is more useful. Thus many firms try to provide 360° feedback to help the person and the organization assess improvements over time.[57]

Practice.   The goal of training is to ensure that the desired behavior occurs not just one time but consistently. This is most likely to occur when trainees are able to practice and internalize standards of performance. Even mental practice appears to help improve performance.[58] Practicing the wrong behaviors is detrimental; therefore, practice must follow specific feedback.

For some jobs, tasks must be overlearned. *Overlearning* involves internalizing responses so that the trainee does not have to think consciously about behavior before responding. For example, if a plane is losing altitude rapidly, a pilot must know immediately how to respond. The pilot has no time to think about what should be done. The emergency routine must be second nature and internalized. Repeated practice sessions are needed for overlearning to occur.

Maintaining Performance After Training

Following employees' exposure to socialization, training, and development experiences, the environment needs to support the transfer of new behaviors to the job, and their maintenance over time.

Learning Points.   New skills and information are more likely to be retained when learning points are developed. Learning points summarize key behaviors—particularly those that aren't obvious—and serve as cognitive cues back on the job. Although learning points can be written by trainers, trainee-generated learning points—even if they're of lower quality—enhance recall and lead to better skill acquisition and retention.[59]

Specific Goals.   Without goals, people have little basis for judging how they're doing.[60] Specific goals for subsequent performance should be challenging but not so difficult as to be perceived impossible. They also shouldn't be set too early in the learning process.

Reinforcers.   Learning new behaviors is difficult and threatening. To ensure that trainees continue to demonstrate the skill they have learned, behavior must be reinforced. Reinforcement can be positive (e.g., praise and financial rewards) or negative (e.g., "If you perform as desired, I will quit screaming at you."), but it must be contingent on performance.

Significant Others.   Trainers must also teach significant others to look for and reinforce desired changes. If a person labeled a troubled employee continues to be viewed as such, the person has no incentive to display new behavior. If, however, a supervisor or coworker responds positively to a positive change in behavior, the frequency with which the new behavior will be displayed is likely to increase.

Self-Reinforcement.   Because it isn't always possible for significant others to reinforce an individual worker, a long-term objective should be to teach employees how to set their own goals and administer their own reinforcement. When people create self-incentives for their efforts, they're capable of making self-satisfaction contingent on their own performance. The challenge here is to ensure that personal goals are congruent with organizational goals, which leads to self-management.

Longer-Term Follow-up.   All too often, even when training has been successful, participants who want to change their behavior get back to work and then slowly slip back into their old patterns. This results in a significant loss of effectiveness of the training program. One approach to help prevent

■□*fast fact*

The average Trident employee receives special recognition 10.6 times per year for behaviors that fit the new culture.

this from happening is an action plan. At Eaton Corporation, Nick Blauwiekel feeds back the results of the Eaton Audit Survey to the plant managers and asks each manager to develop an action plan to remove any deficiencies.

Another approach is a contract. Each participant writes an informal agreement near the end of a training program, stating which aspects of the program he or she believes will have the most beneficial effect back on the job and then agreeing to apply those aspects. Each participant is also asked to choose another participant from the program, to whom a copy of the contract is given and who agrees to check up on the participant's progress every few weeks.

TOP MANAGEMENT LEADERSHIP AND THE PROCESS OF CHANGE

"If you're not thinking all the time about making every person more valuable, you don't have a chance."

Jack Welch
CEO
General Electric

It's now widely recognized that for change to occur in organizations, leaders must get others to change *and* they themselves must also change.[61]

New Leadership Behaviors

CEOs and all other managers must change before other employees will. Managers have to move from the command-and-control style to empowering, visioning, cooperating, and supporting. They must also change the way they behave with respect to suppliers and customers outside the organization, the environment, social and ethical issues of business and society, and the strategy and direction of the organization. These changes in leadership are seen as vital to many organizations today, and they aren't likely to occur unless systematic strategies are in place to help managers make them. Companies like Eaton Corporation, General Electric, Levi Strauss, Federal Express, and Weyerhaeuser are systematically linking specific on-the-job experiences and training and development programs to the new behavioral competencies required in the new organizational forms. Some companies are even establishing leadership institutes.

"TI owes its success to the thousands of TI people who are making the networked society come to life. This is why we will continue to develop our skills, ensure that we have the best tools to do the job, develop our leadership, and make the most of our teams."

Jerry R. Junkins
Chairman, President, and Chief Executive Officer
Texas Instruments

Leadership Institutes.   In the late 1980s, Weyerhaeuser's Forest Products Company (FPC) established its own leadership institute to help its managers change their behaviors. Within FPC, Chief Executive Charles W. Bingham, his executive team, and the director of strategic education, Horace Parker, concluded that a major strategic repositioning called for upgrading the firm's human capabilities through executive development.

> *"How the organization was sold on the worth of an executive development program is an important lesson. The trump card used in closing the deal was to involve the executives at various levels of the organization in the planning stages. During those stages, they came to see, as did the executive team, that an intensive development program such as the Leadership Institute was not an expensive frill but a prerequisite for survival. The Leadership Institute, top management was convinced, would be a powerful catalyst that could accelerate the normal process of change—of everything from a corporate culture to how a salesperson deals with customers."[62]*

Working with others in human resource management and with the top management team, FPC created a leadership institute where managers could come to discuss the new strategy and its implications for them. In addition, the institute offered training to help managers acquire needed competencies and leadership styles. A success, this institute grew into a total quality company program. Today, the entire Weyerhaeuser Company uses the institute to help managers learn new leadership behaviors. The new leadership behaviors identified as critical for total quality management and customer-focus flow directly from what leadership means to the company, including:

- Leadership behavior and standards are well defined and understood throughout the organization and are linked with company values.
- Leaders set clear goals and expectations and inspire others to meet them.
- Development is provided for existing and current leaders.
- Leaders seek and use feedback to improve their leadership competencies.
- A key measure of leadership success is the development of others.

Management Development On-the-Job. When systematically developed and coordinated by the HR department, education and job experiences can go a long way toward helping managers change themselves and, in the process, change their organizations.

The Weyerhaeuser Company has gone from a centralized structure to a decentralized structure and now to a decentralized structure coordinated through shared vision, values, and leadership philosophy. At the same time, it has moved from a maker of undifferentiated commodity products to one of customer-focused, total quality products. Continuous management development helps ensure that all these changes last and continue to filter down in the company. Frequent meetings between top managers are one type of activity facilitating on-the-job development. Working as a team develops, shares, and coordinates efforts to help each individual manager learn more about the company as a whole. A deeper understanding of the business puts each manager in a better position to lead in ways that are consistent with the several separate businesses, yet coordinated to reflect the functions of these businesses as part of one larger company. In addition, the Weyerhaeuser Company, like the Eaton Corporation, uses surveys to measure whether managers exhibit leadership behaviors that are consistent with the company's strategy, values, and vision.

Survey Development and Feedback. As Nick Blauwiekel at the Eaton Corporation understands, constant and continuous change and improvement need measurement systems. Eaton uses surveys to systematically gather information about total quality management in its plants, and feeds the results back to the plant managers and all the plant employees. This is all a part of the Eaton Philosophy Audit Process. Although the data are collected by interview teams rather than written surveys, the team asks specific questions and records this information very systematically. Here, the HR department plays a critical role in determining what information is needed, how to get it, and who to feed it back to. And again, the line managers are working in partnership with the HR department and the employees to make this all happen.

Weyerhaeuser also uses data to support its change efforts. Believing that people are central to instituting total quality management and making other changes in the organization, former CEO Jack Creighton and current CEO Steve Rogel, and his top senior management team developed and use a leadership behaviors survey. The survey items reflect all the values of the com-

■□*fast fact*

Corporate training revenues were less than $1 billion in 1994; then they tripled in the next five years.

■□*fast fact*

Using their intranets, companies can suggest training and development activities for "fast track" employees and tailor the suggestions to each person's individual needs.

pany. Each executive gives the survey to her or his subordinates and asks them to evaluate the boss (anonymously, of course). The surveys are sent to an outside firm that scores them and sends the executives the results. The executives subsequently identify action plans for self-improvement. Through their own improvement, these executives also serve as role models for other managers in the company. As this leadership survey process cascades down the organization, more and more managers exhibit behaviors that are consistent with the needs of total quality management. The success of the process is built upon involvement, data collection, feedback, and development plans for improvement.

Knowledge Management

Companies such as Booz-Allen and Hamilton Consulting, Andersen Consulting, General Electric, Dell, Cisco, KMPG, and Sara Lee are increasingly concerned about being as effective and efficient as possible. This is resulting in the need to systematically manage knowledge in the company. Knowledge management is about making sure that knowledge from employees, teams, and units within an organization is captured, remembered, stored, and shared with others. This knowledge can be about successes and failures. It can be about contacts, potential customers, and environmental trends. Booz-Allen believes so strongly in the value of knowledge management that they have created libraries to store such information so that others can go in and learn from the experiences of others. They, and other organizations as well, have created a position responsible for knowledge management. Typically, the position is titled Chief Learning Officer or Chief Knowledge Officer.

Knowledge management is only as effective as the employees want it to be. They must be willing to share their knowledge and experiences; and they must be willing to use the ideas and knowledge of others. These behaviors don't come automatically. Companies need to reward employees for sharing their knowledge so that others can benefit. They also need to reward employees for using information and knowledge that are in a common stored database, the knowledge management library. Managers need to encourage their employees to share all their information and knowledge, not just certain parts of them. By doing so, they develop an organizational culture that values and encourages sharing, openness, and using the ideas of others. The culture can be further supported by knowledge management technology. The new technology makes knowledge management both more efficient and more feasible.[63]

TEAM TRAINING AND DEVELOPMENT

Management often rushes to form work teams without considering how the behaviors needed for effective teamwork differ from those needed for effective individual contributions. Team members may receive little or no training to ensure that they can perform the required tasks and achieve the goals set. As Displaymasters discovered, this approach to work teams often leads to failure. Displaymasters is a small Minneapolis-based company that manufactures displays. When managers put workers into teams for the first time, they did so without explaining their expectations or defining the team members' new roles. They provided no training in how to be an effective work team member and paid no attention to employees' feelings. The result was chaos. Employees became skeptical of teamwork and frustrated with the managers. Displaymasters has since regrouped and offered team training. Although the company is organized into cross-functional work teams, no one dares to call them that because of their initial failure. Instead, they're called departments to avoid any negative associations with the chaos that "teams" caused in the past.[64]

Team training can take many forms. Three main goals of team training programs are to develop team cohesiveness, effective teamwork procedures, and work team leaders. Although some training efforts address all three of these objectives simultaneously, here we discuss them in sequence for clarity.

Training to Develop Team Cohesiveness

Perhaps more than any other organization, NASA understands that training comes before effective teamwork. Before astronauts are sent into space to live in a community that relies heavily on teamwork for survival, NASA has them working together every day for one to two years to become a team. They share office space, spend countless hours together in flight simulators, and rehearse everything from stowing their flight suits to troubleshooting malfunctions. Formal training in procedures is part of the experience, but it isn't everything. NASA realizes that teamwork training also involves helping teammates get to know each other and developing confidence in each other. Most organizations can't afford to give work team members a year or two of training before the teams begin working on their tasks. They look for quicker ways to achieve the same objectives. Wilderness training, described earlier, is one popular alternative.

Training in Team Procedures

Experiential training is an effective way to develop cohesiveness, but used alone it isn't likely to result in optimal work team effectiveness. Work teams can also benefit from more formal training. For example, team members who are taught about the stages of team development are less likely to become easily frustrated during the early forming and storming stages of team development. They will also realize the importance of norms to their performance and therefore strive to develop norms that aid rather than hinder it. At BP Norge, team members were taught about the characteristics of self-managed teams and provided with information about how such teams have been used in other organizations, as described in the feature, Managing Teamwork: Cultural Change at BP Norge.[65]

Team training programs that develop problem-solving skills can be especially useful. Procedures to be learned include how to

- use a variety of techniques for generating creative ideas (e.g., brainstorming);
- identify and discuss problems and their possible causes (e.g., using fishbone diagrams and other decision-making aids);
- choose one solution from among the many available (e.g., when to resort to voting and compromise); and
- ensure that solutions are implemented on schedule.

MANAGING TEAMWORK

Cultural Change at BP Norge

When the Norwegian arm of British Petroleum (BP Norge) decided that it needed to dismantle its hierarchy and move toward becoming a network of collaborators, it decided to restructure the organization around self-managing teams. If employees were willing to assume leadership and work across functions, the company believed that it could speed up decision making, reduce costs and cycle times, and increase innovation. Despite the strong business argument supporting a change to teamwork, the organization found that pushing the change was difficult.

Nine months of frustration led management to conclude that a systematic training initiative was needed to educate the organization and support the development of new teamwork competencies. The first phase of training focused on changing old thought patterns and helping people understand the link between BP Norge's business strategy and the need for self-managed teams. Because employees had been through many change efforts in the past, they had become skeptical and resistant. To convince them that more change was needed, a team of American and Norwegian facilitators conducted two-day workshops, which were attended by a mix of people from all levels and functional specialties. Oil rig workers and senior managers sat side-by-side, as did Norwegians and Americans—even if they couldn't speak each other's language. Prior to the workshop, everyone completed a prework assignment. First, they watched a video that explained self-managed teams and showed how other organizations had used them successfully. They also interviewed a few colleagues to find out what they thought about self-managed teams. At the workshop, discussion focused on understanding the process through which teamwork develops. Participants were taught that denial about the need for change and resistance to it are natural reactions, but they were also encouraged to share their concerns with each other and seek answers to their questions. Throughout the two-day workshops, participants also used role plays to begin practicing the behaviors that they would need in their new team environment. These behaviors included taking risks, communicating their feelings, and teaching others as well as learning from others.

To learn more about BP Norge, visit the company's home page at **www.bp.com**

For self-managing work teams, formal training may also include company-specific procedures for obtaining resources, cost accounting, progress reports, and team evaluations. When Western Contract Furniture created TQM teams, it hired a consultant to train its managers and associates. The training covered basic teamwork principles and included discussions about the importance of modifying the company's culture to support the new TQM teams. The objective of the training was to prepare managers and employees to work on autonomous ad hoc task forces. The task forces were formed from volunteers interested in addressing an issue needing attention, as identified by the company's quality council. Employees were trained in how to choose a facilitator, research an issue, and develop recommendations. Following this training, almost everyone in the company has served on a TQM team.

Training to Develop Work Team Leaders

New team leaders often misunderstand their role. Good team leaders are receptive to member contributions and don't reject or promote ideas because of their own personal views. Good team leaders summarize information, stimulate discussion, create awareness of problems, and detect when the team is ready to resolve differences and agree to a unified solution. Training in how to support disagreement and manage meetings is especially useful for new work team leaders.

- *Supporting disagreement.* A skillful work team leader can create an atmosphere for disagreement that stimulates innovative solutions while minimizing the risk of bad feelings. Disagreement can be managed if the leader is receptive to differences within the team, delays the making of decisions, and separates idea generation from idea evaluation. This last technique reduces the likelihood that an alternative solution will be identified with one individual rather than the team. The absence of disagreement on a work team may be as destructive to its proper functioning as too much disagreement. The use of decision-making aids, such as the brainstorming, the nominal group technique, devil's advocacy, and dialectical inquiry, creates productive controversy and can result in better quality decisions that are fully accepted by members of the team. Training team leaders to use these simple techniques is a good first step toward stimulating constructive controversy within teams.[66]
- *Managing meetings.* People who resist teamwork often point to time wasted in meetings as a big source of dissatisfaction. True, teams do need to meet, one way or another, but team meetings should never be a waste of time. Training team leaders in the tactics of running meetings can make meetings more efficient. In addition, training can help team leaders learn how to strike a proper balance between permissiveness and control. Rushing through a team session can prevent full discussion of the problem, lead to negative feelings, and poor solutions. However, unless the leader keeps the discussion moving, members will become bored and inattentive. Unfortunately, some leaders feel that pushing for an early solution is necessary because of time constraints. Such a move ends discussion before the team has had a chance to work through a problem effectively.

INTERNATIONAL TRAINING

A few things seem certain, and one is that "globalization" will continue to be an inescapable buzzword. Businesses will operate in an ever more interconnected world. As organizations develop global structures and perspectives, training and development activities should support these changes.

To build the kind of global organization it needs, Pepsico, the cola company, embraces the selection and development of leaders from many different cultures. Its Executive Leadership Program was designed to develop leaders from all over the world. To design this program, an outside consultant and the management development staff compiled a list of 33 leadership practices that reflect the actions leaders and managers are expected to take in running their businesses. The company's top officers have their performance reviewed anonymously by their subordinates against these leadership practices. The results of this review are fed back to senior staff during the Executive Leadership Program. The feature, Managing Globalization: Pepsico Trains Managers for Global Leadership, describes the Executive Leadership Program in more detail.[67]

Expatriate Training

The training and development of U.S. expatriates present special problems. Management development of expatriates should take up where selection leaves off. Although only a few companies provide expatriate training, it's critical. The basic aspects of this training include the

MANAGING GLOBALIZATION

Pepsico Trains Managers for Global Leadership

Pepsico's Executive Leadership Program aims to improve personal leadership behaviors as well as solve practical leadership questions such as those that arise in starting a new bottling plant or dealing with the career development concerns of a specific work unit. During the program, each senior executive receives confidential counseling about specific behaviors that need to change for that executive to manage her or his work group more effectively. Examples of the behaviors executives are expected to develop include communicating the company's vision to all employees, motivating and inspiring people, demonstrating high personal standards, establishing clear and specific performance goals, and helping employees learn new skills. After receiving assessments of how well they are doing in these areas, executives are expected to share their survey results with their work groups and ask for suggestions about how to improve.

In general terms, the leadership program is seen as culturally neutral. Although cultural differences are discussed, the focus is on how best to demonstrate a practice regardless of the country of application. Across countries, the areas needing improvement are likely to vary. For example, an executive in Eastern Europe, where the concept of competition is just taking hold, is less likely than an executive in Japan to hear about goals, targets, and the need to beat the competition.

When this program was initially installed, participants had some significant misgivings about the confidentiality of the data. An outside consultant was called in to ensure confidentiality. The program has now passed the confidentiality hurdle, and many participants are eager to attend and find out how they can improve their personal performance. In general, the program provides an intense forum for the discussion of leadership and management issues; these discussions, in turn, provide data about needed human resource practices and interventions.

A different program, called Excellence in Management, is used for midlevel managers. Questionnaires (translated at local discretion) and feedback are again used, as in the executive program. The midlevel program focuses primarily on basic managerial competencies such as delegating, managing conflict, and being more effective in an organization that's mature, decentralized, and international. The midlevel program is designed more around strategy execution issues.

The two leadership programs focus on improving personal effectiveness and exploring ways to improve executive and managerial effectiveness in an international, culturally diverse organization. The attendees for these programs commonly represent a half dozen different nationalities, which provides a unique opportunity to practice problem sharing and problem solving with a diverse group of colleagues.

To learn more about Pepsico, visit the company home page at **www.pepsico.com**

- development of expatriates before, during, and after foreign assignments;
- orientation and training of expatriate families before, during, and after foreign assignments; and
- development of the headquarters staff responsible for the planning, organization, and control of overseas operations.

This range of training is aimed at bringing about attitudinal and behavioral changes in the expatriates, expatriates' families, and the staff (in the United States and abroad) responsible for the multinational operations. One form of expatriate training is *cross-cultural training*.

Cross-cultural programs usually take the form of a three-to-five-day immersion course in the assigned country's values, customs, and traditions. Most U.S. firms use outside consultants for such instruction. Consultants usually have a basic training module for each country, which they can tailor to a client company's particular requirements. A typical three-day program might cover details about what everyday life in the country is like, typical practices that are important to doing business in the country, the role of women in the foreign culture, and a discussion of the culture shock and the stress that executives and their families are likely to experience.

Cross-cultural training is perhaps the main growth area in the training field, and more and more companies include it as a part of predeparture programs.[68] The primary beneficiaries of this new emphasis on cross-cultural training are departing executives themselves. But companies stress that spouses and children may benefit as much as or even more than executives from this type of instruction, since it's they who are "out" in the local community daily and need to be sensitive to and knowledgeable about the culture. In contrast, most of an executive's time is spent in the somewhat insulated office environment. Therefore, more and more companies have begun offering cross-cultural training to families as well as executives.

By having an extensive development effort, multinational companies can help increase the effectiveness of their expatriate managers. Such a program can also encourage more domestic managers to apply for expatriate positions. To make expatriate positions really attractive, however, multinational companies must also offer commensurate salaries. This makes it expensive for companies to have expatriate managers.

■□ *fast fact*

Procter & Gamble offers overseas employees country-specific information, language and cross-cultural training, and corporate culture training.

ASSESSING TRAINING AND DEVELOPMENT

Many ways of evaluating training and development programs have been proposed, including immediate reactions to the training, changes in productivity, changes in attitudes (e.g., satisfaction with supervisor, satisfaction with diversity programs, satisfaction with job, stress, role conflict, and knowledge of work procedures), cost savings, and benefits gains.[69]

Evaluation Components

Most training experts agree that a systematic approach to training evaluation includes at least four components:

- *Reaction to training:* Did the trainees like the program? Was the instruction clear and helpful? Do the trainees believe that they learned the material?
- *Learning:* Did the trainees actually acquire the knowledge and skills that were taught? Can they talk about things they could not talk about

before? Can they demonstrate appropriate behaviors in training (role-play)?

• *Behavior or performance change:* Can trainees now do things they could not do before (e.g., negotiate, or conduct an appraisal interview)? Can they demonstrate new behaviors on the job? Is performance on the job better?

• *Results:* Did the training produce tangible results in terms of productivity, cost savings, response time, safety, employee retention, and/or customer satisfaction?

The choice of criteria hinges on the level at which the training evaluation is to be conducted. For example, a short attitude survey could be used to assess the response of trainees to a course; it would not provide information on learning, behavior, and results. If the objective is to assess what was learned, then paper-and-pencil tests can be used. It may also be possible to analyze responses to such training exercises as in-basket tests, role-plays, or case analyses.

Although testing for knowledge acquisition may indicate that learning has occurred, it won't reveal whether learning has been transferred to the job. To assess whether behavior or performance has changed, output measures, performance evaluation reports, and employee attitude surveys provide better information. For example, if employees report more positive attitudes toward supervisory communications after supervisors complete an interpersonal skills program, it may be deduced (assuming other factors can be ruled out) that the training resulted in the behavioral change.

Evaluation Designs

Evaluation designs help the manager determine if improvements have been made and if the training program caused the improvements. They also can help the manager evaluate (1) any human resource program to improve productivity and the quality of work life and (2) the effectiveness of any human resource activity. Combining data collection tools, such as organizational surveys, with knowledge of evaluation designs allows human resource departments to demonstrate their effectiveness—and that of specific programs and activities—to the rest of the organization.

The three major categories of evaluation designs are pre-experimental, quasi-experimental, and experimental (see Exhibit 9.7).[70] Each offers advantages and disadvantages. Data collection techniques that can be used include surveys, interviews, and organizational records.

The most rigorous evaluation designs are *experimental designs*, which include the pretest-posttest control group design and the Solomon four-group design. In both types of experimental design, individuals are randomly assigned to groups (Exhibit 9.7) and not all groups receive training (identified as X in Exhibit 9.7). In the Solomon four-group design, some groups are assessed both before and after the training, and others are assessed only after the training. This design allows one to rule out the possible effects of assessing people before they receive training. Evaluation using an experimental design allows the training manager to be more confident that

• a change has taken place—for example, that employee productivity has increased;

• the change is caused by the training program; and

• a similar change could be expected if the program were done again with other employees.

Exhibit 9.7

Three Categories of Evaluation Design

<table>
<tr>
<td valign="top">

Pre-Experimental

1. One-shot case study design

$$X \qquad T_2$$

2. One-group pretest-posttest design

$$T_1 \qquad X \qquad T_2$$

</td>
<td valign="top">

Quasi-Experimental

1. Time-series design

$$T_1 T_2 T_3 \qquad X \qquad T_4 T_5 T_6$$

2. Nonequivalent control groups design

$$T_1 \qquad X \qquad T_2$$
$$T_1 \qquad \qquad T_2$$

</td>
<td valign="top">

Experimental

1. Pretest-posttest control group design

$$T_1 \qquad X \qquad T_2$$
$$T_1 \qquad \qquad T_2$$

2. Solomon four-group design

$$T_1 \qquad X \qquad T_2$$
$$T_1 \qquad \qquad T_2$$
$$\qquad X \qquad T_2$$
$$\qquad \qquad T_2$$

</td>
</tr>
</table>

Note. "T" refers to the time at which the outcomes of interest (e.g., knowledge, attitudes, behavior) are assessed. "X" refers to the training or development experience received by the group.

Organizations generally want all employees in a section trained, not just a few who are randomly selected. Consequently, they're more likely to use *quasi-experimental designs*, which do not involve random selection. In both classes of quasi-experimental design shown in Exhibit 9.7, multiple measures (T_1, T_2, etc.) are taken. In the time-series design, several measures are taken before the training and several after. In the nonequivalent control groups design, two groups receive multiple measurement, but only one receives training.

Again, although to a lesser extent than is true for experimental designs, quasi-experimental designs are time-consuming and constrained by the realities of organizations. Thus, *pre-experimental designs* look most attractive to companies. The two classes of pre-experimental design shown in Exhibit 9.7 are much simpler, far less costly, and far less time-consuming than the other designs. But with ease and low cost come less accuracy and confidence in measuring change that may have been the result of a training program—or any other program to produce change. However, these are the realities of organizations, and reflect the constraints and trade-offs that HR professionals face daily.

■□ *fast fact*

Colgate's People Development process for high potential employees will be evaluated by considering how quickly they can identify qualified people for global placements, how quickly high potentials move up the career ladder, the satisfaction levels of the high-potential employees, and retention rates.

SUMMARY

Rapidly changing technology, illiteracy, foreign competition, and changes in organizational strategy are putting pressure on organizations to socialize, train and develop employees. This requires careful attention to needs assessment, program development and implementation, and evaluation. Four types of needs analysis—organizational, job, person, and demographic—are designed to diagnose systematically the short- and long-term human resource needs of an organization. When actual performance and desired performance differ, training may be needed.

Following effective needs analysis, socialization, training and development activities must be designed and implemented. Setting up these activities involves deciding who will be trained, who will train, where the training will occur, and what methods will be used. Cost considerations, as well as the types of competencies to be acquired (basic, interpersonal, or conceptual) and the location of the training (on the job, on-site, or off the job), affect the selection of appropriate methods.

Regardless of the method chosen, the content of the training should be designed to maximize learning. Principles to consider include clear instructions, proper role models, active participation, feedback, and practice. These should be viewed in relationship to the trainees' self-efficacy or competency beliefs. It's also important to examine the work environment to ensure that new behaviors will be reinforced rather than punished.

The last major phase of socialization, training and development is evaluation. Not only should reactions to training be assessed, but also the degree of learning, the change in job behavior, and organizational outcomes should be examined against objectives.

Globalization creates many new challenges, and developing managers who will be effective everywhere in the world is among the greatest of these. The examples of Pepsico illustrates how the most competitive firms are effectively developing their managers.

TERMS TO REMEMBER

Apprenticeship training	Mentoring
Assessment center method	On-the-job training (OJT)
Assistantships	Orientation
Behavioral modeling	Organizational needs analysis
Business games	Person needs analysis
Demographic needs analysis	Programmed instruction
Development	Reinforcement
Enactive mastery feedback	Role-playing
Evaluation components	Self-efficacy
Evaluation designs	Sensitivity training
Formal course method	Simulation
In-basket exercise	Socialization
Interactive video training	Statistical process control
Internships	Supervisory assistance
Job instruction training	Team training
Job needs analysis	Training
Job rotation	Training transfer
Knowledge management	Vestibule method
Leadership institutes	

DISCUSSION QUESTIONS

1. How is training at SPO in General Motors related to the organization's strategy?

2. Describe and explain the three major phases involved in setting up any training system.

3. Reflect for a moment on your own work experience. What benefits did your former (or present) employer receive by socializing and training you? Why did your employer not just hire someone who could perform the job without training?

4. Explain how and why the socialization, training, and development activities at Boston Consulting Group and at McKinsey Company differ.

5. What design principles can enhance the learning that takes place in training and development programs?

6. As a manager, what indicators would you need in order to decide whether a low-performing subordinate was a selection mistake or merely in need of training? If possible, illustrate this dilemma with an example from your own work experience.

7. Discuss the strategic role of socialization, training and development activities for companies with international operations and markets.

PROJECTS TO EXTEND YOUR LEARNING

1. **Managing Strategically.**   The opening feature of this chapter describes how the SPO division within General Motors uses training and development to help the company achieve its strategic business objectives of better and faster customer service, more efficiently. More and more companies are doing the same thing, that is, learning about what is needed by the business and then tailoring their socialization, training and development activities to serve those needs. This is consistent with the framework that guides an organizational needs analysis. The job and person needs analyses then reflect the strategic business needs of the company. Visit the home pages of a few companies, and then try to identify some of their strategic business needs. With this knowledge, then suggest some socialization, training, and development activities that might be useful. Visit General Motors (**www.gm.com**), General Electric (**www.ge.com**), Cisco (**www.cisco.com**) and Microsoft (**www.microsoft.com**).

2. **Managing Teams.**   More and more companies are turning to the use of teams to get the work done. Consequently, companies turn to their HR departments to help provide the necessary training and development activities to help increase the chances of their teams performing effectively. After switching to team-based management, the Norwegian arm of British Petroleum (BP Norge) decided to conduct such training after nine months of poor team performance. They implemented two-day workshops with employees from all levels of the company and from both countries. At the workshops, they discussed the importance of self-managed teams to BP's business strategy. They also discussed resistance to change and the new behaviors needed in the team environment. Locate other companies that have been using teams or are now switching to team-based management and learn what training needs they had/have. Perhaps visit total quality management companies such as Ford (**www.ford.com**), or Corning (**www.corning.com**) and see if you can determine what team training they have been doing. You may also wish to visit BP to learn more about BP Norge (**www.bp.com**).

3. **Managing Diversity.** Pacific Enterprises (headquartered in Los Angeles) is ranked number one in the hiring, promoting, training, and retaining people of color by the Council of Economic Priorities in New York City, according to a study commissioned by *Fortune* magazine (August 3, 1998, pp. 114–122). Pacific Enterprises allows people to nominate themselves for the company's fast-track management training programs. As a consequence of this, the company has the highest percentage of minority officials and managers of any company in the list of 50 companies. Visit the home page of *Fortune* (**www.fortune.com**), or read the article cited above and describe the training, development, and socialization activities of a few of the other 49 companies on the list.

4. **Managing Change.** Although some companies need to go through major changes, many find it important to change continuously, but in smaller, incremental steps. This creates an environment of continuous change, improvement, and adaptation to the environment. Of course, even businesses planning incremental changes need information to help determine what changes are needed, who needs the change, and what information will be needed to make the changes. Helping in this process of continuous change and information gathering, storage, and distribution is the activity of knowledge management, often under the direction of the chief knowledge officer (CKO) or the chief learning officer (CLO). Many companies have them today, and almost all the public accounting and consulting firms have them. Knowledge is used to help themselves change, improve, and adapt and thereby better serve the customers. Visit the home pages of some firms such as Booz-Allen (**www.bah.com**), Andersen Consulting (**www.ac.com**), and PricewaterhouseCoopers (**www.pricewaterhousecoopers.com**) to learn what these firms do with knowledge management and organizational change. Also visit *Workforce Online* (**www.workforceonline.com**) for a listing of articles to read for further information on knowledge management.

5. **Managing Globalization.** U.S. firms realize that the world is their marketplace. While most firms that do business abroad use employees from the local companies, they still need to use some of their employees (expatriates) for such things as managing the operations, providing technology, or providing a special expertise (e.g., financial management or product marketing). But the success rate of these expatriates is still low. Often the causes cited are lack of preparation for the assignment and lack of family preparation. Visit the home pages of the Society for Human Resource Management (**www.shrmglobal.org**) and the SHRM Global Forum (www.shrmglobal.org) to learn more about expatriate training and development. Then, list five recommendations that you could offer an employer as guidelines for using training as part of the company's predeparture preparation for expatriates.

6. **Integration and Application.** Review the case description of AAL at the end of this text. Critique the approach to socialization, training, and development used by AAL during their organizational change. What were the strengths and weaknesses of this company's use of training?

CASE STUDY

Seeing the Forest and the Trees

The current face of domestic and global competition that the leaders of the Forest Products Company (FPC) and its parent, the Weyerhaeuser Corporation, saw as they surveyed an industry on its knees in the early 1980s was a far different face than the one Weyerhaeuser and its subsidiaries had successfully competed against for so long. They knew how to compete—and win—against a large-firm, commodity lumber business. But that business was in its death throes, and what was emerging from the ashes presented an entirely new set of challenges, one that would require a radical change in Weyerhaeuser's strategy. The new competitors weren't the old monolithic organizations but were instead small mills, lean and mean, configured so they could tailor their products to customer demand and change their product lines rapidly if the need arose. They were nonunion, owner-operated, and entrepreneurial and, in this configuration, were running the lowest-cost, most market-oriented operations around.

Going out of business was not an alternative anyone cared to think about, but if things didn't change it was a definite possibility. So Charley Bingham, the CEO of the Forest Products Company, knew that something had to be done—and sooner, not later. He gathered his top dozen managers, and together they decided that a massive reorganization was called for, accompanied by a radical change in strategy. According to Bingham, the change in strategy went something like this:

"Approximately 80 percent of our sales dollars in 1982 represented products sold as commodities. By 1995, we resolved that we must reverse the proportions."

The massive reorganization at FPC mirrored that occurring at its parent company. The Weyerhaeuser Corporation decided to drastically decentralize. The three operating units, of which FPC was one, were given free reign on how to run their businesses. Given this scenario, Bingham and his team decided they needed to create an organization capable of acting and responding just like their competitors. Thus, they created 200 profit centers with each center largely responsible for its own bottom line.

This restructuring soon proved to be only a first step in the right direction. FPC's ability to implement its new strategy was being undermined by low morale, which was pervasive. In addition, many middle managers, those needed to actually carry out the change, were pessimistic about the possibility of sustained future success. Silently, they even questioned their own ability to operate the profit centers.

With insights from Horace Parker, director of executive development at FPC, the rest of the top team came to realize that there would have to be a total transformation of the organization: the corporate culture, knowledge base, skill levels, style of leadership, and team orientation would all have to change, for all employees. With 18,000 employees across the United States, Parker wasn't sure where to start. The others said they would help, but Horace had to tell them what to do. Horace, of course, is waiting to hear what you have to tell him.

QUESTIONS

1. Where does Horace start? What programs does he put in place to deal with the needs of corporate culture, knowledge, skills, leadership, and team orientation?

2. How does he go about developing the programs that he needs to put in place? Does he do it by himself? Can he buy off-the-shelf programs?

3. What time frame does Horace need to implement the programs to make the change successful? If he deals only with the executive development programs, does he need to be concerned with programs for middle managers and below? How does he do this?

Randall S. Schuler, Rutgers University

CASE STUDY

A Broader View Seizes More Opportunities

Don English, corporate vice president in charge of human resources, is now finally able to take a pause from the stream of "fire fighting" he has been engaged in since he came to Bancroft ten years ago! Like many of his colleagues in other firms, Don's knowledge of HRM came as much from doing it as from formal education.

Because of his workload, Don tended to keep pretty narrowly focused, and he rarely read HRM or attended professional conferences. However, recently, things have been easing up. He has been able to recruit and train almost all the division managers in charge of human resources. Now they can do most of the fire fighting, at least that's what Don is planning on. And he has been doing more reading than ever before. Of course, Don has not been totally out of touch with the rest of the world or the growing importance of HR management planning. When he started filling the slots for division personnel managers, he made sure that it was a learning experience for him. Don always required job candidates to prepare a one-hour talk on the state of research and practice in different areas of HRM, for example, selection, appraisal, compensation, or training. He would even invite MBA candidates who had no course work in HRM and ask them to relate their field of interest to HRM.

Don is planning to become the chief executive officer of Bancroft or some other firm of similar or larger size within the next five to seven years. He thinks he can achieve this if he remains in human resources and does an outstanding job. He will have to be outstanding by all standards, both internal and external to the firm. From his interviews during the past three years, Don knows that it's imperative to move human resources in a strategic direction while at the same time doing the best possible job with the "nuts and bolts" activities.

During a moment of reflection, Don begins to scribble some notes on his large white desk pad. In the middle is Bancroft. To its left are its suppliers and to its right are its customers. In his head are all the HR practices he is so familiar with. He has a hunch that there must be a way to use the firm's expertise in performance appraisal and training to help Bancroft be more effective. Bancroft has been learning tremendously from its five-year drive to improve quality, but during the past year, quality gains have slowed. Bancroft must continue to improve its quality, but large internal quality gains are becoming more and more difficult as Bancroft climbs the learning curve. Don wonders, "How can he help Bancroft experience the excitement of seeing large gains in quality improvement again?" Don circles the list of suppliers and begins to formulate a plan that will improve his chances of becoming CEO. He now seeks your advice in exactly what to do and how to go about doing it.

QUESTIONS

1. Let's assume that Don has gotten the approval from his boss to help Bancroft's suppliers. Should he work with them all or decide to just start with one or two and see how it goes?

2. If Don can do anything to help his suppliers with their HR management activities, what should he focus on?

3. Should Don actually go into the suppliers and do their HR work, or should he train the suppliers' HR professionals at Bancroft?

Randall S. Schuler, Rutgers University.

ENDNOTES

[1] K. Labich, "Is Herb Kelleher America's Best CEO?" *Fortune* (May 2, 1994): 50.

[2] S. R. Davis, J. H. Lucas, and D. R. Marcotte, "GM Links Better Leaders to Better Business," *Workforce* (April 1998): 62–68.

[3] J. Gordon, "The Great Outsourcing Stampede—That Never Happened," *Training* (February 1998): 38–48; "Employee Training: Datagraph," *Bulletin to Management* (January 23, 1997): 28; D. Stamps, "Are We Smart Enough for Our Jobs?" *Training* (April 1996): 44–50; "Industry Report 1997: A Statistical Picture of Employer-Sponsored Training in the United States," *Training* (October 1997): 33–65; D. Stamps, "Wall Street Comes Wooing," *Training* (November 1997): 28–34. For extensive treatment of this topic, see J. K. Ford et al., *Improving Training Effectiveness in Work Organizations* (Hillsdale, NJ: LEA, 1994); I. L. Goldstein, *Training in Organizations*, 3rd ed. (Pacific Grove, CA: Brooks/Cole, 1993); I. L. Goldstein et al., *Training and Development in Organizations* (San Francisco: Jossey-Bass, 1989); S. I. Tannenbaum and G. Yukl, "Training and Development in Work Organizations," *Annual Review of Psychology* 43 (1992): 399–441; W. R. Scott, and J. W. Meyer, "The Rise of Training Programs in Firms and Agencies: An Institutional Perspective," *Research in Organizational Behavior* 13 (1991): 297–326; R. E. Snow and J. Swanson, "Instructional Psychology: Aptitude, Adaptation, and Assessment," *Annual Review of Psychology* 43 (1992): 583–626; R. A. Noe and J. K. Ford, "Emerging Issues and New Directions for Training Research," *Research in Personnel and Human Resource Management* 10 (1992): 345–384.

[4] R. R. Ritti, *The Ropes to Skip and the Ropes to Know: Studies in Organizational Behavior,* 5th ed. (Columbus, OH: Grid Publishing, 1997).

[5] D. C. Feldman, "Socialization, Resocialization, and Training: Reframing the Research Agenda," *Training and Development in Organizations*, Goldstein et al., ed., 376–416.

[6] J. L. Laabs, "Financial Impact: Quality Drives Trident's Success," *Workforce* (February 1998): 44–49.

[7] K. Winkler and I. Janger, "You're Hired! Now How Do We Keep You?" *Across the Board* (July/August 1998): 14–23; J. C. Dannemiller, "How We Keep Good People," *Across the Board* (July/August 1998): 21; A. Baron, "Top Managers Still Don't Get It," *Across the Board* (July/August 1998): 22; M. Budman, "Show Them the Money?" *Across the Board* (July/August 1998): 23; M. R. Buckley, D. B. Fedor, J. G. Veres, D. S. Wiese, and S. M. Carraher, "Investigating Newcomer Expectations and Job-Related Outcomes," *Journal of Applied Psychology*, Vol. 83, No. 3 (1998): 452–461; A. Newman Korn, "Gotcha!" *Across the Board* (September 1998): 30–35; G. T. Chao, "Organizational Socialization in Multinational Corporations: The Role of Implicit Learning," *Creating Tomorrow's Organizations* (New York: John Wiley & Sons Ltd., 1997): Chapter 3; S. J. Ashford and J. S. Black, "Proactivity During Organizational Entry: The Role of Desire for Control," *Journal of Applied Psychology*, Vol. 81, No. 2 (1996): 199–214; A. Colella, "Organizational Socialization of Newcomers With Disabilities: A Framework for Future Research," *Research in Personnel and Human Resources Management*, Vol. 14 (1996): 351–417; C. L. Adkins, "Previous Work Experience and Organizational Socialization: A Longitudinal Examination," *Academy of Management Journal*, Vol. 38, No. 3 (1995): 839–862.

[8] "SHRM – BNA Survey No. 63: Human Resource Activities, Budgets & Staffs, 1997–1998," *Bulletin to Management* (June 18, 1998): 2; "High-Technology Firms Lead the Way in Training," *Bulletin to Management* (February 5, 1998): 376; "1997 Industry Report," *Training* (October 1998): 33–65.

[9] C. C. Morrow, M. Quintin Jarrett, and M. T. Rupinski, "An Investigating of the Effect and Economic Utility of Corporate-Wide Training," *Personnel Psychology* 50 (1997): 91. For a description of how to assess the economic utility of training, see W. F. Cascio, "Using Utility Analysis to Assess Training Outcomes," *Training and Development in Organizations*, Goldstein, ed. (San Francisco: Jossey-Bass, 1989).

[10] K. Kelly and P. Burrows, "Motorola: Training for the Millennium," *Business Week* (March 28, 1994): 158–161.

[11] Industry Report 1998, "Who Gets Trained? Where The Money Goes," *Training* (October 1998): 55–67.

[12] J. P. MacDuffie and T. A. Kochan, "Do U.S. Firms Underinvest in Human Resources? Determinants of Training in the World Auto Industry," *Industrial Relations* (September 1993): 145–160.

[13] C. J. Bachler, "The Trainer's Role: Is Turning Upside Down," *Workforce* (June 1997): 93–105

[14] G. T. Chao et al., "Organizational Socialization: Its Content and Consequences," *Journal of Applied Psychology* 79 (1994): 730–743; E. W. Morrison, "Newcomer Information Seeking: Exploring Types, Modes, Sources, and Outcomes," *Academy of Management Journal* 36 (1993): 557–589; C. Ostroff and S. W. J. Kozlowski, "Organizational Socialization as a Learning Process: The Role of Information Acquisition," *Personnel Psychology* 45 (1992): 849–874.

[15] T. J. Maurer and B. A. Tarulli, "Investigation of Perceived Environment, Perceived Outcome, and Person Variables in Relationship to Voluntary Development Activity by Employees," *Journal of Applied Psychology* 79 (1994): 3–14. See also L. A. Hill, *Becoming a Manager: Mastery of a New Identity* (Cambridge, MA: Harvard Business School Press, 1992); T. A. Scandura, "Dysfunctional Mentoring Relationships and Outcomes," *Journal of Management* 24 (1998): 449–467.

[16] R. Spector and P. D. McCarthy, *The Nordstrom Way* (New York: Wiley, 1995); R. Henkoff, "Finding, Training and Keeping the Best Service Workers," *Fortune* (October 3, 1994): 110–122.

[17] T. A. Stewart, "Brain Power: Who Owns It. . . How They Profit From It," *Fortune* (March 17, 1997): 105–110.

[18] R. Zemke, "How To Do A Needs Assessment When You Think You Don't Have Time," *Training* (March 1998): 38–44; "Lifelong Learning and the Skills Shortage: Policy Guide,"

Bulletin to Management (November 27, 1997): 384; "Technology and Training: A Dynamic Duo," *Bulletin to Management* Vol. 48, No. 10 (March 6, 1997): 80; L. Saari et al., "A Survey of Management Training and Education Practices in U.S. Companies," *Personnel Psychology* 41 (1988): 731–745.

19 Adapted from I. I. Goldstein, *Training: Program Development and Evaluation* (Monterey, CA: Brooks/Cole, 1986): 8.

20 D. Schaaf, "What Workers Really Think About Training," *Training* (September 1998): 59–65; J. J. Laabs, "Training MTA Managers Is An Inside Job," *Workforce* (February 1998): 65–70; M. A. Berman, "Sweating the Soft Stuff," *Across the Board* (January 1998): 39. For a discussion of ethical corporate culture, see F. J. Aguilar, *Managing Corporate Ethics* (Oxford: Oxford Business, 1994); R. W. Rogers and W. C. Byham, "Diagnosing Organization Cultures for Realignment," *Diagnosis for Organizational Change: Methods and Models*, A. Howard et al., eds. (New York: Guilford Press, 1994):; K. Fisher, "Diagnostic Issues for Work Teams," *Diagnosis for Organizational Change*, A. Howard et al., eds.

21 Based on P. Cappelli and A. Crocker-Hefter, *Distinctive Human Resources Are the Core Competencies of Firms*, Report No. R117Q00011-91 (Washington, DC: U.S. Department of Education, 1994).

22 J. Lynch and D. Orne, "The Next Elite: Manufacturing Supermanagers," *Management Review* (April 1985): 49.

23 Douglas Bray, Chairman, Emeritus, Development Dimensions International, Pittsburgh, Pennsylvania, personal communication.

24 For more discussion of the advantages and disadvantages of basic assessment techniques, see I. L. Goldstein, "Training in Work Organizations," *Handbook of Industrial and Organizational Psychology*, Vol. 2 (1991): 507–620.

25 H. Holzer et al., "Are Training Subsidies for Firms Effective? The Michigan Experience," *Industrial and Labor Relations Review* (1994).

26 Modified from J. K. Ford and R. A. Noe, "Self-Assessed Training Needs: The Effects of Attitudes toward Training, Managerial Level and Function," *Personnel Psychology* 40 (1987): 39–53.

27 M. W. McCall, M. M. Lombardo, and A. M. Morrison, *The Lessons of Experience* (Lexington, MA: Lexington Books, 1998); C. D. McCauley et al., "Assessing the Developmental Components of Managerial Jobs," *Journal of Applied Psychology* 79 (1994): 544–560.

28 R. Neil Olson and E. A. Sexton, "Gender Differences in the Returns to and the Acquisition of On-the-Job Training," *Industrial Relations* 35 (January 1996): 59; S. G. Baugh, M. J. Lankau and A. Terri, "An Investigation of the Effects of Protégé Gender on Responses to Mentoring," *Journal of Vocational Behavior* 49 (1996): 309–323; P. J. Ohlott, M. N. Ruderman, and C. D. McCauley, "Gender Differences in Managers' Developmental Job Experiences," *Academy of Management Journal* 37 (1994): 46–67.

29 "Medtronic Expects Managers to Value Differences," *HR Reporter* (February 1993): 3.

30 J. B. Tracey, S. I. Tannenbaum and M. J. Kavanagh, "Applying Trained Skills on the Job: The Importance of the Work Environment," *Journal of Applied Psychology* 80 (1995): 239–252.

31 R. J. Sternberg and E. L. Grigorenko, "Are Cognitive Styles Still in Style?" *American Psychologist* 52 (July 1997): 700–712; K. Kraiger, J. K. Ford, and E. Salas, "Application of Cognitive, Skill-Based, and Affective Theories of Learning Outcomes to New Methods of Training Evaluation," *Journal of Applied Psychology* 78 (1993): 311–328.

32 "Ritz-Carlton Certifies Ladies and Gentlemen," *HR Reporter* (August 1993): 1–4.

33 J. Strandberg, "Training For A Technology Upgrade," *Training* (November 1997): 36–38;

34 L. Rubis, "Show and Tell," *HR. Magazine* (April 1998): 110–117

35 H. W. Marsh, G. E. Richards, and J. Barnes, "Multidimensional Self-Concepts: The Effects of Participation in an Outward Bound Program," *Journal of Personality and Social Psychology* 50 (1986): 195–204; H. W. Marsh, G. E. Richards, and J. Barnes, "A Long-Term Follow-up of the Effects of Participation in an Outward Bound Program," *Personality and Social Psychology Bulletin* 12 (1987): 465–492.

36 J. D. Facteau, G. H. Dobbins, J. E. A. Russell, R. T. Ladd, and J. D. Kudisch, "The Influence of General Perceptions of the Training Environment on Pretraining Motivation and Perceived Training Transfer," *Journal of Management* 21 (1995): 1–25; Goldstein, *Training*; B. M. Bass and J. A. Vaughan, *Training in Industry: The Management of Learning* (Belmont, CA: Wadsworth, 1966): 88.

37 L. A. Ferman et al., *Worker Training: A Legacy for the 1990s* (Madison, WI: Industrial Relations Research Association, 1990); A. P. Carnevale, L. J. Gainer, and A. S. Meltzer, *Workplace Basics Training Manual* (San Francisco: Jossey-Bass, 1990); T. T. Baldwin, R. J. Magjuka, and B. T. Loher, "The Perils of Participation: Effects of Choice of Training on Trainee Motivation and Learning," *Personnel Psychology* 44 (1991): 51–65; A. P. Carnevale, L. J. Gainer, and E. Schulz, *Training the Technical Work Force* (San Francisco: Jossey-Bass, 1990); Goldstein, *Training*.

38 D. Stamps, "Will School-To-Work, Work?" *Training* (June 1996): 72–81; S. Overman, "Apprenticeships Smooth School to Work Transitions," *HR. Magazine* (December 1990): 40–43; K. Matthes, "Apprenticeships Can Support the 'Forgotten Youth'," *HR Focus* (December 1991): 19; "Focus at Ford Is Education for the Sake of Education," *GED on TV* (July–August 1993): 3; E. Kiester, "Germany Prepares Kids for Good Jobs; We Are Preparing Ours for Wendy's," *Smithsonian* (March 1993): 44–55.

39 "Internships Provide Workplace Snapshot: Policy Guide," *Bulletin to Management* 48 (21) (May 22, 1997): 168; "Personnel Shop Talk," *Bulletin to Management* 48 (21) (May 22, 1997): 162.

40 S. L. Willis and S. S. Dubin, eds., *Maintaining Professional Competence: Approaches to Career Enhancement, Vitality and Success throughout a Work Life* (San Francisco: Jossey-Bass, 1990); J. A. Schneer and F.

Reitman, "Effects of Employment Gaps on the Careers of M.B.A.'s: More Damaging for Men than for Women?" *Academy of Management Journal* 33 (1990): 391–406; J. H. Greenhaus, S. Parasuraman, and W. M. Wormley, "Effects of Race on Organizational Experiences, Job Performance Evaluations and Career Outcomes," *Academy of Management Journal* 33 (1990): 64–86.

41 B. Filipczak, "The Executive Coach: Helper or Healer?" *Training* (March 1998): 30–36; J. Waldroop and T. Butler, "The Executive as Coach," *Harvard Business Review* (November–December 1996): 111–117.

42 J. Spiegel Arthur, "Virtual U.," *Human Resource Executive* (March 19, 1998): 44–46; "B-School Faculty Quality Training," *Fortune* (January 13, 1992): 14. See also W. Wiggenhorn, "Motorola U: When Training Becomes an Education," *Harvard Business Review* (July–August 1990): 71–83; L. B. Ward, "In the Executive Alphabet, You Call Them C.L.O.'s," *New York Times* (February 4, 1996): 12; "In the Know," *Human Resource Executive* (February 1997): 31; E. Raimy, "Knowledge Movers," *Human Resource Executive* (February 1997): 32–36; K. F. Clark, "The Right Track," *Human Resource Executive* (May 6, 1997): 52–55; J. Reingold, "Corporate America Goes To School," *Business Week* (October 20, 1997): 66–72; T. Bartlett, "The Hottest Campus on the Internet," *Business Week* (October 20, 1997): 77, 80.

43 Industry Report 1998, "Training By Computer: How U.S. Organizations Use Computers in Training," *Training* (October 1998): 71–76; R. Quick, "Software Seeks to Breathe Life Into Corporate Training Classes," *The Wall Street Journal* (August 6, 1998): B8; B. Roberts, "Via the Desktop://," *HR Magazine* (August 1998): 99–104; A. Pescuric, "Supporting Roles," *Human Resource Executive* (March 5, 1998): 62–64; S.B. Hall, "And the Answer Is..." *Human Resource Executive* (January 1998): 51–54; "Instant Gratification," *Human Resource Executive* (January 1998): 55–57.

44 R. Ganzel, "What Price Online Learning?" *Training* (February 1999): 50–54; S. Fister, "Web-based Training on a Shoestring," *Training* (December 1998): 42–47.

45 A. R. McIlvaine, "Games Employees Play," *Human Resource Executive* (February 1999): 37–39; L. Lorek, "Computers, Cameras, Action," *Human Resource Executive* (January 1998): 36–38; L. Stevens, "Streamlined Training," *Human Resource Executive* (January 1998): 44–46; A. McIlvaine, "Cyber Scholars," *Human Resource Executive* (October 6, 1997): 1, 29–32; D. J. Shadovitz, "Techno Grip," *Human Resource Executive* (October 6, 1997): 4; "1997 Industry Report: Training Technology," *Training* (October 1997): 67–75; E. Santasiero, "Big Game Cyberhunt," *Training: Online Learning* (August 1998): 18–22.

46 R. Becker, "Taking the Misery Out of Experiential Training," *Training* (February 1998): 78–88; M. Hequet, "Games that Teach," *Training* (July 1995): 53–58; T. A. Stewart, "The Dance Steps Get Trickier All the Time," *Fortune* (May 26, 1997): 157–160; G. C. Thornton III and J. N. Cleveland, "Developing Managerial Talent through Simulation," *American Psychologist* (February 1990): 190–199; W. M. Bulkeley, "The World of Work Is A Keystroke Away For Students in Computer-Simulated Jobs," *The Wall Street Journal* (May 7, 1996): B1, B2.

47 For an excellent discussion of assessment centers, see G. C. Thornton III, *Assessment Centers* (Reading, MA: Addison-Wesley, 1992); V. R. Boehm, "Assessment Centers and Management Development," *Personnel Management*, K. M. Rowland and G. Ferris, eds. (Boston: Allyn & Bacon, 1982), 327–362; R. B. Finkle, "Managerial Assessment Centers," *Handbook of Industrial and Organizational Psychology*, M. D. Dunnette, ed. (Chicago: Rand McNally, 1976), 861–888; I. T. Robertson and S. Downs, "Work-Sample Tests of Trainability: A Meta-Analysis," *Journal of Applied Psychology* 74 (1989): 402–410.

48 For an excellent description of the many uses and issues of assessment centers, see the entire special issue, R. E. Riggio and B. T. Mayes, eds., "Assessment Centers: Research and Applications," *Journal of Social Behavior and Personality* 12 (1997): 1–331.

49 E. Brown, "War Games To Make You Better At Business," *Fortune* (September 28, 1998): 291–296; J. Pereira, "Leader of the Pack in Wilderness Training is Pushed to the Wall," *The Wall Street Journal* (July 24, 1997): A1, A6; C. Lawson, "Corporate Bonding Over a Hot Stove," *New York Times* (July 23, 1997): C1, C6; G. M. McEvoy and P. F. Buller, "The Power of Outdoor Management Development," *Journal of Management Development* 16 (3) (1997): 208–217; C. Patton, "In Proper Conduct," *Human Resource Executive* (February 1998): 30–32.

50 C. Lee, "The Adult Learner: Neglected No More," *Training* (March 1998): 47–52; L. W. Hellervich, J. F. Hazucha, and R. J. Schneider, "Behavior Change: Models, Methods, and a Review of Evidence," *Handbook of Industrial and Organizational Psychology*.

51 M. A. Quinones, "Pretraining Context Effects: Training Assignment as Feedback," *Journal of Applied Psychology* 80 (1995): 226–238; V. L. Huber, "A Comparison of Goal Setting and Pay as Learning Incentives," *Psychological Reports* 56 (1985): 223–235; V. L. Huber, "Interplay between Goal Setting and Promises of Pay-for-Performance on Individual and Group Performance: An Operant Interpretation," *Journal of Organizational Behavior Management* 7 (1986): 45–64.

52 J. K. Harrison, "Individual and Combined Effects of Behavior Modeling and the Cultural Assimilator in Cross-Cultural Management Training," *Journal of Applied Psychology* 77 (1992): 952–962.

53 S. J. Ashford and A. S. Tsui, "Self-Regulation for Managerial Effectiveness: The Role of Active Feedback Seeking," *Academy of Management Journal* 34 (1991): 251–280; S. I. Tannenbaum et al., "Meeting Trainees' Expectations: The Influence of Training Fulfillment on the Development of Commitment, Self-Efficacy and Motivation," *Journal of Applied Psychology* 76 (1991): 759–769; M. E. Gist, "The Influence of Training Method on Self-Efficacy and Idea Generation among Managers," *Personnel Psychology* 42 (1989): 787–805.

54 Huber, "Interplay between Goal Setting and Promises of Pay-for-Performance"; J. D. Eyring, D. Steele Johnson, and D. J. Francis, "A Cross-Level Units-of-Analysis Approach to Individual Differences in Skill Acquisition," *Journal of Applied Psychology* 78 (1993): 805–814; P. C. Earley, "Self or

Group? Cultural Effects of Training on Self-Efficacy and Performance," *Administrative Science Quarterly* 39 (1994): 89–117.

55 V. L. Huber, G. P. Latham, and E. A. Locke, "The Management of Impressions through Goal Setting," *Impression Management in the Organization*, R. A. Giacalone and P. Rosenfield, eds. (Hillsdale, NJ: Erlbaum, 1989); D. R. Ilgen, C. D. Fisher, and M. S. Taylor, "Consequences of Individual Feedback on Behavior in Organizations," *Journal of Applied Psychology* 64 (1979): 349–371; E. A. Locke, "Effects of Knowledge of Results, Feedback in Relation to Standards, and Goals on Reaction-Time Performance," *American Journal of Psychology* 81 (1968): 566–575.

56 P. Hogan, M. Hakel, and P. Decker, "Effects of Trainee-Generated vs. Trainer-Provided Rule Codes on Generalization in Behavioral Modeling Training," *Journal of Applied Psychology* 71 (1986): 469–473.

57 W. W. Tornow and M. London, "Maximizing the Value of 360-Degree Feedback: A Process for Successful Individual and Organizational Development," *Center for Creative Leadership* (March 1998); D. E. Coates, "Don't Tie 360 Feedback to Pay," *Training* (September 1998): 68–78.

58 J. E. Driskell, C. Copper, and A. Moran, "Does Mental Practice Enhance Performance?" *Journal of Applied Psychology* 79 (1994): 481–492.

59 W. Honig, *Operant Behavior* (New York: Appleton-Century-Crofts, 1966); Huber, "Interplay between Goal Setting and Promises of Pay-for-Performance"; J. S. Russel, K. Wexley, and J. Hunter, "Questioning the Effectiveness of Behavior Modeling Training in an Industrial Setting," *Personnel Psychology* 34 (1984): 465–482.

60 C. Frayne and G. P. Latham, "The Application of Social Learning Theory to Employee Self-Management of Attendance," *Journal of Applied Psychology* 72 (1987): 387–392.

61 W. C. Byham, "Grooming Next Millennium Leaders," *HR Magazine* (February 1999): 46–50; J. C. Meister, *Corporate Universities: Lessons in Building a World-Class Workforce* (New York: McGraw-Hill, 1998); B. Filipczak, "CEOs Who Train," *Training* (June 1996): 57–64; E. W. Book, "Leadership for the Millennium," *Working Woman* (March 1998): 29–34; L. Thach, "14 Ways To Groom Executives," *Training* (August 1998): 52–55.

62 J. Bolt, *Executive Development* (New York: The Free Press, 1989).

63 S. Greengard, "Will Your Culture Support KM?" *Workforce* (October 1998): 93–94; S. Greengard, "How to Make KM a Reality," *Workforce* (October 1998): 90–91; "In the Know,"

Human Resource Executive (February 1997): 31; E. Raimy, "Knowledge Movers," *Human Resource Executive* (February 1997): 32–37; S. Greengard, "Storing, Shaping and Sharing Collective Wisdom," *Workforce* (October 1998): 82–88.

64 S. Cauldron, "Teamwork Takes Work," *Personnel Journal* (February 1994): 41–49.

65 M. Moravec, O. J. Johannessen, and T. A. Hjelmas, "Thumbs Up for Self-Managed Teams," *Management Review* (July/August 1997); S. E. Prokesch, "Unleashing the Power of Learning: An Interview with British Petroleum's John Browne," *Harvard Business Review* (September–October, 1997); M. Moravec, O. J. Johannessen, and T. A. Hjelmas, "We Have Seen the Future and It Is Self-Managed," *PM Network* (September 1997): 20–22.

66 J. W. Dean, Jr., and M. P. Sharfman, "Does Decision Process Matter? A Study of Strategic Decision Making Effectiveness," *Academy of Management Journal* 39 (1996): 368–396; P. W. Mulvey, J. F. Viega, and P. M. Elsass, "When Teammates Raise a White Flag," *Academy of Management Executive* 10 (1996): 40–49; and R. L. Priem, D. A. Harrison, and N. K. Muir, "Structured Conflict and Consensus Outcomes in Group Decision Making," *Journal of Management* 21 (1995): 691–710.

67 J. Fulkerson and R. S. Schuler, "Managing Worldwide Diversity at Pepsi-Cola International," *Working through Diversity: Human Resources Initiatives*, S. E. Jackson, ed. (New York: Guilford Publications, 1992): 248–278; P. Sellers, "Pepsi Opens a Second Front," *Fortune* (August 8, 1994): 71–76.

68 D. C. Thomas and E. C. Ravlin, "Responses of Employees to Cultural Adaptation by a Foreign Manager," *Journal of Applied Psychology* 80 (1995): 133–146; P. C. Earley, "Self or Group? Cultural Effects of Training on Self-Efficacy and Performance," *Administrative Science Quarterly* 39 (1994): 89–117; O. Tregaskis, "The Role of National Context and HR Strategy in Shaping Training and Development Practice in French and U.K. Organizations," *Organization Studies* 18 (1997): 839–856.

69 G. Gerson and C. McCleskey, "Numbers Help Make a Training Decision That Counts," *HR Magazine* (July 1998): 51–58; G. M. Alliger, S. I. Tannenbaum, W. Bennett, Jr., H. Traver, and A. Shotland, "A Meta-Analysis of the Relations Among Training Criteria," *Personnel Psychology* 50 (1997): 341; K. A. Willyerd, "Balancing Your Evaluation Act," *Training* (March 1997): 52–58.

70 Based on I. Goldstein, *Training: Program Development and Evaluation*, 2nd ed. (Monterey, CA: Brooks/Cole Publishing Co., 1986): 157–167.

TOTAL COMPENSATION: DEVELOPING AN OVERALL APPROACH

Chapter Outline

"Vision and strategy need to lead compensation philosophy and practices. A company's vision and how a person's job relates to it need to be very clear."

**Arthur C. Martinez
Chairman and CEO
Sears, Roebuck and Co.[1]**

MANAGING HUMAN RESOURCES THROUGH PARTNERSHIP
at Sears

Arthur C. Martinez, CEO and Chairman of Sears, sees a close link between the company's business strategy and compensation. "Vision and strategy need to lead to compensation philosophy and practices," he says. "Over the long term, people change their behavior not because of pay practices but because they relate to the organization's vision and strategy. Pay practices need to then reinforce the strategy." With more than 300,000 employees worldwide, finding ways to align employee behavior with the business strategy represents a major challenge.

At Sears, pay practices reward managers who show improvements in customer satisfaction, employee satisfaction, and financial performance. Martinez knows that employee satisfaction, customer satisfaction, and the bottom line are closely related. He also knows that a misguided pay system can do a great deal of harm to the company. The company learned this lesson all too well when an incentive pay system for their auto repair centers resulted in customers being grossly over charged for unnecessary repairs and service. In that instance, the pay system focused employees attention so much on the bottom line that they ignored the concerns of customers.

Sears' current compensation philosophy, which guides pay practices at more than 800 stores, is based on four principles:

- using performance-based pay at all levels in the company,
- using pay to align managers' interests with those of shareholders,
- supporting a culture that is customer- and employee-focused, and
- using pay to attract and retain achievement-oriented, innovative associates and promote management development.

By following these principles, Martinez hopes to eliminate the entitlement mentality that prevailed when he became CEO in 1992. By then, a century of traditional pay practices resulted in a workforce that was paid above the industry average, with no variable element in their compensation. In the competitive retail industry, higher labor costs couldn't be passed on to customers, so profit margins were squeezed year after year. The company would do poorly yet employees never felt it in their pocketbooks. It's not surprising, then, that they also knew very little about how the business worked. The escalating pay within the ailing retail unit was possible because the company's financial services units subsidized the core retail business. Since selling off those units, Sears has had to become more focused on its bottom line.

Martinez hasn't completely abandoned the old compensation system. In fact, to implement the new pay policy, the HR professionals used standard techniques to determine market wage rates. Market rates were then were used to recalibrate the internal pay structure. The company still slots jobs and roles into pay grades, and the variable component of associates' pay is relatively small compared to their fixed wage or salary. But now it's clear that pay raises depend on performance appraisal results and that employees are expected to be actively engaged in the business. Contests with cash prizes create a bit of fun and excitement, and employees receive monetary rewards for achieving company goals. "There's a growing body of evidence that the more you allow idiosyncrasies and creativity into the business process, the more dynamic the discussion and the more creative the solutions," he explains. This applies to the HR professionals, as well as everyone else at Sears. Martinez credits his HR staff with helping drive the cultural change experienced at Sears: "They try to push the envelope and try things that haven't been tried in retailing or in any part of American business. They have a spirit of wanting to find ways to be innovative."[2]

To learn more about Sears, visit the company home page at
www.sears.com

TOTAL COMPENSATION

At Sears and other companies, the total compensation system includes a mix of several elements. As illustrated in Exhibit 10.1, these elements can be categorized using two dimensions.

Forms of Compensation

The horizontal dimension in Exhibit 10.1 reflects the form of the compensation. *Monetary* forms of compensation include *direct* payments such as salary, wages, and bonuses, and *indirect* payments such as payments to cover the costs of private and public insurance plans. *Nonmonetary* forms of compensation include many forms of social and psychological rewards—recognition and respect from others and opportunities

Exhibit 10.1
Elements of a Total Compensation System

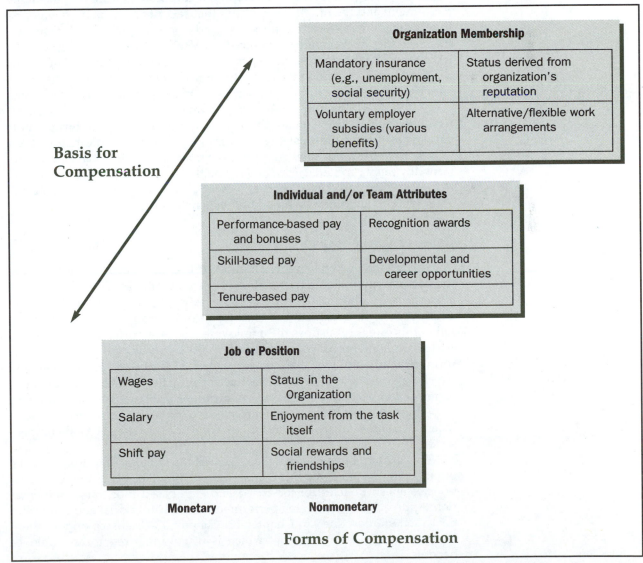

for self development. A total compensation system recognizes that both forms of compensation are valued by employees.

The relative importance of monetary and nonmonetary rewards differs among organizations, as well as among employees. For nine years Steve O'Donnell was David Letterman's head writer. He's the one who came up with the idea of the show's now-famous top ten lists. Did he ever get any special compensation tied to that particular contribution? "No. It never occurred to me," he says. "I did get a couple of thousand dollars to edit the two 'top ten' books that came out, but I did that because I thought it was important to get them to the public the right way. I'm probably the biggest wimp about money of anybody over twelve years old. A pat on the back, making Dave happy, the thrill of hearing the audience laugh—that's what matters most.[3]

Clearly, nonmonetary rewards are important, and there are many sources of such rewards.[4] As noted in Chapter 4, job designs partly determine the social and psychological rewards associated with work. Opportunities for career growth and development, as well as the use of praise and recognition, also contribute to a corporate culture that facilitates recruitment and retention. Recognizing that security may be more valuable to employees than the amount they're paid, some employers offer employment security in exchange for reduced monetary compensation.[5] In cyclical industries, like the airline industry, many companies bulk up on staff during the good times, knowing they'll use furloughs to reduce staff size when business turns down. Herb Kelleher estimates that such downturns occur twice every decade. Unlike most of its competitors, Southwest Airlines has a no-furlough policy. This makes the company cautious about hiring more employees during the upswings, so employees work a little harder then. "There have been times when, in the short-term, we could have been substantially more profitable if we had furloughs. But we didn't because we try to look out five, ten, fifteen years at where Southwest Airlines should be and what kind of institution it should be," explains Kelleher.[6]

Bases of Compensation

The second dimension shown in Exhibit 10.1 reflects the basis for receiving the compensation. Some forms of compensation are based on *organizational membership*. That is, the compensation is received by all, or almost all, employees in the organization. Most forms of insurance and other benefits fall in this category, as does the employment security offered by Southwest Airlines. Other forms of compensation are based on the *job* being performed by an employee. Base wages and salaries fit here, as do social and psychological rewards derived from performing the job itself. Finally, some forms of compensation are based on attributes of the individual employee or perhaps the attributes of an employee's work team. Performance-based incentives and bonuses fit here, as do skill- or knowledge-based compensation.

This chapter begins with a discussion of the strategic importance of the organization's total compensation system. It then describes how organizations establish policies for job-based and skill-based monetary compensation. Approaches to managing performance-based individual and team compensation are described in Chapter 12. Chapter 13 discusses organization-based monetary compensation, which is usually referred to as employee benefits.

THE STRATEGIC IMPORTANCE OF TOTAL COMPENSATION

Like many other aspects of an organization's approach to managing human resources, total compensation can facilitate (or interfere with) achieving many different strategic objectives. Three objectives of particular importance are: (1) attracting and retaining the talent required for a sustainable competitive advantage, (2) focusing the energy of employees on implementing the organization's particular competitive strategy, and (3) controlling costs. Perhaps more than ever, compensation is viewed as key to effectively managing human resources consistent with the needs of the business and the needs of employees. The appropriate blending of direct and indirect compensation makes it possible for companies to address both sets of needs simultaneously.

Attracting and Retaining Talent

In conjunction with an organization's recruitment and selection efforts, the total compensation program can help ensure that the rewards offered are sufficient to attract the right people at the right time for the right jobs.[7] Unless the total compensation program is perceived as internally fair and externally competitive, good employees (those the organization wants to retain) are likely to leave.[8] Effective total compensation systems appeal to employees' sense of fairness. Armed with an understanding of the determinants of pay satisfaction, organizations can develop practices that appeal to applicants and help retain valuable talent.[9] As the value of the monetary rewards being offered decreases, nonmonetary rewards become more important in appealing to employees.

Pay fairness refers to what people believe they deserve to be paid in relation to what others deserve to be paid. People tend to determine what they and others deserve to be paid by comparing what they give to the organization with what they get out of the organization. If they regard the exchange as fair or equitable, they're likely to be satisfied. If they see it as unfair, they're likely to be dissatisfied.[10] Most employers understand the importance of pay fairness, and the procedures they use are intended to create a fair system. But even when employers think they have succeeded in designing "fair" systems, employees may perceive inequities. Three culprits that detract from perceptions of fairness are low pay, pay secrecy, and executive compensation practices.

Low Pay. Employees who are compensated above or on par with the market average are more likely to feel fairly paid than those who are paid below the going rate. In the past, the issue of external equity—fairness relative to the external market—was typically framed as a simple question: "Should we lead, lag, or match the pay rates of labor market competitors?" When almost everyone's pay was predominately a basic salary with few benefits, this simple view made sense. In today's highly competitive environment, however, external equity has become more complex because companies creatively mix several forms of pay. Base salary is no longer the only piece that really matters. For example, to support a high-volume strategy, sales representatives at one company may receive a low base salary ($20,000) with a high bonus potential ($40,000). They enjoy no job security and minimal perks. Employees who focus on the base salary and perks will perceive this as unfairly low pay. Another company couples a high base salary ($50,000) with merit pay increases averaging around 5 percent. Job security is good and the

"To the extent that auto insurance is a commodity, our biggest differentiator is our people. We want the best people at every level of the company, and we pay at the top of the market."

Peter B. Lewis
Chairman
Progressive Corporation

"There are very few people working at Cisco who don't have an opportunity to leave for a 50 percent pay raise any time they want. What keeps them here is that it's fun, it's exciting, you can make a difference."

John T. Chambers
CEO
Cisco Systems

benefits offered are world class. Employees who focus on the maximum direct monetary compensation and place little value on the generous benefits package will view this pay as being unfairly low. When choosing which company to work for, employees consider many aspects of the total pay package: some focus on the predictable, guaranteed level of pay; others focus on the maximum potential pay; still others focus on the less tangible aspects of total compensation. Regardless of how employees make their assessments, however, employees will be dissatisfied if they perceive the company's total pay policy as less generous than that offered by competitors.

Pay Secrecy. Perceived inequities sometimes occur because employees have inaccurate and/or incomplete information. Although it's illegal for employers to forbid employee discussions of pay,[11] keeping pay secret is the norm in many U.S. organizations. According to organizational etiquette, asking others their salaries is generally considered gauche. In a study at DuPont, all employees were asked if the company should disclose more payroll information so that everyone would know everyone else's pay. Only eighteen percent voted for an open pay system. At Whole Foods, a grocery retailer, employees are welcome to peruse a notebook that lists every employee's total annual compensation, but the company acknowledges that not all employees like the system. According to Jody Hetch, the company's vice president of human resources, the policy of openness has made some employees so uncomfortable that they've left, while others have decided against taking a job offer.[12] Managers also favor pay secrecy, because it makes their lives easier. Without knowledge of pay differentials, employees are less likely to confront supervisors about inequitable pay, so managers don't have to justify their actions.[13]

Short of full disclosure about pay, employers can minimize misperceptions by involving employees in pay-system design. Traditionally, compensation professionals and managers had the most involvement in the design of compensation systems. Recently, however, employee involvement has increased. Nearly two-thirds of all labor agreements require incumbent involvement, and approximately half of all companies involve their employees in designing and implementing their compensation plans.[14] As discussed in Chapter 3, involving employees in decisions promotes acceptance of the decisions and establishes a sense of procedural justice.

Perceived inequities may also arise due to poor implementation of a well-designed system. Provisions to ensure due process address this potential problem. Union contracts often prescribe a formal appeal system for compensation decisions. Dissatisfied employees first file their complaints with their immediate supervisors. If no satisfactory resolution is forthcoming, the appeal moves forward to a higher level of management. Many nonunion employees have similar opportunities to appeal pay decisions.

A more radical approach to keeping employees satisfied is letting them set their own pay. Romac Industries, a pipe fitting plant, began using this approach nearly 20 years ago. Employees request pay raises by completing a form that includes information about their current pay level, previous raise, requested raise, and reasons for thinking a raise is deserved. The requests are posted, along with photographs of the employees, for several working days. Then employees vote, and the majority rules.[15] AES, an independent power producer based in Arlington, Virginia and operating in twelve countries, is experimenting with this approach for managers. Participants in the experiment are a dozen members of the firm's Silk Road Group,

"Compensation remains a sacred cow. Business owners still worry about how their workers will react when they find out someone else in the same job makes more than they do."

**Kevin Ruble
Managing Director
TranSolution**

"We trust our employees to make decisions about everything else. Why not about their own compensation?"

**Roger Sant
Chairman
AES Corporation**

which oversees projects in Central Asia. Each manager in the group received a list that contained information about all of their salaries, bonuses, and stock options. They also received this information about all AES employees with similar responsibilities. The managers were then asked to submit proposals for their compensation packages in the coming year. After they discussed their proposals and offered comments to other members of the group, they were submitted to the payroll department without interference from any higher level managers.[16]

Executive Compensation.   During the past decade, employees at the middle and lower levels of organizations have watched the pay of those at the top rise rapidly at a time when increases in their own pay have been relatively modest. During the 1980s and 1990s, CEOs have seen their pay increase 514 percent, or twelve times the rate of inflation. During the same period, real wages for lower-level workers have declined steadily.[17] The pattern is stark when looking at CEO pay, but such disparities aren't limited to comparisons between those at the very top and very bottom of the organization. Similar patterns are found by simply comparing the wages of employees who earn above the median with those who earn less than the median. In the U.S. even lower-level executives make far more than their counterparts in other advanced economies, while average workers make comparatively less.[18] Furthermore, disparities found in the U.S. dwarf those found in many other countries. In the U.S., the typical ratio is about $185 paid to the CEO for every $1 paid to the lowest worker.[19] By comparison, the ratio for British, German, and French firms is less than $50/$1, and the ratio in Japan is just $17/$1.[20]

How do workers feel about such disparities? Based on activity at the AFL-CIO's website devoted to this topic (**www.paywatch.org**), many are angry and resentful. Here are examples of how some employees react to data about CEO pay:

> *"No raise for us little guys for three years while the management all got bonuses and 15 percent raises. Do you think they will still get the same quality work from the lower ranks?"*

> *"I was laid off from a small but successful software company in the early '90s at the height of the recession. And over 200 [out of 1000] other employees were also laid off [because] the company didn't want to post a losing quarter that would affect the stock price. The top five executives of the company each received a bonus that was more than my annual salary. Am I resentful? You bet."*

> *"My personal rule is that if the exec is known to receive over one million a year—I will boycott their products, period."*

Do workers also boycott these companies as potential places to work? Are they more likely to leave such organizations when other employment opportunities present themselves? The extent to which such feelings translate into decisions about where to work isn't known, but it seems likely that at least some members of the workforce would prefer to decline a job offer from a firm known to have large pay disparities. As the demand for labor strengthens, others may choose to leave their current employers and move to more egalitarian companies.

CEO pay: "There's nothing like this issue. This one just galvanizes people instantly."

Betsy Leondar-Wright
Spokeswoman
United for a Fair Economy

■■□ *fast fact*

When the Sammi Group, a Korean conglomerate, was forced into bankruptcy, vice chairman Suh Sang Rok quit and entered a waiter-training program to repent. He's starting again at the bottom and will work his way back up.

Implementing the Competitive Strategy

Do you regard a smile and a "Thank you for shopping" from the cashier of the local store as examples of quality customer-oriented service? Many people do and, in fact, are willing to pay more for the goods in stores, such as Nordstrom, that have salespeople who engage in these behaviors. Whereas selection practices, socialization, and training help ensure that employees will be able and willing to engage in courteous, friendly behaviors, compensation systems provide the supporting structure that motivates employees to display these behaviors even under the most trying circumstances.

According to one study of more than 100 business units across 41 corporations, egalitarian pay systems facilitate a quality-driven, customer-focused strategy. Egalitarian systems are characterized by relatively less pay differential between lower-level and upper-echelon employees. As pay differentials increase, employees are less likely to feel fairly treated. At the same time, their attention to quality apparently declines. Thus, in this study, customers' ratings of quality were lower for business units with less egalitarian pay structures.

An effective compensation system enhances employees' feelings of satisfaction while at the same time encouraging the behaviors needed to implement the business strategy. The role of compensation in implementing competitive strategies becomes especially clear when a company changes its strategy and when it acquires or merges with another company.[21]

Changes in Strategy.   Employers like General Electric, Motorola, Sears, and IBM have discovered that a compensation system can encourage employees to embrace organizational change. Instead of handing out automatic annual pay increases based on job title and seniority—a common practice in the old economy—these companies reward teamwork, measurable quality improvements, and the acquisition of new skills.[22] IBM's use of pay to drive its strategy is described in the feature, Managing Change: The IBM Connection.[23]

A survey of over 700 U.S. organizations found that nearly 50 percent were developing new compensation plans to fit newly emerging business strategies. In these new systems, performance-based incentive pay—for individuals and teams—plays a much bigger role, with incentives being earned through results that are clearly tied to the strategy. In fact, 70 percent of the companies had plans to introduce these elements.[24]

Mergers and Acquisitions.   When companies combine, their cultures often clash. Because compensation systems are so closely linked to company cultures, mergers and acquisitions almost always provoke changes in the compensation system of one or both of the companies involved. As described in Chapter 2, when GE Capital acquires a firm, it uses its Pathfinder Model to anticipate and address clashing cultures. Using information uncovered during a Pathfinder investigation, GE is likely to spot major differences in compensation policies. Differences in pension plans, health insurance coverage, paid vacations, and collective bargaining agreements should be quickly spotted. But the Pathfinder Model doesn't directly link difference in compensation practices to differences in corporate cultures. If GE Capital wanted to address this link, they might consider the following five areas for potential cultural conflict:

- *Preference for risk taking vs. risk aversion:* Use of variable pay, uncapped commissions and executive pay that's tied to shareholder value are all indicators of a risk-taking culture.

MANAGING CHANGE

The IBM Connection

When the *Fortune* magazine published its 1993 annual list of the "most admired" companies, they revealed just how far IBM had fallen. In less than a decade, they went from being Number 1 three years in a row to being Number 324. That was the year Lou Gerstner, a former American Express executive, took over as IBM's CEO and began directing its transformation back into a high-performance company. Did compensation play a role in the transformation? According to Pam Odam, Director of Total Compensation Programs for IBM Canada, it did: "Given that we spend several billion dollars on compensation and benefits worldwide, and given that our business was going through a significant transformation, we needed to take a closer look at all of our programs to determine if they were supporting our key business strategies and reflecting the changing dynamics of today's workforce."

Gerstner and his top management team developed a new strategy for IBM, which focused on three key commitments:

- To Win.
- To Execute.
- To Team.

Now the challenge was to find a way for employees to connect to this strategy. What would it mean for them? Day in and day out, what exactly were the implications of the new strategy for employees? Realizing that employees needed an answer to this question, IBM made significant changes in the design, administration, and communication of several aspects of its HR system. These changes were designed to accomplish three objectives:

- Align employees with the strategy and point them in the right direction.
- Engage employees in the new strategy and foster their commitment.
- Provide a means for measuring results.

One major change in the compensation system was to use skills or competencies as a partial basis for determining employees' base pay and their annual pay increases. IBM's new strategy requires new skills. The new compensation system encourages employees to develop those new skills, and rewards them for it when they do so. Business success also partially determines pay. To support the shift in the culture of IBM, flexible benefits and employee-friendly practices like a new casual dress code were added. Casual dress has become fairly common in U.S. business, but for IBM'ers who had grown accustomed to the traditional blue-suit-and-white-shirt company uniform, this change was anything but easy.

Within five years after Gerstner pointed IBM in its new direction, the company's stock value increased five-fold and it had moved up to Number 69 in *Fortune*'s "most admired" list. Of course, the change isn't over. According to Odam, "We're on a journey, and our goal is to continue to make progress each and every day."

To learn more about IBM, visit the company's home page at
www.ibm.com

- *Flexibility and informality vs. rigidity and formality:* The presence of many ad hoc programs, many employees who are paid by exception rather than by the rules, few job descriptions, and the absence of detailed manuals are all indicators of a flexible and informal culture.

- *Decentralized vs. centralized:* Decision-making authority that's been pushed down to the divisions, a small corporate compensation staff, and bonus payouts that reflect division-level results are all indicators of a decentralized culture.
- *Concern for results vs. concern for people:* Few entitlements, wide variations in the bonus and merit pay given to individuals, and retirement contributions based on company performance are all indicators of culture that emphasizes concern for results over concern for people.[25]
- *Team focus vs. focus on individual stars:* Smaller pay disparities between employees at the the top and bottom rungs of the organization, cash incentives based on team performance, broad participation in employee stock ownership plans, skill- or knowledge-based pay, and team recognition programs are all indicators of a culture that promotes teamwork.[26]

Following mergers and acquisitions, cultural clashes frequently stimulate a focused consideration of the compensation systems. Ultimately, resolving the culture clash always requires making adjustments to several aspects of total compensation.

Organizational Life Cycle.   The choice of a specific compensation mix is constrained by an organization's life cycle. As suggested in Exhibit 10.2,[27] firms grow rapidly during some stages and slowly during others. During the start-up phase, they emphasize product and market development. Attracting key contributors and facilitating innovation are the focus issues for managing human resources. Still, risk is high, sales growth is slow, and earnings are low, so the company offers base salary and benefits below the market. Counterbalancing these are broad-based short- and long-term incentives, designed to stimulate innovation and its associated rewards.

During the growth stage, sales grow rapidly, with moderate increases in earnings. To keep up with increased demand for products and services, the organization must grow rapidly. The human resource focus is on rapid recruitment and training to develop the human capital. Bonuses may be offered for innovation and sales growth, and stock options may be offered to encourage employees to think about the long-term growth of the company.

During the maturity stage, growth is slower and more orderly because the market is saturated with the product. High entry costs and exit barriers keep the number of competitors low, so organizations can focus on profitability. During this stage, performance, consistency, and retention of peak performers are the issues that arise in managing human resources. Profit sharing, cash bonuses, and stock awards tied to short- or long-term growth may be offered to retain key contributors, along with competitive base pay and benefits.

During the decline stage, the human resource focus shifts to cutting back as market shares decline. Base salary and benefits are competitive at best, and may drop below market levels as management attempts to reduce expenditures.[28]

Organizational life cycles have received wide attention as a heuristic device for designing compensation systems, but the concept has critics. More than one set of compensation policies may be appropriate for any given stage in the cycle. Furthermore, organizations often have more than one product, each at a different stage of development. This complexity may make it impossible to cleanly classify a firm and its compensation mix according to a particular stage of development.[29]

Exhibit 10.2
Potential Pay Mixes for Different Stages of the Organizational Life Cycle

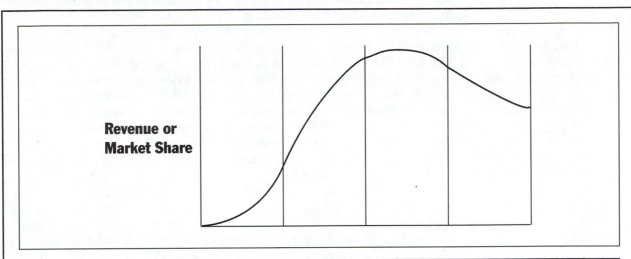

	Life Cycle Stage			
	Start-Up	**Growth**	**Maturity**	**Decline**
Organization Characteristics				
HR management focus	Innovation, attracting key contributors	Recruiting, training	Retention, consistency	Cutting back, cost control
Risk profile	High	Moderate	Low	Moderate to high
Compensation Strategy				
Short-term incentives	Stock bonus	Cash bonus	Profit sharing, cash bonus	Unlikely
Long-term incentives	Stock options (broad participation)	Stock options (limited participation)	Stock purchase	Unlikely
Base salary	Below market level	At market level	At or above market level	At or below market level
Benefits	Below market level	Below market level	At or above market level	At or below market level

Increasing Productivity

Traditionally, total compensation systems in U.S. companies have emphasized cost control and uniformity over productivity improvement. Thus, most hourly workers are paid for the number of hours they work, not their contribution to the bottom line. Merit pay is used widely but the value of merit increases is so low that they have little motivational value. Whereas nonmonetary awards influence employee satisfaction, and thus employee attraction and retention, monetary pay systems influence performance and productivity by linking pay to strategically central criteria.[30] For example,

> "When I came here, they gave you a country ham and a fruitcake at Christmas if you had a good year. Now we're paying [incentives] out in cash on the barrelhead."
>
> **Edward E. Crutchfield**
> **CEO**
> **First Union Corporation**

gainsharing programs link financial rewards to improvements in the performance of a somewhat autonomous plant or facility. Such programs can improve performance by focusing employees' attention on appropriate performance indicators and rewarding employees for improving over time.[31]

Incentive pay programs apply the same principles, but rewards are linked to the performance of individuals or small teams. At First Union, for example, CEO Eddie Crutchfield has put everyone in the branches—from branch managers to tellers—on an incentive system that rewards selling the bank's various products and services. The new incentives are ten times greater than under the old system, making up about 40 percent of an employee's total annual compensation. Some salespeople work on pure commission, with no cap. Crutchfield realizes that some current employees will decide they don't want to sell, and he doesn't mind if they leave. He's happy to replace them with people from outside the industry who understand selling and enjoy reaping their rewards in the form of commissions.[32]

The popularity of performance-based pay (also called variable pay) has exploded in recent years. According to a survey of more than 2,800 companies in the U.S. and Canada, by the year 2000, nearly 80 percent of companies will be using some form of incentive pay.

Although business objectives and employees' preferences shape the many decisions a company makes about how to design pay, they can't be treated in isolation. Other forces from the external environment also come into play.

ROLE OF THE EXTERNAL ENVIRONMENT

Three forces in the external environment that directly shape compensation design decisions are the labor market, legislation, and unions.

Labor Market

Labor market conditions affect the design of compensation in that they drive decisions about the overall level of pay offered and the mix of pay offered.

Pay Level. The degree of competition for labor partly determines the lower boundary or floor for pay level. If a company's pay level is too low, qualified labor won't be willing to work for the company. Thus, shortages in the labor market provide qualified workers the opportunity to negotiate better terms of employment. If employees' wage demands are too high, however, employers may react by hiring fewer people. For example, a 1998 survey of over 500 small businesses revealed that a recent increase in the minimum wage resulted in decreased hiring at about 5 percent of the businesses.[33]

For current employees (the internal labor market), low pay is likely to create turnover, at least under conditions of low unemployment. By jumping ship, valuable employees can increase their total compensation and often their career progress. Under conditions of low unemployment, demand for labor drives labor prices up. Then even burger flippers and java servers may be paid as much as 30 to 40 percent above the minimum wage.[34] High prices, in turn, attract more entrants to the market. At the same time, they push employers to seek alternatives. Introducing new technology that reduces the need for labor is one alternative. Raising prices for products and services is another, as is simply accepting smaller profit margins.[35] Employing lower-priced foreign labor is another alternative. The dynamic interplay between wage prices and hiring has been affecting many Europeans in recent years.

"The pay that the vice presidents get isn't motivating the vice presidents. It's motivating the assistant vice presidents, who want to become vice presidents. Similarly, the CEO's pay isn't motivating the CEO so much—he's already there. Rather, it's serving to motivate the vice presidents who are competing against one another to become CEO."

Edward P. Lazear
Professor
Stanford Business School

■□ *fast fact*

The average hourly wage in the movie business is $32.70, and in the missile production business it's $20.60.

■□ *fast fact*

The median annual earnings for male high school graduates is about $30,000, but they can earn $100,000 a year at Lincoln Electric.

In Germany, for example, the cost of labor and related taxes has been rising. In response, some German companies have moved production out of the country—including to the United States. Arend Oetker, an owner of a food company named Schwartau, explained his company's recent investment in Switzerland this way: "I am a German, and I want to keep employment here as much as possible. But the more the labor costs rise and the more that taxes rise, the more difficult it is to remain in Germany. No one can be astonished that unemployment is going up." Between 1990 and 1998, Germany's unemployment rate has gone from 6 percent to 11 percent.[36] Exhibit 10.3 illustrates the differing costs of labor in several countries.[37]

The procedures employers use to estimate the labor prices of competitors are described later in this chapter, as are other issues related to decisions about how to set base pay levels.

Pay Mix. At American Express and many other companies, the Hudson Institute's *Workforce 2000* report drew sudden attention to the implications of changing employee demographics. The fast-paced, growing American Express business required a large number of new employees each year, so the company's ability to attract and retain qualified employees was a major concern. Yet, the report predicted a shrinking labor supply. The company responded to this potential threat by creating a task force of managers to study the issue. The report documented the high cost of turnover and convinced

Exhibit 10.3

Total Labor Costs for Manufacturing Companies in Selected Countries

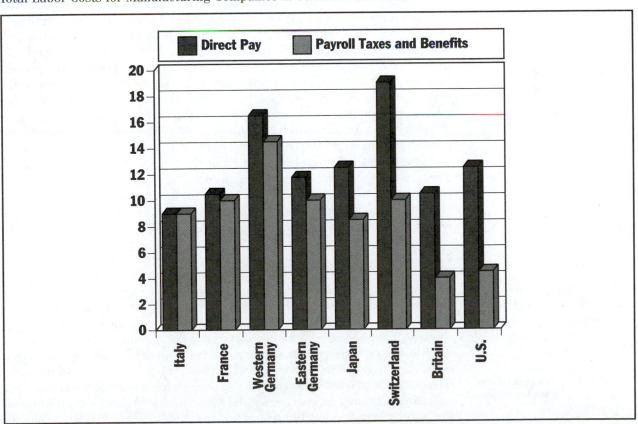

"There are two things
people want more than sex
and money—recognition
and praise."

Mary Kay Ash
Chairman Emeritus
Mary Kay Cosmetics

senior management to take action. With the help of the HR staff, they collected data from employees in order to learn about their needs and concerns. To their surprise, senior managers discovered that employees felt they were unresponsive to employees' needs. Employees wanted to be treated as whole and unique individuals with legitimate interests and needs outside the workplace. For this to occur, a significant departure from the existing culture would be required.

Traditionally, the company maintained an exchange-based relationship with employees—where all employees were treated equally, and family and personal issues were kept separate from work issues. When setting pay policies, the company focused on ensuring that the total value of compensation received was competitive, given market conditions; they paid less attention to the mix of benefits offered. Following the employee survey, employee focus groups were used to identify specific policies and benefits for consideration. The following question was posed: "If you were offered an identical job, for the same pay and in the same city, what would it take, in terms of specific benefits, to make you accept the offer?" Based on employees' responses and an assessment of the competitive advantage that could be gained, the company instituted several new employee benefits. These included family care subsidies, flexible work arrangements, paid sabbaticals for community service, and full benefits for part-time employees.[38]

Employees' preferences are just one of the many factors that influence the mix of compensation elements offered to employees. Competitive pressures to keep costs down and improve productivity are causing many employers to keep fixed pay (wages and salaries) low and link pay increases to gains in productivity and/or profitability, which are variable. With a well-designed variable pay component, a company's labor costs do not increase unless the company can afford it. As part of its turnaround strategy, IBM introduced variable pay to rank-and-file employees. This was a big change for the company. "This is a totally new concept for us," explained HR professional Joseph Mastanunzio. "IBM, as everybody knows, has always been a very traditional type of corporation...So we had to play around with this. We think we've got it to the point now where it's pretty effective. The targets are right [and] the percentages are right." Currently in the U.S., about 90 percent of all executives have some variable incentive pay, compared to only about 25 percent of rank-and-file wage earners.[39]

Companies differ greatly in terms of the mix of pay components they offer employees, and the same company may offer a different mix at different points in time. Likewise, countries differ substantially in terms of the typical pay mix found across all employers. This is illustrated in Exhibit 10.4, which shows the pay mixes typically found in the U.S. and Mexico.[40]

Legal and Social Considerations

"It never dawned on me
that there was a law
against reaching a private
agreement with someone
over work."

Restaurant Owner
Wage Law Violator

Like other aspects of managing human resources, compensation activities are shaped by a plethora of laws and regulations, covering topics such as taxation, nondiscrimination, fair wages, a minimum wage, the protection of children, hardship pay for employees who work unusually long hours, and income security through pension and welfare benefits. A sociological analysis of all congressional bills introduced from 1951 to 1990 revealed that different visions of work and family have been dominant at different periods, reflecting the changing concerns of the labor market.[41] During the middle of the 20th century, barriers between work and family were considered normal

Exhibit 10.4

Comparing the Pay Mix in Mexico and the United States

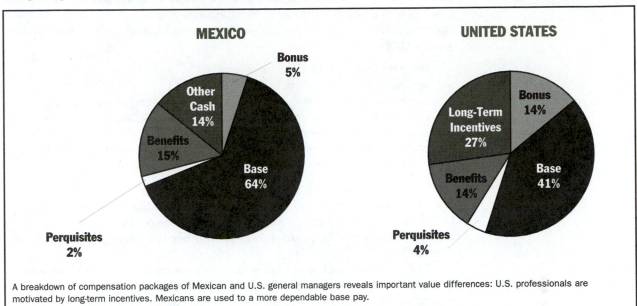

MEXICO

Bonus 5%

Other Cash 14%

Benefits 15%

Base 64%

Perquisites 2%

UNITED STATES

Bonus 14%

Long-Term Incentives 27%

Base 41%

Benefits 14%

Perquisites 4%

A breakdown of compensation packages of Mexican and U.S. general managers reveals important value differences: U.S. professionals are motivated by long-term incentives. Mexicans are used to a more dependable base pay.

and even desirable. Today, legislation such as the *Family and Medical Leave Act* encourages employers to remove such barriers and actively support employees' simultaneous involvement in the spheres of work and family.[42]

Significant changes in our view of what is the normal work week have occurred, as well. A standard workweek now consists of five eight-hour days. In 1840, six thirteen-hour days was considered normal. In 1913, when Henry Ford introduced the eight-hour day at a $5-a-day minimum wage, most of his competitors still expected sixty hours of work a week from employees. Eventually, national legislation governing hours and wages was passed.

Davis-Bacon and Walsh-Healey Acts. The first federal law to protect the amount of pay employees receive for their work was the *Davis-Bacon Act of 1931*. This act required organizations holding federal construction contracts to pay laborers and mechanics the prevailing wages of the majority of the employees in the locality where the work was performed. The *Walsh-Healey Public Contracts Act of 1936* extended the *Davis-Bacon Act* to include all organizations holding federal construction contracts exceeding $10,000 and specified that pay levels conform to the industry minimum rather than the area minimum. The *Walsh-Healey Act* also established overtime pay at one and one-half times the hourly rate. These wage provisions did not include administrative, professional, office, custodial, or maintenance employees, or beginners or disabled persons.

Fair Labor Standards Act. Partly because the coverage of *Davis-Bacon* and *Walsh-Healey* was limited to employees on construction projects, the *Fair Labor Standards Act of 1938*, or *Wage and Hour Law*, was enacted. This set minimum wages, maximum hours, child labor standards, and overtime pay provisions for all workers except domestic and government employees. The Supreme Court extended the coverage to include state and local government employees in 1985.

"Unless a new law has just been passed, wage/hour has always been our No. 1 category for questions."

Deborah Keary
Information Center Director
Society for Human Resource
Management

■□ *fast fact*

Minimum wage laws are among the country's most frequently flouted statutes.

Under the *Fair Labor Standards Act*, the minimum wage began at $0.25 an
hour and had reached $5.15 as of 1999. This totals $10,712 annually, which is
about $2,000 below the poverty line for a family of three and about half the
country's average hourly wage. Note, however, that several states have set
their minimum wage rates above this national rate. Still, subminimum
wages are permitted for

- learners in semiskilled occupations,
- apprentices in skilled occupations,
- messengers in firms engaged primarily in delivering letters and messages,
- handicapped persons working in sheltered workshops,
- students in certain establishments, and
- employees who receive more than $30 a month in tips (up to 40 percent
  of the minimum requirement may be covered by tips).[43]

To prevent abuses regarding children, the act prohibits minors under the
age of eighteen from working in hazardous occupations. For nonhazardous
positions, the minimum age ranges from fourteen to sixteen, depending on
the type of work to be performed and whether the employer is the child's
parent.[44]

The act also establishes who is to be paid overtime for work and who is
not. Most employees covered must be paid time and a half for all work
exceeding 40 hours a week. For wage earners, also called *nonexempt employees*, almost all work-related activities required by the employer must be compensated at the hourly rate or as overtime. Below are some of the activities
that employers often fail to count when they calculate the hours their
employees work:

- down time or on-call time during which the employee is not free to pursue personal business;
- preparation and clean-up before or after a shift;
- mandatory classes, meetings, and conventions;
- unscheduled or unauthorized work;
- travel time between job sites;
- rest breaks shorter than 20 minutes; and
- time worked by trainees who are being prepared for, but do not yet hold,
  managerial positions.

Failure to accurately count and compensate for all of the hours worked by
nonexempt employees is a legal violation, regardless of whether or not
employees consent to the arrangement. Furthermore, compensation must be
in the form of direct pay. Employers may not use a barter system. Thus, if a
restaurant owner asks employees to come in on their days off and help spruce
up their workplace, it's not legal to compensate them by giving a free pizza-
and-beer party instead of overtime pay. Employers can't get around this
requirement simply by claiming the work wasn't required. If an employer
permits someone to work, they're obligated to pay them for that work.[45]

Several types of workers are considered exempt employees. *Exempt
employees* are paid on a salary basis, and they aren't covered by overtime and
minimum wage provisions. Executives and administrators are one type of
exempt employee. To meet the salary criteria, exempt workers must be paid
a fixed, predetermined salary, regardless of the precise number of hours they
work in a given week. The job-content criteria for exempt status as an executive or administrator include spending at least 80 percent of work time in
the following tasks:

- undertaking management duties;
- directing the work of two or more employees;
- controlling or greatly influencing hiring, firing, and promotion decisions; and
- exercising discretion.

Professionals are another major category of exempt employees. Their work requires a college-level or post-graduate degree in a field of *specialized* study. In addition, professionals must spend 80 percent of their work hours in the following tasks:

- doing work requiring knowledge acquired through specialized, prolonged training,
- exercising discretion or judgment, and
- doing work that is primarily intellectual and nonroutine.[46]

Job title alone is not a sufficient basis for treating these jobs as exempt. A comprehensive job analysis is necessary to document the activities involved in executive, administrative, or professional jobs.[47]

Other exempt employees include workers in seasonal industries, certain highly paid commission workers, workers in motion picture theaters, as well as some others.

Equal Pay Act.   A fourth provision of the *Fair Labor Standards Act* was added as an amendment in 1963. Called the *Equal Pay Act*, this extension prohibits an employer from discriminating "between employees on the basis of sex by paying wages to employees . . . at a rate less than the rate at which he pays wages to employees of the opposite sex . . . for equal work on jobs the performance of which requires equal skill, effort and responsibility, and which are performed under similar working conditions."

To establish a prima facie case of wage discrimination, the plaintiff needs to show that a disparity in pay exists for males and females performing substantially equal, not necessarily identical, jobs. The amount of skill, effort, and responsibility and the working conditions required by each job must be assessed through careful job analysis. Job contents rather than the window dressing of job titles should be examined. If jobs are found to be substantially equal, wages for the lower-paid job must be raised to match those for the higher-paid position. Freezing or lowering the pay of the higher-paid job is unacceptable.

Four exceptions can be used to legally defend unequal pay for equal work: the existence and use of a seniority system, a merit system, a system that measures earnings or quality of production, or a system based on any additional characteristic other than gender. If the employer can show the existence of one or more of these exceptions, a pay differential may be found to be justified.

Comparable Worth.   The heart of the comparable worth theory is the contention that, although the "true worth" of nonidentical jobs may be similar, some jobs (often held by women) are paid a lower rate than others (often held by men). Several state and local governments and unions have passed comparable worth or pay-equity legislation, and many businesses have also taken action on pay-equity issues. The feature, Managing Diversity: Pay Equity Pays Off, describes these issues and how they can be addressed.[48]

A recent analysis of entry level pay found that women earned 84 cents for every dollar earned by men. About fourteen percent of this difference is

On pay for female movie stars: "Maybe the glass ceiling has been raised a bit. But when a woman hits her head on it, she can look up and see men's loafers."

Elaine Goldsmith-Thomas
Talent Agent
International Creative Management

MANAGING DIVERSITY

Pay Equity Pays Off

Pay equity is a policy that provides businesses the competitive edge to meet the challenges of the 21st century, according to the National Committee on Pay Equity. A consistent, fair pay policy whereby all workers are paid equally for work of equal value produces a more productive and better-motivated workforce, which, in turn, promotes recruitment and retention of good workers. "Smart employers recognize that future profits depend on current investment in their most vital resource: their people," says the coalition of labor, women's, and civil rights groups in its report, *Pay Equity Makes Good Business Sense.*

Women and people of color are concentrated in lower-paying jobs. When women and people of color occupy traditionally white-male-dominated positions—even after accounting for legitimate reasons for pay differences such as differing skills, work experience, and seniority—women and people of color are still paid less. Discriminatory wage practices account for between one-quarter and one-half of this disparity in wages.

What Is Pay Equity?

Pay equity is a means of eliminating race, ethnicity, and gender as wage determinants within job categories and between job categories. Many businesses pay women and people of color less than white males due to wage structures that retain historical biases and inconsistencies that are, in fact, discriminatory. A pay-equity policy examines existing pay policies that underpay women and people of color and activates steps to correct the discrimination.

How to Achieve Pay Equity

A comprehensive audit is the first step in implementing a pay equity policy. The audit should examine the following areas for inequities and needed changes:

- job evaluation,
- external market pay levels,
- pay administration procedures, and
- recruitment practices.

In the area of pay administration, the audit should scrutinize each individual component of a compensation system, including salary range design, salary grades, and pay differentials. Additional items to be examined for inequities include promotion rates, merit increases, incentive programs, and performance and seniority elements in the pay system.

Pay Equity Is Not Costly

Following the lead of public employers, many private-sector businesses incorporate pay-equity analyses in their annual budget proposals. The cost of pay equity adjustments usually has been between two and five percent of payroll. In no cases have the wages of any workers been lowered in order to achieve pay equity. The objective of pay equity is to remedy wage inequities for underpaid workers, not to penalize another group of employees.

To learn more about comparable worth and pay equity, visit the web site for Canada's Pay Equity Commission at **www.gov.on.ca/lab/pec**

due to differences in the skills of men and women, and another fifteen percent is due to differences in career aspirations.[49] Comparable worth theory holds that the remaining differential in entry level wages reflects wage discrimination. For example, men are placed into better-paying job categories and are more likely to have mentors, although they're equivalent on all qualifications.[50] Or, in the case of hollywood stars, movie studios simply offer male stars higher salaries than they offer female stars, despite similar box office appeal. According to comparable worth advocates, legal protection should be provided to ensure pay equity.[51]

Labor Unions

The presence of a union in a private-sector firm is estimated to increase wages by 10 to 15 percent and benefits by about 20 to 30 percent. The wage differential between unionized and nonunionized firms appears to be greatest during recessionary periods and smallest during inflationary periods. Whether the increased compensation costs in unionized firms translate into higher output is widely debated. Some researchers contend that, by improving employee satisfaction, lowering turnover, and decreasing absenteeism, unions have a positive effect on net productivity. Others contend that the gains in productivity aren't equivalent to the increased compensation costs.[52]

Unions also have pushed for wage escalation clauses, which increase wages automatically during the life of a contract. One way unions have accomplished this is to tie wage increases to changes in the consumer price index. However, whereas cost-of-living adjustments (COLAs) were popular in the 1960s and 1970s, the number of workers covered by COLAs declined during the 1980s and early 1990s, when the consumer price index decelerated and concerns about job security increased in priority during contract negotiations.

In addition to determining how much employees are paid, unions have shaped the way total pay is allocated among wages, performance-based pay, and benefits.[53] For example, the International Association of Machinists opted to set aside $0.10 an hour for skill retraining rather than take a $0.05-an-hour increase in direct pay. Retraining was viewed as a route to long-term job security, which was valued more than short-term gains in salary. Thus, the union established a Career Mobility program to provide funds to retrain members for higher-level jobs that also pay better.

The nature of union-management relationships within a firm have important implications for pay system design and administration also. Some unions take an active part in job evaluation to protect their interests. Others preserve customary relationships, seeking job security and resisting changes in job content and wage rates. (Chapter 15 describes the changing dynamics of union-management relationships in more detail.)

MANAGING COMPENSATION THROUGH PARTNERSHIP

Total compensation is linked to the needs and characteristics of a business when top management believes that compensation affects the company's overall performance. It's linked to the interests and preferences of employees when they have the means to voice their concerns and the power to negotiate on behalf of their interests. A compensation system that balances the interests of all concerned stakeholders is most likely when compensation is managed

■□ *fast fact*

Members of the International Longshoremen's and Warehouse Union working on the West Coast averaged $97,000 in pay for 1997. Foremen averaged $148,000.

through a true partnership. If designed and implemented well, compensation policies and practices encourage and reward desired employee behaviors while at the same time treating employees fairly.

Many companies actively involve employees in the design of new compensation systems. Although involving only managers is still the norm, about one-third of companies also involve nonmanagement employees in the design process. Employee participation is especially important as a means for assuring that the diverse needs of all employees are met. Involving employees at all levels takes longer, but the investment seems to pay off. Several studies show that plans designed by a task force produce both higher satisfaction and better performance.[54]

Guidelines for forging a partnership among managers, employees and HR professionals are summarized in The HR Triad: Partnership Roles and Responsibilities for Total Compensation feature.

THE HR TRIAD: PARTNERSHIP ROLES AND RESPONSIBILITIES FOR TOTAL COMPENSATION

Line Managers	HR Professionals	Employees
Work with HR professionals to ensure alignment of pay system with strategic objectives.	With line managers, ensure alignment of pay system with strategic objectives.	Take responsibility for understanding the total compensation system.
Work with employees to ensure pay system satisfies and motivates them.	Assess employees' preferences and reactions to pay systematically and regularly.	Indicate preferences for forms of pay.
Participate with HR professionals to determine how to value jobs and people.	Monitor and analyze trends in the external market.	May participate in job evaluation.
Communicate pay system principles and abide by them.	Develop processes to measure performances and/or skills.	May assess the levels of performance and/or skill of self and others.
Make and communicate decisions about direct pay given to individuals and small teams.	Design processes for job evaluation to involve line managers and job incumbents.	Accept responsibility for actively managing indirect compensation plans and accounts.
Communicate and fairly implement indirect components of the pay system.	Ensure employees have access to due process and are free to appeal pay decisions.	Communicate own perceptions of equity and due process.

Addressing employees' perceptions of equity is central to the design of an effective monetary compensation system. To completely address equity issues, a compensation system should address four policy issues:

1. **Pay-level policy:** How much should the organization pay, *relative to competitors*?
2. **Job-based pay policy:** How much should the organization pay employees in each *job*?
3. **Skill-based pay policy:** How much should the organization pay employees with different *skills*?
4. **Performance-based pay policy:** How much should the organization pay employees who exhibit different levels of *performance*?

The pay-level policy addresses the issue of external equity, as already described. The other policy components deal with internal equity—that is, equity among employees within the organization. They are described next.

JOB-BASED PAY POLICY

Job evaluation involves the systematic, rational assessment of jobs to determine their relative internal worth. Internal job worth reflects a job's importance or its contribution to the overall attainment of organizational objectives. By design, job evaluation focuses internally, on the structure of the organization; it does not take into account market forces, individual skills, or individual performance.

Job evaluation is closely related to job analysis, but they're not identical. As described in Chapter 6, the objective of job analysis is to determine the content of jobs: what tasks are performed, what responsibilities do employees have, and what competencies are required? Obtaining this information is an essential prior step to job evaluation. Job evaluation then asks, "What is the relative value of jobs with various contents and responsibilities involving the use of various competencies?"

As with any administrative procedure, job evaluation invites give and take. Consensus building is often required among stakeholders (incumbents, managers, HR professionals, union officials) to resolve conflicts that inevitably arise about the relative worth of jobs. The use of group judgments throughout the job evaluation process helps ensure that these conflicts are addressed, producing a compensation system that is congruent with organizational values and strategic objectives and not based solely on external market valuations of worth.[55]

The three major decisions to be made when conducting job evaluation are

- whether to use a single plan or multiple plans,
- what job evaluation method to follow, and
- how to set up a process to drive the plan.

Single Plan Versus Multiple Plans

Traditionally, organizations have used different job evaluation plans for different job families (e.g., clerical, skilled craft, and professional). This approach assumes that the work content of jobs in different families is too diverse to be captured by one plan. For example, manufacturing jobs may vary in terms of working conditions and physical effort, whereas professional jobs usually vary in terms of technical skills and knowledge. Proponents of multiple plans contend that these differences require the use of unique evaluation systems tailored to the job.

Persuasive arguments against using multiple job evaluation systems have been made, however. From a strategic perspective, using multiple systems is incongruent with the objective of communicating a coherent message about the organization values. For example, if the strategy is to focus on customers, it may be logical to use potential for affecting customers as a factor when determining the relative worth of all jobs within the company. Also, the use of a single system for valuing all jobs has been proposed as a partial solution to the problem of sex-based inequities. Proponents of pay equity assert that only if jobs are evaluated using the same criteria can the relative value of all jobs be fairly determined. When separate plans are used, it's much easier to discriminate against specific classes of jobs (e.g., clerical versus skilled) because direct comparisons of segregated jobs can be avoided.

Developing a firm-specific job evaluation system with universal factors selected in accordance with the company's strategy and culture is clearly more difficult than adopting off-the-shelf job evaluation systems developed for specific occupational groups. Nevertheless, companies such as Cisco and Hewlett-Packard have concluded that the extra effort of developing a tailored system pays off. Thus, these companies use a set of core factors to provide some common basis for evaluating all jobs, and they supplement this with another set of factors unique to particular occupational groups.

Job Evaluation Methods

Traditional job evaluation methods focus on the job as the unit of interest. Some methods evaluate the whole job, whereas others evaluate components of jobs using compensable factors. Some methods evaluate jobs directly in dollar worth, whereas others assign points to jobs, and points are then converted to dollar values.

Ranking Method. The simplest, and least specific job evaluation method is ranking. One approach is to simply rank jobs according to their perceived overall value. Alternatively, jobs can be ranked on the basis of such factors as difficulty, criticality to organizational success, and the competencies required. The ranking method is convenient when only a few jobs need to be evaluated and when one person is familiar with them all. As the number of jobs increases, it becomes less likely that one person will know them all well enough to create a meaningful rank order. Thus, as the number of jobs to be ranked increases, detailed job analysis information becomes more important, and input is more likely to be sought from several members of a committee.

One difficulty in the ranking method is that all jobs must be different from each other. Making fine distinctions between similar jobs can lead to arbitrary evaluations, which may then result in disagreements over the ranks and less acceptance of the results. Such problems undermine perceptions of internal equity and fairness.

Job Classification Method. The job classification method is similar to the ranking method, except that it first establishes job classes—usually referred to as pay grades—and then groups job descriptions within these broader categories. Classification standards specify the kinds and levels of responsibilities assigned to jobs in each grade, the difficulty of the work performed, and the required employee qualifications. The pay grade descriptions serve as the standard against which the job descriptions are compared. The description of a grade captures some of the details of the work that falls within the grade, yet it's general enough that several jobs can be slotted into the grade.

No matter how lengthy and comprehensive the pay grade narratives, the placement of a specific job into a pay grade can be tricky. Two steps can be taken to make this process easier: (1) make sure the job descriptions are accurate and complete and (2) identify benchmark jobs for each pay grade. *Benchmark jobs* are common across a number of different employers. Because the job content is relatively stable, external wage rates for these jobs are used for setting internal pay. Benchmark jobs can serve as reference points or judgment anchors against which the content of other jobs can be compared. For example, many organizations have computers that are linked together through an intranet, and they have a person assigned to act as the intranet administrator. Regardless of the company, an intranet administrator is likely to install, maintain, and monitor the operation of the system. The job would also involve evaluating vendor hardware and software products, recommending purchases of telecommunications equipment, and developing policies to ensure the system's security. Specifying the job of intranet administrator as a benchmark job that fits into a particular pay grade helps the job classification process by making abstract grade descriptions more concrete and easier for job evaluators to understand.

A particular advantage of the job classification method is that it can be applied to a large number and a wide variety of jobs. As the number and variety of jobs increase, however, the classification process becomes more subjective. This is particularly true when employees work at several locations and in jobs that have the same title but not the same job content. In such cases, it's difficult to attend to the true content of each job, so job evaluators tend to rely on the job title for making a job classification.[56] Employees in these jobs may be more attuned than their managers to differences in the contents of jobs with similar titles, which is a good reason to involve them in the job classification process.

Point Rating Method. The most widely used method of job evaluation is the point rating (or point factor) method. This consists of assigning point values for previously determined compensable factors and then adding them to arrive at the overall worth of a job. Compensable factors may be adapted from existing point evaluation plans or may be custom designed to reflect the unique values of an organization. The system for allocating points to jobs includes a weighting method so that more important factors count more in determining the job's pay level. For example, a research-and-development firm may assign more points to education and experience factors than would a manufacturing facility. Conversely, the manufacturing facility may assign more points to a working conditions factor than would an accounting firm.

The point system presented in Exhibit 10.5 has six compensable factors. The total maximum number of points in this system is 1,000, and the total minimum number of points is 225. Notice that the maximum points assigned to the factors can easily be translated into weights expressed in percentages. In practice, job evaluators usually work with a set of points like the one shown, where factor weights are built into the points but aren't explicitly shown. The factor weights can be easily computed, however. To obtain the factor weights, simply divide the maximum points for each factor by the total points possible (1,000). This yields the following weights for factors 1 to 6, respectively: 20 percent, 26 percent, 24 percent, 5 percent, 10 percent, and 15 percent.

Once factors are chosen and weighted, the next step is to construct scales reflecting the different degrees within each factor. Exhibit 10.6 shows descriptions for five degrees of problem-solving. Notice that each degree is anchored by a description of the typical tasks and behaviors associated with that degree.

Exhibit 10.5

Sample Point Evaluation System

Compensable Factor	First Degree	Second Degree	Third Degree	Fourth Degree	Fifth Degree
1. Job knowledge	50	100	150	200	NA
2. Problem solving	50	100	150	205	260
3. Impact	60	120	180	240	NA
4. Working conditions	10	30	50	NA	NA
5. Supervision needed	25	50	75	100	NA
6. Supervision given	30	60	90	120	150

Note: NA = Not Applicable, which means that this degree level is not used for the relevant compensable factor

---

Exhibit 10.6

Example of a Compensable Factor and Related Degree Statements

Problem Solving

This factor examines the types of problems dealt within your job. Indicate the one level that is most representative of most of your job responsibilities.

Degree 1: Actions are performed in a set order according to written or verbal instructions. Problems are referred to a supervisor.

Degree 2: Routine problems are solved and various choices are made regarding the order in which the work is performed, within standard practices. Information may be obtained from various sources.

Degree 3: Various problems are solved that require general knowledge of company policies and procedures applicable within own area of responsibility. Decisions are made based on a choice from established alternatives. Actions are expected to be within standards and established procedures.

Degree 4: Analytical judgment, initiative, or innovation is required in dealing with complex problems or situations. Evaluation is not easy because there is little precedent or information may be incomplete.

Degree 5: Complex tasks involving new or constantly changing problems or situations are planned, delegated, coordinated, or implemented, or any combination of these. Tasks involve the development of new technologies, programs or projects. Actions are limited only by company policies and budgets.

After factors and underlying degrees are delineated, a job's worth can be assessed. Typically, a compensation committee is chosen to assess job worth. The committee includes a cross-section of stakeholders (e.g., managers, union officials, hourly workers, and workers from various job families) who are trained in the use of the job evaluation process. They independently evaluate each job—that is, they determine the degree level for each factor for each job. Committee members usually discuss their evaluations, and debate continues until consensus is reached on the value of each job. At the end of the process, each job has a total point value that reflects its relative worth.

Like other job evaluation plans, the point factor method incorporates the potential subjectivity of the job analyst. Thus, it has the potential for wage discrimination. Bias or subjectivity can enter (1) in the selection of the compensable factors, (2) in the assignment of relative weights (degrees) to factors, and (3) in the assignment of degrees to the jobs being evaluated. To make sure its point system is free from potential bias and is implemented as objectively as possible, organizations may solicit the input of job incumbents, supervisors, and job evaluation experts, as well as that of human resource professionals.[57]

One widely used point system is the Hay Guide Chart-Profile. It's been particularly popular for evaluating executive, managerial, and professional positions, but it's also widely used for technical, clerical, and manufacturing positions. The Hay Guide Chart-Profile system relies on three primary compensable factors: problem solving, know-how, and accountability. Point values are determined for each job, using the three factors. In addition, jobs are compared to each another on the basis of each factor. According to Hay Associates, which developed this method, a major advantage of this system has been its wide acceptance and usage. Because organizations worldwide use the system, Hay can provide clients with comparative pay data by industry or locale. Another advantage of the system is that it has been legally challenged and found acceptable by the courts.

The Hay Guide Chart-Profile Method, like any canned, or standardized, system, may not reflect a particular organization's true values, however. Thus, each organization needs to consider whether the Hay system's problem-solving, know-how, and accountability factors are truly congruent with the organization's values. In recognition of the idea that different companies are likely to value different aspects of a job, Hay Associates now works with companies to create tailored point systems that fit specific organizations. The feature, Managing Change: Bayer's Job Evaluation System Reflects its Values,[58] describes how one company adapted the Hay Guide-Chart Profile method to fit its organizational change efforts.

Competency-Based Job Evaluation. The alterations Bayer made to the Hay point system involve a partial shift toward the competency-based method for assigning points to jobs. Competency-based systems keep the focus on the *job*, but the emphasis is on the competencies needed to perform the job rather than the job activities. In Bayer's new system, points assigned for "Improvement opportunity" and "Contribution" reflect job activities. The points assigned for "Capability" reflect competencies.

Many companies have adopted competency-based job evaluation systems in recent years. Often the shift to a competency-based system coincides with the adoption of a broadbanding approach (described in Chapter 6). Used together, competency-based job evaluation and broadbanding provide a

■□ fast fact

In 1998, about 12 percent of medium and large U.S. companies used competency-based pay and 30 percent were considering it.

MANAGING CHANGE
Bayer's Job Evaluation System Reflects Its Values

Bayer Corporation is a Pittsburgh-based subsidiary of the German firm named Bayer Group AG. Today Bayer Corp. is one corporation with three major divisions, but back in 1991, it was three separate operating companies: a chemical producer called Mobay Chemical Corp., a healthcare organization called Miles, Inc., and an imaging company called Agfa. In the aftermath of the merger that created Bayer Corp., the top executive team set out to develop a vision that would bring together the diverse workforces of the original three firms. Their vision states that Bayer Corp. will be a leader in the markets it serves and it will be a major contributor to its parent firm. To reach this vision, Bayer would operate according to a new set of values, which emphasized the importance of

- maintaining a diversified and highly motivated workforce that was fairly compensated for its performance;
- satisfying internal and external customers through innovative problem-solving, while also adhering to ethical standards;
- managing the organization in a way that minimizes bureaucracy, delegates authority, and fosters teamwork and cooperation; and
- being a good citizen of the communities in which employees work and live.

To succeed, the new organization needed employees who embraced the new values. Bayer's managers realized that employees would be more likely to embrace these new values to the extent they received a clear and consistent message about their importance. Redesigning the job evaluation systems used within the company was high on the agenda. CEO Helge Wehmeier put this challenge to the Job Advisory Committee—a task force of fourteen senior vice presidents: "Whatever you do, I want the work-valuing process you come up with to be responsive to what we're doing as a business, and I don't want to increase costs."

Prior to the merger of the three companies, jobs at Mobay had been relatively unstructured. Miles and Agfa had each used the Hay Guide-Chart Profile method, but in recent years they had grown dissatisfied with it because they felt it did not reflect the business values in their specific companies. The old system was too oriented toward functional and hierarchical values. People often felt that jobs were valued according to the degrees and credentials required for the job rather than the contribution or the way those degrees and credentials were used. Another problem with the old system was the way responsibility was assessed, i.e., according to the size of one's budget and one's staff. Clearly, the Job Advisory Committee had to make a choice: Choose a completely new method for evaluating jobs *or* revise the content in the old Hay Guide-Charts. They chose the latter alternative. Instead of valuing jobs according to know-how, problem-solving, and accountability, the new job evaluation system used the following dimensions:

Improvement opportunity	How much opportunity is there for people in this job to improve the company's performance?
Contribution	How strong are the requirements for people in this job to achieve results?
Capability	What are the total proficiencies and competencies required in the job? Three categories were considered:

- Expertise and complexity
- Leadership and integration
- Relationship-building skills

This new job evaluation system is now used throughout Bayer Corporation. There is one pay system that values work in the same way, regardless of whether that work involves healthcare, chemicals, or imaging technology. This helps managers and employees alike because it facilitates easy cross-business transfers and promotions.

To learn more about Bayer Group AG, visit the company home page at **www.bayer.com**

method for defining career paths that are defined by the objective of individual development instead of climbing the corporate ladder.

SmithKline Beecham began shifting to a competency-based organization in 1994. The first unit to make the change was Pharm Tech—a small unit that employs about 400 scientists and support staff in the United States and the United Kingdom. Like many organizations, Pharm Tech had just redesigned its organization. It replaced its old functional structure with process-driven teams. In the old structure, career advancement meant moving up the hierarchy within one's functional area. In the new organization, career advancement was conceptualized as moving through four stages. To move through the four stages, employees needed to progress through jobs that required increasing levels of seven key competencies. These seven competencies, identified as central to Pharm Tech's business strategy and culture, are

- innovation,
- teamwork,
- communication,
- use of resources,
- decision making/perspective,
- customer satisfaction, and
- technical ability.

At career stage 1, the work being performed requires relatively low levels of these competencies. At career stage 2, higher levels of competencies are required by the work, and so on. By categorizing jobs according to their fit with the four career stages, Pharm Tech structured its jobs into four broad competency bands. Salaries are tied to these four bands.[59] Exhibit 10.7 illustrates how competency-based advancement can be mapped onto salary levels.

Companies often adopt the competency-based approach for valuing work because it promotes individual development and growth through lateral moves in the organization. Growth through lateral moves is consistent with flatter, team-based structures. This approach does have some drawbacks, however. According to a study by Hewitt and Associates, an HR consulting firm, broadbanding may meet stiff cultural resistance in many countries. In Brazil, for example, status symbols and titles that differentiate people according to their status are highly valued forms of recognition. Similarly, in India, work often is organized hierarchically. Promotions up through the hierarchy are a major form of reward and recognition for employee loyalty. People typically expect promotions every three or four years. In Singapore, people depend heavily on clear structures and rules as guides to behavior. In contrast, competency-based broadbanding was developed to promote flexibility. It eschews rigid rules, and thus may be less culturally comfortable for Singaporeans to understand and accept.[60]

Exhibit 10.7
Using Competency-Based Broadbanding to Establish Base Pay Levels

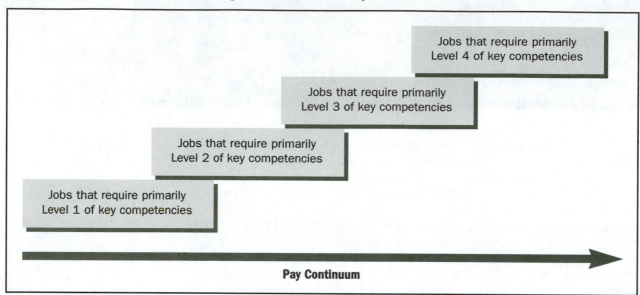

Within the U.S., the corporate cultures of many organizations reflect some of these same cultural values—they're still hierarchical, bureaucratic, and rule-driven. When companies with such corporate cultures attempt to introduce competency-based broadbanding, the effort may ultimately fail. The most common reasons for failed implementation appear to be that

- the new system results in low morale;
- managers and their subordinates are frustrated by the system;
- managers and other employees don't understand the system;
- employees do not trust management to make fair evaluations of the competencies needed in various jobs; and
- managers continue to base their pay decision on the old, hidden pay grade system.[61]

SKILL-BASED PAY

As just described, competency-based job evaluation systems begin to shift the focus of pay systems toward the competencies of employees. Skill-based pay is an even more radical approach to paying people based on competencies. Companies using skill-based pay, which is also called pay-for-knowledge or multiskilled pay, determine people's pay by measuring their competencies directly. With skill-based pay, the question asked isn't, "What level of competency is required to perform your job?" The relevant question becomes, "At what competency level *can* an employee perform?" In this system, employees are paid based on their personal skill or competency level regardless of what level of competency is required in their current position.

Skill-based pay rewards employees for the range, depth, and types of skills they're capable of using. This is a very different philosophy from the conventional job-based approaches. It moves the compensation of workers toward the approaches used to evaluate many types of professionals.[62] Research-and-development firms have valued the contributions of engineers and scientists using a related approach, called maturity curves, since the 1950s. With this method, a series of curves is developed to provide differing levels of worth to individuals. The underlying principle is that professionals with more experience and knowledge are more valuable to the organization. Similar approaches are used to pay elementary and secondary school teachers and apprentices in skilled crafts, who receive pay increments based on educational levels and seniority.

Skill-based pay is premised on the same assumption, namely, that a person who can do more different tasks or who knows more is of greater value and should be paid according to capabilities, not according to job assignment. The important distinction between skill-based pay and the maturity curve approach is that with maturity curves, pay increases occur automatically at particular time intervals. With skill-based pay, pay goes up only after the worker demonstrates an ability to perform specific competencies. In one version of skill-based pay, pay goes up as distinct tasks or knowledge areas are mastered. This is a multiskill system. For a machine operator, the relevant skills might include an assembly task, a material handling and inventory task, and maintenance tasks. Alternatively, pay may be pegged to the employee's level of skill or knowledge within a job domain. For example, supervisors might demonstrate increasing skills and knowledge in job domains such as budget planning and analysis, employee performance management, and developing client relationships. Exhibit 10.8 summarizes several differences between skill-based and job-based pay systems.[63]

Exhibit 10.8
Comparison of Skill-Based and Conventional Job-Based Pay Systems

Component	Skill-Based System	Job-Based System
1. Determination of worth	Tied to evaluation of skill blocks	Tied to evaluation of total job
2. Pricing	Difficult because the overall pay system is tied to the market	Easier because wages are tied to benchmark jobs in the labor market
3. Pay ranges	Extremely broad; one pay range for entire cluster of skills	Variable, depending on type of job and pay grade width
4. Evaluation of performance	Competency tests	Job performance measures
5. Salary increases	Tied to skill acquisition as measured by competency testing	Tied to seniority, performance appraisal ratings, or actual output
6. Role of training	Essential to attain job flexibility and pay increases for all employees	Necessitated by need rather than employee's desire
7. Pay growth opportunities	Greater opportunities; anyone who passes competency test advances	Fewer opportunities; no advancement unless there is a job opening
8. Effect of job change	Pay remains constant unless skill proficiency increases	Pay changes immediately to level associated with new job
9. Pay administration	Difficult because many aspects of pay plan (training, certification) demand attention	Contingent upon the complexity of job evaluation and pay allocation plan

Although skill-based pay is relatively new, preliminary research shows that it can be very effective. Skill-based pay creates an environment that facilitates worker rotation. This may reduce absenteeism and may ease job assignment pressures for management. Because workers are motivated to learn higher-level skills, they will likely be paid more than the job evaluation rate of the specific jobs to which they're assigned. Nevertheless overall labor costs may be lower owing to enhanced workforce flexibility and productivity.[64]

Skill-based pay systems represent a truly different approach to designing a compensation system. The approach may not fit all situations. In fact, a large study comparing *Fortune* 1000 companies to companies using skill-based pay found substantial differences in many other aspects of their cultures and their total systems for managing human resources, as shown in Exhibit 10.9.

MANAGING THE PROCESS USED TO VALUE JOBS AND EMPLOYEES

"In addition to absolute levels of pay, people are interested in equity—how they're paid, how they're graded, and how they're evaluated relative to other employees."

Herb Kelleher
CEO
Southwest Airlines

Organizations have many choices when developing a system for establishing the relative worth of individual employees. They may attach worth based on the job being performed, the skills of the employee, and/or the results produced by the employee. None of these approaches is foolproof, nor are they wholly objective. Ultimately, they all rely on evaluators making judgments about jobs and people based on the facts presented to them.[65] The acid test of any scheme's value is whether it produces results that are acceptable to both jobholders and managers, and are perceived as fair and reasonable. Formal job and skill evaluation schemes are capable of meeting these objectives when they promote genuine participation by all employees—including job incumbents and their managers, as well as union representatives, where appropriate. Participation also smooths the process of communicating and justifying results to employees.

Job, competency, and skill evaluation judgments, like other human resource decisions, can be made by a variety of constituents including HR professionals, managers, and job incumbents. Traditionally, compensation experts and managers had the most involvement in the design of compensation systems. Recently, however, employee involvement in job evaluation has increased. For example, 64 percent of all labor agreements require incumbent involvement. As many as half of all companies involve their employees in designing and implementing their compensation plans.[66]

Participation alone isn't sufficient to ensure the system's effectiveness, however. The people participating in the evaluation process should be trained in how to make valid judgments. They may also need to be trained to correctly use, interpret, and know when to question the results produced by commercial software. Such software is designed to reduce the burden of making the calculations involved in designing a pay structure. But unless one fully understands the calculations being made, one can't be certain that the results the program yields match the design decisions that were intended by the user.

Employees who are ultimately expected to live with the system also need to understand how judgments are made. When managers and employees alike understand both the objectives of the system and the business objectives used to design the system, the system is more likely to be effective. Exhibit 10.10 illustrates some of the key principles that should be followed when creating an internal pay structure.

Exhibit 10.9
Skill-Based Pay Users Versus *Fortune* 1000 Companies

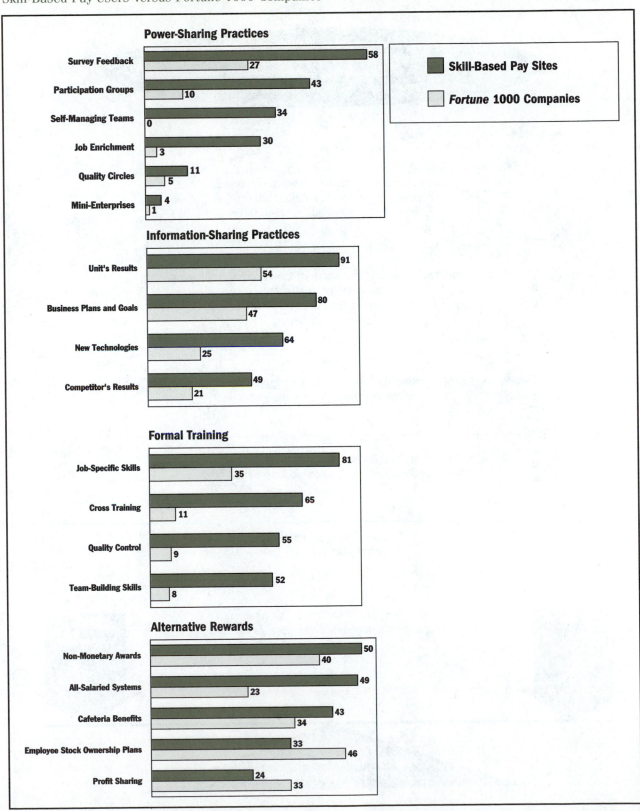

Power-Sharing Practices

Survey Feedback — Skill-Based Pay Sites: 58; *Fortune* 1000 Companies: 27
Participation Groups — Skill-Based Pay Sites: 43; *Fortune* 1000 Companies: 10
Self-Managing Teams — Skill-Based Pay Sites: 34; *Fortune* 1000 Companies: 0
Job Enrichment — Skill-Based Pay Sites: 30; *Fortune* 1000 Companies: 3
Quality Circles — Skill-Based Pay Sites: 11; *Fortune* 1000 Companies: 5
Mini-Enterprises — Skill-Based Pay Sites: 4; *Fortune* 1000 Companies: 1

Legend:
■ **Skill-Based Pay Sites**
□ *Fortune* **1000 Companies**

Information-Sharing Practices

Unit's Results — Skill-Based Pay Sites: 91; *Fortune* 1000 Companies: 54
Business Plans and Goals — Skill-Based Pay Sites: 80; *Fortune* 1000 Companies: 47
New Technologies — Skill-Based Pay Sites: 64; *Fortune* 1000 Companies: 25
Competitor's Results — Skill-Based Pay Sites: 49; *Fortune* 1000 Companies: 21

Formal Training

Job-Specific Skills — Skill-Based Pay Sites: 81; *Fortune* 1000 Companies: 35
Cross Training — Skill-Based Pay Sites: 65; *Fortune* 1000 Companies: 11
Quality Control — Skill-Based Pay Sites: 55; *Fortune* 1000 Companies: 9
Team-Building Skills — Skill-Based Pay Sites: 52; *Fortune* 1000 Companies: 8

Alternative Rewards

Non-Monetary Awards — Skill-Based Pay Sites: 50; *Fortune* 1000 Companies: 40
All-Salaried Systems — Skill-Based Pay Sites: 49; *Fortune* 1000 Companies: 23
Cafeteria Benefits — Skill-Based Pay Sites: 43; *Fortune* 1000 Companies: 34
Employee Stock Ownership Plans — Skill-Based Pay Sites: 33; *Fortune* 1000 Companies: 46
Profit Sharing — Skill-Based Pay Sites: 24; *Fortune* 1000 Companies: 33

Exhibit 10.10
Developing the Pay Structure

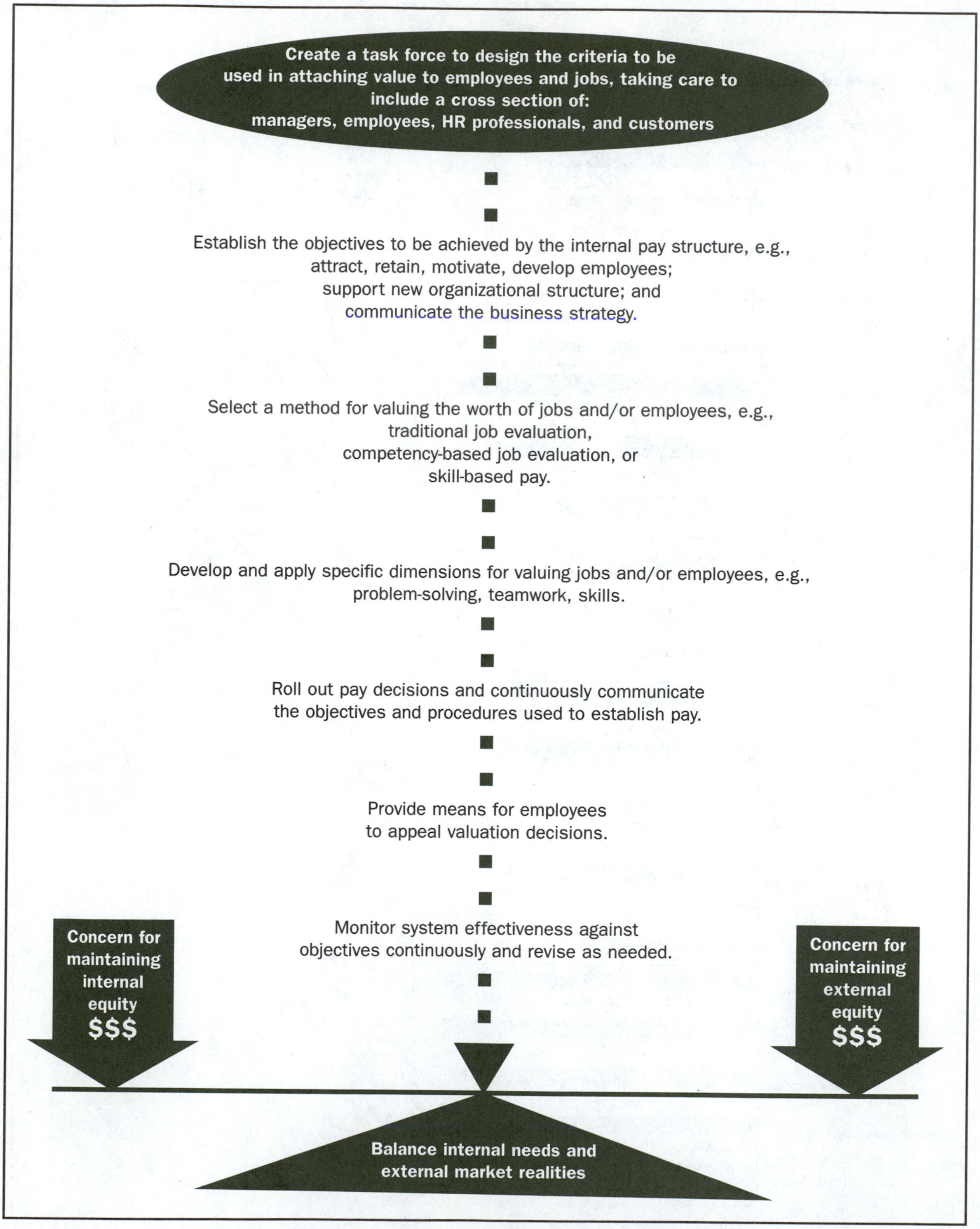

Create a task force to design the criteria to be
used in attaching value to employees and jobs, taking care to
include a cross section of:
managers, employees, HR professionals, and customers

Establish the objectives to be achieved by the internal pay structure, e.g.,
attract, retain, motivate, develop employees;
support new organizational structure; and
communicate the business strategy.

Select a method for valuing the worth of jobs and/or employees, e.g.,
traditional job evaluation,
competency-based job evaluation, or
skill-based pay.

Develop and apply specific dimensions for valuing jobs and/or employees, e.g.,
problem-solving, teamwork, skills.

Roll out pay decisions and continuously communicate
the objectives and procedures used to establish pay.

Provide means for employees
to appeal valuation decisions.

Monitor system effectiveness against
objectives continuously and revise as needed.

Concern for
maintaining
internal
equity
$$$

Concern for
maintaining
external
equity
$$$

Balance internal needs and
external market realities

EXTERNAL EQUITY: ENSURING COMPETITIVENESS

As already noted, an effective compensation system attracts and retains qualified employees. To do so, it must take into account the realities of the external labor market. Achieving external equity involves (1) conducting a wage survey of the external market, (2) setting the overall wage policy, and (3) linking market information to the internal pay structure.

Conducting a Wage Survey

To make use of data from a wage survey, an organization first needs to select appropriate benchmarks. Traditionally, benchmarks have been jobs that are commonly found across a range of organizations. For competency-based pay systems, however, the appropriate benchmarks would be competency profiles. For skill-based pay, the appropriate benchmarks would be identifiable skill levels. In practice, however, most companies must still rely on benchmarking against common jobs because that is the method usually used to collect market wage data.

Next, the organization defines the relevant labor market for each benchmark job.[67] Three variables are commonly used to determine the relevant market: the occupation or skill required, the geographic location (the distance from which applicants would be willing to relocate or commute), and the other employers competing for labor. The relevant geographic labor market for a vice president of sales for Microsoft Corporation may be the entire United States; by comparison, the relevant labor market for an accounts receivable clerk may be Greater Seattle. In global companies, the relevant labor market for some jobs is the entire world!

Once the labor market is defined for each benchmark job, survey data must be collected. In some cases, companies conduct their own wage and salary surveys, but they purchase a survey from a consulting firm or use labor market data from government sources. Regardless of how survey data are obtained, the process is filled with subjective judgments and the results are likely to depend in part on idiosyncratic issues taken into account by the people conducting the analysis.[68] Thus, as is true for other steps in the process of designing the pay system, involving multiple people with multiple perspectives is a good strategy. Exhibit 10.11 illustrates a portion of a typical market survey questionnaire.

With the appropriate market wage and salary information in hand, market pay rates are plotted against the company's evaluation points or rankings. This establishes a policy line for pay in the external market, as shown in Exhibit 10.12. Why does an organization need to calculate the external market's policy line? Because market data won't be available for all jobs. The market policy line makes it possible to estimate what the market pays for jobs that are similar to those in the company but aren't among the benchmark jobs included in the market survey.

Deciding on a Pay Policy

After calculating the market's policy line, an organization has sufficient data to set its own pay policy line. If the company wants simply to match the market, it may set its policy line equal to the line for the external market. Alternatively, the company may choose to pay somewhat above the market or somewhat below the market. The choice of a pay policy is influenced by the pay rates of major competitors, the firm's profits or losses, surpluses or

■□ *fast fact*

Canadian techies who move across the border to work for Microsoft can often increase their base pay 200 percent.

■□ *fast fact*

The cost of living in San Francisco is 31 percent higher than the national average.

Exhibit 10.11

Sample Questions from a Market Survey Questionnaire

Position Title	Code	Level	No. of Employees in Position	SALARY & SALARY RANGE			ANNUAL BONUS			OTHER CASH COMPENSATION		
				Average Annual Salary as of 3/1/99	Annual Salary Range (Do not report actual low and high paid)		No. of Employees Receiving Annual Bonus	Average Annual Bonus Paid in $	Average Annual Bonus Paid as % of Sal.	No. of Employees Receiving Other Cash	Avg. Annual Other Cash Paid in $	Avg. Annual Other Cash Paid as % of Sal.
					Minimum	Maximum		Complete Either Column			Complete Either Column	
Industrial Health Care												
Industrial Physician	150											
Head Industrial Nurse	160											
Industrial Nurse—RN (Full-Time)	170											
Industrial Nurse—LPN	180											
Industrial Hygienist	190											

Variable Pay

1. Do you currently have any of the variable pay programs listed below in place as part of your pay program? (Check "Yes" if plan was in place even if no awards or payouts were granted) . . . . ☐ Yes   ☐ No

2. Do you plan to install any new or additional programs within the next 2 years? (Check "Yes" if you intend to add a plan of the same type that already exists) (If you answered "no" to both questions 1 and 2, go to next section.) . . . . ☐ Yes   ☐ No

3. Please complete the following by checking the appropriate boxes:

	a. Plan is currently in place	b. Intend to install new or additional plan within next 2 years
a. Annual bonus	☐	☐
b. Current cash profit sharing (exclude retirement plans)	☐	☐
c. Small group/team incentives.	☐	☐
d. Individual incentives	☐	☐
e. Spot awards	☐	☐
f. Technical achievement awards.	☐	☐
g. Gainsharing awards	☐	☐
h. Lump sum merit pay (not added to base)	☐	☐
i. Lump sum merit pay (added to base)	☐	☐
j. Commission	☐	☐
k. Key contributor retention awards	☐	☐
l. Skill/knowledge-based pay	☐	☐
m. Other: (please specify)	☐	☐

4. Indicate which measurements are used to determine bonus and/or variable pay awards (Check any that apply)
   - a. ☐ Sales/revenues
   - b. ☐ Profits
   - c. ☐ Productivity
   - d. ☐ Quality
   - e. ☐ Innovation
   - f. ☐ Cost reduction
   - g. ☐ Safety
   - h. ☐ Achievement of project milestones
   - i. ☐ Customer service
   - j. ☐ Length of service
   - k. ☐ Other (Explain)

5. During 1999, did you adjust your approach to compensation to place greater emphasis on bonus or other variable pay programs? . . . . ☐ Yes   ☐ No

6. In 2000, do you plan to adjust your approach to compensation to place greater emphasis on bonus or other variable pay programs? . . . . ☐ Yes   ☐ No

Exhibit 10.12

Pay Rates Based on Market Survey Results for Benchmark Jobs

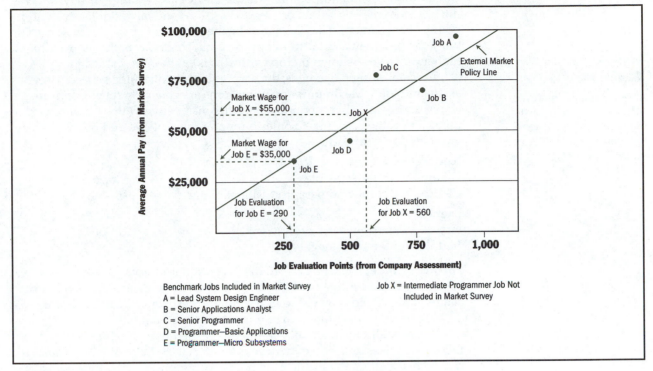

Benchmark Jobs Included in Market Survey
A = Lead System Design Engineer
B = Senior Applications Analyst
C = Senior Programmer
D = Programmer—Basic Applications
E = Programmer—Micro Subsystems

Job X = Intermediate Programmer Job Not
Included in Market Survey

shortages of qualified workers, the stage of the firm's development, the role of performance-based pay, the strength of union demands, the organizational culture, and so forth.[69]

A lead policy, paying somewhat above the market rate, maximizes the company's ability to attract and retain quality employees and to minimize employee dissatisfaction with pay. A lead policy signals that the firm values employees as a source of competitive advantage. A concern is whether the additional pay attracts and retains the best or merely the most applicants. It's also uncertain how much a firm needs to lead others to gain a distinct competitive advantage. Finally, the pay rates of other firms tend to escalate and eventually match the leader's rates.

By far the most common policy is to match the competition. Although this approach does not give an employer a competitive advantage, it does ensure that the firm isn't at a disadvantage. When Sears restructured its pay system, they discovered from market survey data that past decisions about pay had resulted in an unintended policy of substantially leading the market. For the company, a lead policy was too costly, so the new system was designed to gradually lower the company's internal pay line in order to more closely match the market. The option to lag the market may hinder a firm's ability to attract potential employees unless other variables—such as job security, benefits, locale, and job content—compensate for the low base pay.[70]

Developing a Pay Grade Structure

With the pay policy set, a pay structure can be developed.

Job-Based Pay Grade Structure.   Exhibit 10.13 shows a pay grade structure for a conventional job-based pay system. The boxes are associated with a spread of job evaluation points (the job grade) and a range of pay. Several different jobs may be within one box. These jobs will have similar evaluation points, if not content. The boxes may be the same size or may vary in height, but generally they ascend from left to right. This reflects the association of higher pay levels (shown on the vertical axis) with more valued jobs.

In establishing pay ranges, the corporate pay policy line generally serves as the midpoint. Maximums and minimums are generally set at a percentage above and below that amount. The difference between the maximum and minimum is the pay range. Some common ranges above and below the pay grade midpoint include

Nonexempt

Laborers and tradespeople	Up to 25%
Clerical, technical, and paraprofessional workers	15—50%

Exempt

First-level managers and professionals	30–50%
Middle and senior managers	40—100%

For the firm depicted in Exhibit 10.13, six equal-interval pay grades were established, each with a width of one hundred points. Each grade has a pay range of $1,000. For pay grade II, the range goes from $2,250 (minimum) to $3,250 (maximum) a month; the midpoint is $2,750 a month.

Occasionally, jobs fall outside the established pay structure. When a job falls *below* the established minimum (see job A in Exhibit 10.13), it's *blue circled*, and usually an adjustment is made to bring the job within the established pay range. When a job is *overpaid* (see job B in Exhibit 10.13), it may be *red circled*—that is, as long as the current incumbent remains in the job, the pay rate remains unchanged; when the incumbent leaves the job, the rate will be adjusted downward to put the job back in the established range.

Exhibit 10.13

Pay Grade Structure for a Conventional Job-Based Pay System

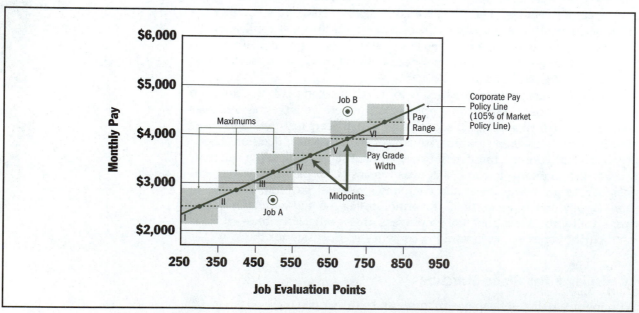

Compa-Ratio.   To determine how management is actually paying employees relative to the pay line midpoint, managers often rely on an index called a compa-ratio:

$$\text{Compa-Ratio} = \text{Average Rate of Pay for Employees Within a Pay Grade} \div \text{Range Midpoint}$$

A compa-ratio of less than 1.00 means that on average, employees in the pay grade are being paid below the midpoint. Translated, this means that on average, employees are being paid below the intended policy. A valid reason for this may be that employees as a group were hired relatively recently, are poor performers, or are promoted so rapidly that they aren't in their jobs long enough to reach the upper half of the pay range.

A compa-ratio greater than 1.00 means that, on average, the organization is paying more than the stated policy. This might occur when employees as a group "top out" because they stay in the same job a long time without getting promoted to jobs in higher grades.

Pay Grades for Skill-Based Pay.   The establishment of external equity is more complex with skill-based pay systems than with job-based pay systems. Companies often find it difficult to directly compare particular pay levels in a skill-based pay plan with pay levels of other firms using job-based pay. Although organizations using skill-based pay rely on the market to set pay levels, they use market data to set minimum, maximum, and average pay levels for the entire job family, not to peg each particular skill step in the pay system to jobs found in the outside markets.

As with job-based pay, organizations employing skill-based pay differ in their pay policies relative to the external market. HR officials at a Honeywell ammunition plant in Joliet, Illinois, adopted a policy that was below the market for entry-level skills but above the market for advanced skills. Traditionally, the ammunition industry has been a low-wage industry. However, average wages in the area of the Honeywell plant were relatively high, owing partly to the number of unionized industrial plants in the region. According to Honeywell's HR manager, this meant that paying locally competitive wages would make the organization uncompetitive in its business market. Skill-based pay was viewed as a way out of this pricing nightmare. Entry wages were pegged at a rate that was low for the area but competitive within the industry. Pay rates rose sharply as employees reached higher skill levels—that is, each new skill was worth an additional $0.90 an hour. With a total of five levels, this produced a pay range of $4.50 on an hourly basis. Level 3 was pegged at slightly above the area average, and level 4 was priced at well above the area average. Company officials believed that by the time employees reached level 4, they would be so productive that the facility could afford to pay them the higher rate.[71]

BALANCING INTERNAL AND EXTERNAL EQUITY

External and internal data as well as a firm's compensation strategy differentially affect job worth decisions. As Exhibit 10.10 illustrates, every organization must find the appropriate balance. Sometimes differences between market rates and job evaluation results can be resolved by reviewing the basic decisions associated with evaluating and pricing particular jobs. Sometimes survey data can be ignored or benchmark jobs can be changed or jobs can simply be reevaluated. In cases where the disparities persist, judgment is required to resolve them.

As the feature, Managing Globalization: Borderline Pay at Nortel, describes, the challenge of balancing internal and external equity has become acute for Canadian firms. The technical skills of Canadians are much in demand in the United States, where salary levels can be much higher. To keep Canadians home, many companies must be responsive to an external market that includes the United States, but doing so can create problems of internal equity. Nortel's solution represents a compromise that favors external equity while still acknowledging the importance of internal equity concerns.[72]

MANAGING GLOBALIZATION

Borderline Pay at Nortel

Northern Telecom, Ltd. (Nortel) is Canada's leading telecommunications company. Its 63,000 employees are spread around the world, so dealing with pay differences between countries is nothing new for Nortel. Ironically, however, the company found that some of its most difficult motivation and reward problems arise from pay differences between Canada and its nearest neighbor, the United States. Like other Canadian companies, Nortel faces a significant challenge in deciding what is equitable pay for managers and professionals.

Demand for managers and professionals is strong in the United States, so many Canadians consider the option of moving across the border. Typically, Canadian professionals and managers earn one-third less than their U.S. counterparts, as shown in Exhibit A. In contrast, employees who hold jobs at lower pay levels are paid more in Canada than in the United States.

Exhibit A   Examples of Pay Differences in Canada and the United States

Job	Canada	United States	Canadian Pay as a Percentage of U.S. Pay
CFO of $300-million packaging company	$161,000	$247,500	65%
Information system executive	$98,000	$150,300	65%
Treasurer	$109,100	$153,200	71%
Machine operator	$27,000	$19,900	136%
Salesclerk	$24,500	$16,800	146%

Note: Amounts are in Canadian dollars.

A Canadian manager comparing inputs and outcomes to those of a similar executive in the United States may conclude that she is underpaid and seek employment across the border. As more Canadian professionals and managers seek employment in the United States, companies such as Nortel face the possibility of a "brain drain."

In order to attract new talent and avoid losing its best employees, Nortel has adopted a new approach to setting salaries. Because Nortel employees use their U.S. counterparts when assessing whether they're paid fairly, Nortel now utilizes a formula that blends the pay levels in the United States and Canada to set salaries for higher level jobs, giving more weight to U.S. salary levels. An example of the formula used to determine the salary of a top information systems executive, who the company believes is vulnerable to offers from the United States, is as follows:

Weighted blending. A weight of 0.2 is given to pay rates in Canada, and a weight of 0.8 is given to pay rates in the United States. The exchange rate used to convert U.S. to Canadian dollars is 1.37. Thus

$$(0.2 \times \$98,000) + (0.8 \times \$110,000 \times 1.37) = \$140,160 \text{ Canadian}$$

Using this formula, Nortel hopes to prevent the perception of two types of inequity. First, the new formula takes into account the manager's natural tendency to compare his or her inputs and outcomes to those of similar U.S. managers. Second, the Canadian manager who has subordinates in the United States knows that they're paid at U.S. rates. Using the blended approach to setting the manager's pay helps reduce any perceived inequity that might arise from a manager's comparing inputs and outcomes and knowing that subordinates are being paid as much as or more than the manager.

To learn more about Northern Telecom, visit the company's home page at
www.nortel.com

To learn more about issues of international compensation, visit the home page of the American Compensation Association at
www.acaonline.org

Pay Differentials

One way the discrepancy between internal and external pay equity can be resolved is to establish temporary market differentials. Consider the dilemma confronting a television broadcast company. The broadcast firm conducted a job evaluation study and collected market data for key positions. The job evaluation positioned the job of a broadcast engineer technician in pay grade VI. When designing the pay structure, the pay rate for this grade had been set well below the average pay rate in the external market. The discrepancy persisted even following a check of the job evaluation and wage survey data. Because engineers with broadcast experience are difficult to find, company executives considered reassigning the job to a higher pay grade (they had done this in the past). Although this would provide a "quick fix," the long-term consequences—particularly if other employees found out about the reclassification—could be disastrous, threatening the validity of the entire compensation system. To preserve the integrity of the system while meeting market demands, engineering jobs were left in the appropriate grades and a market differential was paid to employees in these jobs. As long as the external market rate of pay was higher than the station's policy line, engineers would receive the 10 percent market differential; when the labor market imbalance corrected itself, the differential would be eliminated.

Pay Compression

Pay compression results when wages for jobs filled from outside the organization are increasing faster than wages for jobs filled from within the organization. As a result, pay differentials among jobs become very small, and the traditional pay structure becomes compressed. Compression is an issue for professional organizations—such as engineering and law firms and colleges and universities—where new graduates command salaries equal to or above those of professionals with more experience.

The problem of compression has no one correct solution. Ultimately, a company considers the costs and consequences of eliminating compression problems (e.g., by raising the pay of more senior job incumbents to keep pace with the changing market) versus letting compression drive employee behavior (e.g., through psychological withdrawal or active job hunting among employees with compressed pay), and chooses the course of action that has the least negative consequences.

COMMUNICATING THE PLAN

"The worst-kept secret in any plant is what people make. Everybody ends up finding out anyway, so we just post."

Jim Larkin
CEO
Romac Industries

A recent study by Hewitt and Associates found that failure to adequately communicate with employees was a major source of problems when employers introduced new pay systems. Although most (73 percent) companies reported that they communicated during the introduction of a new compensation system, most (82 percent) did not continue to communicate about the system after its initial introduction. With new employees continually being hired, such communication lapses undermine the value of even the most well-designed pay structures. When employees don't fully understand how their pay is determined, they're not motivated by the way their pay is structured.

When Allstate's board decided to restructure executive pay packages, they paid a great deal of attention to explaining the bases for the new packages. Allstate Insurance Company was established in 1931 by Sears, Roebuck and Company. Sixty years later, Sears spun it off to pursue a more focused strategy. Allstate came face-to-face with the demands of Wall Street for the first time. When Allstate went public, an outside board of directors was established. Evaluating executive pay packages was among its first tasks. The board commissioned a study of key executives to learn how they perceived their pay and their views about how pay should be determined. The study revealed a weak link in the system. Because the pay of Allstate executives was tied to the stock movement of Sears, they felt that they had little control over it. "In many cases, our executives were not really motivated by Sears' executive pay," concluded the assistant vice president of compensation.

Allstate needed a new, simpler plan that linked pay directly to Allstate's business results. When the new pay plan was ready, experts were brought in to develop a communication strategy. They collaborated with a team of Allstate managers who hadn't been involved in developing the pay plan and who represented a variety of specialty areas. The communication strategy developed by this team focused on conveying to executives how great the future could be for them individually and collectively if adequate results were achieved.

Before devising its formal communication strategy, team members began by making sure they understood the new pay plan themselves. "We ripped (the plan) apart, we took the staples out if it—we literally ripped it apart, not figuratively—and stuck the pages up on the walls. . . . We tried to understand the plan and draw it on the board," explained one of the communication experts.

Once the team members were sure that they understood the new pay plan, the principle that proved most important as they developed the formal communication strategy was "Keep it Simple." Rather than overwhelm people with all the details, the communicators emphasized the link between achieving business objectives and the pay that the executives would receive. To ensure that the executives could see "the big picture," the written material included a foldout page showing how all the pieces of the package fit together. To give personal meaning to the package, each executive received an individualized statement that showed the maximum amounts that he or she could earn if individual and group targets were achieved.

A second survey conducted after the new package was explained revealed that 85 percent of the executives felt that they now had a better understanding than before of their annual incentive pay, their stock options, and the total pay package.[73]

COMPENSATION IN THE CONTEXT OF GLOBALIZATION

As the environment for many business firms in the United States becomes more global, international compensation becomes a more significant element of total compensation.[74] When developing international compensation policies, the basic objectives are the same as in a domestic context. The policy should be consistent and fair in its treatment of all employees. It should help attract and retain personnel in the areas where the company has the greatest needs and opportunities. It should motivate employees. And, it should facilitate the transfer across locations of employees in the most cost-effective manner.

Basic Compensation Philosophy

In general, the first issue facing multinational corporations (MNCs) when designing international compensation policies is whether to establish an overall policy for all employees or to distinguish between parent-country nationals and third-country nationals. This differentiation may diminish in the future, but in the 1990s, it was very common for MNCs to distinguish between these two groups. Furthermore, separate policies may be established based on the length of assignment (temporary transfer, permanent transfer, or continual relocation). Cash remuneration, special allowances, benefits, and pensions are determined in part by such classification. Short-term expatriates—for example, those whose two- or three-year tours of duty abroad are interspersed with long periods at home—may be treated differently than career expatriates, who spend most of their time working in various locations abroad. Both these groups are different from third-country nationals (TCNs), who often move from country to country in the employ of a MNC headquartered in a country other than their own. For example, a Swiss banker may be in charge of a German branch of a British bank. In effect, TCNs are the real global employees, the ones who can weave together the far-flung parts of an MNC. As the global MNC increases in importance, TCNs will likely become more valuable and command higher levels of compensation.

For parent-country expatriates, the most widely used policy emphasizes "keeping the expatriate whole"—that is, maintaining a pay level comparable to that of the PCN's colleagues plus compensating for the costs of international service. Foreign assignees shouldn't suffer a material loss owing to their transfer. Many companies use the balance sheet approach to equalize the purchasing power of employees at comparable position levels living overseas and in the home country, and to provide incentives to offset quali-

■□ *fast fact*

The Australian government mandates that all organizations must provide employees with benefits equivalent to 9 percent of their salary, effective in 2002.

tative differences between assignment locations.[75] The objective of this approach is to provide a level of net spendable income in the new destination that is similar to that received in the previous (usually home) location.

Base Pay

Employers usually pay expatriates in the employee's home currency at the home rate, but some companies pay in the local currency at the local rate paid for the same job. Similarly, salary adjustments and promotional practices may be fashioned according to either home-country or local standards. U.S. and Canadian companies usually pay according to the home rate, while European companies use both approaches about equally. Increasingly, however, MNCs are developing global salary and performance structures that can be applied without concern for where work is performed.[76]

The development of the European Union has brought greater use of the euro within business. This common currency will make it easier to develop a global policy that applies regardless of the organization's national origin, recognizing the need to treat European operations as truly one market and employees as truly all Europeans.

"The euro will be one of three major currencies in the world, after the dollar and the yen."

Alain Johnson
Employee Benefits Director
PriceWaterhouseCoopers, Paris

Relocation Premiums

Five major categories of expenses incurred by expatriates and their families are:

Goods and Services: Items such as food, personal care, clothing, household furnishings, recreation, transportation, and medical care.

Housing: The major costs associated with the employees' principal residences.

Income Taxes: Payments to federal and local governments for personal income taxes. For U.S. employees, tax liabilities usually increase when they go abroad, so most U.S. employers adopt a tax equalization policy for assignment-related income.

Reserve: Contributions to savings, payments for benefits, pension contributions, investments, education expenses, Social Security taxes, and so forth.

Shipment and Storage: The major costs associated with shipping and storing personal and household effects.

Not all these aspects of international compensation come into play for every expatriate; nevertheless, most U.S. companies pay expatriates a premium to cover such costs, and many also provide free housing. Consequently, the cost of posting an expatriate can be anywhere from three to seven times the expatriate's home base salary.

ASSESSING COMPENSATION EFFECTIVENESS

For domestic and multinational firms alike, the following major purposes of total compensation should drive an organization's approach to assessing the effectiveness of their total compensation system:

- attracting potentially qualified employees,
- motivating employees to exhibit behaviors consistent with the business strategy and corporate culture,
- retaining qualified employees, and
- administering pay within legal constraints.

To achieve these purposes, employees need to be satisfied with their pay. This means the pay levels should be competitive, employees should perceive internal pay equity, and the compensation program should be properly administered. It also means that compensation practices must adhere to the various state and federal wage and hour laws, including comparable worth considerations.

Organizations assess their total compensation system by comparing pay levels with those pay levels of other organizations, by analyzing the validity of the organization's job evaluation method, by measuring employee perceptions of pay equity and performance-pay linkages, and by determining individual pay levels within jobs and across jobs.

Total compensation should also be assessed according to how well it helps attain strategic business objectives. Lincoln Electric, a leader in small motors and arc welders, has a compensation system tied to the company's profits. This system has resulted in an average Lincoln worker making as much as $80,000 a year. In addition to having a high motivation to produce, Lincoln workers rarely quit; their turnover rate is less than one percent. The result of Lincoln's compensation system is a cost-efficient competitive advantage that allows it to price its products below those of competitors yet maintain equal, if not better, quality.

■□ *fast fact*

The AFL-CIO set up at web site at *www.paywatch.org* to help people monitor executive pay levels.

SUMMARY

Organizations develop strategic compensation in a cost-conscious, competitive business environment that demands high quality and a continuous flow of new products. A total compensation system that's consistent with the organization's culture and the needs of the business improve the organization's ability to compete successfully. In addition, compensation practices must adhere to the *Fair Labor Standards Act*, the *Equal Pay Act* and all other relevant regulations.

Total compensation includes many components. Monetary and non-monetary forms of pay are part of a total compensation system. And both forms of pay can be offered on a variety of bases. Some compensation elements (e.g., mandatory insurance coverage) are offered to everyone in the organization simply on the basis of organizational membership. Other elements (e.g., base wage and salary pay) are offered on the basis of the job in which one works. Finally, pay may be offered contingent on individual or team attributes (e.g., skill-based pay and bonuses).

When designing the base pay component of a compensation system, employers can opt for one of many alternative approaches. Two basic choices are job-based and skill-based pay. The job-based approach is grounded in job evaluation. Job evaluation involves a systematic assessment of the value of jobs in the organization. It's intended to establish internal equity in jobs. Ranking and job classification methods focus on evaluating the whole job. These methods rely heavily on intuitive judgments about job worth. Preferable methods include point evaluation and competency-based evaluation.

In conducting a job evaluation study, a decision needs to be made regarding whether to custom design or buy a system. Although it may be more expedient to buy a standardized system, such a system may not reflect organizational needs and values. Another decision is whether to use one or several evaluation plans. To ensure systemwide equity, a single job evaluation plan is usually preferred over multiple plans. Still another decision is who should evaluate the worth of jobs. The greater the involvement of incumbents, the more likely they are to accept the results of the job evaluation study. Job- and skill-evaluation procedures establish the relative values of jobs and skills, but used alone, they do not yield actual wage rates. To establish actual wage rates, organizations use market survey data. Market survey data can be used to accurately set pay at a level that leads, matches, or lags the pay offered by competitors.

Organizations can also let employees set their own pay levels. In the few companies that have tried this approach, employees have set their own wages responsibly without management's altering the procedures or changing decisions. The method is most successful in organizations where employees and management have mutual trust and where employees are provided with information to help them understand the business objectives and financial status of the company.

An organization operating beyond domestic borders faces additional challenges when designing its compensation system. The basic objectives to be achieved by compensation remain essentially the same, but achieving them usually requires a more complex pay system. The system must be responsive to country differences in pay practices and take into account cultural differences in the values and expectations of employees around the world.

TERMS TO REMEMBER

Base pay
Benchmark jobs
Comparable worth
Compensable factors
Compensation based on
    organization membership
Competency-based job evaluation
Davis-Bacon Act
Direct compensation
Exempt employees
External equity
External market
Fair Labor Standards Act
Hay Guide Chart-Profile Method
Incentive pay
Indirect compensation
Internal equity
Job-based pay
Job classification method
Job evaluation

Job ranking method
Maturity curves
Minimum wage
Nonexempt employees
Nonmonetary compensation
Pay compression
Pay differentials
Pay fairness
Pay grade
Pay level
Pay mix
Performance-based pay
Point rating method
Ranking method
Self-determined pay
Skill-based pay
Total compensation
Wage and salary surveys
Walsh-Healey Act

DISCUSSION QUESTIONS

1. What purposes can total compensation serve? Can the purposes vary across different organizations? Explain.

2. What forms of pay make up total compensation?

3. What basic wage issues must any job evaluation system address?

4. Describe the basic mechanics of the traditional job evaluation methods.

5. Describe the similarities and differences of skill-based pay and traditional job-based pay systems.

6. Are the CEOs of U.S. firms overpaid? Are most employees underpaid? What issues should be considered in setting pay rates for CEOs?

7. What are the components of the typical expatriate's compensation package?

PROJECTS TO EXTEND YOUR LEARNING

1. **Managing Strategically.** You have just been hired as the head of administrative services for a nonprofit charity fund located in Portland, Oregon. With unemployment in the area being so low, they're having more difficulty than usual finding people to fill their open positions. At the moment, groundskeepers and accounting clerks are the jobs that need to be filled. You wonder whether the pay level is too low, so you decide to investigate. Use the internet to locate information about wage levels in the local external market. Then make a proposal for a total compensation system approach that will succeed in attracting qualified applicants. Include in your proposal some brief suggestions about where and how to recruit for these jobs.

2. **Managing Teams.** Imaginative Design Center (IDC) is a small business that does commercial interior design work. They specialize in renovations for the hospitality industry, providing designs for everything from bed and breakfast inns to major hotels and restaurant chains. Employees almost always work in teams, with each team having a variety of specialists. When business is booming, staffing these teams becomes difficult. The owner, Bea N. Bee, thinks this problem could be eliminated if staff members would develop a broader range of skills. She is considering changing to a skill-based pay system. Currently, employees are paid a base salary supplemented by a bit of merit pay. The merit pay is too small to make much difference, however, and usually everyone gets the same raise. IDC has hired you to provide advice. Is skill-based pay a good idea? What are the advantages and disadvantages of this approach? Regardless of whether or not you think skill-based pay is a good idea, Bea wants you to provide her with some information about the experiences of two or three other companies that have used skill-based pay.

    You decide to begin by visiting the American Compensation Association's home page at
    www.acaonline.org.

3. **Managing Diversity.** This project is to be completed in a group of four to six students.

Step 1: Preparation for Group Meeting

Individually, read the instructions to the Employee Profile Sheet shown in the exhibit, and decide on a pay increase for each of the eight employees. Write your decisions in both dollars and percentages. Be prepared to explain your decisions to your group.

Step 2: Group Meeting

In a group, share the recommendations you made in step 1 and explain your reasons. After all group members have reported, analyze and try to explain differences among everyone's recommendations. Then develop a set of recommendations that the group can agree on. Appoint a spokesperson to present the group's recommendations to the class.

The group may also decide to totally re-vamp the current pay system, e.g., make it more incentive-based. Describe what changes you recommend here.

Employee Profile Sheet

You must make salary increase recommendations for the eight individuals whom you supervise. They have just completed their first year with the company and are now to be considered for their first annual raise. Keep in mind that you may be setting precedents that will shape future expectations and that you must stay within your salary budget. Otherwise, there are no formal company policies to restrict you as you decide how to allocate raises. Write the raise you would give each person in the spaces to the left of each name. You have a total of $50,000 in your budget for pay raises.

$ _____ % _____   Arnold J. Adams. Adams isn't, as far as you can tell, a good performer. You have discussed your opinion with others and they agree completely. However, you know that Adams has one of the toughest work groups to manage. Adams' subordinates have low skill levels and the work is dirty and hard. If you lose Adams, you aren't sure that you could find an adequate replacement. Current salary: $60,000.

$ _____ % _____   Bruce K. Berger. Berger is single and seems to lead the life of a carefree swinger. In general, you feel that Berger's job performance isn't up to par, and some of Berger's "goofs" are well known to other employees. Current salary: $63,750.

$ _____ % _____   Carol C. Carter. You consider Carter to be one of your best subordinates. However, it's quite apparent that other people don't agree. Carter has married into wealth and, as far as you know, doesn't need any more money. Current salary: $67,000.

$ _____ % _____   Ellen J. Ellis. Your opinion is that Ellis just isn't cutting the mustard. Surprisingly enough, however, when you check with others to see how they feel you find that Ellis is very highly regarded. You also know that Ellis badly needs a raise. Ellis was recently divorced and is finding it extremely difficult to support a young family of four as a single parent. Current salary: $60,750.

$ _____ % _____

Fred M. Foster. Foster has turned out to be a very pleasant surprise, has done an excellent job, and is seen by peers as one of the best people in your group of managers. This surprises you because Foster is generally frivolous and doesn't seem to care very much about money or promotions. Current salary: $62,700.

$ _____ % _____

Gloria K. Gomez. Gomez has been very successful so far. You are particularly impressed by this because Gomez has one of the hardest jobs in your company. Gomez needs money more than many of your other subordinates and is respected for good performance. Current salary: $65,250.

$ _____ % _____

Julio Hernandez. You happen to know from your personal relationship that Hernandez badly needs more money because of certain personal problems. He also happens to be one of your best managers. For some reason, your enthusiasm isn't shared by your other subordinates, and you have heard them make joking remarks about his performance. Current salary: $64,000.

$ _____ % _____

Harriet A. Hunt. You know Hunt personally. This employee seems to squander money continually. Hunt has a fairly easy job assignment, and your own view is that Hunt doesn't do it especially well. You are thus surprised to find that several of the other new managers think that Hunt is the best of the new group. Current salary: $61,500.

Adapted from material copyrighted by Edward E. Lawler, III.

4. **Integration and Application.** After reviewing the end-of-text cases, compare and contrast Lincoln Electric and Southwest Airlines on the following:
   a. The objectives of their total compensation systems
   b. The role of compensation in achieving competitive advantage
   c. The approach used to establish base pay rates
   d. The pay mix and employees' reactions to the pay mix.

Which compensation system would you prefer? Explain why.

CASE STUDY

Pacific Coast Electric Company

Pacific Coast Electric Company (PCEC) is a public utility company located in San Francisco. The company is so successful that it's considered a model for other utility companies. Over the past two years, however, PCEC management has become concerned with increasing payroll costs. Cost containment and a "lean and mean" structure are key ingredients in the company's success. Management wants to study this problem and, if warranted, take corrective action.

Roger Waters is a compensation specialist with PCEC. Roger has been assigned to study PCEC's compensation practices and determine whether any action is required. He decides to compile compensation data for the past five years using the company's human resource information system (HRIS). Five years will reveal any trends, and the HRIS allows him to break down the data by department, length of service, gender, exempt versus nonexempt employees, and the like.

Roger has uncovered a startling situation. The data indicate that certain nonexempt employees are receiving compensation far in excess of their base pay rate. It seems that these employees are working excessive overtime because of the specific expertise they possess. Overtime rates are one-and-one-half times through 48 hours and double time after that. Employees who work overtime also receive additional compensation, including meal and travel allowances. The base salary for these employees averages $33,000 per year. With overtime, these employees make between $45,000 and $49,000 a year. This situation would be less of a concern if it involved only a few individuals, but hundreds of employees are in this situation. It should be noted that PCEC initiated the overtime policy because of the high cost of consultants—besides, the company feels that its own employees are better skilled and more capable than most consultants.

The employees in question make more than their superiors. First-line supervisors, for example, make approximately fifteen percent more than the base compensation of the top craft employees. In other words, supervisors are making approximately $38,750 on the average. Supervisors can receive merit pay, but only a small number of supervisors are eligible for merit awards. Further, supervisors aren't paid overtime and receive no meal allowances. Fortunately for PCEC, thinks Roger, our supervisors aren't aware of the extent of the pay inequities.

Aside from the obvious problem of employees making a great deal more money than their supervisors, another problem becomes apparent. Examination of the internal labor market reveals that all of the first-line supervisors have come from outside the company. The qualified employees aren't accepting "promotions" because they do not want to take a cut in pay. The long-term consequences of this situation could be very serious.

Then Roger looks at a breakdown of the data by gender for the nonexempt employees in question. Women have an average base salary of $30,500 while the average base salary for men is $35,900. Furthermore, not one of the employees receiving high salaries resulting from overtime is female. Roger is very concerned about the differences in compensation for men and women who are doing essentially the same jobs, especially because PCEC prides itself on its equal employment/affirmative action reputation.

Roger becomes lost in thought as he contemplates his findings. He knows that it will be difficult to frame a report around the compensation issues that he has uncovered. He suspects that it will be even more difficult to recommend changes that will resolve these thorny issues.

QUESTIONS

1. Are there cases in which employees should be paid more than their supervisors?

2. Does PCEC have a pay-equity problem?

3. What recommendations should Roger make?

4. How should he make compensation changes?

CASE STUDY

Comparable Worth Finds Rockdale

Bill Starbuck was proud to be assigned to the city beat of *The Rockdale Times*. Bill, a newspaper reporter for two years now, was paying his dues at a small-town newspaper, hoping to work his way up to a larger circulation daily. The city beat would mean that Bill could draw on his background in journalism and political science at Wabash College to write news stories with substance. His prior assignment to the features section of *The Rockdale Times* was interesting but not intellectually stimulating.

Bill's first major assignment was coming up in two days with an invitation to cover a breakfast meeting with the city council. Clyde Langston, Rockdale's city manager, was scheduled to present the revised city budget. Bill prepared for the meeting by calling one of his contacts in the city office for some "inside" information. Bill had been dating Jill Bateman, a secretary to the HR executive director, and he was confident he could learn something about the breakfast meeting agenda.

As Bill hung up from his call to Jill, he wondered what the rumor of a pay raise for some city employees could mean. If anything, the city was expected to trim its budget because of a slowdown in the local economy and loss of revenues due to the shutdown of two plants in the community within the past year. According to Jill, the rumor was that some of the clerical and administrative staff employees were scheduled for midyear pay adjustments. The figure working the hallways was a three percent pay raise, which would come as a pleasant surprise to the 95 employees in the administrative-office clerical positions.

As Bill arrived at the Wednesday morning breakfast meeting, he quickly scanned the room to identify the four city councilmen and one councilwoman. Bill wanted to interview at least three of the members for his story, which was due by 1:00 p.m. After Mayor Jim Earnie arrived, the city council, city manager, and local news reporters finished a quick and cordial breakfast.

Clyde Langston called the group to attention with a rap on his water goblet, and the cordial bantering quickly subsided. Clyde distributed a five-page report of the preliminary budget. Bill quickly scanned the report and noted that the $13.7 million total was considerably trimmed down from last year's budget of $16.4 million. Then, as Bill anticipated, Clyde pointed out a $41,000 line item increase in salaries within the pared-down budget.

Clyde proceeded to explain that the city had done an analysis of their 95 administrative-office clerical positions and their 350 technical-craft positions and decided to make some pay adjustments. All but one of the administrative-office clerks are women, while only 27 of the technical-craft workers are women. The pay range for office workers ranges from a low of $5.79 per hour to a high of $11.17 per hour, with an average of $6.30 per hour. The technical-craft jobs begin at $5.83 per hour and max out at $13.85 per hour, with an average of $9.69 per hour. The net effect of the $41,000 increase was to provide about a three percent increase to the administrative-office clerical workers.

Clyde pointed out that a recently conducted job evaluation study had resulted in the merger of the previously separated job families, such that all jobs were to be evaluated on a common set of attributes. Clyde elaborated further that the impetus of this change was to avoid any litigation over the comparable-worth issue. After completing the budget review briefing, Clyde offered to answer questions. When the council members sat quietly, Jim Earnie thanked the council for their time and adjourned the meeting.

Bill scurried to the door to intercept the council members as they prepared to leave, hoping to get a few reactions to this surprise comparable-worth initiative by the city government. Bill caught all five of the city council members and the mayor and proceeded to ask them what they thought of Clyde's proposal for the pay adjustments. Mayor Jim Earnie, along with three of the council members, indicated that they did not understand the rationale for the raises. After Bill questioned them, they even agreed that they thought that the issue deserved some further discussion.

"I did not know we were using that standard," councilman Jim Maloney said. "If we're applying comparable worth throughout the system, it would be good to know that, and on what basis it's being done."

Councilwoman Marcie Rivera said she was in accord with the approach. "I'm inclined to agree with the way Clyde put it out," she said, "to avoid any problems in discrimination. If that's the concern here, I feel like it's a step in the right direction."

Amazing, thought Bill as he headed to his car with notes in hand. I just attended a city council breakfast meeting to review the upcoming city budget, and comparable worth is proposed by the city manager. And the mayor and city council hardly noticed until after the meeting was adjourned!

QUESTIONS

1. Has Rockdale really implemented a comparable-worth standard?
2. How do you think the technical-craft workers will react to the announced pay raise?
3. What other approaches are available for achieving pay equity between men and women?
4. Why have state and local governments shown more interest in comparable worth than have private employers?

ENDNOTES

[1] M. A. Thompson, "Supporting Sears' Turnaround with Compensation: An Interview with Chairman and CEO Arthur C. Martinez, *ACA Journal* (Autumn 1997): 8.

[2] Thompson, "Supporting Sears' Turnaround with Compensation," 8–17.

[3] A. Farnham, "How to Nurture Creative Sparks," *Fortune* (January 10, 1994): 98.

[4] T. B. Weiss, "Show Me More Than The Money," *HR Focus* (November 1997): 3–4; "Employees' Views on Work," *Bulletin to Management* (September 16, 1993): 289.

[5] J. Fierman, "When Will You Get a Raise?" *Fortune* (July 12, 1993): 34–36.

[6] F. E. Whittlesey, "CEO Herb Kelleher Discusses Southwest Airlines' People Culture," *ACA Journal* (Winter 1995): 8–24.

[7] D. M. Cable and T. A. Judge, "Pay Preferences and Job Search Decisions: A Person-Organization Fit Perspective," *Personnel Psychology* 47 (1994): 339–348; A. B. Krueger, "The Determinants of Queues for Federal Jobs," *Industrial and Labor Relations Review* 41 (1988): 567–581.

[8] C. O. Trevor, B. Gerhart, and J. W. Boudreau, "Voluntary Turnover and Job Performance: Curvilinearity and the Moderating Influences of Salary Growth on Promotions," *Journal of Applied Psychology* 82 (1997): 44–61; S. J. Motowidlo, "Predicting Sales Turnover from Pay Satisfaction and Expectation," *Journal of Applied Psychology* 68 (1983): 484–489.

[9] M. P. Miceli and M. C. Lane, "Antecedents of Pay Satisfaction: A Review and Extension," *Research in Personnel and Human Resource Management* 9 (1991): 235–309; P. Capelli and P. D. Sherer, "Satisfaction, Market Wages, and Labor Relations: An Airline Study," *Industrial Relations* 27 (1988): 56–73; H. G. Heneman III, "Pay Satisfaction," *Research in Personnel and Human Resources Management*, vol. 3, Rowland and Ferris, eds. (1985): 115–139; N. Weiner, "Determinants and Behavioral Consequences of Pay Satisfaction: A Comparison of Two Models," *Personnel Psychology* 33 (1980): 741–757;

V. Scarpello, V. L. Huber, and R. J. Vanderberg, "Compensation Satisfaction: Its Measurement and Dimensionality," *Journal of Applied Psychology* (May 1988): 163–171; R. W. Rice, S. M. Phillips, and D. B. McFarlin, "Multiple Discrepancies and Pay Satisfaction," *Journal of Applied Psychology* 75 (1990): 386–393.

[10] L. A. Witt and L. G. Nye, "Gender and the Relationship Between Perceived Fairness of Pay or Promotion and Job Satisfaction," *Journal of Applied Psychology* 77 (1992): 910–917.

[11] B. S. Murphy, W. E. Barlow, and D. D. Hatch, "Manager's Newsfront," *Personnel Journal* (December 1992): 22.

[12] A. Markels, "Blank Check," *The Wall Street Journal* (April 9, 1998): R11

[13] E. E. Lawler III, *Pay and Organizational Development* (Reading, MA: Addison-Wesley, 1981).

[14] "Employee Involvement in Compensation Plans," *Bulletin to Management: Datagraph* (May 19, 1994): 156–157.

[15] M. Zippo, "Roundup," *Personnel* (September–October 1980): 43–45.

[16] A. Markels, "Blank Check."

[17] J. K. Galbraith, *Created Unequal: The Crisis in American Pay* (New York: Free Press, 1998); J. M. Schlesinger, "Wages for Low-Paid Workers Rose in 1997," *The Wall Street Journal* (March 28, 1998): A2; L. R. Gomez-Mejia, "Executive Compensation: A Reassessment and a Future Research Agenda," *Research in Personnel and Human Resource Management* 12 (1994): 161–222.

[18] J. S. Lublin, "Pay for No Performance," *The Wall Street Journal* (April 9, 1998): R1–R19 ; R. B. Freeman, "How Labor Fares in Advanced Economies," *Working Under Different Rules*, R. B. Freeman, ed. (New York: Russell Sage, 1993); K. Bradsher, "Widest Gap in Incomes? Research Points to U.S.," *New York Times* (October 27, 1995): D2.

[19] "Readers on CEO Pay: Many Are Angry, A Few Really Think the Big Guy Is Worth it," *Fortune* (June 8, 1998): 296;

J. Reynolds and R. Grover, "Executive Pay," *Business Week* (April 19, 1999): 72–90.

20 For additional data, see *American Compensation Association,* "CEO Pay: A Comprehensive Look" (Scottsdale, AZ: American Compensation Association, 1997).

21 M. Bloom, "The Performance Effects of Pay Dispersion on Individuals and Organizations," *Academy of Management Journal* 42 (1999): 25–40; "Aligning Compensation with Quality," *Bulletin to Management* (April 1, 1993): 97.

22 For reviews of strategic compensation, see E. E. Lawler III, *Strategic Pay: Aligning Organizational Strategies and Pay Systems* (San Francisco: Jossey-Bass, 1990); E. E. Lawler III and G. D. Jenkins, Jr., "Strategic Reward Systems," *Handbook of Industrial and Organizational Psychology,* vol. 3, Dunnette and Hough, eds. (1991); C. L. Weber and S. L. Rynes, "Effects of Compensation Strategy on Job Pay Decisions," *Academy of Management Journal* 34 (1991): 86–109; L. R. Gomez-Mejia, "Executive Compensation: A Reassessment and a Future Research Agenda," *Research in Personnel and Human Resource Management* 12 (1994): 161–222; L. R. Gomez-Mejia, "Structure and Process of Diversification, Compensation Strategy, and Firm Performance," *Strategic Management Journal* 13 (1992): 381–397.

23 W. Fox, "Staying a Step Ahead of the Competition with Outstanding Total Compensation," *ACA News* (October 1998): 20–22.

24 S. O'Neal, "Study Shows Compensation Programs Becoming More Strategic," *ACA News* (November–December 1996): 19–21.

25 C. J. Cantoni, "Mergers and Acquisitions: The Critical Role of Compensation and Culture," *ACA Journal* (Summer 1996): 38–45.

26 P. Pascarella, "Compensating Teams," *Across the Board* (February 1997): 16–22; E. E. Lawler, III, "Teams, Pay and Business Strategy: Finding the Best Mix to Achieve Competitive Advantage," *ACA Journal* (Spring 1996): 12–25; D. G. Shaw and C. E. Schneier, "Team Measurement and Rewards: How Some Companies Are Getting It Right," *Human Resource Planning* 18 (3) (1995): 34–49.

27 See D. B. Balkin and L. R. Gomez-Mejia, "Compensation Systems in High Technology Companies," *New Perspectives in Compensation,* Balkin and Gomez-Mejia, eds. (Englewood Cliffs, NJ: Prentice-Hall, 1987): 269–277.

28 D. B. Balkin and L. R. Gomez-Mejia, "Entrepreneurial Compensation," *Readings in Personnel and Human Resource Management,* Schuler, Youngblood, and Huber, eds., 14–23.

29 G. T. Milkovich, "A Strategic Perspective on Compensation Management," *Research in Personnel and Human Resources Management,* Rowland and Ferris, eds., 263–288.

30 P. E. Platten and D. A. Hofrichter, "The Compensation Lag," *Across The Board* (May 1996): 27–31; L. M. Kahn and P. D. Sherer, "Contingent Pay and Managerial Performance," *Industrial and Labor Relations Review* 43 (1990): 107S–120S; M. L. Weitzman and D. L. Kruse, "Profit Sharing and Productivity," *Paying for Productivity,* A. S. Blinder, ed. (Washington, DC: Brookings Institute, 1990);

R. A. Guzzo, R. D. Jette, and R. A. Katzell, "The Effects of Psychologically Based Intervention Programs on Worker Productivity: A Meta-Analysis," *Personnel Psychology* 38 (1985): 275–291.

31 T. M. Welbourne, "Gainsharing: A Critical Review and a Future Research Agenda," *Journal of Management* (1995): 559–609.

32 D. Greising, "Fast Eddie's Future Bank," *Business Week* (March 23, 1998): 74–77.

33 "Myth and the Minimum Wage," *Business Week* (October 12, 1998): 6.

34 J. Laabs, "What Goes Down When Minimum Wages Go Up," *Workforce* (August 1998): 54–58.

35 J. M. Brett and L. K. Stroh, "Jumping Ship: Who Benefits from an External Labor Market Career Strategy?" *Journal of Applied Psychology* 82 (1997): 331–341; J. Laabs, "What Goes Down When Minimum Wages Go Up;" B. S. Klaas and J. M. McClendon, "To Lead, Lag, or Match: Estimating the Financial Impact of Pay Level Policies," *Personnel Psychology* 49 (1996); M. L. Williams and G. F. Dreher, "Compensation System Attributes and Applicant Pool Characteristics," *Academy of Management Journal* 35 (1992); 571–595; R. B. Freeman and J. L. Medoff, "Substitutions Between Production Labor and Other Inputs in Unionized and Nonunionized Manufacturing," *Review of Economics and Statistics* 64 (1982): 220–233.

36 E. L. Andrews, "Germans Cut Labor Costs with a Harsh Export: Jobs," *New York Times International* (March 21, 1998): A3.

37 Andrews, "Germans Cut Labor Costs with a Harsh Export: Jobs."

38 E. W. Morrison and J. W. Herlihy, "Becoming the Best Place to Work: Managing Diversity at American Express Travel Related Services," *Diversity in the Workplace: Human Resources Initiatives,* S. E. Jackson, ed. (New York: Guilford Press, 1993).

39 D. J. McNerney, "Compensation: Spreading the Wealth," *HR Focus* (March 1997): 4–5.

40 Hewitt Associates, as presented in G. Flynn, "HR in Mexico: What You Should Know," *Personnel Journal* (August 1994): 36. Used by permission.

41 P. Burstein, R. M. Bricher, and R. L. Einwohner, "Policy Alternatives and Political Change: Work, Family, and Gender on the Congressional Agenda," *American Sociological Review* 60 (1995): 67–83.

42 V. Peckham, "The Value of Being A Child-Friendly Company," *Solutions* (October 1996): 28–29; S. J. Boyd, "Will Compensatory Time Become Law?" *ACA News* (May 1997): 18–19.

43 R. Kuttner, "So Much For The Minimum-Wage Scare," *Business Week* (July 21, 1997): 19; "Crackdown on Child Labor Violations," *Fair Employment Practices Guidelines* 299 (June 6, 1990); "FLSA Amendments of 1989: Higher Federal Minimum Wage, Plus New Training Wage," *Bulletin to Management* (December 28, 1989): 1–3.

[44] "Youth Employment: Child Labor Limitations Reviewed," *Bulletin to Management* (May 19, 1994): 153.

[45] G. Flynn, "Pizza as Pay? Compensation Gets Too Creative," *Workforce* (August 1998): 91–96.

[46] "White-Collar Exemptions under FLSA," *Bulletin to Management: Datagraph* (February 13, 1992): 44–45; "Ask the Experts—Questions and Answers on Classifying White-Collar Employees as Exempt from Overtime Regulations," *Fair Employment Practices Guidelines* (April 10, 1994): 8.

[47] See "Record Settlement under Fair Labor Standards Act," *Bulletin to Management* (August 12, 1993): 249.

[48] A. Bernstein, "Pay Equity Makes Good Business Sense," *Fair Employment Practices* (August 30, 1990): 103.

[49] M. M. Marini and P-L Fan, "The Gender Gap in Earnings at Entry Level," *American Sociological Review* 62 (1997): 588–604.

[50] G. F. Dreher and T. H. Cox, Jr., "Race, Gender, and Opportunity: A Study of Compensation Attainment and the Establishment of Mentoring Relationships," *Journal of Applied Psychology* 81 (1996): 297–308; M. M. Marini and P-L Fan, "The Gender Gap in Earnings at Entry Level."

[51] For an explanation of the analytic methods used to evaluate the role of gender in determining pay levels, see M. O'Malley, "Testing for Gender Difference on Pay," *ACA Journal* (Summer 1998): 16–28; P. England, *Comparable Worth: Theories and Evidence* (Hawthorne, NY: Aldine de Gruyter, 1992); J. A. Jacobs, "Women's Entry into Management: Trends in Earnings, Authority, and Values Among Salaried Managers," *Administrative Science Quarterly* 37 (1992): 282–301; L. A. Jackson, P. D. Gardner, and L. A. Sullivan, "Explaining Gender Differences in Self-Pay Expectations: Social Comparison Standards and Perceptions of Fair Pay," *Journal of Applied Psychology* 77 (1992): 651–663.

[52] A. Bernstein, "Why Workers Still Hold A Weak Hand," *Business Week* (March 2, 1998): 98; Bureau of National Affairs, "Employment Cost Index—Second Quarter 1997," *Bulletin to Management: Datagraph* (August 7, 1997): 252–254; D. C. Johnston, "On Payday, Union Jobs Stack Up Very Well," *New York Times* (August 31, 1997): Section 3; H. C. Bentiam, "Union–Non-Union Wage Differential Revisited," *Journal of Labor Research* 8 (1987): 381; D. Lewin, "Public Sector Labor Relations: A Review Essay," *Public Sector Labor Relations: An Analysis and Readings,* D. Lewin, P. Feuill, and T. Kochan, eds. (Glen Ridge, NJ: Thomas Horton & Daughters, 1977): 166–184; R. Flanagan, R. Smith, and R. G. Ehrenberg, *Labor Economics and Labor Relations* (Glenview, IL: Scott Foresman, 1984).

[53] R. Freeman and J. Medoff, "What Do Unions Do?" (New York: Basic Books, 1984); T. A. Kochan, H. C. Katz, and R. B. McKersie, *The Transformation of American Industrial Relations* (New York: Basic Books, 1986).

[54] P. L. Gilles, "Enhancing the Participatory Process of Compensation Design," *ACA News* (May 1998): 27–29.

[55] P. Cappelli and W. F. Cascio, "Why Some Jobs Command Wage Premiums: A Test of Career Tournament and Internal Labor Market Hypotheses," *Academy of Management Journal* 34 (1991): 848–868; S. R. Rynes, C. L. Weber, and G. T. Milkovich, "Effects of Market Survey Rates, Job Evaluation, and Job Gender on Job Pay," *Journal of Applied Psychology* 74 (1989): 114–123; D. Gleicher and L. Stevans, *A Classical Approach to Occupational Wage Rates* (Westport, CT: Praeger, 1991).

[56] R. Sneigar, "The Comparability of Job Evaluation Methods in Supplying Approximately Similar Classifications in Rating One Job Series," *Personnel Psychology* (Summer 1983): 371–380.

[57] D. Doverspike, "An Internal Bias Analysis of a Job Evaluation Instrument," *Journal of Applied Psychology* (November 1984): 648–650; S. L. Fraser, S. F. Cronshaw, and R. A. Alexander, "Generalizability Analysis of a Point Method Job Evaluation Instrument: A Field Study," *Journal of Applied Psychology* (November 1984): 643–647.

[58] J. J. Laabs, "Job Evaluation Redesign: Rating Jobs Against New Values," *Workforce* (May 1997): 39–49.

[59] J. A. Green and R. W. Keuch, "Contribution-Driven Competency-Based Pay," *ACA Journal* (Autumn 1997): 62–71.

[60] K. S. Abosch and B. L. Hmurovic, "A Traveler's Guide to Global Broadbanding," *ACA Journal* (Summer 1998): 38–46.

[61] B. Parus, "Broadbanding Highly Effective, Survey Shows," *ACA News* (July/August 1998): 40–41.

[62] N. Gupta et al., "Survey-Based Prescriptions for Skill-Based Pay," *ACA Journal* (Fall 1992): 48–58; M. Rowland, "It's What You Can Do That Counts," *New York Times* (June 6, 1993): F17; M. Rowland, "For Each New Skill, More Money," *New York Times* (June 13, 1993): F16.

[63] Adapted from G. J. Ledford, "Three Case Studies on Skill-Based Pay: An Overview," *Compensation and Benefits Review* (April 1990): 11–23; H. Tosi and L. Tosi, "What Managers Need to Know About Knowledge-Based Pay," *Organizational Dynamics* (Winter 1986): 52–64.

[64] B. Murray and B. Gerhart, "An Empirical Analysis of a Skill-Based Pay Program and Plan Performance Outcomes," *Academy of Management Journal* 41 (1998): 68–78; Ledford, "Three Case Studies on Skill-Based Pay;" H. Tosi and L. Tosi, "What Managers Need to Know about Knowledge-Based Pay."

[65] D. Doverspike, "An Internal Bias Analysis of a Job Evaluation Instrument," *Journal of Applied Psychology* (November 1984): 648–650; S. L. Fraser, S. F. Cronshaw, and R. A. Alexander, "Generalizability Analysis of a Point Method Job Evaluation Instrument: A Field Study," *Journal of Applied Psychology* (November 1984): 643–647.

[66] "Employee Involvement in Compensation Plans," *Bulletin to Management: Datagraph* (May 19, 1994): 156–157.

[67] J. Domat-Connell, "Labor Market Definition and Salary Survey Selection: A New Look at the Foundation of Compensation Program Design," *Compensation and Benefits Review* (March–April 1994): 38–46.

[68] C. Viswesvaran and M. R. Barrick, "Decision-Making Effects on Compensation Surveys: Implications for Market Wages," *Journal of Applied Psychology* 77 (1992): 588–597.

[69] Ledford, Tyler, and Dixey, "Skill-Based Pay Case Number Three."

[70] J. C. Kail, "Compensating Scientists and Engineers," *New Perspectives on Compensation,* Balkin and Gomez-Mejia, 278–281; G. T. Milkovich, "Compensation Systems in High-Technology Companies," *New Perspectives on Compensation,* Balkin and Gomez-Mejia, eds., 269–277; C. F. Schultz, "Compensating the Sales Professional," *New Perspectives on Compensation,* Balkin and Gomez-Mejia, eds., 250–257.

[71] G. E. Ledford, "Three Case Studies in Skill-Based Pay."

[72] C. Gedvilas, "Recognizing and Addressing International Pay Differences," *ACA News* (October 1996): 9–10.

[73] A. M. Healey, "Grabbing Attention for Total Compensation Plans," *ACA News* (October 1996): 11–13.

[74] Adapted from P. Dowling, D. Welch and R. S. Schuler, *International Dimensions of Human Resource Management,* 3rd ed. (Cincinnati, Ohio: South-Western, 1999).

[75] V. Frazee, "Is the Balance Sheet Right for Your Expats?" *Global Workforce* (September 1998): 19–26; C. Reynolds, *Compensating Globally Mobile Employees: Approaches to Developing Expatriate Pay Strategies for the Evolving International Corporation* (Scotsdale, AZ: American Compensation Association, 1995).

[76] C. M. Gould, "The Impact of Headquarters Location on Expatriate Policy," *HRM Magazine* (April 1998): 9–12; S. Spencer, "The Euro Is Coming!" *ACA Journal* (Autumn 1998): 37–44.

Chapter

11

"To embed our values, we give our people 360-degree evaluations, with input from superiors, peers, and subordinates. These are the roughest evaluations you can get, because people hear things about themselves they've never heard before."

Jack Welch
CEO
General Electric Company[1]

PERFORMANCE MANAGEMENT: APPRAISAL AND FEEDBACK

Chapter Outline

MANAGING THROUGH PARTNERSHIP

at Con-Way

Con-Way Transportation Services is a subsidiary of CNF, the giant shipping company. It's a company in which teams are prevalent, yet the company has no centralized approach to evaluating team effectiveness. So the Information Systems (IS) department decided to become trailblazers. To evaluate themselves, they developed the Team Improvement Review (TIR). According to Debbie Blanchard, the name TIR was chosen quite deliberately—they wanted to avoid having the words "performance" or "appraisal" attached in any way to their new creation. That fact alone provides good insight into how this group feels about traditional performance appraisal systems!

Since its inception in 1995, the IS department has been concerned with team performance. Daily life is guided by their Team Agreement, a document they crafted as a means for defining excellence. "The Agreement sets out how we do things," explains the department manager. "It's pretty much the common law around here." Although the department was comfortable developing its own performance standards, they decided to bring in a consultant to help design the review process. Like many traditional appraisal systems, the TIR separates feedback sessions from salary reviews. Their reasoning was that people might not be candid in evaluating each other if they knew it would affect salaries. Many experts agree with that reasoning.

Unlike traditional performance appraisals, which often happen only one a year, the TIR takes place every three months. This scheduling fits well with the department's desire to improve continuously. Before a team meets, members rate each other on 31 criteria. To ensure that the feedback environment is "safe," the TIR feedback sessions usually take place with no managers present. In their place is an expert facilitator who helps the team manage the delicate process of providing feedback that improves rather than destroys team functioning. One trick the team has learned is to let the individual's own assessment of strengths and weaknesses serve as the centerpiece for conversation. Each team member begins by listing a few of his or her strengths and weaknesses on a sheet of paper. The sheets are then passed around the group. By the time each sheet gets back to its owner, the sheet has comments from the other team members indicating whether they agree or disagree with the list, and suggestions for how and where to focus improvement efforts. The process encourages people to be honest with themselves and, at the same time, creates a network of support for self-initiated change efforts.[2]

To learn more about CNF Transportation, visit the company home page at **www.cnf.com**

To learn more about Con-Way Transportation, visit the company home page at **www.con-way.com**

In this chapter and the next, we describe the objectives and design of performance management systems. Performance management systems *direct* and *motivate* employees to maximize the effort they exert on behalf of the organization. Two components of performance management systems are: (a) performance appraisal and feedback processes, and (b) performance incentives. A well-designed performance appraisal and feedback process *directs* employees' attention toward the most important tasks and behaviors.[3] At Con-Way, the 31 criteria used in the TIR provide a clear road map for team members. A performance incentive system *motivates* employees to perform at the level of their maximum potential. At Con-Way, a deliberate decision was made to base salary and incentive decisions on something other than feedback from team members.

The general steps in developing a performance management system are shown in Exhibit 11.1.[4] Those relevant to everything except rewards are discussed in this chapter. Chapter 12 addresses linkage between performance and rewards.

Exhibit 11.1
The Performance Management System

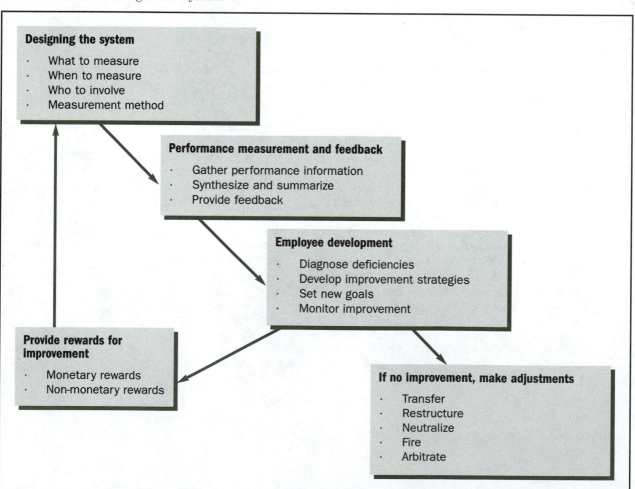

Designing the system
- What to measure
- When to measure
- Who to involve
- Measurement method

Performance measurement and feedback
- Gather performance information
- Synthesize and summarize
- Provide feedback

Employee development
- Diagnose deficiencies
- Develop improvement strategies
- Set new goals
- Monitor improvement

Provide rewards for improvement
- Monetary rewards
- Non-monetary rewards

If no improvement, make adjustments
- Transfer
- Restructure
- Neutralize
- Fire
- Arbitrate

Employees may learn about how well they're performing through informal means, such as by favorable comments from coworkers, but *performance appraisal* refers to a formal, structured system for measuring, evaluating, and influencing an employee's job-related attributes, behaviors, and outcomes. Its focus is on discovering how productive the employee is and whether he or she can perform as or more effectively in the future, so that the employee, the organization, and society all benefit. The terms performance appraisal and performance evaluation can be used interchangeably. Or, as Con-Way employees chose to do, they can be replaced by other terms that better capture the reasons for assessing performance.

THE STRATEGIC IMPORTANCE OF PERFORMANCE APPRAISAL AND FEEDBACK

Performance appraisal information can be used in many ways. As shown in Exhibit 11.2,[5] the two most frequently reported uses of performance appraisal information are providing feedback to employees and salary administration.

Exhibit 11.2
Top Twenty Uses of Performance Appraisal Information

Use	Rating*	Rank
Between-Person Evaluation		
Salary administration	5.6	2
Recognition of individual performance	5.0	5
Identification of poor performance	5.0	5
Promotion decisions	4.8	8
Retention and termination decisions	4.8	8
Layoffs	3.5	13
Within-Person Development		
Performance feedback	5.7	1
Identification of individual strengths and weaknesses	5.4	3
Determination of transfers and assignments	3.7	12
Identification of individual training needs	3.4	14
Systems Maintenance		
Development of individual and corporate goals	4.9	7
Evaluation of goal attainment by individuals, teams, and strategic business units	4.7	10
Human resource planning	2.7	15
Determination of organizational training needs	2.7	15
Reinforcement of authority structure	2.6	17
Identification of organizational development needs	2.6	17
Human resource system auditing	2.0	20
Documentation		
Documentation of HR management decisions	5.2	4
Meeting legal requirements	4.6	11
Criteria for validation research	2.3	19

*Ratings were based on a seven-point scale measuring the effect of appraisal on different organizational decisions and action, where 1 = No Effect, 4 = Moderate Effect, and 7 = Primary Determinant.

The uses of performance information can be grouped into four categories:

- *Evaluation:* Here the emphasis is on making between-person comparisons, which then serve as the basis for basic employment decisions.
- *Development:* Here the emphasis is on helping the individual improve over time.
- *Systems maintenance:* Here the emphasis is on using performance information to assess organizational needs and goal attainment. The focus is on improving the organization as a whole.
- *Documentation:* For legal reasons, organizations should maintain records of performance in order to document the reasons for various decisions, which may some day be contested in court.

In the U.S., managers and employees alike place great emphasis on making employment decisions based on merit, so evaluational uses of performance appraisals are particularly salient. In Korea, promotions are based primarily on seniority, so performance appraisals are conducted primarily for counseling and development. Many Koreans believe that the cooperative nature of work makes it impossible to differentiate performance levels between employees with any degree of accuracy. As a result, variables such as seniority, loyalty, proper attitude, and initiative are at least as important as actual job performance. In some companies, the appraisal review consists of nothing more than informal individual counseling sessions. At others, it's more formalized. Practices at Sunkyong are representative of the more formalized approach to appraisal in Korea. The appraisal process begins with an extensive self-assessment inventory that's completed by the employee. Results are discussed with the employee's immediate supervisor and later with the supervisor's supervisor. Extensive peer assessments are also used.[6]

■□*fast fact*

The best performing employees can produce up to three times as much as the worst performing employees.

Aligning Performance Appraisal with the Business

The performance appraisal system achieves its purposes when the organization aligns and integrates performance appraisal with strategic business objectives. Strategic performance appraisal, as it's called when linked to the business, aligns the goals of the individual with those of the organization; that is, it embodies the description of actions employees must exhibit and results they must achieve to make a strategy come alive.[7] At Pepsi-Cola International, for example, performance information pointed to a deficiency in corporate training. To address the deficiency, the firm established an umbrella organization to deliver training programs around the world. Performance deficiencies revealed in appraisal data also led to a program that brings non-U.S. citizens to the United States for eighteen months of training in the domestic Pepsi system. The program provides in-depth experiential training that builds the competency base among expatriate employees. Having a knowledgeable workforce was viewed as a necessary first step in attaining Pepsi-Cola International's overall growth objective and its underlying business goal of developing talented people to drive the growth in Pepsi brands.[8]

At Mrs. Fields' Original Cookies, the performance management system is fully integrated with the company's production and administrative operations. As described in the feature, Managing Strategically: Mrs. Fields Has the Right Ingredients,[9] some companies understand that their best chance for attaining peak performance at the individual, team, and organization levels lies with establishing a strategically aligned performance management system that includes monitoring performance *and* giving employees feedback as quickly as possible on how well they're doing. Although performance management systems are as individual as the goals and objectives of organizations, to be successful, they must mesh with key aspects of the organizations' overall approaches to managing human resources.

Performance measurement, which necessarily reflects the past, isn't an end to be achieved. Rather, it's a means for moving into a more productive future. For performance appraisals to achieve their potential, it's not sufficient to just *do* them; employees must *act* on them. Usually, supervisors have responsibility for communicating the results of appraisals to their subordinates and helping their subordinates improve in the future. Conversely,

> *"Managers are solely responsible for evaluating their employees. No specific, company-side evaluation forms are used for salespeople and managers. Rather, each manager designs his or her own evaluation system."*
>
> **Mary Kim Stuart**
> **HR Manager**
> **Nordstrom's**

MANAGING STRATEGICALLY
Mrs. Fields Has the Right Ingredients

Debbi Fields opened the first Mrs. Fields Original Cookies store in 1977. Today, more than eight million people are employed by this organization. With a new franchise location opening up somewhere in the world every eight minutes, maintaining a consistent product is a true challenge. Nevertheless, this is a thriving business. Sales for the year 2000 are projected to top $1 trillion. How does a rapidly growing company, which generates 60 percent of its sales outside the U.S., manage performance? Very carefully.

When she founded her company in Palo Alto, California, Fields set hourly sales quotas for herself and baked up the day's inventory based on daily experience. Today, state-of-the-art software networks all retail outlets to the company's headquarters and allows corporate officials to communicate with all store managers and vice versa. On demand, Fields can pull up daily sales figures for hundreds of cookie emporium outlets located throughout the world. Fields can tell which stores did the best and which did the worst, or which stores met their sales projections and which did not. Armed with this information, Fields regularly calls store managers to congratulate them on their performance. Information obtained through the system is used to motivate managers and staff. A manager of a Mrs. Fields' store in Costa Mesa, California, provides her employees with individualized, daily bonus reports to let them know how close they are to reaching their goals. The computer even flashes reinforcing messages such as "Congratulations, you're doing great" as employees reach performance milestones.

The system also helps diagnose performance deficiencies and develop high-potential employees. Once hired, employees participate in computerized skill assessment. Immediate grading with on-line tutorials for questions incorrectly answered is provided.

The ROI system supports a lean and flat organizational structure, freeing managers to focus on managing people. "If you're supposed to be the expert and the manager who's going to build sales, the last thing you should be doing is sitting at your desk working numbers," explained one store manager. "You should be developing your team."

To learn more about Mrs. Fields Original Cookies, visit the company home page at **www.mrsfields.com**

subordinates usually have responsibility for seeking honest feedback and using it to improve their performance. Human resource professionals can facilitate the effective use of appraisal by training supervisors in the art of feedback and by providing competency-building resources to employees. These principles may seem straightforward, yet few organizations can claim to have perfected their performance management systems. Numerous hindrances to performance maximization are inherent in organizational life.

Roadblocks in Aligning Performance Appraisal with the Business

Organizations aren't always successful in using performance appraisals strategically. One reason is that line managers do not fully understand performance appraisal basics. Most managers spend far more time acquiring technical competencies (e.g., in the areas of accounting, marketing, and operations management) for entry into an organization than they do learning to manage human resources. Yet, skillfully managing performance appraisals can help line managers achieve their corporate mandate to get things done through other people.

Another roadblock to the effective use of performance appraisals is that managers fail to see the payoff for conducting them. Most organizations offer no obvious organizational incentives for managers to do a good job of appraising employee performance. In fact, many managers so dislike the associated excessive paperwork and unpleasant confrontations with employees that they try to avoid the process entirely. This, of course, is shortsighted.

A third reason performance appraisals fall short of achieving strategic objectives is the ambiguity around who owns responsibility for managing human resources. Does performance management fall in the domain of human resource departments or line departments?[10] But debates about who is responsible miss the point. Line managers, HR professionals, and employees all need to work in partnership to ensure that appraisals are effective and fair to everyone concerned as described in the feature, The HR Triad: Roles and Responsibilities for Performance Appraisal and Feedback.

Performance appraisal is an emotionally charged activity. When everything is going well, appraisal is easy. Everyone wants to give and get feedback that says "You do not need to change." But today's competitive environment does not usually accept the status quo. Instead, it mandates improvement. Improvements often come slowly, in part because of conflicts inherent in the appraisal process. These conflicts interfere with honest data gathering, data sharing, and data use. The result? Employees, employers, and experts alike all give the typical appraisal system low marks.

Often, appraisal systems reflect larger systemic problems. Appraisals lead to conflict if employees' and managers' goals aren't aligned with the organization's overall objectives. If human resource issues aren't fully addressed during strategic planning, the performance management system evolves in isolation from strategic initiatives—rather than in anticipation of them. Even when managers recognize problems of strategic misalignment, they may not be willing to commit the resources needed to fix the problem without assurances for an immediate payoff. Developing an effective performance management system requires involvement and buy-in from everyone affected. Achieving this ideal takes time and determination, but the improved feelings of trust that a good system promotes seems well worth the investment.[11]

■□ *fast fact*

The courts have held that fair performance evaluations are tangible job benefits, and employees are protected from interference with those benefits in the form of "indefensibly harsh" evaluations.

■□ *fast fact*

Two separate surveys of HR professionals revealed that fewer than 10 percent were very satisfied with their company's performance management system.

■□ *fast fact*

Employees who perform well on specific job tasks also tend to be good organizational citizens.

THE HR TRIAD: ROLES AND RESPONSIBILITIES FOR PERFORMANCE APPRAISAL AND FEEDBACK

Line Managers	HR Professionals	Employees
Work with HR professionals and employees to develop business-relevant criteria for appraisals.	Work with line managers and employees to develop the criteria for appraisals.	Work with line managers and HR professionals to develop criteria for appraisals.
Develop an understanding of how common appraisal errors can be avoided.	Train everyone who provides appraisal information (e.g., peers, subordinates, and supervisors) how to avoid errors in appraisal.	Candidly appraise the work of other employees (boss, peers, etc.).
Fill out appraisal forms carefully and conscientiously.	Coordinate the administrative aspects of the appraisal process.	Participate in self appraisal.
Give constructive and honest feedback to employees.	Train line managers to give feedback.	Seek and accept constructive and honest feedback.
Seek and accept constructive feedback about personal performance.	May train self-managing teams to give feedback.	Learn to give constructive and honest feedback to others.
Use performance information for decision making.	Monitor managerial decisions to ensure they're performance-based.	Develop accurate understanding of performance expectations and appraisal criteria.
Diagnose performance deficiencies.	May train self-managing teams to diagnose performance deficiencies.	Learn to diagnose causes of own performance deficiencies.
Work with employees to develop performance improvement strategies, and monitor performance changes.	Ensure managers and employees are aware of all possible ways to deal with performance deficiencies (e.g., training, EAPs, arbitration).	Work with managers to develop performance improvement strategies.
Provide resources/remove constraints as needed for improvement.	Develop and administer appeals process.	Develop goal-setting and self-management skills.

DECIDING WHAT TO APPRAISE

Performance *criteria* are the dimensions against which the performance of an incumbent, a team, or a work unit is evaluated. They're the performance expectations individuals and teams strive for in order to achieve the organization's strategy. If jobs have been designed well, with attention paid to how job demands relate to strategic business needs, then conducting a job analysis should ensure that performance appraisals reflect strategic concerns. The job analysis should capture both performance on specific tasks and the employee's more general performance as an organizational citizen.[12] Examples of *organizational citizenship* behaviors (sometimes referred to as contextual performance) include

- volunteering to carry out task activities that aren't formally a part of the job;
- persisting with extra enthusiasm or effort when necessary to complete task activities successfully;
- helping and cooperating with others;
- following organizational rules and procedures even when doing so is inconvenient; and
- endorsing, supporting, and defending organizational objectives.[13]

Three types of performance criteria often assessed are trait-based criteria, behavioral criteria, and outcome-based criteria. Regardless of which types of criteria gets measured during the appraisal process, the performance management system becomes strategic to the extent that these criteria are clearly linked to organizational goals. This linkage almost always involves an inferential leap. Consider the job of assistant vice president in a bank. The performance criteria for this job may include "Phones arbitrageurs and traders within ten minutes of order receipt" and "Generates $5 million in sales each month." For both criteria, the strategic linkage assumes that an aggregation of these individual performances relates to total profitability of the bank for a specific quarter.

Trait-Based Criteria

Trait-based criteria focus on personal characteristics. Loyalty, dependability, conscientiousness, and leadership exemplify traits often assessed during the appraisal process. Criteria such as these address what a person is, not what a person does or does not accomplish on the job. For jobs that involve work that's difficult to observe, trait-based appraisal instruments may be the easiest to construct. Unfortunately, they may not be valid indicators of job performance. To one person, being dependable may mean showing up to work on time every day; to another person it may mean staying late when the boss requests it; to a third person, it may mean not using sick days even when you are really sick. Because of these concerns, court decisions often penalize employers who rely on trait-based performance measures when making employment decisions.[14]

The philosophy of meritocracy is a distinctively American societal value. *Meritocracy* emphasizes evaluating people on their work-related contributions. In work settings, merit is further constrained by the short-term orientation of annual appraisals, which focus on only the recent past. In other cultures, meritocracy isn't so firmly established as a guiding principle. In its place is more concern for status, family ties, and loyalty to the supervisor or organization. Recent performance isn't always the most important criterion. Valued more are behavior over time and the potential for the future.[15]

Does the position of the courts and the importance of meritocracy in U.S. culture mean that difficult-to-measure personal qualities shouldn't be evaluated as part of the performance appraisal process? Can employers still build corporate cultures around having the right kinds of people as defined by personal qualities that extend beyond job skills? The answer is that personal qualities can be appropriately assessed by shifting the focus from traits to behaviors.

"An employer has no business with a man's personality. Employment is a specific contract calling for specific performance and for nothing else."

**Peter Drucker
Management Guru**

Behavioral Criteria

Behavioral criteria focus on how work is performed. Such criteria are particularly important for jobs that involve interpersonal contact. Whether cashiers are friendly and pleasant with Au Bon Pain's customers is critical to the image of the store in the minds of customers. To assess employees' friendliness, the company generated a list of specific behaviors that employees should engage in. Performance is measured by mystery shoppers, who are hired to buy meals and fill out behavior-based appraisals.

As organizations struggle to create a culture in which diversity is valued and respected, behavioral criteria are proving useful for monitoring whether managers are investing sufficient energy in their own development. Imagine how difficult it would be to evaluate whether a manager achieved a trait-like criterion such as "Values the diversity of subordinates." A performance criterion like this provides little guidance to the manager about what actually to *do*. It would be equally difficult for the manager's superior to interpret. (Subordinates, on the other hand, may be quite willing to express their opinions!). For the purpose of performance management, more effective criteria would be specific behaviors. For example, one company uses the following items to assess management accountability for diversity:

- Does your business plan include a diversity strategy?
- Are you a member of a diversity focus group or steering committee?
- Have you attended a diversity workshop or seminar during the past twelve months?
- What percentage of employees in your organization have individual development plans?
- Has your organization formed a diversity focus group?
- Has anyone in your organization filed complaints of discrimination or harassment during the past twelve months? If yes, what is their current status?

When combined with performance feedback, behavioral criteria are particularly useful for employee development. With behaviors clearly identified, an employee is more likely to exhibit the acts that lead to peak performance. Behavioral criteria are less appropriate for jobs in which effective performance can be achieved using many different behaviors. Still, even in these jobs, the identification of the most appropriate behaviors serves as a useful guideline for most employees' actions.

Outcome-Based Criteria

With the increased emphasis on productivity and international competitiveness, outcome-based criteria are enjoying rising popularity. These criteria focus on *what* was accomplished or produced rather than on *how* it was accomplished or produced. Outcome-based criteria may be appropriate if the company does not care how results are achieved, but they're not appropriate for every job. They're often criticized for missing critical aspects of the job that are difficult to quantify. For example, the number of cases handled annually by a lawyer can easily be counted, but the result won't indicate the quality of legal counsel given or the resolution of the cases. On the other hand, a results-at-all-costs mentality may plague outcome-based appraisals. A collection agency used the outcome-based criterion "Collects large sums of money" as its sole measure of performance. Large sums of money were collected, but the agency ended up being sued because its agents used threats and punitive measures to amass collections.

Single or Multiple Criteria

Most jobs are composed of many different duties and related tasks. The primary duty for the assistant vice president of a market research firm, to coordinate market activities, may be accompanied by other duties such as staying abreast of current events and closing out daily market activities. If job analysis identifies all these duties as important, all should be measured by the performance appraisal instrument.

If the performance appraisal doesn't measure job behaviors and results that are important and relevant to the job, the measure is *deficient*. If the form appraises anything either unimportant or irrelevant to the job, it's *contaminated*. Unfortunately, many performance appraisal methods used in organizations today are both deficient and contaminated.

One theory of performance suggests that a limited set of performance domains can be used to capture all aspects of nearly any job. This theory defines performance in terms of what people do, not what they produce. The eight domains thought to capture all aspects of performance are shown in Exhibit 11.3.[16] Not all jobs will include all these activities. Nevertheless, the taxonomy serves as a useful checklist when thinking through the types of criteria that might be relevant to a particular job.

Weighting the Criteria

For jobs involving multiple performance criteria, another question must be asked: "How should these separate aspects of performance be combined into a composite score that facilitates comparisons of incumbents?" One way is to weight all the criteria equally. But if some criteria are much more important than others, then weights should be assigned to reflect these differences. The simplest approach to assigning weights is to use job analysis information—such as ratings of task frequency and importance. Statistical procedures also can be used to determine appropriate weights for each job dimension. With these procedures, greater weights get assigned to dimensions that are most strongly associated with overall performance evaluations.

TIMING

The timing of performance measurement *should* reflect strategic considerations. But often the timing of performance appraisal and feedback activities is driven by convenience and tradition.

Focal-Point System

Many organizations conduct formal review sessions at regular intervals, such as every six months or annually. In a focal-point system, all employees are appraised at approximately the same time, usually the end of the fiscal or calendar year. The major advantage of this system is that supervisors can look at all individuals, report to them, and get a sense of how their performances compare during the same time period. Similarly, top management can compare the performances of different strategic business units to assess how well they're meeting corporate objectives. Such comparative information is particularly important if performance information is used for compensation decisions. Because the link to compensation is central to Lincoln Electric,

Exhibit 11.3
A Taxonomy of Performance Domains

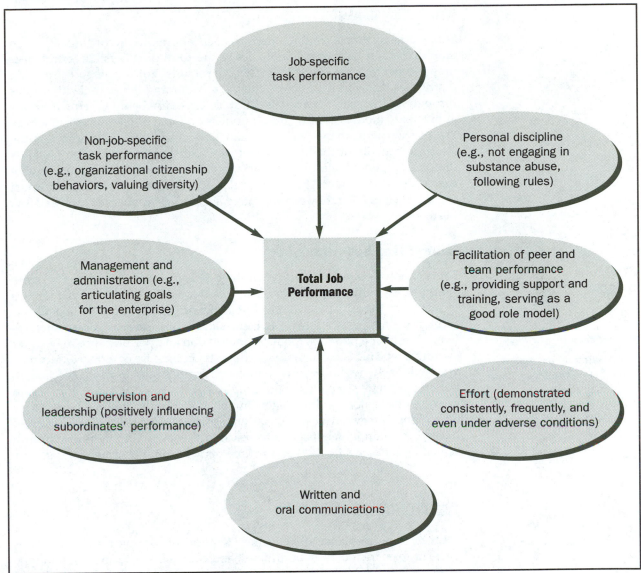

its line managers spend up to two weeks doing appraisal. The HR department spends several weeks before this making sure the line managers have all the necessary data, for instance, on absenteeism and productivity.

Focal-point reviews produce a tremendous workload for a concentrated period of time, which can be burdensome. The burden can be reduced in two ways: first, by having clear criteria against which to evaluate performance, and second, by ensuring that subordinates share with their supervisors the responsibility for defining performance criteria and documenting accomplishments relative to performance standards. Focal-point reviews also may create artificial productivity cycles that reflect merely the timing of appraisals. For example, if a law firm measures performance each year at the end of November, an employee's billable hours may begin to peak in the weeks immediately preceding the appraisal, and then drop below normal as everyone takes time to recover from the frenzy.

Anniversary Model

Some organizations conduct performance appraisals according to when employees join the organization. As in the focal-point system, employees may receive reviews every six or twelve months. But the *anniversary model* distributes the workload across the year. Assuming the organization hires throughout the year, the appraisal task is less overwhelming. However, the anniversary model typically does not tie individual or team performance to the overall performance of the organization, and thus compromises the strategic benefits of the appraisal process. Furthermore, research suggests that ratings given to employees early in the year are higher or more lenient than ratings given later. This is particularly likely if raters or appraisers must use a "curve" so that they can allocate only specific numbers of high and low ratings.

Natural Time Span of the Job

Some experts argue that a better timing rule is to schedule reviews to correspond to the natural time span of the job, that is, the length of time it takes to recognize the performance level of someone who is doing the job. If performance is assessed before it can be reasonably measured, misassessment is likely. If the time period is too long, motivation and performance may suffer significantly. This is particularly detrimental in the case of a poor performer, who will likely not know how to improve performance until it's too late. In the case of some simple jobs, the time span may be only a few minutes; in the case of a senior-level management job, the appropriate time period may be as long as several years. In an advertising agency, account executives receive evaluation feedback after each presentation. In a research firm searching for a genetic marker, the time period would be much longer.

PARTICIPANTS

Sources of performance data include supervisors, employees themselves, peers or team members, subordinates, and customers. The amount and type of work contact each source has with the person being evaluated should determine who participates in the appraisal process.[17] Team members, customers, and subordinates see different facets of an individual's task behavior than do supervisors.[18] A customer is more likely to observe the behavior of a sales representative—for instance, greeting the customer or closing the sale—than is a first-level supervisor. No one—not even the employee—has complete information. A worker may know what he or she has done but not be aware of the results of that behavior in terms of customers' reactions or the bottom line. On the other hand, a supervisor has access to more information about results and comparative sales performance than do employees or customers. Thus, involving multiple raters in the evaluation process generally is the best approach. When evaluations from supervisors, subordinates, peers, and employees themselves are all used, they're often referred to as 360-degree appraisals. Such appraisals are especially useful for providing developmental feedback.

Appraisal by Superiors

The term *superior* in this context refers to the immediate boss of the subordinate being evaluated. Many companies assume that the superior knows the subordinate's job and performance better than anyone else and so give all the responsibility for appraisal to this person. Supervisors do appear to produce more reliable performance judgments than other sources, perhaps because they have knowledge about several aspects of employees' performance.[19] However, appraisal by superiors alone has drawbacks. Besides having only partial information, superiors usually have power to reward and punish. Thus subordinates may feel threatened and not really hear any negative feedback they're given.

Because of the potential legal liabilities and the desire to have the best appraisal data possible, organizations often invite other people to share in the appraisal process. This increases the reliability and perceived fairness of the appraisal process. In addition, it creates greater openness in the performance appraisal system and enhances the quality of the superior-subordinate relationship. These benefits aren't without cost, however. Evaluations obtained from other sources often bypass natural lines of authority (organizational hierarchy) or reverse the usual authority structure (upward evaluations) and may be prohibited by contractual agreements (e.g., union-management contracts).[20]

Self-Appraisal

When employees assess their own performance, they conduct a self-appraisal. The use of self-appraisal gained popularity as a component of management by objectives, often referred to as MBO. *Management by objectives* combines the assessment of past performance with goal setting for the future. Subordinates who participate in the evaluation process become more involved and committed to the goals. Subordinate participation also clarifies employees' roles and may reduce role conflict.[21]

Self-appraisals increase employees' satisfaction with the appraisal process,[22] and promote self-development, personal growth, and goal commitment. When self-appraisals are compared to the appraisals provided by others, they often reveal blind spots that need attention. Interestingly, high performing employees appear to have fewer such blind spots than do low performing employees.[23] However, self-appraisals are subject to systematic biases and distortions. Self-ratings often are more lenient than those obtained from supervisors. Providing extensive performance feedback and including some objective performance data are two ways to reduce this problem.[24]

For global firms, and even domestic firms with a culturally diverse workforce, the use of self assessment raises another concern—do employees from different cultures approach self assessment differently? If some cultures are more likely to be modest in their self-assessments, the use of this approach may be detrimental to their personal development and advancement. The feature, Managing Diversity: Cultural Differences in Self Assessment?, describes what research says about this concern.[25]

Peers

The use of team-member appraisals is likely to increase in the 21st century in light of corporate America's focus on employee participation, teamwork, and empowerment. Within team-based organizations, peer involvement in

■■ *fast fact*

In *Byrd v. Ronayne*, an employer successfully defended their decision to fire an attorney using the attorney's candid self-evaluation that acknowledged performance deficiencies.

MANAGING DIVERSITY

Cultural Differences in Self Assessment?

Are self-evaluations of performance always lenient? Do workers in collective cultures, which discourage boasting about individual accomplishments, evaluate performance the same way as American workers do? Or is the leniency bias merely a product of Western culture's emphasis on individuality? As the world economy becomes globalized and more multinational firms find themselves operating in many different countries, these questions become more important. Also, a growing portion of the U.S. labor force includes people with non-Western cultural backgrounds. How will this diversity affect the performance evaluations used by companies to make important decisions?

In Western cultures, subordinates tend to evaluate themselves more favorably than do their supervisors. This effect occurs across different types of employees (clerical, managerial, blue-collar) for different types of rating scales, and for appraisal done for different purposes. Leniency in self-ratings is consistent with the notion that people view themselves in a positive light. The tendency to have a positive self-image and to project a positive self-image to others is common in Western culture, which stresses individual achievement, self-sufficiency, and self-respect. In contrast, collectivistic cultures encourage interpersonal harmony, interdependence, solidarity, and group cohesiveness. They do not draw attention to individual achievements in the interest of interpersonal harmony.

Are workers in collectivistic cultures more modest than their American counterparts when it comes to rating their own job performance? To find out, an international team of researchers examined the performance ratings of over 900 pairs of supervisors and their subordinates. The ratings of people working in the Republic of China (Taiwan) were compared with those of American supervisors. In conducting this cross-cultural research, English-language versions of the rating scales were translated into Chinese and then translated back into English to be sure that a good translation had been achieved.

When Chinese workers evaluated their own job performance and their own desire to work, they gave themselves lower ratings than did their supervisors. Their ratings were also lower than the ones American workers gave to themselves. Consistent with the belief of collectivistic cultures that wisdom comes with age, younger workers rated themselves lower than did their supervisors, and the self-ratings of younger workers were lower than those of older workers.

The researchers concluded that the use of self-ratings by multinational firms may create bias against Chinese employees and against other employees from collectivistic cultures. Such employees may rate themselves lower than equally performing Anglo-Americans. Also, Chinese employees may be reluctant to engage in impression management behaviors and self-promotion (e.g., making sure their supervisor knows about their accomplishments). As a result, their supervisors may give them lower ratings than they deserve. If the ratings are used for evaluation purposes, the result may be unintended discrimination and unfair treatment, as well as lower morale and ineffective use of the best talent.

performance appraisal is growing. Research showing that appraisals by peers are useful predictors of future performance is consistent with this trend.[26] Also consistent with this trend is research showing that, for managerial employees, the ratings of peers and subordinates tend to be consistent with each other.[27]

Peer involvement in performance management takes many forms. It may be limited to making appraisals for developmental feedback purposes only, or it can serve as the foundation for a team's self-management processes. Jamestown Advanced Products Incorporated, a small metal fabrication firm, had to deal with the issue of employee tardiness. According to the team members' assessment of the problem, one person's late arrival disrupted everyone else's schedule, reduced team performance, and consequently lowered financial bonuses. Traditionally, a tardy employee lost some wages but could still receive a quarterly performance bonus. Team members thought this was unfair. The work team was encouraged to set performance standards for its members and to identify consequences for low performance. After the team batted around the issue of how much lateness or absenteeism it could tolerate and how punitive it should be, it reached agreement: employees could be tardy—defined as one minute late—or absent without notice no more than five times a quarter. Beyond that, they would lose their entire bonus. In addition to defining performance expectations, Jamestown team members commonly serve as evaluators; the coworker who is at an individual's side all day has an excellent opportunity to observe that individual's behavior. Common performance dimensions on which team members have evaluation expertise include

- attendance and timeliness (e.g., "Attends scheduled group meetings"),
- interpersonal skills (e.g., "Is willing to give and take on issues," "Isn't unreasonably stubborn"),
- group supportiveness (e.g., "Offers ideas or suggestions for the group to use on the project," "Supports group decisions"), and
- planning and coordination (e.g., "Contributes input to help other team members perform their assignments").

Subordinates

Organizations such as Johnson & Johnson and Sears have been surveying employees for their opinions of management for years, but in general, this type of appraisal, called *upward appraisal,* is still catching on. Major firms that are out in the front of this movement include Amoco Corporation, Chrysler, Cigna, and DuPont. They all use subordinates' ratings in order to improve operations, reduce hierarchy, and develop better managers. Amoco adopted an upward appraisal system in response to suggestions from employees. A voluntary, computer-scored employee questionnaire solicits feedback on a supervisor's participative leadership, creativity, and performance management. Feedback results are incorporated into Amoco's training sessions for middle-level managers.[28]

Although subordinates often don't have access to information about all dimensions of supervisory performance, they do have frequent access to information about supervisor-subordinate interactions. One drawback to upward feedback is that subordinates don't always evaluate performance objectively or honestly, especially if their ratings aren't anonymous.[29] To protect anonymity, evaluations need to be made by several subordinates, and someone other than the supervisor should combine the subordinates' ratings.

Customers

At a medical clinic in Billings, Montana, patients routinely rate desk attendants and nursing personnel on behaviors such as courtesy, promptness,

■□ *fast fact*

To encourage participation in
its customer performance
appraisal process, Xerox
Business Services plants a
tree for each customer that
returns a completed form.

and quality of care. Domino's Pizza hires mystery customers who order piz-
zas and then evaluate the performance of the telephone operator and delivery person. The owner of a carpeting firm in Utah uses a customer checklist
to monitor the on-site performance of carpet installers. The use of customers
as appraisers has the additional advantage of educating customers in what
the organization expects from employees. This can help create greater alignment between customers' and employers' expectations. A potential difficulty in using real customers is getting a fair sampling of customer experiences.
Customers who have had particularly bad experiences may be more likely
to complete a questionnaire.

360-Degree Appraisals

Increasingly, major companies are using 360-degree appraisal and feedback
systems.[30] These systems recognize that each of the potential sources of
information just described has strengths and weaknesses. In contrast to the
traditional approach, where a single person—usually a supervisor—rates
employee performance, 360-degree systems collect performance information
from a set of colleagues and internal customers who form a circle around the
employee. Multiple-source evaluations are perceived as more fair than single-source approaches. The evaluation process produces more valid results
because it involves a group of people who interact with the employee in
many different ways. For the same reason, the process should be less susceptible to gender and ethnicity biases than are single-source evaluations.[31]

Because the practice is relatively new, little research exists to guide organizations in developing the most appropriate 360-degree practices. However,
the limited evidence that's available does suggest that the raters' identities
should remain anonymous, when possible. Also, it appears that this technique works best when the full circle is represented—not just one portion of
it (e.g., including only subordinates or only peers). In most other respects,
the principles for developing an effective appraisal system are essentially the
same for single-source and multi-source assessment.[32]

PERFORMANCE APPRAISAL FORMATS

The development of a rating format follows systematic job analysis, the
identification of criteria and appropriate raters, and decisions about the timing of appraisals. Although direct measures for performance appraisal are
available for some jobs, by far the most widely used formats are judgmental.
Judgmental formats vary in how they specify the standards for judging performance. Some formats are norm-referenced, some use absolute behavioral
standards, and some focus on output.

Norm-Referenced Appraisals

For many types of human resource decisions, the fundamental questions
often are: Who is the best performer in the group? Who should be retained,
given that we have to cut our workforce? Who should be assigned a specific task? For these types of decisions, norm-referenced formats are appropriate. With norm-referenced methods, the rater is forced to evaluate the individual, team, or strategic unit in relation to similar others. The two most
commonly used are straight ranking and forced distribution.

Straight Ranking.   In straight ranking, the appraiser lists the focal employees (or teams of employees) in order, from best to worst, usually on the basis

*"With 360-degree
feedback, we capture input
from people with whom the
employee works on a
regular basis. We call it
their 'knowledge network.'
The person who receives
the evaluation views it as
very accurate."*

Ann J. Ewen
President
TEAMS, Inc.

■□ *fast fact*

Park View Medical Center in
Pueblo, Colorado, doesn't
believe in forms. It has an
appraisal called the Annual
Piece of Paper (APOP), but its
only purpose is to document
that a conversation focused
on performance took place.

of overall performance. Employees can also be ranked with regard to specific duties. Rankings may be appropriate when only a few employees need to be evaluated. As the number increases, it becomes increasingly difficult to rank employees because the majority tends to be about average. A problem with straight ranking is assigning a unique rank. This suggests that no two subordinates perform exactly alike. Although this may be true, many supervisors believe that some incumbents perform so similarly that individual differences can't be discerned.

Forced Distribution. The forced distribution method is one way to deal with the problem of having several employees who all perform about the same. Instead of assigning each employee to a unique rank, the forced distribution format asks the appraiser to distribute the employees across several categories of performance. A typical format would use five categories, with a fixed percentage of all subordinates in the group falling within each category, as illustrated below.

Lowest Performers	Next Lowest	Middle	Next Highest	Highest Performers
10%	20%	40%	20%	10%
(5 people)	(10 people)	(20 people)	(10 people)	(5 people)

The forced distribution method creates problems for evaluators who believe that the pattern of performances from people being evaluated does not conform to the fixed percentages. Regardless of the approach, norm-referenced methods usually measure performance using one criterion—overall performance. This global measure isn't anchored in an objective index, such as units sold, so results can be influenced by subjective biases that have little to do with actual performance. Because the rankings lack behavioral specificity, they may be subject to legal challenge.[33] Other problems with norm-referenced approaches are that they provide no information about the absolute level of performance, and they provide no useful information for the job incumbent to act on.

Absolute Standards

Formats that use absolute standards allow evaluators to assess performance in relation to specified criteria. Graphic rating scales, behaviorally-anchored rating scales, and behavior observation scales are three widely used formats that involve absolute standards.

Graphic Rating Scales. Introduced in the 1920s, graphic rating scales were touted as useful because direct output measures were not needed, and the rater was free to make as fine a judgment as desired. The scales consist of performance descriptions and unbroken lines with various numbers positioned along the lines and sometimes with descriptive adjectives below. Graphic rating scales vary considerably in terms of the clarity with which the performance dimension is delineated, the number of rating categories, and the specificity of the anchors (short definitions) associated with the rating categories. Exhibit 11.4 illustrates several alternative graphic rating scales that might be used to assess the quantity of work a person completed. In this exhibit, scales A to C require the rater to define the dimension. This obviously leads to different interpretations by different raters. Although scales D and E do a better job of defining work quantity, they still provide

Exhibit 11.4

Sample Graphic Rating Scales for Work Quantity

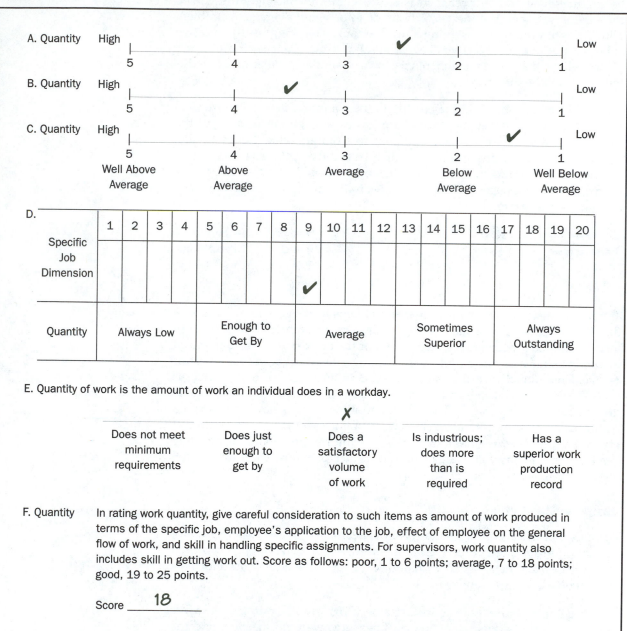

E. Quantity of work is the amount of work an individual does in a workday.

Does not meet minimum requirements	Does just enough to get by	Does a satisfactory volume of work	Is industrious; does more than is required	Has a superior work production record

F. Quantity   In rating work quantity, give careful consideration to such items as amount of work produced in terms of the specific job, employee's application to the job, effect of employee on the general flow of work, and skill in handling specific assignments. For supervisors, work quantity also includes skill in getting work out. Score as follows: poor, 1 to 6 points; average, 7 to 18 points; good, 19 to 25 points.

Score _____ 18 _____

latitude for disagreement. Scale F is problematic in a different way: although it provides the most extensive definition of work quantity, the rater must consider more than one aspect of quantity. In addition, scale F provides anchors for only three general groups of scale values, although 25 discrete scale values can be used. The primary advantage of the graphic rating scale format is its simplicity. The major disadvantage is its lack of clarity and definition. Even when raters are trained, they still might not define the performance dimensions in the same way.

Behaviorally Anchored Rating Scales. Dissatisfaction with graphic rating scales led to the development of formats that include more specific behavioral criteria. Behaviorally anchored rating scales (BARS) were developed to provide results that employees could use to improve their performance, which in turn allows the appraiser to feel more comfortable in giving feedback.

To develop a BARS performance measure, one begins collecting descriptions of incidents that illustrate very competent, average, and incompetent work behaviors. These incidents are then grouped into broad overall categories or dimensions of performance—for example, administrative tasks and interpersonal tasks. Each dimension serves as a criterion for evaluating performance. Exhibit 11.5 shows one such criterion—transacting loans—and the critical incidents pertinent to it. This exhibit also shows the next step: assigning a numerical value. A higher number means higher performance. BARS provides a format for assigning scale values to performance levels in a way that's less ambiguous in meaning, understandable, justifiable, and easy to use.

Like any format, the BARS format has limitations. One problem is that the scales can be difficult and time-consuming to develop. This means they're more difficult to modify as jobs change and performance expectations shift. From a cost-benefit perspective, the development of behavioral formats should be restricted to jobs that have many incumbents or for which

A hospitality checklist reminds Red Lion Hotel employees of their company's customer-service goals:

1. *Greet the guest.*
2. *Show the guest that you care.*
3. *Show the guest that you can help (by going out of your way to accommodate the guest's needs).*
4. *Appreciate the guest's business.*

Exhibit 11.5

Sample Behaviorally Anchored Rating Scale for One Dimension of the Work Performance of a Corporate Loan Assistant

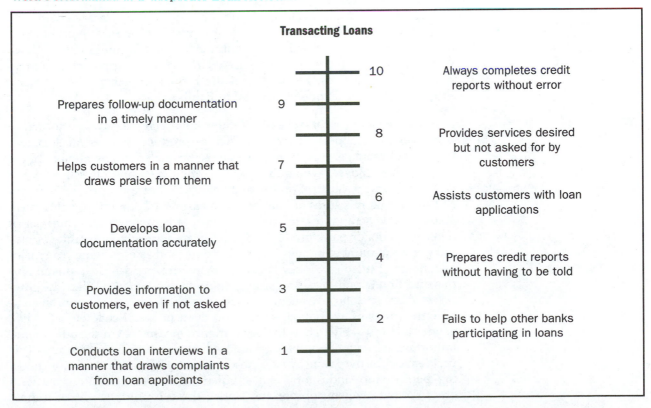

the job *processes* (versus outcomes) are critical to job success. In the service sector, success often depends on *how* work is performed, so its worthwhile to invest in the effort required to develop clear behavioral standards.

For raters, problems occur when the incidents shown on the form don't correspond to any behavior the rater has observed, or when the rater has observed the employee displaying behaviors associated with both high and low performance. For example, a corporate loan assistant could prepare follow-up documentation in a timely manner and also receive complaints from loan applicants about rudeness and inappropriate questioning. In such situations, it's difficult to decide whether to give a high or low rating.[34]

Behavioral Observation Scales.   A more recent development in behavioral scales is called the behavioral observation scale (BOS). Like BARS, these scales are derived from critical incidents of job behavior. But the format used to rate performance is different. Raters aren't asked to indicate the level of performance; they're asked to report how frequently employees engage in certain behaviors. Exhibit 11.6 illustrates the BOS format.[35] When adding all the ratings together, items that describe ineffective performance are reverse scored. BOS is just as expensive and time-consuming as BARS to develop, but raters find it easier to use. Unfortunately, however, raters often don't have sufficient time or ability to accurately assess the frequency with which behaviors are observed.

Output-Based Formats

For some jobs, the way work is performed is less important than the results achieved. For these types of jobs, measuring actual outputs produced—regardless of the behaviors used to obtain them—may be the most useful approach for assessing performance.

Output-based formats focus on job products as the primary criteria. As is true for the norm-referenced and absolute standards approaches, job analysis should guide the choice of outputs selected for measurement. Two widely used output-based formats are the direct index approach and management by objectives. Regardless of the format, effective output criteria should include the components listed in Exhibit 11.7.

Direct Index Approach.   The direct index approach measures performance using objective, impersonal criteria, such as productivity, absenteeism, and turnover. A manager's performance may be evaluated by the number of the manager's employees who quit or by the employees' absenteeism rate. For nonmanagers, measures of productivity may be more appropriate. These can be broken into measures of quality and measures of quantity. Quality measures include scrap rates, number of customer complaints, and number of defective units or parts produced. Quantity measures include units of output per hour, number of new customer orders, and sales volume. The major advantage of the direct index approach is that it provides clear, unambiguous direction to employees regarding desired job outcomes. When the criteria used are specific, extraneous variables such as the ratee's prior evaluation, the order of evaluation, salary, and even personal characteristics like gender are less likely to bias the performance measures. On the other hand, important job behaviors may be ignored in the evaluation process. This problem can be overcome by using job analysis results as the basis for choosing performance indicators, and supplementing the direct indexes with other formats, when appropriate. Under these conditions, direct indices

Exhibit 11.6
Sample Behavioral Observation Scale Items for a Maintenance Mechanic

In completing this form, circle
0– if you have no knowledge of the employee's behavior
1– if the employee has engaged in the behavior 0 to 64 percent of the time
2– if the employee has engaged in the behavior 65 to 74 percent of the time
3– if the employee has engaged in the behavior 75 to 84 percent of the time
4– if the employee has engaged in the behavior 85 to 94 percent of the time
5– if the employee has engaged in the behavior 95 to 100 percent of the time

Customer Relations   **Behavior Frequency**

1. Swears in front of customers (e.g., operators and vendors) (R) — 0 1 2 3 4 5
2. Blames customer for malfunction (R) — 0 1 2 3 4 5
3. Refers to customers by name or asks for his or her name when first introduced — 0 1 2 3 4 5
4. Asks operator to demonstrate what she or he was doing at the time of the malfunction. — 0 1 2 3 4 5

Teamwork

1. Exhibits rude behavior that coworkers complain about (R) — 0 1 2 3 4 5
2. Verbally shares technical knowledge with other technicians — 0 1 2 3 4 5
3. As needed, consults fellow workers for their ideas on ways to solve specific problems — 0 1 2 3 4 5
4. Given an incomplete assignment, leaves a clear, written tie-in for the next day shift to use — 0 1 2 3 4 5
5. Works his or her share of overtime — 0 1 2 3 4 5

Planning

1. Estimates repair time accurately — 0 1 2 3 4 5
2. Completes assigned jobs on time — 0 1 2 3 4 5
3. Is able to set job priorities on a daily or weekly basis — 0 1 2 3 4 5
4. Even when the job is not yet complete, cleans up area at the end of the shift — 0 1 2 3 4 5
5. Identifies problems or potential problems that may affect repair success or completion time — 0 1 2 3 4 5

Planned Maintenance Repairs

1. Executes planned maintenance repair, requiring no follow-up — 0 1 2 3 4 5
2. Adjusts equipment according to predetermined tolerance levels; commits no errors — 0 1 2 3 4 5
3. Replaces components when necessary rather than when convenient or easy — 0 1 2 3 4 5
4. Takes more time than allotted to complete a planned maintenance repair (R) — 0 1 2 3 4 5

Note: "R" denotes item is reverse scored.

Exhibit 11.7
Components of Effective Output-Based Performance Criteria

- *Specific Parameters:* Identify how well the behavior must be performed or how high the output must be to be considered acceptable. Specificity reduces variability in performance and in ratings.
- *Deadlines:* Identify the deadline for completion of the task or attainment of the output level.
- *Conditions:* Point out any qualifications associated with attaining the standard—for example, whether the production schedule is adhered to—because many circumstances beyond the control of the incumbent may hamper goal attainment.
- *Priorities:* Ensure that incumbents understand which standards are most important. Supervisors and incumbents can weight them, or weights can be derived from the job description.
- *Consequences:* Specify the consequences of attaining or not attaining the specified level of performance.
- *Congruent Goals:* For employees performing similar jobs, assign comparable goals.

formats are useful tools for making between-employee comparisons, developing employees, and documenting organizational actions.

Management by Objectives (MBO). MBO begins with the establishment of goals or objectives for the upcoming performance period. In some organizations, superiors and subordinates work together to establish goals; in others, superiors establish goals for work groups or individuals; in still others, goals are derived from time-and-motion studies. In organizations with self-managed work teams, the team may set its own goals. Regardless of how goals are established, a strategy for goal attainment is developed next. Experienced employees can develop their strategies on their own. For less experienced employees, the supervisor may need to assist with the strategy development. Clearly delineating how a goal is to be attained reduces ambiguity and makes goal attainment more likely. Strategy development includes outlining the steps necessary to attain each objective, as well as any constraints that may block attainment of the objective.

At the conclusion of the performance period, actual performance is evaluated relative to the pre-established objectives. Performance against each objective should be scored separately. Scoring algorithms can be either simple (indicating whether the objective was or was not met) or complex (signaling how far above or below the objective actual performance was). After evaluation, the reasons goals were not attained or were exceeded should be explored. This step helps determine training needs and development potential.

The final step is to decide on new goals and possible new strategies for goals not previously attained. At this point, subordinate and superior involvement in goal setting may change. Subordinates who successfully reached the established goals may be allowed to participate more in the goal-setting process the next time. Exhibit 11.8 illustrates goals set by a graphic artist.[36]

Exhibit 11.8
Performance Goals and Subgoals for a Graphic Artist

Project: Logo Development for Casper County Park System
1. Meet all agreed-on deadlines.
2. Keep costs within the agreed-on budget.
3. Bill final hours within plus or minus 10 percent of the agreed-on budget.
4. Achieve supervisor's criteria for logo development. Subgoals include:
   a. Reproduces well in various sizes and in three dimensions
   b. Can be used in one color, line art, and halftone versions
   c. Has a strong identity
   d. Uses type in a unique manner
   e. Has high-quality art
5. Meet client's criteria for logo. Subgoals include:
   a. Conveys desired public image
   b. Message is clear
   c. Logo is easily recognizable
   d. Typeface matches the personality of the park system
6. Strive to exceed client expectations. Indicators that this goal is met include:
   a. Logo design wins an award
   b. Customers express excitement about using the logo
   c. Public learns to recognize the logo without text within one year.

Management must be clearly committed to the process if the MBO system is to be effective. When management is committed and goals cascade from the top down, supervisory complaints are reduced by more than 20 percent and employee satisfaction increases. In addition, productivity gains average 56 percent. Without management commitment and a shared vision, productivity gains average a meager 6 percent. Even under the best conditions, MBO systems don't lead to immediate increases in productivity. On average, it takes about two years after implementation for MBO systems to work effectively.[37] At Etec Systems, goal setting and management by objectives are credited with helping the company engineer a major turnaround, as described in Managing Change: The Goal Is a Turnaround.

MANAGING CHANGE

The Goal Is a Turnaround

Stephen Cooper, CEO and Chairman of Etec Systems, a high-tech manufacturer of expensive electronic equipment, used a combination of goal setting and MBO to turn around that company. In 1993, when Cooper took over, the company was losing $1 million a month. Believing in the power of goals both to motivate employees and to direct their attention, he set the goal of generating annual revenues of $500 million by 2000. To get there, he made sure that 800 employees had written personal plans to guide their daily work. These one-page plans included five to seven goals, to which employees assigned priority rankings. For each goal, the employee had to state how progress would be measured. Cooper views this system as essential to the company's success. He explains, "We operate on the leading edge of technology with very demanding customers. If you're going to be a technology leader, you have to execute on schedule."

For Phil Arnold, a precision optics manager, executing on schedule means achieving goals such as increasing production volume by 30 percent and reducing cycle times by 10 percent. The six junior managers who report to him, in turn, each have goals that they must achieve. And the people supervised by the junior managers all have daily checklists that reflect the junior managers' goals. Every Monday, the junior managers give a four-minute status report to Arnold. Problems are identified and solutions for dealing with them are developed immediately.

Arnold learned the hard way to monitor progress and identify problems before they turn into crises. Before he began holding his Monday meetings, Arnold didn't find out about a problem with a vendor until it was far too late to take corrective actions. He then had to spend months dealing with the damage caused by the vendor. With the current system, every week everyone knows what they should be doing, how much weight to give each assignment, and how their goals relate to the goals of other people in the company. The company operates efficiently, yet can respond quickly to changes in the environment.

Cooper says that the key to Etec's success is doing the little things right: "You do the big things by doing the little things right. If you execute, you can do anything. When a company has a clear mission, and people know how their individual mission fits into the big picture, everyone paddles in the same direction." In this case, Cooper and everyone else at Etec Systems paddled themselves out of their decline and have returned to their former status as a fast growing, highly profitable company.[38]

To learn more about Etec Systems, visit the company's home page at
www.etec.com

When used appropriately, MBO goals serve as guidelines that facilitate two-way communication. Goals can refer to desired outcomes to be achieved, means for achieving those outcomes, or both. They may be related to the routine activities that constitute day-to-day duties or to the identification and solution of problems that hamper individual and organizational effectiveness; they may also be innovative or have special purposes. Importantly, they can and should be changed when the job or situation changes.

THE RATING PROCESS

Despite the prevalence of potentially effective performance appraisals, organizations and employees are still somewhat uneasy about using them. This uneasiness centers on the vulnerability of these measures to intentional as well as unintentional bias, both of which threaten the accuracy of the final results. Unintentional cognitive errors often occur simply because human beings are imperfect information processors. In addition, the social setting and specific organizational circumstances may come into play.

The quality of performance judgments depends, in part, on the information processing capabilities or strategies of the person making the evaluation.[39] As shown in Exhibit 11.9, the evaluator first attends to and recognizes relevant information, and then aggregates and stores the information in short-term memory. As time passes, information is condensed further for storage in long-term memory. When a performance judgment needs to be made, information relevant to the category to be rated is retrieved from memory. Recalled information about behaviors and outputs is then compared against the rater's standards. An evaluation is made based on aggregated data retrieved from memory and any additional information used by the rater either intentionally or unintentionally. Finally, before the evaluation is recorded officially, it may be revised depending on possible reactions of the incumbent or higher-level managers, the goals the rater hopes to achieve through the appraisal process, and even organizational norms.[40] Unfortunately, the fallibility of managers combines with this process to create numerous types of errors.[41]

Rating Errors

When criteria aren't clearly specified and no incentives are associated with rating accuracy, a variety of errors occur during the rating process. These errors, which are described in Exhibit 11.10, can affect all stages of the process, but their effects are most clearly seen at the final stage, after ratings have actually been recorded.[42]

Strategies to Improve Rater Accuracy

Even the best performance management system may not be effective when so many extraneous errors impinge on the performance appraisal process. Fortunately, several strategies can be used to minimize appraisal errors.

Design an Effective Appraisal System. Performance ratings tend to be more accurate when the rating criteria, the record of performance accomplishments, and the rating scales are precise. When all three of these elements are in place, evaluators aren't only more accurate in their ratings but also more confident about their ratings. Features of an effective system include:

Exhibit 11.9
The Performance Appraiser's Rating Process

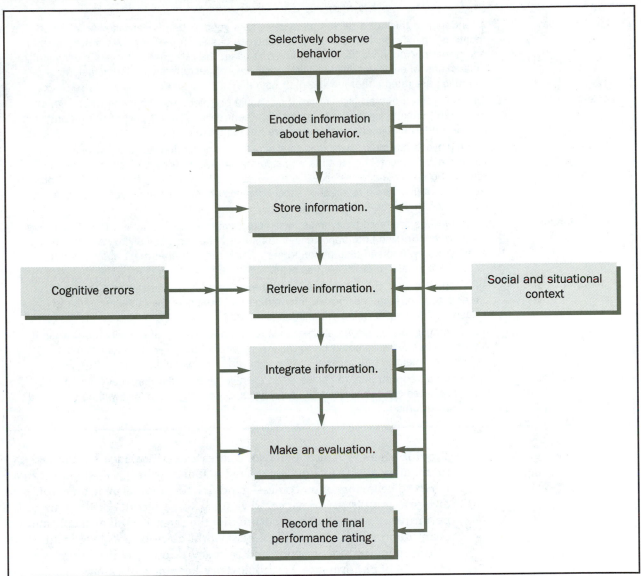

- Each performance dimension addresses a single job activity, rather than a group of activities.
- Each performance dimension is rated separately, and the scores are then summed to determine the overall rating.
- The raters can observe the behaviors of ratees on a regular basis while the job is being accomplished.
- Terms like *average* aren't used on rating scales because different raters have various reactions to them.
- Raters don't evaluate large groups of employees, especially all at the same time.[43]

Exhibit 11.10
Common Rating Errors

Halo and Horn	A tendency to think of a person as more or less good or bad is carried over into judgments of specific performances. Or stereotypes based on the employee's sex, race, or age affect performance judgments. In either case, the rater doesn't make meaningful distinctions when evaluating specific dimensions of performance. All dimensions of performance are rated either low (horn) or high (halo).
Leniency	All employees are rated higher than they should be rated. This happens when high ratings aren't sanctioned by the organization, when rewards aren't part of a fixed and limited pot, and when dimensional ratings are not required.
Strictness	All employees are rated lower than they should be. Inexperienced raters who are unfamiliar with environmental constraints on performance, raters with low self-esteem, and raters who have themselves received a low rating are most likely to rate strictly. Rater training that includes a reversal of supervisor-incumbent roles and confidence building can reduce this error.
Central Tendency	All employees are rated as average, when performance actually varies. Raters with large spans of control and little opportunity to observe behavior are likely to use this "play-it-safe" strategy. A forced distribution format, which requires that most employees be rated average, also may create this error.
Primacy	As a cognitive shortcut, raters may use initial information to categorize a person as either a good or a bad performer. Information that supports the initial judgment is amassed, and unconfirming information is ignored.
Recency	A rater may ignore employee performance until the appraisal date draws near. When the rater searches for cues about performance, recent behaviors or outputs are most salient, so recent events receive more weight than they should.
Contrast Effects	When compared with weak employees, an average employee will appear outstanding; when evaluated against outstanding employees, an average employee will be perceived as a low performer.

Provide Memory Aids. Behavior diaries and critical incident files are useful memory aids.[44] Everyone involved in making appraisals should regularly record behaviors or outcomes—good or bad—that relate to an employee's or work group's performance. Reviewing these records at the time of the performance appraisal helps ensure that the rater uses all available and relevant information. Consulting a behavioral diary or a critical incident file before rating reduces recency and primacy errors, yielding more accurate measures of performance. Electronic diary-keeping software makes this task easier than ever.

Provide Rater Training. Rating accuracy can also be improved through training that focuses on improving the observation skills of raters. Frame-of-reference training is one of the most useful approaches.[45] A comprehensive frame-of-reference training program might include the following steps:

1. The raters are given a job description and instructed to identify appropriate criteria for evaluating the job.
2. When agreement is reached, the raters view a tape of an employee performing the job.
3. Independently, the raters evaluate the videotaped performance, using the organization's appraisal system.
4. The raters' evaluations are compared with each other and with those of job experts.

5. With a trainer as a facilitator, the raters present the rationales for their ratings and challenge the rationales of other raters.

6. The trainer helps the raters reach a consensus regarding the value of specific job behaviors and overall performance.

7. A new videotape is shown, followed by independent ratings.

8. The process continues until consensus is achieved.[46]

Building raters' confidence levels should be another objective of training. A good training experience helps raters see that they *can* rate accurately and *can* handle the consequences associated with giving negative feedback. Confidence can be increased through observing someone else's success in handling the appraisal process, practicing the behaviors, and receiving coaching and feedback on how to do it better.

Reward Accurate and Timely Appraisals. One cause of rating inaccuracy is a lack of rater motivation. Without rewards, raters may find it easier to give high ratings than to give accurate ratings.[47] A straightforward strategy for increasing rater motivation is to base salary increases, promotions, and assignments to key positions partly on performance as a rater. Ratings done in a timely and fair manner (as measured by employee attitude surveys) should be rewarded.

Use Multiple Raters. Often, the ratee believes that the rater is solely responsible for a poor evaluation and any subsequent loss of rewards; the rater may also believe this. Research suggests that this negative effect can be minimized by relying on the judgments of multiple raters.[48] The diffusion of responsibility frees each rater to evaluate more accurately. Furthermore, an employee is less likely to shrug off negative information when multiple raters are involved.[49] Multiple raters acting as a group may be especially effective in producing accurate ratings, because discussion among members of the group helps overcome the various errors and biases of individuals.[50]

PROVIDING FEEDBACK

Performance management is an ongoing process, punctuated by formal appraisals and formal feedback sessions. During the feedback sessions, supervisors and subordinates meet to exchange information, including evaluations of performance and ideas for how to improve.[51] Setting goals for the future may also be on the agenda. If one's only objective for obtaining performance information were to use it for evaluation purposes, the difficult task of providing effective feedback might be avoided. But organizations collect performance data in order to provide feedback, which in turn improves future performance.[52] Many managers feel uncomfortable providing feedback to employees, in part because the process often stimulates conflict. Understanding the sources of conflict associated with performance feedback is the first step in managing it successfully.

Understanding Potential Sources of Conflict

Stakeholders' Goals. Goal conflict between the various constituents who have a stake in the appraisal process may hinder attempts to maximize performance. From organizational and individual goals come two sets of conflicts. One is between the organization's evaluative and developmental goals. When pursuing an evaluative goal, a superior makes judgments that

■□*fast fact*

When multiple raters are used, usually only the person being rated sees all the results because the objective is development rather than evaluation.

affect the subordinate's career and immediate rewards. Communicating these judgments can create an adversarial, low-trust relationship between superior and subordinate. This, in turn, precludes the superior from performing as a problem solver and coach, which is essential to serving developmental goals.

The second set of conflicts arises from the various goals of the employees who are being evaluated. On the one hand, these individuals want valid feedback that gives them information about how to improve and where they stand in the organization. On the other hand, they want to verify their self-image and obtain valued rewards. Supervisors must strive to be both open and protective, to help employees meet both sets of goals.[53]

Perceptual Focus.   Another source of conflict is the differing perspectives that the players bring to the process. For the subordinate (the actor), the perceptual focus is outward. Most salient are environmental forces (the supervisor, availability of supplies, coworkers) that interfere with the subordinate's ability to perform. For the supervisor (observer), the perceptual focus is on the subordinate and her or his motivation and ability. These differences can lead to conflict when it comes to identifying the causes of poor performance. Low-performance situations accentuate a natural tendency that we all share, which is to account for performance in a self-serving manner. To protect their egos, employees attribute their own poor performance to external circumstances—a difficult task, unclear instructions, lack of necessary equipment, and other situations that often implicate the supervisor. Supervisors also wish to protect their egos, which may mean denying responsibility for the subordinate's poor performance and instead attributing causes to the employee's own deficiencies.

Similar self-serving perceptual biases may also dampen the expected effects of positive appraisals. When we perform well, the natural tendency is to take full credit for our performance. We use positive evidence to reinforce our high opinion of ourselves, discounting the role external forces may have played. The self-interested perspective of observers, however, leads them to view our success as due to such things as chance or luck and the support we received from others.[54] Add to this our general feeling that we are better-than-average performers, and the scene is set for a potentially dysfunctional cycle: Employees believe they perform well and deserve credit for having done so; their supervisors often evaluate their performance less favorably, and these evaluations are perceived as unfair. When supervisors do recognize good performance, employees may perceive the recognition as merely what they deserved, leaving supervisors to wonder why their subordinates aren't more grateful.

Of course, not all subordinates or all employees are equally susceptible to these perceptual biases, but few are completely immune, either. So all experience some of the negative consequences. Also, all can improve by understanding these dynamics.

Consequences of Inherent Conflicts.   Among the several consequences of the conflicts inherent in performance appraisal are ambivalence, avoidance, defensiveness, and resistance. The organization demands that superiors act as judge and jury in telling subordinates where they stand, and subordinates expect it. Nevertheless, supervisors may feel uncertain about their judgments and anxious about how subordinates will react to negative feedback. This latter feeling is intensified when superiors haven't been trained in giving feedback. Subordinates are equally ambivalent because they want honest feedback, yet they also want to receive rewards and maintain their self-image. In addition, if they're open with their superiors in identifying undeveloped potential, they risk the chance that the superiors may use this to evaluate them unfavorably.

Timing

The delivery of performance information needs to be well-timed. Performance expectations should be established at the beginning of the appraisal period and then reinforced with feedback. In general, immediate feedback is most useful. Feedback also should involve the amount of information the receiver can use rather than what the evaluator would like to give. Overloading a person with information reduces the possibility that he or she will use it effectively. An evaluator who gives more data than can be used is most likely satisfying a personal need (e.g., pride in not holding anything back) rather than helping the other person.[55] Providing continuous feedback is the best way to avoid information overload and maximize the value of the feedback given.[56]

"Doing annual reviews is like dieting only on your birthday and wondering why you're not losing weight."

Anne Saunier
Principal
Sibson & Co.

Preparation

To signal that performance matters, the interview needs to be scheduled in advance. In setting up the interview, the manager and employee should reach agreement regarding its purpose and content. For example, will the subordinate have an opportunity to evaluate the performance of the supervisor, or will the evaluation be one way? Will the interview be restricted to evaluating past performance or to mapping out a strategy for future performance, or will it be open to both tasks? By discussing these issues before the actual interview, both participants have time to prepare. If subordinates are empowered, advance notice will give them sufficient time to update their performance records and do a self-review.

"Schedule an appointment and have a meeting. Don't give important feedback in the hallway."

Rick Maurer
Consultant

Content of Discussion

Initiating and carrying out an effective interview session requires both coaching and counseling skills. Supervisors need to listen to and reflect back what subordinates say with regard to performance, its causes, and its outcomes. Too often, the interview process breaks down and supervisors end up telling employees how well or poorly they're doing and selling them on the merits of setting specific goals for improvement. This may seem efficient for the supervisors, but subordinates feel frustrated trying to convince their superiors to listen to justifications for their performance levels. As a result, they discount feedback and become entrenched in past behavior.

A more effective approach is to use the appraisal interview as a problem-solving session. This approach centers on sharing perceptions and identifying solutions to problems. Active and open dialogue is established between superior and subordinate. Goals for improvement are established mutually by supervisor and subordinate. This type of interview is difficult for most supervisors, so prior training in problem solving and in giving and receiving feedback should be provided.

Follow-Up

Follow-up is essential to ensure that the behavioral contract negotiated during the interview is fulfilled. Because changing behavior is hard work, supervisors as well as subordinates tend to put behavioral agreements on the back burner. Consequently, supervisors should verify that subordinates know what is expected, have strategies to perform as desired, and realize the consequences of good or poor behavior. They should also monitor behavior, provide feedback, and immediately reinforce new behaviors that match desired objectives. In the absence of feedback and reinforcement, new behaviors will probably not become habit. Reinforcement can be as simple as a pat on the back or a compliment ("That was nice work, George"), or as tangible as a note placed in the employee's file.[57] For some behaviors, constant monitoring may be needed. Consider this example:

> *"I'm inclined to yell. I know I shouldn't. So I got a gadget, a mechanical daisy with sunglasses and guitar that sits in a glass and oscillates with the volume of my voice. It tells me when I'm yelling. Also, I instructed my secretary to hold up a stop sign when I'm screaming at someone. Like a recovering alcoholic, I take it one day at a time. Patience, patience. Tolerance, tolerance."*
>
> *A 49-year-old banker*

Designing performance management systems with all the characteristics needed to maximize performance won't guarantee perfect performance—in some cases, for example, individuals may lack the ability to perform—but it should improve performance in most cases. Also, satisfaction with the system may go up.

Identifying Causes of Performance Deficiencies

To uncover the reasons for performance deficiencies, a number of questions can be asked, based on a model of the determinants of employee behavior in organizations.[58] This model enables HR professionals and line managers to diagnose performance deficiencies and correct them in a systematic way. In general, the model says employees perform well if the following performance facilitators are present:

- ability,
- interest in doing the job,
- opportunity to grow and advance,
- clearly defined goals,
- certainty about what is expected,
- feedback on how well they're doing,
- rewards for performing well,
- punishments for performing poorly, and
- power to get resources to do the job.[59]

Exhibit 11.11[60] shows most of these determinants and specific questions to ask in pinpointing the causes of performance deficiencies. Negative responses indicate that an item is probably a cause. Based on a series of such responses, the likely causes of a performance deficiency can be established. Then, action plans for improvement can be developed.

Whether the manager believes performance problems are caused by the situation or the employee influences the strategy for performance improvement selected by the manager.[61] If problems are attributed to the employee, the manager is more likely to select strategies aimed at changing the employee, such as retraining or reprimands. If problems are attributed to the situation, the manager is more likely to select strategies that modify the environment, such as changing the job design or bringing in more rewards and punishments.

Exhibit 11.11
Sample Checklist for Diagnosing the Causes of Performance Deficiencies

Check the determinants of performance or behavior that apply to the situation you are analyzing.

	Yes	No
I. Knowledge, Skills, and Abilities		
A. Does the incumbent have the skill to perform as expected?	_____	_____
B. Has the incumbent performed as expected before?	_____	_____
C. Does the incumbent believe he or she has the ability to perform as desired?	_____	_____
D. Does the incumbent have the interest to perform as desired?	_____	_____
II. Goals for the Incumbent		
A. Were the goals communicated to the incumbent before the performance period?	_____	_____
B. Are the goals specific?	_____	_____
C. Are the goals difficult but attainable?	_____	_____
III. Certainty for the Incumbent		
A. Has desired performance been clearly specified?	_____	_____
B. Have rewards or consequences for good or bad performance been specified?	_____	_____
C. Is the incumbent clear about her or his level of authority?	_____	_____
IV. Feedback to the Incumbent		
A. Does the incumbent know when he or she has performed correctly or incorrectly?	_____	_____
B. Is the feedback diagnostic so that the incumbent can perform better in the future?	_____	_____
C. Is there a delay between performance and the receipt of the feedback?	_____	_____
D. Can performance feedback be easily interpreted?	_____	_____
V. Consequences to the Incumbent		
A. Is performing as expected punishing?	_____	_____
B. Is not performing poorly more rewarding than performing well?	_____	_____
C. Does performing as desired matter?	_____	_____
D. Are there positive consequences for performing as desired?	_____	_____
VI. Power for the Incumbent		
A. Can the incumbent mobilize the resources to get the job done?	_____	_____
B. Does the incumbent have the tools and equipment to perform as desired?	_____	_____

Team Appraisal and Feedback

As organizations restructure around teams, responsibility for performance management is shifting from supervisors to team members. Experienced teams frequently take full responsibility for constructing and conducting their own performance appraisal and feedback process. Team members are well acquainted with each other's strengths and weaknesses, so it makes sense that they become the primary performance evaluators. And simply knowing that team members will be called on to rate one's performance may in itself be motivation to perform up to the level of one's full potential. Conversely, if an organization trumpets the importance of team work but never asks team members to assess each other's performance, employees might reasonably wonder how important team work really is.

Team appraisal and feedback is fraught with challenges. In addition to all the challenges of traditional appraisal and feedback are a few that cause particular problems for teams. One such challenge is specifying the criteria to be assessed. When work is done by a team, clear goals and objectives may be given to the team as a whole with the expectation that the team will work out the specific responsibilities of individual members. In many teams, the responsibilities of individuals are very fluid. They shift as team members come and go, as customers come and go, and as the preferences of the team fluctuate. If the team never clarifies the responsibilities of individual members, the process of rating individuals against specific individual performance criteria is likely to create anxiety on the part of raters and ratees alike. Ensuring that teams develop a set of appraisal criteria—including both behaviors and outcomes—early on is one way out of this dilemma. Regardless of the criteria developed by the team, the process of defining standards benefits the team by clarifying performance standards while also creating greater cohesiveness among members.[62]

When team members evaluate each other, how should they use the information to provide feedback? Should someone outside the team conduct the appraisal interview? Should a team leader be designated for this task? Or should everyone on the team be involved in every feedback session? The reality is that different teams handle feedback in different ways. At Con-Way, everyone on the team participates in providing feedback to everyone else, and feedback is provided in a group discussion format. The goal is to incorporate feedback sessions into the normal work routine. Many other organizations provide feedback in a more private setting. Often the manager to whom the team reports is responsible for collecting performance information from the team and discussing it with each team member.

More important than who delivers the feedback is how they deliver it. Ideally, anyone who gives feedback has been trained in how to do so effectively. At Con-Way, teams are learning this invaluable skill by involving a professional facilitator in their feedback sessions. With sufficient practice and guidance, Con-Way teams may eventually develop enough skill and self-confidence to hold feedback sessions spontaneously and unassisted.

STRATEGIES FOR IMPROVING PERFORMANCE

When performance deficiencies are found, line managers and HR professionals can do many things to improve employees' performance. They can use the following suggestions for acting on the causes of deficiencies identified in Exhibit 11.11.

Positive Reinforcement

Positive reinforcement involves the use of positive rewards to increase the occurrence of the desired performance. It's based on two fundamental principles: (1) people perform in ways that they find most rewarding to them; and (2) by providing the proper rewards, it's possible to improve performance. Positive reinforcement focuses on the job behavior that leads to desired results, rather than on the results directly. It uses rewards rather than punishment or the threat of punishment to influence that behavior, and attempts to link specific behaviors to specific rewards. Positive reinforcement operates according to the law of effect, which states that behavior that leads to a positive result tends to be repeated, whereas behavior that leads to a neutral or negative result tends not to be repeated. Thus, an effort is made to link behavior to its consequences.[63]

The six basic rules for using positive reinforcement are:

Do not reward everyone the same way. Using a defined objective or standard, give more rewards to the better performers.

Recognize that failure to respond also has reinforcing consequences. Managers influence subordinates by what they do not do as well as by what they do; a lack of reward thus can also influence behavior. Managers frequently find the job of differentiating between workers unpleasant but necessary. One way to differentiate is to reward some and withhold rewards from others.

Tell people what they must do to be rewarded. If employees have standards against which to measure the job, they can arrange their own feedback system to let them make self-judgments about their work. They can then adjust their work patterns accordingly.

Tell people what they're doing wrong. Few people like to fail; most want to get positive rewards. A manager who withholds rewards from subordinates should give them a clear idea of why the rewards aren't forthcoming. The employees can then adjust their behavior accordingly rather than waste time trying to discover what behavior will be rewarded.

Do not punish anyone in front of others. Constructive criticism is useful in eliminating undesired behavior; so is punishment, when necessary. However, criticizing or punishing anyone in front of others lowers that person's self-respect and self-esteem. Furthermore, other members of the work group may sympathize with the punished employee and resent the supervisor.

Be fair. Make the consequences equal to the behavior. Do not cheat an employee out of just rewards; if someone is a good worker, say so. Some managers find it difficult to praise; others find it difficult to counsel an employee about what is being done wrong. A person who is overrewarded may feel guilty, and one who is underrewarded may become angry.

Self-Management

Self-management is a relatively new approach to resolving performance discrepancies. It teaches people to exercise control over their own behavior. Self-management begins when people assess their own problems and set specific (but individual), hard goals in relation to those problems. Next, they discuss ways in which the environment facilitates or hinders goal attainment. The challenge is to develop strategies that eliminate blocks to performance success. Put another way, self-management teaches people to observe their own behavior, compare their outputs to their goals, and administer their own reinforcement to sustain goal commitment and performance.[64]

LeRoy Pingho, a vice president at Fannie Mae, is a model self-manager. In the mid-1980s, he began his own, personal crusade to collect 360-degree feedback about his own performance and then use it to improve. He selects a cross-section of colleagues and asks them to assess his performance. Recently, he decided to make 50 copies of his results to share with everyone. He also chooses a few people each year to work with him on his "flat spots"—areas where he finds it difficult to improve on his own even when he tries. His helpers don't deliver rewards or punishments; they simply tell him when he's engaging in a behavior he has told them he wants to change. Pingho limits the number of areas targeted for improvement to only about four at a time.

Punishment

Even though most employees want to conduct themselves in a manner that's acceptable to the organization and their fellow employees, problems of

"When people identify something that they need to work on, it's usually what everyone else wishes they'd work on too."

Darcy Hitchcock
Consultant

absenteeism, poor work performance, and rule violation do arise. When informal discussions or coaching fails to neutralize these dysfunctional behaviors, formal disciplinary action is needed. The objective of punishment is to decrease the frequency of an undesirable behavior. Punishments can include material consequences, such as a cut in pay, a disciplinary layoff without pay, a demotion, or, ultimately, termination.

Punishment is frequently used by organizations because it can achieve relatively immediate results. It's effective for several reasons. Besides alerting the marginal employee to the fact that his or her low performance is unacceptable, punishment has vicarious power. When one person is punished, it signals other employees regarding expected performance and behavioral conduct. In addition, when the punishment is viewed as appropriate by other employees, it may increase their motivation, morale, and performance.

Punishment can also have undesirable side effects, however. For example, an employee reprimanded for low performance may become defensive and angry toward the supervisor and the organization. As many news reports attest, this anger may result in sabotage (destroying equipment, passing trade secrets) or retaliation (shooting the supervisor). Punishment also frequently leads only to a short-term suppression of the undesirable behavior, rather than its elimination. Another concern is that control of the undesirable behavior becomes contingent on the presence of the punishing agent. When the manager isn't present, the behavior is likely to be displayed. Finally, the employee may not perceive the punishment as unpleasant. For example, an organization with a progressive disciplinary procedure may send an employee home without pay for being late one too many times. If this occurs at the beginning of the fishing season, the employee may relish the excuse not to go to work.

The negative effects of punishment can be reduced by incorporating several principles, including the following:

Provide ample and clear warning. Many organizations have clearly defined disciplinary steps. For example, the first offense might elicit an oral warning; the second offense, a written warning; the third offense, a disciplinary layoff; the fourth offense, discharge.

Be quick. If a long time elapses between the ineffective behavior and the discipline, the employee may not know what the discipline is for.

Be consistent. Administer the same discipline for the same behavior to everyone every time. Discipline has to be administered fairly and consistently.

Don't get personal. It's best to administer the discipline impersonally. Discipline should be based on a specific behavior not a specific person.

Because the immediate supervisor or manager plays an integral role in administering discipline, HR professionals should educate managers and supervisors about the organization's disciplinary policies, and train them to administer the policies.[65]

Employee Assistance Programs

Overall, American organizations invest as much as $798 million annually in EAPs. But for every dollar employers invest, recovery of loss is estimated at $5. That's $3.9 billion recovered from loss annually, according to statistics compiled by the Employee Assistance Professionals Association (EAPA), based in Arlington, Virginia. Recovery from loss is money that otherwise would have been spent on absenteeism, sick benefits, and work-related accidents. EAPs were originally created to battle alcoholism but have since expanded to address family, financial, and legal problems—all of which can cause unsatisfactory work performance.

Demographics—and geography—play a large role in determining the type of EAP a company adopts; but, no two are exactly the same. Carpenter Technology Corporation in Reading, Pennsylvania, for example, happens to be located about 100 miles from Atlantic City, New Jersey. Their proximity to the casinos makes gambling and associated financial problems more of a problem than it might be elsewhere. The company's EAP helps employees stop seeking short-term solutions such as cash advances or loans and achieve a long-term solution through counseling or referral.

Marital and family relationship problems are the most common problems employees bring to their EAPs. But substance abuse continues to have more of an effect on job performance and costs more to treat. Employees who generally perform well but also drink too much can greatly benefit from EAP counseling and assistance. They may be productive, but also end up with their foot in their mouth at the worst times and places. Rather than punish such employees, EAPs focus on rehabilitating them, which often benefits their work and their personal life.[66]

EAPs can provide valuable assistance to employees, yet many employees in need fail to use them unless faced with the alternative of being fired. When so confronted, however, the success rate of those who receive EAP assistance is high. Successful results can translate into substantial gains in employee performance and reductions in absenteeism that far outweigh the costs of an EAP.[67]

■□ *fast fact*

Marital and family problems account for 40 to 50 percent of referrals to EAPs.

When Nothing Else Works

Helping employees—especially problem ones—to improve their work performance is a tough job. It's easy to get frustrated and to wonder if we are just spinning our wheels. Even when we want our efforts to work, they sometimes don't. Still, when we conclude that "nothing works," we are really saying that it's no longer worth our time and energy to help the employee improve. This conclusion shouldn't be made in haste, because the organization has already invested a great deal of time and money in the selection and training of its employees. Nevertheless, some situations may require drastic steps, including when

- performance actually gets worse,
- the problem behavior changes a little—but not enough,
- the problem behavior doesn't change, and/or
- drastic changes in behavior occur immediately, but improvements don't last.

If, after repeated warnings and counseling, performance doesn't improve, then five last recourses are available.

Transfer.   Sometimes, the employee and the job are just not well matched. If the employee has useful skills and abilities, it may be beneficial to transfer her or him. Transferring is appropriate if the employee's performance deficiency would have little or no effect on the new position. The concern is that a job must be available for which the problem employee is qualified.

Restructure.   Some jobs are particularly unpleasant or onerous, causing employees to behave as if they too are unpleasant and onerous. For these positions, the solution may be redesigning the job, rather than replacing the employee. It may also make sense to redesign a position to take advantage of an employee's special strengths. For example, if an employee has extraordinary technical expertise, job redesign might add duties that utilize this expertise.

Neutralize.   Neutralizing a problem employee involves restructuring that employee's job in such a way that his or her areas of needed improvement have as little effect as possible. It means assigning noncritical tasks in which the employee can be productive. Because group morale may suffer when an ineffective employee is given special treatment, neutralizing should be avoided whenever possible. However, temporary neutralizing may be practical and even benevolent for a valued employee who is close to retiring or suffering unusual personal distress due to illness or family problems.[68]

Terminate.   Termination is generally warranted for dishonesty, habitual absenteeism, substance abuse, insubordination including flat refusals to do certain things requested, and consistently low productivity that can't be corrected through training. Termination, even for legitimate reasons, is unpleasant. In addition to the administrative hassles, documentation, and paperwork, supervisors often feel guilty. The thought of sitting down with an employee and delivering the bad news makes most supervisors anxious, so they put off firing and justify the delay by saying that they won't be able to find a "better" replacement. Still, when one considers the consequences of errors, drunkenness, or being under the influence of drugs on the job, firing may be cost-effective. Ensuring that the process is seen as fair will go a long way toward getting even this unfavorable decision accepted.

Arbitrate.   Arbitration has long been used in unionized environments, and its popularity is spreading. Some companies have initiated their own in-house arbitration where a panel composed of one's peers hears an appeal. By ensuring due process, such systems enhance employee and manager satisfaction and appear to reduce turnover.[69] Arbitration is viewed as an effective alternative to costly legal suits that often evolve following the last step in the disciplinary process—termination. Some say, however, that by turning to arbitration, an employee may actually give up the protection legally afforded in some cases, such as that offered under the *Age Discrimination in Employment Act*. The experience of the Marriott Hotel Corporation suggests, however, that by entering into arbitration, an employee is almost as likely as the employer to win. In addition, both the employer and employee learn the results of in-house arbitration in weeks rather than in years as might happen in a case passing through the judicial system.

LEGAL CONSIDERATIONS IN PERFORMANCE APPRAISAL AND FEEDBACK

As shown in Exhibit 11.1, performance information partly determines pay, promotions, terminations, transfers, and other types of key decisions that affect both the well-being of employees and the productivity of a company. Thus, society has a vested interest in seeing to it that high-quality information is used for these important decisions. Numerous pieces of legislation and court decisions provide guidance in how to collect and use performance information that serves the legitimate concerns of business while protecting the rights of employees. Particularly relevant are the *Civil Rights Acts of 1964 and 1991,* the *Americans with Disabilities Act of 1990,* and the *Age Discrimination in Employment Act of 1967.*

When employment decisions are based on performance assessments, the performance assessment is being used, in effect, as a selection criterion. Thus, the appraisals must be based on identifiable job-related criteria. For example, the U.S. circuit court in *Brito v. Zia Company* (1973) found that Zia Company was in violation of Title VII when a disproportionate number of employees of a protected group were laid off because of low performance scores. The critical point was that the performance scores were based on the supervisor's best judgments and opinions, not on important components of doing the job. The best way to determine whether appraisal criteria are job related is to do a job analysis and ensure that performance scores reflect the important components of the job.

A condensed set of recommended actions for developing and implementing a legally defensible appraisal system is detailed in Exhibit 11.12.[70] All of these recommendations are consistent with the development of an effective performance management system that's linked strategically to business objectives. They also are consistent with creating a system that is perceived as fair and just. Following the guidelines shown requires careful record keeping and may limit managers' decisions to make unilateral evaluations. Nevertheless, research indicates that managers respond favorably to the introduction of procedurally just performance management systems, in part because procedurally fair performance appraisal systems improve relationships between managers and their direct reports.[71]

Exhibit 11.12
Prescriptions for Legally Defensible Appraisal and Feedback

1. Job analysis to identify important duties and tasks should precede development of a performance appraisal system.
2. The performance appraisal system should be standardized and formal.
3. Specific performance standards should be communicated to employees in advance of the appraisal period.
4. Objective and uncontaminated data should be used whenever possible.
5. Ratings on traits such as dependability, drive, or attitude should be avoided or operationalized in behavioral terms.
6. Employees should be evaluated on specific work dimensions rather than on a single global or overall measure.
7. If work behaviors rather than outcomes are to be evaluated, evaluators should have ample opportunity to observe ratee performance.
8. To increase the reliability of ratings, more than one independent evaluator should perform appraisals whenever possible.
9. Behavioral documentation should be prepared for extreme ratings.
10. Employees should be given an opportunity to review their appraisals.
11. A formal system of appeal should be available for appraisal disagreements.
12. Raters should be trained to prevent discrimination and to evaluate performance consistently.
13. Appraisals should be frequent, offered at least annually.

SUMMARY

Human variability is a fact of life, especially in organizational life. Much of human resource management involves attending to this variability. This chapter and the next discuss how organizations manage performance variability and use that variability as the basis for making employment decisions.

The strategic use of performance management seeks to direct and motivate employees to invest effort that contributes to the achievement of business objectives. Employees tend to do what is expected and what they believe is valued by "the system," as generally defined by the performance management system. When firms develop performance appraisal criteria that communicate the company's concern about teamwork and customer satisfaction, they're more likely to get teamwork and customer satisfaction from their employees.

The activity of performance appraisal is part of a performance management system that evolves over time. Such systems are premised on the beliefs that the performances of individuals vary over time and that individuals can exert some influence over their performance. Effective performance appraisal and feedback generally serve two purposes: (1) an evaluative purpose of letting people know where they stand and (2) a developmental purpose of providing specific information and direction to individuals, so that they can improve their performance. Performance appraisal is, therefore, linked to other human resource activities such as compensation, promotion, planning, development and training, and validating selection systems.

The importance of using job analysis results to develop job-related performance criteria can't be emphasized too much. In general, the more subjective the performance appraisal approach, the more vulnerable the performance appraisal system is to legal challenge. Despite well-laid plans for a performance management system, human resource professionals are often frustrated by the failure of line managers to conduct performance appraisals consistently. A number of obstacles contribute to resistance from managers: they may not have opportunities to observe subordinates' performance; they may not have clearly specified performance standards to use when making judgments; as human judges, they realize they are prone to errors and may be concerned about how these errors get translated into consequences for their subordinates' lives; and they may view performance appraisal as a conflict-producing activity and therefore avoid it. For these reasons and others, it's important to examine not only why and how performance appraisal data are gathered but also how they're used.

The dual purposes of evaluation and development mean conflicts in the appraisal and feedback process are inevitable. These conflicts, if unaddressed, will cripple the effectiveness of any performance management system. From a design perspective, effective performance appraisal minimizes conflicts by (1) focusing on behavior and outcomes rather than on subjective traits; (2) using multiple sources to improve reliability and validity and thus ensure that the process is fair; (3) delegating appraisal responsibility to employees; (4) establishing goals that integrate the needs of all parties; and (5) conducting effective problem-solving appraisal interviews.

Although many motivation theories explain human performance in organizations, a single diagnostic framework has been provided to help appraisers get at the root cause of a performance problem. Using this framework to understand performance gaps provides a basis for choosing different strategies to improve performance. From a developmental perspective, strategies that involve participation and job clarification encourage self-directed improvement. Ultimately, problem employees may require outside assistance through counseling or EAPs. It may be necessary in some cases to neutralize the negative behavior or in extreme cases to terminate the employee, but these strategies should be used only when all else fails.

TERMS TO REMEMBER

360-degree appraisal
Anniversary model
Absolute standards
Behavioral criteria
Behavioral observation scales
Behaviorally anchored rating scales
Contaminated
Contrast effects
Criteria
Deficient
Developmental purpose of appraisal
Direct index approach
Employee assistance programs
    (EAPs)
Evaluative purpose of appraisal
External attribution
Focal-point system
Forced-distribution method
Graphic rating scale
Halo error
Horn error

Internal attribution
Law of effect
Leniency error
Management by objectives (MBO)
Meritocracy
Neutralizing
Norm-referenced appraisal
Organizational citizenship
Outcome-based approach
Performance appraisal
Performance management
Positive reinforcement
Primacy error
Problem-solving interview
Punishment
Recency error
Reinforcement
Self appraisal
Self management
Team appraisal
Trait-based criteria

DISCUSSION QUESTIONS

1. Why does employee performance vary even after employees have successfully passed rigorous recruitment, selection and placement procedures? How can a performance management system address this performance variability?

2. Assume, in turn, the identity of each of the following persons: a subordinate, a superior, and a human resource professional. Answer this question for each person: "What purpose can performance appraisal and feedback serve for me?" Are the purposes served by performance appraisal and feedback for these three people congruent or conflicting? Explain.

3. Why is job analysis essential for the development of a performance appraisal and feedback system?

4. What are the three major approaches to performance appraisal? Give an example of each approach. What advantages are offered by each of these approaches? What disadvantages?

5. How does the performance appraisal approach called BARS function? BOS?

6. How does Mrs. Fields Original Cookies make its feedback system impersonal yet helpful?

7. What are the advantages and disadvantages of having a 360-degree feedback system?

8. What are the possible causes of performance deficiencies? What strategies can be used to correct those performance deficiencies?

9. Assume you are supervising employees who fall into one of three categories: (1) effective performers who have lots of potential for advancement; (2) effective performers who lack motivation or ability, or both, for potential advancement; and (3) ineffective performers. It's performance appraisal time, and you must plan interviews with subordinates from each of these three categories. How will your interviews differ? How will they be similar?

10. What are the advantages of self-management for the organization? for the individual?

11. Should a global organization attempt to use the same approach to performance appraisal and feedback in each of its locations, or are different approaches needed in different cultures? Explain.

PROJECTS TO EXTEND YOUR LEARNING

1. **Application and Integration.** Review the cases of Lincoln Electric and AAL at the end of the text.
   a. Compare Lincoln Electric and Aid Association for Lutherans with respect to the major purposes of performance appraisal and feedback. Which organization seems more concerned with evaluation? Which focuses more on development? What other uses does performance appraisal and feedback serve in these two companies?
   b. Which of the three major types of criteria are included in Lincoln Electric's performance management system? How well do the criteria fit with the company's strategic objectives? Identify potential sources of deficiency and contamination in the company's performance measures.
   c. Compare the sources of appraisal information used at Lincoln Electric and Aid Association for Lutherans. Would you recommend that these organizations use 360-degree feedback? Why or why not?

2. **Managing Change.** Three years after the IS department at Con-Way began using their Team Improvement Review (TIR) process, the company's top management team decided it wanted the entire organization to adopt this model of performance management. The management team asked the IS group to help implement the change by serving as internal consultants to other departments as they developed their own Team Improvement Review processes. Suppose you were asked to serve as a consultant to the public relations department. Briefly outline the key steps you would advise the department to take. Then list the three most difficult challenges the department is likely to face as they implement their TIR. What recommendations do you have regarding how to deal with these challenges? To stimulate your thinking, you may find it useful to visit the home page of Zigon Performance Group, a consulting

company that specializes in managing team performance, at
www.zigonperf.com

3. **Managing Diversity.**   As the HR Director for one of the major public accounting firms, you've been concerned about the turnover rates for women and people of color. You know that the college graduates hired into the firm are all equally qualified. You also know that, on objective performance measures, they continue to perform equally well. Yet for some reason, women and people of color are promoted more slowly. Understandably, many get frustrated and leave to work elsewhere. You've been conducting exit interviews and believe that the slower promotion rates reflect problems with the performance appraisal and feedback process. People who leave complain that their managers don't appreciate their efforts and seem to base promotion decisions too much on "personality." Describe how you'll proceed to address this issue. You aren't sure whether you need to make fundamental changes to the performance appraisal process. Perhaps managers simply need to be trained in how to conduct appraisals and provide feedback. Or, perhaps the problem is that managers aren't using performance appraisal results when making key employment decisions.

If you aren't familiar with the types of jobs performed by entry-level college graduates in public accounting firms, you can learn more by visiting these sites:

Ernst & Young at **www.ey.com**
Deloitte & Touche at **www.dttus.com**
Arthur Andersen at **www.arthurandersen.com**
PricewaterhouseCoopers at **www.pwcglobal.com**

4. **Managing Globally.**   You work for Teresa's Tee's, which makes promotional T-shirts that sport unusually high-quality artwork. Demand for the shirts is strong, with orders now coming in from all over the world. To get closer to your customers, the company has decided to go international and open offices in several foreign countries. You plan to employ host-country nationals for all positions. Staff from headquarters will help each location get started, but then local managers will take over. The company is organized around customer-focused teams. You use 360-degree appraisals for everyone in the company, including top-level executives. The results are used for developmental purposes only, but, in the future, it's likely that the company will begin using the results for pay and promotion decisions. The CEO is committed to using 360-degree appraisals at all international locations. You're responsible for ensuring that the performance appraisal and feedback process is effective. Your first international assignment is Mexico, where you'll be staying for six months. Map out a detailed plan of action. State the objectives that you need to accomplish during your six-month assignment. You may be able to learn more about Mexican culture by visiting
www.public.iastate.edu/~rjsalvad
and/or
mexico.web.com.mx/

CASE STUDY

Improving Performance Appraisal at Saginaw Regional Bank

Saginaw Regional Bank, located in Michigan, has been having difficulty with its performance evaluation program. The organization has a program by which all nonmanagerial employees are evaluated semiannually by their supervisors. Their evaluation form (shown in Case Exhibit 1) has been in use for ten years. It's scored as follows: excellent = 5, above average = 4, average = 3, below average = 2, and

Case Exhibit 1
Performance Evaluation Form for Saginaw Regional Bank

Performance Evaluation

SUPERVISORS: When you are asked to do so by the HR department, please complete a form for each of your employees. The supervisor who is responsible for 75 percent or more of an employee's work should complete this form for him or her. Please evaluate each facet of the employee's performance separately.

	1	2	3	4	5	Score
Quality of Work	Excellent	Above Average	Average	Below Average	Poor	
Quantity of Work	5 Poor	4 Below Average	3 Average	2 Above Average	1 Excellent	
Dependability	1 Excellent	2 Above Average	3 Average	4 Below Average	5 Poor	
Initiative at Work	5 Poor	4 Below Average	3 Average	2 Above Average	1 Excellent	
Cooperativeness	1 Excellent	2 Above Average	3 Average	4 Below Average	5 Poor	
Getting Along with Co-Workers	5 Poor	4 Below Average	3 Average	2 Above Average	1 Excellent	
					Total	

Supervisor's Signature: _____

Employee Name: _____

Employee Number: _____

poor = 1. The scores for each question are entered in the right-hand column and totaled for an overall evaluation score.

The procedure used has been as follows: each supervisor rates each employee on June 1 and February 1. The supervisor discusses the rating with the employee, then sends it to the HR department. Each rating is placed in the employee's HR file. If promotions come up, the cumulative ratings are considered at that time. The ratings are also supposed to be used when raises are given.

The system was designed by the HR manager who retired two years ago, Mary Bensko. She was replaced by Lillian Meyer, who graduated fifteen years ago with a degree in business from the University of Michigan. Since then, she's had a variety of work experiences, mostly in the automobile industry, and she has done HR work for about five years.

Lillian has been reviewing the evaluation system. Employees have a mixture of indifferent and negative feelings about it. An informal survey has shown that about half of the supervisors fill out the forms, give about three minutes to each form, and send them to HR without discussing them with the employees. The rest spend more time completing the forms but communicate the results only briefly and superficially with their employees.

Lillian has found out that the forms are rarely retrieved for promotion or pay-raise analyses. Because of this, most supervisors feel the evaluation program is a useless ritual. Lillian had seen performance evaluation in her previous employment as a much more useful experience; it included giving positive feedback to employees, improving future employee performance, developing employee capabilities, and providing data for promotion and compensation. Lillian hasn't had much experience designing performance management systems, so she's seeking your advice on what to do.

QUESTIONS

1. Write a report summarizing your evaluation of the strengths and weaknesses of the present performance management system.

2. Recommend some specific improvements or data-gathering activities to Meyer that would help her develop a better system.

3. Since Meyer does not have much experience in this area, she may need to educate herself about the basic principles for effective appraisal and feedback. What's the best way for her to quickly develop more competency in this area?

CASE STUDY

So You Want to Be a Manager?

Wally Reibstein was beginning to get the hang of his job, having survived a grueling six months as a newly appointed division engineering manager for a large aerospace firm located on the West Coast. Wally graduated with a degree in engineering from Rensselaer Polytechnic Institute in the early 1990s. He worked first for an industrial fan manufacturer located in the Midwest, the closest job he could find related to his aeronautical engineering training. When his wife decided to pursue an advanced degree in economics at a prestigious West Coast university, Wally found employment with his current employer, and they moved.

During the first five years, Wally demonstrated considerable skill in working with others and suc-

cessfully completed three different projects on time. One year ago, he was promoted to project engineering manager. Within six months, his immediate boss, a division head, was selected for promotion and recommended Wally to fill his position. Because of his past successes, he got the job, and as division manager he is in charge of a staff of over 50 professional and technical personnel. Five of these professionals are designated as project engineers responsible for specific contracts. The remaining staff of engineers and technicians are about equally distributed over five projects.

Wally has a challenging week ahead of him. He has decided that this is the week for the "rubber to meet the road" in his performance as a division manager. He has scheduled two performance appraisal interviews that promise to challenge his human relations skills. The first review is scheduled on Tuesday with Jerry Masters, a 52-year-old project engineering manager with a Ph.D. in electrical engineering and two masters degrees in computer science and business administration. In Wally's estimation, Jerry is a degree collector and a poor manager. Jerry's project has fallen far behind schedule and is headed for disaster. After reviewing Jerry's past performance ratings, which Wally pulled off the company's intranet, Wally has decided that Jerry must be reassigned. Jerry's past reviews indicate that he seldom met stated objectives despite repeated verbal counseling. Wally's former boss confided that he would have reassigned Jerry himself, but his head count was frozen and he had no one readily available to replace him. Wally has no such constraints. His overhead budget has been increased 10 percent as a result of three consecutive successful quarters of billings for his division. He has also recently interviewed a 45-year-old engineer who, in his judgment, possesses all the qualities needed to succeed where Jerry is failing.

Wally agrees with his former boss's counsel that Jerry is a valued citizen but terribly mismatched in his job; he simply can't manage a project. Tuesday morning arrives, and Wally decides to level with Jerry and tell him that he isn't working out and that he will be reassigned to another project. When Wally informs Jerry of his reassignment, he reacts by launching into a protracted emotional outburst accusing Wally of violating the trust he (Jerry) had placed in him to support his efforts. Jerry reminds Wally of his twelve years of service and the considerable influence he wields. Storming out, Jerry informs Wally that he intends to write a letter to the division president detailing the shoddy treatment he has received. Great, thought Wally, just what he needs to make an impression on the top brass.

QUESTIONS

1. Is Jerry justified in his emotional outburst?
2. How should Wally have told Jerry about the reassignment?
3. Where did Wally go wrong?
4. What would you have done if you were in Jerry's shoes?

ENDNOTES

[1] J. F. Welch, "A Master Class in Radical Change," *Fortune* (December 13, 1993): 83.

[2] G. Imperato, "How to Give Good Feedback," *Fast Company* (September 1998): 144–156.

[3] R. D. Arvey and K. R. Murphy, "Performance Evaluation in Work Settings," *Annual Review of Psychology* 49 (1998): 141–168; C. G. Banks and K. E. May, "Performance Management: The Real Glue in Organizations," *Evolving Practices in Human Resource Management*, A. I. Kraut and A. K. Korman, eds. (San Francisco: Jossey-Bass, 1999): 118–145.

[4] Based on J. N. Cleveland, K. R. Murphy, and R. E. Williams, "Multiple Uses of Performance Appraisal: Prevalence and Correlates," *Journal of Applied Psychology* 74 (1989): 130–135.

[5] Based on J. N. Cleveland, K. R. Murphy and R. E. Williams, "Multiple Uses of Performance Appraisal: Prevalence and Correlates," *Journal of Applied Psychology* 74 (1989): 130–135.

[6] R. Steers, Y. K. Shin, and G. Ungson, *The Chaebol: Korea's New Industrial Might* (Reading, PA: Harper & Row, 1990); see also, S. Faison, "China Pins Economic Hopes On An Obsolete Asian Model," *New York Times* (February 20, 1998): A1, D3; D. D. Davis, "International Performance Measurement and Management," *Performance Appraisal: State of the Art in Practice*, J. W. Smither, ed. (San Francisco: Jossey-Bass, 1998): 95–131.

[7] M. Rozek, "Can You Spot a Peak Performer?" *Personnel Journal* (June 1991): 77–78.

[8] P. Sellers, "Pepsi Opens a Second Front," *Fortune* (August 8, 1994): 71–76; J. Fulkerson and R. S. Schuler, "Managing Worldwide Diversity at Pepsi-Cola International," *Diversity in the Workplace: Human Resources Initiatives*, S. E. Jackson, ed. (New York: Guilford Publications, 1992); also see J. R. Fulkerson and M. F. Tucker, "Diversity: Lessons from Global Human Resource Practices," *Evolving Practices in Human Resource Management*, A. I. Kraut and A. K. Korman, eds. (San Francisco: Jossey-Boss, 1999): 249–271.

[9] J. September, "Mrs. Fields' Secret Weapon," *Personnel Journal* (September 1991): 56–58; A. Prendergast, "Learning to Let Go," *Working Woman* (January 1992): 42–45.

[10] R. D. Pritchard, *Measuring and Improving Organizational Productivity: A Practical Guide* (New York: Praeger, 1990); R. D. Pritchard et al., "The Evaluation of an Integrated Approach to Measuring Organizational Productivity," *Personnel Psychology* 42 (1989): 69–115; J. Hogan and

R. Hogan, "How to Measure Employee Reliability," *Journal of Applied Psychology* 47 (2) (1989): 273–279; J. A. Weekley and J. A. Gier, "Ceilings in the Reliability and Validity of Performance Ratings: The Case of Expert Raters," *Academy of Management Journal* 32 (1989): 213–222.

11 H. Lancaster, "Your Year-End Review Doesn't Have to Be Quite that Horrible," *The Wall Street Journal* (December 23, 1997): B2; R. C. Mayer and J. H. Davis, "The Effect of the Performance Appraisal System on Trust for Management: A Field Quasi-Experiment," *Journal of Applied Psychology* 84 (1999): 123–136; M. S. Taylor, S. S. Masterson, M. K. Renard, and K. B. Tracy, "Managers' Reactions to Procedurally Just Performance Management Systems," *Academy of Management Journal* 41 (1998): 568–579.

12 P. M. Podsakoff, M. Ahearne, and S. B. MacKenzie, "Organizational Citizenship Behavior and the Quantity and Quality of Work Group Performance," *Journal of Applied Psychology* 82 (1997): 262–270; T. D. Allen and M. C. Rush, "The Effects of Organizational Citizenship Behavior on Performance Judgments: A Field Study and a Laboratory Experiment," *Journal of Applied Psychology* 83 (1998): 247–260; S. B. MacKenzie, P. M. Podsakoff, and R. Fetter, "Organizational Citizenship Behavior and Objective Productivity as Determinants of Managerial Evaluations of Salesperson's Performance," *Organizational Behavior and Human Decision Processes* 50 (1991): 123–150; T. McDonald, "The Effect of Dimension Content on Observation and Ratings of Job Performance," *Organizational Behavior and Human Decision Processes* 48 (1991): 252–271; D. W. Organ, *Organizational Citizenship Behavior: The Good Soldier Syndrome* (Lexington, MA: Heath, 1988); D. W. Organ, "The Motivational Basis of Organizational Citizenship Behavior," *Research in Organizational Behavior* 12 (1990): 43–72.

13 W. C. Borman and S. J. Motowidlo, "Expanding the Criterion Domain to Include Elements of Contextual Performance," *Personnel Selection in Organizations,* N. Schmitt et al., eds. (San Francisco: Jossey-Bass, 1993): 71–99; J. M. Conway, "Distinguishing Contextual Performance from Task Performance for Managerial Jobs," *Journal of Applied Psychology* 84 (1999): 3–13.

14 H. S. Field and W. H. Holley, "The Relationship of Performance Appraisal System Characteristics to Verdicts in Selected Employment Discrimination Cases," *Academy of Management Journal* (1982): 392–406.

15 J. Sargent, "Performance Appraisal 'American Style': Where It Came from and Its Possibilities Overseas" (working paper, University of Washington, September 1991); A. Nimgade, "American Management as Viewed by International Professionals," *Business Horizons* (November–December 1989): 98–105.

16 J. P. Campbell et al., "A Theory of Performance," *Personnel Selection in Organizations,* Schmitt et al., eds., 35–70.

17 S. Gruner, "Feedback from Everyone," *Inc.* (February 1997): 102–103; "Teams Introduce 360-degree Feedback for Employees After a Corporate Culture Change at Porsche Cars," *Human Resource Executive* (September 1997): C10; "Despite Hitches, Multisource Feedback Moves Ahead," *Bulletin to Management* 47 (January 18, 1996): 17.

18 Note, however, that research on managers suggests that subordinates and peers often agree in the evaluations. See T. J. Maurer, N. S. Raju, and W. C. Collins, "Peer and Subordinate Performance Appraisal Measurement Equivalence," *Journal of Applied Psychology* 83 (1998): 693–702.

19 C. Viswesvaran, D. S. Ones, and F. L. Schmidt, "Comparative Analysis of the Reliability of Job Performance Ratings," *Journal of Applied Psychology* 81 (1996): 557–574.

20 H. J. Bernardin and J. Abbot, "Predicting (and Preventing) Differences between Self and Supervisory Appraisals," *Personnel Administrator* (June 1985): 151–157; W. C. Borman et al., "Models of Supervisory Job Performance Ratings," *Journal of Applied Psychology* 76 (1991): 863–872.

21 S. J. Ashford, "Self-Assessments in Organizations: A Literature Review and Integrative Model," *Research in Organizational Behavior* 11 (1989): 133–374; T. H. Shore, L. M. Shore, and G. C. Thornton III, "Construct Validity of Self- and Peer Evaluations of Performance Dimensions in an Assessment Center," *Journal of Applied Psychology* 77 (1992): 42–54; J. L. Farh, G. H. Dobbins, and B. S. Cheng, "Cultural Relativity in Action: A Comparison of Self-Ratings Made by Chinese and U.S. Workers," *Personnel Psychology* 44 (1991): 129–147.

22 B. D. Cawley, L. M. Keeping, and P. E. Levy, "Participation in the Performance Appraisal Process and Employee Relations: A Meta-Analytic Review of Field Investigations," *Journal of Applied Psychology* 83 (1998): 615–633; M. A. Korsgaard, L. Roberson, and R. D. Rymph, "What Motivates Fairness? The Role of Subordinate Asssertive Behavior on Managers' Interactional Fairness," *Journal of Applied Psychology* 83 (1998): 731–744.

23 A. H. Church, "Managerial Self-Awareness in High-Performing Individuals in Organizations," *Journal of Applied Psychology* 82 (1997): 281–292; K. M. Nowack, "Congruence Between Self-Other Ratings and Assessment Center Performance," *Journal of Social Behavior and Personality* 12 (1997): 145–166; M. A. Korsgaard, L. Roberson, and R. D. Rymph, "What Motivates Fairness? The Role of Subordinate Assertive Behavior on Managers' Interactional Fairness," *Journal of Applied Psychology* 83 (1998): 731–744.

24 L. E. Atwater, C. Ostroff, F. J. Yammarino, and J. W. Fleenor, "Self-Other Agreement: Does It Really Matter?" *Personnel Psychology* 51 (1998): 577–598; J. L. Farh and J. Werbel, "Effects of Purpose of the Appraisal and Expectation of Validation on Self Appraisal Leniency," *Journal of Applied Psychology* 71 (1986): 527–529; R. P. Steel and N. K. Ovalle, "Self Appraisal Based on Supervisory Feedback," *Personnel Psychology* 37 (1984): 667–685.

25 J. L. Farh, G. H. Dobbins, and C. S. Cheng, "Cultural Relativity in Action: A Comparison of Self-Ratings made by Chinese and U.S. Workers," *Personnel Psychology* 44 (1991): 129–147.

26 Shore, Shore, and Thornton, "Construct Validity of Self- and Peer Evaluations"; R. Saavedra and S. K. Kwun, "Peer Evaluation in Self-Managing Work Groups," *Journal of Applied Psychology* 78 (1993): 450–462.

27 T. J. Maurer, N. S. Raju, and W. C. Collins, "Peer and Subordinate Performance Appraisal Measurement Equivalence," *Journal of Applied Psychology* 83 (1998): 693–702.

28 "Upward Appraisals Rate Highly," *Bulletin to Management* (March 31, 1994): 104.

29 D. Antonioni, "The Effects of Feedback Accountability on Upward Appraisal Ratings," *Personnel Psychology* 47 (1994): 349–360.

30 D. A. Waldman and L. E. Atwater, *The Power of 360 Feedback: How To Leverage Performance Evaluations For Top Productivity* (Houston, TX: Gulf Publishing Co., 1998); A. H. Church and D. W. Bracken, eds., *360-Degree Feedback Systems* (Thousand Oaks, CA: Sage Publications, Special Issue of *Group & Organization Management,* June 1997); R. Lepsinger and A. D. Lucia, *The Art and Science of 360° Feedback* (San Francisco: Pfeiffer, 1997).

31 M. R. Edwards and A. J. Ewen, *Providing 360-Degree Feedback: An Approach to Enhancing Individual and Organizational Performance* (Scottsdale, AZ: American Compensation Association, 1996).

32 For detailed practical advice, see A. T. Dalessio, "Using Multisource Feedback for Employee Development and Personnel Decisions," *Performance Appraisal: State of the Art in Practice,* J. W. Smither, ed. (San Francisco: Jossey-Bass, 1998): 278–330.

33 W. F. Cascio and H. J. Bernardin, "Implications of Performance Appraisal Litigation for Personnel Decisions," *Personnel Psychology* 34 (1981): 211–226.

34 In some forms of BARS, the anchors are stated as expected behaviors (e.g., "Could be expected to develop loan documentation accurately"). When expected behaviors are included, the BARS is more appropriately labeled a BES—Behavioral Expectation Scale. For further discussion, see F. J. Landy and J. L. Farh, "Performance Rating," *Psychological Bulletin* (January 1980): 72–107; K. R. Murphy and J. I. Constans, "Behavioral Anchors as a Source of Bias in Rating," *Journal of Applied Psychology* (November 1987): 573; S. Zedeck, "Behavioral Based Performance Appraisals," *Aging and Work* 4 (1981): 89–100.

35 Adapted from V. L. Huber, *Validation Study for Electronics Maintenance Technical Positions* (Washington, DC: Human Resource Development Institute, AFL-CIO, 1991).

36 To learn more about how goals setting improves performance, see E. A. Locke and G. P. Latham, *A Theory of Goal Setting and Task Performance* (Englewood Cliffs, NJ: Prentice-Hall, 1990); P. C. Earley, T. Connolly, and G. Ekegren, "Goals, Strategy Development and Task Performance: Some Limits on the Efficacy of Goal Setting," *Journal of Applied Psychology* 74 (1989): 24–33; R. E. Wood and E. A. Locke, "Goal Setting and Strategy Effects on Complex Tasks," *Research in Organizational Behavior* 12 (1990): 73–109; C. E. Shalley, "Effects of Productivity Goals, Creativity Goals, and Personal Discretion on Individual Creativity," *Journal of Applied Psychology* 76 (1991): 179–185; T. R. Mitchell and W. S. Silver, "Individual and Group Goals When Workers Are Interdependent: Effects on Task Strategies and Performance," *Journal of Applied Psychology* 75 (1990): 185–193; J. M. Phillips and S. M.

Gully, "Role of Goal-Orientation, Ability, Need for Achievement, and Locus of Control in the Self-Efficacy and Goal-Setting Process," *Journal of Applied Psychology* 5 (1997): 792–802.

37 For a comprehensive review, see R. Rodgers and J. E. Hunter, "Impact of Management by Objectives on Organizational Productivity," *Journal of Applied Psychology* 76 (1991): 322–336.

38 E. Matson. "The Discipline of High Tech Leaders," *Fast Company* (April/May 1997): 34–36.

39 A. S. DeNisi and K. Williams, "Cognitive Approaches to Performance Appraisal," *Research in Personnel and Human Resource Management,* G. R. Ferris and K. M. Rowland, eds. (Greenwich, CT: JAI Press, 1988): 109–156; A. S. DeNisi, T. P. Cafferty, and B. M. Meglino, "A Cognitive View of the Appraisal Process: A Model and Research Propositions," *Organizational Behavior and Human Performance* 33 (1984): 360–396.

40 J. N. Cleveland and K. R. Murphy, "Analyzing Performance Appraisal as Goal-Directed Behavior," *Research in Personnel and Human Resource Management* 10 (1992): 121–185; T. A. Judge and G. R. Ferris, "Social Context of Performance Evaluation Decisions," *Academy of Management Journal* 36 (1993): 80–105.

41 DeNisi and Williams, "Cognitive Approaches to Performance Appraisal;" D. R. Ilgen and J. M. Feldman, "Performance Appraisal: A Process Focus," *Research in Organizational Behavior,* B. Staw and L. Cummings, eds. (Greenwich, CT: JAI Press, 1983): 141–197.

42 A. L. Solomonson and C. E. Lance, "Examination of the Relationship Between True Halo and Halo Error in Performance Ratings," *Journal of Applied Psychology* 82 (1997): 665–674; M. Foschi, "Double Standards in the Evaluation of Men and Women," *Social Psychology Quarterly* 59 (1996): 237–254; S. J. Wayne and R. C. Liden, "Effects of Impression Management on Performance Ratings: A Longitudinal Study," *Academy of Management Journal* 38 (1995): 232–260; K. R. Murphy, R. A. Jako, and R. L. Anhalt, "Nature and Consequences of Halo Error: A Critical Analysis," *Journal of Applied Psychology* 78 (1993): 218–225; C. E. Lance, J. A. LaPointe, and A. M. Stewart, "A Test of the Context Dependency of Three Causal Models of Halo Rater Error," *Journal of Applied Psychology* 79 (1994): 332–340; W. K. Balzer and L. M. Sulsky, "Halo and Performance Appraisal Research: A Critical Examination," *Journal of Applied Psychology* 77 (1992): 975–985; I. M. Jawahar and C. R. Williams, "Where All The Children Are Above Average: The Performance Appraisal Purpose Effect," *Personnel Psychology* 50 (1997): 905–926; J. S. Kane, H. J. Bernardin, P. Villanova, and J. Peyrefitte, "Stability of Rater Leniency: Three Studies," *Academy of Management Journal* 38 (1995): 1036–1051.

43 R. L. Dipboye, "Some Neglected Variables in Research on Discrimination in Appraisals," *Academy of Management Review* (January 1985): 118–125; B. R. Nathan and R. A. Alexander, "The Role of Inferential Accuracy in Performance Rating," *Academy of Management Review* (January 1985): 109–117.

44 T. J. Maurer, J. K. Palmer, and D. K. Ashe, "Diaries, Checklists, Evaluations, and Contrast Effects in

Measurement of Behavior," *Journal of Applied Psychology* 78 (1993): 226–231.

45 N. M. A. Hauenstein, "Training Raters to Increase Accuracy of Appraisals and the Usefulness of Feedback," *Performance Appraisal: State of the Art in Practice*, J. W. Smither, ed. (San Francisco: Jossey-Bass, 1998): 404–442.

46 D. T. Stamoulis and N. M. A. Hauenstein, "Rater Training and Rating Accuracy: Training for Dimensional Accuracy versus Training for Ratee Differentiation," *Journal of Applied Psychology* 78 (1993): 994–1003; R. M. McIntyre, D. E. Smith, and C. E. Hassett, "Accuracy of Performance Ratings As Affected by Rater Training and Perceived Purpose of Rating," *Journal of Applied Psychology* (February 1984): 147–156; D. V. Day and L. M. Sulsky, "Effects of Frame-of-Reference Training and Information Configuration on Memory Organization and Rating Accuracy," *Journal of Applied Psychology* 80 (1995): 158–167; L. M. Sulsky and D. V. Day, "Frame-of-Reference Training and Cognitive Categorization: An Empirical Investigation of Rater Memory Issues," *Journal of Applied Psychology* 77 (1992): 501–510. H. J. Bernardin and M. R. Buckley, "Strategies in Rater Training," *Academy of Management Review* 6 (1981): 205–212.

47 K. R. Murphy and J. Cleveland, *Understanding Performance Appraisal: Social, Organizational, and Goal-Based Perspectives* (Thousand Oaks, CA: Sage Publications, 1995); C. G. Banks and K. R. Murphy, "Toward Narrowing the Research-Practice Gap in Performance Appraisal," *Personnel Psychology* 38 (1985): 335–345.

48 M. K. Mount, M. R. Sytsma, J. Fisher Hazucha, and K. E. Holt, "Rater–Ratee Race Effects in Developmental Performance Ratings of Managers," *Personnel Psychology* 50 (1997): 51; G. J. Greguras and C. Robie, "A New Look at Within-Source Interrater Reliability of 360-Degree Feedback Ratings," *Journal of Applied Psychology* 83 (1998): 960–968; T. J. Maurer, N. S. Raju, and W. C. Collins, "Peer and Subordinate Performance Appraisal Measurement Equivalence," *Journal of Applied Psychology* 83 (1998): 693–702.

49 K. R. Murphy, "Difficulties in the Statistical Control of Halo," *Journal of Applied Psychology* 67 (1982): 161–164; L. Hirshhord, *Meaning in the New Team Environment* (Reading, MA: Addison-Wesley, 1991); Murphy and Cleveland, *Understanding Performance Appraisal*.

50 R. F. Martell and M. R. Borg, "A Comparison of the Behavioral Rating Accuracy of Groups and Individuals," *Journal of Applied Psychology* 78 (1993): 43–50.

51 M. London, *Job Feedback: Giving, Seeking, and Using Feedback for Performance Improvement* (Mahwah, NJ: Lawrence Erlbaum Associates, 1997).

52 L. Atwater, P. Roush, and A. Fischthal, "The Influence of Upward Feedback on Self- and Follower Ratings of Leadership," *Personnel Psychology* 48 (1995): 35–59.

53 M. Beer, "Performance Appraisal: Dilemmas and Possibilities," *Organizational Dynamics* (Winter 1981): 26; A. Zander, "Research on Self-Esteem, Feedback and Threats to Self-Esteem," *Performance Appraisals: Effects on Employees and Their Performance*, A. Zander, ed. (New York: Foundation for Research in Human Behavior, 1963).

54 M. Ross and G. J. O. Fletcher, "Attribution and Social Perception," *Handbook of Social Psychology,* 3rd ed., vol. II, G. Lindzey and E. Aronson, eds. (New York: Random House, 1985): 73–122.

55 D. R. Ilgen, C. D. Fisher, and M. S. Taylor, "Consequences of Individual Feedback on Behavior in Organizations," *Journal of Applied Psychology* 64 (1979): 349–371; J. L. Pearce and L. W. Porter, "Employee Responses to Formal Performance Appraisal Feedback," *Journal of Applied Psychology* (May 1986): 211.

56 K. Kirkland and S. Manoogian, *Ongoing Feedback: How to Get It, How to Use It* (Greensboro, NC: Center for Creative Leadership, 1998); V. U. Druskat and S. B. Wolff, "Effects and Timing of Developmental Peer Appraisals in Self-Managing Work Groups," *Journal of Applied Psychology* 84 (1999): 58–74.

57 M. M. Kennedy, "So How'm I Doing?" *Across the Board* (June 1997): 53–54.

58 R. F. Mager and P. Pipe, *Analyzing Performance Problems, or 'You Really Oughta Wanna'* (Belmont, CA: Fearon Pittman, 1970).

59 M. J. Martinko and W. L. Garner, "Learned Helplessness: An Alternative Explanation for Performance Deficits," *Academy of Management Review* (1982): 195–204; M. E. Kanfer and F. H. Kanfer, "The Role of Goal Acceptance on Goal Setting and Task Performance," *Academy of Management Review* (1983): 454–563; S. E. Jackson and R. S. Schuler, "A Meta-Analysis and Conceptual Critique of Research on Role Ambiguity and Role Conflict in Work Settings," *Organizational Behavior and Human Decision Processes* 36 (1985): 16–78; J. L. Pearce and L. W. Porter, "Employee Responses to Formal Performance Appraisal Feedback," *Journal of Applied Psychology* (1986): 211; H. H. Kelly, "Attribution in Social Interaction," *Attribution: Perceiving the Causes of Behavior.* E. Jones et al., eds. (Morristown, NJ: General Learning Press, 1972).

60 R. F. Mager and P. Pipe, *Analyzing Performance Problems, or 'You Really Oughta Wanna'*.

61 V. L. Huber, P. Podsakoff, and W. Todor, "An Investigation of Biasing Factors in the Attributions of Subordinates and Their Supervisors," *Journal of Business Research* 4 (1986): 83–97.

62 D. Harrington-Mackin, *The Team Building Tool Kit: Tips, Tactics, and Rules for Effective Workplace Teams* (New York: AMACOM, 1994); K. A. Guion, "Performance Management for Evolving Self-Directed Work Teams," *ACA Journal* (Winter 1995): 67–75.

63 A. Bandura, *Principles of Behavior Modification* (New York: Holt, Rinehart & Winston, 1969); R. Beatty and C. Schneier, "A Case for Positive Reinforcement," *Business Horizons* 2 (April 1975): 57–66.

64 C. Frayne and G. P. Latham, "The Application of Social Learning Theory to Employee Self-Management of Attendance," *Journal of Applied Psychology* 72 (1987): 387–392; F. H. Kanfer, "Self-Management Methods," *Helping People Change: A Textbook of Methods*, P. Karoly and A. Goldstein, eds. (New York: Pergamon Press, 1980), 334–389; P. Karoly and F. H. Kanfer, *Self-Management and*

Behavior Change: From Theory to Practice (New York: Pergamon Press, 1986).

[65] "Policy Guide: 'Positive Discipline' Replaces Punishment," *Bulletin to Management* (April 27, 1995): 136; L. K. Trevino, "The Social Effects of Punishment in Organizations: A Justice Perspective," *Academy of Management Review* 17 (1992): 647–676; R. Bennett and L. L. Cummings, "The Effects of Schedule and Intensity of Aversive Outcomes on Performance: A Multitheoretical Perspective," *Human Performance* 4 (1991): 155–169; J. M. Beyer and H. M. Trice, "A Field Study of the Use and Perceived Effects of Discipline in Controlling Work Performance," *Academy of Management Journal* 27 (1984): 743–764; R. D. Arvey, G. A. Davis, and S. M. Nelson, "Use of Discipline in an Organization: A Field Study," *Journal of Applied Psychology* 69 (1984): 448–460; R. D. Arvey and A. P. Jones, "The Use of Discipline in Organizational Settings: A Framework for Future Research," *Research in Organizational Behavior* 7 (1985): 367–408; M. E. Schnake, "Vicarious Punishment in a Work Setting," *Journal of Applied Psychology* 71 (1986): 343–345.

[66] "Alcohol Misuse Prevention Programs: Department of Transportation Final Rules," *Bulletin to Management* (March 24, 1994): 1–7.

[67] "Productivity and Performance EAP-Improved," *Bulletin to Management* (July 23, 1987): 1.

[68] B. P. Sunoo, "This Employee May Be Loafing, Can You Tell? Should You Tell?" *Personnel Journal* (December 1996): 54–62; "Jury Awards Manager Accused of Theft $25 Million," *Bulletin to Management* (March 27, 1997): 97; P. Carbonara, "Fire Me. I Dare You!" *Inc.* (March 1997): 58–64.

[69] S. W. Gilliland and J. C. Langdon, "Creating Performance Management Systems that Promote Perceptions of Fairness," *Performance Appraisal: State of the Art in Practice,* J. W. Smither, ed. (1998): 209–243; M. A. Korsgaard and L. Roberson, "Procedural Justice in Performance Evaluation: The Role of Instrumental and Non-Instrumental Voice in Performance Appraisal Discussions," *Journal of Management* 21 (1995): 657–669; M. S. Taylor, K. B. Tracy, M. K. Renard, and S. J. Carroll, "Due Process in Performance Appraisal: A Quasi-Experiment in Procedural Justice," *Administrative Science Quarterly* 40 (1995): 495–523.

[70] S. B. Malos, "Current Legal Issues in Performance Appraisal," *Performance Appraisal: State of the Art in Practice,* J. W. Smither, ed. (San Francisco: Jossey-Bass, 1998): 49–94; H. J. Bernardin and W. F. Cascio, "Performance Appraisal and the Law," *Readings in Personnel and Human Resource Management,* 3d ed., R. S. Schuler, S. A. Youngblood, and V. L. Huber, eds. (St. Paul: West Publishing Co., 1988): 239.

[71] M. S. Taylor, M. K. Renard, and K. B. Tracy, "Managers' Reactions to Procedurally Just Performance Management Systems," *Academy of Management Journal* 41 (1998): 565–579.

PERFORMANCE MANAGEMENT: REWARDING EMPLOYEES' CONTRIBUTIONS

"Often, it seems that the best managerial intentions wash away into flat, indistinct merit increases for performers who meet expectations and those who exceed them."

Steve Scholl
Compensation Director
Allstate Insurance Company[1]

Chapter Outline

Managing Through Partnership

at Lincoln Electric

When Donald Hastings became president of Lincoln Electric Co., he brought with him a passion for total quality management. His goal was to build quality into the production process rather than test it at the end of the production line. Donald Hastings' efforts have paid off: today, employees assume responsibility for quality. With employee-caused errors down by 50 percent, fewer inspectors are used. This saves the company and customers both time and money. Because quality is such an important part of Lincoln's strategy, employees are rewarded for their efforts to maximize quality. Quality is one of the four criteria included in the performance rating system.

Output is another criterion in the performance rating system. To keep costs low, Lincoln Electric needs highly productive workers, and they have them! Lincoln's productivity level is two to three times that of comparable organizations. High productivity benefits customers and employees alike. Customers like the lower prices, and employees like the profits the company is able to generate. Average employee compensation is $55,000. More unusual is how much variation there is in the pay received by production workers. Some earn only $40,000 while as many as 10 percent earn over $100,000. These differences in pay reflect the substantial differences in the productive contribution employees make. Much of the variation in pay reflects employees' decisions about how much overtime they put in. Business conditions have been good in recent years, and when business is good, Lincoln Electric counts on employees working overtime to keep up with demand. The company does everything possible to not bulk up with more employees as a means to meet demand. Why? Because the company also believes in employment security. Lincoln guarantees workers that they will have a job even during economic downturns. It does not cope with lean times by laying people off. In order for the company to keep its promise of employment security, however, it must also be able to count on workers to work harder and longer when demand for products is high. When business activity exceeds the number of workers, the incentive system encourages workers to work overtime.[2]

THE STRATEGIC IMPORTANCE OF PERFORMANCE-BASED PAY

As Chapter 11 explained, performance appraisal and feedback *direct* employees' attention. Performance incentives and rewards *motivate* employees to exert effort. Effective performance management systems do both. Performance-based pay—the topic of this chapter—recognizes that people working in the same job can differ greatly in terms of the value they contribute to the organization and seeks to provide employees with an incentive for maximizing the value they contribute.

The case of Lincoln Electric illustrates the importance of viewing performance-based pay as just one component of a total system of practices for managing human resources. Many observers of the company believe that Lincoln's performance-based pay system would be far less successful if the company didn't promise employment security. Furthermore, the system could be counter-productive if it didn't ensure that employees maintain high quality standards as they strive to push up their level of production. Thus, as you consider the uses of performance-based pay, remember that it takes several HR practices working together to achieve highly effective employee behavior.[3] Performance-based pay is a powerful cornerstone, but it alone can't hold up the entire organization.

Decisions about how to design pay systems should follow a careful weighing of all the possible consequences associated with alternative forms of pay. Three consequences of particular importance are those related to cost, employee satisfaction with the plan, and effects on performance. In recent years, consideration of all of these pay-related consequences has led to greater use of pay incentives. Dial, a consumer products company, is one company making this change in the way they manage performance. Beginning in the year 2000, their 1,400 nonunion staff members are no longer eligible for merit raises. Instead, they're eligible for an annual cash bonus. The size of the bonus will depend on the company's performance, as measured by net revenue growth, operating margin, and asset turnover.

Cost Considerations

Cost considerations have spurred many organizations to reevaluate the most widespread and familiar form of performance-based pay—the merit raise. Suppose Rhonda Brown, an x-ray technician at Community General Hospital, is earning $20.00/hour. At her annual performance review, her supervisor gives her an overall performance rating of 6 on a 7-point scale. Subsequently, she receives a 10 percent pay raise. The technician will now always be paid at the higher rate, regardless of her performance levels in the future. The next year, for whatever reason, the employee does not perform as well, or even adequately. Nevertheless, last year's salary increase is a permanent cost for the organization.

In order to deal with the problem of rising compensation costs that are unrelated to improvements in employee performance, many companies are replacing merit pay raises with other forms of performance-based pay. A key objective is to ensure that any increases in compensation costs are paid for by improvements in productivity or profitability. An extreme approach is to simply discontinue offering any guarantee of a pay increase—base pay increases aren't even indexed to keep pace with inflation. Over time, this causes the pay policy line to fall below the market. Lord Corporation in Cary, North Carolina took this approach. After years of generous merit increases, employees were paid well above the prevailing rates. So in 1993, Lord stopped giving merit increases to its 1,000 nonunion employees. To soften the blow of this wage freeze, the company offered annual bonuses of up to 10 percent. Cost considerations become more and more salient as more and more of the budget is spent on compensation. In service companies, compensation can account for up to 80 percent of the operating budget. Thus, banks, hospitals, and other labor-intensive service providers companies place high priority on controlling compensation costs and using compensation wisely.

Employee Satisfaction

Besides being economically unsound, merit increases can demotivate the best performing employees because an employee who has performed well previously may have a higher base pay rate than an employee who is currently performing well. Designing pay systems that satisfy the best performers is another objective that drives many organizations to experiment with new forms of performance-based pay. With traditional pay plans, the pay differences received by the best and worst performers within the same

Comment on new pay practices: "We are on the precipice of a very major change."

Sandra O'Neal
Principal
Towers Perrin

■□ *fast fact*

It invariably costs more to give bonuses out more frequently.

job category are often quite small. Many managers believe that this is demotivating for high performers.[4] In industries where labor is abundant, some organizations are willing to risk feelings of dissatisfaction among lower performing employees (who are paid less) in order to adequately reward and satisfy the better performers.

Not all organizations accept this logic, however. At PECO Energy Company, the satisfaction of *all* employees is considered important. PECO is a high wage payer, paying at the 75th percentile and above. The company was certified as a world class performer by the Nuclear Regulatory Commission. PECO wants to maintain its outstanding level of performance, and it also wants to maintain a union-free workplace. When PECO considered whether to follow the crowd and replace its traditional approach to performance-based pay, it considered how employees were likely to react. For PECO, cost considerations are less important than the safety and reliability of its operations. In this context, changing its pay system was viewed as very risky. If any employees disliked a new plan, their dissatisfaction could easily translate into lower service reliability and lower safety. Such dissatisfaction might also lead employees to consider unionization. Thus, until cost considerations became more pressing, PECO decided employee satisfaction with its pay system was the more important consideration to attend to.[5]

As discussed in Chapter 10, pay satisfaction is affected by many factors—including the degree of discrepancy between the compensation paid to top executives and that paid to other workers. Compensation plans that link pay to the performance of the total company have long been used for top-level managers. Under such plans, when a company performs well, managers often receive greater rewards than the rank-and-file employees, causing dissatisfaction among non-executives. Increasingly, upper-level managers have realized that giving all employees rewards based on the performance of the total organization is one way to ensure that everyone's standard of living goes up when the company prospers.

Motivating Strategic Behavior

Effective human resource management systems direct the attention and efforts of employees toward achieving strategic objectives. At PECO, everyone understands that the pay system as well as all other management practices must focus employees on maintaining the highest possible level of safety and reliability of service. An incentive pay system isn't needed to reinforce this point. But in many other organizations, performance-based pay is viewed as essential to communicating the strategic objectives of the firm and motivating employees toward achieving them. Dissatisfaction with the strategic usefulness of merit pay has led companies to experiment with other approaches to performance-based pay.[6] For example, at Corning Incorporated, a leader in creating a corporate culture that embraces diversity, executives receive an extra 10 percent if they meet their goals for diversity management.[7] New goals are set each year. Managers must achieve the new goals in order to re-earn the 10 percent of pay that's tied to this strategic objective.

Growing awareness that traditional pay plans often do a poor job of aligning behavior with the firm's strategic objectives is probably the most important reason that more and more companies have introduced incentive pay. If organizations are to achieve their strategic objectives, then pay needs to be linked to performance in such a way that it aligns the goals of individual employees with the goals of the organization. As described in the feature,

"The more the formula for payouts reads like the fine print in a contract, the more it seems as if management is trying to slip something by."

Don Barksdale
Communications Consultant
Knoxville, Tennessee

Managing Change: A New Pay Plan for Owens Corning, performance-based pay can be especially useful for organizations that are undergoing major strategic change.[8]

DESIGNING PERFORMANCE-BASED PAY SYSTEMS

Substantial research supports the conclusion that performance-based rewards can substantially improve productivity. For example, when a major retailer introduced an incentive plan into half its outlets, those outlets experienced increased sales, customer satisfaction, and profits. The positive effects of incentives were especially great for outlets experiencing intense

MANAGING CHANGE

A New Pay Plan for Owens Corning

Back in the early 1990s, Toledo-based Owens Corning was in a bit of trouble. Glen Hiner, the new CEO, walked into a company that had seen sales of their construction materials decline. Costly asbestos litigation had strained both cash flow and employee morale. As part of his turnaround strategy, Hiner created a new set of corporate goals, referred to as Vision 2000. The vision included achieving a $5 billion sales target and changing the culture to one that valued customer satisfaction, employee dignity, and shareholder value.

The HR group looked at the new business plan and decided they should reconsider their entire HR system. "We started with a very simple, systematic strategy that begins with the business results we want to produce. Then [we] used all of the human resource systems and processes as levers for change or drivers of the business strategy," explained Greg Thomson, senior vice president of HR. Naturally, the compensation system was included as a candidate for change. Rick Tober was the team leader in charge of redesigning compensation. "We looked at all the programs, threw them in the hopper, and asked ourselves how we could design an overall compensation plan that met our guiding principle," explained Tober. To cut fixed costs, the company made several changes in its benefits program. To counterbalance those changes, it added new ways for employees to share in the future successes of the company. For example, the company contributed less to the employees' long-term savings, and counterbalanced this change with the addition of a profit-sharing plan that linked payouts to individual performance. They reduced their total expenditures for benefits by offering a cafeteria-style plan, and counterbalanced this change by adding a broad-based stock option plan. They converted retirement benefits to a cash balance plan with a guaranteed annual interest rate, and counterbalanced this with stock bonuses tied to company performance.

So far, the new approach seems to be working. Whether it will succeed in the long run remains to be seen. The biggest challenge may be the complexity of the changes. Developing understanding and buy-in from the entire HR staff, all the line managers, and all employees is an enormous communication task. To get their message out, the HR staff created outlines of the key pay elements, prepared individualized charts for employees, held dozens of meetings, and even created a board game that teaches employees about the balance of risks and rewards built into the new system. According to one staff member, "They're starting to get it, but it takes time."

To learn more about Owens Corning, visit the company home page at
www.owenscorning.com

competition.[9] Numerous other studies have found similar results. However, research also shows that, under some conditions, performance-based rewards have no effects or even detrimental effects.[10] Results from these latter studies serve as ammunition for critics of performance-based pay.

Author Alfie Kohn has been a particularly vocal critic, stating that "any incentive or pay-for-performance system tends to make people less enthusiastic about their work and therefore less likely to approach it with a commitment to excellence."[11] Although well-publicized, Kohn's assertion about the effect of performance-based rewards is inconsistent with the findings of empirical research. While it's true that performance-based rewards do not always improve performance, the research indicates that effective rewards systems are caused by poor design and implementation; their failure isn't due to a widespread negative psychological effect of performance-based rewards.[12]

To be effective, performance-based pay systems must successfully deal with four major issues: specifying and measuring performance, specifying the level of aggregation for reward distribution, specifying the type of reward, specifying eligibility for rewards, and gaining employee acceptance.[13] Of course, decisions about each of these issues also must be sensitive to legal considerations.

Specifying and Measuring Performance

"If you can't measure it, you can't manage it, and if you can't do either, you sure as heck shouldn't pay for it."

Steven J. Berman
Managing Director
PricewaterhouseCoopers LLP

A valid and transparent performance measurement system is central to any system that links pay to performance. The practice of linking pay to performance can quickly highlight and exacerbate any flaws in the performance measurement system.

What Gets Measured Gets Rewarded. A company may tell employees that speed, efficiency, quality, and customer satisfaction warrant equal attention, and they may really mean it. But if speed and efficiency are easier to measure than quality and customer satisfaction, the incentives may weight them more heavily, leading employees to give them priority when situations force a trade-off. If the performance measurement system focuses on one component of performance and incentives are given for a different component, employees will be confused and managers will wonder why the incentives do not work. In recent years, the use of the balanced scorecard approach to measuring organizational performance has put the spotlight on precisely this issue. When it comes to paying for performance, many companies have relied heavily on financial performance measures while ignoring other performance indicators that reflect the perspectives of employees, customers, and other strategic partners. The result is a mismatch between the incentive system and the company's full understanding of what it takes to be effective in the long run.[14]

Measuring Results Versus Measuring Behaviors. E. I. DuPont de Nemours and Co. planned to improve the relationship between pay and performance on tasks of strategic importance when the Fibers Department initiated a major change in its pay system. The department shifted from straight hourly- or salary-based pay to an incentive plan that tied employees' compensation to their unit's overall performance. Employees were viewed as stakeholders. Managers thought that incentive pay would reinforce this stakeholder philosophy and build a greater sense of teamwork. The compensation plan, which took a thirteen-member task force two years to design, tied an individual's pay to the department's profits and losses. One of the 20,000 employees covered by the plan described it as a shift from being paid for "coming to work" to being paid for how well a business unit succeeds. The plan sounded good in theory, but it was soon scrapped. To cope with a downturn in business, the company had to reduce the workforce by 25 percent. Those who remained worked harder than ever to turn things around. Despite their efforts, however, employees fell short of their profit goal. Rather than withhold the 6 percent pay-for-performance bonus it had designed, DuPont pulled the plug on the plan to avoid demoralizing its workforce. As DuPont's experience illustrates, the strategic value of incentive-pay depends on whether the pay plan supports the behaviors that are most important to the company's success. During an economic recession, Dupont needed employees who would put in their best efforts, even if that effort didn't immediately translate into increased profitability. An incentive plan that defined the strategic objectives of smaller work groups and tied pay to outcomes that workers really could control may have worked more effectively for DuPont.

TRW ensures that employees can control the results on which their performance incentives depend by using behavior-based goals rather than results-based goals. In their Cleveland-based automotive plant, project teams start-up and disband as project needs come and go. To support team efforts, team members establish specific behavioral goals that are tightly related to the team goals. Incentives ranging in size from 10 to 25 percent of their base pay are tied to the team-driven individual goals.[15]

Short-Term Versus Long-Term Perspective.   As more and more companies consider paying for knowledge or skill acquisition, they come face-to-face with the question of how much value they should place on performance in the current job versus behaviors that prepare employees for future jobs. Motorola discovered this conflict when it introduced pay for developing reading and math skills. Team members resented it when their colleagues disappeared to school for weeks, at full pay, leaving the teams weaker. The workers complained about the mixed message they were getting and the conflict between self-development and teamwork. They went to the compensation director and said, "Would you guys get a grip? Make up your minds what you really want from us."[16]

Finding the appropriate balance between rewarding for current performance versus rewarding for long-term performance is a difficult balancing act. Many critics of performance-based incentive plans point to this as a common problem. Executive incentives that focus attention on short-term movements in the company's stock price, for example, may lead managers to make decisions that protect the stock price in the short-term but with negative longer-term consequences. In sales jobs, balancing short-term and long-term performance objectives also poses a challenge. Traditional commissions focus the attention of a sales staff on the short-term objective of selling goods and services, and do nothing to ensure the customer is satisfied with the purchase. Yet building customer loyalty and repeat business are important strategic objectives for most organizations. Thus, incentives for sales organizations increasingly include measures of customer satisfaction.[17]

Specifying the Method for Linking Pay to Performance

As shown in Exhibit 12.1, three basic approaches to linking pay to performance are available. These options differ in the level of guaranteed base pay,

"If organizations pay people based on what they bring to the work place (e.g., knowledge, skills, and the capabilities to exhibit specific behaviors), they run the risk of rewarding potential even when no return on their investment is realized."

Robert J. Green
Consulting Principal
James & Scott Associates

Exhibit 12.1

Total Compensation Under Merit, Incentive, and Earnings-at-Risk Pay Plans

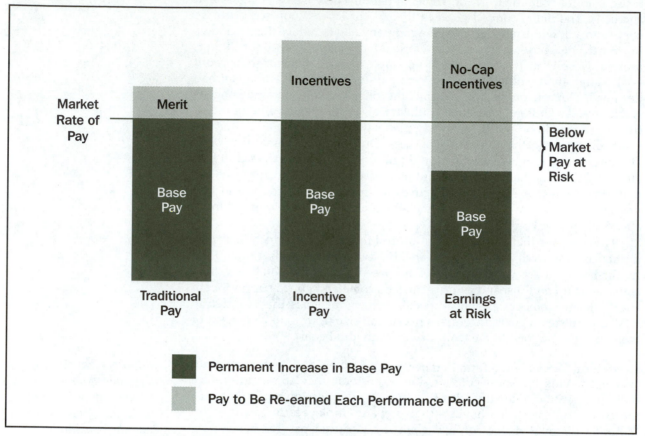

the relationship of base pay to the market, the amount of performance-based pay, the method used to allocate performance-based pay, the permanence of performance-based pay, and the portion of total pay that's at risk.

Merit Pay Plans. With merit pay plans, base pay (the entitlement to be received regardless of performance) is set at the market rate. A small pool of money is set aside to reward performance. Under such plans, performance is usually assessed through subjective ratings. In addition, the size of merit pay adjustments typically is smaller than that awarded under the incentive and earnings-at-risk plans. With traditional merit pay plans, even if subsequent performance remains the same or declines, merit increases awarded in a preceding year aren't revoked. Therefore, traditional merit pay entails little risk for the employee. From the organization's perspective, however, this approach *is* risky. Merit raises permanently increase wage costs without guaranteeing permanent increases in performance.

■□*fast fact*

A 1998 survey of 2,800 firms in the U.S. and Canada found that two out of three companies use variable pay.

Variable Pay Plans. Plans that reward past performance without changing the level of future base pay are often referred to as *variable pay*. Variable pay plans reduce a company's total fixed costs. They offer a means for organization to ensure that any increases in compensation costs vary with a company's ability and willingness to pay. Two types of variable pay are *incentive pay* and *earnings at risk*.

Incentive Pay Plans.   Like merit pay plans, incentive plans peg base pay at the market rate. Additional compensation is available through bonuses or other forms of payment for peak performance. Typically, a cap is placed on incentive pay. Even with a cap in place, however, the maximum earnings potential is usually greater with an incentive plan than with a traditional merit plan. In such plans, the risk is that the incentive pay supplement must be re-earned each performance period. Even in the worst-case scenario, however, the employee earns what the market pays for the job.

Under some incentive plans, compensation of a specified amount is tied to specific goals established and communicated to participants before the start of the performance period. The emphasis is on specific actions performed in pursuit of the goals. The feature, Managing Diversity: Rewarding the Achievement of Diversity Goals, describes how this approach is being used to ensure that the talents of all employees are fully utilized.[18] In other plans, the incentive payment is based on an after-the-fact assessment of the outcomes, with no precise agreement made concerning how payments will be allocated. Because employees do not know the expectations in advance, this type of incentive system may not be effective in achieving specific strategic objectives.

> *"Put bluntly, we should get rid of, fix, or not hire leaders who cannot manage diversity."*
>
> **Roger Wheeler**
> **Chief Tax Officer**
> **General Motors**

MANAGING DIVERSITY
Rewarding the Achievement of Diversity Goals

According to a 1998 study by the Society for Human Resource Management, most *Fortune* 500 companies either do not measure performance against diversity goals or they measure this performance but do not use compensation to reward success. Apparently, these organizations simply hope that the use of fair hiring methods and sending managers to diversity training programs will produce a truly multicultural organization. But about 30 percent of the *Fortune* 500 and (and about 10 percent of firms in general) take a bolder, and more controversial approach: They pay managers to achieve diversity objectives. Tenneco, the oil company, was one of the mavericks. Back in the mid-1980s, Tenneco was among the first organizations to begin linking a portion of managers' bonuses to how many women and people of color they hired and moved up the ladder. Since then, the number of professional women and people of color in the company has more than doubled. At the same time, some managers lost out when it came time for bonuses: "We've all had some of our bonus subtracted because of this program," explained one human resource manager.

Managers who are perfectly comfortable using incentives to achieve other types of strategic objectives—such as increasing ROI and improved customer satisfaction—often balk at this practice. For some critics, the practice seems misguided because it ties pay to something other than improved financial performance. Measuring the bottom-line consequences of diversity is difficult. Companies that link bonuses to effective diversity management are saying they value this objective even if the financial benefits of diversity can't be directly measured. Hoechst Celanese used incentives to reward diversity planning. The result was an increased percentage of women and minority professionals in the company during a time when the total number of its professional staff declined nearly 25 percent. In 1992, it began asking managers to set five- and ten-year diversity goals. Since then, the company has seen modest but steady gains in the diversity of their professional workforce.

Deloitte & Touche, the accounting firm, also uses incentives to achieve diversity goals. Within two years of tying managers' bonuses to increasing the rate at which women were promoted, the company experienced a 50 percent increase in the number of women partners in the firm. Sara Lee Corporation also ties executive bonuses to meeting objectives for the advancement of women. At Motorola, a belief in the strategic importance of managing diversity is reflected in the CEO's bonus formula, which includes goals for managing diversity, EEO, and affirmative action. Such practices are still rare, and their future is unknown. Some experts think the practice is just another fad. Others predict it will eventually become a standard feature in the performance management systems of leading firms.

To learn more about how organizations use rewards to manage diversity, visit the home page of the Society for Human Resource Management at
www.shrm.org

Earnings-at-Risk Pay Plans. Merit and incentive pay systems provide performance-based rewards as a supplement to historically guaranteed base pay amounts that equal the market rate. By comparison, earnings-at-risk (EAR) plans, also called pay-at-risk, involve reductions in base pay to below-market levels. In essence, employees must earn their way back to the level that would have been guaranteed under a traditional or incentive pay plan. The worst case scenario is that employees who do not reach their performance goals experience a lowered standard of living relative to the market of employees in similar jobs. Conversely, the best case scenario allows employees to have the potential for much greater earnings.[19] Such plans may not be acceptable to employees who are used to more traditional reward structures that ensure earnings stability.[20] Yet, for salespeople who work on straight commission, placing their earnings at risk is just considered normal. Increasingly, top-level executives are being asked to accept compensation packages that put greater portions of their earnings at risk.[21] By putting pay at risk, employers effectively buy insurance that protects the company from precipitous declines in performance.

Comparing the Plans. From the employees' perspective, the degree of upside and downside risk is a key factor that differs among these three performance-based approaches. Merit and incentive plans involve primarily upside risk. Employees can count on receiving wages and salaries that meet or nearly meet the market pay level, and they can earn additional pay based on their performance. In an earnings-at-risk plan, employees can't assume they will receive pay that meets the market-level average.

The terms "merit," "incentive," and "earnings at-risk" are regularly used by compensation specialists to describe different philosophies about how much risk employees should be exposed to. This terminology clearly distinguishes these forms of pay. In practice, however, the differences among pay plans is a matter of degree. For example, to deal with the problem of escalating pay, some organizations have adopted merit pay plans that allocate zero raises to poor performing employees, and force managers to identify a specific percentage of poorly performing employees.[22] These merit pay plans function very much like incentive plans. Similarly, it's sometimes difficult to tell the difference between incentive plans and earnings-at-risk. How far below the market must a company set its policy line before we say they have adopted an earnings-at-risk approach: 5 percent? 10 percent? 20 percent? And under what conditions do employees really feel that their pay is "at risk?" Lincoln Electric employees clearly work under an earnings-at-risk plan. Yet,

"I try to remember that people—good, intelligent, capable people—may actually need day-to-day praise and thanks for the job they do."

John Ball
Service Training Manager
American Honda Motor Company

year after year, most employees know that they can expect above-market compensation. From the employees' perspective, perceptions of risk reflect not only the formal plan but also their beliefs about how likely it is that they will perform at the level needed to be compensated at or above the average market level.

The distinction between incentive pay and earnings at risk is further blurred by the fact that pay decisions may reflect the performance of the individual and/or a team and/or the organization. In other word, there are many variations in methods of paying for performance. Furthermore, different methods often are combined within the same plan. Later in this chapter, we describe in more detail a few of these variations.

Specifying the Level of Aggregation for Reward Distribution

Performance can be measured at the individual, work team, department, plant, strategic business unit, or organization level. One variable influencing the aggregation decision is the ease with which performance can be objectively measured. If individual performance can be only evaluated by subjective supervisory ratings, then it may be appropriate to move to a higher level of aggregation—for example, the team or strategic business unit. Moving to a higher level tends to yield more objective measures of performance, such as labor costs, profits, and cost savings. The trade-off is that the tie to individual performance is less direct; the gain is that the tie to achieving the company's business objectives is more clear. Despite this potential weakness, team-based pay systems are proving to be quite effective. In a recent Hay survey, respondents rated the effectiveness of several forms of performance-based pay. As Exhibit 12.2 reveals, team-based pay was consistently viewed as helpful, while ratings of other approaches showed mixed results.[23]

Technological constraints may dictate the appropriate level of aggregation. Team or business unit incentives are more appropriate than individual incentives when work flows are interdependent (as in small-batch manufacturing or the development of an advertising campaign) or when the work flows are machine paced (as on an assembly line). Systems in which work outputs are conditional on the receipt of information or materials from others are good candidates for team-level or business unit-level incentive plans.[24]

A third variable affecting the choice of aggregation level is the type of behavior an organization needs in order to attain its strategic initiatives. Nordstrom's managers want the salespeople to be entrepreneurs. Therefore, they use individual incentive plans, which produce greater competition, increased performance pressure, and greater risk taking.[25] Team incentive plans, on the other hand, reinforce behaviors that promote collective rather than individual success. They encourage each team member to help the team attain its objectives. Even when work is organized around individuals, however, cooperation among employees can be beneficial. Incentive systems that pit employees against each other in order to win rewards, instead of encouraging each employee to compete against an objective performance goal, are likely to cut off information sharing and other forms of coworker support. Not surprisingly, when incentives are tied to one's own job performance, concern about organizational citizenship fades.[26]

Specifying the Type of Reward

Rewards for performance can be of many types, ranging from a feeling of personal satisfaction, to public recognition and small tokens, all the way to substantial monetary payments and stock ownership.

"Individuals don't accomplish anything, teams do."

The Late W. Edwards Deming
TQM Guru

Exhibit 12.2

Responses of Managers When Asked Whether Each Pay Practice Improved Performance

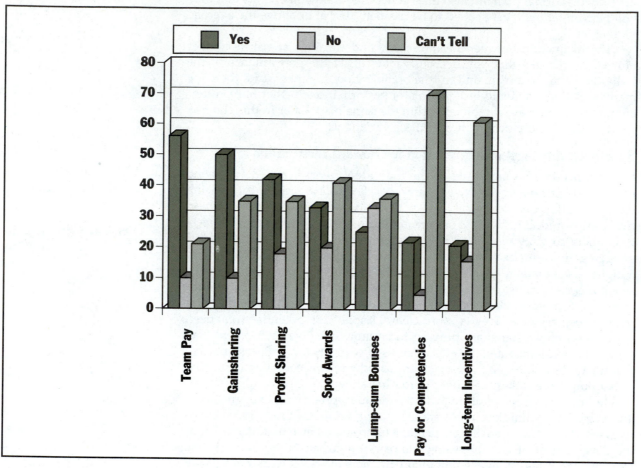

Recognition Versus Money. The terms performance-based pay and incentive pay are generally not used to refer to rewards that consist mostly of social recognition. In practice, however, no clear line separates such rewards from those that are primarily monetary. Regardless of the specific form of the reward, for it to be effective, it must be valued by employees. Because the value of a reward is only partly a function of its monetary worth, judging "how much is enough" is mostly a matter of speculation or trial and error. Perhaps the best advice is to intentionally use both recognition and monetary incentives. This is what Au Bon Pain does.

Au Bon Pain uses mystery customers to evaluate the performance of its restaurants and their employees. To establish a direct relationship between performance and rewards, managers whose employees score 100 percent in all twelve of the categories that are evaluated receive an on-the-spot bonus of twenty Club Excellence Dollars—dubbed CDs. These dollars can be traded for items in a company catalog. Most items are in the $10-$70 range and include such things as Au Bon Pain sunglasses and portable cassette players. In addition, winners' names are posted on the store's bulletin board next to a list of the criteria for the program. All winners receive personal letters of congratulations from company officials. Thus, it isn't clear whether Au Bon

"Our managers wouldn't use a non-cash recognition program if it didn't bring value to employees."

Kathy Charlton
Manager of Workplace Vitality
Texas Instruments

Pain's employees are motivated more by the monetary worth of these rewards or by the social recognition that goes with them.

Size of Reward.   Companies clearly make different choices in the sizes of the incentives they offer.[27] Although the average for nonexecutives is about 7 percent, at Lincoln Electric incentives can amount to 100 percent. Even within the same company, employees in different jobs usually have different percentages of their pay placed "at risk," with the general pattern being proportionately more incentive based for employees who are higher up in the hierarchy. As noted in Chapter 10, market wage and salary surveys typically include questions designed to assess the proportion of pay that's fixed versus performance-based. The results of one recent salary survey indicated that for exempt salaried employees in the U.S., about 8 percent of their pay was tied to performance, compared to about half that figure for nonexempt employees.

Form of Payment.   Besides cash, a company may choose to give employees large prizes (e.g., all-expenses-paid vacations), direct stock awards, stock options, or any combination of these.

Timing of Rewards.   Generally speaking, the more quickly rewards follow desirable behavior, the more potent the rewards are in evoking subsequent desirable behavior.[28] Delayed rewards may decrease desired behavior because the employee doesn't see an immediate consequence. Delayed rewards also may increase dissatisfaction and frustration among high performers. Nevertheless, task cycles seldom conveniently match calendar cycles. Also, the longer the company delays paying the incentive, the longer it can use the money for its own purposes. Thus, in most companies, incentive pay is received from several weeks to a year after the performance being rewarded.

One way to minimize the problems associated with delayed rewards entails developing performance contracts. Upon completion of agreed-upon work at an agreed-upon date, the performance pay is distributed. Feedback or supervisory recognition can be provided intermittently until the formal reward is delivered.[29]

International Considerations.   If a multinational corporation utilizes any type of incentive system, a special policy is usually established. Incentives may be paid according to either parent- or host-country policies. Actual payments can be made in local or foreign currency—or some combination of the two. Some companies let the recipient make the decision about which currency to use. For example, most U.S. financial services companies have an overall policy of paying PCNs according to the U.S. salary structure, including its bonus programs and salary increase practices. This compensation usually is paid partly in U.S. dollars and partly in the local currency. The local-currency portion is generally pegged to pay ordinary living expenses, and bonuses are typically paid in U.S. dollars. When U.S. MNCs use incentives such as stock options, third-country nationals and host-country nationals may not be adequately rewarded for performance since these plans are only tax advantaged in the United States.

Cultural norms and values may also affect a MNC's use of performance-based pay. Although popular in the United States, performance-based pay may ruffle a few feathers in Mexico, especially among line employees. Why? Workers receiving more pay could be viewed as having connections to the higher echelons. Variable pay creates distance, according to Alejandro Palma, intercultural business specialist for Clarke Consulting Group. Palma

■□*fast fact*

Sixty percent of MNCs in China give discretionary bonuses to local employees.

believes it's much more important for a Mexican person to have a congenial working environment than it is to make more money. In fact, he has seen cases where very good workers, ones who have performed well and received pay for that, have felt ostracized by their coworkers and have even left the company because of it. Other consultants argue that incentive pay can work, but because it's less familiar in Mexico, it works only if the company does a very good job of communicating the system to employees. Palma suggests other reward strategies can be more effective in Mexico than performance-based pay. He suggests making the outstanding worker a team leader. This plays into the desire for respect without isolating the worker. Employees-of-the-month programs also seem to be effective, because everyone has a chance. Other valued incentives include family days or other activities including workers' relatives.[30]

Predicting in advance how employees in different countries will react to different pay plans is seldom easy. When management professor Chao Chen compared the preferences of American and Chinese employees, he expected to find that the Americans would prefer unequal, performance-based distribution of rewards and the Chinese would prefer more equal distribution. Instead, his research showed that Chinese and American employees both preferred to have material rewards distributed unequally, based on performance. To his surprise, the Chinese also preferred to see socioemotional awards—such as parties and managerial friendliness—distributed unequally, whereas the Americans felt these socioemotional awards should be distributed to everyone equally.[31] Similarly, one might predict that Americans and Russians would have different preferences for how to allocate rewards, but recent research suggests that managers in both countries place primary emphasis on individual performance when allocating rewards, while showing less concern for treating everyone equally or worrying about how the reward allocations might affect coworker relations.[32]

Specifying Eligibility for Rewards

As is true for many other HR practices, different parts of an organization may be subjected to differing forms of performance-based pay. As described in Chapter 10, for example, the percentage of total pay earned in the form of base pay generally decreases as one moves from lower to higher levels in the organization. Conversely, the percentage of pay that's clearly tied to performance generally increases as one moves up the organizational hierarchy. Another common pattern is to offer higher level employees—but not lower level employees—rewards for improved organizational performance. The rules used to determine which employees are covered by various components of a total pay plan are called *eligibility rules.* Many of the ongoing changes in the use of performance-based pay reflect changes in the eligibility rules used by employers rather than the introduction of truly new forms of pay. When company-wide profit sharing is adopted, for example, the change usually involves going from a situation in which only a limited pool of employees share the profits (top-level executives) to making all employees eligible to receive this form of pay. The same is true for other forms of performance-based pay, such as bonuses and stock options.

Gaining Employee Acceptance

Employee opposition can be a major obstacle to the successful implementation of performance-based pay, especially variable-pay plans. Employees may worry, for example, that incentives will result in work speedups or will put some percentage of the workforce out of a job. Another legitimate concern may be that performance targets will be too difficult or out of the employees' control. When group performance serves as a criterion for variable pay, individualistic U.S. employees may resent having to depend on others for their rewards. And if trust in management is low, employees may not believe the figures when management tells them how the financial performance of their business unit translates into the size of the pool available for bonuses. Several conditions that improve employee acceptance and thus the effectiveness of variable pay are shown in Exhibit 12.3. Assuming that these issues are successfully addressed, a viable performance-based pay system can be developed.[33]

Legal Considerations

Legal considerations must also be taken into account when designing pay-for-performance systems. Issues of discrimination and tax laws are particularly important.

Discrimination. By definition, pay "discrimination" based on performance—not job title, rank, or status—is an inevitable and appropriate outcome of a properly administered performance-based pay system. Performance-based compensation is intended to create behaviors that lead to the accomplishment of organizational goals. Rewards that are administered contingently—that is, according to performance—cause increases in subsequent employee performance and expressions of satisfaction among high performers. They encourage low performers to perform at a higher rate or to exit the organization. The legal issue, then, isn't whether to discriminate in pay but how to do so fairly.

Under Title VII of the *Civil Rights Act of 1964*, the *Civil Rights Act of 1991*, and the *Equal Pay Act of 1963*, a supervisor may be charged with unlawful

fast fact

Until recently, Japanese companies were not permitted to issue their stock as compensation.

Exhibit 12.3
Conditions That Build Support for Employee Acceptance of Performance-Based Pay Plans

- The plan is clearly communicated.
- The employees believe they're being treated fairly.
- The plan is understood, and bonuses are easy to calculate.
- The employees have a hand in establishing and administering the plan.
- The bonuses are awarded as soon as possible after the desired performance.
- The employees have an avenue of appeal if they believe they're being treated unfairly.
- The employees believe they can trust the company, and therefore believe they have job security.

discrimination by an employee in a protected group who believes that a pay raise, bonus, or other incentive was denied on a basis not related to performance. Such problems are most likely to arise when performance measures are subjective and when the size of rewards given is left to managerial discretion rather than being driven by a fixed formula.[34] What is critical for both merit and variable pay is that the same rules be used to give raises fairly and consistently among all employees. Data showing persistent pay differences between men and women, and between Caucasians and people of color, cause many people to believe that unfair pay discrimination persists in many organizations today. Although some of the pay differentials can be explained by years in the labor market, study after study has shown that human capital variables such as education, experience, and performance do not fully account for them.[35]

Taxes and Accounting Rules.   A full discussion of tax and accounting rules is beyond the scope of this chapter, but the importance of these should not go without comment. Particularly in the specialized arena of executive compensation, changes in taxation and accounting rules can dramatically alter the methods companies use to administer performance-based pay. For example, when tax rates for long-term capital gains are low relative to tax rates for ordinary income, incentive stock options become more popular. But when the differential is removed, cash incentives become more popular than stock options. Likewise, laws that require taxes to be paid at the time a stock option is granted—as is true in Norway—discourage the use of stock as a form of reward; laws that defer taxation until the option is exercised have the opposite effect.

THE PARTNERSHIP PERSPECTIVE

"You have to start with your supervisors buying into the goals and incentives. They're the people who are going to whisper sweet things to the people who are producing."

Emanuel Weintraub
Management Consultant

As the examples of the Lincoln Electric Company and Owens Corning illustrate, designing and administering an effective performance-based pay system requires close cooperation among all partners in the HR Triad. In particular, line managers and HR professionals must work together to ensure that performance-based pay practices support the overall strategic objectives of the organization, as well as the specific strategic goals of smaller units and teams within the organization.

Changes in strategic objectives often trigger organizations to scrutinize and redesign their compensations systems. In recent years, changes in total compensation systems have often been directed toward creating a tighter link between performance and pay. In many organizations, such efforts represent major changes in the organization's culture. Thus, for many line managers and HR professionals, the roles and responsibilities associated with performance-based pay systems include those associated with organizational change and learning, as described in Chapter 5.

As is true for any component of the HR system, the ultimate effectiveness of any performance-based pay system depends on whether employees fully understand and accept the system. Thus, seeking and using the input of the employees who will be affected by performance-based pay is an important responsibility of line managers and HR professionals. The importance of involving employees in the design of performance-based systems is amplified when the employees who will be affected come from diverse national cultures. Continuous monitoring of employee satisfaction, as well as changes in key behaviors and performance results, is needed to detect whether the pay plan has its intended effects. The introduction of new performance-based pay systems often leads to unintended consequences, which can be quite disruptive if not detected quickly. These issues are summarized in the feature, The HR Triad: Roles and Responsibilities for Rewarding Employees' Contributions.

MERIT PAY

Traditional performance-based pay has been the cornerstone of public and private compensation systems for many years. It's best exemplified by merit

---

THE HR TRIAD: ROLES AND RESPONSIBILITIES FOR REWARDING EMPLOYEES' CONTRIBUTIONS

Line Managers	HR Professionals	Employees
Work with HR professionals to establish the strategic objectives of performance-based pay (PBP).	Work with line managers to establish the strategic objectives of PBP.	Develop a comprehensive understanding of the strategic objectives of PBP.
Work with HR professionals to establish the performance criteria to be linked to pay and the methods to assess performance.	Work with line managers to establish the performance criteria to be linked to pay and the methods to assess performance.	Make sure you accurately understand the performance criteria that will be used to determine your PBP.
Understand the alternative methods of PBP.	Provide expert knowledge regarding the available methods of PBP.	Assist line managers and HR professionals in identifying potential negative consequences of specific PBP plans.
Assist with communicating the objectives and processes for PBP.	Work with accounting and finance staff to assess the cost implications of PBP.	Be alert to dysfunctional attempts to "game" PBP systems, and work to improve PBP plans that cause such dysfunction.
Work with HR professionals to ensure strategic alignment and integration among all PBP plans used throughout the organization.	Monitor the effects of PBP on employee satisfaction, behavior and results, and recommend revisions to the PBP plan as needed.	Perhaps assist in administering PBP plans for team members.
Implement PBP fairly.	Ensure the PBP plan is integrated and consistent with other components of the total HR system.	Be aware of your own reactions to risk and choose employment setting accordingly.
Assist HR in monitoring and revising PBP as needed.	Develop and deliver training and communications to ensure that line managers and other employees understand the PBP system's objectives and procedures.	

pay plans. Many organizations use some form of merit pay. Merit pay plans differ along several dimensions. First, some plans include other variables besides performance—such as cost of living, job or organizational seniority, or comparability in pay grade—in the pay adjustment formula. Second, plans differ in the way the merit increase is calculated: some award an absolute amount, others award a percentage of base salary, still others rely on merit grids (discussed later in this chapter). Third, merit increases may be distributed more often than once a year or delayed in times of budget crisis.[36]

Performance Assessment

Fundamental to an effective merit pay system is a credible and comprehensive performance appraisal system. Without a reliable assessment of performance, it's impossible to relate pay to performance in a way that's motivating. Much of the dissatisfaction with merit pay plans stems from the fact that they link performance rewards to subjective performance measures. The criteria may be contaminated or deficient. Supervisors all too frequently evaluate incumbents according to preconceived biases. Regardless of the appraisal form—whether it's based, for instance, on behavior, output, or traits—rating errors such as leniency and halo are rampant. Therefore, supervisors and employees often disagree on their performance ratings. When pay hinges on those ratings, confrontation and mistrust often escalate.

Many of the performance measurement problems associated with merit plans are fixable. As the New York Convention & Visitors Bureau (NYCVB) learned, sometimes it's better to fix a poorly designed merit plan than to replace it with variable pay. In 1993, 60 employees at the NYVCB began participating in an incentive pay program that had been carefully designed to measure and weigh every possible aspect of performance. While the incentive plan looked rational on paper, it was so complicated that many supervisors couldn't even explain it. Within five years, the plan was abandoned. Most employees saw the plan replaced with a new and improved merit-based system. (Direct marketers and sales staff continued to be eligible for some performance-based incentives). At the core of the new merit system was a revised, performance appraisal system.[37]

Merit Increase Size

Under merit pay plans, pay raises are recommended by the department heads for the employees being supervised. This is usually carried out within the constraints of a merit pool budget. Since the total of all increases can't exceed the budget percentage for the department, small merit pay pools are problematic. Charles Peck, a compensation expert with the Conference Board, based in New York, has explained some of the other problems often associated with merit plans:

> "Merit increases tend to be expensive and, contrary to their intent, not strongly related to performance. Usually everybody gets something. This so dilutes the salary increase budget that the top performer's increase isn't large enough to be significant (especially after it is prorated over the number of pay periods in the year and subjected to withholding). On the other hand, the poor performer is getting more than he or she should have, which is nothing. The result of all this is that the employees who are most dissatisfied are the ones the company wants satisfied—the top performers."[38]

Allstate's Monoline Matrix Merit Guidelines illustrate this principle.[39] It assigns merit increases as follows:

Performance Level	Merit Increase
Performance consistently and significantly exceeds position requirements	Minimum of 6% increase
Performance consistently meets position requirements	0–4%
Performance requires improvement to meet position requirements	0%

In this system, managers have considerable discretion. To help managers use their discretion wisely, Allstate provides them with a table that clearly lays out several different reward allocation scenarios. Using the table, managers can easily figure out how to fund larger merit raises for outstanding performers by allocating smaller increases for average and poor performers. Suppose the budget provides for an average merit increase of 4 percent. One option for the manager would be to distribute merit increases as follows:

	Exceeds	Meets	Requires Improvement
Employees at the performance level	40%	55%	5%
Average increase given to employees with this level of performance	6.0%	2.9%	0.0%

In this scenario, the best performers receive the minimum required increase of 6 percent. But suppose a manager feels this is too little. Can funds be allocated to give the best performers as much as an 8 percent increase? The answer is yes. Two possible ways to do it are shown below:

Option 1

	Exceeds	Meets	Requires Improvement
Employees at the performance level	30%	70%	0%
Average increase given to employees with this level of performance	8.0%	2.3%	0.0%

Option 2

	Exceeds	Meets	Requires Improvement
Employees at the performance level	40%	55%	5%
Average increase given to employees with this level of performance	8.0%	1.5%	0.0%

Exhibit 12.4 illustrates a more complex system for allocating raises based on both performance and an individual's position in the salary range. At any performance rating higher than Below Average, an employee whose current base pay is lower will receive a larger percentage increase in pay than an employee whose current base salary is higher. Although the percentage of merit increase is greater in the lower quartiles, the absolute size of the merit increase is often larger in the higher quartiles, provided the merit budget is large enough and the grid is designed correctly. Since employees tend to confuse market adjustments and performance pay, they may perceive this approach as unfair because equally performing employees do not get equal

Exhibit 12.4

Merit Increase Based on Current Position in the Salary Range

	Percentage Increase in Annual Salary			
Performance Rating	**First Quartile**	**Second Quartile**	**Third Quartile**	**Fourth Quartile**
1. Unacceptable	0%	0%	0%	0%
2. Below Average	2%	0%	0%	0%
3. Competent	8%	6%	4%	2%
4. Above Average	10%	8%	6%	4%
5. Superior	12%	10%	8%	6%

percentage increases in pay. Although employee education may help to minimize this problem, a more practical approach is to uncouple performance-based and market-based pay adjustments and award each type of increase separately.

Critics of merit pay contend that even the most well-designed merit pay systems are ineffective. According to Edward E. Lawler III, an expert on reward system design, merit increases don't work well because they're plugged into antiquated pay systems. He believes that the one thing shown by 40 years of researching reward systems is that merit pay isn't effective for increasing productivity—particularly for the service, information-processing, and high technology-based industries of the 21st century. Still, many U.S. workers are paid under merit systems. Many others, however, work in organizations that have abandoned the use of merit increases in favor of incentive pay plans.

INCENTIVE PAY

As already noted, one major difference between merit pay and incentive pay is that merit pay is a permanent increase but incentive pay is a one-time increase. Measurements of performance often differ, also. Whereas merit pay plans typically rely on subjective performance appraisal ratings, incentive pay is often paid based on the achievement of performance that can be quantified more easily. As is true for merit pay, performance measures used for incentive pay should be based on a clear vision of the organization's strategy and culture—that is, they should tie rewards to behaviors and outcomes that support business priorities. Finally, compared to merit pay plans, incentive plans often give managers more latitude to make large distinctions in the rewards received by employees, and in any one pay episode, they offer employees the opportunity to earn relatively larger performance-based pay rewards.

Incentive pay takes many forms and may be administered as either incentive pay or earnings at risk. While recognizing that distinguishing incentive pay from earnings at risk is not straightforward, in this section we review the following: individual incentives, team incentives, special achievement awards, profit sharing, and gain sharing.

Individual Incentives

Individual incentives are among the oldest and most popular form of incentive pay. In this type of plan, individual standards of performance are established and communicated in advance, and rewards are based on individual

■□ *fast fact*

Since Martinez took over as CEO at Sears, incentives have gone up more rapidly than base pay for all salaried employees.

output. Individual incentives are used by a significant minority of companies in all industry groups except utilities. Utility firms have been slow to implement such plans owing to their history of regulation, which limits workforce autonomy.

A variety of individual incentive plans exist. These plans differ in terms of the method of rate determination. When the work cycle is short, units of production generally serve as the method of rate determination. For long-cycle jobs, the standard is typically based on the time required to complete a unit. Individual incentive systems also vary with regard to the constancy with which pay is a function of production level. One option is to pay a consistent amount at all production levels, for instance, $0.25 a carton for all cartons shipped. Alternatively, pay may vary as a function of production level. For example, employees may be paid $0.25 a carton for up to 1,000 units a day, and $0.37 a carton beyond this threshold.

Individual incentive plans also share a common job-analysis foundation. For example, time-and-motion studies are often employed to determine how wages are tied to output. The challenge is to identify a "normal" rate of production.

Piecework Plan.   Piecework, like Lincoln Electric's, is the most common type of individual incentive pay. In this plan, employees are paid a certain rate for each unit of output. Under a *straight piecework plan*, employees are guaranteed a standard pay rate for each unit. The standard pay rate is based on the standard output and the base wage rate. For example, if the base pay of a job is $40 a day and the employee can produce at a normal rate 20 units a day, the standard rate may be established at $2 a unit. The normal rate is more than what time-and-motion studies indicate is typical because it is supposed to represent 100 percent efficiency. The standard rate that is agreed to may also reflect the bargaining power of the employees, the economic conditions of the organization and industry, and the amount the competition is paying.

In a *differential piece rate plan*, more than one rate of pay is set for the same job. This plan can be set up in several different ways. Taylor Differential Plans are one example. In Taylor plans, employees receive a higher rate of pay for work completed in a set period of time. For work that takes longer to complete, the rate of pay is lower. For example, an employee may be paid $2 per piece if they complete five pieces per hour, but they would be paid only $1.80 per piece if they completed only four pieces per hour.

When used appropriately, piecework pay can be very effective in raising individual performance, but there is no panacea. Consider what happened when a group of bank processing operators went to a per-item-processed reward system. The staff of twelve operators increased the items processed from an average of 980 items per hour to more than 3,000 items per hour. Their take-home pay increased an average of 50 percent over their former hourly pay. The program seemed to be a success—until the bank president made a visit to the unit. One operator cut off her conversation with the president after a brief time telling him that he was costing her money. The president also could see that operators were unwilling to help each other out because it would reduce their own pay. As in this case, when piece-rate incentives reward individual employees without regard to the consequences for the larger organization, their disadvantages may outweigh any benefits.[40]

Standard Hour Plan.   The standard hour plan is the second most common type of individual incentive plan. This approach is based on setting a standard time for each unit of production. Tasks are broken down by the amount of time it takes to complete them, which can be determined by historical records, time-and-motion studies, or both. The normal time to perform each task becomes a standard.

If you go into an automobile repair shop, you will probably see a chart indicating the labor rates associated with various types of repair. These reflect the use of standard hour plans. Each rate includes the rate paid to the mechanic who does the work plus the premium charged by the owner of the shop. The rate is fixed regardless of how long it actually takes to do the repair. Thus, the mechanic and the shop owner both have incentives to ensure that the work is completed in a shorter amount of time than that used to set the standard rate. Consider a standard time of two hours and a rate of $16 an hour, of which the mechanic is paid $12 an hour. In this system, the mechanic receives $24 for each unit of work completed, regardless of the actual time spent. If the mechanic completes six units in an eight-hour day, he or she receives 6 × $24, or $144. This is substantially more than $96, which would be the "expected" rate of pay for eight hours based on four units.

Executive Incentive Plan. As already noted, individual incentives are commonly used to award top-level managers. Executive incentive plans use a formula to relate incentives to the attainment of corporate or strategic business unit goals, with the various goals weighted. In addition to cash, incentive pay includes such things as restricted stock grants (free shares given to the CEO for staying with the company), performance shares or performance units (free shares or cash for achieving multiyear goals), and stock option grants.[41]

Debate over the effectiveness of executive incentives has raged for many years. For one thing, the pay of U.S. executives seems excessive relative to the pay of rank-and-file employees and of CEOs in other countries. In 1999, the ratio of the pay of CEOs to the pay of rank-and-file employees was 70 to 1 in the United States, compared with 17 to 1 in Germany and only 10 to 1 in Japan. These are the types of figures that make news, but "the relentless focus on how much CEOs are paid diverts public attention away from the real problem—how CEOs are paid," according to compensation experts Michael Jensen and Kevin J. Murphy. After studying the pay of CEOs in 1,400 companies over an eight-year period, the researchers contend that the "incentive" compensation of top executives is virtually independent of corporate performance and is no more variable than that of hourly workers. Unfortunately, current incentive pay for CEOs too often is treated as an entitlement program rather than as a way to motivate outstanding performance. To rectify the problem, the researchers recommend building greater performance variability into executive pay, restructuring incentive pay so that salaries, bonuses, and stock options provide big rewards for superior performance and big penalties for poor performance.[42]

As is true for other employees, a fundamental challenge in designing executive incentive plans is choosing the most appropriate way to measure performance. The performance measures that drive executive incentive pay, and thus performance, are as varied as those that drive nonexecutive pay. One approach that's gained popularity in recent years is paying executives for the value they create for shareholders. This approach was popularized by the consulting firm Stern Stewart & Co., which developed a performance indicator called Economic Value Added (EVA). Those who champion the use of EVA as a basis for awarding executive pay argue that it's the best way to

"It's the underlying philosophy which is the key thing. Three years ago we paid bonuses on sales. Then we moved to profit. Now we're looking for something which more accurately reflects the shareholder's position."

**Andrew Higgins
Finance Director
Burton (a UK retailer)**

align the interests of managers with those of shareholders. Compared to other financial performance measures—including return on equity, operating margins, and earnings per share—EVA is more closely aligned with shareholders' net return on capital. Among the many companies that use EVA measures as a basis for incentive pay are Coca-Cola, AT&T, Quaker Oats, and CSX.[43]

Team Incentives

Team incentives fall somewhere between individual plans and whole-organization plans such as gain sharing and profit sharing. Performance goals are tailored specifically to what the work team needs to accomplish. Strategically, they link the goals of individuals to those of the work group (typically ten people or fewer), which, in turn, are usually linked to financial goals.[44] An insurance company that was encountering friction between its data processing and claims departments used team incentives to focus the departments on the company's strategic needs. The claims people said the data processing staff never met its deadlines. The data processing people said the claims people kept changing their minds and made unreasonable demands. A team-incentive plan was devised to link the performance of the people in these two departments to how well they worked together to meet customer needs. The award amount depended on how quickly and how well the team goal was met. This new team incentive plan made it clear that the conflicts between the departments detracted from everyone's self-interest. In order to improve their chances of earning their incentives, soon the claims group had outlined the specifications and timetable necessary to meet customer service needs. They discussed these with data processing. Data processing developed a project plan and shared it with claims. Now both groups are working together to achieve a common goal.

When designed appropriately, team-based incentives offer four major advantages compared with individual incentive systems. First, the mere presence of team members who have some control over rewards evokes more vigorous and persistent behavior than is evidenced when individuals work alone. Second, the likelihood that conflicting contingencies (peer pressure) will evoke counterproductive control over behavior is reduced. Third, the strength of the rewards is increased, since they're now paired with group-administered rewards, such as praise and camaraderie. Research also suggests that the performance of a group is higher than that attained by individual group members—although not as high as that of the best person in the group. Fourth, the performance of another group member (usually the high performer) can serve as a model, encouraging other team members to imitate successful behavior.[45]

But just as it takes more than piecework to ensure high productivity at Lincoln Electric, it usually takes more than just a team-based incentive plan at most companies. For example, at AAL a team-based incentive plan is integrated with an individual incentive program, market survey data, and a skill-based pay plan.

Types of Teams.   As more and more companies restructure work around teams, new team structures are likely to proliferate. Different team structures may require different forms of pay. For example, three types of teams are commonly found in today's organizations:

- **Parallel Teams.**   These teams operate in a structure that functions in parallel to the regular organization chart. Often staffed by volunteers

"Our experience has been that the group award alone does not do enough. Individuals want to be rewarded for group performance and for the individual contribution as well."

Judy H. Edge
Compensation Manager
Federal Express

who serve the team on a temporary assignment, the typical tasks of such teams include creating reports and making suggestions for improvements in the company. The team's work is usually a small portion of each member's full responsibility.

- **Project Teams.** Project teams may operate in a parallel structure or they may be integrated as part of the formal organization structure. Such teams often have a somewhat stable core of members with diverse areas of specialized expertise. They often are self-managing and have a broad mandate to develop innovative products or services. The team's work may be a part- or full-time responsibility for each member.

- **Work Teams.** Work teams are fully integrated into the organization structure. They have clear, narrow mandates, which usually focus on producing products or providing services. Membership in these teams is usually stable, and the team's work is each member's full-time responsibility.

The very different natures of these team types mean that no single approach to rewarding the performance of team members would fit all three. Exhibit 12.5 shows how two leading experts recommend structuring the performance-based pay for these three types of teams.[46] In many organizations, multiple team types operate side-by-side. By implication, multiple forms of team pay should also be used.

Team-Pay Design Issues.   Although team-based incentives are promising, they involve administrative responsibilities that are as great as those associated with individual incentive plans. Job analysis is still necessary to identify how to structure the teams and to ensure that workloads are equivalent among teams. Also, team incentives may produce unintended side effects, including competition between groups, that may or may not compliment goal attainment. Exhibit 12.6 summarizes several issues to be addressed when designing performance-based pay for teams.[47]

Exhibit 12.5
Pay Systems for Different Types of Teams

Feature	Type of Team		
	Parallel	Project	Work
Base pay	Job based	Skill based	Skill based
Pay for performance			
Individual	Merit pay for job performance	Possible if team assessed	Unusual but possible if team assessed
Team	Recognition or cash for suggestions	Possible at end of project	Possible if team independent
Unit	Possible gain sharing	Profit sharing or gain sharing	Profit sharing or gain sharing
Participation	Design of gain sharing plan	Assessment of individuals	All aspects of design and administration
Communication	Open about rewards for improvement	Open about skill plan and rewards for performance	Highly open

Exhibit 12.6
Design Challenges for Performance-Based Pay for Teams

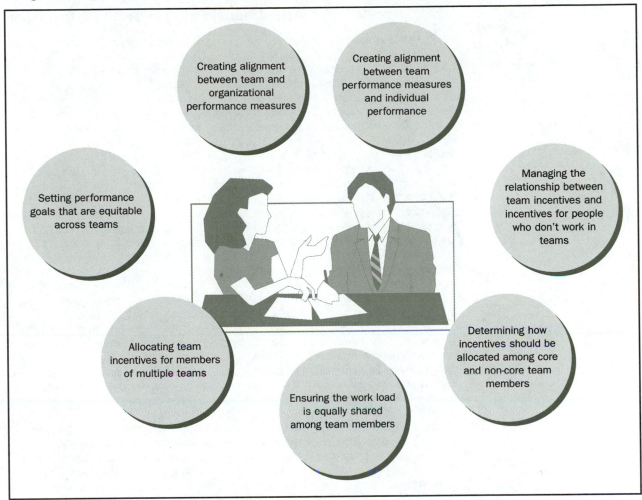

AlliedSignal faced many of these challenges when it began using account teams as the primary vehicle for driving organizational change. As described in the feature, Managing Teams: AlliedSignal Pays for Team Performance, the combination of restructuring around teams and adopting incentive pay for team performance proved to be a powerful way to improve customer satisfaction.[48]

To date, research on how to best design performance-based pay for work teams is scarce, so it's difficult to propose solutions to these challenges.[49] However, case studies of the experiences in three companies—Honeywell Defense Avionics, Solectron California, and XEL Communications provide several insights. For example, one solution to the challenges of changing team membership, multiple team memberships, and interteam relationships is to fund the incentive pool at the business unit level. This reminds employees that ultimately, their team should strive to enhance the organization's performance. Another lesson suggested by the experiences of these companies is that it's best to keep the pay system simple and plan to make adjustments to it as the team and company gain more experience with this

MANAGING TEAMS

AlliedSignal Pays for Team Performance

AlliedSignal Aerospace manufactures components for the aerospace industry. Their customers include the military as well as commercial firms in the private sector, such as Boeing. In an industry where cuts in defense budgets have caused overall contraction and downsizing, AlliedSignal has been growing rapidly through mergers and acquisitions. But as earnings stalled, this company reassessed its strategy and concluded that focusing on customers was the only way to keep the company from going into a tailspin. This change in strategy represented a major shift in focus. Driven by an engineering mentality, historically the company had focused inward. With its new external focus, the company would need to build a strong sales and service organization.

The new organization is structured around account teams, which draw together employees from different business units, regions, and markets. Typically, a core team includes a sales representative, a customer support manager, field service engineers, and one or more business unit representatives. In conjunction with this new structure, AlliedSignal adopted a new pay plan that put earnings at risk. The task of designing the new pay plan was itself carried out through teamwork. It required partnership among business managers, HR generalists, compensation specialists, and systems experts. Among the key decisions made by the design team was to calculate pay outs on a quarterly basis. According to James Harvey, a Sales Support Operations Manager, this helped create "a brutal understanding of the reality." It also ensured that rewards were linked directly to satisfying customers. "Before account teams were set up, our customers told us that we were difficult to work with," explains Harvey. "Typically, AlliedSignal employees acted independently and were only concerned about their own products." Another decision concerned eligibility for team incentives. At AlliedSignal, core teams are supported by "virtual teams" that work as needed to address technical product issues and help with credit, contracts, and warranties. However, virtual team members aren't eligible for team-based incentive awards. The design team also determined which performance measures would be used to evaluate the teams. The measures selected have been a source of some difficulty in the company because some managers believe they put too much emphasis on total sales, without recognizing that some sales are more profitable than others. To ease employees into the new system, and, hopefully, increase their trust and satisfaction levels, the design team also chose to gradually increase the proportion of pay that was put "at risk." During the first six months, there was no downside risk associated with failing to meet performance targets. During the next six months, employees were subjected to "recoverable" downside risk. That is, if they didn't make their target, they could make up for that by exceeding their target in the subsequent quarter. In the final phase, the full at-risk plan went into effect, with performance-based payouts made each quarter.

At AlliedSignal, the introduction of teams and performance-based team pay was at the center of a change effort that had many other important elements. These included developing formal business plans focused on customers, creating new inventory monitoring and tracking systems, training in problem solving and teamwork skills, and adopting a philosophy of continuous improvement. To deal with the fact that account teams link together employees from more than 20 nations and payroll systems, new HR software systems were introduced. And finally, even the customers had to change. At first, some customers were reluctant to get involved with the new approach. They just wanted to order their parts and receive them on time. Gradually, customers learned that they could benefit from being more involved. By defining their needs and expectations, they not only are more likely to have those needs and expectations satisfied, they also help ensure the long-term survival of a major supplier.

To learn more about AlliedSignal, visit the company home page at **www.allied.com**

approach to pay. Third, using 360-degree appraisals as the basis for developing or evaluating individuals should be resisted early in the life of the team. Until a team has matured and developed a level of trust in the team-based incentives, 360-degree appraisals may be threatening to employees, resulting in lack of candor and/or low team cohesiveness.[50]

Special Achievement Awards

Awards for achievement usually target performance in areas of particular strategic value, such as safety, customer service, productivity, quality, or attendance. Recipients typically are nominated by peers or supervisors to receive awards including gifts, savings bonds, dinner certificates, and cash incentives ranging from $150 to more than $1,000.

When designed well, the activities associated with these bonuses effectively focus attention on core values and business objectives. Data I/O Corporation, an electronics manufacturing company in Redmond, Washington, makes extensive use of achievement bonuses. For example, all members of a computer-aided electronics software development team—such as engineers, technical writers, shippers, and quality assurance personnel—garnered $60 dinner certificates when the product was released. Two high achievers also earned weekend trips for two to San Francisco, including $1,500 in airline and motel expenses. On other occasions, recognition plaques, mugs, T-shirts, and pen sets have been distributed. Monthly, an employee is recognized for her or his contribution to Data I/O. Recognition brings a parking place by the front door, an engraved plaque, and verbal acknowledgment in a company meeting.

To encourage more innovative ideas, many companies have suggestion systems that involve some form of instant incentive. Crowley Maritime Corporation's Ship Us an Idea is typical of most suggestion plans. The shipping company receives an average of 20 suggestions a month from its 1,000 employees. Employees earn between $50 and $150 for most ideas and may earn up to 10 percent of the cost savings for significant ideas. A presidential award of $1,000 is given annually for the best idea. According to Moon Hui Kim, program developer, the benefits far outweigh the $6,000-$10,000 annual program administration costs.[51]

Profit Sharing

Introduced first in the Gallatin glasswork factory in New Geneva, Pennsylvania, in 1794, profit-sharing plans in American business now number approximately half a million. As defined by the Council of Profit Sharing Industries, these plans include any procedure under which an employer pays or makes available to regular employees special current or deferred sums based on the profits of the business, in addition to their regular pay.[52]

Profit-sharing plans fall into three categories. *Current distribution plans* provide a percentage of profits to be distributed quarterly or annually to employees. *Deferred plans* place earnings in an escrow fund for distribution upon retirement, termination, death, or disability. These are the fastest-growing type of plans owing to tax advantages. About 20 percent of firms with profit-sharing programs have *combined plans*. These distribute a portion of profits immediately to employees, setting the remaining amount aside in a designated account.

Profit-sharing plans are designed to pay out incentives when the organization is most able to afford them. Other than sharing profits, these plans often do not have clear strategic objectives. Furthermore, employee involvement isn't necessarily an important component of them. The motivational potential of deferred plans is questionable also because employees may not see the relationship between their performance and the profitability of the firm. Critics of profit sharing argue that tying pay to achieving more specific strategic objectives is preferable to tying pay directly to profitability. For example, over a period of fourteen years, Springfield remanufacturing has selected fourteen different goals based on their analysis of the key weaknesses that interfere with profitability. Their goals have included debt-to-equity ratios, inventory accuracy, return on assets, and diversification. Each time a new goal is adopted, employees are educated about why achieving the goal is important to long-term profitability and what they can do to help the company achieve the goal. The objective of this approach is to motivate employees to improve profits by working differently—not just harder.[53]

Rob Rodin, CEO of Marshall Industries, argues that it's exactly because so many different specific goals must be met that profit sharing is the way to go. "How do you design an incentive system robust enough to accommodate every change in every customer and every product and every market every day?" he asks. "You can't—you'd be designing it the rest of your life," he concludes. That's why Rodin eliminated all incentives, commissions, bonuses, and achievement awards and replaced them with a simple profit-sharing plan. After six years of experience with profit sharing, he still loves the new system. In his mind it has helped rid the organization of all the gamesmanship he used to see—shipping early to meet quotas, pushing costs to the next quarter, and fighting over how to allocate computer system costs, just to name a few.[54]

Despite its critics, results such as those at Lincoln Electric, Nucor Corporation, Chrysler, Wal-Mart, and Hallmark, suggest that profit sharing can be very motivational when it's accompanied by employee participation and feelings of involvement.[55] Under the Lincoln Electric Incentive Plan, employees receive profit-sharing bonuses based on their productivity. The bonuses are determined by a simple bonus-factor formula. First, the board of directors sets the amount of the year's bonus pool, based on a recommendation by the chair. The chair looks at such factors as how much money the company has made, how much seed money is needed, and how much money is needed for taxes and dividends. The average bonus pool during a recent ten-year period was 10.6 percent of sales revenue. The company then divides this bonus pool amount by the total wages paid. This quotient is the bonus factor. A bonus factor of 1.00 means that the bonus pool is the same as the total company-wide wages. A typical bonus pool might be 75 percent of wages paid. Once the bonus factor has been determined, the company calculates bonuses by multiplying the bonus factor by individual earnings and merit ratings. Here is an example: A production worker earned $35,000. His merit rating is 110 percent, or 1.10. The bonus factor is 0.75. The formulae for determining his bonus are as follows:

1.	$35,000	×	1.1	=	$38,500	
	(earnings)		(merit rating)		(pay for individual performance)	
2.	$38,500	×	.75	=	$28,875	
			(bonus factor)		(bonus)	

Employees must pay for their own hospitalization insurance, which costs approximately $3,000. The company deducts this money from employees' year-end bonuses. Thus, this production worker receives a bonus of $25,875 (before taxes), bringing annual pay to $64,375.

Gain Sharing

Gain-sharing plans are premised on the assumption that it's possible to reduce costs by eliminating wasted materials and labor, developing new or better products or services, or working smarter. Typically, gain-sharing plans involve all employees in a work unit or firm. The median gain-sharing payout is 3 percent, substantially less than the average 5 percent merit increase.[56]

Three generations of gain-sharing plans have evolved.

First-Generation Plans. Two plans—Scanlon and Rucker—were developed in the Depression Era. Both focus on cost savings relative to historical standards. The Scanlon and Rucker Plans are built around the following four principles:

- A management philosophy emphasizing employee participation;
- A formula to share the benefits of productivity-generated savings among employees and the employer;
- Employee committees to evaluate ideas; and
- A formal system for gathering and implementing employee suggestions on ways to increase productivity or reduce costs.[57]

Even though the Scanlon and Rucker Plans share a common philosophy, they differ in one important aspect: the Scanlon Plan focuses only on labor cost savings. Suppose that the historical costs of labor for your firm are $1 million a year. If actual labor costs are less than anticipated costs ($800,000), a portion ($50,000) of the money saved is placed in a set-aside fund in case labor costs soar in subsequent quarters. The remaining savings ($150,000) is split among the company and the employees. In contrast, the Rucker Plan ties incentives to a wide variety of savings.

Both plans are appropriate in small, mature firms employing fewer than 500 workers. Since standards are based on past performance, simple and accurate measures of performance are needed. Because of the heavy involvement of all employees, the culture must be open, trusting, and participative.[58]

Second-Generation Plans. Beginning in the 1960s, a second generation of gain-sharing plans began to emerge. These differ from first-generation plans in several respects. First, they focus on labor *hours* saved, rather than labor *costs* saved. Detailed time-and-motion studies are conducted to develop engineered standards of physical production. Because of the depth of analysis required, employees typically aren't involved in the development of the plan. This may reduce perceptions of fairness.

Unlike first-generation plans, second-generation plans include nonproduction workers in the measurement of the organization's productivity and in the distribution of variable pay realized from cost savings. ImproShare (which stands for improved production through sharing) is typical of second-generation plans. Developed by industrial engineer Mitchell Fein, ImproShare has been adopted in a wide array of firms, including service-sector firms such as hospitals and financial institutions. Exhibit 12.7 compares the details of the calculations of the Scanlon, Rucker, and ImproShare plans.

Third-Generation Plans. According to Marc Wallace, who studied new pay practices in 46 firms, a third generation of gain-sharing plans emerged during the 1980s. These plans are "so different from first and second generation models that the term gain-sharing may no longer be appropriate."[59]

Exhibit 12.7
Calculations for Selected Gain Sharing Plans

Scanlon Plan Base Ratio

[(Sales Dollars − Returned Goods) ± Inventory] ÷ [(Cost of Work and Nonwork Time Paid + Pension + Insurance)]

Rucker Plan Base Ratio

(Cost of All Wages and Benefits) ÷ (Sales Dollar Value of Product − Goods Returned − Supplies, Services, and Material)

ImproShare Plan Base Formula

[(Standard Value Hours Earned, Current Period) × (Total Actual Hours Worked, Based Period ÷ Total Standard Value Hours Earned, Based Period)] ÷ [(Total Hours Worked, Current Period)]

Third-generation plans encompass a much broader range of organizational goals.[60] They have definite terms, which support the current business plan. A plan adopted by a Cleveland steel manufacturer called L-S Electro-Galvanizing Co. illustrates third-generation plans. L-SE, as the company is known, is a joint venture between the American steel company LTV Corp. and Japan's Sumitomo. The two firms joined forces after American automakers made known their intention to use rust-resistant, electro-galvanized steel in their cars. The technology was available only in Japan at the time the venture was created. L-SE began as a nontraditional workplace with high levels of participation. An important motivator was a gain-sharing plan administered by a labor-management committee and applied to all team members equally. The plan capped payouts at 25 percent of an employee's wages and overtime. Objectives, which were defined twice annually and amended if necessary, reflected goals considered important by management and reasonable by employees. Gain-sharing payouts have been based largely on production levels. Over time, as productivity levels improved, the formula was gradually adjusted.[61] This tailored approach to the design of gain-sharing plans is widespread. The new plans have their roots in Scanlon, Rucker, and Improshare plans, but the variations that have been introduced yield so many different approaches that customized plans are now almost idiosyncratic to each company.[62]

As with Lincoln Electric's plan, this method of compensation works because of other aspects of the total system used for managing human resources in the company. The conditions that support the use of gainsharing include team-based work, broadly defined job responsibilities, and a management philosophy that values employee involvement.

PAY THAT PUTS EARNINGS AT RISK

Merit-based and incentive-based pay systems apply to a large percentage of the workforce. However, they're generally not used for sales personnel and high-level executives, who frequently have their earnings placed at risk.

Some companies have pushed the notion of at-risk pay throughout the organization. Nucor, a steel mill, is well-known as a pioneer of this approach. At year end, the company distributes 10 percent of pretax earnings to employees. Factory workers at Nucor's steel mills earn wages set at less than half the typical union rate. But bonuses based on the number of tons of acceptable quality steel produced bump total pay to about 10 percent more than that of comparable unionized workers. The bonuses reflect company productivity levels, but they also encourage individuals to behave responsibly. Workers who are late lose their bonus for the day; workers who are more than 30 minutes late lose their bonus for the week. Managers at Nucor earn bonuses also. The bonuses of department managers are based on return on plant assets, and those of plant managers are based on return on equity. The system seems to work. Nucor turns out more than twice as much steel per employee than larger steel companies.[63]

Arguably, Lincoln Electric's pay plan also puts employees' earnings at risk, as does any incentive plan that does not guarantee income that's near the market average. In other words, earnings at risk is a matter of degree. Usually, the degree of risk is most extreme for employees paid on commissions.

Implementing an earnings-at-risk pay plan can be difficult, especially when employees are not familiar with the concept. Thus, prudent organizations introduce such changes cautiously. The feature, Managing Strategically: Bankers Prefer to Avoid Risk, describes the experience of one organization that experimented with putting pay at risk.

MANAGING STRATEGICALLY

Bankers Prefer to Avoid Risk

Earnings-at-risk (EAR) systems have gained popularity in many industries including retail banking because of their potential to reduce fixed costs and ensure long-term employment stability. In banks, EAR systems cut base pay levels to below market levels and reward employees for selling new services, loan packages, and even insurance. EAR systems create a wider range of possibilities for total take-home pay, but they also add risk and uncertainty—job conditions that historically have been foreign in the conservative retail banking industry. Thus, when a large, publicly-held retail bank decided to implement a new EAR pay plan, it decided to let two researchers examine employees' reactions to the change

The bank was in extremely good financial health at the time it decided to change its pay plan. But they could see that changes were in the wind. Consolidation within the industry had begun. It was clear that the industry was changing, and only the strongest institutions would survive in the long run. By changing its pay plan, the bank officers hoped they could boost productivity and strengthen the bank's position in the market.

Before the new pay plan was introduced, bank employees completed a survey. They completed a second survey six months after the new plan went into effect. At the time of the first survey, a traditional "upside earnings" incentive pay plan was in place. Employees received a base salary set at the market rate, and they were eligible for quarterly bonuses based on branch performance.

The survey data showed that implementing the EAR pay plan significantly altered employees' pay satisfaction. Employees were moderately satisfied with how much they earned before the EAR system was implemented (Average = 4.43). They were significantly less satisfied once it was in place (Average = 3.05). The change in pay administration procedures also led to a decline in satisfaction (Time 1 Average = 3.77; Time 2 Average = 2.88). Under the old system, employees were more satisfied with how much they earned than with the pay administration process. Under the new system, employees were equally dissatisfied with both how much they earned and how the pay system was administered. Employees who had been with the bank a long time showed the biggest declines in satisfaction. Surprisingly, dissatisfaction was just as great among employees who were making more money under the new system, compared with those making the same or less.

Apparently, changing a pay system can create dissatisfaction even among employees who benefit from the change—i.e., the best performing employees. At least at this bank, the opportunity to earn higher pay was overshadowed by having the steady portion of their paychecks reduced. Further analysis of the survey results showed that, under the EAR plan, employees no longer felt that their individual efforts determined how much pay they earned. They found it difficult to understand how their behavior affected the financial performance measures that were used to measure the organization's success. Based on the level of dissatisfaction revealed by the surveys, the bank officers discontinued the EAR plan and reinstated the incentive pay plan that was previously in effect.

Commissions

■□ *fast fact*

With commissions, a men's clothing salesperson at Nordstrom can earn $90,000 even without a profit-sharing bonus.

Because a large part of a salesperson's job is unsupervised, performance-based compensation programs are useful in directing sales activities. More than half of all sales plans use a combination of salary and individual or group incentives.[64] Only 20 percent of all sales personnel are paid by straight incentives, however.

As companies rethink their strategic objectives, they often evaluate their current pay system for salespeople, who represent the company to their valued customers. IBM's restructuring provides a vivid example. Under Lou Gerstner, IBM has stressed the importance of both customer satisfaction and increased profits. To implement the company's strategy, Gerstner needed salespeople to begin thinking about the implications for IBM of the deals they cut with customers. Simply making a sale to generate revenue wasn't sufficient. To focus the attention of the sales force, IBM restructured their commission system. Instead of tying only 6 percent of commission pay to profits, the new system tied 60 percent of pay to profits. The other 40 percent was tied to customer satisfaction, in order to reduce the temptation to simply push fast-turnover, high-profit products. The firm supports the pay system by giving salespeople access to relevant information—such as margins for the products they sell.

Exhibit 12.8 shows the types of components most commonly found in pay plans for salespeople.[65] Note that approximately 30 percent of all sales personnel are paid a straight salary. This may be appropriate when the major function of the salesperson is providing customer service or prospecting new accounts under low-success conditions. Straight salary plans are also appropriate in jobs demanding high technical expertise but little ability to close sales. Consider the job of a product engineer for a software publishing house. Duties of this job might include developing and executing sales and product training programs, participating in trade shows, promoting new products, and meeting with distributors to encourage them to push product lines. In such jobs, a high salary to attract technically competent individuals is more critical than incentives to close the sale.

Exhibit 12.8
Incentive Pay for Field Sales Personnel

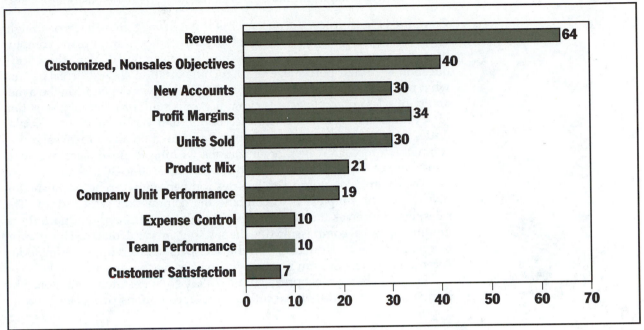

The advantages of a straight salary program are several. From the salesperson's viewpoint, it takes the ambiguity out of the salary process. It's also simpler to administer. If nonsales functions (e.g., paperwork and customer support) are important, salaried sales personnel are more willing to perform them. The drawback is that straight salaries reduce the connection between performance and pay. Commissions make this link directly.

Straight Commission. Usually, the term *commission* refers to pay based on a percentage of the sales price of the product. The percentage received by the salesperson depends on the product being sold, industry practices, the organization's economic conditions, and special pricing during sales promotions. In establishing a sales commission program, the following questions need answering:

- What are the strategic objectives to be achieved?
- What criteria will be used to measure performance?
- Are territories equivalent in sales potential?
- Will commission rates vary by product or vary depending on sales level?
- Will earnings have a cap?
- What will be the timing of commission payments (e.g., monthly or quarterly)?

Once these questions are answered, a program can be set up.

Under commission-only plans, responsibility for generating an income rests directly on the salesperson. The more sales, the greater the earnings; no sales means no income. When employees accept these as legitimate pay plans, their effect on behavior is enormous. At Nordstrom, where salespeople work entirely on commission, the salespeople earn about twice what they would at a rival's store. Unfortunately, such incentives can be so powerful that they elicit unintended behaviors, as when Sears Auto Centers in California were caught for making unnecessary repairs on customers' cars.

Combined Plans.   Because of concerns about the negative effects of straight commission plans, more than half of all sales compensation plans combine base salary and commissions. In setting up a combined plan, the critical question is, "What percentage of total compensation should be salary and what percentage should be commission?" The answer depends on the availability of sales criteria (e.g., sales volume, units sold, product mix, retention of accounts, and number of new accounts) and the number of nonsales duties in the job. Commonly, these plans are based on an 80-to-20 salary-to-commission mix. However, organizations wishing to push sales over customer service functions may utilize different ratios: 60-to-40 or even 50-to-50.

The commission portion of the sales compensation can be established in two ways. The simplest is to combine the commission with a draw. The salesperson receives the draw, or specific salary, each payday. Quarterly or monthly, the total commission due the salesperson is calculated. The amount taken as a draw is deducted, with the salesperson receiving the remainder. Alternatively, bonuses can be given when sales reach a specific level.

Bonuses are the most prevalent nonsalary compensation device used by companies to reward their executives, but stock options run a close second in popularity.

Stock Ownership

Companies use many different approaches to encourage their employees to buy company stock and so take part as an owner of the company. Only some of these approaches represent performance-based pay plans, however. And fewer still truly qualify as earnings-at-risk pay plans.

Broad-Based Plans.   Broad-based stock ownership plans are designed to make stock ownership appealing to all employees. Each year, 15 percent of UPS's pretax profit is used to buy company stock that's distributed to entry-level supervisors on up. Employee stock ownership plans (ESOPs) are one type of broad-based stock-ownership plan. ESOPs grant shares of stock to employees as a means of long-term savings and retirement. They usually do not link the amount of stocks that can be purchased or the purchase price to individual or group performance indicators. Thus, ESOPs are usually treated as an employee benefit rather than as a performance-based reward.

In contrast to ESOPs, stock option plans give employees the opportunity to buy the organization's stock at a later date but at a price established when the option is granted. Over a period of years, employees are given the right to buy stock in the future at today's price. Most options last ten years, with executives typically allowed to exercise half their options after two years and the entire grant after three.[66] Companies with broad-based stock option plans include Pfizer and Eli Lilly. Broad-based stock option plans—that is, those designed to distribute stock as a reward for all employees—seldom put earnings at risk. At best, such plans use stock options as an incentive that's added on to a pay plan that ensures employees are paid at near-market rates.

Stock Options for Executives.   When used as a form of executive compensation, stock options often are designed as true earnings-at-risk plans. The backbone of executive compensation programs, the awarding of stock options is premised on the assumption that the plans encourage executives to "think like owners." After all, they profit only if the stock price goes up. However, critics contend that companies without stock option plans do as well as companies with them. Despite such critics, many companies expect executives to forgo salary increases and cash bonuses and take instead stock options as their rewards. When stock option plans use performance measures to determine the distribution or vesting of stock options, they're using stock ownership as a form of pay for performance.

According to a 1997 survey by KPMG, performance measures used most frequently to determine stock options are traditional accounting measures, such as cumulative profit and return on equity. This same survey revealed that the size of stock options have exploded in recent years. For senior executives, the total value of stock awards often exceeds the combined value of their base salaries and all annual incentives. Another trend identified in the survey was increased eligibility for stock options among employees at deeper levels in the organization. These trends are fueled partly by advantageous accounting and tax rules, and in part by a belief in the motivational value of stock ownership.[67]

Performance-Based Plans. Three common approaches to performance-based options are performance-vesting, premium-priced options, and indexed options.[68]

Performance Vesting and Performance-Accelerated Vesting. In most cases, employees are required to work a set period of time—usually three to five years—before they are vested in the plan. An alternative approach is to tie vesting to the achievement of performance goals. For example, 1,000 options could be vested according to a schedule determined by increases in the price of the stock. The first 200 shares might vest after a $5 increase in stock price, the next 200 might vest after a $10 increase, and so on. Pegging the vesting schedule to growth in earnings per share is another method of performance-vesting. Though straightforward, the problem with this approach is that, under current accounting rules, performance-based vesting requires a charge to earnings, while service-based vesting does not. To get around this problem, some companies use performance-accelerated vesting. With this approach, the basis for vesting is still defined by length of service, but the length of service required before vesting is shortened if performance hurdles are met. In recent years, about 10% of *Fortune* 200 companies used performance vesting or performance-accelerated vesting. Typical performance hurdles include stock price and performance relative to peer companies.

Premium-Priced Options. The principle behind premium pricing is similar to performance vesting, but the mechanism is slightly different. With this method, employees are granted options at an above-market price. Thus, employees won't want to exercise their option until the price advances to a level above that price. For example, if options are granted with an exercise price of $50, but the current market price is only $40, employees would not be able to realize any reward until shareholders realized a 25 percent gain. To further motivate employees, the company might place a time limit on the performance goal. For example, the option could expire in five years if the premium price hasn't been obtained. This approach is used by about 5 percent of *Fortune* 200 companies.

■■□ *fast fact*

A survey of nearly 3,000 companies revealed that more than 50 percent give stock grants to officers and executives, fewer than 10 percent give them to nonexempt employees, and about 25 percent give them to exempt employees.

Indexed Options.   Index options are designed to ensure that employees aren't rewarded (or, in theory, punished) merely due to a robust or retreating economy. They achieve this by indexing the exercise price to an external standard, such as the Russell 2000, the S&P 500, or the Dow Jones Industrial Average. This approach would seem to be the best method for motivating employees to ensure that shareholders receive the best possible return on their investment. But it's seldom used, presumably because it requires a charge to earnings.

SUMMARY

Performance-based pay systems continue to attract the attention of many human resource managers, and line managers continue to ask whether pay can be used to motivate their employees. The success of many variable pay plans indicates that pay can motivate job performance. Nevertheless, many problems can arise because of the myriad issues associated with the design and implementation of performance-based pay systems. To be effective, performance-based pay systems must successfully address several challenges. Perhaps most importantly, a valid and fair performance measurement system serves as the foundation of a performance-based pay system. Other challenges include aligning employee behaviors and performance results with the organization's strategic objectives, gaining employee acceptance and buy-in for the system, and accurately predicting the cost implications of performance-based pay. If organizations can measure performance, and if everyone thinks the system is fair and tied to the objectives of the organization, paying for performance should increase profitability.

Performance-based pay can take many forms. Some forms link pay to the performance of individuals, while others link pay to the performance of teams or the entire organization. Some forms permanently affect the base pay of employees, while other forms have no implications for base pay. Some forms create opportunities for upside rewards without creating any downside risks, while others put a substantial portion of an employee's expected pay at risk. Some forms emphasize short-term performance and offer employees immediate rewards, while others focus employees on longer-term results and defer rewards far into the future. Choosing the best methods of performance-based pay can be difficult because the effects of any of the available methods depend on many factors: the level at which job performance can accurately be measured (individual, department, or organization), the extent of cooperation needed between departments, the willingness of managers to take the time needed to design, implement, monitor, and continuously improve one or several systems, and the culture and degree of trust in the organization. Add to these the need to ensure alignment between the performance-based pay system and all other components of the HR system, and the true magnitude of the challenge becomes apparent. Nevertheless, if the current trend continues, employees in many different industries can expect to see increasing use of performance-based pay.

TERMS TO REMEMBER

Commission
Current distribution plans
Deferred distribution plans
Differential piece rate plan
Earnings-at-risk
Eligibility rules
Employee stock ownership plan
   (ESOP)
Gain-sharing plans
Improshare
Incentive pay plans

Lump-sum bonuses
Merit pay
Performance-based pay
Performance bonuses
Profit-sharing plans
Scanlon and Rucker plans
Standard hour plan
Stock grant
Stock option
Straight piecework plan
Team-based incentives

QUESTIONS FOR DISCUSSION

1. Describe in detail all the parts of compensation linked to performance at Lincoln Electric. How much credit for Lincoln's success do you give to the incentive system?

2. How can performance-based pay help an organization achieve its strategic objectives?

3. Describe an experience you have had in which pay was linked to your performance. Explain the key features of the system used to determine your performance and pay. Did the system work? If not, why not?

4. Under what conditions would you expect a performance-based pay system to have the greatest likelihood of success?

5. Debate the following assertion: If selection and placement decisions are made effectively, differences in the level of performance exhibited by employees should be relatively small; therefore, a performance-based pay system isn't needed and may even be disruptive.

6. When you work on projects as a member of a team, what percentage of the rewards you receive do you prefer to have depend on your own individual performance versus the performance of the team as a whole? Explain why. Does the type of team or the type of project affect your preference? Explain.

7. What does it mean to put earnings at-risk? Why do you think organizations seldom put the earnings of mid- to lower-level employees at risk? List the potential costs and benefits of placing a substantial percentage of pay at risk for *all* employees in the following types of organizations: a hospital, a restaurant, a brokerage firm, a fashion design house.

PROJECTS TO EXTEND YOUR LEARNING

1. **Managing Diversity.** Interview two or three employees of a company in your area. Ask whether they're paid on the basis of their performance.

If so, ask how performance is measured and what percentage of total pay is based on performance. If they aren't so paid, find out if the employees would like to be paid for performance, and if so, under what type of plan—merit, incentive, or earning at risk. Identify the reasons employees use to explain why they prefer one type of plan over another.

2. **Managing Strategically.**   Visit the website of Southwest Airlines and three of its competitors. Locate the annual report for each company and determine what percentage of the company's total stock is held by employees. Then read each annual report. Can you determine why some companies have more employee-owned stock than do others? Does employee stock ownership appear to have any strategic importance to any of these companies? Explain. To begin, visit the following company home pages:

Southwest Airlines at **www.iflyswa.com**
Delta Airlines at **www.delta-air.com**
Continental Airlines at **www.flycontinental.com**

3. **Application and Integration.**
   a.   Compare and contrast the use of incentive pay at Lincoln Electric and Nordstrom. Overall, which plan do you think is more effective? Why?

   b.   Don Hastings has said that Lincoln Electric will gradually move toward having a more traditional pay plan. What do you think he means by this? What strategic objectives would lead this company to conclude that a more traditional pay plan would be more effective? How do you think Lincoln Electric's employees would react to such a change? Why?

CASE STUDY

The Time Clock

Susan Crandall was feeling good about her new position at Western National Bank. Susan, a seven-year employee at Western, had come a long way from her starting position as a teller to her present position as human resource manager, thanks in many respects to her predecessor, Anna Bavetti.

Anna had recently resigned from the bank to take a position with a local computer software company, which was experiencing explosive growth. This company recognized they needed to systematize their staffing practices, so when Anna learned of the opportunity, she jumped. Anna was frustrat-ed by what she considered conservative and stodgy management at the bank, so a change in scenery was a welcome relief.

Anna had begun at Western as an assistant to the then HR manager Nancy Hyer. Anna had an MBA degree from North Carolina and an undergraduate degree from Grinnell College. Anna quickly realized that her technical skills were superior to Nancy's, but she admired Nancy's street smarts and willingness to battle the CEO of the bank over new initiatives in the HR area. Nancy had put in a performance appraisal plan and an absenteeism plan before transferring to the trust department with what was touted as a promotion.

Anna, though, didn't see the move as a promotion. In her estimation, Nancy had gotten too strong and was creating a lot of waves for the top brass at the bank, who were unwilling to move at the pace that Nancy had set. When the president of Western, Larry Wilson, asked Anna to assume the role of assistant vice president of HR, Anna welcomed the opportunity to continue the initiatives begun by Nancy.

Anna decided that she was going to undertake two goals immediately. First, she was going to begin developing Susan. Nancy was too hard on Susan in Anna's estimation. Although Susan didn't have a college degree (she had had to drop out because her mother was ill), she had common sense and extremely good people skills. Over the next year, Anna progressively increased Susan's responsibilities by involving her in applicant screening and interviewing and including her on project assignments. Over time, Susan and Anna developed a teamlike approach to their work and learned to rely on each other to keep the HR management office functioning smoothly.

When Susan learned of Anna's departure, she was saddened but not surprised. Anna always seemed too liberal and progressive for upper management of the bank. Anna valued people and looked for the best in them. Anna, more than the other officers at the bank, seemed genuinely concerned about the welfare of the employees, especially the mostly nonexempt employee workforce. Susan was flabbergasted, though, when Larry Wilson called her into his office and asked her to assume Anna's job. Her pay would increase by 150 percent. Although the job would mean longer hours and more responsibilities, under Anna's tutelage, Susan felt confident that she could rise to the occasion.

Susan wanted more than anything to carry through on Anna's second goal, which was to link the performance evaluation system developed by Nancy to the annual pay increases. The bank had entered an era of competition with other banks and savings and loans, so productivity was a major concern for the bank. Besides cutting staff to the minimum, Susan believed that in the long run, linking pay to effort and performance would encourage productivity among all employees. Susan believed that Western's staff were hard working and would welcome the opportunity to see their pay linked to their performance.

Susan noticed it was almost 5 p.m. and she needed to speak with Gerry Latham, vice president for operations, regarding her proposed merit plan, which would influence his group the most. As she passed by the elevators, she noticed several employees waiting beside the time clock. It was common practice for the nonexempts to wait for a seemingly inordinate amount of time for the elevator to arrive on the fifth floor of the bank building. A common practice was to wait until the elevator bell chimed and the doors began to open before clocking out.

As several of the employees hurriedly punched the clock and dashed to the elevator, Larry Wilson appeared behind Susan. Larry called out to Susan, who was deep in thought about how to present her merit plan to Gerry Latham. "Susan, did you see that?" questioned Larry. "I'm sorry, Larry, I was lost in thought. What are you talking about?" replied Susan. As the elevator doors closed, Larry picked up his voice in obvious irritation. "I think those employees would just as soon cheat us if they're charging their wait time on the elevators. How do we know that they're not trying to cheat us in the morning when they clock in or when they return from lunch late and have a coworker punch them in? Susan, I want you to investigate this tomorrow, first thing. This kind of fraud has got to stop immediately." Oh boy, thought Susan. How am I going to defuse this bomb? As Susan started back down the hall toward Gerry Latham's office, she began to understand the frustration that occasionally leaked through Anna's otherwise calm exterior when she occupied Susan's job.

QUESTIONS

1. What strategic considerations support the concept of a performance-based pay plan in banking?

2. At a minimum, what HR activities must exist prior to implementing a performance-based pay plan in a bank or elsewhere?

3. Does the culture at Western support a performance-based pay plan?

4. How should Susan respond to Larry's directive to investigate the time clock fraud?

CASE STUDY

Merit or Demerit?

BLTC is a firm engaged in the manufacture and distribution of chemicals. Because many of the manufacturing, storage, and distribution processes of BLTC are monitored and controlled by computer technology, the firm's computer operations expenditures are substantial. Tod Jenkins, the director of the firm's computer operations division, estimated that the projected annual budget for his division would be in the neighborhood of $2,500,000. The comptroller of BLTC felt that this amount was excessive and directed Jenkins to reduce costs wherever possible. To accomplish this objective, Jenkins assigned a number of systems analysts to review the current level and type of computer services provided to the organization. These analysts were instructed to streamline operations and eliminate unnecessary or infrequently used management reports and computer equipment.

Stan Cook is one of the best and brightest systems analysts who works for Jenkins. After weeks of intensive investigation, Cook submitted a proposal that permitted a $450,000 reduction in the computer operations budget. These budgetary reductions were accomplished by:

1. Consolidating the existing elements of the management/production control monitoring system
2. Eliminating redundant reporting and data collection procedures
3. Utilizing less expensive "batch" computer processing where possible
4. Eliminating unnecessary or infrequently used computer equipment
5. Increasing utilization and coordination of existing computer resources

Thus, Cook was able to reduce operational costs without reducing the level or quality of services provided to management.

Jenkins was greatly impressed by Cook's activities and felt that he deserved some special form of recognition. Therefore, he informed Cook that he was recommending him for a special merit award (SMA). These SMAs, which are administered by the comptroller's office, constitute an important part of the firm's motivational program. Under this program, the employee's supervisor makes a recommendation as to the amount of the cash award to be received by the employee. In general, the dollar value of the SMA is a percentage of the amount of the cost savings for which the employee was responsible. Jenkins recommended that Cook receive a monetary bonus equivalent to three percent of the cost savings he generated, or $13,500.

Two months after Jenkins recommended Cook for the SMA, Jenkins received a letter from the comptroller indicating that Cook didn't qualify for an award. The comptroller justified his decision by stating that the development of plans to reduce computer operation costs was an integral part of Cook's job and, therefore, didn't warrant additional compensation. Jenkins felt that this decision was both unjustified and characteristic of an "accounting mentality." For the next several months, he and the comptroller exchanged letters and telephone calls arguing for their respective viewpoints. When Cook inquired as the status of his SMA, Jenkins was forced to tell him of the long-running dispute with the comptroller. However, Jenkins assured Cook that the SMA would be awarded even if the firm's president had to be brought in to settle the dispute.

Approximately sixteen months after Jenkins submitted the original SMA recommendation, a compromise agreement was worked out with the comptroller. According to this agreement, Cook was to receive $250 and a printed certificate of achievement. At the awards ceremony, Cook accepted the monetary award and certificate from the comptroller. The following day, Cook informed Jenkins that he was submitting his resignation in order to accept a job offered to him by another firm.

QUESTIONS

1. Was the bonus of three percent a fair amount?
2. What are the real problems with BLTC's suggestion system?
3. Was Cook's response justified?
4. What would you do if you were Cook?

ENDNOTES

1 S. Scholl, "Allstate Pay for Performance Methodology Rewards Excellence," *ACA News* (September 1998): 28–31.

2 R. Hodgetts, "A Conversation with Donald F. Hastings of the Lincoln Electric Company," *Organizational Dynamics* (Winter 1997): 68–74; C. Wiley, "Incentive Plan Pushes Production," *Personnel Journal* (August 1993): 86–92.

3 B. L. Hopkins and T. C. Mawhinney, *Pay for Performance: History, Controversy and Evidence* (Binghamton, NY: Haworth Press, 1992).

4 J. S. Kane and K. A. Freeman, "A Theory of Equitable Performance Standards," *Journal of Management* 23 (1) (1997): 37–58.

5 S. J. Macey and J. M. Sabounghi, "A Roundtable Discussion on Defining, Designing and Evaluating Pay at Risk Programs," *ACA Journal* (Winter 1996): 8–19.

6 S. Kerr, "Risky Business: The New Pay Game," *Fortune* (July 22, 1996): 94–96; J. S. Lublin, "Why More People Are Battling Over Bonuses," *The Wall Street Journal* (January 8, 1997): B1, B7; B. B. Buchholz, "The Bonus Isn't Reserved for Big Shots Anymore," *New York Times* (October 27, 1996): 10.

7 A. Morrison, M. N. Ruderman, and M. Hughes-James, *Making Diversity Happen: Controversies and Solutions* (Greensboro, NC: Center for Creative Leadership, 1993): 11.

8 C. M. Solomon, "Using Cash Drives Strategic Change," *Workforce* (February 1998): 77–81.

9 R. D. Banker, S-Y Lee, G. Potter, and D. Srinivasan, "Contextual Analysis of Performance Impacts of Outcome-Based Incentive Compensation," *Academy of Management Journal* 39 (1996): 920–948.

10 G. D. Jenkins, Jr., A. Mitra, N. Gupta, and J. D. Shaw, "Are Financial Incentives Related to Performance? A Meta-analytic Review of Empirical Research," *Journal of Applied Psychology* 83 (1998): 777–787; N. Gupta and A. Mitra, "The Value of Financial Incentives," *ACA Journal* (Autumn 1998): 58–65.

11 S. Hays, "Pros and Cons of Pay for Performance," *Workforce* (February 1999): 69–72; A. Kohn, *Punished by Rewards* (Boston MA: Houghton Mifflin, 1998); A. Kohn, "Why Incentive Plans Cannot Work," *Harvard Business Review* (September–October 1993): 54–63.

12 R. Eisenberger and J. Cameron, "Detrimental Effects of Reward," *American Psychologist* 51 (November 1996): 1153–1166; see also W. Van Eerde and H. Thierry, "Vroom's Expectancy Models and Work-Related Criteria: A Meta-Analysis," *Journal of Applied Psychology* 81 (1996): 575–586.

13 R. J. Greene, "Effective Variable Compensation Plans," *ACA Journal* (Spring 1997): 32–39.

14 S. J. Berman, "Using the Balance Scorecard in Strategic Compensation," *ACA News* (June 1998): 16–19.

15 P. Pascarella, "Compensating Teams," *Across the Board* (February 1997): 16–22.

16 J. Fierman, "The Perilous New World of Fair Pay," *Fortune* (June 13, 1994): 58–59.

17 J. B. Wood, "Customer Satisfaction and Loyalty," *ACA Journal* (Summer 1998): 48–60.

18 P. Digh, "The Next Challenge: Holding People Accountable," *HR Magazine: Diversity Agenda* (October 1998): 63–69; S. N. Mehta, "Diversity Pays," *The Wall Street Journal* (April 11, 1996): R12.

19 S. J. Macey and J. M. Sabounghi, "A Roundtable Discussion on Defining, Designing and Evaluating Pay at Risk Programs."

20 K. A. Brown and V. L. Huber, "Lowering Floors and Raising Ceilings: A Longitudinal Assessment of the Effects of an Earnings-at-Risk Plan on Pay Satisfaction," *Personnel Psychology* 45 (June 1992): 279–311.

21 I. T. Kay, "High CEO Pay Helps the U.S. Economy Thrive," *The Wall Street Journal* (February 23, 1998): A22.

22 R. J. Greene, "Improving Merit Pay Plan Effectiveness," *ACA News* (April 1998): 26–29.

23 Hay Group, *The Hay Report: Compensation and Benefits for 1998 and Beyond* (New York: The Hay Group, 1998).

24 J. M. Newman, "Selecting Incentive Plans to Complement Organizational Strategy," *Current Trends in Compensation Research and Practice,* Balkin and Gomez-Mejia, eds. (Englewood Cliffs, NJ: Prentice Hall, 1987):14–24.

25 J. Kerr, "Diversification Strategies and Managerial Rewards: An Empirical Study," *Academy of Management Journal* 28 (1985): 155–179; G. T. Milkovich and J. M. Newman, *Compensation* (Homewood, IL: BPI-Irwin, (1999); E. E. Lawler III, *Pay and Organizational Development* (Reading, MA: Addison-Wesley, 1981).

26 P. M. Wright et al., "Productivity and Extra-Role Behavior: The Effects of Goals and Incentives on Spontaneous Helping," *Journal of Applied Psychology* 78 (1993): 374–381.

27 B. Gerhart and G. T. Milkovich, "Organizational Differences in Managerial Compensation and Financial Performance," *Academy of Management Review* 33 (1990): 663–691.

28 B. Flannigan, "Turnaround From Feedback," *HR Focus* (October 1997): 3.

29 T. R. Hinkin, P. M. Podsakoff, and C. A. Schriesheim, "Mediation of Performance Contingent Compensation: A Reinforcement Perspective," *New Perspectives on Compensation,* Balkin and Gomez-Mejia, eds. (Englewood Cliffs, NJ: Prentice Hall, 1987): 196–210; Milkovich and Newman, *Compensation.*

30 G. Flynn, "HR in Mexico: What You Should Know," *Personnel Journal* (August 1994): 44.

31 C. C. Chen, "New Trends in Rewards Allocation Preferences: A Sino–U.S. Comparison," *Academy of Management Journal* 38 (1995): 408–428; see also Y. P. Hau and R. M. Steers, "Cultural Influences on the Design of Incentive Systems: The Case of East Asia," *Asia Pacific Journal of Management* 10 (1996): 71–85; C. E. Rusbult,

C. A. Insko, and Y-H W. Lin, "Seniority-based Reward Allocation in the United States and Taiwan," *Social Psychology Quarterly* 58 (1995): 13–30.

[32] J. K. Giacobbe-Miller, D. J. Miller, and V. V. Victorov, "A Comparison of Russian and U.S. Pay Association Decisions, Distributive Justice Judgments, and Productivity Under Different Pay Conditions," *Personnel Psychology* 51 (1998): 137–163.

[33] "Policy Guide: Incentive Pay Can Bring Many Rewards," *Bulletin to Management* (June 5, 1997): 184; "Policy Guide: Employers Use Pay to Lever Performance," *Bulletin to Management* (August 21, 1997): 272.

[34] G. Flynn, "Your Grand Plan for Incentive Compensation May Yield a Grand Lawsuit," *Workforce* (July 1997): 89–92.

[35] T. Lewin, "Women Losing Ground to Men in Widening Income Difference," *New York Times* (September 15, 1997): A1, A6.

[36] R. Heneman, "Merit Pay Research," *Research in Personnel and Human Resource Management*, vol. 8, K. Rowland and G. Ferris, eds. (1990): 204–263; R. Heneman, *Pay for Performance: Exploring the Merit System* (New York: Pergamon Press, 1984).

[37] T. J. Hackett, "Back to Basics: Why A Non-Profit Agency Abandoned Incentives," *ACA News* (January 1998): 23–25.

[38] C. Peck, *Variable Pay: New Performance Rewards* (New York: Conference Board, 1990).

[39] S. Scholl, "Allstate Pay for Performance Methodology Rewards Excellence," *ACA News* (September 1998): 28–31.

[40] W. B. Abernathy, "Linking Performance Scorecards to Profit-Indexed Performance Pay," *ACA News* (April 1998): 23–25.

[41] I. T. Kay, "High CEO Pay Helps the U.S. Economy Thrive."

[42] J. Reingold, "Executive Pay: Tying Pay to Performance is a Great Idea. But Stock-Option Deals Have Compensation Out of Control," *Business Week* (April 21, 1997): 58–66; T. A. Stewart, "CEO Pay: Mom Wouldn't Approve," *Fortune* (March 31, 1997): 119–120; J. Reingold, "Even Executives Are Wincing At Executive Pay," *Business Week* (May 12, 1997): 40–43; J. A. Byrne, "Smoke, Mirrors, and the Boss's Paycheck," *Business Week* (October 13, 1997): 63.

[43] S. Tully, "A Better Taskmaster Than The Market?" *Fortune* (October 26, 1998): 277, 286; T. Jackson, "How EVA Measures Up," *Financial Times* (October 7, 1996): 10; S. Tully, "The Real Key to Creating Wealth," *Fortune* (September 20, 1993): 38–44.

[44] E. E. Lawler III and S. G. Cohen, "Designing Pay Systems for Teams," *ACA Journal* (Autumn 1992): 6–18; C. Meyer, "How the Right Measures Help Teams Excel," *Harvard Business Review* (May/June 1994): 95–103.

[45] B. Nelson, "Does One Reward Fit All?" *Workforce* (February 1997): 67–70.

[46] Lawler and Cohen, "Designing Pay Systems for Teams," 6–16.

[47] J. S. DeMatteo, L. T. Eby, and E. Sundstrom, "Team-Based Rewards: Current Empirical Evidence and Directions for Future Research," *Research in Organizational Behavior* 20

(1998): 141–183; P. K. Zingheim and J. R. Schuster, "Best Practices for Small-Team Pay," *ACA Journal* (Spring 1997): 40–49; J. S. DeMatteo, M. C. Rush, E. Sundstrom, and L. T. Eby, "Factors Related to the Successful Implementation of Team-Based Rewards," *ACA Journal* (Winter 1997): 16–27.

[48] R. K. Platt, "Driving Change — 'Account Teams' Help Company to Fly into the Next Century," *ACA News* (January 1996): 17–21.

[49] There have been hundreds of laboratory studies on the effects of team-based rewards, and these suggest that they can be effective. But studies in the field show mixed results, due perhaps to challenges in addressing all of the key design issues. For a complete review, see J. S. DeMatteo, L. T. Eby, and E. Sundstrom, "Team-Based Rewards: Current Empirical Evidence and Directions for Future Research."

[50] P. K. Zingheim and J. R. Schuster, "Best Practices for Small-Team Pay."

[51] R. Rose, "Kentucky Plant Workers Are Cranking Out Good Ideas," *The Wall Street Journal* (August 13, 1996): B1; J. Birnbaum, "Recognition Programs Are Widespread," *HR News* (November 1991): 2.

[52] Bureau of National Affairs, "Incentive Pay Schemes Seen as a Result of Economic Employee Relation Change," *BNA Daily Report* (October 9, 1984): 1; Milkovich and Newman, *Compensation*; G. W. Florkowski, "The Organizational Impact of Profit Sharing," *Academy of Management Review* (October 1987): 622–636.

[53] J. Stack, "The Problem With Profit Sharing," *Inc.* (November 1996): 67–69.

[54] G. Colvin, "What Money Makes You Do," *Fortune* (August 17, 1998): 213–214.

[55] D. E. Tyson, *Profit Sharing in Canada: The Complete Guide to Designing and Implementing Plans that Really Work* (New York: Wiley, 1997); "Productivity Boosters in Employee-Owned Firms," *Bulletin to Management* (May 5, 1994): 137; "Profit Sharing Plans Scarce but Successful," *Bulletin to Management* (June 2, 1994): 169; S. Greengard, "Leveraging a Low-Wage Work Force," *Personnel Journal* (January 1995): 90–102.

[56] Peck, *Variable Pay*, 6.

[57] B. E. Moore and T. L. Ross, *The Scanlon Way to Improved Productivity: A Practical Guide* (New York: Wiley, 1978); R. J. Schulhof, "Five Years with a Scanlon Plan," *Personnel Administrator* (June 1979): 55–63; L. S. Tyler and B. Fisher, "The Scanlon Concept: A Philosophy As Much as a System," *Personnel Administrator* (July 1983): 33–37.

[58] B. Graham-Moore and T. Ross, *Productivity Gainsharing* (Englewood Cliffs, NJ: Prentice-Hall, 1983); R. J. Bullock and E. E. Lawler III, "Gainsharing: A Few Questions and Fewer Answers," *Human Resource Management* 23 (1984): 23–40; D-O Kim, "Factors Influencing Organizational Performance in Gainsharing Programs," *Industrial Relations* 35 (April 1996): 227.

[59] M. J. Wallace, *Rewards and Renewal: America's Search for Competitive Advantage through Alternative Pay Strategies* (Scottsdale, AZ: American Compensation Association, 1990): 15.

[60] Huret, "Paying for Team Results," 41.

[61] "Work Redesign, Empowerment Touted," *Bulletin to Management* (August 4, 1994): 248.

[62] T. M. Welbourne and L. R. Gomez Mejia, "Gainsharing: A Critical Review and a Future Research Agenda," *Journal of Management* 21 (1995): 559–609.

[63] S. Baker, "Why Steel Is Looking Sexy," *Business Week* (April 4, 1994): 106–108.

[64] C. F. Schultz, "Compensating the Sales Professional," *New Perspectives on Compensation,* Balkin and Gomez-Mejia, eds. (Englewood Cliffs, NJ: Prentice Hall, 1987): 250–258.

[65] Based on a survey conducted by Hewitt Associates, as represented in G. Fuchsberg, "Selling Isn't Everything," *The Wall Street Journal* (April 1994): R8; see also J. A. Colletti and M. S. Fiss, "Rewarding New Sales Roles With Incentive Pay," *ACA Journal* (Autumn 1998): 45–57.

[66] G. B. Paulin, "Building Blocks in Total Compensation: Granting Stock Options" (American Compensation Association, 1996); K. Capell, "Options For Everyone," *Business Week* (July 22, 1996): 80–88; K. Labich, "When Workers Really Count," *Fortune* (October 14, 1996): 212; J. R. Blasi and D. L. Kruse, *The New Owners: The Mass Emergence of Employee Ownership in Public Companies and What It Means to American Business* (New York: HarperCollins, 1991); K. J. Klein, "Employee Stock Ownership and Employee Attitudes: A Test of Three Models," *Journal of Applied Psychology* 72 (1987): 319–332; M. Quarrey, J. Blasi, and C. Rosen, *Taking Stock: Employee Ownership at Work* (Cambridge, MA: Ballinger Publication Co., 1986): 66.

[67] P. T. Chingos and M. M. Engel, "Trends in Stock Option Plans and Long-Term Incentives," *ACA Journal* (Spring 1998): 13–18; J. Fox, "The Next Best Thing to Free Money," *Fortune* (July 7, 1997): 52–62; L. Jereski, "At a High-Tech Firm, The Daily Stock Price Is Everyone's Business," *The Wall Street Journal* (September 10, 1996): A1; D. C. Johnston, "New Twist Makes Corporate Stock Options Even Sweeter," *New York Times* (July 5, 1997): 35.

[68] This section is based on data reported in M. J. Halloran, "Performance-based Options: An Upcoming Debate," *ACA News* (Spring 1998): 28–30.

Chapter

13

> "People come here for the benefits, and they stay for them. . . . Turnover is very expensive, and our benefits keep our rate down."

Bradley Honeycut
Director of Compensation and Benefits
Starbucks Coffee Company[1]

INDIRECT COMPENSATION: PROVIDING BENEFITS AND SERVICES

Chapter Outline

MANAGING THROUGH PARTNERSHIP

at Steelcase

Steelcase, headquartered in Grand Rapids, Michigan, is the world's leading provider of high-performance workplaces. It serves virtually every country of the world through 900 independently owned dealers. Its own workforce of almost 20,000 employees is also spread throughout the world. It has over 30 manufacturing plants in the United States, six in France, three in the United Kingdom, and one each in seven other countries, including Mexico, Japan, and Germany.

Steelcase is a business totally focused on the customer, quality improvement, and continuous innovation. This focus translates into their mission: "We are committed to helping your people work more effectively. How? By integrating the goals of your organization, the technology you use, and how your people work in the space they occupy. This focus governs all our research efforts and the products, services, and expertise we provide through our independent, worldwide dealer network."

Although Steelcase is a big operation with about $3.5 billion in sales, it has many competitors. One of its most significant competitors is another Michigan-based firm, Herman Miller. Others include Haworth, Inc., and Hon, Inc. Consequently, Steelcase is very concerned about managing and reducing its costs. For example, in the 1990s it focused on reducing the costs of workers' compensation, essentially the costs associated with having people hurt, injured, and out-of-work. Under medical services, Steelcase developed and implemented a "return-to-work" program that has reduced the average cost per claim. The plan has two major concepts:

- A medical review board systematically examines the injured person and the injury situation to make the correct diagnosis of the claim. The intent here is to uncover all the facts and build an atmosphere of trust and understanding between worker and company.
- A return-to-work component enables workers to get back to work as soon as possible: once the injury has been diagnosed, the biggest manageable expense is the time in getting the worker back to work. By setting up therapy centers and accommodating working conditions, Steelcase reduced time away from work for most injuries by 50 percent in six years. Their average cost per claim went from $1,552 to $1,213.

This program has resulted in cost savings of over $44 million since the program's inception. Little wonder it received strong support from the CEO, Jim Hackett. Cost reduction in this area is a crucial issue for most companies because workers' compensation costs have risen dramatically. Payouts in the United States have climbed from $22 billion in 1980 to $70 billion in 1996! While this is smaller than the $250 billion that employers currently pay for health care costs, workers' compensation is rising faster.[2]

To learn more about Steelcase, visit the company home page at
www.steelcase.com

This feature, Managing Through Partnership at Steelcase, addresses a mounting crisis in cost containment for American business. As international competition increases, U.S. firms struggle to contain their costs. For many firms, total compensation costs are a significant part of the problem. But as many firms are discovering, these costs, although significant, are manageable. Steelcase's approach is an excellent example of what firms can do to reduce their workers' compensation costs. Firms are also attempting to reduce other compensation costs by asking workers to contribute to some of the expenses—for example, to pay for some of their health care. In some cases, firms are just cutting back on what they are willing to offer employees.

Although the specific elements of plans vary, employee benefits and services are generally defined as in-kind payments to employees for their membership or participation in the organization. These payments provide protection against health and accident-related problems and ensure income at retirement. Legally required public protection programs include Social Security, unemployment compensation, and workers' compensation; private protection programs include health care, life insurance, and disability insurance. Retirement income is provided through pensions and savings plans. Benefits programs also include pay for time not at work—for instance, vacations, holidays, sick days and absences, breaks, and washup and cleanup. A growing category of benefits enables employees to enjoy a better lifestyle or to meet social or personal obligations while minimizing employment-related costs. Discounts, educational assistance, and child and elder care fall into this category. Exhibit 13.1 illustrates the cost of benefits as a share of the total labor costs associated with the "average" U.S. employee.[3]

■□ *fast fact*

Nearly one out of four companies allow employees to buy and/or sell vacation time.

Exhibit 13.1

Average Annual Employee Benefits and Earnings

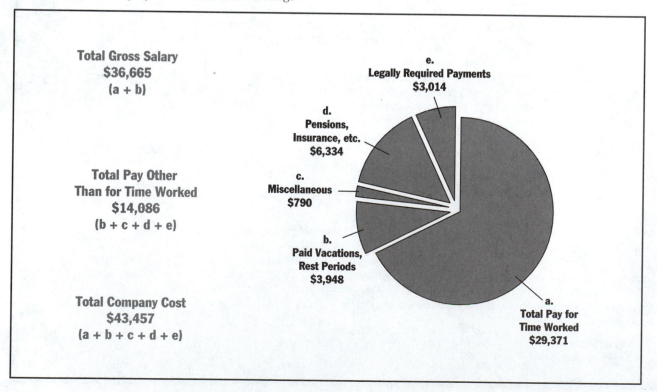

Total Gross Salary
$36,665
(a + b)

Total Pay Other
Than for Time Worked
$14,086
(b + c + d + e)

Total Company Cost
$43,457
(a + b + c + d + e)

e.
Legally Required Payments
$3,014

d.
Pensions,
Insurance, etc.
$6,334

c.
Miscellaneous
$790

b.
Paid Vacations,
Rest Periods
$3,948

a.
Total Pay for
Time Worked
$29,371

This chapter discusses indirect compensation—also called employee benefits and services—and the role it plays in fulfilling organizational objectives. First, it outlines the objectives and organizational and environmental influences affecting the strategic management of benefits. Then, it looks at legal considerations. Next, it reviews public and private protection programs, such as workers' compensation and pension plans. It also focuses on health care benefits, paid leave, and life cycle benefits such as child and elder care. It concludes with a discussion of administration issues, including cost-benefit analyses, and some international comparisons.

THE STRATEGIC IMPORTANCE OF BENEFITS AND SERVICES

Companies provide benefits and services primarily to attract and retain valued employees. Until recently, employers were relatively generous; now, the tide is shifting for several reasons. First, benefits and services are a major, increasingly costly part of total compensation. In 1929, total benefits payments averaged 5 percent of total pay. By 1999, they had risen to an average of almost 40 percent of wages and salaries, or roughly $8 a payroll hour, or $14,659 a year for each employee. Although these numbers vary across industries and by type of worker, the cost of benefits to organizations is, in general, enormous.[4] While wages and salaries increased 40 times from the mid-1940s to the mid-1990s, benefits increased 500 times.[5]

Why do organizations pump so much money into benefits programs? Because they believe that benefits help

- attract good employees,
- increase employee morale,
- reduce turnover,
- increase job satisfaction,
- motivate employees, and
- enhance the organization's image among employees and in the business community.

Unfortunately, ample research demonstrates that these objectives are not always attained, owing largely to inadequate communication. Many, perhaps most, employees don't really know which benefits they receive or how much those benefits are worth. Realizing this, firms such as Hewlett Packard and Starbucks have begun aggressively marketing their benefits packages to tell employees what the company provides to them.[6] If employees don't know they receive a benefit, they won't stay with the company in order to retain that benefit.

Indirect compensation also may fail to help a company achieve its objectives if employees regard it as a condition of employment to which they are entitled. Rather than appreciating their employer's concern, employees may view benefits as a social responsibility the employer is obligated to provide.[7]

Even when indirect compensation is regarded as an inducement to work in a particular company, its importance relative to other job factors—for example, opportunity for advancement, salary, geographic location, responsibilities, and prestige—may be low. Furthermore, some of the potential value of a company's benefits package is often lost because each employee values only some of the benefits offered, and may even resent the company's decision to spend money on benefits used only by other employees. Allowing employees to choose their indirect compensation packages is one solution to this problem. As some firms reduce or even eliminate benefits

■■☐ *fast fact*

FedEx estimates that its day care center in Dallas reduces turnover by 10 percent.

"Balancing the benefit needs of both the company and employees can certainly be a challenge, but the rewards of sound, cost-effective benefits programs, and employee understanding and appreciation are certainly worth the effort."

Cheryl Poulson
Management of Benefits Planning
Glaxo Wellcome

and ask workers to share or even assume their costs, many employees are beginning to realize how expensive benefits can be. Also, they are being forced to decide which benefits are of most personal value,[8] and are thus beginning to learn the range of benefits they can and do receive.

External Influences

The growth in the types and costs of employee benefits can be traced to several environmental trends.

Wage Controls.   Under normal business conditions, employers compete for labor primarily through the wages they offer. During times of major crisis, such as World War II and the Korean War, the government curtailed such activity in order to prevent runaway inflation. Throughout the 20th century, the imposition of wage controls in times of war forced organizations to offer more and greater benefits in place of wage increases to attract new employees.

Health Care Costs.   Health care costs have been increasing over the years, although at a decreasing rate. In 1940, U.S. health care expenses were $4 billion, about 4 percent of the GDP. In 1999, they were more than $1 trillion, or almost 20 percent of the GDP. For employers, the average health benefits cost for each employee was almost $4,000 in 1999. Regardless of their causes, these increases have had a major effect on indirect compensation.[9]

Union Bargaining.   From 1935 into the 1970s, unions were able to gain steady increases in wages and benefits for their members. Practically all benefits are now mandatory bargaining items, which means that employers must bargain in good faith on union proposals to add them. Companies without union representation may offer similar benefits in order to remain attractive to job applicants.

Federal Tax Policies.   Employers prefer not to cover benefits expenses that, for tax purposes, can't be counted as business costs. Employees, on the other hand, want to receive benefits without the burden of increased taxation. Thus, employers' benefits packages regularly change as the tax codes change.

Inflation.   Employee benefits managers, more so than compensation managers, must anticipate the effects of inflation on medical service, education, and pension benefits. For example, double-digit inflation in the 1980s eroded the purchasing power of some retirees' benefits and resulted in adjustments in the retirees' levels of benefits. Inflation is now much lower, but companies are constantly managing their health care costs.

Competition.   In their recruitment ads and literature, most companies label their benefits packages as competitive. Owing to increased competition, being competitive without spending more often means developing innovative packages to attract and retain employees. Wellness programs, health screenings, stock options, and employee assistance programs are examples of relatively new benefits options. Other responses to competitive pressures include flexible benefits plans and cash options offered in place of prepaid benefits packages.[10]

"I sincerely believe employers who find the answers to the questions [surrounding work/life] are going to be leading employers in the future. These leaders will attract and retain the very best people. This is the competitive advantage."

**Lew Platt
CEO
Hewlett-Packard**

fast fact

Of the "100 Best Companies to Work For," 75 percent offer elder care, child care, relocation services, and casual dress everyday.

Social Legislation.   A variety of laws significantly affect the administration and offering of indirect compensation, including the *Family and Medical Leave Act of 1993*, the *Americans with Disabilities Act of 1990*, and the *Employee Retirement Income Security Act of 1974* (ERISA). These are described more fully later in this chapter.

Expansion of Social Security.   In 1935, the *Social Security Act* covered 60 percent of all workers. Subsequently, the scope of benefits and the percentage of eligible workers increased substantially. Today 95 percent of all workers are covered and are eligible to receive disability and health benefits in addition to retirement pay.

Internal Influences

The scope of employee benefits has also been affected by organizations and their stakeholders. Initiatives such as major medical insurance, long-term disability plans, and child and elder care allowances reflect a general concern for employees. All were implemented by organizations in response to employee needs. Provisions such as educational assistance benefits, employee assistance programs, and wellness programs have been inspired by pressures to improve productivity and worker skills. More recently, benefits such as offering auto and home insurance, matching funds for charitable giving, and work-family balance programs have been prompted by private businesses' desire to be socially responsible and attract good workers.[11]

Employee Wants.   Traditionally, employers have adopted a "father-knows-best" attitude toward benefits; the company has assumed it knows what is the most appropriate coverage for its employees. As we begin the 21st century, this attitude is being replaced with one of high employee involvement and choice, consistent with employee empowerment. "Choice accounts" that provide various benefits options and allow employees, rather than the company, to allocate benefits dollars are increasingly popular.[12] Exhibit 13.2 shows how employees evaluate the relative importance of several types of benefits.[13]

Human Resource Philosophy. An organization's fundamental beliefs about its employees and the employer-employee relationship set the stage for benefits management. The benefits manager must understand the underlying basis of the philosophy and the extent to which management supports human resources generally and benefits specifically. Some firms adopt an egalitarian approach to benefits and services by insisting that the same set of benefits be provided to all employees. Other firms adopt a more competitive approach, varying benefits with organization level. Some firms adapt their benefits to the needs of their workers in order to attract and retain them. The feature, Managing Strategically: Avon Listens To Its Workers,[14] illustrates what is possible. Such benefits policies communicate the organization's culture and values to employees.

Business Strategy and Objectives. Human resource planning involves assessing external threats and internal forces, setting and ranking goals, establishing timetables, and integrating benefits planning with human resource planning specifically. These in turn can be linked with the company's strategic direction and specific business objectives. Exhibit 13.3 provides some other examples of business objectives and possible responses from the benefits area.

■□*fast fact*

Illegal drug users have more on-the-job accidents and file twice as many workers' compensation claims.

"In the work/life equation, attitude is far more important than any particular policy or equation."

**Paul Allaire
Chairman and CEO
Xerox**

Exhibit 13.2
Benefits Employees Consider Most Important

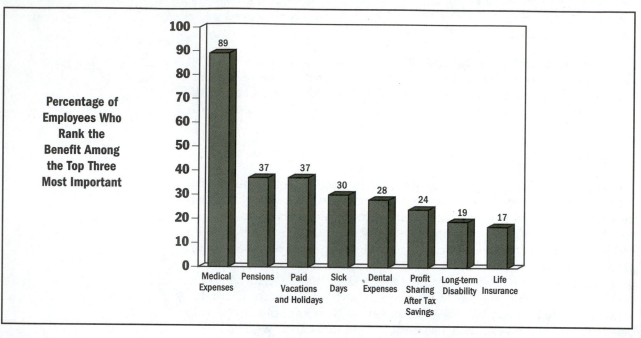

MANAGING STRATEGICALLY

Avon Listens to Its Workers

More and more companies are seeing that benefits can be a very powerful tool in the management of their human resources. As a consequence, many companies are re-examining the ways they provide benefits and the types of benefits they provide. They are looking at the workforce and asking them what they need and want. They know that the result of this is a much more motivated employee who is likely to be satisfied with the firm and likely to work productively. The needs of the companies and the employees will be served at the same time. With this philosophy in mind, Avon Products, Inc., in New York City, developed a new retirement program. It began with a better understanding of its workforce. Most Avon employees are engaged in sales and marketing of beauty products; and about 75 percent of them are female. In these jobs Avon found that employees tend to drop in and out of its workforce. As a result, they never were able to qualify for the traditionally defined benefit retirement plans. In other words, the workers were never able to gain a benefit that most people now regard as critical in their joining and working for a company! So Avon remodeled its retirement benefits to make them more available and more portable. Avon combined the values of defined-benefit and defined-contribution plans into a single-cash balance to be taken as a lump sum at retirement or termination of work. The matching contributions of Avon to the 401(k) plan are immediately vested and the pension benefits are available to anyone chosen by the employee, not just the surviving spouse. Now the needs of Avon's workforce are better served and, thus should be the customers of Avon and its stockholders.

To learn more about Avon visit its home page at
www.avon.com

Exhibit 13.3
Business Objectives and Potential Benefits Responses

Business Objective	Benefits Response
1. To unify the company acquired from the merger, from independent subsidiary to integrated division status, by year-end.	1. Perform an analysis of an immediate versus a gradual transfer of subsidiary employees into the corporate benefits plan.
2. To develop a working environment that is founded on integrity, open communication, and individual growth.	2. Develop an employee career-counseling system that provides employees with an opportunity to assess skills and develop competencies. Establish a tuition reimbursement program.
3. To establish the division as a recognized leader in support of its community.	3. Establish a corporate-giving matching fund.
4. To complete the downsizing of the company by the end of the third quarter.	4. Develop various termination subsidies such as severance pay, outplacement assistance, and early retirement benefits.
5. To cut accident rates 10 percent by year-end.	5. Establish an employee assistance program by year-end. Set up a free literacy training program to ensure that all employees can read job safety signs.

PUBLIC PROTECTION PROGRAMS

Protection programs are designed to assist employees and their families if and when the employees' income (direct compensation) is terminated, and to alleviate the burden of health care expenses. Protection programs required by the federal and state governments are referred to as public programs, and those voluntarily offered by organizations are called private programs. Exhibit 13.4 provides examples of comparable public and private protection programs.

Social Security System

Public protection programs are the outgrowth of the *Social Security Act of 1935*. This act initially set up systems for retirement benefits, disability, and unemployment insurance. Health insurance, particularly Medicare, was added in 1966 to provide hospital insurance to almost everyone age 65 and older.

Funding of the Social Security system is provided by equal contributions from the employer and employee under terms of the *Federal Insurance Contributions Act* (FICA). Initially, employee and employer each paid 1 percent of the employee's income up to $3,000. In 1999, each paid 6.2 percent of the first $68,400 of the employee's income for retirement and disability and 1.45 percent of the total income for hospital insurance through Medicare. The average annual Social Security benefit is about $9,100 for a single person and about $15,500 for a married couple, with adjustments routinely made for increases in the consumer price index.[15]

■□*fast fact*

Almost all economists agree that businesses pass along the cost of Social Security in the form of lower wages.

Unemployment Compensation Benefits

To control costs, the *Social Security Act* dictates that unemployment compensation programs be jointly administered through the federal and state governments. The federal rate is the same for everyone. But because income levels vary from state to state, unemployment compensation also varies by

Exhibit 13.4
Protection Programs

Issue	Public Programs	Private Programs
Retirement	Social Security old-age benefits	Defined benefit pensions Defined contribution pensions Money purchase and thrift plans [401(k)s and ESOPs]
Death	Social Security survivors' benefits Workers' compensation	Group term life insurance (including accidental death and travel insurance) Payouts from profit-sharing, pension, or thrift plans, or any combination of these Dependent survivors' benefits
Disability	Workers' compensation Social Security disability benefits State disability benefits	Short-term accident and sickness insurance Long-term disability insurance
Unemployment	Unemployment benefits	Supplemental unemployment benefits or severance pay, or both
Medical and dental expenses	Workers' compensation	Hospital surgical insurance Other medical insurance Dental insurance

state. The level of benefits paid to unemployed workers ranges from 50 percent to 70 percent of base salary up to a specified maximum weekly amount, which also varies by state. Since passage of the *Tax Reform Act of 1986*, unemployment compensation has been fully taxable, making actual benefit levels much lower.[16]

Corresponding to variations in compensation paid to unemployed workers are variations in the total tax liability of employers. The tax rates for employers vary according to the number of unemployed people drawing from the fund. Consequently, employers who dismiss many workers who later draw unemployment benefits pay higher taxes than employers with better employment records.

Workers' Compensation and Disability

■□ *fast fact*

Steelcase is rated four times safer than the national average for the light-metal industry by the National Safety Council.

As described in the feature, Managing Through Partnership at Steelcase, workers' compensation costs are a major concern to companies. Of the more than six million job-related injuries reported annually in the private sector, about half are serious enough for the injured worker to lose work time or experience restricted work activity, or both. In addition, hundreds of thousands of new occupational illness cases are reported each year. More than 90 percent of these illnesses—most of which are back related—are associated with repetitive motions such as vibration, repeated pressure, and carpal tunnel syndrome. Most require medical care and result in lost work time.[17]

When injuries or illnesses occur as a result of on-the-job events, workers may be eligible for workers' compensation benefits. Administered at the state level and fully financed by employers, these benefits cover costs and lost income due to temporary and permanent disability, disfigurement, medical care, and medical rehabilitation. Survivors' benefits are provided following fatal injuries.

Proactive workers' compensation administrators such as Libby Child at Steelcase are applying a variety of health care cost-containment strategies to workers' compensation, such as

- developing networks of preferred provider organizations,
- specifying fees for treating workers' compensation claimants,
- limiting payments to medically necessary or reasonable procedures,
- requiring precertification of hospital admissions,
- establishing concurrent review of inpatient hospital stays, and
- routinely auditing hospital and health care bills.[18]

PRIVATE PROTECTION PROGRAMS

Private protection programs are offered by organizations but are not required by law. They include retirement income plans, capital accumulation plans, savings and thrift plans, and supplemental unemployment benefits and guaranteed pay. Some firms also offer work options for retirees, including temporary full-time and permanent part-time employment.

The various retirement income plans can be classified in terms of whether they are qualified or nonqualified. A *qualified plan* covers a broad, nondiscriminatory class of employees, meets Internal Revenue Code requirements, and consequently is qualified to receive favorable tax treatment. For example, the employer's contributions to the plan are tax deductible for the current year and employees pay no taxes until retirement. *Nonqualified plans* don't adhere to the strict tax regulations, cover only select groups of employees, and consequently don't receive favorable tax treatment.[19]

Pension Plans

The largest category of private protection plans is pensions. Four out of five employees in medium and large firms are covered by some type of private pension or capital accumulation plan and rely on these plans to provide future security. A less well known fact is that the twenty largest pension funds hold one-tenth of the equity capital of America's publicly owned companies. All told, institutional investors—primarily pension funds—control close to 40 percent of the common stock of the country's largest businesses. Pension funds also hold 40 percent or more of the medium- and long-term debt of the country's bigger companies. Thus, employees, through their pension funds, have become America's largest retirement bankers, lenders, and business owners.[20]

Defined Benefit Plans. With a defined benefit pension plan, the actual benefits received on retirement vary by the employee's age and length of service. For example, an employee may receive $50 a month for each year of company service. Some employers and unions prefer defined benefit plans because they produce predictable, secure, and continuing income. Another advantage of such plans is that they are carefully regulated by the *Employee Retirement Income Security Act*. In addition to reporting rules, disclosure guidelines, fiduciary standards, plan participation rules, and vesting standards, defined benefit plans must adhere to specific funding-level requirements and be insured against termination due to economic hardship, mis-funding, or corporate buyouts. The Pension Benefit Guaranty Corporation (PBGC) administers the required insurance program and guarantees the payment of basic retirement benefits to participants if a plan is terminated. The PBGC also can terminate seriously underfunded pension funds.

Defined Contribution Plans.   Eighty percent of new plans are defined contribution plans. With this type of plan, each employee has a separate account to which employee and employer contributions are added. If only the employer contributes, it's a *noncontributory plan.* When both contribute, it's a *contributory plan.* Typically, the employee must activate a contributory plan by agreeing to contribute a set amount of money; the employer then matches the percentage contribution to a specific level.

The two most common types of defined contribution plans are money purchase and tax-deferred profit-sharing plans. With *money purchase plans,* the employer makes fixed, regular contributions for participants, usually a percentage of total pay. Employees may also make voluntary contributions. The maximum amount for any employee is equal to 25 percent of earned income, up to a maximum of $30,000 for all defined contribution plans combined. Monies are held in trust funds, and the employee is given several investment options that differ in terms of the degree of risk and growth potential. At retirement, accumulated funds are used to provide annuities. In some cases, lump-sum distributions may be made.

Tax-deferred profit-sharing plans allow employees to share in company profits using a predetermined formula. Monies contributed to these plans are set aside until retirement, when the employees can cash in their profits. From the employer's perspective, tax-deferred profit-sharing plans are useful because employers may deduct up to 15 percent of each participant's compensation (up to an income level of $200,000) for contributions. In addition, the employer passes on the investment risk to employees.[21]

Supplemental Plans

In addition to Social Security and standard pension plans, large firms often offer a supplemental defined contribution plan or a supplemental savings plan. Currently, more than 30 percent of all employees participate in supplemental plans. Such plans function as the third leg of the retirement income stool; they also provide additional retirement income or serve as a source for accumulating funds to meet short-term needs and goals. These plans take one of two forms: savings plans that work as defined contribution plans, called 401(k) plans, and employee stock ownership plans.[22]

Individual Retirement Accounts

Under current law, an employee who isn't an active participant in an employer-sponsored pension plan during any part of a year may contribute up to $2,000 to an individual retirement account (IRA). Employees involved in employer-sponsored pension plans also may participate, providing their income does not surpass limits set by the IRS.

Stock Options

Giving individuals an option to buy the stock of the company at a fixed price (which is a benefit only if the actual stock price increases) has, until recently, been a benefit mainly for senior managers. Today, as many as 35 percent of large corporations offer broad-based stock option programs that cover almost

---

■□ *fast fact*

"Cash balance plans" are a relatively new type of defined contribution pension. It is good for younger workers but is being challenged as possibly discriminatory against older workers who don't benefit from many years of compounded returns.

■□ *fast fact*

Under 401(k) plans both the employer and the employee contribute and the employee is responsible for the investment decisions.

■□ *fast fact*

The turnover rate at Starbucks is 60 percent per year versus 300 percent for the industry.

all employees. Starbuck's program, BEAN STOCK, covers virtually all of its 30,000 employees.[23] With a tight labor market, firms are finding that offering stock options is a competitive necessity.

HEALTH CARE BENEFITS

Coverage for medical expenses—including hospital charges, home health care, physician charges, and other medical services—is the core of a group health plan. Companies also may provide wellness programs, employee assistance programs, and short- and long-term disability insurance. Health benefits—particularly medical insurance—cost far less than what employees would pay on their own. Most employees underestimate the cost of health benefits to the organization and view coverage as an entitlement rather than a discretionary benefit offered by employers.

In reality, health care costs more than $1 trillion, and that figure continues to rise faster than inflation. Health care consumed about 14 percent of the U.S. gross domestic product in the mid-1990s; today, the figure is about 20 percent. Companies that buy health insurance for their employees spend, on average, more than thirteen cents of every dollar they make to pay for this coverage. This is 35 to 40 percent more than in other industrialized countries. As a consequence, companies have been very aggressive at reducing health care expenses, sometimes at the cost of reducing employee choice and even coverage.[24]

Medical Care Approaches

Employers usually finance and provide medical expense benefits to employees and employees' dependents through insurance companies. However, a variety of other approaches are gaining in popularity as businesses attempt to thwart rising costs.

Insurance Companies. Insurance carriers offer a broad range of health care services from which employers can select coverage. Premiums are set and adjusted depending on usage rates and increases in health care costs. The insurance company administers the plan, handling all the paperwork, approvals, and problems. Proponents of this approach argue that insurers protect the plan sponsor against wide fluctuations in claim exposure and costs and offer opportunities for participation in larger risk pools. Insurance companies also have administrative expertise related to certification reviews, claim audits, coordination of benefits, and other cost-containment services.

On the downside, the insurance company, not the employer, makes decisions regarding covered benefits. Its decisions may go against the corporation's ethics and sense of social responsibility. Companies that subscribe to a specific insurance plan don't have the luxury of ignoring the insurer's advice and doing what they feel is ethical. The insurance company makes all the tough calls.

Provider Organizations. Blue Cross and Blue Shield are nonprofit organizations that operate within defined geographic areas. Blue Cross plans cover hospital expenses, and Blue Shield plans cover charges by physicians and other medical providers. Typically, these associations negotiate arrangements with their member providers to reimburse the providers at a discounted rate when a subscriber incurs a charge. As originally established,

■□ *fast fact*

In the past ten years, there has been a sharp decline in health insurance provided by small businesses to their employees.

■□ *fast fact*

Only 51 percent of the 37 million workers in companies with fewer than 25 employees have company-paid health insurance.

the rate represented full payment for the service, and no additional charge was levied. However, as a result of skyrocketing health care costs, employees may now be asked to pay deductibles ($50 to $250 a year for each person) or a share of the cost of service (10 to 20 percent), or both.

Health Maintenance Organizations (HMOs). About one-third of all eligible employees, or about 60 million people, participate in HMO plans.[25] The growth in HMOs was stimulated by the passage of the *Health Maintenance Organization Act of 1973*. This act requires that companies with at least 25 employees living in an HMO service area must offer membership in that organization as an alternative to regular group health coverage, provided the HMO meets federal qualification requirements. HMO amendments of 1988 relaxed many of the federal rules governing HMOs and specifically repealed the dual-choice mandate, effective October 1995. This shift in legislative direction is designed to make the HMO field more competitive and, as a result, employers more receptive to using HMOs.

One successful HMO is operated by Deere and Company, a farm machinery manufacturer. Realizing 20 years ago that its own health care costs were skyrocketing, Deere brought its health care operations in-house and thereby established its own HMO, called the Heritage National Healthplan. Deere has been so successful that it has attracted more than 300 other company clients, such as Monsanto, Sundstrand Corporation, and Chrysler.[26]

Preferred Provider Networks. *Preferred provider organizations (PPOs)* are another form of managed health care delivery. Introduced in the 1980s, these plans covered over 99 million participants in 1999. With these programs, employers contract directly or indirectly through an insurance company with health care providers (physicians, dentists, laboratories, hospitals, and so forth) to deliver discounted services to program participants. Because the rates and requirements for these plans are relatively unregulated, employers have a great deal of flexibility in structuring an arrangement.

Unlike HMO participants, employees in a PPO are not required to use the plan's providers exclusively. However, they are usually offered incentives, such as a lower deductible or lower cost-sharing percentage, to use a PPO provider. For example, the employer may cover all the costs of health care provided by a PPO but only 80 percent of the costs of health care provided by physicians outside the PPO network. A concern with PPOs is the potential for antitrust legislation, since these plans ask providers to agree on standard charges for health care services.[27]

Self-Funded Plans. Like Steelcase, a growing number of companies are opting for self-insured or self-funded plans as a way to control medical plan costs and gain relief from state insurance regulations. By eliminating or reducing insurance protection, the employer saves on carrier retention charges (the amount of money not utilized to pay claims), such as state premium taxes, administrative costs, risk and contingency expenses, and reserve requirements. Typically, the employer creates a voluntary employee beneficiary association and establishes a trust whose investment income is tax exempt as long as it is used to provide benefits to employees and their dependents.

Cost-Containment Strategies. To further control costs, firms employ a variety of other strategies such as the following:

■□ *fast fact*

More employees with health insurance coverage are joining managed care programs: 48 percent in 1992 versus 83 percent in 1998.

■□ *fast fact*

The Camberley Hotel in Atlanta reduced health care costs and employee turnover when it became self-insured.

- *Hospital utilization programs.* Employers set up a system to review the necessity and appropriateness of hospitalization prior to admission, during a stay, or both.
- *Coordination of benefits.* Employers coordinate their benefits with those of other providers to prevent duplicate payment for the same health care service.
- *Data analysis.* Employers analyze the available information to determine the most viable cost management approach. Simulations and experience-based utilization assumptions are used to develop models.
- *Managed care.* Many employers are active participants in case management. Interventions include requirements for second opinions and peer reviews.
- *Cost sharing with employees.* By raising deductibles and contribution levels, employers hold the line on overall expenses.[28]
- *Incentives to take care.* By offering incentives, such as bonuses to employees who lose weight, some firms hope to change employees' behaviors so that employees are healthier.[29]

Wellness Programs

Frustrated with efforts to manage health care costs for employees who already are sick, a growing number of employers are taking proactive steps to prevent health care problems. Moving beyond employee exercise classes and stress management classes, a handful of firms implement well-designed wellness programs to produce significant savings on the bottom line.[30]

Coors Brewing Company spent ten years fine-tuning its wellness program. For every $1.00 spent on wellness, Coors sees a return of $6.15, including $1.9 million annually in decreased medical costs, reduced sick leave, and increased productivity. According to William Coors, past chairman and CEO, the secret to Coors's success is really no secret: "Wellness is an integral part of the corporate culture." Coors's commitment to wellness includes a health risk assessment, nutritional counseling, stress management, and programs for smoking cessation, weight loss, and orthopedic rehabilitation.

Overweight Coors employees learn about the long-term risks associated with their condition through a health hazard survey. They are educated about the effect of excess weight on the cardiovascular, endocrine, and musculoskeletal systems. Then they receive an individual plan that may include individual counseling, group classes, and medical programs. The company even gives employees a financial incentive if they participate in the program and achieve and maintain their weight loss goal during a twelve-month period. To further encourage involvement, classes are held on-site.

Coors has been sensitive to the ADA requirements (a) that entry into a wellness program can't be a condition for passing a medical exam and (b) that facilities must be accessible to all. "At Coors Co. persons with disabilities have complete access to all of the company's facilities and its wellness center," says corporate communications manager Joe Fuentes. Part of the wellness program includes a medical questionnaire that determines employees' "health age" in relation to their chronological age. The program is totally voluntary for employees. The questionnaire asks employees whether they smoke, wear a seat belt, have high blood pressure, and exercise, and also includes questions about the employees' medical history. All Coors employees are covered by their health insurance at 85 percent. Employees who pass the questionnaire are then covered at 90 percent. If employees fail the test,

"Large portions of the health care industry have undergone revolutionary change, and not for the purpose of improving health care, but in order to reduce the cost of doing business for large corporations."

New England Journal of Medicine

"Sharing costs is a way of getting the workforce involved in the effects of health care delivery costs. If it's a free lunch, people tend to treat it that way."

**Don Morford
Director of Benefits
Kmart**

■■ *fast fact*

Synovus pays employees $50 to take an annual physical and offers a $200 reward if vital signs are okay.

■■ *fast fact*

Dow's "Backs in Action" program encourages exercise, dieting, and ergonomics. The company has decreased on-the-job strains and sprains up to 90 percent.

they can have a plan of action recommended by the community outreach person who runs the program. Test results are confidential and made available only to the community outreach person who administers the survey. Employees can choose not to follow up on the test results.[31]

Employee Assistance Programs

Whereas wellness programs attempt to prevent health care problems, *employee assistance programs* are specifically designed to assist employees with chronic personal problems that hinder their job performance and attendance. EAPs often serve employees with alcohol or drug dependencies, or both, or those with severe domestic problems. EAPs also help employees cope with mental disorders, financial problems, stress, eating disorders, smoking cessation, dependent care, bereavement, and AIDS. Because the job may be partly responsible for these problems, some employers are taking the lead in establishing EAPs for affected workers.[32] Thus, EAPs serve as a form of indirect compensation that benefits the individual and the firm.

PAID LEAVE

Paid leave is not as complex to administer as benefits from protection programs, but paid leave is more costly, accounting for more than 10 percent of the total payroll. If absenteeism policies are not designed correctly, costs may escalate even further. The two major categories of paid leave are time not worked while off the job and time not worked while on the job.

Off the Job

The most common paid off-the-job times are vacations, holidays, sick leaves, and personal days. The challenge in administering these benefits is to contain costs while seeking better ways to tailor the benefits to fit employees' needs and preferences.

Vacations and Holidays. Vacations give employees time to recuperate from the physical and mental demands of work. Vacation time is also viewed as an appropriate reward for service and commitment to the organization. Recently, a small number of firms have granted sabbaticals to employees (similar to those in academia), which, after a stated period of service, can be used for self-improvement, community work, or teaching. Tandem Computers, for example, grants six-week sabbaticals plus normal vacation time at full pay. Tandem found that in the short term, such programs have a negative effect on productivity, but in the long term, they enhance productivity.

In setting up vacation programs, several issues need to be addressed: (1) Will vacation pay be based on scheduled hours or on hours actually worked? (2) Under what circumstances can an employee be paid in lieu of a vacation? (3) Can vacations be deferred, or will they be lost if not taken? (4) What pay rate applies if an employee works during a vacation? The trend is toward vacation banking, with employees able to roll over a specified period of unused vacation days into a savings investment plan. Keep in mind that in the U.S. firms are not legally required to offer vacation days. In other countries, however, the government mandates these minimum number of days per year:

Brazil	30	Spain	22
Sweden	25	Australia	20
Germany	24	Mexico	6[33]

fast fact

More than 80 percent of workers receive paid holidays and vacations, but less than 10 percent of those in the bottom tenth receive paid leave of any kind.

Paid Absences. On any given day, one million American workers who are otherwise employed won't attend work; they will be absent. In the United States, the absenteeism rate ranges from 2 percent to 3 percent of total payroll, but some organizations report absenteeism in excess of 20 percent. An estimated 400 million person-days are lost each year as a result of employee absenteeism. This is almost ten times the number of person-days lost to strikes over a ten-year period.[34]

Employees fail to show up for work for many reasons—health problems, family problems, bad weather, transportation difficulties, and so forth. Nevertheless, absences are greatly influenced by an organization's formal policies. As the number of paid days off increases, the number of days of actual absence increases proportionally. Because of lax policies, many organizations unwittingly not only tolerate or accept absenteeism but actually reward it. Their policies make it easier to be absent than to come to work.[35]

Negative strategies to control absenteeism include disciplinary procedures against employees who are absent once a week or once every two weeks without a physician's excuse, before or after a holiday, after payday, without calling in, or for personal business. This discipline ranges from oral warnings for first offenses to discharge. Unfortunately, these policies appear to be generally ineffective in controlling absenteeism among habitual offenders.

Programs that reward attendance—with, for instance, cash prizes, bonuses, or conversion of a proportion of unused absence days to vacation days—appear more promising. To prevent unscheduled absenteeism, many organizations grant personal days, or personal time off (PTO). The employees can use these days during the year for any reason. The logic here is that employees must notify supervisors in advance that they will be absent. Self-management programs for habitual offenders also offer some hope for controlling excessive absenteeism.

On the Job

Time not worked on the job includes rest periods, lunch periods, washup times, and clothes-changing and getting-ready times. Together, these are the fifth most expensive indirect compensation benefit. Another benefit that's growing in popularity is paid time for physical fitness. This is clearly pay for time not worked, but organizations often offer it because of its on-the-job benefit: healthy workers.

LIFE CYCLE BENEFITS

In response to a growing number of single-parent families, two-earner families, aging parents in need of care, and nontraditional families, employers are expanding their benefits packages to address new priorities.[36] Some of these benefits are offered by only a handful of firms. However, employers are realizing that a failure to address these needs in the future may restrict their ability to compete. Thus, it's anticipated that many employers will add these benefits. Life cycle benefits include child care, elder care, and other benefits.

Child Care Services

Recognizing that child care is a shared responsibility, more and more employers are providing some type of child care assistance to their employees. In fact, a survey of more than 10,000 firms employing ten or more work-

■□ *fast fact*

On average, absenteeism costs employers $740 for each employee in their workforce.

■□ *fast fact*

At Johnson & Johnson, employees can bring their infants in for free tests and checkups six times annually. Prevention saves $13 million a year.

ers showed that 63 percent of those firms offered some type of assistance benefits, scheduling help, or services related to child care.[37] Thus, to be competitive in the labor market, firms at least need to survey their employees to find out their preferences and may need to offer a variety of options to meet employee needs.[38] Options employers may want to develop include any or all of the following:

- Scholarships for dependents
- Summer employment for dependents
- Subsidized tutoring for dependents
- Sick-child care
- On-site child care
- Flexible scheduling
- Child care referrals
- On-site child care
- Family care leave
- Adoption benefits[39]

Some employers fear that childless employees may resent progressive policies to assist families. In fact, the formation of The Childfree Network, which is an advocacy group that serves as a voice for childless workers, is one indication that there is good reason to be prepared for some possible backlash from employees who feel they are not able to benefit as much as their peers who can utilize these valuable services. A recent study of employee attitudes revealed some disparity in the reactions of employees with and without children. However, the study failed to find any evidence that the more negative attitudes of the childless employees translated into concrete behaviors.[40] Other research indicates that any backlash that occurs tends to be of limited scope and does not create generalized job dissatisfaction.[41]

Even if some backlash occurs, the benefits associated with child care initiatives may outweigh the disadvantages. Prudential Insurance Company estimates that its child care center saves the company $80,000 annually through reduced absenteeism.[42] Families and society as a whole reap even more valuable gains. A recent study of nine Western European countries indicates that parental leave-taking is correlated with children's health and survival. In the countries studied, on average, eligible employees (men and women) used 32 weeks of parental leave benefits. Longer leaves significantly reduced deaths among infants and young children.[43]

Dependent Care Reimbursement Accounts. Dependent care reimbursement accounts have become the most prevalent type of child care benefit in the 1990s. According to a survey by Buck Consultants, this benefit is offered by nearly 60 percent of medium- and large-sized companies.[44] These accounts allow employees to pay for qualified expenses with pretax dollars subject to a use-it-or-lose-it rule. They benefit employees greatly, yet involve minimal administrative costs for the sponsoring organization. The maximum amount an employee can channel into one of these accounts is $5,000 a year. For an employee to participate in a reimbursement account, the child must be under the age of thirteen. The expense must be necessary to permit an employee to work, to permit both husband and wife to work, or to permit a spouse to attend school full-time.[45]

Resource and Referral Programs. Twenty-nine percent of firms offer child care information and referral assistance. These company-sponsored programs counsel employees about day care options and refer them to pre-screened local providers. Prescreening helps to ensure that the centers in the network meet minimum care standards and are financially responsible.

On-Site Care Facilities. By 1998, thousands of employer-sponsored on-site or near-site care centers were in operation. In San Francisco, office and hotel complexes with more than 50,000 square feet must either provide an on-site facility or pay into a city child care fund. Although the operation of such centers can be costly, a growing number of employers now accept it as a social and business necessity.

Consider the comments of Dick Parker, director of administrative services for Merck and Company, at groundbreaking ceremonies for its $8 million child care center: "You don't provide child care just because you want to be a good guy. You do it for business reasons. Merck decided to build the center for three reasons: retention, recruitment, and productivity. Child care will become more and more of a recruitment issue in the future. If employees are worried about their child care services[,] that will affect their productivity and retention."[46]

Campbell Soup Company's child care center is located across the street from its corporate headquarters and cares for 110 children. Contending that on-site care cuts absenteeism, reduces distractions for employees, and helps with hiring, the company picks up 40 percent of the weekly expense for each child.[47] The Hacienda Child Development Center in Pleasanton, California, serves multiple employers, including Hewlett-Packard, Computerland Corporation, and Prudential Insurance Company. Operating costs are funded from parent fees and business fees.

Elder Care Services

Twenty-eight percent of employees over the age of 30 spend an average of ten hours a week giving care to an older relative. For a significant faction, this commitment equals a second job. Some 12 percent of workers who care for aging parents are forced to quit their jobs to do so. With aging of the baby boomers, more and more employers are considering ways to help workers who are caring for elderly relatives. Assistance ranges from information and referral programs to specialized care insurance. *The Family and Medical Leave Act of 1993* supports employee time off for both child care and elder care.

Information and Referral Programs. In 1990, only 11 percent of employers offered information and referral programs for elder care; now the number exceeds 50 percent. Like dependent-care referral programs, company-operated elder-care referral programs are designed to help the caregiver identify appropriate community resources.[48]

Long-Term Care Insurance. One new and fast-growing option for elder care is long-term care insurance. Although fewer than 15 percent of firms offered this benefit in the mid-1990s, nearly 70 percent offer it now. This type of insurance covers medical, social, custodial, and personal services for people who suffer from chronic physical or mental illnesses or disabling injury or disease over an extended period of time. Typically, coverage is offered to employees on an employee-pay-all basis. Premium rates are age based, and some plans set a maximum age (typically 79) for participation. Benefit maximums are related to care site (e.g., nursing home versus day care center) and include lifetime limits.

■□ *fast fact*

Serving a largely female workforce, First Chicago pays for about 800 deliveries a year. Coaching pregnant women has drastically reduced C-sections and underweight babies.

■□ *fast fact*

One out of four households provides informal care to a relative or friend age 50 or older.

Other Life Cycle and Life Style Benefits

With demographic and value shifts, a wider array of lifestyle choices is now available. As a consequence, a rising percentage of workers—such as unmarried couples, divorced people, and single parents—don't fit into conventional benefits packages. Recognizing that people are assets to the organization and that the world of work can never be fully separated from the rest of life, companies on the cutting edge are redesigning their benefits packages to address the needs of all employees.[49]

"Domestic partner benefits isn't a gay and lesbian issue. It's a business issue. We believe that by providing domestic partners access, we are enhancing our ability to recruit and retain the best employees."

Bill Shelley
Health and Welfare Supervisor
Pacific Gas & Electric

Benefits for Spousal Equivalents. About one out of ten companies extend "spousal" benefits to same-sex partners and to unmarried opposite-sex partners, and another 20 percent were considering it in 1999.[50] Lotus, now a unit of IBM, modified its insurance and benefits policy to offer gay and lesbian partners the same benefits accorded heterosexual spouses. According to Russell J. Campanello, vice president for human resources, "This is fair and equal." To be eligible, unmarried partners of the same sex must live together and share financial obligations. If they break up, the employee must wait one year before registering a new partner. In addition to health care, the plan includes life insurance, relocation expenses, bereavement leave, and a death benefit.[51] Such benefits are optional for most employers, but they are required for some. In 1997, the San Francisco Board of Supervisors mandated that all employers who do business with the city must offer registered domestic partners—who may be either same-sex or opposite-sex couples— the same benefits they offer married couples. The San Francisco 49ers football team, television stations, airlines that lease space at the airport, and many other employers have been affected. During the 1980s and early 1990s, many employers shunned domestic partner benefits, due in part to cost concerns. Back then, insurance companies often added surcharges for domestic-partner coverage, because they thought that costs would go up. Since then, however, data have become available and they show the surcharges were unnecessary. Surcharges have largely disappeared, making domestic partner benefits no more expensive than benefits for spouses.[52]

Educational Expense Allowances. Faced with skill obsolescence, downsizing, and retraining demands, most medium and large firms provide some form of educational expense assistance. Most plans cover registration fees, and some assist with graduation, laboratory, entrance examination, professional certification, and activity fees. Typically, these programs require a relationship between the course and some phase of company operations. For example, National Healthcorp, which is headquartered in Murfreesboro, Tennessee, offers tuition assistance to any aide who wishes to become a nurse. The company will pay for up to two years of school in exchange for the aide's promise to stay on staff that long after graduation.

■ *fast fact*

To help an executive relocate across the country, one company arranged for the family to visit a pet shop every 300 miles to ensure the safety and health of the children's two pet goldfish.

Relocation and Housing Assistance. As housing costs continue to soar, more employers are considering housing assistance as an employee benefit. Seventy-five percent of surveyed New Jersey employers with 500 or more employees attributed hiring and retention problems to the high cost of housing; seventy-one percent of surveyed California manufacturers said high housing costs were limiting their business expansion abilities.[53]

Relocation assistance traditionally has consisted of financial help for travel expenses and the cost of moving possessions. If needed, the company might also pay for furniture storage for a limited time as well as for temporary housing. A growing number of firms also offer a variety of allowances and services for transferred employees and high-demand new hires. These benefits include cost allowances for selling a house, expenses for finding a new residence, assistance in finding employment for a spouse, and temporary living expenses.[54]

ADMINISTRATIVE ISSUES

Although organizations tend to view indirect compensation as a reward, recipients don't always see it that way. This conflict causes organizations to become concerned with how they administer their packages of indirect compensation benefits.

Determining the Benefits Package

The benefits package should be selected on the basis of what is good for the employee as well as for the employer. Knowing employee preferences can often help organizations determine what benefits should be offered. For example, employees in one company indicated a strong preference for dental insurance over life insurance, even though dental insurance was only one-fourth the cost to the company. As workers get older or their incomes increase, the desire for higher pension benefits steadily increases.

Even if employers know what employees prefer, they may not be able to offer it. According to Jordan Shields, owner of a consulting firm specializing in benefits, a company's size may constrain the benefits it can provide. Companies with fewer than 10 employees may have difficulty finding an insurance carrier. Dental and vision care insurance options aren't very good. Disability plans for these small companies will be either very restrictive or very expensive. Only after a company has at least 25 employees can it begin to offer a choice of medical plans, according to some experts.

Companies having more than 50 employees, and certainly those with more than 100, have more options and can even participate in partial self-insurance programs. If you self-insure, then you, as the employer, act partially as the insurance company. This means that, if your employees stay fairly healthy and don't file a lot of claims, you won't pay as much in premiums. As companies grow, they encounter fewer limitations. A firm that has 300 to 400 employees can choose from among many options and carriers and can establish a large plan that can be modified easily. However, a firm that grows from 10 to 150 employees within a year or two will have major changes to make. Unfortunately, like many other functions at young, fast-growing firms, benefits management tends to lag behind the more urgent line functions.[55]

Providing Benefits Flexibility

When employees can design their own benefits packages, both they and the company come out ahead. At least that's the experience at companies such as Quaker Oats, Ex-Cello, TRW Incorporated, Educational Testing Service (ETS), and Morgan Stanley Dean Witter.[56] ETS provides a core package of benefits to all employees, covering basic needs such as personal medical care, dental care, disability, vacation, and retirement. In addition, each individual can choose, cafeteria style, from optional benefits or can increase those in the core package. Employees are allowed to change their packages once a year. At Morgan Stanley Dean Witter, about two-thirds of all eligible

> *"Companies are having to offer spouse employment assistance now, just to be competitive with the top companies."*
>
> **Laura Herring**
> **CEO and President**
> **The Impact Group**

employees elect their own benefits package over the standard no-choice plan. The options themselves were developed by the employees working in small discussion groups. This is happening in many companies today because their workforces are becoming so diverse, and their needs for benefits rather varied. This fact, in addition to the fact that providing benefits flexibility is so effective, most companies now offer at least some variable benefits.[57] Having benefits accessible through call centers or on the Web makes it easier than ever to offer this flexibility. The feature, Managing Diversity: Providing More Diversity in Benefits, illustrates just how big a trend this is.[58]

Communicating the Benefits Package

Considering that most benefits program objectives are not attained, assessment of communication effectiveness would probably produce unfavorable results. This may be partly due to the communication techniques used. Almost all companies use impersonal, passive booklets and brochures to convey benefits information; only a few use more personal, active media, such as slide presentations and regular employee meetings. An especially good technique communicates the total compensation components every day. Increasingly, firms are offering voice response benefits systems, or call centers. Employees in firms such as Cummins Engine Company in Columbus, Indiana, telephone in to learn about and manage their benefits. Employees at Oracle, Boeing, and Charles Schwab & Co. can manage their own benefits through Web sites that describe the firms' benefits programs.[59]

Through communicating the benefits package and providing benefits flexibility, the positive image of indirect compensation can be increased. Hewitt Associates found that 75 percent of all employees who understand its compensation program perceive it as fair, whereas only about 33 percent of all employees who do not understand the system think it is fair. Providing clear information about how to file claims and where to get services tends to bring more employees into the positive-perception camp.

Managing and Reducing Benefits Costs

The trend is clear: more and more organizations are managing and reducing benefits costs. Managing costs means having second opinions and fewer choices in health care coverage. It means making sure that a disability is really a disability and that workers get back to work as soon as possible. It means being proactive and seeking ways to prevent sickness and injury, as well as helping employees recover more quickly by offering more home health care.[60]

Does managing and reducing benefits costs mean eliminating benefits? Certainly, firms are asking workers to share the expenses of their own health care and even retirement. This is consistent with employee empowerment and self-management. Workers are capable of understanding business and cost conditions. By having benefits information, they may be able to help reduce costs without eliminating benefits. For coverage that each individual needs, employers are likely to find ways to not only reduce costs but also maintain employee commitment to the organization. Experiences at Steelcase, Johnson and Johnson, Levi Strauss, and Deere show that win-win situations, with extensive employee involvement and understanding, are possible.

Employers in the United States are not the only ones dealing with benefits costs. The issue is also of growing importance in Europe, although

"American companies have failed to realize that there's tremendous value in inspiring people to share a common purpose of self-esteem, self-respect, and appreciation."

Howard Schultz
CEO
Starbucks

■□ *fast fact*

At Sky Chefs Kitchen in El Paso, Texas, each morning begins with an employee-led stretching session designed to curb back injuries.

■□ *fast fact*

Quaker grants bonuses of as much as $500 for families who exercise, shun smoking, and wear seat belts. Employees can keep the money or invest in added benefits.

MANAGING DIVERSITY

Providing More Diversity in Benefits

Employers are faced with the multiple challenges of maximizing their benefit dollars, meeting the needs of an increasingly diverse workforce, and designing a benefit program that helps motivate employees in ways that improve business results, according to Hewitt Associates, the benefits consulting firm headquartered in Lincolnshire, Illinois. To meet these challenges, many employers are designing flexible programs that include new benefits, many of which companies can offer at a relatively small cost to themselves. Examples include

1. group financial planning (a benefit that's one of the fastest growing as the workforce ages and plans for retirement);
2. alternative work arrangements such as flextime, job sharing, and telecommuting;
3. long-term care insurance (again older workers planning for retirement); and
4. group auto and home insurance.

According to Hewitt Associates, many of these benefits can be offered at relatively low or even at no cost to the employer. Employers also gain because it allows employees to focus on their jobs. In the case of many of these benefits—for example, auto insurance—employees actually find it more convenient, cheaper, and more efficient to buy them from their employer-sponsored group plans. Companies also find that in the face of all the options presented in flexible benefit plans, employees can still choose wisely and in their own best interest. Parkview Hospital in Fort Wayne, Indiana, however, found that employees only choose wisely when the variety and quality of the benefits are fully communicated to them. For companies to really gain from offering flexible benefits, they owe it to themselves and their employees to communicate as fully and as frequently as possible about them. Increasingly, information about benefits is being communicated electronically. At Oracle, Boeing, and Charles Schwab, workers can surf company intranets to learn about and self manage 401(k) plans, health care benefits, and even tax withholding options. Hard Rock Café International makes information available through an interactive CD that can be played at publicly available monitors in the employee break rooms.

Outside the U.S., flexible benefits are not as common. Guinness Limited, a brewery headquartered in the U.K., has operations in nearly 50 countries. Flexible benefits are well-established in the U.K., but attempts to spread this practice have met with mixed success. In some countries, for example, high levels of mandatory benefits makes flexibility less feasible. In other countries, there are so few sophisticated service-providers to offer the full range of services that employees might desire. In some countries, restrictive tax laws reduce the appeal of offering a wide range of benefits. Yet another challenge faced by Guinness has been cultural norms that favor a paternalistic approach to benefits administration rather than the self-directed approach that often is used to administer flexible benefits programs.

To learn more about Hewitt Associates, visit the company home page at
www.hewittassoc.com

employers there face a somewhat different situation. In Europe, most of the health care and pensions are provided by governments. Today, however, these governments are seeking ways to balance their budgets, and one way is to get out of the health care- and pension-providing roles. If they do this, employees and governments are likely to look to employers for relief at a time when many of those employers are already paying some of the highest wages in the world. Thus, the pressure on European employers to manage and reduce benefits costs is likely to be even greater than it is on U.S. employers.

LEGAL CONSIDERATIONS

Indirect compensation grew rapidly during the Depression, which produced the first major legislation involving benefits. The *Social Security Act*, passed in 1935, provided old-age, disability, survivors', and health benefits and established the basis for federal and state unemployment programs. The *Wagner Act*, or *National Labor Relations Act of 1935* (NLRA), helped ensure the growth of benefits by strengthening the union movement in the United States. Both the *Social Security Act* and the *Wagner Act* continue to play significant roles in the administration of benefits. Since the 1960s, Congress has passed several acts that make this legal environment more complex, including the *Equal Pay Act of 1963*, the *Americans with Disabilities Act of 1990*, and the *Age Discrimination in Employment Act of 1967* (which were discussed in previous chapters).

Pregnancy Discrimination Act of 1978

The *Pregnancy Discrimination Act of 1978* states that pregnancy is a disability and qualifies a person to receive the same benefits as afforded for any other disability. Applying this statute, a state appeals court in Michigan ruled that a labor contract between General Motors and the United Auto Workers was illegal. The contract provided sickness and accident benefits of up to fifty-two weeks but limited childbearing disability to six weeks.[61]

Although the *Pregnancy Discrimination Act* does not explicitly address this issue, it's interpreted as also requiring companies to offer the same pregnancy benefits program to wives of male employees and to husbands of female employees. The U.S. Supreme Court ruled in *Newport News Shipbuilding and Dry Dock Company v. EEOC* (1983) that employers who provide to spouses of employees health care insurance that includes complete coverage for all disabilities except pregnancy are violating Title VII of the *Civil Rights Act of 1964*. In essence, employers must provide equal benefits coverage for all spouses.

Family and Medical Leave Act of 1993

The *Family and Medical Leave Act of 1993* requires employers with fifty or more workers to grant an employee up to twelve weeks' unpaid leave annually "for the birth or adoption of a child, to care for a spouse or an immediate family member with a serious health condition, or when unable to work because of a serious health condition. Employers covered by the law are required to maintain any preexisting health coverage during the leave period."[62] The employee taking leave must be allowed to return to the same job or a job of equivalent status and pay—with the exception of some highly paid executives. To be eligible, employees must have worked at a company for at least twelve months and have put in at least 1,250 hours in the year before the leave.[63] Some 67 million employees are eligible for family leave, if and when they need it, and two out of five working Americans anticipate needing family and medical leave over the next five years.

This act is entirely consistent with what some companies have been doing for some time in their efforts to accommodate an increasingly diverse workforce and make themselves more "family friendly." However, family-friendly policies are more prevalent within a few industries and less prevalent elsewhere. In particular, the chemical, pharmaceutical, commercial banking, and life insurance industries seem to lead the way.[64]

ERISA and Private Employers' Pensions

Building on the foundation of the *Revenue Act of 1942*, the *Employee Retirement Income Security Act of 1974* was designed to protect the interests of workers covered by private retirement plans, especially plans that promise the workers a certain monthly dollar amount upon retirement. It does not require an employer to offer a pension fund. When companies choose to offer pension plans, employees are eligible for private pension fund participation after one year of service or at age 25.

ERISA also established provisions regarding vesting, which refers to the time when the employer's contribution belongs to the employee. Three basic options are

- full vesting after ten years of service;
- twenty-five percent vesting after five years of service, with 5 percent additional vesting for years 6 to 10 and then 10 percent additional vesting for years 10 to 15; and
- fifty percent vesting after five years of service and when age plus years of service equals 45, with 10 percent additional vesting for each subsequent year of service.

In the past, some companies set up pension funds but then, when necessary, drew upon those funds to pay for operating expenses. Such activity put employees' pensions at great risk. To protect employees against such risk, ERISA prohibits the use of unfunded pension programs that rely on the goodwill of the employer to pay retirement benefits out of current operating funds when needed. Money paid into a pension fund must be earmarked for retirees whether paid in part by the employee or paid solely by the employer (as in noncontributory programs).

Under ERISA, employers are not required to accommodate new or transferred employees who wish to deposit funds into their retirement plans. On a voluntary basis, employers can allow employees to transfer money to individual retirement accounts. When this occurs, the pension funds are said to be *portable*. Increasingly, employers are making it possible for employees to transfer their retirement funds to another firm.

Because ERISA covered only single-employer firms, the *Multi-Employer Pension Plan Amendment Act of 1980* was passed to broaden the definition of defined benefit plans to include multi-employer plans. If employers withdraw from multi-employer plans, they, rather than the employees, face liability for doing so and must reimburse employees for money lost.[65]

Economic Recovery Tax Act of 1981

A major provision of the *Economic Recovery Tax Act of 1981* is that employees can make tax deductible contributions of up to $2,000 to an employer-sponsored pension, profit-sharing, or savings account, or to an individual retirement account. The act also makes it possible for employers to provide company stock to employees and pay for it with tax credits or to establish a payroll-based plan that facilitates employee stock ownership. Both approaches are referred to as *employee stock ownership plans* (ESOPs).

Because these plans are attractive to organizations, over ten million employees have gained direct ownership of stock in their own companies. By the year 2000, 25 percent or more of all U.S. workers will own part or all of their companies.

The appeal of ownership programs goes far beyond the tax breaks available to ESOPs. At a time when competitive pressures are forcing companies to keep a lid on labor costs, many are using stock plans as a substitute for cash compensation. Stock is being used to fund bonuses, pension and savings plans, and even retiree medical benefits.

Such programs are not without risk, particularly if corporate sponsors go belly-up in future years. But they can help make companies more competitive, enhance productivity, and bolster morale when wage hikes need to be deferred. Because workers are concerned with job security, they represent a source of patient capital that's likely to value long-term performance over short-term profits.

The most intriguing aspect of this trend is the possibility that workers who own a significant share of their companies will want a voice in corporate governance, as has already happened in the case of United Airlines and Northwest Airlines. Employers who prepare for this development by setting up mechanisms for dialogue can lay the groundwork for productive cooperation between labor and management in future decision-making. Those who don't may find worker ownership a mixed blessing.[66]

Tax Reform Act of 1986 and Revenue Reconciliation Act of 1993

The *Tax Reform Act of 1986* and the *Revenue Reconciliation Act of 1993* essentially cap the tax-exempt deferred contribution employees can make to a qualified pension plan that receives favorable tax treatment, such as a 401(k) plan or defined benefit plans. These acts put into force provisions to reduce the disparity of benefits provided high- and low-income employees, to ensure that all employees are treated in a roughly equal manner. Referred to as *nondiscrimination tests*, these provisions essentially limit the absolute amount of money that employees and employers can contribute to their qualified pension plans. The percentage of salary an employer can contribute is based on a maximum employee salary of $150,000. Employees can set aside, tax deferred, roughly 6 percent of their salaries, to a maximum of approximately $9,500. Prior to 1993, the maximum had been $30,000. Because this cap imposed a reduction in benefits for highly paid employees, some firms have set up supplemental executive retirement plans, which do not receive favorable tax treatment.[67] Furthermore, under these acts, for the top five executives in a company, annual pay above $1 million isn't tax deductible for the business unless it's performance related.

Health Insurance Portability and Accountability Act of 1996

The provisions of this act aid workers in keeping track of their health care coverage and in transferring this coverage to another employer. By providing certificates of coverage to employees who leave their jobs, employees can more easily obtain individual or group health insurance without restrictions on pre-existing conditions or coverage gaps.[68]

Crossing the Border

Companies operating outside the U.S. must comply with many other laws besides those reviewed in this chapter. A look at Mexico offers a glimpse into

■□ fast fact

The cost of health care for each citizen in the United States is $2,668. In Great Britain, it's $1,043, and in Canada, it's $1,915.

this challenging area of human resource management. The *Mexican Federal Labor Law* governs all benefits matters in Mexico. The state labor boards oversee the enforcement of the law. These boards have representatives from the government, labor, and management. The law states that full-time employees should get certain fringe benefits, including six days' paid vacation yearly, a minimum wage (about $15 a day), a 25 percent vacation pay premium, seven paid federal holidays, a profit-sharing plan, social security, and an employer-paid payroll tax that funds employee day care centers. Other legal considerations employers should be aware of in doing business in Mexico are described in the feature, Managing Globalization: Benefits in Mexico.[69]

SUMMARY

From the mid-1940s to the mid-1990s, indirect compensation grew substantially more than did direct compensation. This increase occurred despite the lack of evidence that indirect compensation helps to attain the purposes of total compensation. Money, job challenge, and opportunities for advancement appear to serve the purposes of compensation as much as, if not more

MANAGING GLOBALIZATION

Benefits in Mexico

In Mexico, the employer has 28 days to evaluate the employees' work ethics. After that period, the worker is granted job security and termination becomes difficult. This is especially true in terms of financial liability. For example, an employer that decides to fire a worker who has been with the company for six months could be charged for an additional six weeks, plus vacation pay and bonuses accordingly.

An employee is considered tenured after one year of employment. A tenured worker may be dismissed only for causes specifically set out in the *Mexican Federal Labor Law*. Such causes include falsifying employment documents, or committing dishonest or violent acts during working hours. For a dismissal to be valid, a written notice of the firing and complete documentation of the offenses must be given.

Certain border plants, the maquiladoras, are short of good workers because of the infrastructure of nearby cities. Most northern towns have grown quickly, and housing shortages and transportation difficulties cause problems. These conditions haven't really affected industry as a whole, but people tend to change jobs in order to work closer to home. The solution for some maquiladoras is to locate in a central area so that most employees are within walking distance.

Most maquiladoras pay the Mexican legal minimum wage, which varies about 10 percent throughout the country. Owing to the pay, turnover may range from 30 percent to 100 percent a year in major cities. The effects of this turnover are higher production costs, poor quality, and higher wages in the local industry. Some maquiladoras have to pay their employees above minimum wage to keep their good workers. Some firms prevent high turnover by making employees feel that they can move up in the company, and offer an increase in salary after a certain amount of service time given to the company. In the future, however, employers are likely to follow the pattern established in the United States: to attract and retain the best talent, they will find they need to develop new benefit plans that address employees' personal needs.

than, pension benefits, disability provisions, and services, especially for employees aspiring to managerial careers.

This isn't to say that employees don't desire indirect benefits. Organizations are offering them at such a rapid rate in part because employees want them. Unfortunately, the specific indirect benefits offered by an organization are not always valued by all employees, and all employees may not even know what benefits are offered. As a result, some organizations now solicit employee opinions about their preferences for compensation programs. Organizations are also becoming more concerned with the communication of their benefits programs. Current evidence suggests that employees' lack of awareness of the contents and value of their benefits programs may partially explain why these programs are not always perceived favorably.

These benefits don't come without costs. To ensure that an organization is getting the most from its indirect compensation, thorough assessments must be made of what the organization is doing, what other organizations are doing, and what employees prefer to see the organization doing. To improve the motivational value of indirect compensation, organizations should try to provide what employees want. As with direct compensation, employees apparently will continue to want more benefits like the ones they now have, as well as some they presently don't have. For example, employees want greater private retirement benefits, more health and insurance coverage, and more time off. Demands for dental coverage, vision care, and legal services will probably increase. Greater educational and career development opportunities are also likely to be demanded by employees.

As more U.S. firms move into international markets, the need to understand international compensation increases in importance. Although practices in countries such as Canada are similar to those in the United States, practices in Mexico are not. Mexican employees rely more on seniority than do U.S. and Canadian employees, and have many benefits set by the government.

TERMS TO REMEMBER

Cost-sharing
Defined-benefit plan
Defined-contribution plan
Employee assistance programs (EAPs)
Employee Retirement Income Security Act (ERISA)
Flexible spending plans
Health maintenance organizations (HMOs)
Indirect compensation
Individual Retirement Account (IRA)
Money purchase plans
Noncontributory programs

Nonqualified plan
Pension Benefit Guaranty Corporation (PBGC)
Portable pensions
Preferred-provider organization (PPOs)
Private protection programs
Public protection programs
Qualified plan
Supplemental unemployment benefits
Tax-deferred profit-sharing plans
Vesting
Workers' compensation insurance

DISCUSSION QUESTIONS

1. What is Steelcase doing to manage its workers' compensation costs?

2. As a manager, how can you use indirect compensation to improve productivity?

3. Describe the various components of indirect compensation.

4. Distinguish between public and private protection programs, and give examples of each.

5. How are unemployment benefits derived? What is the status of unemployment compensation?

6. How would you rationalize to your employer the costs of providing a physical fitness facility? How would you assess and compare benefits and costs?

7. Should more companies follow the example of Coors and establish a wellness program? Why or why not?

8. Should more companies follow the example of Lotus and provide ample family-friendly benefits? Why or why not?

9. In this chapter, we did not explicitly list the Partnership Roles and Responsibilities for Providing Benefits and Services. This gives you a chance to think through the implications of the partnership perspective. Prepare a chart showing the roles and responsibilities of line managers, HR professionals, and other employees.

PROJECTS TO EXTEND YOUR LEARNING

1. **Managing Strategically.** Your company is debating whether or not to offer stock options to all of its employees. Currently, only senior managers receive them, as is typical in many U.S. companies. The CEO and senior management think that granting options might increase the feeling of ownership and thus result in a greater commitment to work harder for the company, as it seems they do at Southwest Airlines. However, some managers are concerned that granting options might backfire if the company's stock price does not increase. Without the increases, employees may feel less commitment to work hard. A question raised by some is "Do employees really think that they have control or influence over the price of the stock, or is it really subject to broader market forces?" Furthermore some ask, "Once employees start owning stock, will they be more interested in watching the price of the stock than in working hard?" What are your recommendations? Visit the National Center for Employee Ownership to learn more at **www.nceo.org.**

2. **Managing Teams.** A problem that some companies have is the lack of awareness and understanding amongst employees of the value and cost of the benefits they receive. In some cases, employees don't even know what benefits they receive or what they are entitled to receive. With the cost of benefits so high, companies are literally throwing away good money! Your first assignment is to change this situation in your company. You are now a firm believer in partnership in managing human resources. You know that through partnership better practices can be developed. You also believe that partnership is a good way to spread the understanding

and awareness of what human resource practices exist. Therefore, you decide to establish a team to work on the general assignment of increasing all employees' awareness and understanding of the value and cost of the benefits provided by the company. Who will be on the team? What will they do? When and to whom will they report? How will you manage conflicts that might result from differences in worker age, functional area, or level in the company? Visit the American Compensation Association for further reading at **www.acaonline.org**.

3. **Managing Globally.** Steelcase has operations worldwide, just like Lincoln Electric does. Steelcase has wholly-owned operations, subsidiaries, and joint ventures. A major question companies have today is "Should we offer the same benefits to employees worldwide?" While you might think this isn't necessary, after further research you might conclude that a "truly" global company should treat its workers the same regardless of location. For example, if Steelcase were to offer stock options to its employees in the U.S., it should do this for all of its employees outside the U.S. as well, just like PepsiCo does. Of course, there may be local laws or provisions that might make it unnecessary to provide some benefits, e.g., health care in Canada because it is provided by the government. Research the types of benefits that might be provided by some countries and not others. Then make recommendations about whether employers should consider having a "global benefits package" and if so, which benefits would be included in it. For useful information see
www.mercer.com
www2.homefair.com
www.classnet.com

4. **Managing Change.** As the cost of benefits increased in the early 1990s, companies sought to manage these as best they could. Global price competition and pressure from the stock market also encouraged companies to reduce their costs as much as possible in order to maximize their earnings. The competitive conditions and pressures from the stock market still exist. And experience from the early 1990s provided evidence that benefit costs can be managed. So now your company, which has resisted these forces, has decided it must also manage (i.e., reduce) its benefit costs. This will be a major change for the employees. In some cases employees will lose benefits and in other cases they will be asked to share the cost for some benefits that were previously covered fully by the company. How will you implement this change without the workers thinking something is being taken away and, therefore, be less committed to working as hard? For more articles on change, visit the Human Resource Planning Society at **www.hrps.org**.

5. **Managing Diversity.** Your company has one of the most diverse workforces in the country. Diversity exists on a variety of characteristics including age, marital status, organizational level, family status, gender, ethnicity, religion, and physical condition. First of all, should your company try to design a benefits package that is adaptable to a variety of employees? Should employees have the right to choose? If yes to these, then how will you go about designing such a "set" of benefits packages? See what has been done by Microsoft by visiting them at **www.microsoft.com**.

6. **Integration and Application.** After reviewing the Lincoln Electric and Southwest Airlines cases at the end of the book, answer the following questions.

a. What are the objectives of their indirect compensation plans?

b. How well are the indirect benefits plans serving the business objectives and the needs of employees? Which plan would you prefer? Explain why.

c. How can each company's indirect compensation activities be improved? *Note:* For these projects, use your "best guesses," because the cases don't cover indirect compensation extensively. Your responses here might reflect what effective companies in general do with respect to indirect compensation.

CASE STUDY

Who's Benefiting?

Jack Parks is a benefits manager in the auto electronics division of USA Motors, a major manufacturer of audio systems and auto electronic ignition systems. He is very concerned after analyzing the impact of absenteeism on the division's staffing costs for the previous quarter. What troubles Jack is an agreement that the national union negotiated with USA Motors ten years ago that, in effect, paid workers for being absent. Of course, the "paid absence" agreement was not supposed to work quite that way. In theory, workers were given one week of paid absence against which they could charge their personal absences. Presumably, this system would encourage workers to notify their supervisors so that staffing arrangements could be made and production maintained.

In practice, workers discovered that by not charging off any "paid absences," they could receive a full week's pay in June when the company paid off the balance of the unused paid absences for the previous year. This cash bonus, as workers had come to think of it, often coincides with the summer vacation taken by many of the 8,000 hourly employees when USA Motors shuts down for inventory.

As Jack learned, employees with chronic absentee records had figured out how to charge off absences using the regular categories, which permits sick days, excused and unexcused absences. In Jack's mind, USA Motors might just as well have negotiated a cash bonus for hourly workers or given them another ten to fifteen cents per hour.

After reviewing the division's absenteeism rates for controllable absences—that is, those categories of absences believed to be of the employee's own choice—Jack concludes that the company could reduce this rate from the previous year's figure of eleven percent. And then Jack has a brainstorm: what USA Motors needs to negotiate is an incentive plan for reducing absenteeism. The plan Jack has in mind entails a standard for the amount of controllable absence deemed acceptable. If a chronically absent employee exceeds the standard, then vacation, holiday, and sickness/accident pay would be cut by ten percent during the next six months. If worker absence continues to exceed the allowable limits, then vacation, holiday, and sickness pay would be cut during the next six months by the actual percentage of absent days incurred by the chronic absentee. Hence, if a worker misses fifteen percent of scheduled work days during the first six-month period, vacation pay for the next six-month period would be reduced by ten percent. If the employee continues to be absent at the fifteen percent rate, then vacation pay would be reduced by fifteen percent during the next six months.

Jack immediately drafted a memorandum outlining the program and submitted it to the corporate HR manager of USA Motors for inclusion in the upcoming bargaining session. To Jack's surprise and delight, the memorandum received strong corporate support and is scheduled as a high priority bargaining topic for the fall negotiations.

QUESTIONS

1. Will the incentive plan to reduce absenteeism succeed?

2. How much absenteeism is really under the employee's control?

3. Why didn't the "paid absence" plan work?

4. What plan would you suggest to USA Motors?

CASE STUDY

Flowers or Fiasco?

Although secretaries, like any group of good employees, should be complimented and recognized for good work throughout the year, many organizations save their plaudits for secretaries' week. Generally, secretaries' week occurs in the spring, just at the time the doldrums of winter are leaving and the fragrances of the new season are most inviting. Thus, the secretaries of a particular university were especially delighted to be given a day off during secretaries' week last year. Like the students and faculty, they were able to enjoy a beautiful, sunny spring day. Though this fringe benefit of a day off was not planned nor formally agreed to, the secretaries were looking forward to the same thing this year. This was especially true because the winter was a severe one, and many of the secretaries had put in extra hours without pay during the year.

Consequently, the secretaries were extremely displeased, some even angry, when, on the first day of secretaries' week, the dean of the school sent them flowers. Since last year they received a day off, but no flowers, they assumed that this gesture meant they would not get a day off. And they were right! Offended and angered, they "forgot" to send the dean a note thanking him for the flowers. Several weeks passed, and the dean realized he had not received the traditional thank-you note. Puzzled, the dean related what had happened to Professor Freedman, a human relations specialist on the faculty. Professor Freedman, sensitive to the needs of both the dean and the secretaries, later that day asked the head secretary to tell him about secretaries' week. After learning the secretaries' interpretation of what had happened, Professor Freedman shared this with the dean. After the professor left, the dean muttered to himself, "It doesn't pay to try to be nice to people nowadays."

QUESTIONS

1. Do you agree with the dean's final statement?
2. Where did the dean go wrong?
3. Do you think the secretaries should have been happy with the flowers? Were they ungrateful?
4. What should the dean do next year? Is there anything he should do now?

CASE STUDY

You're Darned If You Do and Darned If You Don't

Sally Yuen, director of HR for Dough Pineapple's (DP's) Maui, Hawaii, cannery, returns to her office deep in thought. She has just spent the last hour and a half in a lengthy and somewhat heated discussion with cannery manager Danny Sackos. Shrugging her shoulders, Sally wonders if Danny is right. Maybe the company's employee problem is her fault—well, the fault of her department, that is. According to Danny, if she had done a better job selecting employees in the first place, DP would not be in its current mess. "You hired quitters," he argued, pointing to the high turnover among temporary and permanent full-time employees.

DP maintains a regular workforce of 200 employees. Depending on the harvest, as many as 150 temporary employees are also employed. Temporary workers are paid a higher base salary than regular employees—$6.25 an hour. However, they are not eligible for any benefits, including vacation leave, day care, and sick leave. If they are sick, they have to take time off without pay. They also can't participate in DP's highly successful profit-sharing program and matching pension fund.

Full-time, regular cannery workers are paid $5.00 an hour, $10,400 a year. Although DP's hourly rate is below the industry average of $6.00, employees more than recoup the difference in performance bonuses. To date, DP is the only cannery on the islands to have a state-of-the-art incentive pay program. In fact, it's the only cannery that shares organizational profits with employees at all.

Last year, employees received approximately $2,000 each in bonuses. This amount was lower than usual owing to a hurricane that destroyed almost all of one harvest. Since the program was implemented in 1986, annual bonuses have averaged $8,000 for each employee. And this year, they are expected to be back on target: Sally anticipates that they will be in the range of $10,000 for each employee. Employees have the option of taking the money in one lump sum, in quarterly installments, or in even distributions throughout the next year. According to company policy, employee bonuses will be announced at the next semiannual employee's meeting, which is to be held in six weeks.

Sally also is proud of DP's benefits. Employee benefits as a percentage of payroll average 30 percent in the industry; DP's average 45 percent. All full-time employees with one year's seniority (tenured employees) are eligible to participate in DP's extensive benefits program, which includes such innovations as an on-site day care center (Sally's brainchild, which took her two years to get approved) and an employee assistance program, including free legal assistance. The company also matches, dollar for dollar, employee contributions to a retirement fund and offers two college scholarships annually to employees' children. Sally is par-

ticularly proud of DP's fitness center, which can be used by all tenured employees and their families. Swimming lessons are provided free of charge to family members of employees.

Vacation days also are above the industry average. Employees with one to two years of seniority earn one-half day of paid vacation a month; with three to five years' seniority, three-fourths day a month; and with more than five years' service, one day a month. Personal days accrue at the same rate for tenured employees. To prevent abuse, employees calling in absent before or after a holiday or after a payday are charged with an absence of one and one-half days. Employees with less than one year's service and temporary employees are not reimbursed for absences. Any employee who fails to report an absence at least four hours before his or her shift starts faces disciplinary procedures.

By having a core of permanent, tenured employees, DP is assured of having enough workers to meet average production demands. By paying temporary employees base salaries slightly above the labor market average, DP has traditionally had its pick of new employees. The system has been cost-effective because the salaries of temporary employees were only 18 percent over the base pay for cannery employees and well under the hourly rate, with benefits, for permanent tenured employees (estimated at $7.98).

With all this going for DP, Sally wonders where things went wrong. She starts looking for causes by asking her assistant, Mark George, to interview some employees about their view of the situation. He also prepares a report on causes of turnover at DP (see Case Exhibit A).

According to Mark, the following comments are representative of the feelings of full-time permanent employees:

Case Exhibit A   Reasons for Turnover Among Employees

	Higher Pay	Better Benefits	Supervision	Moving	Better Job	Job Security	Fired
Permanent Employees							
<1 year	40	22	1	2	3	1	2
1–2 years	10	0	3	3	2	4	1
>2 years	1	0	5	4	4	2	0
Temporary Employees							
<6 months	10	45	4	3	10	17	3
6–12 months	12	23	1	0	2	32	2
>1 year	5	15	2	3	15	19	0

NOTE: An employee could list more than one reason for quitting.

- "Sure, it's a great place to work, but I'm tired of those young kids walking in off the street and making more than I do."

- "I know, I know, we're eligible to get bonuses, but they just can't make up for a weekly salary—at least not when you have three kids to support."

- "I worry that things are going to be the same as last year. I hung in there, and look what I got, a lousy $2,500. The bottom line is that I still made less than temporary employees and those at the other canneries. I don't like it one bit."

These comments are typical of permanent untenured workers (full-time employees with less than one year of seniority):

- "I got really steamed last month when they docked my pay for being sick. I mean, I was really sick. I was down flat in bed with the flu. Why should I work hard here if I can't even get a lousy day off when I'm sick?"

- "I've worked here seven months already, and I'm pulling my own weight around here. Know what I mean? Well, it doesn't seem right that I should be paid less than those part-timers."

Among temporary workers, characteristic comments are:

- "Yeah, we make a good rate of pay, but that's not everything. My wife had to have a C-section last month. Without insurance, it cost me a bundle."

- "I work just as hard as everyone else, so why shouldn't I have the same benefits? I'm getting up there in years. It'd be nice to have a little bit set aside."

In reading these comments, Sally begins to think she can't win. Maybe the most current employee attitude survey will help (see Case Exhibit B); at least, it's worth a try. All she knows is that if she does not come up with a strategy for reducing turnover soon, DP won't have enough trained workers to meet its canning quotas, and the employee bonuses will be lost forever.

QUESTIONS

1. What does the employee attitude survey reveal that is helpful in understanding the turnover problem at DP?

2. What should be Sally's bottom-line response to resolve the current crisis? Are more benefits and services the answer?

3. Describe the relationships between employee status (years in the company) and satisfaction with items 1—7 (Case Exhibit B).

Case Exhibit B   Results of the Employee Attitude Survey

Satisfaction with:	Permanent			Temporary
	< 1 year	1–2 years	>2 years	
1. Pay level	2.1	2.3	2.4	3.4
2. Pay system	1.5	2.4	3.2	3.3
3. Benefits	1.0	3.2	4.1	1.1
4. Supervision	3.4	4.1	3.7	3.3
5. Job	2.4	2.7	3.1	2.3
6. Co-workers	3.3	4.0	4.7	2.3
7. Work environment	3.4	4.1	3.6	2.7

Key: 1 = very dissatisfied, 5 = very satisfied.

ENDNOTES

[1] R. McGarvey, "Something Extra," *Entrepreneur* (May 1995): 70; Further details of Starbuck's benefits, such as BEAN STOCK are in N. Weiss, "How Starbucks Impassions Workers to Drive Growth," *Workforce* (August 1998): 60–64.

[2] Personal Communication with Libby Child, Manager, Managed Claims and Disability Management Services, Steelcase (October 1998); Steelcase: See web site **www.steelcase.com**; J. J. Laabs, "Steelcase Slashes Workers' Comp Costs," *Personnel Journal* (February 1993): 72–87; "Workers' Comp Strategy Saves $4 Million Yearly," *Personnel Journal* (January 1993): 55; B. Croft, "Wiring Up Workers' Comp Claims," *Personnel Journal* (April 1996): 153–157; Steelcase Annual Reports (1993–1998).

[3] "Chamber of Commerce Benefits Survey," *Bureau of National Affairs* (1998).

[4] "Chamber of Commerce Benefits Survey;" P. Passell, "Benefits Dwindle Along With Wages for the Unskilled," *New York Times* (June 14, 1998): A1; J. Eisinger, "Best and Worst," *The Wall Street Journal* (October 24, 1996): R9.

[5] L. Uchitelle, "For Employee Benefits, It Pays to Wear the Union Label," *New York Times* (July 16, 1995): F10; R. Brookler, "HR in Growing Companies," *Personnel Journal* (November 1992): 80B–O.

[6] "Employee Benefits—March 1995;" "Not So Fringe Anymore;" Uchitelle, "For Employee Benefits, It Pays to Wear the Union Label."

[7] G. Flynn, "Hallmark Cares," *Personnel Journal* (March 1996): 50–61; S. Caudron, "Andersen Is at Employees' Service," *Personnel Journal* (September 1995): 88–96; "Amenities Help Workers Simplify Life," *Bulletin to Management* (July 20, 1995): 232.

[8] K. Madigan, "Here Come Hefty Hikes in Benefits," *Business Week* (May 18, 1998): 170; "Employer-Based Health Coverage Declining," *Bulletin to Management: Datagraph* (June 23, 1994): 196–197; M. Hequet, "The People Squeeze in Health Care," *Training* (July 1994): 35–39; M. D. Fefer, "Tailored Health Plans Take Off," *Fortune* (June 27, 1994): 12; B. P. Noble, "Surprise: Bigger Isn't Always Better," *New York Times* (June 19, 1994): F21.

[9] "Health-Care Inflation Kept in Check in '97," *The Wall Street Journal* (January 20, 1998): B6; "Slow Rise in Health Care Costs Continues," *Bulletin to Management: Policy Guide* (February 6, 1997): 48; "Health Benefit Costs Hold Steady," *Bulletin to Management: Policy Guide* (January 29, 1998): 32; S. Caudron, "Health-Care Reform: Act Now or Pay Later," *Personnel Journal* (March 1994): 57–67; M. Porter, E. Teisberg, and G. Brown, "Innovation: Medicine's Best Cost-Cutter," *New York Times* (February 27, 1994): F11; "Health Care Cost Sharing: Coating the Pill," *Bulletin to Management* (March 10, 1994): 73.

[10] M. L. Williams and G. F. Dreher, "Compensation System Attributes and Applicant Pool Characteristics," *Academy of Management Journal* 35 (1992): 571–595.

[11] J. Cole, "Auto and Home Insurance: The New Employee Benefit," *HR Focus* (December 1997): 9; J. Landauer,

"Bottom-Line Benefits of Work/Life Programs," *HR Focus* (July 1997): 3.

[12] "Benefits Values from the Employee's Perspective," *ACA News* (June 1998): 14–16; A. M. Rappaport, "The New Employment Contract and Employee Benefits: A Road Map for the Future," *ACA Journal* (Summer 1997): 6–15; A. Karr, "They're Young, But New College Grads Value Retirement, Health Benefits, *The Wall Street Journal* (May 5, 1998): A1; A. McIlvaine, "In The Mainstream," *Human Resource Executive* (August 1997): 48–49; J. E. Santora, "Employee Team Designs Flexible Benefits Program," *Personnel Journal* (April 1994): 30–39.

[13] Based on responses from 500,000 employees surveyed by Hewitt Associates, as reported in *Employee Benefits in 1995* (Lincolnshire, IL: Hewitt Associates, 1994).

[14] R. K. Platt, "Aligning Benefits With Employee, Organizational Goals," *ACA News* (June 1998): 11–13; L. Strazewski, "Strategic Link" *Business Week* (May 5, 1998): 30–34; F. Foulkes, *Personnel Policies in Large Nonunion Companies* (Englewood Cliffs, NJ: Prentice-Hall, 1980), 209–229.

[15] M. McNamee, "Yes: The Private Market Offers Better Returns," *Business Week* (March 23, 1998): 36; C. Farrell, "No: Why Let Wall Street Gamble With Our Nest Egg," *Business Week* (March 23, 1998): 37; G. Koretz, "How Not to Fix Social Security," *Business Week* (March 23, 1998): 24; R. J. Barro, "Don't Tinker With Social Security, Reinvent It," *Business Week* (June 8, 1998): 24; K. Feldstein, "Social Security's Gender Gap," *New York Times* (April 13, 1998): A27; "Calculating Social Security Benefits," *Bulletin to Management: Datagraph* (March 27, 1997): 100; A. Borrus and M. B. Regan, "How Should We Fix Social Security?" *Business Week* (January 20, 1997): 24–26; "How to Resecure Social Security," *Business Week* (January 20, 1997): 104; A. Bernstein, "Social Security: Is the Sky Really Falling?" *Business Week* (February 10, 1997): 92.

[16] "State Unemployment Insurance Funds," *Bulletin to Management: Datagraph* (October 2, 1997): 316; B. DeClark, "Cutting Unemployment Insurance Costs," *Personnel Journal* (November 1983): 868–872; McCaffery, *Employee Benefits Programs*; B. S. Murphy, W. E. Barlow, and D. D. Hatch, "Unemployment Compensation and Religious Beliefs," *Personnel Journal* (June 1987): 36–43; L. Uchitelle, "Jobless Insurance System Aids Reduced Number of Workers," *New York Times* (July 26, 1988): 1.

[17] T. Vander Neut, "Charting the Tides," *Human Resource Executive* (November 1997): 60–61; R. Kirsch, "Oh My Achin . . ." *Human Resource Executive* (June 6, 1997): 25; M. Weinstein, "Ably Assisted," *Human Resource Executive* (June 6, 1997): 27; J. A. Nixon, "Protected Plans," *Human Resource Executive* (June 6, 1997): 30–32; "Paradigm Shift," *Human Resource Executive* (June 6, 1997): 36–37; J. G. Kilgour, "Twenty-Four Hour Coverage: Melding Group Health Insurance with Workers' Compensation," *ACA Journal* (Spring 1997): 56–64; A. McIlvaine, "State of Workers' Comp," *Human Resource Executive* (November 1996): 52; B. Croft, "Wiring Up Workers' Comp Claims," *Personnel*

Journal (April 1996): 153–157; "Posttraumatic Stress Disorder, Workers' Comp, and the ADA," *Fair Employment Practices Guidelines* (August 10, 1997): 6–8.

[18] J. J. Laabs, "Steelcase Slashes Workers' Comp Costs," *Personnel Journal* (February 1993): 72–87. See also "Workers' Comp Strategy Saves $4 Million Yearly," *Personnel Journal* (January 1993): 55; T. Vander Neut, "Step By Step," *Human Resource Executive* (September 1998): 86–88; B. A. Morris, "Injury 101," *Human Resource Executive* (September 1998): 77; T. Thompson, J. F. Burton, Jr., and D. E. Hyatt, eds., *New Approaches to Disability in the Workplace* (Madison, WI: Industrial Relations Research Association, 1998).

[19] McCaffery, *Employment Benefits Programs*, 130–131.

[20] Hylton, "Don't Panic about Your Pension—Yet"; P. F. Drucker, "Reckoning with the Pension Fund Revolution," *Harvard Business Review* (March–April 1991): 106–114.

[21] D. E. Logue and J. S. Rader, *Managing Pension Plans* (Boston: Harvard Business School Press, 1998); S. Blakely, "Pension Power," *Nation's Business* (July 1997): 12–20; Martin E. Segal Co., *Pension Issues: A Fifty Year History and Outlook* 33 (3) (February 1990); T. F. Duzak, "Defined Benefit and Defined Contribution Plans: A Labor Perspective," *Economic Survival in Retirement* (New York: Salisbury Publishing, 1990): 69; U.S. Department of Labor, Bureau of Labor Statistics, *Employee Benefits in Medium and Large Firms,* 1989 (Washington, DC, June 1990).

[22] H. Gleckman, "Gephardt Has A Great Program—For The 30s," *Business Week* (August 14, 1995): 75; J. M. Laderman and M. McNamee, "That 401(k) May Cost More Than You Think," *Business Week* (November 10, 1997): 130; D. L. Browning, "Fortune Tellers," *Human Resource Executive* (November 1997): 1; A. Bernstein, "United We Own: Employee Ownership is Working at the Airline. Can it Travel?" *Business Week* (March 18, 1996): 96–102; "A New Look at Employee Ownership," *Business Week* (March 18, 1996): 124; W. Zellner, "Heavy Weather at American," *Business Week* (January 27, 1997): 32–33; S. Gruner, "You Can't Fire Me, I'm An Owner!" *Inc.* (June 1997): 102.

[23] "Broad-Based Stock Options on the Rise," *Bulletin to Management* (July 9, 1998): 216; L. Sierra, "Growth Strategies: Finding Ways to Create Value," *ACA News* (November–December 1997): 13–16; M. A. Bennett, "Making the Case for Ownership: Employing Workers' Hearts, Not Just Their Hands," *ACA News* (November–December 1997): 18–21; "Employee Stock Options Fact Sheet," **http://www.nceo.org/library/optionfact.html**; J. Fox, "The Next Best Thing to Free Money," *Fortune* (July 7, 1997): 52–62; "Taking Stock of Employee Stock Options," *HR Executive Review* 6 (1) (1998); E. J. Cripe, "Making Performance Management a Positive Experience," *ACA News* (November–December 1997): 22–26; P. Dowling, D. Welch, and R Schuler, *International Dimensions of Human Resource Management,* 3rd ed. (Cincinnati: South-Western College Publishing, 1999).

[24] J. Weber, "Canada's Health-Care System Isn't a Model Anymore," *Business Week* (August 31, 1998): 36; "Cost-Cutting Secrets Unveiled," *Bulletin to Management* 48 (May 8, 1997): 152; "Health Benefit Costs Rise Only Slightly," *Workforce* (April 1998): 19; K. H. Hammonds, "The Healers'

Revenge," *Business Week* (June 15, 1998): 68–73; "Managing Control," *Human Resource Executive* (September 1997): 94; A. Walker, "Manage With Care," *Human Resource Executive* (March 20, 1997): 42–43; J. G. Gray, "Physician Crusaders," *Human Resource Executive* (March 20, 1997): 44, 46; R. Allen, "Size, Skill, Comp, and Care," *Human Resource Executive* (March 20, 1997): 31–35; N. E. Yates, "Guiding Philosophies," *Human Resource Executive* (March 20, 1997): 36–38; G. Jaffe, "Corporate Carrots, Sticks Cut Health Bills," *The Wall Street Journal* (February 3, 1998): B1.

[25] E. Ginzberg, "Healthy Debate," *Human Resource Executive* (May 5, 1998): 57–58; A. Doan, "Unhealthy Premiums," *San Francisco Chronicle* (August 15, 1998): D2; "Benefit Policies: Enrollment in Managed Care Plans," *Bulletin to Management* 47 (August 1, 1996): 247; "Trends: Finding Enough Skilled Trained Workers," *Bulletin to Management* 47 (August 1, 1996): 247; M. Freudenheim, "H.M.O.'s That Offer Choice Are Gaining in Popularity," *New York Times* (February 7, 1994): A1, D3.

[26] B. O'Reilly, "Health Care: Taking on the HMOs," *Fortune* (February 16, 1998): 96–104; B. J. Feder, "Deere Sees a Future in Health Care," *New York Times* (July 1, 1994): D1; J. J. Laabs, "Deere's HMO Turns Crisis into Profit," *Personnel Journal* (October 1992): 82–89.

[27] M. Freudenheim, "(Loosely) Managed Care Is In Demand," *New York Times* (September 29, 1998): C1, C4; "Benefit Policies: Enrollment in Managed Care Plans," *Bulletin to Management* 49 (August 1, 1996): 247; McCaffery, *Employee Benefits Programs,* 130–131.

[28] P. Kerr, "Betting the Farm on Managed Care," *New York Times* (June 27, 1993): 1, 6.

[29] "An Incentive a Day Can Keep Doctor Bills at Bay," *Business Week* (April 29, 1991): 22.

[30] B. Kirsch, "Working Well," *Human Resource Executive* (May 5, 1998): 45–47; N. A. Jeffrey, "'Wellness Plans' Try to Target the Not-So-Well," *The Wall Street Journal* (June 20, 1996): B1, B10; B. P. Sunoo and C. M. Solomon, "Wellness Begins With Compassion," *Personnel Journal* (April 1996): 79–89; "Policy Guide: Wellness Programs Offer Healthy Returns," *Bulletin to Management* (March 7, 1996): 80; S. Caudron, "The Wellness Pay Off," *Personnel Journal* (July 1990): 55–60; "How Healthy Are Corporate Fitness Programs?" *The Physician and Sports Medicine* (March 1989).

[31] "Wellness Plans and the Disabilities Act," *Bulletin to Management* (May 27, 1993): 168.

[32] D. L. Browning, "Mood Indigo," *Human Resource Executive* (January 1997): 60–61; C. M. Steele and R. A. Josephs, "Alcohol Myopia: Its Prized and Dangerous Effects," *American Psychologist* (August 1990): 921–933; P. M. Roman, ed., *Alcohol Problem Intervention in the Workplace: Employee Assistance Programs and Strategic Alternatives* (Westport, CT: Quorum Books, 1990).

[33] P. D. Dowling, D. Welch, and R. S. Schuler, *International Dimension of Human Resource Management,* 3rd ed. (Cincinnati, OH: South-Western College Publishing, 1999).

34 G. Latham and N. Napier, "Practical Ways to Increase Employee Attendance," *Absenteeism: New Approaches to Understanding, Measuring and Managing Employee Absence,* P. Goodman and R. Atkins, eds. (San Francisco: Jossey-Bass, 1984); R. Steers and S. Rhodes, "Major Influences on Employee Attendance: A Process Model," *Journal of Applied Psychology* 63 (1978): 391–407.

35 J. Chadwick-Jones, N. Nicholson, and C. Brown, *Social Psychology of Absenteeism* (New York: Praeger, 1982).

36 S. Zedeck, ed., Work, *Families, and Organizations* (San Francisco: Jossey-Bass, 1992).

37 E. E. Kossek and V. Nichol, "The Effects of On-Site Child Care on Employee Attitudes and Performance," *Personnel Psychology* 45 (1992): 485–509.

38 "Family Friendly Benefits Have Spread Greatly," *Bulletin to Management* 47 (March 7, 1996): 73; A. Halcrow, "Optimas Reflects Changes in HR," *Personnel Journal* (January 1994): 50; C. M. Solomon, "Work/Family's Failing Grade: Why Today's Initiatives Aren't Enough," *Personnel Journal* (May 1994): 72–83.

39 Adapted from B. P. Noble, "Family-Friendly Firms," *New York Times* (May 2, 1993): F25.

40 A. McIlvaine, "Drawing the Lines," *Human Resource Executive* (September 1997): 84; J. Fierman, "Are Companies Less Family-Friendly?" *Fortune* (March 21, 1994): 64–67.

41 T. J. Rothauser, J. A. Gonzalez, N. E. Clarke, and L. L. O'Dell, "Family-Friendly Backlash—Fact or Fiction? The Case of Organizations' On-Site Child Care Centers," *Personnel Psychology* 51 (1998): 685–706.

42 S. VanDerWall, "Survey Finds Unscheduled Absenteeism Hitting Seven-Year High," *HR News* (November 1998):14.

43 "Parental Leave: Healthier Kids," *Business Week* (January 18, 1999): 30.

44 Buck Consultants, *The 1998 Benefits Survey* (Secaucus, NJ: Buck Consultants, 1998).

45 S. J. Goff, M. K. Mount, and R. L. Jamison, "Employer Supported Child Care, Work/Family Conflict, and Absenteeism: A Field Study," *Personnel Psychology* 43 (1990): 793–809; S. Zedeck and K. L. Mosier, "Work in the Family and Employing Organization," *American Psychologist* (February 1990): 240–251; S. Scarr, D. Phillips, and K. McCartney, "Working Mothers and Their Families," *American Psychologist* (November 1989): 1402–1409; E. E. Kossek, "Diversity in Child Care Assistance Needs: Employee Problems, Preferences, and Work-Related Outcomes," *Personnel Psychology* 43 (1990): 769–791; E. E. Kossek, *Childcare and Challenges for Employers* (Horsham, Australia: LRP Publications, 1991); S. L. Grover, "Predicting the Perceived Fairness of Parental Leave Policies," *Journal of Applied Psychology* 76 (1991): 247–255.

46 C. M. Loder, "Merck and Co. Breaks New Ground for Employee Child Care Centers," *Star Ledger* (May 1990): 12.

47 J. J. Laabs, "How Campbell Manages Its Rural Health Care Dollars," *Personnel Journal* (May 1992): 74–81; "Campbell Soup Co.," *Personnel Journal* (January 1992): 56.

48 K. H. Hammonds, "Balancing Work and Family," *Business Week* (September 16, 1996): 74–80; B. Michaels, "A Global Glance at Work and Family," *Personnel Journal* (April 1995) 85–93; E. Smith, "First Interstate Finds an Eldercare Solution," *HR Magazine* (July 1991): 152; A. E. Scharlach, B. F. Lowe, and E. L. Schneider, *Elder Care and the Work Force* (Lexington, MA: Lexington Books, 1991).

49 A. Vincola, "Cultural Change Is the Work/Life Solution," *Workforce* (October 1998): 70–72; E. Sullivan, "Basket Case?" *Human Resource Executive* (May 5, 1998): 42–43; "The Perspectives of Childless Employees," *Bulletin to Management* (May 5, 1994): 144.

50 "Many Employers Considering Domestic Partner Benefits," *HR Magazine* (October 1998): 30–31; "IBM Extends Benefits to Gay Workers' Domestic Partners," *Bulletin to Management* 47 (September 26, 1996): 305; D. J. Jefferson, "Gay Employees Win Benefits for Partners at More Corporations," *The Wall Street Journal* (March 18, 1994): A1, A2.

51 L. Strazewski, "One for All," *Human Resource Executive* (May 5, 1998): 51–53; "Lotus Opens a Door for Gay Partners," *Business Week* (November 4, 1991): 80–81. See also D. Anfuso, "Soul-Searching Sustains Values at Lotus Development," *Personnel Journal* (June 1994): 54–61; M. Rowland, "Hurdles for Unmarried Partners," *New York Times* (May 22, 1994): F15.

52 L. Holyoke, "San Francisco's Mandate Forces Domestic-Partner Benefits Mainstream," *Workforce* (June 1997): 34–41; A. D. Sherman, "Domestic Partner Benefits: Why They Can Succeed," *ACA News* (June 1997): 20.

53 D. G. Albrecht, "Are You Prepared To Relocate," *Workforce* (June 1997): 44–50; J. J. Laabs, "Smooth Moves," *Personnel Journal* (February 1994): 68–76; G. Flynn, "Relocation Has a New Look," *Personnel Journal* (February 1995): 48–60.

54 J. Laabs, "Cool Relo Benefits to Retain Top Talent," *Workforce* (March 1999): 89–94; J. Reese, "Mortgage Help as a Job Benefit," *Fortune* (June 3, 1991): 13; "Housing Aid—Benefit of the 90s?" *Bulletin to Management* (September 5, 1991): 280; *Employer-Assisted Housing Programs* (Lincolnshire, IL: Hewitt Associates, 1991).

55 R. Brookler, "HR in Growing Companies," *Personnel Journal* (November 1992): 802.

56 A. Vincola, "Taking Your Work/Life Policy Abroad," *Global Workforce* (July 1998): 24–27; J. E. Santora, "Employee Team Designs Flexible Benefits Program," *Personnel Journal* (April 1994): 30–39; R. Brookler, "HR in Growing Companies," *Personnel Journal* (November 1992): 802.

57 M. M. Markowich and J. Dortch, "Employees Can Be Smart Benefits Shoppers. Really." *Workforce* (September 1998): 64–70.

58 S. J. Wells, "For Help With a Benefits Package, Help Yourself," *New York Times* (January 7, 1999): G1, 6; "New Benefits Highlight Trend Toward Flexibility," *Bulletin to Management* 49 (April 16, 1998): 113; M. Markowich and J. Dortch, "Employees Can Be Smart Benefits Shoppers. Really." *Workforce* (September 1998): 64–70; R. K. Platt, "One Organization's Journey Into International Flexible

Remuneration," *ACA News* (November–December 1998): 48–49; J. Cole, "Auto and Home Insurance: The New Employee Benefit," *HR Focus* (December 1997): 9–10; J. Landauer, "Bottom-Line Benefits of Work/Life Programs," *HR Focus* (July 1997): 3–4; M. W. Barringer and G. T. Milkovich, "A Theoretical Exploration of the Adoption and Design of Flexible Benefit Plans: A Case of Human Resource Innovation," *Academy of Management Review* 23 (1998): 305–324.

59 B. A. Morris, "Healthier Education," *Human Resource Executive* (May 5, 1998): 36–38; S. Greengard, "Steer Workers: Toward Wise Investments," *Workforce* (April 1998): 71–77; L. Strazewski, "Spreading the Word," *Human Resource Executive* (January 1998): 48–50; S. J. Wells, "For Help with a Benefits Package, Help Yourself," *New York Times* (January 7, 1999): G1, G6.

60 N. Jackson, "Health Care on the Home Front," *Workforce* (March 1998): 30–34; E. Faltermayer, "Getting Health Alliances Right," *Fortune* (May 16, 1994): 82–88; S. Caudron, "Health-Care Reform: Act Now or Pay Later," *Personnel Journal* (March 1994): 57–67; "Employers, Employees Have Different Views on Paying for Health Care Reform," *HR Reporter* (April 1994): 1–3; "Health Care Cost Sharing: Coating the Pill," *Bulletin to Management* (March 10, 1994): 73–74; M. Porter, E. Teisberg, and G. Brown, "Innovation: Medicine's Best Cost-Cutter," *New York Times* (February 27, 1994): F11.

61 "Permissible Pregnancy Practices," *Fair Employment Practices Guidelines* (December 1, 1983): 3. The Pregnancy Disability Amendment also has other provisions; for a description of them, see S. R. Zacur and W. Greenwood, "The Pregnancy Disability Amendment: What the Law Provides, Part II," *Personnel Administrator* (March 1982): 55–58.

62 G. Flynn, "What to Do After a FMLA Leave," *Workforce* (April 1999): 104–107; B. P. Noble, "Interpreting the Family Leave Act," *New York Times* (August 1, 1993): F24. See also D. Gunsch, "The Family Leave Act: A Financial Burden?" *Personnel Journal* (September 1993): 48–57; "Companies Willing to Stretch Employees Still Further," *HR Reporter* (March 1993): 5–6.

63 J. W. Papa, "Sizing Up the FMLA," *Workforce* (August 1998): 38–43.

64 E. Galinsky, D. E. Friedman, and C. A. Hernandez, *The Corporate Reference Guide to Work-Family Programs* (New York: Families & Work Institute, 1991).

65 J. A. LoCicero, "How to Cope with the Multi-Employer Pension Plan Amendments Act of 1980," *Personnel Administrator* (May 1981): 51–54, 68; J. A. LoCicero, "Multi-Employer Pension Plans: A Time Bomb for Employers?" *Personnel Journal* (November 1980): 922–924, 932; C. Del Valle, "Harsh Medicine for Ailing Pension Plans," *Business Week* (September 19, 1994): 91–94; M. Rowland, "An Unseen Trap in Pension Funds," *New York Times* (August 28, 1994): F13; R. D. Hylton, "Don't Panic about Your Pension—Yet," *Fortune* (April 18, 1994): 121–128; "ERISA's Effects on Pension Plan Administration," *Bulletin to Management* (August 9, 1984): 1–2; K. D. Gill, ed., *ERISA: The Law and the Code,* 1985 ed. (Washington, DC: Bureau of National Affairs, 1985); B. J. Coleman, *Primer on Employee Retirement Income Security Act* (Washington, DC: Bureau of National Affairs, 1985).

66 T. A. Stewart, "Will the Real Capitalist Please Stand Up?" *Fortune* (May 11, 1998): 189; D. Leonhardt, "At Northwest, An ESOP in Name Only," *Business Week* (September 14, 1998): 63; D. Leonhardt and A. Bernstein, "Not So United At United These Days," *Business Week* (May 4, 1998): 50; "The Real Strengths of Employee Stockownership," *Business Week* (July 15, 1991): 156. Also see A. Bryant, "Betting the Farm On the Company Stock," *New York Times* (April 16, 1995): Sec 3, 1, 7.

67 M. Rowland, "A Pension Perk with a Lot of Strings," *New York Times* (September 25, 1994): F13; M. Rowland, "Red Flag on Pensions at Nonprofits," *New York Times* (October 2, 1994): F13; D. Schwartz, "The Last Word on Section 89," *Personnel Journal* (January 1989): 48–57; R. E. Johnson and S. J. Velleman, "Section 89: Close the New Pandora's Box," *Personnel Journal* (November 1988): 70–78; J. Ortman, "Section 89: Why You Should Act Now," *Personnel Journal* (November 1988): 78–79.

68 L. Strazewski, "HIPAA Hangover," *Human Resource Executive* (May 5, 1998): 40–41.

69 Based upon G. Smith, S. Baker, and W. Glasgall, "Mexico: Will Economic Reform Survive the Turmoil?" *Business Week* (April 11, 1994): 24–27; S. Baker, G. Smith, and E. Weiner, "The Mexican Worker," *Business Week* (April 19, 1993): 84–92.

OCCUPATIONAL SAFETY AND HEALTH: MANAGING THE INCIDENCE OF DEATHS, INJURIES, AND DISEASES

"In my opinion, the area that requires the greatest attention is this issue of health and safety."

Bennett R. Cohen
Chairman of the Board and CEO
Ben and Jerry's Homemade[1]

Chapter Outline

MANAGING THROUGH PARTNERSHIP

at Ben and Jerry's Homemade

Health and safety get a great deal of attention, yet injuries remain stubbornly high. Any manufacturing company runs the risk, if not certainty, of injury to workers, and Ben and Jerry's of Vermont is primarily a manufacturing company. The type of manufacturing done at the company's three plants offers ample opportunity to hurt a back or to drop a heavy object on a foot or toe. Ben and Jerry's managers have instituted fairly rigorous training methods to prevent these kinds of accidents. But in some areas of the operation, particularly in the Springfield, Vermont plant, jobs involve motions that are repeated all day long, day in and day out, which can lead to other types of injuries. This is especially true with regard to the manufacture of novelty lines such as Peace Pops and Brownie Bars.

Repetitive motion injuries were first recognized more than 200 years ago. In modern parlance, these are called cumulative trauma disorders. They result from motions that, although innocent in themselves, are chronically repeated, usually in an awkward or forceful manner, resulting in musculoskeletal disease, pain, or injury. You don't have to work in a factory to get them. Office workers are at risk, and so too are tennis players and runners. But at Ben and Jerry's, work on the manufacturing line is the primary cause.

Injuries of this sort are the most common workplace injuries, and during the working years, between ages 18 and 64, they are the most common reason for lost work time. Ben and Jerry's has experienced a very high number of workers' compensation claims for these injuries. In 1991, the company paid out 116 percent of workers' compensation premiums on claims, compared with Vermont's average of 17 percent. In 1992, the company's payout percentage soared to 150 percent. In Ben and Jerry's Waterbury plant, injuries rose from 38 to 43 from 1991 to 1992; on the other hand, lost days due to accidents fell significantly from 274 to 148. In Springfield, where the novelty items are made, injuries more than doubled, from 14 to 32 in the same one-year period; lost days due to injuries or accidents rose similarly, from 628 to 1,564. The figures for the two plants together show that from 1991 to 1992, injuries increased over 44 percent and lost days due to accidents or injuries increased over 88 percent—far greater increases than recorded for sales and production. If each injury had occurred to a separate worker, over 15 percent of the workforce would have experienced some type of injury (in fact, some workers experienced more than one injury in the year, meaning a smaller percentage of the workforce was actually affected).

One reason Ben and Jerry's may have higher numbers than other companies is, ironically, because people want to be employed there—so much so that workers repeatedly don't report injuries in the early stages for fear of loss of employment. Employees don't fear termination from their jobs, but some have reported the concern that if they left the company because of disabilities, they might never again get a job that paid as well. Where people have been reluctant to report medical problems, injuries worsened, resulting in longer lost time and greater medical bills.

To address the reluctance to report injuries, Ben and Jerry's began emphasizing and encouraging early reporting of injuries so as to prevent more serious, chronic injuries later on. New employees who suffer injuries are the beneficiaries of a generous short-term disability insurance program. The company also discovered, to its chagrin, that posting consecutive workdays where no one was injured resulted not in greater incentives toward safety, but in an atmosphere where injuries were covered up so as not to break the record.

These experiences and lessons of the early 1990s encouraged Ben and Jerry's to institute a number of changes. The company has discontinued its emphasis on the record of workdays without injuries and is now embarking on education, training, and meetings to encourage early reporting of potential injuries. Furthermore, the company has hired a number of consultants who specialize in ergonomics to visit all the plants' operations and revise tools, posture, seating, and activities so as to prevent repetitive motion injuries. Consequently, the rate of injuries per worker recently began to decline. Nevertheless, the rate is still higher than the industry average, so more improvements are needed. To improve safety performance in 1998, the Waterbury production area was upgraded with new equipment and improved line layouts. Several material handling issues, such as palletizing, were addressed via new equipment and/or improved procedures. At Ben and Jerry's, improving safety and health is a continuing process.[2]

To learn more about Ben and Jerry's Homemade, visit the company home page at **www.benjerry.com**

The feature, Managing Through Partnership at Ben and Jerry's Homemade, illustrates the increased emphasis firms are putting on safety programs. A safe work environment keeps employees healthy and productive, and it reduces the workers' compensation costs that firms pay to the states in which they do business.

This chapter discusses the purposes and importance of occupational safety and health, and then briefly examines the role of the federal government in establishing and enforcing safety standards. Next, it describes the two categories of workplace hazards: (1) the accidents and diseases that produce physiological and physical conditions and (2) the stress and low quality of working life that result when psychological conditions are not optimal. Then, it looks at strategies to improve employee safety and health, including such measures as improved record keeping, job redesign and ergonomics, and educational programs.

THE STRATEGIC IMPORTANCE OF OCCUPATIONAL SAFETY AND HEALTH

Occupational safety and health refers to the physiological-physical and psychological conditions of a workforce that result from the work environment provided by the organization. If an organization takes effective safety and health measures, fewer of its employees will have short- or long-term ill effects as a result of being employed at that organization.[3]

Physiological-physical conditions include occupational diseases and accidents such as actual loss of life or limb, repetitive motion injuries, back pain, carpal tunnel syndrome, cardiovascular diseases, various forms of cancer such as lung cancer and leukemia, emphysema, and arthritis. Other conditions that are known to result from an unhealthy work environment include white lung disease, brown lung disease, black lung disease, sterility, central nervous system damage, and chronic bronchitis.

Psychological conditions result from organizational stress and a low quality of working life. These encompass dissatisfaction, apathy, withdrawal, projection, tunnel vision, forgetfulness, inner confusion about roles and duties, mistrust of others, vacillation in decision making, inattentiveness, irritability, procrastination, and a tendency to become distraught over trifles.

Some observers feel that U.S. companies don't pay enough attention to safety and health issues:

We've reached an accommodation with blue-collar death. Forget that a U.S. worker is five times more likely to die than a Swede. . . . Forget that a U.S.

■□ *fast fact*

Each year there are about 500,000 cases of job-related illnesses and 6 million injuries.

worker is three times more likely to die than a Japanese. The sad reality is that blue-collar blood pours too easily. [Occupational Safety and Health Administration] fines amount to mere traffic tickets for those who run our companies. The small fines are simply buried in the cost of production. Blood can be cash accounted, given a number, and factored with other costs. . . . This has tremendous implications for the union-management relationship, not to mention costs from poor worker morale, lower productivity, and mounting litigation.[4]

Blue-collar workers aren't the only ones to suffer from workplace hazards. White-collar workers, including managers, also do so: "Stress is the most pervasive and potent toxin in the workplace," according to Leon J. Warshaw, executive director of the New York Business Group on Health, a coalition of businesses concerned about health care.[5] The traditional ill effects on the white-collar workforce have been psychological, but concern is now growing over physical conditions relating to the unforeseen effects of the computer terminal (e.g., eyestrain, back strain, miscarriages, and carpal tunnel syndrome) and closed office buildings, where chemical components from sources such as carpeting and structural materials build up and are circulated through the ventilation system.[6]

Just as managers and other employees all pay a personal price for unsafe and unhealthy workplaces, they share responsibility for improving occupational safety and health. Some of the roles and responsibilities of all three members of the HR triad are described in the feature, The HR Triad: Partnership Roles and Responsibilities in Safety and Health.

THE HR TRIAD: PARTNERSHIP ROLES AND RESPONSIBILITIES IN SAFETY AND HEALTH

Line Managers	HR Professionals	Employees
Recognize the strategic consequences of improved workplace safety and health as objectives.	Educate managers to understand the long-term value of improved safety and health.	Participate in the development and administration of safety and health programs.
Support the HR professionals' efforts to train all employees in safety and health.	Ensure that accidents and health-related incidents are accurately monitored, reported and recorded.	Perform in accordance with established safety and health guidelines.
Encourage employees to report unsafe conditions and suggest how to improve workplace safety and health.	Work with other professionals such as medical doctors and industrial engineers to develop new programs.	Take an active role in promoting changes that will enhance workplace safety and health.
Recognize the long-term cost of an unsafe and unhealthy workplace and encourage employees to make true improvements—not merely change their reporting behavior.	Create HR programs that train employees for safe and healthy behaviors and reward them for their success.	Promote workgroup norms that value safety and health.

The Benefits of a Safe and Healthy Work Environment

If organizations can reduce the rates and severity of their occupational accidents, diseases, workplace violence, and stress-related illnesses, and improve the quality of work life for their employees, they can only become more effective. Such an improvement can result in (1) more productivity owing to fewer lost workdays, (2) increased efficiency and quality from a more committed workforce, (3) reduced medical and insurance costs, (4) lower workers' compensation rates and direct payments because of fewer claims being filed, (5) greater flexibility and adaptability in the workforce as a result of increased participation and an increased sense of ownership, and (6) better selection ratios because of the enhanced image of the organization. Companies can thus increase their profits substantially and better serve the objectives of all their stakeholders.[7]

fast fact

Each year nearly one million workers become victims of workplace violence.

The Costs of an Unsafe and Unhealthy Work Environment

Back injuries are the most prevalent of all workplace injuries. Every year an estimated 10 million employees in the United States encounter back pain that impairs their job performance. Approximately 1 million employees file workers' compensation claims for back injuries. Billions of dollars are spent each year to treat back pain—$5 billion in workers' compensation payments alone.[8]

fast fact

According to the International Labor Organization the number of work-related accidents worldwide each year is about 125 million.

Estimates of workplace deaths in the U. S. range from 2,800 to around 10,000 yearly. Workplace-related deaths were about 7 per 100,000 employees in 1999. This is much better than 1970, when the rate was about 18 per 100,000 employees. Homicide is the leading cause of workplace deaths, and nearly one-third of all occupational fatalities are the result of car and truck crashes.[9]

Of course, these rates differ depending on job type, and sometimes even on the state. For example, the accident rate for 100,000 workers in the United States is 7, but for workers in Alaska's fishing industry, it is nearly 700. Another dangerous industry is construction, which places workers in a constantly changing environment. One misstep or forgetful moment can snuff out a life or crush a limb. Pressures to finish a job quickly often push foremen and workers to take risks. A macho culture tends to belittle safety measures and confuse caution with timidity. Construction, mining, and agriculture are typically the three most dangerous industries nationwide, with yearly deaths for every 100,000 employees being around 32, 43, and 40, respectively.[10]

fast fact

About 220,000 workers die around the world every year in work accidents or from illness contracted at work.

The costs of workplace deaths and injuries are estimated to be more than $50 billion. Similar costs are estimated for the more than 100,000 workers who annually succumb to occupational diseases. Enormous costs are also associated with psychological conditions. For example, alcoholism, often the result of attempts to cope with job pressures, costs organizations and society over $65 billion annually. Of this, $20 billion is attributed to lost productivity and the remainder to the direct costs of insurance, hospitalization, and other medical items. Perhaps more difficult to quantify, but just as symptomatic of stress and a poor quality of working life, are workers' feelings of lack of meaning and involvement in their work and loss of importance as individuals.

fast fact

Of the six million workplace injuries, about half result in lost work time.

HAZARDS IN OCCUPATIONAL SAFETY AND HEALTH

As Exhibit 14.1 shows, both physical and sociopsychological aspects of the workplace environment affect occupational safety and health. Traditionally,

"At some of our plants, if there is one accident, everyone's bonus is cut by 25 percent, two accidents means a 50 percent cut, and three accidents means no bonus for anyone."

Dennis Bakke
CEO
AES

hazards in the physical environment have received greater attention. Increasingly, however, both OSHA and companies themselves admit that sociopsychological conditions greatly affect health and safety, and they are doing something about it. At Hoffman-LaRoche, a pharmaceutical company, employees receive after-hours instruction in stress management methods such as meditation, breathing exercises, and biofeedback. Today, efforts to improve occupational safety and health aren't complete without a strategy for reducing psychological work-related stress.

Occupational Accidents

At AES, a global power company, top management is so concerned about safety that they hold everyone in the company accountable for reducing accidents. In 1998, the company had an excellent financial year. Under normal circumstances, the company would have distributed a 12 percent bonus. But because the company had experienced four fatalities around the world, the bonus was reduced 10 percent. By significantly penalizing poor safety performance, AES intends to motivate its employees to examine the causes of accidents and institute changes to prevent them in the future. At AES and elsewhere, the causes of accidents are many so eliminating them completely represents a major challenge.

Organizational Qualities. Accident rates vary substantially by industry. Firms in the construction and manufacturing industries have higher incidence rates than do firms in services, finance, insurance, and real estate. But some high-risk firms are taking steps to beat the odds. Barden Corporation, in Danbury, Connecticut is one of them. Over the years, Barden employees assumed that, because they work in a metal shop, people were going to get hurt. Then Barden created a Safety and Health Committee, which meets monthly to consider its safety and health performance. One of the major objectives is developing programs that strengthen safety awareness and performance. An example of one change made was to eliminate the safety engineering position and transfer its accountabilities to the Medical Department. The occupational health nurse in that department had shown considerable knowledge about safety matters and she aggressively investigated accidents and near-misses. The occupational health nurse was promoted to a new position entitled Manager of Employee Health and Safety.[11]

Exhibit 14.1
Model of Occupational Safety and Health in Organizations

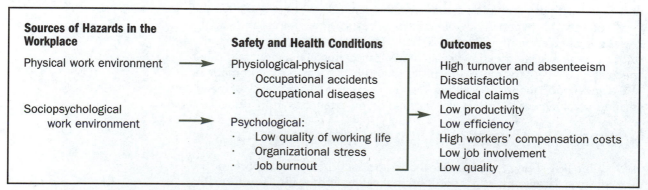

Small (those with fewer than 100 employees) and large organizations (those with more than 1,000 employees) have lower incidence rates than medium-sized organizations. This may be because supervisors in small organizations are better able to detect safety hazards and prevent accidents than those in medium-sized ones. And larger organizations have more resources to hire staff specialists who can devote all their efforts to safety and accident prevention.

In general, however, the working conditions (e.g., outdoors versus indoors), and the tools and technology available to do the job (e.g., heavy machinery versus personal computers) most affect occupational accidents. Next in line are the workers themselves.

The Unsafe Employee.   Some experts point to the employee as the pivotal cause of accidents. Accidents depend on the behavior of the person, the degree of hazard in the work environment, and pure chance. The degree to which a person contributes to an accident can be an indication of the individual's proneness to accidents. No stable set of personal characteristics *always* contributes to accidents. Nevertheless, certain psychological and physical characteristics seem to make some people *more susceptible* to accidents. For example, employees who are emotionally "high" have fewer accidents than those who are emotionally "low," and employees who have fewer accidents are more optimistic, trusting, and concerned for others than those who have more accidents. Employees under greater stress are likely to have more accidents than those under less stress. Substance abusers also experience more job-related injuries, and this is true regardless of whether the substance abuse takes place at work or off-the-job. Older workers may be less likely to have accidents, but more likely to suffer fatalities and recover more slowly.[12] As a consequence the issue of older workers in the workplace is a significant one. This is described more in the feature, Managing Diversity: Safety Issues and the Aging Workforce.[13] People who are quicker at recognizing visual patterns than at making muscular manipulations are less likely to have accidents than those who are just the opposite.

Many psychological conditions that may be related to accident-proneness—for instance, hostility and emotional immaturity—may be temporary states. Thus, they are difficult to detect until at least one accident has occurred. Because these characteristics aren't related to accidents in all work environments and because they aren't always present in employees, selecting and screening job applicants on the basis of accident-proneness is difficult.

The Violent Employee.   Workplace violence is growing rapidly, and employers are being held responsible. Homicide is the major cause of death in the workplace today.[14] Homicide, as well as other less serious forms of violence can be triggered by a number of forces, including being treated unfairly, an organizational culture that accepts aggressive behavior as normal, layoffs and downsizing, and even anger at being monitored too closely.[15] Although it may be difficult to identify the violent employee before the fact, employers are urged to be on the lookout for some common signs such as:

- **Verbal Threats:** Individuals often talk about what they may do. An employee might say, "Bad things are going to happen to so-and-so," or "That propane tank in the back could blow up easily."
- **Physical Actions:** Troubled employees may try to intimidate others, gain access to places they don't belong, or flash a concealed weapon in the workplace to test reactions.

■□ *fast fact*

Small firms cannot afford lost time from accidents: Each employee represents a larger percentage of the workforce than in larger firms.

■□ *fast fact*

A study by the National Institutes of Health shows that the cost of alcohol use is due mostly to productivity loss due to occasional overindulgence, not to problems caused by truly dependent alcohol abusers.

■□ *fast fact*

Nationally, nearly 11 percent of all violent crimes are committed against people at work.

MANAGING DIVERSITY

Safety Issues and the Aging Workforce

"I'm 51 years old, and I know for a fact that there's more risk for me to climb to the top of a rail car today than there was when I was younger and more agile," says Wayne Gordon, general manager of Farmers Cooperative Association in Jackson, Minnesota. Mr. Gordon indicates, however, that it's difficult to get other older workers to always agree with him: "Individuals have a tendency to think they can still do things they did 20 years ago." While he feels that it might be in the worker's interest to be prevented from performing a specific job, it might also violate age discrimination laws. The *Age Discrimination in Employment Act of 1967* suggests that employers can't automatically exclude workers from jobs solely because of age. Older workers, in fact, are among the best performers many companies have. From a safety side, however, the data give employers and society some concern. Federal studies show that older workers (above 54 years and particularly above 64 years of age) are 5 times more likely to die of a fatal transportation accident and 3.8 times as likely to be killed by objects and equipment than are younger workers. There also appears to significant medical differences between older and younger workers: As a group, older workers take nearly twice as long to mend and are more likely to die from injuries than younger workers. The average-per-person cost of health claims per year for workers 65–69 years old is more than double that for 45–59 year olds.

Especially given that the number of older workers is rising (from 3 million to 3.8 million age 65 and over during the past ten years), the question remains, "What can be done about this?" Studies by the *American Journal of Industrial Medicine* suggest that only about 30 percent of those older workers injured in work accidents received safety training. Other studies suggest that relatively simple work place modifications would be helpful, such as painting the steps of ladders with bright colors. Clearly, the answers aren't easily forthcoming. Older workers have better attendance and accident records argues the America Association of Retired Persons (AARP), so tread carefully in labeling older workers "those more likely to be more costly to employ." While the AARP may be sidestepping the reality of older worker fatalities, their concern is legitimate: companies need to treat all workers as individuals, and they also need to help protect and train all workers about safety concerns.

To learn more about the AARP, visit this organization at
www.aarp.org

---

fast fact

Employers may be held liable for the violent action of an employee if they knew, or should have known, that the employee was at risk for committing a violence.

- **Frustration:** Most cases of workplace violence don't involve a panicked individual who perceives the world as falling apart. A more likely scenario involves an employee who has a frustrated sense of entitlement to a promotion, for example.
- **Obsession:** An employee may hold a grudge against a coworker or supervisor, which, in some cases can stem from a romantic interest.[16]

These may be early warning signals for other acts of violence, including assault against coworkers and property damage. Like other forms of unacceptable performance on the job, the options for how to deal with violent employees include employee assistance programs, training in conflict management, and termination.

Occupational Diseases

Potential sources of work-related diseases are as distressingly varied as the symptoms of those diseases. Several federal agencies have systematically studied the workplace environment, and they have identified the following disease-causing hazards: arsenic, asbestos, benzene, bichloromethyl-ether, coal dust, coke-oven emissions, cotton dust, lead, radiation, and vinyl chloride. Workers likely to be exposed to those hazards include chemical and oil refinery workers, miners, textile workers, steelworkers, lead smelters, medical technicians, painters, shoemakers, and plastics industry workers. Continued research will no doubt uncover additional hazards that firms will want to diagnose and remedy for the future well-being of their workforces.[17]

Categories of Occupational Diseases.   In the long term, environmental hazards in the workplace have been linked to thyroid, liver, lung, brain, and kidney cancer; white, brown, and black lung disease; leukemia; bronchitis; emphysema; lymphoma; aplastic anemia; central nervous system damage; and reproductive disorders (e.g., sterility, genetic damage, miscarriages, and birth defects). Chronic bronchitis and emphysema are among the fastest-growing diseases in the United States, doubling every five years since World War II; they account for the second highest number of disabilities under Social Security. Cancer tends to receive the most attention, however, since it's a leading cause of death in the United States (second after heart disease). Many of the known causes of cancer are physical and chemical agents in the environment. And because these agents are theoretically more controllable than human behavior, the Occupational Safety and Health Administration's (OSHA's) emphasis is on eliminating them from the workplace.

OSHA is also concerned with the following categories of occupational diseases and illnesses: occupation-related skin diseases and disorders, dust diseases of the lungs, respiratory conditions due to toxic agents, poisoning (the systematic effect of toxic materials), disorders due to physical agents, disorders associated with repeated trauma, and all other occupational illnesses. OSHA, therefore, requires employers to keep records on all these diseases.

■□*fast fact*

OSHA estimates that more than 100,000 lives have been saved since OSHA was established in 1970.

Occupational Groups at Risk.   Miners, fire fighters, construction and transportation workers, and blue-collar and low-level supervisory personnel in manufacturing industries experience the majority of both occupational diseases and occupational injuries. In addition, large numbers of petrochemical and oil refinery workers, dye workers, dye users, textile workers, plastics industry workers, painters, and industrial chemical workers are also particularly susceptible to some of the most dangerous health hazards. Skin diseases are the most common of all reported occupational diseases, with leather workers being the group most affected.

Nevertheless, occupational diseases aren't exclusive to blue-collar workers and manufacturing industries. The "cushy office job" has evolved into a veritable nightmare of physical and psychological ills for white-collar workers in the expanding service industries. Among the common ailments are varicose veins, bad backs, deteriorating eyesight, migraine headaches, hypertension, coronary heart disorders, and respiratory and digestive problems. The causes of these include too much noise, interior air pollutants, uncomfortable chairs, inactivity, poor office design, and electronic office technology.

A Low Quality of Working Life

For many workers, a low quality of working life is associated with workplace conditions that fail to satisfy important preferences and interests such as a sense of responsibility, desire for empowerment and job involvement, challenge, meaningfulness, self-control, recognition, achievement, fairness or justice, security, and certainty.[18] Organizational conditions and practices that contribute to a low quality of working life include

- jobs with low levels of task significance, variety, identity, autonomy, and feedback;
- minimal involvement of employees in decision making and a great deal of one-way communication with employees;
- pay systems not based on performance, or based on performance that isn't objectively measured or under employee control;
- supervisors, job descriptions, and organizational policies that fail to convey to the employee what is expected and what is rewarded;
- human resource policies and practices that are discriminatory and of low validity;
- temporary employment conditions, where employees are dismissed at will (employee rights don't exist); and
- corporate cultures that aren't supportive of employee empowerment and job involvement.

Although these conditions tend to create feelings of poor work life quality, low quality of working life for one individual may not be so for another individual, because of differences in preferences, interests, and perceptions of uncertainty in the environment.

Organizational Stress

Prevalent forms of organizational stress include "the four Ss," organizational change, work pacing, the physical environment, stress-prone employees, and job burnout.[19]

The Four Ss. Common stressors for many employees include the supervisor, salary, security, and safety.[20] Petty work rules and relentless pressure for more production are major stressors that employees associate with *supervisors.* Both deny worker needs to control the work situation and to be recognized and accepted. *Salary* is a stressor when it's perceived as being distributed unfairly. Many blue-collar workers feel they are underpaid relative to their white-collar counterparts. Teachers may think they are underpaid relative to people with similar education who work in private industry. Employees experience stress when they aren't sure whether they will have their jobs next month, next week, or even tomorrow. For many employees, lack of job *security* is even more stressful than lack of safety—at least, with an unsafe job, they know the risks, whereas with an insecure job, they are in a continual state of uncertainty.[21]

Fear of workplace accidents and their resulting injuries or deaths can also be stressful for many workers. When pressure for production is increased, the fear regarding workplace *safety* can rise to the point where production decreases rather than increases. This result, in turn, may lead to a vicious cycle that is counterproductive for the workers and the organization.

Organizational Change. Changes made by organizations usually involve something important and are accompanied by uncertainty. Many changes

■□ *fast fact*

Managers run double their usual risk of a heart attack during the week after they have fired an employee.

"Now you have to call them change management seminars, instead of stress management…because companies are afraid that by bringing in a stress specialist, the employees will think the company is aware of a problem."

Tim O'Brien
Director
Institute for Stress Management

are made without official warning. Although rumors often circulate that a change is coming, the exact nature of the change is left to speculation. People become concerned about whether the change will affect them, perhaps by displacing them or by causing them to be transferred. The result is that many employees suffer stress symptoms.[22] As a consequence, many companies have adopted stress management programs. An example is described in the feature Managing Change: Stress Management at Adolph Coors Co.[23]

Work Pacing. *Work pacing* may be controlled by machines or people. *Machine pacing* gives control over the speed of the operation and of the work output to something other than the individual. *Employee pacing* gives that control to the individual. The effects of machine pacing are severe, because the individual is unable to satisfy a crucial need for control of the situation. It has been reported that workers on machine-paced jobs feel exhausted at the end of their shifts and are unable to relax soon after work because of increased adrenaline secretion on the job. In a study of 23 white- and blue-collar occupations, assembly workers reported the highest level of severe stress symptoms.[24]

■□*fast fact*

The number of hours worked per year by the average American rose by 66 hours between the late 1960s and 1990s.

MANAGING CHANGE
Stress Management at Adolph Coors Co.

A stress management program at Adolph Coors Co., a Golden, Colorado-based brewery, has expanded to help workers cope with increasing workforce changes. A downsizing of 643 employees through voluntary separations, followed by corporate reorganization, led to a rethinking throughout the company on Coors' direction, says Bob Tank Jr., manager of counseling services. Originally, the stress management program included only a course on anger management and an exercise component. Now, both group programs and individualized help in managing stress are offered through the employee assistance plan. Tank notes that group programs help employees see that they are "not alone" in their need to reduce stress.

Coors' stress management program features 27 different courses, which address family and personal concerns as well as workplace issues such as communication, self-esteem, and how to work together. The program also can be "customized" to address specific problems. For example, a work group requested training because it had been struggling with bickering, strife, and management/worker dysfunction. Instruction was aimed at clarifying roles and redirecting energies. Feedback following the classes showed success in deflating the dysfunctional processes and clarifying team operations.

With so much going on in the company lately, employee participation in the stress management program has dropped off in every area except for a tremendously popular course on dealing with corporate change. To boost participation, Coors integrates more programs into the workplace, makes programs user-friendly, and makes them available to production areas. In addition, information on stress reduction is made available through open houses and notices in cafeterias and individual work sites.

Outreach programs can be an effective, less formal way to help employees deal with change, Tank adds. Companies today need to stay flexible to adapt and do what is necessary to thrive, he says. Coors wants its employees to be able to do the same.

To learn more about Adolph Coors Co., visit the company's home page at **www.coors.com**

Physical Environment.   Although office automation is a way to improve productivity, it has stress-related drawbacks. One aspect of office automation with a specific stress-related characteristic is the video display terminal (VDT); Sweden and Norway have taken the most measures to deal with these devices. Other aspects of the work environment associated with stress are crowding, lack of privacy, and lack of control—for example, the inability to move a desk or chairs or even to hang pictures in a work area in an effort to personalize it.[25] Poor indoor air quality is another aspect of the work environment that employees report being a source of stress. According to one survey, about one out of three managers believes that poor air quality is a significant cause of both illness among employees and lost productivity.[26]

Stress-Prone Employees.   People differ in the ways they respond to organizational stressors. A classic difference is referred to as Type A versus Type B behavior. Type A people like to do things their way and are willing to exert a lot of effort to ensure that even trivial tasks are performed in the manner they prefer. They often fail to distinguish between important and unimportant situations. They are upset, for instance, when they have to wait fifteen minutes to be seated in a restaurant, since this isn't in compliance with their idea of responsive service. In short, Type A people spend much of their time directing energy toward noncompliances in the environment. Still, Type A people are "movers and shakers." They enjoy acting on their environment and modifying the behavior of other people. They are primarily rewarded by compliance and punished by noncompliance.

Type B people are generally much more patient. They aren't easily frustrated or easily angered, nor do they expend a lot of energy in response to noncompliance. Type B people may be excellent supervisors to work for— that is, until you need them to push upward in the organization on your behalf. They probably will permit their subordinates a lot of freedom but also might not provide the types of upward support necessary for effective leadership.[27]

Job Burnout

Job burnout is a particular type of stress that seems to be experienced by people who work in jobs in human services, such as health care, education, police work, ministry, and so on. This type of reaction to one's work includes attitudinal and emotional reactions that a person goes through as a result of job-related experiences. Often the first sign of burnout is a feeling of being *emotionally exhausted* by one's work. An emotionally exhausted employee might express feelings of being drained, used-up, at the end of his or her rope, or physically fatigued. Waking up in the morning may be accompanied by a feeling of dread at the thought of having to put in another day on the job. For someone who was once enthusiastic about the job and idealistic about what could be accomplished, feelings of emotional exhaustion may come somewhat unexpectedly, though to an outsider looking at the situation, emotional exhaustion would be seen as a natural response to an extended period of intense interaction with people and their problems.

Extreme emotional exhaustion can be very debilitating both on and off the job, so people who are experiencing it must find some way to cope. One common coping reaction is to put psychological distance between one's self and one's clients and to decrease personal involvement with them. In moderation, this reaction may be an effective method for creating "detached concern," but when engaged in to excess, the employee begins to dehumanize or depersonalize the clients. People who have reached an extreme state of *depersonalization* report feeling they have become calloused by their jobs and that they have grown cynical about their clients.

In addition to emotional exhaustion and depersonalization, a third aspect of burnout is a feeling of *low personal accomplishment*. Many human service professionals begin their careers with great expectations that they will be able to improve the human condition through their work. After a year or two on the job, they begin to realize they aren't living up to these expectations. There are many systemic reasons for the gap that exists between the novice's goals and the veteran's accomplishments, including unrealistically high expectations due to a lack of exposure to the job during training, constraints placed on the worker through the rules and regulations of an immutable bureaucracy, inadequate resources for performing one's job, clients who are frequently uncooperative and occasionally rebellious, and a lack of feedback about successes. These and other characteristics of human service organizations almost guarantee that employees will be frustrated in their attempts to reach their goals, yet the workers may not recognize the role of the system in producing this frustration. Instead the worker may feel personally responsible and begin to think of himself or herself as a failure. When combined with emotional exhaustion, feelings of low personal accomplishment may reduce motivation to a point where performance is in fact impaired, leading to further experienced failure.

The Consequences of Burnout. Burned out staff members may perform more poorly on the job compared to their counterparts who are still "fired up." Consider as an example the job of an intake interviewer in a legal aid office. For the organization, the intake interview serves as a screening device through which all potential clients must pass. During the interview, specific information about the nature and details of a case must be assessed and an evaluation of the "appropriateness" of the case for the office must be made. Since as many as 40 intake interviews may be conducted per day, it's important that the interviewer work as efficiently as possible. Here the major index of efficiency is the number of forms accurately filled out for further processing. To the extent time is spent talking about problems not relevant for these forms, efficiency decreases.

Now consider the client's perspective. Upon arriving for an interview, the client is likely to be rehearsing the injustices done and planning for retaliation. The client does not consider the precise statutes encompassing the problem nor the essential details that make the case worthy of attention. Rather, the client is concerned with the problems faced as a result of the perceived injustices. The client's primary concern is to return emotional and physical life to normal—the law seems to offer a solution. The intake interview may be the first chance to explain the problems the client is facing. From this perspective, good job performance is displayed by an interviewer who lends a sympathetic ear.

How will the interviewer handle this situation? Typically, the person doing the interview will be a relatively recent graduate of law school with little or no clinical experience to rely on. Socialization has emphasized the supremacy of objectivity. But clearly, adoption of an objective, analytic attitude combined with the pressure to efficiently fill out forms does not add up to the sympathetic ear the client is looking for. The objective interviewer appears unconcerned and the client becomes frustrated. The emotionally

■□ fast fact

Burnout has a negative impact on the customer as well as the employee.

involved client becomes an obstacle to detached efficiency, frustrating the interviewer. Whether or not open hostility erupts, both participants are aware of the antagonistic relationship they have formed.

Another unfortunate consequence of burnout is a deterioration of one's relationships with coworkers. A study of mental health workers found that people who were experiencing calloused feelings toward their clients also complained more about their clients to their coworkers, thereby generating a negative atmosphere within the work unit. These burned out mental health workers were also absent from work more often and took more frequent work breaks.[28]

STRATEGIES FOR IMPROVEMENT

"One thing common to nearly all [stress management] programs in business is they don't do anything about the cause. Instead, they try to make the person more resistant to stress, or able to cope with it better."

Terry Beehr
Stress Expert and Professor
Central Michigan University

Once the cause of a work hazard is identified, strategies can be developed for eliminating or reducing it (see Exhibit 14.2). To determine whether a strategy is effective, organizations can compare the incidence, severity, and frequency of illnesses and accidents before and after the intervention. OSHA has approved methods for establishing these rates.

Monitoring Safety and Health Rates

OSHA requires organizations to maintain records of the incidence of injuries and illnesses. Some organizations also record the severity and frequency of each.[29]

Incidence Rate.   The most explicit index of industrial safety is the incidence rate, which reflects the number of injuries and illnesses in a year. It's calculated by the following formula:

Incidence Rate = (Number of Injuries and Illnesses × 200,000) ÷ Number of Employee Hours Worked

The base for 100 full-time workers is 200,000 (40 hours a week × 50 weeks). Suppose an organization had 10 recorded injuries and illnesses and 500 employees. To calculate the number of employee hours worked, multiply the number of employees by 40 hours and by 50 weeks: 500 × 40 × 50 = 1,000,000. Therefore, the incidence rate is 2 for every 100 workers a year: (10 × 200,000) ÷ 1,000,000 = 2.

Frequency Rate. The frequency rate reflects the number of injuries and illnesses for every million hours worked, rather than in a year as with the incidence rate. It's calculated as:

Frequency Rate = (Number of Injuries and Illnesses × 1,000,000 hours) ÷ Number of Employee Hours Worked

Severity Rate. The severity rate reflects the hours actually lost owing to injury or illness. It recognizes that not all injuries and illnesses are equal. Four categories of injuries and illnesses have been established: deaths, permanent total disabilities, permanent partial disabilities, and temporary total disabilities. An organization with the same number of injuries and illnesses as another but with more deaths would have a higher severity rate. The severity rate is calculated by this formula:

Severity Rate = (Total Hours Charged × 1,000,000 Hours) ÷ Number of Employee Hours Worked

Exhibit 14.2
Sources and Strategies for Improving Occupational Safety and Health

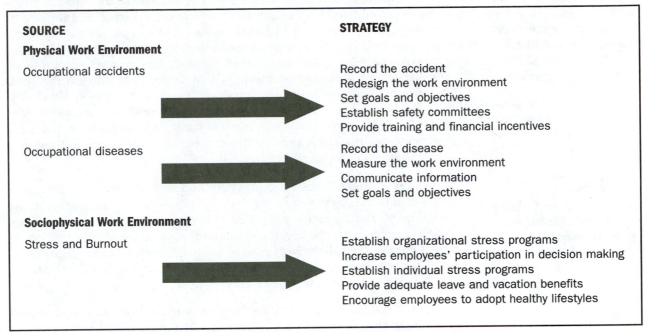

SOURCE

Physical Work Environment

Occupational accidents

STRATEGY

Record the accident
Redesign the work environment
Set goals and objectives
Establish safety committees
Provide training and financial incentives

Occupational diseases

Record the disease
Measure the work environment
Communicate information
Set goals and objectives

Sociophysical Work Environment

Stress and Burnout

Establish organizational stress programs
Increase employees' participation in decision making
Establish individual stress programs
Provide adequate leave and vacation benefits
Encourage employees to adopt healthy lifestyles

Controlling Accidents

Designing the work environment to make accidents unlikely is perhaps the best way to prevent accidents and increase safety. Among the safety features that can be designed into the physical environment are guards on machines, handrails in stairways, safety goggles and helmets, warning lights, self-correcting mechanisms, and automatic shutoffs. The extent to which these features will actually reduce accidents depends on employee acceptance and use. For example, eye injuries will be reduced by the availability of safety goggles only if employees wear the goggles correctly.[30] This is more likely when employees accept the responsibility for safety, as is the trend in some firms. Du Pont employees understand that they bear responsibility for their safety. This responsibility has grown as the company has reduced its organizational levels, which means less supervision and a more participatory approach to management. With self-management and teamwork comes the onus on individuals to assume more responsibility. Teams are expected to work toward common objectives, and these objectives should include excellent safety performance.[31]

Ergonomics.   Another way to improve safety is to make the job itself more comfortable and less fatiguing through ergonomics. Ergonomics considers changes in the job environment in conjunction with the physical and physiological capabilities and limitations of the employees.[32]

In an effort to reduce the number of back injuries, the Ford Motor Company and Eaton Corporation are redesigning workstations and tasks that may be causing musculoskeletal problems for workers. For instance, lifting devices are being introduced on the assembly line to reduce back strain, and walking and working surfaces are being studied to see if floor mats can reduce body fatigue. Videotapes that feature Ford employees performing their jobs both before and after ergonomic redesign are used in training.[33]

In an effort to reduce back injuries, Federal Express instituted a three-pronged prevention program stressing education, exercise, and the use of back belts, for thousands of package handlers. The program begins by using training to raise overall awareness about back injuries through safety training. Awareness is further heightened through tips printed in employee newsletters and weekly group meetings that discuss safe lifting techniques. The second component of the program prepares workers physically. Employees participate in a pre-shift stretching routine that is mandatory for all workers whose jobs involve lifting. Third, all package handlers use flexible back supports. These provide direct protection while also serving as a constant reminder to lift safely.[34]

Safety Committees. Another strategy for accident prevention is the use of safety committees, as they do at Barden. The HR department can serve as the coordinator of a committee composed of several employee representatives. Where unions exist, the committee should have union representation as well. Often, organizations have several safety committees at the department level, for implementation and administration, and one larger committee at the organization level, for policy formulation.

Behavior Modification. Employers have known for a long time that a small percentage of their workforce is responsible for the majority of their health insurance claims. Originally, they tried to encourage their employees to be healthy by offering to subsidize health club memberships and building exercise facilities and jogging trails, but the results were disappointing. Now, many companies are implementing incentive-based health and safety programs.

Reinforcing behaviors that reduce the likelihood of accidents can be highly successful. Reinforcers can range from nonmonetary rewards (such as positive feedback) to activity rewards (such as time off) to material rewards (such as company-purchased doughnuts during a coffee break) to financial rewards (such as bonuses for attaining desired levels of safety).

The behavioral approach relies on measuring performance before and after the intervention, specifying and communicating the desired performance to employees, monitoring performance at unannounced intervals several times a week, and reinforcing desired behavior several times a week with performance feedback.

In two food processing plants, behavior was monitored for 25 weeks—before, during, and after a safety training program. Slides were used to illustrate safe and unsafe behaviors. Employees were also given data on the percentage of safe behaviors in their departments. A goal of 90 percent safe behaviors was established. Supervisors were trained to give positive reinforcement when they observed safe behavior. Following the intervention, the incidence of safe behavior increased substantially—from an average of 70 percent to more than 95 percent in the wrapping department and from 78 percent to more than 95 percent in the makeup department. One year after the program, the frequency rate of lost-time injuries was fewer than 10, a substantial decline from the preceding year's rate of 53.8.[35]

Reducing the Incidence of Diseases

Occupational diseases are far more costly and harmful overall to organizations and employees than are occupational accidents. Because the causal relationship between the physical environment and occupational diseases is often subtle, developing strategies to reduce their incidence is generally difficult.

Record Keeping. At a minimum, OSHA requires that organizations measure the chemicals in the work environment and keep records on these measurements. The records must also include precise information about ailments and exposures. Such information must be kept for as long as the incubation period of the specific disease—even as long as 40 years. If the organization is sold, the new owner must assume responsibility for storing the old records and continuing to gather the required data. If the company goes out of business, the administrative director of OSHA must be told where the records are.[36] Guidelines for record keeping are given in Exhibit 14.3.

Monitoring Exposure. The obvious approach to controlling occupational illnesses is to rid the workplace of chemical agents or toxins; an alternative approach is to monitor and limit exposure to hazardous substances. Some organizations now monitor genetic changes due to exposure to carcinogens—for example, benzene, arsenic, ether, and vinyl chloride. Samples of blood are obtained from employees at fixed intervals to determine whether the employees' chromosomes have been damaged. If damage has occurred, the affected employee is placed in a different job and, where feasible, conditions are modified.

Genetic Screening. Genetic screening is the most extreme, and consequently the most controversial, approach to controlling occupational disease. By using genetic testing to screen out individuals who are susceptible to certain ailments, organizations lower their vulnerability to workers' compensation claims and problems. Opponents of genetic screening contend that it measures predisposition to disease, not the actual presence of disease, and therefore violates an individual's rights.[37]

Controlling Stress and Burnout

Increasingly, organizations are offering training programs designed to help employees deal with work-related stress. For example, J. P. Morgan offers stress management programs as part of a larger supervisory and management development curriculum. Available to supervisors, professional staff, and officers, these courses are designed to introduce supervisory and management material, information skills, and role definition. The emphasis is on providing concrete information to reduce the ambiguity associated with fast-paced, changing work roles.[38]

Increasing Participation in Decision Making. The importance of being able to control, or at least predict future outcomes is well-recognized. Having opportunities to be self-determining, combined with the freedom and the ability to influence events in one's surroundings, can be intrinsically motivating and highly rewarding. When opportunities for control are absent and people feel trapped in an environment that's neither controllable nor predictable, both psychological and physical health are likely to suffer.[39]

In most organizations, employees are controlled by organizational rules, policies, and procedures. Often these rules and procedures are creations from an earlier era of the organization and are no longer as effective as they once were. Nevertheless, their enforcement continues until new rules are developed. Most often, the new rules are created by people in the highest

Exhibit 14.3
OSHA Guidelines for Recording Cases

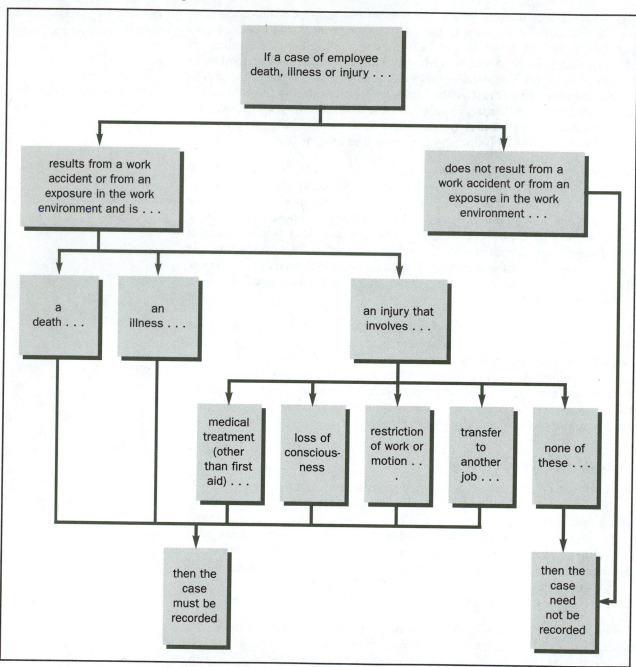

levels of the organization and then imposed upon people at the lower levels.
Sometimes the new rules are an improvement over the old rules, other times
they aren't. Regardless of whether they are an improvement, the new rules
or procedures are likely to be experienced as another event in the organization over which the employees had no control.

Besides giving workers a feeling of control, participation in decision
making gives them the power they need to remove obstacles to effective per-

formance, thereby reducing frustration and strain. One effective use of influence would be to persuade others to change their conflicting role expectations for one's own behavior. Through the repeated interchanges required by participative decision making, members of the organization can also gain a better understanding of the demands and constraints faced by others. When the conflicts workers face become clear, perhaps for the first time, negotiation is likely to begin over which expectations should be changed in order to reduce inherent conflicts. Another important consequence of the increased communication that occurs when an organization uses participative decision making is people become less isolated from their coworkers and supervisors. Through their discussions, employees learn about the formal and informal expectations held by others. They also learn about the formal and informal policies and procedures of the organization. This information can help reduce feelings of role ambiguity. It also makes it easier for the person to perform his or her job effectively.

Finally, participation in decision making helps prevent stress and burnout by encouraging the development of a *social support network* among coworkers. Social support networks help people cope effectively with the stresses they experience on the job.

Individual Stress Management Strategies. Time management can be an effective individual strategy to deal with organizational stress. It's based in large part on an initial identification of an individual's personal goals. Other strategies that should be part of individual stress management include following a good diet, getting regular exercise, monitoring physical health, and building social support groups. Many large organizations such as Coors encourage employees to enroll in regular exercise programs, where their fitness and health are carefully monitored. Finally, encouraging employees to use, not bank, their vacation time and regular days off appears to be another strategy for managing stress and burnout.[40]

Developing Occupational Health Policies

As scientific knowledge accumulates and liabilities rise, more and more organizations are developing policy statements regarding occupational hazards. These statements grow out of a concern that organizations should be proactive in dealing with health and safety problems. For example, Dow Chemical's policy states, "No employee, male or female, will knowingly be exposed to hazardous levels of materials known to cause cancer or genetic mutations in humans."[41]

An example of the growing complexity of the problems associated with workplace hazards is the debate over whether women of childbearing age should be allowed to hold jobs in settings that could endanger fetuses. Johnson Controls Incorporated of Milwaukee, Wisconsin, which makes lead automobile batteries for such customers as Sears and the Goodyear Tire and Rubber Company, responded to this issue by restricting women's access to jobs in its Bennington, Vermont plant. Johnson's management claimed that the factory's air contained traces of lead and lead oxide. Although presumably not high enough to harm adults, the toxin levels were dangerous for children and fetuses. Thus, women were allowed to work in the plant, but only if they were unable to bear children (either because of surgery to prevent pregnancies or because they were too old to have children). According to the company, "The issue was protecting the health of unborn children."

■□ *fast fact*

A safe and healthy workplace is a corporate value at Weyerhaeuser. They say that "All employees are accountable for a safe, clean workplace and are empowered to challenge any activity that compromises safety and/or cleanliness."

Women's advocates and union leaders argued that the firm was guilty of
sex discrimination. Specifically, they claimed that lead levels were too high
for men as well; that the firm was deciding for women rather than allowing
women to decide for themselves whether to take the risk; that such rules
invade women's privacy; and, finally, that the restrictions denied women
access to high-paying jobs (a typical factory job for women in Bennington
paid $6.35 an hour, versus $15.00 an hour in the Milwaukee plant).[42]

The situation was made more complex by the reluctance of many workers to leave their jobs to avoid occupational exposure unless they were guaranteed that their incomes would not suffer. Some workers went so far as to
have themselves sterilized to protect their jobs. When the Supreme Court
heard this case, it ruled in favor of the workers, thus striking down the company's fetal protection policy (*United Auto Workers v. Johnson Controls*, 1991).

The policies of AT&T and Digital Equipment illustrate alternative strategies. These provide for income protection for pregnant production workers
who might be exposed to the toxic gases and liquids used to etch micro-
scopic circuits onto silicon wafers. Other companies are obtaining voluntary
consent agreements from employees who choose to stay on hazardous jobs.
Although these statements can absolve employers from punitive damages in
civil court, they don't alleviate liability under workers' compensation laws
and civil disability suits.

Establishing Wellness Programs

Corporations are increasingly focusing on keeping employees healthy rather
than helping them get well.[43] They are investing in wellness programs at
record rates, and such programs appear to be paying off in terms of morale,
performance, absentee rates, and health care costs.[44]

LEGAL CONSIDERATIONS

The negative consequences of working in unsafe and unhealthy workplaces
can be severe. And often, long periods of exposure occur before any symptoms appear. Thus, to protect workers, the U. S. government actively regulates employers. The legal framework for occupational safety and health can
be divided into four major categories: the Occupational Safety and Health
Administration, workers' compensation programs, the common-law doctrine of torts, and local initiatives.

Occupational Safety and Health Administration

The federal government's primary response to the issue of safety and health
in the workplace has been the *Occupational Safety and Health Act of 1970*, which
created the Occupational Safety and Health Administration and which calls
for safety and health inspections of organizations regardless of size, reporting
by employers, and investigations of accidents and allegations of hazards.
OSHA is responsible for establishing and enforcing occupational safety and
health standards and for inspecting and issuing citations to organizations
that violate these standards. Two other organizations support the role of
OSHA: the National Institute for Occupational Safety and Health (NIOSH)
and the Occupational Safety and Health Review Commission (OSHRC). The
commission reviews appeals made by organizations that received citations
from OSHA inspectors for alleged safety and health violations.[45]

Regardless of whether organizations are inspected, they are required to keep safety and health records so that OSHA can compile accurate statistics on work injuries and illnesses. These records should cover all disabling, serious, or significant injuries and illnesses, whether or not they involve loss of time from work. Excluded are minor injuries that require only first aid and don't involve medical treatment, loss of consciousness, restriction of work or motion, or transfer to another job. Falsification of records or failure to keep adequate records can result in substantial fines. However, the recordkeeping requirement was recently qualified. An employer may withhold injury and illness records from federal safety investigators if it has a legitimate need to keep the records private, and the Occupational Safety and Health Administration has failed to obtain a warrant granting it access to such documents.

The *Access to Employee Exposure and Medical Records Regulation of 1980* requires employers to show or give employees, their designated representatives, and OSHA the employees' on-the-job medical records. This regulation also requires employers to provide access to records of measurements of employee exposure to toxic substances.

Communication Is Key.   The employee's right to know about workplace hazards is supported by the Hazard Communication Standard, which went into effect in 1986. Under this standard, employers are required to provide workers with information and training on hazardous chemicals in their work area at the time of their initial assignment and whenever a new hazard is introduced. According to OSHA, effective communication is the real key and should include information for employees on

- the standard's requirements and workplace operations that use hazardous chemicals,
- proper procedures for determining the presence of chemicals and detecting hazardous releases,
- protective measures and equipment that should be used,
- the location of written hazard communication programs, and
- workers' compensation programs.[46]

Whereas OSHA was established to provide protection against accidents and diseases for workers on the job, workers' compensation was established to provide financial aid for those unable to work because of accidents and diseases. For many years, workers' compensation awards were granted only to workers unable to work because of physical injury or damage. Since 1955, however, court decisions have either caused or enticed numerous states to allow workers' compensation payment in job-related cases of anxiety, depression, and mental disorders.[47]

In 1955, the Texas Supreme Court charted this new direction in workers' compensation claims by stating that an employee who became terrified, highly anxious, and unable to work because of a job-related accident had a compensable claim even though he had no physical injury (*Bailey v. American General Insurance Company*, 1955). In another court ruling (*James v. State Accident Insurance Fund*, 1980), an Oregon court ruled in favor of a worker's claim for compensation for inability to work due to job stress resulting from conflicting work assignments. Determining responsibility is sometimes difficult because determining cause-and-effect relationships is difficult, especially since reactions such as asbestosis or hypertension take a long time to develop or occur only in some people working under the same conditions as others.

Common Law Doctrine of Torts

Much of the legal discussion on human resource management is based on statutory law, that is, the body of laws passed by legislatures at the federal and state levels. For example, the *Civil Rights Act of 1991*, the *Americans with Disabilities Act of 1990*, and the *Occupational Safety and Health Act of 1970* are statutory laws. But the common-law doctrine of torts also plays a role. This body of law consists of court decisions regarding wrongful acts such as personal injuries that were committed by an employee on another employee or even a customer and resulted in a lawsuit against the employer.

Employees and customers can obtain damage awards if they demonstrate that the employers engaged in reckless or intentional infliction designed to degrade or humiliate. Few such cases have been successful, in part because workers' compensation programs were designed to remove workplace accidents and injuries from litigation. The cases that have been successfully brought against employers are notable because of the costs involved. For example, consider the customer in a car rental office who argued with the rental agent. The employee struck the customer with a blow to his head, knocking him to the floor. As the customer lay on the floor, the employee repeatedly kicked him and pummeled him with "judo chops." The customer filed a civil action lawsuit for negligent retention. The evidence showed that the employee had a history of blowing up at and threatening customers. The rental company had not disciplined the employee either before or after the incident. A jury awarded the customer $350,000 in compensatory damages and $400,000 in punitive damages (*Greenfield v. Spectrum Inv. Group*, 1985).

Local Initiatives

State, municipal, and city governments may pass their own safety and health laws and regulations that go beyond the coverage of OSHA. Consequently, employers need to be aware of local regulations. Sometimes, these local initiatives offer a glimpse as to what other area governments or even the federal government might do in the future.

Americans with Disabilities Act (ADA)

Employee layoffs and discharges (terminations) constitute 50 percent of all claims filed under the ADA, and 15 percent of these are for back pain. Victims are entitled to sue for up to $300,000, and many employers are tempted to settle before going to trial in hopes of reaching smaller settlements. Thus, the ADA gives organizations another reason to seek ways to remove hazardous conditions from the work environment.

> *"The law is clear that a landowner does not have a duty to provide for the safety of independent contractors."*
>
> **U.S. Seventh Circuit Court of Appeals**

SUMMARY

Employers are keenly aware of the cost of ill health and the benefits of having a healthy workforce. The federal government, through OSHA, is also making it more necessary for employers to be concerned with employee health. The government's current concern is primarily with occupational accidents and diseases, both aspects of the physical environment. However, organizations can choose to become involved in programs dealing with the sociopsychological environment as well. If organizations choose not to become involved with improving the sociopsychological environment, the government may prescribe mandatory regulations. Thus, it pays for organizations to be concerned with both aspects of the work environment. Effective programs for both environments can significantly improve both employee health and the effectiveness of the organization.

When the adoption of improvement programs is being considered, employee involvement isn't only a good idea but also is likely to be desired by employees. Many things can be done to improve both the physical and sociopsychological work environments. Each is different and has its own unique components. Although some improvement strategies may work well for one component, they may not work for other components. A careful diagnosis is required before programs are selected and implemented.

Assuming that a careful diagnosis indicates the need for a stress management program, the challenge is selecting one from the many available. Programs such as time management or physical exercise could be set up so that employees can help themselves cope, or the organization could alter the conditions that are associated with stress. The latter approach requires a diagnosis of what is happening, where, and to whom before a decision is made on how to proceed. Because so many possible sources of stress exist, and because not all people react the same way to them, implementing individual stress management strategies may be more efficient. However, if many people are suffering similar stress symptoms in a specific part of the organization, an organizational strategy is more appropriate.

For many aspects of safety and health, either pertinent information does not exist or organizations are unwilling to gather or provide it. From a legal as well as a humane viewpoint, it's in the best interests of organizations to seek and provide more information so that more effective strategies for improving safety and health can be developed and implemented. Failure to do so may result in costly legal settlements against organizations or further governmental regulation of workplace safety and health.

TERMS TO REMEMBER

Common law
Doctrine of torts
Employee pacing
Ergonomics
Frequency rate
Incidence rate
Job burnout
Low quality of working life
Machine pacing
National Institute of Occupational
    Safety and Health (NIOSH)
Occupational accidents
Occupational disease

Occupational safety and health
Occupational Safety and Health
    Administration (OSHA)
Organizational stress
Physical/physiological conditions
Physical work environment
Psychological conditions
Safety committees
Severity rate
Sociopsychological work
    environment
Work pacing

DISCUSSION QUESTIONS

1. In what ways are safety and health important issues at Ben and Jerry's?

2. How can strategies to improve the physical work environment and the sociopsychological work environment be assessed?

3. The United States prides itself on freedom, democracy, and free labor markets. Thus, employees should be made responsible for health and safety. In other words, employers who offer riskier employment should simply pay workers more for bearing the risk (a wage premium), and the workers can in turn buy more insurance coverage to cover this risk. Discuss the advantages and disadvantages of this approach.

4. Who is responsible for workplace safety and health? the employer? the employee? the federal government? judges and juries? Explain.

5. How are physical hazards distinct from sociopsychological hazards? What implications do these differences have for programs to deal with these two categories of hazards?

6. Is there such a thing as an unsafe worker? Assuming that accident-prone workers exist, how can effective human resource activities address this problem?

7. What incentives does OSHA provide the employer for promoting workplace safety? Explain.

8. How might a company's strategy to prevent occupational accidents differ from a program to prevent occupational disease? In what ways might the programs be similar?

9. Should all employers institute wellness programs for their employees? Why or Why not?

PROJECTS TO EXTEND YOUR LEARNING

1. **Managing Strategically.** Conduct research by comparing two companies within the same industry. Distinguish them by the level of care they put to the safety of their employees in the workplace. Find out whether the costs incurred in safety procedures create bigger return in overall revenue of the companies. (Hint: Compare fiscal year periods before and after safety procedures were increased. Which period saved more overhead costs? Legal expenses and health expenses? Safety procedure expenses? You might start by visiting 3M, a company that actively promotes safety (**www.3M.com/cws**). Also visit

   Federal Express   **www.fedex.com**
   Ford Motor Company   **www2.ford.com**
   Eaton Corporation   **www.eaton.com**

2. **Managing Teams.** Stress in organizations is a major concern: it can result in ill health and workplace accidents. Thus successful stress management activities are very desirable. Extensive research has shown that teams can be an excellent way employees can manage the stress at work, just as teams can be an excellent way to perform a multitude of complex

tasks. Teams perform this helpful role in stress management by offering "social support." As you now know, it's predicted that if stress is managed well, the ill-health effects and workplace accidents are likely to be reduced. You can investigate the extent of these relationships by identifying companies that are team-based and those that are not. Then relate their ill-health measures and their accident rates to whether or not they are team-based or not. You might consider using firms that use TQM principles versus those that do nott. Do companies that follow TQM principles appear to have better health and safety records?

3. **Managing Globalization.** Multinational corporations operate in a variety of countries, some of which have more restrictive laws than others regarding health and safety. Visit several web sites to learn more about the safety and health conditions, laws and safety concerns in at least ten countries of the world where U.S. multinational corporations operate. You might begin by visiting the ILO at **www.ilo.org** and the International Occupational Safety and Health Information Center at **turva.me.tut.fi/cis/**

4. **Managing Change.** Organizational change is a major event in the lives of many employees. It means that their organizational life will be different. Thus it would seem reasonable for employees to be told about the change that's coming. Such advance notification would help employees deal with one of the biggest sources of resistance to change: uncertainty and fear of the unknown. This uncertainty and fear are the heart of the stress that most of us feel when confronted with organizational change. Little wonder that we tend to prefer the "old" way to the "new" way. At least with the "old" way we know what to expect, we're certain about it, even if it's not a bed of roses. But with the "new" way, even though it might be better, if we don't know this, then we are uncertain about the future. In reality, most of us like predictability. With this in mind, determine the policies and practices that organizations can have about informing their employees of forthcoming organizational changes. Find out why they choose to inform them or why they don't. Visit **www.astd.org** and scan issues of the *Training and Development Magazine* for stories.

5. **Managing Diversity.** A major source of stress for many employees is role conflict and the inability to resolve that conflict. As organizations become more diverse in terms of employee characteristics, there is the potential for more conflict: employees bring different viewpoints, biases, competencies, perceptions, learning styles, and personality preferences. These differences have the tendency to conflict with each other, and if unresolved, may lead to ill will among colleagues, and also ineffectiveness in carrying out tasks, particularly where teams are the basis for most tasks. With diversity in organizations increasing, it's important to learn how companies deal with the situation. Contact companies known for their high quality diversity programs, such as Bank America, Advantica, Computer Associates, and Ryder, to see what they do that enables individuals to deal with differences and manage them for positive gain. Also visit **www.inform.umd.edu/Diversityweb** to learn about diversity programs at universities.

6. **Integration and Application.** After reviewing the AAL, Lincoln Electric, and Southwest Airlines cases at the end of the text, compare and contrast

the threats to health and safety at these three companies. Choose one company and describe the safety and health programs that you believe should be in place. Be specific about the objectives of the programs and be sure to state who should be responsible for them.

CASE STUDY

Safety Net or Death Trap?

Appliance Park is located in Henderson, a small city in western Kentucky near the Ohio River. Appliance Park is aptly named for its major employer, Appliance House, which created 800 manufacturing jobs for this small community. Appliance House manufactures washing machines, dryers, and dishwashers at its Appliance Park location.

Two weeks ago, a tragedy occurred at Appliance Park that was felt throughout the community. Joe Kitner fell to his death at the east plant, where washing machines are assembled. Joe, 24 years old, was a local football star in high school and had worked at Appliance Park full-time since his graduation from Henderson Central High School. An investigation of the accident was conducted by representatives of the corporate safety staff and Teamster local officials, who represent the nonexempt workers at Appliance Park. Although not widely reported, a curious set of factors contributed to Joe's death.

The assembly line at the washing machine division occupies two stories within a large prefab building on the east side of the park. A rope net or mesh is suspended about 30 feet above the ground-level floor to catch accessories and parts that drop from the upper conveyor system where some of the assembly of the washing machines is conducted. Periodically, when model changeovers are scheduled on the line, a changeover crew is assigned to switch the setup of the various machines throughout the assembly line. One of Joe's jobs on the changeover crew was to climb out on the net and retrieve the parts that had dropped from the previous production run. The net, though tightly strung across the ceiling, did have a tear on one side where a bracket that had fallen previously had cut part of the mesh. Although the changeover crew was responsible for inspecting and repairing the net,

they often overlooked minor rips because of the production time lost in making repairs to the mesh net.

An autopsy of Joe Kitner revealed that he died of a brain hemorrhage suffered in the fall to the concrete floor below. The autopsy also revealed that Joe had a small but malignant brain tumor located near the part of the brain that controls the central nervous system. The medical examiner did not discuss whether the tumor was far enough along to affect Joe's judgment or motor abilities. But the other test result from the autopsy indicated that Joe had consumed alcohol a few hours before his death, probably at lunch. His blood alcohol level, however, was not high enough for him to have been ruled intoxicated using the state's DWI standard.

The changeover crew experienced some difficulty in replacing Joe Kitner. Because the plant was unionized, his job was open to bid, but no one would bid for the job. Under these circumstances, the company used seniority to determine who would work the job among the assemblers. Luther Duncan was selected, and he really had little choice because he was low man on the totem pole with only seven years' seniority at the plant. Although the changeover job involved several duties, Luther knew that inevitably he would be asked to climb out on the net.

Luther had been on the job for only eight days when his foreman ordered the assembly line shut down for a model changeover for the next production run. At first, Luther decided not to think about what he eventually would have to do. But when his time came to scale the utility ladder to the rope net, Luther balked. No amount of encouragement, cajoling, or threatening would change Luther's mind; he simply wasn't going up that ladder with the memory of Joe's death fresh in his mind.

Alex Stearns, the Teamster steward, pulled Luther aside and pleaded with him to obey his foreman's order to complete the job. Alex even promised to file a grievance concerning the rip on the side of the net, which still had not been repaired. Luther stood firm and adamantly refused to proceed. Despite Alex's intervention, Luther's foreman suspended him for the remainder of the day and told him to report, along with Alex Stearns, to the plant superintendent's office early the next morning. When Luther reported to the superintendent's office the next day, he was informed of his dismissal for insubordination.

Case written by S. A. Youngblood, Professor of Strategic Human Resource Management, Texas Christian University.

Questions

1. Do you agree with the decision to fire Luther?

2. Who was really at fault in Joe's death?

3. How could Joe's death have been prevented?

4. Why did Alex encourage Luther to obey his foreman?

CASE STUDY

Who's There on the Line?

The telecommunications field is changing very rapidly. In perhaps no other field has the impact of technology had such a significant effect on the jobs of so many workers. Mitch Fields, for example, still remembers that tragic day in November 1963 when President Kennedy was assassinated while Mitch was pulling the afternoon shift as a switchman for Midwest Telephone Company (MTC). As Mitch described it, it sounded like 30 locomotives hammering their way through a large room filled with walls of mechanical switches putting phone calls through to their destination. Today, that room of switches has been replaced by a microchip. Mitch himself has undergone extensive training to operate a computer console used to monitor and diagnose switching problems.

The job of operator has changed from sitting in long rows operating equipment attached to walls of jacks and cords to individual work stations that look like command centers out of a Star Trek spaceship. In addition, the competitive environment of telephone services has changed dramatically because of deregulation and competition from other phone companies offering similar services. The new thrust now is to shift operator performance from being not just fast and friendly but profitable as well, by marketing the company ("Thank you for using MTC")

and selling high-profit-margin services ("Is there someone else you would like to talk to? The person-to-person rate is only additional for the first minute").

The operator's job at MTC remains unchanged in two respects: (1) operators will talk to nearly 600 people in a typical day, some of whom are still abusive, and (2) operator job performance is monitored. Technological innovation has enabled MTC to monitor each operator by computer to produce statistics on numbers of calls handled per shift, speed of the call, and amount of revenue generated by the calls. In addition to computer monitoring, supervisors may also listen in on operators to ensure that proper operator protocol is followed. For example, customers are never told they dialed the "wrong" number, obscene calls are routed to supervisors, and one learns to say "hold the line" or "one moment please" instead of "hang on."

Meeting performance standards based on these criteria does not typically lead to large rewards. A beginning operator usually earns about $12,000 a year working swing shifts that may begin at 8:30 A.M., noon, 2:00 P.M., 4:30 P.M., 8:30 P.M., or 2:00 A.M. Only the highest rated operators have the opportunity to be transferred, promoted, or receive educational benefits.

Steve Buckley, training and development manager for MTC, knows that to change the fast and friendly MTC operator of the past to one who is fast, friendly, and profitable as well is going to be a real challenge. Steve has not figured out yet how to get the operators to conclude each transaction by saying "thank you for using MTC." A recent clandestine supervisor survey revealed that fewer than 20 percent of the operators were using the requested reply. Steve is also being pressured by the local union leaders who represent the telephone operators to reduce the job stress brought on by the high volume of people transactions and the constant, computer-assisted surveillance. One thing is for sure, however, Steve must implement a plan for improvement.

Questions

1. Can Steve really change the behavior of the operators?

2. How can Steve succeed in getting the operators to say "thank you for using MTC?"

3. Is computer monitoring the answer?

4. Should the operators really decide on the change?

ENDNOTES

[1] *Ben and Jerry's Homemade Incorporated Annual Report,* 1992–1998; F. C. Lager, *Ben & Jerry's: The Inside Scoop* (New York: Crown Publishers, 1994); C. L. Hays, "Getting Serious at Ben & Jerry's," *New York Times* (May 22, 1998): 1,3.

[2] L. Johnson, "Preventing Injuries: The Big Payoff," *Personnel Journal* (April 1994): 61–64; R. S. Schuler, "Occupational Health in Organizations: A Measure of Personnel Effectiveness," *Readings in Personnel and Human Resource Management,* 2nd ed., R. S. Schuler and S. A. Youngblood, eds. (St. Paul, MN: West Publishing Co., 1984). See also D. R. Ilgen, "Health Issues at Work: Opportunities for Industrial/Organizational Psychology," *American Psychologist* (February 1990): 273–283.

[3] For detailed discussions of this topic, see J. M. Harrington, *Occupational Health* (London: Blackwell, 1998); S. Sadhra and K. G. Rampal, *Occupational Health: Risk Assessment and Management* (London: Blackwell, 1999); P. A. Erickson, *Practical Guide to Occupational Health and Safety* (New York: Academic Press, 1996); J. K. Corn, *Response to Occupational Health Hazards: A Historical Perspective* (New York: John Wiley & Sons, 1997).

[4] J. A. Kinney, "Why Did Paul Die?" *Newsweek* (September 10, 1990): 11. See also B. J. Feder, "A Spreading Pain, and Cries for Justice," *New York Times* (June 5, 1994): 3–1, 3–6.

[5] "Job Stress a Rising Threat," **www.cnnfn.com/quickenonfn/life/9901/06/q_stress/** (January 6, 1999); "Stress Resides in the Executive Suite," *HR Focus* (October 1996): 19; T. F. O'Boyle, "Fear and Stress in the Office Take Toll," *The Wall Street Journal* (November 6, 1990): B1, B2. See also Bureau of Labor Statistics, *Shifting Work Force Spawns New Set of Hazardous Occupations,* Summary report no. 94-8 (Washington, DC: Bureau of Labor Statistics Office of Safety, Health Conditions, 1994).

[6] K. Tyler, "Sit Up Straight," *HR Magazine* (September 1998): 121–128; L. Himelstein, "The Asbestos Case of the 1990s?" *Business Week* (January 16, 1995): 82–83;

K. Rebello, "It Just May Be the Year of the Apple," *Business Week* (January 16, 1995): 84–85; B. J. Feder, "Apple Settles Lawsuit on Repetitive Stress Injury," *New York Times* (February 28, 1995): D4; "Carpal Tunnel Claims Up, But Cost Per Claim Down," *Bulletin to Management* 47 (30) (July 25, 1996): 233; "Policy Guide: Debate Escalates Over Ergonomics," *Bulletin to Management* (July 10, 1997): 224; "Policy Guide: Ergonomics Moves to the Forefront," *Bulletin to Management* 47 (42) (October 17, 1996): 336.

[7] J. J. Laabs, "Cashing in on Safety," *Workforce* (August 1997): 53–57; E. Raimy, "Safety Pays," *Human Resource Executive* (November 1996): 1, 21–23; C. A. Bacon, "Is There a Nurse in the Office?" *Workforce* (June 1997): 107–113; S. Caudron, "Workplace Violence," *Workforce* (August 1998): 45–52.

[8] "Back Injuries," *Bulletin to Management* (January 9, 1992): 396; "Sprains and Strains Lead Workplace Injuries," *Bulletin to Management* (May 26, 1994): 164–165; "Occupational Injuries and Illnesses," *Bulletin to Management* (January 12, 1995): 12–13.

[9] "Facts and Figures: Safety and Health," *Bulletin to Management* (January 7, 1999): 5. "Occupational Injuries and Illnesses," *Bulletin to Management* (January 15, 1998): 13; "Datagraph: Workplace Fatalities—1997," *Bulletin to Management* (August 28, 1997): 276–277; Datagraph: Workplace Issues Then and Now," *Bulletin to Management* (December 25, 1997): 412–413. See also "ILO Releases New Version of Health and Safety Encyclopedia," *International HR Update* (July 1998): 3. Visit the home page of the Bureau of Labor Statistics (**stats.bls.gov**) and the National Safety Council (**www.nsc.org**).

[10] S. R. King, "Nursing Homes Draw Attention As Worker–Safety Focus Shifts," *New York Times* (August 7, 1996): D1, D5; B. Saporito, "The Most Dangerous Jobs in America," *Fortune* (May 31, 1993): 131–140; "Occupational Injuries and Illnesses," *Bulletin to Management* (January 6, 1994): 4–6. These estimates could be regarded as conservative because they do not include the costs due to stress and to a low quality of working life. See also A. J. Kinicki, F.

M. McKee, and K. J. Wade, "Annual Review, 1991–1995: Occupational Health," *Journal of Vocational Behavior* 49 (2) (October 1996): 190–220; D. A. Hofmann and A. Stetzer, "A Cross-Level Investigation of Factors Influencing Unsafe Behaviors and Accidents," *Personnel Psychology* 49 (1996): 307.

11 Personal correspondence with Donald Brush, President, Bearings Division, Barden Corporation.

12 M. R. Frone, "Predictors of Work Injuries Among Employed Adolescents," *Journal of Applied Psychology* 83 (1998): 565–576.

13 B. A. Lee and R. J. Thompson, "Reducing the Consequences of Disability: Policies to Reduce Discrimination Against Disabled Workers," T. Thomason, J. F. Burton, Jr., and D. E. Hyatt, eds., *New Approaches to Disability in the Workplace* (Madison, WI: Industrial Relations Research Association, 1998): 155–179; M. Moss, "For Older Employees, On-the-Job Injuries Are More Often Deadly," *The Wall Street Journal* (June 17, 1997): A1; "Workplace Deaths Unchanged; Homicides At Six-Year Low," *Bulletin to Management: Facts and Figures* (August 27, 1998): 269; "Occupational Injuries and Illnesses," *Bulletin to Management: Facts and Figures* (January 15, 1998): 13.

14 T. D. Schneid, *Occupational Health Guide to Violence in the Workplace* (Lewis, 1998); K. F. Clark, "On Guard," *Human Resource Executive* (March 19, 1998): 75–78; B. Filipczak, "Armed and Dangerous at Work," *Training* (July 1993): 39–43; "Workplace Violence: When Dissatisfaction Turns to Fury," *HR Reporter* (March 1994): 1–5. See also "Workplace Violence: An Array of Potential Legal Repercussions?" *Fair Employment Practices Guidelines* (August 25, 1994): 6–8.

15 J. H. Neuman and R. A. Baron, "Workplace Violence and Workplace Aggression: Evidence Concerning Specific Forms, Potential Causes and Preferred Targets," *Journal of Management* 24 (3) (1998): 391–419; G. R. VanderBos and E. Q. Bulatao, eds., *Violence on the Job: Identifying Risks and Developing Solutions* (Washington, DC: American Psychological Association, 1996); A. M. O'Leary-Kelly, R. W. Griffin, and D. J. Glew, "Organization-Motivated Aggression: A Research Framework," *Academy of Management Review* 21 (1996): 225–253.

16 S. Caudron, "Target: HR," *Workforce* (August 1998): 44–52; J. Laabs, "What Goes Down When Minimum Wages Go Up," *Workforce* (August 1998): 54–58; D. Bencivenga, "Dealing with the Dark Side," *HR Magazine* (January 1999): 50–58.

17 Visit the library at the National Safety Council (**www.nsc.org**) and the National Center for Health Statistics (**www.cdc.gov/nchswww**) for the latest information.

18 S. Melamed, I. Ben-Avi, J. Luz, and M. S. Green, "Objective and Subjective Work Monotony: Effects on Job Satisfaction, Psychological Distress, and Absenteeism in Blue-Collar Workers," *Journal of Applied Psychology* 80 (1) (1995): 29–42; P. L. Perrewe, ed., *Handbook on Job Stress: Special Issue of Journal of Social Behavior and Personality,* Vol. 6, No. 1 (1991). "Charges of Emotional Distress: A Growing Trend," *Fair Employment Practices Guidelines* 284 (1989): 1–4. See also a set of references identifying and discussing each preference or interest listed here, in R. S. Schuler,

"Definition and Conceptualization of Stress in Organizations," *Organizational Behavior and Human Performance* 23 (1980): 184–215; R. S. Schuler, "An Integrative Transactional Process Model of Stress in Organizations," *Journal of Occupational Behavior* 3 (1982): 3–19.

19 For a recent summary, see R. S. DeFrank and J. M. Ivancevich, "Stress on the Job: An Executive Update," *Academy of Management Executive* 21 (3) (1998): 55–66.

20 A. B. Shostak, *Blue Collar Stress* (Reading, MA: Addison-Wesley, 1980).

21 R. C. Kessler, J. B. Turner, and J. S. House, "Unemployment and Health in a Community Sample," *Journal of Health and Social Behavior* 28 (1987): 51–59; R. C. Kessler, J. B. Turner, and J. S. House, "Intervening Processes in the Relationship Between Unemployment and Health," *Psychological Medicine* 17 (1987): 949–961; R. D. Caplan et al., "Job Seeking, Reemployment and Mental Health: A Randomized Field Experiment in Coping with Job Loss," *Journal of Applied Psychology* 74 (1989): 759–769; S. J. Ashford, C. Lee, and P. Bobko, "Content, Causes, and Consequences of Job Insecurity: A Theory-Based Measure and Substantive Test," *Academy of Management Journal* 32 (1989): 803–829; R. H. Price, "Psychological Impact of Job Loss on Individuals and Families," *Current Directions* (American Psychological Society, 1992).

22 S. Cohen and G. M. Williamson, "Stress and Infectious Disease in Humans," *Psychological Bulletin* 109 (1991): 5–24; S. R. Barley and D. B. Knight, "Toward a Cultural Theory of Stress Complaints," *Research in Organizational Behavior* 14 (1992): 1–48; R. Martin and T. D. Wall, "Attentional Demand and Cost Responsibility as Stressors in Shopfloor Jobs," *Academy of Management Journal* 32 (1989): 69–86; C. A. Higgins and L. E. Duxbury, "Work-Family Conflict in the Dual-Career Family," *Organizational Behavior and Human Decision Processes* 51 (1992): 51–75; S. Parasuraman et al., "Work and Family Variables as Mediators of the Relationship between Wives' Employment and Husbands' Well-Being," *Academy of Management Journal* 32 (1989): 185–201; B. A. Gutek, S. Searle, and L. Klepa, "Rational versus Gender Role Explanations for Work-Family Conflict," *Journal of Applied Psychology* 76 (1991): 560–568; L. E. Duxbury and C. A. Higgins, "Gender Differences in Work-Family Conflict," *Journal of Applied Psychology* 76 (1991): 60–74; K. J. Williams et al., "Multiple Role Juggling and Daily Mood States in Working Mothers: An Experience Sampling Study," *Journal of Applied Psychology* 76 (1991): 664–674; M. F. Frone, M. Russell, and M. L. Cooper, "Antecedents and Outcomes of Work-Family Conflict: Testing a Model of the Work-Family Interface," *Journal of Applied Psychology* 77 (1992): 65–78.

23 Adapted from "Personnel Shop Talk," *Bulletin To Management* (Sept. 4, 1994): 282.

24 M. Frankenhaeuser and B. Gardell, "Underload and Overload in Working Life: Outline of Multidisciplinary Approach," *Journal of Human Stress* 2 (1976): 36–45; M. Pesci, "Stress Management: Separating Myth from Reality," *Personnel Administrator* (January 1982): 57–67.

25 R. Sutton and A. Rafaeli, "Characteristics of Work Stations as Potential Occupational Stressors," *Academy of Management Journal* 30 (June 1987): 260–276.

26 "Please, Somebody! Open a Window!" *Business Week* (January 18, 1999): 8.

27 M. Friedman and R. Roseman, *Type A Behavior and Your Heart* (New York: Alfred A. Knopf, 1974).

28 M. Maslach and M. P. Leiter, *The Truth About Burnout: How Organizations Cause Personal Stress and What to Do About It* (San Francisco: Jossey-Bass, 1997); C. L. Cordes and T. W. Dougherty, "A Review and Integration of Research on Job Burnout," *Academy of Management Review* 18 (1993): 621–656; S. E. Jackson and R. S. Schuler, "Preventing Employee Burnout," *Personnel* (March–April 1983): 58–68.

29 For an overview of OSHA's Strategic Plan for 1997–2002, see its web site: **http://spider.osha.gov/oshainfo/strategic/newplan1.html**.

30 L. Miller, "People on the Move Are Going Back to Driving School," *The Wall Street Journal* (May 20, 1997): A1; "Safety: A Quick Pay-Off, a Long-Term Commitment," *HR Reporter* (October 1990): 6; R. Pater, "Safety Leadership Cuts Costs," *HR Magazine* (November 1990): 46–47.

31 S. Dolan and R. S. Schuler, *Human Resource Management Canada* (Toronto: Nelson, 1993).

32 M. Moss, "For Older Employees, On-the-Job Injuries Are More Often Deadly," *The Wall Street Journal* (June 17, 1997): A1; D. P. Levin, "The Graying Factor," *New York Times* (February 20, 1994): 3-1, 3-3. For extensive discussion of office space and physical design issues, see L. Altman, "Some Who Use VDTs Miscarried, Study Says," *New York Times* (June 5, 1988): 22; "Reproductive Hazards—How Employers Are Responding," *Fair Employment Practices Guidelines* (October 29, 1987): 132; R. S. Schuler, L. R. Ritzman, and V. Davis, "Merging Prescriptive and Behavioral Approaches for Office Layout," *Production and Inventory Management Journal* 3 (1981): 131–142.

33 K. Tyler, "Sit Up Straight," *HR Magazine* (September 1998): 121-128; "National ASPA Conference Highlights," *Bulletin to Management* (July 28, 1988): 239. See also J. R. Hollenbeck, D. R. Ilgen, and S. M. Crampton, "Lower Back Disability in Occupational Settings: A Review of the Literature from a Human Resource Management View," *Personnel Psychology* 45 (1992): 247–278.

34 "Personnel Shop Talk," *Bulletin to Management* (April 25, 1994): 266.

35 J. Komaki, K. D. Barwick, and L. Scott, "Pinpointing and Reinforcing Safe Performance in a Food Manufacturing Plant," *Journal of Applied Psychology* 63 (1978): 434–445. See also G. M. Ritzky, "Turner Bros. Wins Safety Game with Behavioral Incentives," *HR Magazine* (June 1998): 79–83; R. Allen, "Playing It Safe," *Human Resource Executive* (August 1997): 1, 26–30.

36 H. M. Taylor, "Occupational Health Management-by-Objectives," *Personnel* (January–February 1980): 58–64.

37 K. Ridder, "Genetic Testing Raises Fears of Workplace Bias," *Dallas Morning News* (April 26, 1998): 8H; S. Greengard, "Genetic Testing: Should You Be Afraid? It's No Joke," *Workforce* (July 1997): 38–44; J. Olian, "New Approaches to Employment Screening," *Readings in Personnel and Human Resource Management,* 3rd ed., Schuler, Youngblood, and Huber, eds.

38 J. C. Erfurt, A. Foote, and M. A. Heirich, "The Cost-Effectiveness of Worksite Wellness Programs for Hypertension Control, Weight Loss, Smoking Cessation and Exercise," *Personnel Psychology* 45 (1992): 5–27; D. L. Bebhardt and C. E. Crump, "Employee Fitness and Wellness Programs in the Workplace," *American Psychologist* (February 1990): 262–272.

39 D. H. Shapiro Jr., C. E. Schwartz, and J. A. Astin, "Controlling Ourselves, Controlling Our World," *American Psychologist* 51 (December 1996): 1213–1230; T. D. Ludwig and E. S. Geller, "Assigned Versus Participative Goal Setting and Response Generalization: Managing Injury Control Among Professional Pizza Deliverers," *Journal of Applied Psychology* 82 (1997): 253–261; J. Schaubroeck and D. E. Merritt, "Divergent Effects of Job Control on Coping With Work Stressors: The Key Role of Self-Efficacy," *Academy of Management Journal* 40 (1997): 738–754.

40 D. Etzion, D. Eden, and Y. Lapidot, "Relief from Job Stressors and Burnout: Reserve Service as a Respite," *Journal of Applied Psychology* 83 (1998): 577–585; M. Westman and D. Eden, "Effects of Vacation on Job Stress and Burnout: Relief and Fade Out," *Journal of Applied Psychology* 82 (1997): 516–527.

41 "Fetal Protection Policy Struck Down," *Fair Employment Practices Guidelines* (May 1991): 1–2; "Fetal Protection Ruling," *Fair Employment Practices Guidelines* (March 28, 1991): 31.

42 S. B. Garland, "A New Chief Has OSHA Growing Again," *Business Week* (August 20, 1990): 57; P. T. Kilborn, "Who Decides Who Works at Jobs Imperiling Fetuses?" *New York Times* (September 2, 1990): A1, A12; R. Winslow, "Air Polluted by Carbon Monoxide Poses Risk to Heart Patients, Study Shows," *The Wall Street Journal* (September 4, 1990): B4; R. Winslow, "Safety Group Cites Fatalities Linked to Work," *The Wall Street Journal* (August 31, 1990): B8; C. Trost, "Business and Women Anxiously Watch Suit on 'Fetal Protection,'" *The Wall Street Journal* (October 8, 1990): 1.

43 C. Winters, K. Stangler, A. L. Shaffer and B. A. Morris, "Corporate Wellness," *Human Resource Executive* (September 1997): 47–60; "Personnel Shop Talk," *Bulletin to Management* 48 (December 18, 1997): 402. See also The Managed Care Information Center at **www.themcic.com.**

44 D. A. Harrison and J. J. Martocchio, "Time for Absenteeism: A 20-year Review of Origins, Offshoots, and Outcomes," *Journal of Management* 24 (1998): 305–350; "Injury Rates: An Incentive to Cheat?" *Bulletin to Management* (September 17, 1998): 292; M. R. Edwards, "Measuring Team Performance Through a Balanced Model," *ACA News* (November/December 1996): 17–18.

45 "OSHA Levies Second Big Ergo Fine," *Bulletin to Management* 49 (January 8, 1998): 4; "Safety Rule on Respiratory Protection Issued," *Bulletin to Management* 49 (1) (January 8, 1998): 1; "Enforcement Activity Increased in 1997," *Bulletin to Management* (January 29, 1998): 28; "OSHA Seeks 'Cooperative Compliance,'" *Bulletin to Management* (September 4, 1997): 288; "OSHA's Cooperative Program Shoves Off," *Bulletin to Management* (December 25, 1997): 416; "OSHA to Address Ruling on Protective Equipment," *Bulletin to Management* 48 (52)

(December 25, 1997): 409; "Settling Safety Violations Has Benefits," *Bulletin to Management* (July 31, 1997): 248; "OSHA: Reforms and Penalties," *Bulletin to Management* (January 28, 1993): 25; D. Foust, "Stepping into the Middle of OSHA's Muddle," *Business Week* (August 2, 1993): 53; "OSHA Penalties Fall in Fiscal 1993," *Bulletin to Management* (April 21, 1994): 124–125; "Safety and Health Highlights," *Bulletin to Management* (August 11, 1994): 250, 255.

46 C. Patton, "Gray Matters," *Human Resource Executive* (November 1997): 64–68; P. A. Susser, "Update on Hazard Communication," *Personnel Administrator* (October 1985): 57–61; M. G. Miner, "Legal Concerns Facing Human Resource Managers: An Overview," *Readings in Personnel and Human Resource Management,* 3rd ed., Schuler, Youngblood, and Huber, eds., "Hazard Communication Training: Compliance Cues," *Bulletin to Management* (March 13, 1986): 81.

47 M. Novit, "Mental Distress: Possible Implications for the Future," *Personnel Administrator* (August 1982): 47–54.

UNIONIZATION AND COLLECTIVE BARGAINING: NEGOTIATING THE EMPLOYMENT CONTRACT

Chapter Outline

MANAGING THROUGH PARTNERSHIP

UPS and the Teamsters

UPS, an employee-owned company, is the third largest private employer in the United States. Represented by the Teamsters union, the company's 300,000 employees are the highest paid in the industry and have a relatively low turnover rate. Senior managers receive modest pay compared to most other *Fortune* 500 companies. Clearly the history of UPS indicated a strong desire to work in partnership with the employees and the Teamsters union. When the union went on strike in August 1997, it came as a surprise to many observers. The Teamsters had worked collaboratively with the company for 82 years, guided by UPS founder Jim Casey's philosophy that "You can be a good Teamster *and* a good UPSer." What went wrong? What were the issues that divided them? Was the strike worth it?

The two most significant issues were the multi-employer pension plan and the increasing reliance on part-time workers. The pension plan was one in which several companies contributed. UPS's share to the total plan was about $1 billion yearly, a cost they thought they could reduce by administering their own plan. The Teamsters wanted to protect the retirement benefits of the UPS workers as well as the benefits for the other companies in the plan. In another attempt to cut costs, UPS had been hiring more part-time workers. The Teamsters wanted the company to hire more full-time workers who would receive better wages and benefits. To settle the strike, UPS agreed to increase salaries over the five-year life of the agreement by $3.10 per hour for full-timers and by $4.10 per hour for part-timers, combine part-time positions into 10,000 new full-time jobs, and remain in the multi-employer pension plan.

While it appears that UPS has regained the business it lost to competitors during the strike, the long-term impact is difficult to measure. Is the benign partnership among the union, UPS, and the employees now tarnished by distrust? Some say it is too early to tell, but many believe that all parties need to work hard to make sure that ill will is forgotten. Perhaps UPS had underestimated the union's resolve and the workers' belief in the importance of the issues. It certainly underestimated the public support that the union members received. The legacy from this situation is that other companies thinking strategically about the use of part-timers may need to think again.[2]

To learn more about UPS, visit the company home page at
www.ups.com

Unions are present in 28 of *Fortune*'s 100 Most Admired companies.

In retrospect, the events at UPS are a good reminder of how valuable union-management cooperation can be. For 82 years, UPS and the Teamsters union had worked together, producing an employment relationship that benefited both workers and the company. Over the years, service quality had been excellent, absenteeism was low, employees were relatively satisfied with their jobs, they enjoyed employment security and received continual training, and the result was a profitable company. But maintaining such a positive and cooperative relationship takes constant work from everyone involved. Among the roles and responsibilities to be fulfilled are those shown in the feature, The HR Triad—Extended: Partnership Roles and Responsibilities for Unionization and Collective Bargaining.

THE HR TRIAD—EXTENDED: PARTNERSHIP ROLES AND RESPONSIBILITIES FOR UNIONIZATION AND COLLECTIVE BARGAINING

Line Managers	HR Professionals	Employees	Unions
Know and appreciate the historical context of union-management relations.	Train line managers in the legal considerations protecting the unionization rights of employees.	Present their views about working conditions to HR professionals and line managers.	Seek to represent the employees' views to the company.
Support the efforts of HR professionals in making policies and programs for good working conditions.	Develop HR policies and programs that make for good working conditions.	Express views on work place conditions, wages, and working hours.	Offer to improve wages and working conditions for their members.
Know and work with the union-management contract.	Continually survey employees' attitudes so that management knows employees' views and opinions.	Bargain in good faith through union representatives with line managers and HR professionals.	Offer to work with management to improve company profitability and survival.
Manage employees with respect and equality.	Work with line managers in dealing effectively with union representatives.	Fulfill rights and responsibilities in the union contract.	Bargain with line managers and HR professionals.
Know what can and can't be said to employees regarding unionization during an organizing campaign.	Develop mechanisms for effective grievance resolution.	Understand your rights as a union member.	Seek improvements in conditions and wages.
Work cooperatively with HR professionals in developing an effective relationship with union representatives.	Move along such issues as total quality management and quality-of-work-life programs.	Seek to understand the business issues that may drive management's perspective on union activities.	Be willing to adapt to local conditions and changes in technology and economic conditions.
Work with HR professionals and union representatives in resolving grievances.			

As conditions continue to change in the 21st century, the union-management relationship will likely also change. Changes are likely to occur both in unionization efforts and in the bargaining relationships between existing unions and management. For example, the UAW is extending its efforts to unionize nonteaching employees in universities. Changes are also occurring within unions as they consider offering alternative forms of membership such as an associate status.[3] To put into perspective these aspects of union-management relationships, this chapter describes the process of forming a union (unionization) and the characteristics of administering an agreement reached between the union and management (collective bargaining).

THE STRATEGIC IMPORTANCE OF UNIONIZATION AND COLLECTIVE BARGAINING

Unionization is the effort by employees and outside agencies (unions or associations) to act as a single unit when dealing with management over issues relating to their work. When recognized by the National Labor Relations Board (NLRB), a union has the legal authority to negotiate with the employer on behalf of employees—to improve wages, hours, and conditions of employment—and to administer the ensuing agreement.[4]

The core of union-management relations is *collective bargaining.* Collective bargaining generally includes two types of interaction. The first is the negotiation of work conditions that, when written up as the collective agreement (the contract), becomes the basis for employee-employer relationships on the job. The second includes activities related to interpreting and enforcing the collective agreement (contract administration) and resolving any conflicts arising from it.[5]

For employers, the existence of or possibility of a union can significantly influence an employer's ability to manage its vital human resources. Unions can help employees get what they want—for example, high wages and job security—from their employers. For management, unionization may result in less flexibility in hiring new workers, making job assignments, and introducing new work methods such as automation; a loss of control; inefficient work practices; and an inflexible job structure. However, it also may result in greater workforce cooperation with programs such as total quality management.[6]

Unions obtain rights for their members that employees without unions don't legally have. This, of course, forces unionized companies to consider their employees' reactions to a wide variety of decisions. Nevertheless, in some cases, employers who are nonunion and want to remain that way give more consideration and benefits to their employees. Consequently, it may or may not be more expensive for a company to operate with unionized rather than nonunionized employees.[7]

Unions assist employers through wage concessions or cooperation in joint workplace efforts, such as teamwork programs or Scanlon Plans, allowing employers to survive particularly difficult times and, in fact, remain profitable and competitive. This has been particularly true in the automobile, steel, and airline industries. Unions can also help identify workplace hazards and improve the quality of work life for employees.[8] Clearly, unions have an important role to play in the strategic issues of a company. These are described more in the feature Managing Strategically: Unions Get Involved.[9]

■□ *fast fact*

Union Summer was a program put forth by the AFL-CIO in the summer of 1996 to bring the union movement to college students.

"My greatest regret was the relationship, for one reason or another, between myself and the unions."

Robert L. Crandell
CEO
American Airlines (retired)

MANAGING STRATEGICALLY

Unions Get Involved

Labor costs are critical to the success of many companies vis-a-vis their competitors. In many industries today, companies face possible bankruptcy because of high labor costs. Wage reductions reached between unions and management are helping to lower costs. During the 1980s, American Airlines, McDonnell Douglas, Boeing, and Ingersoll-Rand negotiated two-tier wage systems to help reduce total costs by reducing labor costs. Without these jointly negotiated systems, these companies may not have survived. Thus, a company's relationship with its union can be critical to its survival, and the better its relationship, the more likely the company is to gain a competitive advantage.

Ford Motor Company has engaged in a program of more worker involvement and more cooperative labor relations with the United Auto Workers. The results of this program are higher product quality for Ford than for its competitors, and a marketing campaign centered on the slogan "Quality Is Job One." This program of more worker involvement gains competitive advantage through higher product quality and improved efficiencies. Similar results have been obtained at Eaton Corporation, Saturn, AT&T, Xerox, and the Mass Transportation Authority of Flint, Michigan. In these companies, gains in quality and efficiency have resulted from employee commitment associated with quality-circle programs. These companies have also experienced fewer grievances, reduced absenteeism and turnover, lower design costs, higher engineering productivity, and fewer costly changes in design cycles.

It is likely that we will continue to see this strategic involvement. This involvement will generally take a form similar to that at Saturn. It may, however, also take another form: workers actually taking over, or assuming part of the equity ownership of the company. The workers at United, Southwest, and Northwest Airlines got a stake in the company for granting wage concessions.

At National Steel Corporation, Wheeling-Pittsburgh Steel Corporation, and the LTV Corporation, wage concessions resulted in board membership. Giving unions access to the board room is common in Europe, where the unions are stronger, but is still quite novel in the United States. It has generally only been entertained by troubled companies that have had to work closely with their unions to avert bankruptcy or liquidation. Only the future will tell if nontroubled companies also elect to bring worker representation onto their boards.

To learn more about the United Auto Workers, visit the organization's home page at www.uaw.org

"You would see a more militant and adversarial relationship come back if the unemployment rate were two or three percentage points higher than it is today."

**Larry Gigerich
President
Indianapolis Economic
Development Corporation**

Deciding to Join a Union

Unions were originally formed in response to the exploitation and abuse of employees by management. To understand the union movement today, we need to examine why employees decide to join unions and why they decide not to. Three separate conditions strongly influence an employee's decision to join a union: dissatisfaction, lack of power, and union instrumentality.[10]

Dissatisfaction. When an individual takes a job, certain conditions of employment (wages, hours, and type of work) are specified in the employment contract. A *psychological contract* also exists between employer and employee, consisting of the employee's unspecified expectation about reasonable working conditions, requirements of the work itself, the level of effort that should be expended on the job, and the nature of the authority the employer should have in directing the employee's work.[11] These expectations are related to the employee's desire to satisfy certain personal preferences in the workplace. The degree to which the organization fulfills these preferences determines the employee's level of satisfaction.

Dissatisfaction with the implicit terms and conditions of employment will lead employees to attempt to improve the work situation, often through unionization. A major study found a very strong relationship between the level of satisfaction and the proportion of workers voting for a union. Almost all workers who were satisfied voted against the union.[12] Thus, if management wants to make unionization less attractive to employees, it must make working conditions more satisfying.

Lack of Power. Unionization is seldom the first recourse of employees who are dissatisfied with some aspect of their jobs. The first attempt to improve the work situation is usually made by an individual acting alone. Someone who has enough power or influence can effect the necessary changes without collaborating with others. The amount of power the jobholder has in the organization is determined by *exclusivity*, or how difficult it is to replace the person, and *essentiality*, or how important or critical the job is to the overall success of the organization. An exclusive employee with an essential task may be able to force the employer to make a change. If, however, the employee can easily be replaced and the employee's task is not critical, other means, including collective action, must be considered in order to influence the organization.[13]

Union Instrumentality. When employees are dissatisfied with aspects of a work environment—such as pay, promotion opportunity, treatment by supervisor, the job itself, and work rules—they may perceive a union as being able to help improve the situation. If they believe that the union may be able to help, they then weigh the value of the benefits to be obtained through unionization against unionization's costs, such as a lengthy organizing campaign and bad feelings between supervisors, managers, and other employees who don't want a union. Finally, the employees weigh the costs and benefits against the likelihood of a union's being able to obtain the benefits. In other words, they determine union instrumentality.[14] The more that employees believe a union can obtain positive work aspects, the more instrumental employees perceive the union to be in removing the causes of dissatisfaction. When the benefits exceed the costs and union instrumentality is high, employees are more likely to be willing to support a union.[15] However, research suggests that employees' willingness to support a union is also affected by general attitudes about unions formed early in life.[16]

THE HISTORICAL CONTEXT AND UNIONS TODAY

A better understanding of the attitudes and behaviors of both unions and management can be gained through a knowledge of past union-management relations.

The Early Days

The beginning of the labor union movement in the United States can be traced back to the successful attempt of journeymen printers to win a wage increase in 1778. By the 1790s, unions of shoemakers, carpenters, and printers had appeared in Boston, Baltimore, New York, and other cities. The

■■□ *fast fact*

Honda of America, in Marysville, Ohio, is a non-union plant but wages and benefits match the UAW-negotiated agreements.

■■□ *fast fact*

Women see unions as instrumental for issues such as health care, equal pay, and sexual harassment.

Federal Society of Journeymen Cordwainers, for example, was organized in Philadelphia in 1794, primarily to resist employers' attempts to reduce wages. Other issues of concern to these early unions were union shops (companies using only union members) and the regulation of apprenticeships to prevent the replacement of journeymen employees.

The early unions had methods and objectives that are still in evidence today. Although there was no collective bargaining, the unions did establish a price below which members would not work. Strikes were used to enforce this rate. These strikes were relatively peaceful and for the most part successful.

One negative characteristic of early unions was their susceptibility to depressions. Until the late 1800s, most unions thrived in times of prosperity but died off during depressions. Part of this problem may have been related to the insularity of the unions. Aside from sharing information on strike-breakers or scabs, the unions operated independently of each other.

The work situation had undergone several important changes by the end of the nineteenth century. Transportation systems (canals, railroads, and turnpikes) expanded the markets for products and increased worker mobility. Increases in capital costs prevented journeymen from reaching the status of master craftworker (that is, from setting up their own businesses), thereby creating a class of skilled workers. Unionism found its start in these skilled occupations, largely because "the skilled worker . . . had mastered his craft through years of apprenticeship and was no longer occupationally mobile" and the alternatives were "to passively accept wage cuts, the competition of non-apprentice labor, and the harsh working conditions, or to join in collective action against such employer innovations."[17]

Unions continued to experience ups and downs that were largely tied to economic conditions. Employers took advantage of the depressions to combat unions: In "an all out frontal attack . . they engaged in frequent lockouts, hired spies . . . summarily discharged labor 'agitators,' and [engaged] the services of strikebreakers on a widespread scale."[18] These actions, and the retaliations of unions, established a tenor of violence and lent a strong adversarial nature to union-management relations—the residual effects of which are still in evidence today.

Unions Today

Today, the adversarial nature of the union-management relationship has been replaced to a certain extent by a more cooperative one. This change toward relying on collective bargaining has been dictated in part by current trends in union membership, including the shifting distribution of the membership.

Decline in Membership

Union membership in the United States has declined steadily from its high of 35.5 percent of the workforce in 1945. In the mid-1950s, 35 percent of the workforce was unionized. In 1970, the percentage of unionized workers in the labor force was about 25. In 1999, approximately 14 percent of all workers—11 percent in the private sector and 35 percent in the public sector—were represented by unions, down from 23 percent in 1980.[19] These percentage declines resulted in part from an increase in service-sector employment, high technology jobs, and white-collar jobs—all of which historically have had a low proportion of union members. Other contributing circumstances are a decline in employment in industries that are highly unionized, increased decertification of unions, and management initiatives. To counter these trends, union leadership, particularly the AFL-CIO has increased its efforts to expand its membership base.[20] The feature, Managing Diversity: Unions Reach Out, illustrates some recent union efforts to enlist new members.[21]

To gain more organizational ability, power, and financial strength, several unions have merged. Although mergers may not automatically increase membership, they can mean more efficiency in union-organizing efforts and an end to costly jurisdictional disputes between unions. Increased organizational strength from mergers may also enable unions to cover industries and occupations previously underrepresented in union membership, such as health care and telecommunications workers.

Distribution of Membership

Historically, membership has been concentrated in a small number of large unions. In 1976, 16 unions represented 60 percent of union membership, and 85 unions represented just 2.4 percent. Similarly, the National Education Association accounted for 62 percent of all teaching association members. Many employee associations are small because they are state organizations; therefore, their membership potential is limited.

Unions today are exhibiting a substantial and increasing amount of diversification of membership. The most pronounced diversification has occurred in manufacturing. For example, of the 29 unions that represent workers in chemicals and allied products, 26 have less than 20 percent of their membership in a single industry.[22]

■□fast fact

The rates of unionization around the world vary greatly:

- Australia   35%
- Brazil   44%
- Denmark   80%
- France   9%
- Japan   24%
- Mexico   43%
- UK   33%

MANAGING DIVERSITY

Unions Reach Out

Linda Chavez-Thompson is first executive vice-president of the AFL-CIO, a position critical to the future of the union movement. President John J. Sweeney has stated that the union movement has changed, and the union needs to be more responsive in organizing women and minorities, the fastest growing groups of union membership. According to Sweeney, the election of Chavez-Thompson is very significant: "I wanted someone who knew what it was like to go door-to-door organizing and to come home at night dead-tired and foot-sore." In addition to including a greater variety of groups in the top management of the AFL-CIO, the union movement has sought to include more groups in the grassroots labor organizing campaigns. It has expanded its organizing efforts in the South, increased efforts to organize construction and kitchen workers in Las Vegas, signed up asbestos clean-up crews in New York, and signed up more farm workers in California. It is doing this in part with a new crop of workers/organizers who are young, ambitious, college-educated people with a passion for the union movement. "They get to know every nuance of a company's operations and target the weak managers' departments as a way to appeal to employees who may be willing to organize." And with the real wages of many workers remaining stagnant, the voice of appeal may fall on an increasing number of willing ears.

To learn more about the AFL-CIO's efforts at creating more diversity, visit the organization's home page at
www.aflcio.org

The Structure of American Unions

The basic unit of labor unions in the United States is the national (or international) union, a body that organizes, charters, and controls member locals. National unions develop the general policies and procedures by which locals operate, and help locals in areas such as collective bargaining. National unions provide clout for locals because they control a large number of employees and can influence large organizations through national strikes or slowdown activities.

The major umbrella organization for national unions is the American Federation of Labor and Congress of Industrial Organizations (AFL-CIO). It represents about 85 percent of the total union membership, or about 13 million workers. Every two years, the AFL-CIO holds a convention to develop policy and amend its constitution. Each national union is represented in proportion to its membership. Between conventions, an executive council (the governing body) and a general board direct the organization's affairs; a president is in charge of day-to-day operations.

The executive council's activities include evaluating legislation that affects labor and watching for corruption within the AFL-CIO. Standing committees are appointed to deal with executive, legislative, political, educational, organizing, and other activities. The department of organization and field services, for instance, focuses its attention on organizing activities. Three structures organize the local unions: many of the craft unions are represented by the trade department and the industrial department, and the remaining locals are organized directly as part of the national unions, being affiliated with AFL-CIO headquarters but retaining independence in dealing with their own matters. About 60 national unions, representing 4.5 million workers, operate independently of the AFL-CIO. Although this separation is not considered desirable by the AFL-CIO, its effect has been diminished substantially since the Teamsters reaffiliated with the AFL-CIO in 1987. The two largest unions in the AFL-CIO are the Teamsters (1.3 million) and the American Federation of State, County and Municipal Employees (1.2 million).

At the heart of the labor movement are the 70,000 or so local unions, varying in size up to 40,000 members. The locals represent the workers at the workplace, where much of the day-to-day contact with management and the human resource department takes place. Most locals elect a president, a secretary-treasurer, and perhaps one or two other officers from the membership. In the larger locals, a *business representative* is hired as a full-time employee to handle grievances and contract negotiation. Locals also have a *steward*, an employee elected by her or his work unit to act as the union representative at the workplace and to respond to company actions against employees that may violate the labor agreement. The steward protects the rights of the worker by filing grievances when the employer has acted improperly.

How Unions Operate

The activities of union locals revolve around collective bargaining and grievance handling. In addition, locals hold general meetings, publish newsletters, and otherwise keep their members informed. Typically, however, the membership is apathetic about union involvement. Unless a serious problem exists, attendance at meetings is usually about five percent of membership, and the election of officers often draws votes from less than one-fourth of the membership.[23]

■□ *fast fact*

The AFL-CIO has a goal of increasing membership by three percent per year.

■□ *fast fact*

The AFL-CIO's Office of Investment keeps track of CEO compensation levels. It believes that excessive CEO pay is a point around which it can rally the workers.

At headquarters, the AFL-CIO staff and committees work on a wide range of issues, including civil rights, job security, community service, economic policy, union-management cooperation, education, ethical practices, housing, international affairs, legislation, public relations, health care, research, safety, Social Security, and veterans' affairs. A publications department produces various literature for the membership and outsiders. National union headquarters also provides specialized services to regional and local bodies. People trained in organizing, strikes, legal matters, public relations, and negotiations are available to individual unions.

National unions and the AFL-CIO are also active in the political arena. Labor maintains a strong lobbying force in Washington, D.C., and is involved in political action committees at the state and local levels. Recently some large national unions have become active in international politics. For example, the United Auto Workers held discussions with Japanese car manufacturers concerning the level of imports into the United States and the construction of Japanese assembly plants here. They have lobbied in Washington, D.C., to restrict car imports in an attempt to bolster U. S. automakers and to increase jobs. They have also lobbied against NAFTA and for health care reform. Thus, to help their membership, unions are expanding their activities on all levels and, in some cases, working with other organizations to attain mutual goals. Unions are also trying to do a more effective job in their organizing campaigns. Descriptions of these activities in Mexico and Canada are offered in the feature, Managing Globalization: Unionization in Mexico and Canada.[24]

■□*fast fact*

The Amalgamated Engineering and Electrical Union has a single union deal with Nissan in Sunderland, England. By comparison, U.K. firms typically deal with multiple unions in one location.

THE ORGANIZING CAMPAIGN

One major function of the National Labor Relations Board is to conduct the process in which a union is chosen to represent employees. This is accomplished through a certification election to determine if the majority of employees want the union. The process by which a single union is selected to represent all employees in a particular unit is crucial to the American system of collective bargaining. If a majority of those voting opt for union representation, all employees are bound by that choice and the employer is obligated to recognize and bargain with the chosen union.[25]

Because unions may acquire significant power, employers may be anxious to keep them out. Adding to this potential union-management conflict is the possibility of competition and conflict between unions if more than one union is attempting to win certification by the same group of employees. The certification process has several stages, as outlined in Exhibit 15.1, which appears on page 621.[26]

■□*fast fact*

Union salting refers to the practice of union organizers seeking employment in companies without disclosing their true backgrounds in order to establish a base for union organizing activities.

Soliciting Employee Support

In the campaign to solicit employee support, unions generally attempt to contact the employees, obtain a sufficient number of authorization cards, and request an election from the NLRB.[27]

Establishing Contact Between the Union and Employees

Contact between the union and employees can be initiated by either party. National unions usually contact employees in industries or occupations in which they have an interest or are traditionally involved. The United Auto Workers, for example, has contacted nonunion employees in the new automobile plants that have been built in the South by German and Japanese auto companies.

MANAGING GLOBALIZATION

Unionization in Mexico and Canada

In Mexico, unions have the right to organize workers at a business, but only one union represents a given location, covering all employees at that location. When a strike is called, the workplace is closed until the strike is settled—picket lines are unknown. In most manufacturing operations, plant workers are unionized, first-line supervisors are sometimes unionized, and high-level supervisors are seldom unionized.

In case of a dispute, the burden of proof is always on the employer. Also, the labor law is part of Mexico's constitution, and workers aren't allowed to renounce these rights. Therefore, any individual employment contracts or collective agreements that limit these rights are considered invalid.

Since the advent of NAFTA, union organizations in the United States have seen relations with Mexico as a strategic opportunity and necessity. Many U.S. firms such as GE, Honeywell, and General Motors have increased operations in Mexico. The U.S. unions active in these companies are providing support to the local unions in Mexico, such as the Authentic Workers Front, that are trying to organize the workers of these companies. The U.S. union movement is also trying to work through NAFTA to help improve wages and working conditions in Mexico. NAFTA legislation empowers the secretaries of labor in Canada, the United States, and Mexico to impose fines on a country that fails to enforce its labor laws.

Approximately one-third of the Canadian labor force is unionized. About three-fourths of the union members are affiliated with the Canadian Labor Congress (CLC). As in the United States, the union local is the basic local unit. The CLC is the dominant labor group at the national level. Its political influence may be compared with that of the AFL-CIO.

The labor laws in Canada are similar to those in the United States, but there are some noteworthy differences. For example, Canadian labor laws require frequent interventions by governmental bodies before a strike can take place. In the United States, such intervention is largely voluntary. For the Canadian union movement as a whole, the trend toward concessionary bargaining to avoid layoffs and plant closings appears to be less evident than it is in the United States. Canadian labor organizations affiliated with unions dominated by labor organizations in the United States are becoming increasingly autonomous. This trend was highlighted when the United Auto Workers in Canada became independent from the same union in the United States.

To learn more about NAFTA, visit
www.ustreas.gov

In other cases, employees may approach the union, and the union is usually happy to oblige. Employees may have strong reasons for desiring this affiliation—low pay, poor working conditions, and other issues relating to dissatisfaction. Because workers generally tend to be apathetic toward unions, however, their concern must become quite serious before they will take any action.

At the point that contact occurs between the union and employees, the company must be careful and must avoid committing unfair labor practices. Accordingly, employers should *not*:

·   Misrepresent the facts. Any information management provides about a union or its officers must be factual and truthful.

·   Threaten employees. It is unlawful to threaten employees with losses of their jobs or transfers to less desirable positions, income reductions, or

Exhibit 15.1
Certification Process

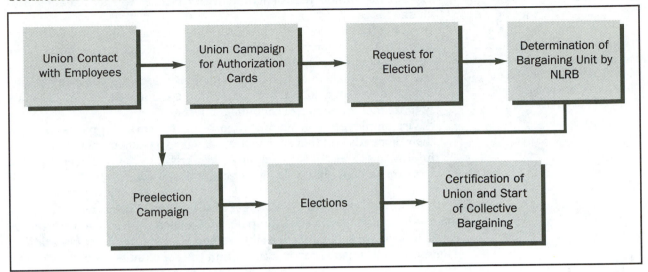

losses or reductions of benefits and privileges. The use of intimidating language to dissuade employees from joining or supporting a union also is forbidden. In addition, supervisors may not blacklist, lay off, discipline, or discharge any employee because of union activity.

- Promise benefits or rewards. Supervisors may not promise a pay raise, additional overtime or time off, promotions, or other favorable considerations in exchange for an employee's agreement to refrain from joining a union or signing a union card, to vote against union representation, or to otherwise oppose union activity.
- Make unscheduled changes in wages, hours, benefits, or working conditions. Any such changes are unlawful unless the employer can prove they were initiated before union activity began.
- Conduct surveillance activities. Management is forbidden to spy on employees' union activities or to request antiunion workers to do so, or to make any statements that give workers the impression they are being watched. Supervisors also may not attend union meetings or question employees about a union's internal affairs. They also may not ask employees for their opinions of a union or its officers.
- Interrogate workers. Managers may not require employees to tell them who has signed a union card, voted for union representation, attended a union meeting, or instigated an organization drive.
- Prohibit solicitation. Employees have the right to solicit members on company property during their nonworking hours and distribute union literature in nonwork areas during their free time, provided this activity doesn't interfere with the work being performed.[28]

Employers *can:*

- discuss the history of unions and make factual statements about strikes, violence, or the loss of jobs at plants that have unionized,
- discuss their own experiences with unions,
- advise workers about the costs of joining and belonging to unions,

- remind employees of the company benefits and wages they receive without having to pay union dues,
- explain that union representation won't protect workers against discharge for cause,
- point out that the company prefers to deal directly with employees (not through a third party) in settling complaints about wages, hours, and other employment conditions,
- tell workers that, in negotiating with the union, the company is not obligated to sign a contract or accept all the union's demands, especially those that aren't in its economic interests,
- advise employees that unions often resort to work stoppages to press their demands and that such tactics can cost workers money, and
- inform employees of the company's legal right to hire replacements for workers who go out on strike for economic reasons.[29]

Authorization Cards and the Request for Elections. Once contact has been made, the union begins the campaign to collect sufficient authorization cards, or signatures of employees interested in having union representation. This campaign must be carried out within the constraints set by law. If the union obtains cards from 30 percent of an organization's employees, it can petition the NLRB for an election. (Procedures in the public sector are similar.) If the NLRB determines there is indeed sufficient interest, it will schedule an election. If the union gets more than 50 percent of the employees to sign authorization cards, it may petition the employer as the bargaining representative. Usually employers refuse, whereupon the union petitions the NLRB for an election.

The employer usually resists the union's card-signing campaign. For instance, companies often prohibit solicitation on the premises. However, employers are legally constrained from interfering with an employee's freedom of choice. Union representatives have argued that employers ignore this law because the consequences are minimal—and by doing so, they can effectively discourage unionism.

During the union campaign and election process, it is important that the HR manager caution the company against engaging in unfair labor practices. Unfair labor practices, when identified, generally cause the election to be set aside. Severe violations by the employer can result in certification of the union as the bargaining representative, even if it has lost the election. This process can determine the quality of labor-management relations in the future.

Determination of the Bargaining Unit

When the union has gathered sufficient signatures to petition for an election, the NLRB will identify the bargaining unit, the group of employees that will be represented by the union. The bargaining unit must be truly appropriate and not contain a mix of antagonistic interests or submerge the legitimate interests of a small group of employees in the interest of a larger group.[30]

To ensure the fullest freedom of collective bargaining, legal constraints and guidelines constrain which groups can be included in bargaining units. Professional and nonprofessional groups can't be included in the same unit, and a craft unit can't be placed in a larger unit unless both units agree to it. Physical location, skill levels, degree of ownership, collective bargaining history, and extent of organization of employees are also considered.

From the union's perspective, the most desirable bargaining unit is one whose members are pro-union and will help win certification. The unit also must have sufficient influence in the organization to give the union some power once it wins representation. Employers generally want a bargaining unit that's least beneficial to the union; this maximizes the likelihood of failure in the election and minimizes the power of the unit.

Pre-Election Campaign

After the bargaining unit has been determined, both union and employer embark on a preelection campaign. Unions claim to provide a strong voice for employees, emphasizing improvement in wages and working conditions and the establishment of a grievance process to ensure fairness. Employers emphasize the costs of unionization—dues, strikes, and loss of jobs. Severe violations of the legal constraints on behavior, such as the use of threats or coercion, are prevented by the NLRB, which watches the preelection activity.

Election, Certification, and Decertification

Generally, elections are part of the process of determining if unions will win the right to represent workers. Elections can also determine if unions will retain the right to represent employees.

Election and Certification. The NLRB conducts the certification election. If a majority votes for union representation, the union will be certified. If the union does not get a majority, another election won't be held for at least a year. Generally, about one-third to one-half of all certification elections certify the union, with less union success in larger companies. Once a union has been certified, the employer is required to bargain with that union.

Decertification Elections. The NLRB also conducts decertification elections that can remove a union from representation. If 30 percent or more of the employees in an organization request such an election, it will be held. Decertification elections most frequently occur in the first year of a union's representation when the union is negotiating its first contract. During this period, union strength has not yet been established, and employees are readily discouraged by union behavior.

THE COLLECTIVE BARGAINING PROCESS

Collective bargaining is a complex process in which union and management negotiators maneuver to win the most advantageous contract. How the issues involved are settled depends on

- the quality of the union-management relationship,
- the processes of bargaining used by labor and management,
- management's strategies in collective bargaining, and
- the union's strategies in collective bargaining.

The labor relations system is composed of several constituencies: employees, management, and the union, with the government influencing interaction between the three. Employees may be managers or union members, and some union members are part of the union management system (local union leaders). These interrelationships are regulated by specific federal statutes.

Typically, the constituencies in the labor relations system have different goals. Workers are interested in improved working conditions, wages, and

■ ▢ fast fact

The number of elections won by unions has been increasing. In 1997, it was over 50 percent for the first time in fourteen years.

opportunities. Unions are interested in these as well as their own survival, growth, and acquisition of power, which depend on their ability to maintain the support of the employees by providing for their needs. Management has overall organizational goals (e.g., increasing profits, market share, and growth rates) and also seeks to preserve managerial prerogatives to direct the workforce and to attain the personal goals of the managers (e.g., promotion or achievement). Government is interested in a stable and healthy economy, protection of individual rights, and safety and fairness in the workplace. All of these factors influence the roles that these groups play.

Adversarial Relationship

Historically, the goals of workers, unions, management, and governments were seen as incompatible. Thus, an adversarial relationship emerged, with labor and management attempting to get a bigger cut of the pie, while government oversaw its own interests. In an adversarial relationship between union and management, the union's role is to gain concessions from management during collective bargaining and to preserve those concessions through the grievance procedure. The union is an outsider and critic.[31]

Unions also adopted an adversarial role in their interactions with management. Their focus has been on wages, hours, and working conditions as they attempted to get "more and better" from management. This approach works well in economic boom times but encounters difficulties when the economy is not healthy. High unemployment and the threat of continued job losses induced unions to expand their role, especially since many of their traditional goals have already been achieved. Consequently, some unions have begun to enter into new, collaborative efforts with employers, which result in a cooperative relationship.

Cooperative Relationship

In a cooperative relationship, the union's role is that of a partner, not a critic, and the union is jointly responsible with management for reaching a suitable solution to business challenges. Thus, a cooperative relationship requires that union and management solve problems, share information, and integrate outcomes.[32]

Cooperative systems have not been a major component of labor relations in the United States, although they have been built into labor relations in other countries such as Sweden and Germany. Increasingly, however, U.S. management and labor are working together cooperatively. As described in the feature, Managing Change: Saturn Employees Swing Back to a More Traditional Philosophy, the future of this recent trend is uncertain.[33] At Saturn, the past decade was a time of experimentation. Management recognizes that most of the programs they undertake to improve their organization need the acceptance of the union to be successful. Active involvement of the union was a good way to gain this acceptance.[34]

Then, suddenly, union members revealed their frustration with the new trail they had blazed. Employees who only recently were considered mavericks chose to return to "the good ol' days."

Yet, at the same time that Saturn seems to be taking a step backward, other companies are embracing cooperation and teamwork.[35] The feature, Managing Teams: Chrysler and the UAW Train in Teams, illustrates what this can mean.[36]

"What we're seeing is a complete lack of respect for workers, for the jobs they do. We're seeing so many examples of how insensitive corporate America can be to their workers."

John Sweeney
President
AFL-CIO

Cooperative agreements are particularly fragile. "A lot of times when they break down it's not because of new economic circumstances. An individual can make a difference—a new plant manager, a new local president."

Douglas Fraser
Past President
UAW

MANAGING CHANGE

Saturn Employees Swing Back to a More Traditional Philosophy

In autumn 1991, when Chairman Robert Stempel of General Motors visited the GM Saturn plant in Spring Hill, Tennessee, the workers, wearing black-and-orange armbands, launched a work slowdown. Another strike to get higher wages? No, a protest against the higher production quotas GM was trying to impose on the plant. Although high quality and high quantity can go hand in hand when everything is working right, they can't be expected to in the early stages of operation. Still in the early stages of their new operation at the Saturn plant, the workers were more concerned about quality—about the car and the customer's satisfaction with it—than they were with quantity of output. They believed that quality was more critical than quantity for the long-term success of the company.

Quality takes commitment, dedication and training—and the United Automobile Workers (UAW) has never been known for being concerned about either quality *or* quantity. Why were the union workers at the Saturn plant behaving contrary to the traditional stereotype of the union member in the auto industry? Because management was behaving contrary to its stereotype. Management was giving workers more say in the production of the automobile, treating workers as co-owners and as members of teams. Any employee who did not want to fit into this new labor-management relationship could collect a generous severance package—$15,000 to $50,000, depending on length of service.

Reflecting on their original agreement, Stempel and the GM management heard the concerns of the workers at the plant and gave them the benefit of any doubt. These managers knew that Saturn was the test case for whether GM could build cars to compete directly with the top-selling Japanese cars, many of which are also made in the United States, some by UAW members and some by nonmembers.

But in the years that followed, things changed. Eventually, the union local leaders who made Saturn famous as an example of cooperative union-management relations were voted out by the members. The new slate of leaders advocated a more traditional and less cozy relationship with management. It appears that members were no longer satisfied with the concessions made to management, which included irregular work weeks, working Saturdays without overtime pay, and linking pay increases to productivity. With management committed to building a car-based sport utility vehicle at the plant, workers may be thinking they can once again demand that management be as responsive to workers' concerns as they are to customers' concerns. Considering that unemployment levels are at historic lows, they may be right.

To learn more about General Motors visit the company home page at **www.gm.com**

Processes of Bargaining

Five types of bargaining are used in contract negotiations: distributive, integrative, concessionary, continuous, and intraorganizational.

Distributive Bargaining. Distributive bargaining takes place when the parties are in conflict over the issue, and the outcome represents a gain for one party and a loss for the other. Each party tries to negotiate for the best possible outcome. The process is outlined in Exhibit 15.2, which appears on page 627.[37] On any particular issue, union and management negotiators

■ *fast fact*

During 1985, Saturn's HR function formed a proactive partnership with the United Auto Workers. This novel idea was a clear statement that people issues and participative, collaborative team behavior would be considered equally important to engineering, manufacturing, and finance.

MANAGING TEAMS

Chrysler and the UAW Train in Teams

Like many manufacturing facilities, Chrysler's Evart Glass Plant division began restructuring around teams during the mid-1990s. "Team effort is what counts," according to plant manager Bert Burtolozzi. "As a society, we have focused on the individual, but in the workplace no one individual can do it—we must focus on our greatest asset: our teams."

Many companies put their top executives through programs such as Outward Bound, but Evart had the entire workforce participate. Union members and managers were trained side by side. They spent the day at a nearby camp learning a variety of teamwork lessons. The training took place during employees' normal work hours, which in this case meant that training took place across three eight-hour shifts. Everyone received normal pay for the time spent in training. The training teams were cross-functional. For example, a hi-lo driver (similar to a forklift operator), a maintenance person, a shift supervisor, and a receptionist found themselves working together as a team throughout their training. After each activity, trainers led a discussion about the experience to identify the lessons to be learned from it. Below are a few of the activities and associated lessons from the specially designed one-day program.

Exhibit A

The Challenging Activity	The Teamwork Lesson
· Juggle several objects simultaneously (e.g., tennis balls, hackey sacs, and koosh balls) as a team.	· Although everyone has a different role, each person touches and affects the outcome.
· Find the path hidden in a carpet maze and move each member through it in a limited amount of time.	· Teams must find and use each individual's hidden strengths (e.g., a good memory and the ability to move quickly). Doing so allows the team as a whole to succeed.
· Balance fourteen nails on the head of a nail that has been pounded into a supporting block of wood, creating a free-standing structure without supports.	· Things that may seem impossible can be achieved when people work together.
· Draw a vehicle that represents the training team and signify which part of the vehicle each member represents.	· To validate the different strengths of each member and recognize that bringing these strengths together leads to success on the task.

each have three identifiable positions. The union has an *initial demand point*, which is generally more than it expects to get; *a target point,* which is its realistic assessment of what it may be able to get; and *a resistance point,* or the lowest acceptable level for the issue. Management has three similar points: an *initial offer point,* which is usually lower than the expected settlement; a *target point,* at which it would like to reach agreement; and a *resistance point,* or its upper acceptable limit. If management's resistance point is greater than

Exhibit 15.2

Distributive Bargaining Process: Example of a Positive Settlement Range

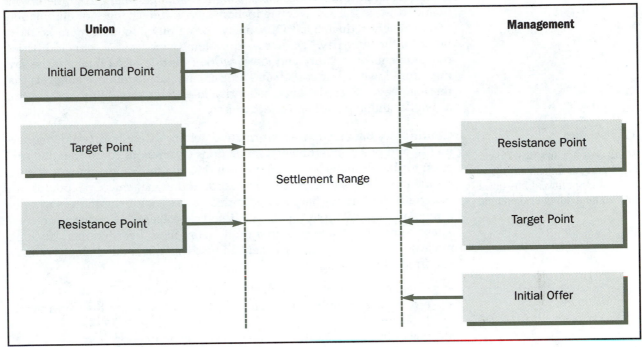

the union's, a *positive settlement range* exists. If, however, management's resistance point is below the union's, a *negative settlement range*, or bargaining impasse, exists, and there is no common ground for negotiation.[38] For example, on the issue of wages, the union may have a resistance point of $8.40 an hour, a target of $8.60, and an initial demand point of $8.75. Management may offer $8.20, have a target of $8.45 and a resistance point of $8.55. The positive settlement range is between $8.40 and $8.55, and this is where the settlement will likely be. However, only the initial wage demand and offer are made public at the beginning of negotiations.

Because many issues are involved in a bargaining session, the actual process is much more complicated. Although each issue can be described by the above model, in actual negotiations, an interaction occurs among issues. Union concessions on one issue may be traded for management concessions on another. Thus the total process is dynamic.[39]

Integrative Bargaining. When more than one issue needs to be resolved, integrative agreements may be pursued. Integrative bargaining focuses on creative solutions that reconcile (integrate) the parties' interests and yield high joint benefit. It can occur only when negotiators have an "expanding-pie" perception—that is, when the two parties (union and management) have two or more issues and are willing to develop creative ways to satisfy both parties.[40]

Concessionary Bargaining. Distributive and integrative bargaining are the primary approaches to bargaining; concessionary bargaining often occurs within these two frameworks. Concessionary bargaining may be prompted by severe economic conditions faced by employers. Seeking to survive and prosper, employers seek givebacks or concessions from the unions, promising job security in return. In the early 1990s, this type of bargaining was

■□ fast fact

More than half of all unions entered the new millennium with web sites in place to serve their members.

prevalent, especially in the smokestack industries, such as automobiles, steel, and rubber, and to some extent in the transportation industry. In these groups of enterprises, concessions sought by management from the unions included wage freezes, wage reductions, work rule changes or elimination, fringe-benefit reductions, COLA delays or elimination, and more hours of work for the same pay. Two-tier wage systems were tried in some industries, but problems of inequity and lower worker morale offset much of the savings from lower labor costs.[41] In addition, available evidence suggests that these agreements erode union solidarity, leadership credibility, and control, as well as union power and effectiveness.

Continuous Bargaining. As affirmative action, safety and health requirements, and other governmental regulations continue to complicate the situation for both unions and employers, and as the rate of change in the environment continues to increase, some labor and management negotiators are turning to continuous bargaining. In this process, joint committees meet on a regular basis to explore issues and solve problems of common interest. These committees have appeared in the retail food, over-the-road trucking, nuclear power, and men's garment industries.[42] Several characteristics of continuous bargaining are

- frequent meetings during the life of the contract,
- a focus on external events and problem areas rather than on internal problems,
- use of the skills of outside experts in decision making, and
- use of a problem-solving (integrative) approach.[43]

The intention of continuous bargaining is to develop a union-management structure that's capable of adapting positively and productively to sudden changes in the environment. This approach is different from, but an extension of, the emergency negotiations that unions have insisted on when inflation or other circumstances have substantially changed the acceptability of the existing agreement. Continuous bargaining is a permanent arrangement intended to help avoid the crises that often occur under traditional collective bargaining systems.

Intraorganizational Bargaining.   During negotiations, the bargaining teams from both sides may have to engage in intraorganizational bargaining—that is, confer with their constituents over changes in bargaining positions. Management negotiators may have to convince management to change its position on an issue—for instance, to agree to a higher wage settlement. Union negotiators must eventually convince their members to accept the negotiated contract, so they must be sensitive to the demands of the membership, as well as realistic. When the membership votes on the proposed package, it will be strongly influenced by the opinions of the union negotiators.

NEGOTIATING THE AGREEMENT

Once a union is certified as the representative of a bargaining unit, it becomes the only party that can negotiate an agreement with the employer for all members of that work unit, whether they are union members or not. Technically, however, individuals within the unit can still negotiate personal deals that give them more than the other members receive, particularly if the agreement is silent on this issue.

The union serves as a critical link between employees and employer. It is responsible to its members to negotiate for what they want, and it has the duty to represent all employees fairly. The quality of its bargaining is an important measure of union effectiveness.

Negotiating Committees

The employer and the union select their own representatives for the negotiating committee. Neither party is required to consider the wishes of the other. For example, management negotiators can't refuse to bargain with representatives of the union because they dislike them or don't think they are appropriate.

Union negotiating teams typically include representatives of the union local—often the president and other executive staff members. In addition, the national union may send a negotiating specialist, who is likely to be a labor lawyer, to work with the team. The negotiators selected by the union don't have to be members of the union or employees of the company. The general goal is to balance skill and experience in bargaining with knowledge and information about the specific situation.

At the local level, when a single bargaining unit is negotiating a contract, the company is usually represented by the manager and members of the labor relations or human resource staff. Finance and production managers may also be involved. When the negotiations are critical, either because the bargaining unit is large or because the effect on the company is great, specialists such as labor lawyers may be included on the team.

In national negotiations, top industrial relations or human resource executives frequently head a team of specialists from corporate headquarters and perhaps managers from critical divisions or plants within the company. Again, the goal is to have expertise along with specific knowledge about critical situations.

The Negotiating Structure

Most contracts are negotiated by a single union and a single employer. In some situations, however, different arrangements can be agreed on. When a single union negotiates with several similar companies, for instance, firms in the construction industry, the employers may bargain as a group. At the local level, this is called *multi-employer bargaining;* at the national level, it is referred to as *industrywide bargaining.* Industrywide bargaining occurs in the railroad, coal, wallpaper, and men's suits industries. When several unions bargain jointly with a single employer, they engage in *coordinated bargaining.* Although not as common as the multi-employer and industrywide bargaining, coordinated bargaining appears to be increasing, especially in the public sector. One consequence of coordinated and industrywide bargaining is *pattern settlements,* where similar wage rates are imposed on the companies whose employees are represented by the same union within a given industry.

In the contract construction industry, a *wide-area and multicraft bargaining* structure arose in response to the unionized employers' need to be more price competitive and to have fewer strikes, and in response to the unions' desire to gain more control at the national level. Consequently, the bargaining is done on a regional (geographic) rather than local basis, and it covers several construction crafts simultaneously. The common contract negotiations resulting from wide-area and multicraft bargaining help lessen the opportunity for unions to *whipsaw* the employer. Whipsawing occurs when one contract settlement is used as a precedent for the next, which then forces

Two people describing Brian Mayhew, negotiator for the Allied Pilots Association:

"He's our nuclear weapon. He's a brilliant man and he fights to the death."

a union official

"This is not a bat-wielding thug. This is a very professional man with a sense of humor, and that kind of person is a real adversary."

aviation consultant

the employer to get all contracts settled in order to have all the employees working. As a result of whipsawing, an employer frequently agrees to more favorable settlements on all contracts, regardless of the conditions and merits of each one, just to keep all employees working.[44]

Preparation for Bargaining

Prior to the bargaining session, management and union negotiators need to develop the strategies and proposals they will use.

Management Strategies. For negotiations with the union, management needs to complete four different tasks, which include

- preparing specific proposals for changes in contract language;
- determining the general size of the economic package that the company anticipates offering during the negotiations;
- preparing statistical displays and supportive data that the company will use during negotiations; and
- preparing a bargaining book for use by company negotiators that compiles the information on issues to be discussed, giving an analysis of the effect of each clause, its use in other companies, and other facts.[45]

The relative cost of pension contributions, pay increases, health benefits, and other bargaining provisions should be determined prior to negotiations. Other costs should also be considered. For instance, management might ask itself, "What is the cost of union demands for changes in grievance and discipline procedures or transfer and promotion provisions?" The goal is to be as well prepared as possible by considering the implications and ramifications of the issues that will be discussed and by being able to present a strong argument for the position taken.

Union Strategies. Like management, unions need to prepare for negotiations by collecting information. Because collective bargaining is the major means by which a union can convince its members of its effectiveness and value, this is a critical activity. Unions collect information on

- the financial situation of the company and its ability to pay;
- the attitude of management toward various issues, as reflected in past negotiations or inferred from negotiations in similar companies; and
- the attitudes and desires of employees.

The first two areas give the union an idea of what demands management is likely to accept. The third area is sometimes overlooked. It involves awareness of the preferences of the union membership. For instance, the union might ask, "Is a pension increase preferred over increased vacation or holiday benefits?" Membership preferences will vary with the characteristics of the workers. Younger workers are more likely to prefer more holidays, shorter workweeks, and limited overtime, whereas older workers are more likely interested in pension plans, benefits, and overtime. The union can determine these preferences by using questionnaires and meetings to survey its members.

Issues for Negotiation

The issues that can be discussed in collective bargaining sessions are specified by the *Labor-Management Relations Act.* This act established three categories of issues for negotiation: mandatory, permissive, and prohibited.[46]

"We no longer accept the view that the only way to make money as shareholders is to ignore the needs of working Americans and their communities."

John Sweeny
President
AFL-CIO

Employers and employee representatives (unions) are obligated to meet and discuss "wages, hours, and other terms and conditions of employment." These are the *mandatory issues*. These critical elements in the bargaining process include the issues that may affect management's ability to run the company efficiently or may clash with the union's desire to protect jobs and workers' standing in their jobs.

Permissive issues are those not specifically related to the nature of the job but still of concern to both parties. For example, decisions about price, product design, and new jobs may be subject to bargaining if the parties agree to it. Permissive issues usually develop when both parties see that mutual discussion and agreement will be beneficial. This is more likely when a cooperative relationship exists between union and management. Management and union negotiators can't refuse to agree on a contract if they fail to settle a permissive issue.[47]

Prohibited issues are those concerning illegal or outlawed activities, such as the demand that an employer use only union-produced goods or, where it is illegal, that it employ only union members. Such issues may not be discussed in collective bargaining sessions.

Direct Compensation. Wage conflicts are a leading cause of strikes. Difficulties arise here because a wage increase is a direct cost to the employer, whereas a wage decrease is a direct cost to the employee. As discussed in Chapters 10 and 12, rates of pay are influenced by a variety of issues, including the going rate in an industry, the employer's ability to pay, the cost of living, and productivity. All of these are debated and discussed in negotiations.

Indirect Compensation. Because the cost of indirect compensation can run as high as 40 percent of the total cost of wages, it is a major concern in collective bargaining. Benefit provisions are very difficult to remove once they are in place, so management tends to be cautious about agreeing to them. Some commonly negotiated forms of indirect compensation are pensions, paid vacations, paid holidays, sick leave, health care and life insurance, dismissal or severance pay, and supplemental unemployment benefits.

Hours of Employment. Although federal labor law requires organizations to pay overtime for work beyond forty hours a week, unions continually try to reduce the number of hours worked each week. Negotiations may focus on including the lunch hour in the eight-hour-day requirement, or on providing overtime after any eight-hour shift rather than after a forty-hour workweek.

Institutional Issues. Some issues not directly related to jobs are nevertheless important to both employees and management. Institutional issues that affect the security and success of both parties include:

- *Union security.* About two-thirds of the major labor contracts stipulate that employees must join the union after being hired into its bargaining unit. However, 20 states that traditionally have had low levels of unionization have passed right-to-work laws outlawing union membership as a condition of employment.
- *Checkoff.* Unions have attempted to arrange for payment of dues through deduction from employees' paychecks. By law, employees must agree in writing to a dues checkoff. A large majority of union contracts contain a provision for this agreement.
- *Strikes.* The employer may insist that the union agree not to strike during the life of the contract, typically when a cost-of-living clause has

fast fact

The wages and benefits of German workers in manufacturing average $30 per hour. However, the rate of unemployment is 10 percent.

been included. The agreement may be unconditional, allowing no strikes at all, or it may limit strikes to specific circumstances.

- *Managerial prerogatives.* More than half the agreements today stipulate that certain activities are the right of management. In addition, management in most companies argues that it has "residual rights" stating that rights not specifically limited by the agreement belong to management.

Administrative Issues. Administrative issues concern the treatment of employees at work. These issues include:

- *Breaks and cleanup time.* Some contracts specify the time and length of coffee breaks and meal breaks for employees. In addition, jobs requiring cleanup may have a portion of the work period set aside for this procedure.
- *Job security.* Job security is perhaps the issue of most concern to employees and unions. Employers are concerned with a restriction of their ability to lay off employees. Changes in technology or attempts to subcontract work impinge on job security. A typical union response to technological change was demonstrated by the International Longshoremen's Association (ILA) in the late 1960s when containerized shipping was introduced. The union operated exclusive hiring halls, developed complex work rules, and negotiated a guaranteed annual income for its members. Job security continues to be a primary issue for most unions.
- *Seniority.* Length of service is used as a criterion for many human resource decisions in most collective agreements. Layoffs are usually determined by seniority. "Last hired, first fired" is a common situation. Seniority is also important in transfer and promotion decisions. The method of calculating seniority is usually specified in order to clarify the relative seniority of employees.
- *Discharge and discipline.* Termination and discipline are tough issues, and, even when an agreement addresses these problems, many grievances are filed concerning the way they are handled.
- *Safety and health.* Although the *Occupational Safety and Health Act* specifically deals with worker safety and health, some contracts have provisions specifying that the company will provide safety equipment, first aid, physical examinations, accident investigations, and safety committees. Hazardous work may be covered by special provisions and pay rates. Often, the agreement will contain a general statement that the employer is responsible for the safety of the workers, so that the union can use the grievance process when safety issues arise.
- *Production standards.* The level of productivity or performance of employees is a concern of both management and the union. Management is concerned with efficiency, and the union is concerned with the fairness and reasonableness of management's demands. Increasingly, both are concerned about total quality and quality of work life.
- *Grievance procedures.* The contract usually outlines a process for settling disputes that may arise during its administration.
- *Training.* The design and administration of training and development programs and the procedure for selecting employees for training may also be bargaining issues. This is particularly important when the company is pursuing a strategy of total quality management.
- *Duration of the agreement.* Agreements can last for one year or longer, with the most common period being three years.

■□ *fast fact*

Harry Bridges, head of the ILA, was in favor of containerized shipping to reduce the workload on his members.

Factors Affecting Bargaining

The preceding discussion suggests that negotiations proceed in a rational manner and end in resolution when a positive contract zone, a set of outcomes that is preferred over the imposition of a strike, exists. Unfortunately, negotiators often fail to reach agreement, even when a positive contract zone exists.

To fully understand the negotiation process, it is important to examine the decision processes of negotiators. If the biases of negotiators can be identified, then prescriptive approaches and training programs can be developed to improve negotiations. The following are common cognitive or mental limitations to negotiator judgments.[48]

The Mythical Fixed Pie. All too frequently, negotiators believe that their interests automatically conflict with the other party's interests. In other words, what one side wins, the other side loses. However, most conflicts usually have more than one issue at stake, with the parties placing different values on the different issues. Consequently, the potential usually exists for integrative agreements. A fundamental task in training negotiators lies in identifying and eliminating this false "fixed pie" assumption and preparing them to look for trade-offs between issues of different value to each side.

Framing. Consider the following bargaining situation. The union claims that its members need a raise to $12 an hour and that anything less will represent a loss due to inflation. Management argues that the company can't pay more than $10 an hour and that anything more would impose an unacceptable loss. If each side had the choice between settling at $11 an hour or going to binding arbitration, they are likely to take the risk and move toward arbitration rather than settlement.

Changing the frame of the situation to a positive one results in a very different outcome. If the union can view anything above $10 an hour as a gain, and if management can view anything under $12 as a gain, then a negotiated settlement at $11 is likely.

As the preceding example emphasizes, the frame (positive or negative) of negotiators can make the difference between settlement and impasse. One solution then to impasses is to alter the frame of reference such that it is positive, rather than negative.[49]

CONFLICT RESOLUTION

Although the desired outcome of collective bargaining is agreement on the conditions of employment, on many occasions, negotiators are unable to reach such an agreement at the bargaining table. In these situations, several alternatives are used to break the deadlock. The most dramatic response is a strike or lockout; indirect responses are also used, and third-party interventions such as mediation and arbitration are common as well.

Strikes and Lockouts

When the union is unable to get management to agree to a demand it believes is critical, it may tell employees to refuse to work at the company. This is called a *strike*. When management refuses to allow employees to work, the situation is called a *lockout*.[50]

In order to strike, the union usually holds a vote to gain members' approval. Strong membership support for a strike strengthens the union

"Cyber unions will put communications in the hands of rank-and-file members: Out go carefully worded newsletters and magazines; in come bulletin boards and chat rooms."

Arthur B. Shostak
Director
Drexel University's Center for Employment Futures

On the Teamsters' strike:
"It was two weeks that felt like two years."

Lea Soupata
Senior VP for HR
UPS

negotiators' position. If the strike takes place, union members picket the employer, informing the public about the existence of a labor dispute and preferably, from the union's point of view, convincing it to avoid this company during the strike. Union members commonly refuse to cross the picket line of another striking union, which gives added support to the striking union.

Employers usually attempt to continue operations while a strike is in effect. They either run the company with supervisory personnel and people not in the bargaining unit or hire replacements for the striking employees. At the conclusion of the strike, employers will be expected to (1) reinstate strikers in all the positions that remain unfilled, unless they have substantial business reasons for doing otherwise, and (2) establish a preferential hiring list for displaced strikers to facilitate their recall as new openings occur.

The success of a strike depends on its ability to cause economic hardship to the employer. Severe hardship usually causes the employer to concede to the union's demands.[51] Thus, from the union's point of view, the cost of the company's lack of production must be high. The union, therefore, actively tries to prevent replacement employees from working. Although it appears that the company can legally hire replacements, the union reacts strongly to the employment of scabs, as these workers are called, and the replacement employees may be a cause of increasingly belligerent labor relations. The hiring of replacement workers has reached a level where companies are keeping them even after the strike is settled—if the strike is settled at all. This tactic has given employers even more power in a strike situation. Thus, the union movement seeks a law to prevent replacement workers from becoming permanent workers.

The timing of the strike is also often critical. The union attempts to hold negotiations just before the employer has a peak demand for its product or services, when a strike will have the maximum economic effect.

Although strikes have been on the decline, they are costly to both the employer, who loses revenue, and employees, who lose income. If a strike is prolonged, the cost to employers will likely never be fully recovered by the benefits gained. In part because of this, employers seek to avoid strikes. Moreover, the public interest is generally not served by strikes. They are often an inconvenience and can have serious consequences for the economy as a whole.

Slowdowns. Short of an actual strike, unions may invoke a slowdown. At the Caterpillar plant, Lance Vaughan usually installed a set of small and large hoses on huge off-highway trucks—small hoses first, then the big hoses. But when a slowdown started, he began to install the big hoses first, and then reach awkwardly around it to attach the other smaller hoses. The result was lost production time. Technically, Vaughan was just doing his job. The instructions furnished by Caterpillar's engineers describe the inefficient procedure. Normally, Vaughan ignores such instructions and makes a note to himself to tell the engineers to fix the mistake. When the slowdown began, he stopped speaking up and began working according to the rules furnished by the company. "I used to give the engineers ideas," explained Vaughan, who has worked at Caterpillar for 20 years. "We showed them how to eliminate some hose clips and save money. And I recommended larger bolts that made assembly easier and faster, and were less likely to come loose."[52]

At Caterpillar, the slowdown was referred to as an "in-plant strategy." Regardless of the name, the result is the same: a reduction of work output, physically and mentally. Slowdowns can be more effective than actual strikes.

Primary Boycotts. Unions sometimes want to make the public more aware of their cause. As a consequence, they may engage in a *primary boycott*. For instance, a union that is striking a soda-bottling company may set up an informational picket line at grocery stores that sell the bottler's products. It has generally been ruled that as long as the picket line is directed at the bottling company, asking customers not to buy its soda, it constitutes a primary boycott and thus is legal. The picket line becomes illegal, however, when it tries to prevent customers from shopping at the grocery store. This action is called a *secondary boycott,* and it is illegal because it can harm an innocent third party—the grocery store.

Corporate Campaigns.   In a *corporate campaign,* a union may ask the public and other unions to write letters to a company, asking it to change the way it bargains with the union.[53]

Mediation

Mediation is a procedure in which a neutral third party helps the union and management negotiators reach a voluntary agreement.[54] Having no power to impose a solution, the mediator attempts to facilitate the negotiations between union and management. The mediator may make suggestions and recommendations and perhaps add objectivity to the often emotional negotiations. To have any success at all, the mediator must have the trust and respect of both parties and have sufficient expertise and neutrality to convince the union and employer that she or he will be fair and equitable.

The U.S. government operates the Federal Mediation and Conciliation Service (FMCS) to make experienced mediators available to unions and companies. A program called Relationships by Objective is offered by the FMCS to eliminate the causes of recurrent impasses and to increase the likelihood of a cooperative relationship between union and management.

Arbitration

Arbitration is a procedure in which a neutral third party studies the bargaining situation, listens to both parties and gathers information, and then makes a determination that is binding on the parties. The arbitrator, in effect, determines the conditions of the agreement.

In *final-offer arbitration,* the arbitrator can choose between the final offer of the union and the final offer of the employer. The arbitrator can't alter these offers but must select one as it stands. Since the arbitrator chooses the offer that appears most fair, and since losing the arbitration decision means settling for the other's offer, each side is pressured to make as good an offer as possible. By contrast, in conventional arbitration, the arbitrator is free to fashion any award deemed appropriate.

The arbitration process that deals with the contract terms and conditions is called *interest arbitration.* This type of arbitration is relatively infrequent in the private sector; it is more common in the public sector, where it becomes a necessary quid pro quo for foregoing the strike option.[55] Only about 20 states have compulsory interest arbitration procedures.

Once the contract impasse is removed, union and management have an agreement. Abiding by it is the essence of contract administration; however, at

■■□ *fast fact*

The real power of the arbitrator's decision was established by three Supreme Court decisions in 1960 referred to as the Trilogy cases and all involving the United Steelworkers.

times, arbitration will again be necessary, namely when a grievance is filed. This type of arbitration is referred to as rights arbitration or *grievance arbitration*.

CONTRACT ADMINISTRATION

Once signed, the collective agreement becomes "the basic legislation governing the lives of the workers."[56] That is, the daily operation and activities in the organization are subject to the conditions of the agreement. Because of the difficulty of writing an unambiguous agreement anticipating all the situations that will occur over its life, disputes will inevitably occur over the contract's interpretation and application. The most common method of resolving these disputes is a grievance procedure. Virtually all agreements negotiated today provide for a grievance process to handle employee complaints.

Grievance Procedures

Basically, a grievance is a charge that the union-management contract has been violated.[57] A grievance may be filed by the union for employees, or by employers, although management rarely does so. The grievance process is designed to investigate the charges and to resolve the problem. Common sources of grievances are

- outright violation of the agreement,
- disagreement over facts,
- dispute over the meaning of the agreement,
- dispute over the method of applying the agreement, and
- argument over the fairness or reasonableness of actions.[58]

Grievance procedures typically involve several stages. The collective bargaining agreement specifies the maximum length of time that can elapse between the incident that is the subject of the dispute and the filing of a grievance on that incident. The most common grievance procedure, shown in Exhibit 15.3,[59] involves the following four steps:

STEP 1. An employee who feels that the labor contract has been violated usually contacts the union steward, and together they discuss the problem with the supervisor involved. If the problem is simple and straightforward, it is often resolved at this level.

STEP 2. If agreement cannot be reached at the supervisor level, or if the employee is not satisfied, the complaint can enter the second step of the grievance procedure. Typically, a human resource representative of the company now seeks to resolve the grievance.

STEP 3. If the grievance is sufficiently important or difficult to resolve, it may be taken to the third step. Although contracts vary, they usually specify that top-level management and union executives be involved at this stage. These people have the authority to make the major decisions that may be required to resolve the grievance.

STEP 4. If a grievance cannot be resolved at the third step, an arbitrator will likely need to consider the case and reach a decision. The arbitrator is a neutral, mutually acceptable individual who may be appointed by the FMCS or some private agency. The arbitrator holds a hearing, reviews the evidence, and then rules on the grievance. The decision of the arbitrator is usually binding.

Exhibit 15.3

Typical Union-Management Grievance Procedure

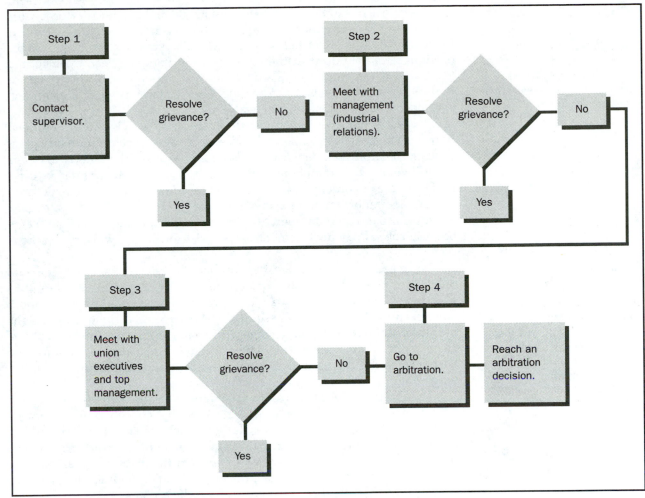

Since the cost of arbitration is shared by the union and employer, some incentive exists to settle the grievance before it goes to arbitration. An added incentive in some cases is the requirement that the loser pay for the arbitration. The expectation behind these incentives is that the parties will screen or evaluate grievances more carefully because pursuing a weak grievance to arbitration will be expensive.

Occasionally, the union will call a strike over a grievance in order to resolve it. This may happen when the issue at hand is so important that the union feels that it cannot wait for the slower arbitration process. Such an "employee rights" strike may be legal; however, if the contract specifically forbids strikes during the tenure of the agreement, it is not legal and is called a *wildcat strike.* Wildcat strikes are not common; most grievances are settled through arbitration.

Grievance Issues

Grievances can be filed over any workplace issue that is subject to the collective agreement, or they can be filed over interpretation and implementation of the agreement itself. The most common type of grievance reaching the arbitration stage involves discipline and discharge, although many grievances are filed over other issues.

Absenteeism can be grounds for discharge, and a grievance procedure may be used to determine whether the absenteeism in question is excessive. Insubordination is either failure to do what the supervisor requests or the outright refusal to do it. If the supervisor's orders are clear, explicit, and legal, and if the employee is warned of the consequences, discipline for refusal to respond is usually acceptable. The exception is when the employee feels that the work endangers health.

Because seniority is usually used to determine who is laid off, bumped from a job to make way for someone else, or rehired, its calculation is of great concern to employees. Seniority is also used as one of the criteria to determine eligibility for promotions and transfers, so management must be careful in this area in order to avoid complaints and grievances.

Compensation for time away from work, vacations, holidays, or sick leave is also a common source of grievances. Holidays cause problems because special pay arrangements often exist for people working on those days.

Wage and work schedules may also lead to grievances. Disagreements often arise over interpretation or application of the agreement relating to such issues as overtime pay, pay for reporting, and scheduling. Grievances have been filed over the exercise of such management rights as the right to introduce technological changes, use subcontractors (outsource), or change jobs in other ways. This type of behavior may also be the source of charges of unfair labor practices, since these activities may require collective bargaining.

The *Taft-Hartley Act* gives unions the right to file grievances on their own behalf if they feel their rights have been violated. It also gives unions access to information necessary to process the grievance or to make sure the agreement is not being violated. In addition, unions may file grievances for violations of union shop or checkoff provisions. On the other hand, employees have the right to present their *own* grievances on an individual basis, and the employer can resolve that grievance without the union's presence. The only qualifying items are that adjustments cannot abrogate the collective agreement, and the union must be given an opportunity to participate in the grievance proceedings at some point prior to the adjustment.

Occasionally, other activities prompt grievances. Wildcat strikes or behavior that functions as a strike (mass absences from work, for example) can result in a management grievance. Increasingly, outsourcing and replacement workers are issues resulting in grievances.

Management Procedures

Management can significantly affect the grievance rate by adopting proper procedures for taking action against an employee. One of the most important procedures involves that of discipline and discharge. The issue of just cause and fairness is central to most discipline grievances. Employers must ensure that the employee is adequately warned of the consequences, that the rule involved is related to operation of the company, that a thorough investigation is undertaken, and that the penalty is reasonable. In areas outside of discipline and discharge, management can avoid grievance problems by educating supervisors and managers about labor relations and about the

■□*fast fact*

Doctors in 46 primary care clinics in Washington State decided to unionize after their H.M.O. employer ordered some doctors to increase their hours of scheduled appointments from 32 to 36 per week.

■□*fast fact*

After Douglas McCarron became president of the United Brotherhood of Carpenters, he followed the advice of a management consultant about how to restructure his staff: he fired or retired a third of his staff and outsourced several functions.

conditions of the collective agreement. It has been found that supervisors with labor knowledge are an important factor in the reduction of grievances.

Union Procedures

The union has an obligation to its members to provide them fair and adequate representation and to process and investigate grievances brought by its members speedily. Thus it should have a grievance-handling procedure that aids in effectively processing grievances without being guilty of unfair representation. Unfair representation, according to the NLRB, is usually related to one of four types of union behavior:

1. *Improper motives.* The union cannot refuse to process a grievance because of the employee's race or gender or because of the employee's attitude toward the union.
2. *Arbitrary conduct.* Unions cannot dismiss a grievance without investigating its merits.
3. *Gross negligence.* The union cannot recklessly disregard the employee's interests.
4. *Union conduct after filing the grievance.* The union must process the grievance to a reasonable conclusion.[60]

Because the employer can also be cited for unfair representation, management should attempt to maintain a fair grievance process. Company labor relations managers should avoid taking advantage of union errors in handling grievances so that this action does not affect fair representation.

Another important influence on the grievance process is the union steward. Since the union steward is generally the first person to hear about an employee's grievance, the steward has substantial influence on the grievance process. A steward can either encourage an employee to file a grievance, suggest that the problem is really not a grievance, or informally resolve the problem outside the grievance procedure. The personalities of stewards may, in fact, influence the number of grievances filed.[61] Because stewards are selected from the ranks of employees and may have little knowledge of labor relations, the union should train them to improve their effectiveness. The company can also be liable in a fair-representation suit and therefore should support such training.

ASSESSMENT OF COLLECTIVE BARGAINING

The effectiveness of the entire collective bargaining process and the union-management relationship can be measured by the extent to which each party attains its goals, but this approach has its difficulties. Because goals are incompatible in many cases and can therefore lead to conflicting estimates of effectiveness, a more useful measure may be the quality of the system used to resolve conflict. Conflict is more apparent in the collective bargaining process, where failure to resolve the issues typically leads to strikes. Another measure of effectiveness is the success of the grievance process, or the ability to resolve issues developing from the bargaining agreement.

Effectiveness of Negotiations

Because the purpose of negotiations is to achieve an agreement, the agreement itself becomes an overall measure of bargaining effectiveness. A healthy and effective bargaining process encourages the discussion of issues and problems and their subsequent resolution at the bargaining table. In addition, the effort required to reach agreement is a measure of how well the process is working. Some indications of this effort are the duration of negotiations, the outcome of member ratification votes, the frequency and duration of strikes, the use of mediation and arbitration, the need for government intervention, and the quality of union-management relations (whether conflict or cooperation exists). Joint programs for productivity and quality-of-work-life improvements could be regarded as successes resulting from effective union-management relations.

Effectiveness of Grievance Procedures

The success of a grievance procedure may be assessed from different perspectives. Management may view the number of grievances filed and the number settled in its favor as measures of effectiveness, with a small number filed or a large number settled in its favor indicating success. Unions may also consider these numbers, but from their point of view, a large number filed and a large number settled in their favor may indicate success.

An overall set of measures to gauge grievance procedure effectiveness may be related to the disagreements between managers and employees. Measures that might be included are frequency of grievances; the level in the grievance procedure at which grievances are usually settled; the frequency of strikes or slowdowns during the term of labor agreements; the rates of absenteeism, turnover, and sabotage; and the necessity for government intervention.

The success of arbitration is often judged by the acceptability of the decisions, the satisfaction of the parties, the degree of innovation, and the absence of bias in either direction. The effectiveness of any third-party intervention rests in part on how successfully strikes are avoided, because the motivation for such intervention is precisely to avert this extreme form of conflict resolution.

SUMMARY

Line managers and HR professionals need to know as much as possible about unionization because the stakes are substantial. Employees are generally attracted to unionization because they are dissatisfied with work conditions and feel powerless to change these conditions. By correcting unsatisfactory work conditions, or by not allowing them to occur in the first place, organizations help prevent unions from becoming attractive. However, once a union-organizing campaign begins, a company cannot legally stop it without committing an unfair labor practice.

Historically, unions and management have operated as adversaries because many of their goals are in conflict, but because conflict is detrimental to both management and unions, effective labor relations have been established to reduce this conflict. Although cooperation is not widespread, it may be the style of union-management relations in the future. Its effects are particularly apparent in collective bargaining, contract negotiation, and grievance processing.

The quality of the union-management relationship can have a strong influence on contract negotiations. Labor and management each select a bargaining committee to negotiate the new agreement. The negotiations may be between a single union and a single company or multiple companies, or between multiple unions and a single company. Bargaining issues are mandatory, permissive, or prohibited. Mandatory issues must be discussed, permissive issues can be discussed if both parties agree to do so, and prohibited issues can't be discussed. The issues can be grouped into wage, economic supplement, institutional, and administrative issues.

Almost all labor contracts outline procedures for handling employee complaints. The most common grievance is related to discipline and discharge, although wages, promotions, seniority, vacations, holidays, and management and union rights are also sources of complaints.

The effectiveness of collective bargaining and contract administration is usually assessed by measures of how well the process is working. Bargaining can be evaluated using measures such as the duration of negotiations, the frequency of strikes, the use of third-party intervention, and the need for government intervention. The effectiveness of the grievance process can be assessed by the number of grievances; the level in the grievance process at which settlement occurs; the frequency of strikes or slowdowns; the rates of absenteeism, turnover, and sabotage; and the need for government intervention.

Finally, as economic conditions in the world have changed substantially, so have union-management relations. Much more cooperation exists. Management sees cooperative relationships as instrumental in the implementation of quality-improvement strategies. Unions see cooperative relationships as instrumental in protecting the jobs and incomes of their members. And society as a whole sees cooperative relationships as necessary and appropriate in these times of intense global competition. Thus, with some exceptions, we are likely to see cooperative relationships continue in the 21st century.

TERMS TO REMEMBER

AFL-CIO
Arbitration
Authorization cards
Bargaining unit
Boycott
Certification election
Collective bargaining
Concessionary bargaining
Coordinated bargaining
Decertification
Distributive bargaining
Essentiality
Exclusivity
Final offer arbitration
Grievance arbitration
Industrywide bargaining
Integrative bargaining
Lockout
Mediation

Multiemployer bargaining
Pattern settlements
Permissible issues
Pre-election campaign
Prohibited issues
Psychological contract
Right-to-work laws
Slowdown
Steward
Strike
Union
Union instrumentality
Union salting
Union shops
Unionization
Wide-area and multicraft
    bargaining
Whipsaw
Work slowdown

DISCUSSION QUESTIONS

1. How can the UAW and UPS work together even more effectively than they are today?

2. Identify and discuss the conditions that make unionization attractive to employees. Are these conditions different today than they were fifty years ago?

3. What is a certification election? a decertification election?

4. What is the structure of unionization in the United States today?

5. What is a bargaining unit? Why is its formation important?

6. Why has there been a trend toward cooperation between unions and management?

7. What are the steps in a typical grievance procedure?

8. Distinguish among mandatory, permissive, and prohibited bargaining issues.

9. Distinguish mediation from arbitration. How does a grievance procedure differ from interest arbitration? What is final-offer arbitration?

PROJECTS TO EXTEND YOUR LEARNING

1. **Managing Strategically.** At Southwest Airlines almost 80 percent of its employees are members of unions. Yet, the employees are among the most productive in the industry and have a tremendous sense of pride and respect for the company and for Herb Kelleher. The company puts a great deal of value on the employees and the unions as key stakeholders in the success of the airlines. And it treats the employees and deals with the unions as if it means it! This fits with the overall model the company uses, which is: employee satisfaction leads to customer satisfaction which leads to profitability. Employees and the unions are strategic partners at Southwest Airlines (**www.iflyswa.com**). Identify other companies that do the same. Perhaps start your search in *Fortune* magazine's Most Admired companies (**www.fortune.com**). Look at the names of the companies in Robert Levering's book *The 100 Best Companies to Work for in America*. Determine what makes company-employee-union relationships so good.

2. **Managing Teams.** Do unions resist team-based job design? Do unions do better when jobs are designed around the individual, and are narrowly defined rather than around the team and are more enriched? UPS designs many of its jobs around the individual using principles of scientific management. Ford Motor Company and the Cadillac division of General Motors design many of their jobs around teams and give the workers opportunity for participation and variety. So is job design really irrelevant to whether or not unions are attractive to the employees? Obtain more information on the relationship between job design and the attraction of unionization. What would you recommend to employers who want to remain union-free to design their jobs around teams? Examine UPS, Ford, and General Motors at
   www.ups.com
   www.ford.com
   www.gm.com

3. **Managing Globalization.** As companies go global, what do unions do? Should they resist the efforts of firms to go global? If firms say they have to move operations to stay competitive, what should unions do? If firms say they have to expand operations abroad to serve distant markets employing local workers, what should unions do? If firms who are unionized here say they have to expand abroad, but would prefer to have no union representation there, what should unions do? If firms say to their unions, "either the workers reduce their wage and benefit demands, or we'll move the operations outside the U.S.," what should the unions do? All of these are difficult but important questions for the union movement. But as importantly, especially if the firms want to treat their unions as strategic partners, how should companies behave in the global marketplace? Should they use the same labor-management practices abroad that they use in the U.S.? To learn about the positions of several labor organizations, visit
   The AFL-CIO at **www.aflcio.org**
   Also visit Labor Net at **www.igc.org**
   and the International Labor Organization at **www.ilo.gov**

4. **Managing Change.** Today's environment requires that firms not only be global, but that they are able to change rapidly. This means they need to move people around, train their employees to have new skills, and manage their employees so they aren't only able to change but willing to change as well. What's the role of the union here? Should companies that are unionized work closely with the union so that together they create a workforce that's ready and willing to change and adapt to new conditions? Are unions responsible for making sure that companies don't expect more from their employees than they are capable of providing? Companies like Ford and Cadillac have successfully adopted total quality management principles working with the unions. What did they do to help ensure that the process went smoothly? Identify companies that have been changing and determine what they do with the unions to help ensure a true cooperative partnership in navigating through organizational change. Visit the web sites of the
   UAW at **www.uaw.org**
   and the National Labor Relations Board at **www.nlrb.gov**

5. **Managing Diversity.** What should be the union's position regarding a firm's effort at developing a highly diverse organization? If they want to be helpful, what can they do? Should they at least serve as a role model, that is, be highly diverse and manage their diversity well? What type of diversity do unions have today? Contact local or national unions such as the AFL-CIO, the Teamsters or the United Auto Workers to discuss these questions.

6. **Integration and Application.** Using the cases at the end of the text, compare and contrast Lincoln Electric and Southwest Airlines with regard to

   - the views of management regarding union representation of their workers,
   - the views of employees regarding union representation, and
   - the consequences of these views for cooperation and conflict between employees and management.

   What changes in the environment or the company might lead Lincoln Electric's employees to become more interested in unionization? How likely do you think such changes are to occur?

CASE STUDY

The Union's Strategic Choice

Maria Dennis sits back and thoughtfully reads through the list of strategies that the union's committee gave her this morning. If her union is to rebuild the power it has lost over the past few years, it's time to take drastic action. If the union continues to decline as it has the last few years, it won't be able to represent the members who voted for it to be their exclusive bargaining representative.

Maria was elected two years ago, at her union's convention, to be the international president of the Newspaper Workers International Union (NWIU). At the time, she knew it would not be an easy job, and she eagerly looked forward to taking on a new challenge. But she had no idea just how difficult it would be to get the union back on its feet again.

The NWIU was founded in the late 1890s, made up of newspaper typographers who were responsible for such tasks as setting type on linotype machines, creating the layout of the newspaper, proofing the articles, and printing the newspaper. Members of the union typically completed a six-year apprenticeship, learning all the different tasks involved in the printing process. Before 1960, printing professionals were considered the elite of the industrial workforce. The craft demanded that typographers be literate at a time when even the middle and upper classes were not. Furthermore, printing was a highly skilled, highly paid craft.

Since the 1970s, however, the union has declined. Literacy is no longer a unique characteristic, and automation has led to a deskilling of the craft. The introduction of video display terminals, optical character recognition scanners, and computerized typesetting has eliminated substantial composing room work, and the demand for skilled union workers has been reduced. The union experienced its peak membership of 120,000 in 1965. During the 1970s, membership began a substantial decline, and in 1988 the total membership was only 40,000. The reduced membership has resulted in other problems for the union. First, fewer members mean fewer dues, which are the union's main source of revenue. Consequently, the union is having some serious financial problems and is being forced to cut some of its services to members.

Second, the union is experiencing a significant loss in bargaining power with newspaper management. In the past, the printers were fairly secure in their jobs because there was a good demand in the labor market for individuals who could run the complicated printing equipment. But the recent switch to automation has eliminated many jobs and has also made it possible for employers to easily replace union employees. Anyone can be trained in a short time to use the new printing equipment. Therefore, if union members decide to strike for better wages, hours, and working conditions, management could easily, and legally, find replacements for them. In essence, the union is unable to fulfill its main mission, which is to collectively represent the employees who voted for it.

To solve the current crisis, Maria is considering five options:

1. Implement an associate member plan through which any individual could join the union for a fee of $50 a year. Although these members would not be fully represented on the job, they would get an attractive package of benefits, such as low-cost home, health, and auto insurance.

2. Attempt some cooperative labor-management relations programs, such as getting member representation on newspaper boards of directors or employee participation programs in the workplace.

3. Put more effort into political action. For example, lobby for labor law reform or for new laws more favorable to unions. Initiate action that would result in harsher penalties against employers that practice illegal union-avoidance activities, such as threatening to move the business if a union is voted in or firing pro-union employees.

4. Appeal to community leaders to speak out in favor of the union in order to improve public relations, to help recruit new members, and to encourage employers to bargain fairly when negotiating with the union.

5. Search for another union with which the printing professionals might merge, thus increasing their membership, strengthening their finances, increasing their bargaining power, and obtaining economies of scale.

Maria realizes that each of these options could have both positive and negative results, and is unsure which strategy, if any, she should recommend for the union to pursue. In less than three hours, however, she will have to present the list to the council with her recommendations.

QUESTIONS

1. What are the strengths and weaknesses of each strategy?

2. What strategies could be employed to get new bargaining units?

3. What other types of services could the union offer to its members?

4. What would be your final recommendation? Justify your response.

Source: K. Stratton-Devine, University of Alberta.

ENDNOTES

[1] R. J. Grossman, "Trying to Heal the Wounds," *HR Magazine* (September 1998): 85–92.

[2] R. J. Grossman, "Trying to Heal the Wounds;" D. A. Tosh, "After the UPS Strike," *ACA News* (October 1997): 11–14.

[3] "GM Saturn Workers Weigh Innovative Labor Accord," *The Wall Street Journal* (February 18, 1998): B6; R. Kuttner, "Unions Are Good For the U.S.—and Clinton Should Say So," *Business Week* (October 7, 1996): 23; A. R. McIlvaine, "The Comeback Trail," *Human Resource Executive* (November 1997): 55–58.

[4] For a more extensive discussion of unionization and the entire union-management relationship, see G. Strauss, D. G. Gallagher, and J. Fiorito, *The State of the Unions* (Madison, WI: Industrial Relations Research Association, University of Wisconsin, 1991); P. C. Weiler, *Governing the Workplace* (Cambridge, MA: Harvard University Press, 1990); J. A. Fossum, *Labor Relations: Development, Structure, Process*, 7th ed. (Plano, TX: Business Publications, 1998).

[5] For an overview and in-depth discussion of collective bargaining, see L. Balliet, *Survey of Labor Relations* (Washington, DC: Bureau of National Affairs, 1981); R. B. Freeman and J. L. Medoff, *What Do Unions Do*? (New York: Basic Books, 1984); R. J. Donovan, "Bringing America into the 1980s," *American Psychologist* (April 1984): 429–431; J. A. Fossum, "Labor Relations," *Human Resource Management in the 1980s,* S. J. Carroll and R. S. Schuler, eds. (Washington, DC: Bureau of National Affairs, 1983); B. E. Kaufman, *The Origins and Evolution of the Field of Industrial Relations* (Ithaca, NY: ILR Press, 1993).

[6] Tosh, "After the UPS Strike; " M. J. Koch and G. Hundley, "The Effects of Unionism on Recruitment and Selection Methods," *Industrial Relations* 36 (3) (July 1997): 349.

[7] Balliet, *Survey of Labor Relations*.

[8] D. P. Twomey, *Labor Law and Legislation* (Cincinnati, OH: South-Western College Publishing, 1998).

[9] C. McDonald, "U.S. Union Membership in Future Decades: A Trade Unionist's Perspective," *Industrial Relations* (Winter 1992): 13–30; A. Gladstone et al., eds., *Labour Relations in a Changing Environment* (New York: Walter de Gruyter,

1992); M. Bognanno and M. Kleiner, "Introduction: Labor Market Institutions and the Future Role of Unions," *Industrial Relations* (Winter 1992): 1–12; T. A. Kochan and P. Osterman, *The Mutual Gains Enterprise: Forging a Winning Partnership Among Labor, Management, and Government* (Boston: Harvard Business School Press, 1994); T. A. Kochan, R. B. McKersie, and P. Cappelli, "Strategic Choice and Industrial Relations Theory," *Industrial Relations* (Winter 1984): 16–38; A. L. Cowan, "Steel Pact Lets Union Name a Board Member," *New York Times* (August 1, 1993): L34.

[10] J. Barling, E. K. Kelloway, and E. H. Bremermann, "Preemployment Predictors of Union Attitudes: The Role of Family Socialization and Work Beliefs," *Journal of Applied Psychology* 75 (5) (1991): 725–731; S. Mellor, "The Relationship between Membership Decline and Union Commitment: A Field Study of Local Unions in Crisis," *Journal of Applied Psychology* 75 (3) (1990): 258–267; C. Fullagar and J. Barling, "A Longitudinal Test of a Model of the Antecedents and Consequences of Union Loyalty," *Journal of Applied Psychology* 74 (2) (1989): 213–227; S. P. Deshpande and J. Fiorito, "Specific and General Beliefs in Union Voting Models," *Academy of Management Journal* 32 (4) (1989): 883–897; G. E. Fryxell and M. E. Gordon, "Workplace Justice and Job Satisfaction as Predictors of Satisfaction with Union and Management," *Academy of Management Journal* 32 (4) (1989): 851–866.

[11] E. H. Schein, *Organizational Psychology* (Englewood Cliffs, NJ: Prentice-Hall, 1965).

[12] J. G. Getman, S. B. Goldberg, and J. B. Herman, *Union Representation Elections: Law and Reality* (New York: Russell Sage Foundation, 1976); "Employee Survey: Unionization and Attitude Measure," *Bulletin to Management* (April 24, 1986): 133–134.

[13] A. Ritter, "Are Unions Worth the Bargain?" *Personnel* (February 1990): 12–14; J. M. Brett, "Behavioral Research on Unions and Union-Management Systems," *Research in Organizational Behavior,* vol. 2, B. M. Staw and L. L. Cummings, eds. (Greenwich, CT: JAI Press, 1980); J. M. Brett, "Why Employees Want Unions," *Organizational Dynamics* 8 (1980): 47–59.

[14] S. A. Youngblood et al., "The Impact of Work Attachment, Instrumentality Beliefs, Perceived Labor Union Image, and Subjective Norms on Union Voting Intentions and Union Membership," *Academy of Management Journal* (1984): 576–590.

[15] T. A. Kochan, *Collective Bargaining and Industrial Relations* (Homewood, IL: Irwin, 1980); J. LeLouarn, *Proceedings of the 32nd Annual Meeting of the Industrial Relations Research Association* (1979): 72–82.

[16] Barling, Kelloway, and Bremermann, "Preemployment Predictors of Union Attitudes: The Role of Family Socialization and Work Beliefs," 725–731.

[17] A. A. Sloane and F. Witney, *Labor Relations,* 5th ed. (Englewood Cliffs, NJ: Prentice-Hall, Inc., 1985): 57.

[18] Sloane and Witney, *Labor Relations,* 62.

[19] J. W. Wimberly, "State of the Unions," *Human Resource Executive* (September 1998): 90–91; G. Burkins, "Union Membership Fell Further in 1997," *The Wall Street Journal* (March 18, 1998): A2, A8; S. Greenhouse, "Gains Put Unions At Turning Point, Many Experts Say," *New York Times* (September 1, 1997): A1, A20; "Union Membership Fell Again in 1997," *Bulletin to Management (February 26,* 1998): 61; "Union Membership By State and Industry," *Bulletin to Management* (June 12, 1997): 188–189; "Union Membership By State and Industry," *Bulletin to Management* (May 29, 1997): 172–173; "Union Membership and Earnings," *Bulletin to Management* (February 13, 1997): 52–53. For an extensive presentation of union membership data, see C. D. Gifford, ed., *Directory of U. S. Labor Organizations,* 1997-98 Edition (Washington, DC: Bureau of National Affairs, 1998); and B. T. Hirsch and D. A. Macpherson, *Union Membership and Earnings Data Book,* 1998 Edition (Washington, DC: Bureau of National Affairs, 1998).

[20] G. Burkins, "Number of Workers in Labor Unions Grew Last Year," *The Wall Street Journal* (January 26, 1999): B2; D. Whitford, "Labor's Lost Chance," *Fortune* (September 28, 1998): 177–182; S. Greenhouse, "Despite Efforts to Organize, Union Rosters Have Declined," *New York Times* (March 22, 1998): 21; "More Women Leading Unions," *Fair Employment Practices Guidelines* (November 22, 1990): 141; J. G. Kilgour, "The Odds on White-Collar Organizing," *Personnel* (August 1990): 29–34.

[21] M. B. Regan, "Shattering the AFL-CIO's Glass Ceiling," *Business Week* (November 13, 1998): 46; A. Bernstein, "Sweeney's Blitz," *Business Week* (February 17, 1997): 56–62; A. Bernstein, "Andy Stern's Mission Impossible," *Business Week* (June 10, 1996): 73; A. Bernstein, "Wireless Workers Get Connected," *Business Week* (May 26, 1997): 160; J. E. Lyncheski and J. M. McDermott, "Unions Employ New Growth Strategies," *HR Focus* (September 1996): 22–23.

[22] Gifford, *Directory of U. S. Labor Organizations, 1997–1998 Edition.*

[23] A. B. Shostak, *CyberUnion: Empowering Labor Through Computer Technology* (M. E. Sharpe, 1999); Balliet, *Survey of Labor Relations,* 72–105.

[24] G. Flynn, "HR in Mexico: What You Should Know," *Personnel Journal* (August 1994): 34, and C. R. Greer and G.

[25] K. Stephens, "Employee Relations Issues for U.S. Companies in Mexico," *California Management Review* 38 (3) (Spring 1996): 121–145; S. Dolan and R. S. Schuler, *Human Resource Management* (Toronto: Nelson, 1994); G. Smith, S. Baker, and W. Glasgall, "Mexico: Will Economic Reform Survive the Turmoil?" *Business Week* (April 11, 1994): 24–27; S. Baker, G. Smith, and E. Weiner, "The Mexican Worker," *Business Week* (April 19, 1993): 84–92; A. R. Myerson, "Big Labor's Strategic Raid in Mexico," *New York Times* (September 12, 1994): D1, D4.

[25] Getman, Goldberg, and Herman, *Union Representation Elections,* 1; B. P. Noble, "At the Labor Board, New Vigor," *New York Times* (September 4, 1994): F21.

[26] Prepared for this chapter by William D. Todor, Professor of HRM, The Ohio State University.

[27] "Unions Won More Representation Elections Than They Lost in 1997," *Bulletin to Management* (June 4, 1998): 173; G. Burkins, "Labor Plans to Shift to Its Foot Soldiers in 1998's Congressional Campaigns," *The Wall Street Journal* (January 20, 1998): A20; S. Greenhouse, "Renewed Push in New York: More Union Cards in Wallets," *New York Times* (May 30, 1997): A1, B2; W. E. Fulmer, "Step by Step Through a Union Campaign," *Harvard Business Review* (July–August 1981): 94–102.

[28] C. R. Fine, "Beware the Trojan Horse," *Workforce* (May 1998): 45–51; "Dealing with Organizing: Do's and Don'ts," *Bulletin to Management* (March 7, 1985): 8.

[29] J. Hoerr, "The Strange Bedfellows Backing Workplace Reform," *Business Week* (April 20, 1990): 57. See also R. Koenig, "Quality Circles Are Vulnerable to Union Tests," *The Wall Street Journal* (March 28, 1990): B1; L. E. Hazzard, "A Union Says Yes to Attendance," *Personnel Journal* (November 1990): 47–49; Twomey, *Labor Law and Legislation,* 134.

[30] Getman, Goldberg, and Herman, *Union Representation Elections,* 72.

[31] Brett, "Behavioral Research on Unions and Union-Management Systems," 200.

[32] M. Estes, "Adversaries Find Common Ground," *Workforce* (March 1997): 97–102; A. Bernstein, "Look Who's Pushing Productivity," *Business Week* (April 7, 1997): 72–73; V. Zinno, "Relations in Labor," *Human Resource Executive* (August 1996): 28–30. See N. Herrick, *Joint Management and Employee Participation: Labor and Management at the Crossroads* (San Francisco: Jossey-Bass, 1990); Brett, "Behavioral Research on Unions and Union-Management Systems;" Brett, "Why Employees Want Unions," 47–59.

[33] K. Bradsher, "Saturn Plant's Union Leaders Voted Out," *New York Times* (February 26, 1999): C1, C5; R. Meredith, "Many at the Saturn Auto Factory Are Finding Less to Smile About," *New York Times* (March 6, 1998): A1, D2; R. Meredith, "Saturn Union Votes to Retain Its Cooperative Company Pact," *New York Times* (March 12, 1998): D1, D4; D. Woodruff, "At Saturn, What Workers Want Is . . . Fewer Defects," *Business Week* (December 2, 1991): 117–118; K. Kerwin, "Why Didn't GM Do More For Saturn," *Business Week* (March 16, 1998): 62; "Saturn Workers to Take Contract Vote," *USA Today* (March

9, 1998); K. Naughton and K. Kerwin, "At GM, Two Heads May Be Worse Than One," *Business Week* (August 14, 1995): 46; B. Vlasic, W. Symonds, and K. Naughton, "The Big Squeeze On GM," *Business Week* (October 21, 1996): 32–34; B. Vlasic and A. Bernstein, "Why Ford is Riding Shotgun For the UAW," *Business Week* (March 17, 1997): 112; J. Fox, "First: The UAW Makes Nice," *Fortune* (October 28, 1996): 28–30; B. Vlasic, "Bracing for the Big One," *Business Week* (March 25, 1996): 34–35.

34 J. T. Delaney, "Workplace Cooperation: Current Problems, New Approaches," *Journal of Labor Research* 17 (1) (Winter 1996): 45–61; T. Kochan, "Creating a Labor Policy for the 1990s," *Boston Globe* (September 12, 1995): 40; D. Q. Mills, *The New Competitors* (New York: Free Press, 1985): 225–242; M. Schuster, "The Impact of Union-Management Cooperation on Productivity and Employment," *Industrial and Labor Relations Review* (April 1983): 415–430; H. C. Katz, T. A. Kochan, and K. R. Gobeille, "Industrial Relations Performance, Economic Performance, and QWL Programs: An Interplant Analysis," *Industrial and Labor Relations Review* (October 1983): 3–17.

35 B. Vlasic and W. C. Symonds, "Sweet Deal," *Business Week* (September 30, 1996): 32–33; J. Flynn, S. Reed, and A. Barrett, "Give a Little, Get a Little in Detroit," *Business Week* (November 18, 1996): 56–57; K. Bradsher, "U.A.W.'s Pact At Ford Aims At Downsizing," *New York Times* (September 18, 1996): A1, D6; B. P. Noble, "More Than Labor Amity at AT&T," *New York Times* (March 14, 1993): F25. See also Chap. 6 in J. Pfeffer, *Competitive Advantage through People* (Boston: Harvard Business School Press, 1994).

36 H. Campbell, "Adventures in Teamland," *Personnel Journal* (May 1996): 56–62.

37 Adapted from R. Walton and R. B. McKersie, *A Behavioral Theory of Labor Negotiations* (New York: McGraw-Hill Book Co., 1965): 43.

38 Fossum, *Labor Relations: Development, Structure, Process.*

39 A. Blum, "Collective Bargaining: Ritual or Reality?" *Harvard Business Review* (November–December 1961): 64.

40 M. H. Bazerman, *Judgment in Managerial Decision Making* (New York: Wiley, 1986); M. H. Bazerman and J. S. Carroll, "Negotiator Cognition," *Research in Organizational Behavior,* vol. 9, Cummings and Staw, eds.; M. H. Bazerman, T. Magliozzi, and M. A. Neale, "The Acquisition of an Integrative Response in a Competitive Market," *Organizational Behavior and Human Decision Processes* 34 (1985): 294–313.

41 M. Winerip, "A Union Standing Fast Now Stands to Lose," *New York Times* (June 12, 1996): A16; K. Jennings and E. Traynman, "Two-Tier Plans," *Personnel Journal* (March 1988): 56–58.

42 Sloan and Witney, *Labor Relations.*

43 Fossum, "Labor Relations," 395–396.

44 P. Hartman and W. Franke, "The Changing Bargaining Structure in Construction: Wide-Area and Multicraft Bargaining," *Industrial and Labor Relations Review* (January 1980): 170–184.

45 Sloan and Witney, *Labor Relations,* 59.

46 Hartman and Franke, "The Changing Bargaining Structure in Construction."

47 Fossum, *Labor Relations.*

48 M. Bazerman and M. A. Neale, "Heuristics in Negotiation: Limitations to Effective Dispute Resolution," *Negotiating in Organizations,* M. Bazerman and R. Lewick, eds. (Beverly Hills, CA: Sage, 1983): 51–67; M. Gordon et al., "Laboratory Research in Bargaining and Negotiations: An Evaluation," *Industrial Relations* (Spring 1984): 218–223; R. E. Walton and R. B. McKersie, *A Behavioral Theory of Labor Negotiations* (New York: McGraw-Hill, 1965).

49 M. Neale, V. Huber, and G. Northcraft, "The Framing of Negotiations: Contextual Versus Task Frame," *Organizational Behavior and Human Decision Processes* 39 (1987): 228–241.

50 "Union Growth–Learn the Signs and How to Prevent It," *HR Reporter* 14 (12) (December 1997): 5; L. Reynolds, "Management—Labor Tensions Spell Union Busting," *Personnel* (March 1991): 7–10; "Teamsters Hope Democracy Brings New Membership," *Personnel* (March 1991): 1–2; B. Schiffman, "Tougher Tactics to Keep Out Unions," *New York Times* (March 3, 1991): F8; "Lockout and Shutdowns," *Labor Relations Reporter* (Washington, DC: Bureau of National Affairs, 1985): 688–691.

51 S. Greenhouse, "Unions, Growing Bolder, No Longer Shun Strikes," *New York Times* (September 7, 1998): A12; B. P. Sunoo, "Managing Strikes, Minimizing Loss," *Personnel Journal* (January 1995): 50–60; D. Mitchell, "A Note on Strike Propensities and Wage Developments," *Industrial Relations* 20 (1981): 123–127; J. Kennan, "Pareto Optimality and the Economics of Strike Duration," *Journal of Labor Research* 1 (1980): 77–94.

52 D. Weimer, "A New Cat on the Hot Seat," *Business Week* (March 9, 1998): 56–61; A. Bernstein, "Why Workers Still Hold A Weak Hand," *Business Week* (March 2, 1998): 98; "Tentative Deal Reached by Caterpillar and the UAW," *Bulletin to Management* 49 (7) (February 19, 1998): 49; L. Uchitelle, "Labor Draws the Line in Decatur," *New York Times* (June 13, 1993): 3-1, 3-6; L. Uchitelle, "Strikes: They Don't Make 'Em Like They Used To," *New York Times* (August 21, 1994): E3.

53 J. Tasini, "For the Unions, a New Weapon," *New York Times Magazine* (June 12, 1988): 24–25, 69–71; C. Perry, *Union Corporate Campaigns* (Philadelphia: Wharton Industrial Relations Center, 1987).

54 S. Briggs, "Labor/Management Conflict and the Role of the Neutral," *Personnel and Human Resource Management,* 3rd ed., R. S. Schuler, S. A. Youngblood, and V. L. Huber, eds. (St. Paul, MN: West Publishing Co., 1988).

55 Johnson, "Interest Arbitration Examined"; "Collective Bargaining Through Diplomacy," *Bulletin to Management* (January 25, 1990): 32.

56 R. L. Blevins, "Maximizing Company Rights Under the Contract," *Personnel Administrator* (June 1984): 75–82; D. A. Hawver, "Plan before Negotiating . . . and Increase Your Power of Persuasion," *Management Review* (February 1984): 46–48; R. J. Colon, "Grievances Hinge on Poor Contract Language," *Personnel Journal* (September 1990): 32–36.

[57] K. E. Boroff and D. Lewin, "Loyalty, Voice, and Intent to Exit A Union Firm: A Conceptual and Empirical Analysis," *Industrial and Labor Relations Review* 51 (1) (October 1997): 50–63; S. Slichter, J. Healy, and E. Livernash, *The Impact of Collective Bargaining on Management* (Washington, DC: Brookings Institution, 1960): 694.

[58] B. Bemmels and J. R. Foley, "Grievance Procedure Research: A Review and Theoretical Recommendations," *Journal of Management* 22 (3) (1996): 359–384.

[59] Prepared by William D. Todor, Professor of HRM, The Ohio State University, for this chapter.

[60] Memorandum 79–55, *National Labor Relations Board* (July 7, 1979).

[61] D. R. Dalton and W. D. Todor, "Manifest Needs of Stewards: Propensity to File a Grievance," *Journal of Applied Psychology* (December 1979): 654–659.

THE HR PROFESSION

> *"Over the past few years, the Levi Strauss organization has linked its HR department and practices closely to the business: HR participates in every major business decision, and every HR program directly supports a business goal. The payoff is enormous."*
>
> **Donna Goya**
> **Senior Vice President of Human Resources**[1]

Chapter Outline

MANAGING THROUGH PARTNERSHIP

at W. L. Gore

W. L. Gore & Associates, the company that manufactures GoreTex® and other fabric-based materials, doesn't have bosses and it doesn't have employees. Instead, consistent with their flat structure and culture of creativity, they employ sponsors and associates who have no specified job titles. Perhaps there is something about this approach to managing people that helps explain why Gore was listed as one of *Fortune*'s "The 100 Best Companies to Work For."

When Bill Gore, a research chemist, left his job of 17 years at DuPont to found the company, he worked out of his home's basement. Now, more than 50 years later, some 200 Gore manufacturing plants operate in 45 countries. Regardless of their location, all Gore work sites reflect the company's core values:

1. Fairness to each other and everyone with whom we come in contact.
2. Freedom to encourage, help, and allow other associates to grow knowledge, skill, and scope of responsibility.
3. The ability to make one's own commitments and keep them.
4. Consultation with other associates before undertaking actions that could impact the reputation of the company by hitting it "below the water line."

HR professionals serve as caretakers of these values. "Day in and day out, we're champions of the culture, guaranteeing the consideration for people plays into business decisions," says HR leader Sally Gore.

At W. L. Gore, the structure of HR activities facilitates their success. Each plant is essentially self-sufficient, with at least one dedicated HR generalist located on-site. In addition to serving as a member of the leadership team, the HR generalist is responsible for staff development, staff allocation, and conflict resolution. "They're the ones who make sure we're being fair (value #1) and creating an environment people want to work in, which is critical to getting business results," observed business leader Terri Kelly.

Supporting the HR generalists out in the plants are HR specialists, located in the corporate headquarters in Delaware. Regardless of where they are located, however, HR generalists and specialists often work together on special project teams. Gore refers to this structure as a "Lattice." Just as a garden trellis might support the growth of a rambling rose, Gore's Lattice structure is designed to support the growth and development of HR practices and decisions that complement the needs of the business.

To understand how the Lattice structure works, consider what happens when a plant leadership position needs to be filled. Recruitment and hiring for the position is carried out by a team that includes other plant leaders, the HR generalist at the plant, and one or more specialists from headquarters. The business leaders define their needs and the HR professionals help them meet those needs through the use of effective recruitment and selection procedures. Those procedures recognize the importance of finding talent that is both technically competent and appropriate for the culture. HR knows that the needs of the business are changing rapidly, so new hires must be agile and willing to learn new skills. When people are hired, they make commitments to perform within a general functional area (value #3)—they aren't hired to fill a specific job title.

Compensation activities are carried out in a similar way. A team comprised of leaders within the company, one or more HR generalists, and compensation specialists make the compensation decisions. HR's role is to ensure the process is fair—that is, it must be based on performance and contribution to the business and it must be externally competitive. "Our compensation practice is a good example of our principle in action day to day," says HR associate Jackie Brinton. "It's our goal to pay people based on the success of the business, and that's fair. People make their own commitments and that affects their contribution." Stock ownership and profit sharing plans further support this philosophy.

As Sally Gore knows, this democratic, high-involvement approach to HR has costs as well as benefits. Conducting HR through partnership takes time and costs money. But in the end, Gore believes "the quality of life is far better than what you'll find in a dictatorship."[2]

To learn more about W. L. Gore & Associates, visit the company home page at **gore.com** (NOTE: There is no "www" in this address.)

As the experience of W. L. Gore highlights, HR professionals can contribute to—even determine—the success (or failure) of an organization. Members of a company's HR staff, working with external HR consultants and vendors, can help ensure that the needs of the business *and* the needs of employees are reflected in HR policies, mission statements, and practices. These are central to the coordination and operation of an organization. At W. L. Gore, HR professionals help the firm satisfy its key stakeholders.

The human resource department is the group formally established by an organization to help manage the organization's people as effectively as possible for the good of the employees, the company, and society. HR professionals include external consultants and service providers with HR expertise. As we have emphasized throughout this book, the managing of human resources gets done through a working partnership of HR professionals, line managers, and employees. At times, this partnership extends outside the organization—for example, as the firm strives to forge better working relationships with its suppliers.[3] It may also venture into local education facilities as the HR staff works with schools to prepare students for internships in the firm. And, increasingly, companies use HR consultants to help with activities such as compensation, benefits, training, recruiting and selection, and implementing large-scale organizational change.[4]

■□ *fast fact*

At Spectrum Signal Processing Inc., there is no HR department. Instead the 180 employees serve as rotating members of the company's HR committee.

HUMAN RESOURCE PROFESSIONALS PLAY MANY ROLES

In 1991, IBM and the internationally recognized HR consulting firm Towers Perrin conducted a study of nearly 3,000 senior HR managers and CEOs worldwide. Results indicated that a majority of HR managers saw the HR department as critical to the success of businesses in 1991, and even more expected it to be critical by the year 2000 (see Exhibit 16.1).[5] Without doubt, these expectations have come true: Charles Nielson, vice president of human resources at Texas Instruments has watched the profession's evolution for more than three decades: "I've been involved in the people business in one way or another for 35 years, and I'm having more fun today than I've ever had. . . . In the past, the HR function has been like a spare tire kept in the trunk. In an emergency, it's taken out, but as soon as the emergency's over, it's put away. Now I feel that we're a wheel running on the ground. We're not the HR we used to be, but in terms of partnering and helping our companies become competitive, we've only just begun. There are fun times ahead," he says.[6]

The fun comes in part from performing a broad variety of activities and playing a variety of roles. The effectiveness with which HR professionals

■□ *fast fact*

According to a poll of HR professionals, a meeting between the head of HR and the CEO occurs at least every day for one-third of companies, several times per week for about one-third of companies, and less than once per week for one-third of companies.

Exhibit 16.1
Expectations of the Effect of the Human Resource Department on Business Success

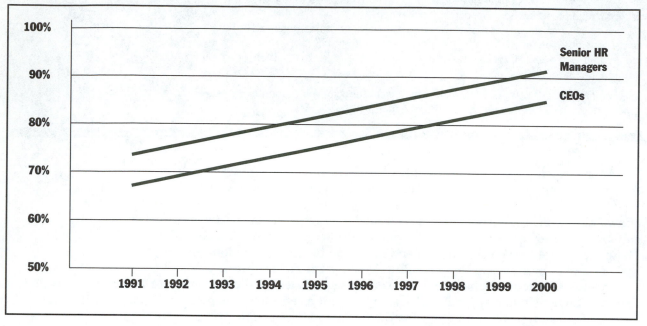

play all these roles depends on leadership effectiveness, the staffing of the department, and the department's organization.

Effective firms in the highly competitive environments of today encourage their HR departments and professionals to play all of the roles shown in Exhibit 16.2. The more roles they play well, the more likely they will be to help improve the organization's productivity, enhance the quality of work life in the organization, comply with all the necessary laws and regulations related to managing human resources effectively, gain competitive advantage, and enhance workforce flexibility, in essence, serve all the multiple stakeholders. Janet Brady, vice president of human resources at The Clorox Company, understands how challenging it can be to address the concerns of many different stakeholders:

> I serve the board of directors, executive management, general office employees, retirees, production and salespeople across the country, every type of function—and they all view HR slightly differently based on their backgrounds, their needs and their histories. That has told me there isn't a one-size-fits all solution. I've got to listen and ask questions, so that we can ultimately do something that's fair for everybody. HR can be very challenging because what we do can affect people at the most personal level and we can't lose sight of that.[7]

> "I'm probably speaking with our senior v.p. of human resources about 40 percent of my time."
>
> **Robert McDonald**
> **CEO, North America Division**
> **Standard Chartered**
> **Bank of New York**

Partnership Role

Traditionally, HR departments had limited involvement in the total organization's business affairs and goals. HR managers were often only concerned with making staffing plans, providing specific job training programs, or running annual performance appraisal programs (the results of which were sometimes put in the files, never to be used). They focused on the short-term—perhaps day-to-day—needs of human resources.

Exhibit 16.2
Key Roles for the HR Professional

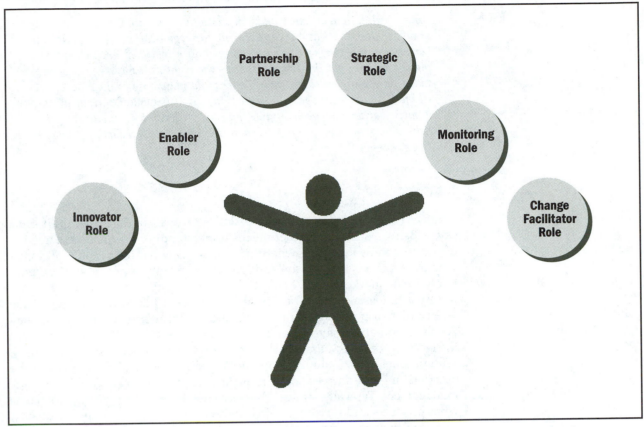

With the growing importance of human resources to the success of the firm (see Exhibit 16.1), HR managers and their departments have become more involved in the organization. They know the needs of the business and are helping address those needs.[8] More typical today, then, is the following observation by Jim Alef, executive vice president and head of human resources at First Chicago Corporation: "All of our HR programs serve the bank's mission. If they didn't, we wouldn't have them. In the last five years, we've become increasingly a part of the decision-making process at the bank," he says. "It's much more rewarding to be a thinking participant on the front end of a decision, rather than someone who undoes the damage created by those decisions."[9]

Throughout this book, we've emphasized the importance of the partnership role because we believe it is the key to long-term success for HR professionals. By performing this role well, HR professionals help organizations balance the sometimes competing concerns of "the business," as defined by line managers, and the employees upon whom business success ultimately depends.

John McMahon, corporate vice president of human resources for Stride Rite Corporation in Cambridge, Massachusetts, describes how his group partnered with the information systems (IS) group to strengthen the information systems department and at the same time improve the work environment for employees. The project involved creating state-of-the-art data

"HR people first get involved in strategic planning in areas that are most closely aligned with HR issues."

Diana Lewis
Vice President of HR
EcoLab

architecture, introducing participative management, creating more effective end-user computing environments, and establishing better business partnerships between IS employees and their internal customers.

What we did, from an HR standpoint, was to work with the vice president of information systems on restructuring his organization. We assessed the bench strength of current IS employees and established a developmental plan to ensure that the department has the right skill mix. Then, we provided counseling on career management and managing change, we assisted the IS management team in their transition from a non-participatory to a participative management style, and we conducted a climate survey to help managers assess the effectiveness and employee satisfaction related to these changes.10

Strategic Role

Tim Harris, senior vice president of HR at Novell in San Jose, California, says, "Being a strategic partner means understanding the business direction of the company, including what the product is, what it's capable of doing, who the typical customers are and how the company is positioned competitively in the marketplace."[11]

By acting as a strategic business partner, the HR department can provide real value to top management. As Richard A. Zimmerman, CEO of Hershey Foods Corporation, says, "There was a time when the HR department was the last to know. Now, the first thing you do is call human resources and say, 'Can you help me do things properly?'"[12] This process of linking HR to the broader, longer-term needs of firms is the essence of *strategic* human resource management. Typically, strategic business needs arise from decisions such as what products and services to offer and on what basis to compete—quality, cost, or innovation, or for purposes of survival, growth, adaptability, and profitability. These decisions are associated with the formulation and implementation of the organization's strategy, so they reflect characteristics of the external and internal environments.[13]

Enabler Role

In reality, human resource policies and practices succeed because line managers make them succeed. The HR professional's bread-and-butter job, therefore, is to enable line managers to make things happen. Thus, in traditional activities such as selecting, interviewing, training, evaluating, rewarding, counseling, promoting, and firing, the HR department is basically providing a service to line managers. In addition, the department administers direct and indirect compensation programs. It also assists line managers by providing information about, and interpretation of, equal employment opportunity legislation and safety and health standards.

To fulfill these responsibilities, the HR department must be accessible, or it will lose touch with the line managers' needs. The HR professionals should be as close as possible to the employees. Being accessible and providing services and products to others (customers) is a practice called customerization. *Customerization* means the state of viewing everybody, whether inside or outside the organization, as a customer and then putting that customer first. Through customerization, the professionals enable line managers and other employees to achieve their objectives. Essential to cus-

---

"We need to understand where our business is going five to six years down the road, and HR is crucial to understanding the changing demographics and expectations of our workforce."

**Mike Goodrich
CEO
BE&K**

■☐ *fast fact*

Two-thirds of senior HR managers are members of a senior policy-making committee and more than half regularly attend board meetings.

"We exist because of customers. They are our raison d'etre."

**Michael Mitchell
Vice-President of Human Resources
Tiffany & Company**

tomerization is the realization that all HR professionals produce and deliver products and have "customers."[14] So, too, is the realization that the products provided to satisfy the customer are determined with the customer. Together, in partnership, the customer and HR professional determine what is best for the situation.

Monitoring Role

Although HR professionals may delegate much of the implementation of HR activities to line managers, they remain responsible for seeing that HR programs are implemented fairly and consistently. Meeting this obligation requires monitoring the outcomes and effectiveness of all HR activities. This is especially true today because of fair employment legislation. Various state and federal regulations make sophisticated demands on organizations. Responses to these regulations are best made by a central group supplied with accurate information, the needed expertise, and the support of top management.

Monitoring the organization's compliance with legal regulations is not the only aspect of this role, however. As we have emphasized throughout the preceding chapters, HR professionals should continuously monitor the effectiveness of HR activities to ensure they are meeting the various and changing needs of both line managers and other employees.

Change Facilitator Role

It is increasingly necessary for organizations to adopt new technologies, structures, processes, cultures, and procedures to meet the demands of stiffer competition. Organizations look to the human resource department for the skills to facilitate organizational change and to maintain organizational flexibility and adaptability. One consequence of this change facilitator role is the need to be more focused on the future. For example, as the external environment and business strategies change, new skills and competencies are needed. To ensure that the right skills and competencies are available at the appropriate time, HR departments must anticipate change. The significant role that the HR department can play in creating organizational change is described in the feature, Managing Change: HR Supports New Business Principles at AT&T.[15]

Innovator Role

Today, organizations are asking their HR departments for innovative approaches and solutions to improve productivity and the quality of work life while complying with the law in an environment of high uncertainty, energy conservation, and intense international competition. They are also demanding approaches and solutions that can be justified in dollars and cents. Past approaches do not always make the cut in this environment; innovation is no longer a luxury, it is a necessity.[16]

As part of the innovator role, HR should do more than help others innovate. It also can serve as a role model. HR departments face the same demands as their organizations. They must continually streamline their operations and redesign the way work gets done. Not waiting for mandated cutbacks, they review and evaluate expenses and implement incremental changes to become, and stay, lean. Flexible HR departments aggressively seek to be perceived as "bureaucracy busters," setting an example for other staff functions and line organizations.

"Retail is really tough right now. It's a quality of life issue. The question that we face is how to improve our employees' lifestyles. People don't want to work weekends and evenings, and that's the lifeblood of retail."

Craig Sturken
CEO
Farmer Jack Supermarkets

MANAGING CHANGE
HR Supports New Business Principles at AT&T

From hiring and firing to training and performance management, every HR activity influences human resources and, thus, the success or failure of most efforts for organizational change. Keeping HR systems aligned with business strategies such as total quality and customer-focused management is a major HR challenge in the 21st century. At AT&T's Global Business Communications Systems (GBCS), HR professionals facilitated the achievement of a new strategy by

- helping formulate the firm's strategic business principles,
- identifying an HR mission or culture consistent with the business needs,
- identifying the key strategic HR imperatives that result from the business principles and strategies, and
- developing and implementing HR initiatives and activities consistent with the HR culture.

HR professionals first helped develop the GBCS's key business principles and a corresponding set of seven organization values. Then, using input from other managers, they identified the key strategic HR imperatives. Line managers contributed by providing answers to questions such as:

- What are the specific HR implications of your business strategy and plan?
- What employee behaviors do you need in order to make the implementation of your business strategy and plan a success?
- What types of competencies not presently available will be needed?
- What action steps are you taking to ensure that these competencies will be available?
- What specific objectives do you have?
- What measures of success vis-a-vis the objectives are you using? What do you need from the HR department to help you be successful?

Based on their conversations with line managers, the HR professionals concluded that their own imperatives included taking ownership of business processes, increasing shareholder value, preparing the organization for global expansion, and maintaining high levels of personal competence, among other things.

At the same time, the HR group developed their own mission statement, which was:

> To create an environment where the achievement of business goals is realized through an acceptance of individual accountability by each Associate and his/her commitment to performance excellence.

With this foundation in place, GBCS's HR professionals then developed specific HR initiatives that would link HR with the business. The details of GBCS's business principles, strategic HR imperatives, HR mission, and HR initiatives are shown in Exhibit 16.3.

To learn about AT&T, visit the company home page at
www.att.com

Exhibit 16.3
GBCS's Human Resource Strategy and Planning Model

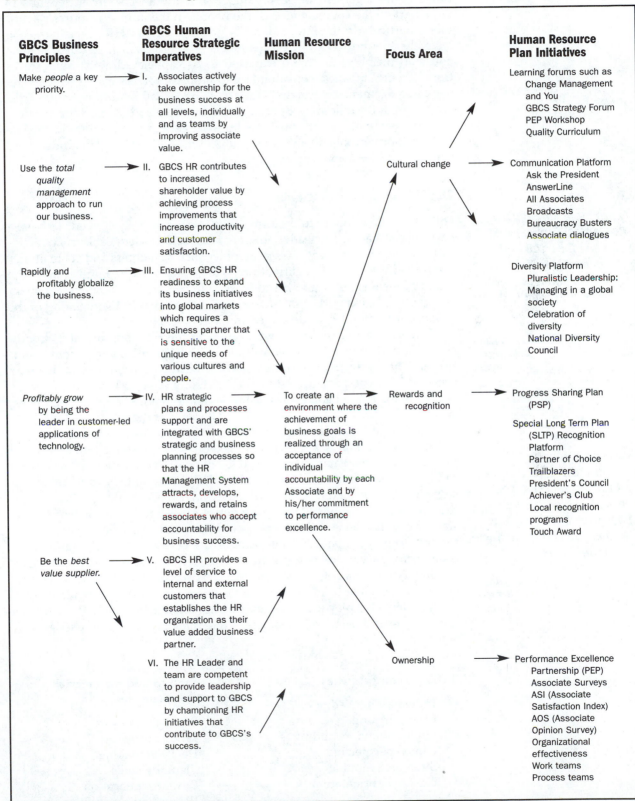

STAFFING THE HUMAN RESOURCE DEPARTMENT

Effective management of an organization's human resources depends in large part on the competencies of the people in the human resource department, particularly the HR leader, HR generalists, and HR specialists—collectively referred to as HR professionals. The top human resource leaders and staff members are often expected to be capable administrators, functional experts, business consultants, and problem solvers with global awareness. Management expects the HR staff "to have it all." Administrative skills are essential for efficiency. Specialized expertise also is important, particularly in combination with business knowledge and perspective. In flexible organizations, problem-solving and consulting skills are vital in guiding and supporting new management practices.

The Human Resource Leader

For the HR department to perform all its roles effectively, it needs to have a very special leader. The leader not only must be knowledgeable in HR activities but also must be well-versed in topics such as mergers and acquisitions, productivity, and total quality efforts. He or she must be familiar with the needs of the business and able to work side by side with line management as a partner. Being part of the management team shapes the meaning of the HR leader's key roles, as described in Exhibit 16.4.[17]

The most effective person who can head the HR department is an outstanding performer in the organization, with both HR management expertise and line management experience. To be a true professional in many areas of HR management, individuals virtually have to have an advanced degree in the subject and spend full time in that field. Areas like compensation have become incredibly complicated because of their close connection to strategic, legal, financial, and tax matters. Nevertheless, with the exception of technical specialists, HR managers need to spend a significant amount of time in line management positions. It is not enough for senior HR managers to have worked in different areas of the HR function; they must have had some line business experience so that they have a first-hand familiarity with the business operations.[18] Line experience gives the HR leader an understanding of the needs of the business and the needs of the department's customers. To prepare potential HR leaders, the HR department's staff should rotate through various line positions over several years. Short of actually serving as a line manager, such individuals could serve as special assistants to line managers or head up a special task force for a companywide project.

To effectively play the roles described in Exhibit 16.4, the HR leader in a highly competitive environment needs the following skills, knowledge, and abilities:

On the topic of effective HR leaders: "To succeed, you must have the ability to be persuasive and move the organization forward and to influence key business decisions."

Mike Bowlin
CEO
ARCO

Commenting on HR professionals:
"To really succeed, you have to be passionate about your work. You have to feel you can make a difference."

Mike R. Bowlin
CEO
ARCO

Business competencies

- Industry knowledge
- Company understanding
- Financial understanding
- Global perspective
- Strategic visioning
- Customer orientation

Leadership and managerial competencies

- Strategic analysis
- Problem solving
- Decision making
- Planning skills
- Resource allocation
- Persuasion capabilities

Exhibit 16.4
The Meaning of Key Roles for the HR Leader

Key Role	What Is Expected on the Job
Partnership	Shows concern for bottom line Understands how money gets made, lost, and spent Knows the market and what the business is Has a long-term vision of where the business is headed
Change Facilitator	Can execute change in strategy Can create sense of urgency Can think conceptually and articulate thoughts Has a sense of purpose—a steadfast focus, a definite value system
Enabler	Has the ability to build commitment into action Responds to organizational needs Recognizes the importance of teamwork Is capable of building relationships
Strategic	Is capable of educating line managers Knows the plan of top executives Is involved in the strategy formulation of the executive committee—is not an afterthought Develops and sells own plans and ideas—is able to get needed resources
Innovator	Sees the movement from an emphasis on strictly the numbers or bodies needed, to the type of talent and skills needed in the organization Sees the emphasis on talent needed for executing future strategies as opposed to today's needs Knows high-potential people and anticipates their concerns—for example, who is bright but bored
Monitoring	Is comfortable using and interpreting both "soft" and "hard" data Can creatively measure effectiveness in own areas of responsibility and other areas of the organization Can use automation effectively

Change management

- Consulting and influencing
- Group process facilitation
- Organization diagnosis
- Partnering and relationship building
- Designing and monitoring planned change efforts
- Assessing impact

Professional and technical competencies

- Organization and job design
- Staffing and workflow management

- Performance management
- Socialization/training/development
- Remuneration/reward/recognition systems
- Employee communications and involvement
- Succession planning
- Union relations
- Safety/health/wellness
- Diversity management
- Technological currency
- Strong personal and professional ethics

"The model I use in leadership is to try to paint a picture. I try to get people to think about what things could look like, so they can visualize it."

Janet M. Brady
Vice President Human Resources
The Clorox Co.

Some firms are now adopting procedures to identify competencies for their HR staff. At Weyerhaeuser, each major division, led by its human resources director, is responsible for developing a list of specific, required competencies. Of course, overlaps occur among major divisions. The HR directors help generate a slate of competencies based on their interviews with the "customers"—others in the organization—and HR professionals, and on their own requirements. The corporation is also aiming to predict future HR issues as a basis for updating human resources strategies and developing future competency requirements for HR staff.

The systematic preparation of a job description that captures all the required competencies helps firms, like Weyerhaeuser, that want to select their HR leaders from outside the organization. Exhibit 16.5 shows the extensive set of responsibilities for the senior HR leader in today's organization.

The Human Resource Staff

"We emphasize that an HR associate needs to understand fully the goals, challenges and financial position of his or her business to be an effective business partner."

Sally Gore
HR Leader
W. L. Gore & Associates

As the HR leader begins to play many of the roles listed in Exhibit 16.4, staff members must recognize this and adapt accordingly. After all, the leader is playing these roles because of the need to form a better link to the business, to be more effective, and to establish a partnership with the employees and the line managers. Just as the department and its leader must change, so must the staff members. Although they do not have the same responsibilities as their leader, the staff members still need to know the business, facilitate change, be conscious of costs and benefits, and work with line managers (this is probably more true for the generalist than for the specialist). The HR staff is active at the operational level and the managerial level, whereas most of the leader's time is spent at the strategic level and some at the managerial level.

In effective organizations, managers like the HR staff to work closely with them in solving people-related business challenges. Although line managers may best understand their own people, many desire the more distant perspective of HR staff in handling problems. As the HR staff actively builds working relationships with line management, the managers will find it easier to work with them as partners.

HR specialists and HR generalists are types of staff positions typically found in larger organizations. Human resource specialists can pursue their fields of specialization within a company and/or sell their expertise to external organizations as consultants. Generalists can remain in human resources and also occasionally serve on companywide task forces for special issues such as downsizing or capital improvement projects. Finally, as U.S. organizations become more global, opportunities for careers in international HR management will increase.[19] Most U.S. firms see growth coming from abroad, thereby, having overseas assignments may be a typical part of any manager's career.

Human Resource Generalists. Line management positions are one source for human resource generalists. HR generalists come from a variety of backgrounds: some are career HR professionals with degrees in business or psychology, some are former line managers who have switched fields, and some are line managers who are on a required tour of duty. As human resources becomes more heavily valued by organizations, required tours of duty by line managers will become more frequent. A brief tour by a line manager in an HR staff position conveys the knowledge, language, needs, and requirements

Exhibit 16.5
Position Description and Candidate Specifications

POSITION:	**Vice President, Human Resources**
COMPANY:	**Nationwide Clothing Retailer**
LOCATION:	**Midwestern United States**
REPORTS TO:	**President**

COMPANY

In an exciting, high growth, publicly held speciality retailer of quality casual, classic American sportswear that appeals to customers of all ages yet specifically targets people in their 20s. As the "keeper of the culture," the ideal candidate must strongly embody and reinforce the Company's unique brand image, which is casual, classic, and all-American.

Given the Company's distinctive culture and strong brand image, the Human Resource Department is critical to the continued success of the Company. The ideal candidate will bring a fresh and creative approach to the Human Resource Department to further the brand position through the recruitment, training, and motivation of all employees. The candidate must also be non-political and able to diplomatically voice his/her opinions while operating in a team-oriented environment.

Ideal Candidate Specifications:

·   Build upon a premiere recruiting program that reflects energy, vitality, and a team-oriented atmosphere.

·   Establish a process to identify and recruit the very best brand representatives (sales associates) to assure an ongoing flow of future talent for the business.

·   Institute a program of design training and establish a reputation in programs that assures that the Company becomes the number one choice of design graduates from the best schools in the country.

Professional Characteristics

·   Has built a strong career with either a "best of class" consumer or technology company that places a premium on attracting top talent or a premiere organizational consulting firm that has a strong human resource focus

·   Quickly understands the critical organizational structure and the Company's unique culture to assure the future growth of the business and its supporting mechanisms, i.e., recruiting, training, and succession planning and other key human resource aspects to accomplish this objective.

·   Successfully tailors a new compensation program that reflects shareholder value, corporate profitability, and individual unit/group objectives.

·   Able to partner with top management to bring a critical human resources perspective that complements the strategic, merchandising, business, and financial acumen of the company.

Personal Characteristics

·   Has a passion for the Company's distinctive and powerful lifestyle brand.

·   Has a "sixth sense" which allows him/her to grasp the inherent uniqueness of the Company's brand image and identify those same great qualities in prospective employees at all levels of the organization.

·   Thrives in a team-oriented and creative atmosphere but yet also has the ability to bring a tough perspective to top management in human resources and other business issues.

·   Takes a creative approach as a leader and partner with the Company's top management team.

of the line in a particularly relevant way. As a result, the HR department can more effectively fill its roles.

Human Resource Specialists. Human resource specialists should have skills related to a particular specialty, an awareness of the relationship of that specialty to other HR activities, and knowledge of where the specialized activity fits in the organization. Since specialists may work at almost any human resource activity, qualified applicants can come from specialized programs in law, organizational and industrial psychology, labor and industrial relations, HR management, counseling, organizational development, and medical and health science. In addition, specialists are needed in the newer areas of total quality management, service technologies, and information systems. With such rapid changes occurring in hardware and software technologies, the HR information systems manager is a particularly important HR specialist.

Typically, when organizations create an HRIS and/or an HR intranet, they need to have a specialist manage the area. Over the years, the role of this leader has changed from that of a project manager to that of a systems manager and now to that of a strategic change partner. An emerging trend is to see the specialist who manages HR technology playing a strategic rather than technical role. This new role asks the technology manager to be concerned not with how efficiently the department can store and retrieve information but with how HR information can be used strategically to create and manage organizational change.[20]

The role changes for the HRIS manager have paralleled those for the HR manager. Not surprisingly, they have also produced the same need for new competencies. Today's HRIS manager needs to be aware of the global environment and of the organization's needs to be global and act local. HR information systems can enable the organization to operate as a global organization and at the same time be sensitive to local conditions and needs. An HRIS can enable managers worldwide to tap into a database giving information about candidates to run an operation in a distant country, without their even knowing the candidates. It also requires managers to become concerned with issues of information security.[21]

According to Marc Tanzer, president of BCI/Information Security in Portland, Maine, "When corporate spies want confidential information, they often infiltrate HR departments first. A well-structured information-security program can keep spies from obtaining your company's secrets."[22] The names of employees, where they work, and what they do can be valuable information to other companies, especially competitors. Such information can be used to plan recruiting efforts to lure these people from their current employment. Organizations that value openness and access to information are especially vulnerable to this threat. Yet, if companies are to empower people, they often need to be open and allow access to information. Tandem Computers in Cupertino, California, handles this concern by

- creating an awareness among managers and employees that others could gain access to company information and data;
- tightening telephone security so that callers need to identify themselves and respond to the right screening questions;
- weeding out bogus job candidates—that is, those who are only going through the motions in order to gain access to information;
- adding more restrictions in confidentiality agreements—for example, when individuals join the firm, they can be asked to sign agreements not to reveal company secrets to others at any time, even if they leave; and

■□*fast fact*

TI's HR re-engineering effort was a total redesign of its HRIS systems. It now has a distributed, decentralized system, rather than a mainframe system, throughout its global operations.

- classifying information and restricting access using a need-to-know basis.

Not only can these programs limit the leakage of corporate information but they also can prevent unauthorized people from obtaining personal information about individual employees—not a trivial concern in today's atmosphere of rising employee violence and credit card scams.

Some say that restricting the type and amount of information collected reduces the potential for invasion of privacy. This solution has to be balanced against the HR department's need for information for its various programs. Family-friendly activities such as drug and alcohol abuse programs cannot take place without a sound database. Nor can the organization's numerous legal obligations be fulfilled without an effective HRIS. Some balance must be struck. The latest security must be used, and the environment must be continually scanned for the latest computer hacking scams—the best defense is a good offense.

Compensation of HR Staff

Human resource management is becoming very attractive as a field of employment. The results of a 1998 compensation survey, by types of jobs in a human resource department, show that HR jobs pay well.[23] In that survey, salaries were generally higher for individuals in larger organizations, for those with more experience, and for those with more education. In addition, salaries were higher in the South and Midwest. In other surveys, the senior HR person, sometimes called senior vice-president, was the highest paid individual in the survey, earning about $200,000 on average, including salary plus cash bonus and profit sharing. As is true for other managerial jobs, incentive pay is becoming a bigger part of the picture for top level HR executives, with about 40 percent being eligible for long-term incentive pay. In comparison, only about 20 percent of other HR managers and 5 percent of HR specialists are eligible for long-term incentive pay.[24]

PROFESSIONALISM IN HUMAN RESOURCE MANAGEMENT

Like any profession, HR management follows a code of ethics and has an accreditation institute and certification procedures. Together, these set standards for behavior that serve as useful guides to HR professionals.

Ethical Issues

The code of ethics for human resource professionals states that:

Practitioners must regard the obligation to implement public objectives and protect the public interest as more important than blind loyalty to an employer's preferences.

More specifically, in daily practice, HR professionals are expected to

- thoroughly understand the problems assigned and undertake whatever study and research are required to ensure continuing competence and the best of professional attention;
- maintain a high standard of personal honesty and integrity in every phase of daily practice;

"I went through a period of really agonizing over the behavior I was seeing—things I didn't expect to encounter."

Anonymous HR Professional

- give thoughtful consideration to the personal interest, welfare, and dignity of all employees who are affected by their prescriptions, recommendations, and actions; and
- make sure that the organizations that represent them maintain a high regard and respect for the public interest and that they never overlook the importance of the personal interests and dignity of employees.[25]

"It's comforting to know that ethical issues are out there and I'm not alone. But it's disheartening to know that they're so commonplace."

**Participant
On-line ethics bulletin board**

Increasingly, HR professionals are becoming involved in ethical issues. Some of the most serious issues center on differences in the way people are treated because of favoritism or a relationship to top management. In a survey conducted by the Society for Human Resource Management (SHRM) and the Commerce Case Clearing House (CCCH), HR professionals agreed that workplace ethics require people to be judged solely on job performance. Ethics requires managers to eliminate such things as favoritism, friendship, sex bias, race bias, or age bias from promotion and pay decisions (it is, of course, also unlawful to take sex, race, or age into account).[26]

Is ethics a "bottom line" issue? It becomes one when we consider that by acting in an ethical manner, companies will, in fact, hire, reward, and retain the best people. This will, in turn, help assure that the company has the best work force possible to achieve its business goals.[27] By adopting a definition of workplace ethics that centers on job performance, HR professionals may be in a better position to persuade others in the organization that making ethical behavior a priority will produce beneficial results.

Not all ethical issues affect the bottom line in the way that favoritism versus employee performance does, however, and to assume that a single policy can be devised to ensure that everyone in the organization always behaves ethically is unrealistic. People with different perspectives will inevitably view some situations differently. Even when they agree about basic values, such as the right of employees to be treated fairly, they may disagree about what constitutes fairness. For example, a Catholic nurse in Erie, Pennsylvania who was fired for refusing to hand out birth control pills and condoms felt she was unfairly terminated because of her religious beliefs, but her employer felt the nurse's behavior was unfair to patients. Such situations are common and unavoidable. Nevertheless, business ethics can be improved in a number of ways.

A good starting point for managing ethical issues is for top management to critically examine practices such as reward systems, managerial style, and decision-making processes. In some organizations, the reward system promotes unethical behavior by encouraging the achievement of organizational goals at almost any cost. Because of HR's traditional involvement in reward systems, HR has a natural role in encouraging ethical behavior.[28] But in the spirit of partnership, encouraging ethical behavior is a responsibility of all parties—the employees, line managers, and HR professionals. A result of this partnership might be the creation of an easy-to-use hot line and dissemination of standards that offer guidance on issues of ethical behavior.

Professional Certification

■□*fast fact*

Approximately 115,000 HR professionals are members of SHRM.

The Society for Human Resource Management (SHRM) has established the Human Resource Certification Institute to certify human resource professionals.[29] The institute's purposes are to

- recognize individuals who have demonstrated expertise in particular fields;

- raise and maintain professional standards;
- identify a body of knowledge as a guide to practitioners, consultants, educators, and researchers;
- help employers identify qualified applicants; and
- provide an overview of the field as a guide to self-development.

The certification institute has two levels of accreditation: basic and senior. The basic accreditation level is appropriate for all HR professionals. This designation requires an examination covering the general body of knowledge and four years of professional experience. A bachelor's degree in HR management or in the social sciences counts for two years of professional experience. The senior level accreditation is designed for the senior leaders in human resources. This accreditation requires a minimum of eight years of experience, with the three most recent years including policy development responsibilities. All professionals receiving accreditation are listed in the *Register of Accredited Personnel and Human Resource Professionals*.[30]

Toward Defining Global Competencies for HR Professionals

The globalization of business is putting HR professionals from around the world in almost daily contact with each other and with line managers representing many different countries and cultures. Coinciding with this globalization of business is the globalization of the HR profession. The World Federation of Personnel Management Associations (WFPMA) links together country- and region-specific professional associations around the world. As a service to its members, the WFPMA investigated the question of how the work of HR professionals is similar and different around the world. Their research revealed how little is known at the global level. Although a few countries have developed national standards for HR professionals, there are no such standards in most countries. To address this information vacuum, the WFPMA decided to conduct a study of its own. Among the questions their study will address are these:

1. How do different countries define the standards that constitute an HR professional? What are the competencies they will need to be able to perform HR activities, from the operational to the most strategic?
2. How do national associations certify the attainment of national standards? What are the learning and development routes they might pursue in order to keep those competencies up to date?
3. Are there generic standards of professionalism in HR common to all or many countries? What standards might be appropriate to certify the attainment of generic competencies?
4. Could standards be expressed in such a way that they would be helpful to emerging professional associations wishing to develop HR professionalism in their country?

Plans call for the initial results from this study to be released in the year 2000, with the possible development of global HR competency standards following in the next year.[31]

ORGANIZING THE HUMAN RESOURCE FUNCTION

In traditional, bureaucratic organizations, HR professionals resided almost exclusively within a centralized functional department. As organizations

"There is no worldwide definition of what an HR professional is, does, or can be expected to contribute."

Judy Whittaker
Director
Institute of Personnel and
Development

have restructured into a variety of newer forms, however, they have often re-evaluated this approach. As is true for many support functions, there is currently much experimenting going on to find the most effective way to organize the HR function. When considering new organizational forms, two major questions that need to be addressed are

1. Where are the HR decisions made?
2. What level of investment will the company make?

The first question has to do with the advantages and disadvantages of centralized and decentralized organizations. The second question has to do with budgets and compensation.

Centralization versus Decentralization

Centralization means structuring the organization so that essential decision making and policy formulation are conducted at one location (at headquarters). Decentralization means structuring the organization so that essential decision making and policy formulation are conducted at several locations (in various divisions or departments of the organization).

Organization of HR departments differs widely from one company to another not only because of the differing requirements of various industries but also because of differing philosophies, cultures, and strategic plans of individual organizations. Compare the centralized structure of Merck with the decentralized structure of TRW. At Merck, large, specialized corporate staffs formulate and design human resource strategies and activities, which are then communicated to the small HR staffs of operating units for implementation. High levels of consistency and congruence with corporate goals are thus attained. At TRW, small corporate staffs manage HR systems for executives and act only as advisers to operating units. Business units take most of the responsibility for their HR policies and activities. TRW operates with a wider divergence in practices and a greater flexibility in addressing local concerns.[32]

The organizational structures used by Merck and TRW are very appropriate for their respective types of businesses. TRW, a high-technology company with a diverse array of businesses, cannot use the consistent, stable approach to HR that Merck, with a more singular product focus, is able to employ.[33]

Because of today's rapidly changing and highly competitive business environment, the trend seems to be toward greater decentralization. This entails a greater delegation of responsibilities to lower HR levels and to the operating units and line managers themselves. Along with this is a trend toward less formalization of policies—that is, fewer rules that are seen as bureaucratic hurdles. Human resource departments and their organizations thus have greater flexibility to cope with the continually changing environment. Diminished bureaucratization can also lead to a greater openness in approaches to problems. On the other hand, it tends to reduce the consistency of HR practices found throughout an organization. When HR practices vary dramatically across different units within an organization, it may become more difficult to maintain a common corporate culture. To address this concern, decentralized organizations generally strive to develop broad policies that state basic principles to be followed by everyone, and then allowing local units to develop practices that fit their specific contexts.

Cost Control

The amount of money that organizations allocate to their HR departments generally rises yearly. In 1998, the average costs allocated to the human resource department for each employee was $1,053. Not surprisingly, department expenditures per employee decrease steadily with company size. For all firms, the median ratio of HR department staff members to workers in 1998 was 1.1 to 100. Among firms with fewer than 250 employees, the median ratio was 1.7 staff for every 100 workers, and among companies with 250 to 499 employees it was 1.2 for every 100 employees. The ratio was substantially lower in organizations with 500 to 2,499 employees, at 0.8 for every 100 workers, and lowest among employers with 2,500 or more workers, at 0.6 for every 100 employees.[34]

Larger organizations generally have been able to spend less per employee because they have taken advantage of the efficiencies associated with standardized policies and practices. As organizations attempt to decentralize their HR function, however, many find that their administrative costs begin to increase. In order to keep administrative costs under control, some organizations have adopted a structure that includes *shared services*. Like a traditional functional department, a shared services unit provides service to units throughout the entire organization. But a major difference is that costs associated with shared services usually are allocated to the specific units that use the services instead of being charged to a general corporate budget.

One approach to shared services is to create *service centers* that handle transaction-based activities such as processing medical claims, answering questions related to retirement planning, and handling tuition reimbursement programs. Such transactions can be efficiently carried out by one unit for the entire firm, often over the telephone or online. IBM's Human Resources Service Center (HRSC) for its North American operations is located in Raleigh, North Carolina. Their mission is to be the "premier centralized service channel for the competitive delivery and administration of HR policies, programs, processes, applications, and database management in support of IBM's quest for industry leadership." The HRSC's 400 employees serve more than 670,000 current and former employees, processing nearly two million calls annually. Among the many activities handled by the service center are payroll transactions, benefits management and problem solving, the design and management of a self-service HR website, establishment of affirmative action plans, OFCCP compliance reviews, processing of job applications, and the dissemination and analysis of employee surveys. IBM's HRSC is considered to be among the best in the world, serving as a benchmark target for other firms. Established in 1995, it has continually evolved over time—leveraging new technologies, adding new services, and at the same time reducing costs.

An alternative way to reduce costs within a decentralized structure is through the use of *centers of excellence*. A center of excellence typically houses a variety of HR specialists who have in-depth expertise in activities that are of significant value to the firm. Such activities include recruitment and selection, compensation, job redesign, reengineering, organizational change, and measuring organizational effectiveness. These specialists essentially work as internal consultants, providing service only to the units that request (and are willing to pay for) them.[35] Like shared services, the objective behind organizing HR activities into centers of excellence is to improve efficiency while also allowing for flexibility and decentralization of HR practices. In

"If you become over-focused on the [bottom-line results], you can get to a point at which you need to do an ROI on conducting an ROI to make sure it's worth the time spent measuring results—it can get a little crazy."

Mark Teachout, PhD
Executive Director of Learning and
Performance Technology
USAA

■■□ *fast fact*

By developing a highly sophisticated HR intranet, Cisco Systems reduced the workload of the HR staff by an estimated 15-20 percent.

1999, AT&T reorganized its HR function from a highly decentralized model to a new structure that utilizes both shared services and centers of excellence.

According to William M. Mercer, the HR consulting firm, changes such as those underway at IBM and AT&T reflect the newly emerging HR organizational model. "The traditional design typically includes a vice president of HR, then a manager of benefits and compensation, a manager of HRIS and payroll, a manager of employment, and so on," explained associate David Hilborn. "However, the emerging model is more like a three-legged stool." As Exhibit 16.6 illustrates, one leg is a service center focused on efficiently performing administrative tasks. A second leg is a center of excellence that focuses on designing the most effective approaches to HR, given the organization's needs. The services provided by these two legs are shared throughout the company. The third leg houses the HR generalists who report directly to line managers within the businesses. They focus on creating strategic fit at the business unit level, and report secondarily to HR. Seated at the top of this three-legged stool is the HR leadership team. They're responsible for coordinating these various activities and ensuring that pressures for centralization and cost-reduction are balanced appropriately with the need for flexibility and change.[36]

Reengineering and Outsourcing

Reengineering the HR department basically means reconsidering what the department is doing to see whether it can do it better and more effectively.[37] Customerization is consistent with this process because it asks, "What are we doing for our customers, what do they want, and how can we fill in the

Exhibit 16.6
The Evolving Structure of the HR Organization

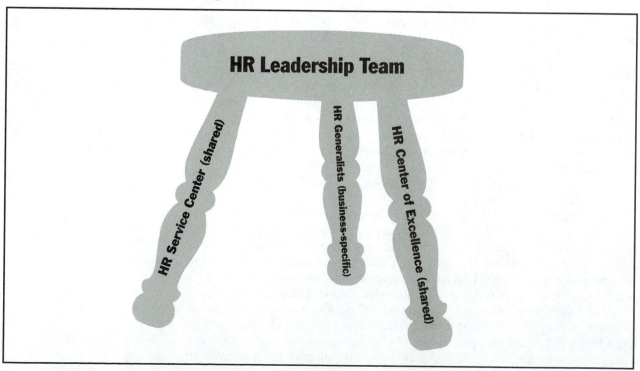

gaps between what they get and what they want?" But reengineering goes much further. It seeks to examine all the parts of the department, asking, "What is the purpose of this group, what does it do and how does it do it, and can it improve the way it does things?" The reengineering process should identify what counts, what adds value, and what can best be done by someone else—particularly a consulting firm that specializes in supplying HR activities, such as pension plan administration.

Reengineering may lead to a decision to outsource some HR activities.[38] Novell, like many other companies, decided that some of its responsibilities were better left to outside vendors. According to Theresa Dadone, director of compensation and benefits for Novell:

> It wasn't long ago that employees had to come to HR and request a loan from their 401(k) plan. They had to talk to an HR person and fill out papers. A committee then had to review the request and decide whether or not to grant the loan. Well, that's not in keeping with customer service. That's treating our employees like children. So, we outsourced that responsibility to an HR consulting firm. There's now a toll-free number for employees to call so they don't have to involve HR in their personal finances. We're out of the loop . . . that isn't where our value is. Our value is in helping employees understand the plan.
>
> Educational assistance is another responsibility that's been outsourced. Employees used to have to come to HR and request approval of a course and receive reimbursement. Today, an HR consulting firm takes care of it. Employees don't have to come begging to HR, hat in hand, to process something. We now spend our time helping employees understand the benefits of educational assistance and how it can serve them in their personal and professional lives.[39]

During the 1990s, many firms began outsourcing a variety of staff functions, including HR. Forecasters predict that as many as 30 percent of firms will outsource all or part of the HR department by the year 2000. The logic underlying this trend is that outside vendors, who might serve dozens of organizations, should be more efficient. Consequently, the cost per employee for their services should be lower. But after a few years of experience, many companies have discovered that outsourcing often results in higher costs.[40] At the same time, service levels from outside vendors often don't match the level formerly provided by the company's own staff. Like all other decisions regarding how to manage human resources, organizations can avoid some of the disappointments associated with outsourcing by treating outsourcing as a key strategic move. The feature, Managing Strategically: Avoiding Common Outsourcing Pitfalls, summarizes several challenges that must be met in order to reap the potential benefits of outsourcing.[41]

STEPPING INTO THE FUTURE: GLOBALIZATION

The 1990s have seen dramatic changes in international trade and business. Once-safe markets are now fierce battlegrounds where firms aggressively fight for their share against both foreign and domestic competitors. It is, therefore, not surprising to find that in an increasing number of firms, a large proportion of the workforce is located in other countries. As a consequence, HR departments and their professionals have to be familiar with concerns and aspects of operating across countries and cultures.

"The optimist says the glass is half full, the pessimist says the glass is half empty, the re-engineer says the glass is too big."

Michael Hammer
Coauthor
Re-engineering the Corporation

■☐ **fast fact**

A 1998 survey of HR professionals revealed that 40 percent had unsatisfactory results with outsourced HR activities.

"About 25 percent of the people who've outsourced [HR activities] that we've talked to this year indicate they've experienced disappointment."

Jack Walsh
Consulting Practice Leader
The Segal Company

MANAGING STRATEGICALLY
Avoiding Common Outsourcing Pitfalls

Common Mistakes	Recommended Solutions
· Begin outsourcing as a tactical solution to an immediate problem.	· Adopt a strategic perspective. Consider what HR should be like five or ten years from now.
· Fail to anticipate resistance to change.	· Recognize that outsourcing is a form of major organizational change and must be managed accordingly.
· Not measuring, or ignoring, current costs *and* service levels.	· Document current costs and service levels for use in future evaluations of outsourcing effectiveness.
· Failing to fully design and specify the "ideal" service delivery model to be achieved.	· Specify the roles and relationships of all partners involved *before* evaluating and contracting with specific vendors.
· Not learning about the outsourcing market in advance.	· Thoroughly research alternative vendors. Understand their differences in business philosophies, technologies, and long-term plans.
· Choosing a vendor that doesn't perform satisfactorily.	· Using a cross-functional team, develop a vendor selection model that includes specific, objective criteria that have been prioritized according to their importance. At the same time, develop performance indicators and a process for evaluating subsequent vendor performance. Then, repeat the competitive bidding process every three to five years.
· Mismanaging the contract negotiation, which can be costly, cause delays, and damage relationships.	· Use experienced negotiators. Be sure that at least one member of the selection design team is involved in the vendor negotiations.
· Underestimating the time and resources required for implementation.	· Establish an implementation team to develop a project plan that includes a clear statement of goals, roles and responsibilities, realistic time lines, and target milestones.
· Underestimating the need for frequent communications with the vendor and for vendor management.	· Identify someone to be responsible for vendor management, and clearly specify his/her roles and activities.
· Not anticipating failure.	· Consider what can go wrong, identify warning symptoms to watch for, and develop contingency plans.

When it comes to operating in a global context, most organizations and most HR professionals are at an early stage of learning. Globalization is forcing managers to grapple with complex issues as they seek to gain or sustain a competitive advantage. Faced with unprecedented levels of foreign competition at home and abroad, operating an international business is high on the list of priorities for top management. So are finding and nurturing the human resources required to implement an international or global strategy.

HR professionals play a critical role in the globalization process by helping companies evaluate the human resource prospects and possibilities involved in moving to different regions of the world. The HR department of Novell helped its senior management decide to establish a technical center in Australia. According to Tim Harris, Novell's HR head:

> We were debating between establishing the center in Australia or Singapore. We had to evaluate local employment laws, the cost and availability of housing and what it would cost to recruit and relocate the multilingual employees needed to staff the center. We also researched tax issues, the competitive salary structure, medical facilities and the healthcare system.
>
> There's a myriad of decisions in which HR must participate—to go back to the business unit and say: "This is what you should do, this is what it will cost, and this is how long it will take to get the new business or division up and running."[42]

The complexities of operating in different countries and of employing people of different nationalities, are the main issues that differentiate domestic and international HR management. Many companies underestimate these complexities, and some evidence suggests that business failures in the international arena are often linked to poor management of human resources.

The primary causes of failure in multinational ventures stem from a lack of understanding of the essential differences in managing human resources, at all levels, in foreign environments. Certain management philosophies and techniques have proved successful in the domestic environment, yet their application in a foreign environment too often leads to frustration, failure, and underachievement. These "human" considerations are as important as the financial and marketing criteria upon which so many decisions to undertake multinational ventures depend.[43]

Increasingly, domestic HR is taking on an international flavor as the workforce becomes more and more diverse. In the future, more and more HR professionals will find that being effective in an international HR work is required for success in their profession. A consideration of how international and domestic HR differ today provides a glimpse of the future.[44]

More Functions and Activities.   To operate in an international environment, the HR department must engage in a number of activities that would not be necessary in a domestic environment: international taxation, international relocation and orientation, administrative services for expatriates, host-government relations, and language translation services.

Broader Perspective.   Domestic managers generally administer programs for a single national group of employees who are covered by a uniform compensation policy and who are taxed by one government. International managers face the problem of designing and administering programs for more than one national group of employees, and they must therefore take a more global view of issues.

More Involvement in Employees' Lives.   A greater degree of involvement in employees' personal lives is necessary for the selection, training, and effective management of expatriate employees. The international HR department needs to ensure that the expatriate employee understands housing arrangements, healthcare, and all aspects of the compensation package provided for the assignment.

More Risk Exposure.   Frequently, the human and financial consequences of failure are more severe in the international arena than in domestic business. For example, expatriate failure (the premature return of an expatriate from an international assignment) is a persistent, high-cost problem for international companies. Another aspect of risk exposure that is relevant to international HR is terrorism. Major multinational companies must now routinely consider this element when planning international meetings and assignments.

More External Influences.   Other forces that influence the international arena are the type of host government, the state of its economy, and business practices that may differ substantially from those of the originating country. A host government can, for example, dictate hiring procedures or insist on a company providing training to local workers.

Mergers and acquisitions that cross country borders are likely to accelerate the blending of domestic and international HR activities. Cisco has pursued the acquisition strategy as well as any company as a means of expanding its product lines. John Chambers, CEO of Cisco, says very clearly that integrating the newly acquired company into the Cisco culture is very important. In fact, Cisco even evaluates the culture of the companies it is thinking about acquiring. The culture for them represents the values of the company and the way it treats people. Given that Cisco manages its people to: (1) allow them to be rewarded for their performance; (2) encourage them to be creative; and (3) facilitate their working effectively in teams, Cisco evaluates the companies it may acquire on these same cultural dimensions. Certainly this is a clear role for the human resource manager, and one the company takes very seriously. When put in a global context with national cultural, language, and legal differences, this cultural evaluation audit becomes even more complex and challenging, and so are the potential costs of any misjudgments.[45]

Beginning in the 1980s, the HR profession began to change. Since then, in most U.S companies, the old "personnel" department has been replaced with one or more "human resource" units. Along with this change in title has been a change in expectations. The primary responsibilities of personnel departments involved carrying out a variety of administrative tasks for which little formal training was required. Increasingly, the responsibilities of HR professionals include ensuring that the organization manages people in a way that contributes to the growth and development of individual employees as well as the growth and development of the organization. Early in the 21st century, HR continues to evolve. During the next two decades, globalization is likely to force even more change in the profession than we've seen during the past two decades. Those who are prepared for this next change will undoubtedly thrive!

SUMMARY

Because of the increasing complexity of human resource management, nearly all mid- to large-size companies employ human resource professionals—as full time employees, as vendors with long-term contracts, and/or as consultants who work on short-term projects. The ways organizations allocate responsibility for HR activities are many. They vary from firm to firm, and even over time within the same firm. Regardless of how HR activities are structured, however, companies that are most concerned with HR management seek professionals who effectively perform the partnership, strategic, enabler, monitoring, innovator, and change facilitator roles. When this occurs, HR professionals can help organizations link their HR activities to the business. In doing so, they demonstrate their value to the organization and help achieve enhanced productivity, quality of work life, competitive advantage, adaptability, and legal compliance—all goals associated with the organization's several stakeholders. Going forward, human resource professionals will increasingly be called upon to perform their roles in a global context. Globalization adds additional challenges for the HR profession, and it may ultimately reshape the professional's role. Regardless of how the roles of HR professionals shift, however, getting everyone involved in human resource management will continue to be essential. Employees, line managers, and HR professionals have to work together in order for organizations to manage human resources effectively.

TERMS TO REMEMBER

Centers of excellence	HR mission statement
Centralization	HR specialist
Change facilitator role	Innovator role
Customerization	Monitoring role
Decentralization	Outsourcing
Enabler role	Partnership role
Ethical behavior	Professional standards
HR department	Service centers
HR generalist	Shared services
HR leader	Strategic role

DISCUSSION QUESTIONS

1. How does W. L. Gore link its HR activities to the needs of the business?

2. Why is the HR profession seen as critical to the success of organizations? Do line managers and HR managers agree with this view?

3. What roles can human resource professionals play in an organization? What specific activities are associated with these roles?

4. How do the roles of the HR leader and the HR staff differ?

5. Why are some human resource management departments centralized and others decentralized?

6. Is outsourcing of HR activities likely to increase or decrease during the next ten years? Explain your opinion.

7. How is the role of HR professionals likely to change as organizations move toward globalization?

PROJECTS TO EXTEND YOUR LEARNING

1. **Managing Strategically.** Your company would like you to link the way it manages its people more closely with the needs of the business, like Southwest Airlines and Lincoln Electric. They want you to be as thorough as possible. As far as you know, when the strategy of the company was formulated two years ago, the human resource department was not involved. Consequently, you may wish to start with an understanding of the strategy of the firm and work through the implications for human resource management. Your company is a relatively new one and is based on the concept that some people would rather take the bus than the train or plane, but bus service just isn't fun, nor very efficient. You strongly believe that your company, Funways Bus Service, definitely can do a better job of linking the people with the needs of the business and serve the transportation needs of the customers. You can't do everything at once, but to start, outline the types of behaviors the company needs from most of its employees and then identify what human resource practices would help attain these behaviors. First you may want to read the next project on **Managing Teams**. For possible ideas, visit Southwest Airlines at
www.iflyswa.com

2. **Managing Teams.** You know the value of teams and the importance of partnership in human resource management. In order to identify the behaviors needed by the employees of Funways Bus Service to successfully implement the company's strategy and serve the customers, you decide to form a team. This team might also be used to help you gain a much better understanding of the company's strategy and what human resource management practices would be acceptable to the company. So with this team you will fulfill the needs of the first exercise, **Managing Strategically**. Accordingly, identify the members of the team and describe how they would work together. What incentives would you give them to be members of the team? How would you motivate them to do a great job? For ideas, visit the website of the American Compensation Association at
www.acaonline.org

3. **Managing Globalization.** Lincoln Electric has learned, much to its credit, that going global is not easy, but something that can be learned. You know this and now your company, Frost Manufacturing, is asking you to help it with its decision as to whether to become a global player. Chad Frost, the founder's grandson and current CEO, wants you to tell him all the human resource implications of going global. He is thinking now of establishing a plant in England, one based upon total quality management principles. His major customers would be the automobile companies in England. You need to tell him such things as: (1) Does he have to change his HR department? (2) Will the department have to do things much

differently from what they are doing now? (3) Will the human resource practices that work so well in Michigan now, also work in England or will new practices be necessary? (4) Can he plan to assign his current HR manager to be the first HR manager in England? (5) Will he be able to convince some of his current managers to become expatriates and uproot their families from the suburbs of Grand Rapids, Michigan for up to three years? Write a memo to Chad outlining your recommendations.

4. **Managing Change.** More than ever, companies need to be flexible and adaptable and ready to change. But even in the best of circumstances, it can be hard to get employees and companies to change. Nonetheless, change they must and you are in charge of the HR department. What would you do to help ensure that the company is able to change when it needs to? That is, what can you do to help ensure that the company is flexible and that the employees are comfortable with change? You may wish to form a team to help you with this investigation, but first you should identify the topics and issues that should be addressed by the team. What types of human resource management practices would be helpful in getting employees comfortable with change? You may even wish to benchmark some companies that do this successfully, companies such as AAL, Southwest Airlines, W. L. Gore, General Electric, and Weyerhauser. You may also wish to contact professional associations such as the American Society for Training and Development at
    www.astd.org
    and the Human Resource Planning Society at
    www.hrps.org

5. **Managing Diversity.** For the projects above, you will most likely be using teams: partnership in human resource management depends upon effective team interaction. But you know that people from different areas of a company have different beliefs, values, knowledge, and biases. Some may not believe that human resource management is as important as you do. Some may not believe that areas other than their own are as valuable as theirs. But they do have knowledge which you know is important to the process of managing human resources, which is why you are using them on the teams for the earlier projects. What will you do to help ensure that your teams, diverse in terms of characteristics such as organizational level, age, functional expertise, gender, and ethnicity, function effectively? How should you go about selecting people for your partnership teams? Should you establish policies, such as being on the teams for only a certain length of time, to ensure that partnership is maximized and that people reluctant to work cooperatively in teams are only on the teams for a limited time?

6. **Managing Globalization and Diversity.** The WFPMA set out to investigate whether there is significant commonality in the work of HR professionals around the world. Of what value would such standards be to the HR profession? To line managers? To employees around the world? Are there any possible negative consequences of establishing worldwide HR standards? Explain your opinions.

    To learn about the current status of their project to establish worldwide HR competency standards, visit the home page of the WFPMA at **wfpma.com.br**

Other associations that may provide progress reports on this and related projects include the Asian Pacific Federation of Human Resource Management, the European Association for Personnel Management, the Interamerican Federation of Personnel Administration, the North American Human Resource Management Association, the Institute of People Management (South Africa) and Association Nationale des Directeurs et Cadres de la Fonction Personnel (France). Search the web to see if you can locate home pages for these.

7. **Integration and Application.** After reviewing the cases at the end of the text, describe the following for each company (Lincoln Electric, Southwest Airlines, and AAL):

     a.   the degree of partnership in managing human resources,
     b.   the role/importance of the HR department,
     c.   the value that the company places on its people, and
     d.   the competencies of the human resource professionals.

CASE STUDY

Bringing the Human Resource Department to the Business

Mike Mitchell left the Bank of Montreal to become vice president of human resources at the North American branch of the Swiss Bank Corporation (SBC) in the autumn of 1993. It was a move up for him in terms of status, responsibility, monetary compensation, and challenge. Of these, it was the challenge that was most intriguing to Mitchell. In his mid-thirties, he saw this as a perfect time to take a risk in his career. He realized that if he succeeded he would establish a prototype that could be marketed to other firms. In addition, success could lead to further career opportunities and challenges. While he had a general idea of what he wanted to do and had gotten verbal support from his superiors, the senior vice president of human resources and the president of SBC, North America, the details of exactly what he was going to do and how he was going to do it remained to unfold.

In 1992, the parent company of SBC (a $110 billion universal bank) headquartered in Basel, Switzerland decided it needed a clearer statement of its intentions to focus its energies and resources in light of the growing international competition. Accordingly, it crafted a vision statement to the effect that the bank was going to better serve its customers with high-quality products that met their needs rather than just those of the institution. While the North American operation was relatively autonomous, it was still expected to embrace this vision. The details of its implementation, however, were in local hands. For the human resource side, the hands became those of Mitchell.

While Mitchell had spent some time in human resources at the Bank of Montreal in New York, the bulk of his work experience was as an entrepreneur in Montreal, Canada. It was this experience that impacted his thinking the most. Thus when he came to the SBC, his self-image was a businessperson who happened to be working in human resources. It was in part because of this image that his stay at the Bank of Montreal was brief: the idea of human resources was still a bit too conservative for his style. Too many of his ideas "just couldn't be done." In interviewing with the top managers at SBC, they warned him of the same general environment. Thus, he knew change would be slow among the 1000 employees, including his own department of 10 employees. He knew, however, that he wanted to reposition and "customerize" the HR department at SBC. He also understood the importance of connecting the HR department to the business.

He identified the four major aspects for his program to reposition and customerize the HR department. The four aspects included: gathering information; developing action agendas; implementing those agendas; and then evaluating and revising those agendas.

Gathering Information

To gather information about the current environment, Mitchell asked the customers, diagnosed the environment, and asked the HR department itself. From the customers, Mitchell learned the nature of the business strategy and how HR currently fit with or helped that strategy. Customers discussed what they now get from the HR department, what their ideal would be, and how the ideal could best be delivered. Each HR activity, as well as the entire department and the staff, were discussed. From the environment, Mitchell learned what other companies are doing with their HR departments and HR practices. He examined competitors and those in other industries in order to gather ideas for the entire department and for each HR activity. From the HR department he learned how they see themselves in relation to servicing their customers, their knowledge of strategy, how they think the customers perceive the department, and their desire to improve and change.

Developing Agendas

Making agendas based upon this information was the second aspect of Mitchell's plan. As the HR staff analyzed the information, they were asked to develop plans (agendas) for resolving any discrepancies between what they are currently doing and what their customers want. As the staff worked, they began to recognize a need to determine a vision of themselves; to formulate a statement of who they are and how they interact with the rest of the organization. They also began to examine if their current ways of operating and the department's current structure were sufficient to move ahead. The need to reorganize began to become apparent. Once the vision began to take shape and the agendas were developed, the HR department established a game plan to get their agendas implemented. Approval by top management and line managers immediately impacted was seen as critical to successful implementation.

Implementing the Agendas

To begin the implementation phase, the HR staff met with the customers to discuss the agendas. In addition to responding to the specific needs of the line managers, it also involved selling the line managers on other activities. With a new focus to be more strategic and customer-oriented, the HR department began to develop programs that went beyond the regular administrative activities and services that it had provided to the line managers. Because these services were new, they had to be sold to their customers, at least at first. So in addition to implementing the specifically agreed upon agendas and contracts, this aspect included developing, selling, and implementing new programs.

Evaluating and Revising

Developed along with the agendas were contracts, specifying what will be delivered to the customer. The customer was given the right to appraise the work delivered. Based on these appraisals by the customers (line managers), the agendas are evaluated. Revisions and adjustments can then be made for continual improvement. In addition to these contracts, the work of the HR department is reviewed internally using such criteria as the reduction in turnover resulting from better selection procedures or an increase in the number of new ideas or innovations resulting from a change in the HR practices to facilitate the innovative strategy of the business.

Implications for the HR Department

There are several implications for the HR department (Mitchell and his staff) in their efforts to reposition and customerize:

- The HR department has been re-oriented to be strategic and customer-oriented.
- The HR department is becoming a constant gatherer of information from the internal and external environments. By knowing the competition, the business strategy, and the current assets of the company, the HR staff can develop new HR activities, implement new ideas, and work to maintain the company's competitive advantage.
- The HR department has identified the level of excellence it wants to attain. The staff is working to become a strategic player while fulfilling their managerial and operational roles.
- HR managers and staff are working closely with the line managers to design systems to gather the needed services and information. They also work with the line managers to develop con-

tracts by which the HR department will be evaluated by the line managers.

- The HR department is changing so that there is more of a generalist rather than a specialist orientation. A greater team orientation is also being built.
- Things will never be the same. The HR professionals in the department will be gathering, servicing, evaluating, revising, and most of all listening. And because the business is always changing, the HR department will continue to evolve and change.

Implications for the Line Managers

There are also several implications in the repositioning and customerization program for the line managers.

- The line managers need to cooperate with Mitchell and his staff as they gather information and implement new ideas and practices. Together, they are becoming partners in the business. The line managers must accept the new role being played by Mitchell and his HR staff.
- The line managers need to work closely with the HR staff in developing the action agendas.
- The line managers must continue to work with the HR staff in appraising the success of the HR efforts.

The Benefits from the Partnership

From Mitchell's perspective, there are several outcomes that result from a repositioning and customerization program. They include

- enhancing the quality and responsiveness of the HR department;
- developing the HR department in terms of new jobs (skillwise), providing new excitement, and building commitment to the company's mission, goals, and strategies;
- linking HR with the business and integrating HR with the corporate strategy;

- becoming market- or customer-oriented with flexibility to respond to and anticipate changes;
- developing criteria by which the behaviors of the HR department can be evaluated and changed;
- gaining an ability to develop and use HR practices to gain competitive advantage;
- gaining an awareness of the potential ways different HR practices can be done by constantly monitoring what other successful companies are doing;
- becoming more keenly aware of the internal and external environments;
- providing standard HR products more efficiently;
- developing new products and services;
- developing technology to deliver the new products and services;
- selling new services and products outside the company;
- changing the HR department dramatically and consequently becoming a catalyst for change with the company; and
- becoming a department where everyone wants to work.

QUESTIONS

1. Who are the customers of Mitchell and his HR staff?

2. What must Mitchell do in order for his staff to be able to do the things necessary to reposition and customerize?

3. Do you think that the line managers will cooperate with Mitchell and his staff? What will it take to see that they do? What would be their reasons for resisting a partnership with the HR department?

4. Develop a matrix with projects, dates, milestones, and people involved (i.e., HR, line managers, and employees) for Mitchell and his staff.

SOURCE: Prepared by Randall S. Schuler, Rutgers University, who expresses his appreciation for the cooperation of Michael Mitchell who moved from SBC to Tiffany and Company.

CASE STUDY

A Broader View Seizes More Opportunities

Don English, corporate vice president of human resources, is now finally able to take a pause from the ongoing stream of "fire fighting" he has been engaged in since he came to Bancroft ten years ago! Like many of his colleagues in other firms, Don's knowledge of HR management came as much from doing it as from formal education.

Because of his workload, Don tended to keep pretty narrowly focused, and he rarely read HR journals or attended professional conferences. However, recently, things have been easing up. He has been able to recruit and train almost all the division managers in charge of human resources. It is Don's intention that the newly trained division managers will put out most of the company's "fires," and he will be freed to look at the "big picture." And he has been doing more reading than ever before. Of course, Don has not been totally out of touch with the rest of the world or the growing importance of HR management planning. When he started filling the slots for division HR managers, he made sure that it was a learning experience for him. Don always required job candidates to prepare a one-hour talk on the state of research and practice in different areas of personnel—for example, selection, appraisal, compensation, or training. He would even invite MBA candidates who had no course work in HR and ask them to relate their field of interest to HR management.

Don is planning to become the chief executive officer of Bancroft or some other firm of similar or larger size within the next five to seven years. He thinks he can achieve this if he remains in human resources and does an outstanding job. He will have to be outstanding by all standards, both internal and external to the firm. From his interviews during the past three years, Don knows that it is imperative to move human resources in a strategic direction while at the same time doing the best possible job with the "nuts and bolts" operational activities.

During a moment of reflection, Don begins to scribble some notes on his large white desk pad. In the middle is Bancroft, a well-established clothing manufacturer. To its left are its suppliers and to its right are its customers. In his head are all the HR practices he is so familiar with. He has a hunch that there must be a way to use the firm's expertise in performance appraisal and training to help Bancroft be more effective. Bancroft has been learning tremendously from its five-year drive to improve quality, but during the past year, quality gains have slowed. Bancroft must continue to improve its quality to gain and sustain competitive advantage, but large internal quality gains are becoming more and more difficult as Bancroft climbs the learning curve. Don wonders, "How can he help Bancroft experience the excitement of seeing large gains in quality improvement again?" Don circles the list of suppliers and begins to formulate a plan that will improve his chances of becoming CEO. He now seeks your advice in exactly what to do and how to go about doing it.

QUESTIONS

1. Is it reasonable for Don and the rest of Bancroft management to think about the suppliers of Bancroft as a source of competitive advantage? Refer to Chapter 1.

2. Should Don go directly to Bancroft's suppliers and talk to them, or should he work with others in his company such as the person in charge of purchasing or even the CEO?

3. Is there really a place here for the corporate vice president of human resources to help his company gain competitive advantage by working with the suppliers?

4. Can Don become a CEO by being effective in human resources?

SOURCE: Randall S. Schuler, Rutgers University

ENDNOTES

[1] S. Sherman, "Levi's: As Ye Sew, So Shall Ye Reap," *Fortune* (May 12, 1997): 104–116.

[2] D. Anfuso, "Core Values Shape W. L. Gore's Innovative Culture," *Workforce* (March 1999): 48–53.

[3] R. S. Schuler and I. C. MacMillan, "Gaining Competitive Advantage Through Human Resource Management Practices," *Human Resource Management* 23 (1994): 241–255.

[4] M. F. Cook, *Outsourcing Human Resources Functions* (New York: AMACOM, 1999).

[5] *Priorities for Competitive Advantage: A Worldwide Human Resource Study* (IBM/Towers Perrin: 1992): 27; see also, A. I. Kraut and A. K. Korman, "The 'Delta Forces' Causing Change in Human Resource Management," *Evolving Practices in Human Resource Management*, A. I. Kraut and A. K. Korman, eds.(San Francisco: Jossey–Bass, 1999): 3–22.

[6] S. Caudron, "HR Leaders Brainstorm," *Personnel Journal* (August 1994): 53–62.

[7] J. J. Laabs, "Painting a Vivid Picture of HR," *Workforce* (October 1998): 26–30.

[8] "HR Outlook: HR's Transformation to Business Partner," *HR Executive Review* 5 (1997): 25–27; D. Ulrich, "The Future Calls for Change," *Workforce* (January 1998): 87–91; F. Kemske, "HR's Role Will Change. The Question is How, HR 2008," *Workforce* (January 1998): 46–60; R. S. Schuler, "Strategic Human Resource Management: Linking the People with the Strategic Needs of the Business," *Organizational Dynamics* (Summer 1992): 18–32; J. Pfeffer, *The Human Equation* (Boston: Harvard Business School, 1998); S. A. Mohrman, E. E. Lawler III, and G. C. McMahan, "New Directions for the Human Resources Organization: An Organization Design Approach," *Center for Effective Organizations* (School of Business Administration, University of Southern California, 1996): 1–38.

[9] S. Caudron, "Strategic HR at First Chicago," *Personnel Journal* (November 1991): 56. See also P. Stuart, "HR and Operations Work Together at Texas Instruments," *Personnel Journal* (April 1992): 64–68.

[10] E. Leinfuss, "Speed Zone," *Human Resource Executive* (February 1998): 56–58; Caudron, "HR Leaders Brainstorm," 56.

[11] Caudron, "HR Leaders Brainstorm," 54.

[12] S. Lawrence, "Voice of HR Experience," *Personnel Journal* (April 1989): 64. For an extensive description of HR's new role at AT&T, see D. Anfuso, "AT&T Connects HR and Business Leaders for Success," *Personnel Journal* (December 1994): 84–94.

[13] A. A. Thompson and A. J. Strickland, *Crafting and Implementing Strategy,* 10th ed. (New York: McGraw-Hill, 1998); J. Pfeffer, *The Human Equation* (Boston: Harvard Business School Press, 1998); P. Cappelli and A. Crocker-Hefter, *Distinctive Human Resources Are the Core Competencies of Firms,* Report no. R117Q00011-91 (Washington, D.C.: U.S. Department of Education, 1994); *High Performance Work Practices and Firm Performance* (U.S. Department of Labor: Washington, D.C., 1993); J. P. MacDuffie and J. Krafcik, "Integrating Technology and Human Resources for High-Performance Manufacturing," *Transforming Organizations,* T. Kochan and M. Useem, eds. (New York: Oxford University Press, 1992): 210–226; B. E. Becker and M. A. Huselid, "High Performance Work Systems and Firm Performance: A Synthesis of Research and Managerial Implications," *Research in Personnel and Human Resources Management,* G. Ferris, ed. (Greenwich, CT: JAI Press, 1998).

[14] M. Voves, "Blazing the HR Trail Alone," *Personnel Journal* (December 1996): 39–45; "Customers for Keeps: Training Strategies," *Bulletin to Management* (March 31, 1988): 8. See also R. L. Desatnik, *Managing to Keep the Customers* (San Francisco: Jossey-Bass, 1987).

[15] M. J. Plevel, F. Lane, S. Nellis, and R. S. Schuler, "AT&T Global Business Communications Systems: Linking HR With Business Strategy," *Organizational Dynamics* (1994): 59–72.

[16] J. J. Laabs, "Why HR Can't Win Today," *Workforce* (May 1998): 62–74; S. Caudron, "Team Staffing Requires New HR Role," *Personnel Journal* (May 1994): 88–94; E. E. Lawler III and J. R. Galbraith, "Staff Organizations: New Directions," *Organizing for the Future: New Approaches to Managing Complex Organizations* (San Francisco: Jossey-Bass, 1995).

[17] Based on N. D. Johnson, "Positioning Your HR Organization to Become a Strategic Business Partner," *ACA News* (March 1998) 20–23; D. Ulrich, M. Losey, and G. Lake, eds., *Tomorrow's HR Management: 48 Thought Leaders Call For Change* (New York: Wiley and Sons, 1997); J. Walker, "What's New in HR Development?" *Personnel* (July 1990): 41; the material in Exhibit 16.2 is adapted from M. J. Plevel et al., "AT&T Global Business Communications Systems: Linking HR with Business Strategy," *Organizational Dynamics* (Winter 1994): 64.

[18] M. A. Huselid, S. E. Jackson, and R. S. Schuler, "Technical and Strategic Human Resource Management Effectiveness as Determinants of Firm Performance," *Academy of Management Journal* 40 (1997): 171–188; L. Davidson, "Measure What You Bring to the Bottom Line," *Workforce* (September 1998): 34–40.

[19] H. Lancaster, "Mike Bowlin Started His Path to Arco CEO From a Personnel Job," *The Wall Street Journal* (September 3, 1996): B1; R. Henson, "Globalization: A Human Resource Mandate," *Solutions* (January 1994): 62–63.

[20] V. Y. Haines and A. Petit, "Conditions for Successful Human Resource Information Systems," *Human Resource Management,* 36, (2) (Summer 1997): 261–276; T. Starner, "Networking HR," *Human Resource Executive* (March 4, 1999): 56–58; T. Starner, "Being Direct," *Human Resource Executive* (March 4, 1999): 44–47; J. N. Mottl, "Links to the Future," *Human Resource Executive* (March 4, 1999): 52–55.

[21] J. Fasqualetto, "New Competencies Define the HRIS Manager's Future Role," *Personnel Journal* (January 1993): 2.

[22] M. Tanzer, "Keep Spies Out of Your Company," *Personnel Journal* (May 1993): 45–51.

681

23 "Human Resource Compensation," *Bulletin to Management* (September 30, 1998): 252–253; A. R. McIlvaine, "Show Me the Money," *Human Resource Executive* (March 19, 1998): 66–68; "Datagraph: Human Resource Compensation Survey," *Bulletin to Management* (September 18, 1997): 300–301.

24 M. Avery, "HR Pay Growth Accelerates," *HR Magazine* (November 1998): 122–126.

25 S. H. Applebaum, "The Personnel Professional and Organization Development: Conflict and Synthesis," *Personnel Administrator* (July 1980): 57–61; F. R. Edney, "The Greening of the Profession," *Personnel Administrator* (July 1980): 27–30, 42; F. R. Edney, "Playing on the Team," *Personnel Journal* (August 1981): 598–600; L. B. Prewitt, "The Emerging Field of Human Resources Management," *Personnel Administrator* (May 1982): 81–87.

26 S. H. Applebaum, *1991 SHRM/CCH Survey* (June 26, 1991); M. T. Brown, *Working Ethics: Strategies for Decision Making and Organizational Responsibility* (San Francisco: Jossey-Bass, 1990).

27 L. Grensing-Pophal, "Walking the Tightrope," *HR Magazine* (October 1998): 112–119; M. T. Brown, *Working Ethics: Strategies for Decision Making and Organizational Responsibility* (San Francisco: Jossey-Bass, 1990). L. L. Nash, *Good Intentions Aside: A Manager's Guide to Resolving Ethical Problems* (Boston, MA: Harvard Business School Press, 1990); L. T. Hosmer, *The Ethics of Management* (Homewood, IL: Irwin, 1991).

28 "HR Staff Feeling, Seeing Ethics Pressure," *Bulletin to Management,* 49 (6) (February 12, 1998): 41.

29 *Certification Information Handbook,* (Alexandria, VA: HR Certification Institute, 1994); D. Yoder and H. Heneman, Jr., *PAIR Jobs, Qualifications, and Careers: ASPA Handbook of Personnel and Industrial Relations* (Washington, DC: Bureau of National Affairs, 1978): 18; W. M. Hoffman, R. Frederick, and E. W. Petry, Jr., eds., *The Ethics of Organizational Transformation: Mergers, Takeovers and Corporate Restructuring* (New York: Quorum Books, 1989).

30 W. W. Turnow, "The Codifications Project and Its Importance to Professionalism," *Personnel Administrator* (June 1984): 84–100; C. Haigley, "Professionalism in Personnel," *Personnel Administrator* (June 1984): 103–106. Also contact the Human Research Certification Institute directly by calling the Society for Human Resource Management at (800) 331–2772.

31 "Global HR 'Competencies' Project Gets Under Way," *Worldlink* (October 1998): 1; "Toward Global Standards," *Worldlink* (October 1998): 4.

32 J. J. Laabs, "Stay a Step Ahead," *Workforce* (October 1997): 56–65; R. A. Eisenstat, "What Corporate Human Resources Brings to the Picnic: Four Models for Functional Management," *Organizational Dynamics* (Autumn 1996): 7–21; C. Gedvilas, "The HR Organization for the Future," *ACA News* (March 1997): 14–15.

33 "Special PPF Survey Report: A Profile of Human Resource Executives," *Bulletin to Management,* 48, (25) (June 19, 1997): 1–8; S. Carroll, "HRM Roles and Structures in the Information Age," *HRM in the Information Age,* R. S. Schuler, ed. (Washington, DC: Society for Human Resource Management and Bureau of National Affairs, 1991): 204–227.

34 "SHRM-BNA Survey No. 63, Human Resource Activities, Budgets and Staffs: 1997–1998," *Bulletin to Management,* 49 (24) (June 18, 1998): 1–27; "SHRM-BNA Survey No. 62, Human Resource Activities, Budgets, and Staffs: 1996–97," *Bulletin to Management,* 48 (26) (June 26, 1997): 1–20.

35 M. C. Ciccarelli, "Calling All Computers," *Human Resource Executive* (March 5, 1998): 32–35; D. Ulrich, "Shared Services: From Vogue to Value," *Human Resource Planning* 18 (3) (1995): 12–23.

36 C. Johnson, "Changing Shapes: As Organizations Evolve, HR's Form Follows Its Functions," *HR Magazine* (March 1999): 41–48.

37 L. Davidson, "Cut Away Noncore HR," *Workforce* (January 1998): 41–45; F. Kemske, "HR's Role Will Change. The Question is How. HR 2008," 47–60; J. A. Byrne, "Has Outsourcing Gone Too Far?" *Business Week* (April 1, 1996): 26–28; "Outsourcing Offers Strategic Advantage," *Bulletin to Management* (June 29, 1995): 208; "HR's Advances in Reengineering and Restructuring," *Personnel Journal* (January 1996): 60; G. Flynn, "Optimas Awards Celebrate Exemplary HR," *Personnel Journal* (January 1996): 50; T. A. Stewart, "Re-engineering: The Hot New Management Tool," *Fortune* (August 23, 1994): 41–48; M. Hammer and J. Champy, *Re-engineering the Corporation* (New York: Harper-Collins, 1993); C. Marmer Solomon, "Working Smarter: How HR Can Help," *Personnel Journal* (June 1993): 54–64.

38 J. Rogier, "Making Every Minute Count," *Workforce* (May 1998): 31–33; R. K. Platt, "Outsourcing the HR Function," *ACA News* (June 1996): 12–15.

39 A. Halcrow, "Survey Shows HR in Transition," *Workforce* (June 1998): 73–80; Caudron, "HR Leaders Brainstorm," 59–60.

40 "Outsourcing: Not Always What It's Cracked Up to Be," *Workforce* (August 1998): 23.

41 J. J. Laabs, "The Dark Side of Outsourcing," *Workforce* (September 1998): 42–48; K. S. Wallace, "Avoid the Ten Major Pitfalls of Outsourcing," *Workforce* (September 1998): 44–45; C. M. Solomon, "Protect Your Outsourcing Investment," *Workforce* (October 1998): 130–132; M. F. Cook, *Outsourcing Human Resources Functions: Strategies for Providing Enhanced HR Services at Lower Cost* (New York: AMACOM, 1999).

42 Caudron, "HR Leaders Brainstorm," 57; B. P. Sunoo, "Amgen's Latest Discovery," *Personnel Journal* (February 1996): 38–45.

43 F. Luthans, P. A. Marsnik, and K. W. Luthans, "A Contingency Matrix Approach to IHRM," *Human Resource Management,* 36 (2) (Summer 1997): 183–200; P. J. Dowling, D. Welch, and R. S. Schuler, *International Dimensions of Human Resource Management,* 3rd ed. (Cincinnati, OH: South-Western College Publishing, 1999).

44 M. S. Schnell and C. M. Solomon, "Global Culture: Who's the Gatekeeper," *Workforce* (November 1997): 35–39; J. J. Laabs, "Getting Ahead By Going Abroad," *Global Workforce* (January 1998): 10–11; J. J. Laabs, "HR Pioneers Explore

the Road Less Traveled," *Personnel Journal* (February 1996): 70–78.

[45] A. Kupfer, "Cisco Systems," *Fortune* (September 7, 1998): 85–94; P. Nakache, "Cisco's Recruiting Edge," *Fortune* (September 29, 1997): 275–276; J. A. Byrne, "The Corporation of the Future," *Business Week* (August 31, 1998): 102–106; C. M. Solomon, "Corporate Pioneers

Navigate Global Mergers," *Global Workforce* (September 1998): 12–17; "HR Has Role in Mergers," *Bulletin to Management* (August 13, 1998): 256; R. E. Numerof and M. N. Abrams, "Integrating Corporate Culture from International M&As," *HR Focus* (June 1998): 11–12.

SOUTHWEST AIRLINES: CAN LUV RULE THE WORLD?

Few industries have experienced the turmoil faced by the U.S. domestic airline business during the past two decades. Once characterized by high wages, stable prices, and choreographed competition, the industry changed swiftly and dramatically when deregulation took effect in 1978. Several of the strongest and greatest airlines (e.g., Pan Am, Eastern) disappeared through mergers or bankruptcies. Strikes and disruptions interfered with companies' attempts to reduce costs. New competitors aggressively swooped into the marketplace; the majority failed. In fact, in 1992, industry losses for the year surpassed cumulative profits since the industry's inception.

The industry is again in a period of high demand and expanding profitability. Despite the volatile conditions and many organizational failures, one carrier grew and prospered throughout this entire period—Southwest Airlines.

Southwest was controversial from its inception. Although the Texas Aeronautics Commission approved Southwest's petition to fly on February 20, 1968, the nascent airline was locked in legal battles for three years because competing airlines—Braniff, TransTexas, and Continental—fought through political and legal means to keep it out of the market. Through the efforts of Herb Kelleher, a New York University law school graduate and the airline's current chief executive officer, Southwest finally secured the support of both the Texas Supreme Court and the United States Supreme Court.

Ari Ginsberg and Richard Freedman wrote this case with the research assistance of Bill Smith. The authors thank Myron Uretsky, Eric Greenleaf, and Bethany Gertzog for their valuable comments and suggestions. They also appreciate the careful review, corrections, and helpful recommendations made by Susan Yancey of Southwest Airlines on an earlier version. The case is intended to serve as the basis for class discussion rather than to illustrate either effective or ineffective handling of an administrative situation. A glossary of key terms appears in the case Appendix.

Southwest emerged from these early legal battles with its now famous underdog fighting spirit. The company built its initial advertising campaigns around a prominent issue of the time as well as its airport location. Thus "Make Love, Not War" became the airline's theme, and the company became the "Love" airline. Fittingly, *LUV* was chosen as the company's stock ticker symbol. Southwest went on to see successful growth through three distinct periods. The "Proud Texan" period (1971–1978) saw the establishment of a large city-service network within its home state of Texas. Because it did not engage in interstate commerce, the fledgling carrier was not subject to many federal regulations, particularly those imposed by the Civil Aeronautics Board (CAB). The second phase, "Interstate Expansion" (1978–1986), was characterized by the opening of service to fourteen other states. Interstate expansion was made possible by, and thus coincided with, the deregulation of the domestic airline industry. The most recent phase, "National Achievement" (1987–1997), has been a time of considerable growth, distinguished recognition, and success.

Despite its past success, Southwest Airlines now faces new challenges that raise concerns about its continued ability to grow. Ironically, many of these concerns are a result of changes brought about by Southwest itself. Some of them are external, such as imitation by competitors who are becoming more efficient and the limited size of the shorter haul flight markets in which Southwest developed a core competency. Others are internal, including the emergent problems of managing a larger, more complex organization, and a culture that may be too dependent on the charisma of a single individual or that may not play well to the new audiences needed for future growth. Will Southwest Airlines be able to continue its remarkable success or will emerging conditions seriously threaten Southwest's future prosperity?

The Airline Industry

The competitive environment in which Southwest operates can be subdivided into different value-added stages, customer and service segments, and competitor groups.

Airlines engage in several value-adding activities. These include aircraft procurement, aircraft maintenance, reservation systems, schedule and route planning, in-flight services, and after-flight services. Competitors may differ in their involvement in these activities. For example, Southwest performs some in-house maintenance but offers no post-flight services. By contrast, American Airlines owns and markets its own reservation system, and Allegis, as United Airlines was known briefly in 1987, at one time operated a car rental agency (Hertz) and two hotel chains (Hilton and Westin).

Airlines compete for three primary types of customers: travel agents, corporate travel managers, and individual travelers. The two major categories of passengers are leisure travelers, who tend to be quite price-sensitive, and business travelers, who are more concerned with convenience. To satisfy the different needs of some or all of these groups, airlines present a wide variety of services, depending on their strategy.

Passenger service can be categorized along a number of dimensions. For example, airlines differ by geographical coverage; some specialize in short-haul service while others provide a vast network of interconnected long-haul and short-haul flights on a global basis through a network of strategic alliances. They also differ in how their routes are structured within the territories they serve. The two extremes are point-to-point and hub-and-spoke. The former is characterized by direct service between two points. The latter is characterized by complex, coordinated routes and schedule structures that channel passengers from numerous far-flung airports (the spokes) through a central airport (the hub). The hub itself has many costly infrastructure requirements (baggage handling systems, large terminals, maintenance facilities, and parts inventories). To address the pricing complexity created by multiple traffic flows through a hub, hub-spoke carriers conduct complicated yield and inventory management calculations. The result of this complexity is that the hub-spoke pricing structure is systematically different from point-to-point pricing. These added complexities allow a carrier to offer flights between more "city-pairs" than it could under a point-to-point network. For a company that relies on a network, like an airline or telephone company, competitive advantage accrues from economies of scope, i.e., the geographic reach of that network. Economies of scope do not necessarily complement economies of scale, and in fact are often achieved at the expense of scale economies and vice versa. Thus, although the hub-and-spoke system is driven by economies of scope, each strategy, hub-and-spoke or point-to-point, has its own inherent cost and organizational implications.

Passenger service can also be characterized in terms of breadth. An airline may choose to provide a broad gamut of services including meals, advance seat assignments, and frequent flier programs (full service), or it can offer only Spartan services (no-frills). A further differentiation is the number of service classes offered. Most airlines have two classes of service, First and Coach. Some offer three classes, First, Business, and Coach (United and American on select flights), others offer only Coach (Southwest), and a few offer only First Class (Midwest Express). In addition to the direct cost of providing differentiated service, amenities such as First Class seating and in-flight meals indirectly affect the cost structure of an airline by limiting the number of seats its aircraft can hold. Because Southwest does not currently offer meals or First Class service, its 737-300 holds 137 seats whereas a United Airlines 737-300 holds only 128 seats.

U.S. airlines can be categorized into three major competitor groups based on geographical coverage. First are the "major" national airlines. They include: America West Airlines, American Airlines, Continental Airlines, Delta Airlines, Northwest Airlines, United Airlines, USAir, Southwest Airlines, and TWA. Second are the regionals, which include Reno Air, Airtran (formerly ValuJet), Frontier Airlines, Alaska Airlines, Horizon Airlines, Western Pacific Airlines, Inc., Kiwi International, Air South, and many others. Third is the commuter or "feed" carriers, most of which operate as extensions of the majors. These carriers use mostly turboprop or regional jet equipment and fly routes that are generally less than 500 miles. Some of these carriers include Atlantic Coast Airlines, which operates as United Express, Atlantic Southeast Airlines, which operates as Delta's Business Express, Comair Holdings, another Delta commuter, Mesa Air Group, which operates its own flights as well as feeder flights for United, Mesabi Holdings, Inc., SkyWest, Inc., and numerous others.

Competitive Environment. The *Airline Deregulation Act of 1978* redefined the industry by eliminating the ability of the CAB to set fares, allocate routes, and control entry and exit into markets. Unfortunately, most airlines were hamstrung by high cost structures, including exorbitant labor costs, and highly inefficient planes and infrastructure facilities. In the aftermath of the complete removal of entry and price controls by 1980, competition intensified considerably as new entrants cherry-picked the large carriers' most profitable routes. This led to an extended period of severe industry shakeout and consolidation.

Structural Characteristics. The industry's structural characteristics make it a tough place to be very profitable. The overall industry is not highly concentrated, although it has become more concentrated since deregulation. Nevertheless, most discrete markets are served by a limited number of carriers. In the oligopolistic markets in which most airlines compete, the pricing actions of one company affect the profits of all competitors. Intense price wars have been a frequent event in the industry. Because competition varies from route to route, a carrier can dominate one market, be dominated in another, and face intense rivalry in a third. As a result of the hub-and-spoke system, airlines face head-to-head competition with more carriers in more markets.

Suppliers tend to have relatively high bargaining power. Certain unions are in a position to shut down airlines. Airplane manufacturers (Boeing, Airbus) have considerable power in altering the terms of purchase for planes. Furthermore, the business is capital intensive and requires very large expenditures for airplanes and other infrastructure.

Despite difficult economics, the industry is still attractive to new entrants. There are few substitutes for long-haul air travel. In addition, most of the incumbents have high cost structures that are exceedingly difficult to improve significantly. Carrier failures and downsizing have also created a large supply of relatively new "used" aircraft and the cost of acquiring aircraft is reduced further by the practice of aircraft leasing. Given high debt levels and low profitability in comparison to other industries, most airlines, including Southwest, have begun to lease their planes rather than purchase them. In light of high debt and low profits, the depreciation tax shield is not as valuable to the airlines. By leasing, carriers can "sell" that tax shield to the leasing company, actually creating value for the carrier. As a result, entry barriers are not as high as one would expect in other capital-intensive industries.

Furthermore, new entrants generally gain significant cost advantage by securing lower labor costs because they are not burdened by the unfavorable union contracts that affect many older airlines. Many of the union contracts agreed to by the major airlines call for higher pay and contain work rule provisions that reduce labor productivity. In addition, new entrants are sometimes able to gain favorable terms by purchasing excess capacity of other airlines, such as training and maintenance.

Profitability.   In order to survive and profit in this tough environment, airlines attempt to manipulate three main variables: cost, calculated as total operating expenses divided by available seat miles (ASM); yield, calculated as total operating revenues divided by the number of revenue passenger miles (RPM); and load factor, calculated as the ratio between RPMs and ASMs, which measures capacity utilization. Thus, profitability, defined as income divided by ASM, is computed as:

$$\text{Profitability} = [\text{yield} \times \text{load factor}] - \text{cost}$$

The major airlines have faced intensive competition from low-price airlines in the 1990s. While these low-priced airlines expanded the market for air travel they also placed great downward pressure on the prices of the majors, thereby reducing their yields. To compete, the majors engaged in great cost cutting efforts. Delta announced the goal of reducing its cost/ASM to 7.5 cents by June 1997. It fell from 9.6 cents in April 1994 to 8.75 cents in March 1997. While this resulted in significant savings, it did not prevent Delta's stock price from falling after the company announced earnings well below Wall Street's expectations. Strains arose between Delta CEO Ronald Allen and the board as a consequence of the damage done to Delta's reputation for stellar service, due in part to the cost cutting. This apparently contributed to the board's decision in May 1997 to replace Allen.

Capacity.   JP Morgan analysts believe that the most important factor influencing pricing in the long-term will be the falling industry cost curve. They point out that low-cost airlines have already lowered and inverted the traditionally downward sloping industry cost curve. "With it they have pressured fares industry-wide, but particularly in short-haul markets where their impact on costs have been most dramatic . . . the airlines that are increasing capacity are those lowest on the industry's cost curve."[1] This shift

has occurred because of the growth in low-cost, short-haul travel.

Outlook.   Lehman Brothers analysts concluded in 1996 that the U.S. airline industry was entering a mature and more stable phase, as the major restructuring it required was largely accomplished. In their view, this restructuring was driven by two key developments. First was the retrenchment of the majors into their core hubs. Second was technology diffusion, which occurred when the weaker airlines upgraded their systems technology regarding pricing and yield management and eliminated many disparities among major carriers.

Arenas of competition have also shifted. Low-cost carriers, including Southwest Airlines and Shuttle by United, dominate short-haul capacity in the west. Expansion of the low-cost carriers seems to be slowing, and competition appears to be stabilizing. Meanwhile the East Coast is still dominated by high-cost carriers such as USAir. Consequently, it is not surprising that the low-cost airlines have targeted the east as a major arena for expansion. Southwest's invasion of Florida and Providence, RI is a noteworthy example. In the Northeast, capacity reduction by high-cost competitors such as American, USAir, and Continental has also enhanced the opportunities for low-cost airlines. As carriers learn to adapt the low-cost formula to the geographic, climatic, and market intricacies of the Northeast, low-cost operations will likely continue to expand.

Southwest Airlines' Mission and Objectives

Southwest Airlines' mission focuses to an unusually large degree on customer service and employee commitment. According to its annual report, the mission of Southwest Airlines is "dedication to the highest quality of Customer Service delivered with a sense of warmth, friendliness, individual pride, and Company Spirit." Indeed, Southwest proudly proclaims, "We are a company of People, not planes. That is what distinguishes us from other airlines and other companies." In many respects, the vision that separates Southwest from many of its competitors is the degree to which it is defined by a unique partnership with, and pride in, its employees. As stated in its *Annual Report*:

> At Southwest Airlines, People are our most important asset. Our People know that

because that's the way we treat them. Our People, in turn, provide the best Customer Service in the airline industry. And that's what we are in business for—to provide Legendary Customer Service. We start by hiring only the best People, and we know how to find them. People want to work for a "winner," and because of our success and the genuine concern and respect we have for each of our Employees, we have earned an excellent reputation as a great place to work. As a result, we attract and hire the very best applicants. Once hired, we train, develop, nurture, and, most important of all, support our People! In other words, we empower our Employees to effectively make decisions and to perform their jobs in this very challenging industry.

The airline's goal is to deliver a basic service very efficiently. This translates into a number of fundamental objectives. A central pillar of its approach is to provide safe, low-price transportation in conjunction with maximum customer convenience. The airline provides a high frequency of flights with consistent on-time departures and arrivals. Southwest's employees also aspire to make this commodity service a "fun" experience. Playing games is encouraged, such as "guess the weight of the gate agent." The fun spirit is tempered so that it is never in poor taste and does not alienate business travelers.

Long-term financial objectives include a 15 percent operating margin, 7.5–8.0 percent net margin, return on equity (ROE) of 15 percent, and a debt/equity ratio below 60 percent.

Southwest Airlines' Strategy

Southwest Airlines is categorized as a Low Fare/No Frills airline. However, its size and importance have led most analysts to consider it to be one of the major airlines despite its fit in the low-fare segment. In a fundamental sense, Southwest's business-level strategy is to be the cheapest and most efficient operator in specific domestic regional markets, while continuing to provide its customers with a high level of convenience and service leveraged off its highly motivated employees. Essentially, Southwest's advantage is that it is low-cost and has a good safety reputation.

Cost Leadership. Southwest operates the lowest cost major airline in the industry. The airline devised a number of clever stratagems to achieve this low-cost structure. For example, by serving smaller, less congested secondary airports in larger cities, which tend to have lower gate costs and landing fees, Southwest can maintain schedules cheaply and easily. Southwest's approach is also facilitated by its focus on the southwest and other locations with generally excellent weather conditions, which leads to far fewer delays. Moreover, by following a point-to-point strategy, Southwest need not coordinate flight schedules into connecting hubs and spokes, which dramatically reduces scheduling complexity and costs.

Route Structure. Historically, Southwest has specialized in relatively short-haul flights and has experienced considerable threat from providers of ground transportation (cars, trains, and buses) because the buyers of these short-haul services tend to be quite price sensitive. Southwest has widened the market for air travel by attracting large numbers of patrons who previously relied on ground transportation. For example, before it entered the Louisville to Chicago market, weekly traffic totaled 8,000 passengers. After Southwest entered the market, that number grew to over 26,000. This increase in traffic is now recognized as "The Southwest Effect." Emphasis on short-haul flights has also allowed them to pare costly services such as food, which passengers demand on longer flights. Passengers are provided with only an "extended snack"—cheese, crackers, and a Nutri-Grain bar.

Turnaround Time. Its route structure has helped Southwest to experience the most rapid aircraft turnaround time in the industry (15–20 minutes versus an industry average of 55 minutes). Interestingly, Southwest's "20 Minute Turnaround" can be traced directly to the carrier's first days of operation in Texas when financial pressures forced the company to sell one of the four Boeing 737s it had purchased for its initial service. Having only three planes to fly three routes necessitated very rapid turnaround.

Rapid turnaround time is essential for short-haul flights because airplanes are airborne for a smaller percentage of time than on long-haul flights. Faster turnaround also allows Southwest to fly more daily segments with each plane, which in turn increases its assets' turnover.

Fleet Composition. Southwest has the simplest fleet composition among the major airlines. The company only flies Boeing 737 planes and has committed to fly the 737 exclusively through 2004. Southwest will add a fourth variation when it introduces the 737-700, the newest generation 737.

In choosing the fuel efficient 737, Southwest developed a close relationship with Boeing that enabled it to develop comparatively favorable purchase terms. Although Southwest flies a number of model variations of the 737, the cockpits of the entire fleet are standardized. Therefore, any pilot can fly any plane, and any plane can be deployed on any route. In addition to helping capture scale economies at a much smaller size than its larger competitors, the homogenous fleet composition reduces the complexities of training, maintenance, and service. It is difficult to calculate the large savings associated with this approach, but they exist in almost all operating areas including scheduling, training, aircraft deployment and use, wages and salaries, maintenance, and spare parts inventories.

Travel Agency Exposure. Southwest sells only 60 percent of its tickets through travel agents (compared to 80–85 percent for the majors), thereby saving the 10 percent commission paid to travel agents. This also alleviates the need to participate in many of the travel agent reservation systems.

While this reduces the company's breadth of distribution, it helps to reduce commission payments and Computer Reservation System (CRS) fees, which are approximately $2.50 per flight segment.

Gates. Access to gates is often a constraining factor in the ability of airlines to expand because major airports have limited numbers of gates and most are already taken by other airlines. An emphasis on less crowded secondary airports has alleviated this problem for Southwest. Southwest purchases or leases gates at airports, as opposed to renting the gates of other airlines, which enables the airline to use its own ground crews.

Connections. Southwest does not offer connections to other airlines, which simplifies its ground operations. However, this also limits access for many passengers, particularly from international flights.

Fare Structure. Southwest also controls costs through its simplified fare structure. While Southwest's major competitors have complex fare structures and use computers and artificial intelligence programs to maximize passenger revenues, Southwest offers no special business or first-class seating. Rather, they generally offer a regular coach fare and a limited number of discounted coach fares.

Labor. Labor is the largest cost component of airlines despite the heavy capital investment demanded in the industry. In 1996, Southwest's labor costs were 30.6 percent of revenue and 32.7 percent of operating expenses. About 85 percent of Southwest's employees are unionized. Given the ability of unions to bring carrier operations to a halt, it is not surprising that they wield considerable power. The International Association of Machinists and Aerospace Workers (IAM) represents customer service and reservation employees; the Transportation Workers Union of America (TWU) represents flight attendants; the Southwest Airline Pilots' Association (SWAPA) represents pilots; and the International Brotherhood of Teamsters (IBT) represents aircraft cleaners, mechanics, flight training instructors, and others. There are also some other smaller unions.

What is unique in the industry is Southwest's partnership between its management and its unions. Southwest's strategy has been a combination of profit sharing and participation. In 1992, employees owned 10 percent of stock, and in 1995, pilots were granted options to purchase 14.5 million shares of stock (an additional 10.1 percent of outstanding common stock). Pilots will be eligible for profit bonuses of up to 3 percent of compensation in three of the first five years and in two of the second five years of the recently signed ten-year contract.

In an industry where unions and management have often been at war—and where unions have the power to resist essential changes—the quality of their relationship is a crucial issue. Perhaps one of the best examples of this is the 1994 agreement between Southwest Airlines and SWAPA. The pilots agreed to keep pay rates at existing levels for five years, with increases of 3 percent in three of the last five years of the ten-year deal (five-year base term, with an additional five years unless it is terminated by the union.). As mentioned, pilots can earn additional pay based on company profits. The pilots also obtained options to acquire up to 1.4 million shares of company stock in each of the ten years, in accord with market prices on the date of the deal. Pilots hired between 1996 and 2003 obtain lesser amounts of options at 5 percent over the then market value of the stock.

Customer Service. Southwest's approach to customer service is one of its core strategies. Its "Positively Outrageous Service" (POS) is different from the customer service associated with other major airlines. Service is provided with friendliness, caring, warmth, and company spirit—staff go out of their way to be helpful. This approach to service leverages Southwest's outstanding relationship with its employees. However, this stellar customer service does not include costly amenities like reserved seats or food service, and only offers very limited automatic baggage re-checking. By emphasizing flight frequency and on-time performance, Southwest has redefined the concept of quality air service. This unusual approach has allowed Southwest to differentiate its service while maintaining its cost leadership strategy.

Culture. Perhaps one of the most unique aspects of Southwest's strategy is the degree to which it has used its unique culture as a major strategic weapon. An atmosphere of cooperation and team spirit characterizes the culture. Workers believe that Southwest's management cares about them, and management tries hard to ensure that personnel are treated properly. This culture provides much of the basis for Southwest's labor relations, customer service, and organizational flexibility.

Marketing. Marketing savvy also plays a key role in Southwest's strategy. Since Southwest's inception, the major elements of the product offering have been price, convenience, and service. As a Texas native serving mostly Texas markets, it has played the role of the hometown underdog, fighting against the majors. Now, when Southwest enters a new market, they use a sophisticated combination of advertising, public relations, and promotions in the belief that once people fly Southwest they will be hooked.

Growth. Despite its remarkable growth in what had been until recently a relatively moribund industry, Southwest has not emphasized growth as an objective. In fact, Herb Kelleher

expresses a "go-slow" philosophy. For example, Southwest will not enter markets unless it perceives favorable conditions, which range from the wishes of the local community to the availability of an appropriate labor supply. Given its record of success and its reputation, it is not surprising that there are many communities that want Southwest to serve their markets. After all, good air service is considered by most communities to be an essential aspect of economic development. However, Southwest's policy prohibits accepting monetary subsidies or other incentives that cities and airports offer to gain air service. Southwest has also demonstrated a remarkable ability to manage its growth, an essential commodity in an industry known for its complexity. The inability to manage rapid growth has been blamed for the failure of many carriers, including Braniff, PeopleExpress, and ValuJet.

Organization

Structure. Southwest, like most airlines, is a formal and centralized organization. Organizationally, Southwest is structured according to functions, as illustrated in Exhibit C.1.1. The nature of operations in the airline business is quite mechanical. That is, airline operations naturally aim for efficiency and consistency. They are not spontaneous—they value clock-like behavior. Planes must be in certain places at certain times and must be operated safely and efficiently. Safety itself requires following very rigorous procedures to ensure proper maintenance and training. The reputation of an airline can be seriously damaged by only one or two serious accidents. Therefore, the organization of Southwest is characterized by a high degree of formalization and standardization.

Reporting to Chief Executive Officer (CEO) Herb Kelleher are three Executive Vice Presidents. Perhaps the most influential is Colleen C. Barrett who is in charge of such key functions as marketing, sales, advertising, human resources, customer relations, and governmental affairs. John G. Denison is Executive Vice President in charge of Corporate Services, which includes finance, legal, facilities, reservations, revenue management (pricing), and systems (including computer services and telecommunications). Gary Barron is Executive Vice President and Chief Operations Officer. His responsibilities include schedule planning, flight

Exhibit C.1.1
Organizational Chart

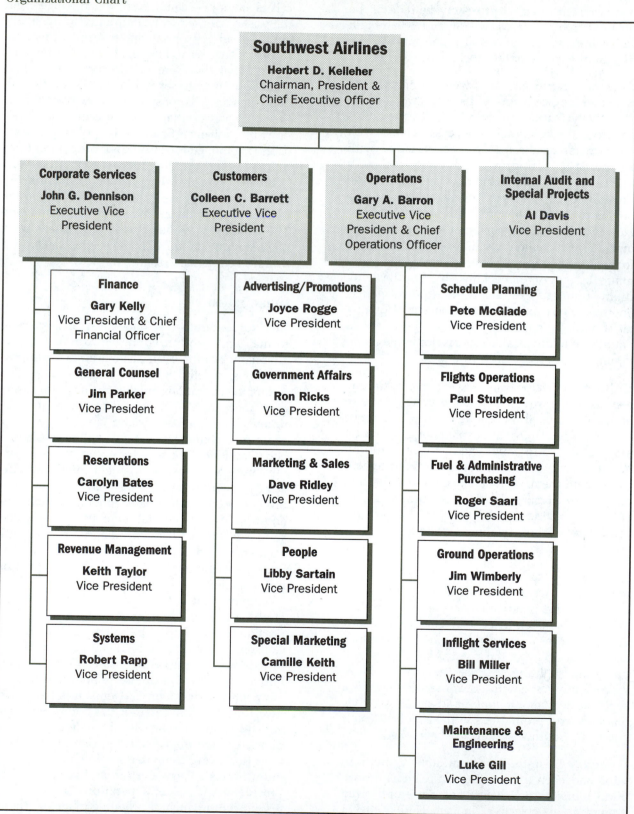

operations, fuel and administrative purchasing, ground operations, in-flight services, and maintenance and engineering. There is one other Vice President reporting to Kelleher, Al Davis, who is in charge of internal auditing and special projects. For operations controller functions he reports to Gary Barron.

How has Southwest Airlines maintained high levels of customer and employee satisfaction in the context of a functional organization? The company uses a number of mechanisms to allow employee participation. The fundamental concept is the notion of a "loose-tight" design. Within the context of tight rules and procedures, employees are encouraged to take a wide degree of leeway. The company maintains rather informal job descriptions and decentralizes decision making regarding customer service. So while there is very high standardization regarding operations, it is low with respect to customer service. Employees are empowered to do what is necessary to satisfy customers. Flight attendants are allowed to improvise cabin instructions and employees play practical jokes on each other and customers. Positively Outrageous Service in action! The company management operates with an informal open door policy that allows employees to circumvent the formal hierarchy. Employees are encouraged to try things, knowing they will not be punished.

Southwest's organization is considerably simpler than its major competitors. Most of its competitors must manage the spatial complexity of far flung international operations and contend with the added intricacies of hub-and-spoke systems. These large international carriers are also involved in complex alliances with other airlines in foreign markets to augment the scope of their services. They manage code sharing arrangements with small regional domestic carriers. In short, the large carriers are complex networks, with more complicated organizational management issues.

Size. Southwest operates in more than 50 cities in 25 states and employs 22,944 people. This consists of 6,228 flight personnel, 1,049 maintenance workers, 13,148 in ground customer service, and 2,519 in management, marketing, accounting, and clerical positions. The company has become such a popular employer that in 1995, 124,000 people applied for 5,500 jobs. Southwest is still a relatively small company compared to the other major airlines. It ranks eighth in revenues and fifth in passenger boardings. Southwest's Available Seat Miles (ASMs) total less than a quarter of American Airlines, and it operates a fleet of only 243 aircraft compared to American's 635. Nevertheless, Southwest is the largest carrier in a significant number of the markets in which it flies and the dominant airline in the short-haul niche of the airline business.

Adaptability. Southwest has been a very nimble organization, quick to take advantage of market opportunities. For example, when American Airlines and USAir scaled back their California operations, Southwest quickly took over the abandoned gates, acquired more planes, and now has 50 percent of the California market. Another example is Southwest's expansion into the Chicago Midway market following the collapse of Midway Airlines. Much of this flexibility stems from the company's remarkable labor relations. In addition, although Southwest is still purely a domestic carrier, it is developing a strategic alliance with Icelandair, a small North-European Carrier.

Human Resource Management. At Southwest Airlines the human resource function is called the People Department. According to the department's mission statement: "recognizing that our people are the competitive advantage, we deliver the resources and services to prepare our people to be winners, to support the growth and profitability of the company, while preserving the values and special culture of Southwest Airlines." The crucial importance of human resources to the strategy of Southwest has made the People Department more organizationally central to the company than its counterparts are at its competitors. Given Southwest's reputation as a great place to work, it is no wonder that so many people apply for each job opening. This allows the company to be extremely selective in its hiring and to look for applicants who are a good "fit." In fact, the company rejects about 100,000 applicants a year, and the turnover rate is less than half of most other airlines. As Kelleher has said, "We draft great attitudes. If you don't have a good attitude, we don't want you, no matter how skilled you are. We can change skill levels through training. We can't change attitude." A new hire's first six months at Southwest are a period of indoctrination and mentoring. These six months are also used to weed out anyone who does not mesh with the culture.

In an organization where attitudes, culture, and fit are so important it is natural that the company places such a great emphasis on socialization and training. McDonald's has its Hamburger University, Southwest has its University for People. Everyone at Southwest has a responsibility for self-improvement and training. Once a year, all Southwest employees, including all senior management, are required to participate in training programs designed to reinforce shared values. Except for flight training, which is regulated and certified, all training is done on the employee's own time. Nonetheless, the training department operates at full capacity, seven days a week. The fun spirit of Southwest emerges in graduates very early. For example, a class of new pilots stumbled into Kelleher's office wearing dark glasses and holding white canes.

The importance of labor relations cannot be underestimated in a company that is almost 85 percent unionized. Here again Kelleher's unusual abilities emerge. Somehow he has been able to convince union members and officials to identify with the company.

It is also noteworthy that in an era when chief executive pay has escalated to huge amounts, Kelleher, in 1994, was named one of the lowest-paid chief executive officers in Dallas on a performance-adjusted basis. Furthermore, company officers do not get the perks often enjoyed by their counterparts in comparable organizations—no cars or club memberships—and they even stay in the same hotels as flight crews. Southwest has refused to compete for executive talent based on salary. This is not to suggest that Kelleher is impoverished. Like many Southwest employees, he has become wealthy from its stock.

Culture and Control.   The most distinguishing feature of Southwest Airlines is its culture. When competitors and outside observers describe Southwest, they tend to focus on its cultural attributes. Herb Kelleher has made the development and maintenance of culture one of his primary duties. The culture permeates the entire organization and sends clear signals about the behavior expected at Southwest. To promote employee awareness of the effects of their efforts on the company's bottom line, *LUV Lines* (the company newsletter) reports break-even vol-

umes per plane. The newsletter informs employees not only of Southwest's issues, but competitor news as well. The belief is that informed employees are better equipped to make decisions.

One of the shared values is the importance of having fun at work. Humor is a significant aspect of the work environment. Such attributes are believed by senior management to enhance a sense of community, trust, and spirit and to counterbalance the stress and pressures of the mechanistic demands of airline operations.

Another characteristic is the cooperative relationship among employee groups. This can be an advantage in functional structures, which are notorious for generating coordination problems. In other airlines, work procedures clearly demarcate job duties. However, at Southwest everyone pitches in regardless of the task. Stories abound of pilots helping with baggage and of employees going out of their way to help customers. In one particularly bizarre story, an agent baby-sat a passenger's dog for two weeks so that the customer could take a flight on which pets were not allowed. Employee cooperation impacts the bottom line. When pilots help flight attendants clean the aircraft and check in passengers at the gate, turnaround time, a cornerstone of the low-cost structure, is expedited.

Because of its team-oriented culture, Southwest is not stifled by the rigid work rules that characterize most competitors. As a result, Southwest has tempered the stringent demands of a functional structure with the liberating force of an egalitarian culture. One excerpt from Southwest's "The Book on Service: What Positively Outrageous Service Looks Like at Southwest Airlines" is rather instructive:

> *"Attitude breeds attitude . . ." If we want our customers to have fun, we must create a fun-loving environment. That means we have to be self-confident enough to reach out and share our sense of humor and fun—with both our internal and external customers. We must want to play and be willing to expend the extra energy it takes to create a fun experience with our customers.*
>
> *Just as the words "it's not my job" can take away the source of life for a consumer-oriented business, the words "it's just a job" are equally as dangerous. Positively Outrageous Service cannot be learned from a book or manual; it cannot be artificially manufac-*

tured; and it is not required by law. It is born and bred in each individual according to his or experiences, attitude, and genuine desire to succeed—both personally and professionally. Service does not start at the beginning of each work day, nor does it end when you go home. It is a very real part of you . . . it's your company; your success; your future.

This approach certainly contributes significantly to the lowest employee turnover rate in the industry (7 percent) and the highest level of consumer satisfaction.

Despite all of the freedom that the culture permits, in some areas the company also employs very stringent controls. Perhaps the best example is that Herb Kelleher himself must approve all expenditures over $1,000!

Forged over 26 years, Southwest's culture has been a source of sustainable competitive advantage. A Bankers Trust analyst put it this way:

> Southwest has an indefinably unique corporate culture and very special management/ employee relationship that has taken years to cultivate. Employees have long had a significant stake in the company; employee ownership and employee contribution to wealth creation are not ideas that are alien to the workforce of Southwest Airlines since it is emphatically not 'just a job.' Then, too, the relationship is not merely spiritual—the employees have come to trust the only company that has a record of 23 consecutive years of earning stability combined with an impressive record of stock appreciation unmatched by virtually any company . . . within or beyond the airline industry. The pilots are well compensated relative to the industry average, and they understand that. The challenge was to find creative ways to tie together the fortunes of the company with those responsible for it without risk or destruction of shareholder value . . . and, unlike the employee groups at other major airlines, the Southwest pilots understand that.[2]

Management. There is no doubt as to who is in charge at Southwest. In this respect Southwest is like most of the other airlines, centralized with a very strong, if not dominating CEO. What sets Herb Kelleher apart is his charismatic nature. His friendly, participative, deeply involved, and caring approach is revered throughout the organization. A very large number of employees know the CEO, and he is reputed to know thousands of them by name. Nonetheless, it is also known that behind the scenes he can be extremely tough, implying that his public and private personae can be quite different.

Herb Kelleher, age 65, started Southwest with a former client, Rollin King, who is still a member of the Board of Directors. King supposedly presented his idea for a low-cost Texas-only airline based on the success of Pacific Southwest Airlines in California to Kelleher over dinner at the St. Antony Club in San Antonio. The original "Love Triangle," the foundation of Southwest's strategy, was drawn on a cocktail napkin.

Kelleher's management style, which has been described as a combination of Sam Walton's thriftiness and Robin Williams's wackiness,[3] seems to have been consistent right from the beginning. Direct, visible, and, some would say, even bizarre, he has attended company parties dressed in drag and appeared in a company ad as Elvis. Known for constantly showing the flag in the field and interacting with large numbers of employees and customers, Kelleher is reputed to have engaged people in conversations for hours, at all hours, about company and industry issues, often with a drink in his hand. He almost always seems ready for a party, and this fun-oriented atmosphere pervades the organization. The company newspaper, *LUV Lines*, has a column, "So, What Was Herb Doing All This Time?" recounting the CEO's activities. Kelleher regularly works 16-hour days and 7-day weeks. Following his example, Southwest employees are well known for going the extra mile. Among the stories of such behavior is that of a customer service representative who stayed overnight at a hotel with an elderly woman who was afraid to stay alone when her flight was grounded due to fog. The agent "knew" that was what Herb would have done.

Kelleher has replaced formal strategic planning with "future scenario generation," arguing that "reality is chaotic, and planning is ordered and logical. The meticulous nit-picking that goes on in most strategic planning processes creates a mental straightjacket that becomes disabling in an industry where things change radically from one day to the next."[4]

One of the most powerful departments is the Customer Department headed by Colleen

Barrett, Executive Vice President, and Kelleher's right-hand. She is the senior female in the airline industry, and provides the organizational balance for Kelleher. While he is reputed to have a chaotic style, she is known to be a stickler for details. She plays another unofficial role, acting as an ombudsman for customers and as an internal management expert.

In the early 1990s Barrett set up a company culture committee, comprised of people from all geographic areas and levels of the company. The committee, which meets four times a year, is charged with preserving and enhancing the company culture. One of the committee's successes is illustrated by the company organization. It is well known that functional structures such as Southwest's are designed to promote specialization and scale economies, but often at the expense of teamwork and coordination. As these organizations grow they become even more difficult to operate in an integrated manner. The committee developed a number of initiatives to improve cross-functional cooperation. One example is that all company officers and directors have to spend one day every quarter in the field—working a real "line job."

Technology. Like all airlines, Southwest is a very heavy user of computer-related technology. This technology supports all activities from scheduling to reservations to general operations support. The network is built on four superservers and a reservations subsystem that connects more than 5,000 PCs and terminals across the country. Remote locations communicate with the servers using TCP/IP across Novell LANs.

This network supports a reservation system that has enabled Southwest to be the first carrier to offer ticketless travel on all of its flights. They now average more than 15,000 ticketless passengers per day, according to Robert W. Rapp, Vice President of Systems. The ticketless system offers significantly improved customer service by eliminating lines at ticket counters. The system also reduces costs; it is estimated that it costs an airline from $15 to $30 to produce and process a single paper ticket.

Customers using the Southwest ticketless system can purchase a seat on a Southwest flight by telephone or on the Internet. Customers receive a confirmation code, which is traded for a boarding pass at the airport. The concept of ticketless travel originated at Morris Air, a Salt Lake City airline acquired by Southwest in 1993. Although policy and operational differences prevented Southwest from adopting the Morris system, the company was able to accelerate the development of its own system with the assistance of Evan Airline Information Services, a consulting firm that helped to develop Morris Air's system. The first ticketless passenger boarded a Southwest plane only four months after development began.

All Internet activities are concentrated under Kevin Krone, Manager of Marketing Support. Marketing activities explicitly build on the Internet as a primary marketing channel. Krone's activities are closely coordinated with the requirements and support facilities of Rapp's department. Southwest was the first carrier to host a web site, **www.iflyswa.com**, which was deemed "Best Airline Web Site" by Air Transport World. It recently launched a joint venture with Worldview Systems to enhance its Internet presence.

Performance

There are many different criteria that can be used to evaluate Southwest's success in achieving its basic objectives. Certainly Southwest's different constituencies look at its performance in different ways. Southwest takes particular pride in the following accomplishments:

- 28 years of safe, reliable operations;
- five consecutive years of Triple Crown Customer Service;
- five consecutive years of record profits and 24 consecutive years of profitability;
- recognition as one of the top ten places to work in Robert Levering and Milton Moscowitz's book, *The Best 100 Companies to Work for in America*;
- top ranking in the Airline Quality Survey conducted by The National Institute for Aviation Research for two of the last three years;
- consistent financial success that provides thousands of jobs in the aerospace industry; and
- a route system that has grown to 52 airports in 25 states, carrying more than 50 million customers on 243 Boeing 737 aircraft.

No issue is more important than safety. One need only to study the checkered history of ValuJet or Air Florida to see what one catastrophic crash can do to an airline when the airline is perceived to have been at fault. Meanwhile, Southwest maintains a 28-year safety record and is generally acknowledged to be one of the world's safest airlines.

Of course, Southwest's customers remain one of the company's main constituencies. Despite its "no-frills" orientation, Southwest consistently receives the highest rankings for customer satisfaction. This is achieved through the successful management of customer expectations. By emphasizing low price and consistency, Southwest has successfully redefined the concept of quality airline service. For example, the "Triple Crown Award" goes to the airline, if any, which has the best on-time record, best baggage handling, and fewest customer complaints according to statistics published in the Department of Transportation (DOT) Air Travel Consumer Reports. First won by Southwest in 1988, the airline has won the award every year since 1992. No other airline has ranked on top in all three categories for even a single month.

Given its mission, employee satisfaction is another important indicator of company success. Personnel are a crucial determinant of organizational performance throughout the industry. Labor costs are about 40 percent of operating costs in the industry, while at Southwest they are considerably lower. As noted, labor relations is an important determinant of company survival. Southwest has one of the lowest personnel turnover ratios in the industry. It began the first profit-sharing plan in the industry, and employees now own more than 10 percent of the stock. *Fortune* has named Southwest as one of the best companies for attracting, developing, and keeping talented people. In 1997, *Fortune* ranked Southwest first on its list of the "100 Best Companies to Work for in America."

Southwest has had generally peaceful and cooperative labor relations throughout most of its history. One salient result of management-labor harmony is that Southwest employees are the most productive in the industry. A single agent usually staffs gates, where competitors commonly use two or three. Ground crews are composed of six or fewer employees, about half the number used by other carriers. Despite the lean staffing, planes are turned around in half the time of many rivals. Southwest pays its pilots wages that are comparable to the major carriers, but pilot productivity (e.g., number of flights per day, number of hours worked) is considerably higher.

Despite its low-cost structure, Southwest is not able to control all costs. Perhaps the most important uncontrollable element is fuel, which has varied from 21.8 percent of operating expenses in 1990 to 14.0 percent in 1995 (it is estimated at 15.3 percent in 1996). One advantage that larger, broader scope carriers have is a more limited exposure to fuel price volatility. Broader scope allows them to take advantage of geographic differences in fuel prices, and deeper pockets allow them to hedge against future price increases. However, Southwest does have the advantage of a younger and more fuel-efficient fleet than its larger competitors.

Southwest has also performed well on many financial criteria. The company's net earnings were $207.3 million in 1996 compared to $182.6 million in 1995, capping five consecutive years of record profits and 24 consecutive years of profitability. This record includes 1991 and 1992, when every other major airline lost money. It has an "A" rating on unsecured debt, and its debt to equity ratio is one of the best in the industry (.25 versus .6 industry average). Its interest coverage is one of the best (6.75 versus an industry average of 2).

Market share is another indicator of an organization's performance. By this criterion, Southwest also ranks at the top of the industry. For example, it consistently ranks first in market share in 80–90 of its top 100 city-pair markets, with a passenger share of 60–70 percent. Because of the "Southwest Effect," the carrier gains this share by growing the size of each of its markets—this is achieved by a fare structure that is on average $60 lower than the majors.

The Challenges Ahead

Southwest Airlines is no Johnny-come-lately. Its basic strategy of consistent low-cost, no-frills, high-frequency, on-time air transportation with friendly service is a recipe that has been refined throughout the company's 28-year life. It has worked for the company in periods of catastrophic losses for the industry as well as in times of abundance. Southwest has been able to compete successfully both with the major airlines and those that have been formed to copy its formula.

Opportunities for Growth. Southwest apparently recognizes the potential saturation of its historic markets and the limited number of attractive short-haul markets. Therefore, it has expanded into some longer-haul markets. Longer-haul not only provides avenues for future growth, but also provides potentially higher margins. On average, the company's cost per ASM is just below 7.5 cents. However, on its longer routes costs are as low as 4 cents per ASM. Furthermore, as mentioned, the 10 percent ticket tax has been replaced with a combination ticket tax and takeoff fee. This increases the attractiveness of longer-haul flights.

Analysts see growth directions in the invasion of new markets, such as Florida, as well as in the addition of new city-pairs to Southwest's point-to-point network. In 1996, Southwest entered four new markets: Tampa, Ft. Lauderdale, and Orlando, Florida, and Providence, Rhode Island. At year-end 1996, 22 percent of the carrier's ASMs were deployed on the west coast; 33 percent in the remainder of the western region (west of Texas); 19 percent in the heartland region (Texas, Oklahoma, Arkansas, and Louisiana); 16 percent in the Midwest region; and ten percent on the east coast (Providence, Baltimore, and Florida). Southwest is adding longer routes, such as the recently inaugurated Albuquerque to Orlando route, and operations from Nashville all the way to the west coast. Seven new nonstop flights from Nashville International Airport began in April 1997, and two additional departures became effective in June. The new nonstop routings are Nashville to Detroit, Los Angeles, Oakland, and Columbus, and enhanced nonstop service from Nashville to Las Vegas and Tampa. Southwest began service to Jacksonville, Florida on January 15, 1997.

Limits to Growth.   As critics have noted, there are many challenges on the horizon. Southwest will eventually saturate its historic niche. The company currently flies into 52 airports with an average of 2,600 flights per day. Its old strategy of focusing on good climates and smaller, less congested airports has contributed to Southwest's low costs. Many believe that poor weather conditions can affect Southwest's ability to maintain on-time performance and can significantly impact down-line operations. This is magnified by a schedule based on a rapid turnaround, which leaves little leeway for flight delays. Southwest entered and then left the Denver market when bad weather forced an unacceptable number of delays and canceled flights.

This puts a limit on growth because there are only a finite number of markets that can satisfy these criteria. Thus, Southwest has begun to enter markets in poorer climates and to introduce longer-haul flights. Providence, Rhode Island, one of the newer locations, is not a good weather location. There are about 56 airports in good weather locations with populations of over 100,000. Southwest currently serves 36. It is unclear how much demand for point-to-point service exists in the remaining 20.

If Southwest decides to introduce food services as an amenity for longer-haul flights, it would require galleys and onboard services that would significantly boost the cost of operation of those airplanes. Longer flights also result in fewer flights per day and may serve to drive down yield. A mixture of galleyed and non-galleyed aircraft will also make fleet scheduling less flexible. Furthermore, there will be a greater need for functions in the organization responsible for new elements such as national marketing, the frequent flyer program, interline agreements, new geographic operations, and possibly food services.

People and culture also are major concerns to further expansion. Southwest is highly selective; it consequently needs a large pool of applicants in order to find a few people good enough for the culture. With labor shortages across the country, it may be difficult to attract large pools of applicants. Without the selectivity, Southwest may not be able to get the human resources it needs in order to differentiate itself from others. The unique culture of Southwest helps make the company really fly. As companies expand, particularly in geographic location, they often find that it becomes increasingly more difficult to maintain the same culture. This is particularly true if the culture is built around the persona of one major leader such as Herb.

Competition.   During the last several years, the gap between Southwest and the rest of the majors has narrowed as other carriers have attempted to emulate Southwest's formula. Larger airlines have developed lower cost short-haul divisions. Continental, United, and Delta have all introduced an "airline within an airline" to lower costs for short-haul flights, and American is likely to follow. These separate divisions may hire their own pilots and ground support at much lower costs under separate contractual relations with unions. Under these arrangements pilots can often be employed for less than half the cost of the parent airline. This, not surprisingly, has led to some bitter disputes between management and unions. For example, at American Airlines the unions have seen this as a management tactic for shifting their members from high- to low-paying jobs with the same duties.

At the same time, Southwest has adopted many of the features that the majors use to support their large networks. As Southwest has grown in scope, it has introduced national advertising, including NFL sponsorship; a frequent flyer program, including a branded credit card; and interline and marketing agreements with international carriers. Southwest's operations at Nashville are developing into a hub. The carrier's average stage length has also increased over the last several years. Southwest has now expanded into geographic markets and climates that are not as compatible with its original fair-weather, low-congestion strategy. Its flights now compete head to head with some of the major carriers.

Succession. Few CEOs are more closely identified with company success than Herb Kelleher. As the company gets larger, and as he gets older—and by the way, he boasts of his passion for bourbon (Wild Turkey) and cigarettes (five packs a day)—will organizational weaknesses begin to emerge? For example, Southwest's boast about hard working employees provoked 92 percent of its flight attendants to reject a new contract in June 1997. As Paul Sweetin, the flight attendants' union chief stated: "After being told for a long time that they were the best employees in the business, flight attendants are saying 'Well show me I'm the best in terms of compensation.'"[5]

Analysts worry about the degree to which Southwest's future is dependent on one person—although the company claims that this is not the case. In fact, articles in *Fortune* and *The New York Times Magazine* have identified the issue as an obstacle to the company's long-term success. Although Kelleher says he won't retire until about 2010, Rollin King, a board member and close friend, predicts he will likely retire at the end of his five-year contract in 2003.[6]

Board members, concerned about his health, cut back on the number of people reporting to Kelleher several years ago and have questioned him about succession planning. However, he still does not have a clear second in command. To some extent, the board also sees his lack of an apparent successor as a virtue, claiming that it keeps contenders from leaving. As a safeguard, Southwest has also put in place a Culture Committee of more than 100 corporate missionaries who have been charged with institutionalizing Kelleher's influence. Still, invoking the case of Walt Disney, analysts wonder whether Southwest's greatest risk after Kelleher is gone might be letting that influence grow too strong.[7]

Whoever will lead Southwest in the coming years will need to deal with significant challenges: a set of increasingly able competitors, potentially weakened labor relations, and the strain of national growth that will accompany Southwest's departure from previously successful strategies. Southwest is committed to introducing "safe, affordable, Triple Crown service to even more Americans in order to allow them to go, see, and do things never before dreamed possible." In effect, this means doing for the United States what the high-speed rail network did for Western Europe. To keep this dream from turning into a nightmare, the company's management will need to think very carefully about the challenges ahead and the actions that will be critical for future success.

ENDNOTES

[1] JP Morgan, *Short-haul Competitive Update* (April 16, 1996): 3.

[2] V. Lee, "Impacts of Deregulation and Recent Trends on Aviation Industry Management," *Bankers Trust Research* (August 30, 1996): 16.

[3] A. R. Myerson, "Air Herb," *New York Times Magazine* (November 9, 1997): 36.

[4] J. Freiberg and K. Freiberg, *NUTS! Southwest Airlines' Crazy Recipe for Business and Personal Success* (Austin, TX: Bard Books, 1996).

[5] Myerson, "Air Herb," 39.

[6] Myerson, "Air Herb," 39.

[7] Myerson, "Air Herb," 39.

Appendix
Glossary of Terms

ARC	Airline Reporting Corporation. An organization owned by the airlines that serves as a clearing house for processing airline tickets.
ASM	Available Seat Mile. One ASM is one sellable seat, flown for one mile. For example, a 138 seat Boeing 737 traveling 749 miles from LGA to ORD (LaGuardia to O'Hare) represents 103,362 ASMs.
Class of Service	The fare level at which a ticket is sold. This does not refer to the cabin in which the passenger flies. For example, a United Airlines' availability display shows the following classes of service for coach: Y B M H Q V. By subdividing coach into classes, airlines can control inventory and manage yield.
Code Share	An interline agreement by which two carriers are able to apply their flight numbers to the same plane. This often includes an interline connection. For example, American Airlines and South African Airlines code share on SAA's flight to JHB (Johannesburg). The flight has an AA flight number and an SAA flight number. AA can sell it as an American Airlines flight.
CRS	Computer Reservation System. Allows airlines and travel agents to reserve and sell seats on airline flights. CRS companies include Apollo, Sabre, System One, and Worldspan.
Direct Flight	Any flight designated by a single flight number. Direct flights can include multiple stops and even changes of aircraft. For example, Pan Am Flight 1 at one time made 11 stops as it flew "round the world" direct from LAX to JFK.
Full Fare	Designated as "Full Y." The undiscounted first, business, or coach fare. For domestic fares, this is used to calculate the level of discounted fares. Full Y is rarely paid for domestic flights, but is common on international flights when inventory is scarce.
IATA	International Air Transport Association. Organization which regulates the relationships between carriers.
Interline Agreement	Refers to various agreements between carriers. Common interline agreements concern the transfer of baggage, the endorsement and acceptance of tickets, and joint airfares (for example, a passenger flies USAir from Albany to JFK and then SAS to Copenhagen).
Inventory	The number of seats available for each class of service for a given flight. For example, a USAir flight may have no K inventory available (seats to sell at K class fare levels) although higher priced H seats may be available. Both seats are in coach.
Load Factor	The percentage of ASMs that are filled by paying passengers. Can be calculated by dividing RPMs by ASMs.
O&D	Origin and Destination. Refers to the originating and terminating airports of an itinerary segment. Connection points are not counted in O&Ds. This is different from city-pair, which refers to the origination and termination of a flight segment. For example, for a passenger traveling on NW from HPN (White Plains) to SMF (Sacramento), the O&D market is HPN-SMF. The city-pairs flown will be HPN-DTW and DTW-SMF (White Plains-Detroit, Detroit-Sacramento)
Restricted Fare	Any fare that has restrictive rules attached to it. Common restrictions include Saturday Night Stayover, Advance Purchase, Day/Time of Travel, Non-Refundability, and Class of Service. Generally, lower fares have greater restrictions.
RPM	Revenue Passenger Mile. One passenger paying to fly one mile. For example, a passenger who pays to fly from LGA to ORD represents 749 RPMs. The class of service and fare paid are not considered in calculating RPMs.
Stage Length	The length of a flight segment. The stage length between LGA and ORD is 749 miles.
Unrestricted Fare	A fare with no restrictions. Often, this is not the full fare. For example, American's Y26 fare is an unrestricted fare, but still lower than the full Y fare.
Yield	Measured as revenue per RPM.

AID ASSOCIATION FOR LUTHERANS

All across the United States, millions of Americans buy a variety of insurance products each year. They buy them from insurers like Metropolitan Life Insurance Company and Prudential Insurance Company of America, the so-called commercial insurers, and from Aid Association for Lutherans (AAL) and Knights of Columbus, the so-called fraternal benefit societies. Unlike commercial insurers, the approximately 200 fraternal benefit societies, which are exempt from certain taxes, serve up a mix of financial products, good works, member services, and sometimes social activities. Generally founded at the turn of the twentieth century by immigrants to provide for each other in tough times, the groups were among the first to offer insurance to working-class people. Although the societies account for less than two percent of the new life insurance policies written each year, they sell life insurance and annuities—and sometimes health insurance, disability insurance, and mutual funds—to about ten million Americans.[1]

A key concern for anyone when buying life insurance is a company's financial soundness. In this regard, fraternal societies appear to be ahead of the pack. Policyholders have suffered no losses in recent memory, says a spokesman for A. M. Best, an independent agency that reviews and rates the insurance industry on the basis of overall performance and financial strength. But a few societies have merged because of declining membership. Of the 42 fraternals rated by the agency, 30 fall in the top six of its fifteen rating categories, and the six largest fraternals, after which size drops off considerably, are in that upper tier. The largest of these is Aid Association for Lutherans.[2]

This case was prepared by Randall S. Schuler with the assistance of Jerome H. Laubenstein and his associates in the IPS Department of AAL. Their contributions are greatly appreciated. Updated, 1999.

Aid Association for Lutherans

AAL provides fraternal benefits and financial security for Lutherans and their families. Individuals who purchase financial products from AAL also become members of AAL and join one of over 8,600 local volunteer service chapters called branches. Through the volunteer efforts of 1.6 million members, branches are provided opportunities to help themselves, their churches, and their communities. Members also receive free educational materials on family and health topics. AAL also offers scholarship opportunities for members as well as grants to help Lutheran congregations and institutions. In total, nearly $65 million was spent on AAL's fraternal outreach in 1997. AAL's financial product's include individual life, disability income, and long-term care insurance, and annuity products. Its subsidiary company, AAL Capital Management Corporation, offers mutual funds to AAL's members. The AAL Member Credit Union is an affiliate that offers members federally insured savings accounts, a credit card, and various types of loans and home mortgages.

AAL assets under management are over $24 billion. Total revenue is over $2 billion. AAL is among the top two percent of all U.S. life insurers and is the nation's largest fraternal benefit society in terms of assets and ordinary life insurance in force. AAL also maintains an A+ rating from A. M. Best, an AAA rating from Duff and Phelps Corporation, and an AAA rating from Standard and Poor's Corporation, all the highest possible.

AAL markets its products and services in all 50 states and the District of Columbia through a sales staff of over 2,400. Corporate headquarters are located in Appleton, Wisconsin, where over 1,400 are employed. (*Note:* Staffing numbers throughout this case study are in terms of full-time equivalents [FTEs]. Since a sizable number of regular part-time workers are retained, the actual number of people employed is greater than stated.)

Organizational Change at AAL

A major organizational change, dubbed Renewal and Transformation, officially began at AAL in December 1985 with the engagement of Roy Walters and Associates as consultants for a diagnostic process. The beginnings of this change effort can be traced back to the early 1980s.

Some seeds were planted during several very successful product introductions in 1982. The focus and energy level of the organization at that time was exciting, even though managers were up to their ears trying to keep up with business owing to the phenomenal success of the organization's universal life product. Company leaders remember saying AAL should have one of these situations every two years or so, for the energizing effects it had on them and the organization.

With the introduction of these new products, AAL also ushered in a new awareness of the shrinking margins in financial services and its need to rein in expenses in order to stay competitive. In addition, the organization's president and CEO had announced his upcoming retirement, and its new president, Richard L. Gunderson, came in September 1985 from another life insurance organization. Studies of the insurance industry convinced Gunderson that the association had to cut costs by over $50 million over the next five years to stay competitive. The question on the minds of some senior managers was; "What choices can be made now to position AAL for the future?" Organizational change or transformation became the answer.

Positive Dissatisfaction. The change effort was difficult in part because AAL was not in crisis. The good news was that this gave the organization time to change and adjust; the bad news was that it made it difficult for employees to motivate themselves to go through the effort of change. Many of the concerns mentioned were like clouds out at the distant horizon; sales, as well as financial and fraternal results, were continuing to grow. Nothing in the status quo pointed to the need for fundamental change. As AAL's consultant Bob Janson pointed out, what employees did need to discover and tap was the sense of what he termed positive dissatisfaction within the organization—the feeling that even if AAL was doing well, it had an even higher potential.

Diagnosing AAL's Strengths and Weaknesses. The first task of the change effort was an organizational diagnosis to seek out this positive dissatisfaction. A team of twelve managers was trained in a structured interview process, then went out and conducted over 200 interviews in a diagonal slice of the home office and field. The team asked people what AAL's strengths and weaknesses were in ten categories: control, culture, management, style, marketing, mission, historic strengths, productivity, quality, structure, and technology.

Those team interviews were a great experience; people in the organization did share their hopes and dreams for what AAL could become and their frustrations that the organization was not working as effectively as it could to reach those dreams. People identified many strengths on which to build: AAL's members and market, financial strength, fraternal focus and reputation, dedicated employees—both home office and field. But as the team reported to a larger management group in May 1986, some areas needed attention. The consultant has since said that he had never seen an organization so "ripe" for change.

Defining AAL's Vision. Working in parallel with the diagnosing team, one hundred of AAL's managers developed a vision statement for the organization. The result was viewed as a reaffirmation of what AAL had become and what it stood for. It reads as follows: "AAL, the leader in fraternalism, brings Lutheran people together to pursue quality living through financial security, volunteer action and help for others."[3]

Identifying the Gaps. So, six months from the start of the transformation process, AAL had both a vision statement and a current snapshot of the organization; when the two were compared, the gaps that needed to be addressed came into clearer focus. The organization was set to launch its efforts to close these gaps in order to position itself even more strongly for the future. The working theme at that time was "Touch tomorrow today."

Closing the Gaps. The first gaps to be addressed were in the areas of organizational structure, management style, and marketing strategy. Efforts to study and recommend ways to close the gaps between AAL's current situation and its vision in these three areas were launched anew, still employing participative methods. For example, for the structure study, a team of six managers was charged to develop alternative proposals for restructuring the organization through the two management levels below the president. Recommendations were developed by the team, with input from a larger circle of man-

agers, then finally delivered to the president. He chose to reorganize AAL using many of the concepts recommended, and the new organization was put into place late in November 1986. The reorganization was significant: 25 of the top 26 positions in the organization had changes in responsibility, including significant changes in senior management.

The efforts in other areas continue to this day. A new marketing strategy was completed in the fall of 1988. Work has progressed at defining a more precise vision of desired management style and having managers assess themselves (and employees assess them) against that vision. AAL has also produced a technology strategy in response to a gap-closing need, and is now wrestling with ways to address productivity and quality variables in a more direct way.

Organizational Change Results. AAL's corporate restructuring, just by its nature, has been the most visible result. Frankly, after restructuring at the top of the organization was over, it was hard to convince employees that the change process was not complete.

In response to AAL's expense challenges, the organization also achieved its downsizing goal of 250 positions by 1990. This was primarily accomplished through an early retirement window offered in 1986, as well as through attrition.

Structure and personnel changes can always be disrupting, but were especially so in this organization. Not only was AAL a part of a very stable industry, it was also one of the largest employers in a relatively small community, with very low turnover. One key element of the change process was the guarantee of continued employment that was built into the change effort. As Robert H. Waterman, co-author of *In Search of Excellence*, says, "stability in motion" must be maintained throughout renewal. AAL strives to give its managers and employees the freedom and courage to reorganize and try new ways of work, by placing a safety net underneath them. Employees whose positions are eliminated during the change process, or who turn out to have a mismatch of skills for new ways of work, become members of a program. The program helps assess skills, finds temporary work assignments, offers support, and looks for internal placements, field transfers, or voluntary outplacements.

For a sharper focus on the planning and implementing of teams within a key service area of AAL, let us look at the transition of the Insurance Product Services Department, set against the backdrop of this larger change effort.[4]

Planning and Implementing Teams in the IPS Department

The Insurance Product Services (IPS) Department at AAL provides all services related to the individual life, long-term care, and disability income insurance product lines, from the initial underwriting of contracts to the ultimate handling of claims. IPS consists of about 426 employees, about 30 percent of the home office employees.

Planning Phase 1: Identifying the Need. The desire for a new organizational design for IPS had its roots in the corporate change study and subsequent corporate reorganization called Renewal and Transformation. As a result, the change efforts of IPS management were fully supported by Dick Gunderson and top management in the spirit of corporate renewal, and IPS management had the freedom to restructure the department without periodic presentations and approvals.

The major concerns that came out of the corporate change study regarding the "old" insurance product services environment were as follows:

- The old environment was not truly focused on the customer, because of its functional rather than wholistic approach to service.
- Most decisions were made very high in a hierarchical organization with as many as six levels of supervision. As a result, decisions were made some distance from the problems, which decreased timeliness. They were also made by people other than those who knew the most about the problems, which reduced the quality of the decisions.
- The skills and abilities of people were underutilized, and many jobs tended to be boring because of their narrow scope.
- Productivity was viewed from a functional perspective rather than from an integrated perspective.
- Recent marketing successes had caused significant growth in staff and related expenses. Top management felt that it was *excessive* growth.

Related to the last point, the change of IPS was addressed in an environment that called for

downsizing the corporate staff by 250 over a five-year period. Corporate staff numbered 1,556 on January 1, 1987. As part of the corporate change action, a new IPS department head was put in place in December 1986. This new leader, Jerome H. Laubenstein, a former marketing executive, was noted for his participative style. He was given the charge to "regionalize" the IPS service function in an effort to get closer to the customer and to address the corporate downsizing goal as it related to the significant growth experienced by IPS in recent years.

Laubenstein brought in a new senior-level departmental management team in January 1987. This team consisted of five individuals to manage five geographic service regions. These people were selected for their active management style, creativity, and demonstrated willingness to take calculated risks (a contrast to the way they were selected in the risk-averse former culture). They were also selected because of their management strengths and highly participative management style. Technical insurance knowledge, though desirable, was not felt to be essential.

Planning Phase 2: Setting Broad Parameters. The second week after selection, the new IPS management team came together in an off-site retreat to address the approach to be used for redesigning the department. The first step was to develop a vision for the new IPS organization. The result was a simple statement—"Regionalization plus 'one-team' processing"—and included the following list of "desired outcomes":

- A "customer-driven" organization. Customers were identified as field staff and members. Being customer driven was perceived to include
  - listening to the customer for wants and needs,
  - being responsive and pro-active to the customer's wants and needs,
  - acknowledging that the customer's problem is the provider's problem,
  - seeing the provider as a problem solver rather than an order taker,
  - informing and educating the customer, and
  - using customer-informed measures to assess how well IPS is meeting customer needs.

- A strong "team" relationship with the field staff and internal support units. The need for "networking" was heavily stressed.
- A "flat" organization with fewer levels of supervision and fewer staff.
- "One-stop" processing as fully as possible to avoid the delays and lack of ownership associated with an assembly line approach.
- A quality management team that would model participative management, more involvement of employees in deciding how work was to be accomplished, and more decision-making authority for employees in carrying out their day-to-day assignments.

A very simple mission statement was also established for the new organization: "To enable the agent, the primary customer, to do an even better job of serving the policyholder, the ultimate customer."

Planning Phase 3: Designing and Developing. The design process did not begin with the self-managing team concept as a goal. It did, however, begin with a strong desire to obtain the employees' appreciation for restructuring. Therefore, a major first task of the new departmental management team was to communicate the reasons for pursuing a change in work design to every employee in the department. The reasons for change really were restatements of what individuals had related to the corporate change interview teams.

Communication. Because AAL had no facility to bring the entire IPS staff (484 people) together at one time, the first attempt at communication to all employees was through the existing functional management structure in the department. The IPS managers were asked to conduct unit meetings, explaining the reasons for and parameters around which a new organization would be developed. Information and support materials were provided to facilitate communication. This approach met with limited success.

More Communication. A second effort was structured around large-group meetings, with approximately 100 employees in each group. Dick Gunderson and Jerry Laubenstein also participated. This attempt met with more success. Periodic unit meetings, led by the new regional managers, were continued. A departmental newsletter was also established. The newsletter was distributed to all IPS employees to provide continuing communication as the redesign progressed through the planning and implementation stages. Good, solid communication cannot be overemphasized in a restructuring process such as AAL experienced.

Design Teams. Because the new management team was committed to a highly participative team style of management, it involved a significant cross section of employees in the departmental redesign. Ten teams, with a total of approximately 125 employees, were appointed from lists of employees nominated by managers, supervisors, and employees. Team members came from all levels within the organization. The teams and their charges were as follows:

- Three Structure Teams. Independently propose a new departmental structure, taking into account several "givens" such as regional organization, and a maximum of three levels of supervision.
- One Physical Resource Team. Address the physical resource issues that need to be dealt with in any reorganization.
- One Management Style Team. Address management style and propose a culture in which employees can grow and perform in the spirit of service excellence.
- One Management Information Team. Evaluate the types of management information needed to lead the operation.
- One Field Input Team. Gain agent (customer) input on IPS's electronic data processing (EDP) support services.
- One EDP Resource Team. Look at the effect of this change on IPS's EDP support services. IPS was a highly mechanized operation, and as a result, the effect was significant.
- One Operations Team. Look after ongoing operations during the renewal effort.
- One Celebration Team. Plan and administer appropriate and timely celebration events to highlight specific milestones and successes along the way.

The results produced by these teams in just three weeks were phenomenal—and were achieved while employees continued to handle normal work activities.

Role Clarification. During planning phase 3, management had to clearly articulate the role of teams within a participative management decision-making process, especially when proposals required modification or rejection. Employees tended to confuse the various teams' roles of providing input with management's accountability for making decisions. Managers, on the other hand, had to remember to explain why team decisions were modified or rejected. It probably would have been better to label the approach high involvement rather than participative management. Doing so may have avoided some misunderstandings.

Phase 4: Decision Making and Implementation. Two of the three structure teams submitted organizational proposals that closely parallel IPS's current design. These proposals, together with input from a variety of sources including a literature search that produced the self-managing team concept, provided the direction for the organizational model. The next step was to contact some proponents of sociotechnical management. As a result, it was recognized that to attain the desired outcomes and accomplish its mission, the department had to move away from a hierarchically arranged, functional, and highly specialized structure that extensively used rules, records, reports, and precedents. Instead, it had to move toward a flat, full-service, self-managing, self-regulating service team structure that placed decision making closer to the transaction and to the customer. Management then created a tentative model of the new organization. This model was worked with all employees, using the nominal group process, in an attempt to get their input on potential pitfalls.

Once the organizational concept was finalized, the number of service teams needed to serve IPS's customers was determined by modeling service activity by region. The goal was to have as many teams (i.e., customer contacts) as could be supported by existing staff capabilities. IPS concluded that the "critical mass" of knowledge and skills currently available in the department could support sixteen service teams. Managers were then selected to lead these teams.

Implementation. The next step was to develop an implementation plan. Implementation teams were named, again using a significant cross section of employees. The teams were charged to do everything necessary to ready the department for a physical move to the new organizational structure. The EDP resource, physical resource, and celebration teams were continued, and additional teams were formed around service functions of the "old" organization. They were to address the disbursement of the three functions of the insurance services: life, medical, and disability.

Employee Assignments. Now, the new management team addressed the issue of employee assignments. After an initial "reallocation" of employees was agreed on, employees were given the opportunity to request a change in tentative team assignment. However, because it was necessary to balance the existing knowledge among the teams, changes in assignments were not made unless exceptional reasons existed. This "assignment issue" was perhaps one of the biggest and least anticipated social issues of the renewal effort. Not since high school had most of these adults had their social choices removed—choices of colleagues, work location, and work environment. As these new "groups" moved through the group formation stages of "forming, storming, norming, and performing," they spent much time and energy in the storming and norming stages.

Security. The period of organizational change—including downsizing—was trying for many employees, even though all were guaranteed employment (not positions). It was especially so for supervisors and managers. The organizational redesign reduced supervisory positions from 62 to 22. By the end of 1987, 57.5 full-time equivalent positions were eliminated. To reduce the negative effect of these changes, stress management sessions were made available to all employees through the medical department. Several hundred employees took advantage of this opportunity. A course on managing change was made available to management through a local technical institute. A career-counseling service was offered to employees whose jobs were eliminated. And the existing corporate Employee Placement Program was strengthened to help employees cope with the loss of positions (not employment) that resulted from the total corporate renewal effort.

The Move. The physical move from a functional structure to one centered around self-managing teams was made in August 1987. This was one of the first opportunities to demonstrate the power of team problem solving. IPS's building services and space management units estimated it would take three to five months to move the department's 484 employees and associated equipment. IPS management could not live with that time frame. The physical resource implementation team, led by its adviser, a newly appointed and creative regional manager, together with the building services people, synergistically arrived at an alternative, which was to move people but not workstations. This required employees to accept inadequacies in their new workstations until those stations could be modified at a later date. The organization's space management staffers also had to accept something less than a "clean" move. The only change in equipment would be the provision of computer terminals at workstations where they had not been required earlier. Employees moved themselves by packing their belongings in boxes, putting the boxes on their chairs, and wheeling both to their new workstations. This was something never before done. An incentive was provided: The move began at noon on a Friday. As soon as the unit was moved, employees would have the rest of the day off. The move was completed in less than two hours. Terminals caught up the following Tuesday.

Self-Managing Work Teams at IPS

Teams Within Teams. The IPS organizational team design has four significant aspects:

- It is a regional organization, with each region providing all services to its designated customers. (These service regions parallel the existing field distribution and management regions.)
- Each region has four service teams, with each service team providing almost all services to a specific group of agencies. Under the old system, a few services were handled by such a small staff that it was difficult to spread them to service teams in the early stages of restructuring. The number of employees sufficient to constitute an adequate "critical mass" to permit disbursement was a major point of discussion. Managers tended to be more inclined to take risks than staff in this area.
- Each service team was initially structured to have three self-managing work teams within

it—one around the underwriting and issue functions; another around service functions such as loans, terminations, dividends, preauthorized check handling; and the third around the claims functions. The goal is to move to more wholistic self-managing teams by encouraging the integration of the three functional teams.
- Finally, IPS had a cadre of functional specialists with responsibility for establishing functional policy and for monitoring the appropriate administration of policy across the regions and teams. These specialists are currently organized by line of business and report to the regional managers.

Self-Managed Teams Defined. The focal point of IPS's current organization is clearly the self-managing work team. The self-managing work team concept, as found in the organization's literature search and adopted by AAL, is as follows:

- Self-managing work teams are semiautonomous groups of workers who share the responsibility for carrying out a significant piece of work and who run their own operations with almost no supervision. Each group has the authority and the technical, interpersonal, and managerial skills to make decisions about how the work should be done.
- Each team is accountable as a group for processing all the work for which it is responsible. Members plan, do, and control their work. The team decides who will do what work, and assigns members to tasks. The group has control over scheduling and coordinating its own work, formulating vacation schedules, monitoring quality, solving technical problems, and improving work methods. Employees have both responsibility and accountability for quantity, quality, and costs. The team meets regularly to discuss goals; to identify, analyze, and solve work-related problems; and to provide improvement ideas.
- Employees typically possess a variety of skills and are encouraged to develop new skills to increase their flexibility. Workers typically learn second and third jobs. The team is responsible for motivating, training, coaching, and developing its members. Team members train each other or arrange for their own training.

- The team is also responsible for employee evaluation and discipline. The group, as a whole, reviews overall team performance, evaluates individual members, and handles problems such as absenteeism and poor performance. Teams need to be skilled in handling the social system as well. This means being able to celebrate their success, recognize each other's efforts, thank each other for help, and in general reinforce positive behavior. As teams mature, they hire new members or do the final selection of new team members.

- Reward systems typically reward teamwork as well as the individual's acquisition of skills and the individual's performance. For example, the team's results may determine the size of the compensation resource pool available to be distributed as increases or bonuses, or both. The team then determines how that pool is allocated to individual team members.

Some aspects of the self-managing work team concept have not been implemented at AAL. For example, peer appraisal is achieved by anonymous input, not direct input, and significant performance problems continue to be turned over to managers for disciplinary action.

Benefits of the Self-Managing Team Concept

Six intrinsic elements of the self-managing team concept that are motivators are

- variety and challenge,
- elbow room for decision making,
- feedback and learning,
- mutual support and respect,
- wholeness and meaning, and
- room to grow; a bright future.

With respect to these motivators, Marvin Weisbord, in his book *Productive Workplaces: Organizing and Managing for Dignity, Meaning, and Community*, says, "The first three must be optimal—not too much, which adds to stress and anxiety, nor too little, which produces stultifying tedium. The second trio are open ended. No one can have too much respect, growing room, or 'wholeness'—meaning a view of both the origin and the customer's use of your work." All this assumes that in place are the "satisfiers," a list of six conditions of employment: fair and adequate pay, job security, benefits, safety, health, and due process. As Weisbord comments, "Only in work-places embodying both lists can the century-old dreams of labor-management cooperation ever come true." The six motivators can be met far more effectively through the self-managing team structure than through the traditional multilevel hierarchical management structure that focuses on one person, one task.

Joseph H. Boyett and Henry P. Conn suggest in their book *Maximum Performance Management: How to Manage and Compensate People to Meet World Competition*, that excellence is a function of the knowledge and skills, motives and abilities of employees. They also suggest that we cannot directly change the internal traits and characteristics that employees bring to the job and thus are stuck with them. They further suggest that we can, however, adjust the work environment to compensate for weaknesses in these attributes. The three leverages they propose for doing this are

- Information
  - shared values and business strategies
  - linked missions and goals
  - measures and feedback
  - identification of critical behaviors
- Consequences
  - social reinforcement
  - contingent awards
  - pay for performance (a variable portion up to 40 percent of total compensation)
- Involvement
  - nonvoluntary
  - management-directed teams
  - cross-functional task forces

AAL's self-managing team approach supported by its pay-for-performance compensation system, which is anchored to team measures and results, takes full advantage of these areas of leverage far better and with far less effort than can be done in a traditional hierarchical structure.

Manager's Role in the Self-Managing Team Environment

The move to self-managing teams required a redefinition of the role of the team manager. This leader is still responsible and accountable for the bottom-line results of the team, but these results are attained differently. In the new work environment, the creative abilities of all team members are used, not just those of the manager.

The redefined role requires managers to

- set direction by creating and focusing the team's efforts toward a common vision;
- coach and counsel, and ensure and support the development of team members;
- lead the team in problem solving;
- make sure the team has needed information and resources; and
- encourage the team to make its own decisions on operating problems.

The new role requires managers to manage through "boundaries" or "parameters" rather than by directive. Key challenges are the need to create a motivating work environment and to remove barriers for team members. The latter is accomplished by managing relationships between teams and between the team and other areas of the organization.

Although the role of the manager in a self-managing team environment differs from the role of a manager in the traditional environment, research has shown that the profile of outstanding managers is very similar regardless of the environment. Successful managers are visionaries, use a participative management style, and can deal with ambiguity and a lack of structure. They share information and responsibility with employees and are committed both to the work and to the individuals on their teams. And they deliver results.

Key Support Systems

Pay-for-Applied-Services for Individuals and Teams. Pay-for-Applied-Services (PAS) is the compensation system designed to support IPS's self-managing work teams. It offers maximum flexibility to meet the unique job design needs of each team.

One significant challenge during the development of PAS was to integrate it into a corporate culture firmly entrenched in the Hay system of job evaluation. This task was uniquely and creatively accomplished by a team including individuals from the service areas and corporate compensation services.

Within IPS, individual position descriptions have been replaced by a team job description and individual personal assignments. Each personal assignment is a listing of the services an individual performs to support the needs of the team and to support her or his own career interests.

Employees have identified approximately 165 services that are being performed within the department.

Compensation is delivered through four components.

1. The first is valued services. As new services are learned and applied, their values are added to the employee's ongoing compensation. The values of individual services are determined using the know-how portion of the Hay system. A matrix has been constructed using Hay know-how values. One axis of the matrix is absolute values representing the minimum AAL would be willing to pay for a service if it were a stand-alone service. The other axis of the matrix is incremental values. The more an individual learns with the same base know-how value, the less additional learning is worth.

2. The second component of pay delivery is the team incentive. Incentive dollars are tied to productivity measures. Allocation is based on a team's contribution to productivity. Distributions to individuals within the team are based on the individuals' support of the team. Incentive dollars are distributed quarterly.

3. The third component is a market adjustment feature. To remain competitive within the marketplace and among comparable jobs within the organization, IPS considers market adjustments annually. These adjustments may be made to either the matrix or the incentive "pot." When adjustments are made to the matrix, the values of individual personal assignments are recalculated. Where appropriate, immediate adjustments are made to pay.

4. The fourth component is an individual-incentive program, in which IPS recognizes outstanding achievement by individual employees. This lump-sum incentive is paid once a year only to employees who are already paid at market value. It is worth as much as six percent of an individual's compensation.

This new compensation system encourages cross training, enhances team flexibility, and encourages team performance, but still permits compensation dollars to be managed and controlled. It was implemented on April 1, 1989, and underwent a degree of modification in 1991 to bring it into closer synchronization with a new incentive compensation plan introduced to the rest of the organization that year.

Training for Self-Managing Work Teams. A comprehensive training program continues to be developed for all employees working in a sociotechnical management environment within the organization. The entire process of program design and delivery to all employees was completed in 1990. The topics covered include

- Team Roles. Typical supervisory responsibilities that teams may take on in their own self-management are
  - planning and scheduling time schedules,
  - securing and allocating resources,
  - scheduling and coordinating work,
  - setting standards and rotating assignments,
  - providing performance data,
  - recruiting, selecting, and firing,
  - disciplining and rewarding,
  - celebrating successes,
  - motivating and training,
  - coaching and developing, and
  - solving problems and resolving conflicts.

Management allocates these tasks to team members as the team is ready for them. A part of the preparation for this passing of responsibilities includes training and development relevant to each team's needs.

- Team Manager's Role. Service team managers must play a stronger coaching and counseling role than do traditional managers. They find themselves being facilitators, empowerers, and consultants, responsible for "managing the culture." Therefore, the training program developed for managers pays special attention to the development of these skills.

Performance Appraisal

- Peer (Individual) Appraisal. Self-managing work teams require a new concept in performance appraisals. Members of the team use an anonymous peer appraisal concept. In addition, teams "certify" their members' skill levels.
- Group (Team) Appraisal. Teams are expected to function as teams and not just groups of individuals. Team members receive training in the skill areas required to enable this. The individual's *ability* to function as a team member is evaluated as part of the training process. The *team's* actual *behavior* in this area is assessed by managers. The team's progress is assessed by the team itself, against the standards and goals that contribute to bonus results.

Success and Challenges of Change and Self-Managed Teams in the IPS Department

External Visibility. The concept of a self-managing work team initially found only a modest level of credibility within the rest of the AAL organization because, in the minds of many, it still had to be proven. The attention given IPS's efforts helped support the validity of this concept. Examples include a *Business Week* article about IPS's efforts; several references by Tom Peters in his syndicated newspaper column; several other references in other national and local publications; requests for and subsequent site visits by many organizations; and invitations to make presentations about the team concept from organizations such as the Association for Quality and Participation and the Work in America Institute. Subsequently, demonstrated improvements in productivity and customer satisfaction made it more difficult to criticize the concept. However, the one soft spot that plagued IPS for some time was overall employee satisfaction. This was probably most affected by the introduction of an incentive compensation system with pay at risk while the rest of the organization remained on the traditional merit system.

Employee Successes and Challenges. Employee reactions to the redesigned organization are monitored by a number of approaches. First, monthly employee feedback sessions are sponsored and hosted by the department head. Employees are randomly selected from throughout the department and offered the opportunity to air their concerns, ask questions, and suggest changes. This approach is also used by regional managers.

In addition, in July 1987, a survey instrument was introduced to monitor employee attitude as IPS implemented the new design. The survey continues to be used on a periodic basis. Results are evaluated on a regional and service team level as well as on a departmental level. Employee attitude goals are established for service teams and actual results versus goals are used in evaluating managers' overall performance. The first reading was taken in July 1987, just prior to the physical move. The second was taken in October 1987, shortly after the physical move, followed by the third in May 1988, the fourth in September 1989 following the introduction of the Pay-for-Applied-Services compensation system, and the last in August 1990. A few comparative readings from the old organization were available from several years before. Some results are shown in Exhibit C.2.1. The significant effect of *change* can be noted in the overall satisfaction of employees. A very stable, "comfortably staffed" functional organization in 1983 resulted in a relatively high level of overall satisfaction. Surprisingly, the design stage and, not so surprisingly, the implementation stage of the new design resulted in a significant deterioration in overall employee satisfaction even though employees were heavily involved in developing and implementing the design. However, employees, for the most part, still respond that they would not want to go back to the old structure and organization, even though they dislike some things about the new system.

The Tough Spots. Two specific problem areas identified by the survey were:

- lack of *advance* training for the new roles and duties employees were being asked to assume and
- employees' inability to measure how well they were doing in their new roles.

The first area, the training issue, was an enormous challenge for both management and employees. Enlarging jobs put a tremendous strain on training capabilities during the early stages of transformation. That, together with not having a compensation system in place to support the cross-training concept, may have led to low employee morale owing to a lack of adequate incentives. It is understandable that employees did not feel very good about this aspect of the renewal effort. The second area, moving from individual standards to measuring and rewarding individuals on the basis of team results, is a difficult change for some to accept in a culture in which individuality has been lauded and many prefer to be fully in control of their own destiny.

In addition, the approach used to assign employees to new work teams significantly unbalanced the existing social system. This was further compounded in January 1989 when the department moved from a five-region structure to a four-region structure to parallel a similar move in the field distribution system.

Another major effect on employees' satisfaction was the installation of a new compensation

Exhibit C.2.1
Employee Satisfaction Survey Results

	1983	July 1987	October 1987	May 1988	September 1989	August 1990	August 1991
				Percentage Agreeing			
Overall satisfaction	70%	56%	47%	41%	51%	58%	65%
Employees . . .							
Are encouraged to innovate	—	58%	73%	69%	66%	70%	69%
Receive adequate training	—	60%	49%	51%	57%	58%	58%
Are permitted to use judgment	—	81%	90%	88%	89%	89%	88%
Enjoy good communication between the field staff and headquarters	30%	58%	66%	58%	54%	66%	68%
Are familiar with measures for doing a good job	—	64%	38%	42%	45%	52%	57%

system that puts a part of their compensation at risk based on performance.

The aggregation of these changes has lowered employees' overall satisfaction level. It is doubtful that the negative effect of change can be avoided, but it is possible to avoid drawing the change out over an extended period of time. In IPS's case, the design was begun in January 1987 and the last piece, the compensation program, was implemented in 1989 and 1991. This is probably an excessive time frame.

Nevertheless, the changes have had some positive results in the IPS Department. For example, communication between employees and customers has improved. Employees now feel challenged to innovate. And employees feel free to use their own rather than a supervisor's judgment. IPS also has a very large number of employees who favor the new compensation system because it has increased their ability to influence their earnings.

One noteworthy result is a gain in productivity (which is addressed later in this case study). An additional, "nice-to-see," result is the rapidity with which the organization is moving from the concept of three functional self-managing work teams within a service team to that of a more integrated, functionally inclusive self-managing team. This evaluation is a longer-range design goal that is being realized much sooner than anticipated.

Customer Successes and Challenges. Perhaps the most visible success thus far is the favorable effect the new self-managed design is having on

IPS's customers, the field staff. Input gathered from them, as part of a field renewal effort and reported in March 1988, indicated that the field staff felt that the new IPS organization was one of the four best things about AAL. A survey instrument was implemented to measure the satisfaction of the field staff, and the results are shown in Exhibit C.2.2. An improvement in customer attitude occurred between August 1985 and March 1988. This improvement was probably primarily related to: (1) the promise of better service; (2) the pairing of specific service teams with specific customers (agencies); (3) field visits where members of service teams would attend agency meetings; and (4) an experimental partnership program in which specific IPS employees would work with specific agents. A slight deterioration in October 1988 was probably somewhat related to the establishment of higher expectations and to field renewal activity that was taking place. Speed, for example, showed a fairly significant deterioration in level of satisfaction when, in fact, IPS was providing better service than earlier in the renewal process. Other "anecdotal evidences" of customer satisfaction are numerous letters and other communications about how pleased individuals are with the support they are getting from their home office service team; flowers, candy, and other treats received by service teams from their field customers; and customer-hosted celebrations for successful sales results.

Looking at "Percentage Disagreeing" results for the customer satisfaction survey, rather than "Percentage Agreeing" results, suggests an even better outcome:

Exhibit C.2.2
Customer Satisfaction Survey Results

			Percentage Agreeing			
Overall, IPS . . .	August 1985	September 1987	October 1988	September 1989	September 1990	October 1991
Understands the field staff	27%	47%	45%	48%	57%	60%
Wants to help the field staff	—	83%	78%	79%	84%	89%
Will respond	—*	84%	82%	85%	85%	89%
Responds with satisfactory speed	61%	68%	61%	65%	77%	73%
Responds with accuracy	76%	79%	74%	77%	85%	84%

*No survey data are available, but this area was the focus of a high number of complaints from the field staff.

	Percentage Disagreeing		
Overall, IPS. . .	**Sept. 1989**	**Sept. 1990**	**Sept. 1991**
Understands the field staff	19%	12%	13%
Wants to help the field staff	2%	2%	2%
Will respond	4%	5%	2%
Responds with satisfactory speed	14%	8%	13%
Responds with accuracy	6%	2%	4%

Productivity Successes and Challenges

Very tangible productivity gains have been realized. IPS Department was initially rightsized by eliminating 59 positions (12 percent of the workforce), resulting in a savings of over $1 million in salaries and benefits. Additional reallocation of employee resources has since occurred. On the other hand, business processing has continued to increase. A macro productivity model developed to monitor IPS's progress shows a cumulative productivity increase of approximately 29 percent through 1990. This means that if IPS had been operating at the same standard of productivity as in 1985 and 1986, it would have required about 120 more positions than it had at the end of 1990. IPS anticipates additional productivity gains as cross training progresses and teams mature. However, the amount of time and energy it takes to cross train while continuing to process business should not be underestimated. A significant commitment of time and resources is required.

Future Design Changes

The first phases of the sociotechnical design was implemented in IPS in August 1987. A review of the original design decisions, in view of the knowledge gained from a little over a year of operation, took place in December 1988. As a consequence, IPS implemented several modifications to the organization in March 1989 and introduced the individual-incentive modification (PAS) to the compensation system in 1991. First, the department moved from a five-region to a four-region design to match a similar change that was made in the alignment of its field distribution organization effective January 1989. Second, it moved the reporting relationship between spe-

cialists and service team managers to one between specialists and regional managers. This was done to recognize that specialists have a departmental role, not a service team role, and thus are a part of the departmental management team. IPS later reorganized the specialists by line of business, with each regional manager taking responsibility for one major area. Third, IPS moved from sixteen service team managers to fifteen, further broadening the spans of control of the managers. This was possible because of the progress made in the self-managing capabilities of employees.

This "fine-tuning" of the organization resulted in employee reassignments and as a result was followed by some deterioration in the morale of employees who were looking for stability.

CEO Diagnostic Intervention

IPS contracted with the Center for Effective Organizations (CEO), University of Southern California, in October 1992, to learn how to better understand the effect of IPS structure and support systems on team performance and employee satisfaction. The department felt that it needed to understand the employee concerns voiced in the November 1991 corporate employee survey, and needed to address those concerns. Also, it had been five years since IPS had been reorganized into teams, and it was time to reassess the department's direction. IPS selected CEO to do the research because it would be a neutral third party, was an internationally known organization in the study of teams and teamwork, and employed some of the leading thinkers on compensation, particularly skill-based pay.

As IPS began its research in the fall of 1992, it had four key objectives:

- Assess the current status and design of the team-based IPS organization.
- Specifically address the issue of why improvements in employee morale lagged improvements in productivity and customer satisfaction.
- Suggest possible innovations in IPS's team-based design, which could be implemented and tested for their influence on the effectiveness of teams and the department as a whole.
- Assist with the design, implementation, and assessment of innovations related to new

ways of doing business that were planned for at least some of the work teams.

Here is what IPS learned from a year of intensive self-scrutiny:

- Despite its hypothesis that employee quality of work life (QWL) lagged improvements in productivity and customer satisfaction, QWL for IPS employees was in fact above average compared with that for employees in other organizations.
- IPS's efforts at empowerment were effective, but room for continued progress remained.
- Employee QWL was not strongly related to either productivity or customer satisfaction. In other words, changes in employee QWL were not likely to have major effects on either productivity or customer satisfaction. This was a surprising finding, but is consistent with findings from other CEO research into the relationship of QWL to organizational performance.
- The need for communication was strong.
- Overall satisfaction with pay was high, but not all employees agreed with AAL's compensation system or the philosophy behind it. Most employees demonstrated a good understanding of the PAS compensation system (base pay, team incentives, and individ-

ual incentives) and the corporate Success Share incentive program. However, they indicated some dissatisfaction with nonannuitized incentive compensation (they would prefer annual base salary increases over annual bonuses), and felt that the compensation system does not effectively reward good performers.
- The visibility of the service team director was low; the supervisory style of the manager was not related to the team's performance. Most employees reported that they did not see their managers frequently and would appreciate more contact. A second finding on this issue was that management style had no correlation to team results in employee QWL, productivity, or customer satisfaction.

These findings led IPS to convene the department management team (regional managers, service team directors, and lead specialists) so that it could communicate the issues to them and involve them in developing a work plan for addressing areas for improvement. The work of fine-tuning the organization based on the CEO findings was begun in August 1993. Exhibit C.2.3 shows the resulting organizational structure of AAL and Exhibit C.2.4 shows the structure of the Member Insurance Services Unit, which houses the IPS department.

Exhibit C.2.3

AAL Corporate Organization Chart, September 1994

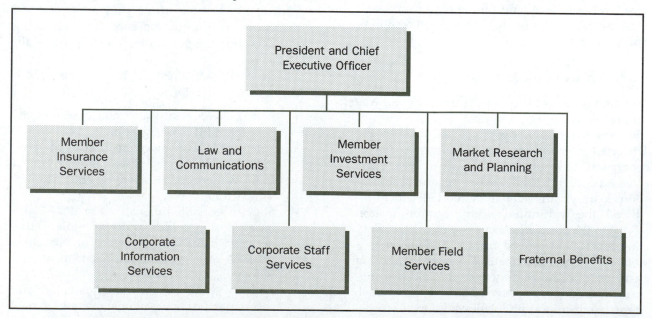

Exhibit C.2.4

Member Insurance Services Division and IPS Department, September 1994

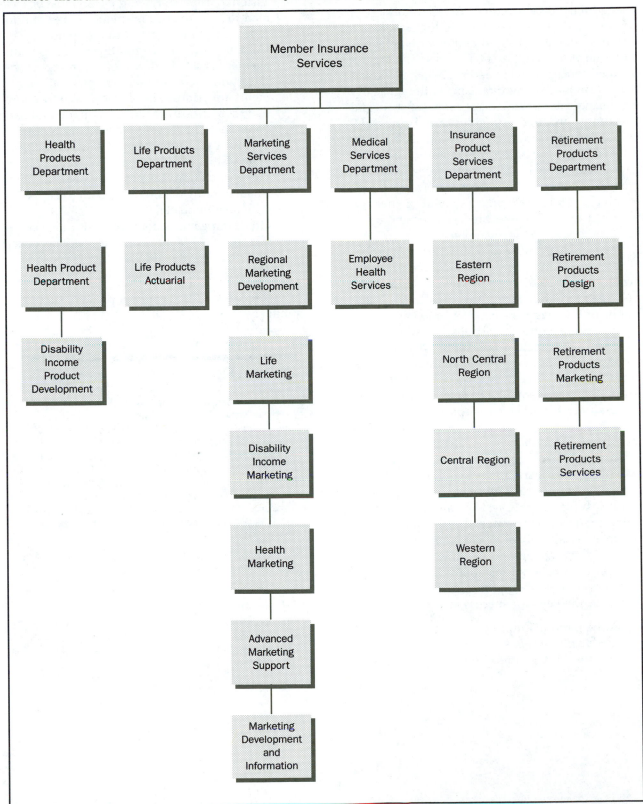

SUMMARY

The primary driving forces for the redesign of IPS were a desire to get closer to the customer, a desire to enlarge jobs and empower employees, and a need to right-size staff levels. The organizational concept used to accomplish the task was the self-managing work team. Although early results indicate customers are more satisfied, and corporate productivity goals are being met, employee satisfaction goals are not being fully achieved. The transition from traditional hierarchical management to sociotechnical management has not been without a lot of pain for all involved. Thus, IPS management is heavily involved in the change process even though it has been going on for several years.

The greatest value of restructuring is probably derived from undergoing the process of organizational diagnosis, establishing a vision, and *participatively* discovering the gaps between the results of the diagnosis and the vision and creating the organizational response. Also, creating positive dissatisfaction is healthy when it helps unfreeze employee attitudes so that they will permit change to occur. This process is preferably led by top management example; in AAL's case, it took place through the corporate change that preceded the IPS effort. IPS's managers suggest that it is impossible to overcommunicate to employees as the process unfolds, that affected employees must participate, and that the effect of change on employees cannot be underestimated. It is helpful if support systems are implemented concurrently with the renewal efforts and, if at all possible, it is probably best to implement all aspects of the change at one time to avoid prolonged organizational instability and the associated suppression of employee morale.

Thus, the keys for success include

- Participation. Employee involvement at all levels will help ensure employee acceptance and the best results. The more brainpower applied to the problem, the better the chance that the emerging solution will be successful.
- Vision. A clear energizing vision must be created to gain the commitment of staff and to motivate them through times of pain.
- Commitment. The commitment of top management and the support of other key corporate staff, such as human resource management, are critical. Employees have to know that their efforts are part of a larger strategy.
- Patience. If the focus is on short-term results, the effort will probably not achieve the ultimate vision. If the goal is to avoid all pain in the organization, it is probably unachievable. Change brings pain, but pain disappears with newfound stability.
- Time. Implementation and cultural change take time. Although some immediate benefits will occur, the ultimate payoff may not be realized for several years.

If these conditions are not present, success is unlikely.

ENDNOTES

[1] J. H. Boyett and H. P. Conn, *Maximum Performance Management: How to Manage and Compensate People to Meet World Competition* (London: Glenbridge Publishing Ltd., 1988); S. Caudron, "Team Staffing Requires New HR Role," *Personnel Journal* (May 1994): 88–94; J. Hoerr, "The Payoff from Teamwork," *Business Week* (July 10, 1989): 56–62; M. R. Weisbord, *Productive Workplaces: Organizing and Managing for Dignity, Meaning, and Community* (San Francisco: Jossey-Bass, 1987); R. S. Wellins, W. C. Byham, and J. M. Wilson, *Empowered Teams* (San Francisco: Jossey-Bass, 1991).

[2] S. Scherreik, "Off the Beaten Path in the Insurance Field," *New York Times* (December 25, 1993): L45.

[3] This vision statement later became the organization's mission statement.

[4] The IPS group is now titled the Member and Employee Service group, but this group is still headed by Jerome H. Laubenstein, Sr. VP. The current CEO and President of AAL is John O. Gilbert.

THE LINCOLN ELECTRIC COMPANY

People are our most valuable asset. They must feel secure, important, challenged, in control of their destiny, confident in their leadership, be responsive to common goals, believe they are being treated fairly, have easy access to authority and open lines of communication in all possible directions. Perhaps the most important task Lincoln employees face today is that of establishing an example for others in the Lincoln organization in other parts of the world. We need to maximize the benefits of cooperation and teamwork, fusing high technology with human talent, so that we here in the USA and all of our subsidiary and joint venture operations will be in a position to realize our full potential.

George Willis
former CEO
The Lincoln Electric Company

Today, the Lincoln Electric Company under the leadership of Donald Hastings, is the world's largest manufacturer of arc welding products and a leading producer of industrial electric motors. The firm employs almost 4,000 workers in three U.S. factories near Cleveland and almost an equal number in factories located in other countries. This does not include the field sales force of more than 200. The company's U.S. market share (for arc-welding products) is estimated at more than 40 percent.[1]

The Lincoln incentive management plan has been well known for many years. Many college management texts make reference to the Lincoln plan as a model for achieving higher

This case was written by Arthur Sharplin and appears in R. S. Schuler and P. D. Buller, eds., *Cases in Management, Organizational Behavior and Human Resource Management*, 5th ed. (St. Paul, MN: West Publishing, 1996). It is adapted here by R. S. Schuler and used with the permission of Arthur D. Sharplin.

worker productivity. Certainly, the firm has been successful according to the usual measures.

James F. Lincoln died in 1965 and there was some concern, even among employees, that the management system would fall into disarray, that profits would decline, and that year-end bonuses might be discontinued. Quite the contrary, since Lincoln's death, the company appears as strong as ever. Each year, except the recession years 1982 and 1983, has seen high profits and bonuses. In 1995, Lincoln Electric's centennial, sales for the first time surpassed $1 billion. While there was some employee discontent about relatively flat bonuses in 1995, employee morale and productivity remain very good.[2] Employee turnover is almost nonexistent except for retirements. Lincoln's market share is stable. The historically high stock dividends continue.

A Historical Sketch

In 1895, after being "frozen out" of the depression-ravaged Elliott-Lincoln Company, a maker of Lincoln-designed electric motors, John C. Lincoln took out his second patent and began to manufacture his improved motor. He opened his new business, unincorporated, with $200 he had earned redesigning a motor for young Herbert Henry Dow, who later founded the Dow Chemical Company.

Started during an economic depression and cursed by a major fire after only one year in business, the company grew, but hardly prospered, through its first quarter century. In 1906, John C. Lincoln incorporated the business and moved from his one-room, fourth-floor factory to a new three-story building he erected in east Cleveland. He expanded his workforce to 30 and sales grew to over $50,000 a year. John preferred being an engineer and inventor rather than a manager, though, and it was to be left to another Lincoln to manage the company through its years of success. In 1907, after a bout with typhoid fever forced him from Ohio State University in his senior year, James F. Lincoln, John's younger brother, joined the fledgling company. In 1914 he became the active head of the firm, with the titles of General Manager and Vice President. John remained president of the company for some years but became more involved in other business ventures and in his work as an inventor.

One of James Lincoln's early actions was to ask the employees to elect representatives to a committee that would advise him on company operations. This "Advisory Board" has met with the chief executive officer every two weeks since that time. This was only the first of a series of innovative personnel policies that have, over the years, distinguished Lincoln Electric from its competitors.

The first year the Advisory Board was in existence, working hours were reduced from 55 per week, then standard, to 50 hours a week. In 1915, the company gave each employee a paid-up life insurance policy. A welding school, which continues today, was begun in 1917. In 1918, an employee bonus plan was attempted. It was not continued, but the idea was to resurface later.

The Lincoln Electric Employees Association was formed in 1919 to provide health benefits and social activities. This organization continues today and has assumed several additional functions over the years. In 1923, a piecework pay system was in effect, employees got two weeks' paid vacation each year, and wages were adjusted for changes in the Consumer Price Index. Approximately 30 percent of the common stock was set aside for key employees in 1914. A stock purchase plan for all employees was begun in 1925.

The Board of Directors voted to start a suggestion system in 1929. The program is still in effect, but cash awards, a part of the early program, were discontinued several years ago. Now, suggestions are rewarded by "additional points" which affect year-end bonuses.

The legendary Lincoln bonus plan was proposed by the Advisory Board and accepted on a trial basis in 1934. The first annual bonus amounted to about 25 percent of wages. There has been a bonus every year since then. The bonus plan has been a cornerstone of the Lincoln management system and recent bonuses have approximated annual wages.

By 1944, Lincoln employees enjoyed a pension plan, a policy of promotion from within, and continuous employment. Base pay rates were determined by formal job evaluation and a merit rating system was in effect.

In the prologue of James F. Lincoln's last book, Charles G. Herbruck writes regarding the foregoing personnel innovations:

They were not to buy good behavior. They were not efforts to increase profits. They were not antidotes to labor difficulties. They did not constitute a "do-gooder" program. They were an expression of mutual respect for each person's importance to the job to be done. All of them reflect the leadership of James Lincoln, under whom they were nurtured and propagated.

During World War II, Lincoln prospered as never before. By the start of the war, the company was the world's largest manufacturer of arc-welding products. Sales of about $4,000,000 in 1934 grew to $24,000,000 by 1941. Productivity per employee more than doubled during the same period. The Navy's Price Review Board challenged the high profits. And the Internal Revenue Service questioned the tax deductibility of employee bonuses, arguing they were not "ordinary and necessary" costs of doing business. But the forceful and articulate James Lincoln was able to overcome the objections.

Certainly since 1935 and probably for several years before that, Lincoln's productivity has been well above the average for similar companies. The company claims levels of productivity more than twice those for other manufacturers from 1945 onward. Information available from outside sources tends to support these claims.

Company Philosophy

James F. Lincoln was the son of a Congregational minister, and Christian principles were at the center of his business philosophy. The confidence that he had in the efficacy of Christ's teachings is illustrated by the following remark taken from one of his books:

The Christian ethic should control our acts. If it did control our acts, the savings in cost of distribution would be tremendous. Advertising would be a contact of the expert consultant with the customer, in order to give the customer the best product available when all of the customers needs are considered. Competition then would be in improving the quality of products and increasing efficiency in producing and distributing them; not in deception, as is now too customary. Pricing would reflect efficiency of production; it would not be a selling dodge that the customer may be sorry he accepted. It would be proper for all concerned and rewarding for the ability used in producing the product.

There is no indication that Lincoln attempted to evangelize his employees or customers—or the general public for that matter. Neither the former chairman of the board and chief executive, George Willis, nor the current one, Donald F. Hastings, mention the Christian gospel in their recent speeches and interviews. The company motto, "The actual is limited, the possible is immense," is prominently displayed, but there is no display of religious slogans, and there is no company chapel.

Attitude Toward the Customer

James Lincoln saw the customer's needs as the *raison d'etre* for every company. He wrote, "When any company has achieved success so that it is attractive as an investment, all money usually needed for expansion is supplied by the customer in retained earnings. It is obvious that the customer's interests, not the stockholder's, should come first." In 1947 he said, "Care should be taken . . . not to rivet attention on profit. Between 'How much do I get?' and 'How do I make this better, cheaper, more useful?' the difference is fundamental and decisive." Willis, too, ranked the customer as management's most important constituency. This is reflected in Lincoln's policy to "at all times price on the basis of cost and at all times keep pressure on our cost . . . ." Lincoln's goal, often stated, is "to build a better and better product at a lower and lower price." James Lincoln said, "It is obvious that the customer's interests should be the first goal of industry."

This priority, and the priority given to other groups, is reflected in the Mission and Values Statement and the set of Goals shown in Appendix 3A.

Attitude Toward Stockholders

Stockholders are given last priority at Lincoln. This is a continuation of James Lincoln's philosophy: "The last group to be considered is the stockholders who own stock because they think it will be more profitable than investing money in any other way." Concerning division of the largess produced by incentive management, he wrote, "The absentee stockholder also will get his share, even if undeserved, out of the greatly increased profit that the efficiency produces."

Attitude Toward Unionism

There has never been a serious effort to organize Lincoln employees. While James Lincoln criticized the labor movement for "selfishly attempting to better its position at the expense of the people it must serve," he still had kind words for union members. He excused abuses of union power as "the natural reactions of human beings to the abuses to which management has subjected them." Lincoln's idea of the correct relationship between workers and managers is shown by this comment: "Labor and management are properly not warring camps; they are parts of one organization in which they must, and should, cooperate fully and happily."

Beliefs and Assumptions About Employees

If fulfilling customer needs is the desired goal of business, then employee performance and productivity are the means by which this goal can best be achieved. It is the Lincoln attitude toward employees, reflected in the following comments by James Lincoln, which is credited by many with creating the success the company has experienced:

> He is just as eager as any manager is to be part of a team that is properly organized and working for the advancement of our economy. He has no desire to make profits for those who do not hold up their end in production, as is true of absentee stockholders and inactive people in the company.

> If money is to be used as an incentive, the program must provide that what is paid to the worker is what he has earned. The earnings of each must be in accordance with accomplishment.

> Status is of great importance in all human relationships. The greatest incentive that money has, usually, is that it is a symbol of success. The resulting status is the real incentive. Money alone can be an incentive to the miser only.

> There must be complete honesty and understanding between the hourly worker and management if high efficiency is to be obtained.

These beliefs and assumptions have helped shaped Lincoln's human resource objectives. These are shown in Appendix 3B.

Lincoln's Business

Arc-welding has been the standard joining method in shipbuilding for decades. It is the predominant way of connecting steel in the construction industry. Most industrial plants have their own welding shops for maintenance and construction. Manufacturers of tractors and all kinds of heavy equipment use arc-welding extensively in the manufacturing process. Many hobbyists have their own welding machines and use them for making metal items such as patio furniture and barbecue pits. The popularity of welded sculpture as an art form is growing.

While advances in welding technology have been frequent, arc-welding products, in the main, have hardly changed. Lincoln's Innershield process is a notable exception. This process, described later, lowers welding cost and improves quality and speed in many applications. The most widely-used Lincoln electrode, the Fleetweld 5P, has been virtually the same since the 1930s. The most popular engine-driven welder in the world, the Lincoln SA-200, has been a gray-colored assembly including a four-cylinder continental Red Seal engine and a 200 ampere direct-current generator with two current-control knobs for at least four decades. A 1989 model SA-200 even weighed almost the same as the 1950 model, and it certainly was little changed in appearance.

The company's share of the U.S. arc-welding products market appears to have been about 40 percent for many years. The welding products market has grown somewhat faster than the level of industry in general. The market is highly price-competitive, with variations in prices of standard items normally amounting to only a percent or two. Lincoln's products are sold directly by its engineering-oriented sales force and indirectly through its distributor organization. Advertising expenditures amount to less than three-fourths of a percent of sales. Research and development expenditures typically range from $10 million to $12 million, considerably more than competitors.

The other major welding process, flame-welding, has not been competitive with arc-welding since the 1930s. However, plasma-arc-welding, a relatively new process which uses a conducting stream of super heated gas (plasma) to confine the welding current to a small area, has made some inroads, especially in metal tubing manufacturing, in recent years. Major advances in technology which will produce an alternative superior to arc-welding within the next decade or so appear unlikely. Also, it seems likely that changes in the machines and techniques used in arc-welding will be evolutionary rather than revolutionary.

It is also reasonable to observe that Lincoln Electric's business objectives, shown in Appendix 3C, are likely to change in an evolutionary rather than a revolutionary way.

Products

The company is primarily engaged in the manufacture and sale of arc-welding products—electric welding machines and metal electrodes. Lincoln also produces electric motors ranging from one-half horsepower to 200 horsepower. Motors constitute about eight to ten percent of total sales. Several million dollars have recently been invested in automated equipment that will double Lincoln's manufacturing capacity for one-half to 20 horsepower electric motors. The electric welding machines, some consisting of a transformer or motor and generator arrangement powered by commercial electricity and others consisting of an internal combustion engine and generator, are designed to produce 30 to 1,500 amperes of electrical power. This electrical current is used to melt a consumable metal electrode with the molten metal being transferred in super hot spray to the metal joint being welded. Very high temperatures and hot sparks are produced, and operators usually must wear special eye and face protection and leather gloves, often along with leather aprons and sleeves. Lincoln and its competitors now market a wide range of general purpose and specialty electrodes for welding mild steel, aluminum, cast iron, and stainless and special steels. Most of these electrodes are designed to meet the standards of the American Welding Society, a trade association. They are thus essentially the same as to size and composition from one manufacturer to another. Every electrode manufacturer has a limited number of unique products, but these typically constitute only a small percentage of total sales.

Welding electrodes are of two basic types: coated "stick" electrodes and coiled wire. Coated "stick" electrodes, usually 14 inches long and smaller than a pencil in diameter, are held in a special insulated holder by the operator, who must manipulate the electrode in order to maintain a proper arc-width and pattern of deposition of the metal being transferred. Stick electrodes are packaged in 6- to 50-pound boxes.

Thin coiled wire is designed to be fed continuously to the welding arc through a "gun" held by the operator or positioned by automatic positioning equipment. The wire is packaged in coils, reels, and drums weighing from 14 to 1,000 pounds and may be solid or flux-cored.

For more information on products visit the Web site **http://www.lincolnelectric.com.**

Manufacturing Process

The main plant is in Euclid, Ohio, a suburb on Cleveland's east side. The layout of this plant is shown in Exhibit C.3.1. There are no warehouses. Materials flow from the half-mile long dock on the north side of the plant through the production lines to a very limited storage and loading area on the south side.

Materials used on each work station are stored as close as possible to the work station. The administrative offices, near the center of the factory, are entirely functional. A corridor below the main level provides access to the factory floor from the main entrance near the center of the plant. *Fortune* declared the Euclid facility one of America's ten best-managed factories

Another Lincoln plant, in Mentor, Ohio, houses some of the electrode production operations, which were moved from the main plant. Electrode manufacturing is highly capital intensive. Metal rods purchased from steel producers are drawn down to smaller diameters, cut to length, and coated with pressed-powder "flux" for stick electrodes or plated with copper (for conductivity) and put into coils or spools for wire. Lincoln's Innershield wire is hollow and filled with a material similar to that used to coat stick electrodes. As mentioned earlier, this represented a major innovation in welding technology when it was introduced. The company is highly secretive about its electrode production processes, and outsiders are not given access to the details of those processes.

Lincoln welding machines and electric motors are made on a series of assembly lines. Gasoline and diesel engines are purchased partially assembled, but practically all other components are made from basic industrial products, e.g., steel bars and sheets and bar copper conductor wire.

Exhibit C.3.1
Main Factory Layout

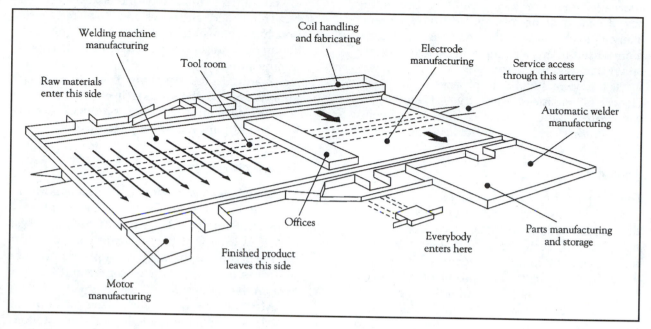

Individual components, such as gasoline tanks for engine-driven welders and steel shafts for motors and generators, are made by numerous small "factories within a factory." The shaft for a certain generator, for example, is made from raw steel bar by one operator who uses five large machines, all running continuously. A saw cuts the bar to length, a digital lathe machines different sections to varying diameters, a special mining machine cuts a slot for the keyway, and so forth, until a finished shaft is produced. The operator moves the shafts from machine to machine and makes necessary adjustments. Another operator punches, shapes, and paints, sheetmetal cowling parts. One assembles steel laminations onto a rotor shaft, then winds, insulates, and tests the rotors. Finished components are moved by crane operators to the nearby assembly lines.

Worker Performance and Attitude

Exceptional worker performance at Lincoln is a matter of record. The typical Lincoln employee earns about twice as much as other factory workers in the Cleveland area. Yet the company's labor cost per sales dollar is well below industry averages. Worker turnover is practically nonexistent except for retirements and departures by new employees. Turnover is less than four per-

cent for employees who have been on the jobs for at least 18 months.[3]

Sales per Lincoln factory employee currently exceed $150,000. An observer at the factory quickly sees why this figure is so high. Each worker is proceeding busily and thoughtfully about the task at hand. There is no idle chatter. Most workers take no coffee breaks. Many operate several machines and make a substantial component unaided. The supervisors are busy with planning and record keeping duties and hardly glance at the people they "supervise." The manufacturing procedures appear efficient—no unnecessary steps, no wasted motions, no wasted materials. Finished components move smoothly to subsequent work stations. Appendix 3D includes summaries of interviews with employees.

Organizational Structure

Lincoln has never allowed development of a formal organization chart. The objective of this policy is to ensure maximum flexibility. An open door policy is practiced throughout the company, and personnel are encouraged to take problems to the persons most capable of resolving them. Once, Harvard Business School researchers prepared an organization chart reflecting the implied relationships at Lincoln. The chart became available within the company, and present management feels that had a disruptive effect. Therefore, no organizational chart appears in this case.

Perhaps because of the quality and enthusiasm of the Lincoln workforce, routine supervision is almost nonexistent. A typical production foreman, for example, supervises as many as 100 workers, a span-of-control that does not allow more than infrequent worker-supervisor interaction.

Position titles and traditional flows of authority do imply something of an organizational structure, however. For example, the Vice President, Sales, and the Vice President, Electrode Division, report to the President, as do various staff assistants such as the Personnel Director and the Director of Purchasing.

Using such implied relationships, it has been determined that production workers have two or, at most, three levels of supervision between themselves and the President.

Human Resource Policies

As mentioned earlier, it is Lincoln's remarkable human resource practices which are credited by many with the company's success.

Recruitment and Selection

Every job opening is advertised internally on company bulletin boards and any employee can apply for any job so advertised. External hiring is permitted only for entry-level positions. Selection for these jobs is done on the basis of personal interviews—there is no aptitude or psychological testing. A committee consisting of vice presidents and supervisors interviews candidates initially cleared by the Personnel Department. Final selection is made by the supervisor who has a job opening. Nonetheless, it is increasingly desirable that factory workers have some advanced math skills and understand the use of computers. Out of over 20,000 applications received by the Personnel Department during a recent period, relatively few were hired in 1994–1995. Consequently, Lincoln's expansion is becoming increasingly dependent upon getting employees qualified to work in the Lincoln environment, within the famous incentive system.[4]

Job Security

In 1958 Lincoln formalized its guaranteed continuous employment policy, which had already been in effect for many years. There have been no layoffs since World War II. Since 1958, every worker with over two years' longevity has been guaranteed at least 30 hours per week, 49 weeks per year.

The policy has never been so severely tested as during the 1981 to 1983 recession. As a manufacturer of capital goods, Lincoln's business is highly cyclical. In previous recessions the company was able to avoid major sales declines. However, sales plummeted 32 percent in 1982 and another 16 percent the next year. Few companies could withstand such a revenue collapse and remain profitable. Yet, Lincoln not only earned profits, but no employee was laid off and year-end incentive bonuses continued. To weather the storm, management cut most of the nonsalaried workers back to 30 hours a week for varying periods of time. Many employees were reassigned, and the total workforce was slightly reduced through normal attrition and restricted hiring. Many employees grumbled at their unexpected misfortune, probably to the surprise and dismay of some Lincoln managers. However, sales and profits—and employee bonuses—soon rebounded.

Performance Evaluations

Each supervisor formally evaluates subordinates twice a year using the cards shown in Exhibit C.3.2. The employee performance criteria, "quality," "dependability," "ideas and cooperation," and "output" are considered to be independent of each other. Marks on the cards are converted to numerical scores which are forced to average 100 for each evaluating supervisor. Individual merit rating scores normally range from 80 to 110. Any score over 110 requires a special letter to top management. These scores (over 110) are not considered in computing the required 100-point average for each evaluating supervisor.

Suggestions for improvements often result in recommendations for exceptionally high performance scores. Supervisors discuss individual performance marks with the employees concerned. Each warranty claim is traced to the individual employee whose work caused the defect. The employee's performance score may be reduced, or the worker may be required to repay the cost of servicing the warranty claim by working without pay.

Compensation

Basic wage levels for jobs at Lincoln are determined by a wage survey of similar jobs in the

Exhibit C.3.2
Merit Rating Cards

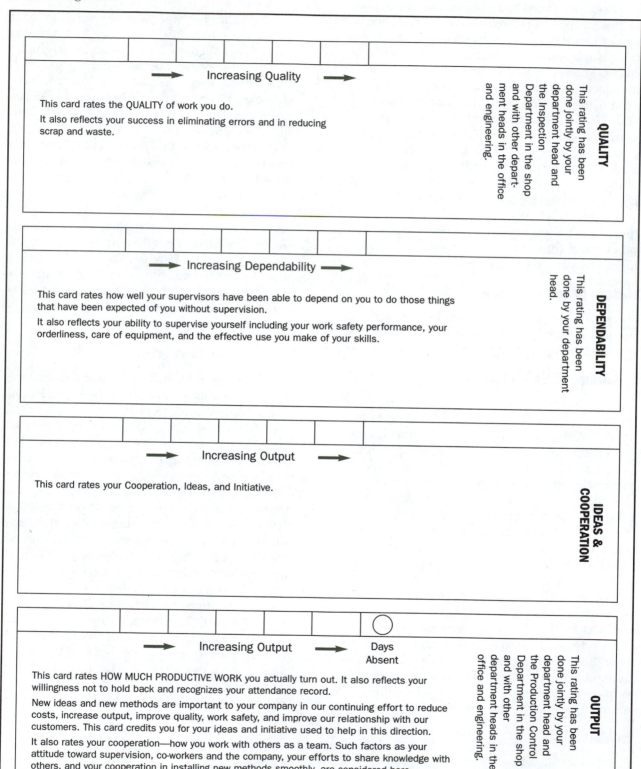

Increasing Quality

QUALITY

This card rates the QUALITY of work you do.

It also reflects your success in eliminating errors and in reducing scrap and waste.

This rating has been done jointly by your department head and the Inspection Department in the shop and with other department heads in the office and engineering.

Increasing Dependability

DEPENDABILITY

This card rates how well your supervisors have been able to depend on you to do those things that have been expected of you without supervision.

It also reflects your ability to supervise yourself including your work safety performance, your orderliness, care of equipment, and the effective use you make of your skills.

This rating has been done by your department head.

Increasing Output

IDEAS & COOPERATION

This card rates your Cooperation, Ideas, and Initiative.

Increasing Output   Days Absent

OUTPUT

This card rates HOW MUCH PRODUCTIVE WORK you actually turn out. It also reflects your willingness not to hold back and recognizes your attendance record.

New ideas and new methods are important to your company in our continuing effort to reduce costs, increase output, improve quality, work safety, and improve our relationship with our customers. This card credits you for your ideas and initiative used to help in this direction.

It also rates your cooperation—how you work with others as a team. Such factors as your attitude toward supervision, co-workers and the company, your efforts to share knowledge with others, and your cooperation in installing new methods smoothly, are considered here.

This rating has been done jointly by your department head and the Production Control Department in the shop and with other department heads in the office and engineering.

Cleveland area.[5] These rates are adjusted quarterly in accordance with changes in the Cleveland area wage index. Insofar as possible, base wage rates are translated into piece rates. Today the average Lincoln factory worker earns $16.54 an hour versus the average $14.25 manufacturing wage in the Cleveland area. Practically all production workers and many others—for example, some forklift operators—are paid by piece rate. Once established, piece rates are never changed unless a substantive change in the way a job is done results from a source other than the worker doing the job.

In December of each year, a portion of annual profits is distributed to employees as bonuses. Incentive bonuses since 1934 have averaged about 90 percent of annual wages. The average bonus for 1995 was $18,887. Even for the recession years 1982 and 1983, bonuses had averaged $13,998 and $8,557, respectively. Individual bonuses are proportional to merit-rating scores. For example, assume the amount set aside for bonuses is 80 percent of total wages paid to eligible employees. A person whose performance score is 95 will receive a bonus of 76 percent (0.80 × 0.95) of annual wages. While these percentages have often resulted in high total compensation, some employees believe that their bonuses are not rising fast enough, despite rising profits. This reflects the firm's decision to use profits to expand the operations rather than put them into higher bonuses. It also reflects the fact that there are more workers today sharing in a bonus pool that is only a little higher than in many years in the 1980s.[6]

Vacations

The company is shut down for two weeks in August and two weeks during the Christmas season. Vacations are taken during these periods. For employees with over 25 years of service, a fifth week of vacation may be taken at a time acceptable to superiors.

Work Assignment

Management has authority to transfer workers and to switch between overtime and short time as required. Supervisors have undisputed authority to assign specific parts to individual workers, who may have their own preferences due to variations in piece rates. During the 1982-1983 recession, 50 factory workers volunteered to join sales teams and fanned out across the country to sell a new welder designed for automobile body shops and small machine shops. The result: $10 million in sales and a hot new product.

Employee Participation in Decision Making

Thinking of participative management usually evokes a vision of a relaxed, non-authoritarian atmosphere. This is not the case at Lincoln. Formal authority is quite strong. "We're very authoritarian around here," says Willis. James F. Lincoln placed a good deal of stress on protecting management's authority. "Management in all successful departments of industry must have complete power," he said. "Management is the coach who must be obeyed. The men, however, are the Players who alone can win the game." Despite this attitude, there are several ways in which employees participate in management at Lincoln.

Richard Sabo, Assistant to the Chief Executive Officer, relates job enlargement/enrichment to participation. He said, "The most important participative technique that we use is giving more responsibility to employees. We give a high school graduate more responsibility than other companies give their foremen." Management puts limits on the degree of participation which is allowed, however. In Sabo's words:

> When you use 'participation,' put quotes around it. Because we believe that each person should participate only in those decisions he is most knowledgeable about. I don't think production employees should control the decisions of the chairman. They don't know as much as he does about the decisions he is involved in.

The Advisory Board, elected by the workers, meets with the chairman and the president every two weeks to discuss ways of improving operations. As noted earlier, this board has been in existence since 1914 and has contributed to many innovations. The incentive bonuses, for example, were first recommended by this committee. Every employee has access to Advisory Board members, and answers to all Advisory Board suggestions are promised by the following meeting. Both Willis and Hastings are quick to point out, though, that the Advisory Board only recommends actions. "They do not have direct authority," Willis says, "and when they bring up something that management thinks is not to the benefit of the company, it will be rejected."

Under the early suggestion program, employees were awarded one-half of the first year's savings attributable to their suggestions. Now, however, the value of suggestions is reflected in performance evaluation scores, which determine individual incentive bonus amounts.

Training and Education

Production workers are given a short period of on-the-job training and then placed on a piece-work pay system. Lincoln does not pay for off-site education, unless very specific company needs are identified. The idea behind this latter policy, according to Sabo, is that everyone cannot take advantage of such a program, and it is unfair to expend company funds for an advantage to which there is unequal access. Recruits for sales jobs, already college graduates, are given on-the-job training in the plant followed by a period of work and training at one of the regional sales offices.

Fringe Benefits and Executive Perquisites

A medical plan and a company-paid retirement program have been in effect for many years. A plant cafeteria, operated on a break-even basis, serves meals at about 60 percent of usual costs. The Employee Association, to which the company does not contribute, provides disability insurance and social and athletic activities. The employee stock ownership program has resulted in employee ownership of about 50 percent of the common stock. Under this program, each employee with more than two years of service may purchase stock in the corporation. The price of these shares is established at book value. Stock purchased through this plan may be held by employees only. Dividends and voting rights are the same as for stock that is owned outside the plan. Approximately 75 percent of the employees own Lincoln stock.

As to executive perquisites, there are none—crowded, austere offices, no executive washrooms or lunchrooms, and no reserved parking spaces. Even the top executives pay for their own meals and eat in the employee cafeteria. If the CEO arrives late due to a breakfast speaking engagement, he has to park far away from the factory entrance.

Financial Policies

James F. Lincoln felt strongly that financing for company growth should come from within the company—through initial cash investment by the founders, through retention of earnings, and through stock purchases by those who work in the business. He saw the following advantages of this approach:

1. Ownership of stock by employees strengthens team spirit. "If they are mutually anxious to make it succeed, the future of the company is bright."
2. Ownership of stock provides individual incentive because employees feel that they will benefit from company profitability.
3. "Ownership is educational." Owner-employees "will know how profits are made and lost; how success is won and lost. There are few socialists in the list of stockholders of the nation's industries."
4. "Capital available from within controls expansion." Unwarranted expansion would not occur, Lincoln believed, under his financing plan.
5. "The greatest advantage would be the development of the individual worker. Under the incentive of ownership, he would become a greater man."
6. "Stock ownership is one of the steps that can be taken that will make the worker feel that there is less of a gulf between him and the boss. Stock ownership will help the worker to recognize his responsibility in the game and the importance of victory."

Until 1980, Lincoln Electric borrowed no money. Even now, the company's liabilities consist mainly of accounts payable and short-term accruals. The unusual pricing policy at Lincoln was succinctly stated by Willis: "At all times price on the basis of cost and at all times keep pressure on our cost." This policy resulted in the price for the most popular welding electrode then in use going from 16 cents a pound in 1929 to 4.7 cents in 1938. More recently, the SA-200 Welder, Lincoln's largest selling portable machine, decreased in price from 1958 through 1965. According to Dr. C. Jackson Grayson of the American Productivity Center in Houston, Texas, Lincoln's prices increased only one-fifth as fast as the Consumer Price Index from 1934 to about 1970. This resulted in a welding products market in which Lincoln became the undisputed price leader for the products it manufactures. Not even the major Japanese manufacturers, such as Nippon Steel for welding electrodes and Saka Transformer for welding machines, were able to penetrate this market.

Substantial cash balances accumulated each year preparatory to paying the year-end bonuses. Modest success with international expansion put some pressure on what was basically a conservative financial philosophy. However, the company borrowed money in 1992 to pay for employee bonuses in the United States. In 1995 Lincoln issued $119 million of new stock. This sale created greater public ownership. As a consequence, Don Hastings remarked that the company must now consider not only the employees but its shareholders, customers, and suppliers.[7] For more current financial information, visit Lincoln's web site.

How Well Does Lincoln Serve Its Stakeholders?

Lincoln Electric differs from most other companies in the importance it assigns to each of the groups it serves. Hastings identifies these groups, in the order of priority ascribed to them, as: (1) customers, (2) employees, and (3) stockholders. As suggested, the 1995 stock issue increased the salience of the stockholders.

Certainly the firm's customers have fared well over the years. Lincoln prices for welding machines and welding electrodes are acknowledged to be the lowest in the marketplace. Quality has consistently been high. The cost of field failures for Lincoln products was recently determined to be a remarkable 0.04 percent of revenues. The "Fleetweld" electrodes and SA-200 welders have been the standard in the pipeline and refinery construction industry, where price is hardly a criterion, for decades. A Lincoln distributor in Monroe, Louisiana, says that he has sold several hundred of the popular AC-225 welders, which are warranted for one year, but has never handled a warranty claim.

Perhaps best-served of all management constituencies have been the employees. Not the least of their benefits, of course, are the year-end bonuses, which effectively double an already average compensation level. The foregoing description of the personnel program and the comments in Appendix 3D further illustrate the desirability of a Lincoln job.

While stockholders were relegated to an inferior status by James F. Lincoln, they have done very well indeed. Recent dividends exceeded $11 a share and earnings per share have approached $30. In January 1980, the price of restricted stock, committed to employees, was $117 a share. By 1989, the stated value, at which the company will repurchase the stock if tendered, was $201. A check with the New York office of Merrill Lynch, Pierce, Fenner and Smith at that time revealed an estimated price on Lincoln stock of $270 a share, with none being offered for sale. Technically, this price applies only to the unrestricted stock owned by the Lincoln family, a few other major holders, and employees who have purchased it on the open market. Risk associated with Lincoln stock, a major determinant of stock value, is minimal because of the small amount of debt in the capital structure, because of an extremely stable earnings record, and because of Lincoln's practice of purchasing the restricted stock whenever employees offer it for sale. The 1995 stock sale has changed this situation dramatically. The stock now trades freely on the NASDAQ stock exchange.

A Concluding Comment

It is easy to believe that the reason for Lincoln's success is the excellent attitude of the employees and their willingness to work harder, faster, and more intelligently than other industrial workers. However, Sabo suggests that appropriate credit be given to Lincoln executives, whom he credits with carrying out the following policies:

1. Management has limited research, development, and manufacturing to a standard product line designed to meet the major needs of the welding industry.
2. New products must be reviewed by manufacturing and all producing costs verified before being approved by management.
3. Purchasing is challenged to not only procure materials at the lowest cost, but also to work closely with engineering and manufacturing to assure that the latest innovations are implemented.
4. Manufacturing supervision and all personnel are held accountable for reduction of scrap, energy conservation, and maintenance of product quality.
5. Production control, material handling, and methods engineering are closely supervised by top management.

6. Management has made cost reduction a way of life at Lincoln, and definite programs are established in many areas, including traffic and shipping, where tremendous savings can result.

7. Management has established a sales department that is technically trained to reduce customer welding costs. This sales approach and other real customer services have eliminated nonessential frills and resulted in long-term benefits to all concerned.

8. Management has encouraged education, technical publishing, and long-range programs that have resulted in industry growth, thereby assuring market potential for the Lincoln Electric Company.

Sabo writes, "It is in a very real sense a personal and group experience in faith—a belief that together we can achieve results which alone would not be possible. It is not a perfect system and it is not easy. It requires tremendous dedication and hard work. However, it does work and the results are worth the effort."

Appendix 3A

Mission and Values Statement of the Lincoln Electric Company

Mission and Values Statement

The mission of The Lincoln Electric Company is to earn and retain global leadership as a total quality supplier of superior products and services.

Our Core Values

As a responsible and successful company in partnership with our customers, distributors, employees, shareholders, suppliers and our host communities, we pledge ourselves to conduct our business in accordance with these core values:

- Respond to our customers' needs and expectations with quality, integrity, and value.
- Recognize people as our most valuable asset.
- Maintain and expand the Lincoln Incentive Management philosophy.
- Practice prudent and responsible financial management.
- Strive continually to be environmentally responsible.
- Support communities where we operate and industries in which we participate.

continued next page

Appendix 3A, cont.
Mission and Values Statement of the Lincoln Electric Company

To Realize Our Mission and Support Our Core Values, We Have Established the Following Goals:

Respond to Our Customers' Needs and Expectations With Quality, Integrity and Value

- Assure value through innovative, functional, and reliable products and services in all the markets we serve around the world.
- Exceed global standards for products and service quality.
- Provide our customers with personalized technical support that helps them achieve improvements in cost reduction, productivity and quality.
- Lead the industry in aggressive application of advanced technology to meet customer requirements.
- Invest constantly in creative research and development dedicated to maintaining our position of market leadership.
- Achieve and maintain the leading market share position in our major markets around the world.

Recognize People As Our Most Valuable Asset

- Maintain a safe, clean, and healthy environment for our employees.
- Promote employee training, education, and development, and broaden skills through multi-departmental and international assignments.
- Maintain an affirmative action program and provide all employees with opportunities for advancement commensurate with their abilities and performance regardless of race, religion, national origin, sex, age, or disability.
- Maintain an environment that fosters ethical behavior, mutual trust, equal opportunity, open communication, personal growth, and creativity.
- Demand integrity, discipline, and professional conduct from our employees in every aspect of our business and conduct our operations ethically and in accordance with the law.
- Reward employees through recognition, "pay for performance," and by sharing our profits with incentive bonus compensation based on extraordinary achievement.

Maintain and Expand the Lincoln Incentive Management Philosophy

Promote dynamic teamwork and innovation as the most profitable and cost-effective way of achieving:
- A committed work ethic and positive employee attitudes throughout the Company.
- High quality, low-cost manufacturing.
- Efficient and innovative engineering.
- Customer-oriented operation and administration.
- A dedicated and knowledgeable sales and service force.
- A total organization responsive to the needs of our worldwide customers.

Practice Prudent and Responsible Financial Management

- Establish attainable goals, strategic planning, and accountability for results that enhance shareholder value.
- Promote the process of employee involvement in cost reductions and quality improvements.
- Recognize profit as the resource that enables our Company to serve our customers.

Strive Continually To Be Environmentally Responsible

- Continue to pursue the most environmentally sound operating practices, processes, and products to protect the global environment.
- Maintain a clean and healthy environment in our host communities.

Support Communities Where We Operate and Industries In Which We Participate

- Invest prudently in social, cultural, educational, and charitable activities.
- Contribute to the industries we serve and society as a whole by continuing our leadership role in professional organizations and education.
- Encourage and support appropriate employee involvement in community activities.

Appendix 3B
Lincoln Electric's HR Objectives

What Are the HR Objectives of Lincoln Electric?

- To maintain and expand the Lincoln Incentive Management Philosophy
- To recognize people as [the company's] most valuable asset
- To promote training, education and development that broaden employee skills
- To maintain an affirmative action program and provide all employees with opportunities for advancement commensurate with their abilities and performance regardless of race, religion, national origin, sex, age or disability

Appendix 3C
Lincoln Electric's Business Objectives

Business Objectives of Lincoln Electric

- To be a global leader in price and quality and serve the customers first
- To achieve and retain global leadership as a total quality supplier of superior products and services
- To respond to our customers with quality, integrity, and value
- To practice prudent and responsible financial management
- To strive continually to be environmentally responsible
- To support communities where we operate and industries in which we participate
- To maintain an environment that fosters ethical behavior, mutual trust, equal opportunity, open communication, personal growth and creativity.
- To promote feedback
- To demand integrity, discipline and professional conduct from our employees in every aspect of our business and conduct operations ethically and in accordance with the law
- To reward employees through recognition, pay for performance, and by sharing profits with incentive bonus compensation based on extraordinary achievement as a means of motivation
- To promote dynamic teamwork and innovation

Appendix 3D
Employee Interviews

Employee Interviews

Typical questions and answers from employee interviews are presented below. In order to maintain each employee's personal privacy, fictitious names are given to the interviewees.

Interview 1

Betty Stewart, a 52-year-old high school graduate who had been with Lincoln 13 years, was working as a cost accounting clerk at the time of the interview.

Q: What jobs have you held here besides the one you have now?

A: I worked in payroll for a while, and then this job came open and I took it.

Q: How much money did you make last year, including your bonus?

A: I would say roughly around $25,000, but I was off for back surgery for a while.

Q: You weren't paid while you were off for back surgery?

A: No.

Q: Did the Employees Association help out?

A: Yes. The company doesn't furnish that, though. We pay $8 a month into the Employee Association. I think my check from them was $130.00 a week.

Q: How was your performance rating last year?

A: It was around 100 points, but I lost some points for attendance for my back problem.

Q: How did you get your job at Lincoln?

A: I was bored silly where I was working, and I had heard that Lincoln kept their people busy. So I applied and got the job the next day.

Q: Do you think you make more money than similar workers in Cleveland?

A: I know I do.

Q: What have you done with your money?

A: We have purchased a better home. Also, my son is going to the University of Chicago, which costs $13,000 a year. I buy the Lincoln stock which is offered each year, and I have a little bit of gold.

Q: Have you ever visited with any of the senior executives, like Mr. Willis or Mr. Hastings?

A: I have known Mr. Willis for a long time.

Q: Does he call you by name?

A: Yes. In fact, he was very instrumental in my going to the doctor that I am going to with my back. He knows the director of the clinic.

Q: Do you know Mr. Hastings?

A: I know him to speak to him, and he always speaks, always. But I have known Mr. Willis for a good many years. When I did Plant Two accounting I did not understand how the plant operated. Of course you are not allowed in Plant Two, because that's the Electrode Division. I told my boss about the problem one day and the next thing I knew Mr. Willis came by and said, "Come on, Betty, we're going to Plant Two." He spent an hour and a half showing me the plant.

Q: Do you think Lincoln employees produce more than those in other companies?

A: I think with the incentive program the way that it is, if you want to work and achieve, then you will do it. If you don't want to work and achieve, you will not do it no matter where you are. Just because you are merit rated and have a bonus, if you really don't want to work hard, then you're not going to. You will accept your 90 points or 92 or 85 because, even with that you make more money than people on the outside.

Q: Do you think Lincoln employees will ever join a union?

A: I don't know why they would.

Q: So you say that money is a very major advantage?

A: Money is a major advantage, but it's not just the money. It's the fact that having the incentive, you do wish to work a little harder. I'm sure that there are a lot of men here who, if they worked some other place, would not work as hard as they do here. Not that they are overworked—I don't mean that—but I'm sure they wouldn't push.

Q: Is there anything that you would like to add?

A: I do like working here. I am better off being pushed mentally. In another company if you pushed too hard you would feel a little bit of pressure, and someone might say, "Hey, slow down, don't try so hard." But here you are encouraged, not discouraged.

Appendix 3D, cont.
Employee Interviews

Interview 2

Ed Sanderson, a 23-year-old high school graduate who had been with Lincoln four years, was a machine operator in the Electrode Division at the time of the interview.

Q: How did you happen to get this job?

A: My wife was pregnant, and I was making three bucks an hour and one day I came here and applied. That was it. I kept calling to let them know I was still interested.

Q: Roughly, what were your earnings last year including your bonus?

A: $45,000.

Q: What have you done with your money since you have been here?

A: Well, we've lived pretty well and we bought a condominium.

Q: Have you paid for the condominium?

A: No, but I could.

Q: Have you bought your Lincoln stock this year?

A: No, I haven't bought any Lincoln stock yet.

Q: Do you get the feeling that the executives here are pretty well thought of?

A: I think they are. To get where they are today, they had to really work.

Q: Wouldn't that be true anywhere?

A: I think more so here because seniority really doesn't mean anything. If you work with a guy who has 20 years here, and you have two months and you're doing a better job, you will get advanced before he will.

Q: Are you paid on a piece-rate basis?

A: My gang does. There are nine of us who make the bare electrode, and the whole group gets paid based on how much electrode we make.

Q: Do you think you work harder than workers in other factories in the Cleveland area?

A: Yes, I would say I probably work harder.

Q: Do you think it hurts anybody?

A: No, a little hard work never hurts anybody.

Q: If you could choose, do you think you would be as happy earning a little less money and being able to slow down a little?

A: No, it doesn't bother me. If it bothered me, I wouldn't do it.

Q: Why do you think Lincoln employees produce more than workers in other plants?

A: That's the way the company is set up. The more you put out, the more you're going to make.

Q: Do you think it's the piece rate and bonus together?

A: I don't think people would work here if they didn't know that they would be rewarded at the end of the year.

Q: Do you think Lincoln employees will ever join a union?

A: No.

Q: What are the major advantages of working for Lincoln?

A: Money.

Q: Are there any other advantages?

A: Yes, we don't have a union shop. I don't think I could work in a union shop.

Q: Do you think you are a career man with Lincoln at this time?

A: Yes.

Interview 3

Roger Lewis, a 23-year-old Purdue graduate in mechanical engineering who had been in the Lincoln sales program for 15 months, was working in the Cleveland sales office at the time of the interview.

Q: How did you get your job at Lincoln?

A: I saw that Lincoln was interviewing on campus at Purdue, and I went by. I later came to Cleveland for a plant tour and was offered a job.

Q: Do you know any of the senior executives? Would they know you by name?

A: Yes, I know all of them—Mr. Hastings, Mr. Willis, Mr. Sabo.

Q: Do you think Lincoln sales representatives work harder than those in other companies?

A: Yes. I don't think there are many sales reps for other companies who are putting in 50- to 60-hour weeks. Everybody here works harder. You can go out in the plant, or you can go upstairs, and there's nobody sitting around.

Q: Do you see any real disadvantage of working at Lincoln?

A: I don't know if it's a disadvantage, but Lincoln is a spartan company, a very thrifty company. I like that. The sales offices are functional, not fancy.

Q: Why do you think Lincoln employees have such high productivity?

A: Piecework has a lot to do with it. Lincoln is smaller than many plants, too; you can stand

Appendix 3D, cont.
Employee Interviews

in one place and see the materials come in one side and the product go out the other. You feel a part of the company. The chance to get ahead is important, too. They have a strict policy of promoting from within, so you know you have a chance. I think in a lot of other places you may not get as fair a shake as you do here. The sales offices are on a smaller scale, too. I like that. I tell someone that we have two people in the Baltimore office, and they say, "You've got to be kidding." It's smaller and more personal. Pay is the most important thing. I have heard that this is the highest paying factory in the world.

Interview 4

Jimmy Roberts, a 47-year-old high school graduate who had been with Lincoln 17 years, was working as a multiple-drill press operator at the time of the interview.

Q: What jobs have you had at Lincoln?

A: I started out cleaning the men's locker room in 1967. After about a year I got a job in the flux department, where we make the coating for welding rods. I worked there for seven or eight years and then got my present job.

Q: Do you make one particular part?

A: No, there are a variety of parts I make—at least 25.

Q: Each one has a different piece rate attached to it?

A: Yes.

Q: Are some piece rates better than others?

A: Yes.

Q: How do you determine which ones you are going to do?

A: You don't. Your supervisor assigns them.

Q: How much money did you make last year?

A: $53,000.

Q: Have you ever received any kind of award or citation?

A: No.

Q: Was your rating ever over 110?

A: Yes. For the past five years, probably, I made over 110 points.

Q: Is there any attempt to let the others know . . . ?

A: The kind of points I get? No.

Q: Do you know what they are making?

A: No. There are some who might not be too happy with their points and they might make it

known. The majority, though, do not make it a point of telling other employees.

Q: Would you be just as happy earning a little less money and working a little slower?

A: I don't think I would, not at this point. I have done piecework all these years, and the fast pace doesn't really bother me.

Q: Why do you think Lincoln productivity is so high?

A: The incentive thing—the bonus distribution. I think that would be the main reason. The paycheck you get every two weeks is important too.

Q: Do you think Lincoln employees would ever join a union?

A: I don't think so. I have never heard anyone mention it.

Q: What is the most important advantage of working here?

A: Amount of money you make. I don't think I could make this type of money anywhere else, especially with only a high school education.

Q: As a black person, do you feel that Lincoln discriminates in any way against blacks?

A: No. I do not think any more so than any other job. Naturally, there is a certain amount of discrimination, regardless of where you are.

Interview 5

Joe Trahan, a 58-year-old high school graduate who had been with Lincoln 39 years, was employed as a working supervisor in the tool room at the time of the interview.

Q: Roughly what was your pay last year?

A: Over $56,000, salary, bonus, stock dividends.

Q: How much was your bonus?

A: About $26,000.

Q: Have you ever gotten a special award of any kind?

A: Not really.

Q: What have you done with your money?

A: My house is paid for, and my two cars. I also have some bonds and the Lincoln stock.

Q: What do you think of the executives at Lincoln?

A: They're really top notch.

Q: What is the major disadvantage of working at Lincoln Electric?

A: I don't know of any disadvantage at all.

Appendix 3D, cont.
Employee Interviews

Q: Do you think you produce more than most people in similar jobs with other companies?

A: I do believe that.

Q: Why is that? Why do you believe that?

A: We are on the incentive system. Everything we do, we try to improve to make a better product with a minimum of outlay. We try to improve the bonus.

Q: Would you be just as happy making a little less money and not working quite so hard?

A: I don't think so.

Q: Do you think Lincoln employees would ever join a union?

A: I don't think they would ever consider it.

Q: What is the most important advantage of working at Lincoln?

A: Compensation.

Q: Tell me something about Mr. James Lincoln, who died in 1965.

A: You are talking about Jimmy Sr. He always strolled through the shop in his shirt sleeves. Big fellow. Always looked distinguished. Gray hair. Friendly sort of guy. I was a member of the Advisory Board one year. He was there each time.

Q: Did he strike you as really caring?

A: I think he always cared for people.

Q: Did you get any sensation of a religious nature from him?

A: No, not really.

Q: And religion is not part of the program now?

A: No.

Q: Do you think Mr. Lincoln was a very intelligent man, or was he just a nice guy?

A: I would say he was pretty well educated. A great talker—always right off the top of his head. He knew what he was talking about all the time.

Q: When were bonuses for beneficial suggestions done away with?

A: About 18 years ago.

Q: Did that hurt very much?

A: I do not think so, because suggestions are still rewarded through the merit rating system.

Q: Is there anything you would like to add?

A: It's a good place to work. The union kind of ties other places down. At other places, electricians only do electrical work, carpenters only do carpentry work. At Lincoln Electric we all pitch in and do whatever needs to be done.

Q: So a major advantage is not having a union?

A: That's right.

Letter From the CEO

To Our Shareholders

Each of you is aware that your company faced enormous challenges in 1993. Those challenges required a focused, creative and positive leadership approach on the part of your management team. As I write this, first quarter 1994 results indicate that the domestic economy is continuing its upward surge. Because of the many tough decisions we had to make in 1993, we are now poised to take advantage of an improved economic climate. Even though much of my personal time has been devoted to overseeing the situation in Europe, excellent results are being achieved in the U.S.A. and Canada.

During 1993, a thorough strategic assessment of our foreign operations led to the conclusion that Lincoln Electric lacked the necessary financial resources to continue to support 21 manufacturing sites. We did not have the luxury of time to keep those plants operating while working to increase our sales and profitability. As a result, with the endorsement of our financial community, the Board of Directors approved management's recommendation to restructure operations in Europe, Latin America, and Japan.

The restructuring included closing the Messer Lincoln operations in Germany, reducing employment throughout Lincoln Norweld, which operates plants in England, France, the Netherlands, Spain, and Norway; and closing manufacturing plants in Venezuela, Brazil, and Japan. The result was a workforce reduction totaling some 770 employees worldwide. We are not abandoning these markets by any means. Rather, the restructuring will allow us to retain and increase sales while relieving us of the high costs associated with excess manufacturing capacity. Now that the restructuring has been accomplished, we operate fifteen plants in ten countries. This capacity will be adequate to supply the inventory needed to support our customers and an increasingly aggressive marketing strategy. We are internationally recognized for outstanding products and service, and we have been certified to the international quality standard ISO-9002.

It was not easy for Lincoln Electric to eliminate manufacturing capacity and jobs. However, I must point out that the overseas companies were given repeated opportunities to turn their performance around. In all fairness, no one anticipated the depth of the recession that continues to devastate Europe, and particularly Germany. But we could not in good conscience, risk both the continuous erosion of shareholder value and the jobs of our dedicated U.S. employees, by remaining unprofitable in these manufacturing operations.

For the second year in the history of this company, it was necessary to take restructuring charges that resulted in a consolidated loss. The restructuring charge totaled $70,100,000 ($40,900,000 after tax), and contributed to a consolidated net loss for 1993 of $38,100,000, compared to a $45,800,000 consolidated loss in 1992.

continued next page

In 1993 our U.S. and Canadian operations achieved outstanding results with increased levels of sales and profitability and a significant gain in market share. We made a huge step forward by concentrating on the "Top Line" to meet one of our major goals—manufacturing and selling $2.1 million worth of product from our Ohio company each billing day from June 1 through the end of the year. Our Canadian company also made significant contributions with a 38 percent increase in sales. The bottom line automatically moved into greater profitability.

These impressive gains were not made without sacrifice. Lincoln manufacturing people voluntarily deferred 614 weeks of vacation, worked holidays, and many employees worked a seven-day-a-week schedule to fill the steady stream of orders brought in by the sales department as we capitalized on an emerging domestic economy that we felt was being largely ignored by our major competitors.

This remarkable achievement would never have been possible without the expert management of your President and Chief Operating Officer Frederick W. Mackenbach. His leadership consistently inspired our employees and management team alike. The U.S. company's extraordinary performance encouraged the Board of Directors to approve a gross bonus of $55 million, and to continue the regular quarterly dividend payment throughout the year. As you know, the usual course of action for a company reporting a consolidated loss is to cut or defer bonuses and dividends. That these were paid is a tribute to our Board and their steadfast belief in the long-range, proven benefits of the Incentive Management System.

Thinking in the long term is critical to our progress in a world that too often seems to demand instant solutions to complex problems. Your Chairman, your Board, and your management team are determined to resist that impulse. Currently, Lincoln people around the world are working diligently to formulate a Strategic Plan that will carry this company into the next century. An important element of this business plan will be our new state-of-the-art motor manufacturing facility, which is on schedule. Furthermore, we have strengthened our international leadership with the addition of executives experienced in global management to our Board and to key management posts.

While your company is indeed emerging from a very challenging period in its history, we project excellent results for 1994, with strong sales, increased profits, and the benefits of those developments accruing to shareholders, customers, and employees. As the year proceeds, we will be looking forward to our Centennial in 1995. I am confident that you and I will enjoy celebrating that event together.

Sincerely,

Donald E. Hastings
Chairman and Chief Executive Officer (Retired May 1997)

POSTSCRIPT: In Lincoln Electric's centennial year, 1995, sales topped $1 billion for the first time. It was also the year that Hastings eliminated the two-tier wage plan that was instituted in 1993. Under this plan, new hires started at 75 percent of the normal pay rate. This plan increased the turnover among the new hires and was regarded as unfair by senior workers. According to one of them, "If an individual shows he can handle the workload, he should be rewarded." As of 1997, Lincoln Electric appears to be back on track, committed as ever to its philosophy and values.[8] Although Donald F. Hastings has been replaced by Anthony A. Massaro, he continues to be an inspiration for the direction and spirit of Lincoln Electric.

ENDNOTES

[1] T. W. Gerdel, "Lincoln Electric Experiences Season of Worker Discontent," *Plain Dealer* [Cleveland] (December 10, 1995):1-C.

[2] Gerdel, "Lincoln Electric Experiences Season of Worker Discontent."

[3] Z. Schiller, "A Model Incentive Plan Gets Caught in a Vise," *Business Week* (January 22, 1996): 89, 92.

[4] R. Narisetti, "Job Paradox Manufacturers Decry A Shortage of Workers While Rejecting Many," *The Wall Street Journal* (September 8, 1995): A4.

[5] Schiller, "A Model Incentive Plan Gets Caught in a Vise," 89, 92.

[6] Gerdel, "Lincoln Electric Experiences Season of Worker Discontent."

[7] Gerdel, "Lincoln Electric Experiences Season of Worker Discontent."

[8] R. M. Hodgetts, "A Conversation with Donald F. Hastings of the Lincoln Electric Company," *Organizational Dynamics* (Winter 1997): 68–74; M. Gleisser, "Lincoln CEO's Formula: Mutual Trust and Loyalty," *Plain Dealer* [Cleveland] (June 22, 1996): 2-C.

Appendix

A

LEGISLATION, COURT AND NLRB DECISIONS AFFECTING HUMAN RESOURCE MANAGEMENT

EMPLOYMENT LEGISLATION/BASIC PROVISIONS

Act	Jurisdiction	Basic Provisions
Fair Labor Standards Act (1938) and subsequent amendments—FLSA	Most interstate employers, certain types of employees, are exempt from overtime provisions—executive, administrative, and professional employees and outside salespeople	Establishes a minimum wage; controls hours through premium pay for overtime; controls working hours for children
Minimum Wage Law (1977)	Small businesses	Sets graduated increases in minimum wage rates
Equal Pay Act (1963 amendment to the FLSA)	Same as FLSA except no employees are exempt	Prohibits unequal pay for males and females with equal skill, effort, and responsibility working under similar working conditions

Act	Jurisdiction	Basic Provisions
Civil Rights Act (1964) (amended by EEOA 1972)	Employers with fifteen or more employees, employment agencies, and labor unions	Prevents discrimination on the basis of race, color, religion, sex, or national origin; establishes EEOC
Civil Rights Act of 1991	Same as the *Civil Rights Act of 1964*	Protects groups against discrimination (as does the 1964 act), but makes provision for jury trials and punitive compensation
Equal Employment Opportunity Act (1972)—EEOA	Adds employees of state and local government and educational institutions, reduced number of employees required to fifteen	Amends Title VII, increases enforcement powers of EEOC
Executive Order 11246 (1965) as amended by Executive Order 11375 (1966)	Federal contractors and subcontractors with contracts over $50,000 and 50 or more employees	Prevents discrimination on the basis of race, color, religion, sex, or national origin; establishes Office of Federal Contract Compliance (OFCC)
Revised Order Number 4 (1971)	Federal contractors	Defines acceptable affirmative action program
Executive Order 11478 (1969)	Federal agencies	Prevents discrimination on the basis of race, color, religion, sex, or national origin
Age Discrimination in Employment Act (1967)—revised 1978; 1986	Employers with more than 20 employees	Prevents discrimination against persons age 40 and over, and states compulsory retirement for some workers
Rehabilitation Act (1973) as amended 1980	Government contractors and federal agencies	Prevents discrimination against persons with physical and/or mental handicaps and provides for affirmative action
Americans with Disabilities Act (1990)	15 or more employees	Protects against discrimination of individuals with disabilities
Older Worker Benefit Protection Act of 1990	Same as the *Age Discrimination in Employment Act* as amended	Employers are prohibited from discriminating with regard to benefits on the basis of age
Immigration Act of 1990	*Immigration Reform and Control Act of 1986*—IRCA	Amends the employer-verification and unfair-immigration—related employment practices as defined by the IRCA
The Family and Medical Leave Act of 1993	Employers with 50 or more employees	Allows workers to take up to 12 weeks unpaid leave for pregnancy or illness of close family member
Glass Ceiling Act of 1991	Same as the 1991 *Civil Rights Act*	Empowers the Glass Ceiling Commission to focus greater attention on eliminating artificial barriers for advancement of women and minorities
Prevailing wage laws— 1. *Davis-Bacon Act* (1931) and 2. *Walsh-Healey Act* (1935)	Employers with government construction projects of $2,000 (Davis-Bacon) and government contracts of $10,000 or more	Guarantees prevailing wages to employees of government contractors

Act	Jurisdiction	Basic Provisions
Legally required fringe benefits— 1. OASDHI (1935 and amendments)	Virtually all employers	Provides income and healthcare to all retired employees and income to the survivors of employees who have died
2. Unemployment compensation (1935)	Virtually all employers	Provides income to employees who are laid off or fired
3. Workers' compensation (dates differ from state to state)	Virtually all employers	Provides benefits to employees who are injured on the job and to the survivors of employees who are killed on the job
Occupational Safety and Health Act (1970)—OSHA	Most interstate employers	Assures as far as possible—safe and healthy working conditions and the preservation of our human resources
Employee Retirement Income Security Act (1974)—ERISA	Most interstate employers with pension plans (no employer is required to have such a plan)	Protects employees covered by a pension plan from losses in benefits due to: · mismanagement · plant closings and bankruptcies · job changes
Freedom of Information Act (1966)	Federal agencies only	Allows individuals to review employers' records on them and bring civil damages
The Pregnancy Discrimination Act of 1978	Same as *Civil Rights Act* (1964)	Identifies pregnancy as a disability and entitles the woman to the same benefits as any other disability
Privacy Act of 1974 (Public Law 93-579)	Federal agencies only	Allows individuals to review employer's records on them and sue for civil damages
Uniform Guidelines on Employee Selection Procedures (1978)	Same as EEOA (1972)	Updates EEOC 1970 guidelines to more clearly define adverse impact and test validation
Guidelines on Sexual Harassment (1980)	Same as EEOA (1972)	Defines standards for what constitutes harassment
Vietnam Era Veterans Readjustment Act (1974)	Government contractors with contracts in excess of $10,000	Provides for affirmative action in the employment of Vietnam era veterans
Civil Rights Act of 1866, Section 1981	All citizens	Gives all persons, regardless of race, age, and national origin, the same contractual rights as "white citizens." Does not apply to sex-based discrimination.
Civil Rights Act of 1871, Section 1983	All citizens	Applies to sex-based discrimination
The First Amendment, U.S. Constitution	All citizens	Guarantees freedom of speech and religion
The Fifth Amendment	All citizens	Guarantees due process of law
The Fourteenth Amendment	All citizens	Prohibits abridgment of federally conferred privileges by actions of the state
Employee Polygraph Protection Act (1988)	Private employers	Prohibits most employees from polygraph testing without reasonable suspicion

Act	Jurisdiction	Basic Provisions
Drug-Free Workplace Act (1988)	Federal contractors with contracts exceeding $25,000	Requires employers to maintain drug-free workplace
Worker Adjustment and Retraining Notification Act of 1988	Employers with more than 100 employees	Requires 60 days notice of plant or office closing
Railway Labor Act (1926)—RLA	Railroad workers and airline employees	Provides right to organize, provides majority choice of representatives, prohibits "yellow dog" contracts, outlines dispute settlement procedures
Norris-LaGuardia Act (1932)	All employers and labor organizations	Prohibits yellow dog contracts, injunctions for nonviolent activity of unions (strikes, picketing, and boycotts), provides limited union liability
National Labor Relations Act (1935)—*Wagner Act*	Nonmanagerial employees in private industry not covered by *Railway Labor Act* (RLA)	Provides right to organize, provides for collective bargaining, requires employers to bargain, unions must represent all members equally
Labor Management Relations Act (1947)—*Taft-Hartley Act*	Nonmanagerial employees in private industry not covered by RLA	Prohibits unfair labor practices of unions; outlaws closed shop; prohibits strikes in national emergencies; requires both parties to bargain in good faith
Labor Management Reporting and Disclosure Act (1959)—*Landrum-Griffin Act*	Labor organizations	Outlines procedures for redressing internal union problems
Amendments to *Taft-Hartley Act* (1974)	Labor organizations	Specifies illegal activities within union
Executive Order 10988 (1962)	Federal employees	Recognizes employee's right to join unions and bargain collectively, prohibits strikes. Requires agency to meet and confer with union on policy practices and working conditions

COURT AND NLRB DECISIONS PROVISIONS

United Steelworkers of America v. Warrior & Gulf Navigation Co. (1960); *United Steelworkers of America v. American Manufacturing Co.* (1960), and *United Steelworkers of America v. Enterprise Wheel & Car Corp.* (1960)
    Referred to as the "Trilogy" cases, these three cases upheld the arbitrator's authority to remedy violations of collective bargaining agreements. The court, however, could decide the question of arbitrability. If the court determines that a collectively bargained contract calls for arbitration, then the arbitrator can arbitrate it. This was further upheld in *AT&T Technologies, Inc. v. Communications Workers of America* (1986).

Stringfellow v. Monsanto Corporation (1970)
    Established the precedent for giving credit to the employer for making performance appraisal-based decisions on the basis of evidence that the appraisal uses definite identifiable criteria based on the quality and quantity of an employee's work.
Phillips v. Martin Marietta Corp. (1971)
    Whether a BFOQ exists depends on whether it can be shown that the qualification is demonstrably more relevant to job performance for a woman than a man.
Diaz v. Pan American World Airways, Inc. (1971)
    The primary function of an airline is to transport passengers safely from one point to another

Therefore, not hiring males for flight attendants is discriminatory. Business necessity is established.

Griggs v. Duke Power (1971)

Test for hiring cannot be used unless job related. Organizations must show evidence of job relatedness. Not necessary to establish intent to discriminate.

Board of Regents of State Colleges v. Roth (1972)

Protects workers from discharge when due process hasn't been given.

Richardson v. Hotel Corporation of America (1972)

Dismissal on grounds of conviction record resulted in adverse impact; but since conviction record argued (not shown) to be related to business necessity (not job performance), dismissal is okay.

Spurlock v. United Airlines (1972)

Use of college degree as a selection criterion valid because job related, even though no performance data provided.

Rowe v. General Motors Corporation (1972)

All white supervisory recommendations were based on subjective and vague standards which led to a lack of promotions for black employees. Identified five discriminatory factors.

Hodgson v. Robert Hall Clothes, Inc. (1973)

Pay differentials between salesmen and saleswomen justified on the basis of profitability of area in which employees work.

McDonnell Douglas Corporation v. Green (1973)

Employer's test device constitutes prima facie case of racial discrimination under four different criteria (see Chapter 7).

Brito v. Zia Company (1973)

Zia violated Title VII because they laid off a disproportionate number of a protected group on the basis of low performance scores on measures that were not validated.

Sugarman v. Dougal (1973)

The due process and equal protection clauses of the Fifth Amendment also apply to aliens in public employment.

Hodgson v. Greyhound Lines, Inc. (1974)

Could discriminate without empirical evidence on basis of age. Good faith used to show older people would make less safe drivers.

Corning Glass Works v. Brennan (1974)

The *Equal Pay Act* is violated by paying male inspectors on the night shift a higher base wage than female inspectors on the day shift.

Baxter v. Savannah Sugar Refining Co. (1974)

Subjective appraisal form is viewed as discriminatory.

Green v. Missouri Pacific R. R. Co. (1975)

Applying the lessons from *Griggs v. Duke Power*, the court and the EEOC have found it unlawful to refuse to hire job applicants because of their arrest record except for certain circumstances (*Richardson v. Hotel Corporation of America*).

Kirkland v. New York Department of Correctional Services (1975)

The use of quotas was rejected as a method of determining promotions except as an interim measure to be used until nondiscriminatory procedures to determine promotion are established.

Stamps (EEOC) v. Detroit Edison (1975)

Title VII does not provide for an award of punitive damages. Back pay and attorney fees are the explicit provisions of Title VII.

Rogers v. International Paper Company (1975)

Subjective criteria are not to be condemned as unlawful per se because some decisions about hiring and promotions in supervisory and managerial jobs cannot be made using objective standards alone. This opinion, however, is somewhat contrary to those in *Albemarle Paper Company v. Moody* (1973); *Baxter v. Savannah Sugar Refining Corporation* (1974); and *Rowe v. General Motors* (1972).

Albemarle v. Moody (1975)

Need to establish evidence that test is related to content of job. Could use job analysis to do so, but not evidence from global performance ratings made by supervisors.

McDonald v. Santa Fe Trail Transportation Co. (1976)

Requires consistency in dismissal policies due to absenteeism.

Mastie v. Great Lakes Steel Corporation (1976)

As with Stringfellow, the court said that the objectivity of evaluation can be established by demonstrating that the company performed and relied on a thorough evaluation process intended to be used fairly and accurately.

Smith v. Mutual Benefit Life Insurance Company (1976)

Employer is not discriminating if refusing to hire male appearing to be effeminate.

Chrysler Outboard v. Dept. of Industry (1976)

Employer refuses to hire a worker who had leukemia because he was prone to infection. Court said he had to be hired because he was qualified.

Watkins v. Scott Paper Company (1976)

Performance data to validate tests that are derived from graphic scales are too vague and easily subject to discrimination.

Robinson v. Union Carbide Corporation (1976)

These two require written standards for promotion to help prevent discrimination.

Wade v. Mississippi Cooperative Extension Service (1976)

Performance scores used to decide promotions and salary issues not valid because no job analysis.

Washington v. Davis (1976)

When a test procedure is challenged under constitutional law, intent to discriminate must be established. No need to establish intent if filed under Title VII, just show effects. Could use communication test to select applicants for police force.

Castaneda v. Partida (1977)

Prima facie evidence of discrimination established when evidence of both statistical disparity and discriminatory selection procedures vis-a-vis the gross population figures.

Barnes v. Costle (1977)

Sexual harassment is a form of sex discrimination under Title VII, and employer is responsible if he takes no action on learning of events.

Mistretta v. Sandia Corporation (1977)

Employment decisions suspect when based on evaluations that reflect only best judgments and opinions of evaluators rather than identifiable criteria based on quality or quantity of work or specific performances that are supported by some kind of record.

Hazelwood School District v. U.S. (1977)

Labor market comparisons must be based on relevant labor market and not general labor market.

International Brotherhood of Teamsters v. United States (1977)

Bona fide seniority systems maintained without discriminatory intent are exempt from Title VII liability if established before 1964.

United Air Lines, Inc. v. McMann (1977)

Employer can force retirement before age of 65 if it has bona fide retirement plan.

Yukas v. Libbey-Owens-Ford (1977)

All practices against nepotism, especially close relatives and spouses, are nondiscriminators, especially in same department and/or as in supervisor-subordinate relationship.

Flowers v. Crouch-Walter Corporation (1977)

Plaintiff established prima facie evidence that a discharge was discriminatory and not based on performance.

Donaldson v. Pillsbury Company (1977)

Requires clear establishment and communication of job requirements and performance standards.

James v. Stockman Values and Fittings Company (1977)

White supervisors without formal guidelines selecting applicants to apprenticeship program is discriminatory. Need more discrete performance appraisal.

Dothard v. Rawlinson (1977)

Height requirements not valid, therefore constitutes discriminatory practice.

Bakke v. Regents of the University of California (1978)

Reverse discrimination not allowed. Race, however, can be used in selection decisions.

Affirmative action programs permissible when prior discrimination established.

United States v. City of Chicago (1978)

Specific promotion criteria must be used that are related to the job to which being promoted.

Detroit Police Officers Association v. Coleman Young (1979)

Court holds in favor of goals and quotas to reverse previous discrimination.

NLRB v. Wright Line, Inc. (1981)

In cases where an employee is fired for what may appear to be union-related activities, the employer must show (to be vindicated in the dismissal) that the discipline imposed is the same as in other cases where union activity was not an issue.

American Textile Manufacturers Institute v. Donovan (1981)

OSHA need not do cost-benefit analyses before issuing working health standards.

Tooley v. Martin-Marietta Corporation (1981)

Must be religious accommodation for employees who object to union membership or support (as long as no undue hardship on union).

Los Angeles Dept. of Water v. Manhard (1981)

Rules against department rule of having female employees contribute more to a retirement plan than men.

Clayton v. United Auto Workers (1981)

When a union member feels unfairly represented and only the employer can grant the relief requested, the employee need not exhaust internal union remedies before suing the employer.

Lehman v. Yellow Freight System (1981)

Informal affirmative action not permissible although formal voluntary one such as Weber is okay.

Northwest Airlines, Inc. v. Transport Workers (1981)

An employer found guilty of job discrimination cannot force an employee's union to contribute to the damages, even though the union may have negotiated the unequal terms.

County of Washington, Oregon v. Gunther (1981)

It can be illegal (under Title VII and EPA 1963) to pay women unfairly low wages even if not doing same work as men (not a comparable worth case).

First National Maintenance v. NLRB (1981)

Management does not have to negotiate with unions in advance over closing plants or dropping lines.

Texas Department of Community Affairs v. Joyce Ann Burdine (1981)

A defendant in a job discrimination case need only provide a legitimate, nondiscriminatory explanation for not hiring or promoting a woman or minority, and need not prove that the white man hired was better qualified. The burden of proving intentional discrimination rests with the plaintiff.

Fernandez v. Wynn Oil Company (1981)

Title VII does not permit employers to use stereotypic impressions of male and female roles as a BFOQ defense to sex discrimination. Employer can't use customer preferences for working with male employees as a defense of discrimination.

Connecticut v. Teal (1982)

Employers must defend each part of a selection process against adverse impact and not just the end result of the entire process (the bottom line).

Spirit v. TIAA/CREF (1982)

Retirement annuities must be equal, regardless of sex.

Borg Warner Corp. v. NLRB (1982)

Distinction between mandatory and permissible. Terms depend on whether topic regulates the employer-employee relation.

American Tobacco v. Patterson (1982)

Bona fide seniority systems without discriminating intent are exempt from Title VII liability.

Newport News Shipbuilding and Dry Dock Co. v. EEOC (1983)

If an employer supplies any level of health benefits to female workers' husbands, the employer must also supply the same level of benefits to male workers' wives, and that includes pregnancy benefits. This, in effect, reverses the Supreme Court's ruling in *General Electric v. Gilbert,* where the court said that pregnancy benefits need not be given the same treatment by employers as other health and disability programs.

Arizona Governing Committee v. Norris (1983)

Pension payouts by employers should be equal for women and men, and past unequal treatment of women must be cured by retroactive funding of pensions. This decision is in essence the other half of the issue. The first half was rendered in the Supreme Court decision of *Los Angeles Department of Water and Power v. Manhart,* where the decision was made that requiring larger contributions by females than males into pension programs is discriminatory.

NLRB v. Transportation Management (1983)

Employees are protected by the NLRA when helping organize employees. If an employee claims to be fired for trying to organize a union but the employer claims it was poor performance, the employer has the burden of proof. In cases where such "mixed" motives for employer action may exist, the employer must prove the case.

Firefighters Local Union No 1784 v. Stotts (1984)

In this decision, the Supreme Court upheld the bona fide seniority system over an affirmative action consent decree in a situation of layoffs. Thus, the employees most recently hired could be subject to layoff even though this action could compromise the affirmative action efforts.

Otis Elevator v. NLRB (1984)

Employees need not bargain over a transfer of operation if move is based on economics, not labor cost consideration.

AFSCME v. State of Washington (1985)

State had systematically paid jobs dominated by women less than their value according to job evaluation. Court of appeals overturned this decision saying state could not be forced "to eliminate an economic inequality that it did not create."

Pattern Makers' League v. NLRB (1985)

Employees may resign from a union at any time, even during a strike or when one is imminent.

Garcia v. San Antonio Transit Authority (1985)

Extends coverage of FLSA to state and local governments.

Scott v. Sears Roebuck (1985)

Woman unsuccessful in sex harassment suit based on acts by coworkers. Woman did not complain to supervisors. Court ruled only responsible for acts of coworkers if they knew or should have known of acts and took no action.

Horn v. Duke Homes (1985)

Court endorsed principle that employers have strict liability for sexual harassment by supervisors (company claimed that it was not liable because it was not aware of the behavior). Court supported full back pay (plaintiff had been terminated).

Glasgow v. Georgia Pacific Corp. (1985)

Court accepts sexual harassment argument on basis of creating hostile work environment (no quid pro quo). Company was found by Court to have made sexually harassing environment a condition of employment because harassment went on for a long period of time with organization doing nothing. Court outlined four-point test for sexually harassing work environment.

1. Harassment was unwelcome
2. Harassment was because of sex
3. Harassment affected terms and conditions of employment
4. Knowledge of harassment is "imputed" to employer

Wygant v. Jackson Board of Education (1986)

The Court ruled that white teachers were illegally dismissed in order to hire minority teachers in the School Board's efforts to fulfill a voluntary affirmative action program.

Barns v. Washington Natural Gas (1986)

Employer fires an employee because he was believed to have epilepsy. Awarded two years back pay and reinstatement.

Local 28 of the Sheet Metal Workers v. Equal Employment Opportunity Commission (1986)

The Court approved a lower court order requiring a New York City sheet metal workers' local to meet a 29 percent minority membership goal by 1987. The Court also held that judges may order racial preferences in union membership and other context if necessary to rectify especially "egregious" discrimination.

Local 93 of the International Association of Firefighters v. City of Cleveland (1986)

The Court held that lower Federal courts have broad discretion to approve decrees in which employers, over the objections of white employees, settle discrimination suits by agreeing to preferential hiring or promotion of minority-group members. It upheld a decree in which Cleveland agreed to settle a job discrimination suit by African-American and Hispanic firefighters by temporarily promoting African-American and Hispanic workers ahead of whites who had more seniority and higher test scores.

Meritor Savings Bank v. Vinson (1986)

The Court held that sexual harassment is a form of sex discrimination prohibited by Title VII of the *Civil Rights Act* and that employers may be liable for condoning a hostile work environment. However, the Court made it clear that employers will not be automatically liable for sexual harassment by supervisors or employees.

Philbrook v. Ansonta Board of Education (1986)

An employer may choose its own method of religious accommodation over a plan suggested by the worker as long as the employer's plan is reasonable.

Johnson v. Transportation Agency, Santa Clara County (1987)

The U.S. Supreme Court ruled that the county was justified in giving a job to a woman who scored two points less on an exam than a man. The county had an affirmative action plan that was flexible, temporary, and designed to correct the imbalance of white males in the workforce.

School Board of Nassau County, Fla. v. Airline (1987)

The U.S. Supreme Court ruled that contagious diseases are not automatically excluded from coverage of the handicap provisions of Section 504 of the 1973 *Rehabilitation Act.*

Luck v. Southern Pacific Transportation Company (1987)

The court ruled that the company wrongfully discharged Barbara Luck for refusing a drug test on the grounds that it violated her rights to privacy. Subsequently, the company stopped its random drug-testing program.

U.S. v. Paradise (1987)

The U.S. Supreme Court affirmed the affirmative action plan for the state troopers at Alabama in which promotion and hiring quotas were established in order to correct racial imbalances even though it may result in discrimination against an individual because of race or color.

Chalk v. U.S. District Court for Central District of California (1987)

Although handicapped because of AIDS, the teacher was otherwise able to perform his job within the meaning of the *Rehabilitation Act* of 1973 and, therefore, should be allowed to teach.

O'Connor v. Ortega (1987)

Supreme Court recognized workplace privacy for the first time.

EEOC v. Commonwealth of Massachusetts (1987)

A Massachusetts law requiring entry-level motor vehicle examiners to be aged 35 or younger does not violate *Age Discrimination in Employment Act* because it is a bona fide occupational qualification (BFOQ).

Watson v. Fort Worth Bank and Trust (1988)

The U.S. Supreme Court held that all selection procedures—objective or subjective, scored or unscored—should be subject to adverse impact analysis, compelling a demonstration by the employer that the procedure is job related if adverse impact is shown.

Kraszewski v. State Farm (1988)

Out of court settlement firm agrees to set aside half of its new sales jobs to women for ten years and to pay damages and back pay.

Arrow Automotive Industries v. NLRB (1988)

Company does not have to bargain on plant closings even if based on labor-cost considerations.

Wards' Cove Packing v. Atonio (1989)

Concentration statistics were used to prove adverse impact. Court ruled that burden of proof should not shift to employer unless it can be proved that a specific policy created the disparity.

Hopkins v. Price Waterhouse (1989)

The court upheld the award of a partnership to the female accountant who successfully claimed that sexual stereotyping prevented her promotion.

Dimaranan v. Pomona Valley Hospital (1991)

The court essentially ruled that employers can restrict the use of foreign languages only when there is a compelling business-related necessity to do so.

EEOC v. Arabian American Oil Co. (1991)

The U.S. Supreme Court decided that Title VII has no application to U.S. employers employing U.S. citizens to work abroad. ADEA and the *Civil Rights Act* of 1991, however, have application.

Gilmer v. Interstate/Johnson Lane Corp. (1991)

The Supreme Court ruled in favor of alternative dispute resolution (ADR) by stating that employees can be required to go to arbitration before pursuing litigation.

Electromation Inc. v. NLRB (1992)

The Board held that 'action committees' at Electromation were illegal "labor organizations" because management created and controlled the groups and used them to deal with employees on working conditions in violation of Section 8 (a) 2 of the NLRA.

Stewart v. Jackson & Nash (1992)

A truth-in-hiring lawsuit in which the appeals court declared that the law firm's misrepresentations caused Stewart to join a firm in which her skills as an environmental lawyer were not used although promised to be so.

Soroka v. Dayton Hudson Corporation (1991)

A California court ruled against the use of pre-employment psychological tests by Target Stores (a division of Dayton Hudson). The company had been using the tests to screen retail store security officers for emotional stability. The court found that the tests represented an invasion of privacy under California law.

Stender v. Lucky Stores (1992)

The court ruled that the use of interest surveys as a defense in disparate treatment and disparate impact cases by Lucky Stores is permitted. "Even in a situation where gender stereotypes about work interest patterns reflect reality, it is unlawful for an employer to discriminate against those whose work interests deviate from the stereotype," the court decides.

E. I. DuPont de Nemours and Company v. NLRB (1993)

The Board concluded that DuPont's six safety committees and fitness committee were employer-dominated labor organizations and that DuPont dominated the formation and administration of one of them in violation of Section 8 (a) 2 of the NLRA.

St. Mary's Honor Center v. Hicks (1993)

The Supreme Court ruled in this disparate treatment case, that the suing employee has to produce evidence that the employer's true motive is not a discriminatory one. This increases the burden of proof on the employee to demonstrate that the employer intentionally discriminated.

EEOC v. AIC Security Investigations (1993)

The court ruled in favor of a director of a security firm who was discharged after he was diagnosed with terminal brain cancer and awarded the individual $572,000. The first case under ADA.

Harris v. Forklift Systems (1993)

The Supreme Court affirmed the "reasonable women" standard by sending the case back to the appeals court stating that Harris did not have to prove that she was psychologically damaged by her boss' behavior to claim sexual harassment.

Electromation Inc. v. NLRB (1994)

The court upheld the NLRB's ruling in the 1992 decision of the same case.

Black Fire Fighters Association of Dallas v. City of Dallas (1994)

Race-conscious promotion remedies must be narrowly tailored to remedy past discrimination, the appeals court explains. Finding that the 28 blacks are slated for promotion without regard to whether anyone is the victim of past discrimination, that the city is not the type of "particularly egregious" employer that a court must force to promote minorities through broad, race-conscious remedies, and that the benefits of having more minority supervisors does not justify imposing racial classifications with such loose connections to remedying past discrimination, the court concludes that the remedy unnecessarily harms other firefighters.

Ensley Branch, NAACP v. Seibels (1994)

"The goal of eliminating discrimination may justify some interim use of affirmative action, but affirmative action selection provisions are themselves a form of discrimination that cannot continue forever. An end to racial discrimination demands the development of valid, nondiscriminatory selection procedures to replace race-conscious selection procedures," the court rules.

Grant v. Lone Star Co. (1994)

The court held that private employees are exempt from personal liability under suits brought under Title VII. This extends the exemption that had been given earlier to public employees. The reasoning here was that Congress probably did not want to impose the burden of costly litigation upon individuals nor businesses with fewer than 15 employees.

Dirschel v. Speck (1994)

The court held that individual employees may be personally liable under suits brought under Title VII when they act as agents of the employer and when they possess independent authority to make employment decisions regarding the employee who claims bias. Thus a CEO (Speck) had independent authority over the female executive (Dirschel) and was acting as the hospital's agent when allegedly making offensive and hostile remarks.

National Labor Relations Board v. Town & Country Electric Inc. (1995)

In a reversal of a lower court decision, the Supreme Court ruled individuals paid by labor unions to find employment at nonunion job sites and to organize the workforce (salting) were still considered employees and entitled to protection under the NLRA.

United Food and Commercial Workers Union Local 751 v. Brown Group Inc. (1996)

A union has the right to sue for damages on behalf of the members who don't receive sufficient notice of a plant closing as stated under the *Worker Adjustment and Retraining Notification (WARN) Act,* according to this Supreme Court ruling. And the union isn't required to show injury to itself.

STATISTICS FOR MANAGING HUMAN RESOURCES

This book refers to numerous research studies, which provide documentation for its assertions. Readers who wish to learn more about the studies cited are encouraged to consult the original sources, listed in the notes for each chapter. Much of this literature requires some basic familiarity with the statistics and research methods used in human resource management. This appendix describes some of the basic concepts needed to understand the original research reports. Although this appendix uses examples relevant to selection and placement (described in Chapter 8), the basic concepts described here also apply to research on most other topics.

MEASUREMENT

Regardless of the method or site used to study human resource issues, researchers need to be concerned about the reliability and validity of measurement devices. *Reliability* refers to the consistency of measurement and *validity* relates to the truth or accuracy of measurement. Both are expressed by a *correlation coefficient* (denoted by the symbol r).

Correlation Coefficient

A correlation coefficient expresses the degree of linear relationship between two sets of scores. A positive correlation exists when high values on one measure (e.g., a job knowledge test) are associated with high scores on another measure (e.g., overall ratings of job performance). A negative correlation exists when high scores on one measure are associated with low scores on another measure. The range of possible correlation coefficients is from +1 (a perfect positive correlation coefficient) to -1 (a perfect negative correlation coefficient). Several linear relationships represented by plotting actual data are shown in Exhibit B.1.

Lockheed Corp. v. Spink (1996)

This case involved the legality of employment waivers for employees electing to choose early retirement. Because of the number of employers instituting early-retirement incentive plans, the Supreme Court's decision was much anticipated by the HR/benefits community.

The high court ruled that the *Employee Retirement Income Security Act* (ERISA) of 1974 does not necessarily prevent an employer from conditioning an employee's receipt of early retirement benefits upon a plan participant's waiver of employment claims.

Oncale v. Sundowner (1998)

Supreme Court unanimously voted to define sexual harassment to include by people of their own gender. The case was based upon a male worker who worked on an offshore oil rig who claimed sexual harassment by his co-workers and supervisors.

Piscataway Board of Education v. Waxman (1998)

The Third Circuit Court ruled that "the goal of achieving or maintaining diversity can never justify a racial preference." Affirmative action can only be justified as a remedy for a precisely identified discrimination. The case involved an African-American teacher who was retained during a layoff while an equally qualified white teacher was not retained. The case was settled out of court before reaching the Supreme Court.

This set of court cases is meant to provide a sampling of those mentioned in the text. For descriptions of these and other cases, see V. C. Smith, "Supreme Decisions," *Human Resource Executive* (May 6, 1997): 34–37; J. Ledvinka, and V. G. Scarpello, *Federal Regulation of Personnel and Human Resource Management*, 2nd ed. (Boston: Kent, 1991); M. McCarthy, ed., *Complete Guide to Employing Persons with Disabilities* (Albertson, NY: National Center on Employment of the Handicapped at Human Resources Center, 1985); D. P. Twomey, *Employment Discrimination Law: A Manager's Guide* (Cincinnati: South-Western, 1998); H. H. Perritt, *1998 Wiley Employment Law Update* (New York: Wiley Law, 1998); W. L. Keller and T. J. Darby, eds., *International Labor and Employment Laws* (American Bar Association, 1997); M. P. Posner, ed., *The Developing Labor Law: The Boards, the Courts, and the National Labor Relations Act: 1997 Cumulative Supplement* (Washington, DC: BNA, 1998); S. L. Wilborn, J. F. Burton, Jr., and S. J. Schwab, *Employment Law: Cases and Materials* (Lexis Law, 1998).

Exhibit B.1

Scatterplots Indicating Possible Relationships Between Selection Test Scores and Job Performance Scores

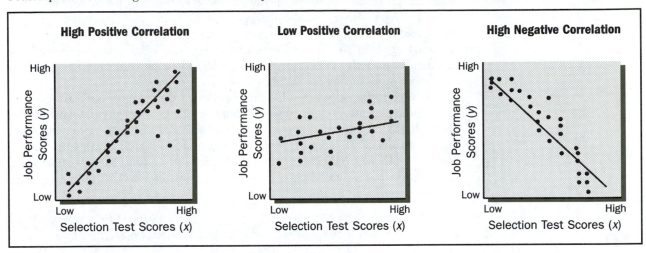

The correlation between scores on a predictor (x) and a criterion (y) is typically expressed for a sample as r_{xy}. If we did not have a sample but were able to compute our correlation on the population of interest, we would express the correlation as ρ_{xy} (ρ is the Greek letter *rho*). In almost all cases, researchers do not have access to the entire population. Therefore, they must estimate the population correlation coefficient based on data from a sample of the population. For instance, an organization may desire to know the correlation between a test for computer programming ability (scores on a predictor, x) and job performance (scores on a performance appraisal rating form, y) for all its computer programmers, but decides it cannot afford to test all computer programmers (i.e., the population of interest). Instead, the organization may select a sample of computer programmers and estimate the correlation coefficient in the population (ρ_{xy}) based on the observed correlation in the sample (r_{xy}).

For each scatterplot in Exhibit B.1, a solid line represents the pattern of data points. Each line is described by an equation, which takes the general form for a straight line: $y = a + bx$, where a is the point at which the line intercepts the y-axis and b is the slope of the line. Such equations, called *prediction equations*, allow researchers to estimate values of y (the criterion) from their knowledge of x (the predictor). For example, we may conduct a study to determine the correlation between sales performance (i.e., dollar sales volume) and number of years of sales experience, for a group of salespeople. Once we have developed a prediction equation, we can then estimate how well a sales applicant might perform on the job.[1] The equation might read,

Dollar Sales per Month = $50,290 + $2,000 × Years of Sales Experience

Using this equation, we would predict that a salesperson with ten years' of experience will generate $70,290 a month in sales. A new salesperson with only one year of experience will be expected to generate only $52,290 a month in sales.

As you might expect, decision makers often employ more than one predictor in their equations. For example, organizations often use multiple predictors when making selection and placement decisions. Similar to that of the single-predictor approach, the purpose of multiple prediction is to estimate a criterion (y) from a linear combination of predictor variables ($y = a + b_1x_1 + b_2x_2 + \ldots + b_mx_m$). Such equations are called *multiple-prediction equations* or *multiple-regression equations*. The bs are the regression weights applied to the predictor measures. The relationship between the predictors and the criterion score is referred to as the *multiple-correlation coefficient* (denoted by the symbol R).[2]

For example, suppose a manager believed that sales were a function of years of experience, education, and shyness (scored 0 for people who are not very shy to 7 for people who are very shy). To determine whether the manager's intuition was correct, we might conduct a research study. Information on each of these predictors could be collected, along with sales performance, or criterion, data. A multiple-regression equation such as the following could be generated:

Dollar Sales per Month = \$25,000 + (\$1,500 × Years of Experience) + (\$500 × Years of Schooling) - (\$25 × Score on Shyness)

This equation would indicate that a salesperson who scored low on shyness (1) and had ten years of experience plus a college degree (sixteen years of schooling) will be expected to generate \$47,975 in sales [\$25,000 + (\$1,500 × 10) + (\$1,500 × 16) - (25 × 1)].

Multiple regression analysis has been used to determine how to combine information from multiple selection devices. Multiple regression has also been used to assess such things as the effects of rater and ratee characteristics (e.g., sex, experience, prior performance rating, and rate of pay) on performance appraisal and pay decisions and to measure the effects of organizational characteristics (e.g., size, industry, and sales) on human resource planning and policies.

Reliability

If a measure such as a selection test is to be useful, it must yield reliable results. As pointed out in Chapter 8, the reliability of a measure can be defined and interpreted in several ways. Each of these methods is based on the notion that observed scores (x) comprise true scores (T) plus some error (E) or $x = T + E$ where T is the expected score if there were no error in measurement.[3] To the extent that observed scores on a test are correlated with true scores, a test is said to be reliable. That is, if observed and true scores could be obtained for every individual who took a personnel selection test, the squared correlation between observed and true scores in the population is (ρ^2_x) would be called the reliability coefficient for that selection test.

One means of estimating reliability is *test-retest reliability* (ρ_{xx}). This method is based on testing a sample of individuals twice with the same measure and then correlating the results to produce a reliability estimate.

Another means of estimating the reliability of a measure is to correlate scores on alternate forms of the measure. *Alternate test forms* are any two test forms that have been constructed in an effort to make them parallel; their observed score means, variances (i.e., measures of the spread of scores about the means), and correlations with other measures may be equal or very similar.[4] They are also intended to be similar in content.

A problem with test-retest reliability and alternate forms reliability is the necessity of testing twice. In contrast, *internal consistency reliability* is estimated based on only one administration of a measure. The most common method, *coefficient* α (alpha), yields a *split-half reliability* estimate. That is, the measure (e.g., a test) is divided into two parts, which are considered alternate forms of each other, and the relationship between these two parts is an estimate of the measure's reliability.

Researchers are interested in assessing the reliability of measures based on one or more of these methods because reliability is a necessary condition for determining validity. The reliability of a measure sets a limit on how highly the measure can correlate with another measure, because it is very unlikely that a measure will correlate more strongly with a different measure than with itself.

Estimating Population Coefficients

If we were able to assess the relationship between a predictor and a criterion in a population of interest with no measurement error, then we would have computed the true correlation coefficient for the population, ρ_{xy}. Because we almost never have the population available and almost always have measurement error, our observed correlation coefficients underestimate the population coefficients. That is, predictor and criterion unreliability are statistical artifacts that lower predictor-criterion relationships.[5]

Two other statistical artifacts that obscure true relationships are sampling error and range restriction. A *sampling error* is an inaccuracy resulting from the use of a sample that is smaller than the population when computing the validity coefficient. A *range restriction* is a correlation or validity coefficient computed between the predictor and criterion scores for a restricted group of individuals. For example, suppose you were interested in determining the correlation between height and weight. If you had data that reflected the entire range of human variability, the correlation would be fairly substantial. However, if you studied only retired adult men, the correlation would be artificially low owing to the restricted range of heights and weights represented in your sample.

Formulas have been developed to remove the effects of predictor unreliability, criterion unreliability, and range restriction, and for determining sampling error variance. Researchers can use these correction formulas to remove the influence of statistical artifacts and, consequently, obtain a better idea of the predictor-criterion relationship in the relevant population. A number of studies have examined the effects of variations in sample size, range restriction, and reliability on the size and variability of observed validity coefficients. These studies have improved our understanding of how observed validity coefficients are affected by measurement error and statistical artifacts.

Validity

As defined in the American Psychological Association's *Principles for the Validation and Use of Personnel Selection Procedures*, validity is the degree to which inferences from scores on tests or assessments are supported by evidence. This means that validity refers to the inferences made from the use of a measure, not to the measure itself. Two common strategies used to justify the inferences made from scores on measures are criterion-related validation and content-oriented validation.

Criterion-Related Validation. *Criterion-related validation* empirically assesses how well a predictor measure forecasts a criterion measure. Usually, predictor measures are scores on one or more selection "tests" (e.g., a score from an interview or a score to reflect the amount of experience), and criteria measures represent job performance (e.g., dollar sales per year or supervisory ratings of performance). Two types of criterion-related validation strategies are concurrent validation and predictive validation. These are shown in Exhibit B.2. *Concurrent validation* evaluates the relationship between a predictor and a criterion for all participants in the study at the same time. For example, the HR department could use this strategy to determine the correlation between years of experience and job performance. The department would collect from each person in the study information about years of experience and performance scores. All persons in the study would have to be working in similar jobs, generally in the same job family or classification. Then, a correlation would be computed between the predictor scores and criterion scores.

The steps in determining predictive validity are similar, except that the predictor is measured sometime before the criterion is measured. Thus, *predictive validity* is determined by measuring an existing group of employees on a predictor and then later gathering their criterion measures.

The classic example of a predictive validation analysis is AT&T's Management Progress Study.[6] In that study, researchers at AT&T administered an assessment center to 422 male employees. Then, they stored the scores from the assessment center and waited. After eight years, they correlated the assessment center scores with measures of how far the same individuals progressed in AT&T's management hierarchy. For a group of college graduates, the predictions were highly accurate; a correlation of .71 was obtained between the assessment center predictions and the level of management achieved.

Content-Oriented Validation. On many occasions, employers are not able to obtain sufficient empirical data for a criterion-related study. Consequently, other methods of validation are useful. One of the most viable is *content-oriented validation.* It differs from a criterion-related strategy in that it

Exhibit B.2
Criterion-Related Validation Strategies

Concurrent Study

Time 1	Time 1	Time 1
Test (predictor) scores are gathered.	Criterion scores are gathered.	The correlation between scores on predictor measures (x) and criterion measures (y), r_{xy}, is calculated.

Predictive Study

Time 1	Time 2	Time 2
Test (predictor) scores are gathered.	Criterion scores are gathered.	The correlation between scores on predictor measures (x) and criterion measures (y), r_{xy}, is calculated.

uses subjective judgments and logic as the basis for arguing that a predictor is likely to be effective in forecasting a criterion. To employ a content validation strategy, one must know the duties of the actual job. As discussed in Chapter 6, information about job tasks and duties can be obtained using one or more job-analysis procedures. Once the duties are known, then logic is used to argue that a predictor is relevant to performance in the job. For example, if a job analysis showed that word processing duties were a substantial portion of a job, then you might logically conclude that a test of word processing skills would be a valid predictor of job performance. For this type of validation, the most important data are job-analysis results.

Validity Generalization

Since the mid-1900s, hundreds of criterion-related validation studies have been conducted in organizations, to determine the predictive effectiveness of HR measures (e.g., ability tests) for selecting and placing individuals. Often, the validity coefficients for the same or a similar predictor-criterion relationship differed substantially from one setting to another. Although researchers were aware that these differences were affected by range restriction, predictor unreliability, criterion unreliability, and sampling error, only recently were corrections for these statistical artifacts integrated into systematic procedures for estimating to what degree true validity estimates for the same predictor-criterion relationship generalize across settings.

A series of studies has applied validity generalization procedures to validity coefficient data for clerical jobs, computer programming jobs, petroleum industry jobs, and so on.[7] In general, these investigations showed that the effects of range restriction, predictor unreliability, criterion unreliability, and sample size accounted for much of the observed variance in validity coefficients for the same or similar test-criterion relationship within an occupation (i.e., a job grouping or job family). Thus, the estimated true (corrected) validity coefficients were higher and less variable than the observed (uncorrected) validity.

The implications of these findings are that inferences (predictions) from scores on selection tests can be transported across situations for similar jobs. That is, if two similar jobs exist in two parts of an organization, a given selection test may have approximately the same validity coefficients for both jobs. If validity generalization can be successfully argued, an organization can save a great deal of time and money developing valid, job-related predictors when the inferences from a predictor for a job have already been established.

The concept of validity generalization, or *meta-analysis,* has also been applied to other areas of HR research.[8] Such research has led to a better understanding of the effectiveness of interventions such as training programs, goal-setting programs, and performance measurement (appraisal) programs.

Cross-Validation

HR researchers are also interested in how stable their prediction equations are across samples. Cross-validation studies address this concern. For the prediction equations developed by researchers to be of any practical use, they must produce consistent results. *Cross-validation* is a procedure for determining how much capitalization on chance has affected the prediction equation, (or *regression weights*). In the case of HR selection research, for example, one is interested in how well the regression weights estimated in a sample of job incumbents will predict the criterion value of new job applicants not tested in the sample.

Traditional or empirical cross-validation typically involves holding out some of the data from the initial sample and then applying the equation developed in the initial sample to the holdout sample to evaluate the equation's stability. In general, this procedure is less precise than one using a formula for estimating the stability of regression equations. The reason for this is that in formula-based estimates, all the available information (the total sample) is used at once in estimating the original weights.[9]

UTILITY ANALYSIS

Armed with tools to determine the reliability and validity of measurement devices, researchers have become concerned about demonstrating the usefulness of the methods and procedures they use. This is particularly important when human resource activities and programs are vying for scarce financial resources. To justify funding, human resource activities must be cost-effective. The process used to assess the costs and benefits of human resource programs is called *utility analysis.* Although it is not yet used by many organizations, utility analysis helps human resource managers compare the economic consequences of two alternative HR practices. For example, you might compare the consequences of relying on a single interview to select people into a job, versus giving applicants a written ability test. Or you might compare the economic consequences of a three-week off-site training session versus a six-month on-the-job approach to training.[10]

In HR selection, most applications of utility analysis are premised on the assumption that supervisors can estimate the dollar values associated with performance at the 50th percentile, the 85th percentile, and the 15th percentile. This is called the *standard deviation* (SD_y) of the performance in dollars. Studies have been conducted in which supervisors have provided estimates of the SD_y for such jobs as sales manager, computer programmer, insurance counselor, and entry-level park ranger. The research indicates that the SD_y usually ranges from 16 to 70 percent of wages, with values most often being in the 40 to 60 percent range. This means that an estimate of the SD_y for a job paying \$40,000 a year typically ranges from \$16,000 to \$24,000. Utility analysis also considers other variables (e.g., the number of employees, tax rates, and the validity coefficient of the selection device) that affect the value or utility of a selection process. The following equation, which incorporates these economic concepts, can be employed when comparing two alternative selection procedures or other human resource options:

$$\Delta U = N_s \sum_{t=1}^{T} \{[1/1 + i)^t] \ SD_y(1 + V)(1 - TAX)(\hat{\rho}_1 - \hat{\rho}_2)z_s\} - \{(C_1 - C_2)(1 - TAX)\}$$

where

ΔU = the total estimated dollar value of replacing one selection procedure (1) with another procedure (2) after variable costs, taxes, and discounting

N_s = the number of employees selected

T = the number of future time periods

t = the time period in which a productivity increase occurs

i = the discount rate

SDy = the standard deviation of job performance in dollars

V = the proportion of SD_y represented by variable costs

TAX = the organization's applicable tax rate

$\hat{\rho}_1$ = the estimated population validity coefficient between scores on one selection procedure and the criterion

$\hat{\rho}_2$ = the estimated population validity coefficient between scores on an alternative selection procedure and scores on the criterion

z_s = the mean standard score on the selection procedure of those selected (this is assumed to be equal in this equation for each selection procedure)

C_1 = the total cost of the first selection procedure

C_2 = the total cost of the alternative selection procedure[11]

For illustration, let us employ a portion of the utility analysis information collected at a large international manufacturing company, which we will call company A. Company A undertook a utility analysis to obtain an estimate of the economic effect of its current procedure for selecting sales managers as compared with that of its previous program. The current procedure is a managerial assessment center. Although the assessment center had been in operation for seven years at the time of the utility analysis, a value of four years was used because this was the average tenure (T) for the 29 sales managers (N_s) who had been selected from a pool of 132 candidates. A primary objective of the utility analysis was to compare the estimated dollar value of selecting these managers using the assessment center with what the economic gain would have been if the managers had been selected by an interviewing program.

The values -.05 for V and .49 for TAX were provided by the accounting and tax departments, respectively. V was the proportion of dollar sales volume compared with operating costs. Its value was negative because a positive relationship existed between combined operating costs (e.g., salaries, benefits, supplies, and automobile operations) and sales volume. The value for i, .18, was based on an examination of corporate financial documentation. The accounting department also provided the figure for C_1 (the total cost of the assessment center), $263,636. Based on 29 selected individuals, the cost of selecting one district sales manager was computed to be about $9,091. The estimated total cost to select 29 sales managers by the previous one-day interviewing program (C_2) was $50,485.

The estimated population validity coefficient for the assessment center, $\hat{\rho}_1$, was obtained by correlating five assessment dimension scores (i.e., scores for planning and organizing, decision making, stress tolerance, sensitivity, and persuasiveness) with an overall performance rating. The multiple correlation between the measures was .61. Next, the cross-validated multiple correlation for the population was calculated, using the appropriate formulas. The resulting value, .41, was corrected for range restriction and criterion reliability to yield an estimated value of .59 for $\hat{\rho}_1$

Because Company A had not conducted a criterion-related validity study for the interviewing selection program, a value was obtained from the validity generalization literature; the resulting $\hat{\rho}_2$ for the interviewing program was .16. In addition, the standard score on the predictor (z_s) was determined to be .872. This value was assumed to be the same for both the assessment center and the interviewing program.

The final, and traditionally the most difficult, component to estimate in the equation was SD_y. This expression is an index of the variability of job performance in dollars in the relevant population. The relevant population for evaluating a selection procedure is the applicant group exposed to that procedure. When evaluating the economic utility of organizational interventions, however, the relevant group is current employees. Because the intervention at company A would be applied to current employees, the appropriate value of SD_y was for this group. Thus, if SD_y were estimated from the applicant group, it could be an overestimate. Consequently, the approximate value for a sales manager, $30,000, was used for SD_y.

Placing all these values into the utility analysis equation gave approximately $316,460 as the estimated present value, over four years, to the organization from the use of the assessment center in place of an interviewing program to select 29 sales managers. Although the cost of the interviewing program was only about one-fifth that of the assessment center, the estimated dollar gain from use of the assessment center instead of the interviewing program was substantial. This result was primarily due to the greater predictive effectiveness (i.e., higher validity coefficient) of the assessment center.

Despite the potential usefulness of utility analysis, very few firms have adopted its procedures. Several circumstances may explain this failure. First, practice tends to lag theory. Because utility analysis is rather new, it may not yet have filtered down to organizations. Second, opponents of utility analysis question the viability of measuring the standard deviation of performance by using managerial estimates. However, this concern may be alleviated by a new utility approach that does not require the direct estimation of SD_y.[12] Finally, validation studies have not been conducted as often as they should be. Without information regarding the validity of selection, training, safety, or absenteeism programs, utility analysis cannot be conducted.

ENDNOTES

[1] For a summary of the conditions under which each type of correlation coefficient is used, refer to M. J. Allen and W. M. Yen, *Introduction to Measurement Theory* (Monterey, CA: Brooks/Cole, 1979), 36–41.

[2] G. V. Glass and J. C. Stanley, *Statistical Methods in Education and Psychology* (Englewood Cliffs, NJ: Prentice-Hall, 1970).

[3] F. M. Lord and M. R. Novick, *Statistical Theories of Mental Test Scores* (Reading, MA: Addison-Wesley, 1968).

[4] E. E. Ghiselli, J. P. Campbell, and S. Zedeck, *Measurement Theory for the Behavioral Sciences* (San Francisco: Freeman, 1981).

[5] P. Bobko, "An Analysis of Correlations Corrected for Attenuation and Range Restriction," *Journal of Applied Psychology* 68 (1983): 584-589; R. Lee, R. Miller, and W. Graham, "Corrections for Restriction of Range and Attenuation in Criterion-Related Validation Studies," *Journal of Applied Psychology* 67 (1982): 637–639.

[6] A. Howard, "College Experience and Managerial Performance," *Journal of Applied Psychology* 53 (1968): 530–552. For a discussion of the *AT&T Management Progress Study,* as well as an overview of assessment centers, see A. Howard, "An Assessment of Assessment Centers," *Academy of Management Journal* 17, (71) (1974): 115–134. See also A. Howard and D. W. Bray, *Managerial Lives in Transition: Advancing Age and Changing Times* (New York: Guilford, 1988).

[7] For a review of validity generalization research, see M. J. Burke, "A Review of Validity Generalization Models and Procedures," *Readings in Personnel and Human Resource Management,* 3rd ed., R. S. Schuler, S. A. Youngblood, and V. L. Huber, eds. (St. Paul, MN: West Publishing Co., 1988). See also F. L. Schmidt and J. E. Hunter, "Development of a General Solution to the Problem of Validity Generalization," *Journal of Applied Psychology* 62 (1977): 529–540. Alternative validity generalization procedures have been presented in J. C. Callender and H. G. Osburn, "Development and Test of a New Model for Validity Generalization," *Journal of Applied Psychology* 65 (1980): 543–558; N. S. Raju and M. J. Burke, "Two New Procedures for Studying Validity Generalization," *Journal of Applied Psychology* 68 (1982): 382–395.

[8] G. V. Glass coined the term *meta-analysis* to refer to the statistical analysis of the findings of many individual studies, in "Primary, Secondary, and Meta-Analysis of Research," *Educational Researcher* 5 (1976): 3–8. Numerous articles and books have been written on the subject of meta-analysis (of which validity generalization can be considered a subset);

two original and frequently cited texts in this area are G. V. Glass, B. McGaw, and M. L. Smith, *Meta-Analysis in Social Research* (Beverly Hills, CA: Sage, 1981), and J. E. Hunter, F. L. Schmidt, and G. Jackson, *Meta-Analysis: Cumulating Research Findings Across Settings* (Beverly Hills, CA: Sage, 1982).

[9] P. Cattlin, "Estimations of the Predictive Power of a Regression Model," *Journal of Applied Psychology* 65 (1980): 407–414; J. G. Claudy, "Multiple Regression and Validity Estimation in One Sample," *Applied Psychological Measurement* 2 (1978): 595–607; K. R. Murphy, "Cost-Benefit Considerations in Choosing among Cross-Validation Methods," *Personnel Psychology* 37 (1984): 15–22.

[10] W. Cascio, *Costing Human Resource Management,* 3rd ed. (Boston: PWS-Kent, 1991); G. R. Jones and P. M. Wright, "An Economic Approach to Conceptualizing the Utility of Human Resource Management Practices," *Research in Personnel and Human Resource Management,* 10th ed., K. Rowland and G. Ferris, eds. (1992): 271–299.

[11] A study that employed this full equation and provides useful information for estimating economic components as well as true validity coefficients is presented in M. J. Burke and J. T. Frederick, "A Comparison of Economic Utility Estimates for Alternative SD, Estimation Procedures," *Journal of Applied Psychology* 71 (1986): 334–339.

[12] N. S. Raju, M. J. Burke, and J. Normand, "A New Approach for Utility Analysis," *Journal of Applied Psychology* 75, (1) (1990): 3–12.

Glossary of Web Site Links

Web sites and domain names are subject to change. These site addresses were current as of the date of publication.

A

Academy of Management	www.aom.pace.com
Adolph Coors Company	www.coors.com
Aetna Life and Casualty Company	www.aetna.com
AFL-CIO	www.aflcio.org
AFL-CIO Executive PayWatch	www.paywatch.org
Aid Association for Lutherans	www.aal.com
AlliedSignal Aerospace	www.allied.com
American Association of Retired Persons	www.aarp.org
American Compensation Association	www.acaonline.org
American International Group	www.aig.com
American Society for Training & Development	www.astd.org
American's Job Bank	www.ajb.dni.us
Andersen Consulting	www.ac.com
Arthur Andersen	www.arthurandersen.com
	www.arthuranderson.com /bus-info/services/IES
AT&T	www.att.com
Avon Products, Inc.	www.avon.com

B

Barden Corporation	www.mai.net /~barden01/home
Bavarian Motor Works	www.bmw.com
Bayer Corporation	www.bayer.com
Ben & Jerry's Homemade	www.benjerry.com
Booz-Allen	www.bah.com
Boston Consulting Group	www.bcg.com

British Petroleum   www.bp.com

Brush Wellman   www.brushwellman.com

Bureau of Labor Statistics   stats.bls.gov

Bureau of National Affairs   www.bna.com

C

Caligiuri & Associates   www.caligiuri.com

Canada's Pay Equity Commission   www.gov.on.ca/lab/pec

Career Mosaic   www.careermosaic.com

Case Swayne Co.   www.case-swayne.com

Chicago Tribune   www.chicago.tribune.com

Chubb Corporation   www.chubb.com

Cirque du Soleil   www.cirquedusoleil.com

Cisco Systems   www.cisco.com

ClassNet   www.classnet.com

CNF Transportation   www.cnf.com

Coca-Cola   www.cocacola.com

Computer Mediated Communications Magazine   www.december.com/cmc/mag

Continental Airlines   www.flycontinental.com

Con-Way Transportation   www.con-way.com

Corning   www.corning.com

D

Deloitte & Touche   www.dttus.com

Delta Airlines   www.delta-air.com

Department of Labor   www.doleta.gov
                                     /programs/onet/

Diversity Web   www.inform.umd.edu
                                     /Diversityweb

E

Eastman Kodak Company   www.kodak.com

Eaton Corporation   www.eaton.com

Eddie Bauer Company   www.eddiebauer.com

Equal Employment Opportunity Commission   www.eeoc.gov

Ernst & Young   www.ey.com

Etec Systems   www.etec.com

F

Family and Medical Leave Act	www.dol.gov/dol/esa/fmla
Fannie Mae	www.fanniemae.com
FastCompany	www.fastcompany.com
Federal Express	www.fedex.com
Ford Motor Company	www.ford.com
	www2.ford.com
Fortune Magazine	www.fortune.com
Freddie Mac	www.freddiemac.com

G

Gateway, Inc.	www.gateway.com
Genentech	www.gene.com
General Electric	www.ge.com
General Motors	www.gm.com

H

Hallmark Cards, Inc.	www.hallmark.com
Hewitt Associates	www.hewittassoc.com/resc
Hire Quality	www.hire-quality.com
HispanStar	www.hispanstar.com
Human Resource Planning Society	www.hrps.org

I

IBM	www.ibm.com
IBM's *Annual Report*	www.ibm.com/AnnualReport
International Association for Human Resource Information Management	www.ihrim.org
International Labor Organization	www.ilo.gov
International Labour Organization	www.ilo.org
International Occupational Safety & Health Information Center	turva.me.tut.fi/cis/
International Personnel Management Association	www.ipma-hr.org

K

Kinko's	www.kinkos.com
Kinko's Atlanta Learning Center	www.tlckinkos.com
Kinko's Document Solution Division	www.edp.com
KPMG Consulting Firm	www.us.kpmg.com /ethics
Kraft General Foods	www.kraftfoods.com

L

Labor Net	www.doleta.gov/programs /onet/onet_hp.htm
Levi Strauss & Company	www.levi.com
Lincoln Electric	www.lincolnelectric.com

M

Malcolm Baldrige National Quality Award	www.nist.gov /public-affairs/bald97
McKinsey & Company	www.mckinsey.com
Mercer Consulting Group	www.mercer.com
Metropolitan Life Insurance Company	www.metlife.com
Mexico Web	mexico.web.com.mx/
Microsoft Corporation	www.microsoft.com
Motorola	www.motorola.com
Mrs. Field's Cookies	www.mrsfields.com
Munroe, Nelson, & Pearl Immigration Attorneys	www.immigrationlaw.com

N

National Center for Employee Ownership	www.nceo.org
National Center for Health Statistics	www.cdc.gov/nchswww
National Labor Relations Board	www.nlrb.gov
National Safety Council	www.nsc.org
New Balance	www.newbalance.com
Nike	www.nike.com
Northern Telecom	www.nortel.com

O

Online Career Center	www.occ.com
Owens Corning	www.owenscorning.com

P

Pepsico	www.pepsico.com
Pharmacia & Upjohn	www.pharmacia.se
Pratt & Whitney	www.pratt-whitney.com
PricewaterhouseCoopers Global	www.pwcglobal.com
PricewaterhouseCoopers	www.pricewaterhouse coopers.com
PRT Company	www.prt.com

R

Reebok	www.reebok.com
Ritz-Carlton Hotels	www.ritzcarlton.com

S

Sears, Roebuck & Company	www.sears.com
Shearman & Sterling	www.shearman.com
Sherwin Williams Company	www.sherwinwilliams.com
SHRM Global Forum	www.shrmglobal.org
Signicast Corporation	www.signicast.com
Society for Human Resource Management	www.shrm.org
Society for Human Resource Management Global Forum	www.shrmglobal.org
Southwest Airlines	www.iflyswa.com
Southwest Airlines Flight Attendant Recruitment	www.iflyswa.com/people /fltattend.html
Steelcase	www.steelcase.com

T

Teamsters	www.teamster.org
Texaco	www.texaco.com
The Federation of European Employers	www.euen.co.uk
The Managed Care Information Center	www.themcic.com
The Monster Board	www.monster.com
The Web of Culture	www.worldculture.com
3M	www.3M.com/cws
Time Work Web	www.vcn.bc.ca/timework /worksite.htm

U

U.S. Department of Treasury	www.ustreas.gov
U.S. Government's Glass Ceiling Commission	www.dol.gov/dol/_sec /public/media/reports/ceiling
United Auto Workers	www.uaw.org
United Parcel Service	www.ups.com

V

Verifone	www.verifone.com

W

W.L. Gore & Associates	gore.com
Walt Disney Company	www.disney.com
Weyerhaeuser Company	www.weyerhaeuser.com
WFPMA	wfpma.com.br
Windham World	www.windham.com/expat
Workforce Online	www.workforceonline.com

X

Xerox Business Services	www.xerox.com/XBS
Xerox Press Release	www.xerox.com/PR /NR970915-family

Z

Zigon Performance Group	www.zigonperf.com

Index